Charles Masson: Collections from Begram and Kabul Bazaar, Afghanistan, 1833–1838

Elizabeth Errington

With contributions by Joe Cribb, Lauren Morris, Piers Baker, Paramdip Khera, Chantal Fabrègues, Kirstin Leighton-Boyce and Wannaporn Kay Rienjang

The British Museum

To all the volunteers and co-workers on the Masson Project

Research funded by the Neil Kreitman Foundation 1993–2011

This project has received funding from the European Research Council (ERC) under the European Union's Seventh Framework Programme (FP7/2007–2013) (grant no. 609823)

Publishers
The British Museum
Great Russell Street
London WC1B 3DG

Series editor
Sarah Faulks

Charles Masson: Collections from Begram and Kabul Bazaar, Afghanistan, 1833–1838

Elizabeth Errington

ISBN 978 0861592197
ISSN 1747 3640
https://doi.org/10.48582/charlesmasson_vol3

© 2021 The Trustees of the British Museum

Text © 2021 individual contributors as listed on p. iii

Front cover: Aerial image of the site of Begram in June 2012 (US Buckeye Program, courtesy of the Afghan Heritage Mapping Partnership, University of Chicago Oriental Institute)

Printed and bound in the UK by 4edge Ltd, Hockley

Papers used by The British Museum are recyclable products made from wood grown in well-managed forests and other controlled sources. The manufacturing processes conform to the environmental regulations of the country of origin.

All British Museum images illustrated in this book are
© 2021 The Trustees of the British Museum

All British Library images illustrated in this book are
© British Library Board

All other drawings and maps where copyright is not specified are
© E. Errington

Further information about the British Museum and its collection can be found at britishmuseum.org

Contents

Acknowledgements	v
Preface	1

Part 1: Begram – Excavation and Collection History

1. Charles Masson and Begram *Elizabeth Errington*	3
2. The Excavations of the Délégation archéologique française en Afghanistan at Begram (1936–46) *Lauren Morris*	20

Part 2: The Masson Collections from Begram and Kabul

3. Masson Manuscript F526/1a: Analysis of the Begram Coins with Reference to Plates *Piers Baker with Elizabeth Errington*	35
4. The Monetary History of Begram *Joe Cribb*	81

Part 3: Catalogue of Coins Elizabeth Errington and Paramdip Khera with Joe Cribb, Kirstin Leighton-Boyce and Wannaporn Kay Rienjang	127
Part 4: Catalogue of Gems, Seals and Amulets Elizabeth Errington, Wannaporn Kay Rienjang and Chantal Fabrègues	211
Part 5: Catalogue of Ornamental Metalwork and Miscellaneous Artefacts Chantal Fabrègues with Elizabeth Errington, Kirstin Leighton-Boyce and Wannaporn Kay Rienjang	232

Concluding Remarks	303
Appendices	304
Appendix 1: Masson's Annotated Copy of *Ariana Antiqua* *Piers Baker with Elizabeth Errington*	305
Appendix 2: F526/1m. EIC Receipt of Masson's Collections 19 October 1836 to December 1838	329
Appendix 3: F526/1n. Masson's Summary List of Collections 1833–8	331
Appendix 4: List of Standardised Spelling and Transcribed Names	334
Appendix 5: British Museum, India Museum and South Kensington Museum Inventories	336
References	340
Contributors	354
Index	355

Acknowledgements

Someone once said that I make no impression initially, but I get there in the end. This has been of immense comfort over the years, not least because never a truer word has been spoken with regard to the Masson Project. That I have finally reached the end is entirely due to the help of many volunteers and co-workers who have contributed their time and expertise to this long overdue attempt to publish the work and collections of Charles Masson.

As already stated in the previous two Masson volumes, the Project would never have happened without the initiative of Joe Cribb and Neil Kreitman, or the extensive financial support of the Neil Kreitman Foundation (1993–2011), to whom I am eternally grateful. Additional funding was provided by the British Museum Research Board and Asia Department, the Townley Group of British Museum Friends (1998–2004) and the Royal Numismatic Society, which *inter alia* financed several additional workers on the Project. In 2018, the European Research Council (ERC) paid for work on completing this specific volume and its publication through the *Beyond Boundaries* project (project number 609823). I thank them all. I am also obliged to Michael Willis for arranging the ERC funding.

By authorising the transfer of *c.* 10,000 coins and fragments uncovered in the India Office Collections of the British Library on indefinite loan to the British Museum in 1995, Graham Shaw single-handedly released a vast quantity of new numismatic data for the study of Begram and Afghanistan. In 2004, further caches of coins, still in their original bags (marked 'A', 'F' and 'k'), were found at the Library by Jennifer Howes and transferred to the Museum in 2007.

Many people have worked on processing these India Office Loan Collection (IOLC) coins and separating those acquired by Masson (*c.* 7,300 coins) from those from other sources, notably South India, Kashmir and various Indian Sultanates. I am extremely grateful to them all.

The mammoth task of conserving and cleaning all the IOLC coins was undertaken by British Museum conservators Celestine Enderley, Simon Dove and Pippa Pearse.

Numerous volunteers, including Maria Fernandez, Setsuko Kuga-Cornish, Anna McIlreavy, Clair Joy and Henry Lythe helped with the subsequent sorting, weighing, measuring, registration and scanning of the coins and objects. There were however several long-term key workers who accomplished much of this essential documentation.

John Perkins worked on the pre-Islamic coins down to the Later Kushans and created the initial entries for the British Museum's Collection Online database.

Paramdip Khera extracted and identified all the Masson Islamic coins and contributed to the coin catalogue (see pp. 200–10 below).

Gul Rahim Khan identified all the later Kushan coins and arranged them in order. Sushma Jansari was also a great help, even though she wrote herself out of the Project by demonstrating – with the help of Sam Moorcroft – that almost all the IOLC Roman coins were from South India, the remainder being from the Near East and Egypt, not Begram.

The Project and this volume would never have been completed without the assistance of Kirstin Leighton-Boyce

Opposite: Views from Begram in 2019.
Top: view from the New Royal City looking north to the Burj Abdullah and the Ghorband and Panjshir rivers; bottom: view of Koh-i Pahlawan from the east fortification wall of the New Royal City.
© Lauren Morris, courtesy of Noor Agha Noori

and Kay Rienjang who did much of the practical work, such as processing the coin images and putting them on the Museum's Collection Online database. They were also responsible for extracting the online text and images of the coins and objects included in the catalogues here.

I am also indebted to my fellow authors for expanding the scope of this publication on Begram: Joe Cribb (not least for checking and correcting the coin catalogue); Lauren Morris, Piers Baker and Chantal Fabrègues.

I have to thank Kathryn Franklin, Project Manager of the Afghan Heritage Mapping Partnership, University of Chicago Oriental Institute for supplying the satellite images of Begram; Pierfrancesco Callieri for making his research on the seals available to me; and also Claudia Wagner, Senior Researcher, Beazley Archive Gem Programme, the Classical Art Research Centre in Oxford, for organising and photographing the seal impressions made under the direction of Nathan Harrison in the Department of Asia. Alexsandr Naymark generously supplied the information and translation of the contemporary account of Masson by the Russian agent Ivan Vitkevich; he was also kind enough to correct and standardise the transliteration and translation of all the Russian bibliographic references.

I greatly appreciate the unflagging support I have received from my former colleagues in the Museum's Department of Coins and Medals, especially the former Keeper Philip Attwood, Vesta Curtis, Robert Bracey and above all, Helen Wang, who has always been at hand to help in every way, far beyond the call of duty or friendship.

Last but not least, my thanks go to Michael Alram for reviewing the volume and to Sarah Faulks for organising its publication.

Preface

This is the third and final volume dealing with the discoveries and collections of Charles Masson (1800–53) in the British Museum and British Library. It focuses on tracking down the vast collection of over 60,000 coins and other small ornamental artefacts Masson records making primarily at the urban site of Begram, and supplemented by purchases in the Kabul bazaar (1842, III, p. 149). It is preceded by *Charles Masson and the Buddhist Sites of Afghanistan: Explorations, Excavations and Collections 1832–1835*, which also contains the main biography of Masson and a general history of the collection (**Vol. I**, pp. 1–27). Both volumes **I** and **III** are linked to the online publication of selected manuscript documents, *The Charles Masson Archive: British Library, British Museum and Other Documents Relating to the 1832–1838 Masson Collection from Afghanistan* (**Vol. II**). There are several other archival sources of information on Masson's excavations and collections which are excluded from **Vol. II**. For example, the papers of Henry Pottinger in the National Archives at Kew include copies of the same correspondence (Garg 2016). There are also duplicated records in the East India Company's *Bombay Dispatches* and *Political Proceedings*, copies of which abound in both the national and regional archives of India as well as in the British Library.

References marked in bold (e.g. **F526/1f** or **E161/VII f. 30**) link directly to the relevant archival records in **Vol. II**. However, Masson's treatise 'Analysis of the Begram coins with reference to plates'– which appeared in a severely abridged form in the *Journal of the Asiatic Society of Bengal* (Masson 1836a-b) – is reproduced in full here, rather than in **Vol. II**, as it provides a comprehensive illustrated survey of the coins from the site (**F526/1a**, see pp. 35–80 below). **F526/1a** 'plates' are cited in bold, while 'figures' are in italics (e.g. **Pl. 2**, *Fig. 45*), thereby differentiating between Masson's references and those in the rest of the volume (**Figs 1–142**).

Masson's copiously annotated personal copy of *Ariana Antiqua* survives in the Bodleian Library in Oxford and his annotations are reproduced in Appendix 1 in this volume (pp. 305–28).

Two further documents are also included: an East India Company Bombay Government receipt of coins collected between October 1836 and December 1838, and a summary list of coins, seals and ornamental artefacts collected between 1833–8 (Appendix 2–3: **F526/1m-n**, pp. 329–33).

It was the discovery in 1995 of the fully illustrated document **F526/1a** that expanded the potential for new numismatic research on Begram. At the same time over 10,000 coins – including the residue of Masson's vast collection – were unearthed in the old India Office Library and transferred on loan to the Museum. Together they transformed the Masson Project. Begun on small scale involving the identification of Masson coins and artefacts in the British Museum from a few hundred illustrated in *Ariana Antiqua* (Wilson 1841), it became a major enterprise encompassing over 7,400 coins and some 2,000 miscellaneous objects.

On turning to the catalogued artefacts in the present volume, it will immediately be apparent that the scope of information – especially on the non-coin objects – ranges from simple listings to lengthy discussions. This is partly due to the fragmentary nature of most of the artefacts, as well as the general lack of comparable dated or provenanced material. But the publication does not aspire to be definitive; rather it aims to make all the material easily accessible as a study collection for further research. The finds – in particular, coins – collected and recorded by Masson provide unique and comprehensive numismatic evidence for reconstructing the history of the lost city of Begram, as only a small area was ever excavated (see pp. 20–34 below).

The site of Begram lies near the confluence of Ghorband and Panjshir Rivers, *c.* 80km to the north-east of Kabul (lat. 34°59'N, long. 69°19'E; **Figs 1–2**). It is quite close to the military air base of Bagram, and at one point in the 1990s Google Earth satellite images revealed Burj Abdullah (its citadel) being used as a parking area for armoured vehicles. The outlined structures excavated by the French between 1937 and 1946 were also still clearly visible in the same satellite images. But these remains have greatly eroded since, mainly due to necessary mine clearance in recent years (**Figs 3–4**).

In all probability a high percentage of the British Museum's own India Office coin collection (IOC) also originated from Masson (see pp. 119–26, **Table 23**) but Museum coins included in this catalogue have been limited to those that are identified by drawings in *Ariana Antiqua* or **F526/1a**, and the East India Company donations of 1838 and 1845, which are certainly from Masson. Since the entire Masson collection is available with images online (https://research.britishmuseum.org/research/collection_online/search.aspx), only a representative selection of all the British Museum objects and India Office Loan Collection (IOLC) coins from Begram and Kabul bazaar have been included here.

For simplicity the diverse spellings of place and personal names have been standardised in the text; the variations are listed in Appendix 4.

Part 1: Begram – Excavation and Collection History

Chapter 1
Charles Masson and Begram

Elizabeth Errington

Pioneer numismatist and archaeologist, reluctant spy

A single impetuous act by James Lewis – his desertion from the East India Company Bengal Artillery regiment in 1827 and his assumed identity as an American named Charles Masson – has resulted in a number of flights of fantasy about who he actually was. It has been variously alleged, for example, that he was French or a spy for the Russians (**Vol. I, pp. 4, 12–13**; Murray 2016, pp. 343–4), while in the introduction to Masson's *Narrative of Various Journeys in Balochistan, Afghanistan and the Panjab* (1974, pp. xi–xiii), Gavin Hambly imaginatively remarks that:

> The East India Company's European regiments always included among the private soldiers a handful of social out-castes, for whom enlistment under an assumed name was an escape from crime, debt or family misfortune. Much later they were to be immortalised in Kipling's *Gentlemen Rankers*. Masson probably fell into just such a category, a desperate young man who enlisted in England in the Company's Artillery, with the prospect of a lifetime of brutal soldiering in the East ahead of him. If such was the case, an additional twist must be added to the mystery. In 1830 ... he submitted to the Government of Bombay a memorandum ... describing the prevailing conditions in Afghanistan, including an account of Herat. No dates are given, but it is certain that, from 1826 [*sic* 1827] onwards ... he never visited Herat. ... It is possible, therefore, that his personal account ... was a fabrication but if it were not, the question arises, when was he ever in that city? Presumably, before 1826 and thus, by inference, before he enlisted in the Bengal Artillery, which in turn implies that he made his way to India overland through Herat and Kandahar, ... and then went on to enlist in the Company's army in Bengal, a most unusual procedure at that period. If true, was it purely love of adventure which led him to undertake this hazardous journey across unknown lands, only to become a private soldier at the end of it, or was he perhaps a fugitive of some kind? Was the name of James Lewis also assumed?

The reality is more mundane (**Vol. I, pp. 3–4**). The paper trail of archival records in the British Library and elsewhere leaves no doubt that Charles Masson was born James Lewis on 16 February 1800 in the City of London, the son of George Lewis, a respectable tradesman and member of the Worshipful Company of Needlemakers, and Mary Hopcraft, daughter of a substantial yeoman farmer (Kaye and Johnston 1937, pp. 1272–3; **B191**: **Vol. II, p. 1**; Whitteridge 1986, pp. 1–2). After receiving a good classical education, he worked as a clerk for Durant & Co., silk and insurance brokers in the City. He initially enlisted as an infantryman in the East India Company on 5 October 1821 in London, sailed to Calcutta in January 1822 and served in the Bengal European Artillery from 6 July 1822 to 4 July 1827 (**Vol. II, pp. 1–2, 4, 123**). The negative view of the EIC army is contradicted by Whitteridge (1986, p. 2): the Company's Artillery, in particular, was relatively well paid and held excellent prospects for promotion to clerical appointments for men of some education like Masson. In fact, this was the route followed by two fellow enlisters who had sailed with Masson on the *Duchess of Atholl* to Calcutta: Charles Brownlow (who bought his discharge from the army in 1826) and George Jephson (who became Registrar of the Adjutant-General's Office). Both men resumed contact with Masson once his whereabouts became known following his royal pardon in 1835 (Whitteridge 1986, p. 5). Intriguingly, both men also changed their names: from Brown to Brownlow, and from Morton to Jephson.

It may be partly on the strength of Masson's imaginary overland journey via Russia and Herat that has inspired the fantasy that he was Russian spy. However, his knowledge of Herat also has a simple explanation: he gleaned the information of the city and environs from people he met who had been there and had travelled overland from Europe. The most likely source and time for acquiring this intelligence was the 1929 monsoon season (June–October), which he spent in Lahore as the guest of General Jean-François Allard (1765–1839) and in the company of the other European officers in the service of Ranjit Singh (1799–1839). Following Napoleon's defeat at Waterloo in 1815, a number of Bonapartist officers – notably Allard himself and Claude-Auguste Court (1793–1880) – faced with little prospect for advancement under the restored French monarchy, left France to seek their fortunes in the East. They initially found employment in the early 1820s in Iran, before migrating to the Sikh court in the Punjab.

Court's 'Voyage à travers la Perse centrale et l'Afghanistan' (*Mémoires* MSS vol. III; Lafont 1992, p. 47; 2007, pp. 144–6), gives a detailed account of the road between Yazd and Peshawar as it was in 1826, including a description of the monuments and surroundings of Herat, and a reference to the city in the time of Alexander the Great. It also illustrates coins from Begram (Lafont 1987, vol. III, no. 53, pp. 152–87; 1992, p. 326; Grey 1929, appendix III, pp. xxvii–xlviii). It would have been only natural for Masson to cross-question Court in particular about Herat, having failed in his own attempt to reach the city from Kandahar earlier in 1829 (**Vol. I, p. 6**). It is also tempting to think that Court was the first to tell him about Begram and the quantities of coins and artefacts found there.

The closest Masson got to Herat and Central Asia was Tabriz in north-west Iran, which he reached in November–December 1830 by sea from Karachi to the Persian Gulf, then overland in the company of British officers (**Vol. I, p. 6**). Be that as it may, it was his account of his fictitious overland journey via Herat and his actual travels through Afghanistan and Baluchistan – submitted to the East India Company in Bombay (**E/4/1057** *Bombay Dispatches* 1834, p. 790) – that first brought him to the attention of the British authorities in India. Indeed, the Chief Secretary, William Hay Macnaghten (1793–1841) declared in January 1835, that this 'Memoir of Mr Masson is in my opinion by far the most important state paper I have read since I have been in India' (*cf.* Lafont 1992, p. 61, n. 373; NAI Political Consultations, § 13). The date suggests that Macnaghten was voicing his support for the recommendation by the Governor-General of India to grant Masson a royal pardon for his desertion (**PRO 30/12/29/1 nos 54, 69**: Vol I, pp. 13–14; Vol. II, p. 4).

Macnaghten – later Envoy to Kabul (1838–41) – played a crucial, ultimately catastrophic role in the formation of British policy in Central Asia in the 1830s (Yapp 1980, pp. 245–9, 424), which led to the misguided invasion of Afghanistan in support of Shah Shuja (**Vol. I, pp. 12–13**). There is a certain irony in the realisation that had he continued in his high opinion of Masson's judgement, and more importantly, had acted upon it, war with Afghanistan and his own murder in Kabul might not have taken place.

From June 1832 – May 1838 Masson had been based in Kabul exploring the ancient remains in the region (**Vol. I, pp. 59–214**). In this he was funded initially by John Campbell (British Envoy to Persia), then James Gerard (on his return from accompanying Alexander Burnes to Bukhara) and subsequently by the Bombay branch of the East India Company, via Henry Pottinger (1789–1856), British Political Agent in Kutch and later Sind.

However, once Masson's true status as a deserter was revealed in 1835, everything changed. In return for his pardon, he was summarily appointed 'news-writer' for the East India Company in Kabul, directly responsible to Claude Wade (1794–1861), Political Agent at Ludhiana (**Vol. I, pp. 11–13**). As a result of his appointment, he found his freedom of movement severely curtailed and largely restricted to Kabul. So in addition to buying coins and other artefacts from Kabul bazaar, he depended on local Afghans to make collections on his behalf, principally at Begram.

As news-writer Masson joined a network of informants for the British, not only in Kabul and Kandahar, but also in Bukhara. Ivan Vitkevich (actually Jan Witkiewicz, 1808–39), who was sent on a Russian intelligence mission to Bukhara in 1836, reported that (1983, pp. 105–6; quotation courtesy of Alexsandr Naymark):

> The English keep in Bukhara a Kashmiran [named] Nizametdin and pay him 20 thousand rupees, i.e. 40 thousand roubles per year. For four years already, he has lived under the guise of a trader in Bukhara and pretends that up to now he has been unable to sell his shawls at good prices. He is a very clever man, knows everybody and is munificent towards the Bukharan nobility. Every week or more often he sends letters to Kabul with secret messengers, where an Englishman [named] Masson lives [and] who [then] delivers these tidings further on. The strangest [aspect of this] is that Dost Muhammad Khan, the ruler of Kabulistan, knows the function of Masson quite well; the Khan has even intercepted his letters, but does not touch the spy saying 'what can one man do to me!' It seems, that Dost Muhammad, who always wants to treat the Europeans excellently, does not want to cause their discontent and tolerates Masson as well, because of his respect of Europeans in general. This man [Masson] lives in Kabul under the pretext of searching for ancient coins. Before him a Persian [named] Karamat 'Ali occupied the post. … But the English were not content with him, recalled him to Ludhiana and sent him about his business. Nizametdin keeps in Bukhara a relative, who is actually doing the writing. They both live in the Saroy [either saroi, i.e. palace, or a caravanserai] of Kushbegi [chief minister of the Khanate]. They treat the nobility in a way that by local standards is [considered] splendid; Nizametdin is dressed foppishly and is extremely handsome; his friend is very smart, though is not that good-looking, and plays a role of a subordinate, although it is clear that he is the one who does all the business. They receive their money from Indian bankers. Immediately on my arrival, Nizametdin tried to get acquainted with me and asked me about everything: … about the New Line [i.e. the Russian military frontier posts], about the relationship with Khiva, etc. Being forewarned, I did not give him any definite answers. He sent, nevertheless, a messenger through Karshi to Kabul on the very next day after these inquiries. Being aware of European etiquette, he expected me to pay him a visit in return and, being afraid of attracting the

suspicions of the Bukharans, he came himself to my place in the evening, in other words, secretly, and asked me, through a third [party] not to visit him.

There is one glaring error in this account: searching for ancient coins was not a 'pretext' but an overwhelming passion and *raison d'être* for Masson. Nevertheless, he was conscientious regarding his political duties, reporting to Wade the initial overtures between Dost Muhammad, the Shah of Persia and Count Ivan Simonich, Russian minister in Tehran (Whitteridge 1986, pp. 108, 118–19). In December 1837, Vitkevich was sent by Simonich to Kabul with written instructions only to negotiate a commercial agreement between Russia and Dost Muhammad, but possibly with verbal authorisation to exceed this remit (Yapp 1980, pp. 234–9; Meyer and Brysac 2001, pp. 84–5, 106). What is clear is that both he and Alexander Burnes (on behalf of the British) offered Dost Muhammad far more than either of their governments were prepared to agree to. It was the British refusal to meet any Afghan requests that resulted in the Amir's acceptance of Vitkevich's offer on 21 April 1838 and the failure of Burnes' personal mission to achieve a political alliance between Britain and Kabul. Vitkevich's agreement was subsequently also repudiated by the Russian Foreign Minister, Count K.R. Nesselrode (1780–1861; Yapp 1980, p. 196). Masson had no role in this apart from advising Burnes and sending his required reports to India. He left Kabul for Peshawar with Burnes on 27 April 1838.

After Macnaghten failed to re-employ Masson in any capacity in Afghanistan in 1838, the latter spent a large part of 1839–40 staying with Henry Pottinger in the British Residency at Tatta, and was so out of touch with the political reality that he thought it safe to go back to Kabul as a private individual and continue his research. Instead he got no further than Kalat, where he was taken prisoner by locals rebelling against revenue arrangements implemented by Lieutenant Loveday, the British Political Agent. When sent by the 'rebels' to convey their demands to the British in Quetta, Masson was arrested on suspicion of being their spy by the officer in charge, Captain J.D.D. Bean (Yapp 1980, pp. 470–1).

The recent branding of Masson as a spy for the Russians (Murray 2016, pp. 343–4) is based on the self-serving 'evidence' of Bean, who subsequently tried to justify his wrongful imprisonment of Masson (as a spy for local insurgents only), and on a passing mention by Mohan Lal linking Masson with Vitkevich. However, there is certainly no reason why Vitkevich should have had any need to enrol Masson as a spy in Kabul, or that Masson would have been privy to any meetings between Vitkevich and Dost Muhammad as subsequently suggested by Mohan Lal (Burnes' former secretary and an interpreter for the British forces in Afghanistan). Like Bean, Mohan Lal can be suspected of trying to divert attention from his own actions. Yapp remarks that 'efforts at concealment failed to hide all the activities of Mohan Lal in Afghanistan' and the mischief he caused with claims that 'Macnaghten and John Conolly had ordered him to arrange the murder of various Afghan chiefs' (1980, pp. 524–5).

The only active role Masson ever took regarding Central Asia was numismatic and that was at a distance. In the winter of 1837, he commissioned some Hindu traders to purchase coins from Turkestan for him. The possibility that one of them was Nizametdin cannot be ruled out. However, Masson wrote in May 1838 from Peshawar (**E161/VII f. 34**, Masson to Pottinger, 8–5–1838) that:

> One of them, a long time since, wrote that he had 17 golden, and a number of silver coins, which if true, up to this time he must have got many more. These Hindus were to reach Kabul by the second Kafila [caravan] of the season, but when we left, the first had not made its appearance. I left three of my servants at Kabul to make arrangements respecting these coins and other matters.

In June he speaks from Peshawar of sending 'two of my young men to Kabul with Rs 300 to secure, if possible, the coins coming from Turkestan' (**E161/VII f. 38**, Masson to Pottinger, 24–6–1838), but shortly afterwards he informed Pottinger that 'On the close of July my man sent to Kabul returned to me, but without having succeeded in making the purchases from Turkestan I had hoped for, the Hindu to whom he looked having not appeared with the spring Kalifa although his goods were sent by it' (**E161/VII f. 40**, Masson to Pottinger, 10–9–1838). There is no record of Masson ever receiving any of these coins from Central Asia. There are also 11 Sogdian Hyrcodes silver coins (*c*. 1st century AD) in the Masson collection (**Fig. 33.9–20**). Only one is specifically recorded as having been acquired in Kabul bazaar in 1836 (**E161/VII f. 29**); but a further eight are included in Masson's 'List of Coins A' (**F526/1f**) of the 1837–8 collections of coins from Kabul bazaar which he was allowed to retain (**Vol. II, pp. 65, 92, 100**: 'Kodes').

Masson's discovery of Begram

In July 1833, Masson left Kabul to explore the districts to the north, at the base of the Hindu Kush mountains in Parwan and Kapisa provinces. He says 'A primary object of my rambles into the Kohistan of Kabul was to ascertain if any vestiges existed which I might venture to refer to Alexandria ad Caucasum, the site [founded by Alexander the Great 329 BC] of which, I felt assured, ought to be looked for at the skirts of the Hindu Kush in this quarter' (1842, III, p. 140). He was rewarded (1834, p. 153; **Fig. 1**)

> by the discovery of numerous interesting objects, and among them of the site of an ancient city of immense extent, on the plain now called Begram, near the confluence of the rivers Ghorband and Panjshir, and at the head of the high road leading from Khwaja Khedari of Kohistan to Nijrau, Tagau [districts/valleys of Kapisa province], Laghman and Jalalabad.

According to Masson (1842, III, pp. 140–3):

> I had before reached the borders of the plain of Begram, and had heard strange stories of the innumerable coins and other relics found on the soil, but had been unable to procure a specimen, all to whom I applied, whether Hindu or Muslim, denying that they had any such things in possession. I now purposed to obtain from Mir Saiyad Khan a party of his retainers to enable me to traverse and survey the plain, which is dangerous to do, owing to the marauders infesting it. He provided half a dozen horsemen, a sufficient escort, as, being known to the robbers, they are not interrupted by them. Having passed the large ruinous village Ghulam Shah, we arrived at Killa Bolend, on the brink of the Kohistan basin and at the commencement of the plain [**Fig. 1**]. There were seven considerable Hindu traders here, but we applied to them for

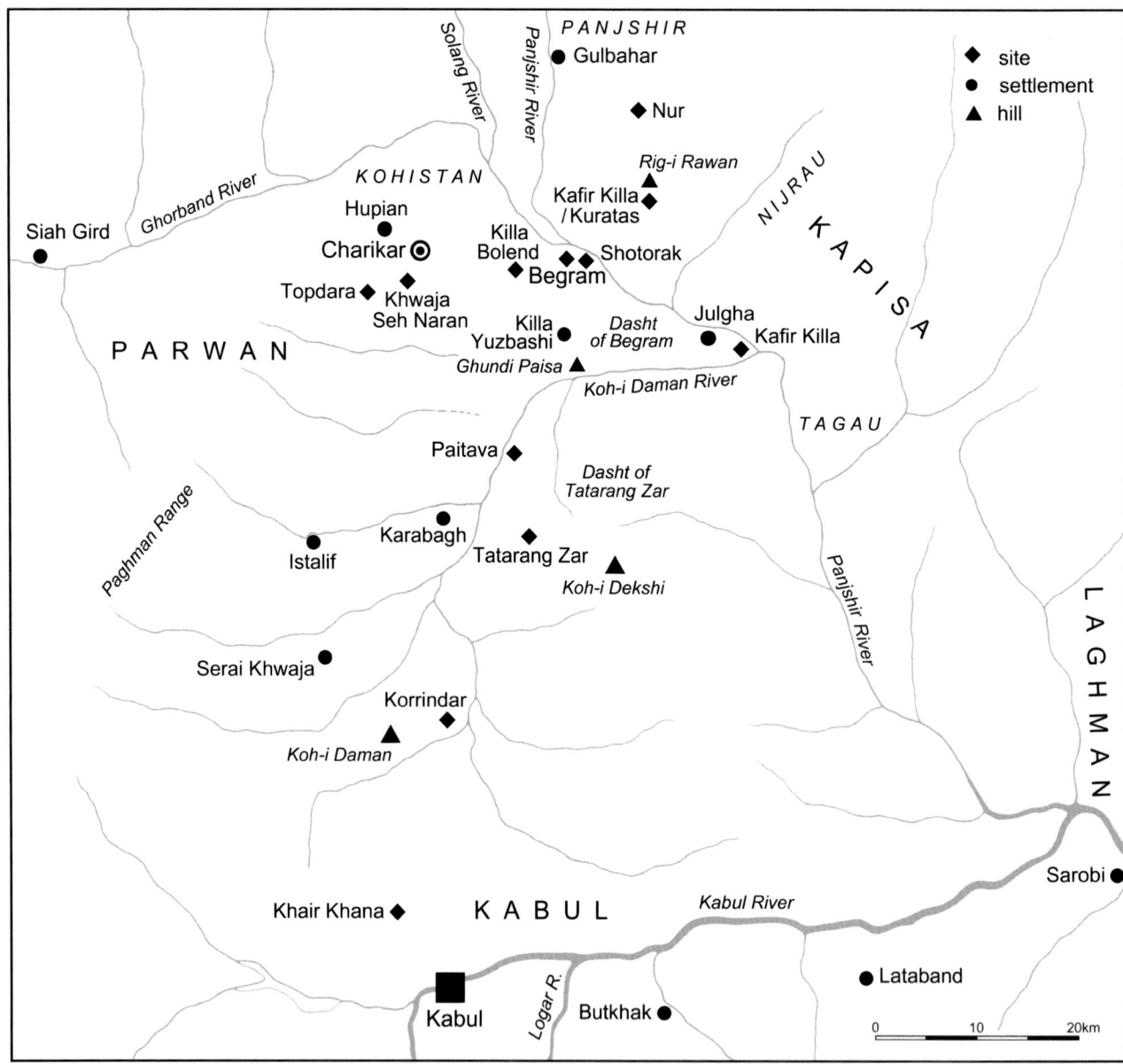

Figure 1 Map of the Kabul–Begram region

coins in vain. We then proceeded across the plain until we reached a tope at the eastern extremity of Koh-i Bacha [Koh-i Top, see Fussman 2008, pp. 157–60, pl. 96]. ... Of this monument I made a sketch [**Vol. I, Fig. 74**], and noted my observations of the country. When we were well back ... [at] Killa Khwaja ... we heard fresh tales of Begram and the treasures found there, and my curiosity was so intensely excited that I determined to revisit it, taking with us Mir Afzil, the [Killa Khwaja] malik's son, who had friends in the vicinity. ... [At] Killa Bolend ... I repaired to the roof of the dyer's house and wished to take bearings, but the wind was too violent to permit me to remain at ease. Mir Afzil returned with Baloch Khan, a fine honest young man, who brought me a present of melons and grapes. This was the commencement of an acquaintance which continued as long as I remained at Kabul; and Baloch Khan greatly assisted me in my subsequent researches, as I could always, when needed, call upon him and his armed followers to attend me in my excursions and to protect the people I sent. He now exerted himself to procure coins; and at last an old defaced one was produced by a Muhammadan, for which I gave two pais, which induced the appearance of others, until the Hindus ventured to bring forth their bags of old monies, from which I selected such as suited my purpose. I had the satisfaction to obtain in this manner some eighty coins, of types which led me to anticipate bright results for the future. The fears and scruples of the owners had been overcome, and I remained some time at Killa Bolend, securing their confidence. It had been feared that I should employ *bigaris*, or forced labourers, to scour the plain in search of antique relics, on which account it had been determined to conceal from me, if possible, their existence. I afterwards learned from a *zirghar*, or goldsmith, of Charikar, that at the time I applied to him he had three *charaks*, or about fifteen pounds [6.8kg] in weight of old coins by him, which his companions deterred him from exhibiting. I made myself well informed as to the mode, and by whom these coins were found; and the clue to them once discovered, the collection became an easy matter, although it subsequently proved that a long time was necessary before I became fully master of the plain. While this traffic was carried on, the report spread that a Feringhi had come to engage soldiers, and crowds came from the neighbouring castles to ascertain the truth, and what pay was given. I now thought it better to leave, and accordingly we retraced our steps to Killa Khwaja.

[Masson 1842, III, p. 154] The boundaries of the *dasht* of Begram are the lands of Julgha to the east, the level plain of

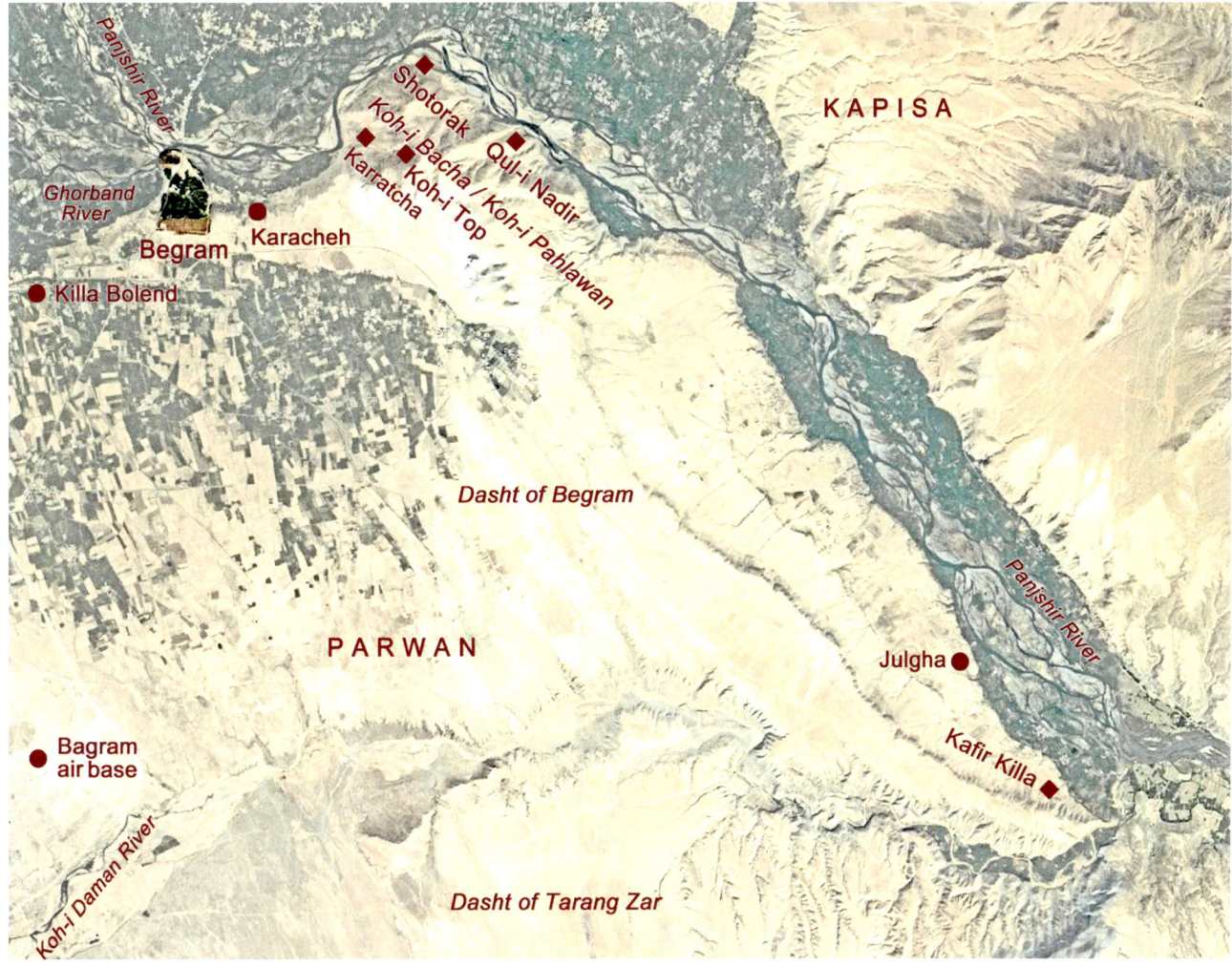

Figure 2 Begram region (Digital Globe Corporation WorldView-3 satellite image, courtesy of the Afghan Heritage Mapping Partnership, University of Chicago Oriental Institute)

Mahighir [now the site of Bagram air base] to the west, the river of Kohistan to the north [i.e. Ghorband River], and to the south what is called the river of Koh-i Daman [**Fig. 2**]. At the north-west angle of the *dasht* is the small village of Killa Bolend, ... and at the south-west angle are three castles, called Killa Yuzbashi [lat. 34°55´N, long. 69°15´E], distant from Killa Bolend about four miles [6.45km].

[Masson 1836a, pp. 1–2] The *dasht* or plain of Begram bears N15E from the modern city of Kabul [lat. 34°59´N, long. 69°19´E]; ... the direct distance may probably be about 25 British miles [40km]. It is situated at the south-east point of the level country of the Kohistan, in an angle formed by the approach of a lofty and extensive mountain range, radiating from the superior line of the Caucasus [Hindu Kush] on the one side, and by the inferior range of [the] Siah Koh on the other. The former range separates the Kohistan from the populous valley of Nijrau, and the latter, commencing about 15 miles [24km] east of Kabul, gradually sinks into the plain of Begram. East of the Siah Koh is a hilly, not mountainous, tract called Koh-i Safi, which intervenes between it and the extensive valleys of Tagau. Through the open space, extending from west to east, between these two hill ranges, flows the [Panjshir] river formed by the junction of the streams of Ghorband and Panjshir, and which forms the northern boundary of the site of Begram. ... The *dasht* of Begram is comprised in an extensive district of the Kohistan called Khwaja Khedari; to the north, the plain has an abrupt descent into cultivated lands and pastures ... which at the north-western point interpose between it and the river for the extent of perhaps a mile [1.6km], or until the river leaves the base of a singular eminence called Burj Abdullah, which from the vast mounds on its summit was undoubtedly an appurtenance of the ancient city [**Figs 3–4**]. East of this eminence another small space of cultivated land with two or three castles, called Karacheh interposes between a curvature in the direction of the abrupt boundary of the *dasht*, and the direct course of the river [Qaracha: see https://forum.valka.cz/attachments/5461/bagram_1_.pdf. Hiebert and Cambon 2011, p. 134: Qaracheh; 'Bagram District Parwan Province 2004']; east of Karacheh rises a low detached hill, called Koh-i Bacha, which has an extent of about a mile and a half [2.4km], intruding for that distance between the level *dasht* and the river; at the eastern extremity of Koh-i Bacha is one of those remarkable structures we call *topes* [**Vol. I, p. 83, Fig. 74**].

According to Ball and Gardin, Killa Bolend comprises many mounds, including a large one that may have been a stupa (1982, no. 838, Qal'a-i Buland, lat. 34°59´N, long. 69°17´E). Karratcha – a variation of Karacheh and Qaracha – is the name of a Buddhist monastery near the site of Shotorak, 1km east of Begram on the western escarpment of the hill ranging west to east, called 'Koh-i Bacha' by Masson (now known as Koh-i Pahlawan). The site was excavated by Barthoux in 1925 (Cambon 1996, pp. 20–6). The 'tope' Masson mentions is identified as Koh-i Top by Fussman (2008, pp. 157–60, pl. 96). It is located on the south-eastern

Charles Masson and Begram | 7

Figure 3 (above) Aerial image of the site of Begram in June 2012 (US Buckeye Program, courtesy of the Afghan Heritage Mapping Partnership, University of Chicago Oriental Institute)

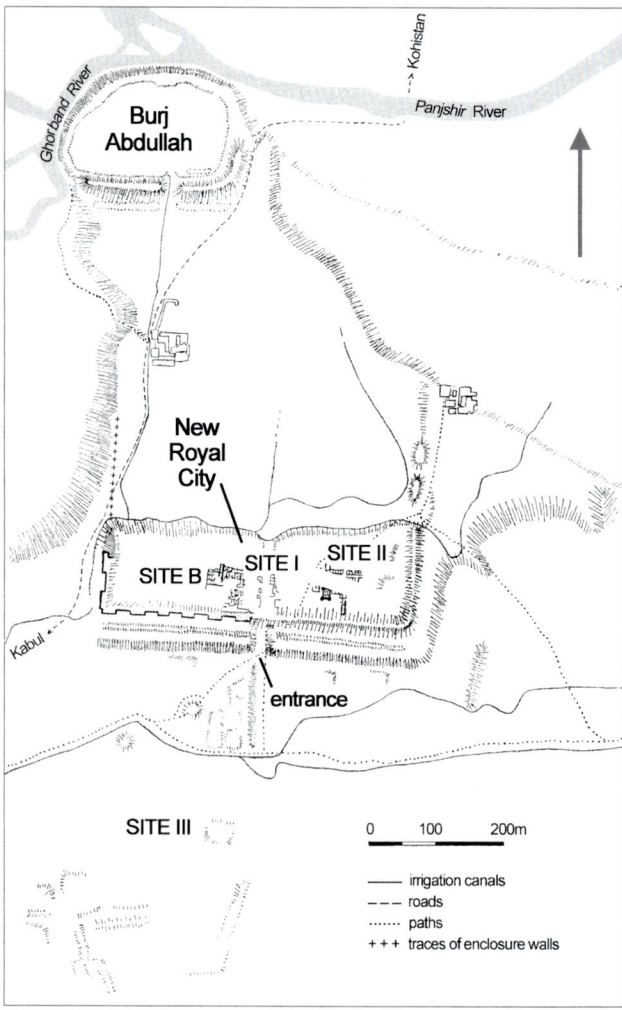

Figure 4 (right) Plan of Begram (after Ghirshman 1946, pl. XXIV; Ball and Gardin 1982, p. 425, pl. 9)

slope of Koh-i Bacha. Shotorak and Qul-i Nadir lie on the north-eastern slopes bordering the Panjshir River (Fussman 2008, pp. 162–9). Masson continues (1836a, pp. 2–4):

> Parallel to Koh-i Bacha, on the opposite [eastern] side of the [Panjshir] river, are the castles and cultivated lands called Muhammad Rakhi [Maḥmūd Raqi], and beyond them a sterile sandy tract gradually ascending to a celebrated hill and ziyarat, named Khwaja Raig Rawas [Rig-i Rawan], and thence to the superior hill range before mentioned; east of Koh-i Bacha, the level plain extends for about a mile [1.6km], until the same character of abrupt termination sinks it into the low lands of Julgha, where we find numerous castles, much cultivated land and, as the name Julgha implies, a large extent of *chaman* or pasture. The lands of Julgha to the east form the boundary of the *dasht* of Begram, to the south its boundary may be considered the stream called the river of Koh-i Daman, which after flowing along the eastern portion of Koh-i Daman and receiving what may be spared after the irrigation of the lands from the streams of Shakr Dara, Beydak, Tugah, Istalif, &c. falls into the joint river of Ghorband and Panjshir at a point below Julgha. Beyond the river of Koh-i Daman, a barren sandy soil ascends to the skirts of the Siah Koh [the range of hills separating the *dasht* of Begram from that of Tarang Zar: **Fig. 2**] and Koh-i Safi [a hilly tract between the Tagau valley and Panjshir River]. Among the topographical features of the *dasht* of Begram may be noted three small black hills or eminences, detached from each other, which in a line and contiguous to each other, arise from the surface of the soil a little north of the river of Koh-i Daman. To the west of Begram are the level lands of Mahighir; at the north-west angle of the plain is the small village of Killa Bolend. … From Killa Bolend to Julgha a distance occurs of about four and a half to five miles [7.2–8km]; from Julgha to the skirts of the Siah Koh, about six miles [9.65km]; from the termination of Siah Koh to Killa Yuzbashi may also be about six miles [9.65km], and from Killa Yuzbashi to Killa Bolend about four miles [6.45km] as just noted [**Fig. 1**]. The whole of the intermediate space between these points, and even beyond to the south-east and south-west, is covered with fragments of pottery, lumps of dross iron &c. and here are found the coins, seals, &c. … Notwithstanding the vast numbers of such relics discovered on this extent of plain, we have hardly any other evidence that a city once stood on it, so complete and universal has been the destruction of its buildings. But in many places, we may discover, on digging about the depth of a yard [91.4cm], lines of cement, which seem to denote the outlines of structures and their apartments; on the edge of the plain where it abruptly sinks into the low lands of Baltu Khel, from Killa Bolend to Karacheh, is a line of artificial mounds; on the summit of the eminence called Burj Abdullah are also some extraordinary mounds, as before noted, and contiguous to the south is a large square described by alike surprising mounds; on one side of this square, the last year, a portion sank or subsided, and disclosed that these mounds were formed or constructed of huge unburnt bricks, two spans square [45.7cm] and one span [22.8cm] in thickness. This circumstance also enabled me to ascertain that the original breadth of these stupendous walls … could not have been less than sixty feet [18.29m]; probably much more.

[Masson 1842, III, pp. 156–8] In specifying the extensive limits over which coins and other relics are brought to light, we must not be understood as conveying the notion that the entire space defined by them was once filled by a city. … If asked to assign the site of the city, I should, fixing the enormous square enclosure south of Burj Abdullah as the fort, or citadel, locate it between those remains and the western portion of the plain, or towards Killa Bolend and Mahíghír, in which space coins are found in far less number, while scoriae [slag], lumps of iron, fragments of glazed earthenware (the latter a peculiar token, in opposition to the common baked pottery which is scattered over the whole plain) are found more abundantly than in other spots. In this part also, besides the remains of walls, may be traced the courses of ancient canals, by their parallel lines of embankment. The presence of mounds, the casual discovery of coins, and other antiques, are generally supposed to indicate the site of a city … great numbers of coins and other relics, discovered on the *dasht* of Begram … were mingled with … rings, seals, beads, ear-rings, small images, &c., [and frequently] arrowheads. … The collections from Begram have furnished a great variety of engraved signets, and many gems, curious as specimens of art, with multitudes of small sculptured animals, particularly of birds. … [An] immense distribution of fragments of pottery [has] by the abrasion of the surface of the soil … become exposed; hence we discover the fragments mixed with the soil, and the coins and other relics originally deposited with them. … Entire jars are, indeed, sometimes found: and the lines of cement, before noted, as discoverable about a yard below the surface, if horizontal, may indicate the floors on which these jars were placed; and, if perpendicular, the separation of one deposit from the other.

The traditions of the country assert the city of Begram to have been the Sheher Yunan, or Greek city, overwhelmed by some natural catastrophe, and the evidence of its subterranean lines and apartments is appealed to support them.

[Masson 1836a, p. 4] It is not however improbable that this city, like many others, may owe its destruction to the implacable rage of the barbarous and ruthless Genghis [Khan 1162–1227]. That it existed for some time after the Muhammadan invasion of these countries is evidenced by the numerous coins of the Caliphs found on the site.

Skirting the south-eastern limits of the plain of Koh-i Daman, Masson noted (1842, III, p. 143):

Under the hills parallel to our course is the site of a city, called, by tradition, Tatarang Zar [Ball and Gardin 1982, no. 1154, lat. 34°49′N, long. 69°13′E]. It extends for a long distance, but appears to be a continuation of the ancient sepulchral grounds of Begram, from which it is separated only by the river of Koh-i Daman. Coins, trinkets, &c., are frequently picked up on the surface.

Initiating the system of coin and artefact collections at Begram

Masson's first visit to Begram in July 1833 put him 'in possession of about eighty' coins (1834, pp. 154–5), which

were of such a type and description as naturally increased my ardour in their research; and, succeeding in allaying the mistrust of the finders, I obtained successive parcels until up to this time [28 November 1833], I have accumulated 1865 copper coins and fourteen gold and silver ones, the latter Brahmanical and Kufic. Of course many of these are of no value, but I persevered in my collection, under the hope of obtaining ultimately perfect specimens of every type and variety of coin; in this I have but partially succeeded, so great is the diversity of coins found in this place, that every fresh parcel of 100 or 150 coins yields me one or more with which I was not previously acquainted. … I suppose that no less a number than thirty thousand coins, probably a much larger number, are found annually on the *dasht* or plain of Begram, independently of rings, seals and other trinkets. Gold and silver coins occur but rarely. … The antique treasures of Begram, until their diversion this present season, have been melted in the mint at Kabul, or by the coppersmiths of that city and of Charikar. The collection of them is made by Afghan shepherds, who sell them by weight at a very low price to itinerant *misghurs* or coppersmiths who occasionally visit their tents, and these again melt them down themselves, or vend them at a small profit to the officers of the mint.

The coins of Begram comprise five grand classes, viz. Greek, Indo-Scythic [Kushan], Parthian, and Guebre [Kushano-Sasanian, see **Pl. 11.1–16**] … which are found in considerable numbers … Brahmanical [Hindu Shahi] and Muhammadan [Ghaznavid, Ghurid, Timurid, Khwarazm Shah], and each of these classes contains many varieties or series. … As Sasanian coins are also discovered, it would seem probable that these countries were also at some period dependent on the princes of the house of Sasan. The Brahmanical [Hindu Shahi] coins, that is, such as are clearly so from their [Deva]nagari inscriptions, I calculate may chronologically be placed in succession to the Sasanian ones; and that they formed the circulating specie of these countries at the period of the Muhammadan invasion is proved by coins with Nagari legends on one side and Kufic on the other.

Elsewhere he describes the finds as (1842, III, pp. 49, 148–50, 158, 160)

coins of ages in regular succession from Alexander to the Muhammadan era [**Figs 21–64**], … arrowheads [**Fig. 133**], … very large numbers of engraved seals, some of them with inscriptions, figures of men and animals, particularly of birds, cylinders, and parallelogramic amulets [box seals] with sculptured sides [**Figs 72–5**], rings [**Figs 78–92**], and a multitude of other trinkets, and miscellaneous articles, generally of brass and copper [including] … a great variety of engraved signets, and many gems [**Figs 65–71**], curious as specimens of art, with multitudes of small sculptured animals, particularly of birds [**Figs 100–4, 106, 130**]. …

The discovery of so interesting a locality as that of Begram imposed upon me new, agreeable, and I should hope, not unprofitable employment. I availed myself of every opportunity to visit it, as well with a view to secure the rich memorials of past ages it yielded as to acquire a knowledge of the adjacent country.

Before the commencement of winter [1833], when the plain, covered with snow, is of course closed to research, I had accumulated one thousand eight hundred and sixty-five copper coins [1865], besides a few silver ones, many rings, signets, and other relics. The next year, 1834, the collection amounted to one thousand nine hundred copper coins [1,900], besides other relics. In 1835 it increased to nearly two thousand five hundred copper coins [2,500], and in 1836 it augmented to thirteen thousand four hundred and seventy-four copper coins [13,474; *sic*: **F526/1n**: 3,474 coins, see Appendix 3, pp. 331–3 below]. In 1837, when I had the plain well under control, and was enabled constantly to locate my people upon it, I obtained sixty thousand copper coins [60,000], a result at which I was well pleased, having at an early period of my researches conjectured that as many as thirty thousand coins [30,000] might be annually procured. The whole of the coins, and other

1. Begram (total coins: 72,252)

Collections sent to East India Company							Retained by Masson	Total
Coins	1833	1834	1835	18–10–36	15–10–37	EIC Total	8–5–38 + 30–6–38	Total
Gold	1					1	7 + 1 = 8	9
Silver	13	?	?	3,500	3,087	6,00	2,898 + 142 = 3,040	9,640
Copper	1,865	1,930	2,500	3,474	30,345	39,614	20,689 + 1,800 = 22,489	62,603
Total	1,879	1,930	2,500	6,974	33,432	46,715	25,537	72,252
Gems					9	9	53 + 4 = 57	65
Silver rings							32	32
Copper rings		?			256	256	816 + 148 = 964	1,072
Copper seals		?	8			8		156
Ornaments					370	370		370

2. Kabul bazaar (total coins: c. 4,614)

Collections sent to East India Company							Retained by Masson	Total
Coins	1833	1834	1835	18–10–36	15–10–37	EIC Total	8–5–38 + 30–6–38	Total
Gold			32	31	70	133	45	178
Silver		192	501	369	462	1524	[301 + 22 = 323] 324	1,848
Copper		410		c. 1,000	400–500	c. 1,910	678	c. 2,588
Total		602	533	c. 1,400	c. 1,032	c. 3,567	1,047	c. 4,614
Gems		8	3		33	44	9	53
Ornaments					1	1	9	10

3. Coins from elsewhere (c. 4,951 coins)

Coins	1833	1834	1835	1836	1837	1843	Total
Hazarajat silver	120						120
Charikar copper		?					?
Jalalabad copper	117	248		c. 500	204		c. 1,069
Ghazni gold	102						102
Charikar, Jalalabad, Ghazni copper			c. 3,000				c. 3,000
Peshawar copper			c. 400				c. 400
Total	339	248+	c. 3,400	c. 500	204		c. 4,691
Cairo copper						260	260
Total							c. 4,951

4. Sum of entire collection

Coins	1833–43
Begram	72,252
Kabul	c. 4,614
Elsewhere	c. 4,951
Total	c. 81,817
Gems	118
Rings	1,104
Seals	156
Ornaments	380

Table 1 Masson's recorded quantities of coins, gems, rings, seals and ornaments collected 1833–43. Sources: Masson 1834, p. 154; 1836a, pp. 10–13, 15; E161/VII ff. 21, 24, 30, 33, 36, 38; F526/1e, m. See also Appendix 2, pp. 329–30 below

---

antiquities from Begram, with several thousands of other coins, brought to light in various parts of Afghanistan, have been forwarded to the Honourable the East India Company. …

It may be superfluous to dwell upon the importance of the Begram collections; independently of the revelation of unknown kings and dynasties, they impart great positive knowledge, and open a wide field for speculation and inquiry on the very material subjects of languages and religions prevailing in Central Asia during the dark periods of its history. … The reasons which confine me to a mere allusion to the results of my researches at Begram [i.e. the fact that all the finds had been forwarded to London] need not restrict me as regards the locality, which, besides its pretensions to be considered Alexandria ad Caucasum, has other claims to notice.

Masson's identification of Begram as one of the cities founded by Alexander was considered correct by Paul Bernard (1982, pp. 217– 42), with Ai Khanum being identified as Alexandria on the Oxus.

Summary of collections from Begram and elsewhere (Table 1)

It is impossible to arrive at an exact total for the numbers of coins collected from Begram in the years 1833–8, since Masson clearly had problems keeping track of the amounts himself. For instance, in his first 'Memoir', he initially gives a total for 1833 of 1879 coins (1865 + 14, see **Table 1.1**), but a few pages later includes an additional 568 Greek coins, giving a grand total of 2447 coins for that year (1834, pp. 154, 163. See also **F526/1n**: Appendix 3 below).

According to Masson's second 'Memoir' (1836a, p. 10):

> It had been my intention this year to have secured every coin of every description that should be picked up from the *dasht* of Begram. [A young man was dispatched to Kohistan] and to him was confided the collection of all he might be able to procure. On my eventually reaching Kabul [from Jalalabad], the young man joined with 1320 coins, from the appearance of which it was evident he had selected, and not, as ordered, taken all that were offered. [Due to the unsettled political state of

Kohistan the nomadic shepherds – 'the principal finders of these coins' – had not visited the plains as usual]. … I twice repaired to Begram, and at various intervals despatched my young men, and the total result … this year was 5 silver and 1900 copper coins.

In the Proceedings of the Asiatic Society of Bengal for 6 January 1836, it is recorded that 'the memoir had been detained in Capt. Wade's possession, since the month of June last [1835], in consequence of some official correspondence with Col. Pottinger to whom the coins to which it relates have been finally forwarded for the Bombay Government' (Proc. ASB 1836, p. 54). This indicates that Masson was compiling the account in late 1834 or early 1835. The question as to which year he is referring is answered by a letter dated September 1834, where the same figure of 1,320 coins is mentioned and he adds 'since my arrival I have personally collected 1000 more' (**P/387/71** 6–9–1834), thereby producing a total of 2,320 coins for 1834. The figures given elsewhere for 1835 are 2,393 and 2,500 coins respectively (**F526/1a**, k: **Vol. II, pp. 81, 101** and p. 332 below), whereas the figures for 1834 – 1,928 and 1,930 coins – while also not exact, relate more closely to the 1,900 recorded above (**E161/VII, f. 20**; **F526/1a**, k: **Vol. II, pp. 81, 101**; **F526/1n**, Appendix 3, p. 332 below). There is further confusion in **F526/1k, f. 3**, where the Begram coins for 1833 are listed as 1930, while the coins collected for 1834 number 2,220. The largest discrepancy in the numbers of copper coins however occurs for 1836: in **F526/1n** the figure given is 3,474, while elsewhere the figure of 'thirteen thousand four hundred and seventy-four copper coins' is spelled out (i.e. 13,474: Masson 1842, III, p. 148).

It is probably safe to assume that the totals given for the coin collections for 1833–5 included in the first two parcels, dispatched on 11 December 1834 and 18 October 1836 respectively, are more or less accurate (see **E/4/1062** §§ 7, 10; **Vol. I, pp. 22–3**). Both collections were forwarded to the India Museum in London, but with extractions en route (see below). The muddle in quantities first seems to arise from the split of the 1836 collections (January–18 October and 19 October–31 December) between the second and third dispatched collections. On arrival at the Asiatic Society in Calcutta in December 1838, the second parcel was estimated to contain 'four to six thousand' coins. This 'magnificent collection' is described as being 'large enough to supply all the museums in Europe … and in one bag there are about two thousand copper coins' (Proc. ASB 1838, pp. 1047–8). Later the amount is estimated as 'some hundred gold and silver coins and several thousand copper coins' (Proc. ASB 1839a, p. 74). Discrepancies in quantities aside, the other point worth noting is Masson's instruction in 1835 not to select, but indiscriminately to take 'all that were offered', evidently regardless of condition. This could be a reason why the coin numbers jump from 3,474 (elsewhere estimated as c. 5,000: **F526/1k f. 3**; **Vol. II, p. 101**) for 1836, to 33,432 for 1837 and to 25,537 for 1838.

The third parcel of 33,432 coins, comprising the collections made after 18 October 1836, was sent from Kabul to Kutch for the East India Company on 15 October 1837 (**P/389/18** 10–9–1839). This package included any coins acquired between October and December 1836, so could conceivably account for the 10,000 coins added to 3,474 for 1836. But this means that 10,000 is duplicated by being included in the total for 1837. As already noted, the figure for October–December 1836 is also said to be only c. 5,000 coins (**F526/1n**; 1842, III, p. 148; **F526/1k f. 3**). So the additional prefix of '1' (i.e. 10,000) to 3,474 is probably an error, but there is no way of checking.

A fourth group, comprising coins collected after October 1837, was taken to Peshawar by Masson when he relocated there with Alexander Burnes at the end of April 1838 (Whitteridge 1986, p. 131). However, he continued to receive parcels of coins from Kabul until he left Peshawar towards the end of the year: the latest reference is to coins from Kabul bazaar 'collected since 11 November 1838' (Appendix 2, p. 329, **F526/1m**, Bag 'F'). He appears to have brought this fourth and final collection himself to Pottinger at Tatta in Sind. He spent 1839 between here and Karachi, writing his account for *Ariana Antiqua* and the first draft of his *Narrative of Various Journeys* (**Vol. I, p. 13**).

Questioning the reality and fate of the estimated 60,000 to 80,000 coins

A letter to Pottinger from the Government of India, dated 6 March 1839 (**E/4/1065** 25–3–1840, §§ 2, 4) states that:

> With regard to the dispatch of any future collections … we approve of the arrangement … that instead of being exposed to the risk and delay of being sent to England via Bengal [as had happened with the second dispatch of 1836], they shall be sent to us direct, after a selection shall have been made from them by qualified persons in Bombay, of duplicate specimens for transmission to the Supreme Government.
>
> … respecting the copper coins which Mr Masson … states it to be his wish to retain on his own account after they shall have been transmitted to us, and a selection shall have been made from them of any we may think it desirable to place in our cabinets. Mr Masson estimates the number at 60,000, of which 35,000 were sent from Kabul in October 1837, and the rest are in his hands. The cost of procuring them he calculates at 960 rupees, for which he holds himself answerable. We have no objection to comply with his desire, and shall be prepared, when the coins reach us, and have been examined for the purpose of selection, to transfer all that we do not require to any person authorised by Mr Masson to receive them on his account.

In the correspondence between Masson and the East India Company from 1839 onwards, the fate of the '60,000 coins' collected from Begram between 18 October 1836 and 30 June 1838 is raised several times (**E/4/1065** 25–3–1840, § 4; **E161/VII f. 74**: 27–11–1847, §§ 2–3), but the sum is never questioned by the Bombay authorities, suggesting that it was accepted as correct. This lends authenticity to Masson's figures. Moreover, as he is a reliable witness in everything else regarding his collections, why should he exaggerate here, especially since the estimated figures could be checked? Yet the fact also remains that we can now only account for less than c. 10,000 coins and the fate of the rest can only be guessed at.

The Supreme Government of India clearly agreed to the proposal that Masson should be allowed to keep all items acquired after 15 October 1837 (25,537 coins: see **Table 1.1**; **E/4/1065**, 6–3–1839, § 4; **E161/VII f. 74**, Masson to

Box I	Year	Quantity	Total weight	1 tola = 11.664g	Average weight
Bag IV	1836	3,500 silver coins	25¼ tolas		294.52g	0.08g (F526/1e)
Bag V	1837	3,087 silver coins	173 tolas	2.02kg		0.69g
Bag XVI	–	copper coins	3,013¼ tolas	35.15kg		
Bag B	1838	very small coins	117¼ tolas	1.37kg		
		silver fragments	4½ tolas		52.48g	
		silver coins	3¾ tolas		43.74g	
		[Total]	3,337 tolas	38.92kg		
Box II	–	18,953 copper coins	4041¼ tolas	47.14kg		2.49g
		[Total Boxes I–II]	7,378¼ tolas	86.07kg		

Table 2 Weighed coins in Boxes I and II: collections 19 October 1836–December 1838 (F526/1e, m)

Melvill, 27-11-1847, §§ 2–3; **BM-OP 20-6-1847**). He lists these as 8 gold, 3040 silver and 22,489 copper coins; 32 silver rings; 963 copper seals, rings, figures '&c.'; 57 gems and beads (**Table 1.1**; **E161/VII f. 33**, where there are slight discrepancies, i.e. 56 gems rather than 57 gems and beads, and '964 copper seals, rings etc'. instead of 963). There is again a lack of correspondence with the tallies cited in **F526/1n** (Appendix 3), of 18,559 copper coins, 9 intaglios, 30 silver rings, but the total of 964 seals and rings is the same. However some of his figures are clearly only estimates for he admits that the quantities for the 1836 and 1838 collections 'are unknown, but as they continually increased, it may be reckoned that the bazaar of Kabul supplied altogether from 20,000 to 25,000 copper coins' (**F526/1n**, Appendix 3, p. 332 below).

Back in London in the 1840s, Masson attempted to quantify the number of coins collected between 1833 and 1838 and produced the following figures for Begram (**F526/1e: Vol. II, p. 68**):

Coins	1833	1834	1835	1836	1837	1838
Silver	13	?	?	3,500	3,087	3,040
Copper	1,865	1,930	2,500	? [3,474]	30,345	22,489

He says further that:

> This account very imperfectly sets forth the extent of the Begram collections as to silver and copper coins. The numbers of silver coins for 1835 and 1836 I cannot learn from the lists furnished to me [by the Bombay authorities] (my own having been lost at Kabul) and the collections of 1838 only include coins up to the month of May of that year, whereas the collections continued to October. Allowing moderately for these collections the aggregate of coins procured from Begram from 1833 to 1838 will not be less than silver coins 7,500 [and] copper coins 80,000 [**Table 1.1** 9,640 and 62,603 respectively]. Besides these a few gold coins, engraved stones, and a vast number of miscellaneous articles were obtained – the numbers of each variety I cannot state from the lists, which yet enable me to set down some of them by which the remainder may be inferred.

The last collection recorded by Masson is dated 30 June 1838, not October (when he quit Peshawar). The entire amount for 1838 is given above (2,898 + 142 = 3,040 silver coins; 20,689 + 1800 = 22,489 copper coins: **Table 1.1**). The extant archival records list a sum of 9 gold coins, 9640 silver coins and 62,603 copper coins, i.e. a grand total of 72,252 coins from Begram (Masson 1834, p. 154; 1836a, pp. 10–13, 15; **E161/VII ff. 21, 24, 30, 33, 36, 38; F526/1e, P/387/71 6-9-1834**). Computation of all the data from Begram, Kabul bazaar and elsewhere (**Table 1.2–4**) gives a final figure of c. 81,817 coins, 118 gems, 1104 rings, 156 copper seals and 380 miscellaneous ornaments. But as the contradictory figures cited above make clear, this is a very rough estimate at best, not an exact total.

Apart from Masson's records, an independent list (already mentioned above) survives among his papers (Appendix 2 pp. 329–30: **F526/1m**, ff. 1–3). This was compiled by J.P. Willoughby, Secretary to the Bombay Government, and witnessed by J. Williams (President), L.R. Reid (Chief Secretary) and P.M. Melvill, Political Agent in Kutch, who signed in person. It is written on paper watermarked 1838. However, since Melvill only served as Agent in Kutch from March 1840 until June 1841, the document must have been created during that specific period. It was apparently compiled by the Bombay authorities, prior to sending the collections to London. The latest items included are 59 gold, 131 silver and 6 copper coins '&co. from Bazaar Kabul collected since 11 November 1838' (Appendix 2, **F526/1m**: 'Bag **F**'). This means that Masson's personal collection, i.e. everything acquired after 15 October 1837, was also forwarded with the October 1836–15 October 1837 collections destined ultimately for the India Museum in London.

Masson notes that 'the greater portion' of the 3,087 silver coins from Begram in 1837 'are minute coins' (**E161/VII f. 31**). The 15 October 1837 – 30 June 1838 collections similarly included 216 minute silver coins procured from Begram and 16 minute coins from Kabul bazaar (**F526/1c-d**). Also among the Kabul bazaar purchases after 15 October 1837 are 496 minute unidentified silver coins, possibly a hoard, 'found in one spot with the 36 Sasanians … of a singular and novel type' (**E161/VII f. 32**).

The question is how many of these 'minute silver coins' were actual coins and, secondly, how small does a coin have to be to qualify as 'minute'? Coins now in the collection which weigh less than a gram and could conceivably fit this category are 9 silver Hyrcodes (0.45g–0.97g); 17 silver and 57 copper alloy Amirs of Sind (0.18g–0.55g); and 77 copper alloy Hun issues (0.18g–0.98g). There are also 130 copper alloy quarter-drachms of Huvishka weighing between 0.95g and 1.95g.

Willoughby (**F526/1m**: Appendix 2, **Fig. 136** below) lists some of the contents of Box **I** (Bags **I–XVII** and **A–G**) and

Box **II** both in quantity and also tola weight (**Table 2**). For example, Box **II** is said to hold two large bags of copper coins weighing 4041¼ tolas (47.14kg, where one tola equals 11.664g) and to have contained 24 smaller bags with a total of 18,953 coins (giving an average coin weight of *c.* 2.49g). But if it is assumed that the bags included, for instance, 2,953 coins with an average weight of 8.5g (total weight: 25.1kg), the average weight of the remaining 16,000 coins would be 1.38g (total weight: 22.04kg).

In another case (Box **I**, Bag **V**), 3,087 'minute' silver coins, 'with 17 or 18 Bactrians and a large number of punched square coins and many cubic ones' from Begram 1837 are said to weigh 173 tolas (2.02kg). If 18 'Bactrians' are interpreted as Indo-Greek drachms, with an average weight of 2.28g (total weight 41.15g; a calculation derived from 22 silver drachms now in the Masson collection), the remaining 3,069 coins had a total weight of 1.98kg and an average of 0.64g per 'minute' coin. In addition, a large quantity of both silver and copper tiny fragments of coins and other artefacts survive, which could further account for the huge numbers recorded by Masson in 1837–8 (**Fig. 6**).

Two bags unearthed in the British Library's India Office Collections in 2004 seem to relate to Willoughby's list, for they are labelled in ink respectively '**F**' and '**k**' (**Fig. 5**) in the same handwriting (**F526/1m**, ff. 2–3; see **Fig. 142**). There is no reference to Bag '**k**' in the list, but the fact that it is not written as a capital letter suggests that it was a subsidiary bag. Bag **E**, for example, contained twelve subsidiary bags (**a–l**?); Bag **F** contained nine (**a–i**?). The contents of Bag **k** – a mix of 811 coin and ornament fragments (registered as 321 groups and individual items: IOLC.5410–5486, IOLC.7513–7628; IOLC.7634–7732) – confirms that they are part of the Masson collection, while the distinctive patina of their uncleaned state confirms a Begram provenance (**Fig. 6**).

The situation with Bag **F** is more complicated. According to **F526/1m**, the bag contained '9 Bags Gold, Silver coins &co. from Bazaar Kabul collected since 11 November 1838'. This included 60 gold, 131 silver and 6 copper coins. But in 2004 it contained only 121 copper alloy coins, which suggests that the original contents had been removed and the bag reused. This is confirmed by a faded note in a different handwriting on the back of the bag: 'Jas. Prinsep 118 Coins Kanerkos [Kanishka] Types'. Apart from five coins (Azes II: IOLC.7513; Yaudeya, Kota and two from Kashmir: IOLC.7629–7633), the remainder are all Kushan issues (116 coins) ranging from Kujula Kadphises to Kanishka II, but are predominantly of Kanishka I and Huvishka, so broadly fit the description on the bag.

A further complication is that Bags **D** and **E** each list four bags of copper coins which bear the suffix T.H.P. and H.P. respectively. Given the subsequent Bag **F** connection with James Prinsep, it is tempting to equate these initials – albeit in the first instance in the wrong order – with his brother, Henry Thoby Prinsep (1792–1878), Secretary to Government (i.e. Willoughby's counterpart) in the Bengal Civil Service and Vice-President of the Asiatic Society of Bengal, who had chaired the Society's meeting in May 1839, when Masson's 1835–6 'large collection of coins and relics' had been exhibited (Proc. ASB 1839a; **Vol. II, p. 78**). So although

Figure 5 Bag k (contained 118 coin and ornament fragments collected from Begram *c*. 1838). India Office Loan Collection

documentation is lacking, it is possible that eight subsidiary bags of copper alloy coins from Bags **D** (2,544 coins) and **E** (105 coins) were extracted for Bengal before the remaining coins were sent on to London, as suggested in the Government of India letter of 6 March 1839 (**E/4/1065** 25–3–1840, § 2, see above p. 11).

In his letter of 27 November 1847, Masson specifically mentions his claim 'to the particular coins contained in the Bag A' (**E161/VII f. 74**). This comment links directly to Bag **A** in Willoughby's list, which is said to contain 25 gold coins, a bag of silver coins and 26 copper coins, with the additional comment that 'In Mr Masson's note of 7 December 1838, stating that they cost Rs 270 and were purchased from his own funds, the 26 copper coins are not mentioned'. In the same letter Masson says that

> I would farther profit by this opportunity to urge upon the Honourable Court's attention, that of the 60,000 copper coins &co. which the Honourable Court by their public dispatch to the Bombay Government, in the first instance, and afterwards by letter to my own address of the 4 September 1845, engaged to make over to me, I have only received 35,340, and these I dare to assert were not the coins for which I applied. It is true that I have since received a letter from the Honourable Court, expressing that it was never intended to give me any other, but [as] the statement must have been made unmindful of the dispatch to the Bombay Government, I would rather imagine the Honourable Court's instructions upon the subject have been neglected.

> It might appear absurd to point out to the Honourable Court with regard to these 60,000 coins, that when I permitted a selection of all unique specimens and even of other specimens in better condition than had previously been acquired, I would never have conceived it possible that 25,000 coins should be abstracted, and I need at notice that the large number, so abstracted or withheld, comprise, of course, all the better coins, and indeed all of any value as coins at all. Yet this has been

Figure 6 Sample of the numerous copper alloy object and coin fragments collected from Begram. British Museum, 1880.4118.b

unblushingly done by those directed to carry out the Honourable Court's intentions. This ungenerous treatment is moreover aggravated to me, by the knowledge that not more than 2000 copper specimens are preserved in the Honourable Court's Museum, which I was so anxious to render complete.

After the deaths of Masson on 5 November 1853 and his wife in September 1855 (**FR4–5**), the East India Company paid £100 for all his papers, drawings and coins which were deposited in the Company's Library (**IOR/B/233**). This theoretically brought all 60,000 coins together in one place. But is 60,000 a real or illusory total? To summarise: Willoughby's list includes seven instances of weighed coins, but in only three instances are the quantities given and their average weight fluctuates between a miniscule 0.08g and 2.49g.

It can feasibly be assumed that only the bags in Willoughby's list said to contain huge quantities of 'minute' coins and fragments were generally weighed, although the 18,953 copper coins in Box **II** which were both weighed and counted refutes this. The key phrase in Masson's letter above seems to be 'all of any value as coins at all', suggesting that some may have been too worn to enable identification, or even that a vast quantity were merely fragments. It is difficult to account for huge escalation of coin numbers from 1836 onwards in any other way. Lists 'A' and 'B', inventories of Masson's personal coin collection, compiled in the 1840s, only include a total of 8,157 coins (**F526/1**f-g), a huge reduction of the figure of 35,340 coins cited above. It is also worth noting in the same letter of November 1847, Masson says that 'not more than 2,000 copper specimens are preserved in the Honourable Court's Museum', a figure which doubtless included coins from Kabul bazaar and elsewhere.

Surviving records therefore show that four coin collections were dispatched in total from Kabul via Bombay to London. The first, sent on 11 December 1834 (**E161/VII f. 20**) reached London in May 1838 (**E/4/1062**, §10; **Vol. II, p. 71**). The second, sent on 18 October 1836 (**E161/VII f. 27**), travelled via Calcutta, reaching London in March 1840 (**E/4/1065**, §1; **Vol. I, p. 23**). The third was sent on 15 October 1837 (**E/4/1065**, §3); and the fourth, comprising the collections made between 16 October 1837 and *c.* 7 December 1838, Masson appears to have brought himself to Tatta. Both the third and fourth collections were then included in a single package dispatched to London *c.* 1840–1 (**F526/1m**). There was also a fifth collection of 260 Roman coins purchased by Masson in Cairo while travelling back to London in early 1843 (**F526/1**j).

The dispersal of the coin collections

There are three separate collections acquired by the British Museum, which indicate the dispersal of the coins started almost immediately. On 10 February 1938, 116 coins (Indo-Greek, Indo-Scythian, Indo-Parthian and Kushan from the first dispatch) were donated by the East India Company to British Museum (1838,EIC.1–116). Coins of Menander and Apollodotus, for example, in the group are illustrated in Masson's 1835 manuscript and confirm this attribution (1838, EIC.7, 10, 19, 24, 30: **F526/1a**, see below **Pl. 1**, *Figs 14, 13, 17, 16, 6* respectively). On 18 July 1843, nine coins (including Kushan issues) were donated by the East India Silk Company (1843,0718.1–9), followed by a further 59 silver Hun, countermarked Sasanian and Arab-Sasanian coins from the East India Company in 1845 (1845,EIC.1–59).

The Proceedings of the Asiatic Society of Bengal in December 1839 record that 'duplicates' were extracted from the second (1836) collection in Calcutta although no details were given (Proc. ASB 1839b). It is also possible that the eight bags tagged 'T.H.P.' or 'H.T.' (**F526/1m**) were extracted for the Asiatic Society of Bengal prior to the dispatch of the final collections to London in 1840–1.

As already noted above, in his letter of 27 November 1847, Masson complains of only receiving 35,340 coins from the authorities in London, while the '25,000' they retained were 'all the better coins, and indeed all of any value as coins at all'. This appears to be corroborated by his catalogued lists 'A' and 'B' of his own collection, which – as already mentioned – include only 8,157 coins (**F526/1**f-g: **Vol. II, pp. 81–93**). Although in October 1847 he tried to sell the coins to the Austrian government and also to the Norwegian orientalist Christian Lassen (1800–76), professor of ancient Indian languages and literature in Bonn (**E161/VII ff. 71–3**), he does not appear to have had any success. In his letter to Lassen he also says 'if unable to preserve the cabinet complete by handing it over to some institution, I shall then dispose of it by auction here'. There is, however, no record of his having done so and the coins were still in his possession at the time of his death in November 1853. This is confirmed by the illustration in his 'Descriptive Catalogue of Select Coins in the Cabinet of Mr Masson' (**F526/1h**) of a small coin imitating Greek issues (helmeted head of Athena/double-bodied owl) of which there are two examples in the India Office Loan Collection (**Fig. 23.1**; IOLC.110–11). The 'Select Coins' also lists a rare, small, square Eucratides/Bonnets of the Dioscuri coin which has the Greek legend only on the reverse (**Fig. 24.9**; IOLC.202; respectively **Vol. II, pp. 93, 96–7, Figs 101.1–3, 102.15**).

Following the death of his wife in 1855, the East India Company bought all the 'papers, drawings and coins' in Masson's possession at the time of his death (**IOR/B/233**; **Vol. I, p. 14**; **II, Fig. 2**). These were deposited, together with the collections acquired earlier, in the India Museum at East India House, Leadenhall Street, in the City of London. When the East India Company was disbanded in 1858, they came under the jurisdiction of the India Office, a British Government department handling affairs relating to British India. In 1860–1, East India House was sold and demolished. The collections moved temporarily to Fife House near the Embankment, and in 1869 to cramped quarters in the new building in Whitehall housing the India Office (now the Foreign and Commonwealth Office). From 1875 the Museum occupied rented rooms in the South Kensington Museum (now the Victoria and Albert Museum) and in 1879 it closed. A letter, dated 8 July 1879, to the British Museum Trustees announced 'that the Secretary of State for India in Council had decided to remove the contents of the India Museum to other institutions of a kindred nature, their special Indian character to be preserved; proposing that some portion of the collections be placed in the British Museum on terms to be agreed to' (**BM-TM 12–7–1879**; **Vol. II, pp. 106–19**). Ultimately, the collections were divided between the British Museum (antiquities and archaeological collections), Kew Gardens and the South Kensington Museum, while the India Office retained some objects, although these continued being exhibited in the South Kensington Museum (**BM-TM 11–7–1885**; **BM-TM 10–3–1900**; **BM-Asia 22–2–1881**).

After the India Museum closed in 1879, its coin collections were deposited temporarily in the British Museum. In October 1882, a letter from Louis Mallet, Under Secretary of State for India, proposed (**C&M 14–10–1882**):

> on the subject of the collection of coins belonging to the India Office which have been recently placed in deposit at the British Museum, I am directed by the Secretary of State for India in Council to inform you that his Lordship has decided to comply with the request of the Trustees of the British Museum to be allowed to retain permanently in their Department of Coins, such of the India Office pieces as are wanting, or represented by inferior examples, in the Museum collection. …
>
> When the selection of coins required for the National Collection has been duly made by the Museum authorities, and the work of cataloguing has been completed, Lord Hartington requests that the residue of the coins with list attached may be returned to the India Office for subsequent disposal as His Lordship in Council may decide.

A selection of *c.* 2420 coins was made and registered as India Office Collection (IOC). It included an unspecified and unidentified number from the Masson collections. There are also coins from other sources, only a few of which have a traceable provenance, e.g. IOC.158 (**Fig. 29.1A**), a coin of Maues, is recorded as having been acquired from the collection of General Jean-Baptiste Ventura (1795–1858), via the Royal Asiatic Society (Wilson 1841, p. 314, no. 1, Coins pl. VIII.10).

Unlike the coins, the objects from Begram, Kabul bazaar and the Buddhist relic deposits largely retained a record of their association with Masson on transfer to the British Museum, thanks in no small measure to the interest taken in them by A.W. Franks (1826–97), Keeper of British and Medieval Antiquities and Ethnography (**Vol. II, pp. 106–19**). In contrast, the coin collection has had to be reconstructed by identifying coins from Masson's sketches, particularly his 1833–5 manuscript (**F562/1a** below) and above all, from the accurate machine-made drawings in *Ariana Antiqua* (Wilson 1841). Through this process 264 coins have been identified as originating from Begram and Kabul bazaar (116 coins IOC; 50 coins EIC 1838; 9 coins EIC Silk Co. 1843; 59 coins EIC 1845; 14 coins from other sources; 16 coins Asia Department). There are also 118 coins from various Buddhist stupa deposits (**Vol. I, Figs 86.7–8, 13; 117.1–4; 129.1–2; 215; 256.13–23; 281–2**).

The 'residue' of coins retained by the India Office seem to have been dispersed in several ways. A letter from F.W. Thomas, India Office librarian in 1906, describes them as 'mainly copper: the more precious parts of the collection having been withdrawn in the years 1882–7 for presentation to the British Museum and the Indian Museum in Calcutta, while a first remainder was disposed of by sale' (**Vol. II, p. 122: FW 19–11–1906**).

Vincent Smith's *Catalogue of the Coins in the Indian Museum* (1906, p. xvi) states only that its coin collections 'have been dependent almost wholly on presentations of treasure trove made by the central and provincial governments and the Calcutta mint'. However, he includes 885 coins ranging from Greco-Bactrian to Indo-Scythian, Indo-Parthian and Kushan issues of the types only found in Afghanistan and north-west Pakistan. There is thus a strong possibility that their source was the Masson collections, particularly as 465 of the 885 were donated by the Asiatic Society of Bengal, a known recipient of 'duplicates' from the packages sent from Kabul in October 1836 (Proc. ASB, 1839a-b; **Vol. II, p. 78**).

In 1887 the London auctioneers Sotheby, Wilkinson and Hodge sold an unspecified quantity of 'Indo-Scythic [Kushan], Hindu and Indian coins', on behalf of the Government of India (the 'first remainder' mentioned above: 2–6 August 1887, pp. 54–62). The coin groups in the sale identified as originating from the Masson collections are punch-marked and local issues, 'Bactrian' (primarily Indo-Greek and Indo-Scythian), 'Indo-Scythic' (Kushan), Sasanian, 'Indo-Sasanian' (Hun), Arab-Sasanian, Hindu Shahi, Ghaznavid and Khwarazm Shah coins. Also listed are 45 'false Greek and Bactrian coins' (p. 61, lot 868). The Masson coins were sold in 58 lots (out of a total of 148) and comprise 1850+ coins, 3.03kg of 'broken oriental coins' and five 'large' job lots of uncounted 'copper Bactrian, Indo-Scythic &c. coins' (1887, p. 61, lots 874–9). A copy of the sales catalogue in the Department of Coins and Medals is annotated with the names of the purchasers, most notably Alexander Cunningham (p. 45, lot 604: miscellaneous coins including 'Bactrian'; p. 55, lot 753: 48 'Indo-Sasanian' i.e. Hun) and Walter Stanley Talbot (pp. 55–6, lot 746: 51 Sasanian; lot 755: 30 silver Bactrian and Indo-Greek coins including Demetrius, Agathocles, Eucratides, Apollodotus and Antimachus). Alexander Cunningham (1814–93) specifically says that 'a few' (actually 48) of his Hun coins 'were purchased at the sale of the remains of the Masson collection' (1895, pp. 106, 111). Some of these have been identified from Masson's sketches as coins from Hadda stupa 10 (**Pl. 14**; **Vol. I, pp. 185–7**). A Talbot donation to the Museum (1903,1106.1–34) also included coins of Agathocles, Aspavarma and Mujatria which could have been part of the Masson collections.

However, most of the auction bidders for the Masson coins were dealers: particularly Lincoln, Talbot-Ready, Spink and Rollin. W.S. Lincoln & Son subsequently sold 289 Sasanian coins (1913,0411.1–289) to the British Museum, but the Sotheby annotated *Catalogue* makes it clear that the dealer did not acquire any such coins from the 1887 sale. However, 14 coins originally collected by Masson were evidently bought by individual collectors from dealers afterwards and were then sold or donated to the Museum later. They include a unique coin of Menander (**Fig. 26.1**, head of king/dolphin; 1926,0502.1), which shows that the original Museum selection of 2320 IOC coins was not very thorough. Two coins of Gondophares in the Ashmolean Museum were similarly acquired from independent collectors (**Fig. 32.5, 15**: Wilson 1841, p. 339, no. 1, pl. V.14, donated by H.E. Stapleton; Wilson 1841, p. 343, no. 7, pl. VI.2, H. de S. Shortt bequest 1975).

In July 1906 the India Office offered to transfer the whole remaining collection of coins to Cambridge, 'leaving the Fitzwilliam Museum to make what selection may seem good' (**FW 27–7–1906**). On 19 November four boxes of 'mainly copper' coins were duly dispatched, with a request that 'the rejected coins may … be returned' (**FW 19–11–1906**). Eventually in 1912, the residue consisting of a 'considerable mass of mere rubbish' was sent back to the India Office (**FW 15–11–1912**). The *c.* 500 predominantly copper alloy coins retained by the Fitzwilliam do include some of silver, specifically several of the Indo-Greek drachms from the Hazarajat hoard (MacDowall 1991) and a few of the Hun coins from the Hadda stupa 10 relic deposit (**Vol. I, Figs 281.15; 282.4–6, 9, 13–14**). The coins were not registered and are principally recognised from drawings in *Ariana Antiqua* (Wilson 1841) and by type.

As noted by A.W. Franks, a proportion of the non-coin artefacts also appear to have been dispersed in the period between the publication of *Ariana Antiqua* and the closure of the India Museum in 1878 (**Vol. II, pp. 114–18, Figs 103–5**). However, apart from the more spectacular objects (like the Hadda stupa 10 reliquaries **Vol. I, pp. 178–9, Fig. 278.30, 37–8**), these were never documented, so the original extent of the collections can only be imagined from Masson's partially recorded quantities (**Table 1**; **F526/1n**, Appendix 3, pp. 331–3 below; **Vol. II, pp. 66–8**). Like the coins, some of the objects entered the Museum subsequently.

There are 100 seals/intaglios from the collection of Henry Haversham Godwin-Austen (1834–1923), topographer for the Indian Survey (1852–77), donated by his niece Miss Godwin-Austen on 10 August 1943 (Asia Department 1943,1009.1–51; Middle East Department 1943,1009.1–49: the registration numbers are duplicated). According to the Middle East acquisition register 'some' of the 49 'Sasanian rings and gems' are from Masson. The Asia draft acquisition register for this date similarly records 51 seals 'from the collection of the donor's uncle, said to have been collected in N.W. India by "Mason [sic] of the Calcutta Museum" (17 inscribed; 25 of classical type; 9 magical)' (see **Fig. 65**). The reference to Calcutta Museum is best explained as the result of confusing the defunct India Museum in London with the Indian Museum in Calcutta. Secondly, it is inferred that Godwin-Austen acquired them in Calcutta. However, no seals were included in the collections dispatched from Kabul on 18 October 1836 (**E161/VII f. 27**; **Vol. II, p. 64**) and sent via Calcutta, so they could not have numbered among the so-called 'duplicates' extracted by the Asiatic Society of Bengal before the collection was forwarded to London in December 1838. Masson in fact acquired most of the 'engraved gems' or intaglios between October 1837 and June 1838 (**Table 1**; **F526/1k**, **Vol. II, p. 101**; **F526/1n**, Appendix 3, pp. 332–3 below).

A study collection of artefacts from Begram has also recently come to light in the Cambridge Museum of Archaeology and Anthropology. It was acquired from Sir William Ridgeway (1853–1926), Disney Professor of Archaeology in Cambridge, and although not documented, must have originally been gifted by the India Office. Many of the objects (1927.1192) have counterparts in the Masson material from the site in the British Museum. They also have the distinctive Begram patina, caused by a mud coating (the result of being washed out during the rains) which has then undergone a chemical reaction when baked in the hot sun.

Investigations at the start of the Masson Project led to the discovery in 1995 of the 'residue' mentioned in correspondence with the Fitzwilliam Museum. Over 10,000 coins came to light in the India Office Library, by then already part of the British Library, but still located separately in a building at Waterloo. It was decided that these should all be transferred on loan to the Department of Coins and Medals where they were all cleaned and conserved prior to sorting. Three small bags (Bags 'A', 'F' and 'k' discussed above) followed in 2007. These contained 535 coins and 270 groups of small finds (mostly all fragments). Now collectively known as the India Office Loan Collection (IOLC), the coins broadly divide into several distinctive groups: those clearly from Afghanistan collected by Masson; Indian Sultanate and Princely States; 328 Kashmir coins; c. 4,000 South Indian coins; 428 EIC Madras Presidency cash; 117 Roman and 317 silver coins from Java.

Work on the Roman coins by Sushma Jansari showed that they were predominantly types found in South India and Sri Lanka. Further research led to the conclusion that the South Indian and Javanese coins as a whole belonged to the long-lost collection of Colin Mackenzie (1754–1821), which was sold to the East India Company after his death (Jansari 2012, p. 93; 2013, p. 178). Although based for much of his career in Madras and the Deccan, Mackenzie also served as Commanding Engineer in the British capture of Sri Lanka in 1795, was part of the British occupying force in Java in 1811–13, and was appointed the first Surveyor General of India in 1816. Since he also visited numerous places in northern India, including Delhi and Calcutta, it is quite possible that the IOLC Sultanate and Kashmir coin collections can also be assigned to him.

The Masson collection from Begram and Kabul now in the British Museum

Even when using the Collection Online database (www.britishmuseum.org/collection), it is difficult to determine exactly how many coins and artefacts from Masson are now in the British Museum since quantities are dependent on the search parameters, which can vary widely each time. A search on 'coin' for example will include all entries where the word is mentioned even if the object is not a coin. A search for 'Charles Masson' comes up with 9,387 items. Deducting 618 coins and objects from the Buddhist relic deposits produces a total of 8,769 from Begram and Kabul bazaar. But these figures include groups of fragments with a single registration number. 1880.4118.b for example, comprises 347 miscellaneous silver and copper alloy fragments (**Fig. 6**). These groups have been roughly sorted prior to registration: 1880.3742.a includes 75 small fragments of thin-walled metal vessels, while 1880.3716.a consists of 71 copper alloy fragments of pin shafts, bangles and miscellaneous ornaments.

A search specifically on 'coin' and 'Begram' returns 6,864 results (**Figs 21–64**). This includes 667 coins assigned 'Begram or Kabul bazaar', to which should be added 67 coins from Kabul alone, giving a combined total of 7,297 coins (plus 108 stupa coins equals 7,405). There are approximately 1,982 groups of other objects, including c. 550 from relic deposits, leaving c. 1,432 from Begram and Kabul (**Figs 66–134**). The largest groups are 79 intaglios from Kabul, 105 copper alloy seals, many pins, buttons and stoppers in the shape of birds from Begram, as well as 257 finger- and 158 signet-rings from Begram or Kabul bazaar, elsewhere calculated as 1168 (**Vol. II, p. viii**).

Masson's legacy

Masson favoured the identification of Begram as Alexandria ad Caucasum, the city founded by Alexander the Great (336–323 BC) in this region, a suggestion that receives modern support (Masson 1836a, pp. 8–9; Bernard 1982). He therefore dated occupation of the site from the late 4th century BC to the Mongol invasion in the early 13th century (1836a, pp. 3–4):

> The traditions of the country assert the city of Begram to have been overwhelmed by some natural catastrophe, and … the outlines of buildings discoverable beneath the surface seem not to discountenance the tradition. It is not however improbable that this city, like many others, may owe its destruction to the implacable rage of the barbarous and ruthless Genghis [Khan, 1206–27], who … described himself as the 'Scourge of God'.

> That it existed for some time after the Muhammadan invasion of these countries [7th–8th century] is evidenced by the

numerous coins of the Caliphs found on its site. That it [had] ceased to exist at the period of Timur's expedition into India, we have negative proof furnished by his historian Sharaf al-dīn ['Ali Yazdī, *Ẓafarnāmah*], who informs us, that Timur [1370–1405], in his progress … to Kabul, encamped … on the plain of Baran (the modern Bayan, certainly) and that while there, he directed a canal to be cut, which was called Mahighir [see pp. 7–9 above], by which means, the country, before desolate and unproductive, became fertile and full of gardens. … The canal of Mahighir exists at this day. … A considerable village, about one mile [1.6km] west of Begram, has a similar appellation. This canal, derived from the river of Ghorband, at the point where it issues from the hills into the level country, irrigates the lands of Bayan and Mahighir, and has a course of about ten miles [16.09km]. Had the city of Begram then existed, these lands immediately to the west of it would not have been wasted and neglected, neither would Timur have found it necessary to cut his canal, as the city when existing must have been supplied with water from the same source, that is, from the river of Ghorband; and from the same point, that is, at its exit from the hills into the level country.

Masson was also the first to realise that the reverse legends in an unknown script and language (the Indian Prakrit Gandhari) on the bilingual coins of the Indo-Greeks and their successors were direct translations of the Greek on the obverse (**F526/1a f. 30, Pl. 18**). This was the starting point to deciphering Kharoshthi, initially called 'Pahlavi' or the 'Bactrian alphabet' (Prinsep 1838, p. 636). In a note sent in 1834 to Prinsep, Masson pointed out (Prinsep 1835, p. 329)

> the Pahlavi signs which he had found to stand for the words ΜΕΝΑΝΔΡΟΥ, ΑΠΟΛΛΟΔΟΤΟΥ, ΕΡΜΑΙΟΥ, ΒΑΣΙΛΕΩΣ and ΣΩΤΗΡΟΣ. When a supply of coins came into my own hands, sufficiently legible to pursue the inquiry, I soon verified the accuracy of his observation; found the same signs, with slight variation, constantly to recur; and extended the words thus authenticated, to the names of twelve kings, and to six titles or epithets. It immediately struck me that if the genuine Greek names were faithfully expressed in the unknown character, a clue would, through them, be formed to unravel the value of a portion of the alphabet, which might, in its turn, be applied to the translated epithets and titles, and thus lead to knowledge of the language employed.

The original note from Masson demonstrating his discovery – and annotated by Prinsep – survives in one of the bound volumes of Prinsep's manuscripts in the Ashmolean Museum (MSS III, f. 16v). In it Masson transcribes the inscription on the steatite casket from Bimaran stupa 2 (**Vol. I, p. 104, Fig. 117.5**; Appendix 1, **Fig. 138**) and notes 'the commencement of the inscriptions, if they be Pahlavi, read from the right'. He further comments: 'the word Basileos (ΒΑΣΙΛΕΩΣ) or its equivalent in Pahlavi, if such be the language on the Greek Bactrian coins, does not occur here' (i.e. on the Bimaran reliquary). He goes on to list the identified words on coins – Basileos, Soteros, and the genitive case of Menander, Apollodotos and Hermaeus – together with their correct Kharoshthi equivalents.

A folio in Masson's 1835 coin manuscript entitled 'Names, titles and epithets of Bactrian kings in Greek and Bactrian characters' (watermarked G. Wilmot 1832) expands this initial list to fourteen kings ranging from Apollodotus to Wima Kadphises (**F526/1a f. 30, Pl. 18**), with some titles such as *maharajasa* correctly transliterated.

Following up on Masson's discovery, Prinsep independently arrived at a similar result (1835a, pl. XX). His progress can also still be traced in his manuscript notes. Several pages show the variants of Kharoshthi letters – some again evidently supplied by Masson (MSS III, f. 18) – or Prinsep's efforts to determine what the actual language was (MSS III, ff. 16v–24). In the mistaken assumption that the inscriptions were in a Semitic or Iranian language (Salomon 1998, pp. 210–11), he tried to equate Kharoshthi with Hebrew, as well as with all known Indian and Iranian scripts (MSS III, f. 17). Only in 1838 did he realise that ΒΑΣΙΛΕΩΣ was consistently expressed in the genitive, as in *maharajasa* 'of the great king', that the word-ending character Ᵽ was *sa*, and that the initial vowel signs were 'formed by modification of the alif as in Arabic'. He also identified the diacritics for the post-consonantal vowels *i*, *e* and *u* (Prinsep 1838, pp. 640, 643; Salomon 1998, p. 212). Working concurrently in Europe, Lassen also managed to identify a number of characters, realised that the vowel *a* was inherent in all consonants, and that the language was an Indian Prakrit (1838, pp. 18, 26–9, 55). Both 'suspected the absence of long vowels' (Salomon 1998, p. 212).

However, the primary source for deciphering Kharoshthi was the rock inscription near Shahbazgarhi in the Peshawar Valley, which was not available until after Prinsep's death in 1840. In October 1838, Masson spent five days at the site and made the first complete and accurate copy of the inscription by coating the rock surface with ink and then taking impressions on cotton cloth (1846, pl. facing p. 298). The impressions covered 50 yards of calico which, together with written copies of the inscription, were presented to the Royal Asiatic Society on Masson's return to London in 1842. Only in May 1845 was it realised that the Shahbazgarhi inscription was another edict of the Mauryan emperor Ashoka, with the same text as his edicts in Brahmi already deciphered and translated by Prinsep (Proc. ASB 1845). Masson's 'labours' thus made possible a 'nearly perfect' transcription of the edict by Edwin Norris, Assistant Secretary of the Royal Asiatic Society (1846, pp. 303–14). This was later completed by Horace Wilson, by then Professor of Sanskrit at University College, London (1850). James Prinsep's manuscripts therefore contain at least one posthumous insert in the form of a page entitled 'Arian alphabet from Asoka's edict on the rock at Kapoordigiri 40 miles NE from Peshawar decyphered [*sic*] by Mr Norris, Royal A. Society, from Masson's cloth and lamp black impressions & manuscript' (MSS III, f. 16v).

A second issue regarding Masson and his contemporaries' translation of coin legends (from the time of Kanishka I onwards) is that they thought the language used was still Greek, when it is actually Bactrian, a local dialect that continued to use Greek script, but with additional letters to denote pronunciations not present in the original language. So they mistook the Bactrian 'Þ' (sh) for the Greek 'Ρ' (rho), resulting in, for example, ΚΑΝΗÞΚΙ (Kanishka) being misread as 'Kanerkes' and ΚΟÞΑΝΟ (Koshano, i.e. Kushan) as 'Korano'. In some instances, Masson also misreads Bactrian 'H' as a K, so ΟΗÞΟ (Oesho) becomes 'Okro' (see pp. 61, 310, 323–5). It was only in 1890 that the distinction between the Bactrian Þ and Greek P was finally established by Cunningham (1890, pp. 6–7; p. 288).

When it is remembered that the quantities of coins collected between January 1835 to 18 October 1836 alone were said to be 'large enough to supply all the museums in Europe' (Proc. ASB 1838), the realisation sinks in that even if the estimate of 60,000 is hypothetical, most public and private collections in Europe must nevertheless include a high percentage of coins from Afghanistan collected by Masson. Starting from scratch, the study of such a huge quantity of coins enabled him by 1835 to construct a numismatic sequence which was essentially correct although the details understandably needed some refinement (**F526/1a** below).

His greatest contribution is not just the quantity of coins and artefacts from Begram and the Buddhist sites, but above all, his records, which have created a study collection that can be understood in context of the history of Afghanistan.

Chapter 2
The Excavations of the Délégation archéologique française en Afghanistan at Begram (1936–46)

Lauren Morris

Introduction

Over a century after Charles Masson reached the *dasht* of Begram for the first time, the Délégation archéologique française en Afghanistan (DAFA) began excavations at the fortified urban site there. Work at Begram proved to be central to the DAFA's early activities, with various operations undertaken under the tenure of each of its first four directors: Alfred Foucher (1922–34), Joseph Hackin (1934–40), Roman Ghirshman (1941–3), and Daniel Schlumberger (1945–65). The excavations proper focused primarily on the southern tepe conventionally known as the New Royal City (**Fig. 7**), but the citadel (the Burj Abdullah) and an extramural fort were also explored (**Fig. 4**). Not only did these excavations shed light on a site which flourished under the Kushans, but they also uncovered one of the most evocative discoveries in the archaeology of Afghanistan: the Begram hoard. This find consisted of over 400 objects produced largely in the Roman Mediterranean, Han China, and the Indian Subcontinent, and was primarily recovered in two sealed rooms within what appears to have once been an elite residence at Site II of the New Royal City. Yet the date and significance of this hoard has been subject to contention since it came to light, which is largely due to the difficulties of interpreting the published excavation data. Indeed, the socio-historical context of the DAFA excavations at Begram has had such a profound impact on the data and knowledge produced about this site, that any discussion of the excavations must not be dissociated from this backdrop.

The present contribution first synthesises the results of the DAFA excavations at Begram and clarifies central difficulties with the published data. Then, the chronology and cultural connections of the archaeological material from Begram are considered, particularly in light of Masson's coin collections on the *dasht* of Begram.

Surveys (1923–5)

After the establishment of the DAFA in 1922, Alfred Foucher set out to delineate micro-regions and sites for future archaeological investigation, arriving to the Kohistan in April 1923. Here, he looked to features of the landscape and the distribution of Buddhist monuments to identify Begram as the capital of the country of Kapisa mentioned by Xuanzang (Foucher 1925, pp. 255–73; 1942, pp. 138–45). Foucher further hypothesised that the Burj Abdullah was the location of an older, original 'royal city', and that the palace was transferred at a later date to the southern tepe, becoming a 'new royal city' (Foucher 1925, p. 270). Although these designations were made without excavation, the latter became conventional in the work of Foucher's successors, but given with prophylactic inverted commas (Ghirshman 1946, p. 1; Hackin and Hackin 1939, p. 7). Foucher also disagreed with Masson's identification of Begram as the location of Alexandria in the Caucasus, with Hackin and Ghirshman following suit. They considered Hopian or Parwan to be more viable candidates (Ghirshman 1946, p. 6; Hackin and Hackin 1939, p. 4), although scholars now tend to agree with Masson's view (Bernard 1982).

Foucher wanted to get further survey and excavations rapidly underway, but was compelled by the excavation commission in Paris to begin his ill-fated excavations at

Balkh (Bernard 2002, pp. 1291–300). Foucher thus invited Gabriel Jouveau-Dubreuil, an archaeologist specialising in south India, for a mission to Afghanistan, tempting him with the strong possibility of excavations in Kapisa (Fenet 2010, no. 168). Jouveau-Dubreuil's ensuing mission to Kapisa in 1924 envisaged a month of work at Begram, but the dangers posed to foreigners by the Khost Rebellion heightened, and the disappointed archaeologist was sent back to India before commencement (excerpt of unpublished report in Cambon 2006, p. 86; Fenet 2010, no. 198; De Saxcé 2011, pp. 296–301).

In December of 1925, Jules Barthoux was delegated to undertake some soundings and execute a topographic plan of the site and extramural microreliefs south of the New Royal City (Cambon 1996, fig. 15). Although further work was envisaged for 1926 (Fenet 2010, no. 309), this did not eventuate. Neither Jouveau-Dubreuil's nor Barthoux's reports were published, serving only to inform later excavation plans. Foucher's full account of his observations at the Kohistan and Koh-Daman appeared only two decades after his travels (Foucher 1942).

The Hackin excavations (1936–40)

During Joseph Hackin's directorship, permission to excavate at Begram was obtained from the Afghan Ministry of Public Instruction in 1936. In April of that year, Jean Carl and Jacques Meunié (both DAFA architects) were tasked with opening Site I, also known as the 'Bazar' (**Fig. 8**), in the

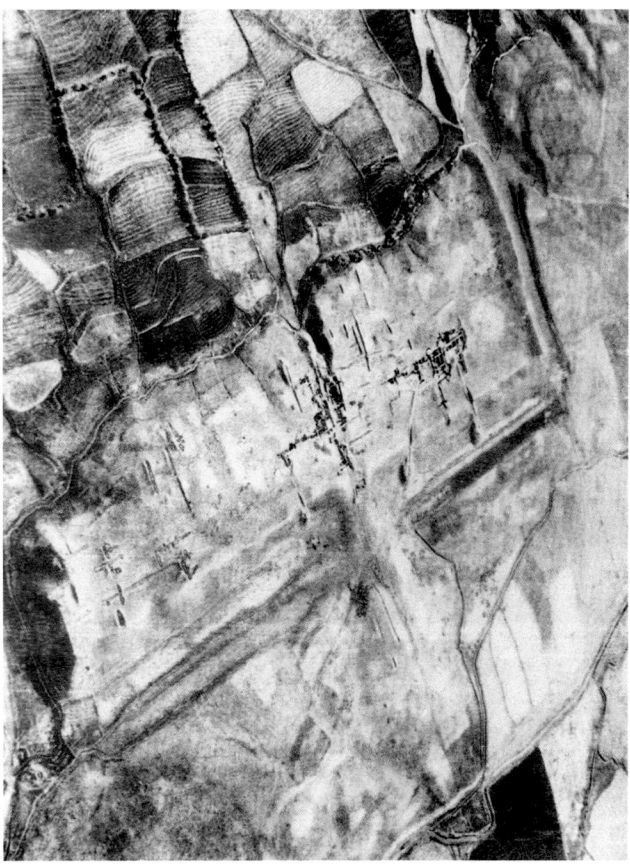

Figure 7 Aerial photograph of the New Royal City, 1939 (Ghirshman 1946, pl. I)

Figure 8 Plan of Site I (Hackin *et al.* 1959, Plan K)

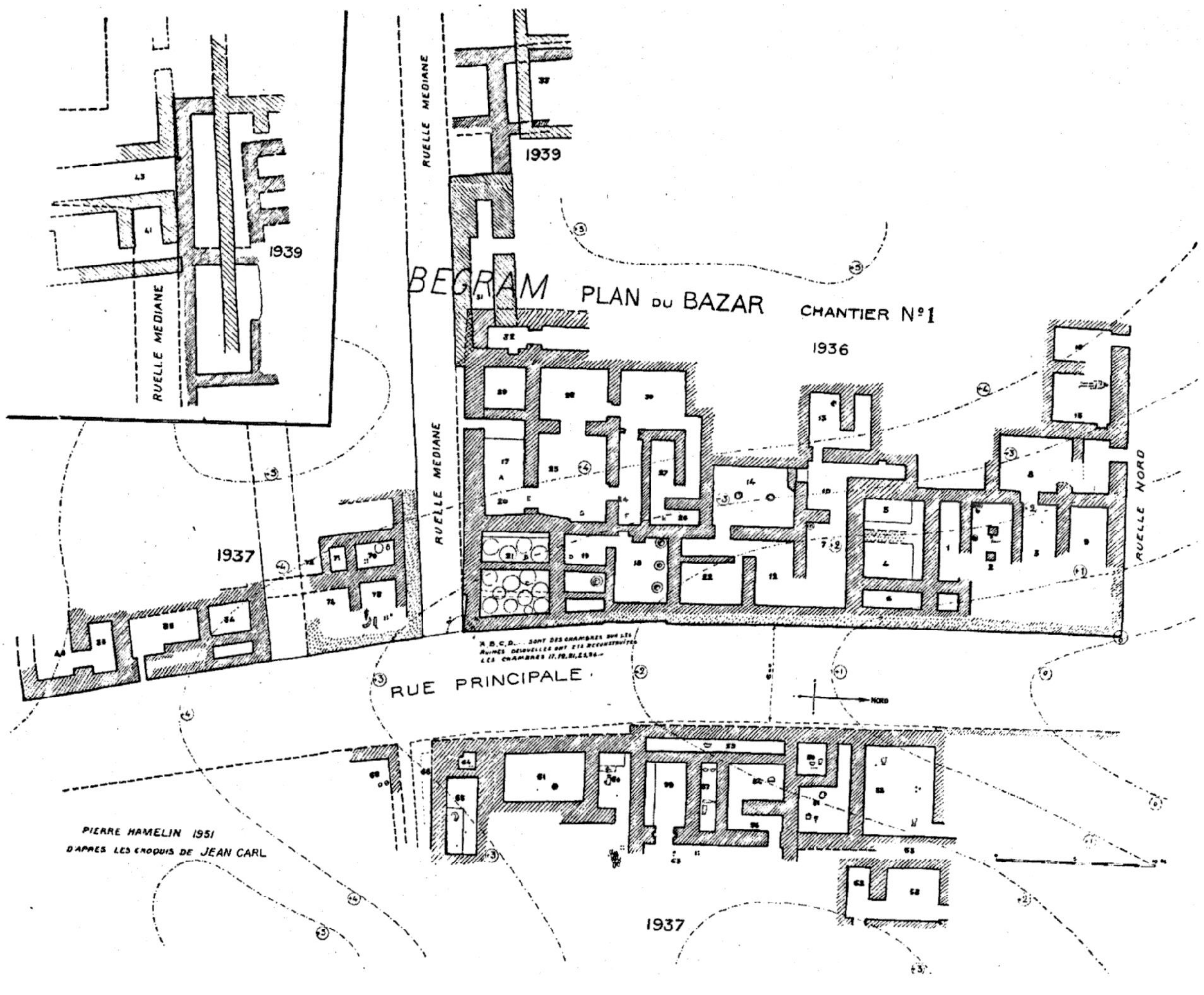

Figure 9 Examples of stamped medallion designs on pottery found at Site I (after Hackin *et al.* 1959, pl. VII)

centre of the New Royal City. Here, Carl and Meunié followed a north-south depression, marking the line of a main street which led to the city's south entrance, then worked from the west to the east in April to May of 1937 (Carl 1959). This area was comprised of blocks of houses with varying numbers of rooms, set around the city's central intersections. Two sufficiently distinct occupation levels were noticed (Carl 1959, p. 102, partially indicated on Plan K). Finds from this area were characterised as the debris of domestic life (Carl 1959, p. 102) including articles of bodily adornment, instruments for personal grooming, some copper and iron implements, some arrow and lance heads, a copper vessel, pottery including specimens impressed with distinct medallion shapes (**Fig. 9**), and copper coins. From the coins they were able to identify, the excavators associated the first level with Hermaeus, Soter Megas, Wima Kadphises, and the second with Kanishka I, Huvishka and Vasudeva I (Carl 1959, p. 85).

It is difficult to work with the limited documentation of this campaign, which was published posthumously only in 1959. This publication included a site plan depicting structures exposed in 1936 and 1937, but also within a small extension made in 1939 for which no further information is provided. The report for 1936 included a partially illustrated find catalogue with virtually no contextual information, and a summary of the coin finds, the majority of which were unidentified. The report from 1937 consisted of two laconic paragraphs. The finds were divided between Paris and Kabul according to Article 7 of the convention establishing the DAFA (Olivier-Utard 1997, pp. 35–44), an agreement with various advantages and disadvantages from heritage and scientific perspectives. Yet, after the purge of the Kabul Museum's coin collection during the Afghan Civil War, the fact that part of the coin collection from Begram was held in Paris has been instrumental for subsequent research. For instance, the excavators' conclusions about the date of the occupation levels at Site I were incorrect, as Bopearachchi's study of the coins preserved in the Musée Guimet identified numerous later issues (Bopearachchi 2001).

Although the methodology of the Hackin-era excavations at Begram was never explicitly clarified in print, it can be generally sketched. The unpublished finds catalogue for Site I in 1937 is preserved in the Musée Guimet (Fonds Hackin/DAFA) and demonstrates that the documentation format seen at Site II during 1937, 1939, and 1940 was also in use at Site I in 1937, if not earlier. Contextual data from this documentation format included room numbers and the depth at which almost every artefact was found below a fixed ground level point, rounded to the nearest 10cm increment. Carl's notebooks preserved in the Musée Guimet (43810 S.P.) indicate that a Sanguet Model no. 1 Tachymeter was employed to survey Begram and its hinterland during 1936–7; perhaps the find depth measurements were also taken with the aid of this instrument. These measurements were recorded precisely and quite consistently, producing what appears to be a surprisingly coherent dataset. Yet, interpreting these data remains difficult. On the one hand, they cannot be translated directly into stratigraphic data, occupation periods, or floor levels, especially across broad areas. On the other hand, when clusters of several objects around certain horizons in single rooms are evident (such as in the hoard rooms), these can probably be interpreted as indicating the presence of a floor. Otherwise the excavators cleared fill within rooms as they were encountered, and finds were catalogued in each. Judging from the surviving documentation, it appears that only pot sherds with remarkable decorative features were recorded, and recorded finds were biased towards the whole rather than fragmentary. The bulk of the excavation labour was undertaken by local workers.

In April 1937, another area was opened 200m to the east of Site I, which was called Site II or Site R, for Ria Hackin (Joseph Hackin's collaborator and wife) who led excavations there (**Fig. 10**). This excavation area was dominated by the remains of a probably residential rectangular edifice (hereafter the Site II structure), and superimposed by a Qala, i.e. a rectangular ediface with four circular bastions. Excavations in 1937 began close to the south rampart,

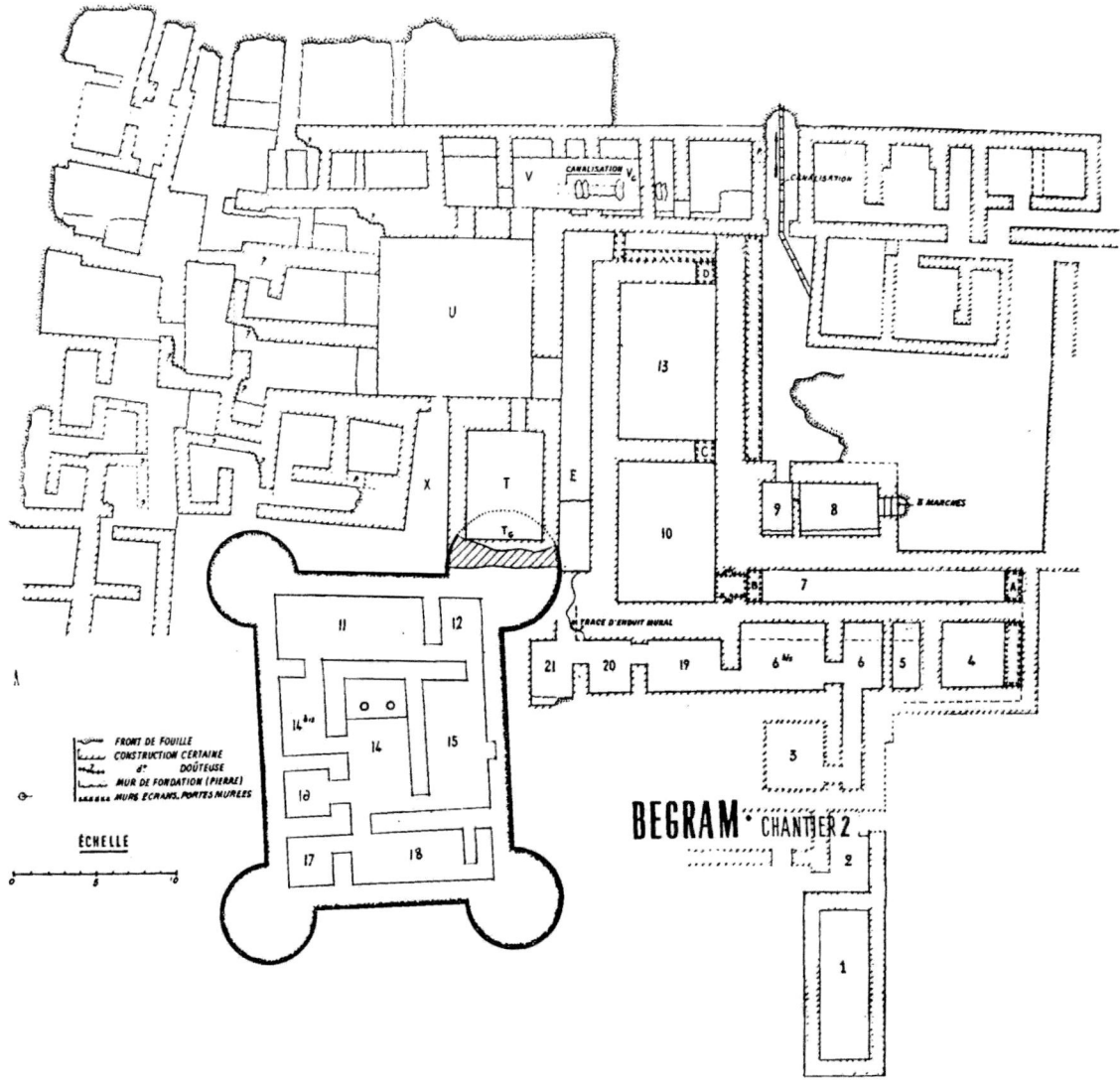

Figure 10 Plan of Site II by Marc Le Berre, 1947 (Hackin *et al.* 1954, p. 9)

moving progressively north. The Site II structure's walls were composed in its foundations and first courses of large irregular quarried stones interspersed with smaller ones, completed with rammed earth (pakhsa) then covered with an earthen plaster, which was lime-washed and bore traces of remnants of red or green pigment in places (Hackin and Hackin 1939, p. 9). Only few finds were encountered in rooms 1–9, including some copper coins and pottery, but corridor 7 was found to terminate in a curious wall of mud bricks. Delineating the outline of a spacious room – what would be the first hoard room, room 10 (8.4m x 6m) – on the other side, Ria Hackin began clearing this from its northwest corner and northern wall. Working here until June, hundreds of finds were removed (**Fig. 11**). These included ornate and unusual glass vessels (some found in a fragmentary state and dispersed, while others were still relatively intact in bag or basket-shaped deposits), alabaster vessels, worked ostrich eggs, bronze basins, figural balsamaria, and carved ivory or bone elements either found in isolation or in association with wooden furniture frames that had since decayed. Two plain pottery lamps and eight copper coins were also found here, the latest identified in the report attributed to Kanishka I (Hackin and Hackin 1939, no. 275 [129]).

In 1938, Hackin rapidly signalled their sensational finds in French, German, Dutch and English (see Rosu 1969, nos 101–2, 106, 108–10), then published what was intended to be the preliminary report covering the finds from room 10 (Hackin and Hackin 1939). This included indications of some finds from other rooms of the Site II structure in 1937. Additionally in 1938, in Hackin's absence, Meunié was delegated to excavate the Qala and extended Site II to the west (Meunié 1959a, pp. 103–5). The Qala was constructed in stone in the lower courses, with pisé laid above, and had featured a central open court. The few finds here included two unidentified copper coins, fragments of pottery with stamped decoration, a terracotta pitcher, and a gilded, painted plaster face of a Buddha, evidently in a secondary find context (Meunié 1959a, p. 104). The western extension of Site II revealed what was apparently a continuation of the

Figure 11 Ria Hackin in the south-west corner of room 10 during excavation (81311/62). Photo © MNAAG, Paris, Dist. RMN-Grand Palais / image Musée Guimet

rooms of the Site II structure, with very few finds. There was some evidence of renovation, transitioning around room 34 into habitation areas featuring domestic pottery analogous to that found at Site I (Meunié 1959a, p. 105). Finally, Meunié opened a feature located around 400m to the south of the New Royal City's ramparts. This revealed a structure similar to the Qala with four circular bastions, but with thicker walls and different internal organisation (Meunié 1959a, pp. 105–6).

From May to August of 1939, excavations at Site II continued under Ria Hackin's direction, focusing primarily on room 13 (9m x 6m), which was found directly north of room 10; other rooms were excavated but they are poorly documented (**Fig. 12**). As in room 10, the entrance of room 13 at its north-east corner had also been walled in (Meunié 1954, p. 8). The objects found here were of the same character as those found in the first hoard room, but even more diverse in variety; besides glassware, carved ivory and bone furniture elements (**Fig. 13**), and a range of copper alloy vessels, there were vessels carved from porphyry and from rock crystal, a range of bronze utensils, figurines and cast elements from composite devices, as well as cast plaster relief emblemata, and lacquered vessels and boxes. Fifteen coins were found at a range of depths within this room. Few were identified, but the latest that appeared to be associated with the hoard deposit was a copper of Wima Kadphises (Hackin *et al.* 1954, no. 208). Regarding the interpretation of the hoard, Hackin observed that most of the objects were dated to the 1st and 2nd centuries AD, which was understood to be a heightened period of international exchange that Begram had benefited from by virtue of its geographical situation (Hackin 1954, p. 14).

The last campaign at Begram of Joseph Hackin's directorship ran from April to July of 1940 at Site II (Meunié 1954, p. 8). The primary focus was room T within the Site II structure, directly to the north of the north-east bastion of the later Qala, although they also opened other rooms and ambiguously defined areas (**Fig. 14**). Room T exhibited some finds similar to those from room 13, mostly bronze decorative elements and figurines, while finds elsewhere from the Site II structure included a diverse mix of domestic pottery (primarily drinking vessels and lamps), spindle whorls, zoomorphic terracotta figurines and coins.

All in all, the documentation and publication record of the Hackin excavations at Begram as they survive today is patchy and problematic. Multiple factors are responsible for this, foremost the outbreak of World War II, the political complexities of Kabul during this time, the involvement of the DAFA archaeologists in the Free France movement, and ultimately the tragic deaths of the Hackins and Carl in 1941 (see Olivier-Utard 1997, pp. 119–24; Cambon *et al.* 2018, pp. 92–123). Joseph Hackin had fought in the French infantry in

Figure 12 Excavations in process at room 13, 1939 (81315791/4). Photo © MNAAG, Paris, Dist. RMN-Grand Palais / image Musée Guimet

World War I and earned the Legion of Honour and Croix de Guerre, remaining a reserve officer thereafter. When war was declared in 1939, he felt strongly morally obliged to join the fight in France, but various authorities intervened to place him on special assignment to remain in Kabul as an intelligence officer. During the 1940 excavation season at Begram, German forces rapidly advanced through the Low Countries and France, culminating in General de Gaulle's appeal for a French Resistance and the armistice at Compiègne between Nazi Germany and the French Third Republic.

Excavations were closed on July 3, and three days later, Joseph Hackin declared the allegiance of himself and his companions to Free France in a telegraph sent through the British Legation in Kabul. In the following weeks, in recognition of Hackin's valuable knowledge of local politics and his connections, the new Vichy regime attempted unsuccessfully to install him as a diplomatic agent at the French Legation at Kabul. Nonetheless, he resigned his directorship of the DAFA in August of 1940, leaving for London shortly afterwards with Ria Hackin and Jean Carl. During this tumultuous period, Joseph Hackin astonishingly found time to publish short notices about their work at Begram in 1939 in French, Persian (translated by their collaborator, Ahmad Ali Kohzad of the Kabul Museum), and English (see Rosu 1969, nos 119, 122). Before departing Kabul, Hackin had entrusted his manuscripts and notes to the British Legation, via his friend and colleague, Kenneth de Burgh Codrington, a British archaeologist and art historian.

After liaising with General de Gaulle at his headquarters in Carlton Gardens, Joseph and Ria Hackin departed Liverpool on 20 February 1941 on a mission to make contact with Free French communities around the world. Four days later, the ship on which they were travelling was torpedoed west of the Faroe Islands in the early hours of the morning by a U-Boat, and the Hackins perished. Learning the news, Carl took his own life.

The trajectory of much of the excavation documentation from this point is not clear. A portion of Carl's notes and the site plan for 1940 were determined to be lost (Carl 1959, p. 85; Meunié 1954, p. 9). However, Hackin's documents had been conveyed from the British Legation to the Warburg Institute in London in 1941. Apparently, following Hackin's orally

Figure 13 Chair back 34 fitted with carved ivory and bone panels in situ, centre of room 13 (Hackin *et al.* 1954, fig. 7)

expressed wish, the Institute had intended to publish the results of the Begram excavations in English, which provoked a dispute in 1942 with the French archaeologist Claude Schaeffer (Olivier-Utard 1997, p. 128). After the liberation of France in 1944, the documents were returned to the Musée Guimet. The journey of Carl's notebooks now preserved in the Musée Guimet is less clear; a note inside one reads that it was returned to the Guimet in 1951 by a former member of the British Legation in Kabul (43810 S.P. Carnet 1).

In the following years, a publication programme followed, with the main volume for the 1939 and 1940 seasons (i.e. foremost the hoard finds in room 13) appearing in 1954. This included contributions from, among others, personnel of the DAFA, the Musée Guimet, and the Warburg Institute (Hackin *et al.* 1954, xi–xii; Olivier-Utard 1997, p. 128). Roman Ghirshman was not involved. Rather significantly, this publication featured the only surviving complete plan of the Site II excavation area, executed in 1947

Figure 14 Site II after the Hackin excavations (81311/93 bis). Photo © RMN-Grand Palais / image Musée Guimet

The Excavations of the Délégation archéologique française en Afghanistan at Begram (1936–46) | 25

Figure 15 Excavations at Site B showing three occupation phases (Ghirshman 1946, pl. VI.1)

by Marc Le Berre from the decaying exposed excavated structures (**Fig. 10**). Despite the admirable effort involved in producing this volume, it is marred by two major errors. The first is that the published catalogue stated that the objects nos 1–229 were found in room 13, but the typed manuscript thereof (Hackin/DAFA Fonds, Musée Guimet) reveals that a dozen objects originally had a different findspot indication ('Chantier no. [blank]') which were simply removed for publication. Second, comparison of the published catalogue with the original handwritten catalogue and the typed manuscript thereof for the finds from the 1940 season (Hackin/DAFA Fonds, Musée Guimet) reveals that the findspot indication for each catalogue entry was accidentally moved to the previous entry for the publication.

Additionally, Pierre Hamelin, conservator at the Musée Guimet and participant in the 1939 excavation season, published three articles on the glassware from the hoard, which also included plans of the distribution of finds in rooms 10 and 13 and information about the architecture of the Site II structure (Hamelin 1952; 1953; 1954). Extremely brief reports at Site I, the western extension of Site II in 1938, Site III and the city entrance appeared in only 1959, in an edited volume of unpublished excavations from Hackin's directorship (Hackin *et al.* 1959).

The Ghirshman excavations (1941–2)

Roman Ghirshman took up the mantle as director of the DAFA. Between 1941 and 1942, he expanded excavation at Begram to a number of new areas (Ghirshman 1946). Two sondages were taken at the Burj Abdullah. The first, at the centre of the citadel, reached sterile earth at a depth of 2m, but revealed no traces of construction, as apparently any structures had been razed and their stone foundations dismantled. Yet dozens of pottery sherds were found, which according to Ghirshman covered a date range from the first centuries AD to the Middle Ages, as well as two fragments taken from schist Buddhist sculpture (Ghirshman 1946, pp. 2–3). The south rampart of the Burj Abdullah was studied, and found to be comprised of retaining walls built from mud bricks (40 x 40 x 14cm) with no foundation, filled with earth and stone (Ghirshman 1946, p. 3). This method of construction differed from the fortification wall of the New Royal City, which Ghirshman also explored. The latter wall exhibited a stone foundation along its south side, was constructed also of mud bricks (40 x 40 x 12cm) marked with a character resembling a Greek *theta*, and featured regular 16.6m long rectangular bastions (Ghirshman 1946, p. 16).

Ghirshman's main excavations at Begram were at a site marked as 'B' on his published plan (hereafter Site B), on the western side of the New Royal City, which was chosen deliberately to establish the chronology and stratigraphy of the site (Ghirshman 1946, p. 23). In this area dominated by simple habitations, Ghirshman observed three phases of occupation (**Fig. 15**). He dated these from the distribution of coins he observed in each. Begram I was thus dated from Apollodotus I (?) to Wima Kadphises; Begram II from Kanishka I to Vasudeva I, and Begram III to Vasudeva I imitations (rev. Oesho and bull) and Kanishka II types (rev. seated Ardochsho) (Ghirshman 1946, pp. 85–6; Morris 2017, pp. 77, 97). Unfortunately, Ghirshman did not publish his coins specifically according to occupation phase.

Begram I, constructed on sterile ground between a depth of 3.7m and 4.5m, was characterised by stone walls, with mud bricks (40 x 40 x 10cm) sometimes present beneath, indicating to Ghirshman that the latter acted as foundations for levelling uneven ground (Ghirshman 1946, pp. 23–4). These walls survived to a height of 2 to 3m. Pottery of this level was grey-black/black ware or finer red ware covered with a red slip, featuring limited decoration, usually incised (Ghirshman 1946, pp. 44–6).

Begram II was characterised by renovations and mixed patterns of re-use and adaptation of walls from Level I, or the construction of entirely new walls on stone foundations of 60–70cm topped with pakhsa laid in 30–50cm layers (Ghirshman 1946, pp. 26–7). Pottery of this level did not exhibit much change; it primarily constituted red ware with few examples of grey-black ware, but notably saw the appearance of goblets painted with painted black triangle motifs (Ghirshman 1946, pp. 54–7). Ghirshman judged this level to have ended with a disaster and an abandonment lasting one to two decades. This was based on traces of destruction and fire in certain houses, and thick layers of ash covering the ground along the interior of the fortification wall, followed by a rubble and a thin accumulation layer (Ghirshman 1946, p. 30). Ghirshman proposed that this was instigated by an invasion of Shapur I, putatively taking place between AD 241–50 (Ghirshman 1946, p. 100).

Begram III was marked by new constructions oriented slightly towards north-north-west. Walls were built on foundations of river stones rather than the irregular quarried stone of previous levels, then completed in mud bricks (38 x 38 x 8cm or 40 x 40 x 10cm), plastered with clay mixed with straw and covered with a light green whitewash (Ghirshman 1946, p. 32). The houses of Site B did not follow a homogenous plan, but often featured earthen benches as well as niches protruding from the walls (Ghirshman 1946, pp. 35–7, pl. VIII.1–6). At least one terracotta lamp was found in association with most niches, and the additional finds of a fragmentary terracotta horse-riding figurine (room A 4), a piece of low relief Buddhist sculpture, clearly repurposed (room G 3), and a statuette of seated Ardochsho (room E 3) led Ghirshman to suggest that these niches served loci for private worship (Ghirshman 1946, p. 37). The pottery of this level is marked by a few changes: the predominance of red ware with few examples of grey-black ware, the phasing out of painted decoration, the introduction of stamped decoration in circular medallions, and zoomorphic terracotta figurines, notably representing elephants (Ghirshman 1946, pp. 69–74). Some objects of value were found buried beneath floors, such as a hoard of bronze vessels (Ghirshman 1946, p. 41; pl. XXI.7–12). Ghirshman attributed the end of this occupation layer to an abandonment in anticipation of invasion by the 'Chionites-Hephthalites', i.e. Huns (Ghirshman 1946, p. 41).

Ghirshman also expanded excavations at the Site II structure with the express objective of establishing its stratigraphy and comparing this with his findings at Site B (Ghirshman 1946, p. 28). Working on ambiguously defined areas north and north-west to the site under the Hackin excavations, he found coins only of the 'second Kushan dynasty' (i.e. Kanishka I – Vasudeva), and stated that the main structure was built in the 'first or … second Kushan dynasty', dating to Begram II (Ghirshman 1946, p. 28). In one area, around 'V' indicated on Le Berre's plan (see **Fig. 10**), a waste-water drain was identified running across a court, where a number of mortars were also found, adjoined to five narrow rooms. Ghirshman identified this area as a food reserve (Ghirshman 1946, p. 28). Clearing the northern part of the north-east tower of the Qala, new finds in this expansion of room T included bronze finds similar to those found in room 13, such as a bronze figurine of a grotesque or comedic figure, and separate decorative elements (Ghirshman 1946, pp. 67–9).

Ghirshman's approach differed to that of his predecessors', which affects the possibility of comparing and interpreting their results. Hackin's work featured limited interpretation, while Ghirshman's ran in the opposite direction. Characterising occupation phases and material features in broad sweeps without much contextual precision, the reader is left to trust his assessments. Ghirshman also paid attention to pottery, while Hackin's excavations documented very little. Ghirshman was also distinctive in that he had linguistic access to the products of Russian imperial and Soviet archaeology, suggesting Sarmatian jewellery and Khwarazmian architecture as parallels for material at Begram. Additionally, Ghirshman's work was far more historically oriented than Hackin's; indeed, research on the Kushans was still in its infancy at this time, and a third of Ghirshman's excavation report was occupied by a new chronology and reconstruction of Kushan history (Ghirshman 1946, pp. 99–184). At the time, this constituted an important new contribution to the field, even if many of Ghirshman's hypotheses are now untenable.

Ghirshman also had unacceptable obstacles placed in front of him which directly shaped the results of his excavations. The first is that he had to operate blindly to his predecessors' fieldwork. When he was appointed as Hackin's successor and set about continuing excavations at Begram, the new British Minister at Kabul, Sir Francis Verner Wylie, reportedly refused to give him Hackin's documents (Olivier-Utard 1997, p. 134). Accordingly, Ghirshman had to undertake excavations and publish his findings with knowledge only of what had been published thus far and what had been left by his predecessor in Kabul Museum. Finally, the anti-Semitic and Russophobe politics of the Vichy regime contributed to Ghirshman's dismissal in 1943 (Olivier-Utard 1997, p. 137), bringing his promising work at Begram to a premature close.

Meunié's final campaign (1946)

Finally, after the DAFA resumed operations in 1945, in agreement with the Minister of Public Instruction, it was decided in 1946 to resume excavations at Begram with Meunié's work at the south city gate between September and October (Meunié 1959b). On sterile ground, three stages of construction were documented, which gradually restricted access through the gate. By the last stage, Meunié determined a rising path, an elevated threshold accessed by one or two side ramps, what may have been two square stupa bases on either side of the gate, and the apparent spread of habitations outside of the gate (Meunié 1959b, pp. 108–10). On the city side of the gate, habitations pressed against the rampart in two layers of occupation, the upper floor being 70–80cm below modern soil, and the older floor c. 90cm below that. Coins of Huvishka and Vasudeva were reported in the upper layer, and of Wima Kadphises and Kanishka in the lower (Meunié 1959b, pp. 110–11). All earlier coins were found in the waste water canal running under the road of the city gate, and a hoard of 65 copper coins attributed by Raoul Curiel to Vasudeva (Oesho with bull and seated Ardochsho types) was found directly in the centre of the city gate 'on the floor' attributed to the last phase of occupation (Meunié 1959b, pp. 111–12).

Yet Schlumberger's private correspondence reveals he found the site to be 'not very promising' and 'exhausted by Hackin's extraordinary find' (Olivier-Utard 1997, p. 181). Faced with multiple new obligations, including the enormous parallel task of publishing the results of the Hackin campaigns and working through the material preserved the Kabul Museum from the excavations through the autumn and winter – some fragmentary, some since restored, but without labels (see notes, for example, in Hackin *et al.* 1954, pp. 248, 262) – excavations at the site were not resumed. Perhaps it did not help that a visit to the excavations by the Indian Cultural Mission – which included, among others, Mortimer Wheeler and M.A. Shakur of the Peshawar Museum – was followed by an undiplomatic appraisal of Meunié's methodology in print (Shakur 1947, pp. 36–7):

> Nothing by way of scientific excavation has yet been done at the site. The present dig of Mon Meunie [*sic*], as seen by members of the mission, is nothing less than the destruction of valuable evidence … His work to all intents and purposes was in search of treasures, as is done by 'common' people. It was not conducted in the light of the science of Field Archaeology … [continuing at some length].

Figure 16 Coins from room 10, Site II in the Musée Guimet. Photo © Osmund Bopearachchi, Musée Guimet

Recalibrating some debates

In view of Begram's complex excavation and publication record, it is no surprise that many scholars have sought to nuance or dispute the excavators' interpretations. The most prominent debate has been concerned with the date of the hoard from Site II, which has occurred largely in isolation from its archaeological context. Positions on this matter can be divided into two camps. The first, initially supported by Joseph Hackin (Hackin and Hackin 1939, pp. 10, 22) advocates for a late dating of at least some of the hoard objects, with the implication that they were produced over an extended time period, the 1st–3rd or even 4th centuries AD (Coarelli 1962, p. 319; Menninger 1996, p. 91; Rütti 1998, pp. 196–200; Nehru 2004, p. 124; Rosen Stone 2008, p. 48). The second position argues for an earlier date and a more limited time frame of production, the 1st or 1st–early 2nd centuries AD. After the excavation of room 13, Hackin leant towards this interpretation (Hackin 1954, p. 14), which was also supported by the case studies in *Nouvelles recherches archéologiques à Begram* (Hackin et al. 1954, pp. 54, 108, 155) and has since been revived with wide acceptance (Mehendale 1997, 5.5; 2011, p. 143; Whitehouse 1989, p. 99; 2001, p. 444). A linchpin of this position in more recent scholarship has been the belief that the latest coin associated with the hoard was of Kanishka I, found at a depth of 2.6m in room 10 (Hackin and Hackin 1939, no. 275 [129]). Yet, three previously-unidentified coins kept in the Musée Guimet, found at the same depth in the same room, were already published by Bopearachchi almost twenty years ago, who identified them as late emissions of Vasudeva I (Bopearachchi 2001, nos 117, 119, 120). The significance of these coins (**Fig. 16**) for dating purposes was not acknowledged by contemporary scholarship. Recent re-analysis identifies them as Vasudeva I imitations (see pp. 177–8 below), based on types from copper coins of Vasudeva and Kanishka II, first issued contemporary to the reigns of Kanishka II or Vasishka. Due to the low weights of nos 119 and 120 (2.39g and 2.57g respectively), the *terminus post quem* of the hoard's deposition was judged to have taken place at least after *c.* AD 260 (Morris 2017, pp. 87–9).

Broader issues with the New Royal City's chronology as published have also been raised, foremost by Kuwayama (1974; 1991b; 2010) who rightly observed that the upper level of Site I must be contemporary with Ghirshman's Begram III, as they share the same variety of pottery with stamped medallion decorations, some even with the same dies. Distrusting the numismatic evidence as published, he has argued that Begram III, including Site I and the Qala at Site II, should be dated much later than Ghirshman proposed. He holds that the New Royal City was part of the town visited by Xuanzang in the 7th century, and – supported by analysis of the occurrence of stamped medallion pottery and round bastions at sites in the vicinity of Kapisa, Kabul, and Ghazni – that occupation at Begram III dates from the mid-6th to mid-8th century (Kuwayama 1991b, pp. 112, 117–118), and certainly not earlier than the 6th century (Kuwayama 2010, p. 291). The dates of these features have been discussed elsewhere, leaving open the possibility of an earlier date for Begram III (see MacDowall and Taddei 1978, pp. 266–7; Fussman 2008, p. 156). Furthermore, the numismatic evidence for this phase, as it is currently understood, would appear to be earlier and provide a chronological link between the deposition of the Begram hoard and Begram III (Morris 2017, pp. 97–101). However, as the archaeology of this period is subjected to renewed scholarly attention, Kuwayama's interpretation appears increasingly plausible. We will return to these issues below. Another relevant point worth raising is that the overall irregular form of the site of Begram, as seen clearly in Ghirshman's plan (**Fig. 4**), appears to have been transformed by water erosion. It is fully possible that this process also impacted the survival and integrity of remains closer to the surface, including those of Begram III.

For now, it should be reiterated that a careful re-examination of the archaeological data produced by the DAFA can help to address such questions in part and form broader hypotheses, but ultimately does not allow for an appropriately subtle analysis of this complex site. Nonetheless, one productive way to recalibrate these debates is through the lens of the coinage collected by Masson from the *dasht* of Begram, which is now possible due to the work of Elizabeth Errington, in addition to the chronology of political control of Begram seen through the prism of its monetary history laid out by Joe Cribb in this volume. Through these data, we can access a broader view of the place of the New Royal City within Begram's hinterland, which was clearly settled for a longer period than the structures uncovered by the DAFA.

The earliest remains and Begram I

It is difficult to pinpoint the earliest archaeological material documented in the DAFA excavations. As discussed above, Ghirshman dated the occupation phase of Begram I as spanning between the Indo-Greek period to the reign of Wima Kadphises, although as Ghirshman did not publish his coin finds by occupation layer, it is perhaps better not to take this too literally. The New Royal City's fortification wall was probably raised early on in this phase. Although Ghirshman considered the structures of Begram I to have been created on sterile ground, Bernard rightly pointed out that the occasional mudbricks noticed beneath the stone walls of this phase may derive from earlier, dismantled structures. Bernard also agreed with Ghirshman's suggestion that the fortification wall of the Burj Abdullah was possibly earlier than that of the New Royal City, perhaps dating to the 3rd century BC or even earlier (Bernard 1982, p. 242).

Yet material culture that might be characterised as Indo-Greek remains somewhat ephemeral. Rapin has proposed that the Site II structure may have developed from an orthogonal, monumental edifice of the Hellenistic period (Rapin 1992, pp. 383–5). This is plausible, but impossible to verify as the excavators did not systematically document the structure's architectural development. The same might be suggested for a partially exposed structure of Begram I revealed by Ghirshman at Site B, which – apparently monumental and orthogonal – is distinct to houses lying just to the south. Room 27 seems to be a long peripheral corridor surrounding three parallel rooms (28–30), recalling the domestic architecture of Ai Khanum, which had strong local and broadly Iranian roots (Lecuyot 2013, pp. 205–7).

It is interesting that Cribb's contribution in this volume amply demonstrates that Begram and its hinterland was a politically contested space during the 1st century BC to the 1st century AD – changing between Indo-Greek, perhaps Indo-Scythian, and Kushan hands, with the additional possibility of an Indo-Parthian incursion – but the long occupation phase of Begram I as thus far revealed does not seem to reflect conflict instigated by these regime changes. This is also a good reminder that the end of archaeological phases need not be aligned with political events. In addition to the potential links with the architectural tradition of Bactria noted above, some small finds that Ghirshman reported from Begram I further reflect a complex cultural milieu, which may be explained in part by Kapisa's political history, but moreover by the region's status as a dynamic borderland situated geographically, economically, and culturally between Bactria, Arachosia, and Gandhara. To cite some examples, a small terracotta head of a woman was found, clearly inspired by stylistic norms of the Hellenistic world (Ghirshman 1946, pp. 49–50, BG 452, pl. X.1–3, pl. XXVIII). An inscribed potter's tool known as a dabber in South Asian archaeology was reported in this phase (Ghirshman 1946, BG 444, pl. XXIX) featuring a name written in Gandhari (*Pa[śa]medasa* + ?, CKI 181), apparently a mark of ownership. However, it is possible that the context of this find was misinterpreted, as another dabber inscribed with the same name (Ghirshman 1946, BG 169, pl. XXXVIII) was found in the phase Begram II (Fussman 1970, p. 53). Nonetheless, these finds indicate both an Indic component to Begram's secular onomastics in the early phases of settlement in the New Royal City (Fussman 1970, pp. 44–5), in addition to the existence of pottery production in the Indic tradition at the site, albeit at a location not yet identified in the excavated areas.

Begram II, a city of the Kushan empire

Judging from the available data, it would appear that Ghirshman's second level at Site B, and the main Site II structure may belong to the occupation phase of Begram II. The dating of the lower level observed at Site I and the second level at the city gate remains unclear. As noted above, the structures of Begram II sometimes re-used and renovated those of Begram I, and the material culture between the two phases is likewise broadly similar. During the time of Begram II – the height of Kushan power – the city's cultural ties with Gandhara and Bactria-Tokharistan also appear to increase.

From the east, the spread and increasing popularity of Buddhism is reflected in the foundation of certain monasteries and stupas around the Koh-i Pahlawan which served the urban population. The monasteries of Karratcha, Shotorak and Qul-i Nadir – all excavated by the DAFA and with similar documentation problems as Begram – were perhaps founded in the latter half of the 1st century AD, but appear to have been developed around the phase of Begram II and later (see Fussman 2008, pp. 161, 163, 168–9; on the date of Qul-i Nadir's relic deposit, see **Vol. I, p. 36**).

From the north, pottery forms of the Yuezhi-Kushan period in Bactria-Tokharistan appear to have infiltrated the local repertoire at Kapisa. For example, distinctive pedestaled goblets seem to have been introduced to Bactria during the 'Nomadic' period, perhaps by the Yuezhi (Lyonnet 1997, pp. 161–4), indicating also a change in drinking practice (Maxwell-Jones 2015, pp. 496–7). Becoming ubiquitous under the Kushans, these goblets appear to have inspired a common new type of carinated goblets at Begram with distinctive painted triangular decoration (Ghirshman 1946, pls XL, XLIV). The same type has been also found at the site of Tapa Skandar, c. 40km to the south-west of Begram (Kuwayama 2010, p. 289, fig. 5).

Likewise, as noted above, the architecture of the Site II structure may suggest an earlier Hellenistic-period structure, or even links with the successors of Hellenistic domestic architecture in Bactria-Tokharistan during the Yuezhi-Kushan period. Comparisons include, for example, the elite residence of Saksanokhur, with its central courtyard, peripheral corridor, and sets of subsidiary rooms (Litvinsky and Mukhitdinov 1969, fig. 3), and the Kushan-period elite houses at Dal'verzin Tepe (DT-5 and DT-6) which featured central reception rooms (Pugachenkova and Rtveladze 1978, figs 15, 26). Certainly, the Site II structure was grander than other habitations excavated at Begram, with much larger dimensions and two central reception rooms. One of these, room 13, was originally decorated with a wall painting depicting a draped colonnade, a motif clearly originating in the Greco-Roman world (**Fig. 17**).

Yet, while the Site II structure appears to have been built during Begram II, its internal chronology is more

Figure 17 Wall painting room 13 (81314/3). Photo © MNAAG, Paris, Dist. RMN-Grand Palais / image Musée Guimet

complicated. The depth measurement data appear to indicate multiple levels of beaten earth floors – both above and below the floor level of *c.* 2.6m upon which the hoard was deposited – and the slightly-askew additions to the main structure on the plan suggest renovations. Most problematic are the presence of coins that Ghirshman considered characteristic of Begram III, including at least six post-Vasudeva issues associated with various rooms of the Site II structure (Morris 2017, pp. 87–9, 99). This indicates that the Site II structure was occupied for a long time, well past the reign of Vasudeva, and the possibility that the phase Begram II was abandoned later than Ghirshman believed.

The items in the Begram hoard had been produced during the phases of both Begram I and Begram II, and after *c.* AD 260, the hoard was deposited and concealed in what had once been the central reception rooms of an elite residence, and never recovered. It is tempting to connect this hoard with the owner of the house, but the number of objects found in rooms 10 and 13 (including over 180 glass vessels) seem too numerous to have been used by one family alone. Rather, the hoard may have been assembled at the moment of deposition from multiple origins, including an atelier (MacDowall and Taddei 1978, p. 257). The production date of the lacquerwares, i.e. the latter 1st century BC to the very early 1st century AD (Zhang 2011), means that these objects would have been *c.* 250 years old by the time of deposition, presumably constituting heirlooms of some kind. While the Kushan Empire fostered conditions for heightened connectivity across Eurasia, comparative objects to those found in the Begram hoard are very rare in the archaeological record of Central Asia and north-west India. As so little of Begram was excavated, it remains difficult to place these objects within their context of consumption among the city's social elite.

Begram III and the end of the New Royal City

Begram III was the most widely documented occupation phase at the New Royal City, apparently including the upper layer of remains revealed by Ghirshman, in addition to the majority of the structures in Site I, the final stage of constructions at the city gate, and perhaps features emergent from the Site II structure. Wall construction was coarser and the dimensions of dwellings were smaller in this phase, while some links with material culture and religious beliefs fermented in Bactria-Tokharistan may be apparent. For example, the terracotta figurines found in this phase representing a horse and rider with pointed cap (Ghirshman 1946, pl. XX.1–3, 7, 9) have perhaps distant antecedents in Bactria-Tokharistan of the Yuezhi-Kushan period, which apparently relate to the worship of a steppe ancestor (Pugachenkova 1989, p. 16).

Yet the historical context of Begram III remains elusive, as such vastly different appraisals of its date have been offered. Ghirshman dated Begram III to the last decades of the 4th century AD (Ghirshman 1946, pp. 78–82), which, as discussed above, was extensively disputed by Kuwayama in favour of the 6th to 8th centuries. The stakes of this debate have attained rather more urgency in recent years with the publication of excavated material – including pottery with stamped medallions – from Buddhist monastic sites with significant late phases, including Tepe Narenj (Paiman and Alram 2013), Qul-i Tut (Paiman 2018), and Mes Aynak (Lerner 2018). A future study of pottery with stamped medallions would be beneficial to more finely assess the dating and seriation of specific designs, ideally through a study of precise 'die' links between pottery from different sites, from Kapisa to Ghazni and the vicinity of Gandhara, alongside critical appraisals of all relevant archaeological contexts. For now, some clues as to the date of Begram III and its pottery may be obtained from the *c.* 873 coin finds produced by the DAFA excavations at Begram (presented here in **Table 3**) when analysed in tandem with the numismatic data collected by Masson.

It is not possible to study the entire corpus of coins collected from the DAFA excavations anew; all of the coins found in 1936 and 1937 that were allocated to Paris have been published and studied (Bopearachchi 2001; Morris 2017), but all specimens allocated to Kabul are presumed lost. The corpus of coins from the excavations thus must be reconstructed through multiple sources of legacy data, some of which are seriously problematic. For example, images of the coins from the Hackin and Meunié excavations were never published, and the coins were not cleaned and categorised at the time, resulting in few published identifications, some of which are probably dubious. In a few cases, comparative published types for coins were given, which can be classified according to more recent typologies.

The situation is slightly better for the coins from later excavations. Ghirshman, at least, published photographs and drawings of certain coins (Ghirshman 1946, pp. 85–97, pls XXII–XXIII), which reveal that some of his identifications were also incorrect and thus all cannot be taken at face value. Additionally, although Ghirshman cleaned and studied 47 coins from 1937 and 1938 in the Kabul Museum (Ghirshman 1946, p. 86), it is not possible to attribute these finds to specific seasons/sites. After the 1937 and 1938 seasons, there should have been 68 coins in Kabul Museum, but as Ghirshman studied 47, this might not have included the 20 coins collected by Meunié at the extramural fort (Site III) in 1938. Accordingly, Ghirshman's figures are not included in the working sum of coins for the DAFA excavations, but are cited as they demonstrate clearly that previously unidentified coins from the 1937 and 1938 seasons included numerous specimens of types (official and/or imitation?) inaugurated by Vasudeva and Kanishka II.

An important further source is Robert Göbl's notes from his study of coins held in the Kabul Museum in 1962, including the finds from Ghirshman's excavations and those from Meunié's 1946 campaign at the city gate. Göbl relied here on pre-existing classifications, which limited some of the specificity of his identifications. For example, both lifetime and imitation issues of Vasudeva were subsumed under the classification PMC 216, with qualifications such as 'late' and 'type', and likewise lifetime and imitation coins of Kanishka II were presumably subsumed under PMC 228. Nonetheless, the identifications in these documents certainly supersede those published by Ghirshman.

Another way Göbl's documents are valuable are in providing a reliable representative sample of coins throughout occupation at the New Royal City; although only just over two thirds of the coins from the excavation have been identified, Göbl was able to identify almost all of the coins from three different campaigns that explored all three occupation periods at the New Royal City. According to the current understanding of the local numismatic sequence, the latest coins Göbl identified here were six Kushano-Sasanian coppers, only three of which could be classified more specifically as issues of Peroz I and Hormizd II. The only later known coins from the DAFA excavations include a single silver Sasanian coin of Khusrau II from the spoil of the sondage at the Burj Abdullah, and a copper Shri Shahi coin (after the type from de Morgan cited in Hackin *et al.* 1954, no. 117), found at a depth of 70cm in – according to the typed manuscript, see above – an unspecified excavation area, which could well have been an accidental loss.

The virtual absence of coins after the early Kushano-Sasanians from the New Royal City would seem to provide a case for dating the end of Begram III to around the mid-4th century AD, which is nonetheless a form of *argumentum e silentio*. Here, Masson's collection provides an indispensable comparative corpus for monetary circulation in Begram and its hinterland for the following centuries. In this collection, Kidarite and Alkhan coins are represented in smaller numbers, in addition to larger numbers of Shri Shahi coins, as well as those of the Turkic Kabul Shahis and Hindu Shahis (see Cribb, this volume). Thus, according to our current understanding of Begram's overall numismatic sequence and the available numismatic data from the DAFA excavations, it would appear that the absence of post-Kushano-Sasanian coins at the New Royal City is significant for dating purposes.

However, one significant complicating factor must be raised. Copper imitations of types of Vasudeva and Kanishka II (especially with the reverse type Oesho and bull), the production and circulation of which is currently attributed to the Kushano-Sasanian period (see pp. 105–6 below) have been documented in later archaeological contexts. The clearest example of this is from Tapa Sardar. Here, layer 4 (of the Late Period, which follows on from an abandonment phase) yielded such coins, ranging also to Hunnic coinage of the 8th century, in addition to one Kushano-Sasanian coin. However, the red clay-coated sculptures of this layer are of the Fondukistan type, indicating that their production should be dated to the 7th–8th centuries (Taddei 1999, pp. 392–3). Likewise, ongoing excavations at Barikot are furnishing Vasudeva and Kanishka II imitations in similarly late archaeological contexts (Luca Maria Olivieri, personal communication).

Thus, the numismatic evidence relating to Begram III is ultimately not necessarily at odds with Kuwayama's hypothesis for the date of this phase, but future research on patterns of circulation of the Vasudeva and Kanishka II imitations in such late contexts is also necessary. In particular, clarifying the economic conditions of these patterns of circulation should require assessing whether the relevant coins found in late contexts possess a distinctive, internal metrological and typological coherence, whether a metrological consistency with stratigraphically co-circulating coinage can be observed, and whether these specific coins truly had remained in prolonged circulation since the Kushano-Sasanian period, or may have been minted later. Sadly, from the surviving archaeological and numismatic documentation, undertaking this kind of study in relation to Begram III is impossible.

Conclusion

Reviewing the DAFA excavations at Begram, it is clear that the results these campaigns produced are just as extraordinary as they are problematic, providing us with a significant yet partial view into life at the urban site at Begram. The incompleteness of the data should not be forgotten; surface remains at the site have likely been impacted by surface erosion, those at the lower city (between Burj Abdullah and the New Royal City) as well as at the Burj Abdullah have been impacted by later human occupation, and beyond the products of Masson's collections from the *dasht* of Begram, we know almost nothing about the apparently rich history of occupation in the city's suburbs and agricultural hinterland. The most light was shed by the DAFA on the New Royal City, although the interpretation

Begram excavations	1936 – Site I (Bop. 2001 for MG coins). 65 in KM	1937 – Site I (Bop. 2001 for MG coins). 36 in KM	1937 – Site II (RAB, F1937; Bop. 2001; Morris 2017). 7 in KM	1938 – Site II + Qala (Meunié 1959). All in KM	1938 – Site III (Meunié 1959). All in KM	47 coins 1937–8 :in KM – Site I/II 1937 + Meunié Site II + Qala? (Ghirshman 1946, 86)
Euthydemus						
Pantaleon		2				
Local lion/elephant					1	
Eucratides I					1	
Eucratides imitation	1	1				
Menander I						
Strato						
Apollodotus I						
Antialcidas						
Diomedes						
Parthian imitation						
Hermaeus lifetime or imitation	1					
Spalahores and Spalagadama				1		
Gondophares						
Abdagases						
Indo-Parthian?						
Mujatria						
Azes I imitation						
Kujula Kadphises	4		2			2
Heliocles imitation		1				
Soter Megas	1					4
Wima Kadphises	9		1		1	1
Kanishka I	17	3	3			
Huvishka	17		4			
Vasudeva I (including imitations)	16	4			1 (imitation?)	16 (including imitations)
Vasudeva imitations	2	1	5			
Kanishka II	3	9	1			17
Vasishka	1					
Kushano-Sasanian						1
Sasanian						
Shri Shahi						
illegible	7 + 65 in KM	12 + 36 in KM	+ 5 in KM	4	16	6

Table 3 Synthesis of coin finds from the DAFA excavations. Abbreviations: Bop. = Bopearachchi; MG = Musée Guimet; KM = Kabul Museum

1939 – Site II (NRAB). KM	1939 – Site? (MS NRAB) KM	1940 – Site II (NRAB) KM	1941 – NRC and Burj Abdullah (Göbl) KM	1942 – NRC (Göbl) KM	1946 – city gate (Göbl) KM	Summary (minus coins from 1937–8)-Kabul Museum
				1		1 Euthydemus
						2 Pantaleon
				1		2 Local lion/elephant
			2	13 (including imitations)		16 Eucratides I (including imitations)
						2 imitations
			1	1		2 Menander I
				1		1 Strato
				2	1	3 Apollodotus I
			1			1 Antialcidas
			1			1 Diomedes
				1		1 Parthian imitation
			8 (or lifetime?)	11 (or lifetime?)	2 (or lifetime?)	22 Hermaeus lifetime or imitation
						1 Spalahores and Spalagadama
1			5	15		21 Gondophares
			1	4		5 Abdagases
			1			1 Indo-Parthian?
				1		1 Mujatria
			1			1 Azes I imitation
1			13	56	4	80 Kujula Kadphises
				3		4 Heliocles imitation
			6	21	3	31 Soter Megas
1			5	18	5	40 Wima Kadphises
			13	30	8	74 Kanishka I
		3 (imitations?)	22	36	12	90 Huvishka
6 (imitations?)			7 (including imitations)	31 (including imitations)	21 (including imitations; 4 from hoard)	86 Vasudeva I (including imitations)
						8 Vasudeva imitations
			4	10	65 (including imitations? 61 from hoard)	92 Kanishka II (including imitations?)
						1 Vasishka
				2	4	6 Kushano-Sasanian
			1			1 Sasanian
	1					1 Shri Shahi
54	5	46	7	16	2	275 illegible
					Total: identified unidentified	873 598 275 (see commentary)

of certain remains excavated there – foremost the hoard and the phase of Begram III – have been debated for decades. As we have seen, such uncertainty is primarily caused by documentation issues that were shaped profoundly by the socio-historical context of the excavations, although these can be partly resolved with archival research. The continuing re-examination of the archaeological data produced by the DAFA excavations, if not the distant possibility of future exploration at the site, will help to resolve further longstanding points of concern. But at least now we have an important piece of the puzzle in Masson's collections from the site and its hinterland. With the full publication of these crucial data, it is finally possible to give the urban site of Begram – and especially the New Royal City – some firmer historical context.

Acknowledgements

This contribution draws from doctoral research partly funded through a fellowship in the DFG GSC 1039 and defended in 2017 at Ludwig-Maximilians-Universität Munich, currently in preparation for publication. I am thankful to Osmund Bopearachchi, Pierre Cambon, and the staff of the Musée Guimet's library and photographic archives for their assistance during my research. I am also grateful to Michael Alram and Nikolaus Schindel for making Robert Göbl's notes available to me, a fuller publication of which is intended. Special thanks are due to Luca Maria Olivieri for his comments on an earlier version of this text.

Part 2: The Masson Collections from Begram and Kabul

Chapter 3
Masson Manuscript F526/1a: Analysis of the Begram Coins with Reference to Plates

Piers Baker with Elizabeth Errington

Introduction

Masson submitted three memoirs on the ancient coins found at Begram to James Prinsep, which were published in the *Journal of the Asiatic Society of Bengal* in April 1834, January and May 1836 respectively. The last of these articles (1836b, p. 546) included a rider by Prinsep to the effect that:

> Mr Masson confesses in this memoir that he has been too ready on former occasions to draw inferences which subsequent researches have either failed to confirm or have overthrown. The more he avoids such speculations, the more confidence will be placed in his results, because they will be freed from the suspicion of any bias. We could not, however, have ventured to prune his essays without danger of cutting off what was really valuable, or of robbing him perhaps of some happy conjecture which might hereafter prove well founded. On the same grounds we have formerly allowed names to stand in his list (like *Ausios* [Lysias], &c,), which were evidently wrong, and which his further research has led him to correct. His present elaborate memoir is hardly free from the same objections, for it is yet too early to generalise: nevertheless we do not like to keep back a line of his introduction, replete as it is with valuable information. The list of coins to which it is a prelude includes the whole of his former collection, with additional light thrown on them by other essays published in the *Journal*. It would be a useless and expensive repetition to republish these drawings at length, especially when we have not the coins themselves to engrave from.
>
> We trust, therefore, the author will excuse our limiting an insertion of figures and descriptions to those that are new in name or in type.

In 1995 the original 'elaborate memoir' submitted to Prinsep was unearthed in a box of then still uncatalogued Masson Papers in the India Office Collections of the British Library (**F526/1a**). In direct contrast to Prinsep's opinion, it is now considered the most comprehensive and valuable contribution on coins from Afghanistan, particularly Begram, made by Masson. It has also proved to be invaluable for identifying individual coins in the collection. For these reasons it is published in full below (with the spelling of place names standardised as in Appendix 4; and personal names standardised on modern usage).

The original manuscript plate and figure numbers have been retained here, but are expressed in a specific format (e.g. *Fig. 1*, **Pl. 1.3**) in order to differentiate between **F526/1a** and the **Figs 1–142** of the main body of text. The folios are shown in square brackets e.g. [f. 2]. The text discusses all the coins illustrated in **Plates 1–13**. However Masson includes two further pages of coin drawings without any commentary. These illustrate the coins from the relic deposit of Hadda stupa 10 (**Pls 14–15**) and have been used to reconstitute the numismatic evidence from the site (see **Vol. I, pp. 25–6, 185–8, Figs 9, 281–2**). The manuscript also has three addenda, one illustrating monograms and tamghas (here designated **Pl. 16**); another of monograms on Bactrian and Indo-Greek coins (**Pl. 17**); and a third of Greek and Kharoshthi coin inscriptions (**Pl. 18**). The chapter concludes with two tables, the first an enumeration of the coins collected from Begram (**Table 5**), the second a table of correspondence between the coins illustrated by Masson and those held in the British Museum collections and/or generally recognised published coins types (**Table 6**).

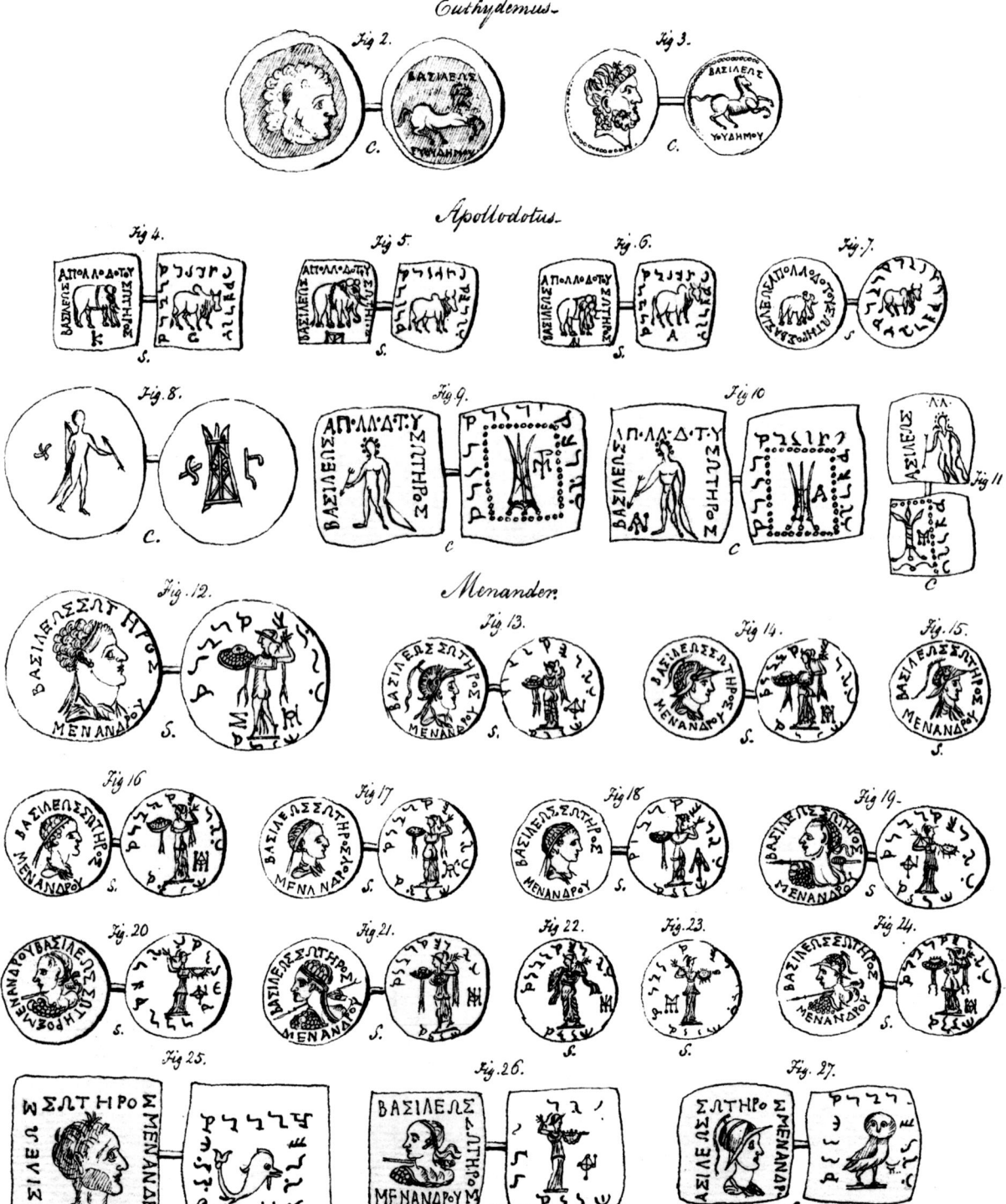

Plate 1 Recorded Greek Bactrian kings. Antiochus (1), Euthydemus (2–3), Apollodotus I (4–11), Menander I (12–27)

[f. 1] **Plate 1. Class 1. Greek Series 1.**
Recorded Kings of Bactria [*Figs 1–27*].
[*Fig. 1*] **Antiochus** [**III** Megas, 223–187 BC][1]

Fig. 1 [IOLC.112 (**Fig. 23.3** below)]. *Reverse* – Apollo, standing, right hand extended and holding an arrow, left hand resting on a bow. Legend Greek CIΛEΩ ANTIOX.

The obverse of this coin found at Begram is not represented, for although obviously a bust, it was too corroded and defaced to be otherwise intelligible. It can refer only to one of the Greek Syrian princes, under whose authority the Bactrian provinces continued from Seleucus to Antiochus III and probably to the latter sovereign. It would seem to be of provincial coinage. The only other circumstance connected to this coin worthy of notice, is that the obverse has a raised or convex surface, to be observed also on some of the copper monies of Euthydemus, the third independent monarch of Bactria, from which we may infer that those of Theodotus and Theodotus II, when discovered, will show the same peculiarity [i.e. Diodotus I and II, *c*. 250–230 BC, see Kovalenko 1995/6].

[*Figs 2–3*] **Euthydemus** [**I**, *c*. 230–200 BC; Wilson 1841, Coins pl. I.14–15]

Fig. 2. Obverse – Bust of King, head bound with fillet. *Reverse* – Horse at speed. Legend Greek ΒΑΣΙΛΕΩΣ ΕΥΘΥΔΗΜΟΥ.

Fig. 3. Obverse / Reverse and legend same as preceding.

These figures represent the copper coins of Euthydemus, the third king of Bactria; they are found at Begram but sparingly. 1833 gave one, 1834 two, and 1835 three. Single coins have also been found at Jalalabad and Ghazni. That this prince could have governed at Begram only at the close of his reign, is evident, because it was necessary that he should first expel Sophagasenus [*c*. late 3rd-century BC Indian king, allied to Antiochus III: see Polybius, XI.34.11–12], who was his contemporary at the time of the invasion of Antiochus, and held authority in the Paropamisadae and at Ghazni, and by inference at Begram also.

Fig. 2 has the obverse on a raised or convex surface, as alluded to above, and is the description of coin generally found.

Fig. 3 has not this peculiarity and is a single specimen. The style and execution of the coins are excellent. We have not hitherto been so fortunate as to procure silver medals of Euthydemus, but the nature of these will be seen by reference to Mr Prinsep's delineations [1833b, p. 312, pl. VII (Thomas 1858, p. 29, pl. II); Prinsep 1835a, p. 337, pl. XXV (Thomas 1858, p. 185, pl. XIII)].

[*Figs 4–11*] **Apollodotus** [**I**, *c*. 180–160 BC; with one coin (*Fig. 8*) of the Khaharata satrap **Higaksha** (*c*. late 1st century AD) copying a coin of **Apollodotus II**, *c*. 80–65 BC].

Fig. 4 to *Fig. 7* represent silver coins of King Apollodotus, and *Fig. 8* to *Fig. 11* represent his copper coins. The former have an elephant with Greek legend on the obverse, and a humped bull with native inscription on the reverse. *Fig. 4, 5, & 6* are square and not uncommon [*Fig. 6*: 1838,EIC.30 (**Fig. 23.24** below)].

Fig. 7 [IOC.68 (**Fig. 23.23**)] is circular and a single specimen. These coins have monograms, sometimes on both obverse and reverse, sometimes only on the reverse. *Fig. 7* has no monogram. The Greek legend is ΒΑΣΙΛΕΩΣ ΑΠΟΛΛΟΔΟΤΟΥ ΣΩΤΗΡΟΣ and the native or Bactrian [Kharoshthi] is correspondent

𐨨𐨱𐨪𐨗𐨯 𐨀𐨤𐨫𐨜𐨟𐨯 𐨟𐨿𐨪𐨟𐨪𐨯 or agreeably to Mr Prinsep's plan *malakáo apaladado rakako* [*sic*: *maharajasa apaladatasa tratarasa*]. The native equivalent for ΣΩΤΗΡΟΣ is also frequently found on these coins, 𐨟𐨿𐨪𐨟𐨪.

The copper coins of Apollodotus, so far as hitherto discovered, agree in the nature of their devices, having the figure of Apollo, with bow and arrow on the obverse, and a singular tripodical emblem on the reverse. The circular coins at *Fig. 8* are of rare occurrence in Afghanistan. *Fig. 9* has the head of Apollo surrounded with dots or rays of glory, but numerous coins are found without such distinctions. The monograms on the copper coins of Apollodotus exceedingly vary – they generally occur only on the reverse of the square coins, but occasional coins have them both on reverse and obverse as *Fig. 10* which is a single specimen. Another coin of this description has ⴺ for [the] monogram on the obverse and ⴽ for that of the reverse. The circular coins would appear to have monograms formed of native characters, which are sparingly to be found on the square ones. Of the latter coins *Figs 9* and *10* are of the largest size and *Fig. 11* of the smallest. Coins of intermediate sizes are found. The numbers in which the coins of Apollodotus are found, may authorise the belief that his reign was rather a long than a short one. We have met with none of them which display his bust, but such coins have been found east of the Indus, and are delineated by Mr Prinsep in his journal [1835a, pl. XX. 6–8]. They are distinguished by the additional epithet of ΦΙΛΟΠΑΤΟΡΟΣ [father-loving], recording his filial affection. It is a source of regret that we can only conjecture as to the father so honoured. If Euthydemus be he, then Apollodotus will have been the founder of Euthydemia, as we perhaps too positively advanced in a memoir last year, and which may have been published in the journal [Masson 1836a, p. 13] – for if Demetrius, as it would seem, general opinion credits, ruled in the North-western provinces of India – Euthydemia may fairly be ascribed to him, and perhaps Apollodotus may have been his son. The expulsion of his father by Eucratides, would have afforded Apollodotus on the death of the latter, both with an opportunity to signalise himself, and in the recovery of the kingdom with a cause for the assumption of the title of Saviour, which was arrogated indiscriminately by his successors, would nevertheless have been adopted with reason in the first instance, and if Apollodotus, as supposed, preceded Menander, so his coins will be the earliest [f. 2] which exhibit that epithet.

[*Figs 12–33*] **Menander** [*c*. 155–130 BC]

[*Fig. 12*: IOC.90 (**Fig. 25.1** below); *Fig. 14*: 1838,EIC.7 (**Fig. 25.5**); *Fig. 16*: 1838,EIC.23 (**Fig. 25.4**); *Fig. 17*: 1838. EIC,1838.19 (**Fig. 25.3**); *Fig. 23*: 1838,EIC.20 (**Fig. 25.12**)]. The coins of the celebrated Menander numerously occur at Begram, and generally in Kabul and the dependent districts. *Fig. 12* to *Fig. 24* exhibit the various types of his silver coinage we have met with, and *Fig. 25* to *Fig. 33* will explain the nature of his copper coins.

[*Figs 12–24*] The silver coins essentially agree in having on the obverse the bust of the prince, with the Greek legend ΒΑΣΙΛΕΩΣ ΣΩΤΕΡΟΣ ΜΕΝΑΝΔΡΟΥ, and on the reverse

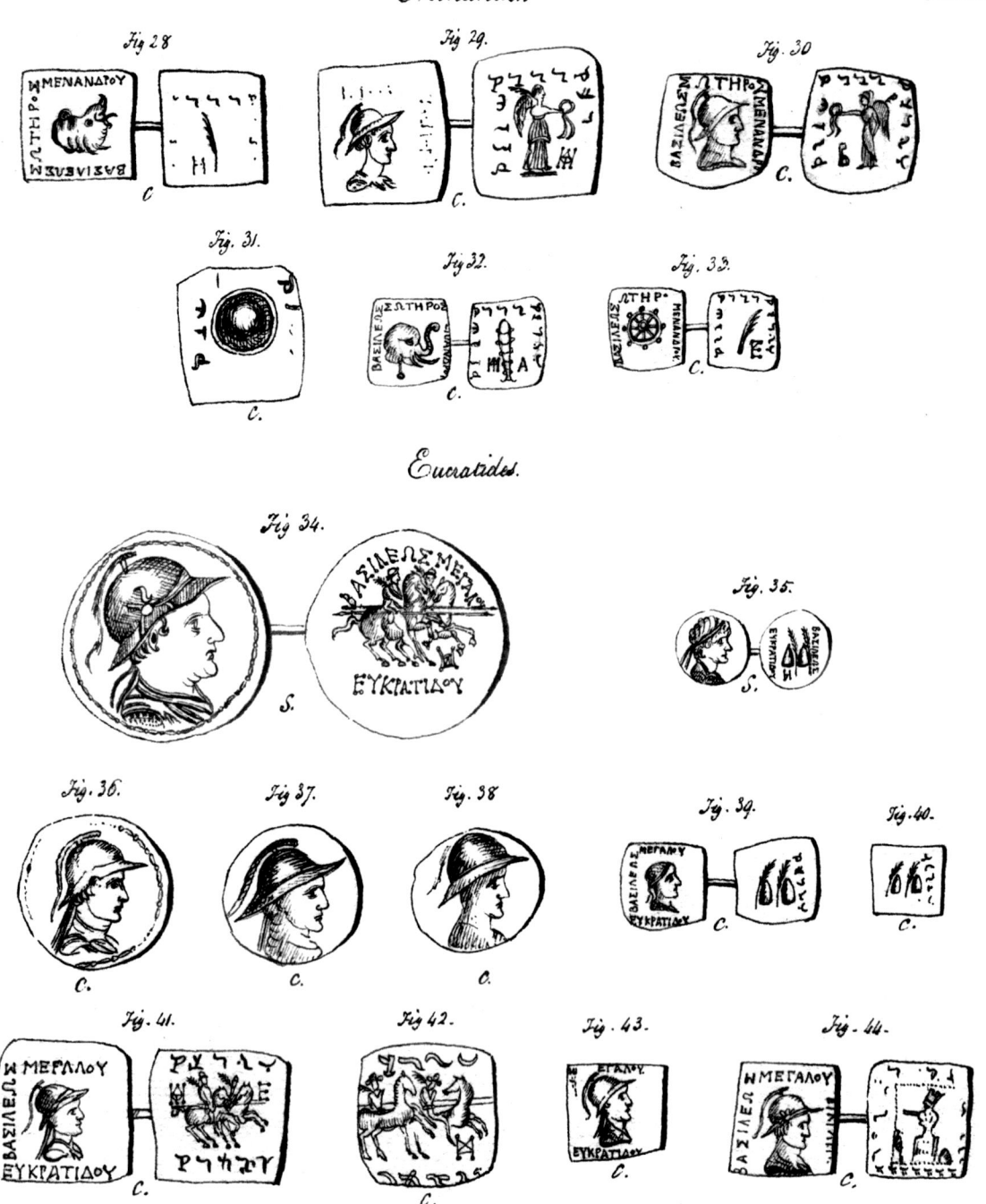

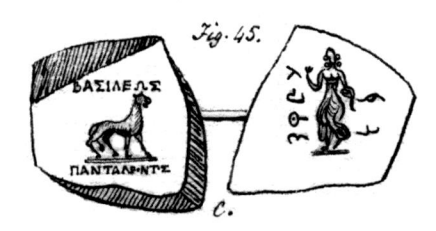

Plate 2 Menander (28–33), Eucratides (34–44), Pantaleon (45)

a warrior, or as Mr Prinsep hints, Minerva, in the act of hurling a bundle of darts with the right hand [Athena hurling a thunderbolt], while the left grasps an embossed buckler [*aegis*]. The same device is found on certain coins of Apollodotus. These silver coins may be reduced into three classes, with reference to the obverse – the first, as *Fig. 13* to *Fig. 15* displaying a helmed bust – the second, as *Fig. 16* to *Fig. 18*, having a plain bust with head bound with the fillet or diadem – and the third, as *Fig. 19* to *Fig. 23*, exhibiting a bust, the head also bound with [a] fillet, but contrary to the two former classes looking to the left, while the right arm raised behind the shoulder is in the act of ejecting a dart or lance. The right shoulder is moreover naked, the left one, is protected with a buckler. *Fig. 24* is a unique specimen of this latter class of coins in which the bust is helmed.

The coins of no prince present so great variety in the devices, as those of Menander, which is particularly evinced by his copper coinage. *Fig. 25* [1926,0502.1 (**Fig. 26.1**)] is a unique specimen procured from Charikar in 1834, having a bust on the obverse, and a fish, probably a dolphin, on the reverse.

Fig. 26 [IOC.96 (**Fig. 26.2**)] has a bust on the obverse, and warrior on the reverse, being analogous to the third class of silver coins – it occurs but rarely, one or two during each year.

Fig. 27 [IOC.102 (**Fig. 26.10**)] has a helmed bust on the obverse, and an owl on the reverse; it is a unique specimen, found in 1833 at Begram.

[**Plate 2**, *Figs 28–43*]

Fig. 28 [IOLC.376 (**Fig. 26.15**)] is alike unique – has a boar's head on the obverse, and a palm branch on the reverse. Begram produced it in 1835. The disposition of the Greek legend on this coin may be remarked.

Fig. 29 and *Fig. 30* [IOC.100 (**Fig. 26.9**)] give the types of a class of coins more abundantly found, particularly as *Fig. 29*. The obverse has a helmed bust and the reverse a winged figure of victory, holding a palm branch in the hand, looking or standing to the right as in *Fig. 29*, or to the left as in *Fig. 30*.

Fig. 31 [IOLC.371 (**Fig. 26.8**)] gives the reverse of a unique coin, whose obverse has a helmed bust – it was found at Begram in 1835, but does not satisfactorily enable to determine, what the orb [*aegis* or shield] was intended to represent.

Fig. 32 shows the type of a small class of coins, which like *Fig. 29* are of ordinary occurrence. They have on the obverse an elephant's head, and on the reverse a long figure, perhaps a fish [*sic*: club].

Fig. 33 [IOC.104 (**Fig. 26.4**)] is a unique specimen from Begram in 1834, the obverse has a wheel [*chakra*], and the reverse a palm branch.

The monograms on the copper coins as on the silver ones of Menander remarkably vary – both are noted in the Table of Monograms [**Pls 16–17**, pp. 69–70]. The copper coins also as the silver ones, have on their obverses the Greek legend ΒΑΣΙΛΕΩΣ ΣΩΤΕΡΟΣ ΜΕΝΑΝΔΡΟΥ and on their reverses the equivalent native or Bactrian 𐨨𐨱𐨪𐨗𐨯 𐨟𐨿𐨪𐨟𐨪𐨯 or as read by Mr Prinsep *malakáo rakako minano* [*maharajasa tratarasa Menamdrasa*] – the Bactrian equivalent for Menander is variously rendered, principally as affects the second letter – we find 𐨨𐨅𐨣𐨯, 𐨨𐨅𐨣𐨯, 𐨨𐨅𐨣𐨯, 𐨨𐨅𐨣𐨯.

Although we have copper coins of Menander, whose analogous silver ones have not been found, it is probable that the whole of the silver ones have correspondent copper ones. It may be also observed, that chance has not hitherto brought to light either a circular copper or a square silver coin of this prince.

The name of no one of the Bactrian princes has been so honourably transmitted to posterity as that of Menander – and in proportion to the interest excited by the knowledge that he was one of the most illustrious princes who ever swayed a sceptre, will be our regret at the absence of historical records, relative to his actions and the events of his life. The only facts, we believe, known of the history of this great monarch, are, that he was the first of the Greek Bactrian sovereigns, who in his course of conquest penetrated to the river Jumna [in the Punjab], and that he died in camp. For the first we are indebted to Strabo [XI.6.1; XV.1.27] and Trogus Pompeius [*Justin Prologues XLI*], for the last to Plutarch [*Moralia* 28.6]. Pliny [VI.100], if memory deceive not, relates that in his time monuments of Menander were to be seen at Barygaza or Bharuch [see also *Periplus*, ch. 47: Casson 1989]. [f. 3] From the number of his coins found annually at Begram, we may however infer that his reign was a long one, or, from twenty to twenty five years – a circumstance confirmed by his coins themselves, on which his busts enable us to trace the various gradations in age, from youth to confirmed manhood. We have before remarked, that the scant historical data we have, are as much against as for the belief, that Menander preceded Eucratides. If the opinion be well founded, that he ruled in some part of India previous to his conquest of Bactria, (an opinion, however liable to objection,) he must have done so, subsequent to Demetrius – and if it be matter of fact, that the latter prince, was despoiled by Eucratides, the same Eucratides must have preceded Menander. That Apollodotus moreover ruled before Menander appears probable if not certain. So far as the execution of coins, may be a criterion of precedence, those of Menander may perhaps collectively be deemed equal to those of Eucratides, some of whose monies (but these are probably of provincial mints) are very irregular in this respect – but there are coins, as we shall presently show, of Eucratides, which surpass as specimens of art, the finest we have hitherto discovered of Menander.

[f. 3: *Figs 34–44*] **Eucratides** [**I**, *c*. 174–145 BC]

Fig. 34 and *Fig. 35* represent silver coins and *Fig. 36* to *Fig. 44* represent copper coins of King Eucratides the Great of Bactria.

Fig. 34. Obverse – Helmed bust of king, in magnificent relief. *Reverse* – Two horsemen at charge [the Dioscuri], with lances and palm branches. Monogram ⋈. Legend Greek – ΒΑΣΙΛΕΩΣ ΜΕΓΑΛΟΥ ΕΥΚΡΑΤΙΔΟΥ.

This splendid coin of a splendid prince, although procured in the bazaar of Kabul, was probably brought from Turkestan.[2]

Fig. 35. Obverse – Bust of a king, head bound with fillet. *Reverse* – Two conical emblems, probably beehives [bonnets of the Dioscuri], with two palm branches. Monogram ⋈. Legend Greek. ΒΑΣΙΛΕΩΣ ΕΥΚΡΑΤΙΔΟΥ.

This small coin was procured from Charikar in the Kohistan of Kabul and may be of importance, as in conjunction with analogous copper ones, it seems to establish a connection of descent or succession between Eucratides and a prince Antilakides [Antialcidas], who will afterwards be noticed – a connection, if allowed, of high value, as history leaves to be supplied by conjecture, both the predecessor and successor to Eucratides. The bust on this coin, from the deficiency of the helm[et], is what Mr Prinsep designates 'the peaceful bust', and the legend in conformity exhibits not the epithet ΜΕΓΑΛΟΥ – however both the helm[et] epithets are found on copper coins whose reverses bear the same emblematical figures.

Figs 36, 37, 38. Obverse – Helmed bust of king. The reverses of these coins are not given, because they are identical with that of *Fig. 34*, as are the legends. These circular coins appear [to be] of a peculiar coinage consecutive to a silver one, of which *Fig. 34* may be a member. The three coins here given are of various sizes, according to their respective ratios of value. Similar coins occur but rarely at Begram; two, three or four only are elicited during the year.

Fig. 39. Obverse – Bust of king, head bound with fillet. Legend Greek ΒΑΣΙΛΕΩΣ ΜΕΓΑΛΟΥ ΕΥΚΡΑΤΙΔΟΥ. *Reverse* – Two conical emblems [bonnets of the Dioscuri] with two palm branches. Legend Bactrian [Kharoshthi], portion visible 𐨤𐨪𐨸𐨯 [*maharajasa*].

Fig. 40. Reverse – Same as preceding. The coin [is] a smaller one.

These two coins, it will be seen, are analogous to the small silver one *Fig. 35*. Coins of this class are not abundant, two, three or four, being found during each year at Begram.

Fig. 41. Obverse – Helmed bust of king. Legend Greek ΒΑΣΙΛΕΩΣ ΜΕΓΑΛΟΥ ΕΥΚΡΑΤΙΔΟΥ. *Reverse* – Two horsemen at charge [Dioscuri], similar to *Fig. 34*. Monogram 𐅽E. Legend Bactrian [Kharoshthi] 𐨤𐨪𐨸𐨯 𐨀𐨿𐨬𐨁𐨐𐨿𐨪𐨟𐨁𐨡𐨯.

Fig. 42. Reverse – Same as preceding, represented to show the irregularity in execution of these coins.

Fig. 43. Obverse – as *Fig. 41*. This is of a smaller series of coins.

[f. 4] These three figures show the type of the ordinary variety of Eucratides coin so numerously found at Begram – analogous indeed to the circular variety, from which however the present differs, both in being square and having native or Bactrian legends – besides in other minor points. We have previously requested that it might be held in remembrance that Begram will have been generally only a provincial capital, and it might be suspected that many of the earlier Bactrian princes had distinct provincial coinages. In the instance of Eucratides, we would believe that the square copper coinage was the produce of a provincial mint or mints, as the circular coinage was of metropolitan origin. There may be the same relations between the circular and square coins of Apollodotus and of Antilakides [Antialcidas] and these circumstances, although trivial, may perhaps be useful as enabling us to conjecture as to the seats of government of these princes. For if a spot be found where the circular coins of these princes should be ascertained to predominate in number over the square ones, supposing our assumptions of distinct coinages correct, we might venture to conclude that we were near their seats of government or within the sphere of circulation of metropolitan currency.

The native or Bactrian legend on these coins has no equivalent for ΜΕΓΑΛΟΥ being simply 𐨤𐨪𐨸𐨯 𐨀𐨿𐨬𐨁𐨐𐨿𐨪𐨟𐨁𐨡𐨯 according to Mr Prinsep, *malakao eukratido* [*maharajasa Evukratidasa*] – or the King Eucratides[3] – the equivalent for Eucratides is sometimes given a slight variation affecting the third letter.

Fig. 44. Obverse – Helmed bust of king. Legend Greek ΒΑΣΙΛΕΩΣ ΜΕΓΑΛΟΥ ΕΥΚΡΑΤΙΔΟΥ. *Reverse* – Seated figure, on head, crown turreted as of Cybele [*sic*: Tyche, city goddess]. Behind the figure a conical emblem or beehive – figure enclosed in a dotted square – beneath the lower line of which is a parallel line of ornaments. Legend Bactrian, but obscure.

This represents a unique coin of Eucratides, found in 1833 at Begram. The Bactrian legend, if legible, as being carried on three sides, would probably have included the equivalent for ΜΕΓΑΛΟΥ and have been 𐨤𐨪𐨸𐨯 𐨐𐨐𐨯 𐨀𐨿𐨬𐨁𐨐𐨿𐨪𐨟𐨁𐨡𐨯 or *malakáo kákáo eukratido*. [*sic*: *kavishiye nagara devata* 'goddess of the city of Kapiśi'].

It may be mentioned in support of Mr Prinsep's reading of *kákáo*, that the same word, or *káká* is still in use among the Afghans, as a term of honour and respect – and they are much flattered by its application to them. To soothe and to command the attention of the rude inhabitant of the wild, it is but prudence to elevate him into a superior by addressing him as *káká*.

While the coins of Eucratides so plentifully occur at Begram, they are found rarely at Jalalabad, a collection of above 500 coins from that vicinity having yielded merely one or two – and the Ventura[4] collection made in the Punjab, or [the] country east of the Indus, had only five, two of which were silver medals. The scarcity of this prince's coins in the regions east of Kabul might authorise the belief that, in his time, an independent Greek Kingdom existed at Nysa or the modern Jalalabad. It may however be urged that Eucratides could have ruled over the countries bordering on the Indus, only towards the very close of his reign or after the expulsion of Demetrius; this allowed, the less frequency of his coins in them may be accounted for. The narrative of the division between Eucratides and his ally Mithridates, of the kingdom of Demetrius, is very obscure, and it is singular that the coins of King Demetrius, should not be found in the countries where conjecture fixes his reign, and which endured for so long a period as 49 years. According to the chronological data of Schlegel [1808], Eucratides reigned so long as 35 years – a term which we have ventured to suggest may be curtailed ten years. The date of his death, assumed as 146 BC, receives some confirmation from the silver medal in the Pembroke cabinet, depicted by Pinkerton, whose monogram is HP or 108, which if indicating the Bactrian era, is of the last year of his reign. Mr Prinsep [1835a, p. 339] has been the first to hint at the identity of Eucratides and the Indian hero Vikramaditya, which if established, may render it necessary to antedate the common era of the Hindus. [Pompeius] Trogus, who mentions Eucratides, flourished in the century before Christ – and Artemidorus, who calls him the Great King, the historian of Ephesus, flourished about 104 BC.

[f. 5] **Class 1. Greek Series 2. Unrecorded Greek Bactrian Kings** presumed to have reigned over Begram, from the regular and constant occurrence of their coins on its site, and from the numbers in which they are found.

[Fig. 45] **Pantaleon** [*c.* 190–185 BC]

Fig. 45. Obverse – Figure of lion [panther]. Legend Greek ΒΑΣΙΛΕΩΣ ΠΑΝΤΑΛΕΟΝΤΟΣ. *Reverse* – Female deity [Krishna's sister Subhadra] with flower in right hand. Legend native [Brahmi] 𑀤 𑀧 𑀟 𑀬 𑀠 𑀲 𑀰.

The coins of this prince, although of regular occurrence at Begram, are found in small numbers, only two or three during each year – indicative of a short reign. We are not allowed to suspect the fact of his having ruled there, from the strict accordance of his coinage, with that of the next prince to be noted.

[Plate 3, *Figs 46–66*]

[Figs 46–7] **Agathocles** [*c.* 190–180 BC]

Fig. 46 [IOC.18 (**Fig. 23.17**)] and *Fig. 47. Obverse* – Figure of lion [panther]. Legend Greek ΒΑΣΙΛΕΩΣ ΑΓΑΘΟΚΛΕΟΥΣ. *Reverse* – Female deity [Subhadra]. Legend native [Brahmi] 𑀤 𑀧 𑀟 𑀬 𑀠 𑀲 𑀰.

The coins of Agathocles are found at Begram in sufficient numbers to authorise the belief that they were certainly once current there, but not to induce the notion that his reign was a very long one. The purity of the Greek legend allows us to place both him and his predecessor Pantaleon, very high on the list of Bactrian princes. The coins of both princes present a singularity in the characters of the native legends, suggested by Mr Prinsep to resemble those found on the several pillars of India, and on the coins of the early princes of Kanauj – and it is remarkable that a series of coins extensively prevalent at Begram, and apparently connected with those of Pantaleon and Agathocles, depicted as *Fig. 76* and *Fig. 77* of Plate 24 [*sic*: **Plate 4**], should exhibit the identical emblems or symbolical characters so conspicuously displayed on the ancient coins elicited at Kanauj and Behat [both in Uttar Pradesh: Prinsep 1835b]. Had we not disclaimed any very particular adherence to method in this Memoir, these coins would have been introduced subsequent to those of Agathocles – as it is, it is sufficient in this place to point out the connection between them. To have introduced them would moreover have involved the necessity of succeeding them by the analogous coins represented as *Fig. 68* to *Fig. 75*, **Plate 4**, which however cannot be conceded the same antiquity which must be granted to those of the sovereigns before us.

The Ventura collection, it may be remarked, included not one of the copper coins of Pantaleon or Agathocles, but it brought to knowledge a fine silver medal, no doubt referring to the later prince, and depicted by Mr Prinsep [1835a, pl. XXV.3]. The monogram on this coin is Bactrian and found on the square coins of a prince ΕΡΜΑΙΟΥ (see *Fig. 66*, **Plate 3**). Subsequent collections in the regions bordering on the Indus, may however produce coins of these princes, and we infer such will be the case, as *Fig. 75* of the connected coins, represents a coin brought to us from Peshawar.

It would be superfluous to speculate as who Agathocles may have been, or whether he should stand before or after Eucratides. The peculiarity of the native legend on the coins of him and of his predecessor, seem to intimate some revolution in authority, which our knowledge, limited as it is, affords not the means to explain. It is possible that the Greeks, whose footing in the Gangetic provinces may be conjectured to have been firmly established, should have at some period seized upon the sovereignty of Kanauj, and that Pantaleon one of their princes should have extended his arms to the Hindu Kush? Or, in what manner are we to account for a King of Bactria, having stamped on his coins the characters of Kanauj?

[Fig. 48] **Lysius** [**Lysias** *c.* 120–110 BC]

Fig. 48 [IOC.57 (**Fig. 27.6**)]. *Obverse* – Bust of prince, a pad, or it may be a palm branch, projecting from behind the shoulders [*sic*: Heracles and club]. Monogram C. Legend Greek ΒΑΣΙΛΕΩΣ ΑΝΙΚΗΤΟΥ ΛΥΣΙΟΥ. *Reverse* – Elephant. Monogram 𐤠𐤔. Legend Bactrian 𐨤 𐨌 𐨱 𐨀 𐨤 𐨁. 𐨤𐨱𐨱 𐨤 𐨍 𐨁 𐨪 𐨮

The coins of Lysias are found but in small number yet regularly at Begram, two, three or four during each season – but as in the instance of Pantaleon and Agathocles, the connection between the coins of Lysias and his successor Antialcidas warrant the conviction that he reigned in these countries, as the latter must have done – and moreover lead to the supposition that his reign was a short one. The Ventura collection intimates that the coins of Lysias and Antialcidas are found in the Punjab in the same relative numerical proportion – as it contained one of the former and seven of the latter. The monogram 𐤠𐤔 of the Lysias coin, occurs also on some of Antialcidas.

[f. 6] The native legend [Kharoshthi] on these coins is read by Mr Prinsep, *malakai, apatilado, lisati* or *litato* (?) [*sic*: *maharajasa apadihatasa Lisikasa* 'of the great king Lysias the invincible'] – the equivalent for Lysias is however given by him 𐨤𐨌 𐨌𐨍 which varies from the form we observe on the coins (three only) before us – on these it is 𐨤 𐨱 𐨌 𐨍 which upon the same gentleman's plan, we should read *litikao* – were it possible to read *lilitao* – we should discover a name borne by a conqueror of Kashmir, Lilita-ditya [Lalitaditya], mentioned in the *Rajatarangini* – we mean not however to suggest that our Lysias is the Kashmirian conqueror.

[Figs 49–53] **Antilakides** [**Antialcidas** *c.* 115–95 BC]

Fig. 49 [IOC.57 (**Fig. 27.6**)]. *Obverse* – A helmed bust. Legend Greek ΒΑΣΙΛΕΩΣ ΝΙΚΗΦΟΡΟΥ ΑΝΤΙΛΑΚΙΔΟΥ. *Reverse* – A deity seated on throne, right hand supporting a small winged figure, left hand holding a staff [Zeus with Nike]. Monogram ℞. Legend Bactrian [Kharoshthi] but incomplete.

This Figure represents a silver drachma of King Antialcidas. The figure on the reverse, as regards the smaller figure supported in the right hand, may be thought to have some affinity to the reverse of the silver coin of Agathocles, in the Ventura collection before alluded to. The monogram we also find on coins of Apollodotus. It is to be regretted that the native legend is incomplete, as it would seem to have been longer than that found on the copper coins.

Fig. 50. Obverse – Bust of King, pads depending from back of head [Zeus with thunderbolt over shoulder]. Legend Greek – portion visible ΝΙΚΗΦΟΡΟ [ΒΑΣΙΛΕΩΣ

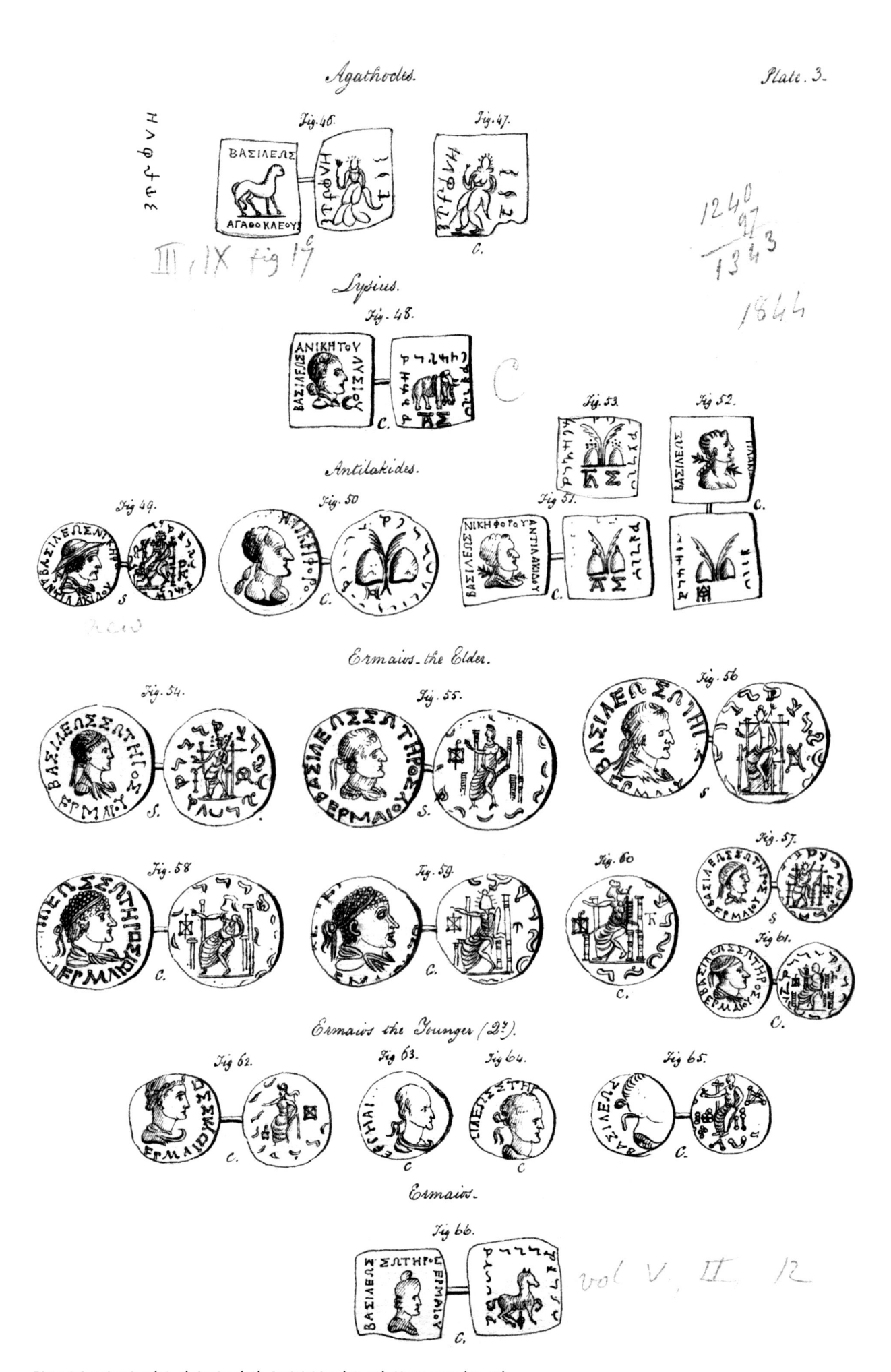

Plate 3 Agathocles (46–7), Lysias (48), Antialcidas (49–52), Hermaeus (53–66)

ΝΙΚΗΦΟΡΟΥ ΑΝΤΙΑΛΚΙΔΟΥ]. *Reverse* – Two beehives [bonnets of the Dioscuri] with palm branches. Monogram ⌶ Legend Bactrian [Kharoshthi], but indistinct.

This represents a circular copper coin, and the only one we have met with, procured in 1834 from Begram. It may be of importance, as in conformity to our notions of distinct coinages, it may refer to the metropolitan currency of King Antialcidas – the monogram is somewhat analogous to that on the coin of a prince Diomedes [*c.* 95–90 BC].

Figs 51, 52, 53. Obverse – Busts of king with palm branch extending across the shoulders – or it may be darts [Zeus with thunderbolt]. Legend Greek as *Fig. 49. Reverse* – Beehives [bonnets of the Dioscuri] and palm branches. Monograms ⌶Σ ⌶ Legend Bactrian [Kharoshthi] *maharajasa jayadhatasa atialikudasa* [*sic*: *maharajasa jayadharasa Amtialkidasa*] 𐨿𐨪𐨿𐨗𐨭𐨿𐨪𐨞𐨿 𐨪𐨗𐨳𐨁 𐨀𐨁𐨮 𐨪𐨁𐨥.

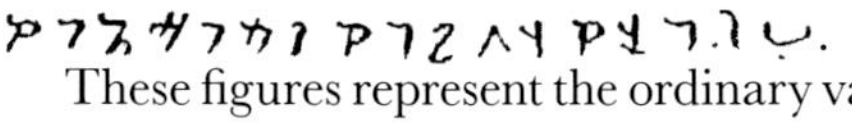

These figures represent the ordinary varieties of the square copper coinage of Antialcidas. The reverse of *Fig. 53*, showing the swarms of bees [*sic*: palm fronds] above the conical emblems, is decisive as to their character – and the reverse of the coins therefore displays the symbols of industry, plenty and victory. The native legend Mr Prinsep reads *malakáo, ajalado, atilikado* or *átikatikado* – the latter reading of the name, we should prefer, – or it may be *átiálikado*.

It merits attention, that the copper coins of Antialcidas, have similar reverses to those of certain coins both silver and copper of Eucratides, seeming to imply a connection of descent or succession. In the latter case, it might be supposed that we had discovered the parricide and successor of the Great King, but we think that circumstances may be adduced as evidence, that Antialcidas was prior to Eucratides and may have immediately preceded him. The coins of the latter prince, with these emblems, may be those of the early part of his reign. The silver drachma *Fig. 49* may have an affinity to the silver medal of Agathocles, and the latter coin authorises us to place the sovereign high on the list of Bactrian sovereigns, as do his copper coins, from the great purity of their Greek legends – not withstanding their uncouth form. Lysias would also seem to have been prior to Antialcidas, and Pantaleon and Agathocles to both.[5]

The discovery of such silver coins as these of Agathocles and Antialcidas, warn us to be cautious in drawing inferences from copper coins, which may be, as before hinted of metropolitan or provincial coinage. A satisfactory adjustment of the descent and succession of the Bactrian monarchs, if ever to be effected, will only be attainable when we shall have before us the entire series of their coins, particularly those of the precious metals; and for this object time is necessary, and chance must be concurring.

[f. 7. *Figs 54–61*] **Ermaios the Elder** [**Hermaeus** *c.* 90–70 BC; lifetime and anonymous issues in the name of Hermaeus].

Fig. 54 to *Fig. 57* represent silver [lifetime] coins and *Fig. 58* to *Fig. 61* represent copper coins [in the name] of King Ermaios [imitations and posthumous issues, possibly produced by the Yuezhi]. As they all agree in their general character, it becomes unnecessary to designate them separately. The obverses exhibit the bust of a king with a Greek legend ΒΑΣΙΛΕΩΣ ΣΩΤΕΡΟΣ ΕΡΜΑΙΟΥ, and the reverses, Jupiter [Zeus] enthroned, the right hand supporting an eagle, the bird of Jove, and the left holding a staff or sceptre. The monograms vary, and may be seen in the Table of Monograms [**Pls 16–17** below]. The copper coins have behind the enthroned figure, also Bactrian monograms, as 𐨁, 𐨨, &c. The Bactrian [Kharoshthi] legend is 𐨪𐨗 𐨀𐨁𐨮 𐨪𐨗𐨳 𐨗𐨪𐨗 𐨗𐨪𐨗, according to Mr Prinsep, *malakáo, rakako, ermayo* [*sic*: *maharajasa tratarasa Heramayasa* of great king Hermaeus the saviour].

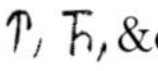

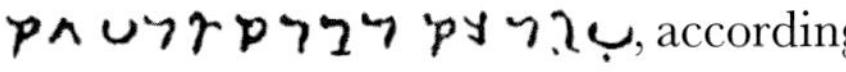

We corrected in our memoir of 1834, published in the *Journal As. Soc.* the opinion that Hermaeus was the founder of the dynasty of Nysa, as set forth in our Memoir of the preceding year – and therein suggested that he might be the successor to Menander. Indeed a striking resemblance exists between the better silver coins of the two princes, particularly in the parity of their style and execution – see *Fig. 54* [IOC.133 (**Fig. 28.1**)] of Hermaeus and *Fig. 12* **Plate 1** [IOC.90 (**Fig. 25.1**)] of Menander. *Fig. 55* and *Fig. 56* of inferior execution are obviously of provincial coinage. We also noted in our last year's memoir, that the coins of Hermaeus found at Begram, represent him in advanced life, but his silver coins manifestly show that he commenced his reign when young, and it is just to observe, that an occasional copper coin is elicited at Kabul or Jalalabad, which displays the same youthful features, and this description of coin is always of superior execution, and may be from the mints of his capital which may possibly have been distant from Begram. The coins of Hermaeus seem to testify that he enjoyed a long reign, and his bust seems to denote a sovereign of ability.

Ermaios the Younger (?) [**Hermaeus posthumous imitations** *c.* mid 1st century BC – early 1st century AD].

Fig. 62 [IOC.148 (**Fig. 28.8**)] to *Fig. 65* represent a series of coins of annual occurrence at Begram, and analogous to those Hermaeus preceding, and whose name they also bear – they would also in size and consequent value, seem to occupy the space between the larger coins of Hermaeus the Elder as *Fig. 58*, and the smaller ones as *Fig. 61*. On the other hand, their style is somewhat different and the Greek legend runs ΒΑΣΙΛΕΩΣ ΣΤΗΡΟΣΣΥ ΕΡΜΑΙΟΥ – the same as occurs on the coins of a prince of the same name, to be hereafter mentioned. The few specimens of this type of coin before us, do not enable us to give with precision the native legend.

Ermaios [**Hermaeus lifetime** copper issue, *c.* 90–70 BC].

Fig. 66 [IOC.150 (**Fig. 28.4**)]. *Obverse* – Bust of king, with pad on crown of head [*sic*: Mithras wearing a Phrygian cap]. Legend Greek ΒΑΣΙΛΕΩΣ ΣΩΤΕΡΟΣ ΕΡΜΑΙΟΥ. *Reverse* – Naked horse. Monogram ⊕. Legend Bactrian [Kharoshthi] 𐨪𐨗 𐨀𐨁𐨮 𐨪𐨗 𐨪𐨗𐨪𐨗 – *maharajasa dadátsa ermayasa*. [*sic*: *maharajasa tratarasa Hermayasa* of great king Hermaeus the saviour].

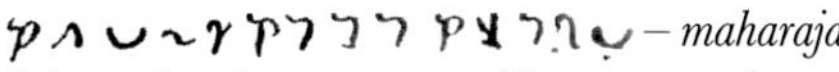

This figure represents a square species of coin, of which Begram in 1833 gave two specimens, and in 1834, 1835 none. Jalalabad gave in 1833, one specimen and a very fine one, which we regret we did not delineate, as our representation would then have been of a perfect coin, as it is now of a defaced one. The Jalalabad coin rivalled the better

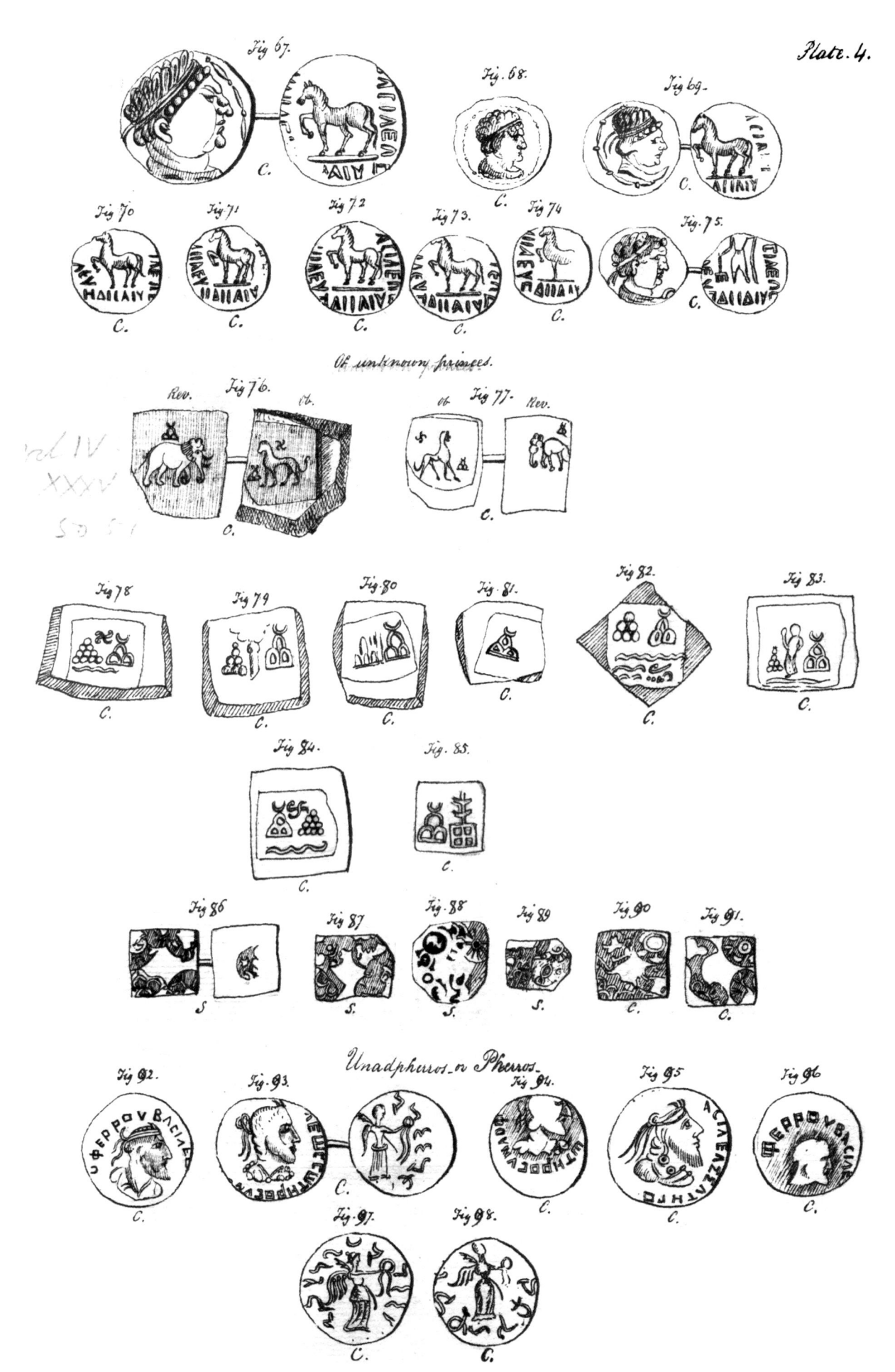

Plate 4 Heliocles imitations of Wima Takto (67–75), Local coins (76–85), Punch-marked (86–91), Gondophares (92–8)

specimens of Menander in execution. One other defaced but recognisable coin of this species, we extracted with sundry others from a Tope at Hadda near Jalalabad, where of course it was a curiosity at the time of deposit [Hadda stupa 3; see **Vol. I, Fig. 256.24**]. Whether this coin refers to Hermaeus the Elder or not, we cannot determine, the principal argument against it may be the pad on the head. The monogram, or a very analogous one, is found on the silver coin of Agathocles in the Ventura collection.

[f. 8] The device, on the reverse of the coins, of a naked horse, is only again found, on the coins of the prince we shall next notice and it may be remarked that as in these coins the animal stands to the left, so in those of Hermaeus it stands to the right, as if it were thought necessary to adopt the same device, and yet constitute a distinction – the animals on both species of coin have also the peculiarity of the fore-foot raised. In other respects, the coins of Hermaeus and those of the succeeding prince, have no points of agreement, and we introduce them next not from the supposed analogy, but rather from the necessity of introducing them somewhere.

[**Plate 4**, *Figs 67–98*]
[*Figs 67–75*] **Diæus, Dicæus or Dicaio (?)** [ΔΙΚΑΙΟΥ ('the Just'): **Heliocles I** (*c.* 120–90 BC) **imitations**. The tamgha – ⚌ – on the rump of the horse in good specimens identifies the coins as issues of Wima Takto (AD 90–113), see Cribb 2014, p. 125, figs 20–1].

Fig. 67 to *Fig. 75* represent the varieties of a type of coin, aptly described by Mr Prinsep, as 'sui generis' and is the one alluded to in the preceding remarks.

Fig. 67. Obverse – Bust of king, enclosed in an ornamental circle. *Reverse* – Naked horse standing to the left with fore-foot raised. Legend corrupt Greek and incomplete [ΒΑΣΙΛΕΩΣ ΔΙΚΑΙΟΥ ΗΛΙΟΚΕΟΥΣ 'of King Heliocles the Just'].

Fig. 68. Obverse – This, a superior coin, was found at Begram in 1835. Coins of this size occur but rarely and seldom in so good preservation. The execution is very tolerable.

Fig. 69 [misnumbered *Fig. 68* in **F526/1a, f. 8**]. *Obverse* of a coin of the same prince, the reverse has a horse as is clearly recognisable, although nearly worn smooth, with the line of the legend to the right ΒΑΣΙΛΕΩC. This coin is a unique specimen of the type, yielded by Begram in 1835, and very thin. The reverse is hollowed by the relief of the obverse, as is the case with early Sasanian coins.

Fig. 70 to *Fig. 74* [misnumbered *Figs 59–74* in **F526/1a, f. 8**] represent the types of the coins of this prince ordinarily found, the multiplied reverses are exhibited for the purpose of attempting the identification of the legend.

Fig. 75. Obverse – Bust of prince. *Reverse* – Erect figure [Zeus]. Legend corrupt obscure Greek. This is a unique specimen from Begram 1835. The reversed trident, from the state of the coin, may be either a detached emblem or held in hand.

There are some peculiarities to be noticed on these coins, as the general character of the bust, especially on the larger coin – the wart or excrescence on the nose – with the nature of the head-dress. The absence of a native legend and the obscurity of the Greek one, also claim attention. The present year 1835, had furnished two novel varieties of this species of coin, and it is therefore possible that others may yet be elicited. It being of primary importance to become acquainted with the name of a prince whose coins we detect, the reverses containing the legends of our most intelligible specimens are submitted. The name or epithet it may be, is evidently concealed in the lower line of the legend – the side lines being ΒΛCΙΛΕVC ΒΑCΙΛΩC as is clear from the united specimens – in *Fig. 70* the lower line would appear ΗΔΙCΑΙΥ, but the first letter is obviously the C the last letter of the left side line – as the other specimens show, particularly *Fig. 74* – the name or epithet becomes reduced therefore to six letters, of which the first is satisfactorily a Δ and the second an I, the third may be an I also, but it may be a C, as this letter occurring in the left side lines in the word ΒΑCΙΛΕVC, is represented with scarcely any distinction from I, as in *Fig. 71* and *Fig. 74* especially. The fourth letter might be read Δ in *Fig. 75* but in all other examples it is manifestly an A – the two final letters are not to be mistaken in any of the specimens, being I and V. We may therefore be allowed to read this lower line of the legend ΔΙΙΑΙV or perhaps more correctly ΔΙCΑΙV. If we ventured to anglicise these terms Diiæus or Diæus and Dicæus may be admitted to be Greek names, while Dicaiu or Dicaio has a great affinity in sound at least to Dikaios, an epithet liberally assumed by many princes, particularly of the Parthian dynasty. A strong Parthian tinge pervades the character of the coinage of the prince we comment on, but it may be the effect of imitation.

[Marginal note] 'These coins are barbarous or provincial coins of Heliocles a king of Bactria – a coin subsequently procured I believe by Court[6] [BM OR.5996] and figured by Prinsep [1836a, p. 550, pl. XXXV.4] decided the matter, as the reverse gave the same figure which the celebrated coin described by Mionnet [1837, pp. 460–506] bears – a copy of the latter I saw in the Penny Cyclopedia'.

[f. 9. *Figs 76–91*] **Of unknown princes** [**local issues and punch-marked coins**, *c.* 3rd–1st century BC].

Fig. 76 and *Fig. 77* represent a species of coins [so-called 'local Taxila' issues], having lions on the obverses [*sic*: reverses], and elephants on the reverses [*sic*: obverses] – distinguished by peculiar symbols ⚘ and ⚛ the latter called by Mr Prinsep, the swastika mark – the only variations to be noted in these coins, are the positions of the animals, as they stand to the right or left – and in the style of execution. The specimens selected for delineation are of the superior kind. It will be noted that the lion [panther] is the obverse [*sic*: reverse] figure on the copper coins of Agathocles and Pantaleon and their coins bear so much analogy, to these under consideration, in form and appearance, that upon receiving a new supply of coins from any quarter, we are at sight enabled to select the three sets, while it is necessary to remove their coverings of earth to distinguish the one from the other. All that we dare to speculate upon these monies, in the absence of legends, is that they may refer to the two princes just named, these being also two varieties of them – should they not, they may commemorate two nameless princes, who will certainly have governed at Begram, where the coins constantly occur in considerable number.

Fig. 78 to *Fig. 85* represent the types of a series of coins, which the generic symbolical characters ☸ and ⚕ connect with the preceding series. They are distinguished by the reverse exhibiting a plain smooth surface, without any marks or characters, as far as we can judge from the few specimens we have before us [*Fig. 81*: IOC.1053 (**Fig. 22.8**); *Fig. 82*: IOC.1052 (**Fig. 22.3**); *Fig. 84*: IOLC.1051 (**Fig. 22.1**)]. *Fig. 78* to *Fig. 84* are from Begram and *Fig. 85* from Peshawar. In addition to the generic symbols, these coins display some novel ones, and in *Fig. 83* a female figure is apparently introduced. These coins are not abundant in Begram, those here figured are all that it yielded in 1835, and in the two former years either none were found or only one or two unintelligible specimens which escaped our detection. In form, they resemble the lion and the elephant coins, with less clumsiness.

Fig. 86 to *Fig. 91* represent the types of an additional series of [punch-marked] coins, connected with the two preceding by the generic symbol ☸, and presenting new ones, such as the sun, moon, stars &c. On *Fig. 88* [*sic*: *Fig. 86*; Gupta and Hardaker 2014, p. 180, type GH 574] is the figure of a cow or some animal. These coins have the smooth surface on the reverse, stamped with some impress, as represented in *Fig. 86*, but too obscure to be intelligible. They have not the clumsy form of their prototypes. *Fig. 86* to *Fig. 89* are of silver, and *Fig. 90* and *Fig. 91* of copper. These coins are found more frequently in the bazaars of towns, as Kabul, Ghazni &c than at the site of Begram, where being of only very casual occurrence, we would not venture to affirm that they have been ever current there. They are evidently the more modern of the several varieties of the grand series we meet with in Afghanistan, and it will be seen that the silver coins are more frequent than the copper ones, and both of them rare.

Coins of the two last species have been found at Kanauj, Benares and Behat – to the east – in the maritime provinces of Kutch and Gujarat – to the south west of Hindustan, while besides being discovered at Ujjain and other spots in the central provinces, they are detected not only in the regions bordering on the Indus, but, as is evident from the above examples, in the provinces west of that river, so far as the modern Kabul – seeming to imply that they had once circulation over the whole continent of India, accepted in its widest sense. The lion and elephant coins must be excluded in these remarks, their circulation having been probably more limited, none of them, so far we know, having been found in Hindustan Proper. Although the coins we have met with of this class have no legends, an analogous one found at Behat, and depicted by Mr Prinsep [1834, pp. 227–8, pl. IX.1] has a legend in the characters we call Bactrian [Kuninda silver coin depicting a deer and Lakshmi, *c*. 1st century BC, with Brahmi inscription]. Coins, of a different character indeed, but preserving the generic symbol ☸, (see fig. 19 of pl. IX just noted [Prinsep 1834, pl. IX.19, Thomas 1858, p. 86, pl. IV.19: silver Western Satrap coin of Rudrasena I, AD 200–22]) have fortunately fallen under Colonel Tod's observations, and he ascribes them to [f. 10] the Balla Raes of Anhalwára Patan [Tod 1826; Thomas 1858, p. 86]. It may be suggested whether the quotation from the Arabian traveller, happily given by the Colonel with reference to his coins, may not somewhat explain those before us. 'He, the Balhara prince, has of these pieces of silver, called Tartarian drams'. This remark implies that the Balhara coinage had for prototype a Tartarian one, and Bactrian or Scythian would naturally be called Tartarian by an Arabian. The question remains whether these coins we have under consideration, be not those Tartarian and Bactrian prototypes.

[Figs 92–8] **Unad-Pherros or Pherros (?)** [**Gondophares**, Indo-Parthian king *c*. AD 32–58]

Fig. 92 to *Fig. 98* represent the type of the copper coinage of King Pherros or Unad-Pherros [Gondophares]. The obverses have the bust of the king – the head, bound with a fillet the ends dependent behind, and crowned with a tuft or tufts, probably the jiker [?]. The legend in corrupt Greek ΒΑCΙΛΕШΙC CШΤΗΡΟC VΝΑΔΦΕΡΡΟV. The reverses exhibit a winged figure of victory [Nike], with a chaplet or wreathe in the right hand, and a palm branch in the left, resting on the shoulder. The legend native or Bactrian [Kharoshthi] appears to be 𐨤𐨫 𐨨𐨱𐨪𐨗𐨯 𐨒𐨂𐨢𐨤𐨱𐨁𐨯 𐨟𐨿𐨪𐨟𐨪𐨯 which Mr Prinsep [1835a, p. 147, pl. XXIV.5–8] suggests may be read *malakáo fareto nanado* [*sic*: *maharajasa Gudaphanisa tratarasa* of the great king Gondophares the saviour]. This prince, will have reigned over the provinces east of the Indus as well as those west of it as far as the Ghazni at least. The Ventura collection possessed 23 of them.

Mr Prinsep first intimated that Pherros might be the Phraates or Phraortes visited by Apollonius [of Tyana] at his capital of Taxila east of the Indus, at the commencement or early part of the first century of our era [Philostratus II.26]. Although this intimation be founded on a similarity of nomenclature, it may be worthwhile to examine whether it may be supported by other circumstances – because if our Pherros be Phrahates [Praates], we gain a fixed point, useful in our reflections upon the chronology of our coins. Besides the evidences as to Pherros, which his own coins supply, accidental circumstances have contributed but little towards a better acquaintance with him – yet that little is available. [Marginal note] 'The native legend of these coins is actually read by Prinsep *Phráhatasa* [1835a, p. 147]'.

Among the coins, some thirty extracted from a Tope called Jani Tope [Bimaran stupa 5] by M. Honigberger, was one of Pherros [see **Vol. I, pp. 118–19**]. The monument undoubtedly referred to a prince of the dynasty, whose coins have the figure of Hercules on the reverse [Kujula Kadphises] – and the presence of the coin of Pherros, proved that he flourished anterior to the erection of the structure and by inference to the dynasty. The coin found was of that particular coinage represented by *Fig. 96* – and like all coins of that coinage we meet with, much worn. As Pherros must have governed at Begram, we set ourselves to calculate the probable reigns of those princes, whose coins are also found on its site, and who must have preceded him in rule – and began from the death of Euthydemus stated by Schlegel [1808] to have occurred 195 BC. From that time to 50 AD, assumed as about the age of Taxila, is a period of 245 years, to be filled up by the reigns of princes whose coins probably we possess. On the first glance, we have fifteen or sixteen princes who must or may have preceded Pherros, and roundly estimating the reign of each at fifteen years, we are

Princes who must have reigned at Begram between the epochs 195 BC, that of the death of Euthydemus, and 50 AD assumed as that of Pherros [Gondophares].		Probable duration of reign	Comments
1.	Apollodotus [I]	15	Assumed from his coins – possibly underrated.
2.	Menander	25	Assumed from his coins – possibly within a year or two of the fact.
3.	Eucratides [I]	35	Asserted historically – confirmed by great numbers of his coins found.
[f. 11]	*Carried forward*	75	
4.	Pantaleon	5	Assumed from his coins – found in small numbers.
5.	Agathocles	12	Assumed from number of coins found.
6. 7.	Two unknown princes, whose coins have the lion and elephant type [local so-called 'Taxila' issues]	20	Assumed from number of coins found, should this variety of coin refer to the two former princes, the amount must be carried to their reigns.
8.	Lysius [Lysias]	5	Assumed from small number of coins found.
9.	Antilakides [Antialcidas]	12	Assumed from number of coins found – possibly underrated.
10.	Ermaios the Elder [Hermaeus lifetime issues]	25	Assumed from coins – perhaps underrated.
11.	Dicaio (?) [Heliocles imitations – Wima Takto]	15	Assumed from coins.
	Total	94	
	Brought forward	75	
	Total	169	
Princes who may have reigned before Pherros [Gondophares]			
12.	The great prince whose coins bear the legend ΒΑΣΙΛΕΩΣ ΣΩΤΗΡ ΜΕΓΑΣ [Wima Takto]	27	Proved by results of his cenotaph – confirmed by coins [stupas misidentified as cenotaphs].
13.	A successor of above	4	Proved by results of his cenotaph – confirmed by coins.
14.15.16.	Successors of above	30	Whose cenotaphs exist, but yielded no results – their reigns therefore merely conjecturably fixed.
	Total	230	
17.	Hermaios of Nysa [Kujula Kadphises]	20	Introduced if necessary – because his coins are superior to those of Pherros [Gondophares]
	Total	250	

Table 4 Masson's chart of rulers and estimated reigns

at once brought to his epoch or to that of Phrahates of Taxila – but as some of these princes reigned longer than fifteen years, and some we may conclude to have reigned a less term – we drew up the accompanying list in detail of the princes and their reigns, as authorised by their coins and other circumstances – a list however liable to all and every correction.

It is not improbable that Pherros [Gondophares] should have flourished in the interval between the fall of the dynasty, whose princes we have numbered 12 to 16, and the accession of the dynasty of the Nysian Hermaeus [Kujula Kadphises] – that period would no doubt have been one of revolutions in these countries, but of these, we have no more profitable notions, than conjecture may afford. The princes just alluded to preceded the dynasty of the Nysian Hermaeus as did Pherros – for if other proof were wanting, the same monument which yielded a coin of Pherros, gave two others of the prince we number 13 [see **Table 4**]. It is also very singular that [Wima] Kadphises should have claims to be considered about this period – the Greek legends of his coins being identical, even to the forms of the corrupt characters used, with those of the great prince No. 12 and his successors. It is necessary, in this place, however only to show the probability that our Pherros, whether Phrahates or not, may have flourished about 50 AD – nor does the probability in our estimation, lack confirmation, when we consider that the numerous princes of the dynasty of Hermaeus of Nysa, who must have succeeded him in authority, will reasonably fill up a period of 250 years, which brings us down to 200 AD, an epoch which we have ever been fain to believe is about that of Kanerkos [Kanishka].

[f. 11. **Plate 5**, *Figs 99–121*]
[*Figs 99–106*] **Princes of Nysa. Azus Dynasty** [Indo-Scythian, **Azes I**, c. 46–1 BC; *sic*: Kushan, **Wima Takto**, c. AD 90–113].
Fig. 99 to *Fig. 103* represent the types of the copper coinage of a prince, but without disclosing his name, who we suppose to have had his capital at Nysa (*hodie* Jalalabad)[7] from the circumstance of his cenotaph in that vicinity having been opened by M. Honigberger [Bimaran stupa 3; see **Vol. I, pp. 111–13**].

Fig. 99 shows the obverse of a variety of coin, but rarely found, in which the king is helmed, it has also a peculiar emblem ꟼ, which if possibly a literal one, will be equivalent to *ti* [*vi*]. The reverse of these coins, differs in no respect, from that on the succeeding specimens figured.

Fig. 100 to *Fig. 103* represent the ordinary varieties of coinage so plentifully found at Begram and generally in Western [*sic*: eastern] Afghanistan. The obverse gives the bust of the monarch, the head bound with a fillet, and surrounded with rays, while the right hand upraised holds a sceptre, sword or

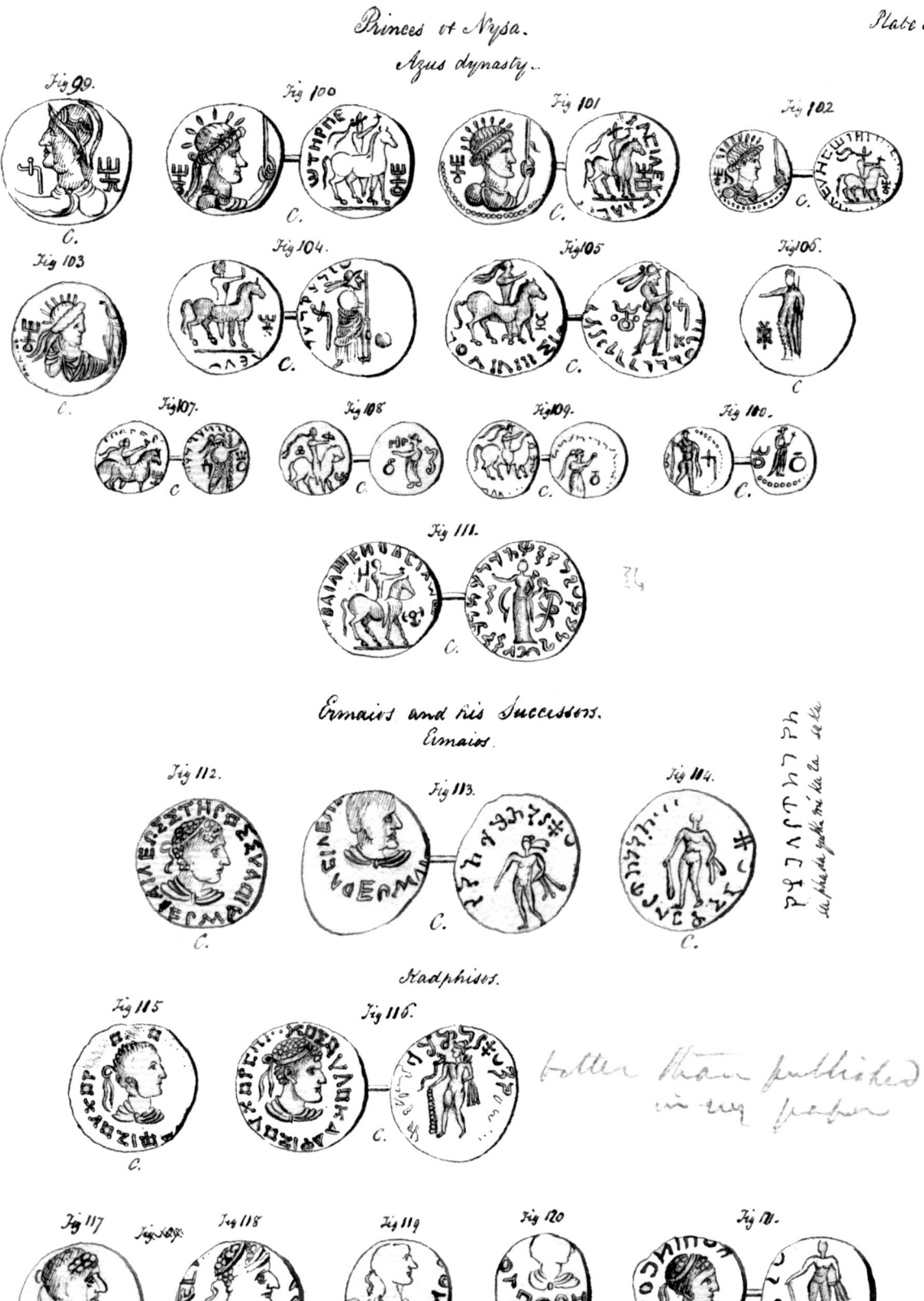

Plate 5 Soter Megas (99–106), Azes II (107–11), Kujula Kadphises (112–21)

48 | *Charles Masson: Collections from Begram and Kabul Bazaar, Afghanistan, 1833–1838*

emblem of authority, behind the bust is a tridental monogram ⛥ here first observed. The reverse exhibits a horseman, his head bound with a fillet, the ends flowing at length behind, while the right hand sustains, what has been supposed a hawk, but probably some weapon [an arrow] – in front of [f. 12] the horse is the same tridental monogram as on the reverse. The legends on the reverses of these coins, which only present them, are Greek in more or less corrupted characters.
ΒΑΣΙΛΕΥΣ ΒΑΣΙΛΕΩΝ ΣΩΤΗΡ ΜΕΓΑΣ is the purest form, the more corrupt is
ΒΑΣΙΛΕΥΣ ΒΑΣΙΛΕΩΝ ΣΩΤΗΡΜΕΓΑΣ, in some ΒΑΣΙΛΕΩΝ appears ΒΑΣΙΛΕΥΩΝ and many coins show other incongruities and transpositions of letters. On the smaller coins, for want of space, the legend is confined to ΒΑΣΙΛΕΩΣ ΒΑΣΙΛΕΩΝΣΩΤΗΡ.

We esteem it a great misfortune not to be acquainted with the name of a prince, whose coins are found in vast numbers, not only in western [*sic*: eastern] Afghanistan and the Punjab, but also over all of the north-western provinces of Hindustan – whence we are allowed to infer that his empire was most extensive, and that he was a monarch of great capacity. His cenotaph [Bimaran 3] opened near Jalalabad produced twenty-seven copper coins, from which we deduce that his reign was of twenty-seven years duration, a fact fully confirmed by his coins, and the multitudes in which they are discovered. That there may exist no doubt that the monument in question, was in reality the cenotaph of this prince, it may be mentioned, that we subsequently opened a small dilapidated Tope [Bimaran stupa 4; see **Vol. I, pp. 113–16**] about two hundred yards behind, or west of it, seated amid a number of connected small tumuli, the whole with the great Tope or cenotaph having probably been originally surrounded with a common wall. In this smaller Tope, with other relics, we found six copper coins of this prince, from which we inferred the structure to be the cenotaph of one of his sons, who was six years of age at the time of death. The coins themselves, so far as they could, corroborated this inference, having been struck in the early part of the prince's reign, as was evident from the youthful busts on them.[8]

The horseman on the reverse of these coins connects them with a series of coins, numerously found east of Kabul, in the countries immediately bordering on the Indus, denominated by Mr Prinsep the Azes Group, from the name observed on great numbers of them. In spite of this connection, we cannot introduce the Azes coins we have found in this place, because we feel confident that the monarchs they commemorate never governed at Begram, or why should we not meet with their coins on its site? Our theory, with respect to these coins, is, that they relate to an independent Greek dynasty [Indo-Scythian], of which Azes was the founder[9] and whose name was borne or assumed by his descendants, that the original seat of their empire was in the mountainous and difficult regions on either side of the Indus, in the northern part of its course, or the north-eastern districts of Afghanistan and the north-western districts of the Punjab. In these countries they would have been supported by the posterity of the numerous colonies planted by Alexander, and from them according to the personal character of their monarchs, or the circumstances of the times, they may have exercised an influence over the surrounding or adjacent countries. That this dynasty flourished coeval with the Bactrian cannot be affirmed, but the better coins of its early princes seem to prove that it may have been established no long time after. It may also be inferred from the presence of the early coins of this dynasty at Peshawar and in the provinces of the Punjab, while they merely casually occur to the west, that the aggressions of their princes were towards the south and south-east, until the epoch of the prince whose coins have led to these remarks [i.e. Wima Takto]. This warlike sovereign, perhaps 'le grand conquérant' of his dynasty, would appear to have increased the empire received from his ancestors, by the subjugation of all the countries from the Hindu Kush to Benares – and that he not only retained, as well as subjugated them, would also appear from the numbers in which his coins are to this day found in them, incontestably proving that they were current. His capital we presume he fixed at Nysa or Dionysiopolis, where at this time we beheld the cenotaphs of himself and his successors, but the latter do not seem to have supported their authority in the extended empire of their predecessor, for we search in vain for their coins at points distant from Nysa – and even there, they appear to have been shortly displaced by another dynasty.[10]

[f. 13] *Figs 104, 105 and 106* show the types of varieties of the Azes coin. *Fig. 104* is the same as fig. 23, pl. XXIII, Mr Prinsep [1835a]; it very probably is a coin of the preceding prince – on it is however observed a novel globular emblem, which we cannot however concede to be a fire altar [Wima Takto: horseman/Zeus with sceptre and *pūrṇaghaṭa* (vase of plenty)].

Fig. 105 we might also have supposed a coin of the same prince, but for the part of the legend preserved, which both distinct and unintelligible has no similarity to the legend on the coins of our great king [Indo-Parthian: Sasan; prototype for *Figs 104, 107, 109*].

Fig. 106 is the reverse of a coin of this class, which from the monogram, may refer to some other monarch of the dynasty, perhaps an earlier one [Azes II: horseman/Zeus Nicephorus]. These coins are casual ones from Begram and the bazaar of Kabul.

Fig. 107 to *Fig. 110* exhibit types of various small coins procured from Begram, the three first in some number [*Figs 107, 109–10*: Wima Takto; *Fig. 108*: Azes II imitation] – the last [*Fig. 110*: standing Oesho/Ardochsho] is a single specimen of 1835 [Cribb 2014, type 2, fig. 31].

Fig. 111 [Mujatria *c.* AD 80–90 (1838,EIC.90, from Bimaran stupa 5: **Vol. I, p. 120, Fig. 136.23**)] is the type of a variety of the Azes coin, which we are able to appropriate to a successor of the great king above – and whose cenotaph has been opened by ourselves.[11] It stood about two hundred yards south from that of its predecessor. Four copper coins extracted from it [Bimaran stupa 2 (**Vol. I, p. 104, Fig. 117.1-4**)], informed us, as we conjectured, that the prince ruled as many years, and this is not without proof, so few of his coins being discernible, two or three only occurring each season. The obverse Greek legend of this coin is so unintelligible from the corrupt form and transposition of the letters, that from about twelve specimens which may have passed through our hands in three years, we have been able to learn no more than that it contains what is intended for ΒΑCΙΛΕШC ΒΑCΙΛΕШΝ. The native or Bactrian legend on the reverse is more evident, and on the specimen depicted is 𐨨𐨫𐨐𐨂 𐨨𐨫𐨐𐨯... 𐨐𐨟𐨁𐨐𐨂 𐨀𐨗 or *malakáo malako… kátikáo ajo* [Marginal note] '*maharajasa maharaja dhamika rajatirajasa âyasa*'. We may here notice the introduction of 𐨟𐨁 or *ti* [sic: vi] in the word equivalent for *megalou*, which we have been accustomed to find 𐨪𐨗𐨪𐨗 or *kákáo* simply [*rajarajasa*], and again the substitution of apparently a novel equivalent for ΣΩΤΗΡ or 𐨢𐨨𐨁𐨐 [*dhramika*], which however is also found on the native legend of a prince Archelius [Archebius *c.* 80–60 BC] to be subsequently brought to notice – here it has the additions of the final 𐨯 and stands 𐨢𐨨𐨁𐨐𐨯 – which may perhaps be read *omekao* [*dhramikasa*] – the initial 'o' may be a long one. The obverse monogram of these coins, is valuable, from being again apparent on the coins of Kadaphes Choranus [Kujula Kadphises, Kushan] as depicted by Mr Prinsep [1835a, pl. XXIV.13–15]. It is very singular, that no one of this prince's coins has fallen into our hands, although I remark that they have been found at Kabul.

We shall close our remarks on these coins, by observing that a cenotaph contiguous to that of the prince whose coins we have now considered, very probably referred to his predecessor or successor – but it unfortunately yielded no evidences of its origin. There are also two or three other cenotaphs which from circumstances of contiguity and position we should incline to appropriate, but from such evidence only, to princes of the same family. The cenotaphs of this family occupy the same site with those of their successors in authority – the princes, whose coins are next brought to view.

Ermaios and his successors [imitations in the name of Hermaeus (*c.* 90–70 BC)]
[*Figs 112–31*] **Ermaios of Nysa** [**Kujula Kadphises** (*c.* AD 50–90): obverse in name of Hermaeus; reverse in own name].

Fig. 112 to *Fig. 131* represent the types of a very numerous series of coins, distinguished by the not to be mistaken figure of Hercules with his club on the reverse, encompassed by a native or Bactrian [Kharoshthi] legend, while the obverse is marked by a bust, the head bound with a fillet or diadem and the legend Greek.

These coins may satisfactorily be ascribed to a dynasty of princes whose capital was the ancient Nysa – near which their cenotaphs are yet to be seen. There is no series of coins, we should have been more gratified to have identified as to the nomenclature of their princes, than this before us, but the obscurity of both Greek and native legends opposes considerable difficulty. It is obvious, from the great numbers in which these coins are found, that they must have been current for a considerable period in the countries from whence this Memoir is written – that they refer to a succession of princes, is as palpable from the mere appearance of the coins, which excepting those of Ermaios, present on scarcely any two of them, similar legends – and unfortunately it happens, that these [f. 14] discordant legends, are so incomprehensible, that it can be hardly believed, that they were ever intended to be read or deciphered – indeed Mr Prinsep has suggested that they have the semblance of copies, which might be credited, were their originals recognisable. We have however to speculate upon the coins as we find them, and to avail ourselves of any circumstances, which may tend to throw a light upon them. At Darunta near Jalalabad, where the cenotaphs of princes of this family have been actually examined, we have six, seven or eight that may fairly be referred to them. These will of necessity imply as many sovereign princes. Unhappily these cenotaphs do not all yield tokens decisive of the identity of the princes, they were intended to commemorate – but from those which do, we may be justified in appropriating those which do not. With this allowance, the cenotaphs of three princes of this family, identified by examination, will allow us to appropriate four or five others to princes of their race. Of course, our chief object with this numerous and mysterious series of coins, is to ascertain the names and number of the sovereigns they represent – to effect this, exceeds our ability; all we can do, will be to infer from the coins themselves, assisted by the accidental circumstances concerning them which have transpired. Let us revert to the coins whose figures are delineated.

Plate 5 *Figs 112*, *113* and *114* are specimens which exhibit a clear legend in pure Greek characters ΒΑΣΙΛΕΩΣ ΣΤΗΡΟΣΣΥ ΕΡΜΑΙΟΥ – here we have a Greek name, and one borne by one or more preceding princes, and it will be observed that the word ΣΤΗΡΟΣΣΥ, occurs on the coins of the prince, we have called, liable to correction ΕΡΜΑΙΟΥ the Younger. The cenotaph of our present ΕΡΜΑΙΟΥ has not been identified at Darunta, and we style him ΕΡΜΑΙΟΥ of Nysa, because his coins are the most intelligible and obviously have precedence of the series of the group or family, of whose members, the cenotaphs of some, have been verified. *Fig. 112*, represents the obverse of a coin, on which the whole Greek legend, as rarely happens, is clear. *Fig. 113* shows both obverse and reverse of a coin of the same prince, and *Fig. 114* displays the reverse of another, which was necessary to explain the native or Bactrian legend, which would seem to be 𐨢𐨨𐨁𐨤𐨂𐨡𐨯 𐨯𐨂𐨗𐨂𐨫𐨐𐨯 𐨟𐨐𐨯-𐨐𐨧𐨯 – of which I dare not attempt the explanation – *dhamípúdasa sujulakasa takasa-kayadaphasa* [*kujula kasasa yavugasa dharmathidasa* 'of Kujula Kadphises Kushan *yabgu* steadfast in the law'].

The coins of Ermaios, besides having plain legends, are of fair execution and readily distinguishable from the remainder of the group – those which must nearly approach them, also fortunately enable us to recognise the name of their prince.

Kadphisos [**Kujula Kadphises** in own name]
Fig. 115 and *Fig. 116* show the types of this variety of coin – which bears the name ΚΑΔΦΙCΟC – one rather Indian than Greek, and singular as being that of a remarkable prince, hereafter to be considered, and who stands at the head of our Indo Scythic [Kushan] dynasties. Mr Prinsep, was the first to detect the name of Kadphisos on coins of this type, and it is gratifying to be able to give two specimens, where the characters are evident and expressed in perspicuous Greek. These coins also give indications of the word ΧΟΡΑΝΟΥ [Kushan],[12] as a substitute or equivalent for ΒΑΣΙΛΕΩΣ, afterwards adopted on Indo-Scythic coins, still however the

legends are not quite distinct on this point – as well as we can make them out from comparison, they stand ΧΟΡϹΠΟ ΚΟΣΟΥΛΟ ΚΑΔΦΙϹΟϹ. If the fourth letter of the first word could have been read A, it might have been concluded to be *chorano* – but with the coins before us, we cannot do so. The two following letters are also doubtful – the name ΚΑΔΦΙϹΟϹ is indubitably distinct on the first specimen, and on the second the traces of the initial letters K A and Δ are obvious. Some coins of this peculiar type are found, where the legends exhibit a variety of transpositions of the letters ΟΥΛΟ as occurring, in the epithet, it may be – from the examples given, it may be hoped future specimens may be found, which will remove the obscurity attached to the title and epithet of the legend on these coins – the native or Bactrian legend appears, in nowise, to differ from that found on the coins of ΕΡΜΑΙΟΥ.

[f. 15] *Fig. 117* and *Fig. 118* show the obverses of two coins, the first copper, the last copper silver, not merely plated, but cased with the superior metal – so decided a similarity is observable on the two coins, that we can have no doubt that they refer to the same prince – and to a distinct one – among some hundred copper coins we could only detect two which we could rank with the silver copper one – the last was brought from Ghazni.

Fig. 119 [IOC.261 (**Fig. 34.19**)] and *Fig. 120* represent the types of ten coins extracted from a tope or cenotaph at Darunta [Kotpur stupa 2, see **Vol. I, pp. 89–90, Fig. 85.7**], as they were all identical, and have on the legends, otherwise illegible, the common characters ΟΦΟ not to be found on other varieties of this class of coins, we consider them to refer to a distinct prince. Analogous coins occur at Begram and at the other spots.

Fig. 121 displays the type of coins extracted from a celebrated tope or cenotaph at Darunta, called Jani Tope [Bimaran stupa 5] – first by M. Honigberger, afterwards by some natives and ultimately by ourselves – of these coins no two were perhaps identical, but all had the same general appearance, were nearly of the same size – and no one of them was more perfect or intelligible than this before us [see **Vol. I, pp. 120–1, Fig. 136.4–20**]. The monument, in which they were deposited, was one of the most substantial of the kind, where we might have expected to have found the coins of the earlier rather than the later of the princes of this family – however facts are incontestable, and the structure must have been erected subsequent to the coinage of the monies it contained. The prince it commemorates we presume a distinct one.

We have thus endeavoured to distinguish five princes of this large family – of necessity there will have been many more – eight of the Darunta topes may reasonably be referred to this dynasty – as may possibly some tumuli, nearly as important in size and construction as the first named monuments. The coins themselves will authorise the notion of a far greater number of sovereigns.

[**Plate 6**] To show the difficulty of identifying them *Fig. 122* to *Fig. 130* are delineated, being so many obverses of specimens – the strange arrangements of their incomprehensible legends will not fail to be noted, and to have exhibited all the variations to be found on the coins of this group, it would have been necessary to have figured every individual coin in our hands, excepting those of ΕΡΜΑΙΟΥ and ΚΑΔΦΙϹΟϹ which alone present intelligible names.

Fig. 131 represents a variety of this type and the only specimen we have met with, where the bust looks to the right instead of to the left.

The figure of Hercules on these coins, may perhaps intimate that the founder of the dynasty was originally a hill prince; as we learn from ancient authorities, alluding to these regions, that Hercules was the deity worshipped in the hills, and Bacchus the one adored in the plains.

[f. 16] Class 1. Greek Series 3. Unrecorded Kings of Bactria

[Kings] whose coins occasionally found on the site of Begram, are seemingly of casual and accidental occurrence, while they are neither regularly found or in number, leaving it a matter of doubt whether they actually governed there or not. Under this series are included any other coins procured at Kabul or the vicinity thereof, which are manifestly Greek Bactrian.

Archelius [Archebius *c.* 90–80 BC**]**
Fig. 132 [**Pl. 6**, *Fig. 122*].[13] *Obverse* – Bust of king, head bound with fillet or diadem. Legend Greek ΒΑΣΙΛΕΩΣ … ΝΙΚΗΦΟΡΟΥ ΑΡΧΕΛΙΟΥ. *Reverse* – Figure of male deity (Jupiter?) standing, bundle of darts [thunderbolt] in right hand, staff or sceptre in left. Monogram ₭. Legend native, Bactrian [Kharoshthi]

𐨤𐨫𐨐𐨩𐨂 𐨤𐨩𐨌𐨨𐨏 𐨤𐨱𐨭𐨗 𐨤𐨩𐨒𐨪𐨆.

This figure represents a beautiful silver drachma, a unique specimen, found at Begram in 1835. It is evident that King Archebius must stand high on the royal lists of these countries – but we are perplexed to locate his empire – if it extended to Begram, why do we not meet with his copper coins? One of the epithets on the Greek legend is not quite distinct, and its equivalent in the native legend is the obscure 𐨤𐨱𐨭𐨗. This is also found on the native legend of one of the Nysian coins *Fig. 111* **Plate 5** – and we ventured to read it *omekao* [*sic*: *dhramikasa*]. In the instance before us, however, the initial 𐨗 of this word, and the medial letter 𐨗 of the native equivalent for ΝΙΚΗΦΟΡΟΥ appear identical, and the latter would appear to stand for *la*. The epithet in question may therefore be *lamekao* – and the reading of the entire native legend, *malakáo lamekao ájalado achatijo* or *achalijo* [*sic*: *maharajasa dhramikasa jayadharasa arkhebiyasa*].

Diomedes [*c.* 95–90 BC]
Fig. 133 [**Pl. 6**, *Fig. 123*]. *Obverse* – Two warriors standing to the front, with spears in right hands – swords by side. Legend Greek [ΒΑΣ]ΙΛΕΩΣ [Σ]ΩΤΗΡΟΣ ΔΙΟΜΗΔΟΥ. *Reverse* – Brahmanical or humped bull. Monogram ₭. Legend native, Bactrian [Kharoshthi]

𐨤𐨗𐨭𐨀𐨩 𐨤𐨩𐨩𐨩.. 𐨩𐨫𐨂 —

This figure represents a square copper coin of King Diomedes, and a unique specimen elicited from Begram in 1834. The purity of the Greek legend permits us to assign this prince, like Archebius, a high date – and we are left in the same doubt as to the seat of his empire. The native

Class 1. Greek. Series 3 – Unrecorded Greek Bactrian Kings.

whose coins occasionally found on the site of Beghram, are seemingly of casual and accidental occurrence, while they are neither regularly found or in number, leaving it a matter of doubt whether they actually governed there or not –

Under this head are included any other coins procured at Kabul or its vicinity, which from their legends are manifestly Greek Bactrian.

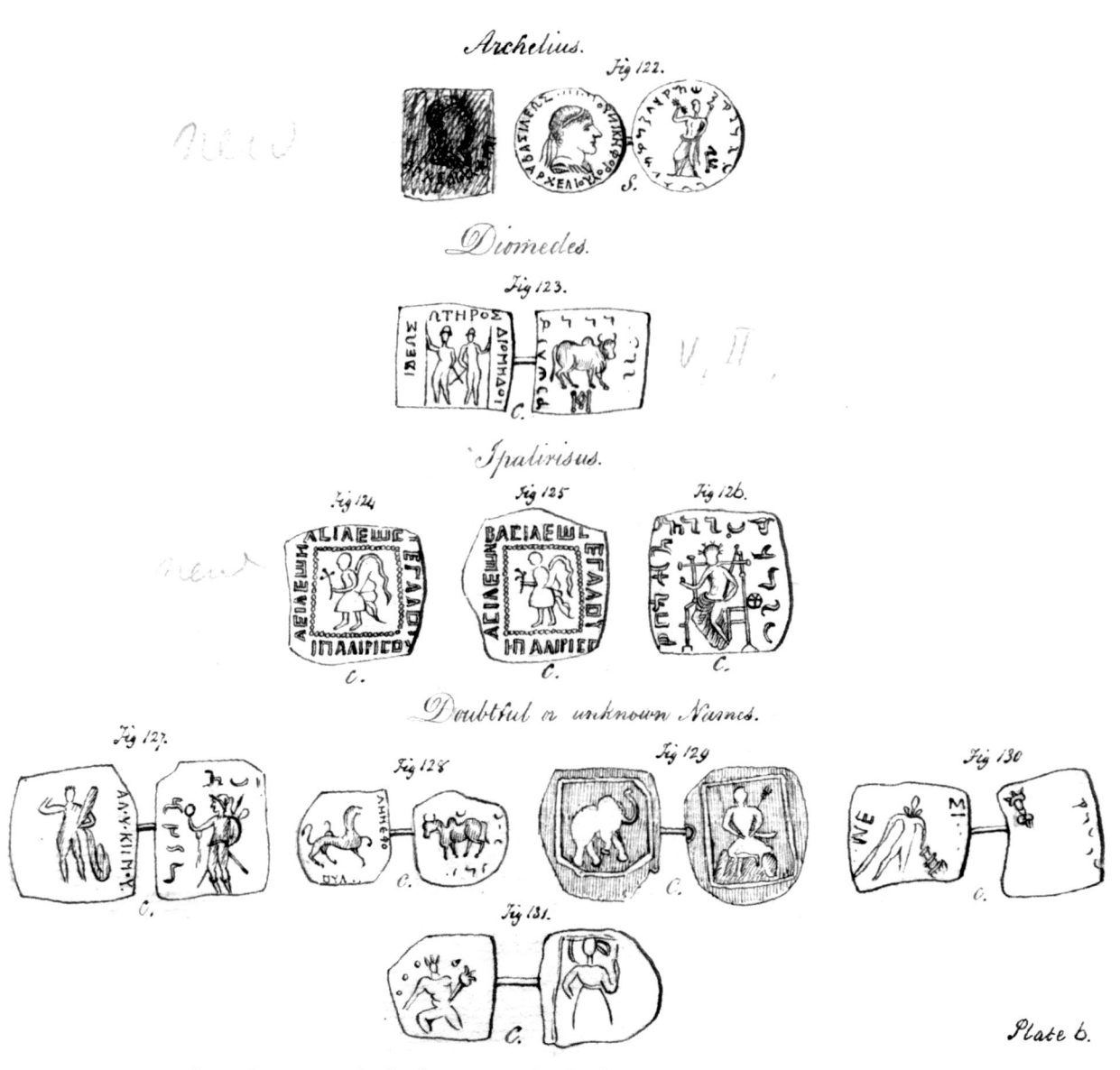

Archelius.
Fig. 122.

Diomedes.
Fig. 123.

Spalirisus.
Fig. 124. Fig. 125. Fig. 126.

Doubtful or unknown Names.
Fig. 127. Fig. 128. Fig. 129. Fig. 130. Fig. 131.

Plate 6.

Plate 6 Kujula Kadphises (122–31), Archebius (122 [132]), Diomedes (123 [133]), Spalirises (124–6 [134–6]), 'doubtful or unknown' (127–31 [137–41])

legend may prove important. It may obviously be read *malakáo rakako ajamedo* [*sic*: *maharajasa tratarasa diyumitasa*] – the equivalent for ΔΙΟΜΗΔΟΥ therefore expressed in Sanskrit, would be Aja-Medha, which we learn was the name of a prince of the Lunar race who reigned at Kanyakubja [modern Kanauj]. This remark is made, having observed in the Rev. Dr Mill's 'Supplement to the historical remarks on the Allahabad inscription no. 2' [1834, p. 340], that the chronicles of Marwar, according to Colonel Tod [1829] – represent Nayn Pal or Nayana Pala as having conquered Kanauj in the year of Vikramaditya 526 or AD 470 from King Aji-Pala, a descendent of Aja-Medha of the Lunar race – which race they represent as having held the sovereignty of Kanyakubja or Gadhipura [name of the city under Yashovarman], from the fabulous times of Gadhi, father of Vishvamitra. We here find a dynasty of princes apparently bearing the common name Aja, identical with our Greek Azes – to be hereafter noticed – and who will have reigned about the same time with Azes and his descendants – and that Colonel Tod suspects Scythic sovereigns, and Bactrian or Greek Bactrian would easily be deemed such, to have reigned at Kanauj, at least, as early as the 5th century, or perhaps long before. We pretend not that our Diomedes is the Aja-Medha of the Lunar race, and know not that his coin will farther instruct us than that ΔΙΟΜΗΔΟΥ and Aja-Medha are synonymous terms – but of this Colonel Todd and other eminent orientalists must decide.

[Marginal note] 'Prinsep printed some of these remarks, but objected that the native legend might probably be read Dayamida. I am not sure of it, but even then it would equally suit my purpose – as the name in the Puranas is variously given Aja-Medha Daya-Medha etc. I have other testimony in favour of the intimation here hinted at that Diomedes may be the Aja-Medha of the Puranas – a most important fact if brought to bear upon the chronology of those books'.

[f. 17] **Ipalirisus** [**Spalirises** *c.* 50–40 BC (Indo-Scythian)] *Figs 134, 135* and *136* [**Pl. 6**, *Figs 124–6*] will exhibit the type of the copper coins of King Ipalirisus [Spalirises] – the two first represent the obverses, on which is a figure standing to the left, with a cross-shaped emblem [battle-axe] in the hand – the robes flow loosely behind, where is also a bow. The legend Greek ΒΑCΙΛΕШΝ ΒΑCΙΛΕШC ΜΕΓΑΛΟΥ ΙΠΑΛΙΡΙCΟC. *Fig. 136* shows the reverse – an enthroned deity, probably Jupiter [Zeus], the head surrounded by rays – the right hand extended – the left sustaining a staff or sceptre. Monogram ⊕. Legend native of Bactrian 𐨩𐨣𐨱𐨗 𐨯 𐨱𐨎𐨓𐨿𐨪𐨯 𐨯𐨩𐨎𐨮 which may perhaps be read *malakáo malak-kao kalitijo* [*sic*: *maharajasa mahatakasa spalirihasa*].

This species of coin is rarely met with. Begram in 1833 yielded but one and in 1834 and 1835 none – a parcel of six were sent me from Munderaus of Laghman; they had been evidently exhumed, the one side of each having adhering to it, the gutch or cement on which the whole had been deposited. They were fortunately in excellent preservation.

Doubtful or unknown names
Fig. 137 [**Pl. 6**, *Fig. 127*: **Vonones** (*c.* 65–50 BC) with nephew Spalagadama]. *Obverse* – Figure standing to the front probably of Hercules [Heracles with club]. Legend Greek but uncertain. *Reverse* – Infantry soldier [Athena], right hand holding a wreath. Legend native or Bactrian [Kharoshthi] but uncertain.

This is a rare coin at Begram, which gave in 1833 but one,[14] and in 1834, 1835 none. It is Mr Prinsep's [1835a] fig. 10. pl. XXI and he ascribes it, liable to doubt, to a prince called Nonus.

Fig. 138 [**Pl. 6**, *Fig. 128*: **Azes II** (*c.* AD 16 – 30), probably posthumous]. *Obverse* – Lion rampant [*sic*: walking to right]. Legend Greek but uncertain [(ΒΑΣΙΛΕΩΣ ΒΑΣΙΛΕ)ΩΝ ΜΕΓ(ΑΛΟΥ ΑΖΟ)Υ]. *Reverse* – Humped bull. Legend Bactrian [Kharoshthi], but uncertain [*maharaja* (*sa rajadirajasa mahatasa*) *aya*(*sa*)].

This is a unique coin afforded by Begram in 1833, since which we have met with no other. The Greek legend would appear to disclose the name ΔΗΜΕΦΟΡΟΥ [*sic*] but it is not certain.

Fig. 139 [**Pl. 6**, *Fig. 129*: **Maues** [*c.* 75–65 BC]. *Obverse* – Elephant. *Reverse* – Seated figure.

This is a unique specimen from Begram 1834 – it is the same as Mr Prinsep's [1835a] fig. 11, pl. XXII.

Fig. 140 and *141* [**Pl. 6**, *Figs 130–1*] – represent obverses and reverses of two unique coins procured in 1835 at Kabul, they convey little information, but are obviously Greek.

Fig. 140 [**Apollodotus I**. *Obverse* – Apollo standing with arrow and bow. *Reverse* – tripod].

Fig. 141 [**Azes I**. *Obverse* – Poseidon trampling a human figure. *Reverse* – Yakshi].

[**Plate 7**, *Figs 142–60*]
Fig. 142 [**Hermaeus** (*c.* 90–70 BC) **posthumous imitation**]. *Obverse* – A bust, head bound with fillet or diadem. Legend Greek but uncertain – the letters ΝΤ…Ш being only distinct [ΒΑΣΙΛΕΩΣ ΣΩΤΗΡΟΣ ΕΡΜΑΙΟΥ]. *Reverse* – Enthroned deity, Jupiter [Zeus] probably. Monogram ⊕. Legend Bactrian but imperfect 𐨩𐨣𐨱𐨗 . . . . 𐨱𐨎𐨿 [*mahara*(*jasa tratarasa*) *hermayasa*].

This is a unique coin from Kabul in 1834 – it has some analogy to the coins of Ermaios [Hermaeus] and in the native equivalent for the name of the prince, may be faintly traced the characters which stand for Ermaios – if the letter preceding the final one of the native name be an 𐨩 as it would seem, the whole might be read *radamao* – but nothing is gained from it.

Fig. 143 [**Hermaeus posthumous imitation**]. *Obverse* – Rude bust. Legend Greek, portion visible ΔΗΤΟΡΟ. *Reverse* – Enthroned deity [Zeus]. Legend Bactrian but uncertain. This is a unique coin from Begram in 1834.

Figs 144, 145 and *146* [**Kujula Kadphises** (*c.* AD 40–90)] represent the types of a variety of coin, occurring sparingly at Begram, one, two or three during each season. The obverses show a peculiarly helmed bust, with a Greek legend, but perfect on no coin yet found, and the reverses have a helmed warrior, with spear and shield, surrounded with a Bactrian legend, which also none of the specimens affords entire [*Obverse* – ΚΟΖΟΥΛΟ ΚΑΔΟΒΙΚΕΙ ΚΟΡΣΑΝ. *Reverse* – *kushana yavu'asa kuyula ka'usa*].

Fig. 147 [**Kujula Kadphises** silver 'Heraus' obol].

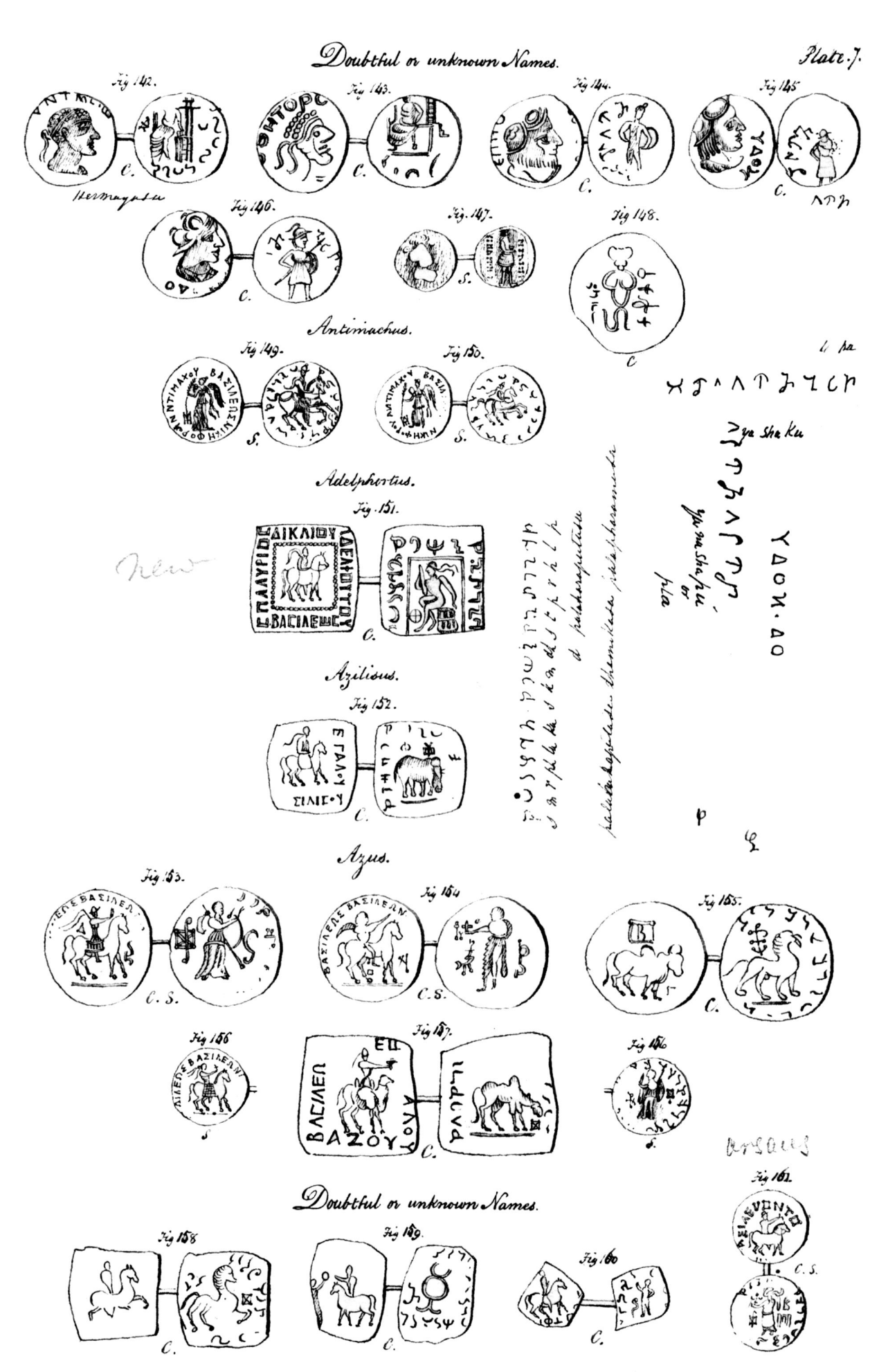

Plate 7 Hermaeus posthumous imitations (142–3), Kujula Kadphises (144–7), Vatashvaka (148), Antimachus II (149–50), Spaladagama (151), Azilises (152), Azes (153–7), Kharahostes (158), Gondophares (159), Mujatria (160), Azes II (161)

Obverse – Bust, but defaced. *Reverse* – Standing figure [soldier with wreath]. Legend Greek but uncertain [HIAOY KOPPANOY 'of Kushan *yabgu*'].

Type of a small coin of silver from Charikar in 1835. The Greek legend is in pure characters but, from the minuteness and dotted form employed, it has baffled us in our efforts to decipher it.

Fig. 148 [**Vatashvaka** (*c.* 2nd century BC): the image is inverted]. *Reverse* – of a coin, the obverse of which having been hammered is unintelligible. The figure may be intended for a human being or deity, but the nature of the legend deserves most attention.

[Uniface copper alloy coin, IOC.1058 (**Fig. 22.4**): a three-arched hill and crescent above a triangular 'hill' of six dots, with, to right, a female figure facing it, hands clasped in worship and standing on a taurine. Vertical Brahmi inscription in the left field *vaṭaśvaka* Wilson 1841, pl. XV.30; Allan 1936, p. 264, BMC.2, pl. XXXIX.3].

[f. 18] **Antimachus II** [*c.* 160–155 BC]
Fig. 149 and *Fig. 150* represent the silver coins of King Antimachus – they evidently are entitled to precedence of many of the coins before noted, but as we disclaim system, we were willing to exhibit the coins, distinguished by the horsemen on the obverse, in one view – it being possible that they may have a connection with each other, if it be only that of locality – a series of coins of the Azes dynasty, we have been willing to locate at Nysa, but we apprehend that the mystery concealed in the major part of the coins will have to be explained by collectors east of the Indus.

The coins of Antimachus we have met with are silver drachma and hemi-drachma. Begram in 1834 gave one, and 1835 another. We have picked up one or two in the bazaar of Kabul – in 1834 with a huge parcel of coins of Menander and Apollodotus were two or three of Antimachus, and this year 1835, having again fallen in with a similar large parcel of coins of the same two princes, we also gained with them another two or three of Antimachus. They are eminent for beauty of design and execution – the obverses displayed a winged figure of Victory with a palm branch in hand – the monograms ⋈ and ⋈ – the legend Greek ΒΑΣΙΛΕΩΣ ΝΙΚΗΦΟΡΟΥ ΑΝΤΙΜΑΧΟΥ – the reverses exhibit a horseman at speed encircled with a Bactrian legend 𐨀𐨯𐨿𐨨𐨿 𐨀𐨗𐨡𐨡𐨆 𐨀𐨟𐨁𐨨𐨕 or *malakáo ájadado atimacho*. We have found no copper coin of Antimachus. Mr Prinsep appropriates to him his fig. 4 [1835a, pl. XXI.4].

The beautiful silver medal of Philoxenus [*c.* 100–95 BC] in the Ventura collection depicted by Mr Prinsep [1835a, pl. XXI.1] has in the nature of the reverse a considerable affinity to the coins of Antimachus. Of Philoxenus, we have not met with any trace at Begram or any other place.

Adelphortus [**Spalagadama** (*c.* 50–46 BC) son of Spalahores; nephew of Vonones].
Fig. 151. Obverse – Horseman. Legend Greek ΒΑCΙΛΕШC CΠΑΛΥΡΙΟC ΔΙΚΑΙΟΥ ΑΔΕΛΦΟΡΤΟΥ. *Reverse* – Seated naked female deity, with club in hand – Fortune (?). Monogram ⊕. Legend Bactrian 𐨀𐨯𐨿𐨨𐨿 𐨀𐨗𐨡𐨡𐨆 𐨀𐨟𐨁𐨨𐨕 / – which is by no means very intelligible [marginal note] '*alahara putasa dhamiasa*

palarahayasa'. This is a rare coin in these countries, Begram in 1833 gave one, and another in 1834 and 1835.

Azilisus [**Azilises**, Indo-Scythian king *c.* 1 BC–AD 16].
[*Fig. 152*]. *Obverse* – Horseman. Legend Greek, portion distinct [ΒΑΣΙΛΕΩΣ ΒΑΣΙΛΕΩΝ Μ]ΕΓΑΛΟΥ [Α]ΖΙΛΙΣΟΥ. *Reverse* – Elephant. Monograms 𐅉 and 𐅊. Legend Bactrian – portion distinct 𐨀𐨗𐨁𐨫𐨁𐨮 or *ajiliso* [*sic*: (*maharajasa rajarajasa mahatasa*) *ayilishasa*].

This is also a rare coin [IOC.215 (**Fig. 29.10** below)]. Begram in 1834 yielded one.

Azus [**Azes I** (*c.* 46–1 BC) and **Azes II** (AD 16–30)]
Fig. 153 to *Fig. 157* display the varieties of the Azes coin we have met with, they are generally single specimens, and not found at Begram. *Figs 153* and *154* are copper silver or billon,[15] *155* and *157* are copper, while *156* is a pure silver drachma and was brought to us from Khulm [also known as Tashqurghan] in Turkestan.

Fig. 157. [IOC.197 (**Fig. 29.7** below). Azes I]. *Obverse* – King riding camel. *Reverse* – Bull.

Mr Prinsep [1835a, pls XXII and XXIII] has exhibited the numerous types and varieties of the Azes coins, afforded by a collection of coins, and not a large one, in the Punjab. The numbers in which they are in those quarters found, while east of Peshawar they seem to be rare ones, serve to point out the regions in which their princes held authority. The great diversity in the devices of these coins, as well as circumstances of style and execution, seem to prove that they refer to a numerous race of princes, of whom the first was of so much importance that his name was continued by his descendants. The whole of these coins agree in having on the obverse a Greek legend ΒΑΣΙΛΕΩΣ ΒΑΣΙΛΕΩΝ ΜΕΓΑΛΟΥ ΑΣΟΥ [*sic*: AZOY] and on the reverse a Bactrian or native one 𐨨𐨫𐨐𐨀𐨆 𐨐𐨐𐨀𐨆 𐨨𐨫𐨐𐨆 𐨀𐨗𐨆 or *malakáo kákáo malako ajo*. The Branch of this dynasty who ruled at Nysa have coins with varying legends, as before noted – the name ΑΣΟΥ [*sic*] being rendered in Bactrian *ajo*, consequently in Sanskrit *aja* – may perhaps be identical with the Hebrew *asa* – and it will be, if Asa have in Hebrew the signification of the victor or the victorious, which meaning the *ajo* or *aja* of our coins may have, being found in *ajalado* or conquest bearing.

[f. 19] We have previously, when considering the coin of Diomedes or Aja-Medha, alluded to the fact of a dynasty of Ajas having ruled at Kanauj. It does appear singular that no traces should be found in ancient Sanskrit history of so many dynasties of princes, some of whom must have been powerful, and probably acted a more conspicuous part in the affairs of Hindustan than native authors were willing to acknowledge. The Azes dynasty seated in the regions on either side of the Indus, at the point where it emanates from the hills, was from that position, most interested in and most likely to interfere with, the affairs of India proper.

Unknown princes of the Azes dynasty
Fig. 158. [**Kharahostes** (Indo-Scythian satrap; *c.* 1st century AD)] *Obverse* – Horseman. Legend defaced. *Reverse* – Lion or monstrous animal. Monogram ⊠. Legend Bactrian [Kharoshthi] but indistinct and incomplete.

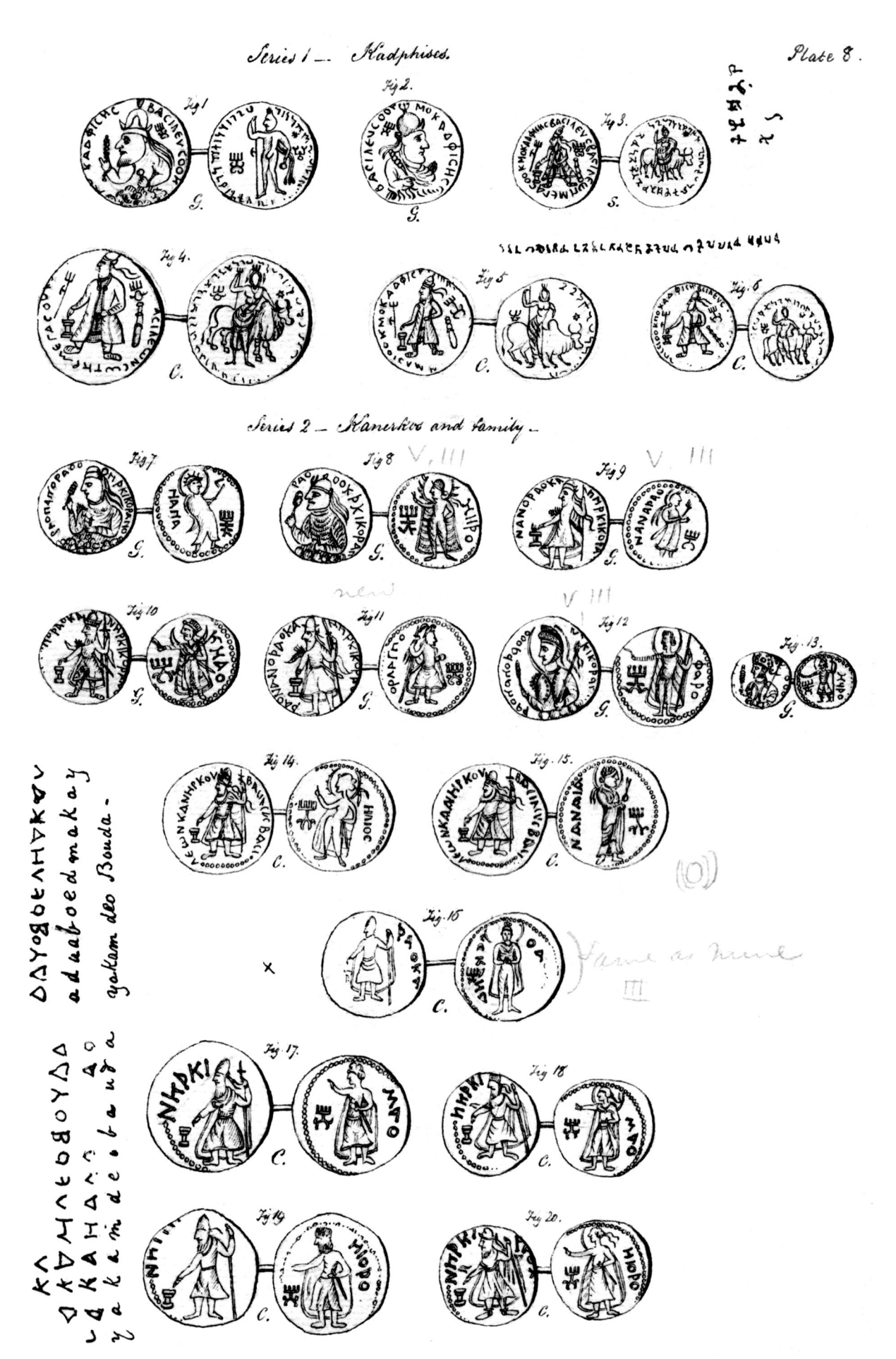

Plate 8 Kushan: Wima Kadphises (1–6), Huvishka (7–8, 12–13), Kanishka I (9–11, 14–20)

Fig. 159. [**Gondophares** (*c.* AD 32–58)] *Obverse* – Horseman receiving a wreath or chaplet from Victory. Legend defaced. *Reverse* – A singular emblem [⚲] (to be observed on Parthian coins). Monogram 卜 perhaps the Bactrian characters *ka*. Legend Bactrian, but indistinct and incomplete.

Fig. 160. [**Mujatria** (Indo-Scythian satrap; *c.* AD 80–90)] *Obverse* – Horseman. Legend Greek, letters distinct ΤΦ. *Reverse* – Standing figure [Heracles]; Monogram the Bactrian character 𐨯 [*sa*]. Legend Bactrian, but indistinct and incomplete.

Fig. 161. [**Azes II** (AD 16–30)] *Obverse* – Horseman. Legend Greek, portion visible [Β]ΑΣΙΛΕΥΟΝΤΟ. *Reverse* – Standing figure. Monograms ⊕ and obscure native characters. Legend incomplete, 𐨨𐨖𐨪𐨗 or *malakáo* [*sic*: *maharajasa*] distinct.

This last coin is of copper, silver or billon. These four figures are from defaced coins picked up at Kabul and Ghazni – they prove however that we are not yet acquainted with all the varieties of this class of coins – the two last probably exhibit other names than that of Azes.

With these coins terminate the class of coins which we call Greek or Greek Bactrian, and of whose several varieties we believe we have brought to notice every type which chance has afforded us, during the researches of three years at Begram and other places in western [*sic*: eastern] Afghanistan – whatever has been affected – we are far from having attained a sufficient acquaintance with the antiquities of Bactria – much, very much remains to be done.

Plate 8 [*Figs 1–20*].
Class Indo-Scythic [Kushan] or Mithraic. Series 1.
[Wima] Kadphises [*c.* AD 113–27]
Fig. 1 to *Fig. 6* represent the types of the gold, silver and copper coinages of King Kadphises.

Fig. 1. Obverse – Bust of King, crowned with a peculiarly formed cap – right hand holding a knobbed sceptre – left hand what may be the top of a staff. Monogram ⚏. Legend Greek ΒΑΣΙΛΕΥΣ ΟΟΚΜΟ ΚΑΔΦΙΣΗΣ. *Reverse* – Erect figure with staff in right hand, left hand holding a ball. Monograms ⚏ and ⚐; a star to the right side of the figure. Legend Bactrian.

Fig. 2. Obverse – Bust of King, looking to the right. Monogram same as preceding – also legend but varying in arrangement.

These two figures exhibit the types of the gold coins of this king. The first specimen discovered was extracted from a cenotaph near Kabul by M. Honigberger [Kamari stupa 2; see **Vol. I, pp. 75–6**, **Fig. 59.7**], and was the same as *Fig. 1*. Another cenotaph [Guldara stupa; see **Vol. I, pp. 77–80, Fig. 69.1–5**] opened by ourselves, yielded with gold coins of a later date, so many as six of Kadphises – they all essentially agreed as to the nature of the devices, the principal difference being in the position of the bust, as looking to the right or left – the legends on all were identical.

Fig. 3. Obverse – Full length figure of king, right hand placed over an altar, which has been supposed to be a fire altar – and which first appears on the coins of Kadphises – left of the king is a tridental staff, and to his right the monogram ⚏ and what appears to be a truncheon or sceptre. Legend Greek ΒΑΣΙΛΕΥΣ ΒΑΣΙΛΕΩΝ ΜΕΓΑΣ ΟΟΚΜΟ [*sic*: ΟΟΗΜΟ] ΚΑΔΦΙΣΗΣ. [f. 20] *Reverse* – Full length figure, (female ? [Oesho]) standing to the front, apparently reclining on a humped bull – right hand holds a staff surmounted with a trident, left hand reposes on the animal. Monogram ⚏ over the hind quarters of the bull and a star over his head. Legend Bactrian [Kharoshthi]

𐨨𐨱𐨪𐨗𐨯 𐨪𐨗𐨟𐨁𐨪𐨗𐨯 𐨯𐨪𐨿𐨬𐨫𐨆𐨐 𐨁𐨭𐨿𐨬𐨪𐨯 𐨨𐨱𐨁𐨭𐨿𐨬𐨪𐨯 𐨩𐨁𐨨 𐨐𐨠𐨿𐨞𐨁𐨭𐨯 𐨟𐨿𐨪𐨟𐨪

[Marginal note] '*maharajasa rajatirajasa rapehiphalikusa mahipetara katiyasa*' [*sic*: *maharajasa rajatirajasa sarvaloga iśvarasa mahiśvarasa yima kathpiśasa tratara* 'of the great king, king of kings, lord of the world, great lord, Wima Kadphises, saviour'].

This figure represents a fine silver drachma of Kadphises, procured from Charikar. The Greek legend included not the epithet ΣΩΤΗΡ to be found on the larger copper coins of the prince – and the native legend while distinct, is perplexing – the two first words appear *malakáo kátikáo*, and in the last but one the four final letters may be rendered perhaps *katijo* – while the last characters 𐨞𐨣𐨡 seem to be the same as occur on the native legend of the Unadpherrus [Gondopherres] coin – and may be read *nanad* – or may be conjectured an equivalent for ΣΩΤΗΡ – which however in this instance is omitted on the Greek legend.

Figs 4, 5 and *6* represent the copper coins of King [Wima] Kadphises. The obverses and reverses agree with that of the silver drachma. The Greek legend is however fully developed on them – ΒΑΣΙΛΕΥΣ ΒΑΣΙΛΕΩΝ ΣΩΤΗΡ ΜΕΓΑΣ ΟΟΚΜΟ [*sic*: ΟΟΗΜΟ] ΚΑΔΦΙΣΗΣ. The native legends are not so complete or distinct that we can note them with precision.

The above coins are those of a remarkable prince, whose cenotaph we may safely presume to be at Kabul, where it was opened by M. Honigberger and yielded one of his gold medals [Kamari 2]. Although another cenotaph [Guldara] examined by ourselves, yielded more gold medals of this sovereign, yet as they were accompanied by others of subsequent princes, our monument related to them and not to Kadphises. The coinage of Kadphises is curious from its superior execution, and it is singular that the Greek legend should not only be nearly identical with that found on the coins of the first Nysian princes of the Azes dynasty, as to the titles and epithets, but exactly so as to the corrupt forms of the Greek characters employed. It is farther singular that the names should occur on the coins of the second dynasty of the Nysian princes. The gold medals of this king fortunately exhibit his portrait, and this as everything else connected with him, has its singularity. The name Kadphises, or as it possibly really was, Kadphis, is perhaps Indian, the termination being so, as proved by the example of Omphis. Whoever our king may have been, inferring from his coins, he was a monarch of considerable ability and power – and from the numbers in which they are found will have ruled for a considerable period. On the silver and copper coins of this prince, the fire altar is first decidedly noted, illustrative of the worship of the prince and of his age – we had once doubted whether a fire altar or simply an altar had been intended, but incline now to the former opinion, from the nature of the reverses of these coins, the figure and bull, being probably, as Mr Prinsep suggests, Mithra and his bull. Gold coins of later princes, having the same figures, with the epithet OKPO [OHÞO – Oesho, supreme Kushan god] which we learn is also that of the sun.

Series 2. Kanerkos and family
[**Kanishka I** (*c.* AD 127–51); **Huvishka** (*c.* AD 151–90)]
Fig. 7 to *Fig. 13* represent the various types of gold coins of this family that we have met with.

Fig. 7. Obverse – Bust of prince [Huvishka], sceptre in right hand. Legend [Bactrian] Greek PAONANOPAO OOHPKI KOPANO [ÞAONANOÞAO OOHÞKI KOÞANO, king of kings Huvishka Kushan]. *Reverse* – Figure [Nana] standing to the right, head surrounded with halo. Monogram ꤊ. Legend Greek NANA.

Fig. 8. Obverse – Bust of prince [Huvishka], as preceding. Legend Greek, incomplete [ÞAONANO]PAO OOHPKI KOPANO. *Reverse* – Figure [Miiro] looking to the left, head surrounded with radiated halo. Monogram ꤊ. Legend Greek MIIPO.

Fig. 9. Obverse – Full length figure of prince [Kanishka I], standing to the left, clothed in flowing robes, staff in left hand, right hand over fire altar. Legend Greek [ÞAO] NANOPAO KANHPKI KOPANO [ÞAONANOÞAO KANHÞKI KOÞANO, king of kings Kanishka Kushan]. *Reverse* – Figure [royal Nana] looking to right. Monogram ꤊ. Legend Greek NANAPAO.

Fig. 10. Obverse – Figure of prince [Kanishka I]. Legend Greek as preceding. *Reverse* – Figure [Mao] standing to the left. Legend MAO.

[f. 21] *Fig. 11. Obverse* – Figure of prince [Kanishka I]. Legend Greek PAONANOPAO KANHPKI KOPANO. *Reverse* – Figure [Orlagno] standing to right with eagle hovering over the head. Staff in hand and sword by side. Legend Greek OPΛAΓNO. This curious legend is peculiar to this coin.

Fig. 12. Obverse – Helmed bust of prince [Huvishka], head surrounded with halo – sceptre in right hand, knobbed mace in left. Legend Greek but corrupt PAONANOPAO OO…KI KOPANO. *Reverse* – Figure [Pharro] robed looking to left, staff in left hand, right hand extended. Monogram ꤊ. Legend Greek ΦAPO.

Here is another peculiar legend, but evidently signifying the sun as source of light and majesty. *Pharos* was the term applied to the Alexandrian light house, and Pharaoh is the well-known scriptural title of the old kings of Egypt. The bust on this coin affords a remarkable contrast to other coins of this family.

Fig. 13. Obverse – Helmed bust as preceding. Legend indistinct. *Reverse* – Figure [Miiro] standing to left. Monogram ꤊ. Legend Greek corrupt ℋꝎ PO (MIIPO ? [MYPO]). This is a smaller gold coin of the same prince.

Fig. 14. Obverse – Figure of prince [Kanishka I]. Legend Greek BACIΛEVC BACIΛEIIIN KANEPKOV. *Reverse* – Figure [Helios] standing to the left. Legend Greek HΛIOC.

Fig. 15. Obverse – Figure of prince and legend as in preceding coin. *Reverse* – Figure [Nana] standing to the right. Legend Greek NANAIA.

Fig. 14 and *Fig. 15* represent the varieties of type and the only ones found of the king of kings Kanerkos – a prince, the fine execution of whose coins, the retention of the Greek titles and other circumstances, entitle to be considered the founder of a dynasty of monarchs, – who assumed his name. Mr Prinsep suggested that Kanerkos was the conqueror Kanishka of the *Rajatarangini*, and although he has subsequently expressed a contrary opinion, their eras may not unlikely have been the same or about 200 AD. It may also be noticed that Abhi-manya the successor of Kaniska is said in the Ayin Akberri [*Ain-i Akbari* of Abū al-Faẓl b. Mubārak] to have been named Nerk which is a considerable portion of the term Ka-nerk-i. We are not positive that the cenotaph of Kanerkos is at Kabul, where many of his successors have been interred – indeed rather suppose it is not. The sepulchral monuments of this numerous dynasty are found scattered in the countries from Kabul to the river Jhelum – and in the east were probably their original seats. The inscription cut on the silver disc found in the casket of the Manikyala Tope 𐨤𐨝𐨴𐨎𐨤𐨯𐨐 is read by Mr Prinsep *samaro Kanadako*[16]. The second word we might read *Kanarakao* or even *Kanarkao* which is identical with Kanerkos, but this monument will not refer to the prince of that name, the founder of a dynasty, but to one of his later successors.

[Marginal note, dated by 'Cunningham' reference to post 1845] '𐨤𐨝𐨴𐨎𐨤𐨯𐨐 *sa-ka-va-dra-ka-sa-na-ma-ga – Gamanasa Kandra Vakasas / Chandra Vaka*'.

Cunningham [1845, pp. 430–1] announces that he has made a brilliant discovery and that the reading on the silver disc disclose the name of Kanerkes. He would seem to forget that I here pointed out the circumstance, and that he read this paper is recorded by Prinsep'.

The coins of Kanerkos are farther remarkable from being the last which exhibit the Greek titles BAΣIΛEΩΣ BAΣIΛEΩN, his successors adopting the Indian ones of RAONANO RAO and KOPANO [*sic*: ÞAONANOÞAO KOÞANO] and they are first on which the native or Bactrian characters cease to be employed [i.e. the bilingual Greek/Kharoshthi legends are replaced by monolingual Bactrian Greek].

The reverses of these coins exhibit figures manifestly personifications of the sun and moon with the Greek legends HΛIOC [Helios] and NANAIA, and these personifications distinguish the coins of the successors of Kanerkos but under very varying legends.

Fig. 16. Obverse – Figure of prince [Kanishka I]. Legend [Bactrian] Greek PAO KA … [(ÞAONANO)ÞAO KA(NHÞKI)]. *Reverse* – Figure [Buddha] standing to front, with hands joined in attitude of prayer or supplication. Monogram ꤊ. Legend Greek but illegible [CAKAMANO BOYΔO, Śākyamuni Buddha. IOC.296 (**Fig. 40.25** below)].

This type rarely occurs, during three years we have met with only one specimen – it has fallen under Mr Prinsep's notice, and he depicted the reverse of the coin of this type [1834, pl. XXV.11] – he was unable like ourselves to decipher the legend. The specimen we found in execution rivals the coins of Kanerkos.

[**Plates 8–9**] *Fig. 17* to *Fig. 27* represent the various types of the copper coins of the descendants perhaps the immediate ones of Kanerkos [Kanishka]. They all agree in having on

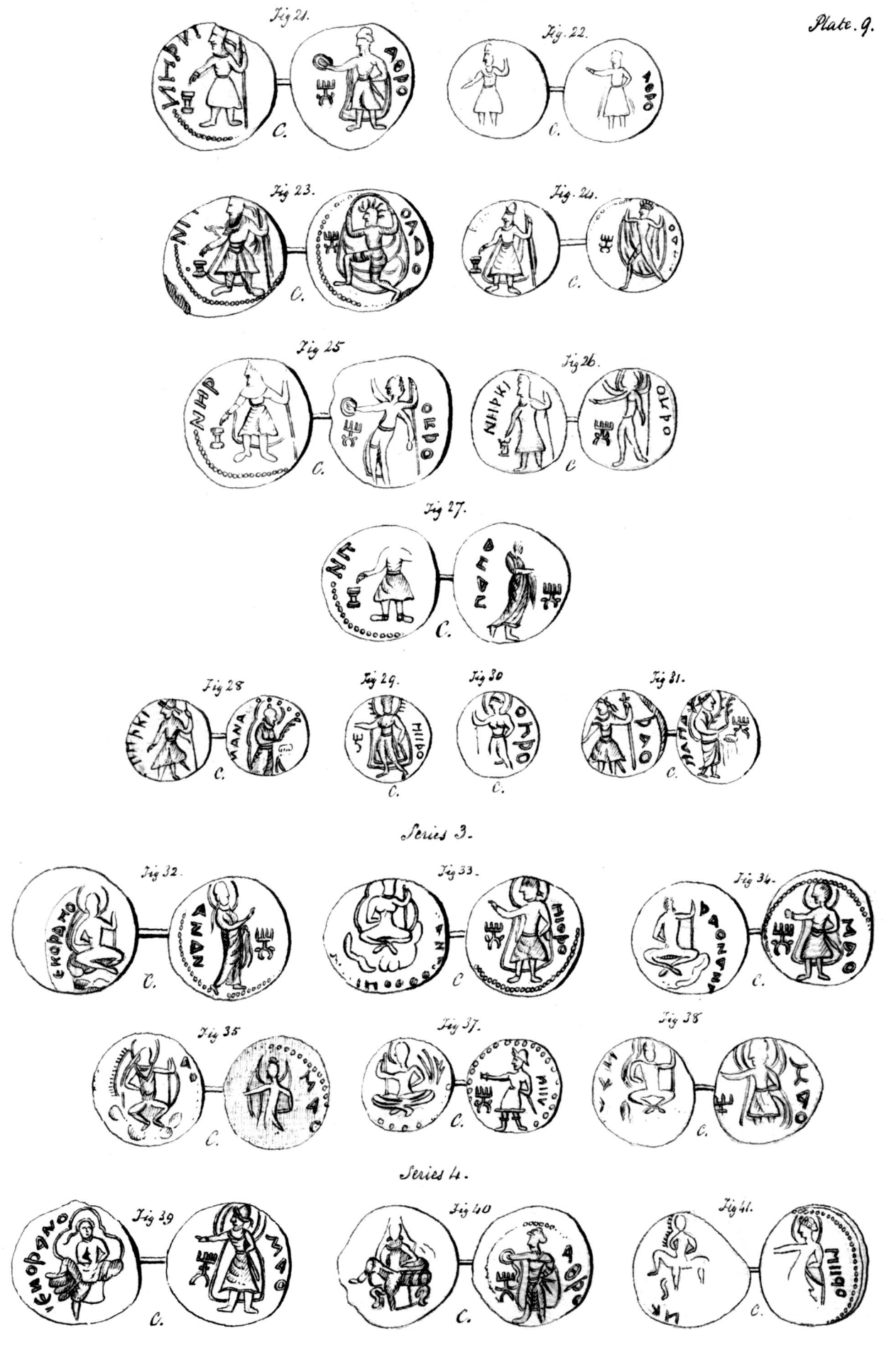

Plate 9 Kanishka I (21–31), Huvishka (32–41)

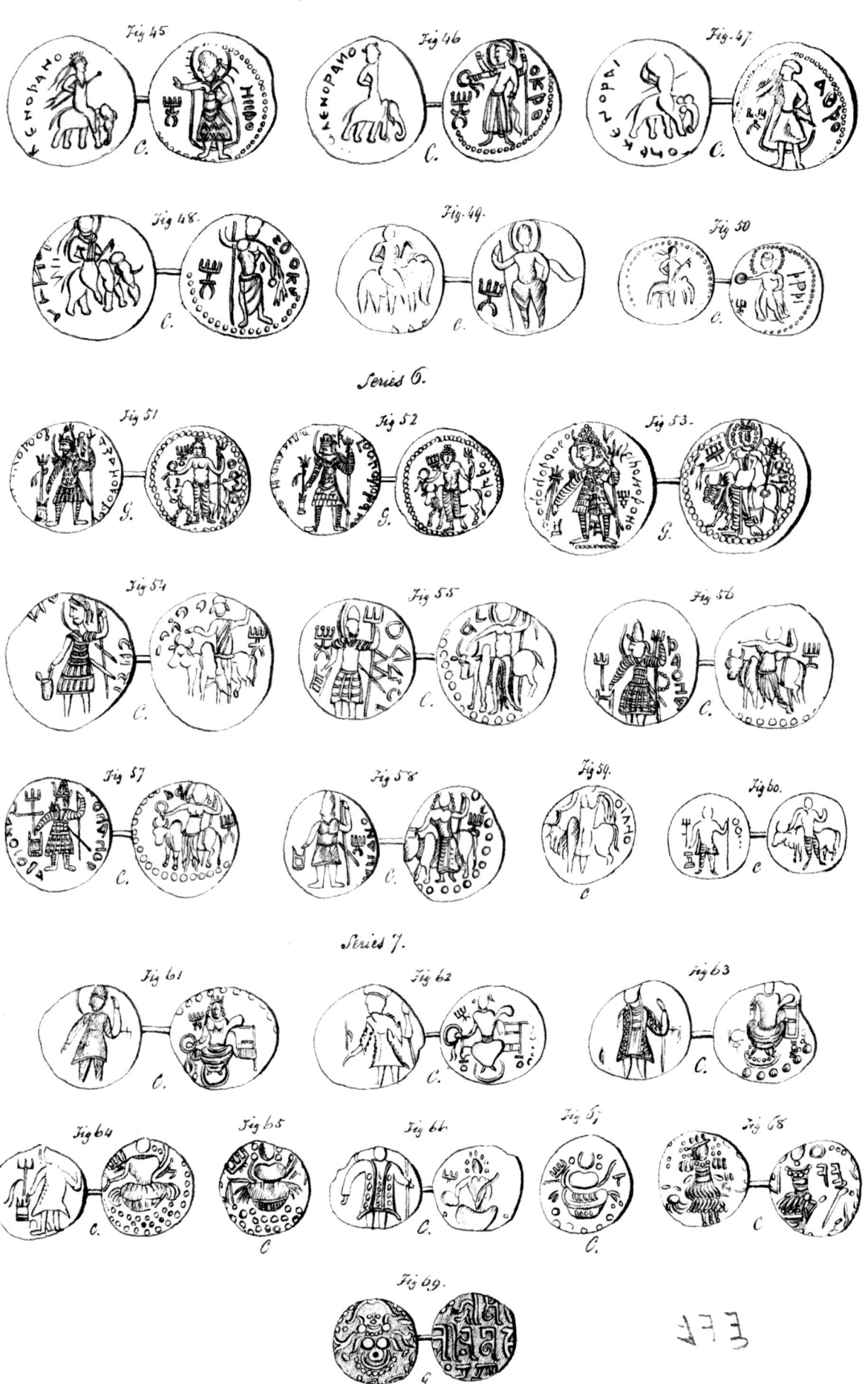

Plate 10 Huvishka (45–50), Vasudeva I (51–60), Kanishka II (61–3), imitation (66), Kanishka III (64–5, 67), Kashmir (68), Muḥammād b. Sām (69)

the obverse the figure of the prince and the fire altar and the Greek legend PAOKANHPKI. The reverses exhibit a variety of figures in sundry positions, with the several legends MAO, MIOPO, AΘPO, OAΔO (?), OKPO [OHÞO] and NANA, and all have the common monogram or symbol ☥. We have represented a large and smaller coin of each type, to show the [f. 22] ratios in size and consequently value of these coins, and probably to them may be united a smaller series represented as *Fig. 28* to *Fig. 31* which show on their reverses the legends NANA, MIIPO and OKPO [OHÞO].

[**Plate 9**] Series 3
[**Huvishka** (*c.* AD 151–90), king seated cross-legged]
Fig. 32 to *Fig. 38* represent the types of a series of coins whose obverses are distinguished by a figure seated cross-legged after the Indian manner, on clouds or it may be a throne or *musnud*, surrounded by a [Bactrian] Greek legend in corrupt characters, which although not distinct on any one coin, from a comparison of many specimens would appear to be PAONANA PAONANA KENOPANO [ÞAONANOÞAO OOHÞKE KOÞANO]. The reverses exhibit the same mythological figures as on the preceding series, with similar legends NANA, MIOPO, MAO &c.

Series 4
[**Huvishka**, king seated on couch]
Fig. 39 to *Fig. 44* [*Figs 42–4* are not illustrated] display the types of another series, where the obverse exhibits a figure seated on a throne, *cum otis et dignitate*, or with the right leg thrown over a cushion – the [Bactrian] Greek legend appears identical with that on the preceding series PAONANA PAONANA KENOPANO. The reverses have also the same mythological devices and legends MAO, AΘPO, MIIPO &c.

[**Plate 10**] Series 5
[**Huvishka** (*c.* AD 151–90), elephant rider]
Fig. 45 to *Fig. 50* show the types of a series of coins, strongly marked by the figure seated on an elephant which distinguish the obverses. The Greek legends seem not to differ from those of the two preceding series, neither do the figures and legends on the reverses – if we except that in the two former series, we find no coin with the four-armed figure of Okro [Oesho].

Series 6
[**Vasudeva I** (*c.* AD 190–230) and imitations]
Fig. 51 to *Fig. 60* represent the gold and copper coins of a series which of all others are found in greater numbers. *Fig. 51* to *Fig. 53* are of gold, *Fig. 54* to *Fig. 60* of copper. It may be remarked that of the Indo Scythic [Kushan] sovereigns we find of the precious metals only gold coins (a silver drachma of [Wima] Kadphises excepted [**Pl. 8**, *Fig. 3*]), while of the Greek Bactrian princes, we have hitherto found only silver coins. The coins now before us are of very variable execution, but all agree in having on the obverse the figure of the prince armed in coat of mail and with his right hand placed over a fire altar – which, by the by, is omitted on the three preceding series. The reverses show a figure standing in front of the sacred bull, sometimes with a chaplet in the left hand and always with a staff crowned with a trident in the right, the legend as seen in the gold coins is very corrupt Ο٩ႸΟ or ΟႬPΟ which we presume to be intended for OKPO [OHÞO]. This is important, because it explains the figure on the reverse of the coins of [Wima] Kadphises – which want the legend – the identity of the reverses of the coins of that prince and those of this Series, would have induced us to have introduced them in succession to him, but the wide difference in their style and execution, the corrupt and ambiguous nature of the legend on the obverse, with many other circumstances did not allow it – besides, possessing the gold coins of [Wima] Kadphises and of the early princes of the Kanerki dynasty [Kanishka I and Huvishka], their connection with and descent into each other becomes evident – moreover it is as manifest that the series under consideration were current to a comparatively late period – a gold coin of this series has been depicted by Mr Prinsep where the prince on the obverse has his head crowned with a pair of wings – this coin, somewhat similar to *Fig. 53* [Kushano-Sasanian, imitating a coin of Vasudeva I: 1838,EIC.3], is of the very latest princes of the series, and being in imitation of the latest of the Sasanian princes we may reasonably conjecture as to the period when the dynasty whose coins we speculate upon ceased to dominate.

[f. 23] Series 7
[*Figs 61–3*: **Kanishka II** (*c.* AD 230–46); *Fig. 66*: Kanishka II imitation; *Figs 64–5, 67*: **Kanishka III** (*c.* AD 267–72)]
Fig. 61 to *Fig. 68* represent the type of a Series of coins very abundantly found in western [*sic*: eastern] Afghanistan – the reverse [*sic*: obverse] has a rude figure of the prince clad in mail, with the accompaniment of the fire altar, and on the reverse a figure seated upon a throne with her feet upon a foot-stool [Ardochsho] – on no one coin of this class have we been able to detect the legend, although they appear in some instances to have had characters intended for such – *Fig. 61* to *Fig. 63* are the types generally found at Begram [Kanishka II]. *Fig. 64* [1838,EIC.116 (**Fig. 49.2**)] to *Fig. 68* are the types prevalent on the banks of the Indus and in the Punjab – the latter are of better execution [Kanishka III]. *Fig. 68* [Kashmiri coin of Toramana I (?) *c.* early 5th century] is perhaps a valuable coin, as, evidently related to this class, it shows the first signs of a Nagari inscription; it was brought from Peshawar; analogous coins are not to be found at Begram. *Fig. 67* shows the obverse of a coin from the same place, the two may serve to explain the gold coin depicted after them. *Fig. 69* [gold Lakshmi coin of Muḥammād b. Sām (AD 1171–1206), see also **Fig. 59.18** below] – the obverse of which has a close affinity to *Fig. 67* and the reverse has the same character visible on the reverse of *Fig. 68*. Coins of the type *Fig. 69* have been sketched by Professor Wilson [1832, p. 585, nos 48–50, pl. III.48–50; 1841, pp. 435–6, nos 1–7, Coins pl. XX.22–7: coins of the Gahadavala dynasty Govindachandradeva (*c.* 1114–55); Kalachuri dynasty Gangeyadeva (*c.* 1015–40); Yadava dynasty Kumarapaladeva (*c.* 1145–71); and Muḥammād b. Sām, 1173–1206] – although we doubt not their connection with the series of coins under consideration, we do not venture to affirm that the princes to whom they refer governed in western [*sic*: eastern] Afghanistan – but they possibly may in the regions east of

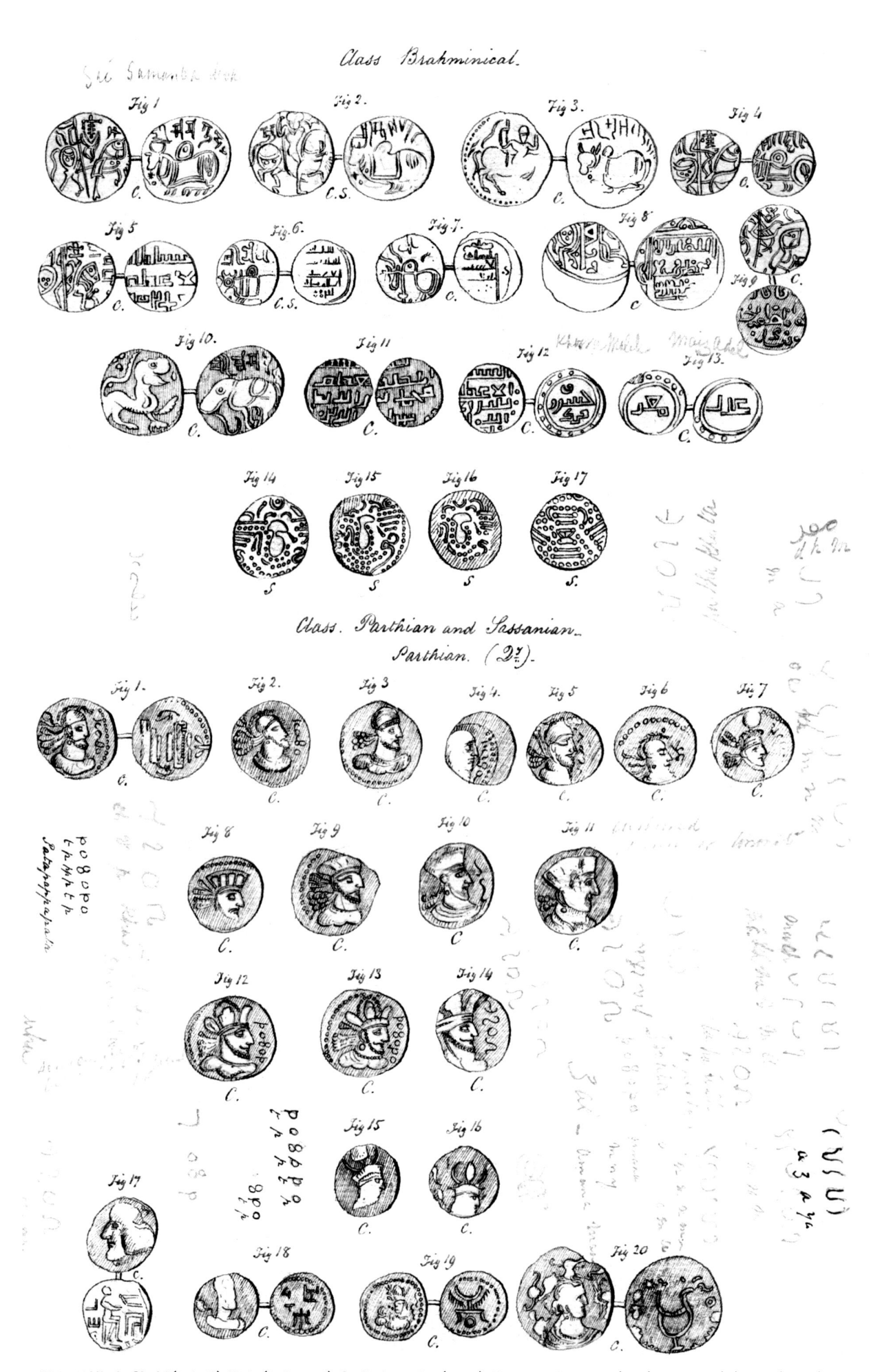

Plate 11 Hindu Shahi (1–3, 10), jitals (4–9, 11–13), Gadhaiya paisa (14–17). Kushano-Sasanian (1–16), Parthian (17), Hun (18–20)

the Indus. At Kabul coins of this peculiar type are met with occasionally in the bazaar, generally of gold – a large parcel was dug out of the soil three or four years since near Korrindar, a village of Koh Daman. It is probable, from the presence of the Nagari character, that this series of coins (7) is the least ancient of the several Indo-Scythic [Kushan] series.

[Plate 11] Class Brahmanical[17]

Fig. 1 to *Fig. 10* represent the types of a species of coin numerously found in Afghanistan – they are either silver, billon or copper. The silver coins are to be always procured in the bazaar of Kabul, and in quantity or in parcels of many, occasionally one or two have been picked up at Begram, where the copper coins occur freely as they do at Jalalabad. The first coin depicted of this type was by Mr Prinsep from a specimen detected by Dr Swiney, and being termed unique, we may infer that such coins are rare in India. Mr Prinsep referred it to the Andhra Bhritya dynasty which reigned anterior to the Muhammadan invasion. To this there can be no objection, should not some of the coins here delineated seem to suggest that they refer to a subsequent epoch.

Fig. 1 [**Shahi – Samantadeva** (c. AD 850–1000)] represents the generic type of this class of coins, the obverse having a horseman, and the reverse a recumbent humped bull – the first has the legend ⁄⁄⁄⁄ in front of the horse, and the last the legend श्रीमद्रूपक over the animal.[18]

Fig. 2 [**Spalapatideva** (c. AD 750–850)] is a billon coin of the same type and *Fig. 3* and *Fig. 4* are copper coins.

Fig. 5 [**Ghurid – Muʿizz al-dīn Muḥammād b. Sām** (1173–1206; IOLC.6724 (**Fig. 62.27**)] shows a coin with the horseman on the obverse, while the reverse has an undoubted Kufic legend.

Fig. 6 and *Fig. 7* [**Ghaznavid** (?) – **Masʿūd III** (1099–1115)] represent coins having on the obverses the recumbent bull, and on the reverses the legends in Kufic.

Fig. 8 [**Khwarazm Shah – ʿAla al-dīn Muḥammād b. Tekish** (1200–20)] shows a coin on which the figure of the horseman on the obverse is intersected perpendicularly by a line of Nagari character, the reverse being also filled by a Kufic legend.

Fig. 9 [**Khwarazm Shah** (?) – **ʿAla al-dīn Muḥammād b. Tekish**] displays a small copper coin, having on the obverse the horseman and on the reverse a legend which appears to be Persian. We exhibited this coin to many mullahs at Kabul, and while no one could decipher the characters, all of them agreed they were Persian.

Fig. 10 [**Shahi – Samantadeva**] is a coin of very rude and inferior execution, having a lion or some monstrous animal on the obverse, and an elephant on the reverse – with a Nagari legend.

Figs 11, 12 and *Fig. 13* are introduced, although properly Kufic coins, from the similarity which the legend of *Fig. 11* bears to that of *Fig. 5* and the reverse of *Fig. 12* allows the exhibition of *Fig. 13*. [*Figs 11, 13*. **Ghurid – Muʿizz al-dīn Muḥammād b. Sām**. *Fig. 12*. **Ghaznavid – Khusrau Malik** (1160–86)].

The presence of Kufic and Persian legends on coins of this class, suggests that they [f. 24] may be the princes who reigned in eastern Afghanistan between the periods of the expulsion of the governors of the Caliphs and the rise of the Ghaznavid dynasty. It is understood here, that Hindu [Shahi] supremacy was established in these countries so far west as Kabul, until the age of Sultan Maḥmūd [AD 998–1030] whose father [Sebuktegin (AD 993–7)] indeed was besieged in Ghazni by a raia or rajah of Lahore [Hindu Shahis of Ohind] in whose empire the provinces west of the Indus were included or were tributary.

[Marginal note] 'These remarks gave Prinsep the idea of his Taxila coins – they have since been borrowed by Professor Wilson – perhaps I ought to say adopted'.

Sultan Maḥmūd it is well known subverted the Hindu authorities in these countries and restored the Muhammadan ascendancy along the line of the Indus. The Persian legend on *Fig. 9* may serve to fix the era at which the Persian language became used in Afghanistan, which by this evidence will be immediately prior to or coeval with that of the Ghaznavid princes, whose coins we shall hereafter show have Persian legends.

Fig. 14 to *Fig. 17* [**Gadhaiya paisa**] exhibit the type of a variety of coin, sometimes met with in the bazaar of Kabul, and always in small parcels of two, three, four, six &c. *Figs 14–16* show the obverse and *Fig. 17* the reverse. These coins have been depicted by Professor Wilson [1832, p. 588, nos 71–3, pl. III.71–3], whence we find that they are common enough in India, and are frequently found of copper. At Kabul they generally occur of silver. Copper ones have however been exhumed at Koh Daman in company with coins similar to **Pl. 10**, *Fig. 69*. Begram has yielded no coin of this type.

Class Parthian & Sasanian

Parthian (?) [**Kushano-Sasanian**, c. AD 233–370]

Fig. 1 to *Fig. 16* will serve to explain slightly the nature of an extensive series of coins found numerously and constantly at Begram. We call them Parthian conditionally because they are certainly not Arsakian, and we are not sure that the presence of the fire altar does not prove them to be Sasanian, as it does demonstrate, that the princes to whom they refer, were adorers of Mithra – but they will then appear to have been other than the Sasanians of Persia.

[Marginal note] 'These highly important coins have been passed over lightly by Prinsep and subsequently by Professor Wilson. Neither was bold enough to grapple fairly with them'.

From the numbers in which these coins occur at Begram, it may be inferred that they were once current there, and consequently that the sovereigns commemorated by them once ruled over it. The difficulty then presents itself to determine at what period to introduce their sway, with the mass of Greek and Indo-Scythic [Kushan] coins before us which we have gone through – we state the difficulty without being able to solve it. As for the coins themselves, however numerous, they may be reduced into three series, with reference to the nature of the head-dress.

Fig. 1 to *Fig. 7* show the type of the first series [Gandharan issues of satraps Kavad and Meze], where the obverse displays a bust – the head helmed [*sic:* crowned] – with a Pahlavi [Bactrian] legend [*Figs 1–3*: Crown of Hormizd I (c.

AD 270–300), inscribed καβαδ. *Figs 4–6*: inscribed μεζε]. *Fig. 7* is a variety where an orb, probably the sun or moon, is above the helm [crown with orb and diadems of Peroz II (*c.* AD 303–30), inscribed μεζε]. The reverses of all these and of the other two series agree in having a plain fire altar as represented in *Fig. 1* – without the two defenders as with the true Sasanians.

Fig. 8 to *Fig. 11* give the type of the second series, where the helm is replaced by a compact crown of which *Fig. 8* shows the most perfect example [Crown of Peroz I (*c.* AD 245–70)].

Fig. 12 to *Fig. 14* display the type of the third series, the bust distinguished by a tripartite crown, the centre portion adorned by a semicircle of jewels [Shapur II (*c.* AD 309–79), *Figs 12–13* inscribed þαβoρo; *Fig. 14* inscribed καβαδ].

Fig. 15 and *Fig. 16* show the coins, probably of a single prince, found annually at Begram in small numbers, whose head is graced by being surmounted by a pair of cow's horns between which is an orb [crown of Peroz II (*c.* AD 303–30), inscribed μεζε].

[f. 25] *Fig. 17* to *Fig. 20* show the types of four coins either Parthian or Sasanian.

Fig. 17 [**Parthian Phraates V** (2 BC–AD 4) imitation?] is never found at Begram – a parcel of some hundreds of these coins was picked up in the bazaar of Kabul, probably brought from Turkestan – they were all of copper – this type may perhaps be genuine Arsakian.

Fig. 18 [**Kidarite** *c.* 4th century] and *Fig. 19* [**Alkhan** *c.* 5th century] are single specimens from Begram, and curious from the characters and symbols on the reverses [Vondrovec 2014, pp. 115–16, type GC-K 20 (?); pp. 179, 231, fig. 3.24, type 37].

Fig. 20 [**Hun** (*c.* AD 700; 1902,0614.55 (**Fig. 53.7**)] is a coin from the bazaar of Kabul, the bust on the obverse is surrounded with the heads of bulls, and the reverse is distinguished by a remarkable emblem; it is a unique specimen, and may possibly be Indo-Sasanian [Vondrovec 2014, pp. 519, 602, 881, type 204].[19]

[Plate 12]
Sasanian [includes Alkhan Hun and Arab-Sasanian coins]
We have introduced a variety of figures here, not so much with the view of entering into particular discussion respecting them, as to show the descent into each other which these coins permit, and thereby to facilitate more serious investigation. Coins of this class, excepting the three first types *Fig. 21, 22* and *Fig. 23* [Alkhan coins from Hadda 10 stupa deposit; see **Plate 14**, *Figs 4, 7* and *12*], are very numerously found in the bazaars of Kabul, but never at Begram, where we have indeed found two or three copper coins similar to *Fig. 21, 22* and *23*, and one or two from which we have designated *Fig. 37*. As these coins, so plentiful in the bazaar of Kabul, are all of silver, there can be little doubt of their being importations, probably from Turkestan – the mint at Kabul being indebted for her silver to other countries, large quantities of bullion are annually imported.[20] It has however happened that very large parcels of Sasanian silver coins have been discovered by chance in various parts of Afghanistan.

Fig. 21 to *Fig. 29* will explain the types of the first series of these Sasanian coins. The three first figures are from coins extracted from a Tope at Hadda [stupa 10] and introduced here as they manifestly stand at the head of the series, the helmed head in these coins is replaced by a decorated crown in the other figures, but the reverses of all agree in having the fire altar surmounted with a bust or it may be the figure of Mithra. [*Fig. 24*: Alkhan imitation of Shapur II; *Figs 25–9*: Shapur II (AD 309–79)].

Fig. 30 to *Fig. 32* [IOC.440 (**Fig. 54.13**)] represent a second series, where the bust is no longer seen over the fire altar, and the crescent and star are introduced [Varhran V (AD 420–38); Yazdagird II (AD 438–57); Kavad I (AD 488–96) 1st reign].

Fig. 33 and *Fig. 34* are coins of the same series, where the crescent and star are introduced at opposite points on the margin [Khusrau I (AD 531–79); Hormizd IV (AD 579–90)].

Fig. 35 [IOC.664 (**Fig. 59.8**)] exhibits a coin of this class, where we first discover the wings over the crown of the bust [Khusrau II (AD 591–628)].

Fig. 36 [IOC.2367 (**Fig. 57.9**)] is a remarkable variety of the winged coin on which the legend on the obverse appears Sanskrit [Turkic ruler: Sandan (*c.* AD 700–50); obverse inscriptions: Brahmi *śrī candāna vakhudevaḥ* 'his Perfection Candana, Lord of the Oxus'; Bactrian: σρι βαγο αζροβδδιγο σανδανο βαγο χοαδηο 'his Perfection the Lord the Chiliarch Sandano, his Perfection the Lord'. Vondrovec 2014, p. 643, type 244].

Fig. 37 is the obverse of a copper coin of this type procured at Begram [unknown Alkhan Narana–Narendra (*c.* 540–80) uniface issue. Vondrovec 2014, p. 346, type 150, var. 3].

Fig. 38, 39 and *Fig. 40* [IOC.509 (**Fig. 54.22**)] give the type of the species of Sasanian coin most abundant, and which manifestly closes the series, these figures are of the better executed coins [Arab-Sasanian 'Abd al-Aziz b. 'Abdallāh b. 'Āmir (*c.* AD 685); Khurshid (*c.* AD 766); Khusrau II (year 36: *c.* AD 625)].

They are succeeded by coins of inferior execution as *Fig. 41, 42* and *43* – which have invariably one or more marks or characters on the margin, which have obviously been struck or punched on them after coinage [Arab-Sasanian Salm b. Ziyād (*c.* AD 680), Muṣ'ab b. al-Zubayr (AD 686–91) and 'Ubaydallāh b. Ziyād (*c.* AD 672–82) with Hun and other counterstrikes] – if any of these additions could be recognised to be Muhammadan, there would be no difficulty in admitting the better sort of these coins to be those of the last of the Khusraus, and those with the distinguishing marks, those struck under the first Caliphs – the nature of these stamped marks will be best explained by noting some of them:

[Plate 13]
Indo-Sasanian [Alkhan Hun, Nezak and Turkic coins]
Fig. 44 to *Fig. 51* are the types of a class of coins, which we call Indo-Sasanian, from the strongly marked Indian countenances of the busts, and from the great probability that the princes ruled in these countries; their copper monies plentifully occurring at Begram, which is not the case with other Sasanian copper coins. The one, two or three coins

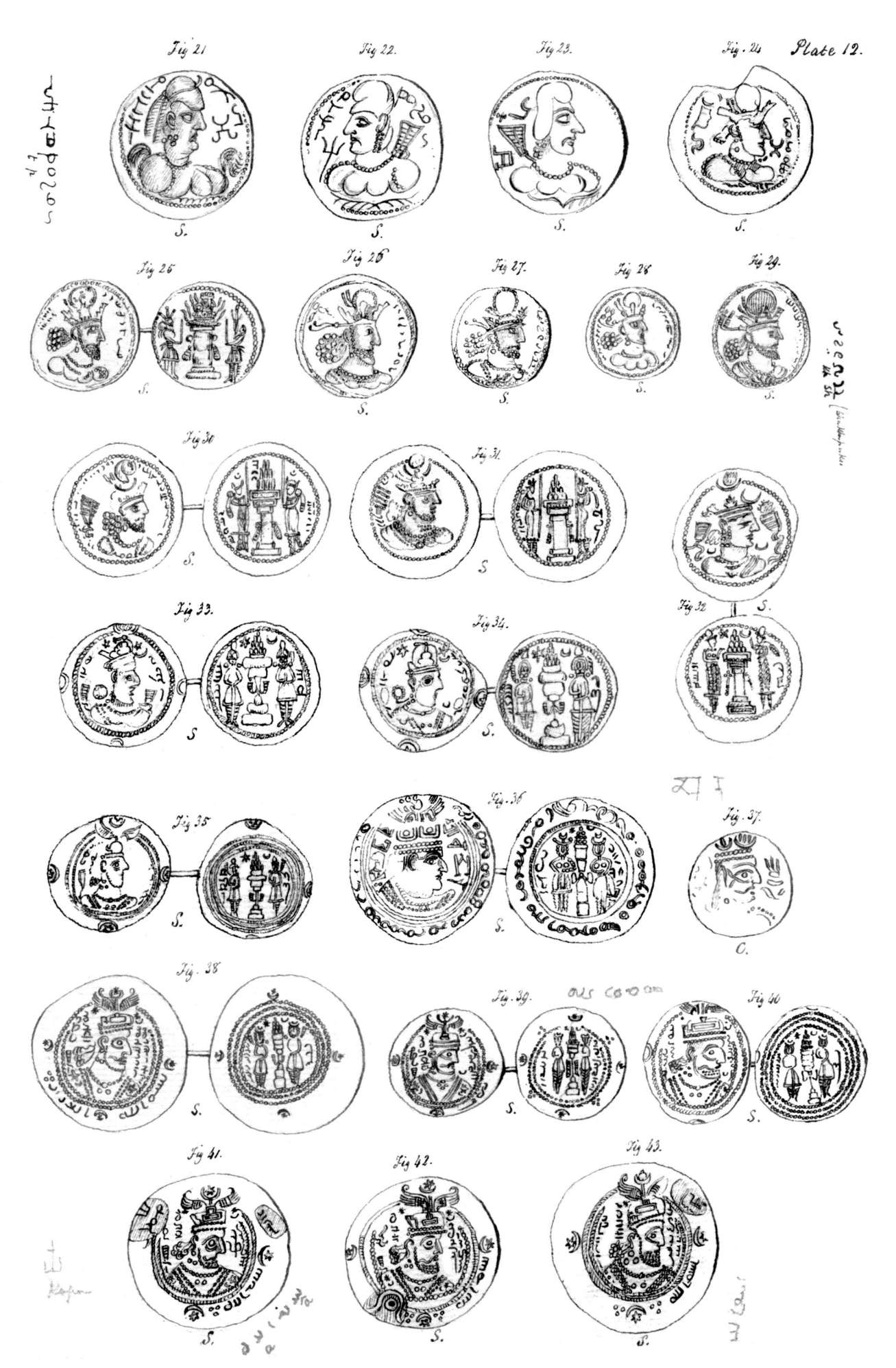

Plate 12 Alkhan Hun (21–4), Sasanian (25–35, 38–40), Turki Shahi (36), Nezak uniface (37), Arab-Sasanian/Hepthalite (41–3)

Masson Manuscript F526/1a: Analysis of the Begram Coins with Reference to Plates | 65

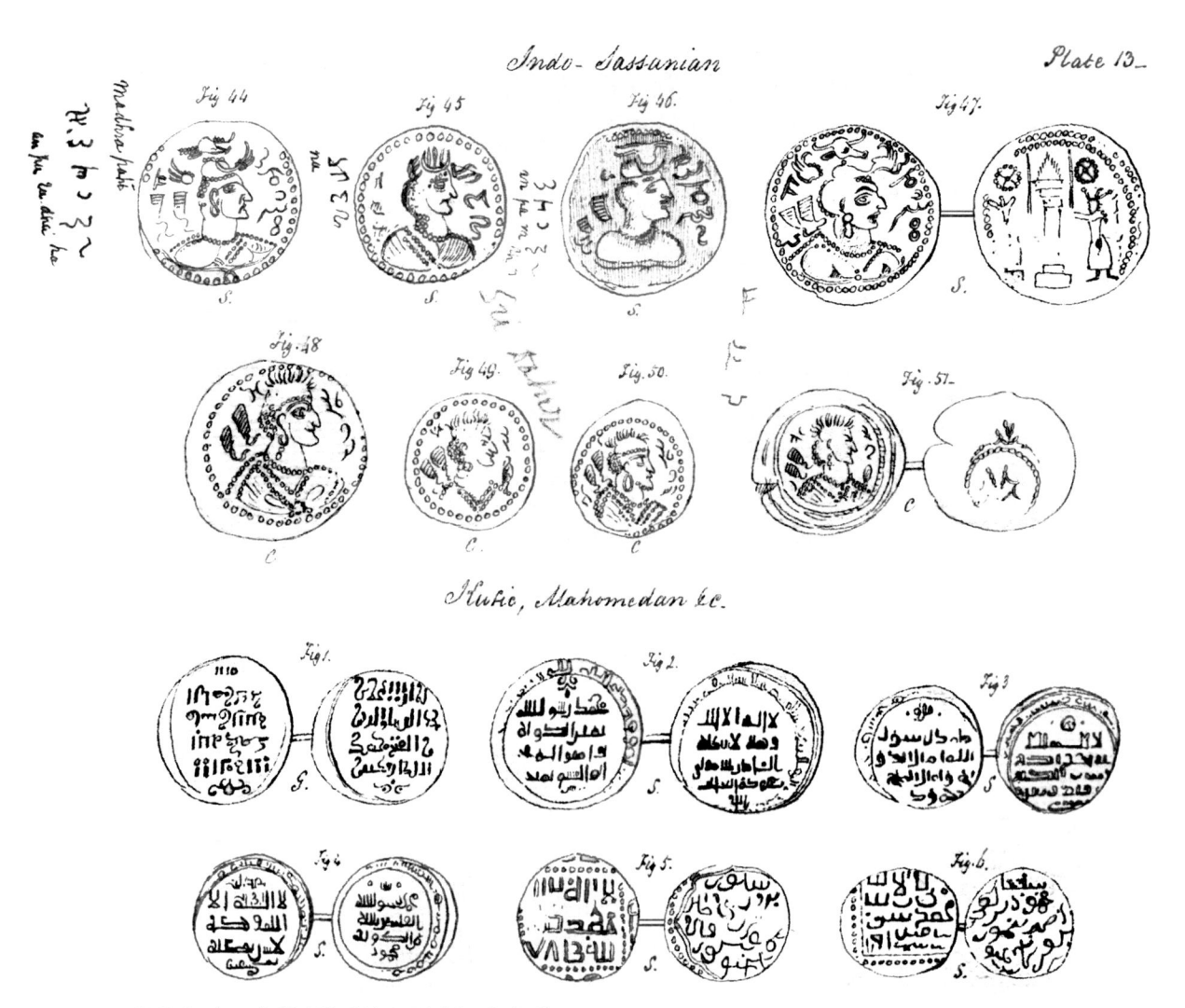

Plate 13 Napki Malka (44–7), Shri Shahi (48–51), Islamic (1–6)

occasionally found of them, as before noted, being to be considered as casualties. *Fig. 44* to *47* are of silver and *Fig. 48* to *51* are of copper. The busts are remarkable for the bulls' heads around it, on which account *Fig. 20* of **Plate 11** should perhaps have been included with these coins. The silver coins appear to show but two varieties of legends – ɜ ʅ ϭ ʒ ∞ and ʃ ט ζ ϟ – and the copper coins but one variety ϟ ∩ ɔ. The reverses of these coins are distinguished by the emblem ۞ over the [f. 26] heads of the altar defenders. *Fig. 51* has a peculiar reverse, found however on other Sasanian coins, and also on one or two of those we call Greek Bactrian.

[*Figs 44, 46–7*: Napki Malka (*nycky MLKA* 'king Nezak'; *c.* AD 500–50). *Fig. 45*: Turkic (*c.* early 8th century). *Figs 48–51*: Alkhan-Nezak (with Alkhan tamgha; *c.* AD 500–50)].

Class Kufic, Muhammadan &c.
The appearance of Kufic coins in these countries in very considerable numbers, is explained by the early conquests of the Caliphs, whose generals reduced the countries on the Indus and west of it, in the first century of their era. Without reference I cannot determine how long they preserved authority in them, but it appears certain that so far as Kabul was recovered from them by the Hindu powers east of the Indus. The sway of the Caliph must however have been of some duration, if we judge from the quantities of their currency found at Begram. This currency appears to have been of gold, silver, billon and copper. The silver coins of the Caliphs are abundant in the bazaar of Kabul, being brought from Turkestan.

The figures represented as *Fig. 1* to *Fig. 6* are given, merely to show the nature of the Kufic coins found in these countries, and as necessary to complete the view of the coins found at Begram and Kabul. A few specimens are therefore presented only, as we are unable to decipher them [*Fig. 1*: Khwarazm Shah or Ilkhanid (?). *Figs 2–4*: Ghaznavid. *Figs 5–6*: Timurid]. *Fig. 6* shows the type of the silver coins of the celebrated Sultan Maḥmūd of Ghazni [*sic*: Timurid, Sultan Maḥmūd (*c.* AD 1494)].

Kabul. 31st December 1835

[Masson includes two additional plates without commentary of the coins excavated from Hadda stupa 10 (Plates 14–15; see **Vol. 1, pp. 185–8, Figs 281–2**)].

Plates 14–15
Types of Sasanian coins discovered in the principal Tope of Hadda near Jalalabad … These represent the various types of 187 silver Sasanians found in the same Tope – No. 1 to 14 single specimens, the others more numerous, the latter types more so, particularly [*Figs*] *25, 26, 27*.

Types of Sassanian Coins discovered in the principal Tope of Haddah near Jelalabad. Plate 14.

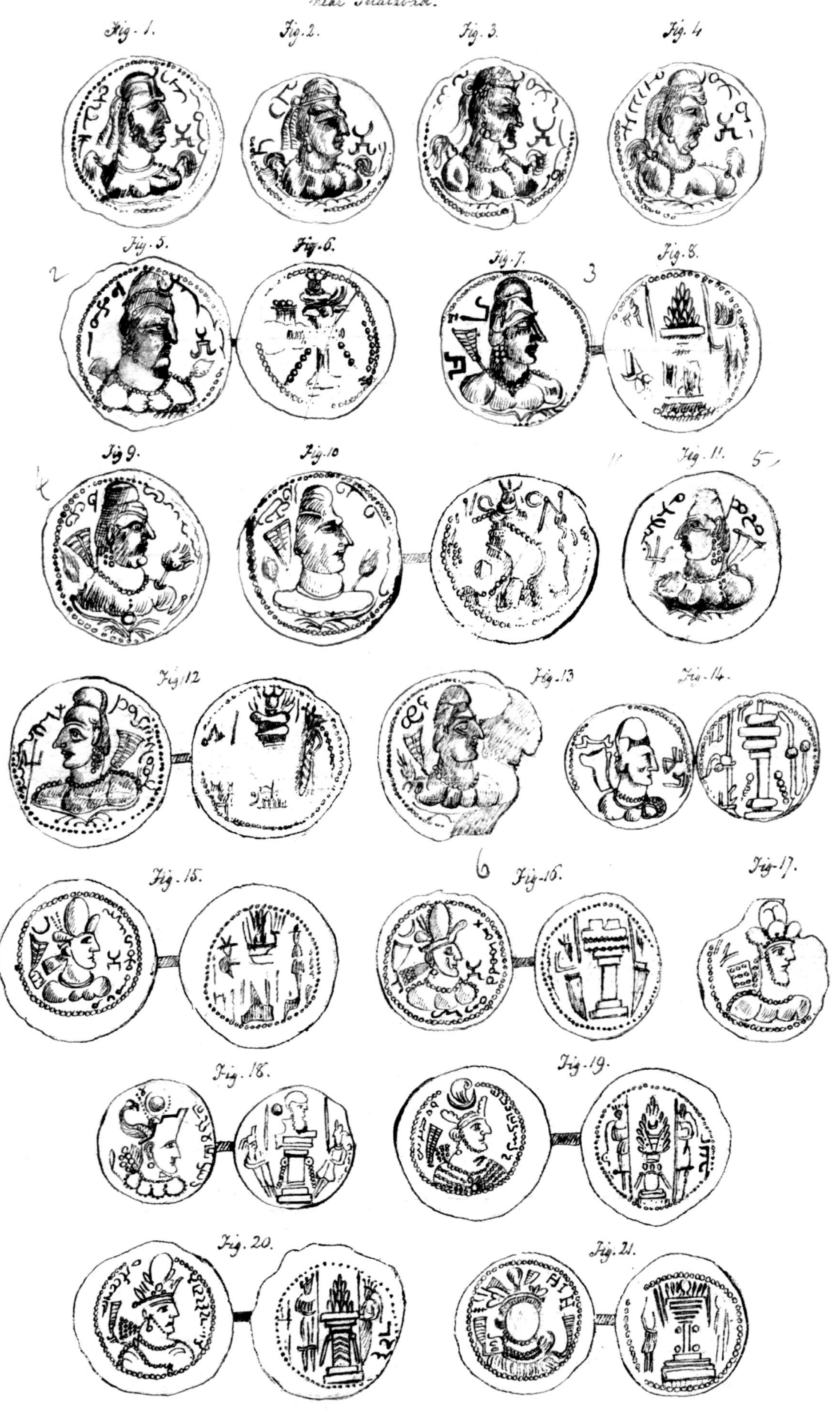

Plate 14 Hadda stupa 10 coins (see Vol. I, pp. 185–7, Fig. 281)

Plate 15 Hadda stupa 10 coins (see Vol. I, pp. 185–7, Fig. 281)

The coins are now identified as follows:

Alkhan
Figs 1–4, 14. Khingila (*c.* AD 440–90).
Figs 1–4. Bactrian inscription χιγγιλο αλχανο (*xiggilo alxano* 'Khingila Alkhan').
Fig. 14. Brahmi inscription: *khigi* in right field.
Figs 5–10. Anonymous Alkhan king.
Figs 5–6, 13. Bactrian inscription þαυο (written backwards) αλχα (?).
Figs 7–8. Brahmi inscription *ṣā-hi*.
Figs 9–10. Bactrian inscription þαυο (written backwards) αλχα (*šauo alxa[no]* 'king Alkhan').
Figs 11–12. Bactrian inscription αλχα (written backwards) þαυο ζαοβ[(*alxa[no] šauo zaob[* 'Alkhan king Zaob').

Figs 15–17. Shapur II imitations (*c.* AD 309–79).
Fig. 15–16. Bactrian inscription, respectively χμοιαδβο ανονο (*xmoiadbo anono*) and χσοιαδβο ανονο (*xsoiadbo anono*), with Alkhan tamgha.

Sasanian
Figs 18, 26–7. Varhran IV (AD 388–99).
Figs 19–20, 22–3. Yazdagird II (AD 438–57).
Figs 24–5. Peroz (AD 457–84).

Kidarite
Fig. 21. Kidara (*c.* AD 355–85). Brahmi inscription *kidara kuṣānaṣā[ha]*.

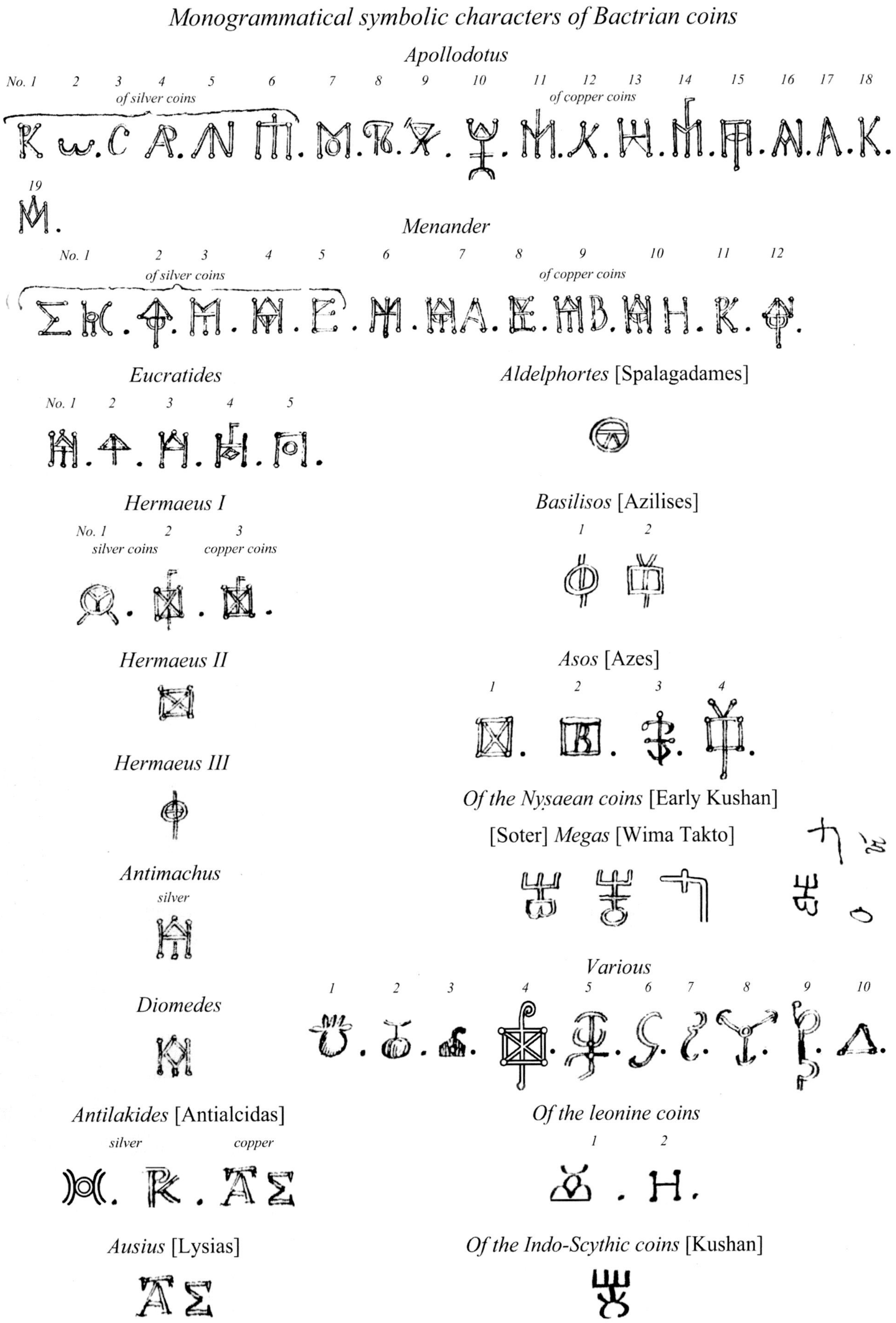

Monogrammatical symbolic characters of Bactrian coins

Apollodotus

No. 1   2   3   4   5   6   7   8   9   10   11   12   13   14   15   16   17   18
           of silver coins   *of copper coins*

19

Menander

No. 1   2   3   4   5   6   7   8   9   10   11   12
       of silver coins   *of copper coins*

Eucratides

No. 1   2   3   4   5

Aldelphortes* [Spalagadames]

Hermaeus I

No. 1   2   3
silver coins   copper coins

Basilisos [Azilises]

1   2

Hermaeus II

Asos [Azes]

1   2   3   4

Hermaeus III

Of the Nysaean coins [Early Kushan]

[Soter] *Megas* [Wima Takto]

Antimachus
silver

Various

1   2   3   4   5   6   7   8   9   10

Diomedes

Antilakides [Antialcidas]
silver   copper

Of the leonine coins

1   2

Ausius [Lysias]

Of the Indo-Scythic coins [Kushan]

Plate 16 Monograms and tamghas

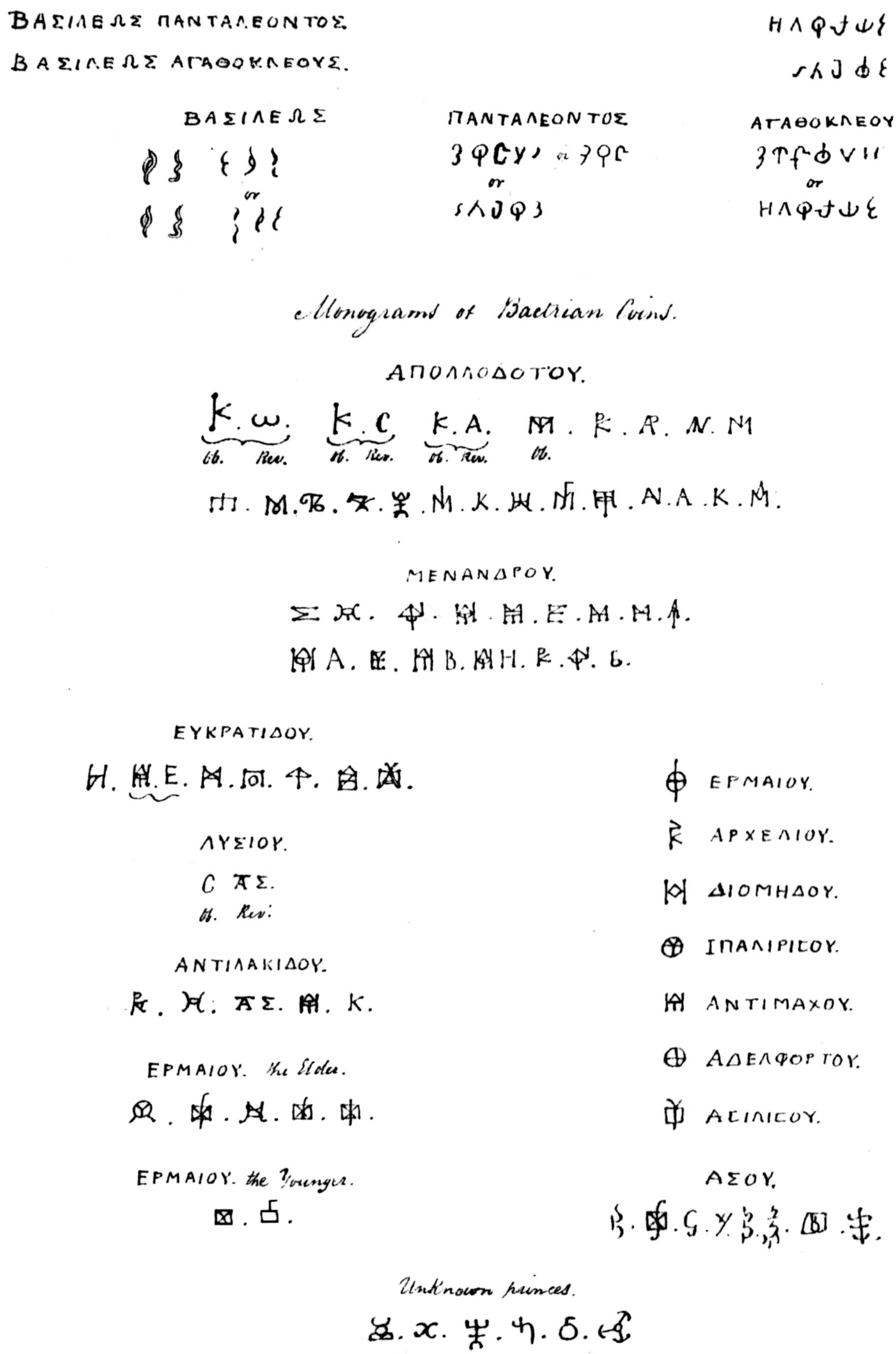

ΒΑΣΙΛΕΩΣ ΠΑΝΤΑΛΕΟΝΤΟΣ

ΒΑΣΙΛΕΩΣ ΑΓΑΘΟΚΛΕΟΥΣ.

ΒΑΣΙΛΕΩΣ   ΠΑΝΤΑΛΕΟΝΤΟΣ   ΑΓΑΘΟΚΛΕΟΥΣ.

Monograms of Bactrian Coins.

ΑΠΟΛΛΟΔΟΤΟΥ.

ΜΕΝΑΝΔΡΟΥ.

ΕΥΚΡΑΤΙΔΟΥ.

ΛΥΣΙΟΥ.

ΑΝΤΙΛΑΚΙΔΟΥ.

ΕΡΜΑΙΟΥ. *the Elder.*

ΕΡΜΑΙΟΥ. *the Younger.*

ΕΡΜΑΙΟΥ.

ΑΡΧΕΛΙΟΥ.

ΔΙΟΜΗΔΟΥ.

ΙΠΑΛΙΡΙΣΟΥ.

ΑΝΤΙΜΑΧΟΥ.

ΑΔΕΛΦΟΡΤΟΥ.

ΑΣΙΛΙΣΟΥ.

ΑΣΟΥ.

Unknown princes.

Plate 17 Monograms on Bactrian, Indo-Greek and other coins

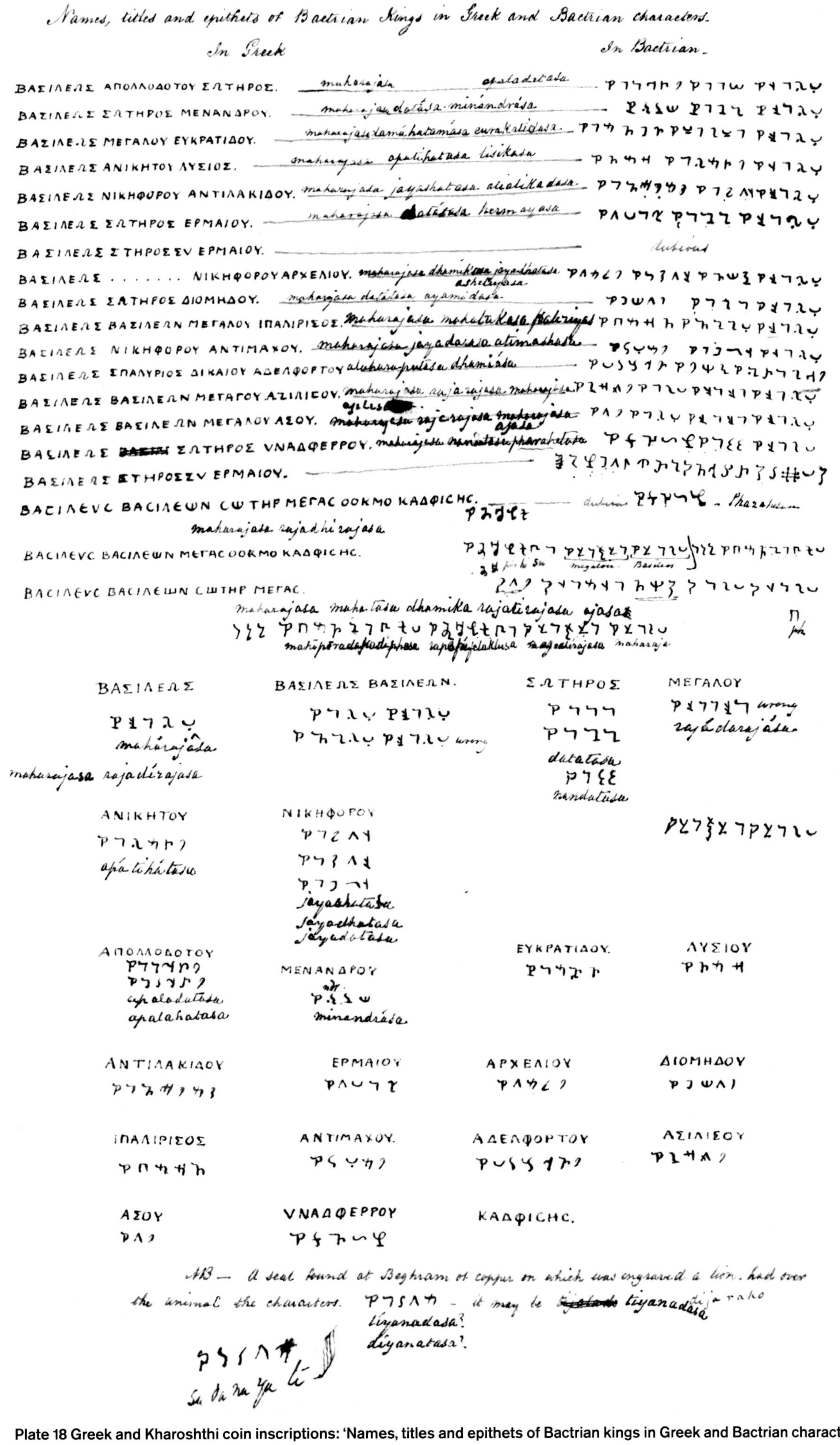

Names, titles and epithets of Bactrian Kings in Greek and Bactrian characters.

In Greek   *In Bactrian*

Greek	Bactrian transliteration	Kharoshthi
ΒΑΣΙΛΕΩΣ ΑΠΟΛΛΟΔΟΤΟΥ ΣΩΤΗΡΟΣ.	maharajasa apaladatasa	𐨥𐨀𐨤𐨐
ΒΑΣΙΛΕΩΣ ΣΩΤΗΡΟΣ ΜΕΝΑΝΔΡΟΥ.	maharajasa datasa minandrasa	
ΒΑΣΙΛΕΩΣ ΜΕΓΑΛΟΥ ΕΥΚΡΑΤΙΔΟΥ.	maharajasa mahatamasa eukratidasa	
ΒΑΣΙΛΕΩΣ ΑΝΙΚΗΤΟΥ ΛΥΣΙΟΥ.	maharajasa apatihatasa lisikasa	
ΒΑΣΙΛΕΩΣ ΝΙΚΗΦΟΡΟΥ ΑΝΤΙΑΛΚΙΔΟΥ.	maharajada jayashatasa atialikadasa	
ΒΑΣΙΛΕΩΣ ΣΩΤΗΡΟΣ ΕΡΜΑΙΟΥ.	maharajasa datatasa hermayasa	
ΒΑΣΙΛΕΩΣ ΣΩΤΗΡΟΣΕΥ ΕΡΜΑΙΟΥ.	*dubious*	
ΒΑΣΙΛΕΩΣ .... ΝΙΚΗΦΟΡΟΥ ΑΡΧΕΛΙΟΥ.	maharajasa dhamikasa jayashatasa asheliyasa	
ΒΑΣΙΛΕΩΣ ΣΩΤΗΡΟΣ ΔΙΟΜΗΔΟΥ.	maharajasa datasa ayamidasa	
ΒΑΣΙΛΕΩΣ ΒΑΣΙΛΕΩΝ ΜΕΓΑΛΟΥ ΙΠΑΛΙΡΙΣΟΥ.	maharajasa mahatukasa palirisyes	
ΒΑΣΙΛΕΩΣ ΝΙΚΗΦΟΡΟΥ ΑΝΤΙΜΑΧΟΥ.	maharajasa jayadarasa atimahase	
ΒΑΣΙΛΕΩΣ ΣΠΑΛΥΡΙΟΣ ΔΙΚΑΙΟΥ ΑΔΕΛΦΟΡΤΟΥ	alahuraputasa dhamiada	
ΒΑΣΙΛΕΩΣ ΒΑΣΙΛΕΩΝ ΜΕΓΟΥ ΑΖΙΛΙΣΟΥ.	maharajasa rajarajasa maharajasa ayilisa	
ΒΑΣΙΛΕΩΣ ΒΑΣΙΛΕΩΝ ΜΕΓΑΛΟΥ ΑΖΟΥ.	maharajasa rajarajasa maharajasa ajasa	
ΒΑΣΙΛΕΩΣ ~~ΒΑΣΙΛΕΩΝ~~ ΣΩΤΗΡΟΣ ΥΝΑΔΦΕΡΡΟΥ.	maharajasa nanatasa pharahatasa	
ΒΑΣΙΛΕΩΣ ΣΩΤΗΡΟΣΕΥ ΕΡΜΑΙΟΥ.		
ΒΑΣΙΛΕΥΣ ΒΑΣΙΛΕΩΝ ΣΩΤΗΡ ΜΕΓΑΣ ΟΟΚΜΟ ΚΑΔΦΙCΗC.	*dubious* — *Pharotasan*	
maharajasa rajadhirajasa		
ΒΑCΙΛΕΥC ΒΑCΙΛΕΩΝ ΜΕΓΑC ΟΟΚΜΟ ΚΑΔΦΙCΗC.	*2nd pub. Sw. megalon Basileon*	
ΒΑCΙΛΕΥC ΒΑCΙΛΕΩΝ CΩΤΗΡ ΜΕΓΑC.		

maharajasa mahatasa dhamika rajatirajasa ajasa
mahipuradaphadiphasa sapasajelaklusa rajatirajasa maharaja

ΒΑΣΙΛΕΩΣ	ΒΑΣΙΛΕΩΣ ΒΑΣΙΛΕΩΝ.	ΣΩΤΗΡΟΣ	ΜΕΓΑΛΟΥ
maharajasa		datatasa	*wrong* rajadarajasa
maharajasa rajadirajasa		nandatasa	

ΑΝΙΚΗΤΟΥ	ΝΙΚΗΦΟΡΟΥ		
apatihatasa	jayashatasa / jayashatasa / jayadatasa		

ΑΠΟΛΛΟΔΟΤΟΥ	ΜΕΝΑΝΔΡΟΥ	ΕΥΚΡΑΤΙΔΟΥ.	ΛΥΣΙΟΥ
apalodatasa / apalahatasa	minandrasa		

ΑΝΤΙΑΛΚΙΔΟΥ	ΕΡΜΑΙΟΥ	ΑΡΧΕΛΙΟΥ	ΔΙΟΜΗΔΟΥ

ΙΠΑΛΙΡΙΣΟΣ	ΑΝΤΙΜΑΧΟΥ.	ΑΔΕΛΦΟΡΤΟΥ	ΑΣΙΛΙΣΟΥ

ΑΖΟΥ	ΥΝΑΔΦΕΡΡΟΥ	ΚΑΔΦΙCΗC.	

NB — A seal found at Begram of copper on which was engraved a lion. had over the animal the characters. 𐨥𐨒𐨯𐨞 — *it may be* ~~tiyatata~~ *tiyanadasa / dijarako / tiyanadasa? / diyanatasa?*

𐨯𐨡𐨞𐨩 *Sa da na ya li*

Plate 18 Greek and Kharoshthi coin inscriptions: 'Names, titles and epithets of Bactrian kings in Greek and Bactrian characters'

Table 5 Enumeration of coins collected from Begram during years 1833, 1834 and 1835 [original manuscript watermarked 'G. Wilmot 1832', published in Masson 1836b, p. 547] * = numbers not preserved

Masson's identification	Corrected identification	1833	1834	1835
Greek Syrio-Bactrian				
Antiochus		-	-	1
Recorded Greek Bactrian				
Euthydemus	not listed in Masson 1834, p. 162	1	2	3
Apollodotus		19	31	23
Menander		39	56	58
Eucratides		70	92	107
Unrecorded Greek Bactrian				
Pantaleon		2	2	3
Agathocles		10	19	14
Lysius	Lysias	6	5	3
Antilakides	Antialcidas	8	16	13
Ermaios the Elder	Hermaeus lifetime & posthumous	34	31	27
Ermaios the Younger (?)	Hermaeus posthumous issues	10	5	13
Ermaios	Hermaeus: 2 listed in Masson 1834, p. 163	1	-	-
Dicaio (?)	1 Heliocles I bust/Zeus; 5 Wima Takto Heliocles imitations	6	14	13
Lion and Elephant Coins	Local 'Taxila' issues; Masson 1834, p. 162: 'Coins without legends'	20	23	24
Symbol Coins	Local hill & crescent	-	-	11
Unadpherros	Gondophares	19	16	20
ΒΑΣΙΛΕVΣ ΒΑΣΙΛΕШΝ ΣШΤΗΡ ΜΕΓΑΣ	Soter Megas issues of Kujula Kadphises/Wima Takto	171	267	257
Analogous Coins, fig. 104 to fig. 106	Wima Takto: horseman/Zeus or Ardochsho	1	1	-
Ditto, fig. 107 to fig. 110	As above: hemidrachms	8	24	20
Ditto, fig. 111	Azes II: horseman/city goddess	1	1	-
Ermaios of Nysa, and his family	Kujula Kadphises Hermaeus imitations	136	179	278
Archelius	Archebius	-	-	1
Diomedes		-	1	-
Ipalirisus	Spalirises as king	1	1	1
Antimachus		-	1	1
Adelphoros	Spalirises with Spalagadama	1	-	1
Azilisus	Azilises	-	1	-
Azos	Azes	-	-	-
Indo-Scythic [Kushan] or Mithraic	E161/VII, f. 20 gives total 1002 for 1834 (**Vol. II, p. 61**)	*	1002	*
Kadphises	Wima Kadphises	37	*	62
Kanerkes	Kanishka I	24	*	4
Kanerkes family	Kanishka I (Masson 1834, p. 163, tetradrachms: 22 Mao and Miiro; 6 Oado; hemidrachms: 16 Nana and Mao	44	*	67
Rao-nano-rao-nano-kero-rano family. Series 3	Huvishka: seated cross-legged (Masson 1834, p. 163: 9 coins)	10	*	19
As fig. 39 to fig. 41. Series 4	Huvishka: reclining on couch	56	*	175
As fig. 45 to fig. 50. Series 5	Huvishka: elephant rider	56	*	73
As fig. 51 to fig. 60. Series 6	Vasudeva I	254		492
As fig. 61 to fig. 68. Series 7	Kanishka II, later Kushan Ardochsho issues; Kashmir coin of Anantadeva (fig. 68)	113	*	161
Parthian and Sasanian				
As fig. 1 to fig. 16 [Masson 1834, p. 163: 'Guebre Coins, Parth. & Sass.'] As fig. 44 to fig. 51	Kushano-Sasanian AE: Peroz (I) flat crown; Hormizd (I) lion-head crown; satraps *Kabod* (Kavad) + *Meze*; Shapur II *Shaboro* Nezak Huns	161	*	278
Kufic and Brahmanical [Masson 1834, p. 163: 122 'Kufic' coins, 34 'Nagree' coins]	AU/AR Ghaznavid, Timurid, Khwarazm Shahs; Hindu Shahi: Spalapatideva, Samantadeva. AE North Indian, Khwarazm Shah, Ghaznavid, Ghurid. Gadhaiya paisa▪ **Vol. II, p. 81** 1835 total:138	122 ▪34	* ▪138	171
Doubtful or unknown names	Illustrated/described in MSS text; omitted from list			
Fig. 108	Azes II (Mitchiner 1976, type 856m-n)	2	-	-
Fig. 127 [=137]	Vonones and Spalahores	-	-	1

Fig. 128 [=138]	Azes II (Mitchiner 1976, type 845)	-	-	1
Figs 129 [=139]	Maues (Mitchiner 1976, type 734)	-	1	-
Fig. 143	Gondophares	-	1	-
Figs 144–146	Kujula Kadphises: helmeted king/soldier	-	-	3
Fig. 148	Taxila: Vatashvaka	-	-	1
Figs 158, 160	Kharahostes (Mitchiner 1976, types 887, 888)	-	-	2
Fig. 159	Gondophares: king on horseback/symbol	-	-	1
Fig. 161	Azes II (Mitchiner 1976, type 859e–f)	1	-	-
	Total	1478	788	2393
'Unintelligible and useless, chiefly Indo-Scythic, as Figs 3–5, of Series, No. 2'	Vasudeva I and Later Kushans (Masson 1834, p. 163, omitted from MSS)	•375	+ *	
	Total (Masson 1834, pp. 162–3: plus 4 'single specimens'; 12 'unarranged and ambiguous' **Total** (+1140 coins **Vol. II, p. 81**, omitted from Masson 1836b)	1853 + 12 1865	1140 1928	

Table 5 continued

Table 6 Correspondence of coins illustrated in Masson's analysis of the Begram coins

Abbreviations

Alram	Alram 1999/2000	GH	Gupta and Hardaker 2014 type no.
BMC	British Museum Catalogue; where the actual coin is in the BM collection, the catalogue number is given	Goron	Goron and Goenka 2001
		Mit. 1	Mitchiner 1977
cf	a coin of the same series, not the actual coin	Mit. 2	Mitchiner 1978
OB	Bopearachchi 1991 série no.	Mit. 3	Mitchiner 1979
JC	Cribb 2007	EE/VC	Errington and Sarkhosh Curtis 2007
EE	Errngton 2010	Senior	Senior 2000
G	Göbl 1984, Kushan type no.	Tye	Tye 1995
Göbl	Göbl 1967, Hun type no.	KV	Vondrovec 2014 type no.

Masson's attribution					
Fig. no.	BM Reg. no.	Type	Wilson 1841 coin plates	Comments	Metal
Plates 1–7: 'Greek'				Plate 1	
Antiochus				Antiochus III (223–187 BC)	
1	IOLC.112				AE
Euthydemus (I)				c. 230–200 BC	
2	cf. IOLC.114	OB 17	pl. I.14		AE
3	cf. IOLC.115	OB 18	pl. I.15		AE
Apollodotus I				c. 180–160 BC	
4	cf. 1838,EIC.27	OB 4	cf. pl. IV.14		AR
5	cf. 1838,EIC.27	OB 4	cf. pl. IV.14		AR
6	1838,EIC.30	OB 4	cf. pl. IV.14		AR
7	IOC.68	OB 2	pl. IV.15		AR
9	cf. IOC.72	OB 6	cf. pl. IV.17		AE
10	IOC.72	OB 6	cf. pl. IV.17		AE
11	cf. IOLC.170	OB 7	cf. pl. IV.19		AE
Apollodotus II				c. 80–65 BC	
8		OB 6(?)	pl. IV.19		AR
Menander				c. 155–130 BC	
12	IOC.90	OB 12	pl. III.13		AR
13–15	14: 1838,EIC.7	OB 16	cf. pl. III.15		AR
16–18	16, 17: 1838,EIC.24, 19	OB 13	cf. pl. III.14		AR
19–20, 23		OB 6	cf. pl. IV.1		AR
21–22		OB 7			AR
24		OB 10	cf. pl. IV.2		AR
25	1926,0502.1	OB 25	pl. IV.3		AE
26	cf. IOC.96	OB 21	cf. pl. IV.7		AE
27	IOC.102	OB 20	cf. pl. IV.8		AE
28	cf. 1888,1208.328	OB 36	pl. IV.9	Plate 2	AE
29		OB 31			AE
30	cf. IOC.99	OB 27	cf. pl. IV.4		AE
31	IOLC.373	OB 19(?)	cf. pl. IV.12		AE
32		OB 28	cf. pl. IV.10		AE
33	IOC.104	OB 37	pl. IV.11		AE
Eucratides				c. 174–145 BC	
34	cf. IOC.24	OB 6	cf. pl. III.1–3		AR
35	cf. IOC.28	OB 3	cf. pl. III.5		AR
36		OB 11	cf. pl. III.8		AE
37		OB 21	cf. pl. III.8	Posthumous issue	AE
38		?	cf. pl. III.8	Same design and size as AR example OB 7	AE

Fig. no.	BM Reg. no.	Type	Wilson 1841	Comments	Metal
39	cf. IOC.42	OB 18	cf. pl. III.12		AE
40		?		As Fig. 39, but a smaller coin	AE
41–2	cf. IOC.37	OB 19	cf. pl. III.9–10		AE
43		OB 20			AE
44	cf. IOC.44a	OB 24	cf. pl. III.11		AE
Pantaleon				c. 190–185 BC	
45		OB 6	cf. pl. VI.11		AE
Agathocles				c. 190–180 BC	
46–7	cf. IOC.16–18	OB 10	cf. pl. VI.7–9	**Plate 3**	AE
Lysius				**Lysias** c. 120–110 BC	
48	cf. 1888,1208.204	OB 8	cf. pl. II.10		AE
Antilakides				**Antialcidas** c. 115–95 BC	
49	cf. IOC.57	OB 13	cf. pl. II.11		AR
50		OB 15	cf. p. 279		AE
51–3	cf. IOLC.609–628	OB 17	cf. pl. II.13		AE
Ermaios				**Hermaeus** c. 90–70 BC; and imitations	
54–6	54: IOC.133	OB 2	p. 54, pl. V.2	Fig. 54: OB 2C	AR
57		OB 3	cf. pl. V.3		AR
58–60	cf. IOC.144	OB 20	cf. pl. V.4	Imitation	AE
61	cf. 1838,EIC.63; IOC.147	OB 21	cf. pl. V.6	Imitation	AE
Kushan					
62–5	cf. IOC.148–9	OB 22	cf. pl. V.11	Kujula Kadphises c. AD 40–90; Su-Hermaeus / Zeus (JC, p. 200)	AE
66	IOC.150	OB 9	pl. V.7	Imitation	AE
67–74				**Plate 4**	AE
67	IOC 364	OB 25–6	cf. p, 311, pl. VIII.15	Wima Takto c. AD 90–113. Heliocles imitation / horse; unit (JC, p. 200)	AE
68–74	cf. IOLC.1563		cf. pl. VIII.14	Wima Takto Heliocles imitation / horse; quarter unit (JC, p. 200)	AE
75	cf. IOLC.1312		cf. pl. VIII.16 (but different denomination)	Wima Takto Heliocles imitation / Zeus quarter unit (JC, p. 200). Wilson 1841 shows possibly a larger coin of this type	AE
Of unknown princes				Mauryan, later punch-marked coins and local issues 3rd–2nd century BC	AR AE
76–91					
76	cf. IOLC.70		cf. pl. XV.26–7	Local uninscribed: elephant / lion	AE
77	cf. IOLC.54		cf. pl. XV.26–7	Local uninscribed: elephant / lion	AE
78	cf. 1894,0507.41, 45			Local uninscribed	AE
79, 80, 83	cf. IOC.1053			Local uninscribed	AE
82	IOC.1052		cf. pl. XV.29	Local uninscribed	AE
84	IOC.1051		cf. pl. XV.28	Local uninscribed	AE
85	cf. 1894,0507.38	BMC 47		Local uninscribed (Allan 1936, p. 220)	AE
86, 90–1	cf. IOLC.18	GH 574		Punch-marked	AR AE
89	cf. 1853,0301.34, 37b; IOLC.11	GH 552		Punch-marked	AR
Unad-Pherros or **Pherros**					
92–98	cf. IOC.362		cf. pl. V.12–13	**Gondophares** c. AD 32–60	AE
Princes of Nysa - Azus [Azes] dynasty [Kushan]					
99–103				**Plate 5 Wima Takto** c. AD 90–113 (JC, pp. 179, 184–5)	**AE**
99	cf. IOC.247		cf. pl. IX.8, 10	Wima Takto – Soter Megas, helmeted bust (JC, p. 200)	AE
100–1, 103	cf. 1850,0305.148		cf. pl. IX.11–12	Wima Takto – Soter Megas, standard issue unit	AE
102			cf. pl. X.3	Wima Takto – Soter Megas, standard issue quarter	AE

Fig. no.	BM Reg. no.	Type	Wilson 1841	Comments	Metal
104–111					AE
104–5	cf. 1894,0506.806; IOLC.1567		cf. pl. IX.20,22	Wima Takto, bilingual unit (JC, p. 200)	AE
106			cf. pl. VI.17		AE
107, 109				Wima Takto, bilingual quarter (JC, p. 200)	AE
108			cf. pl. VIII.4?		AE
110	cf. IOLC.1572			Wima Takto, uninscribed Oesho/Ardochsho (JC, p. 200)	AE
111	1838.EIC.90		cf. pl. VIII.1	Mujatria (Cribb 2015)	AE
Ermaios of Nysa				**Kujula Kadphises** c. AD 40–90	
112–114	cf. IOLC.1006; IOLC.1042		cf. pl. V.8, 9	Kujula Kadphises (obverse in name of Hermaeus)	AE
Kadphisos				**Kujula Kadphises** (JC, p. 200)	
115–21, 123–5, 127, 129–31	cf. IOLC.1084		cf. pl. XI.11	Kujula Kadphises (in own name)	AE
122, 126, 128	cf. IOLC.1468			Kujula Kadphises (in name of Hermaeus)	AE
Archelius				**Archebius** c. 90–80 BC	
132	cf. 1894,0506.1716	OB 3	pl. II.8	**Pl. 6 Fig. 122** duplicated number	AR
Diomedes				c. 95–90 BC	
133	cf. 1857,0813.19	OB 10	pl. V.1	**Pl. 6 Fig. 123** duplicated number	AE
Ipalirisus				Indo-Scythian: **Spalirises** c. 50–40 BC	
134 135 136	– IOC.225 IOC.224	Senior 73	cf. pl. VIII.12	Spalirises **Pl. 6 Figs 124–6** duplicated numbers	AE
Doubtful or unknown names					
137	cf. 1894,0506.700–1 1888,1208.497		cf. pl. VIII.9	Spalahores / Vonones c. 1 BC **Pl. 6 Fig. 127** duplicated number	AE
138	IOC.200		pl. VIII.3	Azes II c. AD 16–30 **Pl. 6 Fig. 128** duplicated number	AE
139	cf. 1860,1220.64	Mit.2 2202		Maues c. 75–65 BC **Pl. 6 Fig. 129** duplicated number	AE
140	cf. 1922,0424.2895	? OB7		? Apollodotus I c. 180–160 BC **Pl. 6 Fig. 130** duplicated number	AE
141	cf. IOC.198	Senior 78		Azes I c. 46–1 BC **Pl. 6 Fig. 131** duplicated number	AE
142–3	cf. OR.5220			Kushan; Hermaeus imitations	
144–6	cf. IOLC.1000			Kujula Kadphises helmeted bust / soldier type (JC, p. 200)	AE
147	cf. 1987,0109.187			Kujula Kadphises Heraus silver obol (JC, p. 200)	AR
148	IOC.1058	BMC.2		Vatashvaka (Allan 1936, p. 264, pl. XXXIX.3)	AE
Antimachus [II]					
149–150	cf. IOC.116	OB 1	pl. II.15		AR
Adelphortus				Indo-Scythian Spalagadama	
151			pl. VIII.13	Spalirises with Spalagadama, c. 50 BC	AE
Azilisus				Indo-Scythian: Azilises	
152	IOC.215		pl. VIII.7	Azilises c. 1 BC–AD 16	AE
Azus				Indo-Scythian: Azes	
153–6				Azes I c. 46–1 BC; Azes II c. AD 16–30	
153	cf. OR.7312		pl. VI.13	Azes I / Aspavarma	BI
154	IOLC.888		cf. pl. VI.15	Azes II	BI
155	IOLC.886		cf. pl. VII.8	Azes II	AE
156	cf. IOLC.752		cf. pl. VI.19	Azes II	AR
157	cf. IOLC.730		cf. pl. VII.6	Azes I	AE
Unknown princes of the Azus dynasty				**Indo-Scythian and Indo-Parthian**	
158	cf. IOLC.897, **Fig. 31.1**			Kharahostes c. 1st century AD	AE
159	Ashmolean Museum cf. 1889,0808.67	cf. EE/ VC fig. 59.3	cf. pl. VI.2	Gondophares c. AD 32–58 (Ashmolean Short Coll.)	AE
160	cf. 1922,0116.32–4			Mujatria son of Kharahostes c. AD 80–90	AE
161	cf. 1922,0424.389			Azes II c. 16–30 Zeus Nicephorus	BI

Fig. no.	BM Reg. no.	Type	Wilson 1841	Comments	Metal
Plates 8–10 'Mithraic or Indo-Scythic' [Kushan]				Plate 8	
Series 1 – Kadphises				Wima Kadphises c. AD 113–27	
1	cf. IOC.271	G15/19	cf. pl. X.10		AU
2	IOC.272	G18	cf. pl. X.13		AU
3	IOC.273	G4	pl. XI.9		AR
4	IOC.277 (?)	G760/762	cf. pl. X.17		AE
5	cf. 1933,1003.1		cf. pl. X.19		AE
6	cf. IOC.281		cf. pl. X.19		AE
Series 2 – Kanerkos & family				Kanishka I c. AD 127–50; and Huvishka c. AD 151–90	
7	IOC.325	G300	pl. XIV.1	Huvishka; Nana	AU
8	IOC.319	G138	pl. XIV.2	Huvishka; Miiro; from the Guldara stupa	AU
9	IOC.290	G54 (?)	pl. XII.2	Kanishka; Nanashao	AU
10	cf. 1860,1220.208	G76 (?)	cf. pl. XII.1	Kanishka; Mao	AU
11	cf. 1857,0813.73	G63	cf. pl. XII.3	Kanishka; Orlagno	AU
12	IOC.338	G206	pl. XIV.3	Huvishka; Pharo	AU
13	–	G276	pl. XIV.10	Huvishka; Myro	AU
14	cf. IOC.283	G766	cf. pl. XI.15	Kanishka; Helios; didrachm*[1]	AE
15	cf. 1846,1027.6	G767	cf. pl. XI.17	Kanishka; Nanaia; didrachm*	AE
16	cf. IOC.296	G787	pl. XIII.1	Kanishka; Buddha; didrachm*	AE
17	cf. IOLC.2644	G774	cf. pl. XII.13	Kanishka; Mao; tetradrachm*	AE
18	cf. IOLC.2796	G775		Kanishka; Mao; didrachm*	AE
19	cf. IOLC.2668	G768 or 770	cf. pl. XII.16	Kanishka; Mioro; tetradrachm*	AE
20	cf. IOLC.2809	G771		Kanishka; Mioro; didrachm*	AE
21	cf. IOLC.2643	G772		Kanishka; Athsho; tetradrachm*	AE
				Plate 9	
22	cf. IOLC.2795	G773		Kanishka; Athsho; didrachm*	AE
23	cf. IOLC.2680	G783	cf. pl. XII.19	Kanishka; Oado; tetradrachm*	AE
24	cf. 1847,1201.200	G784		Kanishka; Oado; didrachm*	AE
25	cf. IOLC.2717	G781		Kanishka; Oesho; tetradrachm*	AE
26	cf. IOLC.2818	G782		Kanishka; Oesho; didrachm*	AE
27	cf. IOLC.2674	G776	cf. pl. XII.12	Kanishka; Nana; tetradrachm*	AE
28	cf. IOLC.2917	G806		Kanishka; Nana; drachm*	AE
29	cf. IOLC.2909	G797	cf. pl. XII.15	Kanishka; Miiro; drachm*	AE
30	cf. IOLC.2972	G813		Kanishka; Oesho; drachm*	AE
31	cf. IOLC.2916	G806		Kanishka; Nana; drachm*	AE
Series 3					
32	cf. 1894,0506.1465	G841	pl. XIII.7	Huvishka; Nana	AE
33	cf. IOLC.3128	G824	cf. pl. XIII.8	Huvishka; Mioro	AE
34–5, 38	cf. IOLC.3195	G837	cf. pl. XIII.	Huvishka; Mao	AE
36	No coin illustrated				
37	cf. IOLC.3200	G822		Huvishka; Miiro	AE
Series 4					
39	cf. IOLC.3175	G836		Huvishka; Mao	AE
40	cf. IOLC.3106	G833		Huvishka; Athsho	AE

* Assumed denominations, derived from Masson's text and illustrations.

Fig. no.	BM Reg. no.	Type	Wilson 1841	Comments	Metal
41	cf. IOLC.3189	G821		Huvishka; Miiro	AE
42–4	No coins illustrated				
Series 5				Plate 10	
45	cf. IOLC.3166	G820	cf. pl. XIII.16	Huvishka; Miiro	AE
46	cf. IOLC.3090	G849		Huvishka; Oesho	AE
47	cf. IOLC.3033	G832	cf. pl. XIII.17	Huvishka; Athsho	AE
48–9	IOLC.3279	G855		Huvishka; Oesho	AE
50				Huvishka imitation; Mao / Athsho?	AE
Series 6					
51	cf. OR.7430			Vasudeva I c. AD 190–230; Oesho	AU
52	cf. 1879,0501.88	cf. G509		Vasudeva I; Oesho	AU
53	cf. 1906,1103.2366	cf. G682	cf. pl. XIV.12	Kushano-Sasanian imitation of Vasudeva I / Oesho	AU
54	cf. 1982,1109.1	cf. G1000–9	cf. pl. XI.3	Vasudeva I; Oesho; tetradrachm	AE
55				Vasudeva I; Oesho; tetradrachm	AE
56				Vasudeva I; Oesho; tetradrachm	AE
57	cf. OR.342	cf. G1005		Vasudeva I; Oesho; didrachm*	AE
58				Vasudeva I; Oesho; didrachm*	AE
59				imitation (?) of Vasudeva I; Oesho; didrachm*	AE
60				imitation of Vasudeva I; Oesho; drachm*	AE
61		cf. G1015 ff		Kanishka II c. AD 230–46; Ardochsho	AE
Series 7					
62	cf. 1981,0322.42			Kanishka II; Ardochsho (?)	AE
63				Kanishka II; Ardochsho	AE
64				period of Kanishka III c. AD 267–72	AE
65				period of Kanishka III	AE
66				Kanishka II or imitation	AE
67				period of Kanishka III	AE
68				Kashmiri	AE
69	cf IOC.652	Goron D6	pl. XX.25	Ghurid: Mu'izz al-dīn Muḥammād b. Sām 1173–1206; Goddess Lakshmi.	AU

Plates 11–13: 'Brahmanical', 'Parthian and Sasanian', 'Indo-Sasanian', 'Kufic, Muhammadan &c.'					
'Brahmanical' – Shahi. Ghaznavid, Ghurid and Khwarazm Shah jitals				Plate 11	
1	cf. IOLC.4652			Shahi: Samantadeva c. AD 850–1000	
2	cf. IOC.814			Shahi: Spalapatideva c. AD 750–850	BI
3	cf. IOLC.6085		pl. XIX.13	Shahi bull and horseman type	AE
4				Shahi bull and horseman type	AE
5	cf. IOLC.6723	Tye 183		Ghurid: Mu'izz al-dīn Muḥammād b. Sām	AE
6	cf. IOLC.5767	Tye 105		Ghaznavid? Masud III 1099–1115	AE
7	cf. IOLC.5767	Tye 105		Ghaznavid? Masud III	AE
8	cf. IOLC.7912	Tye 236.1		Khwarazm Shah 'Ala al-dīn Muhammad ibn Tekish 1200–20	AE
9		Tye 233–5		Khwarazm Shah?	AE
10	cf. IOLC.5389	Tye 19/24	pl. XIX.12	Shahi: Samantadeva elephant and lion type	AE
11	cf. IOLC.7050	Tye 180		Ghurid? Mu'izz al-dīn Muḥammād b. Sām	AE
12	cf. IOLC.6747	Tye 120.3		Ghaznavid: Khusrau Malik 1160–86	AE
13	cf. IOLC.7433	Tye 192		Ghurid: Mu'izz al-dīn Muḥammād b. Sām	AE
14–17	cf. IOC.664	Mitchiner 419		Gadhaiya paisa; mediaeval Indian (Saurashtra/Gujarat), developed from Hun imitations of Sasanian Peroz coins	

Fig. no.	BM Reg. no.	Type	Wilson 1841	Comments	Metal
'Parthian and Sasanian'				**Kushano-Sasanians, Huns**	
1–4	cf. IOLC.4304	JC 2248–94		Hormizd I c. AD 270–300 'Kavad'	AE
5–6	cf. IOLC.4312	JC 2298–336		Hormizd I 'Meze'?	AE
7	cf. IOLC.4354	JC 2350–7		Peroz II c. AD 303–30	AE
8–11	cf. IOLC.4237	JC 2191–202		Peroz I c. AD 245–70	AE
12–13	cf. IOLC.4377–9	JC 2401–5		Shapur II AD 309–79 'Shaboro'	AE
14	cf. 1922,0213.32	JC 2371–82		Shapur II 'Kavad'	AE
15–16	cf. IOLC.4358 1922,0424.3955			Peroz II c. AD 303–30	AE
17	cf. 1894,0506.2144		cf. pl. XV.6	Phraataces (Phraates V) 2 BC–AD 4 imitation (?)	AE
18		cf. Göbl 128		Alkhan	AE
19	cf. IOLC.4500 (?)	Göbl 37	pl. XVII.20	Alkhan	AE
20	1902,0614.55	Göbl 204; KV 204		Turkic c. AD 700 (**Fig. 53.7** below)	AE
				Plate 12	
21	1896,0506.1164	cf. EE/VC, p. 95, fig. 83.5; Göbl 61		Alkhan – Khingila c. AD 440–90 (cf. **Pl. 14.4**)	AR
22	cf. 1894,0506.201	cf. EE/VC, p. 95, fig. 83.3		Alkhan (cf. **Pl. 14.12**)	AR
23	–	cf. EE/VC, p. 95, fig. 83.7		Alkhan (cf. **Pl. 14.7**)	AR
24	cf. 1894,0506.1291	cf. EE/VC, p. 95, fig. 83.2; Göbl 39.2		Alkhan copying Shapur II (cf. **Pl. 14.16**)	AR
25	cf. IOC.441				AR
26		p. 396, no. 5, pl. XVI.1		Shapur II AD 309–79	
27					
28		p. 396, no. 6, pl. XVI.2			
29					
30	cf. 1841,1221.92	cf. EE/VC, fig. 69.10		Varhran V AD 420–38	AR
31	IOC.445	**Vol. I, p. 185, Fig. 281.6**	p. 398, no. 21, pl. XVI.15	Yazdagird II AD 438–57	AR
32	cf. 1862,1004.130	cf. EE/CV, fig. 69.16	p. 397, no. 12, pl. XVI.6	Kavad I AD 488–96; 1st reign	AR
33	cf. 1862,1003.22	cf. EE/VC, fig. 69.19		Khusrau I AD 531–79	AR
34	cf. IOC.472			Hormizd IV AD 579–90	AR
35	cf. IOC.480	cf. EE. VC, fig. 71.3		Khusrau II AD 591–628	AR
36	IOC.2367	KV 244; Göbl 244	p. 400, no. 26, pl. XVII.8	Turkic Sandan c. AD 700–50	AR
37	cf. IOLC.4534–6; 1894,0506.1192	cf. Göbl 150; Alram 2000; KV 150 var. 3		unknown Alkhan (Narana–Narendra c. 540–80); uniface/ trace of fire altar with two attendants	AR
38	Fitzwilliam Museum cf. OR.9022	cf. Walker 192; cf. EE/VC: 98	acq. from India Office 1908	Arab-Sasanian; 'Abd al-Aziz b. 'Abdallāh b. 'Āmir (?) Seistan c. AD 685	AR
39	cf. 1946,0705.9	cf. EE/VC: 98		Tabaristan: Khurshid c. AD 766	AR
40	IOC.509			Khusrau II year 36: c. AD 625	AR
41	cf. IOC.2319	cf.EE/VC 98		Arab-Sasanian governor Salm ibn Ziyad: active AD 680	AR
42	cf. 1845,EIC.37		cf. pp. 401–2, no. 32, pl. XVII.2	Arab-Sasanian governor Muṣ'ab b. al-Zubayr AD 686–91	AR
43	cf. 1845,EIC.46; IOC.2315		cf. p. 402, no. 33, pl. XVII.3	Arab-Sasanian governor 'Ubaydallāh b. Ziyad c. AD 672–82	AR
				Plate 13	**Metal**
44, 46	cf. 1894,0506.1203	cf. Göbl 222; Vondovec 222		Napki Malka: *nycky MLKA*	AR

Fig. no.	BM Reg. no.	Type	Wilson 1841	Comments	
45	cf. 1845,EIC.51	EE/VC 99; cf. Göbl 257		Shri Shahi śrī ṣāhi	AR
47	cf. 1942,0424.3680	cf. Göbl 221		Napki Malka: nycky MLKA	AR
48	cf. 1894,0506.1204 1922,0424.3678	cf. EE/VC 98, fig. 84.2; cf. Göbl 230		Alkhan-Nezak – no legend; Alkhan tamga behind head	AE
49	cf. IOC.2387	cf. Göbl 229.8		Alkhan-Nezak śrī ṣāhi; Alkhan tamga behind head	AE
50	cf. 1922,0424.4644	cf. Göbl 227		Alkhan-Nezak śrī ṣāhi	AE
51	IOC.2389	cf. EE/VC 84.3; Göbl 231.13		Alkhan-Nezak śrī ṣāhi; Pahlavi PK (rev.); Alkhan tamga	AE
'Kufic, Muhammadan &c.'					
1				Ilkhanid?	AR
2				Ghaznavid?	AR
3	cf. IOC.1308	cf. Tye 82		Ghaznavid?	AR
4				Ghaznavid – Maḥmūd AD 998–1030	AR
5		cf. Mitchiner 1948		Timurid?	AR
6				Timurid? - Sulṭān Maḥmūd? c. AD 1494	AR

Notes

1 The Seleucid ruler Antiochus III Megas (the Great) attempted to reassert Seleucid control of Bactria after its secession under Diodotus c. 245 BC, defeating Euthydemus I at the Battle of the Arius in 208 BC and subsequently besieging him in his capital Bactra (modern Balkh). See **Table 6** for this and other coins illustrated in the subsequent *Figures*.

2 Cribb 2003, pp. 209–13 suggests that Eucratides' initial power base was in Margiana. In Masson's time Turkestan (i.e. northern Afghanistan south of the Amu Darya) was under the control of the khanate of Bukhara.

3 Masson did not realise that the Kharoshthi reads *maharajasa* ('of the great king').

4 General Jean-Baptiste Ventura (1794–1858), Italian officer at the court of the Sikh emperor Ranjit Singh (1799–1839).

5 The sequence in the last sentence of this paragraph has been borne out by subsequent research; however, Eucratides (c. 174–145 BC) reigned 30–60 years before Antialcidas (c. 115–95 BC).

6 General Claude-Auguste Court (1793–1880), French officer at the court of the Sikh emperor Ranjit Singh (1799–1839).

7 For the identification of Nysa with Jalalabad, see McCrindle 1893, p. 338.

8 Masson appears here to presume that 'topes' were royal cenotaphs and his relating the number of coins found in a particular stupa to the age or length of reign of the supposed occupant of the 'tomb' compounds the error. This theory was questioned, correctly, by Wilson (1841, p. 45), who supported the developing view that stupas were Buddhist shrines (see Errington 2007, p. 221). However, Masson's letter to Pottinger dated September 1834, shows that he was more open-minded, for regarding the Ishpola stupa in the Khyber, he says that the 'tope … is undoubtedly a Buddhist one and very similar in form to that of Manikyala' (**P/387/71 no. 4** §2). He also fully accepted the Buddhist nature of the monuments after visiting the cave sites at Salsette (Kanheri) and Elephanta near Mumbai in 1841 (**G41** ff. 15, 20; **G43**).

9 Founder of an era in his name, Azes I was the fourth Indo-Scythian king, being preceded by Maues (c. 75–65 BC), Vonones (c. 65–50 BC) and Spalirises (c. 50–40 BC). But here Masson only includes later issues derived from the Indo-Scythian horse rider prototype: a posthumous imitation of Azes II (AD 16–30; *Fig. 108*); two Indo-Parthian coins of Sasan (c. AD 64–70: *Figs 105–6*); and one of the Indo-Scythian satrap Mujatria (c. AD 80–90; *Fig. 111*); the remaining nine being Kushan Soter Megas issues of Wima Takto (c. AD 90–113).

10 Masson did not yet realise that Kujula Kadphises and Wima Takto were 'Indo-Scythians', i.e. Kushan.

11 Masson is referring here to the coins issued in the name of Azes by the Indo-Scythian satrap Mujatria (c. AD 80–90; see Cribb 2015). The *Fig. 111* type occurred in the stupa relic deposits of Kotpur 1, Bimaran 2 and 5, Tope-i Kutchera and Hadda 3 (see **Vol. I, p. 33, Table 1**).

12 Only in 1890 was it finally established that the third letter is an adapted Greek letter 'Þ', not 'P', representing the '*sh*' sound, and that this word is the dynastic name 'Kushan' (Cunningham 1890, pp. 6–7; Cribb 2007a, p. 207).

13 Masson made an error in numbering the figures on **Plate 6**, repeating the numbers 122–131 instead of numbering these coins 132–141; the numbering resumes at 142 on **Plate 7**, but he did not correct the numbers on **Plate 6**. The correct numbering – given in the manuscript text – therefore does not match the numbers appearing on the plate.

14 Masson 1834, p. 171, fig. 39, pl. XI.39 and 43 records one example from Begram and another from Kabul.

15 Masson sometimes used 'billion' for 'billon'.

16 British Museum 1848,0602.3.c. Zwalf 1996, p. 352, no. 666; the correct inscription is 𐨒𐨆𐨨𐨣𐨯 𐨐𐨪𐨬𐨐𐨯 and read by Konow *Gomanasa karavakasa*, '(Gift) of Gomana the architect' (1929, p. 151).

17 Masson's 'Class Brahmanical' is made up of Shahi (*Fig. 1–4*); Ghaznavid (*Figs 6–7, 12*); Ghurid (*Figs 5, 11, 13*); and Khwarazm Shah (*Figs 8–9*) jitals, and Gadhaiya paisa (*Figs 14–17*).

18 The Devanagari legend of **Pl. 11**, *Fig. 1* is correctly marked in pencil as Samantadeva.

19 For related coins see Alram 2016, pp. 126–7, nos 3–5.

20 Silver bearing lead and lead-zinc deposits are widespread in the central Iranian plateau and many show evidence of having been worked in antiquity (Nezafati and Pernicka 2012). This suggests that Sasanian Iran had no need to import silver. In the early Islamic period at least, the Panjshir Valley, to the east of Kabul, was also noted for its silver mines and could well have been another source (see **Vol. I, p. 46**).

Chapter 4
The Monetary History of Begram

Joe Cribb

Charles Masson: coins from Begram

I had before reached the borders of the plain of Begram, and had heard strange stories of the innumerable coins…

The discovery of so interesting a locality as that of Begram imposed upon me new, agreeable, and I should hope, not unprofitable employment…

Before the commencement of winter, when the plain, covered with snow, is of course closed to research, I had accumulated one thousand eight hundred and sixty-five copper coins, besides a few silver ones, many rings, signets, and other relics. The next year, 1834, the collection which fell into my hands amounted to one thousand nine hundred copper coins, besides other relics. In 1835 it increased to nearly two thousand five hundred copper coins, and in 1836 it augmented to thirteen thousand four hundred and seventy-four copper coins. In 1837, when I had the plain well under control, and was enabled constantly to locate my people upon it, I obtained sixty thousand copper coins, a result at which I was well pleased, having at an early period of my researches conjectured that so many as thirty thousand coins might annually be procured…

It may be superfluous to dwell upon the importance of the Begram collections; independently of the revelation of unknown kings and dynasties, they impart great positive knowledge, and open a wide field for speculation and inquiry on the very material subjects of the languages and religions prevailing in Central Asia during the dark periods of its history.

(Masson 1842, III, pp. 140, 148–50; see p. 10 above)

Masson's collections were gathered on the locale of their original issue and subsequent more immediate circulation, and unlike the reserved store of less-freely current foreign coin, or the choice specimens of a miser's hoard, they have, in the majority of instances, been inhumed in detail, apparently, after having been subject to an extensive series of successive transfers in the ordinary commerce of their day. The coins have suffered accordingly; and much of what was probably originally clear, is now often wholly obliterated.

(Edward Thomas 1847, p. 282)

This in no way diminishes the value of the Collection, particularly in view of the information it supplies for Begram.

(Elizabeth Errington 2001, p. 367)

Charles Masson's work stands at the start of our modern understanding of Afghanistan's ancient past. More recent history has not been kind to his legacy. Through bureaucratic misunderstanding and the accidents of time much of what he achieved has been swallowed up into later historical research. Now thanks to Elizabeth Errington's ingenious detective work, it is possible to reassert his role in unlocking the course of events which began with Afghanistan's entry into history as an outpost of the Persian empire of the Achaemenid kings and continued in obscurity until the literary traditions of the Islamic world began to chronicle its conquest and rule by a succession of Arab, Turkish, Iranian, Mongol, Timurid, Mughal and Afghan emirs, sultans, kings and emperors.

Masson's work as an archaeologist, systematically excavating and recording Buddhist monuments in Afghanistan would be enough to earn him a place among the pioneers of creating an understanding of the early history of the region. It is his work as a documenter of the site finds from Begram, however, which raises his contribution to that of the first creator of a detailed understanding of the early history of Afghanistan, unfortunately a status which has been swallowed up by history itself.

Masson's reports on the Begram finds

In his first report on finds from Begram published in the *JASB* (April 1834, pp. 153–75), Masson gave his reasons for collecting material from Begram. Like many of his contemporaries, he was motivated by antiquarian interest. By the time of writing his report of 28 November 1833, he had acquired 1,879 coins from the site. He stated that many were worthless, but he would persist 'under the hope of obtaining ultimately perfect specimens of every type and variety of coin' (1834, p. 154). He also mentioned that collecting from Begram enabled him to avoid competing with two other coin collectors who had cornered the market for coins in Kabul (probably Martin Honigberger, Mohan Lal or Masson's predecessor as news-writer, Karamat 'Ali, all of whom are known to have bought coins in the city at that time). Later, Masson increasingly bought coins and artefacts in the Kabul bazaar himself, but still continued to acquire as many finds as possible from Begram.

Masson was also aware of other benefits from focusing on just collecting from Begram. He first became interested in the site when he visited it earlier in July 1833. He had perhaps heard about Begram from General C.-A. Court, one of the French officers in the Sikh army (see above p. 4) who had earlier acquired coins from there, but his own visit showed that the site represented a vast ancient city. In his memoirs (1842, III, pp. 140–3) he said that he went there as he had heard 'strange stories of the innumerable coins and other relics' which were to be found there. After initial frustration he managed to tap into the market in coins from the site. Previously the coins were collected as scrap metal and sold to metalsmiths or the Kabul mint to be recycled. As his report a few months later showed he quickly accumulated a large number of coins. He immediately saw beyond his antiquarian approach to realising that the coins he assembled opened up the possibility of creating a history of the city he had discovered, 'as my object was not merely the amassing of coins, but the application of them to useful purposes, I hailed with satisfaction the prospect of obtaining a collection from a known spot, with which they could have, of necessity, a definite connection, enabling me to speculate with confidence on the points they involved' (1834, p. 154).

He categorised the collected coins into five classes: 'Greek, Indo-Scythian, Parthian and Guebre, Brahmanical and Muhammedan' (1834, pp. 154–5). His first report only focused on describing and discussing the Greek and Indo-Scythian classes. His 'Greek' class included Indo-Greek, local Indian, Indo-Scythian (in its modern sense), Indo-Parthian and some early Kushan coins, his 'Indo-Scythian' coins were all Kushan issues. He did not illustrate the other classes, but at the end of his commentary (1834, pp. 162–3) he made a summary list of the coins where his terminology is slightly different and gives an indication of the identity of the other classes, expanding 'Parthian and Guebre' to 'Guebre coins, Parth[ian] and Sas[anian]', he referred to the 'Brahmanical' class as 'Nagree' (presumably meaning they were inscribed in Indian script, [*deva*]*nāgarī*, and the Muhammadan class as 'Cufic'. i.e. inscribed in Kufic (*kūfī*), early Arabic script. The 'Guebre' (meaning Zoroastrian) mostly consisted of Kushano-Sasanian coins, 'Brahmanical' were Shahi coins and Ghaznavid and Ghurid Islamic coins with Indian inscriptions and 'Muhammadan' coins were Ghaznavid, Ghurid and Khwarazm Shah coins with Arabic inscriptions.

He saw this classification of the coins as a first step towards 'their application to historical elucidation' (1834, p. 155). His ordering of them was the beginning of an overview of the history of the site, as he was aware that 'the princes whose coins are found on any known spots or site, may fairly be held to have reigned there' (1834, p. 161). He well understood that his discoveries provided 'sufficient evidences and indications … to enable us to decide with certainty, or arrive at a plausible conjecture on, most of the interesting points connected with these countries from the period of the Macedonian conquests to the introduction of the Islam faith' (1834, p. 162).

Through this process of collecting coins from one site and classifying his findings into a chronological system, he was pioneering the archaeological techniques which are now firmly embedded in modern practice and have been refined into techniques such as the chronological mapping of Roman sites through coin finds to understand changes in monetary activity (Reece 2003). In his second report, written late in 1835 (see above pp. 10–11) and published in *JASB* (1836a, pp. 1–28), Masson shows his awareness of the importance of making a full record of the finds, when he bemoans the failure of one of his assistants to pass to him all the coins found, rather than a selection 'It had been my intention this year to have secured every coin of every description that should be picked up from the *dasht of Begram*… On my eventually reaching *Kabul*, the young man joined with 1,320 coins, from the appearance of which it was evident he had selected, and not, as ordered, taken all that were offered' (1836a, p. 10).

As he continued to collect, his understanding of the coinage of Begram grew. In his second report, his Greek class also included some Bactrian Greek coins. He also began to compare his Begram finds with those that he had acquired in Jalalabad, observing for example that the Greek king Menander's coins were common at Begram, but absent from what he had acquired in Jalalabad (1836a, p. 13). He also attempted to create a sequence for the Greek kings whose coins he was finding (1836a, pp. 11–21) and to outline a history using the finds in relation to the meagre references to some of these kings in Classical sources. His finds of coins of kings later than Eucratides and Menander also prompted him to speculate that the Greek kingdom 'in the countries to the west of the Indus' continued to flourish after Bactria was lost to Scythians and Parthians (1836a, p. 19). The editor of *JASB*, James Prinsep, decided not to illustrate all the coins in Masson's second and third reports – which survive in manuscript with the missing drawings in the British Library (see above pp. 35–80: **F526/1a**) – but referred to similar examples he had himself published in the previous year using images of coins received from other collectors (1835a, pp. 327–48; editor notes in Masson 1836a, p. 21, and 1836b, p. 546).

Masson's exploration of the region during 1834 also led him to propose that the site of Begram was the most likely location of the city founded by Alexander the Great as

Alexandria ad Caucasum (1836a, pp. 6–10), and considered it 'not however improbable' that Begram had lasted until the time of the entry of Ghengis Khan's armies into the region c. 1221, as 'it existed for some time after the Muhammedan invasion of these countries' on account of 'the numerous coins of the Caliphs found on its site (p. 4).

By the time of his third report on the coins he was finding at Begram, written in May 1836 and published in part in *JASB* (1836b, pp. 537–47), Masson was able to articulate his broader purpose more clearly (1836b, p. 538):

> It is presumed that coins constantly found and in number on any known spot, afford proofs of their having once been current there, and that the princes whom they commemorate, whether as paramount or tributary sovereigns, held also authority at that spot. The numbers in which coins may be found, may perhaps furnish a criterion upon which we may calculate, first generally, the duration of the dynasties denoted by the various types of coins, and next particularly that of the reign of each individual prince. A collection of one year would not furnish this criterion, a collection of many years might.

In this third report he maintained his broad classification of the coins into five classes, now designated '1st, Greek-Bactrian; 2nd, Indo-Scythic or Mithraic; 3rd, Ancient Persian, whether Parthian or Sasanian; 4th, Hindu or Brahmanical; 5th, Kufic or Muhammadan', classes into which 'the coins of *Begram* fortunately admit of ready classification' (1836b, p. 538). The increasing number of types being brought to light also prompted him to speculate about the survival of 'Greek' issuers into the 1st or 2nd century AD (1836b, p. 539). As his 'Greek' class included what we now call Indo-Scythian and Indo Parthian as well as early Kushan coins, Masson's speculation shows a well-developed understanding on his part of the progression of political entities in the region. He also deduced that the issuers of his 'Indo-Scythic' class, i.e. the Kushans from Wima Kadphises onwards, 'appear to have ruled for a very long time'. He also recognised a Sasanian, rather than Parthian, presence in the region before the arrival of Islam (1836b, pp. 539–40).

Masson concluded his third report with a list of the coin types he had discovered with the numbers so far found (see **Table 5**, pp. 72–3 above). This list shows a progression in the shaping of the history of the region, but also retains some aspects which are residual from his earlier listings. He grouped together the early Kushan issues of Kujula Kadphises and Wima Takto after the coins of the Greek king Hermaeus, which some of them copied. Alongside them he also included the coins of the Indo-Parthian Gondophares, the immediate predecessor of Kujula Kadphises. He had only seen a handful of the Indo-Scythian coinages of Spalirises and Azilises, so not surpisingly they were listed at the end of the 'Greek' class.

The publication of Masson's third report in *JASB* (1836b, pp. 537–48) omitted all of its 13 plates and his 25 foolscap pages of commentary on them. Fortunately the complete original manuscript survives among Masson's papers (**F526/1a, ff. 1–25, Pls 1–13**, see pp. 36–73). In the manuscript further subtleties of his ordering of the coins can be seen, such as his counting of the posthumous Indo-Scythian coins with the name of Azes and some Indo-Parthian coins he had acquired among the Soter Megas coins of Wima Takto. He was only finding small numbers of these coins at Begram, so used material from the Kabul bazaar and his finds from the Jalalabad region, including two plates of coins from Hadda stupa 10 (**F526/1a, Pls 14–15**, pp. 65–6 above) to supplement his discussion, which makes the exact understanding of what was found at Begram slightly confused.

Of the coins he linked with Azes, he remarked 'these coins are casual ones from Begram and the bazaar of Kabul', but one group he clearly identified as from Begram, the base-silver drachms, 'various small coins procured from Begram, the three first in some number' (**F526/1a, f. 13**, p. 49 above). By 'the three first' he was referring to his drawings on **Pl. 5.107–9**, which are two small coins of Soter Megas Gandharan type and an imitation Azes II, which is contemporary with them (Cribb and Bracey at press, type A.S5), and in his list (1836b, p. 547) he included them as 'analogous coins' under the Soter Megas series. The Soter Megas coinage he referred to as 'so plentifully found at Begram' (**F526/1a, f. 11**, p. 47).

In his second and third reports Masson indulged in speculation about the sequencing of the Greek kings whose coins he was finding. In the former he tried to understand the relationship between Menander and Eucratides, the two kings most frequently represented by finds from Begram. His comparisons led him to recognise the contemporaneity of some of the kings, placing Antimachus as reigning between Euthydemus and Eucratides and as a contemporary of Apollodotus and Menander, but he remained uncertain as to whether Eucratides or Menander reigned first (1836a, pp. 15–17), settling at length on the order Menander before Eucratides, 'we have indubitable proof that Eucratides, by some means or other, succeeded Menander in the countries dependent on Bactria ad Caucasum [i.e. the Begram region]' (1836a, p. 17). He also observed that Apollodotus and Menander coins with Kharoshthi inscriptions on the reverse were different from the coins of the Bactrian kings, 'The reverses of the coins of Apollodotus and Menander are not strictly Bactrian' (1836a, p. 15). He therefore suggested Menander [and Apollodotus] ruled territory to the south of the main Bactrian kingdom: that 'he governed in the provinces south of Bactriana is certain … [ruling] in Bactriana Latior and the regions south of the Caucasus' (1836a, pp. 12, 17). This conclusion represented the first suggestion of the distinction between the Bactrian Greek and Indo-Greek kingdoms. By the time of his third report he was again questioning the sequence of Menander and Eucratides (**F526/1a, f. 3**, pp. 39–40 above). His indecision conforms with our modern understanding (Bivar 1970) that they were contemporaries, vying for control of the Begram region.

Prinsep's use of Masson's reports

The editor of *JASB* who made the drastic abbreviation of Masson's third report and omitted images from his second report was James Prinsep. Without doubt he made great use of Masson's coin discoveries, publishing his own article of observations on the finds in the pages following Masson's abbreviated report (1836b: Prinsep 1836a, pp. 548–54). In this article he published only the new types reported by Masson, and in the manuscript (**F526/1a, Pls 6–7**, *Figs 122–6, 151*) one can see Prinsep's handwritten notes 'new' next to the coins he now published (1836a, pl. XXXV.1, 3, 6–7). Prinsep also illustrated (pl. XXXV.12) a coin of Kujula Kadphises from Masson's manuscript, which he annotated 'better than published in my paper' (**F526/1a, Pl. 5.116**). Prinsep's approach somewhat undermined Masson's intention of creating a broad view of the progression of rulers in Begram and the other locations from which he was collecting coins.

Prinsep, however, was the first to make concrete use of Masson's discoveries, picking up on his observation of the relationship between the Greek and undeciphered 'Pahlavi' inscriptions on the coins he was discovering and thereby decipher what became recognised as Kharoshthi script and the Gandhari language it was used to write. He readily acknowledged Masson's first contribution to this (1835a, p. 327–9):

> Mr Masson first pointed out in a note addressed to myself, through the late Dr Gerard, the Pahlavi signs, which he had found to stand for the words *Menandrou, Ermaiou, Basileos*, and *Soteros*. When a supply of coins came into my own hands, sufficiently legible to pursue the inquiry, I soon verified the accuracy of his observations. … It immediately struck me that if the genuine Greek names were faithfully expressed in the unknown characters, a clue would through them be formed to unravel the value of a portion of the Alphabet, which might in its turn be applied to the translated epithets and titles, and thus lead to a knowledge of the language employed.

There was nevertheless a friendly rivalry which Prinsep also acknowledged, 'we are, on the other hand, expecting a fresh memoir from Mr Masson, which might anticipate some of the discoveries I would fain claim for myself, in this fair and highly interesting game of antiquarian research'.

Prinsep, from his base in Calcutta, also had available to him coins being collected further to the east of where Masson was collecting, so had access to a broader set of material, as well as a better library on languages and scripts than Masson. In this way he could build well on some aspects of Masson's discoveries and observations to forward the study of the ancient subcontinent.

Before the arrival of Masson's reports Prinsep had some familiarity with the coins of the north-west of the subcontinent from the articles of Tod (1826) and Wilson (1832) based on collections made in India and on the reports of officers such as Alexander Burnes and Jean-Baptiste Ventura who had collected coins in the north-west, but it was very limited. Prinsep's publications of coins from the north-west before the arrival of Masson's first report covered a small number of coins in the collection of the Asiatic Society (1833a, pp. 27–41: 4 Kushan coins), coins collected by Burnes in the territories of modern Uzbekistan, Afghanistan and Pakistan (1833b, pp. 310–18: 2 Bactrian Greek, 1 Indo-Greek, 2 Indo-Scythian, 1 Indo-Parthian and 3 Kushan coins) and by Swiney in the Punjab (1833c, pp. 405–16: 4 Indo-Greek, 1 Indo-Scythian, 5 Kushan coins). His understanding of them reflected the limited knowledge of the coinage of the region then available. For example, he attributed Kushan coins to 'Greek or Asiatic Princes who inherited the authority of Alexander's successors in the countries watered by the Indus' (1833a, p. 38), or 'may be referred to the reign of Eucratides I' (1833b, p. 314), 'ascribing them to Eucratides' (1833c, p. 411). He did not attempt to move beyond the classification system proposed by Tod (1826, pl. 12): Series 1 Greek kings (Indo-Greeks, Menander and Apollodotus II, Roman Egypt and early Kushan, Wima Takto coins); Series 2 Parthian kings (early Kushan coppers, Wima Takto); Series 3 Parthian or Indo-Scythic kings (Kushan copper, Wima Kadphises to Huvishka); Series 4 Hindu kings (Gupta gold); and Series 5 'a dynasty which ruled from Avanti, or Ujjayan, to the Indus' (Western Satraps and Gupta silver). He did, however, recognise the name Kanishka on a copper coin collected by Burnes (Prinsep 1833b, pp. 314–18; 1833c, pp. 411–12), the first attempt to link Kushan coins with historical sources (Cribb 2007a, pp. 187–8).

Following the arrival of Masson's reports, Prinsep was able to develop a better view of the coinages of the north-west and as well as deciphering Kharoshthi/Gandhari, he began to publish articles showing a more complex sense of the progression of the Greek and later rulers of the region (1835a, pp. 327–48; 1835b, pp. 621–43; 1836a, pp. 548–54; 1836b, pp. 639–57; 1837, pp. 463–7; July 1838, pp. 636–58).

After James Prinsep: Christian Lassen, Henry Thoby Prinsep, Horace Wilson and Alexander Cunningham

The arrival of Masson's collection in Calcutta in December 1838 was unfortunately too late for James Prinsep to pursue the subject further (Proc. ASB 1838, pp. 1047–52), as his failing health had ended his career in Calcutta and in 1840 also ended his life. A succession of scholars in the following decades integrated his discoveries into their accounts of the ancient north-west, but failed to take full account of his purpose in documenting the finds from Begram.

After Prinsep's death his brother Henry Thoby Prinsep used his papers (some of which survive in the Ashmolean Museum: MSS Arch. Ash. fol. 18) to publish a volume in 1844 summarising James Prinsep's discoveries. Henry Thoby readily acknowledged the important role Masson had played in building the picture Prinsep had achieved, 'it is to Mr Masson … that we are indebted for the most complete and best directed local researches that have been made in these regions' (1844, p. 8).

Henry Thoby also referred (1844, pp. 10–11) to two other studies based on Prinsep's work, and therefore ultimately on Masson's discoveries: *Ariana Antiqua* (Wilson 1841) and Christian Lassen's *Zur Geschichte der griechischen und indoskythischen Könige in Baktrien, Kabul und Indien …* (1838), which was translated into English by T.H.E. Röer and H. Torrens in *JASB* (1840, pp. 251–76, 339–78, 449–88, 627–76, 733–65) and then reprinted as a stand-alone volume (references below are to the repaginated version in this volume).

Lassen continued Prinsep's attempts to decipher Kharoshthi/Gandhari using the coins and to construct a historical account of the dynasties and kings ruling in the north-west. Lassen recognised Masson's contribution as a collector of coins, but gave faint praise for his efforts, 'The interpretation of the coins, and the inferences joined to it, prove indeed, that Mr Masson has not enjoyed a learned education … we shall not criticise his deficiencies, and willingly receive from him all that is capable of proof' and ironically refers to his former life, 'Mr Masson, I believe, served first in the artillary, and he knows certainly much better how to deal with numismatic inquiries, than most numismatists would know how to serve a gun' (1840, p. 8). His references to Begram do not fully acknowledge the nature of Masson's approach to the site (1840, p. 77), but only mention the abundance of coins found there and allude to Masson's attribution of the site to Alexandria ad Caucasum (1840, p. 85). In his discussion of individual kings he occasionally mentions that they were found or not found at Begram (1840, pp. 121, 130, 132, 135, 159). His interest was restricted to the coins with Greek inscriptions, so he did not discuss the further discoveries by Masson.

Like Masson and Prinsep, Lassen was keen to create a classification system for breaking up the coins so far discovered into a sequence. His categories were based on the inscriptions on the coins, creating three classes, with subdivisions (1840, pp. 117–45):

I. Greek characters:
  1. With Greek names and titles
  2. With Greek titles but no name
  3. Barbarian names and titles
II. Greek and Indian characters:
III. Greek and 'Cabulian' [i.e. Kharoshthi] characters:
  1. Greek kings
  2. Barbarian kings

This categorisation helped group similar coins, but obscured the historical progression as, for example, it placed the Soter Megas coins of the early Kushan period in his class I.2, but the much earlier coins of Agathocles and Pantaleon in class II, and separated the Bactrian and Indo-Greek issues of Eucratides I. His analysis of the historical evidence, mixing literary and numismatic evidence to construct a chronological sequence from Diodotus to the Kushans and Kushano-Sasanians (1840, pp. 184–5), accordingly made for unrealistic sequences, placing Kujula Kadphises *c.* 120 BC and Azes *c.* 116 BC.

Wilson's volume (1841), on the other hand, made more extensive use of Masson's work, placing in the public realm Masson's detailed accounts of his archaeological endeavours. The volume also presented a full account of the known coinage of the north-west, which was based on Masson's collection, but also drew on other published material from the other collectors, such as Burnes and Ventura. While Wilson acknowledged Masson's contribution as 'the first great step in the series of Bactrian numismatic discovery' and as the 'broad foundation' of 'later investigations', he however suggested that the majority of Masson's coin finds were worthless due to their being 'too much injured by time and corrosion' (1841, p. 12). Outraged at being thus slighted, this comment prompted Masson to annotate his own copy of the volume with 'hardly fair remark – is hardly true – the Begram coins infinitely surpass in presentation those found in India' (see Appendix 1, p. 307 below).

Although Wilson made ready use of the coins collected by Masson, he reverted to a more antiquarian analysis than that suggested by Masson's site find approach. The mixing together of Masson's finds from different locations with those of other collectors is especially apparent in his listings where he often fails to distinguish the Begram finds from those from Kabul, Jalalabad or from India. Like Prinsep and Lassen, Wilson largely deployed the coins collected by Masson to classify the coins into different series, rather than to understand their distribution and to create an outline of the history of the north-west.

In a few instances Wilson used Masson's finds appropriately, pointing to the Eucratides coins collected from Begram to give a view on the nature of this territory on the basis that 'They are found plentifully in Bactria proper, and in immense numbers at Begram, affording evidence both of his Bactrian and his Indian sovereignty' (1841, p. 235). Likewise from Masson's finds of Menander coins and the mention of them in the *Periplus of the Erythraean Sea* (47), he could state that 'he reigned over an extensive tract from the foot of the Paropamisadae mountains to the sea' because 'they are most abundant in the vicinity of Kabul, the Hazara mountains, and at Begram' (1841, p. 281). In other cases he mentions, but ignores, Masson's evidence, as in the case of the Soter Megas coins of the Kushan kings Kujula Kadphises and Wima Takto. Wilson refers to the 'bag-fulls' of this coinage found 'at Begram' (curiously citing Prinsep for this information), but insists that their issuer 'must have reigned chiefly, if not altogether, in India, at least in the Punjab, by the abundance of his coins in the west of Hindustan, on the basis of the reports of stray individual finds in northern India (1841, pp. 332–3).

Alexander Cunningham, a protégé of James Prinsep followed Lassen, Wilson and Henry Thoby Prinsep and, continued the investigation of the coins of the ancient north-west in a series of articles in the *Numismatic Chronicle* (1868, pp. 93–136, 181–213, 257–83; 1869, pp. 28–46, 121–53, 217–46; 1870, pp. 205–36; 1872, pp. 157–85; 1873, pp. 187–219), which were subsequently published as a single volume in 1884. Like his predecessors, Cunningham readily acknowledged Masson's contribution, identifying him as the first to recognise the way to decipher Kharoshthi/Gandhari (1868, p. 125), and crediting him with insights into the absence of the Parthians and the Indo-Scythians Maues and Azes from Begram as evidence that they did not rule there (1868, p. 182). He used Masson's finds from Begram and purchases in Kabul to outline the locations of various Greek kings: Pantaleon and Agathocles (1869, p. 41), Euthydemus (1869, p. 138), Eucratides (1869, pp. 232–4) Antialcidas (1869, pp. 232–4, 293–4), Lysias (1869, p. 311), Menander (1870, pp. 220–1) and Hermaeus (1872, pp. 157–85). In his later essays on Indo-Scythian, Kushan, Kushano-Sasanian and Hun coins in the *Numismatic Chronicle* (1888, pp. 47–58, 199–248; 1889, pp. 268–311; 1890, pp. 103–72; 1892a, pp. 40–82, 98–159; 1893, pp. 93–128, 166–77, 184–202; 1894, pp. 243–93), Masson's finds from Begram are barely mentioned, apart from reference to the coins of Vonones being found at Begram in small numbers (1888, pp. 213–14, 1890, pp. 107, 109), Gondophares coins being found in limited numbers (1890, p. 123) and Azes and Aspavarma coins being absent from the site (1888, p. 242, 1890, pp. 110, 126).

Although all these authors on the coinage and history of the north-west were aware of Masson's collecting and made selective use of his results, the overall effect of their limited use of his results was to push him into obscurity and the evidence he collected to be absorbed virtually unacknowledged into the discourse or to be ignored. Tarn (1938), for example, in his account of the Greek kingdoms in the east published in 1938, made no direct reference to Masson's reports, only picking up a few indications from other sources, reporting that Masson had found coins of Eucratides I (p. 217) and Menander (p. 228) at Begram, and more generally his finds of Greek coins (pp. 441 and 461). He also strangely claimed that Masson found 'thousands' of coins of Eucratides (p. 461), in spite of his reports only mentioning 269 examples (1836b, p. 547). Narain in his account of the Greek kingdoms, in many ways a riposte to Tarn, correctly quoted the number of Menander and Eucratides coins found by Masson at Begram (1957, p. 77) and referred to his finds from Begram as an important tool in the regionalisation of Greek rule (p. 103). He did not, however, pay attention to Masson's actual reports, and quoting him via Cunningham (1890, p. 110), contradicted his reports that Azilises and Azes coins were absent from the Begram finds (1957, p. 163). His reason for this was because Prinsep, in an article on other collections (1835a, p. 344, pl. 32, nos 20–1), had included two imitation Azes coins published in Masson's first report (1834, pl. X.31, 33). Masson had correctly linked these imitation Azes with the period of the early Kushan Soter Megas coins (1834, p. 170). Narain also referred to Masson featuring Azilises and Azes coins in his second report on coins from Begram, but again did not read what Masson had said, i.e. that he acquired these Azes coins in Kabul and Jalalabad, not from Begram (1836a, pp. 25–6, nos 23, 25–6). Whitehead (1950, p. 207) also argued against Masson's conclusion that Azes coins were not current at Begram on the basis of these early Kushan period imitations (1834, pl. 10, nos 31 and 33) and of a single Azes coin (1834, pl. XI, no. 41, Senior 2001, type 111.10), which is also probably a posthumous imitation. The presence of posthumous imitations at Begram cannot be used as evidence of Azes rule at this site, and Masson was clear that he linked them with the early Kushan Soter Megas coinage (*JASB* April 1834, 169–70).

This gradual elimination and devaluing of Masson's contribution from the study of Bactrian and Indo-Greek coin is amply illustrated by his complete absence from the analysis of scholarship on the subject by Olivier Guillaume (1990 [1987]) who seems to be unaware of the collecting practice of Masson and of the Taxila excavations (Marshall 1951), as in his discussion of provenance he asserts 'It is no exaggeration to say that, on the whole, the provenance of BIG [i.e. Bactrian and Indo-Greek] coins is all but unknown' (1990, pp. 43–4).

Begram reconstructed through Charles Masson's archives and collections

The re-discovery of Masson's papers and a large part of his collection in the British Library has opened up the opportunity to reassess his intentions and achievements in documenting the finds from the ancient site of Begram. Thanks to Elizabeth Errington's tenacity, diligence and perceptions, a large part of what Masson achieved has been revealed and reintroduced into the discourse on the ancient history of Afghanistan. His pioneering approach to both archaeology and numismatics lay hidden at the beginnings of modern scholarship on ancient Afghanistan.

The coins he collected, both from Begram and elsewhere in Afghanistan, have long since entered as individual specimens into the reconstruction of the history of the region through their incorporation into the coin collections of the British Museum and the Fitzwilliam Museum in the late 19th century, from the India Museum or through other collectors and by virtue of their appearance in the publications of James and Henry Thoby Prinsep, Lassen, Wilson and Cunningham. In this way they became part of the foundation of our modern understanding of the progression of dynasties and rulers in Afghanistan and the surrounding regions. His work in building a solid documentation of coin finds from the site of Begram has had to rest on his reports published in *JASB*. As discussed above and elsewhere in this volume, Masson's third and best developed report was in large suppressed by James Prinsep, and the illustrations of his second report were not all published, when they duplicated (in Prinsep's opinion) pieces already published. This decision reflected a difference of purpose from Masson's intention to document all coins from the Begram site, as the aim of Prinsep and the other scholars who utilised Masson's material was to document types and varieties of coins in order to construct a full classification and sequence of their issue.

By collecting all the coins and other small finds from Begram, Masson was seeking to create a history for the occupation of the site. In his first report he set out the categories of the coins he was finding with the intention of putting them into a chronological order. The classes he set out: 'Greek, Indo-Scythian, Parthian and Guebre, Brahmanical and Muhammadan' and his categories (1834, pp. 154–63) match our modern understanding of chronology at the site, but they were very loose in comparison with modern classification. Coins in his list which he included for reference, but were collected elsewhere are omitted from the following summary of coins he collected from the Begram site (see **Tables 7–8**).

Using Masson's data to examine the history of Begram and its coinage

Masson's intention in building a comprehensive collection of coins from the site of Begram revealed much to his successors and continues to be a source of information in understanding the history of the city and the region where it was located. Unfortunately the behaviour of his contemporaries and the poor curation of his collections for a century or more have diminished the value of what he achieved. His circumstances meant that he had to rely on East India Company funding to conduct his collecting, and that support came at a price which limited his activities and distracted him from adequately recording his later finds as they came in. His collections were also hostage to the financial and bureaucratic support he received. His former history as a deserter also prejudiced some of his contemporaries, limiting his ability to follow his stated intentions. The transportation of his second collection back to England took it to Calcutta, where Prinsep's ill-health left it without a champion and also prompted the extraction from it of material for the Asiatic Society of Bengal's collection, without regard for its source (mixing Begram finds with Kabul, Jalalabad and Peshawar purchases). That part of Masson's collection was subsequently absorbed in 1866 into the Indian Museum, Calcutta, where it was only labelled as

				1st report	No. of coins	2nd report	No. of coins	3rd report F526/1a	No. of coins	Total
Grecian	1		Antiochus					Pl. 1.1	1	1
		recorded kings of Bactria	Euthydemus [I]		1	pl. II.1–2	2	Pl.1.2–3	3	6
			Menander [I]	pl. VIII.1.2–4	39	pl. II.7	Ar 1 Ae 56	Pl. 1.26–7 Pl. 2.28–33	58	154
			Apollodotus [I] and imitations	pl. VIII.5–7	19		31	Pl. 1.8–11	23	73
			Eucratides [I] and imitations	pl. VIII.8–12	70		92	Pl. 2.36–44	107	269
	2	coins of ΑΝΤΙΛΑΚΙΔΟΣ [sic] and ΛΥΣΙΟΣ	Antialcidas	pl. IX.13–14	8		16	Pl. 3.49 (Ar) Pl. 3.50–3	Ar 1 Ae 12	37
			Lysias	pl. IX.15–16	6		5	Pl. 3.48	3	14
			Antimachus [II]			pl. II.9	Ar 1	Pl. 7.149	1 Ar	2
			Diomedes			pl. II.10	1			1
			Archebius					Pl. 6.132	1 Ar	1
	3	coins of ΑΓΑΘΟΚΛΗΣ, ΠΑΝΤΑΛΕΩΝ, etc.	Agathocles	pl. IX.17	10		19	Pl. 3.46–7	14	43
			Pantaleon	pl. IX.18	2		2	Pl. 2.45	3	7
			anonymous, lion/elephant	pl. IX.19	20		23	Pl. 4.76–7	24	67
			anonymous arched hill					Pl. 4.78–84	11	11
			Vatashvaka			pl. III.21	1	Pl. 7.148		1
	4	coins of the Nysæan Dynasty	imitation Hermaeus	pl. IX.20–1	34	pl. III.18	31	Pl. 3.58–61	27	92
			SuHermaius	pl. IX.22–3	10		5	Pl. 3.62–5	13	28
			Kujula Kadphises	pl. X.24–5	136	pl. III.19–29	179	Pl. 5.112–17 Pl. 6.122–31 Pl. 7.145–6	278	593
			Wima Takto (Soter Megas)	pl. X.26–30, 32	171		267	Pl. 5.99–103	257	695
			Wima Takto Gandharan	pl. X.32				Pl. 5.104, 107, 109–10	[4]	4
			imitation Azes	pl. X.31, 33	8		24	Pl. 5.108	20 [-4]	48
			Gondophares	pl. X.34–6	19		16	Pl. 4.92–8	20	55
			imitation Heliocles	pl. X.37	6		14	Pl. 4.67–75	13	33
	5	unarranged coins	Sasan [perhaps not from Begram]		1		1	Pl. 5.105–6	–	2
			Hermaeus	pl. XI.38	2			Pl. 3.66		2
			Spalagadama	pl. XI.39	1			Pl. 6.137	1	2
			Spalirises	pl. XI.40	1		1	Pl. 7.151	1	3
			Maues					Pl. 6.139	[1]	1
			Azilises					Pl. 7.152	1	1
			Azes [imitation]	pl. XI.41	1			Pl. 6.128		1
		unarranged coins not described	Indo-Scythian?		5					5
Indo-Scythian	1	Kanerkos	Kanishka I, Main mint Greek	pl. XII.1–2	24			Pl. 8.14–15	4	28
			Kanishka I, Main mint	pl. XII.3–5	28			Pl. 8.16–20 Pl. 9.21–7	67 [-3]	92
			Kanishka I, Kashmir mint ¼	pl. XII.6–7	16			Pl. 9.28–31	[3]	19
	2	Kadphises	Wima Kadphises	pl. XII.8–9	37			Pl. 8.4–6	62	99
			Vasudeva I etc.	pl. XII.10–12	254			Pl.10.54–9	492	746

Table 7 Begram finds according to Masson's three reports, omitting material explicitly said to come from Kabul, Jalalabad etc.

				1st report	No. of coins	2nd report	No. of coins	3rd report F526/1a	No. of coins	Total
	3		Huvishka, elephant rider	pl. XIII.13–18	56			Pl. 10.45–50	73	129
			Huvishka, enthroned	pl. XIII.19–21	56			Pl. 9.39–41	175	231
			Huvishka on mountain	pl. XIII.22	9			Pl. 9.32–8	19	28
			Kanishka II	pl. XII.23	113			Pl. 10.61–3	157	271
			Kanishka II imitation					Pl. 10.66	1	
			Kanishka III (p. 23: 'prevalent on the banks of the Indus and in the Punjab')					Pl. 10.64–5, 67	3	3
Guebre	1	Guebre, Parthian and Sassanian	Kushano-Sasanian	–	161			Pl. 10.60 Pl. 11.1–16	278	439
			Hun/ Turkic					Pl. 11.18–19 Pl. 13.44–51	[10]	10
Nagree	1	Nagree [Nagari]	Shahi,	–	34			Pl. 11.1–4, 10	[5]	39
Kufic	1	Kufic	Ghaznavid, Ghurid, Khwarazm Shah, etc.	–	122			Pl. 11.5–7, 8–9, 11–13 Pl. 13.1–6	171	293
ambiguous/ illegible			Kushan		387					387
Indo-Scythic			Kushan				1002			1,002
Kufic / Brahmanic gold / silver					14		138			152
Total					1,880		1,929		2,410	6,219

Table 7 continued

		Begram reports	Manuscripts	IOLC (Begram?)	BM (Begram?)
Achaemenids	bent bar fractions				2
post Alexander	Sophytes etc.			2 Ae	
	Antiochus III	1 Ae		1 Ae	1
Bactrian Greeks	Euthydemus	6 Ae		3 Ae	1
	Demetrius I				1
Bactrian/Indo-Greeks	Pantaleon	7 Ae		7 Ae	
	Agathocles	43 Ae		36 Ae	3
	Pantaleon or Agathocles			5 Ae	
	Eucratides I	269 Ae	6 Ar	91 Ae	5 Ae
	Eucratides I posthumous			76 Ae	
	Heliocles I		5 Ar	1 Ar	
Indo-Greeks	Apollodotus I	73 Ae	4 Ar	24 Ae, 1 Ar	2 Ae, 1 Ar
	Apollodotus I posthumous			18 Ae	2 Ae
	Antimachus II	2 Ar	3 Ar		1 Ar, 1 Ae
	Menander	154	7 Ar	231 Ae, 5 Ar	1 Ar, 9 Ae
	Strato			2 Ae	
	Antialcidas	37 Ae, 1 Ar	5 Ar	20 Ae	2 Ar, 1 Ae
	Lysias	14 Ae		4 Ae	2 Ae
	Heliocles II			1	
	Philoxenus				1 Ae, 1 Ar
	Diomedes	1 Ae			
	Archebius	1 Ar			
	Hermaeus	2 Ae	1 Ar		2 Ae

Table 8 Coins from the India Office Loan Collection, compared with Masson's Begram reports and known pieces from the British Museum

	Apollodotus II			1 Ae	0
	illegible			2 Ae	
Mauryan empire	punch-marked		73Ar	30 Ar	2Ar
	Ae (or plated) punch-marked			6 Ae	1Ae
	Ae cast			5 Ae	1 Ae
Local Indian	anonymous, lion/elephant	67 Ae		63 Ae	1 Ae
	anonymous arched hill	11 Ae		1 Ae	4 Ae
	anonymous arched hill small			7 Ae	
	Vatashvaka	1 Ae			
Indo-Scythian	Spalagadama	2 Ae			
	Spalirises	3 Ae			2 Ae
	Maues	1 Ae			1 Ae
	Azilises	1 Ae		1 Ae	
	Azes I			2 Ae	
	Azes II*			108 Ae	
	imitation Hermaeus	92 Ae		70 Ae	9 Ae
	Zeionises			3 Ae	
	Aspavarma			3 Ar (debased)	
	Kharahostes			1 Ae	
	Mujatria			4 Ar (debased)	
	unidentified	5 Ae	13 Ar		
Indo-Parthian	Gondophares	55 Ae		69 Ae	3
	Abdagases			2 Ae	1
	Sasan	1 Ar (debased)		20 Ar (debased)	1
	Abdagases or Sasan			7	
	Phraataces imitation				1
	Sanabares				4
Kushan	Kujula Kadphises	593 Ae		521 Ae	7 Ae
	Su Hermaeus	28 Ae		24 Ae	2 Ae
	imitation Heliocles	33 Ae		49 Ae	2 Ae
	imitation Azes base Ar	48 Ar (debased)		45 Ar (debased)	1 (Ar debased)
	imitation Azes Ae	1 Ae			1 Ae
	Sapadbizes		1 Ar?		2 Ar
	Soter Megas	695 Ae		853 Ae	7 Ae
	Wima Takto Gandhara	4 Ar (debased)		11 Ar (debased)	
	Wima Takto Kashmir			5 Ae	
	Wima Kadphises	99 Ae	1 Ar	186 Ae	4 Ae
	Kanishka I, Main mint Greek	28 Ae		37 Ae	2 Ae
	Kanishka I, Main mint	92 Ae		197 Ae	6 Ae
	Kanishka I, Kashmir mint ¼	19 Ae		162 Ae	
	Huvishka main mint	388 Ae		246 Ae	8 Ae
	Huvishka imitations			186 Ae	
	Huvishka Gandhara			18 Ae	
	Huvishka Kashmir			2 Ae	
	Huvishka Mathura			3 Ae	
	Vasudeva I etc.	746 Ae		272 Ae	
	Kanishka II	271 Ae	1 Au	153 Ae	
	Kanishka II imitations			59 Ae	
	Vasishka			42 Ae	
	Kanishka III	3 Ae			2 Ae
	Shaka			3 Ae	
	unidentified	1389 Ae			

Table 8 continued

Kushano-Sasanian	Kushano-Sasanian	439 Ae		221 Ae	?
	imitation Vasudeva			156 Ae	?
	Kidarite Kushan			14 Ae	?
	Kidarite/KS			42 Ae	?
	Hun/Turkic	10		55 Ae	?
Shahi-Islamic	Arab-Sasanian		6 Ar		
	Shahi	39 Ar/Ae		400 Ae	?
	Ghaznavid, Ghurid, Khwarazm Shah, etc.	293 Ar/Ae	2632 Ar; 7 Au	96 Ae	?
	unidentified	152 Ar/Ae	216 Ar	138 Ae	
Total		6,219		5,123	106

Table 8 continued

coming from the Asiatic Society (Smith 1906), which mixed it with the coins the society had acquired from other sources, such as Ventura and others, collecting in the Punjab.

The collection that reached England was housed in the East India Company's India Museum, but part of the coin collection was given back to Masson after he had returned to London. From the account which Elizabeth Errington has reconstructed about Masson's life and his collections, we can trace in part what then happened to the collections (**Vol. I**, pp. 3–14, 22–7). After Masson and then his widow had died, his collection and the associated papers were bought back from his estate by the East India Company. The India Museum survived the end of the Company in 1857 and passed to the new India Office. When it was decided in 1879 that the Museum should close, its collections, including the Masson collection was offered to the British Museum and the Victoria and Albert Museum. The British Museum selected and acquired material from his coin collection in 1882 and then residual material from it was passed to other institutions or sold (in 1887). Part of the collection went in 1906 to the University of Cambridge where it is now recognisable in the Fitzwilliam Museum. Other parts are said to have gone to Oxford University (Ashmolean Museum), the Royal Asiatic Society and the Indian Museum Calcutta, but these parts are not traceable. The sold parts are not documentable, but some of that material can be recognised in the collection acquired from London coin dealers by Michael Mitchiner and published in his volumes on ancient Indian and Central Asian coins (1975–6, 1978). As Elizabeth Errington discovered, a large part of the coin collection (*c.* 6,500 pieces) remained buried in the part of the Indian Museum collection which had been retained in the keeping of the India Office Library, and was eventually transferred in 1982 to the care of the British Library and is now on loan to the British Museum.

This careless curation of Masson's collections kept them largely obscured from scholarship until Elizabeth Errington began her marathon task of reconstructing what he had discovered. Among his papers in the India Office Loan Collection in the British Library she rediscovered his original plates for his second Begram report, including the images which Prinsep had omitted, and the missing part of his third report, 13 plates and 25 pages (**F526/1a**, see pp. 36–73 above). The resulting full versions of his three reports on coins found at Begram and a large part of the coins he collected now allow a fuller appraisal of what he set out to achieve.

The surviving coin collection represents a fraction of what Masson reported as having been collected from Begram. Elizabeth Errington has attempted to reconcile the exact numbers as recorded in Masson's papers which suggest that his whole collecting activity enabled him to assemble 72,252 coins from Begram (see above pp. 10, 12). If his figures are to be believed than the surviving coins only represent less than 10% of what he collected.

The surviving coins are also contaminated with coins which he clearly collected elsewhere. In the India Office Loan Collection (IOLC) there are numerous examples of Azes II coins of the types reported from Taxila (Senior 2001: types 107 (75 examples) and 108 (1 example); Marshall 1951) and from Swat (Senior 2001: types 100 (2 examples), 101 (14 examples) and 102 (14 examples), probably Gandharan issues (Göbl 1976; MacDowall and Callieri 2004). These must have been acquired by Masson somewhere other than Begram, as they were only current to the east of the Khyber Pass. A few stray Indo-Scythian coins would be expected in Begram, carried there by merchants as small change, but all the coins in the name of Azes mentioned in his three reports as coming from Begram are later imitations, current in the early Kushan period, probably mixing in circulation with Soter Megas coins. Masson described them along with Soter Megas coins, without distinguishing them (**F526/1a, f. 13**; 1836b, p. 547). Both the collection surviving in the India Office Loan Collection and the coins acquired by the British Museum, Fitzwilliam Museum and Asiatic Society Bengal, all need to be seen in the light of this contamination, so cannot be seen as a precise record of Masson's Begram collection.

The coins purchased by Masson at Kabul and Jalalabad can be viewed as potential finds from these regions, but, as these two cities were on contemporary trade routes with other parts of Afghanistan and the regions to the east of the Khyber Pass, it is impossible to be confident that these coins were in currency in the areas from which they were acquired. Masson's expressed intentions about his acquisitions from Begram give more confidence in accepting what was included in his three reports, covering his collecting from 1833 to 1835, as evidence of currency in that city, and only in so far as the surviving collections correspond with the reports can they also be taken as evidence of the same kind.

There are other limitations on the nature of the evidence of coins Masson acquired as coming from Begram. Setting aside the issue of the integrity of the agents he employed in collecting (see above pp. 5–6, 9–11), the question must also be asked whether site finds without archaeological context give an accurate picture of currency. Masson's agents did not report the contexts of the coins they were buying, other than that they came from the site. Among the coins acquired there may be hoards, which would grossly distort the statistical data. Having three years of reports, however, helps eliminate some of the distortion which hoards would have created. With only a few exceptions the site finds in Masson's three reports were of copper coins, which also only represented part of the currency at most periods.

Silver and gold coins are found more rarely as casual losses at archaeological sites, but if they survive, it is normally in hoards. For example the Taxila excavations yielded only 6 Indo-Greek silver coins in comparison with 290 copper coins (Marshall 1951, pp. 766–767). If any such hoards were found while Masson's agents were acquiring coins from the site during the period covered by his first three reports, then it is more likely that such hoards were melted for their gold or silver, or they were taken to be offered to collectors with more ready cash than Masson. Only one hoard of this kind was acquired by Masson in 1834, but not from Begram (the Hazarajat hoard, 1836b, p. 22). After the period of his reports he seems to have had better access to gold and silver finds, perhaps as he had more ready cash available as he was no longer able to spend it on excavations (**E161/VI, f. 24: Vol. II, p. 62**; Wilson 1841, p. 117). According to his correspondence from 1836 to 1838 he collected from Begram 23 gold and 9642 silver coins (see **Tables 9–10**). It seems that the majority of the silver coins were of the Sasanian, Hindu Shahi and Islamic periods. Another large group were termed by him as 'minute' (see **Vol. II, pp. 66–7, 100–1**). He gives no other information on them. The only coins which can be described as minute which were current in the north-west are either Mauryan period mashaka (Hardaker 1999), which have been reported from Taxila (Walsh 1939) and Mir Zakah (Curiel and Schlumberger 1953, p. 73), but are not present in the India Office collection, or the issues of the Amirs of Sind examples of which are in the India Office collection. The evidence points to the Sind coins, but as they are few in number, it is very likely the numerous coin and other small metal fragments in the surviving collection were also classified as 'minute coins' (see pp. 13–14).

Gold and silver coins found in excavations whether as single finds or hoards can provide useful information about the state of local currency, but unfortuately these coins reported as Begram finds are of limited use as there is insufficient evidence to tell whether they were stray finds or hoards and with a few exceptions we are ignorant of their exact identities. The gold and silver coins published by Wilson from Masson's collection and the list of his holdings after he was back in London are likewise uninformative about whether they were Begram finds or not, so it is probably safer to discount them from any analysis of the site.

The two silver coins of Antimachus II (Nicephorus) he reported as found at Begram (**Fig. 24.27**; 1836a p. 15; **F526/1a, Pl. 7.149–50**; Wilson 1841, p. 274, no. 2, Coins pl. II.15) provide a good example of the problems created by the limitations of his collecting practice, his recording and the later curatorial abuses. Antimachus II's silver coinage is relatively plentiful, but only two had been reported from the site by Masson up to 1836. In subsequent collecting he acquired more Antimachus silver coins, but they could be coins of Antimachus I (Theos) (see above, pp. 54–5). Later in 1836 in his second dispatch, he also sent a single copper coin of this king (**Fig. 24.28**). He did not recognise it as a coin of Antimachus, and it was listed by Wilson as one of Antialcidas (1841, p. 279, no. 7, Coins pl. XXI.11). Based on his discovery of a single silver coin of Antimachus II in 1835 (1836a, p. 15, pl. II.9) he conjectured that 'Among 5000 or more copper coins, procured from the *dasht* of Begram, we have not discovered one of Antimachus, and the detection of a silver coin does not seem to afford evidence that he ruled there, when the absence of his copper coins seem to prove that he did not'. In his unpublished report he also records 'We have found no copper coin of Antimachus' (**F526/1a, f. 18**, p. 55 above).

Antimachus II's copper coins are relatively scarce compared with those of his near contemporaries Apollodotus I, Menander and Eucratides I. Normally copper coins are found more frequently as stray finds on ancient sites, as they normally circulate in larger numbers than precious metal coins and their loss does not so easily prompt a search by their loser because of their lower value. So can we accept Masson's suggestion that the absence of Antimachus copper coins from the site demonstrates his not ruling there? The presence of even the one copper coin he later found might also point to them not being current at the site and therefore him not ruling there. As Antimachus II's copper coins are so scarce, however, the single find could be explained statistically as evidence of his rule there, because his copper coins represented a tiny percentage of the copper coinage of the Indo-Greek kings. Can one make the same argument on the basis of his much commoner silver coins? Their loss at the Begram site suggests they were current in the city. In comparison with the finds of other Indo-Greek coins at the site during Masson's first three years of collecting, they appear to be commoner than the other silver coins he acquired, one each of Menander (1836a, p. 22), Antialcidas (**F526/1a, f. 6, Pl. 3.49**, Prinsep 1836a, p. 549, pl. XXVIII, no. 2) and Archebius (**F526/1a, fig. 132, Pl. 6.122** [*sic*], Prinsep 1836a, p. 549, pl. XXVIII, no. 1). The two large silver coins of Menander and Hermaeus listed in the manuscript for the package of coins collected in Begram in 1834 (**E161/VII f. 20**, **Vol. II, p. 60**) are not Begram finds, but acquired in Kabul (Masson 1836a, pp. 22–3, nos 6, 15 and 16).

So the discovery of two silver coins and a single copper of Antimachus II could be considered evidence of his ruling there, but it is very thin evidence compared with the large number of copper coins of other rulers. It could also be argued that silver (and gold) coins move over larger distances because of their higher value, so the two Antimachus II silver coins could have circulated into Begram from another location where he was issuing coins. In the examination of the quantity of copper coins of the other Indo-Greek kings below, the presence of only one example of Antimachus II's copper coins at the site is anomalous and argues against his ruling there.

In spite of all these limitations on the value of Masson's coins from Begram, his reports and the surviving collection provide a plausible overview of the currency and political chronology of the site. The outcomes from the data collected by Masson for Begram matches well the coins recorded from the French excavations at the site (see **Table 11** and pp. 27–8, **Fig. 16**).

Vol. II: E161/VI mss	p. 50 ff. 3–4 F526/1a	p. 58 f. 15	p. 60 f. 20*	p. 65 f. 29	p. 66 f. 31	p. 67 f. 33 F526/1c	p. 68 f. 33 F526/1e	p. 72 f. 38	p. 75 f. 36	Total
1833	Brahmanic and Kufic 13Ar						13 Ar			13 Ar
1834		Antimachus I Ar								1 Ar
1835										
1836				Demetrius I Ar			3500 Ar			3500 Ar
1837						3087 Ar	3087 Ar		7 Au 2898 Ar	7 Au 3087 Ar
1838					Kanauj Pala 6 Au; 560 Ar	8 Au; 3040 Ar (see **Table 10**)	3040 Ar	1 Au 142 Ar		15 Au 3040 Ar
gold total					6	8		1	7	22
silver total	13	1		1	560	6,127	9,627	142	2,898	9,641

Table 9 Masson archival records of gold and silver coins collected from Begram (* = E161/VII f.20 erroneously records the following coins as from Begram, silver drachms of Menander 111, Apollodotus 7, Antimachus 6, Hermaeus 1, Alexander 1, which are all from the Hazarajat hoard (Masson 1836a, pp. 21–2), two silver tetradrachms of Menander and Hermaeus acquired in Kabul (1836a, pp. 22–3), and a gold coin of the Kushans which he actually found in the relic deposit of the Guldara stupa (1836a, pp. 27–8; Vol. I, p. 79, Fig. 69.1–2))

Series	Attributions	Silver	Attributions	Gold
Bactrian	Eucratides	6*		
	Heliocles	5*		
Mauryan	Punched coins	73		
Indo-Greek	Apollodotus	4*		
	Antimachus	3*		
	Menander	7*		
	Antialcidas	5*		
	Hermaeus	1*		
Indo-Scythian?	Unknown names	13		
Kushan	Kadphises	1*		
	Indo-Scythic	1*	Kanerki family	1
Sasanian or Hun	Sasanian	10		
Shahi	Rajputs	57		
Arab-Sasanian?	Sasanian Muhammadan	6		
Islamic	Kufic	2632	Muhammadan	1
Sind emirates?	Minute coins	216		
Delhi sultanate			Nagari Pala	6
Total		3,040		8

Table 10 Gold and silver coins from Begram 15 October 1837 to 30 June 1838 (F526/1c, Vol. II, p. 67). Figures marked with asterisk* are in the list of coins from Begram according to a dispatch record covering the same period (F526/1k, Vol. II, p. 100)

Begram as revealed by Masson's coin collection

> The discovery of a multitude of coins, which may be classed into many well defined and distinct series, and which were undeniably current in these countries, yield abundant testimony that not only did they undergo a number of political convulsions, and experience considerable alternations in the authority of various dynasties, but that divers religions were introduced, and patronised by the monarchs of the day.

(Masson 1842, I, p. 196).

Masson deduced from the coins being found there that Begram was an important ancient city. He proposed (1836a, pp. 6–10) to attribute its foundation as an Alexandria (of the Caucasus) to the great conqueror Alexander III of Macedon, and modern scholarship (Bernard 1982; Goukowsky 1989; Holt 1995, p. 47; Errington 2001, p. 367; Rapin 2013, p. 53) tends to follow his attribution of this as the city founded by Alexander as he progressed north through the Paramopasidae mountains to capture Bactria in c. 329 BC according to Arrian (III. 28.4), Curtius (VII.3.23) and Diodorus (XVII.83.1–2).

He also thought the city continued to be occupied until the Mongol invasion, 'It is not indeed improbable that this city, like many others, may owe its destruction to the implacable rage of the barbarous and ruthless Genghis' (1842, III, p. 160). The coins he found certainly supported his view of the end of the city as there are no coins later than those of the Khwarazm Shahs from whom Genghis Khan (c. 1206–27) and his army took this region. Unfortunately the histories of the Mongol advance into this region do not mention the destruction of the city.

The coins Masson acquired from Begram provide an index of development of the coinage systems of the region and for the ancient period can be usefully compared with the finds from the excavations at Ai Khanum (Bernard 1985), Taxila (Marshall 1951) and Swat (Göbl 1976; MacDowall and Callieri 2004); and for the later period, with coins collected from Gandhara, especially the Kashmir Smast site and locality (Nasim Khan *et al.* 2008; Errington 2010).

Achaemenid period coins (Fig. 21.1)

Two coins (1880.3733.a-b) which Masson did not recognise and sat in the British Museum among his jewellery fragments until discovered by Elizabeth Errington provide the earliest evidence for the chronology of the site. They are fractions of the silver coinage which circulated in the eastern provinces of the Achaemenid Empire in the period before Alexander the Great's conquests. A hoard found at Kabul contained the examples of the full denomination of this coinage, known to numismatists as 'bent bars', together with Greek coins from the 5th to 4th century and another local coinage struck like Greek coins, but with local designs (Schlumberger 1953; Cribb 1983, 1985).

The discovery of these two coins suggests that Begram may have been in occupation before Alexander passed through. The citadel, for example, could have been an Achaemenid establishment to control the passage from the Kabul plain up into Bactria, like those of the period of Persian rule in Bactria (Leriche 2007, pp. 127–30; Mairs 2014). The foundation of a city from the time of Alexander could have taken advantage of the pre-existence of a citadel.

Post-Alexander period coins (Fig. 23.1–2)

No coins of Alexander have been reported from Begram, but two tiny copper coins from the site seem to represent the period immediately after his death. They have Athenian designs, obverse: the head of Athena in a Corinthian helmet and reverse: two owls with a single head. The reverse design appeared on similar sized Athenian bronze coins in the 4th century BC (BMC pl. VI, no. 6), but with a different obverse design featuring an Athenian helmet. Copper coins with the same helmet and a single owl were found at the Greek site of Ai Khanum on the Oxus (Bernard 1985, pp. 19, 32–4, pl. 2, nos 2–9: from the exacavation; and a-b: local finds). Bernard linked them with the silver coins with Corinthian helmet issued by the post-Alexander local ruler Sophytes (1985, p. 33), whose coins are also linked with the imitation Athenian coins current in Bactria, and it seems plausible to also attribute the two coins from Begram to the same period.

Mauryan period coins (Fig. 21.2–39)

There are no coins from Begram representing the period of Seleucus's succession to Alexander's eastern conquests, but there are plenty of coins from the Mauryan period at the site, both punch-marked silver (**Fig. 21.2–28**) and copper coins (**Fig. 21.30–2**) and cast copper coins (**Fig. 21.33–9**). Such coins are difficult to date precisely as they have no features which link them with the fragments of verifiable political history which survive. The accounts of Strabo (XV, 2.9) and Appian (XI, 55) give Seleucus brief control of the Begram region before he conceded it by treaty to the first Mauryan ruler Chandragupta before *c.* 301 BC, when he used the elephants given him by Chandragupta in battle

Series	Ruler	
Bactrian Greek coins	Euthydemus	1
Post-Mauryan local coins	local uninscribed (lion/elephant)	2
Early Indo-Greek coins	Pantaleon	2
	Eucratides I (incl. imitations)	18
	Menander I	2
Indo-Greek coins	Strato	1
	Apollodotus I	3
	Antialcidas	1
	Diomedes	1
Indo-Scythian	Hermaeus lifetime or imitation	22
	Spalahores and Spalagadama	1
	Mujatria	1
	Azes II imitation	1
Indo-Parthian	Gondophares	23
	Abdagases	5
Parthian	Parthian imitation	1
Kushan	Kujula Kadphises	80
	Heliocles imitation	4
	Soter Megas	31
	Wima Kadphises	40
	Kanishka I	74
	Huvishka	90
	Vasudeva I (incl. imitations)	96
	Kanishka II (incl. imitations)	92
	Vasishka	1
Kushano-Sasanian	Kushanshahs	6
Huns	Shri Shahi	1
	illegible	275
	Total	**871**

Table 11 Coins found at Begram during the French excavations (see pp. 27–8 above)

(Diodorus, XX.113.4). The Mauryan coins from Begram are of the period after the reign of Chandragupta (Gupta and Hardaker 2014, series IV–VII) and continued in currency until at least the mid-2nd century BC (Errington 2003). Such coins were current across Mauryan territory from Bengal to Begram, so may have been made locally or been imported.

Post Mauryan local coins (Fig. 21.40–50; Fig. 22)

One group of coins with Indian designs, which are plentiful at Begram, have often been dated to the Mauryan period, but recently discovered evidence shows that they are contemporary with the Indo-Greeks (Bhandare 2018). The contexts of the excavated examples from Taxila (Marshall 1951, pp. 760–1) also showed that they were current alongside Indo-Greek coins. These coins were made by striking in the same way as Greek coins, normally between two dies, but some are struck only with a single die, so that the reverse is flattened by the surface on which they were struck. They can be dated to the Indo-Greek period because they have been found overstruck on Indo-Greek coins. One of the pieces from Masson in the Fitzwilliam Museum (as **Fig. 22.11–15**) is overstruck on a coin of Apollodotus I (*c.* 180–160 BC). These coins, like the Mauryan period coins, do not have anything in their designs to link them to a political entity. Some of them with elephant and lion designs (**Fig. 22.11–15**) were struck from dies with realistic designs which are stylistically similar to early Indo-Greek coins (like those of Pantaleon and Agathocles, *c.* 190–180 BC), but others have designs which combine into a single die symbols like those appearing on the punch-marked and cast Mauryan period coins. One type collected by Masson (**Fig. 22.4**, Wilson 1841, Coins pl. XV.30) has a Brahmi inscription *vaṭaśvaka* which is either the name of a place or of a people. The location of its issuer is not known (Gupta 1989, pp. 17–18). Several other coins have symbols which link them to the *vaṭaśvaka* coin, as suggested by Allan (1936, p. cxlvi; **Fig. 21.46** and **Fig. 22.1–3, 5–9**; no. 5 appears to be a poorly preserved *vaṭaśvaka* coin). The elephant and lion coins are very numerous at the site, with 67 mentioned in the Masson's reports and 64 now surviving. This type is also well represented at Taxila with 35 examples found (Marshall 1951, p. 761), so was clearly current at both sites, but probably made at Begram. The *vaṭaśvaka* type is represented by two examples illustrated by Wilson and another in the Fitzwilliam Museum, and the related coins by eleven in the reports and four in the British Museum, one in the India Office Loan Collection and sixteen in the Fitzwilliam Museum.

Cunningham (1891, pp. 60–6) and Allan (1936, pp. cxlvi–cxlvii) attributed the *vaṭaśvaka* type and all the other die struck local coins to Taxila on the basis of a hoard from that region acquired by Cunningham. He acknowledged that they were also common in the Kabul Valley, but gave more weight to his hoard in attributing them to Taxila. The hoard also included coins of the Indo-Greek kings Pantaleon and Agathocles. The excavations at Taxila, however, did not yield any of the *vaṭaśvaka* type and related type coins, so they may have been minted at or near Begram, where the Pantaleon and Agathocles coins were also made (see below). Some of the small coins (**Fig. 21.41–3, 45**) of this series are of types better represented at Taxila (Marshall 1951, p. 760, no. 2, 117 examples and no. 3 and 4, 178 examples) and one (**Fig. 21.44**) has a symbol common at Taxila, so all these are probably imports from that area. The other types found at Begram (**Fig. 21.40, 47–50**) are rare and could be local or imported.

The technology used in the production of these local coins is very similar to that used by the early Indo-Greeks, i.e. Pantaleon and Agathocles, to strike their copper coins. The use of square flans is borrowed from the Mauryan punch-marked and cast coins. Some are struck to the same weight standard as the Indo-Greek coins, but some are lighter in weight and others are fractions, perhaps to correspond with the Mauryan period cast coins. The administrative implications of having a local currency parallel to the Indo-Greek issues is more difficult to understand. It has been suggested that the elephant-lion type was issued by the Greek administration, because of its style and because a related coinage with elephant and horse (Allan 1936, pp. 226–7, nos 98–107) is in the same style as the horse design on the coins of the Bactrian king Euthydemus I (**Fig. 23.7–8**). Some of the elephant-horse coins (Allan, var. g, no. 107) have a Greek alpha control mark. Other elephant-horse coins (Allan 1936, var. f, nos 99–106) have a Greek style star control mark and the lotus standard with banners

symbol common on coins found at Taxila (Marshall 1951, pl. 235, nos 11–15). Allan (1936, pp. cxxxiv–cxxxv) suggested that they were Taxilan issues of the Indo-Greek king Agathocles as the symbol appeared on coins found at Taxila (Marshall 1951, pl. 236, nos 46–8) which shared a Kharosthi legend (*hirañasame*, 'golden hermitage' Allan 1936, p. cxxxii) with a local issue in the name of Agathocles (Marshall 1951, pl. 236, nos 43–5). These links have led to speculation about the sequence of the coins in relation to the arrival of Greeks in the region, but the evidence presented by Bhandare makes it clear they are contemporary with the early Indo-Greeks and at Taxila their circulation appears to have persisted well into the Indo-Greek period and perhaps later.

Bactrian-Greek coins (Fig. 23.3–8, 13, 19–20)

While the Mauryans held the territory south of the Hindu Kush, Bactria to the north remained under Greek control and some of the coins issued by the local Greek kings of Bactria were collected from Begram. Most of the Bactrian issues from the site are copper coins of Euthydemus I (*c.* 230–200 BC), six in Masson's reports and four in the surviving collection (**Fig. 23.5–8**). Euthydemus I coins are also the most common Greek issue found at Ai Khanum with 48 examples in the excavations and another 8 from the locality and at Uzundara where at least 104 have been found (Gorin and Dvurechenskaya 2018). They were also the commonest Bactrian coins found at Taxila where three were found (Marshall 1951, p. 766). It seems unlikely that they were issued south of the Hindu Kush, so it is most likely that they were carried there with the army of Euthydemus in his conquests. Euthydemus I's son Demetrius was described as conqueror of India by Strabo (XI.51.6). Another reference to 'Demetrius king of the Indians' by Justin (*Epitome* 41.6.4) may be to a later king of the same name. Demetrius (*c.* 200–190 BC) was already celebrated as a conqueror during his father's life (so his conquests may predate his accession to kingship). Polybius (XI.34) described him as the representative of Euthydemus I in concluding a treaty with the Seleucid king Antiochus III. An inscription said to have been found in Tajikistan, but only recorded through a photograph (Bernard *et al.* 2004, pp. 333–56), also refers to Demetrius during Euthydemus' reign as a conqueror. When Demetrius became king and began to issue his own coins he adopted the elephant scalp previously depicted as worn by Alexander the Great on posthumous coins issued by Ptolemy in Egypt and Seleucus I in Babylon, so perhaps also an indication of his conquests south of the Hindu Kush before his accession. The discovery of a Demetrius I coin in the Masson collection (**Fig. 23.9**), and another at Taxila (Marshall 1951, pl. 236, no. 42), are also suggestive of his penetration into these regions.

A single Seleucid coin of king Antiochus III (223–187 BC) is in Masson's collection (IOLC.112, **Fig. 23.3**) and in the plates of his unpublished report (**F526/1a, Pl. 1.1**). It is an import from Mesopotamia (Seleucia on the Tigris mint). The denomination and fabric of the coin would make it easy to move into the Begram region in circulation with Bactrian coins of Euthydemus I. An imitation Seleucid coin, of the type found in Baluchistan (Rapson 1904), was also among the finds from Begram (1880.3981.g; **Fig. 23.4**).

place of issue/ script	shape/ metal	Kings/types						
		Pantaleon	Agathocles	Antimachus I	Apollodotus I	Antimachus II	Menander I	Eucratides I
BACTRIA Greek	○Ar	K/Zeus	K/Zeus	K/Zeus	[K/Athena]		[K/Athena]	K/Dioscuri *K/star caps* (6)
	○Ae	Dionysus/ panther	Dionysus/ panther	elephant/ Nike				K/Dioscuri
		Stage 1			Stage 2		Stage 3	
BEGRAM	☐Ae				elephant/ thunderbolt			K/star caps
Greek/ Brahmi	☐Ar		Balarama/ Krishna					
	☐Ae	**Sri/panther (7)**	**Sri/panther (43)**					
Kharoshthi	☐Ae		hill/tree [T4] hill/lotus [T3]					
Greek/ Kharoshthi	☐Ar				*elephant/ bull* (3)			
	○Ar				*elephant/ bull* (1)	*Nike/ Alexander on horseback* (6)	Stage 2 Athena/ owl Stage 3 *K/Athena* (7) [T7]	K/Dioscuri
	☐Ae				**Apollo/tripod (73, includes posthumous imitations)**	*aegis/wreath & palm* (1)	Stage 2 Athena/owl (1) *Athena/shield* (1) [T1] *Athena/horse* **Athena/Nike (76)** [T2] Athena/Athena Athena/Horse Heracles/ lionskin *Elephant/Ankus* (1) **Elephant head/ club** (150) [T23] *Bull head/tripod* (1) Camel/bull head Boar/palm *Wheel/palm* (1) Stage 3 *K/Athena* (3) [T1] K/Nike K/dolphin	**K/Dioscuri (269, includes posthumous imitations)** [T3] **K/star caps (10)** [T1]

Table 12 Stages in the development of early Indo-Greek coins. Bold = common at Begram, italic = found at Begram but rare, numbers of examples in brackets. Taxila finds in square brackets [T and number of examples]. K = King's bust. Greek only coins in brackets are special issues

There are no coins reported from Begram of the Bactrian kings after Eucratides I: Demetrius II, Eucratides II, Heliocles I and Plato. The fragment of a silver tetradrachm of Heliocles I (*c.* 145–130 BC; **Fig. 24.26**) in Masson's collection is not documented as a Begram find, but could be from the site and an early Kushan period import, as imitation Heliocles were issued in northern Bactria during the early Kushan period and imported into Begram (see below).

After the conquest of territory south of the Hindu Kush the Greek kingdom in the north continued until Bactria fell to nomad invasion (see below). In Masson's collection there are Bactrian issues of two of the early kings ruling in the south, Agathocles (*c.* 190–180 BC; **Fig. 23.13**) and Antimachus I (*c.* 180–170 BC; **Fig. 23.18–19**), but there is no indication that these were acquired from Begram, so probably bought in the Kabul bazaar.

Early Indo-Greek coins (Fig. 23.9–12, 14–17, 20–4; Fig. 24.1–2, 7–16, 26–8)

The earliest coinages which survived in large numbers at the Begram site are the copper issues of the first Greek kings to issue coins in the region after the period of Mauryan rule. The early Indo-Greek coinage went through three stages distinguished by their inscriptions and by their designs:
1. with religious designs (gods, associated animals, divine attributes), inscribed in Greek and Brahmi, or just Greek, or just Kharoshthi.
2. with religious designs, inscribed in Greek and Kharoshthi.
3. with royal and religious designs, inscribed in Greek and Kharoshthi.

Stage 1 lasted through the reigns of Pantaleon, Agathocles and Antimachus I; stage 2 through the reigns of Apollodotus I, Antimachus II and the early part of Menander's reign;

Early Indo-Greeks	Begram reports	IOLC	BM	Mir Zakah	Swat	Taxila
Pantaleon	7	7		10		
Agathocles	43	36	3	8	1	7
Antimachus I				8		
Apollodotus I	73	24	2	26		1
Antimachus II			1			
Menander I	154	231	9	14	2	34
Eucratides I	269	91	5	13	1	4

Table 13 Comparison of the copper coins of the early Indo-Greeks from Begram. Mir Zakah: Curiel and Schlumberger 1953; Swat: Göbl 1976, MacDowall and Callieri 2004; Taxila: Marshall 1951

stage 3 began under Menander (*c.* 155–130 BC) and Eucratides I (*c.* 174–145 BC) and continued until the end of the Indo-Greek period (see **Table 12**).

The first two stages were largely focused in the Begram region as the issues are plentiful there. There is only one issue, with two varieties inscribed in Kharoshthi in the name of Agathocles at Taxila (Marshall 1951, pl. 236, nos 43–8). Marshall misattributed Apollodotus II (*c.* 80–65 BC) coins found at Taxila to Apollodotus I (Marshall 1951, pl. 236, nos 49–50), so he is not represented further east. The evidence for the first two stages from Begram suggests that this city was initially the centre of the Indo-Greek kingdom. During stage 1 Indo-Greek coins were in the names of kings Pantaleon, Agathocles and Antimachus I, who also issued coins in Bactria. Antimachus I's Indo-Greek copper coins, which have the same fabric as the Indo-Greek issues of Agathocles and Pantaleon, but only have Greek inscriptions, are very rare and finds have only been attested from the Mir Zakah find (Curiel and Schlumberger 1953, p. 75). In Bactria these three kings were the successors of Euthydemus II (*c.* 190–185 BC), the king who succeeded Demetrius I, so appear to have inherited the territory conquered by Demetrius during his father Euthydemus I's reign. Agathocles' control must have briefly reached as far as Taxila, but it is not clear whether control there was continuous. The kings named on stage 2 coins did not issue coins in Bactria, so appear to have only ruled from Begram, and it seems likely that Eucratides I had already started to take over control of Bactria (Cribb 2005), cutting them off from that region. The Bactrian style issues of Apollodotus and Menander were special issues struck in their territory south of the Hindu Kush. Stage 3 seems to begin when Eucratides I captured territory south of the Hindu Kush, and was probably based at Begram where his coins are plentiful. His coinage introduced the Bactrian practice of placing the king's portrait on the obverse of the coinage to the Greek mints south of the Hindu-Kush. Only four Eucratides I coins were recorded from Taxila compared with 37 of Menander I, so there is insufficient evidence from these coin finds to suggest that his conquests reached as far as Taxila for more than a brief period. Menander I's coins are found in sufficient numbers there to think that he withdrew to the East in the face of Eucratides I's invasion, but subsequently reasserted his power in the Begram area and began issuing coins on the model introduced by Eucratides I. Menander I's stage 2 silver coins are rare, but his stage 2 coppers are very common, so it is difficult to determine when in Menander I's reign the interruption by Eucratides I happened. The stage 3 pattern of coinage introduced by Eucratides I and adopted by Menander I was continued by all their Greek successors. The finds from Mir Zakah, Swat and Taxila suggest that the Indo-Greek kingdom in Begram reached further east through Gandhara and Swat to Taxila (see **Table 13**).

Menander I's copper coinage is very diverse in its designs (**Fig. 26.1–20**). Some of these are not represented among the Begram finds and some are only represented by a few examples. There appears to have been considerable experimentation in both the designs and the denomination system of the copper coins. Only two designs and denominations are sufficiently well represented among the Begram finds to confirm that they were a substantial part of the local currency. Masson (1836a, p. 22) suggested that the frequent appearance on the coins of Menander I of one of the Greek monograms was suggestive of its association with the site: 'Were this monogram interpretable, we should have no difficulty in definitely appropriating these coins'. This monogram (see **Fig. 26.1, 3, 5, 7, 10–12, 16–18, 20**) appears on 83 out of 150 Menander I's elephant head and club coins in the India Office loan collection, hence the high incidence of this monogram among the Begram finds has prompted its attribution to the Begram mint (Bopearachchi 1991, pp. 84–5).

The same control mark monogram also appeared on the silver drachms of Menander I (**Fig. 25.8, 15**) and Antimachus II (*c.* 160–155 BC; **Fig. 24.27**), as Masson observed (1836a, p. 22), so these might also be linked with Begram, but the greater mobility of silver coins could equally explain the presence of examples at Begram.

The absence north of the Hindu Kush of the Indo-Greek coins of the kings Pantaleon, Agathocles, Antimachus II and Menander and the rareness there of Apollodotus I, suggests that all these kings had administrations south of the Hindu Kush, and probably at Begram. Pantaleon and Agathocles also issued coins north of the Hindu Kush in the Bactrian style (**Fig. 23.14**) and accordingly represented a period of transition before the establishment of an independent Indo-Greek kingdom. Apollodotus I, Antimachus II and Menander seem to have ruled exclusively south of the Hindu-Kush, perhaps with Begram as their main administrative centre, but Eucratides I seems to have entered this region from Bactria in conflict with Menander, so issued coins both north and south of the Hindu Kush. 'Sans doute, c'est à Kapiçi que se trouva le siège du gouvernement des vice-rois Pantaléon et Agathocle' (Ghirshman 1946, p. 10).

Among the coins in the name of Apollodotus I and Eucratides I are many later imitations, made posthumously as part of the currency of imitation Hermaeus coins issued after the end of Indo-Greek rule in the Begram region (Dobbins 1970, p. 315–16; 1972, pp. 25–31, 40, 203; Senior 1999, pls XX–XXIII, Bopearachchi 1991, pp. 193–4, 213–16; see below).

Later Indo-Greek coins (Fig. 27; Fig. 28.1–5, 21)

The later Indo-Greek coins reported by Masson from Begram represent a limited coverage of the rulers who issued Indo-Greek coins, 8 out of the possible 27 kings known. The only kings whose coins are present in quantity are Lysias and Antialcidas. According to Senior (2006, pp. xxiv–xxxiv) and Bopearachchi (1991, pp. 93–6, 453) both place these rulers soon after Menander, and Bopearachchi, on the basis of Masson's finds (1991, p. 96, fn. 4), places their rule in the Begram region. There are two rulers Zoilus and Theophilus who may have ruled close in time to the reigns of Lysias and Antialcidas, but their coins are rare and, if current at Begram, might simply be absent because of their rarity. The monogram used on the majority of Menander copper coins, as discussed by Masson (see above), also appears on coins of Lysias and Antialcidas and of Zoilus and Theophilus. However, most of the copper coins of Lysias (c. 120–110 BC) and Antialcidas (c. 115–95 BC) reported by Masson have a different monogram (as on **Fig 27.3, 10**), suggesting that more than one monogram was used by the Begram mint.

Another ruler of the period immediately after Menander is Strato I (c. 125–110 BC), whose copper coins are commoner than those of Antialcidas, so one would expect to see them among Masson's reported finds if they were current in the city. Masson doesn't have any examples in his reports of coins collected from Begram for 1833–5, but there are two examples in the India Office Loan Collection (**Fig.27.1**: IOLC.603–604), which he could have acquired elsewhere, so it is possible that Strato I was ruling elsewhere as a contemporary of Lysias and/or Antialcidas.

Masson's reports of coins found at Begram only feature four other Indo-Greek coins, copper coins of kings Diomedes (c. 95–90 BC; one example: **Fig. 27.15**) and Hermaeus (c. 90–70 BC; two examples: **Fig. 28.4–5**) and a silver coin of Archebius (c. 90–80 BC; **F526/1a, Pl. 6.122**). From the manuscript record of the delivery of material collected after 1835, six silver coins can be added, extending the coverage to include Heliocles II (c. 110–100 BC). The movement of silver coins in trade between urban centres does not, however, allow them to be strong evidence of their place of issue. When compared with the coins recovered from Taxila, it suggests that Begram was no longer a centre of Indo-Greek power after Hermaeus. The absence of coins of Zoilus and Theophilus is not indicative of their presence or absence at Begram as their coins are very rare. Nikias's coins are commoner so their absence could indicate that he didn't issue coins at Begram. The copper coins of both Hermaeus and Diomedes (**Fig. 27.15**) continued to use the monogram discussed by Masson as common on the Menander coins found at Begram (see above). The copper coins recovered from finds at Mir Zakah and from the subsequent excavations there (Curiel and Schlumberger 1953) also show a similar cessation of Indo-Greek rule west of the Khyber Pass after Hermaeus.

The Mir Zakah finds in the 1940s largely consist of silver coins (**Table 14**), including Achaemenid, Mauryan, Indo-Greek and Indo-Scythian coins in quantity, reflecting the three major powers controlling this area during the 4th–1st century BC. There are a small number of Greek and Iranian coins, but not of sufficient number to indicate their circulation south of the Hindu Kush. The Indo-Greek silver coins include both issues relating to the copper coins current at Begram and those associated with copper coins issued to the east of the Khyber Pass, such as are represented at Taxila. The Mir Zakah finds therefore include many silver coins imported from further east, including debased silver coins. The composition of the finds suggests an accumulative treasure, of the kind assembled in a religious sanctuary over many centuries. Alongside the silver coins there are many debased coins, Indo-Scythian issues from Gandhara and Taxila, and the Indo-Scythian imitations of Hermaeus from Begram, issued at the end of the silver coinage series, retaining the silver denominations but containing little or no silver. The addition of these to the treasure represented a continuation of the practice of adding silver coins and should be distinguished from the random inclusion of a small number of copper coins, about 1.65% of the Indo-Greek to Indo-Scythian period. These copper coins suggest that the assemblage took place west of the Khyber Pass, either at the spot where they were found or nearer Begram (see **Table 15**). The bulk of the treasure ends with the imitation Hermaeus coinage as current at Begram and the contemporary issues of Azes II (c. AD 16–30), from east of the Khyber Pass. Later coins of the Indo-Parthians and Kushans are mostly copper, with a few debased silver, and in relatively small numbers, suggestive of the currency of the place of assemblage and/or of deposit down to the 3rd century AD. The additions to the treasure after the loss of the region to the Indo-Parthians and Kushans is insignificant (0.54%) and perhaps represents much lower value of additions to the treasure or the casual losses of those guarding the treasure or occupying the site of its deposit. This suggests that the main treasure was active until the Indo-Parthian or the Kushan conquest of Begram. The second find from Mir Zakah shows a similar profile, but are reported as including 'thousands' of Kushan coins down to the time of Vasudeva I (c. AD 190–230) (this probably also includes coins of Kanishka II (c. AD 230–46) as they are not distinguished from Vasudeva I issues in the reports) (Bopearachchi 1995; 2015, vol. 1, pp. 336–8, 636–76). Kushan issues represent about 0.41% of the coins in the first Mir Zakah finds and excavations. If the second Mir Zakah finds in the 1990s are as large as the 300,000–400,000 reported (Aman ur Rahman and Bopearachchi 1995, p. 12) then one would expect 1200–1700 Kushan coins, on the basis of the ratio in the earlier Mir Zakah finds. Unfortunately a full account of the composition of the second set of finds was not possible and is unlikely to ever be available, so any further inferences from it are not likely. Apart from the single Kushano-Sasanian coin from the excavation of the site, significant finds from the site end with Kanishka II, when the region was lost to the Kushano-Sasanians.

The huge quantity of imitations of Hermaeus' silver coins found at Begram, suggests that after his reign the area came under the control of a non-Greek regime which issued imitations. This will be discussed below. In Taxila and further east the Indo-Greek kingdoms continued to flourish until the early 1st century AD. Senior places Hermaeus's reign c. 105–90 BC (2006, p. xxxv) and Bopearachchi places it c. 90–70 BC (1991, p. 453). From the end of Eucratides I's reign, c. 140 BC, the Begram finds show the coinages of Menander, Lysias, Antialcidas, Diomedes and Hermaeus issued before the end of Greek rule, so a date closer to that proposed by Bopearachchi or later seems more likely.

Curiel and Schlumberger 1953	pp. 73–83			pp. 96–8		
	Kabul Museum	S.M. Khan collection	le Berre collection	excavation	Total Ar	Total Ae
ACHAEMENIDS						
bent bars Ar	50				50	
bent bar fractions Ar	547			20	567	
MAURYANS						
5 punch karshapana Ar	4810			182	4992	
mashaka Ar	13				13	
uninscribed Ae	6			4		10
LOCAL INDIAN						
lion/elephant Ae	48			5		53
small uninscribed Ae	23					23
GREEKS						
Greek	2				2	
Seleucus I Ar	1				1	
Lysimachus Ar	1				1	
PARTHIANS						
Phraates III Ar	1				1	
BACTRIAN GREEKS						
Euthydemus Ae	1					1
INDO GREEKS						
Pantaleon Ae sq	8	1	1			10
Agathocles Ae (Bactrian)	1		1			2
Agathocles Ae sq	4		1	3		8
Antimachus I Ae sq	2		6			8
Apollodotus I Ar	496	9	52	16	573	
Apollodotus I Ae	20	1	4	1		26
Antimachus II Ar	113			5	118	
Eucratides I Ae sq	10	1	1			12
Eucratides I Ae round			1			1
Menander Ar	410	19	81	38	548	
Menander Ae	7		7			14
Zoilus I Ar	12			1	13	
Lysias Ar	19	2	6	1	28	
Lysias Ae	2		2	1		5
Antialcidas Ar	84	5		12	101	
Antialcidas Ae	1		2	3		6
Diomedes Ar	1		1		2	
Philoxenus Ar	10	1	5	1	17	
Philoxenus Ae			1			1
Hermaeus (and Calliope) Ar	14	1	7	1	23	
Hermaeus Ae	1					1
Epander Ar	2				2	
Heliocles II Ar	3	1	5		9	
Strato (and Agathocleia) Ar	18		8	2	28	
Archebius Ar	85	2	5	1	93	
Polyxenus Ar	1				1	
Amyntas Ar	3		2	1	6	
Artimedorus Ar			1		1	

Table 14 Coins from Mir Zakah, according to Curiel and Schlumberger 1953

Curiel and Schlumberger 1953	pp. 73–83			pp. 96–8		
Apollodotus II Ar	8		3		8	
Apollodotus II Ae	1		1			2
Hippostratus Ar	1		1		2	
Zoilus II Ar	5				5	
Strato II Ar	1		1		2	
INDO-SCYTHIANS						
Hermaeus uncertain Ar & base Ar, probably mostly imitations	765	15	91	22	893	
Hermaeus imitations Ae	93	7	13	6		119
Spalahores Ar	1		1	1	3	
Spalagadama Ar	1		1		2	
Spalagadama Ae			1			1
Spalirises Ae			1			1
Spalirises and Azes Ar			2		2	
Spalirises and Azes Ae			1			1
Maues Ar	1					1
Azilises Ar	161	1	18	1	181	
Azes I or Azilises Ar	82		5	1	88	
Azes I Ar	2760	19	77		2856	
Azes I Ae	2		1			3
Azes II Ar (and base Ar imitations)	794	6	49	77	926	
Azes II Ae	3		4			7
INDO-PARTHIANS						
Gondophares base Ar	3				3	
Gondophares Ae	5		4			9
Abdagases Ae	2					2
Sasan base Ar	1				1	
Pakores Ae			2			2
KUSHANS						
Kujula Kadphises Ae	7		3	1		11
Heliocles I imitation Zeus			1			1
Su Hermaeus Ae	4					4
Soter Megas base Ar			1		1	
Soter Megas Ae	4		7			11
Wima Kadphises						
Kanishka I Ae	1			1		2
Huvishka Ae	7			4		11
Vasudeva I Ae	3			1		4
Kanishka II Ae	3			2		5
Kushan illegible Ae	3			1		4
KUSHANO-SASANIANS						
Hormizd I Ae	1					1

Table 14 continued

Later Indo-Greeks	Begram reports	IOLC	BM	Mir Zakah	Taxila	Swat
Lysias	14 Ae	4 Ae	2 Ae	5 Ae	3 Ae	
Antialcidas	37 Ae	20 Ae	2 Ae	6 Ae	17 Ae	1 Ae
Zoilus						1 Ae
Theophilus					1 Ae	
Nikias						
Diomedes	1 Ae				1 Ae	
Hermaeus	2 Ae	2 Ae	2 Ae	1 Ae		
Philoxenus			1 Ae	1 Ae	13 Ae	
Heliocles II		1 Ae			8 Ae	
Agathocleia/Strato						
Strato I		2 Ae			9 Ae	2 Ae
Polyxenus						
Demetrius III						
Epander					1 Ae	
Peucolaus						
Archebius					6 Ae	
Amyntas						
Artemidorus						
Menander II						
Apollodotus II		1 Ae		1 Ae	60 Ae	1 Ae
Telephus					1 Ae	
Hippostratus					6 Ae	
Dionysus					1 Ae	
Zoilus II					3 Ae	
Apollophanes						
Strato II					2 Ae	
Strato III						

Table 15 Comparison of finds of later Indo-Greek copper coins from Begram with those from Mir Zakah, Taxila and Swat (Mir Zakah: Curiel and Schlumberger 1953; Swat: Göbl 1976; MacDowall and Callieri 2004; Taxila: Marshall 1951)

Indo-Scythian coins (Fig. 24.3–6, 14–25; Fig. 28.6–7, 10–17; Fig. 30.1–6; 18–23, 25–30)

The demise of Indo-Greek rule in Begram region coincides with the issue of an extensive coinage imitating Indo-Greek prototypes. The coins of three different Indo-Greek kings were imitated, Hermaeus's silver coins, and Eucratides I and Apollodotus I's copper coins. This phenomenon was first recognised by Dobbins (1970) and has since been discussed at length by Bopearachchi (1991, 1993, 1995, 1997; Errington and Cribb 1992, p. 65) and Senior (1999). Masson recognised the continuity of the issue of coins with the name of Hermaeus beyond the end of his reign, but attributed these imitations to successors with the same name. He attributed the copper imitations of Hermaeus silver coins with Zeus reverse to Hermaeus I (1834, p. 167, nos 20–1), those with the part of the Greek inscription spelt ΣΤΗΡΟΣΣΥ in place of ΣΩΤΗΡΟΣ to Hermaeus II (1834, p. 167, nos 22–3) and those with the name of the Kushan king Kujula Kadphises in Kharoshthi on the reverse to Hermaeus III (1834, p. 168, nos 24–5). Because he had found coins of the third type in Buddhist stupas near Jalalabad (**Vol. I, pp. 116–20, 166–7**),

he attributed these three series to what he called the 'Nysaean princes' as he believed the Jalalabad region was the location of the city of Nysa, mentioned in the accounts of Alexander's conquests (Arrian V, 2.3). He later recognised the difference between lifetime coins of Hermaeus and the silver and copper imitations (**F526/1a, ff. 7–8, Pl. 3.54–66**).

In Masson's reports 1833–6 only the posthumous Hermaeus coins can be readily identified (**Fig. 28.6–7, 10–17**), but it is not possible to distinguish the posthumous types of Apollodotus (**Fig. 24.3–6**) and Eucratides (**Fig. 24.15–25**) from their prototypes. A sense of their relative quantities can, however, be achieved because they can be recognised in the surviving India Office Loan and the British Museum collections. There are 92 posthumous Hermaeus in the reports and 79 surviving specimens; this can be compared with 20 posthumous Apollodotus coins and 76 posthumous Eucratides. Senior's analysis of the progression of their issue suggests that Apollodotus types accompany the earlier posthumous Hermaeus and the Eucratides type the later issues (1999, p. 17). The Hermaeus coins with the Greek inscription ΣΤΗΡΟΣΣΥ will be discussed below in the context of the early Kushans.

There are two opinions on the identity of the issuers of these imitations. Dobbins, followed by Senior attributed them to the Indo-Scythians as they parallel the issues of the early Indo-Scythian kings Maues (c. 75–65 BC), Azes I (c. 46–1 BC), Azilises (c. 1 BC–16 AD), Spalirises and Spalagadama (c. 50–40 BC). Bopearachchi attributed them to the Da Yuezhi. Dobbins located the issuers in the Paropamisadae, i.e. the Begram region, and saw it as an 'orderly and centralised currency' (1970, pp. 311, 316, 320), i.e. issued by a stable authority. He identified this authority as Scythian and gave them the title 'pseudo-Hermaios Scythians' (1972, p. 31), a separate group from the Scythians under Maues who succeeded the Indo-Greeks further east (1972, p. 38), but saw them as linked, as both use the title 'king of kings' (as on the imitations of Eucratides; 1972, p. 44). Senior reached a similar conclusion identifying the issuers as a group of Scythians who moved ahead of the Da Yuezhi 'crossed through Afghanistan, crossed the Hindu Kush and settled in the Kabul valley' (2000, p. 2); 'the Scythians who were expelled from north of the Hindu Kush by the Yabghus [i.e. the Da Yuezhi] enter the Kabul valley and many settle in the territory of Hermaios … the migrating Scythians took control of the Kabul valley from the Indo-Greeks and began to strike their coinage in the name of Hermaios' (2000, p. 68). He rejected the attribution of the posthumous Hermaeus coins to the Da Yuezhi on the basis of their difference from Kushan issues (2000, p. 2). Bopearachchi (1991, p. 115) attributed them to 'invading nomads' and remarked on the difference of practice between Maues and his followers who created new designs and the imitative practice of these 'nomads' who shared it with the 'tribes north of the Hindu Kush' who copied Greek designs (1991, p. 121). His identification of these nomads as the Da Yuezhi was made more explicit in later publications (1997, p. 189), again citing the shared practice of imitating Greek prototypes, north and south of the Hindu Kush, 'Greek power in the Paropamisadae and Gandhara came to an end with the Yuezhi invasion' (1997, p. 190).

The arguments presented for the issue of these imitations by Scythians or by Da Yuezhi is thin, both based on similarity of practice. The evidence from classical sources of the 'Scythians' who overthrew the Greeks (Justin *Prologues* XLI; Strabo XI.8.2) referred specifically to the loss of Bactria and do not relate to the loss of the Begram region. Philostratus, a later source of a non-factual kind, has the king of Taxila referring to a mythical king Ganges who repulsed 'Scythians who once invaded this land across the Caucasus', but this cannot be a meaningful source, as suggested by Dobbins (1970, p. 319), of the identity of the issuers of the posthumous coins.

The Chinese history of the Han Dynasty intitially suggest that Gaofu, identified by some as the Kabul region, was under Da Yuezhi control in the 1st century BC (*Han Shu* 96A, 15B; Hulsewé and Loewe 1979, p. 122), but this was contradicted by a later source, the chronicle of the Later Han Dynasty which contradicted the earlier account and named Dumi, identified as the Termez region, as the location being referred to (*Hou Han Shu* 118, sections 13–14; Hill 2009, p. 29; Yu 2014, pp. 386–91). Grenet (2006) has suggested that the naming of Gaofu in the *Han Shu* refers not to the Kabul region, but to Termez and that therefore the writer of the *Hou Han Shu* was confusing the Kabul region with Termez, because the Chinese transcriptions of these regions' names was identical. The *Hou Han Shu* does however throw some light on the history of the Kabul region, and therefore on the rulers of Begram. It states that the way of life in Gaofu was like the way of life in India and that it had been ruled in the past by Tianzhu, Jibin and Anxi. It is generally agreed that these Chinese names identified India, the Indo-Greek kingdom and Parthians. The *Hou Han Shu* concludes its comments on Gaofu by saying it was in the hands of the Parthians before it came under Da Yuezhi rule. The easiest explanation of these statements is that the Kabul valley, i.e. Begram, was ruled by Indians (under the Mauryans), by Jibin and then by Parthians. The 'Anxi' Parthians in this context are usually understood to be the Indo-Parthians, who under Gondophares (*c.* AD 32–58, see Cribb 2018, pp. 14–17) established a kingdom based in Arachosia and Gandhara, defeating the Indo-Scythians who ruled in Gandhara in the 1st century AD. The identity of Jibin is more problema*c*. In later Chinese accounts it signifies Kashmir, but in the *Han Shu* (96A, 10B, Hulsewé and Loewe 1979, pp. 104–12) it is described as flat, whereas Kashmir is mountainous. It also says it is located south-east of the Da Yuezhi and north-east of Wu-i-shan-li, thought to represent Alexandria, meaning Kandahar. This suggests that Jibin is the Kabul valley, Begram region itself, but others suggest it is Gandhara and Taxila. The description is not clear, but in this instance it is unlikely that Kashmir is intended. The *Han Shu* also says it is under the control of the king of Sai, i.e. a Scythian king and describes it as issuing gold and silver coins with a face on one side and a horseman on the other. It is difficult to match this with known coinages, as the Indo-Scythians did not issue gold coins and did not put a face on their coins. The only coins which correspond in design are either late Indo-Greek silver coins of Hippostratus or copper coins of the early Kushans (Soter Megas type). It is possible the Chinese sources are simply confusing information from different periods, as although the chronicle covers the period 206 BC to AD 23, it was written later, by *c.* AD 120 (Hulsewé and Loewe 1979, p. 20).

The *Han Shu* also refers to two kings of Jibin, Wutoulao and Yinmofu, neither of which correspond with any of the king's names in the region known from coins. If Jibin equates with Gaofu and refers to the region where the posthumous coins were issued, then it would explain why these names are not known, but the information is not sufficiently clear. All that we can glean from this is that the Chinese thought the Kabul area was ruled for a time by Scythians, but when the first Kushan king captured the region it was under Parthian rule. There is nothing in these Chinese sources which suggests that it was ruled by the Da Yuezhi before the Indo-Parthians under Gondophares controlled the area. The Greek text, the *Periplus of the Erythraean Sea* (Casson 1989: 74–5, §38), written in the mid-1st century AD in the time of the Parthian rule of Gandhara and perhaps of the Begram region, refers to the Da Yuezhi/Kushans as warlike Bactrians under a king threatening their territory, rather than as occupants of the Paropamisadae, or Kabul region.

From this one can conclude that at the time covered by the *Periplus*, the *Han Shu* and the *Hou Han Shu*, that the Begram area had been under Scythian control and then under Indo-Parthian control until it was conquered by the Kushans. There is no evidence of Da Yuezhi rule in the region before this, so it seems more likely that the posthumous coins were issued during the period of Scythian rule as suggested by Dobbins and Senior. The posthumous coins can therefore be understood as Indo-Scythian iussues, emanating from a different polity to that ruled by Maues and his successors, but contemporary with it.

The posthumous coinage began as close copies of Hermaeus silver coins and Apollodotus I copper coins, but gradually the silver content of the imitation Hermaeus coins was reduced and alongside the more debased coins imitations of Eucratides I copper coins were introduced. No copper coins were issued alongside the last phase of the imitation Hermaeus coinage, which was so debased that they contained no silver. This last phase was followed in the Begram region by copper issues of Gondophares, struck to the same standard as the Hermaeus imitations of the last phase, copper versions of the Indo-Greek silver tetradrachm, weighing *c.* 9.6g.

Among the Eucratides imitations were two types which did not retain the designs of the prototype, but replace the Dioscuri on the reverse with images of Nike (**Fig. 24.15**; IOC.43), or of the goddess of Kapisa, the ancient city of Begram (Masson's example **F526/1a, Pl. 2.44**; **Fig. 24.16**; IOC 44.a). Masson recognised that the design was exceptional, but did not understand the meaning of it as Prinsep's decipherment had not yet sufficiently progressed to enable a clear reading. In his commentary on the coins of Masson's third report (1836b), Prinsep failed to notice this new type (1836a). The identification of the second type as an issue depicting and naming the deity of the city of Kapisa by Rapson (1905, pp. 783–6), linked with Masson's findspot for the type, enabled Kapisa to be identified as one of the ancient names of the site of Begram. Later Whitehead (1947, pp. 92–6) correctly identified the figure of the deity of

Kapisa as a Tyche in the typical Greek style. The Nike type was readily distinguished from Eucratides I's own coins by its Kharoshthi inscription which included the title 'king of kings', not used by Indo-Greek kings and first appearing on coins in this region in the Kushan period, but otherwise the posthumous coins continued the designs and inscriptions of their prototypes. The 'king of kings' title was, however, used by Indo-Scythians further east from the time of their first king Maues, and it is probably copied from them on the imitation-Eucratides coins.

The coins of the Indo-Scythians based further east are very scarce among the Begram finds. Masson was quite clear in his reports that he was of the opinion that these Indo-Scythians did not rule at Begram 'we cannot introduce the Azes coins we have found in this place, because we feel confident that the monarchs they commemorate never governed at Begram, or why should we not meet with their coins on its site?' (**F526/1a, f. 11**). In his chapter on his excavations in Wilson's *Ariana Antiqua*, Masson also stated that 'no moneys of the genuine Azes kings have been discovered at Begram' (1841, p. 73). The reason is clear to us now because these Indo-Scythian kings were contemporaries of the issuers of the posthumous coins.

There are, however, some coins of the Indo-Scythians associated with Azes among the Begram finds. In his reports Masson described coins of Maues (x 1), Azilises (x 1), Spalagadama (x 2) and Spalirises (x 3). The denominations of these coins are similar to the posthumous Apollodotus and Eucratides, so one can imagine that they entered circulation at Begram from the neighbouring Indo-Scythian kingdom as compatible currency. In the India Office Loan Collection there are further examples (**Fig. 29.1–6, 10**), together with similar coins of Azes I (**Fig. 29.7–8**), some acquired in Kabul (1836a, p. 25, nos 22 [Spalirises] and 25 [Azes I]). In this collection, there are also a considerable number of Azes II coins (**Fig. 29.9**; **Fig. 30.1–6, 18–30**), but it seems likely that Masson acquired them elsewhere as they are of the types that were current in Taxila, Swat and Gandhara (see above p. 97) and such coins did not appear in his reports of 1833–6.

There are, however, coins bearing the name of Azes which do appear among the Begram finds (**Fig. 30.7–17, 24**; **F526/1a, f. 13**). In Masson's reports 48 examples copying drachms of Azes from further east are mentioned. Although inscribed with the name of Azes in Greek and Kharoshthi, these are imitations of the Kushan period, linked with the set of posthumous imitations with the Greek inscription ΣΤΗΡΟΣΣΥ, so will be discussed below. Another imitation, a copper coin in the name of Azes (**Fig. 30.23**), is from a different set of imitations and of unknown origin. Like the other Indo-Scythian period coins collected from Begram, it was probably allowed into circulation as compatible currency. Masson's awareness that these were not issues of Azes, but posthumous, is illustrated by his comments on the coins of Mujatria inscribed with the name of Azes which he found during his excavations near Jalalabad (**Vol. I, pp. 88, 103–5, 117–20, 167–8**). He confirmed their posthumous nature: 'they relate to an independent Greek dynasty, of which Azes was the founder and whose name was borne or assumed by his descendants' (**F526/1a, f. 11**).

One copper coin of Mujatria (*c.* AD 60–80), one of the satraps who continued to name Azes II in their coin inscriptions and use his coin designs, was found during the French excavations at Begram (Ghirshman 1946, p. 97, pl. XXII, no. 12). Masson had 11 examples of his coins too, but there is no evidence that any examples were found by him at Begram. He excavated all his examples of Mujatria's base silver coins (**Fig. 31.2–3**), and also copper coins, comparable with Ghirshman's example, from the Darunta stupa relic deposits (see **Vol. I, pp. 97, 103–4, 118, 120, 122, Fig. 142.2-5** and **F526/1a, f. 19, Pl. 7.160**). A coin of Mujatria's father Kharahostes in Masson's collection (**Fig. 31.1**) probably came from the Hadda stupa 3 relic deposit (**Vol. I, p. 167, Fig. 251.25**). Two other issuers of Indo-Scythian style coins in the style of Azes II, Zeionises (*c.* AD 30–50; IOLC.891–893; **Fig. 31.4**) and Aspavarma (*c.* AD 33–64; IOLC.894–896; **Fig. 31.5–6**) are also represented in Masson's collection, but probably collected at Peshawar, not Begram.

A copper coin imitating an issue of the later Indo-Greek king Apollodotus II in Masson's collection has now been identified as a Scythian issue, in the name of Kshaharata Satraps called Higataka and Higaksha (Senior 2006, pp. 23–24; Falk 2016; *Higaksha* is my correction of Falk's reading *Higaraka*). The location of the issuers of this coinage is unknown, but relates to the later Kshaharata satraps Abhiraka, Bhumaka and Nahapana in north-western India. It is possible that Masson acquired it from Begram or at Kabul as he illustrated a crude version of this type with the same reverse monograms, and said of it 'The circular coins at *Fig. 8* are of rare occurrence in Afghanistan' (**F526/1a, f. 1, Pl. 1.8**).

Indo-Parthian and Parthian coins (Fig. 32.1–30; Fig. 33.1–8)

The Begram finds which followed the posthumous coinages in the names of Hermaeus, Apollodotus I and Eucratides I are issues of the Indo-Parthian king Gondophares (**Fig. 32.8–15**; **F526.1a, Pl. 4.92–8: 95–6** are repeats from his earlier report 1834, pl. X, figs 34–5). The denomination of these coins matched that of the posthumous Hermaeus coins current before the territory was invaded by Gondophares (*c.* AD 32–58). Masson collected 55 examples according to his report of 1833–5 and linked him with the Parthian king Phraōtes reported by Philostratus as the 'Indian' king of Taxila *c.* AD 50 (*Life of Apollonius of Tyana*, II.26; Conybeare 1912, p. 185; **F526/1a, f. 10**). There are also two contemporary copies of this coinage (**Fig. 32.19–20**). The other coins of Gondophares in his report (**F526/1a, f. 19, Pl. 7.159**, 'picked up at Kabul or Ghazni', **F526/1a, f. 18**) and in the surviving collection (**Fig. 32.1–7**) do not appear to have been collected from Begram, as they are not a type represented among the coins reported from Begram. They may, however have been issued there as their denomination seems to represent a continuation of that of the imitation Eucratides coins issued during the imitation Hermaeus coinage of Begram.

The large number of these coins suggests that Gondophares ruled at the site. Among the surviving coins in the India Office Loan Collection there is also a coin of Gondophares' successor Abdagases (**Fig. 32.21**; IOLC.994), but it is not clear whether Abdagases (*c*. AD 52–64) also ruled at Begram. He issued coins with the same types as Gondophares, but in a different style, so they may have been minted further east, perhaps at Ghazni.

The surviving Masson collection also includes base silver coins of Abdagases (**Fig. 32.22**; IOLC.968) and Sasan (*c*. AD 64–70; **Fig. 32.27–30**; IOC.235; IOLC.969, 971, 974–993), illegible Abdagases or Sasan (**Fig. 32.23–4**; IOLC.967, 970), but these were probably acquired by Masson at Peshawar or Kabul, as there is no mention of them in his reports. If any were used at Begram, then it would be because they were mistakenly included in a batch of Soter Megas coins of the early Kushan period. In his third report Masson illustrates two Sasan or Abdagases coins, but is unclear about where he got them: 'these coins are casual ones from Begram and the bazaar of Kabul' (**F526/1a, f. 13, Pl. 5**, *Figs 105–6*). Three small copper coins of the series issued by Indo-Parthian kings in the eastern Punjab are also in Masson's collection (**Fig. 32.16–18**; IOLC.963–965). Like the Abdagases and Sasan coins these were probably acquired elsewhere.

Masson's collection contains several copper drachms of a local Parthian ruler Sanabares (*c*. mid 1st century AD; **Fig. 33.2–8**) and a copper imitation of a silver drachm of the Parthian king Phraataces/Phraates V (2 BC–AD 4; **Fig. 33.1**). Wilson said that these were acquired from Begram, but Masson makes it clear that they were not: 'Fig. 17 is never found at Begram – a parcel of some hundreds of these coins was picked up in the bazaar of Kabul, probably brought from Turkestan – they were all copper – this type may perhaps be genuine Arsakian' (**F526/1a, f. 25, Pl. 11.17**). Ghirshman also discussed a group of related coins (Senior 2001, type 200) in his report on Begram (1946, pp. 95–6, pl. XXII.1–5), attributing them to Kujula Kadphises on the basis of a misreading of the inscriptions. However the examples he discussed were not from Begram, but part of the Kabul Museum collection. In the French excavations a countermarked imitation of a Parthian silver drachm (*cf.* Senior 2001, type 199.1), similar to the copper example in Masson's collection, was found, but Ghirshman misattributed it to Spalirises, also on the basis of misreading the inscriptions (1946, pp. 88–93, pl. XXII.7). These imitations and the Sanabares coins based on them are not from the Begram region, but from somewhere on the eastern boundaries of Arsacid Iran, as yet undetermined by finds.

Early Kushan coins – Kujula Kadphises to Wima Kadphises (Fig. 28.8–9, 20; Fig. 30.7–17, 24; Fig. 33.9–10; Figs 34–8)

The largest group of coins Masson collected from Begram consists of the issues of the early Kushan period. These finds largely comprised two types, the Heracles-type imitation Hermaeus coinage of Kujula Kadphises (**Figs 34–5**; about 590 reported by Masson) and the Soter Megas coinage (**Figs 36–7**; about 690 reported by Masson) begun at the end of Kujula Kadphises' reign (*c*. AD 50–90) and continuing through that of his son Wima Takto (*c*. AD 90–113). The quantity and diversity of these finds suggest that Begram was the centre of their issue (Cribb 2014), and one of the most important centres of the Kushan empire south of the Hindu Kush. When the Kushans also captured the Taxila region under Kujula Kadphises, the Hermaeus imitation series was exported there in large numbers and circulated there too (Gul Rahim Khan and Cribb 2012). Later a separate Taxila production of the type was begun and some examples of it flowed back to the Jalalabad region and possibly as far as Begram (e.g. **Fig. 34.18–19**). The Soter Megas coinage, however, seems to have only been produced at Begram, as examples of all the varieties found at Begram are found throughout Kushan territory. The Soter Megas coinage exports to Taxila were much smaller in volume than the earlier Heracles type coins, and all examples come from late in the issue, as it seems likely that Taxila was lost to the Indo-Parthians late in the reign of Kujula Kadphises and only regained after Wima Takto had reasserted Kushan control and driven the Indo-Parthians out of Gandhara (Cribb 2014; Gul Rahim Khan 2014).

Masson curiously attributed the issue of these coins to the region of Jalalabad because examples were found in Buddhist monuments in Darunta to the west of that city (**Vol. I, pp. 96–7, 112–14**). His attribution overlooked what he was finding at Begram and was based instead on his belief that the Buddhist stupas at Darunta were royal tombs, whose occupants were identified as the issuers of the coins found in them (see Masson's own comments Appendix 1, p. 310 below).

A few other coins of these rulers with different types are in the Masson collection. Some may have been acquired elsewhere than Begram, but a few are Begram finds. Masson listed three examples of a rare type of Kujula Kadphises, showing a helmeted head on the obverse and a standing spearman on the reverse (**Fig. 34.1**), in his 1835 report (**F526/1a, f. 17, Pl. 7.144–6**), where he described them as 'occurring sparingly at Begram, one, two or three during each season'. An example was also found in the excavations by Ghirshman (1946, p. 97, pl. XXII, no. 8), suggesting that this type was issued at Begram or nearby, but two examples were also found in the territory north of Taxila (Smith 1898, pp. 133–4), so such an attribution cannot be certain. There is no reason to think that the Masson coins of the bull-camel type of Kujula Kadphises, issued in Kashmir (**Fig. 34.2–4**), were found at Begram, as they are not mentioned in his reports. However, the Taxila issue with Roman designs (**Fig. 34.5**) is specifically mentioned by Masson in his 1835 report as not being found at Begram: 'It is very singular, that no one of this prince's coins has fallen into our hands, although I remark that they have been found at Kabul' (**F526/1a, f. 13**). So it is likely his examples were acquired in the Kabul bazaar or elsewhere. A single silver coin of the 'Heraus' type (**F526/1a, f. 17, Pl. 7.147**) was acquired at Charikar, 11km from Begram.

Among the Soter Megas coins in Masson's collection there are several local issues. In his reports he mentions 33 examples of one series, based on the copper imitation Heliocles imitations (**Fig. 36.32–6; F526/1a, f. 8, Pl. 4.67–75**), which is represented by 49 examples in the India Office Loan Collection and two in the British Museum. These coins appear to have been issued for circulation north of the Hindu Kush, so were probably brought into Begram during Kujula Kadphises' reign through the movement of troops or people following the Kushan conquest. All these coins have the later horse reverse design, except one of the pieces reported by Masson (**F526/1a, Pl. 4.75**) which has a standing Zeus reverse, so is an earlier issue of this series. The imitation Heliocles series seems to have been followed by issues of Wima Takto showing a helmeted bust on the obverse and Masson reported an example of this type from Begram (**F526/1a, f. 8, Pl. 5.99**). An example in the British Museum (**Fig. 37.1**; IOC.247) is from Masson's collection. There are also a few examples of the Gandharan Soter Megas base-silver issues of Wima Takto (**F526/1a, f. 11; Pl. 5.104, 107, 109–10**) which Masson says are from Begram or acquired in Kabul. Six survive in Masson's collection (**Fig. 37.31–3**; IOLC.1566–1568). Likewise Wima Takto's Gandhara copper issue is also represented in Masson's collection by five examples (**Fig. 37.29–30**; IOLC.1571–1575), with one example from Begram illustrated in his third report (**F526/1a, f. 13, Pl. 5.110**). Five Kashmir bull-camel type coins of Wima Takto (**Fig. 37.34–5**, IOLC.1576–1580) are also present in his collection, but there is no evidence of their being Begram finds.

During the early Kushan period there also circulated two series of imitation coins which do not make direct reference to the Kushan authorities, but have features in common with Kushan coins. They share control marks and stylistic features in their Kharoshthi inscriptions. One series (**Fig. 28.8–9**) imitated the Hermaeus imitation coins of Kujula Kadphises, repeating its blundered Greek inscription ΒΑΣΙΛΕΩΣ ΣΤΗΡΟΣΣΥ ΕΡΜΑΙΟΥ, but retaining the enthroned Zeus reverse of the earlier imitation Hermaeus coins. Masson reported 28 examples from Begram (**F526/1a, f. 7, Pl. 3.62–5**) and the surviving collection has 26. Masson attributed them to a king he called 'Ermaios the Younger', to distinguish them from the pre-Indo-Parthian Hermaeus imitations which he attributed to 'Ermaios the Elder'. A related coin type with the same obverse inscription, but a Nike, winged victory, reverse is common at Taxila, having two different reverse inscriptions, naming Hermaeus on some and Azes on others (Cribb and Bracey at press, type A. C7A-iv), but there are no recorded examples from Begram. One example of the Azes reverse variety was in Masson's collection (**Fig. 28.20**) and later came to the British Museum via Sir Alexander Cunningham's collection. The other series of imitations are drachms based on late or posthumous Azes II coins. Their control marks and the style of their Kharoshthi inscriptions link them with the above Hermaeus imitations, and they share with the Soter Megas coinage the representation of the king on horseback holding a pickaxe in place of the whip held on Azes II coins (**F526/1a, f. 11, Pl. 5.108**). There are 48 examples reported by Masson from Begram and 46 examples survive from Masson's collection (**Fig. 30.7–17**). Masson linked them with the Soter Megas coins and thought all were issued by successors of Azes: 'Our theory, with respect to these coins, is, that they relate to an independent Greek dynasty, of which Azes was the founder and whose name was borne or assumed by his descendants' (**F526/1a, f. 11**). Although his ideas about attribution were unrealistic, his understanding of the sequence of coinage showed great perspicacity. The Masson collection also contains a single imitation Azes copper coin (**Fig. 30.24**) issued as a lower denomination of the base-silver drachms,

but it is unlikely that this was from Begram. These series of imitation Hermaeus and imitation Azes coins all appear to have been made at a single mint, perhaps not under Kushan administrative control, but producing coins to be current in the Kushan realm, from Begram to Taxila. Finds suggest this mint may have been located at Akra in Bannu district (Cribb 2002).

Among Kujula Kadphises's Heracles type coins, both at Begram and Taxila, there are many unofficial underweight contemporary copies. At Taxila the locally made official issues appear to have been reduced in weight to match the dropping weight of the currency caused by the unofficial copies. The latter fell in weight to about 3g, so the authorities replaced the Heracles type with a new issue weighing 3.5g and featuring Roman coin designs (Cribb and Bracey at press, type A.C4-i; as Fig. 14, no. 5). Although these circulated at Taxila they also had in turn to be replaced by a smaller version (type A.C4-ii), because unofficial copies of them also began to circulate. Alongside the official currency and the imitations another coinage was also current, the above mentioned imitation Hermaeus with Nike reverse. At the same time the local people cut official and unofficial coins in half or quarters to create units to match the falling weight standard of the official coins and their imitations (Gul Rahim Khan in preparation). At Begram the surviving coinage, as illustrated by Masson's collection, also shows a falling weight standard, with the official copies dropping as much as below 1g. The issue of two versions of the Heracles type with two different obverse inscriptions ΒΑΣΙΛΕΩΣ ΣΤΗΡΟΣΣΥ ΕΡΜΑΙΟΥ and ΚΟΖΟΥΛΟ ΚΑΔΦΙΖΟΥ ΚΟΡΣΝΑΟΥ might reflect an attempt to restabilise the weight standard by issuing new coins at the full standard. Stabilisation was not achieved until a new coinage, which effectively replaced the underweight Heracles type coinage, was introduced towards the end of Kujula Kadphises' reign. This was the Soter Megas coinage which was initially issued in two denominations, *c.* 8.5g and 2.1g. The lower denomination seems to have been designed to substitute for the light unofficial copies of the Heracles type and the higher denomination to reinstate a larger denomination in place of the full-weight Heracles types. This reform was successful and continued into the reign of Wima Takto and by the end of his reign the lower denomination was no longer being issued as the higher denomination sufficed. The success of the Soter Megas coinage also meant that when Taxila came back under Kushan control it became the only currency in use there. Although local varieties were issued for use in territory, Gandhara and Mathura, conquered by Wima Takto, and as an initial substitute for the imitation Heliocles coins current in Bactria, the Begram issues of Soter Megas coins spread to all parts of the empire and was the basis of the new coins issued in the reign of Wima Takto's son Wima Kadphises.

The coins of Wima Kadphises (*c.* AD 113–27) collected by Masson at Begram during 1833–5 number 99, all are copper. An even larger number – 190 – are in the surviving collection (**Fig. 38.4–23**). These copper coins were clearly current in the city and Masson's acquisition of a single silver trial of a copper coin type of this reign at Charikar (**Fig. 38.3**), about 11km from Begram suggests that the mint producing them was located in the city. The discovery of the trial coin suggests that the success of the Soter Megas coinage made Begram the main copper mint of the Kushans, a position it retained until the territory was lost to the Kushano-Sasanians. Like the Soter Megas coins, the Wima Kadphises copper coins found at Begram are the same as those found throughout the Kushan empire.

Two Masson collection silver coins (**Fig. 33.9–10**) from the early Kushan period issued in western Bactria are in the British Museum (IOC.253, 254). These coins were mentioned by Wilson (1841, pp. 352–3, n. 1, Coins pl. XXI.18) as having been included in the 'last dispatch' (i.e. sent in December 1836). They are issues of a local ruler Sapalbizes, thought to have been located in western Bactria in the 1st century AD (Rtveladze 1993/4, p. 83). There is no indication where Masson acquired them, but it is most likely they were bought in Kabul bazaar.

Kushan coins – Kanishka I to the end of the Kushan Dynasty (Figs 39–50)

Kushan copper coins from the reign of Kanishka I (c. AD 127–51) until that of Kanishka II (c. AD 230–46) are represented in large numbers among the Begram finds, both as reported by Masson and in his surviving collection. The majority of these are issues from the main Kushan copper mint at Begram and are therefore the main form of currency in the city.

Kanishka I (**Figs 39–41**) is represented in the surviving collection by 203 coins from the main mint, units of c. 16.5g (**Fig. 39. 11–23**; **Fig. 40.1–14**) and halves of c. 8.25g (**Fig. 39.7–10**; **Fig. 40.15–25**); there are also 162 quarter (**Fig. 41.1–16, 20**) and eighth units (**Fig. 41.21–5**), weighing c. 4.1g and 2g from his Kashmir mint (i.e. about 44% are from Kashmir). The number of surviving Kashmir mint coins is much higher than expected from the proportions in the reports which show 148 main mint coins compared with just 19 of the Kashmir mint coins, i.e. 11.4% of the coins are from Kashmir (a percentage lowered to c. 5% in terms of value by weight), so it is possible that some of the surviving Kashmir mint coins were not collected from Begram. There are also three quarter units from the main mint, all featuring the Buddha on the reverse (**Fig. 41.17–19**). The coins of both the Begram and the Kashmir mints were on the same standard, so could circulate anywhere in the empire, but from finds north of the Hindu Kush it is clear that Kashmir coins did not circulate there, and that nearer to Kashmir the proportion increased, as at Taxila (Gul Rahim Khan 2007).

Most of the copper coins of Huvishka (c. AD 151–90) in both the collection and the reports are issues of the main mint at Begram (**Figs 42–3**; **Fig. 44.1–6**). A few coins from his other mints are also present: 18 from the Gandhara mint (**Fig. 44.7–16**), two from Kashmir (**Fig. 44.17–18**) and three from Mathura (**Fig. 44.19–20**). Under Kanishka I the coins of the different mints were on the same standard so could circulate elsewhere in the empire, but diminished in quantity the further they were from their mint of issue. During the reign of Huvishka there was a monetary crisis of some kind (Cribb and Bracey at press), which resulted first in an outburst of unofficial copies (**Fig. 45**), then a reduction in the official weight standard (**Fig. 43.11–21**) and in the range of designs (**Fig. 44.1–6**). This is reflected in the Begram finds which include many unofficial copies. Masson's reports did not make the distinction (two are illustrated in the 1835 report (**F526/1a, Pl. 9.37** and **Pl. 10.50**), but in the surviving collection 43% of the coins are unofficial copies.

Copper coins (**Fig. 46.4–20**) of Vasudeva I (c. AD 190–230) are present among the finds in similar quantity to those of the previous two kings, but far exceed them in quantity in Masson's reports because he was unaware that there were many later coins with the same designs. Some of these later coins are issues of Vasishka, but the majority are a Kushano-Sasanian imitative series (**Fig. 46.21–8**) combining the reverse of Vasudeva I with the obverse of his successor Kanishka II. Masson also included a Kushano-Sasanian coin of Peroz I among the Vasudeva I coins in his 1835 report (**F526/1a, Pl. 10.60**; cf. **Fig. 51.7–8**). In the surviving collection there is some indication of the ratios in which Masson was collecting Vasudeva I and related coins: Vasudeva I official issues 272, Vasishka official issues 42 and Kushano-Sasanian imitations 156. Vasudeva I's official coins were being issued at the main Kushan mint, so were local to Begram, but the coins of Vasishka (c. AD 246–67) seem to have been issued east of the Khyber Pass (Cribb et al. 2012), so fewer of them would be expected at Begram. It is not clear where the imitations were being issued, but they relate closely to the gold issues of imitation Vasudeva coins being issued by the Kushano-Sasanians in Bactria (**Fig. 50.1–3**). Although the bulk of them were issued in the early Kushano-Sasanian series they continued to circulate until the end of the Kushano-Sasanian period in the 4th century, as well as prompting a lot of unofficial copies. Their presence in quantity at Begram is therefore not surprising.

Copper coins (**Fig. 47**) of Kanishka II (c. AD 230–46) seem to have been the last to have been issued at the main Kushan copper mint at Begram before the city was captured by the Kushano-Sasanian king Peroz I (c. AD 245–70). The 271 examples reported by Masson (1834, pl. XIII, no. 23; **F526/1a, Pl. 10.61–3**) would also have included imitations. In the collection, imitations (**Fig. 47.18–22**) represent about 28% of the Kanishka II coins in the surviving collection, so there probably was a similar proportion among the reported coins (one imitation is featured in his 1835 report: **F526/1a, Pl. 10.66**).

Although missing from his reports it is possible that Masson acquired some copper coins of Vasishka, as there are 42 examples in his surviving collection (**Fig. 48.2–10**). Vasishka is unlikely to have issued coins in Begram as the city came under Kushano-Sasanian rule late in the reign of Kanishka II. They circulated in Gandhara and Taxila alongside Kushano-Sasanian imitation Vasudeva coins, so could easily have circulated with them across the Khyber Pass to Begram, as they are so similar and were struck on the same weight standard, c. 6–5g. Two coins of Vasishka's son Kanishka III (c. AD 267–72) are also in Masson's collection (**Fig. 49**), and three were illustrated in his 1835 report (**F526/1a, Pl. 10.64–5, 67**). Masson says of these (**F526/1a, f. 23**) that they are the types 'prevalent on the banks of the Indus and in the Punjab' and includes with them a copper coin of the 9th century Kashmir king Avantivarman (**F526/1a, Pl. 10.68**), which he says 'was acquired in

		approx. AD	F526/1a nos	F526/1a Plates	IOLC & BM	Plates
Kushano-Sasanian	Ardashir I, Bactria	c. 230–5				
	Ardashir II, Bactria	c. 235–45			1	Fig. 51.4
	Peroz I, Bactria	c. 245–70	1	Pl. 10, *Fig. 60*	5	Fig. 51.6–7
	Peroz I, Begram/Gandhara		5	Pl. 11, *Figs 8–11*	23	Fig. 51.8–12
	Hormizd I, Bactria	c. 270–300			3	Fig. 51.11–13
	Hormizd I, Begram/Gandhara		7	Pl. 11, *Figs 1–7*	81	Fig. 51.14–18
	Hormizd II, Bactria	c. 300–3				
	Hormizd II, Begram/Gandhara				1	Fig. 51.19–20
	Peroz II, Bactria	c. 303–30				
	Peroz II, Begram/Gandhara		2	Pl. 10, *Figs 15–16*	30	Fig. 51.21–3
Sasanian	Shapur II, Begram/Gandhara	c. 309–79	3	Pl. 11, *Figs 12–14*	55	Fig. 51.24–8
illegible	Begram/Gandhara				29	
Kushano-Sasanian	Varhran, Bactria	c. 330–59			3	Fig. 51.29–30
Kidarite	Varhran, Bactria (Kirada)	c. 345–50				
	Varhran, Bactria (Peroz)	c. 350–55			7	Fig. 52.14–15
	Varhran, Bactria (Kidara)	c. 355–85			35	Fig. 52.8–13

Table 16 Kushano-Sasanian and Kushano-Sasanian style Kidarite Hun copper coins from Begram

Peshawar' (**F526/1a, f. 23**). So it is not clear whether the examples in the report and the collection were collected at Begram or east of the Khyber Pass where they circulated. The same can be said for the three copper coins of the late Kushan kings Shaka (c. AD 302–42) and Kipunadha (c. AD 342–52) in the collection (**Fig. 50**). There are no coins of the Kushan emperor Vasudeva II (c. AD 272–97) in Masson's reports and surviving collection, even though they are relatively common to the east of the Khyber Pass.

The continual currency of Kushan coins from the conquest of the city by the first Kushan emperor Kujula Kadphises until its loss late in the reign of the seventh Kushan emperor Kanishka II shows the importance of the city within the Kushan state throughout that period, reflecting its location midway between its territories north and south of the Hindu Kush.

Kushano-Sasanian and Kidarite coins (Fig. 51; Fig. 52.1–16)

A large number of coins now attributed to the Kushano-Sasanian kings, i.e. the Sasanian rulers who adopted the title Kushanshah, were found by Masson at Begram (see **Table 16**): 'From the numbers in which these coins occur at Begram, it may be inferred that they were once current there, and consequently that the sovereigns commemorated by them once ruled over it' (**F526/1a, f. 24, Pl. 11.1–16**). The pieces illustrated by Masson from the 439 examples he reported show coins of the Kushano-Sasanian rulers Peroz I (5), Hormizd I (7) and Peroz II (2). There are also three coins of the Sasanian king Shapur II (AD 309–79) who took over the Kushano-Sasanian territory south of the Hindu Kush and issued Kushano-Sasanian style coins there. One of the coins of Shapur II (**Pl. 11.14**) is exceptional as it has his name in Pahlavi instead of the usual Bactrian inscription (Cribb and Bracey at press). The surviving collection also shows an extensive range of Kushano-Sasanian copper types, with a few examples from the series issued in Bactria (**Fig. 51.4, 6–7, 13–15, 29–30**), but the bulk of the coins are from the series issued south of the Hindu Kush for circulation in the Begram region and Gandhara (**Fig. 51.8–12**). The Kushano-Sasanian conquest of Begram took place in the reign of the third king, Peroz I, and he issued coins weighing about 4g for the region. These were continued by his successors until the region was brought under direct Sasanian control by emperor Shapur II, who also issued coins on the standard initiated by Peroz I. The coins issued north of the Hindu Kush had different designs and were issued on a lighter standard, mostly c. 2g, and one of these was illustrated by Masson as found at Begram, but others in the surviving collection probably also come from the site.

The cause of Shapur II's intervention into the southern Kushano-Sasanian state seems to have been the rise of a Hun kingdom, which took control of Bactria and Gandhara. In Gandhara and the northern Punjab these Huns put an end to both Kushano-Sasanian and Kushan rule. In Bactria they seem to have taken control in the name of Varhran the ruler who seems to have been the last Kushano-Sasanian ruler there. There is no evidence of Varhran ruling in Begram or anywhere south of the Hindu Kush, so it is possible that the Hun takeover happened as his reign began. After their first issue the Bactrian gold coins issued in Varhran's name north of the Hindu Kush began to have a tamgha associated with the Huns (it also appeared on one of the Hun issues in Gandhara, **Fig. 52.16**). The copper coins (**Fig. 52.8–15**) associated with the Hun gold coins from Bactria (**Fig. 52.1**) are well represented in Masson's surviving collection, so are also likely to have been found at Begram. The bulk of them are from the last phase of Kushano-Sasanian style Bactrian copper coinage, corresponding with the reign of the Hun king Kidara, after whom this group of Huns came to be named as the Kidarite Huns. It seems likely that the presence of these coins in Masson's surviving collection represents his takeover of the Begram region in the 380s (Nasim Khan *et al.* 2008, pp. 69–71; Cribb and Bracey at press).

Apart from the Bactrian Kushano-Sasanian style coins of the Kidarite Huns there are also some of their Gandharan issues in Masson's surviving collection. There are 14 examples of one Gandharan series which look like late Kushan coins (**Fig. 52.4–7**), having the same designs as introduced by Kanishka II, but smaller and weighing less than 1.5g. Kidarite copper coins were issued in large numbers in Gandhara (Nasim Khan *et al.* 2008; Vondrovec 2014), but only two other Gandharan types are present in the surviving collection, one with their tamgha (**Fig. 52.16**) and the other in the name of a local ruler *mahadhama* (Vondrovec 2014, type GC-G70). The evidence for the Kidarites among the coins in Masson's collection shows that if they were ever present at the site it was as the result of movement from their bases in Bactria and Gandhara into Begram during a brief invasion in the time of Kidara or soon after. The Tepe Marajan hoard, which contains Bactrian gold coins of Kidara and his Kidarite successor Orōlano along with Sasanian coins of Shapur II (AD 309–79), Ardashir II (AD 379–83) and Shapur III (AD 383–88), suggests that the Kidarite intervention took place just before AD 388 (Cribb 2018, pp. 23–25). There is no evidence of Kidarite coin issue at Begram, which is also reflected in the appearance of Alkhan coinage in the region in the period immediately after the Kidarite intervention, i.e. from *c.* AD 388, or later.

There is no evidence in Masson's surviving collection or reports of the later part of the Sasanian occupation of Begram from the end of the reign of Shapur II in AD 379 until that of Shapur III in AD 388, apart from the Kushano-Sasanian style issues of Shapur II. A handful of early Sasanian coins were in a part of Masson's collection passed to the British Museum by the East India Company in 1845 (**Fig. 54.1–16**). These include silver coins of Shapur, son of Papak, Narseh, Hormizd II, Shapur II and III, Varhran IV and V, Yazdagird I and II and Khusrau I, and a gold coin of Peroz. In the same 1845 EIC donation are many late Sasanian coins, part of a hoard of Sasanian and Arab-Sasanian coins (see below). Masson remarks that these silver coins were 'so plentiful in the bazaar of Kabul, … there can be little doubt of their being importations, probably from Turkestan' and that 'very large parcels of Sasanian silver coins have been discovered by chance in various parts of Afghanistan' (**F526/1a, f. 25**, p. 64 above). Masson also obtained *c.* 200 Sasanian and 16 Alkhan Hun coins from his excavation of Tope Kelan (Hadda stupa 10: **Vol. I, pp. 174–91**), of which 100 are recorded in 1881 as having been included in the India Museum transfer to the British Museum (**BM-Asia 18-2-1881a**, no. 8, see **Vol. II, p. 113** and **Pls 14–15** above, pp. 65–6).

Alkhan Hun, Nezak and Turkic coins (Fig. 52.17–43; Fig. 53)

Masson's reporting for this period is sporadic, largely because he was encountering coins which had not been seen before, so he was less clear about how to list them (see **Table 17**). It is therefore difficult to be certain about their significance in relation to the history of the city of Begram. In his 1835 report he illustrated coins of this period from the site: three attributable to the Huns known in modern scholarship as the Alkhan or Alkhano (**Fig. 52.17–43; Fig. 53.1–3**) and three of the Shri Shahi series (**Fig. 53.8–23**) which is linked by tamgha to the earlier Alkhan coins and by

Coin types	F526/1a from Begram	F526/1a not from Begram/not specified	IOLC and BM	illustrations
Tobazino tamgha bust of Shapur II Ae			3	Fig. 52
Tobazino tamgha bust of Shapur II Ar			1	Fig. 52
Alkhan bust of Shapur II Ar		Pl. 12, Fig. 24*		
Alkhan bust of Shapur II Ae			6	Fig. 52
Alkhan silver Hun bust Ar		Pl. 12, Figs 21–3*		Fig. 52
Alkhan Hun bust Ae	Pl. 11, Figs 18–19		12	Fig. 52
Alkhan Hun bust Toramana Ae			4	Fig. 52
Alkhan: Narendra Ae	Pl. 12, Fig. 37		8	Fig. 53
Nezak Ar		Pl. 13, Figs 44, 46–7	1	Fig. 53
Shri Shahi Ar			4	
Shri Shahi Ae Pahlavi	Pl. 13, Fig. 50		20	Fig. 53
Shri Shahi Ae Pahlavi fish	Pl. 13, Fig. 49		2	Fig. 53
Shri Shahi Ae Pahlavi branch			5	Fig. 53
Shri Shahi Ae Bactrian			8	Fig. 53
Shri Shahi Ae Brahmi			8	Fig. 53
Shri Shahi Ae staff			14	Fig. 53
Shri Shahi Ae conch/tamgha	Pl. 13, Fig. 51			Fig. 53
Shri Shahi Ae illegible			5	Fig. 53
Turkic Nezak Ae		Pl. 11, Fig. 20		Fig. 53
Turkic Ae			10	Fig. 53
Turkic Ar			6	Fig. 54.1–5, 7
illegible Ae			7	

Table 17 Alkhan Hun and Turkic coins from Begram. * Similar additional pieces were found in the relic deposit of Hadda stupa 10 and are illustrated separately. (F526/1a, Pl. 14.15–16; see also Masson 1836a, p. 28, pl. III.1–6; Vol. I, p. 188, Fig. 282)

the inscription to the Nezak series (**Fig. 53.4–7**). Of the Alkhan coins he said: 'Fig. 18 and Fig. 19 are single specimens from Begram, and curious from the characters and symbols on the reverses' and 'Begram, where we have indeed found two or three coppers similar to Fig. 21, 22 and 23 [i.e. the silver Alkhan coins], and one or two from which we have designated Fig. 37' (**F526/1a, f. 24, Pl. 11.18–19, Pl. 12.21–3, 37**). Wilson illustrated two more Alkhan coppers from Masson's collection, which he claimed were from Begram (**Fig. 52.21, 36**; 1841, p. 403, nos 43–4, Coins pl. XVII.20–1). The surviving collection has 33 coins attributable to the Alkhan Huns covering the period from their first issues with the bust of Shapur II (309–379), issued from *c.* AD 390 (**Fig. 52.26**) to the issues inscribed *śrī ṣāhi tora* (Pfisterer 2013, pp. 188, 307; **Fig. 53.1–3**) or a blundered version of the same, which seem to date to the reign of Toramana II in the second half of the 6th century.

The *śrī ṣāhi tora* issues are thought to be contemporary (Vondrovec 2014, pp. 199–202, 459, 485; Alram 1996) with coins with the Pahlavi inscription *nycky MLKA* ('king Nezak'), examples of which were in Masson's collection (**Fig. 53.4–6**; Wilson 1841, p. 403, no. 36, Coins pl. XVII.5, 7), but which he did not report from Begram. The Nezak coinage has been dated from *c.* AD 500 (Vondrovec 2014, pp. 449, 453–4), because it copies issues of the Sasanian emperor Peroz (AD 457, 459–84), but it is more likely to have been initiated later, based on the Hephthalite copies of Peroz's coinage (Vondrovec 2014, pp. 399–406) which continued into the mid-6th century. The later dating of the Nezak coinage also explains why its design was still in use in the late 7th century when it was copied by Turkic rulers (Vondrovec 2014, pp. 598–612, 628–36).

Of the Shri Shahi coins Masson said: 'a class of coins, which we call Indo-Sasanian, from the strongly marked Indian countenances of the busts, and from the great probability that the princes ruled in these countries; their copper monies plentifully occurring at Begram' (**F526/1a, f. 25**). Wilson illustrated one silver and two copper Shri Shahi coin from Masson's collection 'found at Begram' (**Fig. 53.14–15, 23**; 1841, p. 403, no. 36, Coins pl. XVII.10–11, 18). The Shri Shahi coinage is closely related to the Nezak coinage and on some issues retains the Pahlavi inscription *nycky MLKA*, or a corrupted version of the same.

The first Alkhan Hun coins (**Fig. 52.24–6**) copy issues of the Sasanian kings Shapur II and Shapur III (Vondrovec 2014, p. 170). The coins copied are thought to be Sasanian issues from the Kabul mint, so it is likely that the Alkhan centre was Kabul rather than Begram, beginning *c.* 390. Among the silver coins of the first phase, when Alkhan Hun coins copied Sasanian prototypes, one of the issues (**Fig. 52.26**) has a tamgha (Vondrovec 2014, p. 170, type 33), which appears on both the Bactrian issues (Cribb 2018, p. 25) and the Sasanian-style issues (Vondrovec 2014, pp. 392–6) of Kidarite king Tobazino. Two of the Hun coppers in Masson's collection have the same tamgha (with Shapur II's bust) linking them with the silver Alkhan coins and the issues of the Kidarite king Tobazino, *c.* AD 420 (Cribb 2018, pp. 23–5). The other varieties of early Alkhan silver have the tamgha which appears on later Alkhan coins. These connections suggest an initial close relationship between the Kidarite and Alkhan Huns, the nature of which is not yet understood. The use of different tamghas suggests that there may have been different Hun families or clans involved, but the distinctions which are used to classify the coins are based more on the use of coin designs than of tamghas.

The scarce early Alkhan copper coins in Masson's collection do not correspond with the equally scarce Alkhan copper coins reported from Kashmir Smast (Nasim Khan *et al.* 2008, pp. 182–5). They appear therefore to be local issues, perhaps from Kabul.

There are no Nezak coins mentioned in Masson's report as Begram finds, but he acquired examples in the bazaar (**F526/1a, Pl. 13.44–5, 47**; p. 66 above) and a few pieces from his collection were illustrated by Wilson (1841, Coins pl. XVII.6–7; pl. XXI.21; **Fig. 53.4–6**) and one survives (**Fig. 53.6**). The later Shri Shahi coins (**Fig. 53.8–23**), inscribed ΣΡΙΟ ÞΑΗΙ in Bactrian, *śrī ṣāhi* in Brahmi or *nycky MLKA* in Pahlavi, however, are well represented at both Begram and Kashmir Smast (Nasim Khan *et al.* 2008, pp. 18–191), suggesting that a common currency was used west and east of the Khyber Pass in the late 6th to early 7th century. According to Masson 'their copper monies [occur] plentifully at Begram' (**F526/1a, f. 25**), which suggests a resurgence of activity at Begram at this period. The identity of the issuers of the Shri Shahi coins is obscure. On the basis of their use of the Alkhan tamgha, one would expect them to be Huns, but they also use the same inscription as the Nezak coins which do not use the Alkhan tamgha, but are perhaps also Hun issues (Vondrovec 2014, p. 449).

Masson only illustrated one of the Turkic coins, which followed the Nezak coinages (**F526/1a, Pl. 11.20**; **Fig. 53.7**). It was acquired in Kabul. However, in the surviving collection there are 10 copper examples, which are associated by their designs with the silver coinage of the Turkic rulers who took over from the issuers of Nezak-style coins in the early 8th century, and therefore could be Begram finds (**Fig. 53.24–31**). Examples of the silver coinage of this period, issues of the Turkic rulers of Kabul and Ghazni, Tegin (*c.* AD 706–39), Spur (*c.* AD 746–53) and Sandan (*c.* AD 700–50), are included in Masson's surviving collection (**Fig. 57.3–7, 9**). Four pieces from his collection (**Fig. 57.3, 4, 8, 10**), two of which match surviving examples, were also illustrated by Wilson (1841, pp. 399–400, 402, nos 26–7, 35, Coins pl. XVII.6, 8–9, pl. XXI.22). One of the surviving coppers (**Fig. 53.26**) has the same design, but in a cruder form, as some of the silver coins (**Fig. 57.4–7**), the others have portrait types relating to the Turkic copies of Nezak/Shri Shahi period coins (**Fig. 53.27–8**) or to the subsequent Shri Sero or Tegin coins (**Fig. 53.24–5, 30–1**).

The copper coins also feature in Masson's surviving collection, but in small numbers. Similar coins have also been reported from Kashmir Smast (Nasim Khan *et al.* 2008, pp. 189, 192–6). Again a common currency across the Khyber Pass is suggested, but with a stronger presence to the east. The period of early Turkic rule in this region seems to be in the late 7th to mid-8th century, but the evidence from Masson's collection is insufficient to indicate the place of Begram in their polity.

This series of Turkic coins was still current about the same period as Muslims began to penetrate into the area (see below), as a Buddhist dedication in Bactrian found at Tang-i Safedak, to the west of Bamiyan mentions both Turkic (ΔΟΡΚΟ) and Muslim (ΤΑΖΙΓΟ) rulers in the year of its dedication, Bactrian era 492 = *c.* 719 (or 715, see de Blois 2006; Sims-Williams and de Blois 2018; Schindel 2010; de la Vaissière 2019). Found in the same monument were Turkic base silver coins of the series inscribed in Bactrian ΣΗΡΟ (*sero*; Vondrovec 2014, p. 617, type 243B), which closely resemble coins dated year 480 of the Bactrian era (= *c.* 706) of Tegin the Turkic 'king of Khurasan' (Vondrovec 2014, pp.

	Obv./ rev. types	Obv. inscription	Rev. inscription	F526/1a	IOLC	Wilson 1841
Spalapatideva Ar	bull / horseman	ϹΡΙ ϹΠΑΛΒΙΔΟ	śrī spalapatideva	Pl. 11, *Fig. 2*		
Spalapatideva Ae	bull / horseman		śrī spalapatideva	Pl. 11, *Fig. 3*	4	
Vakkadeva Ae	lion / elephant		śrī vakkadeva		14	
Samantadeva Ar	bull / horseman		śrī samantadeva		4	
Samantadeva Ae	lion / elephant		śrī samantadeva	Pl. 11, *Fig. 10*	25	
Pala[deva] Ae	bull / horseman		śrī pala…		6	pl. XIX.13
Pala[deva] Ae	woman / horseman		śrī pala…		1	pl. XIX.14
Samantadeva imitations	bull / horseman		śrī samantadeva	Pl. 11, *Figs 1, 4*	142	

Table 18 Kabul Shahi coins in Masson's collection

651–3, type 240). Related Turkic coins issued by Tegin, his son Fromo Kesaro and grandson Spur continued to be issued until the mid-8th century.

Turkic Kabul and Hindu Shahi coins

Contemporary with the establishment of Muslim rule in parts of this region, a strong Turkic state was established in Kabul from the mid-8th century. This state is known in modern scholarship as the Kabul Shahis (*c*. AD 770–870) and was succeeded by a similar state further east known as the Hindu Shahis, *c*. AD 850–990 (MacDowall 1968; Rehman 1979; Bhatia 1973; Deyell 1990, pp. 51–60). These states issued a distinctive type of coinage, with novel designs and inscriptions, which is represented in Masson's 1835 report (**F526/1a, Pl. 11.1–3, 10**). He says (**F526/1a, f. 23**) that their 'coppers frequently appear at Begram', but unfortunately this statement is less clear than it seems as he includes in his comment later coins with the same design, including both unattributable copies (**F526/1a, Pl. 11.4**) and issues by the Muslim successors of the Turkic Shahis (**F526/1a, Pl. 11.5–9, 11–13**, see below). The main three types of the Shahis are also included in the surviving collection. Many of these examples are imitations and probably later issues, as the designs continued to be used for Islamic coins until the early 13th century.

The evidence for the Shahi kingdoms in Begram is best illustrated by the numerous examples in Masson's collection of the bull/horseman copper coinage, inscribed *śrī splalapatideva* in Devanagari script and ορι σπαλαβιδο in Bactrian (**Fig. 58.5–7**), and the lion/elephant copper coinage, inscribed *śrī vakkadeva* (**Fig. 58.12–14**) or *śrī samantadeva* (**Fig. 58.24–30**) in Devanagari. If the collection reflects what Masson found at Begram then it seems likely that the city was active during the Shahi period. Their silver denominations are less well represented, but this is the normal pattern for what Masson was collecting from Begram.

Six copper coins, with bull and horseman raising a sword over his head, inscribed *śrī pala*… (**Fig. 58.8–10**; Wilson 1841, p. 430, no. 13, Coins pl. XIX.13), and a related type with reclining female and horseman (**Fig. 58.11**; Wilson 1841, p. 430, no. 14, Coins pl. XIX.14), seem to be examples of Shahi types of the same period, but are not otherwise recorded.

The inscriptions on these coins appear to be the names of the rulers, but it is more likely that Spalapatideva, Samantadeva and Vakkadeva are titles (MacDowall 1968, p. 211). MacDowall saw the Spalapatideva and Samantadeva coins as having different geographical distributions, attributing the former to Kabul Shahis and the latter to the Hindu Shahis and the Vakkadeva coins as contemporary with the Spalapatideva coinage (1968, p. 191), but the large number of coppers of all these inscriptions in Masson's collection (see **Table 18**) suggests that they were issued and current while the Shahis were still based in Kabul, i.e. before it was captured by the Saffarid ruler Ya'qub b. al-Layth *c*. AD 870.

The coinage appears to have begun soon after the Turkic issues of Spur and Sandan in the mid-8th century. From the Saffarid conquest through into the following Samanid period the coins current at Begram were all Islamic, so it seems to confirm that the currency of Shahi coins at the city came to an end from *c*. AD 870. The later base-silver and copper copies of Shahi coins, both anonymous and in the names of later Islamic rulers, however, continued to circulate there.

The dating of the Kabul Shahi coins to the 7th–11th century by Bhatia (1973, pp. 53–8) was based on her belief that they began after the coins of Tegin (*c*. AD 706–39), which she misdated to the period AD 633–58, and continued until the end of the Shahi kingdom in 1026. MacDowall (1968) and Rehman (1979, pp. 185–194) gave a shorter chronology from *c*. AD 750–955 or 1002 respectively. Deyell said (1990, p. 55) 'it is risky to hypothesise' the chronology of these coins, but Masson's finds from Begram (**Table 18**) now give a much clearer indication.

Early Islamic coins (Figs 55–6; Fig. 57.1–3; Fig. 60.1–2, 12–17)

Masson's collection, as transferred to the British Museum in 1845 and 1880, his 1835 report (**F526/1a**) and his correspondence contain coins which relate to the Islamic conquests of eastern and northern Afghanistan (Bosworth 1996, 2008) and southern Pakistan (MacLean 1989) in the period before Kabul fell to the Saffarids in AD 870.

From Begram he reported finding large numbers of 'minute' silver coins (**Vol. II, pp. 66–7, 100–1**), but did not illustrate or describe them. The most likely identification of these coins is as issues of the Muslim rulers of Sind, as there are 74 coins of this emirate in the surviving collection (**Fig. 60.12–15**). These are mostly copper or extremely debased silver. The flow of these coins northwards out of Sind is also indicated by two examples found at Kashmir Smast (Nasim Khan *et al*. 2008, p. 214) and a hoard found at Lashkari Bazar in eastern Afghanistan (Fussman and Thierry 2001). The Arab conquest of Sind began in AD 712 and soon after

The Monetary History of Begram | 109

Umayyad style silver and copper coins were being issued. From the reign of the Umayyad governor Tamim b. Zayd al-Qayni, c. AD 726–30, until the Ghaznavid conquest c. 1005, small silver coins were issued in Sind (Fishman and Todd 2018) and it is late examples of this coinage, often debased, which were collected by Masson from Begram.

In 1834 Masson also acquired in the Kabul bazaar what appears to be parts of a hoard of silver coins (see **Table 19**; **Figs 55–6; Fig. 57.1–3**) which bear testimony to the Muslim conquests in north-western Afghanistan (a full report of the hoard is in preparation, Cribb). In his 1835 report of his acquisitions he illustrated four coins (**F526/1a, Pl. 12.38, 41–3**) of the Muslim governors of the eastern provinces. He says of them (**F526/1a, ff. 24–5**):

> Coins of this class are very numerously found in the bazaars of Kabul, but never at Begram. ... As these coins, so plentiful in the bazaar of Kabul, are all of silver, there can be little doubt of their being importations, probably from Turkestan – the mint at Kabul being indebted for her silver to other countries, large quantities of bullion are annually imported. It has however happened that very large parcels of Sasanian silver coins have been discovered by chance in various parts of Afghanistan. ... They are succeeded by coins of inferior execution as *Fig. 41, 42* and *43* – which have invariably one or more marks or characters on the margin, which have obviously been struck or punched on them after coinage – if any of these additions could be recognised to be Muhammadan, there would be no difficulty in admitting the better sort of these coins to be those of the last of the Khusraus [i.e. Sasanians], and those with the distinguishing marks, those struck under the first Caliphs.

These 'coins of inferior execution' appear to be the groups of '125 silver Sasanian coins' costing 72.11.0 rupees and '26 silver Sasanian coins' costing 21.8.0 rupees which he bought in December 1834 (**Vol. II, p. 63: E161/VII f. 25**). They also correspond with the 150 silver Sasanian and Arab Sasanian coins, with the same countermarks and types as featured in his 1835 report, from the surviving Masson collection in the British Museum, the Fitzwilliam Museum and the Indian Museum Calcutta. He also acquired 60 Sasanian silver coins in 1837 (**Vol. II, pp. 65–6: E161/VII f. 30**) which could be a further parcel from the same hoard.

The British Museum samples came in 1845 from the East India Company and in 1882 from the India Museum and also from Sir Alexander Cunningham (1894) who acquired coins in the India Office sale of Masson coins in 1887. The Fitzwilliam Museum coins, acquired in 1908 from the residue of the Masson collection in the India Office (**Vol. II, pp. 121–2**), include pieces seen in the India Museum by Thomas (1849), where he reported 37 coins which are now in the British Museum and Fitzwilliam Museum. The Fitzwilliam Museum group also includes one of the coins illustrated by Masson in 1835 (CM.IS.16 = **F526/1a, Pl. 12.38**). The coins in the Indian Museum Calcutta were probably extracted from Masson's second collection while it was in Calcutta 1838–9 (**Vol. II, p. 78**, *Proceedings of the Asiatic Society Bengal* 1839b) and/or included with 'the more precious parts' of the coin collection presented to that museum by the India Office after 1882 (**Vol. II, p. 122: FW 19-11-1906**).

In the British Museum, Ashmolean Museum and Fitzwilliam Museum there are 64 coins which seem to be from the same hoard as they were collected in Calcutta soon after Masson's acquisitions, perhaps brought there by Mohan Lal Zutshi (Kashmiri), an Indian scholar, who had been Sir Alexander Burnes' secretary and travelled from Kabul to Calcutta in 1834. Other potential sources could have been James Gerard (Burnes' companion to Bukhara) and Karamat 'Ali, Masson's predecessor as news-writer in Kabul, both of whom are recorded as supplying James Prinsep with 'specimens' of 'Bactrian' coins (*JASB* 1834, preface, p. vi).

The British Museum coins came from the collections of James Prinsep (1847), C.S. Steuart (1848) and Emily Eden (1853); while the Ashmolean Museum coins came in 1859 from the collection of J.B. Elliott, who had been a judge in Calcutta and a contemporary of Prinsep. The Fitzwilliam Museum coin is from the J.D. Tremlett (1918), a judge in Bengal and the Punjab.

The British Museum also holds 43 Khusrau II silver drachms (e.g. **Fig. 54.17–22**) acquired from the East India Company or the India Museum which may have been part of the hoard, but they all lack the distinctive countermarks which would make certain their inclusion. There are later un-countermarked coins in the hoard, so the possibility of their presence in the hoard cannot be disregarded. Album also suggested that un-countermarked Khusrau II coins he saw in the market, at the same time as a similar hoard of countermarked coins he published, was suggestive of them being from his hoard (1992, p. 163, n. 7).

Masson's hoard largely consisted of late Sasanian and Arab-Sasanian coins issued between AD 596 and 695. Most of the coins were issues of the rulers of the eastern provinces of the Islamic lands, including coins struck at Merv al-Rudh, Herat and Seistan in western Afghanistan. The hoard also contained coins of a local ruler in north-western Afghanistan, Zhulād Gōzgān (**Fig. 57.1–2**), inscribed in Bactrian with his name (ΖΟΛΑΔΟ ΓΩΖΓΑΝΟ) and title (ΓΑΡΙΓΟ ÞΑΥΟ, king of Ghar) and the name of his mint of Anbēr (ΑΜΒΗΡΟ in Bactrian, *'nbyr* in Pahlavi and *Anber* in Arabic), which has been located in Sar-i Pul to the west of Balkh (Sims-Williams 2008, p. 117). His coins are known in the numismatic literature as Arab-Hephthalite (Walker 1941, pp. lxv–lxix, 127–9; see also Göbl 1967, pp. 186–93), but would now be more appropriately called Arab-Bactrian, as the terminology was originally based on the idea that the Bactrian script was Hephthalite. Zhulād Gōzgān's coins are dated Yazdagird era 69 and AH 84–9, i.e. AD 700–7, but it cannot be ruled out that these dates may simply be copied from Arab-Sasanian coins and do not reflect the exact date of production.

The majority of the coins in the hoard (see **Tables 19** and **23**) are countermarked, often with a punch inscribed with the name of Skag in Bactrian (ΣΚΑΓΟ), who appears to be another king of the same kingdom as Zhulād Gōzgān as he is named in a Bactrian document dated Bactrian era 452 (= c. AD 679) as Skag Gōzgān (Sims-Williams 2012, pp. 92–3, document R, line 18; Sims Williams 2008, p. 120), and in his countermarks used the same tamgha as appears on the coins of Zhulād Gōzgān. Skag Gōzgān's countermarks were used on coins dated as late as AD 695 (Walker 1941, nos 209–10). Zhulād Gōzgān's name also appears in

Province	Mint mark	Mint name	Khusrau II 591–628	651–60	661–70	671–5	676–80	681–5	686–90	691–5	696–700	701–7	Total
Juzjān / Ghar	ANB	Anbēr						1†					1
	ANBYR	Anbēr								3**			3
	MRW/ αμβηρο	Merv/Anbēr								1‡			1
	ANBYR/ αμβηρο	Anbēr									1†	10	11
	PHRZ/ παρ[δο]	Faryab?								1			1
Khurasan	APRŠT	Abrashahr						2†	4*				6
	AYPTK	?						1					1
	BBA	Camp mint?	1						7***				8
	HRA	Haraat						1	10*****				11
	MR	Merv	2*										2
	MRW	Merv						20*******†	18*******	4			42
	MRWY	Merv	1*										1
	MRWRW	Merv al-Rudh							1*				1
	MRWRWT	Merv al-Rudh						3*	2†				5
Sakastan	SK	Sijistān		3	1*	4	1	5					14
	SYCSTAN	Sijistān								1			1
	SYCTAN	Sijistān								1			1
	SYKACTAN	Sijistān						1					1
Kirman	BN	near Kirman	1*			2							3
	KRMAN	Kirman						3*	1				4
	KRMANAN	Kirman								1			1
	KRMANHP	Kirman					1						1
	KRMANNAT	near Kirman								1			1
Fars	ART	Ardashīr Khurrah	3**			1			4*	1			9
	BYŠ	Bīshāpūr	1*			2	4	1	11****	1			20
	DA	Darābjird	5			3	3*	2		1			14
	DAP	Fasā						1					1
	DR	?	1										1
	MY	near Arrajān	2*										2
	RAM	Ramhurmuz?	1*										1
	ST	Ishtakr	1						2				3
	WHYC	Arrajān	2*†						1*				3
	YZ	Yazd	3										3
Khuzistan	AW	Ahwaz?	1										1
	AY	Susa	4****										4
	AYR	Susa	2*										2
	GW?	?				1							1
	WH	?					1*						1
Iraq	BCRA	Baṣra					1	5**	4				10
	DŠT	Dasht Maysān					1	1					2
Jibal	AHM	Hamadān	2										2
	GD	Jayy	2*										2
	RD	Rayy	1		1*			2					4
	RYW	Rev-Ardashir?	1										1
	ŠY	ŠY	1*										1
	WH	Veh-Ardashir	1										1
	WYH	?	1†										1
?	RAPY?	?	1										1
?	PR	?	1*										1
?	?	?								1			1
TOTAL			42	3	3	13	16	48	60	15	1	10	214

Table 19 Distribution by mint and date of the 1834 Kabul hoard. Countermarks: Skag* (57), Besut‡ (1), Zhulād† (7)

Doc	Line	Bactrian era date	AD (BE 1=AD 223)	AD (BE = AD 227)	Persian Kavad drachms	Persian drachms	Kavad drachms	drachms	Muslim (Tazak) drachms
M	3	388	610	614			x		
P	13	446	668	672		x			
Q	14	449	671	675	x				
R	18	452	674	678			x		
S	26	470	692	696			x		
Tt	23, 24	483	705	709			x		
U	25	490	712	716				x	
Uu	29	500	722	726			x		
V	11	507	729	733					x
W	11	525	747	751					x

Table 20 Use of silver coins according to the Bactrian Documents (Sims-Williams 2012)

countermarks on coins issued down to 699 (Malek 2019, no. 860), and on his own coins, dated 700–7 (Malek 2019, nos 16–18, 21). Sims-Williams (2008, p. 120) has suggested that Zhulād Gōzgān and Skag Gōzgān could have been contemporary rulers. The Bactrian document and the countermarked coins suggest that Skag Gōzgān was ruling from at least AD 674/679 until about AD 695. The evidence for Zhulād Gōzgān places him ruling during a period from c. AD 700–7. If the dates on his coins were real dates then his reign began by AD 700, but if the dates are copied from other coins and did not indicate the date of issue, then they also only provide a date after which to place his reign. His issue of coins in his own name suggests that he changed over from a system of countermarking existing coins to creating his own, after the reign of Skag Gōzgān who only countermarked coins. The transition from countermarking to striking new coins was overlapping as Zhulād Gōzgān's own early coins were countermarked with his name (Walker 1941, no. 254). The commoner countermark of Skag Gōzgān does not appear on Zhulād Gōzgān's coins, also suggesting that he preceded him. Album's hoard, deposited after its latest coin dated AH 72/AD 691, contained no coins of Zhulād Gōzgān, but had some pieces countermarked by him (Album 1992, p. 184, no. 93; p. 191, no. 119) which seem to represent the period before Zhulād Gōzgān's transition from countermarking to coin issue. The absence of his coins and any of the preliminary issues which add the mint name Anbēr to coins imitating Sasanian or Arab-Sasanian coins from Album's hoard with its latest coins dateable to 691, suggest that the reign of Zhulād Gōzgān did not begin until after this date and that the dates on his coins are probably reliable. A third name Bēsut (Bactrian ΒΗΣΟΤΟ) appearing in the countermarks (Sims-Williams 2008, p. 119–20) also used the tamgha appearing on Zhulād Gōzgān's coins. It was added to a coin issued in AD 699 (Malek 2019, no. 860), the year before the first coins issued in the name of Zhulād Gōzgān. The logic suggested by Zhulād Gōzgān's transition from countermarking to striking his own coins suggests placing Bēsut between him and Skag Gōzgān.

Zhulād Gōzgān's coins are all inscribed *bismillāh* 'in the name of god' in Arabic in their obverse margin, but it is not clear whether this was a statement of the adherence of this ruler to the Islamic faith, a statement of allegiance to the Arab governor of Khurasan or that it was copied from the Arab-Sasanian coins as part of the design, with no other meaning.

Masson's view that these coins had been brought to Kabul from further north seems the most likely explanation, but it cannot be ruled out that they had been found locally, because a Merv mint Arab-Sasanian coin of 685 (Walker 1941, no. 171), with the same countermark (no. 14) as appeared on many of the hoard coins, was recovered – with coins of Tegin, a Bactrian inscribed ring and a gold reliquary – in a secondary relic deposit in the Manikyala Great Stupa, a Buddhist monument in the northern Punjab excavated by Ventura (Errington and Curtis 2007, pp. 211–12, 214, fig. 177) and came to the British Museum via James Prinsep. The Tegin coin is of the type dated year 77 (Yazdagird era = AD 708) i.e. contemporary with the latest coins in Masson's hoard. Two coins with the same countermark (no. 14), were also found during the excavations at Butkara I (Göbl 1976, nos 265–6). They were a Khusrau II coin of Jayy mint (GD), dated year 35 (AD 624) and a Salm b. Ziyād coin of Merv mint (MRW) dated AH 64 (AD 683). In Masson's surviving collection there is a small copper coin (**Fig. 53.32**), probably found at Begram, with the same tamgha as appears in the margin of Zhulād Gōzgān's silver coins, so the ancient movement of such a hoard to south of the Hindu Kush cannot be ruled out.

The use of silver drachms in northern Afghanistan and particularly the kingdom ruled by Skag Gōzgān and Zhulād Gōzgān is affirmed by the references to payments in the Bactrian documents (**Table 20**), where they were referred to as Kavad drachms δδραχμο κοοαδ[ο] or as Persian drachms δδραχμο παρσαγγο (Sims-Williams 2012, vol. I, pp. 85, 91, 95, 105) from c. AD 610/615 until c. AD 722/725. The coins were named after Kavad, the Sasanian emperor (AD 484, 488–96, 499–531). Before the use of Kavad drachms and overlapping with it, the Bactrian documents express payments in terms of struck gold dinars, i.e. the gold coins of the Kushano-Sasanians, Kidarites and Hephthalites issued in Bactria. Although they do not feature in the documents, there was also a currency of earlier Sasanian silver coins of emperor Peroz (AD 457, 459–84) in northern Afghanistan, which were copied by the Hephthalites at the Balkh mint in the late 5th to early 6th century.

Document R prescribed a fine of 100 Kavad drachms to the treasury of Skag Gōzgān which suggests that the silver coins in this hoard issued by the Sasanian empire and its

Muslim conquerors were current in his kingdom. The term Kavad drachm must refer back to the coinage of the Sasanian emperor Kavad I's third reign (AD 499–531), when the obverse design featuring the star and crescent motifs in the border was introduced, even though this hoard and the similar one published by Album, both containing coins countermarked by the Gōzgān rulers, contained no coins earlier than the reign of Khusrau II (AD 591–628). Kavad I's drachms with star and crescent motifs had penetrated in the region as is demonstrated by the circulation of pieces with Bactrian countermarks (Göbl 1967, type 285), so it is possible the term originated in the circulation of Kavad I coins in northern Afghanistan. The replacement in monetary transactions of the term Kavad drachm by the local name for Muslim dirhems (called Tajik drachms in the Bactrian documents) δδραχμο ταζαγο (or ταζανο), of 'good silver' σιμιγγο ριζδο, and 'locally current' ωδαγο οιζινδδιγο between AD 727 and 734 (Sims-Williams 2012, pp. 119, 125, 133), reflects the eventual replacement of Arab-Sasanian coins with Muslim post-reform dirhems, the issue of which had begun in AH 79 (= AD 698). It seems likely that the preference for Arab-Sasanian drachms in north-western Bactria continued long after the new dirhems became available. This preference for Arab-Sasanian-style coins is also attested by their issue by other local rulers down to the time of Fromo Kesaro, who ruled south of the Hindu Kush *c.* AD 738–45, according to Chinese sources (Kuwayama 1999, pp. 64–5; Vondrovec 2014, p. 568).

Apart from the two series described above current in neighbouring territories during the Shahi period, only one other early Islamic coin survives from Masson's collection, a copper fals of the 'Abbasid caliph al-Manṣūr, minted in Baghdad, dated AH 157 (AD 773/4; **Fig. 60.1**). Masson may have acquired this elsewhere than Begram, probably from the Kabul bazaar, where he also acquired a silver dirhem of the 'Abbasid caliph Hārūn al-Rashīd (**Fig. 60.2**).

Islamic coins from the conquest of Kabul by Ya'qub b. al-Layth *c.* AD 870 until the Mongol invasion 1221 (Fig. 60.3-11, 18-23; Figs 61-3)

> The coins to which the following notice refers form part of the extensive collection made in Afghanistan by Mr Masson, now deposited in the Museum at the India House. Amid the more important relics of the Bactrian successors of Alexander the Great, which constituted the bulk of this acquisition, slight attention was attracted by the medals of a subsequent Mohammedan dynasty, the events of whose rule were comparatively well known, and whose history in itself possessed none of the classic interest attaching to the survival of the Greek monarchies in Central Asia. From this and other causes, Professor Wilson, in his description of the antiquities of Ariana, which the labours of Mr Masson had placed at his command, but briefly referred to the numismatic monuments of the race of Sebuktegin. Such being the case, and adverting both to the numerical amount of these coins now available, and to the very limited number of medals of the Ghaznavi princes yet noticed, either by English or continental writers, it seemed probable that an attempt at a classification of these minor antiquities might not be altogether devoid of interest
>
> (Thomas 1847, p. 267).

The Saffarid conquest of Kabul *c.* AD 870 which put an end to Shahi rule is marked only by a single coin in Masson's surviving collection, a silver coin of 'Amr b. al-Layth, brother and successor of the conqueror Ya'qūb b. al-Layth al-Ṣaffār (IOLC.6028). This coin (**Fig. 60.3**) and some issues of Ya'qūb retained the fabric of the Shahi coins, but there is no evidence of an early Saffarid mint at Kabul or Begram.

'Amr b. al-Layth's reign came to an end when the Samanid ruler Ismā'īl b. Ahmad (AD 892–907) captured him in AD 900, so the Kabul region came under Samanid rule. This period is represented in Masson's collection by falus of the Bukhara mint of Manṣūr I b. Nūh (AD 961–76) dated AH 357 (AD 968. IOC. 6021: **Fig. 60.5**) and of Nūh II b. Manṣūr (AD 965–87), with unclear date (**Fig. 60.10**) and illegible (**Fig. 60.11**); and a set of six copper coins made at the Parwan (or Farwān) mint (IOLC.6781–6786) in the name of Manṣūr I b. Nūh (**Fig. 60.6–7**) and Nūh II b. Manṣūr (**Fig. 60.8–9**). These six Parwan coins were described by Masson in one of his manuscripts (**Figs 18–19**: **F526/1** loose sheets), based on their identification by Thomas (1847, pp. 301–2). A seventh example from Masson's collection, issued by Manṣūr I b. Nūh, is in the Fitzwilliam Museum (CM. IS.364-R). Masson identified Parwan (1842, vol. 3, p. 166) as

> a city of magnitude must have existed at Parwan, about eight miles, bearing north nineteen west, from Begram, consequently that distance nearer to the great range of Caucasus, under whose inferior hills it is in fact found. Coins are discovered there in large numbers.

This referred to a small town on the northern edge of the Begram plain now known as Jabal-e Seraj (http://www.iranicaonline.org/articles/jabal-e-seraj, consulted 28.6.2019). It is likely that these coins were collected at this site or at Begram. At this period Parwan is the only mint operating in this area, so it is possible that this is the mint name for Begram, as a contemporary Arab geographer ibn Ḥawqal described Parwan as being on the banks of the Panjshir River where Begram is located, whereas Jabal-e Seraj is on the Salang River (Ousley 1800, p. 225: 'The river of Panjshir runs… till it comes to Ferouan, and so proceeds into Hindustan'). This suggests that Begram or the region wherein it stood was known at this time as Parwan, and that after the destruction of the city, the name was reused for the township further north (Cribb 2019, p. 9).

Thomas observed that he had found 10 Samanid coins among Masson's collection at India House (1847, p. 299), but that they were probably issues relating to the period when the Ghaznavid dynasty was coming to power south of the Hindu Kush, but still acknowledging the Samanids as their overlords. So he suggested that these coins of Manṣūr I b. Nūh and Nūh II b. Manṣūr were probably issued under the authority of the early Ghaznavids: Alptekin (AD 954–66), Balkategin (AD 966–73), Manṣūr (AD 973–7) and Sebuktegin (AD 977–97). The Ghaznavids were already striking coins in their own names at Ghazni from the reign of Ibrahim b. 'Abd al-Ghaffar (AD 949–56), so the issue of coins at Parwan in the name of Samanid rulers could be the issues of a local governor still loyal to them outside of the control of the Ghaznavids. There had earlier been issues by local rulers from the Parwan mint (Schwarz 1995, p. 64) under Ahmad b. Sahl in AD 918 (Baldwin's Auctions, Islamic Coins 16,

Mahomedan Coins.

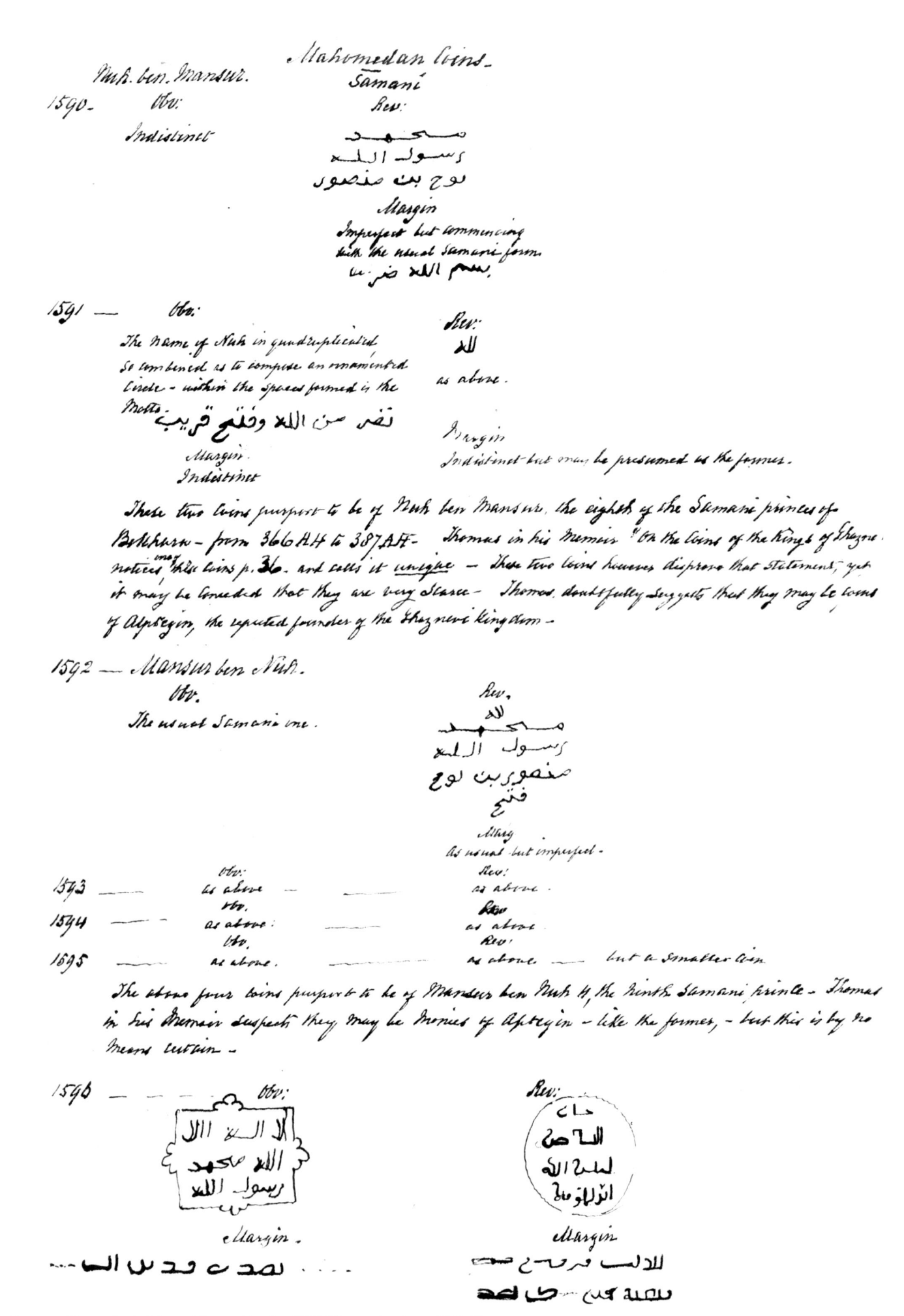

Nuh. ben. Mansur.   *Samani*
1590 —   Obv: Rev:
    Indistinct   محمد
        رسول الله
        نوح بن منصور
        Margin
        Imperfect but commencing
        with the usual Samani form
        بسم الله ...

1591 —   Obv: Rev:
    The name of Nuh is quadruplicated,   لا اله
    so combined as to compose an ornamented
    circle — within the spaces formed is the   as above.
    Motto نصر من الله وفتح قريب
        Margin
        Margin.   Indistinct but may be presumed as the former.
    Indistinct

These two coins purport to be of Nuh ben Mansur, the eighth of the Samani princes of Bokhara — from 366 AH to 387 AH. Thomas in his Memoir "On the Coins of the Kings of Ghazni" notices one of these coins p. 36. and calls it unique — These two coins however disprove that statement, yet it may be conceded that they are very scarce — Thomas doubtfully suggests that they may be coins of Alptegin, the reputed founder of the Ghaznevi kingdom —

1592 —   Mansur ben Nuh.
    Obv.   Rev.
    The usual Samani one.   محمد
        رسول الله
        منصور بن نوح
        فتح
        Marg
        As usual but imperfect.

        Obv.   Rev:
1593 —   as above —   as above.
        Obv.   Rev.
1594 —   as above   as above
        Obv.   Rev:
1595   as above.   as above — but a smaller coin

The above four coins purport to be of Mansur ben Nuh 4, the ninth Samani prince — Thomas in his Memoir suspects they may be monies of Alptegin — like the former, — but this is by no means certain —

1596 —   Obv: Rev:
    [sketch with Arabic inscription   [sketch with Arabic inscription
    لا اله الا   الناصر
    الله محمد   لدين الله
    رسول الله]   ...]
    Margin.   Margin
    [Arabic]   [Arabic]

Figure 18 Masson's sketches of Samanid coins (F526/1 loose sheet nos 1590–6)

Figure 19 Masson's sketches of Samanid coins (F526/1 loose sheet nos 1598–1610)

20.10.2009, lot 537), Yusuf in 935 (Busso Peus Auction 378, 28.3, 2004, lot 1310) and his son Ahmad b. Yusuf in 945–59 (Album 2011, p. 157, V1478; Myntauktioner I Sverige AB Auction 17, 12.3.2016, lot 11416) and issues in the name of the Samanid rulers Ismā'īl b. Ahmad (Myntauktioner I Sverige AB Auction 17, 12.3.2016, lot 1259) and Naṣr b. Ahmad (914–43, Myntauktioner I Sverige AB Auction 17, 12.3.2016, lots 1300, 1302–3). The Parwan mint continued in operation from the Samanid period (earliest dated coin AH 292 = AD 905) until the end of Khwarazm Shah rule in 1221 (last dated coin AH 617 = 1220) (Diler 2009, vol. 2, pp. 891–2).

Under the Ghaznavids Begram again became an important and active centre as is witnessed by the more than 800 coins of this dynasty collected by Masson from Begram. Issues of all the major rulers of the dynasty from the time of its independence from the Samanids under Sebuktegin to its last ruler Khusrau Malik (1160–86) are present in the Masson collection (**Fig. 60.16–23; Fig. 61.1–44**). Many of these coins are probably local products of the Parwan mint.

Among the Museum's IOC coins are a number of silver dirhems minted at Parwan of Sebuktegin, struck in his own name, dated AH 380–4/AD 990–4 (IOC.1306–1308, 1310, 1313–14, 1319–1322), and of Maḥmūd I, AD 998–1030 (IOC.1330, 1332, 1343, 1346, 1357). Only one is recorded as a Masson coin (**Fig. 60.18**), but it is probable that they all were acquired by him in Kabul bazaar. The copper coins in the India Office Loan Collection are not normally inscribed with mint names, but their quantity at Begram suggests they were also mostly minted at the site (Cribb 2019).

The territory of the Ghaznavids came under attack from both the Seljuqs of Iran in 1117 and the emerging Ghurid dynasty in 1150, causing them to lose control of their capital Ghazni. The Ghaznavid coins found at Begram continue down to the end of the dynasty with seven silver coins (IOC.1627–1632, 1634) and nine coppers (IOLC. 6744–7, 6763, 6775, 6777, 6779, 6808) of the last Ghaznavid king Khusrau Malik (**Fig. 61.53–65**). Although Ghazni had been lost, the coins suggest that the Ghaznavids held on to Begram for another one or two decades.

Ghaznavid rule at Begram came to an end when their former vassals in the province of Ghur to the west of Bamiyan attacked the Ghaznavid territories. The coins in Masson's collection suggest that the region of Begram had come under Ghurid control through the Ghurid branch at Bamiyan, as the first Ghurid coinage at the mint of Parwan was struck in the name of Muḥammad b. Mas'ūd of Bamiyan (1163–92). This mint continued to issue coins into the reigns of his successors Sām b. Muḥammad (1192–1206) and 'Alī b. Sām (1206–15; Schwarz 1995, p. 68; Tye 1995, type 153). Alongside the copper coins of the Bamiyan Ghurids in Masson's surviving collection there are also a large number of base-silver and copper coins of the main Ghurid rulers Ghiyāth al-dīn Muḥammad b. Sām (1163–1203; **Fig. 62.1**) and his brother Mu'izz al-dīn Muḥammad b. Sām (1173–1206), who was responsible for laying the foundations of Islamic occupation in India that lasted for several centuries. He reigned as supreme sultan (1203–6) over a territory spanning present day Afghanistan, Pakistan and northern India. After his death, internal squabbles and a lack of manpower resources made it difficult for the Ghurids to sustain the empire. The reign of Tāj al-dīn Yïldïz (1206–15), who governed on behalf of Maḥmūd (1206–12), son of Ghiyāth al-dīn, came to an end when the Begram region was conquered by the Khwarazm Shahs in 1215. There are only about 20 Bamiyan Ghurid coins in Masson's collection (**Fig.62.19–20, 23–26**), but many more of the main Ghurid kingdom, about 100 of Mu'izz al-dīn's coins (**Fig. 62.2–17**) and about 80 of Tāj al-dīn Yïldïz (**Fig. 62.28–34**).

Masson acquired a group of Ghurid gold coins of the type current in northern India (**Fig. 59.17–20**). They have purely Indian designs and Devanagari inscriptions, copying the coins of the earlier Hindu rulers of the Delhi region. Masson also owned some of these earlier Hindu gold coins (**Fig. 59.13–16**) and stated (**F526/1a, f. 23, Pl. 10.69**) that the Ghurid gold coins of this type were 'met with occasionally in the bazaar' and that 'a large parcel was dug out of the soil three or four years since near Korrindar, a village of Koh Daman' to the south-west of Begram (see **Fig. 1**). He did not recognise who issued them, but thought they probably ruled in the locality.

The base silver and copper coins of the Khwarazm Shah Muḥammad b. Tekish (1200–20), in whose reign Begram was conquered, are very plentiful in Masson's collection, with 488 surviving (**Fig. 63.2–9**). Masson also acquired a gold coin of this ruler (**Fig. 63.1**), probably purchased in the Kabul bazaar. The reign of his successor Mangubarni (or Mengubirti, also known as Jalāl al-dīn, 1220–31) at Begram was brief, curtailed by the arrival of the Mongols. In 1221 Mangubarni won a battle at Parwan over an army sent by the Mongol ruler Genghis Khan. Unfortunately this prompted Genghis Khan to send a greater force and Mangubarni fled with his army towards India. He reached the Indus where he was defeated, fled across the river and re-established himself in the Kurram valley. Although he has been recorded as issuing silver coins at Parwan (Album 2011, p. 190), the only coins found in the city which might relate to his reign are a group of seven copper coins (**Fig. 62.21–22**, IOLC.7421–7427) which have the inscription *mālkh al-sharq...* (King of the East...). They all bear the mint name Parwan (thanks to Steve Album for this reading). Tye tentatively attributed this type to the period of Mangubarni (1995, p. 139, type 323), but they could equally be Ghurid issues. Some of the coins are without the ruler's name, but four of Masson's examples have a further inscription, which cannot be read.

Masson's collection contains no significant later coins from Begram and there are no later coins with the mint name Parwan. Genghis Khan appears to have ended the life of the city either on his way through the region following Mangubarni or subsequently.

Miscellaneous coins (Fig. 31.8; Fig. 59.3–20; Fig. 64)

Among Masson's collection there are a few coins which seem to have been found at Begram which one would not expect from the site. The most remarkable are fragments of two Chinese coins, both without doubt Begram finds. The first of these was in Bag k (**Fig. 59.10**: IOLC.5426). It is the lower part, showing the character *yuan* of a two cash coin of the Song dynasty Shaosheng era, 1094–7 (Liu Jucheng 1989, p. 203, type 17). The second fragment (**Fig. 59.11**: 1880.3732) is the left-hand part, showing the character *bao*, of an earlier Song one cash coin, issued in the Mingdao (1032–3), Jingyou (1034–8), or Baoyuan (1039) periods (Liu Jucheng 1989, p.

183, type 5; p. 184, type 4; p. 185, type 10). It was in one of the boxes of unsorted metal ornament fragments definitely from the site. The coins are identified by the calligraphy of the character surviving on each fragment. There is no evidence of Chinese intervention in the region during the 11th century, so they are probably casual losses by traders. The other Chinese coins in the India Office Loan Collection (IOLC.4641–4648) are unlikely to be from Afghanistan, but were probably acquired through 19th-century EIC activity associated with Java, Indonesia and Hong Kong.

An 8th-century Chinese style coin with a Sogdian inscription from the northern Vakhsh valley (**Fig. 59.12**: 1880.3981f; Zeimal 1994, pp. 257–9, figs 14–16) in Masson's collection is however a Begram find, as it was among unsorted metal fragments definitely from the site.

Local Afghan copper coins of the 16th (30 Timurid) and 19th (20 Durrani) centuries in the collection are likely to have been acquired at Kabul (**Fig. 64.4–6, 11–16**). There are also a few coins from Turkey, Iraq and Iran (IOLC.5270, 5183, 5212, 5214, 5278, 5281) which he could have bought in Kabul or collected while in Iran and Iraq in 1830–1 (**Fig. 64. 1–3, 8–10, 17–19**)

A few Indian coins may be from Masson's collection, but it is not clear where he acquired them. The earliest is a silver dramma of the Western Satrap Rudrasena II, AD 256–278 (**Fig. 31.8**; IOLC.4638). According to Prinsep (Thomas 1858, p. 86, pl. IV.19-21), Masson found 20 coins of this type at Begram, but Masson says only that 'two or three occur - rarely' in Afghanistan (Appendix 1, p. 324 below) and there is only one example among the IOLC coins. The movement of these into the Begram region is unlikely, but possible, as Nasim Khan recorded four Western Satrap drammas as coming from Kashmir Smast (2008, pp. 220–1, nos 735–8), including one of Rudrasena II (no. 736). Indian imitation drammas derived from the silver drachms of the Sasanian king Peroz are also in the collection (**Fig. 59.3–9**). One is silver (IOLC.4621) and of the type found in Himachal Pradesh and attributed to the Pratiharas (Maheshwari 2010, pp. 242–3, 'proto-*sri vigra*' type 2). The others are debased (IOLC.4613–4615) and are of the '*sri ha*' series, found in Rajastan and attributed to the Chahamanas (Maheshwari 2010, pp. 175–201). In his 1835 report (**F526.1a, f. 24, Pl. 11, 14–15**), Masson illustrated four examples from the Kabul bazaar and stated that none were to be found at Begram.

General observations

The coin finds assembled by Masson in Afghanistan from 1833 to 1838 are phenomenal, not only in their quantity, but also in the information they convey about the history of Afghanistan and particularly Begram from its entry into history in the period of the Achaemenid kings of Persia down to the cataclysm wrought upon the local polities by the advent of Genghis Khan. The event of that invasion is very visible in the coin record with the hundreds of coins that were current at Begram on its eve. The small change base-silver and copper coinages of the post-Shahi period were struck to a fairly consistent standard meaning that they remained current in the city whoever had issued them. The surviving collection contains over 800 Ghaznavid, 200 Ghurid and 500 Khwarazm Shah of these small change coins. These coins and the many other examples which are now lost from Masson's collection appear to represent the everyday commerce of the city on the day it was sacked by Genghis Khan's army. From this event the city's mint, called Parwan, also ceased to exist. The availability of this research resource suggests many avenues for future study of the monetary systems of this period, particularly as there are many previously unpublished types among these small base-silver and copper coins.

The distribution of Masson's collection by century reveals some other very high peaks of coin survival, some which can be related to military activity, like the Mongol destruction in *c*. 1221 (see **Table 21**). The high density of coins at particular periods could also indicate a change in currency patterns. In this region another factor could be the impact of earthquakes.

The points of conquest, such as the Indo-Scythian defeat of the Indo-Greek rulers of Begram could explain the 2nd century BC peak of Eucratides and Menander coins, but one

Century	Rulers	IOLC & BM	Approx. no. of coins
4th BC	Achaemenid	2	4
	Alexander's Satraps	2	
3rd BC	Seleucid	1	50
	Bactrian	4	
	Maurya	45	
2nd BC	Indo-Greek	409	474
	Local Indian	65	
1st BC	Indo-Greek	38/	208
	Indo-Scythian	170	
1st AD	Indo-Scythian	11	1,608
	Indo-Parthian	75	
	Kushan	1522	
2nd AD	Kushan	1057	1,057
3rd AD	Kushan	478	600
	Kushano-Sasanian	122	
4th AD	Kushano-Sasanian	28	157
	Sasanian	72	
	Kidarite	57	
5th AD	Alkhan Huns	33	33
6th AD	Shri Shahi	60	60
7th AD	Turkic	11	11
8th AD	Turkic	1	29
	Shahi	28	
9th AD	Shahi	25	100
	Saffarid	1	
	Sind	74	
10th AD	Samanid	8	26
	Ghaznavid	18	
11th AD	Ghaznavid	486	486
12th AD	Ghaznavid	343	440
	Ghurid	97	
13th AD until 1221	Ghurid	139	913
	Khwarazm Shahs	494	
	imported Indian	280	
Total			6,256

Table 21 Breakdown of coin quantities from Begram by century

Ruler	Approximate chronology	Locally issued coins	Imported coins
Achaemenids	520–329 BC	local bent bars and die-struck silver	Greek and Achaemenid silver
Alexander the Great	329–323 BC		Greek gold silver and copper coins
Post-Alexander satraps	323–305 BC	imitations of Athenian silver coins and Greek-style local silver and copper coins	
Mauryans	305–180 BC	punch-marked silver and cast copper coins	Hellenistic silver coins
Indo-Greeks	180–60 BC	Greek-style silver and copper coins Local die-struck copper coins	Bactrian Greek silver and copper coins
Indo-Scythians	60 BC–AD 30	imitations of Indo-Greek silver and copper coins	
Indo-Parthians	AD 30–60	copper coins, based on Indo-Greek silver coins	
Kushans	AD 60–250	gold and copper coins	Roman gold and silver coins
Kushano-Sasanians	AD 250–330	gold and copper coins, based on Kushan coins	Kushan gold and silver coins
Sasanians	AD 330–390	silver coins and copper Kushano-Sasanian coins	Sasanian silver coins
Huns	AD 390–600	silver coins based on Sasanian silver and copper coins	Arab-Sasanian silver coins
Turks	AD 600–770		
Shahis	AD 770–870	silver bull and horseman coins and copper coins	
Saffarids	AD 870–900	Islamic gold silver and copper coins	Indian base-silver and copper copies of Shahi bull and horseman coins
Samanids	AD 900–70		
Ghaznavids	AD 970–1150		
Ghurids	AD 1150–1215		
Khwarazm Shahs	AD 1215–21		

Table 22 Summary of the range of coins in the Masson collection

would expect to see more coins of their successors if that was the cause, so it is possible to suggest that an earthquake about the end of Menander's reign is a more likely explanation.

The second large peak falls about the turn of the 1st to 2nd century AD when coins in the name of Kujula Kadphises (c. AD 50–90) and the anonymous coins issued late in his reign and through the reign of his son Wima Takto (c. AD 90–113) were current. There is a direct continuation of Kushan rule in the city from Wima Takto to his son Wima Kadphises (c. AD 113–27), so invasion cannot explain the heavy loss of coin at this period. Again an earthquake could be the cause. At Taxila a similar peak of coin loss occurs a bit earlier, where Kujula Kadphises coins were lost in thousands. Perhaps this was a slightly earlier event further down the same earthquake zone.

The high losses throughout the rest of the Kushan period do not exhibit any specific peaks of loss, so are more likely explained as an increase of activity in the city, where the Kushan kings had their summer residence, according to Xuanzang (Li 1996, p. 40) and the main Kushan copper mint was located (Cribb and Bracey at press). After the Kushan period the rate of loss appears to decline and it is possible that the city became less important as the role of Kabul grew.

The losses during the city's last two centuries suggest a revival of its fortunes, but the extent of coin circulation is difficult to determine accurately, as the same base-silver and copper coins, known to numismatists and in some contemporary sources as *jitals* (Sircar 1966, p. 136; Tye 1995),

continued to circulate throughout the period (Deyell 1990, pp. 207–11), so that old coins continued alongside new throughout the 11th, 12th and early 13th centuries. The higher level of survival for this period can in part be put down to the destruction of the city c. 1221.

The coins collected by Masson provide a broad guide to the political masters of the city, its fluctuating fortunes and open up for future research a broad range of topics (see **Table 22**). This paper provides an introductory guide which it is hoped will inspire others to further investigate what Masson had already achieved when the first steps of ancient Indian historical research had only just begun.

Acknowledgements

I would like to thank my dear friend Elizabeth Errington for all the hard work she has put into making such a study possible and for bearing with my frequent questions about the collection. I also appreciate the hard work which her assistants, Paramdip Khera, Kirstin Leighton-Boyce, John Perkins, Chantal Fabrègues, Kay Rienjang and Piers Baker, have contributed to making this material accessible for research. I also thank my former colleagues Robert Bracey, Vesta Curtis and Helen Wang, and Steve Album, Martin Allan, Michael Bates, Shailendra Bhandare, Graham Shaw and Nicholas Sims-Williams for their help. I also thank my dear partner Linda Crook for putting up with my endless narratives about the wonders of Charles Masson and his collection.

	Ruler	Province	Mint	Mint signature	AD	AH	Other eras	Counter-marks	Collection	BMC Walker
1	Khusrau II	Khurasan	Merv	MR	619		30	11	Masson IOC.504	
2	Khusrau II	Khurasan	Merv	MR	624		35	32, 38 (x2), Göbl 62, 63, ?	Masson IOC.506	
3	Khusrau II	Khurasan	Merv	MRWY	610–618		2x	39	Masson IOC.516	
4	Khusrau II	Kirman	near Kirman	BN	609		20	1, 15, 38 (x 2)	Masson A. Cunningham, 1894,0506.1372	
5	Khusrau II	Fars	Ardashīr Khurrah	ART	620		31		Masson 1845,EIC.30	
6	Khusrau II	Fars	Ardashīr Khurrah	ART	626		37	39?	Masson IOC.532	
7	Khusrau II	Fars	Bīshāpūr	BYŠ	613		24	3, 14, 39	Masson IOC.517	
8	Khusrau II	Fars	Darābjird	DA	609		20	11	Masson IOC.487	
9	Khusrau II	Fars	Darābjird	DA	617		28	14	Masson IOC.522	
10	Khusrau II	Fars	Darābjird	DA	618		29		Masson 1845,EIC.33	
11	Khusrau II	Fars	Darābjird	DA	622		33	14, 29	Masson IOC.503	
12	Khusrau II	Fars	near Arrajān	MY	613		24		Masson 1845,EIC.27	
13	Khusrau II	Fars	near Arrajān	MY	614		25	39	Masson 1845,EIC.31	
14	Khusrau II	Fars	Ramhurmuz?	RAM	605		16	27, Göbl 62	Masson A. Cunningham 1894,0506.1373	
15	Khusrau II	Fars	Ishtakr	ST	598		9	11	Masson IOC.483	
16	Khusrau II	Fars	Arrajān	WHYC	619		30	11, 28	Masson IOC.497	
17	Khusrau II	Fars	Arrajān	WHYC	626		37	33	Masson IOC.510	
18	Khusrau II	Fars	Yazd	YZ	597		8	11	Masson IOC.477	
19	Khusrau II	Fars	Yazd	YZ	605		16	Göbl 56, 66	Masson IOC.485	
20	Khusrau II	Khuzistan	Ahwaz?	AW	616		27	10	Masson IOC.495	
21	Khusrau II	Khuzistan	Susa	AY	624		35	38 (x2), 39, Göbl 56	Masson IOC.507	
22	Khusrau II	Khuzistan	Susa	AYR	619		30	11, 14, 39, 43	Masson IOC.525	
23	Khusrau II	Khuzistan	Susa	AYR	626		37	22	Masson IOC.511	
24	Khusrau II	Jibal	Hamadān	AHM	622		33	15, 22, Göbl 60	Masson IOC.499	
25	Khusrau II	Jibal	Jayy	GD	624		35	2, 12 (x 2), 21 (x 2), 39	Masson 1845,EIC.18	
26	Khusrau II	Jibal	Jayy	GD	625		36		Masson IOC.509 **F526/1a, Pl. 12.40**	
27	Khusrau II	Jibal	Rayy	RD	615		26	1, 4, 11, 15, 20	Masson IOC.493	
28	Khusrau II	Jibal	ŠY?	ŠY	622		33	3, 22 (x 2), 38 (x 2)	Masson IOC.498	
29	Khusrau II	Jibal	Veh-Ardashir	WH	616		27		Masson 1845,EIC.38	
30	Khusrau II	?	PR?	PR	619		30	14, 39	Masson 1845,EIC.26	
31	Khusrau II imitation	Khuzistan	Susa	AY…	626		37	3, 32	Masson IOC.531	
32	Khusrau II imitation	Khuzistan	Susa	AY…	626		37	3, 32	Masson IOC.529	

Table 23 Hoard of Sasanian, Arab-Sasanian and Ghar kingdom silver drachms, nos 1–152 from the coins collected by Charles Masson in Kabul in 1834, nos 153–214 from a separate parcel marketed in Calcutta before 1840. *YE = Yazdagird era

	Ruler	Province	Mint	Mint signature	AD	AH	Other eras	Counter-marks	Collection	BMC Walker
33	Khusrau II imitation	?	?	[RAPY]?	613		24	Göbl 56	Masson IOC.490	
34	anon	Sakastan	Sijistān	SK	651	[31]	YE20	5	Masson Fitzwilliam CM.IS.1	
35	anon	Sakastan	Sijistān	SK	651	[31]	YE20	10	Masson IOC.539	6
36	anon	Sakastan	Sijistān	SK	668	[48]	YE37	45	Masson IOC.546	21
37	anon	Fars	Bīshāpūr	BYŠ	678	[59]	YE47	1, 3, 10, 21	Masson IOC.545	23
38	anon	Fars	Bīshāpūr	BYŠ	680	[61]	YE49	3, 14	Masson 1845,EIC.36	32
39	anon	Fars	Bīshāpūr	BYŠ	681	[62]	YE50	3	Masson IOC.543	34
40	anon	Khuzistan	?	GW?	666	[46]	YE35	2	Masson IOC.542	20
41	anon	Jibal	Rayy	RD	663	[43]	YE32	14, 39	Masson IOC.541	18
42	'Abdallāh b. 'Āmir	Fars	Darābjird	DA?	682–92	?	YE?		Masson **F526/1a, Pl. 12.43**	
43	Ziyād b. Abī Sufyān	Fars	Bīshāpūr	BYŠ	671	51			Masson Fitzwilliam CM.IS.4	
44	Ziyād b. Abī Sufyān	Fars	Bīshāpūr	BYŠ	672	53		4	Masson IOC.2313	51
45	Ziyād b. Abī Sufyān	Fars	Darābjird	DA	672	[52]	YE41	11	Masson IOC.2312	59
46	Ziyād b. Abī Sufyān	Fars	Darābjird	DA	674	[55]	YE43		Masson IOC.2311	61
47	Ziyād b. Abī Sufyān	Iraq	Baṣra	BCRA	674	55			Masson Fitzwilliam CM.IS.3	Cam.2
48	'Abd al-Rahmān b. Zayd	Kirman	near Kirman	BN	672	52		3	Masson IOC.2314	151
49	'Ubaydallāh b. Ziyād	Sakastan	Sijistān	SK	675	56			Masson Fitzwilliam CM.IS.13	
50	Ubaydallāh b. Ziyad	Kirmān	Kirmān	KRMANHP	679	60			Masson IOC.2315 Wilson p. 402, no. 33, pl. XVII, 3; Thomas p. 291, no. 13	95
51	'Ubaydallāh b. Ziyād	Fars	Darābjird	DA	677	[58]	26	14, ?	Masson Fitzwilliam CM.IS.10. Thomas p. 290, no. 8 'Masson'	Cam.5
52	'Ubaydallāh b. Ziyād	Fars	Darābjird	DA	682	[63]	YE 51		Masson 1845,EIC.20	91
53	'Ubaydallāh b. Ziyād	Iraq	Baṣra	BCRA	678	59		14	Masson Fitzwilliam CM.IS.5. Thomas p. 291, no. 10, 'Masson'	T.7
54	'Ubaydallāh b. Ziyād	Khuzistan	?	WH	679	60		33	Masson 1845,EIC.46	98
55	'Ubaydallāh b. Ziyād	Iraq	Baṣra	BCRA	678	61		14, 39	Masson Fitzwilliam CM.IS.6. Walker p. 185 = Thomas p. 291, no. 11?	
56	'Ubaydallāh b. Ziyād	Iraq	Baṣra	BCRA	678	61			Masson Fitzwilliam CM.IS.7. Walker p. 192; Thomas p. 304, no. 35	
57	'Ubaydallāh b. Ziyād	Iraq	Baṣra	BCRA	682	[63]	YE 51	15, 21, ?	Masson Fitzwilliam CM.IS.9	Cam.3
58	'Ubaydallāh b. Ziyād	Iraq	Baṣra	BCRA	682	63		14	Masson Fitzwilliam CM.TM.20, J.D. Tremlett	

Table 23 continued

	Ruler	Province	Mint	Mint signature	AD	AH	Other eras	Counter-marks	Collection	BMC Walker
59	'Ubaydallāh b. Ziyād	Iraq	Baṣra	BCRA	683	64		14, ?	Masson Fitzwilliam CM.IS.8, Walker p. 185 = Thomas p. 291, no. 12?	Cam.4
60	'Ubaydallāh b. Ziyād	Iraq	Dasht Maysān	DŠT	680	61			Masson Fitzwilliam CM.IS.11. Walker p. 106 'Masson'	Cam.6
61	'Ubaydallāh b. Ziyād	Iraq	Dasht Maysān	DŠT	681	62			Masson Calcutta Smith p. 229, no. 1	
62	'Ubaydallāh b. Ziyād	Jibal	Rayy	RD	681	62		14	Masson Fitzwilliam CM.IS.12	
63	Salm b. Ziyād	Khurasan	Abrashahr	APRŠT	683	64		14, 47, 51	Masson 1845,EIC.16	111
64	Salm b. Ziyād	Khurasan	Abrashahr	APRŠT	683	64		27, 34?, 47, 51	Masson 1845,EIC.49	110
65	Salm b. Ziyād	Khurasan	Haraat	HRA	686	67		38 (x 2), 39?	Masson 1845,EIC.22	115
66	Salm b. Ziyād	Khurasan	Haraat	HRA	686	67		14, 33	Masson 1845,EIC.32	116
67	Salm b. Ziyād	Khurasan	Haraat	HRA	686	67		18, 46	Masson IOC.2324	117
68	Salm b. Ziyād	Khurasan	Haraat?	HRA?	686	?		32, 49	Masson **F526/1a, Pl. 12.41** (rev. not seen)	
69	Salm b. Ziyād	Khurasan	Merv	MRW	681	62		14, 52	Masson IOC.2319	123
70	Salm b. Ziyād	Khurasan	Merv	MRW	682	63		?	Masson 1845,EIC.39	131
71	Salm b. Ziyād	Khurasan	Merv	MRW	682	63		12, 39	Masson 1845,EIC.41	126
72	Salm b. Ziyād	Khurasan	Merv	MRW	682	63		14, 47, 51	Masson IOC.2321	128
73	Salm b. Ziyād	Khurasan	Merv	MRW	683	64		14, 39	Masson 1845,EIC.23	134
74	Salm b. Ziyād	Khurasan	Merv	MRW	683	64		1, 39	Masson A. Cunningham 1894,0506.1375	133
75	Salm b. Ziyād	Khurasan	Merv	MRW	683	64		46	Masson IOC.2322	135
76	Salm b. Ziyād	Khurasan	Merv	MRW	684	65		14	Masson Calcutta Smith p. 230, no. 2	
77	Salm b. Ziyād	Khurasan	Merv	MRW	685	66			Masson Thomas p. 294 'Masson'	T.12
78	Salm b. Ziyād	Khurasan	Merv	MRW	686	67		32	Masson Wilson p. 401, no. 32, pl. XVII, 2	
79	Salm b. Ziyād	Khurasan	Merv	MRW	688	69		39, 47, 51	Masson 1845,EIC.25	141
80	Salm b. Ziyād	Khurasan	Merv	MRW	688	69		39, 47, 51	Masson 1845,EIC.42	139
81	Salm b. Ziyād	Khurasan	Merv	MRW	688	69		14, 47, 51	Masson IOC.2325	140
82	Salm b. Ziyād	Khurasan	Merv	MRW	689	62–70		7?, 16	Masson 1845,EIC.43	144
83	Salm b. Ziyād	Khurasan	Merv	MRW	689	70		7	Masson IOC.2326	143
84	Salm b. Ziyād	Khurasan	Merv al-Rudh	MRWRWT	682	63		14, 29	Masson A. Cunningham 1894,0506.1376	147
85	Salm b. Ziyād	Khurasan	Merv al-Rudh	MRWRWT	682	63		7?	Masson IOC.2318	146

Table 23 continued

	Ruler	Province	Mint	Mint signature	AD	AH	Other eras	Counter-marks	Collection	BMC Walker
86	Salm b. Ziyād	Khurasan	Merv al-Rudh	MRWRWT	682	63		6, 14, 39	Masson IOC.2320	145
87	Salm b. Ziyād	Khurasan	Merv al-Rudh	MRWRWT	689	70		14, 28	Masson IOC.2327	148
88	Salm b. Ziyād	Sakastan	Sijistān	SK	675	56			Masson IOC.2316 Thomas p. 293, no. 15	122
89	Salm b. Ziyād	Sakastan	Sijistān	SYKACTAN	683	64			Masson Fitzwilliam CM.IS.14	
90	Salm b. Ziyād	Fars	Ardashīr Khurrah	ART	677	[58]	26	14	Masson IOC.2323	112
91	Salm b. Ziyād	Fars	Darābgird	DA	677	[58]	26	14, 39	Masson 1845,EIC.15	114
92	Qaṭān b. 'Udayy?	Khurasan	Haraat	HRA	686	67		14	Masson Fitzwilliam CM.IS.32. Thomas p. 318, no. 59	Cam.15
93	'Abdallāh b. al-Zubayr	Kirmān	Kirmān	KRMAN	681	62		25, 29, 32	Masson IOC.2329	38
94	'Abdallāh b. al-Zubayr	Kirmān	Kirmān	KRMAN	682	69		43	Masson OR.8912	39
95	Asram b. Sufan	Jibal	Rayy	RD	685	67?			Masson Fitzwilliam CM.IS.31. Thomas p. 317, no. 58	Cam.14
96	Muṣ'ab b. al-Zubayr	Kirmān	Kirmān	KRMAN	690	71			Masson 1845,EIC.37	207
97	'Abdallāh b. Khāzim	Khurasan	Abrashahr	APRŠT	686	67			Masson IOC.2335	154
98	'Abdallāh b. Khāzim	Khurasan	Abrashahr	APRŠT	686	67		14	Masson IOC.2339	155
99	'Abdallāh b. Khāzim	Khurasan	Abrashahr	APRŠT	688	69		14, 39	Masson IOC.2341	156
100	'Abdallāh b. Khāzim	Khurasan	Abrashahr	APRŠT	688	69			Masson IOC.2342	157
101	'Abdallāh b. Khāzim	Khurasan	camp mint	BBA	686	67		20, 21	Masson 1845,EIC.28	161
102	'Abdallāh b. Khāzim	Khurasan	camp mint	BBA	686	67		37, 39, 49	Masson IOC.2336	158
103	'Abdallāh b. Khāzim	Khurasan	camp mint	BBA	686	67			Masson IOC.2338	159
104	'Abdallāh b. Khāzim	Khurasan	camp mint	BBA	687	?		14	Masson **F526/1a, Pl. 12.42**	
105	'Abdallāh b. Khāzim	Khurasan	camp mint	BBA	687	68			Masson 1845,EIC.48	163
106	'Abdallāh b. Khāzim	Khurasan	camp mint	BBA	687	68		14, 32	Masson IOC.2340	164
107	'Abdallāh b. Khāzim	Khurasan	Merv	MRW	684	65		14, 39	Masson IOC.2332	168
108	'Abdallāh b. Khāzim	Khurasan	Merv	MRW	684	65		39	Masson IOC.2333	169
109	'Abdallāh b. Khāzim	Khurasan	Merv	MRW	685	66		27, 41, 51	Masson IOC.2334	170
110	'Abdallāh b. Khāzim	Khurasan	Merv	MRW	686	67		7, ?	Masson IOC.2337	173
111	'Abdallāh b. Khāzim	Khurasan	Merv	MRW	688	69		14, 33, 39	Masson 1845,EIC.24	177
112	'Abdallāh b. Khāzim	Khurasan	Merv	MRW	688	69		14	Masson Fitzwilliam CM.IS.15	
113	'Abdallāh b. Khāzim	Khurasan	Merv	MRW	689	70		14, 39	Masson IOC.2344	186
114	'Abdallāh b. Khāzim	Khurasan	Merv	MRW	691	72			Masson Calcutta Smith p. 230, no. 3	

Table 23 continued

	Ruler	Province	Mint	Mint signature	AD	AH	Other eras	Counter-marks	Collection	BMC Walker
115	'Abdallāh b. Khāzim	Khurasan	Merv	MRW	691	72		14	Masson IOC.2345	188
116	'Abdallāh b. Khāzim	Khurasan	Merv al-Rudh	MRWRW	688	69		39, 47, 51	Masson IOC.2331	189
117	Umayya b. 'Abdallāh	Fars	Ardashīr Khur-rah	ART	689	70		14, 33	Masson Fitzwilliam CM.IS.19	
118	Umayya b. 'Abdallāh	Fars	Ardashīr Khur-rah	ART	689	70		14	Masson Fitzwilliam CM.IS.20	
119	Umayya b. 'Abdallāh	?	?	?	689	?		39?	Masson **F526/1a, Pl. 12.43** (rev. not seen)	
120	'Abdallāh b. ?	Sakastan	Sijistān	SK	685	66		11	Masson IOC.2343	241
121	Umayya b. 'Abdallāh	Sakastan	Sijistān	SYCTAN	692	73		14	Masson Fitzwilliam CM.IS.29	Cam.12
122	'Umar b. 'Ubaydallāh	Kirmān	Kirmān	KRMAN	684	65		14	Masson 1845,EIC.21	203
123	'Umar b. 'Ubaydallāh	Fars	Ardashīr Khur-rah	ART	688	69			Masson Fitzwilliam CM.IS.17	Cam.8
124	'Umar b. 'Ubaydallāh	Fars	Ardashīr Khur-rah	ART	689	70		14	Masson Fitzwilliam CM.IS.18	Cam.9
125	'Umar b. 'Ubaydallāh	Fars	Bīshāpūr	BYŠ	686	68		14, 33, 41, 51	Masson Fitzwilliam CM.IS.21. Thomas p. 303, no. 31a	
126	'Umar b. 'Ubaydallāh	Fars	Bīshāpūr	BYŠ	686	68		14, ?	Masson Fitzwilliam CM.IS.22. Thomas p. 303, no. 31b	
127	'Umar b. 'Ubaydallāh	Fars	Bīshāpūr	BYŠ	686	68		33	Masson Fitzwilliam CM.IS.23. Thomas p. 303, no. 31c	
128	'Umar b. 'Ubaydallāh	Fars	Bīshāpūr	BYŠ	687	69		39	Masson Fitzwilliam CM.IS.24. Thomas p. 303, no. 31d 'Masson'	
129	'Umar b. 'Ubaydallāh	Fars	Bīshāpūr	BYŠ	689	70		7, 14	Masson 1845,EIC.45	199
130	'Umar b. 'Ubaydallāh	Fars	Bīshāpūr	BYŠ	689	70		14	Masson 1845,EIC.47	198
131	'Umar b. 'Ubaydallāh	Fars	Bīshāpūr	BYŠ	689	70		14	Masson A. Cunningham 1894,0506.1377	200
132	'Umar b. 'Ubaydallāh	Fars	Bīshāpūr	BYŠ	689	70		14, 15	Masson Fitzwilliam CM.IS.25	
133	'Umar b. 'Ubaydallāh	Fars	Bīshāpūr	BYŠ	689	70		14	Masson IOC.2346	201
134	'Umar b. 'Ubaydallāh	Fars	Ishtakhr	ST	687	69			Masson Fitzwilliam CM.IS.26. Thomas p. 303 no. 33 'Masson'	Cam.10
135	'Umar b. 'Ubaydallāh	Fars	Ishtakhr	ST	689	70			Masson Fitzwilliam CM.IS.27	
136	Numayra b. Muslih	Fars	Arrajān	WHYC	692	73		39	Masson Fitzwilliam CM.IS.28	Cam.11
137	Ḥumrān b. Abān	Fars	Ardashīr Khur-rah	ART	691	72			Masson Fitzwilliam CM.IS.30. Thomas p. 318, no. 60	Cam.13
138	'Abd al-Malik b Marwān	Khurasan	Merv	MRW	694	75		14	Masson Fitzwilliam CM.IS.2. Thomas p. 312 no. 45 'Masson'	Cam.1

Table 23 continued

	Ruler	Province	Mint	Mint signature	AD	AH	Other eras	Counter-marks	Collection	BMC Walker
139	'Abd al-'Azīz b. 'Abdallāh	Sakastan	Sijistān	SK	685	66			Masson Fitzwilliam CM.IS.16. F526/1a 12, 38	Cam.7
140	al-Muhallab b. Abī Ṣufra	Fars	Bīshāpūr	BYŠ	695	76			Masson IOC.2347	224
141	anon (Gōzgān)	Ghar kingdom	Anbēr	ANB?	681	[62]	YE50	40	Masson IOC.541 Thomas p. 283 'Masson'	T.2
142	in name of Salm b. Ziyād	Ghar kingdom	Faryab?	PHRZ/ παρ[δο]	691	[72]	YE60	12	Masson IOC.2317	150
143	in name of Salm b. Ziyād	Ghar kingdom	Merv	MRW/ αμβηρο	695	[76]	YE64	26	Masson IOC.2328	138
144	in name of 'Abdallāh b. Khāzim	Ghar kingdom	Anbēr	ANBYR	694	[75]	YE63	14, 39	Masson IOC.2330	166
145	Zhulād Gōzgān	Ghar kingdom	Anbēr	ANBYR/ αμβηρο	706	88			Masson A. Cunningham 1894,0506.1378	248
146	Zhulād Gōzgān	Ghar kingdom	Anbēr	ANBYR/ αμβηρο	706	88			Masson Calcutta Smith p. 230, no. 4	
147	Zhulād Gōzgān	Ghar kingdom	Anbēr	ANBYR/ αμβηρο	707	89			Masson 1845,EIC.34	250
148	Zhulād Gōzgān	Ghar kingdom	Anbēr	ANBYR/ αμβηρο	707	89			Masson A. Cunningham 1894,0506.1374	252
149	Zhulād Gōzgān	Ghar kingdom	Anbēr	ANBYR/ αμβηρο	707	89			Masson A. Cunningham 1894,0506.1379	253
150	Zhulād Gōzgān	Ghar kingdom	Anbēr	ANBYR/ αμβηρο	707	89			Masson IOC.2357	251
151	Zhulād Gōzgān	Ghar kingdom	Anbēr	ANBYR/ αμβηρο	707	89			Masson IOC.2358 Wilson p. 402, no. 34, pl. XVII, 4	249
152	Zhulād Gōzgān	Ghar kingdom	Anbēr	ANBYR/ αμβηρο	707	89		34	Masson OR.7562 Walker 'Masson IOC'	254
153	Khusrau II	Khurasan	camp mint	BBA	619		30	39	Emily Eden 1853 OR.142	
154	Khusrau II	Fars	Ardashīr Khurrah	ART	627		38	28?, 39, 56	Emily Eden 1853 OR.166	
155	Khusrau II	Fars	Darābjird	DA	612		23	Göbl 62	Emily Eden 1853 OR.119	
156	Khusrau II	Fars	DR?	DR	625		36	2, 11	Emily Eden 1853 OR.9185	
157	Khusrau II	Fars	Yazd	YZ	624		35	2	Emily Eden 1853 OR.172	
158	Khusrau II	Khuzistan	Susa	AY	626		37	15, 33, Göbl 65	Emily Eden 1853 OR.162	
159	Khusrau II	Jibal	Hamadān	AHM	624		35	2	Emily Eden 1853 OR.9178	
160	Khusrau II	Jibal	Rev-Ardashir?	RYW	625		36	11	Emily Eden 1853 OR.161	
161	Khusrau II	Jibal	?	WYH	621		32	3, 22, 28	Emily Eden 1853 OR.150	
162	anon	Sakastan	Sijistān	SK	651	[31]	YE20	10	Ashmolean J.B. Elliott 1859, Album & Goodwin 357	
163	anon	Sakastan	Sijistān	SK	679	60	YE48	?	Emily Eden 1853 OR.8988	26

Table 23 continued

	Ruler	Province	Mint	Mint signature	AD	AH	Other eras	Counter-marks	Collection	BMC Walker
164	anon	Sakastan	Sijistān	SK	682	63?			Ashmolean J.B. Elliott 1859, Album & Goodwin 372	Ox.1
165	anon	Fars	Bīshāpūr	BYŠ	678	[59]	YE47		Ashmolean J.B. Elliott 1859, Album & Goodwin 119	
166	anon	Fars	Bīshāpūr	BYŠ	679	[60]	YE48	14	Ashmolean J.B. Elliott 1859, Album & Goodwin 127	
167	Ziyād b. Abī Sufyān	Fars	Darābjird	DA	674	55	43		Ashmolean J.B. Elliott 1859, Album & Goodwin 242	
168	Abd al-Rahman b. Zayd	Kirman	Kirman nearby	BN	671	52			Ashmolean J.B. Elliott 1859, Album & Goodwin 108	
169	ʿUbaydallāh b. Ziyād	Sakastan	Sijistān	SK	675	56		14	Emily Eden 1853 OR.9001	92
170	ʿUbaydallāh b. Ziyād	Sakastan	Sijistān	SK	675	56		11	Emily Eden 1853 OR.9002	94
171	ʿUbaydallāh b. Ziyād	Fars	Darābjird	DA	676	[57]	YE45		C.S. Steuart 1848,0803.302	90
172	ʿUbaydallāh b. Ziyād	Iraq	Baṣra	BCRA	676	57			Ashmolean J.B. Elliott 1859, Album & Goodwin 57	Ox.2
173	ʿUbaydallāh b. Ziyād	Iraq	Baṣra	BCRA	679	60		39	Emily Eden 1853 OR.9000	84
174	ʿUbaydallāh b. Ziyād	Iraq	Baṣra	BCRA	681	62			Ashmolean J.B. Elliott 1859, Album & Goodwin 92	Ox.3
175	ʿAbdallāh b. al-Zubayr	Fars	Fasā	DAP	685	]66]	YE54		C.S. Steuart 1848,0803.306	43
176	ʿAṭīya b. al-Aswad	Kirmān	Kirmān	KRMANAN	691	72		48	C.S. Steuart 1848,0803.301	216
177	ʿAṭīya b. al-Aswad	Kirmān	Kirmān nearby	KRMANNAT	694	75		14, 30	C.S. Steuart 1848,0803.304	217
178	Salm b. Ziyād	Khurasan	AYPTAK?	AYPTAK	683	64			Ashmolean J.B. Elliott 1859, Album & Goodwin 43	Ox.4
179	Salm b. Ziyād	Khurasan	Haraat	HRA	686	67		14	Ashmolean J.B. Elliott 1859, Album & Goodwin 306	
180	Salm b. Ziyād	Khurasan	Haraat	HRA	686	67			Ashmolean J.B. Elliott 1859, Album & Goodwin 307	
181	Salm b. Ziyād	Khurasan	Haraat	HRA	686	67		14, 52	Emily Eden 1853 OR.9004	118
182	Salm b. Ziyād	Khurasan	Haraat	HRA	686	67		14, 39, 41, 51, 52	Emily Eden 1853 OR.9005	119
183	Salm b. Ziyād	Khurasan	Haraat	HRA	686	67		29, 39	Emily Eden 1853 OR.9006	120
184	Salm b. Ziyād	Khurasan	Merv	MRW	682	63		14	Ashmolean J.B. Elliott 1859, Album & Goodwin 333	
185	Salm b. Ziyād	Khurasan	Merv	MRW	682	63			Emily Eden 1853 OR.9009	125
186	Salm b. Ziyād	Khurasan	Merv	MRW	682	63		14, 39	Emily Eden 1853 OR.9010	127
187	Salm b. Ziyād	Khurasan	Merv	MRW	682	63		14, 15, 22	Emily Eden 1853 OR.9014	129
188	Salm b. Ziyād	Khurasan	Merv	MRW	682	63		7	Emily Eden 1853 OR.9016	132

Table 23 continued

	Ruler	Province	Mint	Mint signature	AD	AH	Other eras	Counter-marks	Collection	BMC Walker
189	Salm b. Ziyād	Khurasan	Merv	MRW	682	63		14, 40	James Prinsep 1847	124
190	Salm b. Ziyād	Khurasan	Merv	MRW	684	65		33, 47, 51	Emily Eden 1853 OR.9018	137
191	Salm b. Ziyād	Khurasan	Merv	MRW	688	69		14	Emily Eden 1853 OR.9019	142
192	Salm b. Ziyād	Khurasan	Merv al-Rudh	MRWRWT	689	70		14	Emily Eden 1853 OR.9020	149
193	Muḥammad b.'Abdallāh	Khurasan	Haraat	HRA	685	67			Ashmolean J.B. Elliott 1859, Album & Goodwin 308	Ox.5
194	'Abdallāh b. Khāzim	Khurasan	BBA	BBA	686	67		21, 23	Emily Eden 1853 OR.8974	162
195	'Abdallāh b. Khāzim	Khurasan	Merv	MRW	685	66		6, 29	Emily Eden 1853 OR.8975	172
196	'Abdallāh b. Khāzim	Khurasan	Merv	MRW	686	67		32	Emily Eden 1853 OR.8976	174
197	'Abdallāh b. Khāzim	Khurasan	Merv	MRW	688	69		14, 37	Emily Eden 1853 OR.8978	178
198	'Abdallāh b. Khāzim	Khurasan	Merv	MRW	688	69			Emily Eden 1853 OR.8980	180
199	'Abdallāh b. Khāzim	Khurasan	Merv	MRW	688	69		6, 14, 39	Emily Eden 1853 OR.8981	181
200	'Abdallāh b. Khāzim	Khurasan	Merv	MRW	688	69		6	Emily Eden 1853 OR.8983	183
201	'Abdallāh b. Khāzim	Khurasan	Merv	MRW	688	69		14	James Prinsep 1847	175
202	'Abdallāh b. Khāzim	Khurasan	Merv	MRW	688	69		14, 15	James Prinsep 1847	179
203	'Abdallāh b. Khāzim	Khurasan	Merv	MRW	691	72		14, 29	Emily Eden 1853 OR.8984	187
204	Umayya b. 'Abdallāh	Khurasan	Anbēr?	ANBYR	695	[76]	YE64	33	Emily Eden 1853 OR.9025	209
205	Umayya b. 'Abdallāh	Khurasan	Anbēr?	ANBYR	695	[76]	YE64	14, 39	Emily Eden 1853 OR.9026	210
206	Umayya b. 'Abdallāh	Sakastan	Sijistān	SYCSTAN	695	[76]	YE64	14	Emily Eden 1853 OR.9028	212
207	'Umar b. 'Ubaydallāh	Fars	Bīshāpūr	BYŠ	686	68		29, 39	Emily Eden 1853 OR.9023	194
208	'Umar b. 'Ubaydallāh	Fars	Bīshāpūr	BYŠ	689	70		14, 29	Emily Eden 1853 OR.9024	196
209	'Abd al-'Azīz b.'Abdallāh	Sakastan	Sijistān	SK	685	66		14	Ashmolean J.B. Elliott 1859, Album & Goodwin 366	Ox.6
210	'Abd al-'Azīz b.'Abdallāh	Sakastan	Sijistān	SK	685	66		14, 42	James Prinsep 1847	192
211	al-Muhallab b. Abī Ṣufra	Fars	Darābjird	DA	695	76			C.S. Steuart 1848,0803.303	227
212	Zhulād Gōzgān	Ghar kingdom	Anbēr	ANBYR/ αμβηρο	706	88			C.S. Steuart 1848,0803.300	246
213	Zhulād Gōzgān	Ghar kingdom	Anbēr	ANBYR/ αμβηρο	706	88			Ashmolean J.B. Elliott 1859, Album & Goodwin 9	Ox.7
214	Zhulād Gōzgān	Ghar kingdom	Anbēr	ANBYR/ αμβηρο	706	88			Emily Eden 1853 OR.8921	247

Table 23 continued

Part 3: Catalogue of Coins

Elizabeth Errington and Paramdip Khera with Joe Cribb, Kirstin Leighton-Boyce and Wannaporn Kay Rienjang

A comprehensive account of the coin collections from Begram only exists for the period 1833–5. Masson published three articles on the subject in *Journal of the Asiatic Society of Bengal* (1834, 1836a, 1836b). The primary source, however, is the Masson manuscript 'Enumeration of coins collected from Begram during years 1833, 1834 & 1835' and its associated 'Analysis of the Begram coins with reference to plates'. It is reproduced in full here (**F526/1a, Pls 1–15**, pp. 36–73 above) and forms the basis for this catalogue. The original manuscript was submitted for publication in *JASB* 1836, but was severely edited on the grounds that many of the coin drawings had already been published, so only those which were new types or had more legible inscriptions were included. The discussion was also considerably abridged despite James Prinsep claiming that 'the text, in justice to the author, we have inscribed entire' (Masson 1836a, p. 21). Supplementary information exists in various manuscript lists compiled by Masson from 1836 onwards, which survive in the British Library India Office Collections (**Vol. II, pp. 58, 60–3, 66–8, 72, 75, 80–101**; Appendices 2–3, pp. 329–33 below).

There is, of course, also Horace Hayman Wilson's account of a fair number of the coins in *Ariana Antiqua*. Until now this has been the standard work on the subject (1841, pp. 215–439, Coins pls I–XXII). As its coin drawings are crucial to identifying Masson coins in the British Museum and elsewhere, they are included in the catalogue – alongside their actual coins where recognised – in order to provide as comprehensive a survey of the recorded collection as possible.

This inevitably comes with the caveat that only a tiny percentage of the original collection was recorded. Not only is it probable that most of the coins from the Afghanistan region in the India Office Collection, transferred to the British Museum in 1882, originated from Masson, but there is also a strong suspicion that many more acquired from contemporary collectors like Alexander Cunningham originated from the same source. To cite one example: as Joe Cribb's reconstitution of the Arab-Sasanian hoard demonstrates, coins from the same original source have been scattered far and wide (pp. 110–26 above). To subject other groups of coins in known collections to similar scrutiny could be equally productive, but is beyond the present ambition, which aims to provide a survey of identifiable coins in the residue collection now in the British Museum.

There is an inevitable bias towards coins of the pre-Islamic period, which reflects the interests of Masson and his contemporaries. Wilson, for example, only publishes 34 Sultanate coins and 36 copper alloy bull and horseman jitals associated with the successors to the Hindu Shahis, which he says were 'chiefly' from Masson, but were also found by Edward Thomas at Saharanpur in Uttar Pradesh and Karnal in Haryana (1841, pp. 430–9, Coins pls XIX–XX). In Masson's later inventory of the coins in his own collection, he gives a total of 1,449 Ghurid and Ghaznavid coins ('List of coins A', **F526/1f, Vol. II, pp. 86–7, 89, Figs 98–9**). he also attempted to transcribe the inscriptions on Samanid coins (**Figs 18–19**).

The catalogue is arranged roughly chronologically according to issuer, not separated by place of acquisition.

However a broad rule of thumb applies, i.e. most of the gold and silver coins were purchased in Kabul bazaar, while copper alloy coins of the period *c.* 4th century BC to *c.* 10th century AD are primarily from Begram. This includes finds not only from the site, but also from the surrounding plain or *dasht*. It is further possible that the collection area may have included the extensive urban remains of Tatarang Zar to the south, where numerous 'coins, trinkets &co.' scattered the surface (Ball and Gardin 1982, no. 1154; see p. 9 above).

Coins of all metals from *c.* 8th century onwards (Hindu Shahi, Ghaznavid, Ghurid and Khwarazm Shah) were also acquired in Kabul bazaar. Smaller numbers of coins were bought in Jalalabad, Charikar and elsewhere, but are usually not now identifiable. An exception is the silver Hazarajat hoard which was documented as follows.

In 1833 Masson obtained a 'parcel' of 120 'Bactrian' drachms and hemi-drachms from a Hindu trader at Charikar. The coins were originally acquired from a Hazara and are thus thought to be from Hazarajat (central Afghanistan), although Masson was unable 'to ascertain the spot, or under what circumstances these coins were found' (1836a, p. 15). Later in the same article he says he bought '121' coins in Kabul bazaar (1836a, p. 21). The hoard comprised 'seven quadrangular silver coins of Apollodotus, 108 silver coins of Menander, and five silver coins of Antimachus'. However, elsewhere Masson talks of obtaining two large parcels of the coins of the same three rulers in similar proportions, one in 1834 (the Hazarajat hoard) and another in 1835, evidently from Kabul bazaar, but possibly originally part of the same hoard (**F526/1a, f. 18**). Fifty-seven drachms putatively from the Hazarajat hoard have been identified in the Fitzwilliam Museum: 3 Apollodotus I, 48 Menander and 6 Antimachus II (former India Office collection, see **FW 1906**; **Vol. II, pp. 121–2**; MacDowall 1991, pp. 188–98), but it seems probable that Kabul bazaar coins may be included among them.

Masson also acquired two unique coins from one of the coppersmiths at Charikar, namely the large square copper alloy coin of Menander with a dolphin on the reverse (**E161/VII f. 20**; **Vol. II, p. 60**; **F526/1a, Pl. 1.25**, see pp. 36, 39), and a silver drachm of Wima Kadphises (**F526/1a, Pl. 8.3** see pp. 56–7).

Other cited sources of small quantities of coins are Charikar, Ghazni, Jalalabad and Peshawar (**E161/VII ff. 6–7, 13, 20–2, 25, 27, 38**; **E163 Section 19, f. 17**; **F526/1k**; **Vol. II, pp. 45, 48, 52–3, 58, 60–1, 63–4, 72, 101**).

Punch-marked coins

Punch-marked coins are called 'Buddhist' or 'punched' by Masson, who identifies the marks as 'various Buddhist symbols [such] as the chaitya [three-arched hill and

Figure 20 Silver punch-marked coins. GH574 and an unidentified type (F526/1h: Vol. II, Fig. 101.9–10)

crescent], praying wheel [sun], flower vase (bo[dhi]-tree?), an animal &c.' (**Vol. II, pp. 93–4**). However, he also notes that 'it is probable that the symbols and marks on these coins are not constant' and that some of them are silver-plated. He says that 'these coins are found more frequently in the bazaars of towns, as Kabul, Ghazni &c. than at the site of Begram, where being of only very casual occurrence, we would not venture to affirm that they have been ever current there' (**F526/1a, f. 9, Pl. 4.86–91**). He only records acquiring a number of examples from Kabul bazaar: one in 1836 and two lots of thirty-seven and six respectively in 1837 (**E161/VII ff. 29–31**). Subsequently 73 were forwarded to Pottinger on 15 October 1837 (**E161/VII f. 33**), while a further 33 were acquired between November 1837 and June 1838 (**F526/1d**).

The quantity of these coins in the original collection seems to have been far larger than Masson records. At the 1887 coin auction on behalf of the Government of India, 351 silver punch-marked coins were sold in five lots, while a further lot comprised 83 'early punched copper coins of same class; and others, with lion and elephant, &c.' (Sotheby, Wilkinson and Hodge 1887, p. 57, lots 787–92). Presumably the last lot included, in addition, other examples of so-called local issues, i.e. cast coins and coins using the same punched-mark symbols, particularly the three-arched hill, tree in railing and 'taurine'/sun and moon (**Figs 1.33–50, 2.1–20**).

A total of 40 silver, silver-plated and copper alloy punch-marked coins now survive in the Masson collections: five in the Asia Department material from Begram and the remainder in the India Office Loan Collection. They all had the standard Begram baked mud patina and the silver examples were mostly unrecognisable prior to cleaning and conservation. Apart from two *c.* 4th-century BC half shekels (**Fig. 21.1**; uncleaned), the majority have five punch-marks and belong to the later phases of Mauryan coinage (Gupta and Hardaker 2014, series IV–VII: GH361–GH590). There are only a few isolated examples of series IV (**Fig. 21.2–6**) and five of series V (types GH507 and GH510: **Fig. 21.7–11**), with one variant (**Fig. 21.28**, GH526). Series VI forms the largest group: 14 coins (GH552–GH575: **Fig. 21.12–25**). Finally, there are two coins of series VII (GH586, GH590: **Figs 26–7**).

The dominant type is GH574, which occurs in large numbers in hoards from the north-west, stretching from Rajasthan into Haryana, Taxila and Peshawar in north-west Pakistan and Afghanistan. A study of late punch-mark hoards showed that GH574 and GH575 occur in inverse proportion to each other: where there are concentrations of GH574 (like here), there are only small quantities of GH575 and vice versa (Errington 2003, p. 78). GH574 is confirmed as a late type which continued to the end of punch-marked coinage by such factors as the debasement of silver, the introduction of a sixth mark on some coins (**Fig. 21.23**) and – not evident in the Begram sample – the existence of copper alloy examples, lowering weights and the corruption of symbols. These characteristics are also symptomatic of punch-marked derivatives of the post Mauryan period (**Figs 21.31–2**).

One of the copper alloy examples (**Fig. 21.28**) still bears distinct traces of silver plating and it is probable that the remaining five examples were also once plated or had a silver wash. According to Terry Hardaker, 'coins imitating Mauryan types from series V and VI have been noted from widespread hoards (not just in the north-west). … The symbols are faithfully copied from authentic coins [and] there is no chain of progressively degraded derivatives. Such coins may therefore be contemporary forgeries' (Gupta and Hardaker 2014, p. 196).

Achaemenid punch-marked coins
Fig. 21.1 – 1880.3733.a-b. Two unifaced silver alloy, cup-shaped half shekels, with a punch-mark representing a six-armed symbol. Achaemenid, minted in Gandhara, *c.* 4th century BC. **a.** 1.13g, 12mm; **b.** 1.36g, 13mm.

Mauryan period (*c.* 269–187 BC)
Coins with five individually punched symbols, including sun and six-armed symbol. GH types: Gupta and Hardaker 2014.

Total 32 silver coins: 3.23g–3g (9), 2.98g–2.52g (19), 1.99g – 1.38g (4); 2 silver-plated copper alloy coins: 2.71g, 2.26g; 4 copper alloy coins: 2.68g–1.75g.

Fig. 21.2 – IOLC.1. 1.9g, 19mm; GH361.

Fig. 21.3 – IOLC.2. 2.86g, 17mm; GH401.

Fig. 21.4 – IOLC.3. 2.87g, 16mm; GH416.

Fig. 21.5 – IOLC.4. 2.98g, 18mm; GH450 (?) Reverse

Fig. 21.6 – IOLC.5. 2.95g, 16mm; GH468.

Fig. 21.7 – IOLC.6. 2.88g, 15mm; GH507.
Fig. 21.8 – IOLC.7. 2.91g, 12mm; GH507 (?)

Fig. 21.9 – IOLC.8. 3.02g, 13mm; GH510.
Fig. 21.10 – IOLC.9. 3.1g, 15mm; GH510 (?)
Fig. 21.11 – IOLC.5410. 1.38g, 13mm; GH510 (?).

Fig. 21.12 – IOLC.11. 2.98g, 14mm; GH552.

Fig. 21.13 – IOLC.12. 2.23g, 13mm; GH572 *Reverse*
Fig. 21.14 – 1880.3733.d. 3.2g, 14mm; GH572.

Fig. 21.15 – IOLC.14. 2.8g, 17mm; GH573.

Fig. 21.16 – IOLC.15. 2.98g, 14mm; GH574.
Fig. 21.17 – IOLC.16. 2.76g, 19mm; GH574.
Fig. 21.18 – IOLC.18. 3.06g, 16mm; GH574.
Fig. 21.19 – IOLC.17. 3.09g, 19mm; GH574.
Fig. 21.20 – IOLC.19. 2.74g, 15mm; GH574.
Fig. 21.21 – IOLC.20. 2.84g, 19mm; GH574.
Fig. 21.22 – IOLC.21. 3.12g, 15mm; GH574.

Fig. 21.23 – IOLC.10. 2.53g, 13mm; GH574 with 6th symbol (?)

Fig. 21.24 – IOLC.22. 2.74g, 14mm; GH575.
Fig. 21.25 – IOLC.23. 3g, 13mm; GH575.

Fig. 21.26 – 1880.3768. IM 422 / SKM 1122. 3.14g, 15mm; GH586.

Fig. 21.27 – IOLC.24. 2.88g, 15mm; GH590.

Fig. 21.28 – IOLC.26. 2.86g, 17mm. Uncertain type, seems to combine marks 1–3 of GH526a with a caduceus as the 4th mark and tree in railing as reverse mark and possibly also as 5th mark as with GH526.

Five worn coins; punch-marks illegible: **IOLC.13.** 2.52g, 14mm; **IOLC.25.** 2.97g, 16mm; **IOLC.27.** 1.99g, 18mm; **IOLC.28.** 2.88g, 10mm; **IOLC.29.** 1.7g, 12mm.

Figure 21 Silver punch-marked and local copper alloy coins

Silver-plated copper alloy coins – 5 punch-marks

Fig. 21.29 – IOLC.30. Worn, silver-plated copper alloy coin with five punch-marks including sun, zebu standing to right and three-arched hill. 2.26g, 15mm; GH546.

Fig. 21.30 – IOLC.31. Copper alloy punch-marked coin, probably originally silver-plated. 2.71g, 15mm; GH480.

Copper alloy punch-marked coins

Fig. 21.31 – 1880.4117.j. 2.18g, 13mm. Base silver (?) or copper alloy punch-marked coin with a reversed image of peacock on hill and caduceus; late derivative of GH590.

Fig. 21.32 – IOLC.34. Worn copper alloy coin, with four punch-marks; 2.58g, 13mm; GH617–20. The type is a late derivative of series VI, GH566, but appears to have the same reverse mark as **Fig. 21.15–26**, instead of the usual caduceus as on **Fig. 21.9–11**. See Errington 2003, pl. 23.

Three worn copper alloy coins with five illegible punch-marks: **IOLC.32.** 2.68g, 16mm; **IOLC.33.** 2.13g, 16mm; **IOLC.35.** 1.75g, 19mm. Not illustrated.

Local issues (c. 2nd century BC)
These so-called local issues have generally been attributed to Taxila, but appear to be common at Begram. They comprise cast coins (**Fig. 21.33–9**), uniface coins struck with a single die (**Fig. 22.1–10**) and coins struck on both sides (**Fig. 21.40–6**), the largest group being the type with elephant and lion (**Fig. 22.11–15**).

Cast copper alloy coins
Fig. 21.33 – IOC.1056. *Obverse*: Standard (top left), hollow cross (top right); swastika (bottom left), elephant walking to left (bottom right). *Reverse*: Tree in railing (left), three-arched hill and crescent (top right), inverted sun and moon/'taurine' and standard (bottom right). 3.99g, 14mm x 14mm. BMC India (Ancient) p. 87.17, pl.XI.7; Wilson 1841, p. 416, no. 9, Coins pl. XV.32.

Fig. 21.34 – IOLC.36. *Obverse*: Elephant to left before standard, standing on horizontal ladder; swastika and inverted taurine/sun and moon above. *Reverse*: Hollow cross (bottom left), three-arched hill and crescent (top left), tree in railing to right. 2.45g, 12mm.

Fig. 21.35 – IOLC.46. 1.48g, 13mm.
Fig. 21.36 – IOLC.38. 1.02g, 11mm.
Total 3 coins: 2.45g–1.02g. **F526/1h: Vol. II, pp. 93, 95, Fig. 101.19**.

Fig. 21.37 – IOLC.43. *Obverse*: Elephant to left. *Reverse*: Three-arched hill with crescent. 2.19g, 14mm.

Fig. 21.38 – IOLC.42. 1.98g, 12mm.

Fig. 21.39: Wilson 1841, p. 416, no. 8, Coins pl. XV.33. Coin not traced.

Struck copper alloy coins
Fig. 21.40 – IOLC.44. *Obverse*: Three-arched hill with crescent. *Reverse*: Tree in railing, flanked by taurine on either side. 2.73g, 14mm. **F526/1h: Vol. II, pp. 93, 95, Fig. 101.15**.

Fig. 21.41 – IOLC.41. *Obverse*: Three-arched hill with crescent; taurine to right. *Reverse*: Unclear: Three-arched hill with crescent, taurine to right (?). 0.98g, 13mm.

Fig. 21.42–9 – F526/1h: Vol. II, pp. 93–5, Fig. 101.11–14, 16–18. Copper alloy coins illustrated in 'Descriptive catalogue of select coins in the cabinet of Mr Masson'. Not traced. The predominant symbol is the three-arched hill and crescent, with or without the taurine (**Fig. 21.42–7**), tree in railing (**Fig. 21.47–9**), symbol resembling a Brahmi *go* (**Fig. 21.45**) and, in one instance, a plant (**Fig. 21.44**).

Fig. 21.50 – IOLC.40. *Obverse*: Zebu standing to left before tree in railing. *Reverse*: Unclear; probably uniface. 2.54g, 17mm.

Uniface issues
Fig. 22.1 – IOC.1051. Three-arched hill and crescent (left), a swastika, and a triangular 'hill' of ten dots (right); a wavy line below indicates water. 9.82g, 23mm x 21mm. **F526/1a, Pl. 4.84**; BMC India (Ancient) p. 222.69, pl.XXXII.7; Wilson 1841, p. 415, no. 4, Coins pl. XV.28.

Fig. 22.2: **F526/1a, Pl. 4.78**. Reverse image of **Fig. 22.1**. Coin not traced.

Fig. 22.3 – IOC.1052. Top left a triangular 'hill' of nine dots and a three-arched hill and crescent (top right), a wavy line indicating water (middle) and two vine tendrils each with two bunches of grapes (below). 8.83g, 22mm x 18mm. **F526/1a, Pl. 4.82**; BMC India (Ancient) p. 222.66; Wilson 1841, p. 415, no. 5, Coins pl. XV.29.

Fig. 22.4 – IOC.1058. A three-arched hill and crescent above a triangular 'hill' of six dots, flanked to right by a female devotee, hands clasped, standing on a sun and crescent moon. In the left field, a vertical Brahmi inscription: *vaṭaśvaka*. 9.18g, 25mm. **F526/1a, Pl. 7.148**; Masson 1836a, p. 26, no. 32, pl. III.21; BMC India (Ancient) p. 264.2, pl.XXXIX.3; Wilson 1841, p. 416, no. 6, Coins pl. XV.30.

Fig. 22.5. Wilson 1841, p. 416, no. 7, Coins pl. XV.31. Three-arched hill and crescent flanked by a devotee (left) and a club (right). Coin not traced.

Fig. 22.6–7. F526/1a, Pl. 4.79–80. Same coin type as **Fig. 22.8** (?). Coins not traced.

Fig. 22.8 – IOC.1053. Female devotee to left, holding an object in her right hand; facing a triangular 'hill' of six dots. Behind her, to right, a three-arched hill and crescent. 10.4g, 24mm x 19mm. **F526/1a, Pl. 4.81**; BMC India (Ancient) p. 221.56.

Fig. 22.9 – IOLC.45. Vertical line on left, three-arched hill with crescent above on right. 8.03g, 25mm.

Fig. 22.10 – IOLC.39. Elephant to left before standard, taurine symbol above. 2.98g, 15mm.

Figure 22 Local copper alloy coins. Uniface (1–10), elephant and lion issues (11–15)

Elephant and lion issues

Copper alloy coins, die-struck on both sides. *Obverse*: Elephant walking; three-arched hill and crescent symbol above. *Reverse*: Lion standing; three-arched hill and crescent in front; swastika above.

Masson illustrates three examples: **F526/1a**, **Pl. 4.46–7**; **Vol. II, p. 93, Fig. 101.7–8**, while of the two illustrated in Wilson 1841 (Coins pl. XV.26–7), only one has been traced (**Fig. 22.12**). There are 64 coins in the collection. They comprise three variants:

- **Fig. 22.11 – IOLC.54.** *Obverse*: Elephant to left. *Reverse*: Lion to right; 10.77g, 22mm. Five coins: 11.38g–12.04g; **Vol. II, p. 93, Fig. 101.8**; p. 45 above: *Fig. 77*, **F526/1a, Pl. 4.77** (type).
- **Fig. 22.12 – IOC.1054.** *Obverse*: Elephant to right. *Reverse*: Lion to right. 9.17g, 21mm x 18mm. BMC India (Ancient) p. 225.93; Wilson 1841, p. 415, no. 3, Coins pl. XV.27. Five coins: 10.11g–10.9g.
- **Fig. 22.13**: Wilson 1841, p. 415, no. 2, Coins pl. XV.26. *Obverse*: Elephant to right. *Reverse*: Lion to left.
  Fig. 22.14 – IOLC.70. *Obverse*: Elephant to right. *Reverse*: Lion to left. 12.23g, 20mm.
  Fig. 22.15 – IOLC.101. *Obverse*: Elephant to right. *Reverse*: Lion to left. 11 83g, 17mm.
  1838,EIC.112. *Obverse*: Elephant to right. *Reverse*: Lion to left. 10.76g, 20mm x 18mm. BMC India (Ancient) p. 224.85. Not illustrated.

Total 54 coins: 13.42g (1), 12.55g–12.01g (12), 11.98g–11.09g (22), 10.96g–10.08g (14), 9.78g–9.6g (3), 7.9g (1), 6.22g (1 coin).

For another example (illustrated, but not traced), see p. 44, *Fig. 76*: **F526/1a, Pl. 4.76**.

Post-Alexander Greek issues (late 4th century BC)

Fig. 23.1–2 – IOLC.110–111. Two copper alloy coins associated with local imitations of Athenian silver coins. *Obverse*: Head of Athena wearing a Corinthian helmet to right. *Reverse*: A double-bodied owl with a single head. 1.93g, 12.5mm; 6.9g, 10mm. **F526/1h**: **Vol. II, p. 93, Fig. 101.1–3**; similar to BMC Greek (Attica, Megaris, Aegina), vol. 22, pp. 236–9.

Seleucid

Antiochus III (223–187 BC)

Fig. 23.3 – IOLC.112. Copper alloy coin (Attic standard). *Obverse*: Worn and corroded lauriate and draped bust of Apollo. *Reverse*: Apollo standing to left, right hand extended and holding an arrow, left hand resting on a bow. Greek inscription [B]ΑΣΙΛΕΩΣ [ΑΝΤΙ]ΟΧΟΥ (of king Antiochus). 4.76g, 21.5mm. Wilson 1841, p. 227, no. 20, Coins pl. II.1; **F526/1a, Pl. 1.1** (reverse); **F526/1h**: **Vol. II, p. 96, Fig. 102.18**.

Seleucid imitation

Fig. 23.4 – 1880.3981.g. 'Box 4', tray 'B'. Silver coin imitating trophy issues of Seleucus I Nicator (c. 306–281 BC). *Obverse*: Helmeted head to right. *Reverse*: Winged Nike on left, crowning trophy to right. Minted in Syria (?) 0.52g. 8mm. Type: Rapson 1904, p. 317, no. 1.6–7, pl. XVII.6–7.

Figure 23 Greek imitations (1–2), Seleucid (3) and imitation (4), Greco-Bactrian coins of Euthydemus I (5–8), Demetrius I (9), Pantaleon (10–13), Agathocles (14–18), Antimachus I (19–20) and Apollodotus I (21–6)

Catalogue of Coins | 133

Greco-Bactrian

Euthydemus I (c. 230–200 BC)

Fig. 23.5–8. Copper alloy coin (Attic standard). *Obverse*: Bearded head of Heracles to right within dotted border. *Reverse*: Prancing horse to right. Greek inscription ΒΑΣΙΛΕΩΣ ΕΥΘΥΔΗΜΟΥ (of king Euthydemus). Bopearachchi 1991, p. 160, ser. 17, pl. 3.18–26 (type).

Fig. 23.5 – IOC.5. (from Jalalabad). 3.77g, 18mm x 16.5mm. Masson 1836a, p. 21, no. 2, pl. II.2; Prinsep 1836c, p. 721, pl. XLVI.4; Wilson 1841, p. 226, no. 19, Coins pl. I.15; BMC India (Greek and Scythic) p. 5.18. pl. II.8.

Fig. 23.6 – IOLC.114. 4.84g, 21mm.

IOLC.113. 5.56g, 21mm; **IOLC.115.** 5.25g, 21mm. Not illustrated, see **F526/1h: Vol. II, p. 93, Fig. 101.4–5.**

Fig. 23.7–8. Wilson 1841, p. 226, nos 17–18, Coins pl. I.13–14. Coins not traced.

Total 4 coins: 5.56g–5.25g (2), 4.84g (1), 3.77g (1).

Demetrius I (c. 200–190 BC)

Masson records only two silver coins of Demetrius: one found at Begram in 1836 (**E161/VII f. 29**) and the other bought in Kabul bazaar in 1837 (**F526/1k; Vol. II, pp. 65, 100**). He also acquired 'a very fine copper coin of Demetrius' in 1837 (**P/389/18; Vol. II. p. 69**).

Fig. 23.9 – IOC.12. Copper alloy coin. *Obverse*: Bearded and diademed bust of Heracles to right, with club over shoulder. *Reverse*: Radiant standing figure of Artemis, facing, holding a bow in her left hand and drawing an arrow from a quiver with her right. Greek inscription: ΒΑΣΙΛΕΩΣ ΔΗΜΗΤΡΙΟΥ (of king Demetrius). Monogram ☒. 7.96g, 24mm. Wilson 1841, p. 233, no. 5, Coins pl. XXI.3; BMC India (Greek and Scythic) p. 7.14. Bopearachchi 1991, p. 166, ser. 4.f, pl. 5.11 (type).

Pantaleon (c. 190–185 BC)

Fig. 23.10–13. Copper alloy coin (Indian standard). *Obverse*: Female deity Subhadra (Krishna's sister) moving to left, holding a flower. Brahmi inscription *rajane pamtalevasa* (of king Pantaleon). *Reverse*: Panther to right. Greek inscription ΒΑΣΙΛΕΩΣ ΠΑΝΤΑΛΕΟΝΤΟΣ (of king Pantaleon). Masson 1834, p. 166, fig. 18, pl. IX.18; Wilson 1841, p. 300, Coins pl. VI.11; p. 41 above, **F526/1a, Pl. 2.45.** Bopearachchi 1991, p. 182, ser. 6, pl. 9.2–6 (type).

Fig. 23.11 – IOLC.117. 10.78g, 25mm.

Fig. 23.12 – IOLC.118. 9.65g, 23mm.

Fig. 23.13 – IOLC.119. 11.22g, 21mm.

Total seven coins: 13.36g (1), 11.27g–11.22g (2), 10.78g–10.52g (2), 9.65g (1), 8.63g (1).

A further 5 illegible coins (**IOLC.123–127**) could be issues of either Pantaleon or Agathocles. 11.85g (1), 10.64g–10.11g (3), 8.63g (1), 8.17g (1).

Masson only records acquiring 7 coins of Pantaleon and 43 of Agathocles from Begram in 1833–5 (**F526/1a, f. 1**; see p. 72, **Table 5** and p. 86, **Table 7** above). He also appears to have acquired a further 8 coins of Agathocles in 1837–8 (**F526/1j: Vol. II, p. 98**).

Agathocles (c. 190–180 BC)

Fig. 23.14 – IOC.15. Cupronickel coin. *Obverse*: Bust of Greek god Dionysus to right, wearing an ivy-wreath and holding a thyrsus sceptre over his shoulder. *Reverse*: Panther standing to right, touching a vine with his raised paw. Greek inscription [B]ΑΣΙΛΕΩΣ [A]ΓΑΘΟΚΛΕΟΥΣ (king Agathocles). Greek monogram in left field ☒. 7.62g, 23mm. Wilson 1841, p. 299, no. 4, Coins pl. VI.6; BMC India (Greek and Scythic) p. 11.8, pl. IV.8.

Fig. 23.15–18. Copper alloy coin. *Obverse*: Indian goddess Subhadra (Krishna's sister) walking to left, with a flower in her right hand. Brahmi legend *rajane agathuklayasa* inscribed along left side. *Reverse*: Panther standing to right. Greek inscription ΒΑΣΙΛΕΩΣ ΑΓΑΘΟΚΛΕΟΥΣ (of king Agathocles). Bopearachchi 1991, p. 176, ser. 10, pl. 7.14–19 (type).

Fig. 23.15 – IOC.16. 15.92g, 28mm x 20mm. Masson 1834, p. 166; Wilson 1841, pp. 299–300, no. 5, Coins pl. VI.7; BMC India (Greek and Scythic) p. 11.12, pl. IV.9.

Fig. 23.16 – IOC.17. 9.87g, 24mm x 21mm. Wilson 1841, pp. 299–300, no. 5, Coins pl. VI.8; BMC India (Greek and Scythic) p. 11.13.

Fig. 23.17 – IOC.18. 12.57g, 20mm x 18mm. Masson 1834, p. 166, pl. IX.17; p. 41 above, **F526/1a, Pl. 3.46.** Located on wrong ticket 1844,0909.61.

Fig. 23.18: Masson 1834, p. 166; Wilson 1841, pp. 299–300, no. 5, Coins pl. VI.9 (not traced).

Total 40 coins: 15.92g–15.58g (2), 13.89–13.61g (4), 12.68g–12.09g (6), 11.91g–11g (12), 10.89g–10g (4), 9.87g–8.44g (7), 7.46g–6.03g (4), 5.55g (1,), 3.72g (1).

Antimachus I (c. 180–170 BC)

Masson lists a total of 23 silver Antimachus coins acquired in the years 1833–8, but does not differentiate between Antimachus I and II (**F526/1k, f. 1: Vol. II, p. 99**). However, he only records bilingual issues with the title Nicephorus, not Theos, and the monograms ☒ and ☒ of Antimachus II. Only two silver coins of Antimachus I, both from Kabul bazaar, survive in the Masson collection.

Fig. 23.19–20. Silver drachm. *Obverse*: Bust of diademed king to right, wearing a causia. *Reverse*: Poseidon standing facing, wearing a himation and wreath, holding a trident in his right hand and a palm bound by a fillet in his left; flanked by a Greek inscription ΒΑΣΙΛΕΩΣ ΘΕΟΥ ΑΝΤΙΜΑΧΟΥ (of king Antimachus the divine), with a monogram in the right field ☒. Bopearchchi 1991, p. 185, ser. 3–4, pl. 10.A, 11–12.

Fig. 23.19 – 1838, EIC.33. 2.04g, 15mm. BMC India (Greek and Scythic) p. 12.5.

Fig. 23.20 – IOC.19. 0.68g, 11mm. Wilson 1841, p. 274, no. 3, Coins pl. XXI.12; BMC India (Greek and Scythic) p. 11.6.

Apollodotus I (c. 180–160 BC)

Masson collected a total of 16 silver coins of this ruler: four from Begram (which probably included the plated example **Fig. 23.25**); seven from the Hazarajat hoard; and five from Kabul bazaar (**Vol. II, pp. 58, 60, 66–7**). He also acquired three gold coins from Kabul bazaar purporting to be issues of Apollodotus, but adds 'these require inspection as to their being genuine' (**Vol. II, p. 65**). Presumably he decided they were fake as they are not mentioned again.

Silver coins

Fig. 23.21–4. Silver drachm. *Obverse*: Elephant standing to right. Greek inscription: ΒΑΣΙΛΕΩΣ ΑΠΟΛΛΟΔΟΤΟΥ ΣΩΤΗΡΟΣ (of king Apollodotus the saviour); Greek monogram below feet. *Reverse*: Zebu walking to right. Kharoshthi inscription *maharajasa apaladatasa tratarasa* (of great king Apollodotus the saviour); Greek monogram below feet ҟ.

The Hazarajat hoard contained 7 coins with additional monograms ℳ, C and ⊓ (**F526 1a, Pl. 14**, *Figs 4–7*; MacDowall 1991, p. 196). Bopearachchi 1991, pp. 189–91, ser. 4, pls 11.20–12.72 (type).

Fig. 23.21 – 1838,EIC.29. Hazarajat hoard. Monograms ҟ ω. 2.46g, 16mm x 16mm. BMC India (Greek and Scythic) p. 34.3, pl. IX.9.

Fig. 23.22 – 1838,EIC.27. Hazarajat hoard. Monograms ҟ Δ. 2.44g, 16mm x 16mm. BMC India (Greek and Scythic) p. 34.5. A second example with the same monograms is illustrated in Wilson 1841, p. 289, no. 2, Coins pl. IV.14.

Fig. 23.23 – IOC.68. 2g, 15mm. **F526/1a, Pl. 1.7**; BMC India (Greek and Scythic) p. 34.2.

Fig. 23.24 – 1838,EIC.30. Hazarajat hoard. Monograms Λ Α. 2.43g, 16mm x 15mm. BMC India (Greek and Scythic) p. 34.6; **F526/1a, f. 36, Pl. 1.6**

Fig. 23.25 – IOLC.164. Silver-plated copper alloy.coin. *Obverse*: Elephant to left. *Reverse*: Zebu to left. 1.99g, 14.5mm.

Total 5 coins: 2.46g–2g (4), 1.99g (1).

Copper alloy coinage – lifetime issues

Masson records collecting 73 copper alloy coins of Apollodotus I from Begram in 1833–5 (1834, p. 20; 1836b, p. 350; **F526/1a**, p. 72; **Vol. II, pp. 50, 61, 80**).

Figs 23.26, 24.1–6. *Obverse*: Apollo standing facing with bow and arrow. Greek inscription on three sides ΒΑΣΙΛΕΩΣ ΑΠΟΛΛΟΔΟΤΟΥ ΣΩΤΗΡΟΣ (of king Apollodotus the saviour). *Reverse*: Tripod within dotted border. Kharoshthi legend on three sides *maharajasa apaladatasa tratarasa* (of great king Apollodotus the saviour). Bopearachchi 1991, pp. 192–4, ser. 6, pls 12.73–14.99 (type).

Fig. 23.26 – IOC.75. 10.07g, 25mm x 23mm. Masson 1834, p. 164, pl. VIII.6; BMC India (Greek & Scythic) p. 35.22.

Fig. 24.1 – IOC.72. 9.58g, 23mm x 22mm. No monogram. Wilson 1841, pp. 290–1, no. 7, Coins pl. IV.17; BMC India (Greek and Scythic) p. 35.14.

Fig. 24.2 – IOLC.177. *Reverse*: Monogram illegible. 9.17g, 20mm x 20mm.

Total 11 coins: 10.07g (1), 9.99g–9.02g (3), 8.82g–8.1g (2), 7.95g–7.2g (2), 6.77g (1), 4.06g (4), 3.87g (1).

Illegible monogram – Total 13 coins: 12.67g (1), 9.17g (1), 8.13g (1), 6.69g–6.61g (2), 5.95g–5.27g (4), 4.13g–4.05g (2), 3.1g–3.02g (2).

Imitations

Fig. 24.3 – IOC.78. *Reverse*: Monogram in left field ҟ. 8.61g, 20mm x 20mm. Wilson 1841, pp. 290–1, no. 8, Coins pl. IV.18; BMC India (Greek and Scythic) p. 36.31. Senior 1999, p. 17, P-H issue 11.

Fig. 24.4 – IOLC.188. Half unit. *Reverse*: Monogram in right field ℳ. 3.01g, 17mm x 13mm. Senior 1999, p. 17, P-H issue 18.

Fig. 24.5 – 1838,EIC.61. Half unit. *Reverse*: Monogram in right field ℳ. 3.45g, 17mm x 18mm. BMC India (Greek and Scythic) p. 36.34; Masson 1834, p. 164, pl. VIII.7. The 1834 drawing confirms the source of the coins donated to the Museum by the East India Company in 1838 was the 1833–5 Masson collection (see also **Fig. 30.64**).

Fig. 24.6: Wilson 1841, pp. 290–1, no. 9, Coins pl. IV.19. Half unit. *Reverse*: Monogram in right field ℳ. 15mm x 14mm.

Total 18 coins: 9.01g (1), 8.77g–8.29g (4), 7.91g–7.66g (2), 5g (1), 4.27g (1), 3.95g–3.01g (7), 2.49g–2.02g (2).

Eucratides I (c. 174–145 BC)

Masson lists a total of 269 Eucratides coins acquired from Begram in 1833–5, of which 7 appear to have been silver issues. He also acquired seven silver coins from Kabul bazaar in 1837–8 (**Vol. II, pp. 61, 66, 80, 100**). He subsequently included 46 copper alloy coins in the incomplete catalogue of his own collection (**Vol. II, pp. 96–7, Fig. 102.6–16**). This is increased to a total of 62 coins in the list of his '1st Cabinet' (**Vol. II, p. 98**).

Monolingual lifetime issues

Fig. 24.7 – IOC.28. Silver drachm. *Obverse*: Diademed bust of king to right. *Reverse*: Palm branches and pilei of the Dioscuri, flanked by Greek inscription ΒΑΣΙΛΕΩΣ ΕΥΚΡΑΤΙΔΟΥ (of king Eucratides), with monogram Η below. 0.63g, 12mm. Wilson 1841, p. 240, no. 9, Coins pl. III.5; BMC India (Greek and Scythc), p. 15.23.

Fig. 24.8 – OR.11316. Silver drachm (from Charikar). *Obverse*: Helmeted bust of king to right. *Reverse*: Palm branches and pilei of the Dioscuri, flanked by Greek inscription ΒΑΣΙΛΕΩΣ ΕΥΚΡΑΤΙΔΟΥ with monogram Ѩ below. 0.64g, 12mm. Wilson 1841, p. 240, no. 10, Coins pl. III.6; BMC India (Greek and Scythic) p. 15.29.

Total 2 coins: 0.64g, 0.63g.

Fig. 24.9 – IOLC.202. Square copper alloy quarter unit. *Obverse*: Head of Eucratides to right. *Reverse*: Palm branches and pilei of the Dioscuri, flanked by Greek inscription ΒΑΣΙΛΕΩΣ ΕΥΚΡΑΤΙΔΟΥ with monograms ᛇ Ε below. 1.96g, 13mm. Bopearachchi 1991, p. 208, ser. 10, pl. 19.A.

Bilingual lifetime issues

Fig. 24.10 – IOC.42. *Obverse*: Head of king to right. Greek inscription ΒΑΣΙΛΕΩΣ ΜΕΓΑΛΟΥ ΕΥΚΡΑΤΙΔΟΥ (of king Eucratides the great). *Reverse*: Palm branches and pilei of the Dioscuri, flanked by Kharoshthi inscription *maharajasa evukratidasa* (of the great king Eucratides). 1.95g, 13mm x 16mm. Wilson 1841, p. 241, no. 15, Coins pl. III.12; BMC India (Greek and Scythic) p. 18.57.

Total 14 coins: 2.77g–2.14g (7). 1.96g–1.39g (7). *Reverse*: Monogram ᛇ (2 coins); remainder illegible.

Fig. 24.11–14. Square copper alloy coin. *Obverse*: Helmeted and diademed bust of king to right. Greek inscription on three sides: ΒΑΣΙΛΕΩΣ ΜΕΓΑΛΟΥ ΕΥΚΡΑΤΙΔΟΥ. *Reverse*: Dioscuri with lances and palm

Figure 24 Coins of Apollodotus I (1–6), Eucratides I (7–25), Heliocles I (26) and Antimachus II (27–8)

branches on horseback to right. Kharoshthi inscription above and below *maharajasa evukratidasa*. Monogram in either upper left or lower right field. Bopearachchi 1991, pp. 211–13, ser. 19, pls 20.76–21.105.

Fig. 24.11 – 1838,EIC.39. 7.96g, 19.5mm x 20mm. Monogram illegible.

Fig. 24.12– IOLC.234. *Reverse*: Monogram illegible. 8.03g, 22mm x 22mm.

Fig. 24.13: Wilson 1841, pp. 240–1, no. 13, Coins pl. III.9 (not traced). *Reverse*: Monogram in lower right field ⚵

Fig. 24.14 – IOC.37. *Reverse*: Monogram in right field ⚶ 7.96g, 21mm x 20mm. Wilson 1841, pp. 240–1, no. 13, Coins pl. III.10; BMC India (Greek and Scythic) p. 17.49.

Total 26 coins: 8.52g–8.03g (5); 7.75g–7.18g (8); 6.93g–6.11g (9); 5.44g–5.31g (3); 2.55g (fragment). Additional monograms Ε, ⚶ also occur.

IOLC.265. Half unit (not illustrated). *Obverse*: Helmeted head of king to right. Greek inscription ΒΑΣΙΛΕΩΣ ΜΕΓΑΛΟΥ ΕΥΚΡΑΤΙΔΟΥ. *Reverse*: Dioscuri on horseback to right, carrying lances and palm branches. Kharoshthi inscription *maharajasa evukratidasa*. Monogram off flan. 2.62g, 14mm x 20mm. Bopearachchi 1991, p. 214, ser. 20, pl. 21.106–13 (type).

Total 53 coins: 4.47g–4.01 (5), 3.93g–3.04g (10), 2.96g–2.12g (22), 1.89g–1.28g (13), 0.96g–0.69g (3). Monograms illegible; possibly Ε and ⚶.

Posthumous issues (after c. 145 BC)

Fig. 24.15 – IOC.43. *Obverse*: Helmeted and diademed bust of king to right. Greek inscription ΒΑΣΙΛΕΩΣ [ΜΕΓΑΛΟΥ] ΕΥΚΡΑΤΙΔΟΥ. *Reverse*: Winged Nike within a rectangular frame, walking to left, holding a wreath and a palm branch. Kharoshthi inscription [*maharajasa*] *evukratidasa*. Monogram in left field ⚶. 5.04g, 17mm x 19mm. Wilson 1841, p. 242, no. 18, Coins pl. XXI.18; BMC India (Greek and Scythic) p. 18.59. Another example is listed in Masson's own collection (**Vol. II, p. 96, Fig. 102.12**).

Fig. 24.16 – IOC.44.a. *Obverse*: Helmeted and diademed bust of king to right. Greek inscription ΒΑΣΙΛΕΩΣ ΜΕΓΑΛΟΥ ΕΥΚΡΑΤΙ[ΔΟΥ]. *Reverse*: City goddess within a rectangular frame, seated on a throne to left, holding a palm branch. The head of an elephant in the lower left field and a worn M-shaped monogram above a small beehive-shaped pile in the right. Kharoshthi inscription *kavishiye nagara devata* (goddess of the city of Kapishi). 4.53g, 18mm x 16mm. Masson 1834, pp. 164–5, pl. VIII.11; Wilson 1841, p. 241, no. 14, Coins pl. III.11; BMC India (Greek and Scythic) p. 18.63. Another example is included in Masson's own collection (**Vol. II, p. 96, Fig. 102.13**).

Fig. 24.17 – IOC.44. *Obverse*: Helmeted and diademed bust of king to left, with raised hand holding spear (?). Greek inscription on three sides [Β]ΑΣΙΛΕΩΣ [ΜΕΓΑ]ΛΟΥ ΕΥΚΡΑΤΙΔΟΥ. *Reverse*: Winged Nike walking to right, holding diademed wreath and palm branch, flanked by Kharoshthi inscription *maharajasa [evu]kratida[sa]*. Monogram in right field ⚶. 6.97g, 19mm x 21mm. Wilson 1841, p. 242, no. 17, Coins pl. XXI.5; BMC India (Greek and Scythic) p. 18.62.

Fig. 24.18–21. Square copper alloy coins. *Obverse*: Helmeted head of king to right. Greek inscription ΒΑΣΙΛΕΩΣ ΜΕΓΑΛΟΥ ΕΥΚΡΑΤΙΔΟΥ. *Reverse*: Dioscuri on horseback to right, carrying lances and palm branches. Kharoshthi inscription *maharajasa evukratidasa*.

Fig. 24.18 – IOLC.293. *Reverse*: Monogram in lower right field ⚶. 6.91g, 24mm x 23mm.

Fig. 24.19 – IOLC.299. *Reverse*: Monogram in lower right field ⚶. 6.5g, 21mm x.21mm.

Fig. 24.20 – IOLC.339. 4.9g, 20mm x 19mm.

Fig. 24.21 – IOLC.329. *Reverse*: Monogram in lower right field ⚶. 2.03g, 16mm x 17mm.

Total 69 coins: 8.5g (1), 7.77g–7.06g (9), 6.97g–6.11g (25), 5.97g–5.21g (7), 4.89g–4.05g (10), 3.99g–3.09g (17), 2.95g–2.02g (10), 1.31g (1). Additional monograms ⚶ and ⚶ also occur.

Fig. 24.22–4. Circular monolingual copper alloy coins copying silver tetradrachms of Eucratides I. *Obverse*: Helmeted head of king to right. *Reverse*: Dioscuri on horseback to right, carrying lances and palm branches. Greek inscription ΒΑΣΙΛΕΩΣ ΕΥΚΡΑΤΙΔΟΥ (of king Eucratides).

Fig. 24.22 – IOLC.362. 5.07g, 22mm.

Fig. 24.23: Wilson 1841, p. 240, no. 11, Coins pl. III.8 (not traced).

Fig. 24.24 – IOLC.360. 4.37g, 22mm.

Total 4 coins: 5.44g–5.07g (2), 4.44g–4.37g (2).

Masson includes three coins 'of circular form' in the 1834 collection from Begram (**Vol. II, p. 61**). He subsequently lists seven examples in his own collection (**F526/1h; Vol. II, p. 96, Fig. 102.6**).

Eucratides I imitation (c. late 2nd century BC)

Fig. 24.25 – IOLC.364. Quarter unit. *Obverse*: Head of king to right within dotted border. *Reverse*: Debased rendition of the Dioscuri on horseback. 1.79g, 14mm.

Heliocles I (c. 145–130 BC)

Fig. 24.26 – IOLC.365. Silver tetradrachm fragment (Attic standard). *Obverse*: Diademed head of king to right. *Reverse*: Zeus standing to front. Greek inscription [ΒΑΣΙΛΕΩΣ] ΗΛΙΟΚ[ΕΟΥΣ] (of king Heliocles). 7.92g, 29mm. Bopearachchi 1991, p. 222, ser. 1, pl. 24.1–5.

Antimachus II (c. 160–155 BC)

As already noted above, Masson does not describe the coin types of the 23 Antimachus silver coins collected in 1833–8 which would enable the differentiation between issues of Antimachus I and II. However, he illustrates two drachms and records the monograms ⚶ and ⚶ of Antimachus II (**F526/1a, Pl. 7.149–50**). Five drachms were included in the Hazarajat hoard (1836a, p. 15). Begram in 1834 gave one, and 1835 another (**F526/1a, f. 18**), but in the same account he mentions not just one but two large parcels of silver coins of Apollodotus and Menander obtained in 1834 and 1835 respectively, each including two or three of Antimachus. He also says 'Among 5000 or more copper coins, procured from the *dasht* of Begram, we have not discovered one of Antimachus, and the detection of a single silver coin does not seem to afford evidence that he ruled there, when the absence of his copper coins seem to prove that he did not' (1836a, p. 15).

Fig. 24.27–8. *Obverse*: Greek inscription ΒΑΣΙΛΕΩΣ ΝΙΚΙΦΟΡΟΥ ΑΝΤΙΜΑΧΟΥ (of king Antimachus the victorious). *Reverse*: Kharoshthi inscription *maharajasa jayadharasa amtimakhasa* (of the great king Antimachus the victorious).

Fig. 24.27 – IOC.116. Silver drachm. *Obverse*: Winged Nike standing to left, holding palm branch and fillet. Monogram in left field ⋈. *Reverse*: Rider on horseback to right, wearing a causia, diadem and chlamys. 2.48g, 17mm. Masson 1836, p. 22, no. 14, pl. II.9; Wilson 1841, p. 274, no. 2, Coins pl. II.15; BMC India (Greek and Scythic) p. 55.4.

Either collected at Begram, or one of a parcel of 120 Indo-Greek silver coins (5 Antimachus, 7 Apollodotus, 108 Menander) from Hazarajat.

Fig. 24.28 – IOC.60. Copper alloy coin. *Obverse*: Aegis. *Reverse*: Wreath and palm branch, with monogram (?) below centre I ✝ II. 7.66g, 18mm x 20mm. Wilson 1841, p. 279, no. 7, Coins pl. XXI.11; BMC India (Greek and Scythic) p. 28.31, pl. VIII.4 (incorrectly identified as Antialcidas); Cunningham 1840, p. 393.

Indo-Greek

Menander I (c. 155–130 BC)

Silver coins

According to one Masson record, 233 silver coins of Menander were collected from Begram and Kabul bazaar in 1833–8 (**F526/1k, f. 1; Vol. II, p. 99**). Another list gives a total of 153 coins in the period 1833–5 alone (**F526/1a**: 39, 56 and 58 coins respectively, see p. 72, **Table 5** above), but the figures do not tally with the 108 Hazarajat coins of this ruler acquired in 1833–4 (p. 128 above). There are now only 10 drachms in the Masson collection that can be identified from Hazarajat and/or Kabul bazaar: 2.27g (1), 2.41g–2.48g (7), 2.51g–2.52g (2). In addition, there are three worn examples (1.27g, 1.48g, 2.16g) and two silver-plated copper forgeries (1.87g, 2.39g) from Begram (IOLC.266–270).

MacDowall (1991, pp.196–8) divides the silver coinage into period A (continuous legend: **Fig. 25.10–13**), succeeded by period B (divided legend: **Fig. 25.1–9, 14–15**).

Fig. 25.1–17. *Obverse*: Greek legend ΒΑΣΙΛΕΩΣ ΣΩΤΗΡΟΣ ΜΕΝΑΝΔΡΟΥ (of king Menander the saviour). *Reverse*: Kharoshthi legend three sides *maharajasa tratarasa menamdrasa* (of great king Menander the saviour).

Fig. 25.1 – IOC.90. Silver tetradrachm. *Obverse*: Diademed head of king to right. Divided Greek inscription. *Reverse*: Athena standing to left, holding the aegis and hurling a thunderbolt. Greek monograms in left and right fields Σ and ⋈. 9.78g, 27mm. Kabul bazaar. **F526/1a, Pl. 1.12**; Masson 1836a, p. 22, pl. II.4; Wilson 1841, pp. 283–4, no. 1, Coins pl. III.13; BMC India (Greek and Scythic) p. 44.1.

Fig. 25.2–4. Silver drachm. *Obverse*: Diademed head of king to right. Divided Greek inscription. *Reverse*: Athena standing to left, holding the aegis and hurling a thunderbolt.

Fig. 25.2 – IOC.92. No monogram. 2.53g, 17mm. Wilson 1841, p. 284, no. 2, Coins pl. III.14; BMC India (Greek and Scythic) p. 45.14.

Fig. 25.3 – 1838,EIC.19. Hazarajat hoard. *Reverse*: Greek monogram in right field ⋈. 2.41g, 18mm. **F526/1a, Pl. 1.17**; Masson 1836a, p. 22, nos 7–11, pl. II.8; BMC India (Greek and Scythic) p. 45.25.

Two more Hazarajat hoard coins with the same monogram are in the Fitzwilliam Museum, 2.3g, 2.35g (MacDowall 1991, p. 197. nos 48–9).

Fig. 25.4 – 1838,EIC.23. Hazarajat hoard. *Reverse*: Greek monogram in right field ⋈. 2.51g, 17mm. **F526/1a, Pl. 1.16** (type); BMC India (Greek and Scythic) p. 46.30.

Masson **F526/1a, Pl. 1.16** probably illustrates one of four Hazarajat hoard coins with the same monogram in the Fitzwilliam Museum; 2.44g–2.47g (MacDowall 1991, p. 197. nos 44–7).

An additional monogram ⋈ illustrated by Masson (**F526/1a, Pl. 1.18**) is found on two Fitzwilliam Museum coins; weight 2.34g, 2.45g; there is also one coin of this type with the monogram ⋈. 2.27g (MacDowall 1991, p. 198, nos 50–2).

Five drachms in the Fitzwilliam Museum depict the variation of Athena standing to left with monograms ⋈, ⋈, ⋈, ⋈. 2.03g–2.43g (MacDowall 1991, p. 198, nos 53–7).

Fig. 25.5–7. Hazarajat hoard. Silver drachm. *Obverse*: Helmeted and diademed head of king to right. Divided Greek inscription. *Reverse*: Athena standing to left, holding the aegis and hurling a thunderbolt.

Fig. 25.5 – 1838,EIC.7. *Reverse*: Greek monogram in right field ⋈. 2.46g, 16mm. **F526/1a, Pl. 1.14**; BMC India (Greek and Scythic) p. 44.10.

Fig. 25.6: Wilson 1841, p. 284, no. 3, Coins pl. III.15. *Reverse*: Greek monogram in right field ⋈. **F526/1a, Pl. 1.15**. One of two examples with this monogram are in the Fitzwilliam Museum, 2.34g (MacDowall 1991, p. 197, nos 33–4).

Fig. 25.7 – 1838,EIC.10. *Reverse*: Greek monogram in right field ⋈. 2.44g, 17mm. BMC India (Greek and Scythic) p. 45.13.

Masson illustrates another example (1836a, p. 22, nos 7–11, pl. II. 6; **F526/1a, Pl. 1.13**): one of eight coins with this monogram in the Fitzwilliam Museum, 2.34g, 2.41g–2.45g (MacDowall 1991, p. 197, nos 35–42).

Fig. 25.8: Wilson 1841, p. 284, no. 6, Coins pl. IV.2. Hazarajat hoard. *Obverse*: Helmeted bust of king hurling javelin to left. Divided Greek inscription. *Reverse*: Athena standing to left, holding aegis and hurling thunderbolt. Greek monogram in right field ⋈. **F526/1a, Pl. 1.24**. One of two examples with this monogram in the Fitzwilliam Museum, 2.34g (MacDowall 1991, p. 197, nos 33–4).

Fig. 25.9: Wilson 1841, p. 284, no. 4, Coins pl. III.16. Hazarajat hoard. *Obverse*: Diademed bust of king hurling javelin to left. Divided Greek inscription. *Reverse*: Athena standing to left, holding aegis and hurling thunderbolt. Greek monogram in right field ⋈. One of two examples with this monogram in the Fitzwilliam Museum, 2.34g (MacDowall 1991, p. 197, nos 33–4).

Fig. 25.10–13. Silver drachms. Hazarajat hoard. *Obverse*: Diademed bust of king hurling javelin to left. Continuous Greek inscription. *Reverse*: Athena standing to right, holding aegis and hurling a thunderbolt.

Fig. 25.10 – 1838,EIC.14. *Reverse*: Greek monogram in left field ⋈. 2.48g, 18mm. BMC India (Greek and Scythic) p. 47.36.

Figure 25 Indo-Greek silver coins of Menander I (1–17)

Fig. 25.11 – 1838,EIC.17. *Reverse*: Greek monogram in left field ᛗ. 2.45g, 17mm. BMC India (Greek and Scythic) p. 47.41.

Fig. 25.12 – 1838,EIC.20. Hazarajat hoard. *Reverse*: Greek monogram in left field ᛗ. 2.46g, 17mm. **F526/1a, Pl. 1.23**; BMC India (Greek and Scythic) p. 47.42. One example in the Fitzwilliam Museum with the same monogram, 2.25g (MacDowall 1991, p. 197, no. 11).

Fig. 25.13: Wilson 1841, p. 283, no. 5, Coins pl. IV.1. Hazarajat hoard. *Reverse*: Greek monogram in left field.

Fig. 25.14 – 1838,EIC.15. Hazarajat hoard. *Obverse*: Diademed bust of king hurling a javelin to left. Divided Greek inscription. *Reverse*: Athena standing to right. Greek monogram in left field ᛗ. 2.27g, 18mm. BMC India (Greek and Scythic) p. 47.38. Three examples in the Fitzwilliam Museum, 2.29g, 2.31g, 2.47g (MacDowall 1991, p. 197, nos 21–3).

Fig. 25.15 – IOLC.366. Begram. *Obverse*: Bust of diademed king to left, hurling a javelin. Divided Greek inscription. *Reverse*: Athena standing to left. Monogram in right field. 2.16g, 17mm.

Fig. 25.16 – IOLC.367. Worn silver drachm. Begram. *Obverse*: Bust of diademed king to left, hurling a javelin. Divided Greek inscription. *Reverse*: Athena standing to right. Monogram in left field. 1.48g, 10.5mm. Bopearachchi 1991, p. 228, ser. 6, pl. 26.11–18.

Fig. 25.17 – IOLC.369. Silver-plated copper alloy coin. Contemporary forgery, Begram. *Obverse*: Helmeted head of Menander to right. Divided Greek inscription. *Reverse*: Athena standing to left, wielding thunderbolt. Monogram in right field. 1.87g, 18mm. Bopearachchi 1991, p. 236, ser. 16, pl. 29.102–13.

Copper alloy coinage

Fig. 26.1–20. *Obverse*: Greek legend on three sides: ΒΑΣΙΛΕΩΣ ΣΩΤΗΡΟΣ ΜΕΝΑΝΔΡΟΥ (of king Menander the saviour). *Reverse*: Kharoshthi legend on three sides: *maharajasa tratarasa menamdrasa* (of great king Menander the saviour).

Fig. 26.1 – 1926,0502.1. *Obverse*: Diademed bust of king to right. *Reverse*: Dolphin to right. Greek monograms below. 22.19g, 26mm x 26mm. **F526/1a, Pl. 1.25**: acquired Charikar 1834.

Masson 1836a, p. 22, no. 12, pl. II.5; Prinsep 1836c, p. 722, pl. XLVI.8; Wilson 1841, p. 285, no. 7, Coins pl. IV.3. Cunningham recorded the coin in the India Museum *c.* 1876 (1884, p. 249, no. 3), but it was not included in the 1882 transfer to the British Museum: BMC India (Greek and Scythic) Supplement, p. 169, no. 3, pl. XXXI.9. It was purchased by the Museum in 1926 from Captain E.B. Woollet (*C&M Medal Room Reports* 1–5–1926, p. 173).

Fig. 26.2 – IOC.96. *Obverse*: Diademed bust of king throwing a javelin to left. *Reverse*: Athena standing to right, holding the aegis and hurling a thunderbolt. Greek monogram in right field. 8.53g, 22mm x 21mm. **F526/1a, Pl. 1.26**; Wilson 1841, p. 286, no.10, Coins pl. IV.7; BMC India (Greek and Scythic) p. 47.46.

Fig. 26.3 – IOLC.375. Worn coin with traces of design. *Obverse*: Bull's head, facing. *Reverse*: Tripod. Legends and monogram illegible; 20.28g, 22mm. Bopearachchi 1991, ser. 29, p. 243, pl. 32 (type).

Fig. 26.4 – IOC.104. Quarter unit. *Obverse*: Eight-spoked wheel or chakra. *Reverse*: Palm frond. Greek monogram in right field. 1.55g, 13mm x 12mm. **F526/1a, Pl. 2.38**. Masson 1836a, p. 22, no. 13, pl. II.7; Prinsep 1836c,

Catalogue of Coins | 139

Figure 26 Copper alloy coins of Menander I (1–20).

p. 722, pl. XLVI.7; Wilson 1841, p. 287, no. 15, Coins pl. VI.11; BMC India (Greek and Scythic) p. 50.73.

Fig. 26.5 – IOLC.602. Worn coin with traces of design. *Obverse*: Elephant standing to right. *Reverse*: Elephant goad. Legends and monograms illegible. 7.09g, 18mm x 15mm.

Fig. 26.6–8. *Obverse*: Helmeted head of Athena to right. *Reverse*: Shield (aegis) with head of Medusa.

Fig. 26.6 – IOLC.372. *Reverse*: Greek monogram in lower right field. 7.21g, 22mm.

Fig. 26.7: Wilson 1841, pp. 286–7, no. 13, Coins pl. IV.12 (type). Greek monogram. Prinsep 1836c, p. 722, pl. XLVI.5; Bopearachchi 1991, ser. 19, p. 238, pl. 31.

Fig. 26.8 – IOLC.371. *Reverse*: Monogram illegible. 6.95g, 21mm. **F526/1a, Pl. 2.21** (reverse).

Fig. 26.9 – IOC.100. *Obverse*: Bust of king to right wearing a crested helmet. *Reverse*: Athena standing to left, holding the aegis and hurling a thunderbolt. Greek monogram B in left field. 5g, 18mm x 18mm. **F526/1a Pl.2.30**; BMC India (Greek and Scythic) p. 48.58.

Fig. 26.10 – IOC.102. *Obverse*: Bust of Athena to right wearing a crested helmet. *Reverse*: Owl head facing, standing to right, head facing. Greek monogram in right field. 9.36g, 19mm x 19mm. Begram 1833. Masson 1834, p, 164, pl. VIII.4; **F526/1a, Pl. 1.27**; Prinsep 1836c, p. 722, pl. XLVI.6; Wilson 1841, p. 286, no. 11, Coins pl. IV.8; BMC India (Greek and Scythic) p. 49.63.

Fig. 26.11–14. *Obverse*: Bust of Athena to right wearing crested helmet. *Reverse*: Winged Nike standing, holding a wreath and palm frond. Masson 1834, p. 163, pl. VIII.1.

Fig. 26.11 – IOC.99. *Reverse*: Nike standing to left.

140 | *Charles Masson: Collections from Begram and Kabul Bazaar, Afghanistan, 1833–1838*

Greek monograms in left and right fields respectively ⋈ B. 6.30g, 19mm x 18mm. Wilson 1841, p. 285, no. 8, Coins pl. IV.4; BMC India (Greek and Scythic) p. 48.56.

Fig. 26.12 – IOLC.533. *Reverse*: Nike standing to right. Monogram in right field ⟨⟩. 4.3g, 16mm x 17mm.

Fig. 26.13 – IOLC.583. Half unit. *Reverse*: Nike standing to right. Monogram in right field ⟨⟩. 2.74g, 15mm x 13mm.

Fig. 26.14: Wilson 1841, pp. 285–6, no. 9, Coins pl. IV.5–6. Reverse images only: Winged Nike standing to right; monograms in right field ⟨⟩ and ⟨⟩ respectively.

Total 78 coins: 10.48g (1), 9.55g (1), 8.86g (1), 6.31g–6.01g (2), 5.96g–5.01g (25), 4.98g–4.04g (25), 3.97g–3.02g (17), 2.89g–2.39g (4), 1.84g (1).

Fig. 26.15 – IOLC.376. *Obverse*: Boar's head to right. *Reverse*: Palm branch. Monogram illegible; 9.04g, 18mm x 18mm. **F526/1a, Pl. 2.28**: Begram 1835. Prinsep 1836c, p. 722, pl. XLVI.9; Wilson 1841, p. 286, no. 12, Coins pl. IV.9; Bopearachchi 1991, ser. 36, p. 246, pl. 33.

Fig. 26.16–20. *Obverse*: Elephant head with a bell around its neck to right. *Reverse*: Club in centre flanked by Greek monograms.

Fig. 26.16: Wilson 1841, p. 87, no. 14, Coins pl. IV.10; Masson 1834, pp. 163–4, pl. VIII.2–3. *Reverse*: Greek monograms ⋈ A.

Fig. 26.17 – 1838,EIC.53. *Reverse*: Greek monograms ⋈ A. 2.47g, 13mm x 16mm. **F526/1a, Pl. 2.32** (type).

Fig. 26.18 – 1838,EIC.52. *Reverse*: Greek monograms ⋈ Δ. 2.78g, 13mm x 14mm. BMC India (Greek and Scythic) p. 50.68.

Fig. 26.19 – 1838,EIC.54. *Reverse*: Greek monograms A ⟨⟩. 3.16g, 14mm x 15mm. BMC India (Greek and Scythic) p. 50.69.

Fig. 26.20 – 1838,EIC.51. *Reverse*: Greek monograms ⋈ A. 2.47g, 13mm x 16mm. BMC India (Greek and Scythic) p. 50.67.

Additional monograms: ⟨⟩, ⟨⟩, ⟨⟩.

Total 150 coins: 3.52g–3.02g (23), 2.99g–2g (122), 1.98g–1.66g (4), 0.74g (1).

Strato I (c. 125–110 BC)

Fig. 27.1 – IOLC.603. Copper alloy coin. *Obverse*: Apollo standing to left, bow in left, Greek inscription ΒΑΣΙΛΕΩΣ ΕΠΙΦΑΝΟΥΣ ΣΩΤΗΡΟΣ ΣΤΡΑΤΩΝΟΣ (king Strato, the illustrious saviour). *Reverse*: Tripod. Kharoshthi inscription *maharajasa pracachasa tratarasa stratasa* (great king Strato the illustrious saviour). Uncertain monogram in left field. 9.35g, 23mm.

IOLC.604. 9.8g, 23mm. Not illustrated. Bopearachchi 1991, ser. 31, p. 264, pl. 37.

Total 2 coins: 9.8g, 9.35g.

Lysias (c.120–110 BC)

Fig. 27.2–4. *Obverse*: Greek inscription ΒΑΣΙΛΕΩΣ ΑΝΙΚΗΤΟΥ ΛΥΣΙΟΥ (of king Lysias the invincible). *Reverse*: Kharoshthi inscription *maharajasa apadihatasa lisikasa* (of the great king Lysias the invincible).

Fig. 27.2: Silver drachm. *Obverse*: Bust of king with elephant scalp to right. *Reverse*: Radiant nude Heracles standing to front, holding a club, lion-skin and palm fronds in his left hand. Greek monograms ⟨A Σ⟩ in left and right fields respectively. Wilson 1841, p. 270, no. 1, Coins pl. XXI.9. One coin in the 1836 collection (not traced).

Fig. 27.3–4. Copper alloy coins. *Obverse*: Bearded bust of Heracles to right, with club over his shoulder. Greek inscription on three sides. *Reverse*: Elephant walking to right. Greek monograms ⟨A Σ⟩ below. Kharoshthi inscription on three sides.

Fig. 27.3 – 1888,1208.204. 8.72g, 16mm x 18mm. Cunningham collection. Masson 1834, p. 165, pl. IX.16; **F526/1a, Pl. 3.48**. Wilson 1841, p. 270, no. 2, Coins pl. II.10.

Fig. 27.4 – 1838,EIC.72. 8.72g, 16mm x 18mm. Bopearachchi 1991, ser. 8, pp. 269–70, pls 38–9.

14 coins of this type were acquired from Begram 1833–5. In addition to the two illustrated, there are now only four more coins in the collection (IOLC.605– IOLC.608): 4.95g, 7.94g, 7.99g, 8.52g.

Antialcidas (c. 115–95 BC)

Fig. 27.5–6. *Obverse*: Greek inscription ΒΑΣΙΛΕΩΣ ΝΙΚΗΦΟΡΟΥ ΑΝΤΙΑΛΚΙΔΟΥ (of king Antialcidas the victorious). *Reverse*: Kharoshthi inscription *maharajasa jayadharasa amtialkidasa* (of the great king Antialcidas the victorious).

Fig. 27.5 – IOC.55. Silver drachm. *Obverse*: Helmeted and diademed bust of king to right. *Reverse*: Enthroned Zeus Nicephorus holding Nike to left; the forepart of an elephant to right, in front of the throne. Monogram in left field ⟨k⟩. 2.43g, 17.5mm. BMC India (Greek and Scythic) p. 26.12. Wilson 1841, p. 277, no. 3 (?), not illustrated.

Fig. 27.6 – IOC.57. Silver drachm. *Obverse*: Diademed bust of king to right, wearing a causia. *Reverse*: Enthroned Zeus Nicephorus holding Nike to left; with the forepart of an elephant beside the throne, also to left. 2.4g, 16mm. Monogram in right field ⟨k⟩. **F526/1a, Pl. 3.49**; Wilson 1841, p. 277, no. 1, Coins pl. II.11; BMC India (Greek and Scythic) p. 26.8.

Total 2 coins: 2.43g, 2.4g. Masson records three coins of this type in his 1835 collection.

Fig. 27.7–10. Copper alloy coins. *Obverse*: Bust of Zeus to right, with thunderbolt over shoulder. Greek inscription on three sides ΒΑΣΙΛΕΩΣ ΝΙΚΗΦΟΡΟΥ ΑΝΤΙΑΛΚΙΔΟΥ. *Reverse*: Two palm fronds between bonnets of the Dioscuri. Kharoshthi inscription on three sides *maharajasa jayadharasa amtialkidasa* (of the great king Antialcidas the victorious). Monogram below.

Fig. 27.7 – 1838,EIC.74. 8.39g, 15mm x 17mm. Monogram off flan. BMC India (Greek and Scythic), p. 28.29.

Fig. 27.8 – IOLC.613. 4.21g, 18mm x 18mm. Monogram below left ⟨⟩.

Fig. 27.9 – 1859,0301.36. 8.36g, 20m x 18mm. Monogram below left ⟨⟩. Wilson 1841, p. 278, no. 5, Coins pl. II.13; Bopearachchi 1991, ser. 17, pp. 278–9, pl. 41. The coin is now attributed to a purchase from Mrs Brereton in 1859, but may be on the wrong ticket as Wilson records it as part of the Masson collection in the India Museum in 1841. Alternately, it is clear from the finds already missing from the India Museum's holdings when the collection was transferred to the British Museum in 1879–82, that some of

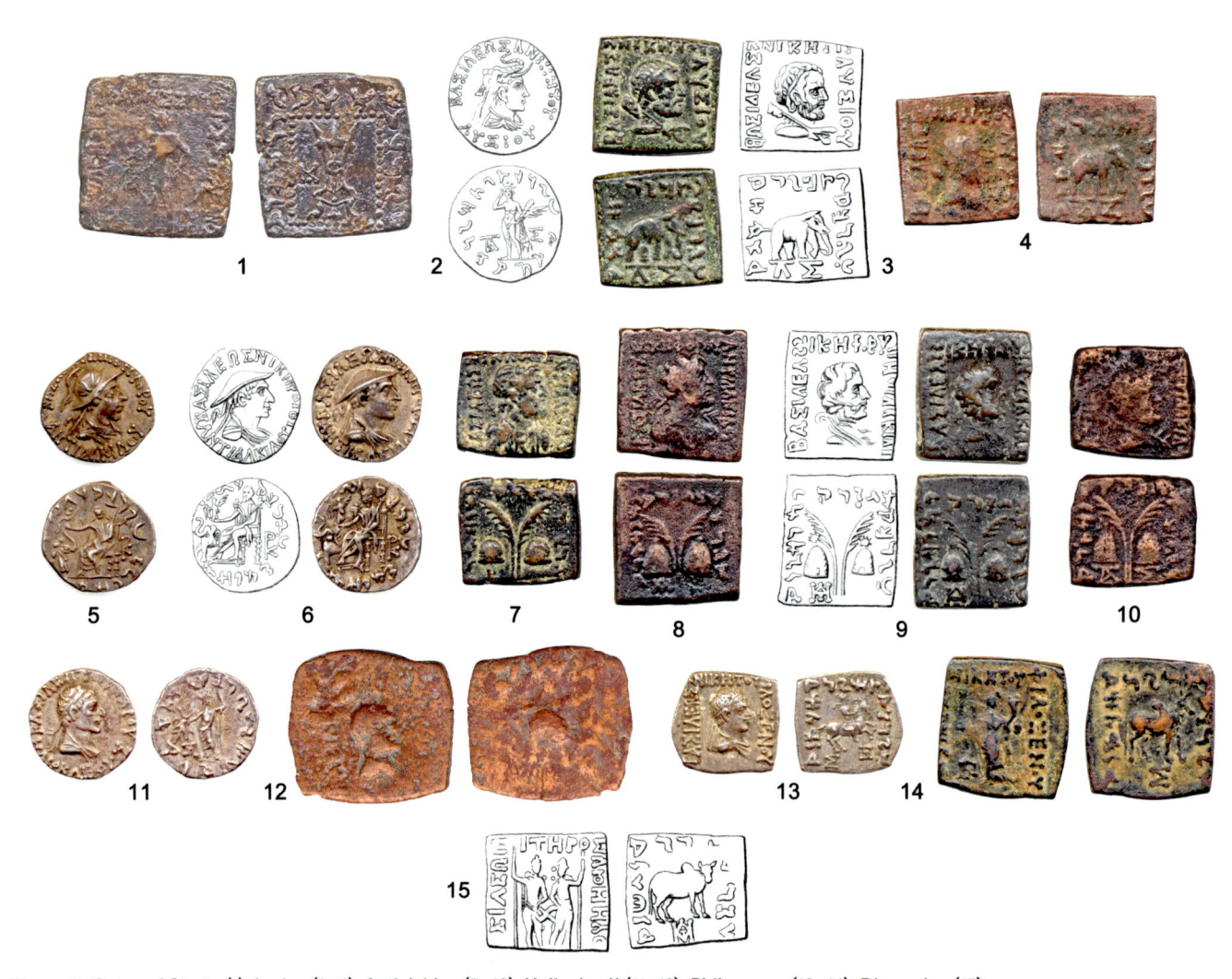

Figure 27 Coins of Strato (1), Lysias (2–4), Antialcidas (5–10), Heliocles II (11–12), Philoxenus (13–14), Diomedes (15)

the material, including possibly this coin, must have been dispersed in the intervening period (**Vol. II, p. vii**).

Fig. 27.10 – IOLC.618. 7.1g, 18mm. Monogram $\overline{A}\Sigma$ below centre.

Total 23 coins: 8.39g–8.24g (3), 7.83g–73g (10), 6.99g–6.11g (4), 5.76g–5.12g (2), 4.82g–4.21g (4). Monograms: $\hat{K}$ (1), ⋈ (3), $\overline{A}\Sigma$ (9).

Heliocles II (c. 110–100 BC)

Fig. 27.11–12. *Obverse*: Greek inscription; ΒΑΣΙΛΕΩΣ ΔΙΚΑΙΟΥ ΗΛΙΟΚΛΕΟΥΣ (of king Heliocles the just). *Reverse*: Kharoshthi inscription *maharajasa dhramikasa heliyakreyasa* (of the great king Heliocles the just).

Fig. 27.11 – IOC.50. Silver drachm. *Obverse*: Diademed bust of king to right. *Reverse*: Zeus standing facing, with a sceptre in his left hand and a thunderbolt in his right. Greek monogram in left field Σ. 2.23g, 16mm. Wilson 1841, p. 268, no. 3, Coins pl. XXI.8; BMC India (Greek and Scythic) p. 23.23.

Fig. 27.12 – IOLC.629. Copper alloy coin. *Obverse*: Diademed head of king to right. *Reverse*: Elephant standing to left. Monogram illegible. 5.95g, 25mm. Bopearachchi 1991, ser. 7, p. 284, pl. 42.

Philoxenus (c. 100–95 BC)

Fig. 27.13–14. *Obverse*: Greek inscription ΒΑΣΙΛΕΩΣ ΑΝΙΚΗΤΟΥ ΦΙΛΟΞΕΝΟΥ (of king Philoxenus the invincible). *Reverse*: Kharoshthi inscription *maharajasa apadihatasa pilasinasa* (of great king Philoxenus the invincible).

Fig. 27.13 – IOC.119. Silver drachm. *Obverse*: Diademed bust of king to right. *Reverse*: Helmeted warrior on horseback to right. Two Greek monograms Σ ⋈ below. 2.14g, 14mm x 15.5mm. Wilson 1841, p. 276, no. 2, Coins pl. XXI.13; BMC India (Greek and Scythic) p. 56.5.

Fig. 27.14 – IOC.125. Copper alloy coin. *Obverse*: Demeter standing to left, right arm outstretched and holding a cornucopia in her left hand. Greek monogram ⋈ in left field. *Reverse*: Zebu standing to right. Greek monogram below centre Σ. 7.51g, 19mm x 18mm. Wilson 1841, p. 276, no. 3 (not illustrated); BMC India (Greek and Scythic) p. 57.17.

Diomedes (c. 95–90 BC)

Fig. 27.15. Copper alloy Indian standard coin. *Obverse*: Dioscuri standing facing, each holding a spear. Greek inscription on three sides ΒΑΣΙΛΕΩΣ ΣΩΤΗΡΟΣ ΔΙΟΜΗΔΟΥ (of king Diomedes the saviour). *Reverse*: Zebu standing to right. Monogram below ⋈. Kharoshthi legend on three sides: *maharajasa tratarasa diyumitasa* (of great king Diomedes the saviour). 18mm x 17mm. **F526/1a, Pl. 6.123**; Masson 1836a, p. 24, fig.17, pl. I.10; Wilson 1841, pp. 291–2, Coins pl. V.1: two examples, coins not traced.

Archebius (c. 90–80 BC)

Masson records only a single Archebius coin – a silver drachm – which was acquired from Begram in 1835.

F526/1a, *Fig. 132*, **Pl. 6**, *Fig. 122*. *Obverse*: Diademed bust of king to right. Greek inscription ΒΑΣΙΛΕΩΣ ΔΙΚΑΙΟΥ ΝΙΚΗΦΟΡΟΥ ΑΡΧΕΛΙΟΥ (of king Archebius, the just, the victorious). *Reverse*: Zeus standing to front holding a thunderbolt in his right hand and a sceptre in his left. Kharoshthi inscription *maharajasa dhramikasa jayadharasa Arkhebiyasa* (of the great king Archebius the victorious. Monogram ꓘ. Coin not traced.

Hermaeus (c. 90–70 BC)

Masson divides Hermaeus coins into three categories: Hermaeus 1 'the elder', i.e. lifetime issues; Hermaeus 2 'the younger', i.e. anonymous posthumous imitations in the name of Hermaeus; and Hermaeus 3 'and dynasty', i.e. Kujula Kadphises coins in the name of Hermaeus (**Vol. II, pp. 50, 60–1, 80**; **F526/1a**, see pp. 50, 72 above). For the period 1833–5, he records collecting 93 lifetime coins; 28 posthumous imitations and 593 Kujula coins of this category.

Lifetime issues

Fig. 28.1 – IOC.133. Silver tetradrachm. *Obverse*: Diademed bust of king to right: Greek inscription ΒΑΣΙΛΕΩΣ ΣΩΤΗΡΟΣ ΕΡΜΑΙΟΥ (of king Hermaeus the saviour). *Reverse*: Enthroned Zeus seated to left, with his right arm outstretched and holding a long sceptre in his left hand. Kharoshthi inscription *maharajasa tratarasa heramayasa* (of great king Hermaeus the saviour). Greek monogram in right field ⚹. 9.76g, 25mm. **F526/1a, Pl. 3.54**; Masson 1836a, pp. 22–3, no. 16, pl. II.11 (2 examples from Kabul: no. 15 not illustrated); Wilson 1841 pp. 292–3, no. 1, Coins pl. V.2; BMC India (Greek and Scythic) p. 62.1.

Fig. 28.2. Wilson 1841, p. 293, no. 2, Coins pl. V.3. Monogram in right field ⚹. 17mm. Coin not traced.

Fig. 28.3 – IOC.153. Silver drachm. *Obverse*: Diademed busts of king and queen to right. Greek inscription ΒΑΣΙΛΕΩΣ ΣΩΤΗΡΟΣ ΕΡΜΑΙΟΥ ΚΑΙ ΚΑΛΛΙΟΠΗΣ (of king Hermaeus the saviour and Calliope). *Reverse*: Diademed rider in a Macedonian helmet on a prancing horse to right; with a bow, quiver and arrow attached to the back of the saddle. Kharoshthi inscription *maharajasa tratarasa heramayasa kaliyapaya* (of great king Hermaeus the saviour and Calliope). Greek monogram in right field ⚹. 2.16g, 15mm. Wilson 1841, p. 293, no. 3, Coins pl.XXI.14; BMC India (Greek and Scythic) p. 66.2.

Fig. 28.4–5. Copper alloy coins. *Obverse*: Bust of Mithras to right. Greek inscription ΒΑΣΙΛΕΩΣ ΣΩΤΗΡΟΣ ΕΡΜΑΙΟΥ. *Reverse*: Horse with front leg raised to right. Kharoshthi inscription *maharajasa tratarasa heramayasa*; Greek monogram ⊕ below.

Fig. 28.4 – IOC.150. 8.96g, 20mm x 19mm. **F526/1a, Pl. 3.66**; Masson 1834, p. 171, fig. 38, pl. XI.38 (2 examples from Begram); Wilson 1841, p. 294, no. 7, Coins pl. V.7; BMC India (Greek and Scythic) p. 66.53.

Masson lists another example 'from Jalalabad' (1836a, p. 25, no. 19, pl. II.12), i.e. from Hadda stupa 3, but this is probably a misidentified Kharahostes coin (**Vol. I, pp. 167–8, Fig. 256.24**).

Fig. 28.5 – IOC.152. *Obverse*: Bust of radiant Mithras to right. 6.39g, 18mm x 18mm. Wilson 1841, p. 294, no. 8, Coins pl. XXI.15; BMC India (Greek and Scythic) p. 66.55.

Total 4 lifetime issues. 2 silver coins: 9.76g, 2.16g; 2 copper alloy coins: 8.96g, 6.39g.

Anonymous imitations in the name of Hermaeus
Fig. 28.6–7. Silver Indian standard drachms.

Fig. 28.6 – IOLC.633. *Obverse*: Diademed head of Hermaeus to right. Greek inscription ΒΑΣΙΛΕΩΣ ΣΩΤΗΡΟΣ ΕΡΜΑΙΟΥ. *Reverse*: Zeus on throne to left. Kharoshthi inscription *maharajasa tratarasa hermayasa*. Monogram illegible; 1.88g, 15mm. Bopearachchi 1991, ser. 17, pp. 336–7, pl. 57.

Fig. 28.7 – IOLC.630. *Obverse*: Worn traces of head of king to right. *Reverse*: Defaced, 1.41g, 15mm.

Fig. 28.8 – IOC.148. [ΒΑΣΙΛΕ]ΩΣ ΣV ΕΡΜΑΙΟΥ (of king Su Hermaeus). *Reverse*: *heramayasa* (of Hermaeus). Monograms in left and right fields ⚹ ⚹. 4.09g, 20mm. **F526/1a, Pl. 3.62**; Masson 1834, p. 167, pl. IX.23; Wilson 1841, p. 310, no. 2, Coins pl. V.11; BMC India (Greek and Scythic) p. 65.45; Cribb and Bracey (at press), Hermaeus imitation.

Fig. 28.9 – IOC.149. *Obverse*: Greek inscription largely off flan. *Reverse*: Kharoshthi inscription *mahara[ja]sa*. Monogram in left field ⚹ ? 5.36g, 18mm. Masson 1834, p. 167, pl. IX.22; BMC India (Greek and Scythic) p. 65.48.

Fig. 28.10–17. Copper alloy Indian-standard tetradrachms. *Obverse*: Diademed head of king to right. Greek inscription ΒΑΣΙΛΕΩΣ ΣΩΤΗΡΟΣ ΕΡΜΑΙΟΥ (of king Hermaeus the saviour). *Reverse*: Zeus seated on a throne to left. Kharoshthi inscription *maharajasa tratarasa heramayasa* (of great king Hermaeus the saviour).

Fig. 28.10 – IOC.143. *Reverse*: Monogram in left field ⚹. 9.11g, 24mm. Wilson 1841, pp. 293–4, no. 5, Coins pl. V.5; BMC India (Greek and Scythic) p. 64.36.

Fig. 28.11 – 1838,EIC.62. *Reverse*: Monogram in left field ⚹; indistinct mark in right field. 9.37g, 24mm. BMC India (Greek and Scythic), p. 64.29.

Fig. 28.12 – 1838,EIC.63. *Reverse*: Monograms in left and right fields ⚹, ⚹. 9.10g, 25mm. BMC India (Greek and Scythic), p. 64.33.

Fig. 28.13 – 1838,EIC.64. *Reverse*: Monograms in left and right fields ⚹, ⚹. 8.39g, 24mm. BMC India (Greek and Scythic), p. 64.31.

Fig. 28.14 – IOC.144. *Reverse*: Monogram ⚹ in left field; indistinct mark in right. 9.42g, 23mm. Wilson 1841, p. 293, no. 4, Coins pl. V.4; BMC India (Greek and Scythic) p. 65.38.

Fig. 28.15 – IOLC.670. *Reverse*: Monogram ⚹ in left field. 9.71g, 21mm. Bopearachchi 1991, ser. 20, pp. 338–42, pls 58–60.

Fig. 28.16 – IOLC.675. *Reverse*: Monogram in left field ⚹. 9.21g, 21mm. Bopearachchi 1991, ser. 20, pp. 338–42, pls 58–60.

Fig. 28.17 – IOLC.693. *Reverse*: Monogram illegible. 2.72g, 18mm.

Fig. 28.18–19. Indian standard copper alloy drachms. *Obverse*: Diademed head of king to right. Greek inscription ΒΑΣΙΛΕΩΣ ΣΩΤΗΡΟΣ ΕΡΜΑΙΟΥ. *Reverse*: Zeus seated on

Figure 28 Coins of Hermaeus (1–20), Apollodotus II (21)

Figure 29 Indo-Scythian coins. Maues (1), Vonones and Spalahores (2), Spalirises and Spalagadama (3), Spalirises (4–6), Azes I (7–9), Azilises (10)

a throne to left. Kharoshthi inscription *maharajasa tratarasa heramayasa*. Monogram in left field ⊠.

Fig. 28.18 – IOC.147. 2.08g, 15mm. Wilson 1841, pp. 293–4, no. 6, Coins pl. V.6. BMC India (Greek and Scythic) p. 65.44.

Fig. 28.19 – IOLC.699. 2.12g, 15mm.

Fig. 28.20 – 1894,0506.1695. *Obverse*: Bust of king facing to left wearing a diadem. Part of Greek inscription. *Reverse*: Goddess Nike to left, holding a diadem in her right hand. Part of Kharoshthi inscription *maharajasa*. Monogram in right field ⊠. 3.13g, 15mm. Cunningham collection. Wilson 1841, p. 339, no. 2, Coins pl. V.15; Cribb and Bracey (at press), Hermaeus imitation.

Total 104 imitations in the name of Hermaeus. 2 silver coins: 1.88g, 1.41g; 102 copper alloy coins: 10.38g–10.1g (2), 9.72g–9.03g (16), 8.98–8.01g (31), 7.92g–7.04g (8), 6.82g–6.02g (3), 5.97g–5g (8), 4.97g–4.01g (11), 3.98g–3.86g (5), 2.99g–2g (12), 1.92g–1.38g (6),

Apollodotus II (c. 80–65 BC)

Fig. 28.21 – IOLC.632. Copper alloy coin: quarter unit, without inscription. *Obverse*: Zebu standing to right within rectangular border. *Reverse*: Tripod within rectangular border. 1.76g, 13mm. Bopearachchi 1991, ser. 19, p. 354, pl. 64.

Indo-Scythians

Maues (c. 75–65 BC)

Fig. 29.1 – IOLC.729. Worn copper alloy coin. *Obverse*: Poseidon standing to left, right foot on a river god, holding a trident in his left hand. Greek inscription ΒΑΣΙΛΕΩΣ ΒΑΣΙΛΕΩΝ ΜΕΓΑΛΟΥ ΜΑΥΟΥ (of the king of kings Maues the great). *Reverse*: Yakshi standing between vines, holding vine in the left hand and bunch of grapes and brazier in the right. Kharoshthi inscription *rajatirajasa mahatasa moasa* (of the king of kings Maues the great). 7.49g, 23mm. The coin is clipped in half. Senior 2000, p. 6, type 26.1.

F526/1a, *Fig. 139*, **Pl. 6.129.** *Obverse*: Elephant walking to right within rectangular frame. Greek inscription ΒΑΣΙΛΕΩΣ ΒΑΣΙΛΕΩΝ ΜΕΓΑΛΟΥ ΜΑΥΟΥ. *Reverse*: King seated cross-legged on a throne, within rectangular frame. Kharoshthi inscription *rajatirajasa mahatasa moasa*. Coin not traced; see p. 53 above.

Vonones and Spalahores (c. 65–50 BC)

Fig. 29.2. Wilson 1841, p. 338, no. 2, Coins pl. VIII.9. *Obverse*: Heracles standing to front, crowning himself with a wreath in his right hand, and holding a club and lion-skin in his left. Greek inscription ΒΑΣΙΛΕΩΣ ΒΑΣΙΛΕΩΝ

ΜΕΓΑΛΟΥ ΟΝΩΝΟΥ (of the king of kings Vonones the great). *Reverse*: Pallas Athena standing left, holding a spear and shield. Kharoshthi inscription *maharajabhrata dhramikasa spalahorasa* (of the brother of the king, Spalahores the just). 20mm x 22mm. Three coins illustrated; none traced, see also Masson 1834, p. 171, pl. XI.39, 43; **F526/1a, fig. 137, Pl. 6.127**; 1836a, p. 25, no. 24, pl. II.24. One example from Begram 1834 and 'several specimens' from Kabul in the 1836 collection (Wilson 1841, p. 338).

Spalirises and Spalagadama

Fig. 29.3. Wilson 1841, p. 318, Coins pl. VIII.13. *Obverse*: King on horseback to right, within a square dotted border. Greek inscription CΠΑΛΥΡΙΟC ΔΙΚΑΙΟΥ ΑΔΕΛΦΟΥΤΟΥ ΒΑCΙΛΕΩC (of Spalirises the just, the king's brother). *Reverse*: Heracles seated on rocks to left, holding a club. Greek monogram in left field ⊕. Kharoshthi inscription:*spalahoraputrasa dhramiasa spalagadamasa* (of Spalagadama the just, son of Spalahores). 22mm x 22mm. Masson 1834, p. 172, pl. IX.44; Masson 1836a, p. 25, nos 21–2, pl. II.13–14: 2 examples from Jalalabad. 'Several very perfect specimens' in the Masson collection (Wilson 1841, p. 318), none traced.

Spalirises (c. 50–40 BC)

Fig. 29.4–6. Copper alloy coin. *Obverse*: King standing to left with battle-axe and bow. Greek inscription ΒΑΣΙΛΕΩΣ ΒΑΣΙΛΕΩΝ ΜΕΓΑΛΟΥ CΠΑΛΙΡΙCΟΥ (of the king of kings Spalarises the great). *Reverse*: Zeus seated on a throne. Kharoshthi inscription *maharajasa mahatakasa spalirihasa* (of the.king of kings Spalirises the great). Monogram in right field ⊕. Three coins collected from Begram 1833–5.

Fig. 29.4. Wilson 1841, p. 316, Coins pl. VIII.12 (drawing has an extra monogram ⊕ in the left field); **F526/1a**, *Fig. 134*, **Pl. 6.124** (without extra monogram). Coin not traced. 24mm x 25mm.

Fig. 29.5 – IOC.224. 8.12g, 22 x 22mm. **F526/1a**, *Fig. 136*, **Pl. 6.126**; BMC India (Greek and Scythic) p. 101.4.

Fig. 29.6 – IOC.225. 8.22g, 23 x 22mm. **F526/1a**, *Fig. 135*, **Pl. 6.125**; BMC India (Greek and Scythic) p. 101.5.

Azes I (c. 46–1 BC)

Fig. 29.7 – IOC.197. Copper alloy coin. *Obverse*: King holding ankus, mounted on Bactrian camel to right. Greek inscription ΒΑΣΙΛΕΩ[Σ ΒΑΣΙΛΕΩΝ ΜΕΓ]ΑΛΟΥ ΑΖΟΥ (of the king of kings Azes the great). *Reverse*: Zebu grazing to right, with a monogram in the right field ⊠. Part of a Kharoshthi inscription [*maharajasa rajarajasa maha*]*tasa ayasa* (of the great king of kings Azes the great) along the left side. 12.9g, 25mm x 26mm. **F526/1a, Pl. 7.157**: procured in Kabul bazaar. Wilson 1841, p. 327, no. 14, Coins pl. VII.6; BMC India (Greek and Scythic) p. 88.179.

Fig. 29.8–9. Worn copper alloy coins. *Obverse*: Greek inscription ΒΑΣΙΛΕΩΣ ΒΑΣΙΛΕΩΝ ΜΕΓΑΛΟΥ ΑΖΟΥ (of the king of kings Azes the great). *Reverse*: Kharoshthi inscription *maharajasa rajarajasa mahatasa ayasa* (of the great king of kings Azes the great).

Fig. 29.8 – IOLC.730. *Obverse*: Azes I on horseback to right holding spear, within a square frame. *Reverse*: Zebu standing to right, with illegible monogram above. 11.1g, 22mm x 24mm. Wilson 1841, p. 330, no. 23, Coins pl. VII.16 (type); Senior 2000, p.48 type 92.4, Reverse die is very close to Senior type 92.5.

Fig. 29.9 – IOLC.733. *Obverse*: Elephant standing to right. *Reverse*: Zebu standing to right. Two illegible monograms above. 10.46g, 25mm. Senior 2000, pp. 73–4, type 100.

Azilises (c. 1 BC–AD 16)

Fig. 29.10 – IOC.215. Copper alloy coin. *Obverse*: King with whip, mounted on horseback to right. Greek inscription [ΒΑΣΙΛΕΩΣ ΒΑΣΙΛΕΩΝ] ΜΕΓΑΛΟΥ [Α]ΖΙΛΙΣΟΥ (of the king of kings Azilises the great). *Reverse*: Elephant standing to right; monograms above. Kharoshthi inscription *maharajasa rajarajasa mahatasa ayilishasa* (of the great king of kings Azilises the great). 5.88g, 19mm x 20mm. Masson 1836a, p. 25, no. 23. pl. II.16: single example, procured in Kabul bazaar 1835. **F526/1a, Pl. 7.152**; Wilson 1841, p. 330, no. 23, Coins pl. VII.16 (type). BMC India (Greek and Scythic) p. 95.26.

Azes II (c. AD 16–30)

Fig. 30.1–2. Silver coins. *Obverse*: King on horseback to right with whip; right hand raised. Greek inscription ΒΑΣΙΛΕΩΣ ΒΑΣΙΛΕΩΝ ΜΕΓΑΛΟΥ ΑΖΟΥ (of the king of kings Azes the great). *Reverse*: Kharoshthi inscription *maharajasa rajarajasa mahatasa ayasa* (of the great king of kings Azes the great).

Fig. 30.1 – 1866.1201.4090. Indian standard tetradrachm. *Obverse*: Monogram X in right field. *Reverse*: Athena standing to right, holding a spear and shield in her left hand, gesturing with her right. Monograms in left Ⱥ and right fields ⚶. 9.38g, 25mm. Bequeathed by James Woodhouse. Wilson 1841, p. 324, no. 2, Coins pl. VI.13; BMC India (Greek and Scythic) p. 81.90, pl.XVIII.8.

Fig. 30.2. Indian standard drachm. *Obverse*: Monogram in right field P. *Reverse*: Athena standing to front, holding a spear and shield in her left hand, right arm raised. Monograms in left ⱦ and right fields ⊠. 16mm. **F526/1a, Pl. 7.156**. Wilson 1841, p. 326, no. 8, Coins pl. VI.19.

Fig. 30.3–17. Silver and copper alloy coins. *Obverse*: King on horseback to right with whip; right hand raised. Greek inscription ΒΑΣΙΛΕΩΣ ΒΑΣΙΛΕΩΝ ΜΕΓΑΛΟΥ ΑΖΟΥ (of the king of kings Azes the great). *Reverse*: Zeus Nikephoros standing to left, sceptre in left hand, right arm outstretched, with wreath-bearing Nike standing on his hand. Kharoshthi inscription *maharajasa rajarajasa mahatasa ayasa* (of the great king of kings Azes the great). Senior 2000, pp. 80–111, type 105.

Fig. 30.3. Indian standard tetradrachm. *Obverse*: Monogram in right field ⴄ. *Reverse*: Monograms in left ⵂ and right fields ⵉ⴯. 9.74g, 22mm. Wilson 1841, p. 325, no. 5, Coins pl. VI.16, BMC India (Greek and Scythic) p. 74.15.

Fig. 30.4 – IOLC.749. Silver Indian standard tetradrachm. *Obverse*: Monogram in right field Ψ. *Reverse*: Monograms in left ⱦ and right fields ⴽP. 9.2g, 23mm.

Fig. 30.5 – IOLC.751. Silver-plated Indian standard drachm. Monograms illegible. 2.37g, 15mm.

Fig. 30.6 –in left ⴽ and right fields ⊠ ⴄ. 2.16g, 15mm.

IOLC.753. 1.81g, 13mm. Not illustrated.

Figure 30 Indo-Scythian coins. Azes II

Fig. 30.7–9. Silver drachms. *Reverse*: Monogram in left field ⌘. Senior 2000, pp. 87–8, type 105.270–4.
Fig. 30.7 – IOLC.754. 2.08g, 13mm.
Fig. 30.8 – IOLC.755. 1.49g, 13mm.
Fig. 30.9 – IOLC.756. 1.79g, 14mm.
Fig. 30.10–17. Silver alloy and copper alloy drachms. *Obverse*: Monogram in right field (where visible) ♆. *Reverse*: Monograms in left ⌘ and right fields ⸙. Senior 2000, p. 88, type 105.275vD–7D.
Fig. 30.10. Wilson 1841, p. 326, no. 11, Coins pl. VII.3. Silver alloy coin. 16mm. Masson 1834, p. 170, pl. X.33.
Fig. 30.11 – IOLC.779. Silver alloy coin. 2.25g, 13mm.
Fig. 30.12 – OR.9168. Copper alloy coin. 1.7g, 13mm. Masson 1834, p. 170, pl. X.31; Cribb and Bracey at press, type B.S2.
Fig. 30.13 – IOLC.759. 1.97g, 13mm.
Fig. 30.14 – IOLC.763. 1.92g, 13mm.
Fig. 30.15 – IOLC.773. 1.46g, 12mm.
Fig. 30.16 – IOLC.757. 1.9g, 13mm.
Fig. 30.17 – IOLC.774. 1.82g, 13.5mm.
Total 48 coins: 2.66g–2.02g (17), 1.99g–1.34g (30), 0.86g (1).

Fig. 30.18–20. *Obverse*: City goddess enthroned to left holding a cornucopia. Greek inscription ΒΑΣΙΛΕΩΣ ΒΑΣΙΛΕΟΝ ΜΕΓΑΛΟΥ ΑΖΟΥ (of the king of kings Azes the great). *Reverse*: Hermes standing to left, holding caduceus in left hand. Kharoshthi inscription *maharajasa rajarajasa mahatasa ayasa* (of the great king of kings Azes the great). Monograms in left ⚹ and right fields ◇.
Fig. 30.18. Wilson 1841, pp. 329–30, no. 22, Coins pl. VII.12. 26mm. Coin not traced.
Fig. 30.19 – IOLC.739. 12.51g, 27mm. Senior 2000, p. 74, type 101.1.
Fig. 30.20 – IOLC.734. 11.47g, 27.5mm. Senior 2000, p. 74, type 101.1. Overstruck on Senior type 100 (Azes I, elephant/zebu: see **Fig. 29.9 – IOLC.733** above).
Total 14 coins: 12.51g–12.16g (2), 11.72g–11.47g (3), 10.47g–10.02g (7), 9.95g–9.6g (2).

Fig. 30.21–2. *Obverse*: Zebu standing to right; monogram above. Greek inscription ΒΑΣΙΛΕΩΣ ΒΑΣΙΛΕΩΝ ΜΕΓΑΛΟΥ ΑΖΟΥ (of the king of kings Azes the great). *Reverse*: Lion standing to right; monogram above. Kharoshthi inscription *maharajasa rajarajasa mahatasa ayasa* (of the great king of kings Azes the great).
Fig. 30.21. Wilson 1841, p. 328, no. 16, Coins pl. VII.8. *Obverse*: Monogram Ā. *Reverse*: Monogram ⚹. 25mm. Coin not traced.
Fig. 30.22 – IOC.190. *Obverse*: Monogram Ⅲ. *Reverse*: Monogram ⚹. 7.21g, 22mm. Wilson 1841, p. 328, no. 17, Coins pl. VII.9; BMC India (Greek and Scythic) p. 86.156.
Total 16 coins: 13.45g–13.05g (3), 12.48g–12.01g (4), 11.74g–11.09g (4), 10.9g–9.72g (2), 7.32g–5.07g (3).

Fig. 30.23 – IOC.200. *Obverse*: Lion standing to right, front paw raised. Monogram ↑ above. Greek inscription [ΒΑΣΙΛΕΩΣ ΒΑΣΙΛΕ]ΩΝ ΜΕΓ[ΑΛΟΥ ΑΖΟ]Υ. *Reverse*: Zebu standing to left. Monogram above ȶ. Kharoshthi inscription *maharaja[sa rajarajasa mahatasa] ayasa*. 2.84g, 15mm x 16mm. **F526/1a, Pl. 6.128**; Masson 1834, p. 171, pl. XI.41; Wilson 1841, p. 331, no. 26, Coins pl. VIII.3; BMC India (Greek and Scythic) p. 90.190. Begram 1833 collection.
Fig. 30.24 – IOLC.748. *Obverse*: Lion standing to right.

Traces of Greek inscription. *Reverse*: City goddess enthroned to left holding cornucopia. Traces of Kharoshthi. 2.21g, 14mm. Senior 2000, pp. 117–18, type 122–3.

Fig. 30.25–30. Copper alloy coins. *Obverse*: Diademed king seated cross-legged to front, head to left, his right hand raised, holding a whip, his left resting on a sword in his lap. Monogram in left field. Greek inscription ΒΑΣΙΛΕΩΣ ΒΑΣΙΛΕΩΝ ΜΕΓΑΛΟΥ ΑΖΟΥ. *Reverse*: Hermes standing to front, head turned to the left. Right hand raised in blessing and a caduceus held in his left. Monograms in left and right fields; Kharoshthi inscription *maharajasa rajarajasa mahatasa ayasa*. Senior 2000, pp. 112–14, type 107.
Fig. 30.25 – IOC.185. *Obverse*: Monogram ⚹. *Reverse*: Monograms ⚹ ⸙. 11.18g, 25mm. Wilson 1841, pp. 328–9, no. 24, Coins pl. VII.14; BMC India (Greek and Scythic) p. 83.116.
Fig. 30.26 – IOLC.835. *Obverse*: Monogram illegible. *Reverse*: Monograms ⌘ ⸙. 7.67g, 22mm.
Fig. 30.27 – IOLC.852. *Obverse*: Monogram ⸙. *Reverse*: Monograms ⌘ ℞ ⸙. 5.85g, 23.5mm.
Fig. 30.28 – IOLC.837. *Obverse*: Monogram ⸙. *Reverse*: Monograms ⌘ ⸙. 8.57g, 23.5mm.
Fig. 30.29. Wilson 1841, pp. 328–9, no. 20, Coins pl. VII.13. *Obverse*: Monogram ⸙. *Reverse*: Monograms ⚹ ℙ. 24mm. Coin not traced.
Fig. 30.30. Wilson 1841, p. 329, no. 21, Coins pl. VII.15. *Obverse*: Monogram ⸙. *Reverse*: Monograms illegible. Coin not traced.
Total 77 coins: 11.41g–11.18g (3), 10.72g–10g (7), 9.99g–9g (14), 8.91g–8.04g (17), 7.71g–7.06g (8), 6.72g–6.04g (9), 5.85g–5.05g (11), 4.86g–4.42g (8).

Indo-Scythian satraps

The coins of the satraps Kharahostes and his son Mujatria are exclusively recorded by Masson as having been found in the Jalalabad region, specifically in the relic deposits of Hadda stupa 3, the Darunta stupas Bimaran 2 and 5, Deh Rahman 1, and as a surface find at Surkh Tope (**Vol. I, pp. 103–4, Fig. 117.1–4; pp. 117–19, Figs 134.5, 136.21–4; p. 122, Fig. 142.2–5; p. 125, Fig. 153; pp. 167–8, Fig. 256.24–8**; see also Cribb 2015). Two more were also excavated at Tope-i Kutchera in Darunta (**Vol. I, p. 131, Fig. 167.3–4**).

Kharahostes (c. early 1st century AD)
Fig. 31.1 – IOLC.897. Copper alloy coin. *Obverse*: Horseman riding to right holding a whip. Blundered Greek inscription ΧΑΡΑΗΩΣΤΕΙ ΣΑΤΡΑΠΕΙ ΑΡΤΑΥΟΙΥ. (Kharahostes the satrap, [son of] Arta[sa]). Monogram illegible. *Reverse*: Lion walking to right. Kharoshthi inscription *kharaostasa artasaputrasa ksatrapasa pra* (the satrap Kharahostes, son of Artasa). Monogram illegible. 6.73g, 22mm. Senior 2000, p. 125, type 143.
F526/1a, Pl. 7.158. 20mm x 18mm.

Mujatria (c. AD 60–80)
Fig. 31.2 – 1838,EIC.90. Copper alloy coin. *Obverse*: King with whip, mounted on horseback to right. Kharoshthi letter *mu* behind the horseman's head; a three-spoked circular device in the right field. Blundered Greek inscription

Figure 31 Indo-Scythian coins. Satraps: Mujatria (1–3), Zeionises (4), Aspavarma (5–6), Higaksha (7), Rudrasena II (8)

ΒΑΣΙΛΕΩΣ ΒΑΣΙΛΕΟΝ ΜΕΓΑΛΟΥ ΑΖΟΥ. *Reverse*: City goddess standing to front, right arm outstretched, cradling a cornucopia in her left. Kharoshthi monogram *shighasa* in right field. Kharoshthi inscription *maharajasa mahatasa dhramiasa rajadirajasa ayasa* (king, great righteous king of kings, Azes). 9.14g, 21mm. Cribb 2015, no. 19. Mitchiner 1975–6, vol. 6, p. 577, type 873.

Fig. 31.3. Wilson 1841, p. 331, no. 25, Coins pl. VIII.1. Massson records 11 coins of this type, which is also the total number recorded from the relic deposits: 9.59g–9g (10), 8.55g (1).

F526/1a, Pl. 7.160. *Obverse*: Horseman riding to right. *Reverse*: Heracles standing, right arm raised. 11mm x 11mm. Coin not traced. Cribb 2015, no. 10, type 2a. See also **Vol. I, pp. 32–4, Fig. 34.2c**.

Zeionises / Jihonika (c. AD 30–50)

Fig. 31.4 – IOLC.892. Copper alloy coin issued as satrap of Chach. *Obverse*: Zebu standing to right. Blundered Greek inscription ΗΑΗΗΙΟΛΟΥ ΥΙΟΥ ΣΑΤΡΑΠΟΥ ΖΕΙШΗΙCΟΥ (satrap Zeionises, son of Manigul). *Reverse*: Lion standing to right. Kharoshthi inscription *manigulasaputrasa chatrapasa jihuniasa* (satrap Jihonika, son of Manigula). 10.35g, 25.5mm. Senior 2000, p. 121 type 133.

Total 3 coins. IOLC.891: 10.08g, 25mm; IOLC.893: 7.29g, 24mm. Coins probably acquired in Peshawar in 1838.

Aspavarma (c. AD 33–64)

Fig. 31.5–6. Copper alloy coins issued in name of Azes as Apraca stratega. *Obverse*: Horseman riding to right holding a whip. Blundered Greek inscription ΒΛΣΙΛΕΩΣ ΒΛΣΙΛΕΑΝ ΜΕΓΛΛΟΥ ΑΖΟV. *Reverse*: Athena standing to right, spear and shield at left side. Kharoshthi inscription *imtravarmaputrasa aspavarmasa stratagasa jayatasa* (of Aspavarma, victorious commander, son of Indravarma). Senior 2000, pp.138–43, type 183.

Fig. 31.5 – IOLC.894. 6.9g, 19.5mm.
Fig. 31.6 – IOLC.895. 9.22g, 20mm.

Total 3 coins. IOLC.896: 8.92g, 20mm. Coins probably acquired in Peshawar in 1838.

Kshaharata Satrap Higaksha (c. late 1st century AD)

Fig. 31.7. Wilson 1841, p. 290, no. 5, Coins pl. IV.16: Misidentified as a coin of Apollodotus. *Obverse*: Apollo standing to right, holding bow; quiver strapped to his back. Greek inscription ΞΑΡΑΤΗΣ ΣΑΤΡΑΦΩ ΒΑΡΑΤΑΣ (of the Kshaharata Satraps brothers). Greek monogram **B** in the left field, in the right field a crescent. *Reverse*: Tripod, flanked by monograms in the left 𐊐 and right fields 𐊑. Kharoshthi inscription *kshaharata kshatapa jayasa higataka higaksha bharata* (of the Kshaharata satraps Higataka and Higaksha brothers). 25mm. Coin not traced. The reverse drawing must be flipped as it shows mirror images of the monograms found on Masson's sketch (**F526/1a, Pl. 1.8**) and on actual coins, see Senior 2006, p. 23, type S67; Falk 2016.

Western Satrap Rudrasena II (c. AD 256–78)

Fig. 31.8 – IOLC.4638. Silver dramma minted in Gujarat. *Obverse*: Bust of ruler to right. *Reverse*: Three-arched hill and crescent flanked by moon and sun, with water below. Worn illegible Brahmi inscription *rajno ksatrapasa Viradamaputrasa rajno mahaksatrapasa Rudrasenasa* (of great satrap king Rudrasena, son of satrap king Viradaman). 1.89g, 14mm.

Indo-Parthians

Gondophares (c. AD 32–58)

A total of 78 Gondophares coins have been identified from the Masson collection (5 British Museum, 69 IOLC, 2 Ashmolean Museum; plus 2 illustrated in *Ariana Antiqua*, but untraced). Masson records collecting 55 coins of Gondophares from Begram in the 1833–5 seasons, all apparently of the bust of king/winged Nike type (**F526/1a, Pl. 4.92–8**; **Fig. 32.8–15** below). Stray coins of this type were also found in the relic deposits of the Jalalabad region

Catalogue of Coins | 149

stupas Bimaran 5 and Hadda 3 (**Vol. I, pp. 118, 167, Fig. 256.23**).

Fig. 32.1 – IOC.231. Silver alloy tetradrachm. *Obverse*: King with whip, mounted on horseback to right. Greek inscription. ΒΑCΙΛΕШΝ ΒΑCΙΛΕШΝ ΓΟΝΔΦΑΡΟΥ (king of kings Gondophares). Monogram in left field ?, Gondopharid tamgha ⚯ in right. *Reverse*: Shiva standing to front, right arm outstretched, holding a trident in his left hand. Monograms in left 🜨 and right fields §. Kharoshthi inscription *maharajasa rajaraja mahata dhramia tratara devavrata gudupharasa* (of the great king, king of kings, Gondophares the saviour, loved of the gods). 9.42g, 23mm. Wilson 1841, p. 342, no. 1, Coins pl. V.16; BMC India (Greek and Scythic) p. 104.10, pl. XXII.9. Mitchiner 1975–6, vol. 8, p. 751, type 1116.1; Senior 2000, p. 153, type 217.

Fig. 32.2 – IOC.228. Copper alloy Indian standard tetradrachm. *Obverse*: King mounted on horseback to right. Gondopharid tamgha in right field ⚯. Greek inscription ΒΑCΙΛΕШC [ΒΑC]ΙΛΕШΝ ΜΕΓΑ[ΛΟΥ] ΥΝΔΟΦΟΟΙΥ (king of kings Gondophares the saviour). *Reverse*: Zeus standing to right, with right arm outstretched. Monograms in left 🜨 and right fields ꓶ ꓬ ꓤ. Kharoshthi inscription *maharajasa gudaphanisa tratarasa* (of the great king Gondophares the saviour). 9.33g, 22mm. Wilson 1841, p.342, no. 3, Coins pl. V.18; BMC India (Greek and Scythic) p. 103.1, pl. XXII.3. Mitchiner 1975–6, vol. 8, p. 758, type 1129.2; Senior 2000, p. 653, type 220.20.

Fig. 32.3 – IOLC.962. Copper alloy Indian standard tetradrachm with traces of silver on the reverse. *Obverse*: King holding whip, riding a horse to left. Tamgha in left field ⚯. Worn Greek inscription largely off flan. *Reverse*: Athena standing to right holding a spear and a shield. Monograms in left ꓶ ꓬ and right fields ⚹. Kharoshthi inscription *maharaja rajatiraja tratara devavrata gudapharasa* (of the great king, king of kings Gondophares the saviour, loved of the gods). 8.75g, 23mm. Senior 2000, p. 155, type 218.6T (same obverse and reverse dies).

Fig. 32.4. Copper alloy coin. *Obverse*: King on horseback to right with right hand raised. Gondopharid tamgha ⚯ in right field. Greek inscription ΒΑCΙΛΕC [ΒΑCΙΛΕШΝ ΜΕΓΑΛΟΥ ΓΟΝΔΟΦ]ΑΡΟΥ (of Gondophares the great king of kings). *Reverse*: Helmeted Athena standing to right with a torque in her raised right hand and a spear over her left shoulder. Monograms in left ⚹ and right fields 🜨. Kharoshthi inscription *maharaja rajadiraja tratara devavrata gudapharasa* (of the great king, king of kings, Gondophares the saviour, loved of the gods). Wilson 1841, p. 342, no. 2, Coins pl. V.17. Senior 2000, type 219.5. Coin not traced.

Fig. 32.5–7. Copper alloy coin. *Obverse*: King mounted on horseback to left, facing Nike standing with a diadem in her raised right hand. Greek inscription only visible on **Fig. 32.7**. *Reverse*: Gondopharid tamgha ⚯ flanked by Kharoshthi monograms. Kharoshthi inscription. Senior 2000, p. 151, type 215.10–33.

Fig. 32.5. Wilson 1841, p. 343, no. 7, Coins pl. VI.2. Ashmolean Museum, H. de S. Shortt bequest 1975. *Obverse*: Traces of a few Greek letters. *Reverse*: Monogram in left field ꓕ. 4.68g, 17mm x 21mm. **F526/1a, Pl. 7.159**; Mitchiner 1975–6, vol. 8, p. 750, type 1114. Wilson misattributes the coin to the Swiney collection.

Fig. 32.6 – IOLC.966. 4.79g, 19.5mm.

Fig. 32.7 – IOC.233. *Obverse*: Greek inscription ΒΑ[CΙΛΕΩC ΒΑCΙΛΕШΝ] ΜΕΓΑΛΟΥ ΓΟΝ[ΔΟ]ΦΑΡΟΥ (of Gondophares the great king of kings). *Reverse*: Kharoshthi monograms in left ꓬ and right ? fields. Kharoshthi inscription *apratihatasa devavratasa gudavharasa [...] dhrami[ka]sa* (of Gondophares, [the great king, the saviour, the just], the invincible, loved of the gods). 6.16g, 21mm x 20mm. Wilson 1841, p. 343, no. 8, Coins pl. XXI.16; BMC India (Greek and Scythic) p. 105.22. Mitchiner 1975–6, vol. 8, p. 750, type 1114.1; Senior 2000 p. 151, type 215.11.

Fig. 32.8–15. Copper alloy Indian standard tetradrachms. *Obverse*: Diademed bust of king to right. Blundered Greek inscription ΒΑCΙΛΕΩC CΩΤΗΡΟC ΥΝΔΟΦΕΡΡΟΥ (of the great king Gondophares). *Reverse*: Winged Nike holding diademed wreath. Kharoshthi inscription *maharajasa gudaphanisa tratarasa* (of the great king Gondophares the saviour).

Fig. 32.8 – IOC.232. *Obverse*: Greek inscription ΒΑCΙΛΕΟΝ … ΥΝΟΔΦΑΡΡΟΥ. *Reverse*: Nike standing to front with wreath. Kharoshthi inscription partly off flan: *gudavhanisa trata[rasa]*. 9.53g, 23mm. Wilson 1841, p. 339, no. 1, Coins pl. V.12; BMC India (Greek and Scythic) p. 105.21, pl. XXII.11. Mitchiner 1975–6, vol. 8, p. 734, type 1084; Senior 2000, p. 150, type 213.

Fig. 32.9 – IOLC.899. *Reverse*: Nike standing to front with wreath.

Fig. 32.10–15. *Reverse*: Nike standing to right with wreath and palm branch. Senior 2000, p. 150, type 213T.

Fig. 32.10. Wilson 1841, p. 339, no. 1, Coins pl. V.13. 21mm. Coin not traced.

Fig. 32.11 – IOLC.898. 10.01g, 23.5mm.
Fig. 32.12 – IOLC.906. 8.64g, 22mm.
Fig. 32.13 – IOLC.901. 8.94g, 25mm.
Fig. 32.14 – 1838,EIC.113. 9.94g, 24mm. Mitchiner 1975–6, vol. 8, p. 734, type 1084.3.
Fig. 32.15. Wilson 1841, p. 339, no. 1, Coins pl. V.14. Ashmolean Museum, 20mm. H.E. Stapleton donation 15-3-1958. **F526/1a, Pl. 4.94**; Mitchiner 1975–6, vol. 8, p. 737, type 1087.

Total 64 coins: 10.01g (1), 9.62g–9.01g (20), 8.97g–8.03g (16), 7.93g–7.09g (10), 6.74g–6.03g (7), 5.84g–5.05g (8), 4.88g (1), 3.71g (1).

Fig. 32.16–18. Worn Indian standard copper alloy drachms of Gondophares. *Obverse*: Crude head of king to right. Illegible Greek inscription. *Reverse*: Athena to right holding a thunderbolt and shield. Illegible Kharoshthi inscription (*maharajasa mahata devavrata gudavharasa*). Mitchiner 1975–6, vol. 8, p. 765, type 1145. Senior 2000, p. 158, type 222.

Fig. 32.16 – IOLC.963. 1.99g, 12mm.
Fig. 32.17 – IOLC.964. 2.11g, 11mm.
Fig. 32.18 – IOLC.965. 2.24g, 11mm.

Contemporary imitations

Fig. 32.19–20. Indian standard copper alloy tetradrachms. *Obverse*: Diademed head of king to right. Corrupt Greek inscription VΛΔOCHΔΟΥ partly off flan. *Reverse*: Winged Nike standing to right, offering diademed wreath. Kharoshthi inscription partly off flan *maharajasa avadagashasa*

Figure 32 Indo-Parthian coins. Gondophares (1–18), contemporary imitations (19–20), Abdagases (21–2), uncertain Abdagases/Sasan (23–4), Sasan (25–30)

Catalogue of Coins | 151

tratarasa (of the great king Abdagases the saviour). Senior 2000, p. 159, type 224.6T.

Fig. 32.19 – 1838,EIC.75. 8.7g, 21mm. BMC India (Greek and Scythic), p. 105.15.

Fig. 32.20 – IOLC.936. 8.79g, 21mm.

Abdagases (c. AD 52–64)

Fig. 32.21 – IOLC.994. Copper alloy Indian standard tetradrachm. *Obverse*: Diademed head of king to right. Traces of Greek inscription partly off flan: ΒΑϹΙΛΕШϹ ϹШΤΗΡΟϹ ΑΒΔΑΓΑϹΟΥ (of king Abdagases the saviour). *Reverse*: Winged Nike standing to right, offering diademed wreath. Traces of Kharoshthi inscription *maharajasa avadagashasa tratarasa* (of great king Abdagases, the saviour). 6.2g, 22mm. Mitchiner 1975–6, vol. 8, p. 759, type 1131. Senior 2000, p. 159, type 224.

Fig. 32.22 – IOLC.968. Copper alloy Indian standard tetradrachm. *Obverse*: King holding whip; on horseback to left. Tamgha ☿ in left field. Blundered Greek inscription ΒΑΣΙΛΕΥΟΝΤΟΣ ΒΑΣΙΛΕШΝ ΑΒΔΑΓΑΣΟΥ (of king of kings Abdagases). *Reverse*: Zeus standing to right, holding winged Nike on outstretched right hand. Traces of Kharoshthi inscription *maharajasa rajadirajasa guduvharabhrataputrasa avadagashasa* (of the great king, king of kings, Abdagases, son of Gondophares) and illegible monograms (✠ in left and ☍ in right field). 9.26g, 22mm. Senior 2000, pp. 162–4, type 229.10–45T.

Uncertain: Abdagases/Sasan (c. AD 52–70)

Fig. 32.23–4. *Obverse*: King holding whip; on horseback to right. Tamgha ☿ in right field. Blundered Greek inscription. *Reverse*: Zeus standing to left, holding winged Nike on outstretched right hand. Traces of Kharoshthi inscription. Monograms in left ✠ and right ☍ fields. Mitchiner 1975–6, vol. 8, pp. 755–6, type 1125–6. Senior 2000, p. 165, type 231.25T, p. 171, type 243.11–16T.

Fig. 32.23 – IOLC.967. 9.75g, 21mm.
Fig. 32.24 – IOLC.970. 9.47g, 20mm.
Total 8 coins: 9.75g–9.21g (6), 8.61g (1), 7.28g (1).

Sasan (c. AD 64–70)

Fig. 32.25–6. Copper alloy Indian standard tetradrachms. *Obverse*: King holding whip, on horseback to right. Tamgha ☿ in right field. Greek inscription ΒΑϹΙΛΕΥΟΝΤΟϹ ΒΑϹΙΛΕШΝ ϹΑϹΟΥ (of king of kings, Sasan). *Reverse*: Zeus standing to front, right arm outstretched. Monograms in left ✠ and right ☍ fields. Kharoshthi inscription *maharajasa rajatirajasa devavratasa gudapharasa sasasa* (of the great king, king of kings, Gondophares Sasan, loved of the gods) partly off flan. Mitchiner 1975–6, vol. 8, p. 755, type 1125.

Fig. 32.25 – IOLC.978. 9.38g, 21mm.
Fig. 32.26 – IOC.235. *Obverse*: Greek inscription off flan. *Reverse*: Kharoshthi inscription *maharajasa raja* ... mostly off flan. 9.58g, 20.5mm. Wilson 1841, p. 343, no. 5, Coins pl. V.19; BMC India (Greek and Scythic) p. 106.31. Mitchiner 1975–6, vol. 8, p. 755, type 1125.7; Senior 2000, p. 171, type 243.

Total 12 coins: 9.67g–9.23g (9), 8.61g (1), 7.28g–7.24g (2).

Fig. 32.27–30. Copper alloy Indian standard tetradrachms. *Obverse*: King holding whip, on horseback to right. Tamgha ☿ in right field. Blundered Greek inscription. *Reverse*: Zeus standing to right holding sceptre. *Nandipada* ☸ in left field and ☍ in right. Kharoshthi inscription *maharajasa mahatasa tratarasa devavratasa guduvharasa sasasa* (of the great king Gondophares Sasan the great saviour, loved of the gods). Senior 2000, pp. 169–71, type 242.601–647T.

Fig. 32.27 – IOLC.982. 7.89g, 20mm.
Fig. 32.28 – IOLC.990. 9.61g, 20mm. Wilson 1841, p.343, no. 6, Coins pl. V.20.
Fig. 32.29 – IOLC.983. 7.65g, 20mm.
Fig. 32.30 – IOLC.992. 9.19g, 20mm.

F526/1a, Pl. 5.105 illustrates a coin of this type from Begram. Total 12 coins: 10.41g (1), 9.61g–9.19g (7), 8.88g–8.53g (2), 7.89g–7.65g (2).

Parthian

Wilson records six Parthian examples 'from a considerable number of similar coins found at Begram' (1841, p. 347). But a note penned by Masson beside this statement in his own copy of *Ariana Antiqua* (Appendix 1 below, p. 323) says categorically that 'They were not found at Begram, but were procured in a large parcel from the bazaar of Kabul, and probably brought from Turkestan'. Five coins are identified from drawings (Wilson 1841, Coins pl. XV.8–11); all were evidently included in the 1887 India Office coin auction and subsequently presented to the Museum by individual collectors. Two coins also survive in the IOLC collection.

Phraataces (2 BC–AD 4)

Fig. 33.1 – 1894,0506.2144. Copper alloy drachm. *Obverse*: Bearded head of king to left, wearing a diadem and torque. Nike flies with a wreath on either side. *Reverse*: Archer with bow seated on a throne to right. Corrupt Greek inscription […]ΥΟ[…]Ω? [Ε]ΠΙΦ[ΑΝΟΥΣ]? (… of the god manifest …). Mint mark Π Margiana (Merv). 4.22g, 17mm. Cunningham collection. Wilson 1841, pp. 346–7, no. 1, Coins pl. XV.6; BMC Greek (Parthia), p. 138.15. Sellwood 1980, 57.14.

Sanabares (c. mid 1st century AD)

This ruler of unknown antecedents set up a secessionist state from the Parthians in Margiana (Merv). The Parthian king Vologases I (AD 51–78) seems to have re-imposed his suzerainty because later coins of Sanabares display the Arsacid tamgha (Sellwood 1980, pp. 304–7).

Fig. 33.2–3. Copper alloy drachm. *Obverse*: Diademed head of king to left. *Reverse*: Figure seated to right.

Fig. 33.2 – 1894,0506.2377. *Reverse*: Part of a corrupt Greek (?) inscription in left field. 3.58g, 14mm. Cunningham collection. Wilson 1841, p. 347, no. 2, Coins pl. XV.7.

Fig. 33.3 – IOLC.4707. 2.93g, 15mm. Sellwood 1980, p. 306, type 93; Senior 2000, p. 183, type 266.2D.

Fig. 33.4–8. Copper alloy drachm. *Obverse*: Bearded head of king to left, wearing a crenelated crown and diadem. *Reverse*: Archer with bow seated on a throne to right.

Fig. 33.4 – IOLC.4708. 3.5g, 15mm. Mint mark Π (?) Margiana (Merv). Sellwood 1980, p. 306, type 93; Senior 2000, p. 183, type 266.4D.

Fig. 33.5 – 1906,1103.2713. *Reverse*: Symbol ♀ possibly derived from Gondopharid tamgha in left field. Mint mark Π Margiana (Merv). 3.14g, 15.22mm. F. Parkes Weber pres. Wilson 1841, p. 347, no. 2, Coins pl. XV.9.

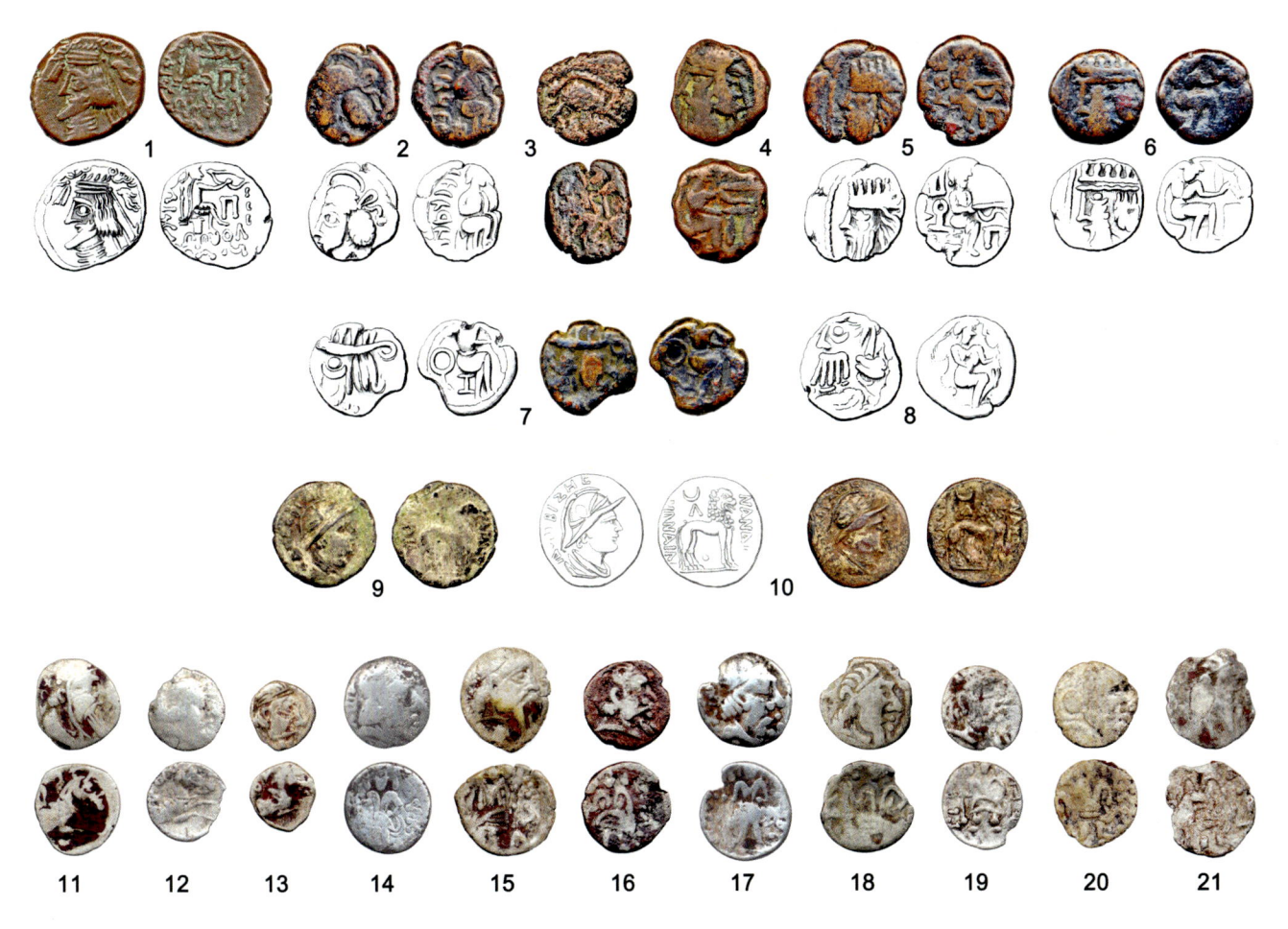

Figure 33 Parthian coins: Phraataces (1), Sanabares (2–8). Bactrian Yuezhi: Sapalbizes (9–10). Sogdia: Hyrcodes (11–21)

Fig. 33.6 – 1938,0413.8. 2.76g, 12mm. W.R. Gourlay pres. Wilson 1841, pp. 346–7, no. 2, Coins pl. XV.8.

Fig. 33.7 – 1906,1103.2715. *Reverse*: Seated figure without bow. Symbol ♀ possibly derived from Gondopharid tamgha in left field. 2.77g, 14.2mm. F. Parkes Weber pres. Wilson 1841, p. 347, no. 2, Coins pl. XV.10.

Fig. 33.8. Wilson 1841, p. 347, no. 2, Coins pl. XV.11. 15mm. Coin not traced.

Total 6 coins: 3.51g–3.14g (3), 2.93g–2.76g (3).

Bactria Yuezhi

Sapalbizes (c. 2 BC–AD 20)

Ruler of one of the Yuezhi tribes who took control of Bactria in the late 1st century BC. His coins are overstruck on issues of the Parthian king Phraates IV (38–2 BC). Masson's 1835–6 collection contained two coins (Wilson 1841, p. 352, n. 1), probably purchased in Kabul bazaar.

Fig. 33.9–10. Base silver coin. *Obverse*: Bust of king in Macedonian helmet to right. Greek inscription CΑΠΑΛΒΙΖΗC (Sapalbizes). *Reverse*: Lion standing to right, flanked on either side by a vertically inscribed NANAIA. Above the back of the lion the Greek letter Λ surmounted by a crescent.

Fig. 33.9 – IOC.253. 1.69g, 15mm.

Fig. 33.10 – IOC.254. 2.02g, 16.7mm. Wilson 1841 p. 352, n. 1, Coins pl. XXI.18; BMC India (Greek & Scythic) p. 119.3.

Total 2 coins: 2.02g, 1.69g.

Sogdia

Hyrcodes (1st century AD)

Masson specifically records purchasing a silver coin of Hyrcodes in Kabul bazaar in 1836 (**MSS Eur. E161/VII, f. 29**) and lists eight coins in his own collections acquired from Kabul bazaar in 1837–8 (**Vol. II, pp. 65, 92, 100**: 'Kodes'). His records do not give any details of coin types. According to Wilson (1841, pp. 345–6), 'The coins are not very rare, though not numerous, and are procured at Kabul or still further north … [They] are identifiable with Bactrian only by the situation in which they are found'.

Fig. 33.11–13. Debased silver coins in name of Hyrcodes. *Obverse*: Head of ruler with diadem and pointed beard. *Reverse*: Forepart of horse to right. Traces of illegible Greek inscription. Cribb 2007b, p. 364; figs 62–73 (type). Total 3 coins.

Fig. 33.11 – IOLC.4616. *Obverse*: Head to left. 2.93g, 15mm.

Fig. 33.12 – IOLC.4617. *Obverse*: Head to right, worn. 0.58g, 11mm.

Fig. 33.13 – IOLC.4618. *Obverse*: Head to right. 0.45g, 9mm.

Fig. 33.14–21. Debased silver coins in name of Hyrcodes. *Obverse*: Head of ruler with diadem and pointed beard. *Reverse*: Warrior standing to front, with spear. Traces of illegible Greek inscription. Cribb 2007b, p. 364; figs 62–73 (type).

Fig. 33.14 – IOLC.4619. 1.3g, 12mm.

Fig. 33.15 – IOLC.4620. 0.97g, 14mm.

Catalogue of Coins | 153

Fig. 33.16 – IOLC.4621. 0.83g, 13mm.
Fig. 33.17 – IOLC.4622. 0.76g, 13mm.
Fig. 33.18 – IOLC.4623. 0.74g, 12mm.
Fig. 33.19 – IOLC.4624. 0.67g, 12mm.
Fig. 33.20 – IOLC.4625. 0.66g, 12mm.
Fig. 33.21 – IOLC.4626. 0.5g, 14mm.
Total 11 coins: 2.93g (1), 1.3g (1), 0.97g–0.45g (9).

Kushan

Kujula Kadphises (c. AD 50–90)

545 copper alloy coins of Kujula Kadphises survive in the collection. Only eight (**Fig. 34.1–6**) have designs other than the principal type (bust of Hermaeus with Heracles reverse). The 537 remaining include 66 coins citing Hermaeus in the obverse inscription. Of the rest – 471 coins in the name of Kujula only – 398 weigh under 6g and appear to be contemporary imitations, with weights ranging down to as little as 0.19g (**Figs 34.21–9, 35.1–12**). This means that only about 73 coins appear to be official issues, which together with the 66 Hermaeus and 8 other examples add up to 147 or 27% of the whole.

Fig. 34.1 – IOLC.1000. Copper alloy coin copying issue of Eucratides I (*c.* 174–145 BC). *Obverse*: Helmeted head of king facing right. Greek inscription ΚΟΖΟΥΛΟ ΚΑΔΟΒΙΚΕ ΚΟΡΣΑΝ (Kujula Kadphises Kushan). *Reverse*: Soldier holding shield to right. Kharoshthi inscription *kushana yavu'asa kuyula ka'usa* (of Kujula Kadphises, Kushan *yabgu*). 4.56g, 20mm. Mitchiner 1978, p. 392, type 2873–4; Jongeward and Cribb 2015, p. 34, type 100–2, pl. 5.100–2. See also Masson 1836a, p. 26, no. 19, pl.III.19 and **F526/1a, Pl. 7.144–6** for three more examples.

Fig. 34.2–4. Worn magnetic copper alloy coins copying issue of Zeionises/Jihonika (*c.* AD 30–50). *Obverse*: Bull standing to right. Blundered Greek inscription largely off flan (ΜΑΝΝΙΟΛΟΥ ΥΙΟΥ ΣΑΤΡΑΠΟΥ ΖΕΙΩΝΙΣΟΥ, of satrap Jihonika, son of Manigula). *Reverse*: Camel standing to right. Illegible Kharoshthi inscription (*maharayasa rayatirayasa devaputrasa kuyula katakaphasa* of great king, king of kings, Kujula Kadphises, son of god). Mitchiner 1978, p. 393, type 2882–90; Jongeward and Cribb 2015, pp 35–6, type 114–24, pls 5.114–6.124.

Fig. 34.2 – IOLC.996. 7.72g, 23mm.
Fig. 34.3 – IOLC.997. 6.98g, 23mm.
IOLC.998. 9.33g, 23mm (not illustrated).
Fig. 34.4 – IOLC.999. 10.06g, 21mm.
Total 4 coins; 10.06g–6.98g.

Fig. 34.5 – IOC.262. Copper alloy issue copying coin design of Roman emperor Augustus (27 BC–AD 14). *Obverse*: Bust of emperor to right. Greek inscription ΚΟΖΟΛΑ ΚΑΔΑΦΕΣ ΧΟΦΑΝΣΥ ΖΑΟΟΥ (of Kujula Kadphises, Kushan *yabgu*). *Reverse*: King seated on Roman-style curule chair to right, right arm raised, left hand resting on pommel of sword. Tripartite circular device ⚹ in upper left field. Kharoshthi inscription *khushanasa ya'u'asa kuyula kaphsasa sacadharmathitasa* (Kujula Kadphises, Kushan *yabgu*, steadfast in the true law). 3.3g, 18mm. Wilson 1841, p. 357, no. 16, Coins pl. XI.14; BMC India (Greek and Scythic) p. 123.4. Mitchiner 1978, p. 392, type 2878–9; Jongeward and Cribb 2015, p, 34, type 103–12, pl. 5.104–12.

IOLC.1001. 3.23g, 17mm (not illustrated).
Total 2 coins: 3.3g, 3.23g.

Fig. 34.6 – IOLC.995. Crude copper alloy imitation of coin of Hermaeus (*c.* 90–70 BC). *Obverse*: Diademed head of king to right. *Reverse*: Zeus seated on a throne. 4.18g, 19mm, Jongeward and Cribb 2015, p, 36, type 131, pl. 6.131.

Fig. 34.7–13. Copper alloy coins in the name of Hermaeus; Kujula Kadphises as *yabgu*. *Obverse*: Diademed bust of king to right, copying obverse coin design of Hermaeus. Greek inscription ΒΑΣΙΛΕΩΣ ΣΤΗΡΟΣ ΣΥ ΕΡΜΑΙΟΥ (of king Su Hermaeus, the saviour). *Reverse*: Heracles standing to front, head turned to left; diademed, with a club in his right hand and a lion-skin in his left. Kharoshthi inscription *kujula kasasa kushana yavugasa dharmathidasa* (of Kujula Kadphises, Kushan *yabgu*, steadfast in the law). Mitchiner 1978, pp. 389–91, type 2844–51; Jongeward and Cribb 2015, pp. 30–1, type 44–56, pl. 3.45–53.

Fig. 34.7. Wilson 1841, pp. 309–10, no. 1, Coins pl. V.8. Coin not traced.
Fig. 34.8 – IOLC.1027. 8.29g, 24mm.
Fig. 34.9 – IOC.256. 8.33g, 23mm. Masson 1834, p. 168, pl. X.24; BMC India (Greek and Scythic) p. 120.4.
Fig. 34.10 – IOC.257. Wilson 1841, pp. 309–10, no. 1, Coins pl. V.9. 6.66g, 22mm. BMC India (Greek and Scythic) p. 120.6.
Fig. 34.11. Wilson 1841, pp. 309–10, no. 1, Coins pl. V.10.
Fig. 34.12 – IOLC.1014. 8.48g, 23mm.
Fig. 34.13 – IOLC.1069. 9.55g, 23mm.
Total 66 coins: 11.32g (1), 9.95g–9.07g (10), 8.98g–8.02g (14), 7.93g–7.05g (26), 6.93g–6.31g (12), 5.91g–4g (3).

Fig. 34.14–16. Copper alloy coin in name of Kujula as *yabgu*. *Obverse*: Diademed bust of king to right. Greek inscription ΚΟΖΟΥΛΟ ΚΑΔΦΙΖΟΥ ΚΟΡΣΝΟΥ (of Kujula Kadphises Kushan). *Reverse*: Heracles standing to front, head turned to left; diademed, with a club in his right hand and a lion-skin in his left. Kharoshthi control mark 𐨢 (*dha*) in upper left field. Kharoshthi inscription *kujula kasasa kushana yavugasa dharmathidasa* (of Kujula Kadphises, Kushan *yabgu*, steadfast in the law). Jongeward and Cribb 2015, p. 32, type 73, pl. 4.73.

Fig. 34.14. Wilson 1841, p. 357, no. 13, Coins pl. XI.10. Coin not traced.
Fig. 34.15 – IOC.258. Wilson 1841, p. 357 (not described), Coins pl. XI.11. 9.31g, 24mm. BMC India (Greek and Scythic) p. 122.1.
Fig. 34.16 – IOLC.1074. *Reverse*: Possible traces of a Kharoshthi control mark in upper left field. 9.21g, 24mm.

Fig. 34.17–20. Copper alloy coins issued in own name. *Obverse*: Diademed bust of king to right. Greek inscription ΚΟΖΟΥΛΟ ΚΑΔΦΙΖΟΥ ΚΟΡΣΝΟΥ (of Kujula Kadphises Kushan). *Reverse*: Heracles standing to front, head turned to left; diademed, with a club in his right hand and a lion-skin in his left. Kharoshthi inscription *kujula kasasa kushana yavugasa dharmathidasa* (of Kujula Kadphises, Kushan *yabgu*, steadfast in the law). Jongeward and Cribb 2015, pp. 32–3, type 74–83, pl. 4.74-83.

Fig. 34.17 – IOLC.1083. 9.42g, 22mm.
1838,EIC.67. 6.03g, 21mm. Not illustrated.
Fig. 34.18. Wilson 1841, p. 357, no. 14, Coins pl. XI.12. Blundered Greek inscription. Coin not traced.

Figure 34 Kushan coins. Kujula Kadphises imitations of Eucratides I (1), Zeionises (2–4), Augustus (5), Hermaeus (7–13). In own name (14–20); unofficial issues (21–9)

Catalogue of Coins | 155

Fig. 34.19 – IOC.261. Wilson 1841, p. 357, no. 15, Coins pl. XI.13. Blundered Greek inscription. 6.41g, 19mm. From the relic deposit of Kotpur stupa 2, Darunta district, west of Jalalabad (see **Vol. I, p. 90, Fig. 85.7**). **F526/1a, Pl. 5.119**; Masson 1836a, pp. 26–7, no. 39, pl. III.28; BMC India (Greek and Scythic) p. 122.8.

Fig. 34.20 – IOLC.1093. 5.74g, 21mm.

Total 134 coins: 10.19g (1), 9.9g–9.14g (11), 8.86g–8g (18), 7.88g–7.07g (13), 6.99g–6.03g (30), 5.98g–5.03g (61).

Fig. 34.21–9. Variable weight unofficial copper alloy imitations with blundered inscriptions.

Fig. 34.21 – 1838,EIC.68. *Obverse*: Diademed bust of king to right. Blundered Greek letters largely off flan. *Reverse*: Heracles standing to front, with a club in his right hand and a lion-skin in his left. Kharoshthi inscription partly off flan. 3.86g, 19mm. BMC India (Greek and Scythic) p. 121.16; Cribb and Bracey (at press), type A.C3f.

Fig. 34.22 – IOLC.1131. 3.02g, 19.5mm.
Fig. 34.23 – IOLC.1287. 2.91g, 19mm.
Fig. 34.24 – IOLC.1290. 3.54g, 17.5mm.
Fig. 34.25 – IOLC.1294. 3.06g, 19mm.
Fig. 34.26 – IOLC.1301. 3.21g, 18mm.
Fig. 34.27 – IOLC.1319. 3.85g, 19mm.
Fig. 34.28 – IOLC.1339. 3.53g, 18mm.
Fig. 34.29 – IOLC.1370. 2.78g, 20mm.

Fig. 35.1–11. Variable weight unofficial copper alloy imitations of Kujula Kadphises coins (continued).

Obverse: Bust of king to right. Blundered illegible inscription. *Reverse*: Heracles standing to front, with a club in his right hand and a lion-skin in his left. Blundered illegible inscription.

Fig. 35.1 – IOLC.1372. 2.95g, 19mm.
Fig. 35.2 – IOLC.1374. 2.77g, 18mm.
Fig. 35.3 – IOLC.1384. 2.3g, 16mm.
Fig. 35.4 – IOLC.1388. 2.22g, 17mm.
Fig. 35.5 – IOLC.1395. 2.97g, 18mm.
Fig. 35.6 – IOLC.1397. 2.61g, 17mm.
Fig. 35.7 – IOLC.1409. 2.41g, 17mm.
Fig. 35.8 – IOLC.1468. 1.44g, 16mm.
Fig. 35.9 – IOLC.1484. 0.86g, 11.5mm.
Fig. 35.10 – IOLC.1505. 0.59g, 11mm.
Fig. 35.11 – 1838,EIC.70. 1.53g, 15mm. BMC India (Greek and Scythic), p.121.21; Cribb and Bracey (at press), type A.c.

Fig. 35.12–15. *Obverse*: Bust of king to left. *Reverse*: Heracles standing to front, holding a club in his right hand and a lion-skin in his left. See also **F526/1a, Pl. 6.121**.

Fig. 35.12 – IOLC.1227. 3.76g, 19mm.
Fig. 35.13 – IOLC.1228. 2.09g, 17mm.
Fig. 35.14 – IOLC.1229. 2.11g, 16.5mm.
Fig. 35.15 – IOLC.1230. 2.09g, 17mm.
IOLC.1231. 1.96g, 16mm (not illustrated).
IOLC.1232. 1.36g, 16mm (not illustrated).

Fig. 35.16 – IOLC.1233. *Obverse*: Schematic head to left. *Reverse*: Heracles standing to front, holding a club in his left hand and a lion-skin in his right. 1.5g, 15mm.

Total 337 coins: 4.97g–4.01g (69), 3.97g–3.02g (82), 2.99g–2.01g (79), 1.96g–1.03g (59), 0.96g–0.19g (32).

Soter Megas issues – Kujula Kadphises and/or Wima Takto

The largest group of coins in the Masson collection are 906 issued by the Kushan 'nameless king' titled Soter Megas (great saviour). There are two denominations: a reduced Attic standard didrachm (9.07g–5.84g) and a hemidrachm (2.36g–1.01g). The coinage seems to divide broadly into three phases determined by the number of prongs on the tamgha found on both sides, and possibly also the lettering style. These groupings are fairly arbitrary, as many of the coins are too worn to enable classification, or the inscription and tamgha are off flan. Nevertheless, approximate totals are 31 with a four-pronged tamgha ⚜ on both obverse and reverse (7 didrachms; 24 hemidrachms); 91 with a four-pronged tamgha on the obverse and a three-pronged one ⚜ on the reverse (17 didrachms, 74 hemidrachms); 648 coins with the three-pronged tamgha only (320 didrachms, 328 hemidrachms), with 136 remaining where the tamgha is uncertain or off flan (3 didrachms, 133 hemidrachms). The first group may perhaps be identified as issues of Kujula; those with both as joint issues of Kujula and his successor Wima Takto; and the last group as Wima Takto alone (Cribb 2014, pp. 100–3).

There are two lettering styles: the four-pronged, four-pronged/three-pronged and some of the three-pronged group all appear to have square letter forms; while the vast majority of the three-pronged variety have cursive letters. A further distinction is the variation in the quantity of rays emanating around the head of Mithra. Examination of the IOLC coins suggests that the square letter style may be earlier and within this group that the number of rays are usually between fourteen and eight. The coins with cursive letters range from twelve down to five rays. It is noteworthy that the tetradrachms of Wima Takto which carry the Kharoshthi letter 𐨬 (*vi*) also have cursive letters (**Fig. 37.1–2**).

Fig. 36.1–3. Copper alloy didrachms. *Obverse*: Diademed, radiate bust of Mithra to right, with 14 to 12 rays, holding an arrow (tied with two pennants on better preserved examples); ⚜ in the left field. *Reverse*: Horse rider in diademed Phrygian cap to right, holding a pickaxe; ⚜ in the right field. Greek inscription with square letters (king of kings, great saviour). Mitchiner 1978, pp. 400–2, type 2978–84.

Fig. 36.1 – IOLC.1581. 14 rays. 7.79g, 20mm.
Fig. 36.2 – IOLC.1582. 12 rays. 7.85g, 20mm.
Fig. 36.3 – IOLC.1584. 12 rays. 8.21g, 20mm.

Total 6 coins: 8.21g–8.18g (2), 7.85g–7.24g (4).

Fig. 36.4–9. Copper alloy hemidrachms. *Obverse*: Diademed, radiate bust of Mithra to right, with 14 to 11 rays, holding an arrow tied with two pennants; ⚜ in the left field. *Reverse*: Horse rider in diademed Phrygian cap to right, holding a pickaxe; ⚜ in the right field. Greek inscription with square letters ΒΑCΙΛΕVC ΒΑCΙΛΕШΝ CШΤΗΡ ΜΕΓΑC. Mitchiner 1978, pp. 403–4, type 2985–3002.

Fig. 36.4 – IOLC.1890. 14 rays. 1.93g, 14mm.
Fig. 36.5 – IOLC.1896. 12 rays. 1.91g, 14mm.
Fig. 36.6 – IOLC.1903. 11 rays? 1.91g, 13mm.
Fig. 36.7 – IOLC.1991. 11 rays. 1.99g, 15mm.
Fig. 36.8 – IOLC.1907. 11 rays. 2.15g, 15mm.

Figure 35 Unofficial imitations of coins of Kujula Kadphises continued (1–16)

Fig. 36.9 – IOLC.1908. 11 rays? 1.92g, 14mm.
Total 24 coins: 2.15g–2.01g (5), 1.99g–1.63g (17).

Fig. 36.10–13. Copper alloy didrachms. *Obverse*: Diademed, radiate bust of Mithra to right, with 12 to 9 rays, holding an arrow tied with two pennants; ⊕ in the left field. *Reverse*: Horse rider in diademed Phrygian cap to right, holding a pickaxe; ⊕ in the right field. Greek inscription with square letters ΒΑΣΙΛΕΥΣ ΒΑΣΙΛΕΩΝ ΣΩΤΗΡ ΜΕΓΑΣ. Mitchiner 1978, pp. 400–3, type 2928–84.

Fig. 36.10. Wilson 1841, p. 335, no. 6, Coins pl. IX.16. 11 rays; 20mm. Coin not traced.

Fig. 36.11 – IOLC.1589. 12 rays. 8.13g, 20mm.

Fig. 36.12 – IOLC.1590. 11 rays. 8.42g, 21mm.

Fig. 36.13 – IOLC.1595. 9 rays. 7.69g, 20mm.
Total 17 coins: 8.42g–8.13g (6), 7.98g–7.24 (11).

Fig. 36.14–17. Copper alloy hemidrachms. *Obverse*: Diademed, radiate bust of Mithra to right, with 13 to 8 rays, holding an arrow tied with two pennants; ⊕ in the left field. *Reverse*: Horse rider in diademed Phrygian cap to right, holding a pickaxe; ⊕ in the right field. Greek inscription with square letters ΒΑΣΙΛΕΥΣ ΒΑΣΙΛΕΩΝ ΣΩΤΗΡ ΜΕΓΑΣ. Mitchiner 1978, pp. 403–4, type 2985–3002.

Fig. 36.14 – IOLC.1925. 11 rays. 1.94g, 14mm.

Fig. 36.15 – IOLC.1926. 11 rays. 1.94g, 14mm.

Fig. 36.16 – IOLC.1933. 10 rays. 1.95g, 14mm

Fig. 36.17 – IOLC.1979. 9 rays. 1.9g, 15mm.
Total 74 coins: 2.35g–2g (24), 1.99g–1.46g (50).

Fig. 36.18–19. Copper alloy didrachms. *Obverse*: Diademed, radiate bust of Mithra to right, holding an arrow; tamgha partly or completely off flan. *Reverse*: Horse rider in diademed Phrygian cap to right, holding a pickaxe; ⊕ in the right field. Greek inscription with square letters.

Fig. 36.18 – 1838,EIC.85. 11 rays. 8.38g, 19mm. Masson 1834, p. 169, pl. X.27; BMC India (Greek and Scythic) p. 115.11; Cribb and Bracey (at press), type B.c.

Fig. 36.19 – IOLC.1601. 10 rays, no pennants on arrow. 8.26g, 21mm. Wilson 1841, p. 335, no. 7, Coins pl. IX.17.

Fig. 36.20–3. Copper alloy didrachms. *Obverse*: Diademed, radiate bust of Mithra to right, with 12 to 8 rays, holding an arrow tied with two pennants; ⊕ in the left field. *Reverse*: Horse rider in diademed Phrygian cap to right, holding a pickaxe; ⊕ in the right field. Greek inscription with square letters.

Fig. 36.20 – IOLC.1632. 12 rays. 9.07g, 21mm.

Fig. 36.21 – IOLC.1603. 10 rays. 8.53g, 18mm.

Fig. 36.22. 8 rays. 21mm. Wilson 1841, p. 334, no. 4, Coins pl. IX.13. Coin not traced.

Fig. 36.23. 8 rays. 20mm. Wilson 1841, p. 334, no. 4, Coins pl. IX.14. Coin not traced.
Total 39 coins: 9.07g (1), 8.8g–8.02g (14), 7.98g–7.19g (23), 6.88g (1).

Fig. 36.24–31. Copper alloy hemidrachms. *Obverse*: Diademed, radiate bust of Mithra to right, with 13 to 7 rays, holding an arrow (tied with two pennants on better preserved examples); ⊕ in the left field. *Reverse*: Horse rider in diademed Phrygian cap to right, holding a pickaxe; ⊕ in the right field. Greek inscription with square letters.

Fig. 36.24 – IOLC.1986. 13 rays. 1.93g, 13mm.

Fig. 36.25 – IOC.245. ? rays. 1.91g, 15mm. Wilson 1841, p. 335, no. 9, Coins pl.X.2; BMC India (Greek and Scythic) p. 115.19.

1838,EIC.89. 11 rays. 1.76g, 14mm. Cribb and Bracey (at press), type B.C1d. Not illustrated.

Fig. 36.26 – IOLC.2127. 11 rays. 2.18g, 13mm.

Fig. 36.27 – IOLC.2117. 9 rays. 2.01g, 13mm.

Fig. 36.28 – IOLC.2157. 8 rays. 1.85g, 12mm.

Fig. 36.29. 8 rays. 16mm. Wilson 1841, p. 335, no. 9, Coins pl. X.3. Coin not traced.

Fig. 36.30. 7 rays. 15mm. Wilson 1841, p. 335, no. 9, Coins pl. X.4. Coin not traced.

Fig. 36.31. ? rays. 15mm. Wilson 1841, p. 335, no. 9, Coins pl. X.6. Coin not traced.
Total 164 coins: 2.36g–2g (52), 1.99g–1.37g (112).

Fig. 36.32–6. Copper alloy reduced Attic standard

Catalogue of Coins | 157

Figure 36 Soter Megas issues. Phase 1 (1–9); Phase 2 (10 – 17); Phase 3 (18–31). Heliocles imitations of Wima Takto (32–6)

158 | *Charles Masson: Collections from Begram and Kabul Bazaar, Afghanistan, 1833–1838*

tetradrachm and drachms imitating a coin type of Heliocles (c. 145–130 BC). *Obverse*: Bust of king to right, wearing a diadem with two ties and a cloak; surrounded by a bead and reel border. *Reverse*: Horse with right foreleg raised, walking to left. Traces of a tamgha on horse's rump; identified on well-preserved specimens as ⚋ (Smith 2001; Cribb 2014, p. 112, figs 20–1). Corrupt Greek inscription on three sides, with cursive letters ΒΑCΙΛΕΩΣ ΔΙΙΑΙΥ ΗΛΙΚΕΥΣ (of king Heliocles the just). Mitchiner 1978, p. 280, type 1879–85.

Fig. 36.32 – IOC.364. Tetradrachm. 12.6g, 27mm. Wilson 1841, p. 311, no. 2, pl. VIII.15; BMC India (Greek and Scythic) p. 22.17.

Fig. 36.33 – IOC.365. Drachm. 3.03g, 18mm. Wilson 1841, pp. 311–12, no. 3, pl. VIII.14; BMC India (Greek and Scythic) p. 22.20.

Fig. 36.34 – IOLC.1563. Drachm. 4.43g, 17mm.
Fig. 36.35 – IOLC.1532. Drachm. 3.21g, 18mm.
Fig. 36.36 – IOLC.1520. Drachm. 3.83g, 17mm.

Total 50 coins: 12.6g (1), 4.55g–4.01g (6), 3.83g–3.03g (21), 2.97g–2.02g (15), 1.97g–1.45g (7).

Wima Takto (c. AD 90–113)

Fig. 37.1–2. Copper alloy reduced Attic standard tetradrachm copying obverse design of Heliocles (c. 145–130 BC). *Obverse*: Bust of king in a Macedonian helmet to left, holding an upright arrow in his right hand. Kharoshthi letter 𐨬 (vi) in the left field, ⚋ in the right. Bead and reel border. *Reverse*: Horseman in diademed Phrygian cap, riding to right, holding a pickaxe in his right hand. Tamgha in right field. Greek inscription with cursive letters ΒΑCΙΛΕVC ΒΑCΙΛΕШΝ] CШΤΗΡ ΜΕΓΑC (king of kings, great saviour).

Fig. 37.1 – IOC.247. 12.52g, 24mm. Wilson 1841, p. 334, no. 2, Coins pl. IX.8; BMC India (Greek & Scythic), p. 116.27, pl. XXIV.6; Masson 1834 p. 169, pl. X.29; Cribb and Bracey (at press), type B.C3.

Fig. 37.2. Wilson 1841, p. 334, no. 2, Coins pl. IX.10. 24mm. Coin not traced.

Fig. 37.3–18. Copper alloy didrachms. *Obverse*: Diademed, radiate bust of Mithra to right, with variable rays emanating around his head and holding an arrow tied with two pennants; ⚋ in the left field. *Reverse*: Horse rider in diademed Phrygian cap to right, holding a pickaxe; ⚋ in the right field. Greek inscription with cursive letters ΒΑCΙΛΕVC ΒΑCΙΛΕШΝ CШΤΗΡ ΜΕΓΑC (king of kings, great saviour). Mitchiner 1978, pp. 400–3, type 2928–84.

Fig. 37.3 – IOC.242. 12 rays. 8.07g, 19mm. Wilson 1841, p. 335, no. 8, Coins pl. IX.18. BMC India (Greek and Scythic) p. 114.5.

Fig. 37.4 – IOC.244. 12 rays. Blundered Greek inscription. 7g, 20mm. Wilson 1841, p. 335, no. 5, Coins pl. IX.15; BMC India (Greek and Scythic) p. 115.12.

Fig. 37.5 – IOLC.1645. 12 rays. 8.33g, 21mm. Jongeward and Cribb 2015, p. 47, no. 178, pl. 7.178.

Fig. 37.6 – IOLC.1763. 12 rays. 8.36g, 20mm.
Fig. 37.7 – IOLC.1649. 12 rays. 8.37g, 20mm.
Fig. 37.8. 10 rays. Wilson 1841, p. 335, no. 9, Coins pl. IX.19. Coin not traced.
Fig. 37.9 – IOLC.1791. 8 rays. 8.45g, 20mm.
Fig. 37.10 – IOLC.1792. 8 rays. 8.46g, 20mm.
Fig. 37.11 – IOLC.1664. ? rays. 8.16g, 20mm.
Fig. 37.12 – IOLC.1707. 6 rays; no pennants on arrow. 8.08g, 19mm.
Fig. 37.13 –1838,EIC.81. 6 rays; no pennants. 7.76g, 22mm. BMC India (Greek and Scythic) p. 115.10; Cribb and Bracey (at press), type B.c.
Fig. 37.14 – IOLC.1760. 5 rays; no pennants. 8.92g, 22mm.
Fig. 37.15 – 1838,EIC.76. 5 rays; no pennants. 8.35g, 23mm. Masson 1834, p. 169, pl. X.26; BMC India (Greek and Scythic) p. 114.8; Cribb and Bracey (at press), type B.c.
Fig. 37.16. 5 rays; no pennants. Wilson 1841, p. 334, no. 3, Coins pl. IX.11. Coin not traced.
Fig. 37.17. 5 rays; no pennants. Wilson 1841, p. 334, no. 3, Coins pl. IX.12. Coin not traced.
Fig. 37.18 – IOLC.1882. 5 rays; no pennants. 8.18g, 20mm.

Total 291 coins: 9.07g (1), 8.92g–8g (145), 7.99g–7.01g (136), 6.93g–6.23g (8), 5.84g (1).

Fig. 37.19–26. Copper alloy hemidrachms. *Obverse*: Diademed, radiate bust of Mithra to right, with 11 to 6 rays, holding an arrow with two pennants; ⚋ in the left field. *Reverse*: Horse rider in diademed Phrygian cap to right, holding a pickaxe; ⚋ in the right field. Greek inscription with cursive letters. Mitchiner 1978, pp. 403–4, type 2985–3002.

Fig. 37.19 – IOLC.2032. 11 rays, 1.86g, 15mm.
Fig. 37.20 – IOLC.2204. 8 rays, 2.09g, 14mm.
Fig. 37.21 – IOLC.2037. 11 rays, 2.09g, 12mm.
Fig. 37.22 – IOLC.2008. 11 rays, 2.04g, 12mm.
Fig. 37.23 – IOLC.2271. 7 rays, 2.21g, 13mm.
Fig. 37.24 – IOLC.2320. 7 rays, 2.12g, 13mm.
Fig. 37.25 – IOLC.2273. 7 rays, 2.35g, 12mm.
Fig. 37.26 – IOLC.2228. 8 rays, 2.1g, 13mm.
Fig. 37.27 – IOC.246. 6 rays, 2.19g, 12mm. Wilson 1841, p. 335, no. 9, Coins pl.X.2; BMC India (Greek and Scythic) p. 115.21.

Total 162 coins: 2.35g–2g (69), 1.98g–1.24g (93).
Additional 136 worn/unidentified coins: didrachms 8.58g–8.33g (3); hemidrachms 2.36g–2g (33), 1.99g–1.01g (100).

Fig. 37.28 – IOLC.1975. Copper alloy variant hemidrachm. *Obverse*: Remains of radiate bust of Mithra to right. *Reverse*: Horse rider to left. 3-pronged tamgha in the left field. Blundered Greek legend. 2.28g, 13mm.

Fig. 37.29–30. Copper alloy uninscribed local issue hemidrachms. *Obverse*: Oesho standing to front, holding a trident in his right hand; an animal skin draped over his left arm. ⚋ in the left field; Kharoshthi 𐨬 (vi) in the right. *Reverse*: Ardochsho standing to front holding a cornucopia, head turned to right. A *nandipada* in the left field; vase of plenty (*pūrṇaghaṭa*) in the right. Mitchiner 1978, p. 399, type 2921–2; Cribb 2014, p. 129, fig. 31.

Fig. 37.29 – IOLC.1572. 1.59g, 13mm.
Fig. 37.30 – IOLC.1573. 1.39g, 12mm.

Total 5 coins: 1.87g–1.34g.

Fig. 37.31–3. Reduced Attic standard tetradrachms imitating issue of Sasan (c. AD 64–70; see Fig. 32.23–6 above). *Obverse*: Diademed king on horseback riding to right, holding a pickaxe. ⚋ in the right field. Corrupt Greek inscription with cursive letters ΒΑCΙΛΕVC ΒΑCΙΛΕШΝ CШΤΗΡ

Figure 37 Kushan coins. Wima Takto Soter Megas issues (1–28); Oesho/Ardochsho (29–30); Sasan imitations (31–3); bull/camel (34–5)

ΜΕΓΑC (of king of kings, great saviour). *Reverse*: Zeus standing to right, right arm raised, left holding a sceptre. A vase of plenty (*pūrṇaghaṭa*) in the right field. Kharoshthi 𐨬 (*vi*) in the left. Kharoshthi inscription *maharajasa rajatirajasa mahatasa tratarasa* (of the great king, king of kings, great lord, great saviour). Mitchiner 1978, p. 399, type 2915–18; Cribb 2014, p. 129, fig. 29.

Fig. 37.31 – IOLC.1568. 8.85g, 20mm.
Fig. 37.32 – IOLC.1566. 9.64g, 22mm.
Fig. 37.33 – IOLC.1567. 9.42g, 22mm.
Total 6 coins: 9.83g–9.42g (3), 8.85g–8.72g (2).

Fig. 37.34 –5. Worn copper alloy coins with illegible inscriptions. *Obverse*: Bull standing to the right. Traces of blundered Greek inscription. *Reverse*: Camel standing to the right. Kharoshthi inscription on better preserved specimens reads *maharajasa rajatirajasa devaputrasa* (of the great king, king of kings, son of the gods), with addition on some examples of *vema takho* (Wima Takto), see Cribb 2014, p. 113–14, figs 33–6; Jongeward and Cribb 2015, p. 48, nos 221–2, pl. 9.221–2.

Fig. 37.34 – IOLC.1576. Didrachm. 8.32g, 21mm. Sims-Williams and Cribb 1995/6, pp. 115–16, type 6.

Fig. 37.35 – IOLC.1580. Hemidrachm. 1.97g, 13mm. Sims-Williams and Cribb 1995/6, pp. 116–18, type 7.
Total 5 coins: 8.32g (1), 5.18g–3.91g (2), 2.76g–1.97g (2).

Wima Kadphises (c. AD 113–27)

In addition to the two coins bought in Kabul bazaar in 1836 (**Fig. 38.1–2**), Masson found six gold coins of Wima Kadphises in the relic deposit of the Guldara stupa to the south-east of Kabul. A single example was also excavated by Honigberger from the nearby Kamari stupa 2 (**Vol. I, pp. 76, 79, Figs 59.7, 69.1–6**). In the Jalalabad valley, ten were contained in the Ahinposh deposit (**Vol. I, pp. 158–9, Fig. 242.1–10**), while Chahar Bagh stupa 4 produced four copper alloy tetradrachms (**Vol. I, p. 146, Fig. 215.1–4**). The Guldara deposit also included a coin of Huvishka (*c.* AD 151–90), while the coins from the last two sites were mixed with both those of Kanishka I (*c.* AD 127–51), Huvishka and in the case of Ahinposh, three 1st–2nd century Roman aurei. There is also a rare silver dram acquired by Masson from a goldsmith at Charikar (**Fig. 38.3**). The remaining 191 copper alloy coins (93 tetradrachms; 3 didrachms; 95 drachms) are from Begram (**Fig. 38.14–23**).

Gold and silver coins
Fig. 38.1 – IOC.268. Reduced Attic standard gold double dinar. *Obverse*: King seated to front on a throne, head turned to the left. His left hand is covered; his right holds a twig with three leaves. A club in the left field, tamgha 𐨲 in the right. Greek inscription ΒΑCΙΛΕΥC ΟΟΗ–ΜΟ ΚΑΔΦΙCΗC (king Wima Kadphises). *Reverse*: Oesho standing to front, holding a trident; head turned to the left. Bull standing behind to right. A *nandipada* 𐨸 symbol in the upper left field. Kharoshthi inscription *maharajasa rajadirajasa sarvaloga iśvarasa mahiśvarasa v'ima kathpiśasa tratarasa* (of the great king of kings, lord of the world, great lord, Wima Kadphises, the great saviour). 15.83g, 24mm. Kabul bazaar. Wilson 1841 p. 354, no. 2, Coins pl. XXI.17; BMC India (Greek & Scythic) p. 124.1. Göbl 1984, type 11.1; Cribb and Bracey (at press), type C.G1iva.

Fig. 38.2. Gold quarter dinar. *Obverse*: Bust of king to right in rectangular frame. Greek inscription ΒΑCΙΛΕ[ΥC ΟΟΗ–]ΜΟ ΚΑΔΦΙCΗC (king Wima Kadphises). *Reverse*: Trident battle-axe combined with a thunderbolt and phallus symbolising Oesho; 𐨲 in the left field, 𐨸 in the right. Kharoshthi inscription *maharaja rajadiraja v'ima kathpiśasa* (of the great king, king of kings, Wima Kadphises). 13mm. Kabul bazaar. Wilson 1841 p. 355, no. 7, Coins pl. XXI.19. Coin not traced.

Fig. 38.3 – IOC.273. Silver drachm. *Obverse*: King standing to front, head turned to left, making an offering with his right hand over a small altar. Trident battle-axe in the left field, club and tamgha 𐨲 in the right. Greek inscription ΒΑCΙΛΕΥC ΒΑCΙΛΕΩΝ ΜΕΓΑC ΟΟΗΜΟ ΚΑΔΦΙCΗC (Great king of kings Wima Kadphises). *Reverse*: Oesho standing to front, holding a trident; bull standing behind to right, with 𐨸 in the upper left field. Kharoshthi inscription *maharajasa rajadirajasa sarvaloga iśvarasa mahiśvarasa v'ima kathpiśasa tratara[sa]* (of the great king of kings, lord of the world, great lord, Wima Kadphises, the great saviour). 3.61g, 18mm. Charikar. **F526/1a, ff. 19–20, Pl. 8.3**; Wilson 1841, p. 355, no. 8, pl. XI.9. BMC India (Greek and Scythic) p. 126.11. Göbl 1984, type 4.1; Cribb and Bracey (at press), type C.c.

Copper alloy coinage
Fig. 38.4–23. Tetradrachms (*c.* 16g), didrachms (*c.* 8g) and drachms (*c.* 4g). *Obverse*: king standing to front, head turned to left, wearing a tall cap, heavy coat and boots. He holds the hilt of a sword in his left hand and makes an offering with his right hand over a small altar. Trident battle-axe in the left field, club and tamgha 𐨲 in the right. Greek inscription ΒΑCΙΛΕΥC ΒΑCΙΛΕΩΝ CΩΤΕΡ ΜΕΓΑC ΟΟΗΜΟ ΚΑΔΦΙCΗC (king of kings, the great saviour, Wima Kadphises). *Reverse*: Oesho with three heads (horned, young, old) and hair tied in a topknot, standing to front and holding a trident. A bull stands behind to right, with 𐨸 in the upper left field. Kharoshthi inscription *maharajasa rajadirajasa sarvaloga iśvarasa mahiśvarasa v'ima kathpiśasa tratara[sa]* (of the great king of kings, lord of the world, great lord, Wima Kadphises, the great saviour). Göbl 1984, type 762, pls 72–3; Perkins 2007, type 1, p. 37, n. 17. Cribb and Bracey (at press), type C.c.

Fig. 38.4–14. Tetradrachms.
Fig. 38.4 – IOC.275. 17.37g, 28mm. Wilson 1841, p. 356, no. 9, pl. X.18; BMC India (Greek and Scythic) p. 126.13.
Fig. 38.5 – IOC.278. 16.73g, 28mm. Wilson 1841, p. 356, no. 9, pl. X.15; BMC India (Greek and Scythic) p. 127.16.
Fig. 38.6. Wilson 1841, p. 356, no. 9, pl. X.16.
Fig. 38.7. Wilson 1841, p. 356, no. 9, pl. X.17.
Fig. 38.8. Wilson 1841, p. 356, no. 9, pl. X.20.
Coins not traced.
Fig. 38.9 – 1838,EIC.98. 16.25g, 26mm. BMC India (Greek and Scythic) p. 127.26.
Fig. 38.10 – IOLC.2440. 16.74g, 28mm.
Fig. 38.11 – IOLC.2436. 17.36g, 28mm.
Fig. 38.12 – IOLC.2494. 16.27g, 28mm.
Fig. 38.13 – IOLC.2437. 17.26g, 26mm.
Fig. 38.14 – IOLC.2493. 16.39g, 26mm.
Total 93 coins: 17.37g–17g (5), 16.95g–16.01g (46),

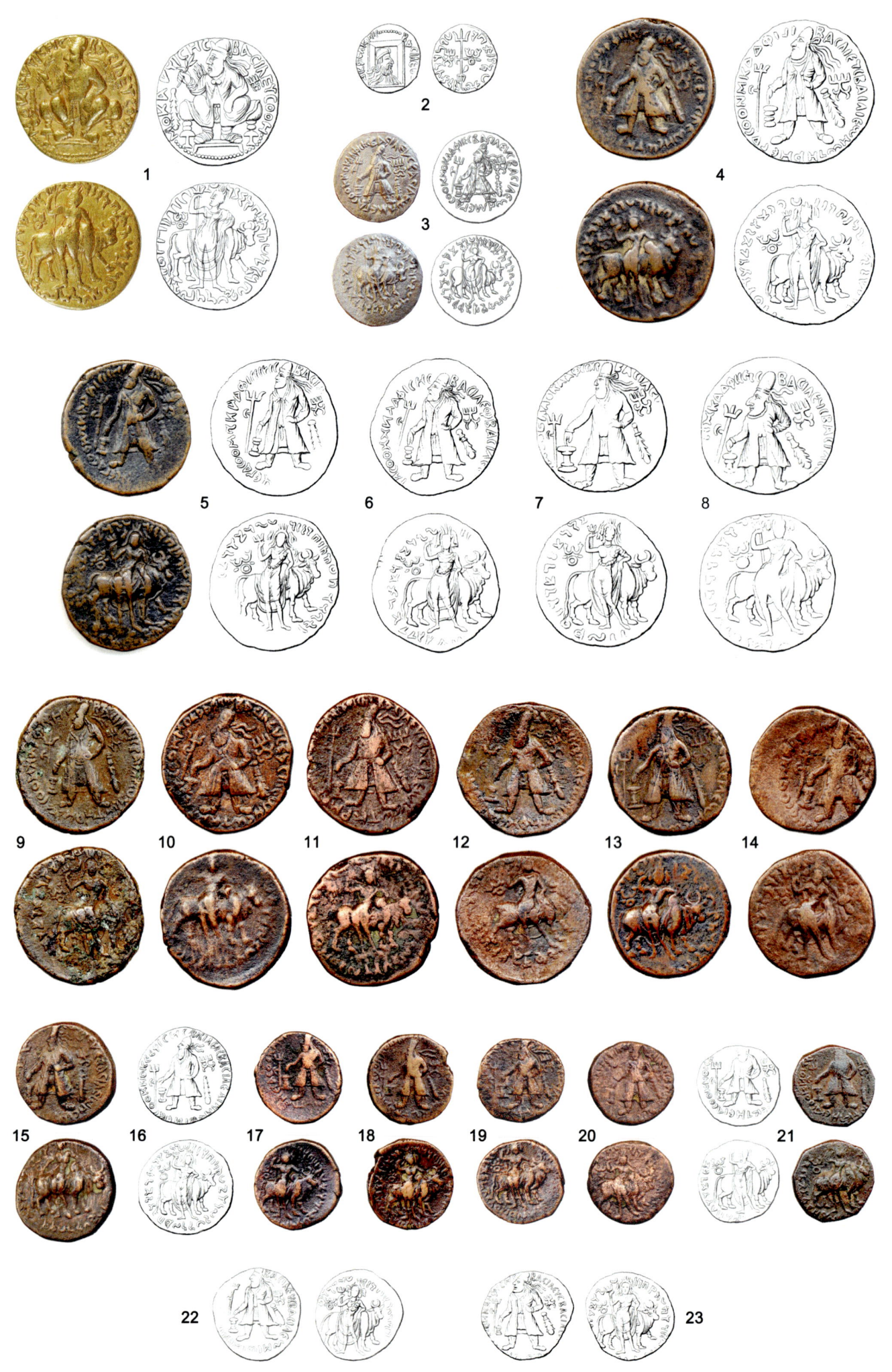

Figure 38 Wima Kadphises gold coins (1–2); silver (3); tetradrachms (4–14); didrachms (15–16); drachms (17–23)

15.94g–15.01g (23), 14.97g–14.1g (16), 13.63g (1), 12.86g–12.82g (2).
Fig. 38.15–16. Didrachms.
Fig. 38.15 – IOLC.2525. 8.22g, 20mm.
Fig. 38.16. Wilson 1841, p. 356, no. 10, Coins pl. X.12. 20mm. Coin not traced.
Total 3 coins (IOLC.2525–IOLC.2527): 8.22g, 8.1g, 7.8g.
Fig. 38.17–23. Drachms.
Fig. 38.17 – IOLC.2555. 4.01g, 19mm.
Fig. 38.18 – IOLC.2538. 4.09g, 18mm.
Fig. 38.19 – IOLC.2561. 3.99g, 18mm.
Fig. 38.20 – IOLC.2599. 3.84g, 17mm.
Fig. 38.21 – IOC.279. 4.4g, 16mm. Wilson 1841, p. 356, no. 10, Coins pl. X.21; BMC India (Greek and Scythic) p. 128.28.
Fig. 38.22. Wilson 1841, p. 356, no. 10, Coins pl. X.19. 18mm. Coin not traced.
Fig. 38.23. Wilson 1841, p. 356, no. 10, Coins pl. X.14; Masson 1834, p. 173, fig. 9, pl. XII.9. Coin not traced.
Total 95 coins: 4.58g–4g (41), 3.99g–3.17g (54).

Kanishka I (c. AD 127–51)

Six gold coins of Kanishka are recorded in *Ariana Antiqua* as having been acquired by Masson in Kabul bazaar (**Fig. 39.1–6**); only two have been located. There are also 418 copper alloy coins, comprising 145 tetradrachms, 88 didrachms, 163 drachms and 22 hemidrachms. Only twelve coins are in the main Museum collection (two quarter dinars, three didrachms, seven tetradrachms). The rest are part of the India Office Loan Collection.

Gold coinage
Fig. 39.1–2. Two Kushan standard gold quarter dinars with Bactrian inscriptions. *Obverse*: ÞAONANOÞAO KANHÞKI KOÞANO (king of kings Kanishka Kushan). *Reverse*: Fire god Athsho, with flaming shoulders, standing to front, head turned to left, holding a diadem in his right hand and fire tongs in his left. Tamgha 🕉 in the left field, inscribed AθÞO in the right.
Fig. 39.1 – IOC.294. *Obverse*: Bust of bearded king to left, wearing a diademed peaked cap and holding a sceptre in his left hand; inscribed ÞA[ONANOÞAO KANHÞ]KI KOÞANO. *Reverse*: Athsho. 1.98g, 12mm. Wilson 1841, p. 367, no. 9, Coins pl.XII.6; BMC India (Greek and Scythic) p. 132.30.
Fig. 39.2 – IOC.287. Worn coin with a broken pierced hole along the top edge. *Obverse*: King standing to front, head turned to the left, sacrificing at a fire altar with his right hand, holding a spear in his left; inscribed [ÞAONA]NOÞAO KANHÞKI K[OÞANO]. *Reverse*: Athsho. 1.78g, 13mm. Wilson 1841, p. 367, no. 15 (not illustrated); BMC India (Greek and Scythic) p. 130.12.
Fig. 39.3–6. Four Kushan standard gold dinars. *Obverse*: King standing to front, head turned to the left, flames issuing from his right shoulder; sacrificing at a fire altar with his right hand and holding a spear in his left. Better preserved examples show that he also holds an elephant goad in his right hand. He wears a tunic, cloak, boots and a sword. Bactrian inscription ÞAONANOÞAO KANHÞKI KOÞANO (king of kings Kanishka Kushan).

Fig. 39.3. Wilson 1841, p. 365, no. 3, Coins pl. XII.1. *Reverse*: Moon god Mao standing to front, head framed by crescents and turned to the left. He wears a cloak and a sword; his right hand outstretched in gesture of blessing, a staff tied with diadems held in his left. 🕉 in the left field, Bactrian inscription MAO in the right. 20mm. Coin not traced.
Fig. 39.4. Wilson 1841, p. 365, no. 4, Coins pl. XII.2. *Reverse*: Kushan royal goddess Nana standing in three-quarters profile to the right; head with a crescent and diadem encircled by a halo. She holds a wand with a lion protome in her right hand. Bactrian inscription NANAÞAO in the left field, 🕉 in the right. 20mm. Coin not traced.
Fig. 39.5. Wilson 1841, p. 365, no. 5, Coins pl. XII.3. *Reverse*: Kushan Orlagno (Verethragna) standing to front, head with bird crown turned to the right. Bactrian inscription OPΛAΓNO in the left field, 🕉 in the right. 20mm. Coin not traced.
Fig. 39.6. Wilson 1841, p. 366, no. 6, Coins pl. XII.4. *Reverse*: Kushan god Oesho with four arms, standing to front, haloed head turned to left. He holds (left to right) a water-pot, thunderbolt, trident and goat. 🕉 in the left field, Bactrian inscription OHÞO in the right. 20mm. Coin not traced.

Copper alloy coins with Greek inscriptions
Fig. 39.7–10. Didrachms. 30 coins. *Obverse*: King standing to front, head turned to left, wearing a diadem with a crescent, sacrificing at a fire altar with his right hand, holding a spear in his left. Greek inscription BACIΛEYC BACIΛEΩN KANHÞKOY (king of kings Kanishka).
Fig. 39.7–8. *Reverse*: Sun god Helios standing to front, head with a rayed halo and diadem turned to the left; right hand raised in a gesture of blessing. 🕉 in the left field, HΛIOC in Greek in the right. Fourteen coins of this type were collected at Begram in 1833–4 (Masson 1834, p. 172).
Fig. 39.7. Wilson 1841, p. 368, no. 16, Coins pl. XI.15. Coin not traced.
Fig. 39.8 – IOC.283. 7.74g, 21mm. Wilson 1841, p. 368, no. 17, Coins pl. XI.16; BMC India (Greek and Scythic) p. 129.2. Masson 1834, p. 172, fig. 2, pl. XII.2.
Total 15 coins: 8.93g–8.01g (4), 7.92g–7.38g (10), 6.74g (1).
Fig. 39.9–10. *Reverse*: Nana standing in three-quarter profile to the right; diademed head encircled by a halo. She holds a wand with a lion protome in her right hand and a bowl in her left. NANAIA in Greek in the left field, 🕉 in the right. Göbl 1984, type 767. Seven coins of this type were collected at Begram in 1833–4 (Masson 1834, p. 172, pl. XII.1).
Fig. 39.9 – IOC.284. 7.8g, 22mm. Wilson 1841, p. 368, no. 18, Coins pl. XI.17; BMC India (Greek and Scythic) p. 129.5.
Fig. 39.10 – IOLC.2773. 7.85g, 21mm.
Total 15 coins: 8.18g–8.01g (4), 7.97g–7.18g (8), 6.78g–6.55g (3).

Copper alloy coins with Bactrian inscriptions.
Fig. 39.11–23. Tetradrachms. 145 coins. *Obverse*: King standing to front, head turned to the left, sacrificing at a fire altar with his right hand, holding a spear in his left; inscribed ÞAO KANHÞKI (king Kanishka).

Figure 39 Kanishka I gold coins (1–6). Copper alloy coins with Greek inscriptions (7–10); with Bactrian inscriptions (11–23)

Fig. 39.11–13. *Reverse*: Nana standing to right, holding a wand with a lion protome in her right hand and a bowl in her left; inscribed NANA in the left field, 𐩏 in the right. Göbl 1984, type 777. Cribb and Bracey (at press), type D. C1-iia/iiia.

Fig. 39.11 – IOC.297. 16.86g, 26mm. Wilson 1841, p. 369, no. 21, Coins pl. XII.12; BMC India (Greek and Scythic) p. 134.54.

Fig. 39.12 – IOLC.2670. 16.8g, 24mm.

Fig. 39.13 – IOLC.2673. 16.8g, 24mm; inscribed ANAN.

Total 12 coins: 16.95g–16.05g (8), 15.82g–15.22g (4).

Fig. 39.14–15. *Reverse*: Moon god Mao standing to front, head turned to left, a crescent emerging behind the right shoulder. The right hand is extended in a gesture of blessing, the left holds a sword. 𐩏 in the left field, inscribed MAO in the right. Göbl 1984, type 774; Cribb and Bracey (at press), type D.C1-iiia.

Fig. 39.14. Wilson 1841, p. 369, no. 22, Coins pl. XII.13. 26mm. Coin not traced.

Fig. 39.15 – IOLC.2644. 16.34g, 25mm.

Total 12 coins: 17.36g (1), 16.23g–16.88g (6), 15.78g–15.25g (4), 13.65g (1).

Fig. 39.16–20. *Reverse*: Sun god Mioro/Miiro, with rayed halo, standing to front, head turned to left, right hand outstretched in gesture of blessing. 𐩏 in the left field; MIOPO or MIIPO in the right.

Fig. 39.16. Wilson 1841, p. 369, no. 23, Coins pl. XII.14. 26mm, inscribed MIOPO. Coin not traced.

Fig. 39.17 – IOLC.2656. 16.91g, 25mm, inscribed MIOPO. Göbl 1984, type 770.

Fig. 39.18 – IOLC.2665. Wilson 1841, p. 369, no. 24, Coins pl. XII.15. 17.11g, 24mm, inscribed MIIPO. Göbl 1984, type 768.

Fig. 39.19 – IOLC.2661. 16.62g, 25mm, inscribed MIIPO. Masson 1834, p. 173, fig. 4, pl. XII.4. Göbl 1984, type 768.

Fig. 39.20 – 1838,EIC.93. 16.86g, 27mm, inscribed MIIPO. BMC India (Greek and Scythic) p. 134.49; Cribb and Bracey (at press), type D.C1-iia.

1838,EIC.94. *Reverse*: Extremely worn. 16.39g, 26mm, inscribed [M]IO[P]O (?) Cribb and Bracey (at press), type D.C1-iia/iiia. Not illustrated.

Total 15 coins: 17.11g (1), 16.91g–16.39g (10), 15.52g–15.22g (4).

Fig. 39.21–3. *Reverse*: Fire god Athsho standing to left, with traces of flames issuing from his shoulders. He holds a diadem in his outstretched right hand and fire tongs in his left. 𐩏 in the left field, inscribed AΘÞO in the right. Göbl 1984, type 772.

Fig. 39.21 – IOLC.2623. 17.53g, 25mm.

Fig. 39.22. Wilson 1841, p. 369, no. 25, Coins pl. XII.16. Coin not traced.

Fig. 39.23 – IOLC.2635. 16.65g, 25mm.

Total 23 coins: 17.53g–17.16g (2), 16.86g–16g (12), 15.96g–15.23g (6), 14.99g–14.86g (2), 13.78g (1).

Fig. 40.1–23. Tetradrachms. *Obverse*: King standing to front, head turned to the left, sacrificing at a fire altar with his right hand, holding a spear in his left; inscribed ÞAO KANHÞKI (king Kanishka).

Fig. 40.1–8. *Reverse*: Wind god Oado running to left, arms outstretched holding billowing cape. 𐩏 in the left field, inscribed OAΔO in the right. Göbl 1984, types 783–4.

Fig. 40.1 – IOC.298. 17.04g, 24mm. Wilson 1841, p. 369, no. 28, Coins pl. XII.19; BMC India (Greek and Scythic) p. 135.62. Cribb and Bracey (at press), type D.C2ii.

Fig. 40.2 – IOLC.2682. 15.21g, 26mm.

Fig. 40.3. – 1838,EIC.96. 16.76g, 23mm. Cribb and Bracey (at press), type D.C1-iia/iiia.

Fig. 40.4. Wilson 1841, p. 369, no. 28, Coins pl. XII.20. 27mm. Coin not traced.

Fig. 40.5 – IOLC.2703. 16.36g, 25mm.

Fig. 40.6–8. Wilson 1841, p. 369, no. 28, Coins pl. XII.21–3. 24mm, 25mm, 26mm. Coins not traced.

Total 39 coins: 17.39g–17.04g (4), 16.87g–16.01g (26), 15.63g–15.01g (5), 14.83g–14.42g (3), 13.54g (1).

Fig. 40.9 – 12. *Reverse*: Four-armed supreme Kushan god Oesho standing to front, head turned to left, holding in his hands a diadem (lower right), a thunderbolt (upper right), a trident (upper left) and a water-pot (lower left). 𐩏 in the left field; OHÞO in the right. Göbl 1984, type 781.

Fig. 40.9. Wilson 1841, p. 369, no. 26, Coins pl. XII.17; Masson 1834, p. 173, fig. 3, pl. XII.3.

Fig. 40.10 – 1838,EIC.92. 16.13g, 24mm. BMC India (Greek and Scythic) p. 135.67. Cribb and Bracey (at press), type D.C1-iia/iiia.

1838,EIC.91. Extremely worn. 16.76g, 23mm. Cribb and Bracey (at press), type B.C1iiia/iii. Not illustrated.

Fig. 40.11 – IOLC.2729. 16.14g, 24mm.

Fig. 40.12 – IOLC.2732. 16.52g, 25mm.

Total 24 coins: 17.58g–17.12g (5), 16.83g–16.01g (14), 15.98g–15.07g (3), 14.72g (1), 13.75g (1).

Fig. 40.13 – IOLC.2739. *Reverse*: Śākyamuni Buddha standing to front, right hand raised in *abhaya mudra* (gesture of reassurance). 𐩏 in the left field; inscribed CAKAMANO BOYΔO. 16.04g, 26mm. Wilson 1841, p. 370, no. 29, Coins pl. XIII.1. Göbl 1984, type 786; Cribb 1999/2000, p. 172, no. 37, pl. 3.37.

Fig. 40.14 – IOLC.2740. Worn coin. *Reverse*: Maitreya Buddha sitting cross-legged to front on a low stool, right hand raised in *abhaya mudra*, the left holding a water-pot; inscribed MHTPAΓO BOYΔO. 16.21g, 26mm. Göbl 1984, type 790; Cribb 1999/2000, p. 177, no. 72, pl. 5.72.

Unidentifiable reverse – total 18 coins: 17.17g (1), 16.79g–16.18g (7), 15.97g–15.09g (5), 14.8g–14.43g (4), 13.43g (1).

Fig. 40.15–25. Didrachms. 58 coins. *Obverse*: King standing to front, head turned to the left, sacrificing at a fire altar with his right hand, holding a spear in his left; inscribed ÞAO KANHÞKI (king Kanishka).

Fig. 40.15 – IOLC.2817. *Reverse*: Nana standing to right, holding a wand with a lion protome in her right hand and a bowl in her left; inscribed NANA in the left field, 𐩏 in the right. 8.5g, 20mm. Göbl 1984, type 777. Cribb and Bracey (at press), type D.C1-iia/iiia.

Total 8 coins: 8.78g–8.14g (5), 7.97g–7.34g (2), 6.8g (1).

Fig. 40.16–17. *Reverse*: Mao standing to front, head turned to left, a crescent emerging from each shoulder. The right hand is extended in a gesture of blessing, the left holds a sword. 𐩏 in the left field, inscribed MAO in the right. Göbl 1984 type 775.

Figure 40 Kanishka I tetradrachms (1–25)

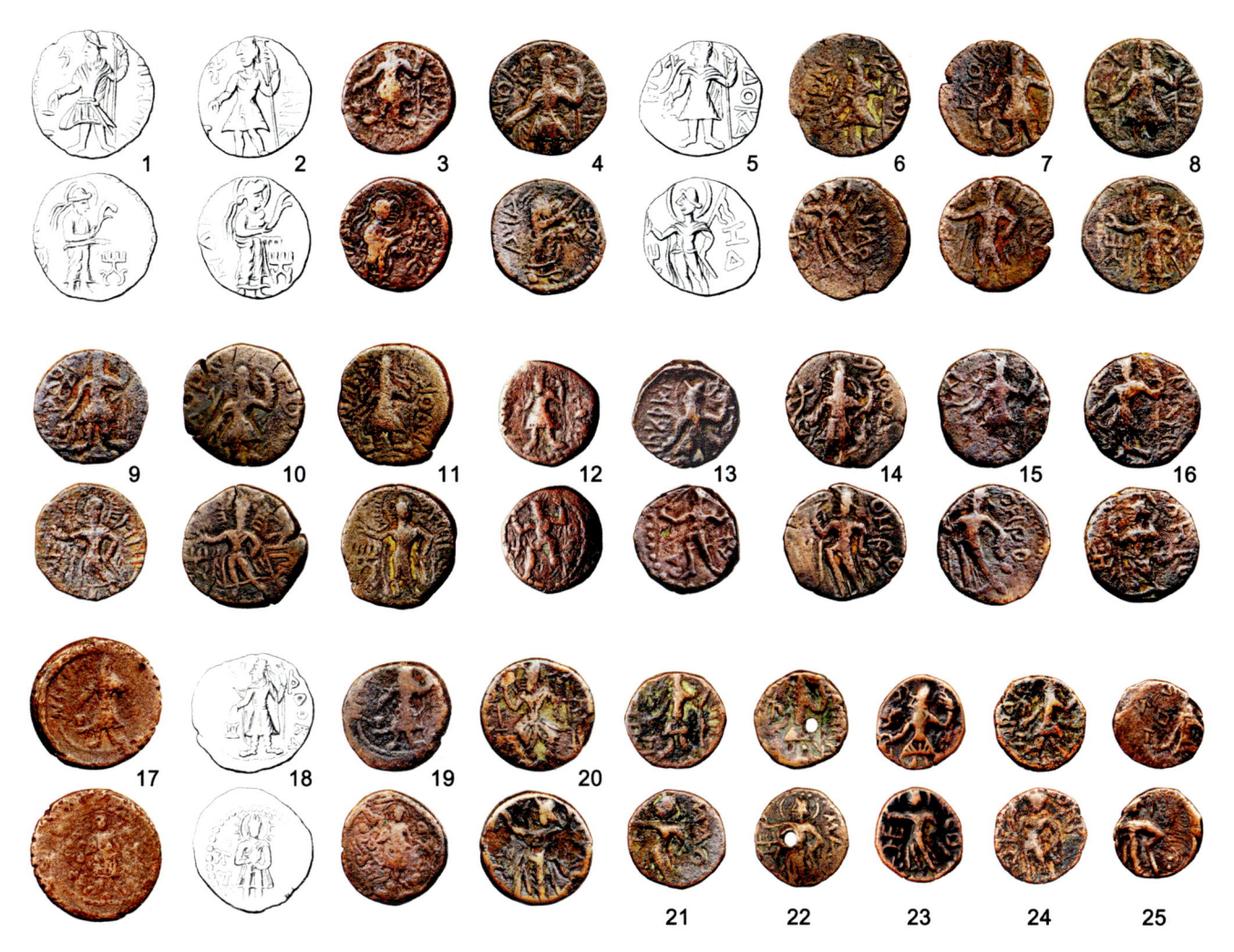

Figure 41 Kanishka I drachms (1–19)

Fig. 40.16 – IOLC.2799. 8.52g, 20mm.
Fig. 40.17 – IOLC.2798. 8.2g, 20mm.
1838,EIC.95. Extremely worn coin. *Reverse*: Mao (?); 7.26g, 22mm. Cribb and Bracey (at press), type D.C1-iia/iiia. Not illustrated.

Total 7 coins: 8.68g–8.14g, 7.26g (1).

Fig. 40.18–19. *Reverse*: Mioro/Miiro with rayed halo, standing to front, head turned to left, right hand outstretched in gesture of blessing. ⛭ in the left field; MIOPO or MIIPO in the right. Göbl 1984, type 775.

Fig. 40.18 – IOLC.2807. Inscribed MIOPO. 8.68g, 20mm.
Fig. 40.19 – IOLC.2805. Inscribed MIIPO. 8.77g, 20mm.

Total 8 coins: 8.09g–8.54g (7), 7.39g (1).

Fig. 40.20–1. *Reverse*: Athsho standing to left, with traces of flames issuing from his shoulders. He holds a diadem in his outstretched right hand and fire tongs in his left. ⛭ in the left field, inscribed AΘÞO in the right. Göbl 1984, type 773.

Fig. 40.20 – IOLC.2788. 8.48g, 20mm.
Fig. 40.21 – IOLC.2787. 8.14g, 20mm.

Total 9 coins: 8.84g–8.14g (8), 7.62g (1).

Fig. 40.22–3. *Reverse*: Oesho standing to front, head turned to left, holding in his hands a diadem (lower right), a thunderbolt (upper right), a trident (upper left) and a water-pot (lower left). ⛭ in the left field; OHÞO in the right. Göbl 1984, type 782.

Fig. 40.22. Wilson 1841, p. 369, no. 27, Coins pl. XII.15. 21mm. Coin not traced.
Fig. 40.23 – IOLC.2818. 8.14g, 21mm.

Total 9 coins: 8.8g–8g (7), 7.82g (1), 6.88g (1).

Fig. 40.24–5. *Reverse*: Śākyamuni Buddha standing to front, right hand raised in *abhaya mudra*, inscribed CAKAMANO BOYΔO. ⛭ in the outer left field. Göbl 1984, type 787.

Fig. 40.24 – IOLC.2827. 8.33g, 20mm.
Fig. 40.25 – IOC.296. 8.25g, 22mm. **F526/1a, ff. 22, 43, Pl. 8.16**; Wilson 1841, p. 370, no. 30, Coins pl. XIII.2; BMC India (Greek and Scythic) p. 133.38. Cribb 1999/2000, p. 174, no. 47, pl. 4.47; Cribb and Bracey (at press), type D.c.

Total 2 coins: 8.33g, 8.25g.

Unidentified reverse – total 15 coins: 9.39g–9.18g (3), 8.87g–8.33g (2), 7.95g–7.02g (7), 6.96g–6.55g (2), 5.79g (1).

Fig. 41.1–19. Drachms. 163 coins. *Obverse*: King standing to front, head turned to the left, sacrificing at a fire altar with his right hand, holding a spear in his left; inscribed ÞAO KANHÞKI (king Kanishka).

Fig. 41.1–4. *Reverse*: Nana standing to right, holding a wand with a lion protome in her right hand and a bowl in her left; inscribed NANA in the left field, ⛭ in the right. Göbl 1984, type 806.

Fig. 41.1–2. Wilson 1841, p. 368, no. 19, Coins pl. XI.19–20. 18mm, 17mm. Coins not traced.
Fig. 41.3 – IOLC.2929. 4.36g, 16mm.

Catalogue of Coins | 167

Fig. 41.4 – IOLC.2938. 3.13g, 17mm.
Total 53 coins: 4.94g–4g (23), 3.98g–3.03g (28), 2.35g (1), 1.68g (1).

Fig. 41.5–8. *Reverse*: Mao standing to front, head turned to left, a crescent emerging behind each shoulder. The right hand is extended in a gesture of blessing, the left holds a beribboned sceptre and a sword. ꙮ in the left field, inscribed MAO in the right. Göbl 1984, type 802.

Fig. 41.5. Wilson 1841, p. 368, no. 19, Coins pl. XI.21. Coin not traced.

Fig. 41.6 – IOLC.2846. 4.57g, 18mm.
Fig. 41.7 – IOLC.2858. 3.58g, 17mm.
Fig. 41.8 – IOLC.2875. 4.25g, 18mm.
Total 55 coins: 4.57g–4g (21), 3.99g–3.07g (33), 2.98g (1).

Fig. 41.9–11. *Reverse*: Mioro/Miiro, with rayed halo, standing to front, head turned to left, right hand outstretched in gesture of blessing. ꙮ in the left field; inscribed MIOPO, MIIPO or MYPO in the right. Göbl 1984, type 797.

Fig. 41.9 – IOLC.2903. Inscribed MIIPO. 3.66g, 17mm.
Fig. 41.10 – IOLC.2905. Inscribed MYPO. 4.45g, 18mm.
Fig. 41.11 – IOLC.2909. Inscribed MIOPO (?). 4.53g, 16mm.
Total 17 coins: 4.53g–4.03g (8), 3.99g–3.26g (9).

Fig. 41.12–13. *Reverse*: Oado running to left, arms outstretched holding billowing cape. ꙮ in the left field, inscribed OAΔO in the right. Göbl 1984, type 817.

Fig. 41.12 – IOLC.2969. 3.39g, 16mm.
Fig. 41.13 – IOLC.2970. 4.23g, 16mm.
Total 2 coins: 4.23g, 3.39g.

Fig. 41.14–16. *Reverse*: Oesho standing to front, holding a trident in his right hand and a water-pot in his left. ꙮ in the left field; OHÞO in the right. Göbl 1984, type 813.

Fig. 41.14 – IOLC.2972. 4.06g, 18mm.
Fig. 41.15 – IOLC.2977. 4.17g, 17mm.
Fig. 41.16 – IOLC.2978. 4.22g, 16mm.
Total 22 coins: 4.79g–4.02g (9), 3.96g–3.06g (12), 2.89g (1).

Fig. 41.17–19. *Reverse*: Śākyamuni Buddha standing to front, right hand raised in *abhaya mudra*, inscribed CAKAMANO BOYΔO. ꙮ in the outer left field. Göbl 1984, type 788.

Fig. 41.17 – IOLC.2993. 4.41g, 19mm.
Fig. 41.18. Wilson 1841, p. 370, no. 31, Coins pl. XIII.3. 18mm. Coin not traced.
Fig. 41.19 – IOLC.2994. 3.75g, 16mm.
Total 2 coins: 4.41g, 3.75g.

Fig. 41.20 – IOLC.2844. *Obverse*: King seated frontally on a throne, head turned to the left; right hand raised; inscribed ÞAO KANHÞKI. *Reverse*: Mao standing to left, right arm outstretched, the ends of a crescent moon encircling his head, with a beribboned sceptre behind him; inscribed MAO. 4.04g, 17mm. Göbl 1984, type 803.

Unidentified reverse – total 11 coins: 4.48g–4.02g (3), 3.82g–3.07g (8).

Fig. 41.21–5. Hemidrachms. 22 coins. *Obverse*: King standing to front, head turned to the left, sacrificing at a fire altar with his right hand, holding a spear in his left; inscribed ÞAO KANHÞKI (king Kanishka).

Fig. 41.21–3. *Reverse*: Mao standing to left, right arm outstretched, the ends of a crescent moon encircling his head, with a beribboned sceptre behind him; inscribed MAO. Göbl 1984, type 804.

Fig. 41.21 – IOLC.3005. 2.03g, 15mm.
Fig. 41.22 – IOLC.3006. 2.5g, 14mm.
Fig. 41.23 – IOLC.3014. 1.9g, 14mm.
Total 10 coins: 3.08g (1), 2.84g–2.03g (7), 1.98g–1.9g (2).

Fig. 41.24 – IOLC.3015. *Reverse*: Oesho standing to front, holding a trident in his right hand and a water-pot in his left. ꙮ in the left field; OHÞO in the right. 2.24g, 14mm, Göbl 1984, type 815.

Fig. 41.25 – IOLC.3025. Unidentified reverse; possibly Mao. 2.22g, 14mm.

Unidentified reverse – total 11 coins: 3.72g (1), 2.77g–2g (7), 1.87g–1.36g (3).

Huvishka (c. AD 151–90)

The coinage of Huvishka appears to have been issued by four mints: a principal one probably at Begram, with a second mint in Gandhara and two minor ones in Kashmir and Mathura (Cribb and Bracey at press).

Gold coinage

Only three gold Huvishka coins are recorded in *Ariana Antiqua* as having been purchased in Kabul bazaar.

Fig. 42.1 – IOC.338. Kushan standard dinar. *Obverse*: Bust of king to left, emerging from a mountain top. A halo encircles his head. He wears a triangular bejewelled helmet with earflaps and a richly ornamented coat; in his right hand is a club; in his left a spear. Inscribed ÞAONANOÞAO OOHÞKI KOÞANO (king of kings Huvishka Kushan). *Reverse*: Pharro standing to front, head turned to left; holding a wreath in his outstretched right hand and a staff in his left. Tamgha with bar ꙮ in the left field; ΦAPO in the right. 8g, 20mm. Acquired Kabul bazaar 1835. Masson 1836, pp. 27–8, no. 5, pl. III.5; Wilson 1841, p. 375, no. 3, Coins pl. XIV.3; BMC India (Greek and Scythic) p. 151.119. Thomas 1858, vol. I, p. 361, pl. XXIX.2; Göbl 1984, type 206.1; Cribb and Bracey (at press), type E.g.

Fig. 42.2 – IOC.336. Quarter dinar. *Obverse*: Bust of king with flaming shoulders to left, emerging from a mountain top. He wears a round helmet with a crescent on the side and holds a club in his right hand. Inscribed ÞAONANOÞAO OOHÞKI KOÞAN[O]. *Reverse*: Gods of war Skanda-kumara and Visakha (Bizago) standing to front, on a platform, heads turned to face each other; tamgha ꙮ in the centre. Inscribed CKANΔO-KOMAPO B[I]ZA[Γ]O. 2.02g, 12mm. Wilson 1841, p. 376, no. 11, Coins pl. XIV.11; BMC India (Greek and Scythic) p. 149.114. Göbl 1984, type 166.11; Cribb and Bracey (at press), type E.G1-iia.

Fig. 42.3 – IOC.314. Quarter dinar. *Obverse*: Bust of king with halo to left, wearing a triangular bejewelled helmet with earflaps and a richly ornamented coat; in his right hand is a club; in his left a spear. Inscribed [ÞAONANO]ÞAO OO[HÞKI KOÞANO]. *Reverse*: Mioro standing to front, head turned to left, with right arm outstretched and holding a staff in his left hand. Tamgha ꙮ in the left field, MYPO in the right. 1.96g, 11mm. Wilson 1841, p. 376, no. 10, Coins pl. XIV.10; BMC India (Greek and

Figure 42 Huvishka gold coins (1–3). Copper alloy coins, Main mint – Begram (?) Phase I (4–23)

Catalogue of Coins | 169

Scythic) p. 142.50. Göbl 1984, type 276.1; Cribb and Bracey (at press), type E.g.

Copper alloy coinage

There are drawings in *Ariana Antiqua* of 10 untraced Huvishka coins (**Fig. 42.4, 15; Fig. 43.3; Fig. 44.1, 9–10; Fig. 45.1, 11, 14, 17**). Actual copper alloy coins number 477 altogether (467 IOLC; 10 British Museum), of which the bulk are either issues of the main mint (268 coins: 258 IOLC; 10 BM) or unofficial underweight imitations (187 coins). The remaining 22 coins belong to the other three mints (17 Gandhara, 2 Kashmir, 3 Mathura).

Main mint – Begram (?)

The weight of copper alloy issues from the main mint was initially c. 17g (Phase I: Cribb and Bracey at press). It is partly a reflection of their worn state that all the 142 Masson coins belonging to this first phase weigh less. Most range between 15.96g and 14g (109 coins) with only three weighing 16.64g–16.46g and the remainder 13.96g–12.33g (30 coins). In addition, however, the weight standard and the quality of engraving both gradually declined during Phase I, culminating in the production of lighter weight coins with badly drawn figures and blundered inscriptions (Phase II: 58 coins).

Phase III comprises a single type: elephant rider with Oesho reverse (68 coins). The engraving of the figures is noticeably consistent in style, while the weight of the majority of coins ranges from 10.62g to c. 7g.

Phase I

Fig. 42.4–15. *Obverse*: King mounted on elephant to right, wearing a diadem with long ribbons and holding a spear or elephant goad in his right hand; inscribed ÞAONANOÞAO OOHÞKE KOÞANO (king of kings Huvishka Kushan).

IOLC.3089. *Reverse*: Extremely worn. Nana standing to right. Legend illegible, ☩ in the right field. 15.4g, 24mm. Göbl 1984, type 839. Not illustrated.

Fig. 42.4–8. *Reverse*: Mao standing to left, wearing a cloak, his right arm outstretched in a gesture of blessing, his left hand holding a sword. A halo and the ends of a crescent moon encircle his head. ☩ in the left field; inscribed MAO in the right. Göbl 1984, type 835.

Fig. 42.4. Wilson 1841, p. 372, no. 12, Coins pl. XIII.15. *Obverse*: King is depicted with a rayed halo and holds a spear. 26mm. Coin not traced.

Fig. 42.5 – IOC.347. 15.74g, 25mm. BMC India (Greek and Scythic) p. 154.147; Cribb and Bracey (at press), type E. C1–i.

Fig. 42.6 – IOLC.3040. 15.63g, 26mm.

Fig. 42.7 – IOLC.3049. 14.64g, 25mm.

Fig. 42.8 – IOLC.3059. 14.45g, 24mm.

Total 43 coins: 16.64g–16.46 (2), 15.74g–15.04g (13), 14.98g–14.04g (20), 13.96g–13.14g (7), 12.96g (1).

Fig. 42.9 – 1838,EIC.108. *Reverse*: Mao or Mioro standing to front, head turned to left, right arm raised. Legend illegible. 15.2g, 25mm.

Fig. 42.10–11. *Reverse*: Mioro with rayed halo, standing to front, head turned to left, right hand outstretched in gesture of blessing. ☩ in the left field; inscribed MIOPO in the right. Göbl 1984, type 823.

Fig. 42.10 – IOLC.3077. 14.45g, 24mm.
Fig. 42.11 – IOLC.3079. 14.45g, 24mm.

Total 19 coins: 16.64g (1), 15.88g–15.03g (5), 14.98g–14.04g (10), 13.76g–13.13g (2), 12.96g (1).

Fig. 42.12–13. *Reverse*: Athsho standing to front, head turned to left and holding a diadem in his outstretched right hand and fire tongs in his left. ☩ in the left field, inscribed AΘÞO in the right. Göbl 1984, type 832.

Fig. 42.12 – 1838,EIC.111. 15.61g, 25mm.
Fig. 42.13 – IOLC.3033. 14.47g, 27mm.

Total 11 coins: 15.61g–15.36g (4), 14.54g–14.34g (5), 13.91g–13.66g (2).

Fig. 42.14 – IOLC.3092. *Reverse*: Oado running to left, arms outstretched holding billowing cape. ☩ in the left field, inscribed OAΔO in the right. 15.28g. 23mm. Göbl 1984, type 852.

Fig. 42.15. Wilson 1841, p. 373, no. 18, Coins pl. XIII.21. *Reverse*: Four-armed Oesho standing to front, head turned to left. ☩ in the left field. 25mm. Coin not traced.

Total 2 coins: 14.66g, 12.41g.

Unidentified reverse – total 7 coins: 15.92g–15.42g (2), 14.93g–14.44g (2), 13.88g–13.87g (2), 12.82g (1).

Fig. 42.16–23. *Obverse*: King sitting cross-legged to front on a mountain top, surrounded by a radiate mandorla; with his head turned to right, holding a short club in his right hand and a trident in his raised left hand. Inscribed ÞAONANOÞAO OOHÞKE KOÞANO (king of kings Huvishka Kushan).

Fig. 42.16 – IOC.354. Wilson 1841, pp. 371–2, no. 4, Coins pl. XIII.7 (obverse drawing misinterprets rays of the mandorla as long diadem ties). *Reverse*: Nana standing to right, head encircled by halo, right hand raised. Inscribed NANA in the left field, ☩ in the right. 15.04g, 25mm. BMC India (Greek and Scythic) p. 158.191. Göbl 1984, p. 86, type 841.

Fig. 42.17–18. *Reverse*: Mao standing to front, head turned to left, a crescent emerging behind each shoulder. The right hand is extended in a gesture of blessing. ☩ in the left field, inscribed MAO in the right. Göbl 1984, p. 86, type 837.

Fig. 42.17 – IOC.350. 15.44g, 24mm. Wilson 1841, p. 372, no. 7, Coins pl. XIII.10. BMC India (Greek and Scythic) p. 156.171.

Fig. 42.18 – IOLC.3140. 14.71g, 25mm.

Total 11 coins: 15.44g–15.02g (4), 14.71g–14.05g (4), 13.93g–13.46g (2), 12.33g (1).

Fig. 42.19 – IOC.353. *Reverse*: Mioro with radiant halo, standing to front, head turned to left, right hand outstretched in gesture of blessing. ☩ in the left field; MIOPO in the right. 15.14g, 24mm. Masson 1834, p. 174, pl. XIII.22; Wilson 1841, pp. 372, no. 5, Coins pl. XIII.8; BMC India (Greek and Scythic) p. 157.182. Göbl 1984, p. 84, type 825.2.

Fig. 42.20 – IOLC.3148. 15.37g, 22mm. Göbl 1984, type 822.

Total 4 coins: 15.37g–15.14g (2), 14.15g (1), 13.82g (1).

Fig. 42.21–2. *Reverse*: Athsho standing to front, head turned to left, with flames issuing from his shoulders; in his outstretched right hand is a diadem, in his left tongs. ☩ in the left field, AΘÞO in the right. Göbl 1984, type 834.

Fig. 42.21 – IOLC.3135. 15.42g, 25mm.
Fig. 42.22 – IOLC.3136. 15.08g, 24mm.
Total 3 coins: 15.42g–15.08g (2), 14.84g (1).
Fig. 42.23 – 1838,EIC.97. *Reverse*: four-armed Oesho standing to front, head turned to left. ⚏ in the left field, OHÞO in the right. 15.08g, 23mm. Göbl 1984, type 851; Cribb and Bracey (at press), type E.C1-i.
Total 2 coins: 15.08g (1), 14.87g (1).

Phase I (continued)
Fig. 43.1–10. *Obverse*: King facing, half reclining, with his right leg and left arm resting on a throne and surrounded by a radiate mandorla; inscribed ÞAONANOÞAO OOHÞKE KOÞANO (king of kings Huvishka Kushan).
Fig. 43.1–2. *Reverse*: Nana standing to right, head encircled by halo, holding a wand with a lion protome in her right hand and a bowl in her left (?). Blundered inscription NANA in the left field, ⚏ in the right. Göbl 1984, type 840.
Fig. 43.1 – IOLC.3132. 15.76g, 26mm.
Fig. 43.2 – IOLC.3133. 13.87g, 24mm.
Total 3 coins: 15.76g (1), 13.87g–13.02g (2).
Fig. 43.3–5. *Reverse*: Mao standing to front, head turned to left, a crescent emerging behind each shoulder. The right hand is extended in a gesture of blessing. ⚏ in the left field, inscribed MAO in the right. Göbl 1984, type 836.
Fig. 43.3. Wilson 1841, p. 371, no. 1, Coins pl. XIII.4. 25mm. Coin not traced.
Fig. 43.4 – IOLC.3113. 15.17g, 25mm.
Fig. 43.5 – IOLC.3116. 15.4g, 25mm.
Total 16 coins: 15.63g–15.17g (6), 14.96g–14.15g (5), 13.9g–13.17g, (4), 12.82g (1).
Fig. 43.6–7. *Reverse*: Mioro with radiant halo, standing to front, head turned to left, right hand outstretched in gesture of blessing. ⚏ in the left field; MIOPO in the right. Göbl 1984, type 836.
Fig. 43.6 – IOLC.3127. 15.38g, 24mm.
Fig. 43.7 – IOLC.3128. Wilson 1841, p. 371, no. 3, Coins pl. XIII.6. 15.49g, 25mm.
Total 7 coins: 15.49g–15.32g (3), 14.09g–14.02g (2), 13.4g (1), 12.92g (1).
Fig. 43.8–9. *Reverse*: Athsho standing to front, head turned to left and holding a diadem in his outstretched right hand and fire tongs in his left. ⚏ in the left field, inscribed AθÞO in the right. Göbl 1984, type 833.
Fig. 43.8 – IOLC.3100. 15.4g, 26mm.
Fig. 43.9 – IOLC.3103. 14.98g, 26mm.
Total 9 coins: 15.89g–15.19g (4), 14.98g–14.75g (5).
Fig. 43.10 – IOC.355. *Reverse*: Four-armed Oesho standing to front, head turned to left, holding in his hands a diadem (lower right), a thunderbolt (upper right), a trident (upper left) and a water-pot (lower left). ⚏ in the left field; OHÞO in the right. 15.29g, 25mm. Wilson 1841, p. 371, no. 2, Coins pl. XIII.5; BMC India (Greek and Scythic) p. 158.194. Göbl 1984, type 850; Cribb and Bracey (at press), type E.c.

Phase II
Fig. 43.11–14. *Obverse*: King mounted on elephant to right, wearing a diadem with long ribbons and holding a spear or elephant goad in his right hand. Traces of an inscription.

Fig. 43.11 – IOLC.3157. *Reverse*: Mao standing to front, head turned to left, a crescent emerging behind each shoulder. The right hand is extended in a gesture of blessing. ⚏ in the left field, inscribed MAO in the right. 9.27g, 23mm.
Total 9 coins: 10.61g (1), 9.75g–9.09g (5), 8.93g–8.49g (2), 7.34g (1).
Fig. 43.12–13. *Reverse*: Miiro standing to front, head turned to left, right hand outstretched. ⚏ in the left field; MIIPO in the right.
Fig. 43.12 – IOLC.3163. 8.94g. 23mm.
Fig. 43.13 – IOLC.3165. 8.94g. 20mm.
Total 6 coins: 9.75g–9.25g (3), 8.94g–8.13g (3).
Fig. 43.14 – IOLC.3167. *Reverse*: Four-armed Oesho standing to front, head turned to left, holding in his hands a diadem (lower right), a thunderbolt (upper right), a trident (upper left) and a water-pot (lower left). ⚏ in the left field; OHÞO in the right. 9.9g, 23mm.
Total 2 coins: 9.9g (1), 6.77g (1).
Unidentified reverse – 1 coin: 11.64g.
Fig. 43.15–17. *Obverse*: King sitting cross-legged to front on a mountain top, surrounded by a radiate mandorla; with his head turned to right, holding a short club in his right hand and a trident in his raised left hand.
Fig. 43.15 – IOLC.3195. *Reverse*: Mao standing to front, head turned to left, a crescent emerging behind each shoulder. The right hand is extended in a gesture of blessing. ⚏ in the left field, inscribed MAO in the right. 10.04g. 23mm.
Total 5 coins: 10.22g–10.04g (2), 9.22g–9.07g (2), 8.81g (1).
Fig. 43.16–17. *Reverse*: Miiro standing to front, head with rayed halo turned to left; right hand outstretched. ⚏ in the left field; MIIPO in the right.
Fig. 43.16 – IOLC.3196. 8.56g, 23mm.
Fig. 43.17 – IOLC.3197. 8.92g, 20mm.
Total 8 coins: 9.88g–9.3g (2), 8.92g–8.56g (3), 7.71g–7.54g (2), 6.25g (1).
Unidentified reverse – total 1 coin: 9.46g.
Fig. 43.18–21. *Obverse*: King facing, half reclining with right leg and left arm resting on a throne.
Fig. 43.18–19. *Reverse*: Mao standing to front, head turned to left, a lunar crescent emerging behind each shoulder; the right hand extended. ⚏ in the left field, MAO in the right.
Fig. 43.18 – IOLC.3170. 9.55g, 23mm.
Fig. 43.19 – IOLC.3174. 8.3g, 25mm.
Total 14 coins: 9.99g–9.43g (4), 8.88g–8.07g (5), 7.89g–7.32g (2), 4.58g–4.39g (2), 3.87g (1).
Fig. 43.20–1. *Reverse*: Miiro standing to front, head with rayed halo turned to left; right hand outstretched. ⚏ in the left field; MIIPO in the right.
Fig. 43.20 – IOLC.3181. 9.63g, 23mm.
Fig. 43.21 – IOLC.3185. 7.9g, 22mm.
Total 10 coins: 9.63g–9.38g (5), 8.08g (1), 7.9g–7.64g (3), 4.8g (1).
Unidentified reverse – total 5 coins: 15.19g, 11.05g, 11.02g, 9.73g, 7.89g.

Phase III
Fig. 44.1–6. *Obverse*: King mounted on elephant to right, wearing a diadem with long ribbons and holding an

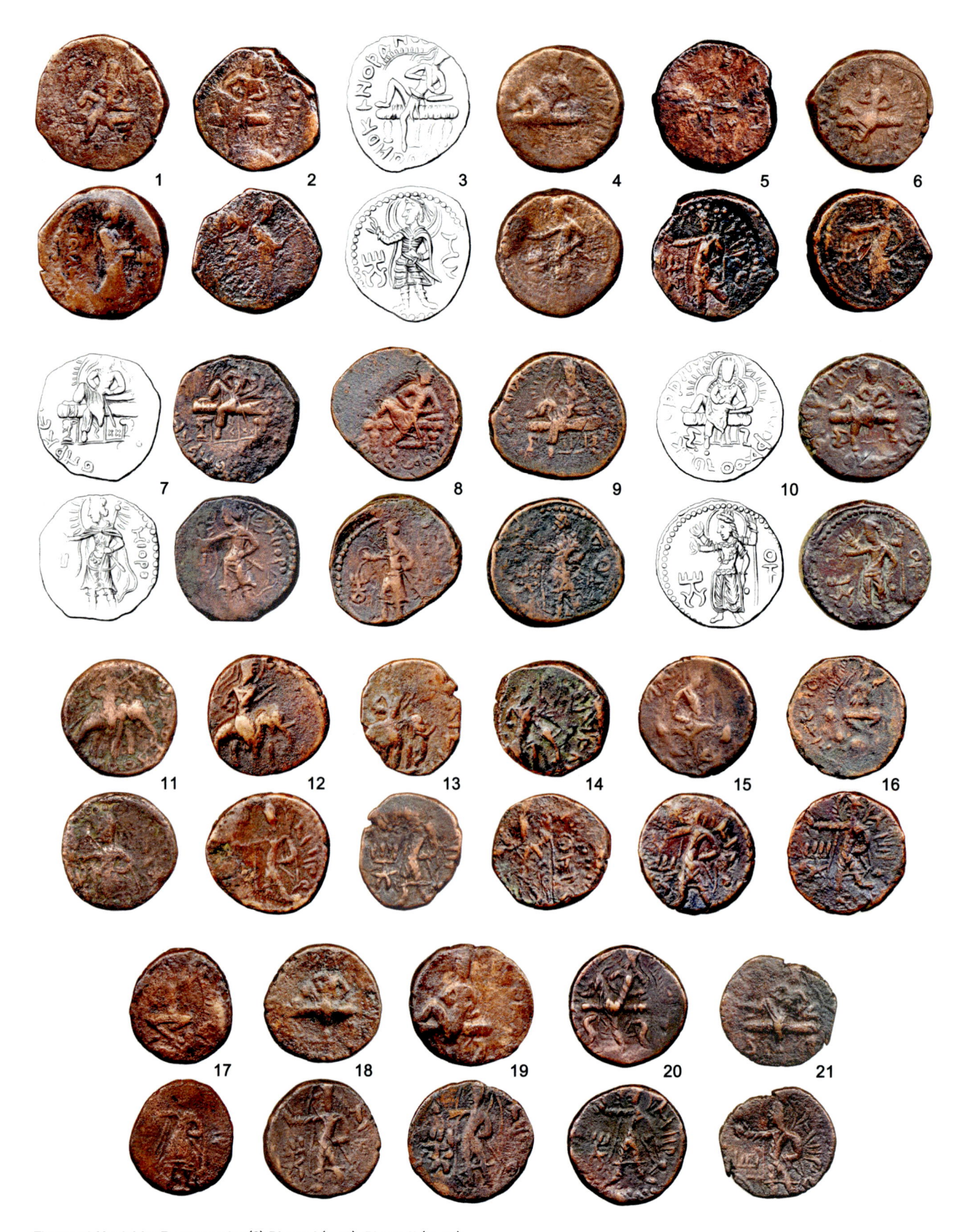

Figure 43 Huvishka Begram mint (?) Phase I (1–10); Phase II (11–21)

elephant goad in his right hand; inscribed ÞAONANOÞAO OOHÞKE KOÞANO (king of kings Huvishka Kushan). *Reverse*: Oesho standing to front, head with rayed halo turned to left. He holds a trident in his right hand and a water-pot or animal skin in his left. ⴲ in the left field; OHÞO in the right.

Göbl 1984, type 855; Cribb and Bracey (at press), type E. C1-iii.

Fig. 44.1. Wilson 1841, p. 373, no. 17, Coins pl. XIII.20. 25mm. Coin not traced.

Fig. 44.2 – 1838,EIC.104. 10.36g, 25mm.

1838,EIC.107. 8.16g, 24mm. Not illustrated.

Fig. 44.3 – IOLC.3215. 8.31g, 24mm.

Fig. 44.4 – IOLC.3245. 10.43g, 24mm.

Fig. 44.5 – IOLC.3251. 10.18g, 25mm.

Fig. 44.6 – IOLC.3255. 9.93g, 22mm.

Total 68 coins: 10.62g–10.09g (11), 9.98g–9.03g (15), 8.96g–8g (27), 7.98g–7.09g (10), 6.82g–6.52g (3), 5.96g (1), 4.94g (1).

Gandhara mint – Peshawar (?)
Copper alloy coins issued by this mint are distinguishable by a crossbar added to the tamgha: ⴲ.

Fig. 44.7–16. *Obverse*: King mounted on elephant to right, holding an elephant goad in his right hand; inscription ÞAONANOÞAO OOHÞKE KOÞANO largely illegible.

Fig. 44.7–8. *Reverse*: Ardochsho standing to right holding a cornucopia. αρδοχþο in the left field, ⴲ in the right. Göbl 1984 type 876.

Fig. 44.7 – IOLC.3281. 11.04g, 23mm.

Fig. 44.8 – IOLC.3282. 10.05g, 23mm.

Total 6 coins: 11.04g (1), 10.78g–10.05g (2), 9.77g–9.69g (2), 5.91g (1).

Fig. 44.9. Wilson 1841, p. 372, no. 14, Coins pl. XIII.17. *Reverse*: Mao standing to front, head turned to left, a crescent emerging behind each shoulder; the right hand extended in a gesture of blessing, the left holding a sword. ⴲ in the left field, μαο in the right. 25mm. Göbl 1984, type 869. Coin not traced.

Fig. 44.10. Wilson 1841, p. 372, no. 13, Coins pl. XIII.16. *Reverse*: Miiro standing to front, head with rayed halo turned to left; right hand outstretched, the left holding a sword. ⴲ in the left field; μιρο in the right. 25mm. Göbl 1984, type 820. Coin not traced.

Fig. 44.11–12. *Reverse*: Athsho standing to front, head turned to left, with flames issuing from his shoulders, his right hand outstretched. ⴲ in the left field, αθþο in the right.

Fig. 44.11 – IOLC.3287. 9.4g, 22mm.

Fig. 44.12 – IOLC.3288. 12g, 24mm.

Total 3 coins: 12g, 11.79g, 9.4g.

Fig. 44.13 – IOLC.3278. *Reverse*: Two-armed Oesho standing to front, head turned to left, holding a trident in his right hand and a water-pot in his left. ⴲ in the left field, blundered inscription in the right. 8.56g, 23mm. Göbl 1984, type 855.

Fig. 44.14 – IOLC.3290. *Reverse*: Oado running to left, arms stretched upwards holding a cloth above his head. ⴲ in the left field, οαδο (?) in the right. 11.01g, 23mm. Göbl 1984, type 852.

Fig. 44.15–16. *Reverse*: Pharro standing to front, head turned to left, holding a staff in his left hand and a bag of money in his outstretched right hand. ⴲ in the left field, φαρο in the right. Göbl 1984, type 863.

Fig. 44.15 – IOLC.3291. 11.16g, 22mm.

Fig. 44.16 – IOLC.3292. 11.04g, 23mm.

Total 5 coins: 11.16g–11.04g (2), 10.59g (1), 9.98g (1), 8.93g (1).

Kashmir mint
Fig. 44.17–18. *Obverse*: King standing to front, head turned to left, holding a staff in his left hand and making an offering to a fire altar with his extended right hand; inscribed OOHÞKE KOÞANOÞAO (Huvishka Kushan king). *Reverse*: Mao standing to front, head turned to left, a lunar crescent emerging behind each shoulder; the right hand extended. Tamgha in the left field, MAO in the right.

Fig. 44.17 – IOLC.3238. 4.14g, 17mm.

Fig. 44.18 – IOLC.3239. *Obverse*: Kharoshthi control mark 𐨧 in the left field. 3.56g, 17mm.

Total 2 coins: 4.14g, 3.56g.

Mathura mint
Fig. 44.19–20. *Obverse*: King seated cross-legged, diademed head turned to right, hands held in front of his chest; inscribed ÞAONANOÞAO OOHÞKE KOÞANO.

Fig. 44.19 – IOLC.3241. *Reverse*: Miiro standing to front, head with a rayed halo turned to left; right arm outstretched; left hand resting on his hip. ⴲ in the left field; inscribed MIIPO in the right. 8.66g, 23mm. Göbl 1984 type 935, pl.98.

Fig. 44.20 – IOLC.3242. *Reverse*: Mao standing to front, head turned to left, a lunar crescent emerging behind each shoulder; the right hand outstretched, holding a diadem, the left holding a sword. ⴲ in the left field, MAO in the right. 8.2g, 21mm. Wilson 1841, p. 372, no. 9, Coins pl. XIII.12. Göbl 1984, type 941.

Unofficial imitations
Approximately 187 coins can be classed as unofficial issues, although – given their generally worn state – it can be difficult to distinguish them from the Phase II examples. They range in weight from 13.54g to 0.97g.

Fig. 45.1–6. *Obverse*: King mounted on elephant to right and holding an elephant goad with a long staff.

Fig. 45.1. Wilson 1841, p. 372, no. 15, Coins pl. XIII.18. *Reverse*: Miiro (?) stands to front, head with plain halo turned to left, his right arm raised offering a diadem with long ribbons. ⴲ in the left field; corrupt legend WHVO in the right. 24mm. Coin not traced.

Fig. 45.2 – IOLC.3345. Dies reversed. *Obverse*: King riding elephant to left. *Reverse*: Unidentified deity standing to front, left hand on hip. Traces of tamgha in right field. 11.57g, 24mm.

Fig. 45.3 – IOLC.3335. *Obverse*: Elephant rider with long-handled trident (?). *Reverse*: Crude, unidentifiable standing figure with halo 7.62g, 24mm.

Fig. 45.4 – IOLC.3336. *Reverse*: Four-armed Oesho (?) standing to front, head turned to the left. ⴲ in the left field. 7.07g, 24mm.

Fig. 45.5–6. *Reverse*: Mao (?) standing to front, head

Catalogue of Coins | 173

Figure 44 Huvishka Begram mint (?) Phase III (1–6). Gandhara mint – Peshawar (?): (7–16). Kashmir mint (17–18). Mathura mint (19–20)

174 | *Charles Masson: Collections from Begram and Kabul Bazaar, Afghanistan, 1833–1838*

Figure 45 Huvishka unofficial imitations (1–18)

turned to left; with right arm outstretched and left hand resting on his hip. 𖤘 in the left field.

Fig. 45.5 – IOLC.3338. 6.17g, 22mm.

Fig. 45.6 – IOLC.3372. 1.19g, 18mm.

Total 31 coins: 13.54g–13g (2), 12.25g (1), 11.63g–11.57g (2), 10.77g–10.26g (3), 8.78g–8.13g (3), 7.84g–7.02g (5), 6.45g–6.17g (2), 5.79g–5.24g (3), 3.01g (1), 2.22g–2.02g (3), 1.45g–1.05g (6).

Fig. 45.7–12. *Obverse*: King sitting cross-legged to front, head turned to right, with one arm raised and the other bent.

Fig. 45.7 – IOLC.3369. *Reverse*: Unidentified deity; 𖤘 (?) in the left field. 5.44g, 23mm.

Fig. 45.8 – IOLC.3359. *Reverse*: Mao standing to front, head turned to left; with right arm outstretched and left hand holding a sword; inscribed MΔO (?) in right field. 7.76g, 21mm.

Fig. 45.9 – IOLC.3363. *Obverse*: Crude seated figure holding a sceptre in his right hand. *Reverse*: Crude standing deity, possibly Mao. 5.09g, 23mm.

Fig. 45.10 – IOLC.3332. *Reverse*: Oado moving to left, both arms raised. 𖤘 (?) in left field; inscribed OAΔO (?) in the right. 6.09g, 22mm.

Fig. 45.11. Wilson 1841, p. 372, no. 10, Coins pl. XIII.13. *Obverse*: Crude seated figure. *Reverse*: Unidentified deity, possibly Oesho; inscribed OH. 19mm. Coin not traced.

Fig. 45.12 – IOLC.3455. *Reverse*: Unidentified deity standing to front, right arm outstretched, left hand resting on hip. 1.61g, 18mm.

Total 82 coins: 10.06g (1), 8.56g–8.2g (2), 7.95g–7.23g (4), 6.46g – 6.06g (6), 5.99g–5.09g (5), 4.76g–4g (9), 3.92g–3.1g (14), 2.97g–2.03g (17), 1.95g–1.16g (22), 0.98g–0.97g (2).

Fig. 45.13–18. *Obverse*: King with rayed mandorla reclining on couch. *Reverse*: Unidentified deity standing to front, with right arm raised and left hand on hip. Tamgha in left field, corrupt inscription in right.

Fig. 45.13 – IOLC.3388. 4.59g, 22mm.

Fig. 45.14. Wilson 1841, p. 372, no. 6, Coins pl. XIII.9. *Reverse*: Flames (?) or lunar crescents issuing from the

Catalogue of Coins | 175

Figure 46 Vasudeva I gold coins (1–3). Copper alloy coins: Phase I (4–10); Phase II (11–15); Phase III (16–20); imitations (21–8)

176 | *Charles Masson: Collections from Begram and Kabul Bazaar, Afghanistan, 1833–1838*

shoulders identify the deity as either Athsho or Mao. 22mm. Coin not traced.

Fig. 45.15 – IOLC.3189. *Reverse*: Tamgha with crossbar in left field; inscribed OIIP (?) in right. 9.66g, 21mm.

Fig. 45.16 – IOLC.3352. 5.21g, 20mm.

Fig. 45.17. Wilson 1841, p. 372, no. 11, Coins pl. XIII.14. 21mm. Coin not traced.

Fig. 45.18 – IOLC.3417. 3.11g, 18mm.

Total 72 coins: 9.66g (1), 7.6g–7.05g (5), 6.86g–6.2g (6), 5.9g–5.15g (6), 4.66–4.04g (6), 3.98g–3.07g (14), 2.96g–2.04g (11), 1.94g–1.19g (21), 0.98g–0.95g (2).

Vasudeva I (c. AD 190–230)

Gold coinage

According to Wilson (1841, p. 378), the Masson collection contained 'several' gold coins of Vasudeva I, doubtless all acquired in the Kabul bazaar. He illustrates three, of which only the quarter dinar is in the British Museum

Fig. 46.1–2. Kushan standard dinar (*c.* 8g). *Obverse*: King standing to front, head with halo turned to the left and flames issuing from his right shoulder. He wears full armour and a triangular helmet (with earflaps in **Fig. 46.1**); and has a sword strapped to his waist. He makes an offering at a small altar with his right hand and holds a sceptre in his left. Inscribed ÞAONANOÞAO BAZOΔHO KOÞANO (king of kings Vasudeva Kushan).

Fig. 46.1. Wilson 1841, p. 378, no. 2, Coins pl. XIV.18. Reverse not illustrated. 23mm. Coin not traced.

Fig. 46.2. Wilson 1841, p. 378, no. 2, Coins pl. XIV.14. *Obverse*: The king is mistakenly depicted holding a trident. The altar is surmounted by a beribboned trident standard. *Reverse*: Oesho standing to front, holding a diadem in his right hand and a trident in his left; behind, a bull standing to left. ☸ in the upper left field; inscribed OHÞO in the right. 23mm. Coin not traced.

Fig. 46.3 – IOC.359. Quarter dinar. *Obverse*: King standing to front, head turned to left; his right hand over a fire altar and holding a sceptre in his left. *Reverse*: Oesho standing to front, holding a diadem in his right hand and a trident in his left; behind, a bull standing to left. ☸ in the upper left field; inscribed OHÞO in the right. 2.02g, 13mm. Wilson 1841, p. 379, no. 3, Coins pl. XIV.15; BMC India (Greek & Scythic) p. 160.17. Göbl 1984, type 510–11; Cribb and Bracey (at press), type F.G1ii b.

Copper alloy coinage

The Masson collection contains 273 copper alloy coins of Vasudeva I (1 BM, 272 IOLC). There is only one standard design of the king in armour, standing before an altar on the obverse, and Oesho with bull on the reverse. The coinage divides into three phases, with the small additions of a trident above the altar (Phase II) and a nandipada (Phase III).

Phase I

Fig. 46.4–10. *Obverse*: King in armour standing to front, with a sword strapped to his waist; head with halo turned to left, making an offering with his right hand at a small altar, and holding a sceptre tied with pennants in his left hand. Inscribed ÞAONANOÞAO BAZOΔHO KOÞANO (king of kings Vasudeva Kushan). *Reverse*: Oesho standing to front; bull standing behind to left. ☸ in the upper right field. Cribb and Bracey (at press), type F.C1.i.

Fig. 46.4 – IOLC.3520. 8.45g, 23mm.

Fig. 46.5 – IOC.360. 10.04g, 24mm. Masson 1834, p. 174, pl. XII.10 (?); BMC India (Greek and Scythic) p. 161.32.

Fig. 46.6 – IOLC.3496. 9.78g, 23mm.

Fig. 46.7 – IOLC.3495. 10.14g, 25mm.

Total 5 coins: 10.14g–10.04g (2), 9.78g–9.72g (2), 8.45g (1).

Fig. 46.8 – IOLC.3497. *Obverse*: A staff with pennants surmounts the altar. 9.81g, 25mm.

Fig. 46.9. Wilson 1841, p. 256, no. 11, Coins pl. XI.1. 25mm. Coin not traced.

Fig. 46.10. Wilson 1841, p. 256, no. 12, Coins pl. XI.5. 25mm. Coin not traced.

Phase II

Fig. 46.11–15. *Obverse*: A trident surmounts the altar. ☸ in the lower right field. *Reverse*: ☸ in the right field.

Fig. 46.11. Wilson 1841, p. 256, no. 12, Coins pl. XI.4. 23mm. Coin not traced.

Fig. 46.12 – IOLC.3623. 9.21g, 24mm;

Fig. 46.12 – IOLC.3501. 9.84g, 22mm.

Fig. 46.14 – IOLC.3542. 8.67g, 23mm.

Fig. 46.15 – IOLC.3639. 7.86g, 21mm.

Total 211 coins: 10.4g–10.09g (3), 9.98g–9.01g (16), 8.98g–8.01g (126), 7.99g–7.04g (57), 6.95g–6g (8), 5.74g (1).

Phase III

Fig. 46.16–20. *Obverse*: Trident not visible above the altar. Nandipada ☸ in the right field.

Fig. 46.16 – IOLC.3642. 9.2g, 22mm.

Fig. 46.17 – IOLC.3659. 6.65g, 22mm.

Fig. 46.18 – IOLC.3684. 8.23g, 19mm.

Fig. 46.19 – IOLC.3686. 8.13g, 21mm.

Fig. 46.20 – IOLC.3693. 7.14g, 20mm.

Total 55 coins: 9.8g–9.2g (2), 8.88g–8.03g (31), 7.95g–7.14g (18), 6.84g–6.05g (3), 5.98g (1).

Vasudeva I imitations (c. AD 230–380)

Many of the coins associated with Vasudeva I were issued after the Sasanians took control of Bactria at the end of his reign. These imitations combine the obverse standing king in a kaftan of Kanishka II, with the Oesho and bull reverse of Vasudeva I. The 182 IOLC coins exhibit a gradual decline in design and weight (from *c.* 7g down to 1g), symptomatic of having been issued over a long period, from the time of Kanishka II until the end of Kushano-Sasanian rule in the late 4th century. The earliest issues have a swastika in the right field (not visible on any of the IOLC coins) or a triangular device under the king's left arm (Cribb and Bracey, at press). See also Wilson 1841, p. 356, no. 11, Coins pl. XI.5-6.

Fig. 46.21–8. *Obverse*: King standing to front, head turned to left, making an offering at a small altar with his right hand, holding sceptre in his left. *Reverse*: Oesho standing to front, bull behind to left. Traces of inscribed OHÞO in the right field

Fig. 46.21 – IOLC.3776. *Obverse*: A trident in the left field; traces of a triangle under the left arm; *c.* AD 230–50. 6.78g, 23mm.

Fig. 46.22 – IOLC.3783. *c.* AD 230–50. 5.67g, 19mm.
Fig. 46.23 – IOLC.3808. *Obverse*: A triangle under the left arm; *c.* AD 230–50. 5.68g, 19mm.
Fig. 46.24 – IOLC.3769. *Obverse*: A trident in the left field. *Reverse*: Traces of inscribed OHÞO in the right field; *c.* AD 230–50. 6.33g, 20mm.
Fig. 46.25 – IOLC.3878. *c.* AD 280–340. 4.41g, 18mm.
Fig. 46.26 – IOLC.3816. *Obverse*: A triangle under the left arm; *c.* AD 310–40. 3.48g, 17mm.
Fig. 46.27 – IOLC.3905. *c.* AD 340–60. 2.26g, 15mm.
Fig. 46.28 – IOLC.3961. *Obverse*: A stick figure representing the king standing with altar to left. *Reverse*: Parallel lines representing Oesho with bull behind; *c.* AD 290–340. 3.76g, 12mm.

Total 66 coins (*c.* AD 230–50): 7.33g–7g (3), 6.98g–6.01g (39), 5.99g–5.4g (24).

Total 27 coins (*c.* AD 250–80): 5.59g–5.03g (16), 4.97g–4.59g (11).

Total 28 coins (*c.* AD 280–320): 4.58g–4.02g (24), 3.87g–3.72g (4).

Total 2 coins (*c.* AD 290–340): 3.76g, 3.56g.

Total 32 coins (*c.* AD 310–40): 3.59g–3.01g (21), 2.98g–2.69g (11).

Total 35 coins (*c.* AD 340–360): 5.41g (1), 4.63g–4.57g (2), 2.87g–2.02g (23), 1.99g–1.48g (9).

Total 4 coins (*c.* AD 360–400): 1.51g–1.1g.

Kanishka II (c. AD 230–46)

In his 1835 manuscript (**F526/1a, f. 23, Pl. 10.61–3, 66**, p. 61 above), Masson observes that the coin series with an enthroned Ardochsho reverse is 'very abundantly found in western [*sic*: south-eastern] Afghanistan'. He illustrates three coins of Kanishka II and one imitation, noting that they represent coin types 'generally found at Begram'.

There appears to have been only one copper mint – functioning probably at Begram – during the reign of this king (Cribb and Bracey, at press, type G.C1-i). It produced a single type – king standing at altar/seated Ardochsho – but with additional control marks. Where visible on the IOLC coins, these are ⟨symbol⟩ and ⟨symbol⟩ (*vi* in Brahmi and Kharoshthi respectively). There are 106 IOLC copper alloy coins, ranging in weight from 9.02g to 4.42g, the majority being *c.* 8.5g–6g (97 coins).

Fig. 47.1–14. *Obverse*: King standing to front, head with halo turned to left, making an offering with his right hand at a small altar and holding a sceptre tied with pennants in his left hand. A standard or trident with pennants emerges above the altar; on some examples a control mark is still visible in the right field. Only traces survive of the inscription ÞAONANOÞAO KANHÞKO KOÞANO. *Reverse*: Ardochsho seated to front on a throne, holding a diadem in her right hand and a cornucopia in her left; inscribed APΔOXÞO in the right field.

Fig. 47.1. Wilson 1841, pp. 380–1, no. 2, Coins pl. XIV.21. Coin not traced, but according to Wilson 'large numbers' of this coin type and **Fig. 47.7** were 'sent home'.
Fig. 47.2–4. *Obverse*: Brahmi control mark ⟨symbol⟩ (*vi*).
Fig. 47.2 – IOLC.3962. Control mark unclear. 8.55g, 22mm.
Fig. 47.3 – IOLC.3963. 8.23g, 21mm.
Fig. 47.4 – IOLC.3965. 7.92g, 19mm.
Total 9 coins: 8.55g–6.72g.
Fig. 47.5. Wilson 1841, pp. 380–1, no. 2, Coins pl. XIV.22.
Fig. 47.6–7. *Obverse*: Kharoshthi control mark ⟨symbol⟩ (*vi*).
Fig. 47.6 – IOLC.3974. 7.91g, 17mm.
Fig. 47.7 – IOLC.3977. 7.15g, 20mm.
Total 8 coins: 8.16g–6.69g. See also **F526/1a, Pl. 10.61, 63**, pp. 61–2 above, for two more examples.
Fig. 47.8 – IOLC.3995. *Reverse*: ⟨symbol⟩ in upper left field. 7.56g, 19mm.
Fig. 47.9 – IOLC.3997. *Reverse*: ⟨symbol⟩ in upper left field. 7.5g, 21mm.
Fig. 47.10–14. No visible tamgha or control marks.
Fig. 47.10 – IOLC.3999. 7.35g, 18mm.
Fig. 47.11 – IOLC.4003. 7.28g, 21mm.
Fig. 47.12 – IOLC.4005. 7.22g, 20mm.
Fig. 47.13 – IOLC.4044. 6.98g, 20mm.
Fig. 47.14 – IOLC.4021. 6.56g, 21mm.

Total 106 coins: 9.02g (1), 8.71g–8g (17), 7.95g–7g (45), 6.99g–6.02g (35), 5.84g–5g (7), 4.98g–4.42g (2).

Kanishka II imitations

Concurrent with the Vasudeva imitations, copper alloy coins copying the Ardochsho reverse of Kanishka II were also produced, probably by the Kushano-Sasanians. The 107 IOLC imitations show the same gradual decline in design and weight (from *c.* 8g to 0.78g).

Fig. 47.15–22. *Obverse*: King standing at altar. *Reverse*: Ardochsho, seated on a throne, wearing a three-pointed crown, holding a diadem and cornucopia; ⟨symbol⟩ in the upper left field.
Fig. 47.15 – IOLC.4090. *c.* AD 230–50. 6.88g, 24mm.
Fig. 47.16 – IOLC.4081. *c.* AD 230–50. 7.19g, 22mm.
Fig. 47.17 – IOLC.4103. *c.* AD 230–50. 6.17g, 19mm.
Fig. 47.18 – IOLC.4137. *c.* AD 280–340. 4.47g, 18mm.
Fig. 47.19 – IOLC.4112. *c.* AD 280–340. 5.92g, 16mm.
Fig. 47.20 – IOLC.4166. *c.* AD 340–60. 1.57g, 15mm.
Fig. 47.21 – IOLC.4164. *c.* AD 340–60. 1.61g, 14mm.
Fig. 47.22 – IOLC.4173. *c.* AD 360–400. 0.78g, 11mm.

Total 60 coins (*c.* AD 230–46): 8.31g–8.02g (4), 7.81g–7.03g (15), 6.94g–6.01g (22), 5.95g–5.53g (19).

Total 13 coins (*c.* AD 250–80): 5.5g–5.02g (7), 4.93g–4.54g (6).

Total 13 coins (*c.* AD 280–340): 4.58g–4.31g (7), 3.87g–3.22g (4), 2.84g–2.52g (2).

Total 12 coins (*c.* AD 340–60): 2.32g–2.04g (6), 1.99g–1.76g (6).

Total 9 coins (*c.* AD 360–400): 1.61g–1.13g (8), 0.78g (1).

Vasishka (c. AD 246–67)

Neither Masson nor Wilson record any coins of Vasishka, but the Masson collection contains a single gold coin and 44 IOLC copper alloy coins of this ruler.

Fig. 48.1 – 1838,EIC.4. Gold dinar from Kabul bazaar. *Obverse*: King in kaftan standing to front, head with halo turned to left, making an offering at a small altar with his right hand and holding a sceptre in his left. A trident with pennants emerges above the altar. Inscription largely off flan. Control marks; ⟨symbol⟩ (blundered Brahmi ā) and Greek A in

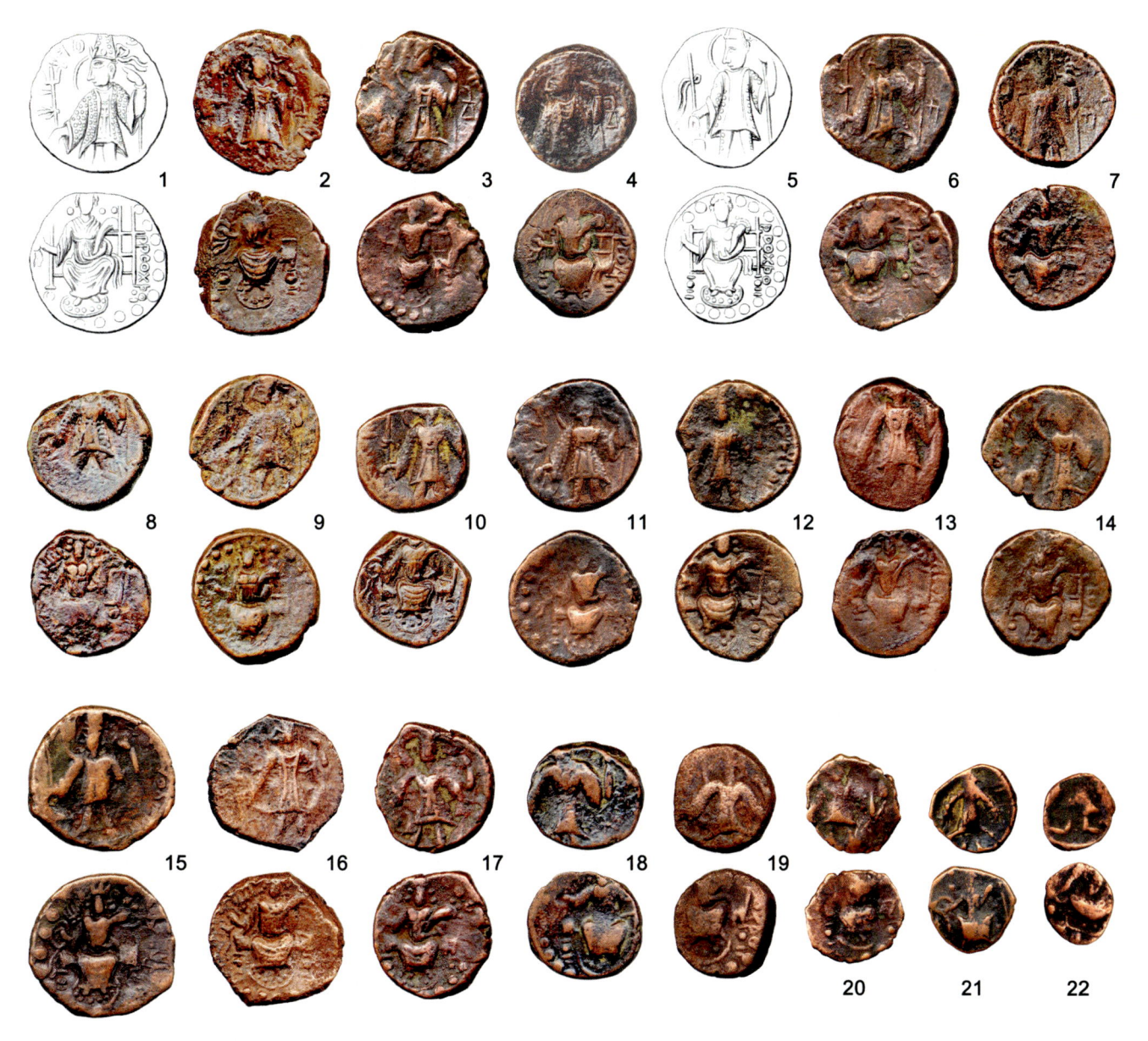

Figure 47 Kanishka II copper alloy coins (1–14); imitations (15–22)

the right field; ổ (Brahmi *tha*) between the legs. *Reverse*: Oesho standing facing; bull behind to left. ẘ in the upper left field; inscribed OHÞO in the right field. 7.83g, 21mm. Göbl 1984, type 626; Cribb and Bracey (at press), type H. G2iii: penultimate issue.

Copper alloy coinage
The 44 IOLC coins are all extremely worn. In only a few instances do traces of the inscriptions or control marks survive.

Fig. 48.2–9. *Obverse*: King in armour standing to front, head turned to left, making an offering at a small altar with his right hand and holding a trident in his left. *Reverse*: Oesho standing facing; bull behind to left; inscribed OHÞO in the right field.

Fig. 48.2 – IOLC.3841. 5.77g, 20mm.
Fig. 48.3 – IOLC.3787. 6.19g, 19mm.
Fig. 48.4 – IOLC.4182. 3.68g, 17mm.
Fig. 48.5 – IOLC.4184. 6.6g, 18mm.
Fig. 48.6 – IOLC.4185. 5.92g, 19mm.
Fig. 48.7 – IOLC.4195. 3.59g, 17mm.

Fig. 48.8 – IOLC.4178. *Obverse*: Brahmi control mark ф (*chu*) in the right field. 4.93g, 18mm. Jongeward and Cribb 2015, p. 167, no. 1619, pl. 43.1619.
Fig. 48.9 – IOLC.4180. *Obverse*: ф (*chu*) in the right field. 4.55g, 19mm.
Fig. 48.10 – IOLC.4200. *Obverse*: King in kaftan. Brahmi ổ (*tha*) between the legs. 5.16g, 20mm. Jongeward and Cribb 2015, p. 167, no. 1618, pl. 43.1618.

Total 44 coins: 8.1g (1), 6.6g–6.26g (4), 5.99g–5.03g (17), 4.93g–4.11g (13), 3.72g–3.02g (9).

Kanishka III (c. AD 267–72)

Masson records three copper alloy coins of Kanishka III in his 1835 manuscript (**F526/1a, f. 23, Pl. 10.64–5, 67**, pp. 61–2 above), which he says are coin 'types prevalent on the banks of the Indus and in the Punjab'. One of these (**Pl. 10.64**) is identifiable from his drawing as a coin donated to the Museum by the East India Company in 1838 (**Fig. 49.2**: 1838,EIC.116). Its inclusion in the manuscript indicates that the source of 1838 EIC coins was the 1833–5 Masson collection (see also **Fig. 44.5**). There are no IOLC coins of this ruler.

Figure 48 Vasishka gold coin (1). Copper alloy coins (2–10)

Figure 49 Kanishka III copper alloy coins (1–2)

Figure 50 Copper alloy coins of Shaka (1–2); Kipunadha (3)

Fig. 49.1–2. Copper alloy coin. *Obverse*: King standing to front, head turned to left, making an offering with his right hand; holding a sceptre with his left. A trident with two pennants in the left field. *Reverse*: Ardochsho seated to front on a throne, holding a diadem in her right hand and a cornucopia in her left. Cribb and Bracey (at press), type I.C1.

Fig. 49.1 – 1838,EIC.114. *Obverse*: The altar is off flan. 5.37g, 19mm.

Fig. 49.2 – 1838,EIC.116. *Obverse*: Traces of possible Brahmi control marks to the right of the altar ∩ (*ga*) and between the legs ⊔ (*gho*). 5.4g, 20mm. **F526/1a, Pl. 10.64**.

Shaka (c. AD 302–42)

There are only two IOLC coins of this ruler.

Fig. 50.1–2. Copper alloy coin with crude designs. *Obverse*: King standing to front before altar to left. Control mark in the right field. *Reverse*: Ardochsho seated to front on a throne.

Fig. 50.1 – IOLC.4205. *Obverse*: Trident above altar? H (Brahmi *sha*) in the right field. 4.08g, 17mm.

Fig. 50.2 – IOLC.4206. 2.77g, 17mm.

Kipunadha (c. AD 342–52)

There is a single IOLC coin of this ruler.

Fig. 50.3 – IOLC. 4207. Copper alloy coin with crude designs. *Obverse*: King standing to front, making an offering at an altar (off flan to left). *Reverse*: Ardochsho seated to front, holding a cornucopia in her left hand. 1.73g, 14mm.

Kushano-Sasanian

Vasudeva imitations (c. AD 235–310)

Following the conquest of Bactria by Ardashir I (AD 223–40), the Sasanian appointed governors of the former Kushan territory adopted the title of Kushanshah. The earliest coins were issued in the name of Vasudeva I (c. AD 190–230) and imitate the Kushan coin designs of a standing king on the obverse, with Oesho and bull or Ardochsho on the reverse (For copper alloy examples, see **Figs 26.18–21; 27.15–22**).

In addition the Kushanshahs minted coins in their own names in Bactria. There are 18 copper alloy IOLC coins in this category: one Ardashir I (?), five Peroz I, three Hormizd I, three Varhran I and six illegible coins of low weight: 1.4g (1), 0.97g–0.4g (5).

Ardashir I (?) Kushanshah (c. AD 230–5)

Compared to the Kushan gold coins of Vasudeva I, the imitations are more debased, have a larger flan and carry additional countermarks. There are three examples recorded from Masson, all purchased in Kabul bazaar.

Fig. 51.1–3. Gold dinars minted in Bactria by the first Kushano-Sasanian ruler, Ardashir I (?), in the name of Vasudeva. *Obverse*: King in armour standing to front, haloed head turned to left; holding a trident in his left hand and making an offering with his right at a small altar surmounted by a trident standard; a swastika between the legs; ⁜ in the right field. Bactrian inscription þαονονοþαο βαζδηο κοþονο (king of kings Vasudeva Kushan). *Reverse*:

180 | *Charles Masson: Collections from Begram and Kabul Bazaar, Afghanistan, 1833–1838*

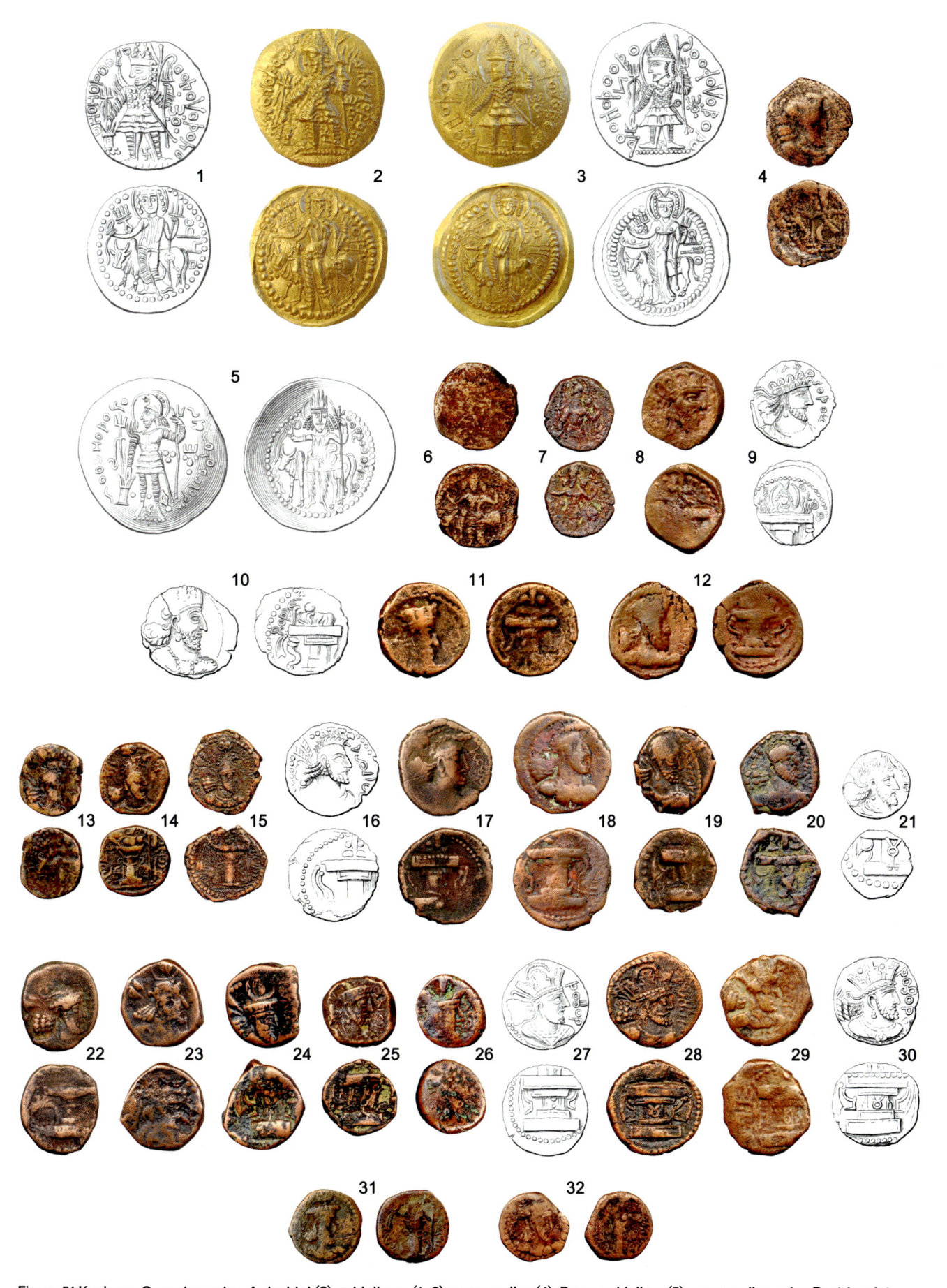

Figure 51 Kushano-Sasanian coins. Ardashir I (?) gold dinars (1–3); copper alloy (4). Peroz gold dinar (5); copper alloy coins Bactria mint (6–7), Begram/Gandhara mint (8–12). Hormizd I Bactria mint (13–15); Begram/Gandhara mint i.n.o. Kavad (16–18); i.n.o. Meze (19–21). Hormizd II (22). Peroz II (23–5). Shapur II (26–30). Varhran (31–2)

Catalogue of Coins | 181

Oesho standing facing; bull behind to left. ⍟ in the upper left field; inscribed οηþο in the right field.

Fig. 51.1. Wilson 1841, p. 378, no. 1, Coins pl. XIV.13. 25mm. Coin not traced.

Fig. 51.2 – 1838,EIC.3. 8.01g, 26mm. BMC India (Greek and Scythic), p. 160.21. Göbl 1984, type 684.2; Cribb and Bracey (at press), type Fimit.Giii.

Fig. 51.3 – IOC.583. 8.06g, 27mm. Wilson 1841, p. 378, no. 1, Coins pl. XIV.12. Göbl 1984, type 691.1; Cribb and Bracey (at press), type Fimit.Giiii.

Fig. 51.4 – IOLC.4217. Copper alloy coin of Ardashir I (?). *Obverse*: Head of king wearing a tripartite crown, to right. *Reverse*: Oesho enthroned, holding a diadem in his right hand and a sceptre in his left. 1.5g, 17mm.

Peroz I (c. AD 245–70)

During the reign of Vasishka (*c.* AD 246–67), the Sasanians gained control of Kushan territory south of the Hindu Kush. They issued a separate series of coins for the region, minted at Begram and/or Peshawar.

Fig. 51.5. Wilson 1841, p. 379, no. 5, Coins pl. XIV.17. Gold scyphate dinar, minted in Bactria: either a late issue of Peroz, or possibly an early issue of Hormizd I who uses the same crown (Cribb and Bracey at press). *Obverse*: King in armour, standing to front, haloed head in a lion-scalp crown turned to left. He holds a trident in his left hand and makes an offering with his right at a small altar surmounted by a trident standard. There is a swastika between the legs; the diamond-shape to the right of the leg is probably a misdrawn Brahmi 𑀧 (*pe*); ⚶ in the right field. Bactrian inscription πιρωζο οοζορκο κοþονο þοvο (Peroz the great, Kushan king). *Reverse*: Deity depicted as Oesho standing facing; bull behind to left; inscribed οορζαοναδο ιαζαδο (exalted god) in the right field. ⍟ in the upper left field. 29mm. Coin not traced. Göbl 1984, type 704.1 Cribb and Bracey (at press), type U.g.

Fig. 51.6–7. Copper alloy coins minted in Bactria. *Obverse*: King standing to front, head in a Kushan-style helmet turned to left; holding a trident in his left hand and making an offering at an altar with his right hand. ⚶ in the right field. Bactrian inscription πιρωζο οοζορκο κοþονο þοvο (Peroz the great, Kushan king). *Reverse*: Oesho standing to front, bull behind to left; inscribed οορζαοναδ*ο* ιαζαδο (exalted god).

Fig. 51.6 – IOLC.4219. *Obverse*: Worn and defaced. 3.15g, 16mm.

Fig. 51.7 – IOLC.4220. 2.05g, 14mm.

Total 5 coins: 3.15g (1), 2.75g–2.05g (2), 1.2g–1.05g (2).

Fig. 51.8–12. Copper alloy coin minted in Begram and/or Gandhara. *Obverse*: Bust of ruler with flat crown, to right. Blundered Bactrian inscription πιρωζο þοvο (king Peroz). *Reverse*: Haloed bust of the exalted god to front above a combined fire altar and lion-legged throne. Blundered Bactrian inscription οορζαοναδο ιαζαδο (exalted god).

Fig. 51.8 – IOLC.4255. 4.08g, 15mm.

Fig. 51.9. Wilson 1841, p. 403, no. 39, Coins pl. XVII.15. 16mm. Coin not traced. **Vol. II, pp. 91–2, Fig. 100.18**.

Fig. 51.10. Wilson 1841, p. 403, no. 37, Coins pl. XVII.12. 20mm. Coin not traced. **Vol. II, pp. 83–4, Fig. 95.52**.

Fig. 51.11 – IOLC.4239. 4.33g, 18mm.

Fig. 51.12 – IOLC.4248. 4.23g, 17mm.

Total 23 coins: 4.63g–4g (11), 3.9g–3.17g (11), 2.84g (1).

Hormizd I (c. AD 270–300)

Fig. 51.13 – IOLC.4223. Copper alloy coin minted in Bactria. *Obverse*: Bust of ruler to right wearing a lion-scalp crown surmounted by a globe. Traces of Pahlavi inscription: *awhrmzdy mlka* (Hormizd great king). *Reverse*: Oesho standing (partly off-flan); bull standing behind to left. Bactrian inscription not visible [βορζαοναδο ιαζαδο (exalted god)]. 2.01g, 13mm. Jongeward and Cribb 2015, p. 212, no. 2219, pl. 57.2219.

Fig. 51.14–15. Copper alloy coin minted in Bactria. *Obverse*: Bust of ruler to right, wearing a lion-scalp crown surmounted by a globe. Traces of Pahlavi inscription: *awhrmzdy mlka* (Hormizd great king). *Reverse*: Bust above fire altar. Traces of Bactrian inscription: βορζαοναδο ιαζαδο (exalted god).

Fig. 51.14 – IOLC.4224. 2.29g, 14mm.

Fig. 51.15 – IOLC.4225. 2.23g, 16mm.

Total 3 coins: 2.29g–2.01g.

Fig. 51.16–18. Copper alloy coin minted in Begram and/or Gandhara in the name of Kavad. *Obverse*: Bust of ruler with lion-head crown, to right. Bactrian inscription καβαδ (Kavad) in right field. *Reverse*: Fire altar.

Fig. 51.16. Wilson 1841, p. 403, no. 40, Coins pl. XVII.16. 20mm. Coin not traced. **Vol. II, pp. 83–4, Fig. 95.51**.

Fig. 51.17 – IOLC.4298. 3.7g, 18mm.

Fig. 51.18 – IOLC.4272. 4.1g, 19mm.

Total 56 coins: 4.71g–4g (15), 3.99g–3.03g (35), 2.98g–2.68g (6).

Fig. 51.19–21. Copper alloy coins minted in Begram and/or Gandhara in the name of Meze. *Obverse*: Bust of ruler with lion-head crown, to right. Bactrian inscription μηζη (Mēzē) in the right field. *Reverse*: Fire altar.

Fig. 51.19 – IOLC.4312. 3.3g, 17mm.

Fig. 51.20 – IOLC.4313. Jongeward and Cribb 2015, p. 215, no. 2298, pl. 59.2298.

Fig. 51.21. Wilson 1841, p. 403, no. 42, Coins pl. XVII.19. 14mm. Coin not traced. **Vol. II, pp. 91–2, Fig. 100.17**.

Total 26 coins: 4.2g–4g (4), 3.96g–3.01g (21), 2.94g (1).

Hormizd II (c. AD 300–3)

Fig. 51.22 – IOLC.4338. *Obverse*: Bust of ruler to right, with winged crown and globe. Bactrian inscription μηζη (Mēzē) in the right field. *Reverse*: Fire altar. 3.91g, 17mm.

Peroz II (c. AD 303–30)

Fig. 51.23–6. Copper alloy coins minted in Begram and/or Gandhara in the name of Meze. *Obverse*: Bust of ruler to right, wearing a flat crown, with a crescent and globe above. Bactrian inscription μηζη (Mēzē) in the right field. *Reverse*: Fire altar.

Fig. 51.23 – IOLC.4354. 3.72g, 17mm.

Fig. 51.24 – IOLC.4358. 3.52g, 17mm.

Fig. 51.25 – IOLC.4361. 3.45g, 15mm.

Total 29 coins: 4.43g–4.21g (2), 3.91g–3.09g (25), 2.95g–2.64g (2).

Shapur II (c. AD 309–79)

Copper alloy coins circulating at Begram c. AD 330–79, and in Gandhara, c. AD 340.

Fig. 51.26 – IOLC.4368. Copper alloy coin in the name of Kavad. *Obverse*: Bust of ruler to right, wearing a tripartite crenelated crown. Bactrian inscription καβαδ (Kavad) in the right field. *Reverse*: Fire altar; illegible; 2.19g, 14mm.

Total 8 coins: 3.89g–3.04g (4), 2.3g–2.17g (3), 1.35g (1).

Fig. 51.27–30. Copper alloy coins in own name. *Obverse*: Bust of ruler to right, wearing a tripartite crenelated crown. Bactrian inscription Þαβορο (Shaboro) in the right field. *Reverse*: Fire altar with flames above.

Fig. 51.27. Wilson 1841, p. 403, no. 38, Coins pl. XVII.13. 20mm. Coin not traced. **Vol. II, pp. 83–4, Fig. 95.53.**

Fig. 51.28 – IOLC.4379. 3.77g, 20mm.

Fig. 51.29 – IOLC.4385. 3.34g, 18mm.

Fig. 51.30. Wilson 1841, p. 403, no. 38, Coins pl. XVII.14. 17mm. Coin not traced. **Vol. II, pp. 83–4, Fig. 95.54.**

Total 40 coins: 5.56g (1), 4.47g–4.01g (5), 3.96g–3.01g (25), 2.95g–2.12g (6), 1.99g–1.72g (3).

Varhran (c. AD 330–59)

Fig. 51.31–2. Copper alloy coins minted in Bactria. *Obverse*: Bust of ruler with flat crown, to right. Traces of Pahlavi inscription *wrhran rba kwshan mlka* (Varhran great Kushan king) *Reverse*: Bust emerging above altar. Traces of Pahlavi inscription *bwlzawndy yzdty* (exalted god).

Fig. 51.31 – IOLC.4226. 1.57g, 13mm.

Fig. 51.32 – IOLC.4228. 1.28g, 15mm.

Total 3 coins 1.57g–1.27g.

Total 19 illegible coins: 4.09g (1), 3.71g–3.05g (13), 2.84g–2.17g (4), 1.83g (1).

Huns

In one of Masson's 1840s inventories of his own collection he noted a series of coins which he identified as 'Sasanian or like Sasanian, chiefly with fire altar of various sizes' (**F526/1g**, 'List of Coins B', **Vol. II, p. 92**), and cites Wilson 'for such as are noticed' (1841, Coins pl. XVII.10–21: 5 Kushano-Sasanian, 2 Alkhan and 4 Nezak coins). He adds

> A few, I think, may be true Sasanian; among others … in some part also contemporaneous – and others again what are called Indo-Sasanian. Amongst the curious types may be instanced one coin with a clearly defined bust of a king, whose usual coins have a fire altar on the reverse, but in this instance, a standing figure sacrificing on an altar … the style of the coin is good, but the legend mostly illiterate and useless. … In other instances … the reverse has a bust as well as the obverse [**Fig. 52.39–41**]. On the reverse of a coin where we look for the plain altar we find a seated figure [**Fig. 52.4–7**], and on others we find shells, flower vases and other singular emblems [**Fig. 52.29–34, 42–3**].

Masson bought several gold Kidarite and silver Alkhan coins in Kabul bazaar (**Fig. 52.1–3, 27–8**). He also found gold and silver coins of Kirada, Kidara and the Alkhan rulers Mepama, Javukha and Khingila mixed with 4 Roman aurei and c. 200 mostly 5th-century Sasanian silver coins in the relic deposit of Hadda stupa 10 (**F526/1a, Pls 14–15**, see pp. 65–6 above; **Vol. I, pp. 185–8, figs 281–2**).

In another list with an 1843 watermark (**F526/1j**, **Vol. II, p. 99**), Begram is said to have produced 123 'Indo-Sasanian' coins, which may be equated with a number of small copper alloy coins (58 Kidarite; 30 Alkhan) and a larger quantity of Nezak issues (67 coins) from the site.

Kidarite

Gold coinage

Varhran imitations

At some point during the reign of Varhran (c. AD 330–59), the Kidarites began minting coins in his name in Bactria, using the same designs, with some modifications e.g. 'ö' was replaced by the Kidarite tamgha ⚛, and the Sasanian control mark, the swastika, was phased out. Some coins bear the mint name Balkh (Cribb and Bracey, in press).

Fig. 52.1 – 1894,0506.174. Scyphate dinar in the name of Varhran, c. mid 4th century. *Obverse*: King in armour, with flaming shoulders, standing to front, head turned to left, wearing a flat crown surmounted by a lotus bud. He has a sword, holds a trident in his left hand and makes an offering with his right at an altar surmounted by a beribboned trident and crescent standard. ⚛ in the right field. Bactrian inscription βαγο οορογρονο οοζορκο κοþανο þαο (Lord Varhran the great Kushan king). *Reverse*: Exalted god with flaming hair standing to front, holding a trident in his left hand; a bull behind standing to left. Blundered Bactrian inscription βορζαοναδο ιαζαδο (exalted god) in the right field. 6.8g, 34mm. Cunningham collection. Wilson 1841, p. 379, no. 4, Coins pl. XIV.16; Göbl 1984, type 719.1. Cribb 2010, pp. 125, 140, table 2, no. 4B, fig. 10; Cribb and Bracey (at press), type O.G1-ii.

Kidara (c. AD 355–85)

Fig. 52.2–3. Dinar of Kidara. *Obverse*: Stylised king standing to the left, holding a trident in his left hand and making an offering at a small altar with his right. Brahmi inscription *kapana* beside altar, *kidara kushana* under arm, in right field. *Reverse*: Stylised Ardochsho with cornucopia seated on throne to front. Göbl 1984, type 616. Cribb 2010, pp. 100–1, 130, 142, table 4, no. B7, fig. 38 (earlier prototype); Cribb and Bracey (at press), type Q.G1-iii.

Fig. 52.2. Wilson 1841, p. 427, no. 26, Coins pl. XVIII.27. 25mm. Coin not traced.

Fig. 52.3 – IOC.556. 7.74g, 23mm. Wilson 1841, p. 427, no. 27, Coins pl. XVIII.28.

Copper alloy coinage

Apart from a single coin bearing the ⚛ tamgha on the reverse (**Fig. 52.16**), evidence for the Kidarites at Begram is limited to Kushan imitations (13 coins) and Bactrian issues copying those of Varhran (35 coins) and the horned crown of Peroz (7 coins). There are also three worn coins of uncertain design.

Kushan imitations (late 4th century)

Fig. 52.4–7. *Obverse*: King standing to left, a spear or

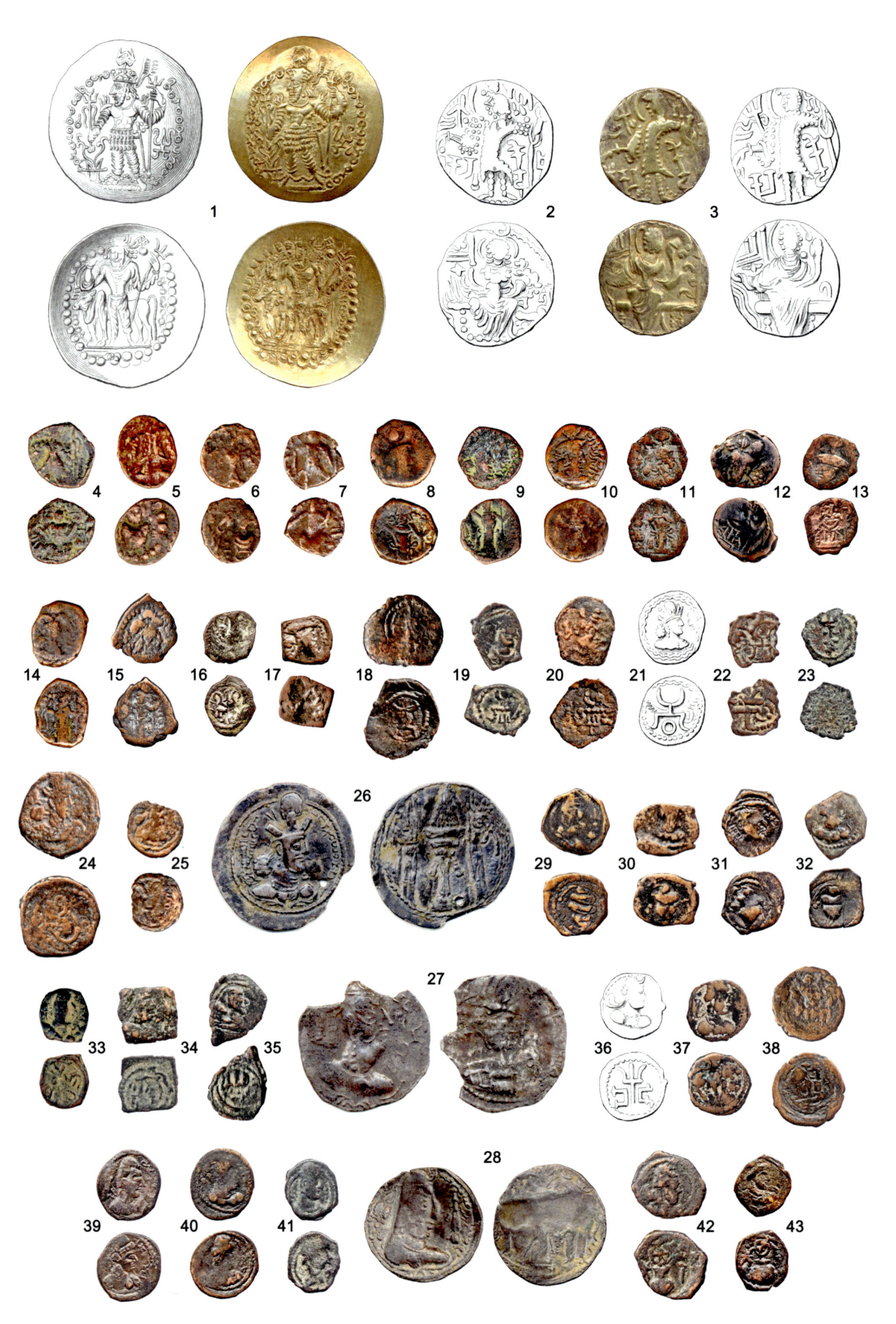

Figure 52 Hun coins. Kidarite gold dinars: Vahran imitation (1), Kidara (2–3). Copper alloy coins i.n.o. Varhran (8–13), Peroz (14–15) Kidara (16). Alkhan anonymous issues (17–25); silver coins (26–8); inscribed copper alloy issues (29–41), Toramana (42–3)

184 | *Charles Masson: Collections from Begram and Kabul Bazaar, Afghanistan, 1833–1838*

sceptre in his left hand. *Reverse*: Ardochsho seated to front, cradling a cornucopia in her left arm and holding a diadem in her right hand.

Fig. 52.4 – IOLC.4438. 1.47g, 15mm.
Fig. 52.5 – IOLC.4439. 1.24g, 12mm.
Fig. 52.6 – IOLC.4446. 1.1g, 13mm.
Fig. 52.7 – IOLC.4448. 1.16g, 13mm.
Total 13 coins: 1.47g–1.1g (10), 0.93g–0.78g (3).

In the name of Varhran (c. AD 330–70)

Fig. 52.8–13. *Obverse*: Bust of ruler to right, wearing a flat crown with ribbons and globe. *Reverse*: Bust above a fire altar. This coin type was also found at Kashmir Smast (Errington 2010, p. 159, fig. 6b-c).

Fig. 52.8 – IOLC.4451. 1.716g, 14mm.
Fig. 52.9 – IOLC.4456. 1.22g, 13mm.
Fig. 52.10 – IOLC.4459. 1.22g, 13mm.
Fig. 52.11 – IOLC.4466. 0.76g, 13mm.
Fig. 52.12 – IOLC.4471. 1.3g, 13mm.
Fig. 52.13 – IOLC.4482. 0.63g, 11mm.
Total 35 coins: 1.71g–1.02g (15), 0.98g–0.37g (20); uncertain 0.66g–0.22g (3).

Peroz (c. AD 340–50)

Fig. 52.14–15. *Obverse*: Bust of ruler, facing to right, with a horned crown. Traces of Bactrian inscription. *Reverse*: Bust above fire altar. This coin type was also found at Kashmir Smast (Errington 2010, p. 159, fig. 6a).

Fig. 52.14 – IOLC.4486. 1.71g, 14mm.
Fig. 52.15 – IOLC.4487. 1.65g, 13mm.
Total 7 coins: 1.71g–1.04g (4), 0.84g–0.6g (3).

Kidara (c. AD 355–85)

Fig. 52.16 – IOLC.4493. *Obverse*: Bust of ruler to right, with the flat crown of Shapur III (AD 383–8). Traces of Brahmi *ṣāhi* in right field. *Reverse*: 🕉 with traces of Brahmi *va* in left field. 0.44g, 12mm. Nasim Khan *et al.* 2008, pp. 196–207; Errington 2010, pp. 149, 158, fig. 4. Vondrovec 2014, I, type 30-36.

Alkhan

Anonymous / affiliated rulers

A small group of 11 anonymous copper alloy coins from Begram exhibit a variety of tamghas which combine additional elements with the Alkhan tamgha ☥.

Fig. 52.17 – IOLC.4497. Copper alloy coin, roughly square in form. *Obverse*: Bust of ruler to right, with a flat crown. *Reverse*: ☥; worn. 0.47g, 12mm. Nasim Khan *et al.* 2008, p. 289; Errington 2010, pp. 149, 158, fig. 4. Vondrovec 2014, I, type 37A-7.

Fig. 52.18 – IOLC.4500. *Obverse*: Bust of ruler to right, with the crenelated crown of Shapur II. *Reverse*: ☥. 1.18g, 17mm. Errington 2010, pp. 149, 158, fig. 4. Vondrovec 2014, I, type 37A-4.

Fig. 52.19–20. *Obverse*: Bust of ruler to right, with the crown of Shapur II. *Reverse*: Alkhan tamgha with trident ☥. Errington 2010, pp. 149, 158, fig. 4.

Fig. 52.19 – IOLC.4501. 0.84g, 13mm. Vondrovec 2014, I, type 37C-4.

Fig. 52.20 – IOLC.4502. 0.73g, 14mm. Vondrovec 2014, I, type 37C-6.
Total 4 coins: 1.37g (1), 0.84g–0.41g (3).

Fig. 52.21. Wilson 1841, p. 403, no. 43, Coins pl. XVII.20. *Obverse*: Bust of ruler to right, with the crown of Shapur II. *Reverse*: Alkhan tamgha with circle. 14mm. Coin not traced. **Vol. II, pp. 91–2, Fig. 100.20**.

Fig. 52.22 – IOLC.4503. *Obverse*: ☥ *Reverse*: Fire altar with stylised flames. 0.4g, 13mm. Vondrovec 2014, I, type 72-8.

Fig. 52.23 – IOLC.4504. *Obverse*: Trident with crossbars within a circle. *Reverse*: Illegible. 0.52g, 12mm; an example from Kashmir Smast has ☥ on the reverse. Nasim Khan *et al.* 2008, type 312; Errington 2010, p. 159, fig. 5.

Fig. 52.24–5. *Obverse*: Bust of ruler to right, with the crenelated crown of Shapur II. Traces of an illegible Bactrian inscription. *Reverse*: ☥; traces of an illegible Bactrian inscription. Göbl 1967, type 34, pl. 14.34.1.

The tamgha is used by the Hephthalites (Alram 2008, pp. 258–60, 268, fig. 50), but it is also found on an imitation Shapur II silver dinar inscribed αλχονο (see **Fig. 52.26**).

Fig. 52.24 – IOLC.4505. 3.37g, 17mm.
Fig. 52.25 – IOLC.4506. 0.58g, 12mm.

Alkhan (c. 4th–5th century)

Silver coinage

Fig. 52.26 – 1845,EIC.3. Drachm, pierced, minted in Kabulistan after *c*. AD 385. *Obverse*: Bust of Shapur II (AD 309–78) to right, with ☥ in the upper left field and the Bactrian legend αλχαννο (*alxanno*) in the right. *Reverse*: Fire altar with diadem ties flanked by two attendants. 3.57g, 30mm. Purchased in Kabul bazaar. Göbl 1967, type 33, tamgha S 2, pl. 24.33; Alram and Pfisterer 2010, p. 16, type 33; Alram 2016, p. 67, no. 5.

Fig. 52.27 – 1845,EIC.58. Broken drachm of Mehama (*c*. AD 450–500). *Obverse*: Cranially deformed bust of king to right above a pair of schematic wings; wearing a diadem topped by a crescent. ☥ in the right field. Trace of Brahmi [*meha*]*ma*. *Reverse*: A fire-altar flanked by two attendants, largely obliterated by the incuse of the obverse. 3.3g, 27mm. Purchased in Kabul bazaar. Göbl 1967, pp. 79–80, type 74, pl. 24.74.1; Vondrovec 2014, I, p. 314, type 74: *ṣāhi mehama*.

Fig. 52.28 – 1845,EIC.59. Dinar of Adomano (*c*. AD 450–500). *Obverse*: Cranially deformed bust of king to right above a pair of schematic wings, wearing a diadem topped by a crescent containing a flower. ☥ in the left field; a diademed club and Bactrian inscription in the right: αδομανο μιιρο σανο βαο (*adomano miirosano šao*: Adomano king of the east). *Reverse*: A fire-altar flanked by two attendants, largely obliterated by the incuse of the obverse. 3.77g, 24mm. Purchased in Kabul bazaar. Göbl 1967, p. 87, type 86, pl. 27.86.5; Vondrovec 2014, I, p. 340, type 86; Alram 2016, p. 86, no. 12.

Copper alloy coinage

Fig. 52.29–32. *Obverse*: Bust of ruler to right. Traces of illegible inscription. *Reverse*: Conch. Göbl 1967, type 165, pl. 37.165.1; Nasim Khan *et al.* 2008, pp. 310–11 (reverse type).

Fig. 52.29 – IOLC.4510. 1.03g, 14mm.

Fig. 52.30 – IOLC.4511. 0.83g, 13mm.
Fig. 52.31 – IOLC.4512. 0.77g, 13mm.
Fig. 52.32 – IOLC.4513. 0.64g, 14mm.
Total 4 coins.

Fig. 52.33 – IOLC.4515. *Obverse*: Bare-headed bust of king to right. *Reverse*: Uncleaned; illegible. 0.7g, 16mm; Göbl 1967, inscription type, pl. 20, no. 54.

Fig. 52.34 – IOLC.4514. *Obverse*: Bare-headed bust of king to right. *Reverse*: Diademed club (?) 0.42g, 15mm. Vondrovec 2014, type 55B: Jayaditya type.

Fig. 52.35 – IOLC.4516. *Obverse*: Bare-headed bust of king to right. *Reverse*: Brahmi inscription [*jayaditya*]. 0.61g, 10mm.

Fig. 52.36. Wilson 1841, p. 403, no. 44, Coins pl. XVII.21. *Obverse*: Bare-headed bust of king to right, with crescent and diadem ties. *Reverse*: Trident. Brahmi inscription *ṣa-hi*. 14mm. Coin not traced. **Vol. II, pp. 91–2, Fig. 100.19**.

Fig. 52.37 – IOLC.4517. *Obverse*: Bare-headed bust of king to right. Bactrian inscription [αλχ]ονο. *Reverse*: Lion to right. 1.04g, 13mm; Göbl 1967, type 48, pl. 17; Errington 2010, pp. 149, 162, fig. 14c; Vondrovec 2014, I, type 48-2.

Fig. 52.38 – IOLC.4518. *Obverse*: Bare-headed bust of king to right, overstruck on bust with winged crown. *Reverse*: Lion to right; overstruck on inscription. 0.93g, 15mm. Vondrovec 2014, type 48-2 o/s type GC-K6.

Fig. 52.39–41. *Obverse*: Bare-headed bust of king to right. Bactrian inscription αλχονο. *Reverse*: Bust with diadem to right. Illegible Brahmi inscription. Göbl 1967, type 45. Errington and Curtis 2007, type p. 93, fig. 81.3.

Fig. 52.39 – IOLC.4519. 1g, 14mm. Vondrovec 2014, I, type 45-9.

Fig. 52.40 – IOLC.4520. 1.05g, 15mm. Vondrovec 2014, I, type 45-7.

Fig. 52.41 – IOLC.4521. 0.94g, 12mm. Vondrovec 2014, I, type 45-10.

Total 3 coins.

Toramana I (? c. AD 485–515)

Fig. 52.42–3. *Obverse*: Bust of king to right. *Reverse*: Water-pot (*pūrṇaghaṭa*) with chakra above. Brahmi inscription (*tora*). Errington and Curtis 2007, type p. 93, fig. 81.2.

Fig. 52.42 – IOLC.4522. 1.29g, 15mm.

Fig. 52.43 – IOLC.4524. *Reverse*: Two overlapping rings above the water-pot. 0.71g, 13mm.

Total 4 coins: 1.29g–0.46g.

Toramana II (c. AD 540–99)

A series of anonymous copper alloy uniface drachms had been attributed to Narana/Narendra, but are now attributed to Toramana II, a successor of Mihirakula (c. AD 515–40), on the evidence that clearly related coins bear the Brahmi inscription *śrī ṣahi tora* (Alram 1999/2000, pp. 136–7, pl. 5B; Pfisterer 2013, pp. 188, 307). In 1997, 447 coins of this type – part of a hoard – were said to have been unearthed 10km north of Kabul (Alram 1999/2000, p. 129). Despite the indication supplied by the hoard that the mint issuing these coins was probably located in the Kabul/Begram vicinity, only eight examples survive in the Masson collection, all apparently of the later 'two plants' type (Vondrovec 2010, p. 175, type 150, variety 3). Masson illustrates an example from Begram (see **F526/1a, f. 25, Pl. 12.37**: pp. 64–5 above).

Fig. 53.1–3. *Obverse*: Bust of ruler to right, holding (where visible) a plant with two stalks. He wears a crown of two crescents with diadem ties and a large circular ear-ring threaded with globular beads. The Brahmi *śrī* in the upper right field is not visible in any of the Masson specimens. Göbl 1967, type 150, pl. 34; Alram 1999/2000, pp. 139–43, pls 2.34–4.90; Vondrovec 2010, pp. 174–5.

Fig. 53.1 – IOLC.4534. The right field is abraded. 2.38g, 25mm.

Fig. 53.2 – IOLC.4536. 3.06g, 25mm.

Fig. 53.3 – IOLC.4541. The coin is pierced through the centre. 4.42g, 24mm.

Total 8 coins: 4.42g (1), 3.81g–3.02g (4), 2.9g–2.38g (3).

Nezak (c. AD 460–650)

Nezak Malka

Silver alloy drachms in the name of Nezak Malka (a.k.a. Napki Malka), are classified as Nezak Group I (c. AD 460–560), Ghazni (?) mint and Nezak Group II (c. AD 515–650), Kabul (?) mint (Alram 1999/2000, p. 148, pl. 7.113–18). As silver coins, they were probably bought in Kabul bazaar (only copper coins were acquired from Ghazni, see **Vol. II, p. 63, E161/VII f. 25**).

Fig. 53.4–5. Group I (c. AD 460–560), Ghazni (?) mint. *Obverse*: Bust of ruler to right, with shoulder diadem ties; wearing a winged crown surmounted by a crescent and buffalo head. Pahlavi inscription *nycky MLK*[*A*] (Nezak Malka) in the right field. *Reverse*: Fire altar flanked on either side by an attendant holding a long staff with a chakra above. Göbl 1967, type 222; Alram 1999/2000, p. 148, pl. 7.113–14; Vondrovec 2010, p. 182, type 222.

Fig. 53.4. Wilson 1841, Coins pl. XXI.21: obverse only; not described; wings of crown omitted (left) and misinterpreted (right) as part of the inscription. 26mm. Coin not traced.

Fig 53.5. Wilson 1841, p. 397, no. 11, Coins pl. XVII.7. 27mm. Coin not traced.

Fig. 53.6 – 1906,1103.5330. Nezak Group II (c. AD 515–650), Kabul (?) mint. *Obverse*: Bust of ruler to right, with shoulder diadem ties; wearing a winged crown surmounted by a crescent and buffalo head. Pahlavi inscription *nycky MLK*[*A*] in the right field. *Reverse*: Fire altar flanked on either side by an attendant holding a long staff with a *chakra* above. Brahmi *la* or *ha* in the left field; Kharoshthi *hi* (?) in the right. 3.03g, 26mm. Donated by F. Parkes-Weber. Wilson 1841, p. 397, no. 10, Coins pl. XVII.5; Göbl 1967, type 198, pls 43–4. Alram 1999/2000, p. 148, pl. 7.115–18; Vondrovec 2014, I, p. 475, type 198.

Fig. 53.7 – 1902,0614.55. Copper alloy coin. *Obverse*: Bust of king to right, encircled by one lion (?) and three buffalo heads to right. *Reverse*: Double struck ⚇ encircled by a Pahlavi inscription *bg'MLKA*. 2.95g, 20mm. Donated by: R.W. Ellis. **F526/1a, f. 25, Pl. 11.20**. Göbl 1967, type 204, pl. 45.

Shri Shahi – Turkic Shahs (6th–7th century)

Fig. 53.8 – IOC.2369. Copper alloy drachm (c. AD 600–20). *Obverse*: Bust of ruler to right, wearing a crown with

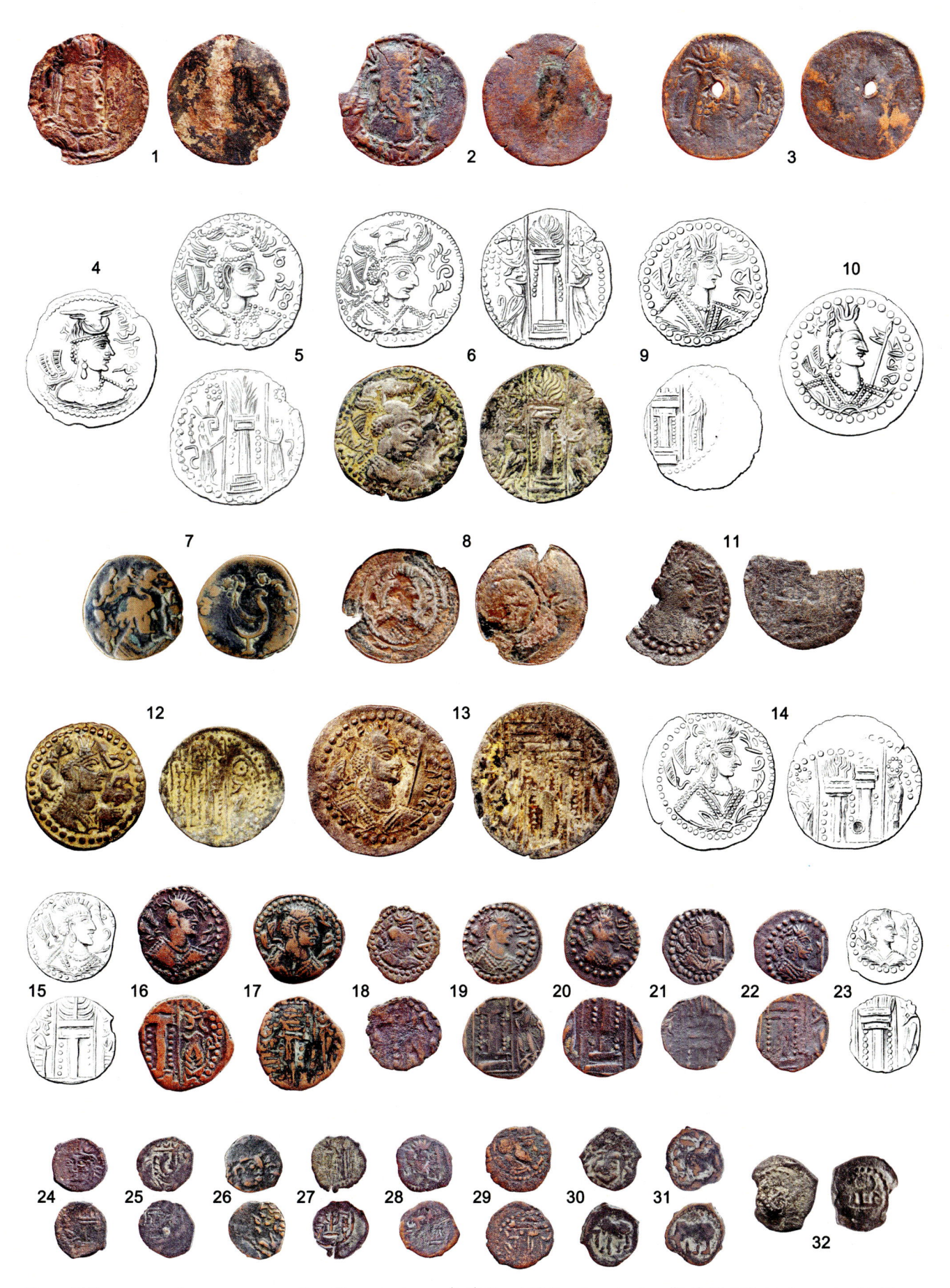

Figure 53 Hun copper alloy anonymous uniface/Narendra issues (1–3). Nezak Malka silver drachms (4–7); Shri Shahi silver coins (9–13); copper alloy coins (8, 14–23); Turkic Shahs (24–31); Zhulād Gōzgān (32)

Catalogue of Coins | 187

three forked crescents and two diadem ribbons attached to the right shoulder. A small Alkhan tamgha ⚵ in the upper left field; a conch and corrupted Pahlavi inscription in the right field. *Reverse*: ⚵ within a double pearl circle, with a star within a crescent at 3 o'clock. Struck partly off flan. 3.68g, 22mm. Vondrovec 2010, p. 183, type 231.

Silver coinage

Fig. 53.9-11. Debased silver drachms in the name of Shri Shahi (*c*. AD 600–50). *Obverse*: Bust of ruler to right, wearing a forked crescent crown and two diadem ribbons; a Brahmi inscription *śrī ṣahi* in the right field. *Reverse*: A fire altar flanked on either side by an attendant. Göbl 1967, type 257–8, pl. 70.

Fig. 53.9. Wilson 1841, p. 400, no. 28, Coins pl. XVII.11. 26mm. Coin not traced.

Fig. 53.10. Wilson 1841, p. 400, no. 29, Coins pl. XXI.20. *Reverse*: obliterated; not illustrated. 28mm. Coin not traced.

Fig. 53.11 – IOLC.4586. Fragment. 1.01g, 24mm.

Fig. 53.12 – 1845,EIC.51. Half drachm (*c*. AD 650–700). *Obverse*: Bust of ruler to right, wearing a forked double-crescent crown and two diadem ribbons attached to the right shoulder. ⚵ in the upper left field and a Brahmi inscription *śrī ṣahi* (lord king?) in the right. *Reverse*: A fire altar comprising three vertical dotted bands; a stylised attendant to right, standing to front, with a dotted circle in place of a head. 2.77g, 24mm. Göbl 1967, type 257, pl. 70. Vondrovec 2014, II, p. 585, type 257.

Fig. 53.13 – 1845,EIC.50. Zabulistan mint (*c*. AD 650–700). *Obverse*: Bust of ruler to right, wearing a forked double-crescent crown and two diadem ribbons attached to the right shoulder; a staff with two pennants in the right field. ⚵ in the upper left field and a Brahmi inscription *śrī ṣahi* in the right. *Reverse*: A fire altar comprising three vertical dotted bands topped by two rectangles each divided into three tiers, flanked on either side by an attendant. 3.34g, 30mm. Göbl 1967, type 252, pl. 68. Vondrovec 2014, II, p. 581, type 252.

Copper alloy coinage

Fig. 53.14. Wilson 1841, p. 403, no. 36, Coins pl. XVII.10. Pierced drachm (*c*. AD 600–20). *Obverse*: Bust of ruler to the right, wearing a crown of three crescents. ⚵ in the upper left field. Pahlavi inscription *pk' mlk* (corrupt *nycky MLKA*) in the right field. *Reverse*: Double-struck. Fire altar flanked by two attendants, each with a dotted circle for a head. 27mm. Coin not traced. Göbl 1967, type 225; Alram 1999/2000, p. 148, pl. 7.121–2; Vondrovec 2010, p. 182, type 225.

Fig. 53.15–17. Hemi-drachms (*c*. AD 560–620). *Obverse*: Bust of ruler to the right, wearing a crown of three crescents. ⚵ in the upper left field. Pahlavi inscription *pk' mlk* (corrupt *nycky MLKA*) in the right field. *Reverse*: Fire altar flanked on either side by an attendant. Göbl 1967, type 227, pl. 59.

Fig. 53.15. Wilson 1841, p. 403, no. 41, Coins pl. XVII.17. 17mm. Coin not traced.

Fig. 53.16 – IOLC.4550. 3.75g, 19mm.

Fig. 53.17 – IOLC.4559. 3.28g, 18mm.

Total 20 coins (Göbl 1967, type 227, pl. 59): 4.18g–4.02g (3), 3.75g–3g (9), 2.99g–2.48g (3), 0.9g–0.62g (5).

Total 10 coins (Göbl 1967, type 231, pl. 61). 2.48g–2.24g (2), 1.92g–1.04g (7), 0.55g (1).

Fig. 53.18 – IOLC.4580. *Obverse*: Bust of ruler to right, wearing a crown of crescents. ⚵ in the upper left field. Bactrian inscription (abbreviated version) σριο βαυιο (*śrī ṣahi*) in the right field. *Reverse*: Illegible (fire altar with attendants). 1.07g, 15mm; Göbl 1967, type 248, pl. 65.

Total 8 coins: 3.04g (1), 1.45g–1.07g (2), 0.98g–0.44g (5).

Fig. 53.19–20. *Obverse*: Bust of ruler to right, wearing a crown of three crescents. ⚵ in the upper left field. Brahmi inscription *śrī ṣahi* in the right field. *Reverse*: Fire altar with attendants (the die used is designed for a larger flan). Göbl 1967, type 257–8, pl. 70.

Fig. 53.19 – IOLC.4587. 1.67g, 16mm.

Fig. 53.20 – IOLC.4594. 1.11g, 16mm.

Total 9 coins: 1.67g–1.01g.

Fig. 53.21–3. Uninscribed. *Obverse*: Bust of ruler to right, wearing crown of crescents, facing a sceptre with two short pennants. ⚵ in the upper left field. *Reverse*: Fire altar with attendants. Göbl 1967, type 253, pl. 69.

Fig. 53.21 – IOLC.4601. 1.31g, 15mm.

Fig. 53.22 – IOLC.4606. 1.01g, 15mm.

Fig 53.23. Wilson 1841, p. 403, no. 41, Coins pl. XVII.18. Coin not traced.

Total 14 coins: 1.59g–1.01g (12), 0.97g–0.75g (2).

Turkic Shahs

Fig. 53.24 – IOLC.4542. *Obverse*: Crowned bust to front. Brahmi inscription. *Reverse*: Fire altar with flames. 0.7g, 12mm. Nasim Khan *et al.* 2008, pp. 616–17; type 655.

Fig. 53.25 – IOLC.4543. *Obverse*: Crowned bust turned three-quarters to right, holding sceptre before him. Brahmi inscription. *Reverse*: Schematic fire altar with flames; worn; 0.27g, 11mm. Nasim Khan *et al.* 2008, type 616.

Fig. 53.26 – IOLC.4546. *Obverse*: Head facing to the right. Traces of illegible inscription. *Reverse*: Head facing to the right, stylised; 0.38g, 12mm. Nasim Khan *et al.* 2008, type 660–1; Göbl 1967, type 210, pl. 51.

Fig. 53.27 – IOLC.4545. *Obverse*: Illegible. The type shows s bust of a ruler to right, with forked sceptre in front. Brahmi inscription. *Reverse*: Fire altar with two attendants. 0.32g, 11mm. Nasim Khan *et al.* 2008, type 629–34; Göbl 1993, p. 238, pl. I.13.

Fig. 53.28 – IOLC.4544. *Obverse*: Bust of ruler facing to right, with forked sceptre in front. Brahmi inscription. *Reverse*: Fire altar with two attendants. 0.31g, 12mm. Nasim Khan *et al.* 2008, type 629–34; Göbl 1993, p. 238, pl. I.13.

Fig. 53.29 – IOLC.4547. *Obverse*: Bust of ruler, crowned, facing to the right. Traces of illegible Bactrian inscription (*śrī togino ṣaho*). *Reverse*: Fire altar with attendants. Illegible inscription; 0.62g, 13mm. Nasim Khan *et al.* 2008, type 658; Göbl 1967, type 207, pl. 46.

Total 6 coins, miscellaneous designs: 0.7g–0.27g.

Fig. 53.30–1. *Obverse*: Bust of ruler to left. *Reverse*: Elephant to left. Errington 2010, pp. 149, 158, fig. 4.

Fig. 53.30 – IOLC.4507. 0.18g, 14mm.

Fig. 53.31 – IOLC.4508. 0.55g, 12mm.

Total 3 coins: 0.55g, 0.41g, 0.18g.

Zhulād Gōzgān of Ghar (c. AD 700–7)
Fig. 53.32 – IOLC.4498. *Obverse*: Worn bust of ruler to left. *Reverse*: ☫. 0.76g, 14mm; Göbl 1967, type IV, pl.19.119. See also **Figs 55.1–5, 57.1–2** below.

Sasanian
Fig. 54.1 – 1845,EIC.35. Hemi-drachm of Shapur, son of Papak, local king of Fars (early 3rd century), minted in Persis. *Obverse*: Bust of king to left, wearing a tiara with earflaps and a diadem. Inscribed *šhpwhr[y] MLKA* (king Shapur). *Reverse*: Head of Papak to left, wearing a cap with a diadem and leaf-shaped headdress. Inscribed *BRE bgy p'[pky] MLKA* (son of the lord king Papak). 1.8g, 18mm. Alram 1986, p. 185, no. 655, pl. 22.

Fig. 54.2–24. Silver drachms, bought in Kabul bazaar. *Obverse*: Bust of king to the right, with a beard and large hair bun, wearing a crown surmounted by a globe with diadem ties. *Reverse*: Fire altar with diadem ties, flanked by two attendants: that on the left wears the king's crown; that on the right a crenelated crown. Pahlavi inscriptions.

Narseh (AD 293–303)
Fig. 54.2 – 1845,EIC.1. *Obverse*: King with a tied beard, wearing a lamellar crown. Inscribed *mzdy...h* (the Mazda-worshipping). *Reverse*: Fire altar with two male attendants each holding a rod. 3.66g, 25mm. Alram and Gyselen 2012, II/6a.

Hormizd II (AD 303–9)
Fig. 54.3 – 1845,EIC.2. *Obverse*: King in a winged crown with a bird protome. Inscribed *mzdysn bgy hwrmzdy...MLKAn MLKA 'yr['n]* (the Mazda-worshipping Lord Hormizd, king of kings of the Iranians). *Reverse*: Fire altar surmounted by a frontal bust with head to left in flames and flanked by two male attendants each holding a rod. Pseudo-legend *NWRA [ZY]; h...* 3.44g, 26mm. Alram and Gyselen 2012, Ia/2b, pl. 51, no. A42, p. 370, no. 10.

Shapur II (AD 309–79)
Fig. 54.4–5. *Obverse*: King in a crenelated crown with diadem ties. Inscribed *mzdysn bgy šhpwhry MLKAn MLKA 'yr'n* (the Mazda-worshipping Lord Shapur, king of kings of the Iranians). *Reverse*: Fire altar surmounted within the flames by the royal bust, head to right, and flanked by two male attendants each holding a rod. Inscribed *šhpwhry* (? Shapur); *l'st* (righteous) on altar shaft.

Fig. 54.4. Wilson 1841, p. 396, no. 5, Coins pl. XVI.1. 26mm. Coin not traced.

Fig. 54.5. Wilson 1841, p. 396, no. 6, Coins pl. XVI.2. Hemi-drachm. 12mm. Coin not traced.

Shapur III (AD 383–8)
Fig. 54.6. Wilson 1841, p. 396, no. 6, Coins pl. XVI.2. *Obverse*: King in a flat-topped crown with diadem ties. Inscribed *mzdysn bgy šhpwhry ZY MLKAn MLK[A 'yr'n]* (Mazda-worshipping Lord Shapur, king of kings of the Iranians). *Reverse*: Fire altar surmounted within the flames by the royal bust, head to right, and flanked by two male attendants each holding a rod. Inscribed *šhpwhry 'twy ZY* (fire of Shapur); *l'st* (righteous) on altar shaft. 25mm. Coin not traced.

Varhran IV (AD 388–99)
Fig. 54.7 – 1845,EIC.7. *Obverse*: King with a tied beard, wearing a crenelated crown with two wings; diadem ties rising from the shoulder. Inscribed *wlhl'n MLKAn MLKA* (Varhran king of kings). *Reverse*: Fire altar with fluted column; throne with schematised lion paws on incense burners; diadems. Inscribed *'twry [ZY] wlhl'n* (fire of Varhran). 4.07g, 23mm. Schindel 2004, Ia2/1a.

Yazdagird I (AD 399–420)
Fig. 54.8 – 1845,EIC.6. Pierced with two holes. *Obverse*: King in a crenelated crown, with a crescent above the forehead surmounted by a globe. Diadem ties above the crown and also rising from the shoulder. Inscribed *mzdsn [bgy l'mštly] yzdklty MLKAn MLKA* (Yazdagird king of kings). *Reverse*: Fire altar with diadem ties, flanked by two attendants, each with a diadem tie falling from shoulder and holding a rod with both hands. Legend unclear ...['twly]? 3.64g, 24mm. Schindel 2004, Ib2/1a.

Fig. 54.9. Wilson 1841, p. 396, no. 8, Coins pl. XVI.4. Clipped drachm. *Obverse*: King wearing a crown with a crenelation to the side and a crescent above the forehead. Inscription off flan. 19mm. Coin not traced. Schindel 2004, Ib1/1a.

Varhran V (AD 420–38)
Fig. 54.10 – 1845,EIC.10. Pierced. *Obverse*: King wearing a crown with a crescent and globe between two crenelations; a diadem attached to the shoulder. Pseudo-legend (?) ...*l'n ML ...* *Reverse*: Fire altar surmounted by royal bust within the flames, head to right, and flanked by two crowned attendants. Inscribed *A[Y]?* (mint: Erran-Khvarrah-Shabuhr) *wlhw*. 3.65g, 27mm. Schindel 2004, Ib1/2.

Yazdagird II (AD 438–57)
Fig. 54.11–13. *Obverse*: King wearing a crenelated crown with diadem ties, crescent and globe above; and a large diadem tie rising from the shoulder. Inscribed 11h: *mzdysn bgy kdy yzdkrty* (the Mazda-worshipping king Yazdagird). *Reverse*: Fire altar with diadem ties flanked by two attendants wearing crenelated crowns, each holding a long rod in both hands.

Fig. 54.11 – 1845,EIC.8. *Reverse*: Inscribed *yzdk[rty] nwky* (Yazdagird the adorer). On altar shaft: *l's[t]* (the just). 3.8g, 29mm. Schindel 2004, Ib1/2b.

Fig. 54.12 – 1845,EIC.9. *Obverse*: partly illegible inscription: *kdy yzdkrty* (king Yazdagird). *Reverse*: inscribed *nwky* (the adorer). *AW* (mint Ohrmazd-Ardaxshir). Illegible letters on the altar shaft. 3.23g, 27mm. Schindel 2004, Ib1/2a.

Fig. 54.13 – IOC.440. *Reverse*: Inscribed *yzdkr* (Yazdagird). *WH* (mint Veh-Ardaxshir?). On altar shaft: *l's[t]* (the just). 4.06g, 27mm. **F526/1a, Pl. 12.32**; Wilson 1841, p. 397, no. 9, Coins pl. XVI.5. Schindel 2004, Ib1/2a.

Peroz (AD 457, 459–84)
Fig. 54.14 – 1845,EIC.11. Gold coin with a broken tang for use as a pendant. *Obverse*: King in a crenelated crown with a wing to each side and a crescent to front; a diadem tie behind each shoulder. Pseudo-legend. *Reverse*: Fire altar with

Figure 54 Sasanian silver coins. Shapur son of Papak (1), Narseh (2); Hormizd II (3); Shapur II (4–5); Shapur III (6); Varhran IV (7); Yazdagird I (8–9); Varhran V (10); Yazdagird II (11–13); Peroz gold coin (14); Kavad (15); Khusrau I (16); Khusrau II (17–22)

diadem ties, flanked by two attendants. Star to left, crescent to right. Inscribed pseudo-legend; *BBA* (itinerant court mint). 0.83g, 11mm. Göbl 1971, III/1; Schindel 2004, IIIb/1c.

Kavad I (1st reign AD 488–96)
Fig. 54.15. Wilson 1841, p. 397, no. 12, Coins pl. XVI.6. *Obverse*: King in a crenelated crown with a crescent to front, a diademed globe and crescent above; a diadem rising from both shoulders. Inscribed *kw'[t]* (Kavad). *Reverse*: Fire altar with diadem ties, flanked by star and crescent moon (upper left and right fields) and two attendants. Inscribed *GW* (mint Gurgan or Qum?); *kw't* (Kavad). 26mm. Coin not traced.

Khusrau I (AD 531–75)
Fig. 54.16 – 1845,EIC.14. *Obverse*: King in a crown with two crenelations and a crescent to front, a diademed globe and crescent above. Three crescent symbols in the outer margin. Inscribed *'pzwn*; *hwslwb* (increase Khusrau). *Reverse*: Fire altar with upturned diadem ties, flanked by two crowned attendants to front, each holding staff. Star to left, crescent moon to right of flames. Inscribed *ML* (Merv mint) *chlchl* (regnal year 44: *c.* AD 574). 4.01g, 32mm. Göbl 1971, II/2.

Khusrau II (AD 591–628)
The group of silver coins donated by the East India Company to the British Museum in 1845 (1845,EIC.1–59) appear to have included part of a large hoard comprising Khusrau II drachms and Arab-Sasanian issues, some with Hun countermarks (see **Table 23**).

Fig. 54.17–22. *Obverse*: King in a cap and crenelated crown surmounted by wings with a star and crescent above. A diadem rises above each shoulder. Two rings; three star and crescent symbols in outer margin. Inscribed *'pzwty GDH hwslwb* (Khusrau has increased the royal glory). *Reverse*: Fire altar with upturned diadem ties. Two crowned attendants to front. Star to left, crescent moon to right of flames. Three rings; four star and crescent symbols in outer margin. Pahlavi inscription: mint and regnal year. Göbl 1971, II/3.

Fig. 54.17 – 1845,EIC.19. Clipped. *Reverse*: Inscribed *WYH* (mint Veh-Kavad or Veh-Ardashir?); *hptwysty* (regnal year 27: *c.* AD 616). 2.48g, 28mm.

Fig. 54.18 – 1845,EIC.27. Clipped. *Reverse*: Inscribed *MY* (mint: near Arraiān) *ch'lwysty* (regnal year 24: *c.* AD 613). 2.46g, 25mm. **Table 23, no. 12**.

Fig. 54.19 – 1845,EIC.38. *Reverse*: Inscribed *WH* (mint Veh-Ardashir?); *hptwysty* (regnal year 27: *c.* AD 616). 3.9g, 30mm. **Table 23, no. 29**.

Fig. 54.20–1. *Obverse*: Inscribed *'pzwty*; *GDH*; *hwslwb* (Khusrau has increased the royal glory); *'pd* (praise).

Fig. 54.20 – 1845,EIC.33. *Reverse*: Inscribed *DA* (mint Darabgird) *nwcwysty* (regnal year 29: *c.* AD 618). 4.06g, 31mm. **Table 23, no. 10**.

Fig. 54.21 – 1845,EIC.30. *Reverse*: *ART* (mint Ardashir-Khurrah) *y'csyh*.(regnal year 31: *c.* AD 620). 3.36g, 29mm. **Table 23, no. 5**.

Fig. 54.22 – IOC.509. Clipped. *Reverse*: *GD* (mint Jayy, Jibal) *ššsyh* (regnal year 36: *c.* AD 625). 1.94g, 23mm. F526/1a, Pl. 12.40. **Table 23, no. 26**.

Total 6 coins: 4.06g (1), 3.9g–3.3g (2), 2.48–2.46g (2), 1.94g (1).

Yazdagird III (AD 632–51)
Fig. 55.1 – IOC.537. *Obverse*: King in crenelated crown with wings and globe above. Inscribed *'pzwty GDH yzdkrty* (Yazdagird has increased the royal glory). *Reverse*: Fire altar with upturned diadem ties. Two attendants standing to front, each holding a staff. Inscribed *SK* (mint Sakastan); *ŠTA* (regnal year 6: *c.* AD 637). 4.06g, 33mm. Wilson 1841, p. 401, no. 31, Coins pl. XVII.1. Göbl 1971, I/1.

Zhulād Gōzgān of Ghar countermarked Khusrau II coins (c. AD 700–7)
Fig. 55.2–5. *Obverse*: King in a cap and crenelated crown surmounted by wings, with a star and crescent above. A diadem rises above each shoulder. Two rings; three star and crescent symbols in the outer margin. Inscribed *'pzwty GDH hwslwb* (Khusrau has increased the royal glory). *Reverse*: Fire altar with upturned diadem ties. Two crowned attendants to front. Star to left, crescent moon to right of flames. Three rings; four star and crescent symbols in outer margin. Pahlavi inscription: mint and regnal year. Göbl 1971, II/3.

Fig. 55.2 – IOC.517. *Obverse*: Inscribed *'pd* (praise). Four countermarks. *Reverse*: Inscribed *BYŠ* (mint Bishapur) *ch'lwysty* (regnal year 24: *c.* AD 613). 3.84g, 31mm. Göbl 1967, vol. IV, pl. 11, marks 3, 14, 39. **Table 23, no. 7**.

Fig. 55.3 – 1845,EIC.31. *Obverse*: Countermark. *Reverse*: Inscribed *MY* (mint near Arrajān) *pncwysty* (regnal year 25: *c.* AD 614). 4.02g, 32mm. Göbl 1967, vol. IV, pl. 11, mark 39. **Table 23, no. 13**.

Fig. 55.4 – 1845,EIC.18. *Obverse*: Six countermarks. *Reverse*: Inscribed *GD* (mint Jayy) *pncsyh* (regnal year 35: *c.* AD 624). 3.45g, 31mm. Göbl 1967, vol. IV, pl. 8, marks 2, 12 (x 2), 21 (x 2), 39. **Table 23, no. 25**.

Fig. 55.5 – 1845,EIC.26. *Obverse*: Two countermarks. *Reverse*: Inscribed *PY* (mint not identified) *syh* (regnal year 30: *c.* AD 619). 3.92g, 33mm. Göbl 1967, vol. IV, pl. 8, marks 14, 39. **Table 23, no. 30**.

Total 4 coins: 4.02g (1), 3.92g–3.45g (3).

Arab-Sasanian (7th century)

Silver drachms of Arab governors copying Sasanian issues of Khusrau II (AD 591–628).
Fig. 55.6–10). *Obverse*: Bust of Sasanian king to right, wearing crenelated crown with wings, crescent and star. Two rings; inscribed in Arabic, with crescent and star symbols in the outer field. *Reverse*: Fire altar flanked by two attendants. Three rings, crescent and star symbols. Date in Pahlavi in the left field; mint signature in Arabic in the right.

Fig. 55.6 – 1845,EIC.36. Silver drachm of an anonymous Arab governor. *Obverse*: Two countermarks. *Reverse*: Inscribed *BYŠ* (mint Bishapur) AH 49 (Yazdagird year 49: AD 680). 3.81g, 31mm. Walker 1941, p. 21.32. Göbl 1967, vol. IV, pl. 8, marks 3, 14. **Table 23, no. 38**.

'Ubaydallāh b. Ziyād (c. AH 52–62 / AD 672–82)
Fig. 55.7 – IOC.2315. *Obverse*: Countermark. *Reverse*: Inscribed *KRMANHP* (mint Kirman) AH 60 (AD 679). 3.99g, 32mm. Wilson 1841, p. 402, no. 33, Coins pl. XVII.3. Göbl 1967, vol. IV, pl. 8, mark 14. **Table 23, no. 50**.

Figure 55 Silver drachms. Sasanian Yazdagird III (1). Turkic Shah Zhulād Gōzgān countermarked Khusrau II (2–5). Arab-Sasanian governors copying Khusrau II: anonymous (6), 'Ubaydallāh b. Ziyād (7–9), Salm b. Ziyād (10–15)

Fig. 55.8 – 1845,EIC.20. *Reverse*: Inscribed *DA* (mint Darabgird) AH 63 (Yazdagird year 51: AD 682). 4.17g, 29mm. Walker 1941, p. 63.91. **Table 23, no. 52**.

Fig. 55.9 – 1845,EIC.46. *Obverse*: Countermark. *Reverse*: Inscribed *WH* (mint not identified) AH 60 (AD 679). 4.01g, 32mm. Walker 1941, p.67.98. Göbl 1967, vol. IV, pl. 8, mark 39. **Table 23, no. 54**.

Salm b. Ziyād (c. AH 60–3 / AD 680–3)

Fig. 55.10 – 1845,EIC.16. *Obverse*: Three countermarks. *Reverse*: Inscribed *APRŠT* (mint Abrashahr) AH 64 (AD 683). 4.06g, 31mm. Walker 1941, p. 74.111. Göbl 1967, vol. IV, pl. 8, marks 14, 47, 51. **Table 23, no. 63**.

Fig. 55.11 – 1845,EIC.49. *Obverse*: Five countermarks (one illegible). *Reverse*: Inscribed *APRŠT* (mint Abrashahr) AH 64 (AD 683). 3.95g, 32mm. Walker 1941, p. 74.110. Göbl 1967, vol. IV, pl. 8, marks 14, 27, 47, 51. **Table 23, no. 64**.

Fig. 55.12 – 1845,EIC.22. *Obverse*: Three countermarks. *Reverse*: Inscribed *HRA* (mint Haraat) AH 67 (AD 686). 4.06g, 32mm. Walker 1941, p. 76.115. Göbl 1967, vol. IV, pl. 8, marks 38 (x 2), 39 (?). **Table 23, no. 65**.

Fig. 55.13 – 1845,EIC.32. *Obverse*: Two countermarks. *Reverse*: Inscribed *HRA* (mint Haraat) AH 67 (AD 686). 4.08g, 32mm. Walker 1941, p. 76.116. Göbl 1967, vol. IV, pl. 8, marks 14, 33. **Table 23, no. 66**.

Fig. 55.14 – 1845,EIC.39. Clipped. *Reverse*: Inscribed *MRW* (mint Merv) AH 63 (AD 682). 1.69g, 22mm. Walker 1941, p. 79.131. **Table 23, no. 70**.

Fig. 55.15 – 1845,EIC.41. *Obverse*: Two countermarks ? . *Reverse*: Inscribed *MRW* (mint Merv) AH 63 (AD 682). 3.71g, 34mm. Walker 1941, p. 78.126. Göbl 1967, vol. IV, pl. 8, marks 12, 39. **Table 23, no. 71**.

Fig. 56.1 – 1845,EIC.23. *Obverse*: Two countermarks. *Reverse*: Inscribed *MRW* (mint Merv) AH 64 (AD 683). 4.04g, 34mm. Walker 1941, p.79.134. Göbl 1967, vol. IV, pl. 8, marks 14, 39. **Table 23, no. 73**.

Fig. 56.2. *Obverse*: One countermark. *Reverse*: Inscribed *MRW* (mint Merv) AH 67 (AD 686). 33mm. Wilson 1841, pp. 401–2, no. 32, Coins pl. XVII.2. Göbl 1967, vol. IV, pl. 8, mark 39. Coin not traced. **Table 23, no. 78**.

Fig. 56.3 – 1845,EIC.25. *Obverse*: Three countermarks. *Reverse*: Inscribed *MRW* (mint Merv) AH 69 (AD 688). 4.09g, 33mm. Walker 1941, p. 81.141. Göbl 1967, vol. IV, pl. 8, marks 39, 47, 51. **Table 23, no. 79**.

Fig. 56.4 – 1845,EIC.42. *Obverse*: Three countermarks. *Reverse*: Inscribed *MRW* (mint Merv) AH 69 (AD 688). 3.99g, 33mm. Walker 1941, p. 81.139. Göbl 1967, vol. IV, pl. 8, marks 39, 47, 51. **Table 23, no. 80**.

Fig. 56.5 – 1845,EIC.43. *Obverse*: Two countermarks ? . *Reverse*: Inscribed *MRW* (mint Merv) c. AH 62–70 (uncertain date). 3.19g, 32mm. Walker 1941, p. 82.144. Göbl 1967, vol. IV, pl. 8, marks 7 (?), 16. **Table 23, no. 82**.

Fig. 56.6 – 1845,EIC.15. *Obverse*: Two countermarks. *Reverse*: Inscribed *DA* (mint Darabgird) (regnal year 26; AH 58/AD 677). 3.66g, 33mm. Walker 1941, p. 75.114. Göbl 1967, vol. IV, pl. 8, marks 14, 39. **Table 23, no. 91**.

Total 11 coins: 4.09g–4.04g (5), 3.99g–3.19g, 1.69g (1).

Muṣʻab b. al-Zubayr (c. AH 70 / AD 690)

Fig. 56.7 – 1845,EIC.37. *Reverse*: Inscribed *KRMĀN* (mint Kirman) AH 71 (AD 690). 3.87g, 31mm. Walker 1941, p. 104.207. **Table 23, no. 96**.

ʻAbdallāh b. Khāzim (c. AH 64–73 / AD 684–92)

Fig. 56.8 – 1845,EIC.28. *Obverse*: Two countermarks. *Reverse*: Inscribed *BBA* (Khurasan camp mint) AH 67 (AD 686). 3.47g, 32mm. Walker 1941, p. 89.161. Göbl 1967, vol. IV, pl. 8, marks 20, 21. **Table 23, no. 101**.

Fig. 56.9 – 1845,EIC.48. *Reverse*: Inscribed *BBA* (Khurasan camp mint) AH 68 (AD 687). 4.00g, 31mm. Walker 1941, p. 89.163. **Table 23, no. 105**.

Fig. 56.10 – 1845,EIC.24. *Obverse*: 3 countermarks. *Reverse*: Inscribed *MRW* (mint Merv) AH 69 (AD 688). 4.32g, 34mm. Walker 1941, p. 93.177. Göbl 1967, vol. IV, pl. 8, marks 13, 33, 39. **Table 23, no. 111**.

ʻUmar b. ʻUbaydallāh (c. AH 67–72 / AD 687–92)

Fig. 56.11 – 1845,EIC.21. *Obverse*: Two countermarks. *Reverse*: Inscribed *KRMAN* (mint Kirman) AH 65 (AD 684). 4.07g, 30mm. Walker 1941, p. 101.203. Göbl 1967, vol. IV, pl. 8, mark 14 x 2. **Table 23, no. 122**.

Fig. 56.12 – 1845,EIC.45. *Obverse*: Two countermarks. *Reverse*: Inscribed *BYŠ* (mint Bishapur) AH 70 (AD 689). 4.09g, 31mm. Walker 1941, p. 100.199. Göbl 1967, vol. IV, pl. 8, marks 7, 14. **Table 23, no. 129**.

Fig. 56.13 – 1845,EIC.47. *Obverse*: Countermark. *Reverse*: Inscribed *BYŠ* (mint Bishapur) AH 70 (AD 689). 3.85g, 31mm. Walker 1941, p. 100.198. Göbl 1967, vol. IV, mark 14. **Table 23, no. 130**.

Zhulād Gōzgān of Ghar (c. AD 700–7)

Fig. 57.1–2. Silver drachm of Zhulād Gōzgān, ruler of the kingdom of Ghar, copying Sasanian issues of Khusrau II. *Obverse*: Bust of king to right, wearing a crown with wings, crescent and star; a diadem behind the right shoulder, a crescent and star on the left shoulder. Pahlavi inscription in the left field *'pzwt GDH* (*farr apzut*: may his splendour increase); Bactrian in the right ζολαδο γωζογανο (zolado gōzogano). In the outer margin, a star and crescent at each quarter point; in the upper right quarter; Pahlavi inscription in the lower left quarter and Arabic *bismillāh* (in the name of God) in the lower right. *Reverse*: Fire-altar with upturned diadem ties, flanked by two attendants. Inscribed AH 68 (AD 688) in the left field; mint signature *ANBYR* / αμβηρο (Anbēr) in the right. Bactrian inscription in outer margin γαριγο þαυο αμβηρο (*garigo šauo ambēro*: king of Ghar/king of the mountains Anbēr), with crescent and star marking the four quarters.

Fig. 57.1 – 1845 5,EIC.34. 3.79g, 32mm. Walker 1941, p. 129.250; Thomas 1858, p. 77.70. **Table 23, no. 147**.

Fig. 57.2 – IOC.2358. 3.73g, 33mm. Wilson 1841, p. 402, no. 34, pl. XVII.4; Walker 1941, p. 128.249; Göbl 1967, vol. IV, pl. 73, type 277.1, pl. 17, mark 71; Davary 1982 pp.102–3, NumH 277/1. **Table 23, no. 151**.

Turkic rulers (c. 8th century)

Fig. 57.3 – IOC.2380. Silver drachm issued in the name of Spur, ruler of Zabulistan and Swat (c. AD 746–53), copying

Catalogue of Coins | 193

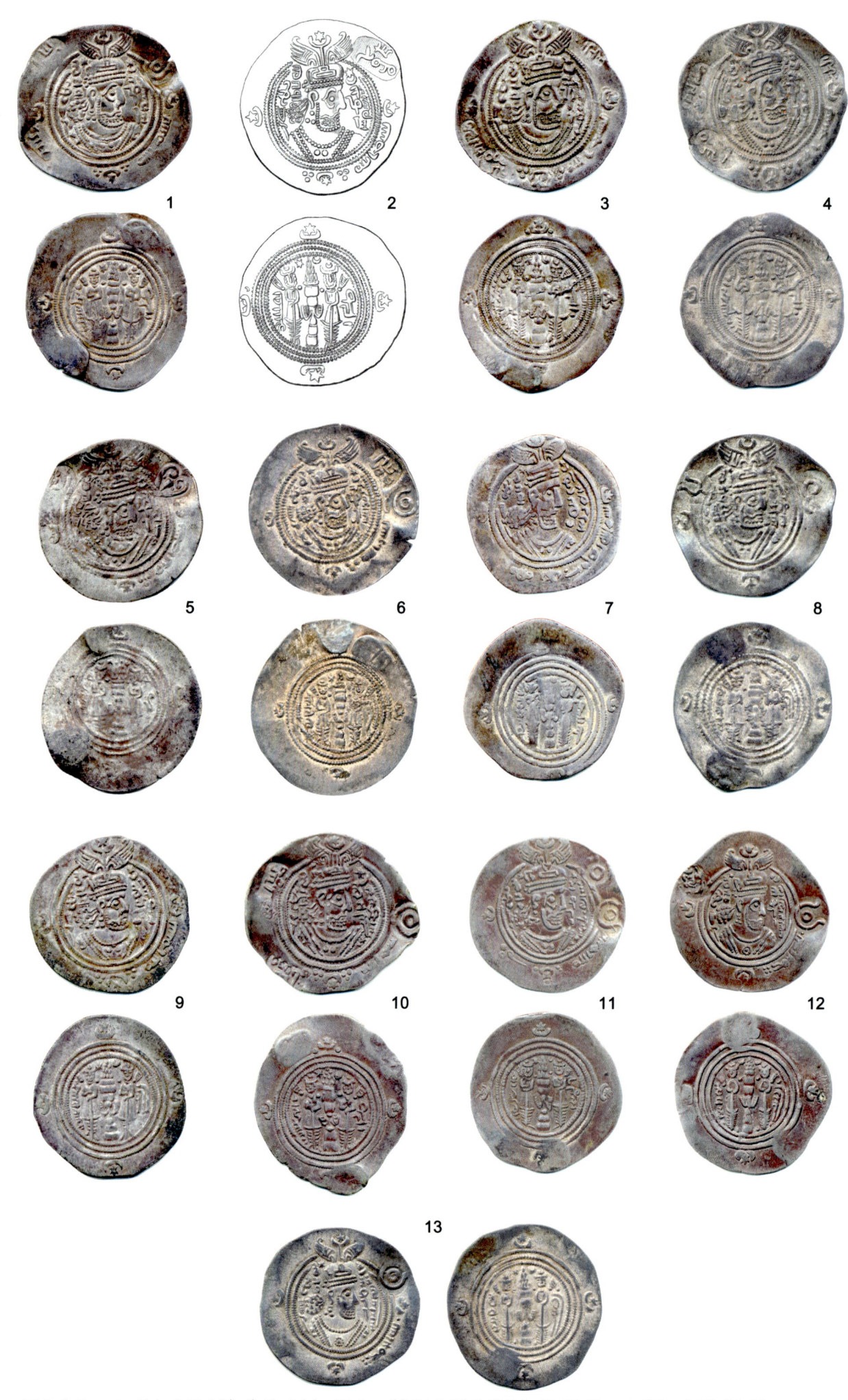

Figure 56 Arab-Sasanian Salm b. Ziyād (1–6), Muṣʻab b. al-Zubayr (7), ʻAbdallāh b. Khāzim (8–10), ʻUmar b. ʻUbaydallāh (11–13)

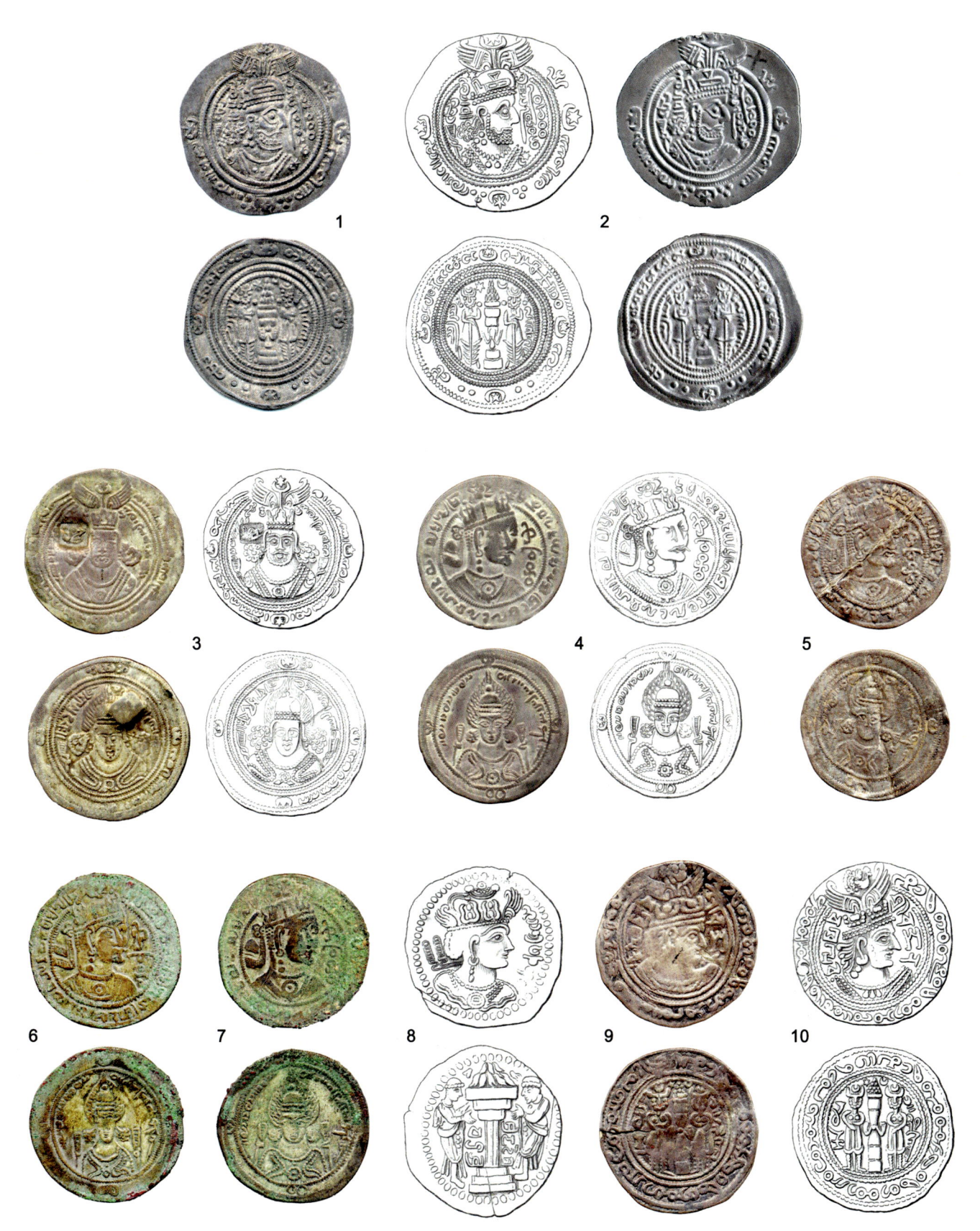

Figure 57 Turki Shahi coins. Zhulād Gōzgān (1–2), Spur (3), Tegin (4–8), Sandan (9–10)

Catalogue of Coins | 195

coins of the Sasanian king Khusrau II (AD 591–628). *Obverse*: Facing bust of a king wearing a crenelated and winged crown with a crescent and star above, and a senmurv in the field to the left of the head. A Pahlavi inscription is ranged on either side of the head *GDH 'pzwt / spwr hwt'p* (may his splendour increase / Spur the ruler), with another inscription in the outer margin *PWN ŠM Y yzdt' whm'n' mrt'n MLKA* (In the name of god, Wahmānāz, king of Mardin). Countermarked in the left field with a senmurv's head. *Reverse*: Bust of Adur to front, with rayed flames ascending to a point. The raised rectangle made by the obverse countermark obliterates part of the head and the Pahlavi inscription in the upper right field *pndh z'wlst'n* (year 15, Zabulistan). In the upper left field is a Brahmi inscription *śrī vāsudevaḥ*. The outer margin contains a Pahlavi inscription in the lower right quarter *splclm'nš'n* (meaning unclear). 3.29g, 30mm. Wilson 1841, p. 400, no. 27, Coins pl. XVII.9; Göbl 1967, pl. 52, type 216.7; Gyselen 2010; Vondrovec 2014, vol. II, p. 669, type 216).

Fig. 57.4–8. Base silver drachm of Tegin (*c.* AD 706–39). *Obverse*: Bust of crowned king to right. Bactrian inscription to right σρι þαυο (*śrī šauo*: his perfection, king); the whole encircled by a Brahmi inscription *śrī-hitivira kharalāva pārame śvara śrī ṣahi tiginadeva kārita* (his perfection Iltäbär of the Khalaj, devotee of the highest divinity, the perfect (?) king, the Shahi Tegin Lord had made this). *Reverse*: Bust of Adur (Vondrovec 2014) to front, with rayed flames ascending to a point; encircled by a Pahlavi inscription: *hpt'hpt't' – tkyn' hwl's'n MLKA* ([year] 77 [post Yazdagird era = AD 728/9?] Tegin king of Khorasan). Göbl 1967, pp. 342–3, type 208, pls 47–51; Alram 2016, p. 137, no. 6; Vondrovec 2014, II, p. 656, type 208.

Fig. 57.4 – IOC.2361. 3.38g, 29mm. Wilson 1841, p. 400, no. 30, Coins pl. XXI.22. 1836 collection, Kabul bazaar.

Fig. 57.5 – 1845,EIC.55. Cracked in half. 3.18g, 28mm.

Fig. 57.6 – 1845,EIC.56. 3.33g, 29mm.

Fig. 57.7 – 1845,EIC.57. 3.37g, 29mm.

Fig. 57.8. Wilson 1841, p. 402, no. 35, Coins pl. XVII.6. Base silver drachm of Tegin (*c.* AD 706–39). *Obverse*: Bust of ruler to right, wearing a winged and diademed crown. Bactrian inscription σρι τογινο þαυο (*śrī togino šauo*) in the right field. *Reverse*: Fire altar flanked by two attendants. Brahmi inscription *śriya devi* to right of altar shaft, *manjuśri* (lady goddess Manjusri) to left. 30mm. Coin not traced. Göbl 1967, type 206.

Fig. 57.9–10. Silver drachm of Sandan (*c.* AD 700–50), copying late issues of the Sasanian king Khusrau II. *Obverse*: Bust of a king to right wearing a crown of two crescents each containing a dot, surmounted by a pair of wings, with a senmurv head above. Brahmi inscription on either side of the head *śrī candāna / vakhudevaḥ* (his perfection Sandana, Lord of the Oxus). Bactrian inscription in the outer margin σρι βαγο αζροβιδιγο σανδαυο βαγο χοαδηο (his perfection, the Lord, the Chiliarch Sandano, the Lord Ruler). *Reverse*: Stylised fire altar flanked by two facing female attendants. Pahlavi inscription in the upper left and right fields *'pzwn'* (increase) / *pwn GDH* (from glory …). Bactrian inscription in the outer margin σρι βαγο δδηβο βαγδδιγγο καγανο σρι βαγι (his perfection, the Lord, his Majesty, the Bactrian Kagan, his perfection, the Lord). Göbl 1967, pp. 166–8, Coins pl. 66, type 244.3; Davary 1982, pp. 99–100, NumH 244/1–16. Vondrovec 2014, II, p. 243, type 244. Sims-Williams 2010, p. 214, no. 412.

Fig. 57.9 – IOC.2367. 3.39g, 31mm. **F526/1a, f. 25, Pl. 12**, *Fig. 36*.

Fig. 57.10. Wilson 1841, p. 400, no. 26, Coins pl. XVII.8: one of two examples in the 1833–5 Masson collection.

Turkic Kabul Shahi/Hindu Shahi

Masson records Hindu Shahi coins in his 'Class Brahmanical' along with post Shahi and Islamic issues utilising bull and horseman imagery as 'the types of a species of coin numerously found in Afghanistan – they are either silver, billon or copper' (**F526/1a, f. 23, Pl. 11.1–10**).

> The silver coins are to be always procured in the bazaar of Kabul, and in quantity or in parcels of many, occasionally one or two have been picked up at Begram, where the copper coins occur freely as they do at Jalalabad.

The collection now has only five silver jitals: two with the title Spalapatideva, three with the title Samantadeva, and two silver-plated contemporary forgeries.

Spalapatideva (c. AD 750–850)

Fig. 58.1–4. Silver jitals. *Obverse*: Humped bull seated to left, with a trident on its rump. Devanagari legend *śrī spalapatideva* above. *Reverse*: Mounted horseman to right, holding a standard, with traces of Bactrian inscription σρι σπαλαβιδο to right. Control marks in the upper left and upper right fields. Procured in Kabul bazaar.

Fig. 58.1 – IOC.795. *Reverse*: ✠ in the upper left field; ✹ in the upper right. 3.06g, 18mm. Wilson 1841, p. 429, no. 6, Coins pl. XIX.6. Tye 1995, p. 90, no. 7.

Fig. 58.2 *Reverse*: ⅓ in the upper left field; ✹ in the upper right. 18mm. Coin not traced. Wilson 1841, p. 429, no. 8, Coins pl. XIX.8. Tye 1995, p. 89, no. 6.

Fig. 58.3. *Reverse*: ⲍ in the upper left field; ✹ in the upper right. 18mm. Coin not traced. Wilson 1841, p. 429, no. 9, Coins pl. XIX.9. Tye 1995, p. 89, no. 6.

Fig. 58.4 – IOC.814. *Reverse*: ⲍ in the upper left field; ✹ in the upper right. 3.10g, 18mm. Wilson 1841, p. 429, no. 7, Coins pl. XIX.7. Tye 1995, p. 89, no. 6.

Fig. 58.5–7. Copper alloy coins. *Obverse*: Humped bull seated to left. Devanagari legend *śrī spalapatideva* above. *Reverse*: Mounted horseman to right, holding a standard.

Fig. 58.5 – IOLC.4649. 3.25g, 18mm.
Fig. 58.6 – IOLC.4652. 2.28g, 18mm.
Fig. 58.7. Wilson 1841, p. 430, no. 13, Coins pl. XIX.13. Corrupt legend (?) 20mm. Coin not traced.
Total 4 coins: 3.25g–3.15g (2), 2.7g–2.28g (2).

Pala... (c. AD 850–1000)

Fig. 58.8–11. *Obverse*: Humped bull seated to left, with a trident on its rump. Devanagari legend *śrī pala…* above. *Reverse*: Mounted horseman to right, holding a sword in his raised left hand.

Fig. 58.8 – IOLC.5672. 1.21g, 14mm. Horseman to left.
Fig. 58.9 – IOLC.5673. 1.06g, 13mm.
Fig. 58.10 – IOLC.5674. 1.07g, 12mm.

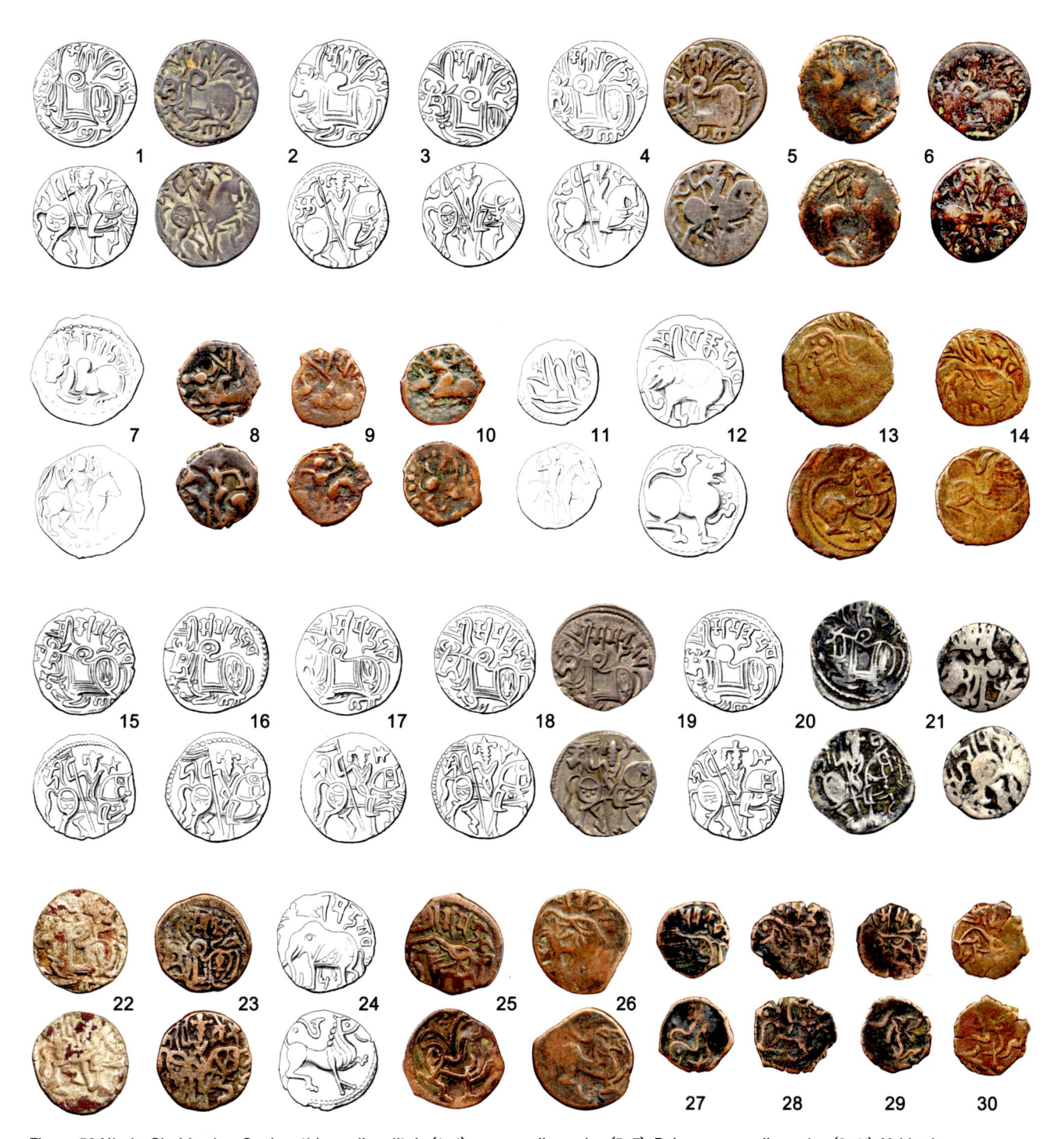

Figure 58 Hindu-Shahi coins. Spalapatideva silver jitals (1–4), copper alloy coins (5–7), Pala... copper alloy coins (8–11), Vakkadeva copper alloy coins (12–14). Samantadeva silver jitals (15–23), silver-plated forgeries (22–3), copper alloy coins (24–6), imitations (27–30)

IOLC.4686. 0.73g, 13mm. Not illustrated.

Fig. 58.11. Wilson 1841, p. 430, no. 14, Coins pl. XIX.14. 15mm. Coin not traced.

Vakkadeva (c. AD 750–870)

Fig. 58.12–14. Copper alloy coins. *Obverse*: Elephant standing to left. Devanagari inscription *śrī vakkadeva*. *Reverse*: Lion standing to right with raised tail.

Fig. 58.12. Wilson 1841, p. 430, no. 12, Coins pl. XIX.12. 20mm. Coin not traced.

Fig. 58.13 – IOLC.4695. *Reverse*: ₹ between the legs. 3.05g, 19mm.

Fig. 58.14 – IOLC.4699. 1.58g, 17mm.

Total 14 coins: 3.63g–3.05g (2), 2.93g–2.22g (7), 1.78g–1.48g (5).

Samantadeva (c. AD 850–900)

Fig. 58.15–23. Silver jitals. *Obverse*: Humped bull seated to left; Devanagari legend *śrī samantadeva* above. *Reverse*: Mounted horseman, holding standard, riding to right. Control marks 🦅 in the upper left field; ✶ in the upper right. Tye 1995, p. 91, no. 14.

Fig. 58.15. Wilson 1841, p. 429, no. 1, Coins pl. XIX.1. 18mm. Coin not traced.

Fig. 58.16. Wilson 1841, p. 429, no. 2, Coins pl. XIX.2. 19mm. Coin not traced.

Fig. 58.17. Wilson 1841, p. 429, no. 3, Coins pl. XIX.3. 20mm. Coin not traced.

Fig. 58.18 – IOC.863. 2.92g, 18mm. Wilson 1841, p. 429, no. 4, Coins pl. XIX.4.

Catalogue of Coins | 197

Fig. 58.19. Wilson 1841, p. 429, no. 5, Coins pl. XIX.5. 18mm. Coin not traced.
Fig. 58.20 – IOLC.4654. *Reverse*: 5 in the upper right field. 2.83g, 19mm.
Fig. 58.21 – IOLC.4656. *Reverse*: Control mark in the right field not visible. 3g, 16mm.

Silver-plated copper alloy contemporary forgeries
Fig. 58.22 – IOLC.4655. Silver flaked off with patches of copper visible. Inscription and control marks not legible. 3.24g, 18mm.
Fig. 58.23 – IOLC.4657. Traces of worn silver still visible. 3.1g, 17mm.

Copper alloy coinage
Fig. 58.24–6. *Obverse*: Elephant standing to left. Devanagari inscription *śrī samantadeva*. *Reverse*: Lion standing to right with tail raised. Tye 1995, p. 91, no. 19.
Fig. 58.24. Wilson 1841, p. 430, no. 11, Coins pl. XIX.11. Coin not traced.
Fig. 58.25 – IOLC.4659. 1.61g, 17mm.
Fig. 58.26 – IOLC.4668. 1.09g, 15mm.
Total 8 coins: 2.03g (1), 1.78g–1.09g (6).

Imitations (c. AD 850–1000)
Fig. 58.27–30. Copper alloy coins. *Obverse*: Schematic elephant standing to left. Incomplete Devanagari inscription *śrī samantadeva*. *Reverse*: Schematic lion standing to right with raised tail.
Fig. 58.27 – IOLC.4669. 0.83g, 13mm.
Fig.38.28 – IOLC.4671. 1.1g, 15mm.
Fig.38.29 – IOLC.4679. 0.74g, 13mm.
Fig.38.30 – IOLC.4680. 1.02g, 13mm.
Total 16 coins: 1.1g–1.02g (3), 0.96g–0.49g (13).
Total 9 illegible coins: 1.78g–1.04g (4), 0.96g–0.68g (5).

Miscellaneous stray coins

Later copy of c. 5th–6th century Kashmir coins
Fig. 59.1 – IOC.577. Gold coin, Kashmir. *Obverse*: Crude stylised figure of king standing to left. *Reverse*: Crude stylised figure of Ardochsho seated to front. 5.6g, 21mm. Wilson 1841, p. 427, nos 24–7, Coins pl. XXI.24. Purchased in Kabul bazaar; Masson's 'last collection' dispatched 1836.

Yasovarman of Kanauj (c. AD 713–36)
Fig. 59.2. Gold coin. *Obverse*: Crude stylised figure of king standing to left. *Reverse*: Crude stylised figure of goddess seated to front. 22mm. Wilson 1841, p. 427, nos 24–7, Coins pl. XXI.23. Acquired in Kabul bazaar. Masson's 'last collection' dispatched 1836. Coin not traced.

Indo-Sasanian imitations (c. 8th–11th century)
Debased coins with stylised designs evolved from the Sasanian royal portrait of Peroz with winged crown / fire altar reverse, issued by various dynasties in northern India.

Gurjara-Pratihara (c. 900–1000)
Fig. 59.3 – IOLC.4612. Silver dramma, 'proto-*śrī vigra*' type 2. *Obverse*: Bust of ruler to right; crudely drawn. Illegible Brahmi inscription. *Reverse*: Fire altar with attendant visible to right; 3.18g, 21mm. Maheshwari 2010, pp. 242–3; Mitchiner 1979, p. 57, type 325–34.

Chahamana dynasty (7th–12th century, Rajasthan)
Fig. 59.4–6. Copper alloy drammas, '*śrī ha*' series. *Obverse*: Traces of stylised head of ruler to right; worn. Illegible Brahmi inscription. *Reverse*: Stylised parallel notched lines denoting a fire altar. Maheshwari 2010, pp. 175–201; Mitchiner 1979, p.59, type 369–72.
Fig. 59.4 – IOLC.4613. 3.47g, 20mm.
Fig. 59.5 – IOLC.4614. 2.96g, 20mm.
Fig. 59.6 – IOLC.4615. 4.15g, 18mm.

Gadhaiya paisa
Fig. 59.7–9. Silver alloy coins issued by the Chaulukya dynasty (c. AD 543–753), ruling in Gujarat, and their successors in northern India (8th–11th century). *Obverse*: Stylised head of ruler to right. *Reverse*: Stylised fire altar. According to Masson (**F526/1a, Pl. 11.14–17**, p. 63 above), these coins were:

> sometimes met with in the bazaar of Kabul, and always in small parcels of two, three, four, six &c. ... they are common enough in India, and are frequently found of copper. At Kabul they generally occur of silver. Copper ones have however been exhumed at Koh Daman [near Korrindar] in company with [Lakshmi coins of Muḥammād b. Sām: **Pl. 10**, *Fig. 69*], Begram has yielded no coin of this type.

Fig. 59.7. 16mm. Wilson 1841, p. 413, no. 10, Coins pl. XV.22. Coin not traced.
Fig. 59.8 – IOC.664. 4.05g, 17mm. **F526/1a, Pl. 11.35**.
Fig. 59.9. 18mm. **F526/1a, Pl. 11.34**. Wilson 1841, p. 413, no. 11, Coins pl. XV.21. Coin not traced.

Chinese and Sogdian coins
Fig. 59.10 – 1880.3732. Fragment of the left side of a cast copper alloy Chinese one cash coin. Uniface, with the character 寶 *bao* (treasure). Song dynasty, Mingdao (1032–3), Jingyou (1034–8), or Baoyuan (1039) periods. 20mm. (Liu Jucheng 1989, p. 183, type 5; p. 184, type 4; p. 185, type 10).
Fig. 59.11 – IOLC.5426. K.53. Fragment of the lower part of a cast Chinese two cash copper alloy coin. Uniface, with the character *yuan*. Song dynasty, Shaosheng era (1094–7). 0.64g, 15mm (Liu Jucheng 1989, p. 203, type 17).
Fig. 59.12 – 1880.3981.f. Box 4, tray B. Copper alloy North Tokharian coin (8th century). *Obverse*: Sogdian legend encircling hole in the centre. *Reverse*: Worn and distorted representations of Chinese characters. 1.18g, 17mm. (type found in excavations at Kafir-qal'a, near Kolkhozabad, Zeimal 1994, p. 258, no. 14).

Gahadavalas of Kanauj

Govindachandradeva (c. 1114–55)
Fig. 59.13. Gold dinar, minted in Kanauj/Delhi. *Obverse*: Goddess Lakshmi seated to front. *Reverse*: Devanagari inscription *śrīmad govindachandra deva*. 20mm. Purchased in Kabul bazaar. Coin not traced. Wilson 1841, p. 435, no. 1, Coins Pl. XX.22. Deyell 1990, no. 145.

Figure 59 Miscellaneous. Later gold Kashmir coin (1). Yasovarman of Kanauj gold coin (2). Indo-Sasanian imitations: Gurjara-Pratihara silver dramma (3), Chahamana copper alloy drammas (4–6), silver alloy Gadhaiya paisa (7–9). Chinese coin fragments (10–11). Sogdian copper alloy coin (12). Gold dinars of Gahadavalas of Kanauj: Govindachandradeva (13); Kalachuris of Tripuri: Gangeyadeva (14); Yadavas of Tribhuvanagiri: Kumarapaladeva (15). Ghurid gold dinars of Muḥammād b. Sām (16–20)

Kalachuris of Tripuri

Gangeyadeva (c. 1015–40)

Fig. 59.14. Gold dinar. *Obverse*: Goddess Lakshmi seated to front. *Reverse*: Devanagari inscription *śrīmad gaṅgeya devaḥ*. 20mm. Purchased in Kabul bazaar. Coin not traced. Wilson 1841, p. 435, no. 2, Coins Pl. XX.23. Deyell 1990, no. 119.

Yadavas of Tribhuvanagiri

Kumarapaladeva (c. 1145–71)

Fig. 59.15. Gold dinar. *Obverse*: Goddess Lakshmi seated to front. *Reverse*: Devanagari inscription *śrīmad kumarapala deva*. 16mm. Purchased in Kabul bazaar. Coin not traced. Wilson 1841, p. 435, no. 3, Coins Pl. XX.24.

Ghurid versions

Muʻizz al-dīn Muḥammād b. Sām AH 569–602 / AD 1173–1206

Fig. 59.16–20. Gold dinar based on Gahadavala coins of Govindachandradeva; issued *c.* 1203–6. *Obverse*: Goddess Lakshmi seated to front. *Reverse*: Devanagari inscription. Purchased in Kabul bazaar. Wilson illustrates four from Masson's 1835 dispatch (**Fig. 59.17–20**) and says that an additional five examples were acquired in Kabul bazaar in 1836 (**Fig. 59.16**).

Fig. 59.16–17. Inscribed *śrī mahamada biṇi sāma*. Deyell 1990, no. 252.

Fig. 59.16 – IOC.652. 4.23g, 20mm.

Fig. 59.17. Wilson 1841, p. 435, no. 5, Coins Pl. XXI.25. 20mm. Coin not traced.

Fig. 59.18–20. Inscribed *śrīma hamīra mahamada sāmaḥ*. Deyell 1990, no. 253.

Catalogue of Coins | 199

Fig. 59.18. Wilson 1841, p. 436, no. 5, Coins Pl. XX.25. 18mm. Coin not traced.

Fig. 59.19. Wilson 1841, p. 436, no. 6, Coins Pl. XX.26. 15mm. Coin not traced.

Fig. 59.20. Wilson 1841, p. 435, no. 7, Coins Pl. XX.27. 15mm. Coin not traced.

Islamic coins

During his explorations in Afghanistan, Charles Masson accumulated a vast number of Islamic coins primarily from Begram and Kabul bazaar. A significant number (approximately 1,730 coins) in the India Office Loan Collection appear to have formed part of this collection. But information is limited, particularly when compared to Masson's comprehensive coverage of the pre-Islamic material. This is partly due to the fact that contemporary interest was focused on the pre-Islamic material and because Masson knew no Arabic, although he did speak Persian. However references in *Ariana Antiqua* and his unpublished papers (**F526/1a**, see pp. 60, 63, 66, **Pls 10.69, 11.5-9, 11-13, 13.1-6** above; **Vol. II, pp. 86–9, Figs 98–9**) shed some light on the types he collected during his time in Afghanistan. Using this material, and the coins themselves, a survey of the IOLC Islamic coins has been carried out by Paramdip Khera and where possible the coin types have been identified.

Masson uses two terms – 'Kufic' and 'Muhammadan' – to classify Islamic coins. Kufic includes all coins using the characteristically elegant angular letter forms of this Arabic calligraphic script. He says (**F526/1a, f. 25**: p. 66 above).

> The appearance of Kufic coins in these countries in very considerable numbers, is explained by the early conquests of the Caliphs, whose generals reduced the countries on the Indus and west of it, in the first century of their era. Without reference I cannot determine how long they preserved authority in them … The sway of the Caliph must however have been of some duration, if we judge from the quantities of their currency found at Begram. This currency appears to have been of gold, silver, billon and copper. The silver coins of the Caliphs are abundant in the bazaar of Kabul, being brought from Turkestan.

Kufic was the main script used in Qurans and on coins until it went out of general use after the 13th century. 'Muhammadan' refers to all later coins utilising other scripts and to Islamic coins in a more general sense.

Most of the Islamic IOLC coins are copper alloy, with only a small number of silver examples (mostly fragments) and no gold. Apart from the 1845 East India Company donation of the hoard of Arab-Sasanian silver coins (pp. 110–26; **Figs 35–6**), recognition of actual Masson Islamic coins in the British Museum permanent collection (IOC) is restricted by the paucity of illustrated examples. Moreover, of the seventeen relevant coin drawings in *Ariana Antiqua*, only five actual coins have been identified (**Figs 39.17, 40.18, 41.3, 42.3–4**). From the comment that some of 'the more precious parts of the [Masson] collection' were presented by the India Office to the Indian Museum in Calcutta c. 1882–7 (**Vol. II, p. 122: FW 19–11–1906**), it can be supposed that many of the gold and silver Islamic coins from Afghanistan and adjoining regions listed in Vincent Smith's *Catalogue* (1906) belong to this donation. But due to the lack of images, this cannot be verified.

'Abbasid (AH 132–923 / AD 749–1258)

al-Manṣūr (AH 136–7 / AD 754–5)
Fig. 60.1 – IOLC.6044. Copper alloy fals, minted in Madinat al-Salam (Baghdad) in AH 157 (AD 773/4). *Obverse*: Arabic inscription. *Reverse*: Arabic inscription. 5.04g, 24mm.

Hārūn al-Rashīd (AH 170–93 / AD 786–809)
Fig. 60.2. Silver coin minted in Madinat al-Salam, AH 188/ AD 804. *Obverse*: Arabic inscription. *Reverse*: Arabic inscription. 246mm. Wilson 1841, p.438, no. 9, Coins pl. XX.36. Coin not traced, acquired in Kabul bazaar.

Saffarid

'Amr b. al-Layth (AH 265–88 / AD 879–901)
Fig. 60.3 – IOLC.6028. Silver coin, unattributed mint. *Obverse*: Arabic inscription in centre and around margin. *Reverse*: Arabic inscription in centre and around margin. 2.90g, 20mm.

Later Saffarid – Seistan

Taj al-dīn Naṣr b. Bahram Shah (AH 618–19 / AD 1221–2)
Fig. 60.4. Silver coin. *Obverse*: Inscription in ornamented cartouche. *Reverse*: Inscription in ornamented cartouche. 19mm. Wilson 1841, p. 438, no. 7, Coins pl. XX.34. Coin not traced, acquired in Kabul bazaar.

Samanid

Manṣūr I b. Nūh (AH 350–65 / AD 961–76)
Fig. 60.5 – IOLC.6021. Copper alloy coin dated AH 357/AD 968; mint not legible, possibly Bukhara (?). *Obverse*: Arabic inscription in centre and around margin. *Reverse*: Arabic inscription in centre and around margin. 1.72g, 21mm.

Fig. 60.6–7. Copper alloy coins, minted in Parwan in the name of Manṣūr I b. Nūh, or Nūh II b. Manṣūr (AH 387–9 / AD 997–9), probably issued by the local governor of Begram, but it is not indicated on the coins. *Obverse*: Rose of four petals with an Arabic inscription on each petal. *Reverse*: Arabic inscription of three lines in the centre encircled by an Arabic inscription in the outer margin.
Fig. 60.6 – IOLC.6784. 2.55g, 18mm.
Fig. 60.7 – IOLC.6785. 2.18g, 18mm.
Total: 4 coins: 2.55g–2.18g (3), 1.24g (fragment).
Fig. 60.8–9. Copper alloy coins, minted in Parwan in the name of Nūh b. Manṣūr (AH 365–87 / AD 976–97),
Fig. 60.8 – IOLC.6782. 1.66g, 16mm.
Fig. 60.9 – IOLC.6783. 2.06g, 17mm.

Nūh II b. Manṣūr (AH 365–87 / AD 976–97)
Fig. 60.10 – IOLC.6022. Copper alloy coin, unknown mint. *Obverse*: Arabic inscription in centre and around margin. *Reverse*: Arabic inscription in centre and around margin. 2.79g, 21mm.

Figure 60 'Abbasid coins. al-Manṣūr copper alloy fals (1), Hārūn al-Rashīd silver coin (2). Saffarid silver coins: 'Amr b. al-Layth (3), Taj al-dīn Naṣr b. Bahram Shah (4). Samanid copper alloy coins: Manṣūr I b. Nūh (5), i.n.o. Manṣūr I b. Nūh or Nūh II b. Manṣūr (6–9), NūhI b. Manṣūr (10), unattributed (11). Amirs of Sind (12–15). Ghaznavid unattributed (16–17), Sebuktegin (18), Ismā'īl b. Sebuktegin (19), Maḥmūd I (20–3)

Unattributed (c. AH 366–582 / AD 977–1186)

Fig. 60.11 – IOLC.6023. Copper alloy coin. Illegible issuer, but very similar in fabric to IOLC.6021 and IOLC.6022 (**Fig. 60.5, 10**); unknown mint. *Obverse*: Arabic inscription in centre and around margin. *Reverse*: Arabic inscription in centre and around margin. 1.43g, 23mm.

Masson's sketch of Samanid coins in his personal collection includes an example which is similar to IOLC.6023 (**Fig. 19** above, no. 1603). Further information about this coin is limited in Masson's notes; however, the drawing suggests it is the same coin type.

Amirs of Sind (AH 256–399 / AD 870–1009)

Da'ud (date unknown)
Fig. 60.12 – IOLC.7897. Copper alloy coin, minted in Brahmanabad. *Obverse*: Encircled. Arabic inscription. *Reverse*: Encircled. Arabic inscription. 0.25g, 6mm. Goron and Goenka 2001, p. xxiii.

'Abd Allāh (date unknown)
Fig. 60.13 – IOLC.7885. Silver coin, minted in Brahmanabad. *Obverse*: Arabic inscription. *Reverse*: Arabic inscription. 0.26g, 7mm. Goron and Goenka 2001, p. xxiii.

Total 1 silver, 11 copper alloy coins: 0.48g–0.43g (2), 6.38g–0.3g (6), 0.29g–0.23g (3).

'Umar b. al-'Ala (?) (date unknown)
Fig. 60.14 – IOLC.7900. Copper alloy coin, minted in Brahmanabad. *Obverse*: Arabic inscription encircled by a dotted border. *Reverse*: Arabic inscription encircled by a dotted border. 0.3g, 6mm. Goron and Goenka 2001, p. xxiv.

Total 3 coins: 0.34g–0.3g (2),: 0.18g (1).

Catalogue of Coins | 201

Unattributed

Fig. 60.15 – IOLC.7904. Silver coin, unknown mint. *Obverse*: Arabic inscription. *Reverse*: Arabic inscription. 0.41g, 9mm.

Total 16 silver alloy coins 0.41g (1), 0.35g–0.3g (9), 0.29g–0.21g (6).

Total 42 copper alloy coins: 0.55g (1), 0.47g –0.4g (5), 0.39g–0.3g (21), 0.29g–0.22g (15).

Ghaznavid

Unattributed (c. AH 350–582 / AD 961–1186)

Fig. 60.16 – IOLC.7876. Copper alloy coin, unknown mint. *Obverse*: Arabic inscription, encircled; worn and illegible. *Reverse*: Arabic inscription, encircled; worn and illegible. 0.36g, 9mm.

Total 150 coins: 1.29g–1.05g (3), 0.88g–0.87g (2), 0.73g–0.7g (4), 0.69g–0.6g (24), 0.58g–0.5g (29), 0.49g–0.4g (32), 0.39g–0.3g (37), 0.29g–0.21g (18), 0.18g (1).

Fig. 60.17 – IOLC.5901. Silver coin, unknown mint. *Obverse*: Arabic inscription encircled by dotted border. *Reverse*: Arabic inscription encircled by dotted border. 0.35g, 7mm.

Total 12 coins: 0.72g (1), 0.6g (1), 0.57g–0.55g (2), 0.49g–0.42g (3), 0.35g–0.32g (2), 0.27g–0.22g (3).

Sebuktegin (AH 366–87 / AD 977–97)

Fig. 60.18 – IOC.1308. Base silver coin minted AH 380/AD 990 in Parwan. *Obverse*: Arabic inscription *lah-llah illa Allāh wadahau la sherik lahu Sebuktigin*. *Reverse*: Arabic inscription *Muḥammād rasul Allāh Nur bin Mansur al-Ta'i-Allāh*. 3.18g, 20mm. Acquired by Masson in 1833–5 in Kabul bazaar. Wilson 1841, p. 438, no. 3, Coins, pl. XX.30; Lane Poole 1876, p. 129.451.

IOLC.6931. Broken base silver coin. 1.35g, 20mm. Not illustrated, see **Fig. 19**, no. 1606.

Total 16 copper alloy coins: 4.01g (1), 3.94g–3.01g (3), 2.99g–2.53g (2), 1.95g–1.08g (6), 0.81g–0.18g (4).

Ismā'īl b. Sebuktegin (AH 387–8 / AD 997–8)

Fig. 60.19 – IOLC.6035. Silver coin minted in Parwan. *Obverse*: Arabic inscription *la ilah ilah Allāh wahdahula sherik lahu al Ta'i Allāh*. *Reverse*: Arabic inscription *Allāh Muḥammād rasul Allāh Mansur b. Nūh Isma'il*. 2.79g, 13mm.

Maḥmūd I (AH 388–421 / AD 998–1030)

Fig. 60.20 – IOLC.6020. Silver alloy coin minted in Ghazni. *Obverse*: Arabic inscription in centre and around margin. *Reverse*: Arabic inscription in centre and around margin. 2.54g, 23mm. Masson illustrates a similar type in his own collection (**Fig. 19**, no. 1607).

Fig. 60.21 – IOLC.6175. Silver alloy coin minted in Ghazni. *Obverse*: Arabic inscription *adl la ilah alla Allāh wahdahula sherik lahu Yamini*. *Reverse*: Arabic inscription *Muḥammād rasul Allāh al-Qadir bi-Allāh Yamin al-daula Maḥmūd*. 1.79g, 13mm. Tye 1995, p. 102, type 85.

Fig. 60.22. Silver coin. 20mm. Wilson 1841, p. 438, no. 4, Coins pl. XX.31. Coin not traced.

Fig. 60.23 – IOLC.6037. Copper alloy coin, unknown mint. *Obverse*: Arabic inscription in centre and around margin. *Reverse*: Arabic inscription in centre and around margin. 2.96g, 18mm.

Total 20 coins: 4.24g (1), 3.08g (1), 2.96g–2.11g (6), 1.7g–1.06g (5), 0.95g–0.36g (7).

Muḥammād b. Maḥmūd (AH 421 / AD 1031; AH 432 / AD 1041)

Fig. 61.1 – IOLC.6059. Copper alloy coin; unknown mint. *Obverse*: Arabic inscription in centre and around margin. *Reverse*: Arabic inscription in centre and around margin. 2.70g, 18mm. Masson illustrates a silver example of similar type (**F526/1a, Pl. 13.3**).

Fig. 61.2 – IOLC.6061. Copper alloy coin. *Obverse*: Arabic inscription within circle. *Reverse*: Arabic inscription within circle. 2.35mm, 17mm.

Total 5 coins: 5.53g (1), 2.7g–2.35g (2), 1.89g–1.82g (3).

Mas'ūd I (AH 421–32 / AD 1031–41)

61 coins including fragments.

Fig. 61.3 – IOC.1426. Silver coin, minted in Warwarliz. 3.42g, 20mm. Wilson 1841, p. 438, no. 4, Coins, pl. XX.32. Lane-Poole 1876, p. 156.522.

Fig. 61.4 – IOLC.6063. Copper alloy coin, unknown mint. *Obverse*: Arabic inscription within dotted border. *Reverse*: Arabic inscription within a circular cartouche, within a square, flanked on each side by an Arabic inscription. 3.91g, 22mm.

Fig. 61.5 – IOLC.6067. Copper alloy coin fragment. *Obverse*: Arabic inscription within a square, encircled by a dotted border. *Reverse*: Arabic inscription within a square, encircled by a dotted border. 2.25g, 20mm. For similar type see **Fig. 19**, no. 1607.

Total 9 coins and fragments: 3.91g (1), 2.49g–2.11g (4), 1.87g–1.23g (3), 0.35g (1).

Fig. 61.6 – IOLC.6092. Copper alloy coin, unknown mint. *Obverse*: Worn Arabic inscription within a circular margin. *Reverse*: Worn Arabic inscription within a circular margin. 1.9g, 15mm.

Total 25 coins: 3.44g–3.02g (7), 2.97g–2.22g (17), 1.9g (1).

Fig. 61.7 – IOLC.7468. Copper alloy coin. *Obverse*: Flower in the centre of a hexagon with curved extensions; a dot in each interstice. *Reverse*: Six-pointed star with a flower in the centre. 2.5g, 15mm.

Total 4 coins: 2.91g–2.5g.

Fig. 61.8 – IOLC.6132. Copper alloy coin, *Obverse*: A six-pointed star with a circle in the centre and dots in the interstices; encircled by a Devanagari legend *śrī Samantadeva*. *Reverse*: A six-pointed star with a star in the centre and dots in the interstices; encircled by an Arabic inscription *Mas'ūd / Maḥmūd*. 2.45g, 13mm. Tye 1995, p. 104, type 89e3.

Total 21 coins: 2.95g–2.01g (20), 1.92g (1).

Mawdūd I (AH 432–40 / AD 1041–50)

55 coins.

Fig. 61.9–10. Silver coin, unknown mint. *Obverse*: Arabic inscription in centre and around margin *adl la ilah illa Allāh wahadahula sherik lahu al-Qa'im bi-amr Allāh*. *Reverse*: Arabic inscription in centre and around margin *fath Muḥammād rasul Allāh Shihab al-daula wa qutb al-millat Mawdūd*. Tye 1995, p. 104, type 90.

Figure 61 Ghaznavid coins. Muḥammād b. Maḥmūd copper alloy coins (1–2); Masʿūd I silver coin (3), copper alloy (4–8); Mawdūd I silver coins (9–11), silver-plated (12–13), copper alloy (14–18); ʿAbd al-Rashid silver alloy coin (19), copper alloy (20); Ibrahim silver jitals (21–2, 25), copper alloy (23–4, 26–7); Masʿūd III copper alloy coins (28–31); Arslan Shah copper alloy coins (32–6); Bahram Shah silver coin (37), copper alloy jitals (38–41); Khusrau Shah copper alloy coin (42); Khusrau Malik copper alloy jitals (43–5)

Catalogue of Coins | 203

Fig. 61.9. 20mm. Wilson 1841, p. 438, no. 6, Coins pl. XX.33. Coin not traced.

Fig. 61.10 – IOLC.6176. Broken, 2.34g, 17mm. Similar type illustrated by Masson (**Fig. 19**, no. 1599).

Fig. 61.11 – IOLC.6145. 2.65g, 15mm.

Total 8 silver coins: 2.95g–2.23g (7), 1.85g (1).

Fig. 61.12 – IOLC.6154. Silver-plated copper alloy coin. 2.59g, 17mm.

Fig. 61.13 – IOLC.6149. Silver-plated. 2.27g 14mm.

Fig. 61.14–16. Copper alloy coin, unknown mint. *Obverse*: Arabic inscription in centre and around margin. *Reverse*: Arabic inscription in centre and around margin.

Fig. 61.14 – IOLC.6137. 3.07g, 18mm.

Fig. 61.15– IOLC 6181. Pierced and broken fragment. 1.37g, 18mm. For a similar type see **Fig. 19**, no. 1606.

Fig. 61.16 – IOLC 6184. 2.35g, 20mm. For a similar type see **F526/1a, Pl. 13.4**.

Fig. 61.17 – IOLC.6157. 1.11g, 14mm. **Fig. 19**, no. 1609.

Total 44 coins: 3.47g–3.16 (2), 2.94g–2g (25), 1.99g–1.11g (15), 0.97g–0.95g (2).

Fig. 61.18 – IOLC.6198. Copper alloy jital, minted in Lahore. *Obverse:* Bull seated to left. Devanagari legend *śrī Samantadeva*. *Reverse*: Arabic inscription *abu'l fath al-amir al-ajalla Shihab-al-daula Mawdūd*. 3.1g, 15mm. Tye 1995 p. 105, type 93.1.

Total 2 coins: 3.1g, 2.85g.

'Abd al-Rashīd (AH 440–3 / AD 1049–52)

Fig. 61.19 – IOLC.6379. Silver alloy coin, minted in Ghazni. *Obverse*: Arabic inscription *fath la ilah ialla Allāh wahdahu la sherk lahu al-Qa'im bi-amr Allāh* encircled by mint and date. *Reverse*: Arabic inscription *sharaf Allāh Muḥammād rasul Allāh 'Izz al-daula wa zain al-millat 'Abd al-Rashīd*. 2.72g, 17mm. Tye 1995, p. 105, type 95.

Fig. 61.20 – IOLC.6294. Copper alloy coin, unknown mint. *Obverse*: Arabic inscription encircled by Arabic inscription. *Reverse*: Arabic inscription encircled by Arabic inscription. 1.9g, 11mm.

Total 42 coins: 2.65g–2g (6), 1.96g–1.24g (36).

Ibrahim (AH 451–92 / AD 1059–99)

81 coins.

Fig. 61.21–2. Silver jital, minted in Lahore. *Obverse*: Bull seated to left. Devanagari inscription *śrī Samantadeva*. *Reverse*: Arabic inscription within dotted margin *'adil al-sultan al-mu'azzam abu'l-muzaffar Ibrahim*. Tye 1995, p. 106, type 103.4.

Fig. 61.21 – IOLC.6197. 3.19g, 15mm.

Fig. 61.22 – IOLC.6200. 3.24g, 14mm.

Total 3 coins: 3.24g, 3.19g, 2.92g.

Fig. 61.23–4. Copper alloy jital, minted in Lahore. *Obverse*: Bull seated to left. Devanagari inscription *śrī Samantadeva*. *Reverse*: Arabic inscription *'adil Nasir al-daula wa zahir al-millat Ibrahim*.

Fig. 61.23. Wilson 1841, p. 438, no. 4, Coins, pl. XX.5. *Reverse*: Arabic inscription within dotted margin. 15mm. Coin not traced.

Fig. 61.24 – IOLC.6445. *Reverse*: Arabic inscription encircled by Arabic inscription. 3.03g, 12mm. Tye 1995, p. 106, type 102–3.

Total 4 coins: 3.99g–3.03g (3), 2.55g (1).

Fig. 61.25 – IOLC.6287. Silver jital, unknown mint. *Obverse*: Arabic inscription in centre and around margin. *Reverse*: Arabic inscription in centre and around margin. 1.42g, 14mm.

Total 7 coins: 1.97g–1.17g (5), 0.65g–0.6g (2).

Fig. 61.26–7. Copper alloy coins, unknown mint. *Obverse*: Arabic inscription in centre and around margin. *Reverse*: Arabic inscription in centre and around margin.

Fig. 61.26 – IOLC.6238. 2.90g, 17mm.

Fig. 61.27 – IOLC.6272. 2g, 13mm.

Total 68 coins: 2.68g–2g (12), 1.97g–1.15g (38), 0.92g–0.37g (18).

Mas'ūd III (AH 492–508 / AD 1099–1115)

66 coins

Fig. 61.28 – IOLC.6383. Copper alloy coin, unknown mint. *Obverse*: Arabic inscription encircled by dotted border; worn. *Reverse*: Arabic inscription encircled by dotted border; worn. 2.78g, 14mm.

Total 52 coins: 3.64g–3.02g (12), 2.99g–2g (34), 1.96g–1.36g (18).

Fig. 61.29 – IOLC.6436. Copper alloy coin, minted in Ghazni. *Obverse*: Arabic inscription in centre *al-Mustazhir la ilah illa llah Muḥammād rasul Allāh billah*, encircled by Arabic inscription. *Reverse*: Arabic inscription in square *al-sultan al-'azam Mas'ūd*, encircled by Arabic inscription. 2.47g, 16mm. Tye 1995, p. 106, type 104.

Total 8 coins: 2.94g–2.28g.

Fig. 61.30 – IOLC.6435. Copper alloy coin, minted in Ghazni. *Obverse*: Arabic inscription. *Reverse*: Arabic inscription. 2.83g, 12mm. Tye 1995, p. 107, type 105e1.

Total 3 coins: 3.09g (1), 2.83g–2.47g (2).

Fig. 61.31 – IOLC.5767. Copper alloy jital, minted in Lahore. *Obverse*: Bull seated to left. Devanagari inscription *śrī Samantadeva*. *Reverse*: Arabic inscription *Khusru al-sultan al-'azam Abu Sa'id Mas'ūd*. 3.08g, 14mm.

Total 3 coins: 3.08g (1), 2.86g–2.37g (2).

Arslan Shah (AH 509–10 / AD 1116–17)

154 coins

Fig. 61.32 – IOLC.6475. Copper alloy coin. *Obverse*: Arabic inscription encircled by double border with dots. *Reverse*: Arabic inscription encircled by double border with dots. 2g, 13mm.

Total 6 coins: 2g (1), 1.99g–1.94g (3), 1.78g–1.74g (2).

Fig. 61.33–7. Copper alloy jitals, minted in Ghazni. *Obverse*: Arabic inscription encircled by rays. *Reverse*: Arabic inscription encircled by rays. Tye 1995, p. 107, type 107e1.

Fig. 61.33 – IOLC.7463. *Reverse*: Worn. 4.16g, 15mm.

Fig. 61.34 – IOLC.6449. 2.53g, 14mm.

Fig. 61.35 – IOLC.6575. 2.49g, 12mm.

Fig. 61.36 – IOLC.6502. 1.47g, 11mm.

Total 148 coins: 4.16g (1), 3.44g–3g (14), 2.94g–2.1g (26), 1.99g–1.02g (103), 0.97g–0.67g (4).

Bahram Shah (AH 511–45; 547–52 / AD 1117–50; 1152–7)

125 coins

Fig. 61.37 – IOLC.6113. Silver alloy coin, minted in Ghazni. *Obverse*: Arabic inscription within a dotted margin

Allāh la ilah illa Allāh al-Mustarshid billah 'Azd al-daula Sinjar. Reverse: Extremely worn, illegible Arabic inscription within a dotted margin [*al-sultan Muḥammād rasul Allāh al-sultan al-'azam Yamin al-daula Bahramshah*]. 2.86g, 16mm. Tye 1995, p. 107, type 108

Fig. 61.38 – IOLC.6604. Copper alloy jital, unknown mint. *Obverse*: Bull seated to left. Devanagari inscription *śrī Samantadeva*. *Reverse*: Arabic inscription encircled by Arabic inscription. 3.08g, 15mm.

Fig. 61.39 – IOLC.5517. Copper alloy jital, minted in Lahore. *Obverse*: Bull seated to left. Devanagari inscription *śrī Samantadeva*. *Reverse*: Arabic word *yamini* with dots above and below, encircled by a border of rays. 3.35g, 9mm. Tye 1995, p. 108, type 111.3.

Total 4 coins: 3.35g–3.14g (3), 2.86g (1).

Fig. 61.40 – IOLC.6605. Copper alloy jital, unknown mint. *Obverse*: Arabic inscription. *Reverse*: Arabic inscription. 3.10g, 13mm.

Fig. 61.41 – IOLC.6606. Copper alloy jital, unknown mint. *Obverse*: Arabic inscription encircled by dots. *Reverse*: Arabic inscription encircled by border of dots and rays. 1.74g, 10mm.

Total 118 coins: 2.79g–2.01g (12), 1.99g–1.03g (105), 0.88g (1).

Khusrau Shah (AH 552–55 / AD 1157–60)

Fig. 61.42 – IOLC.6444. Copper alloy coin, minted in Lahore. *Obverse*: Bull seated to left. Devanagari inscription *śrī Samantadeva*. *Reverse*: Arabic inscription *as-sultan al-'azam Mu'izz al-daula Khusru shah*. 3.18g, 10mm. Tye 1995, p. 108, type 113.

Total 4 coins: 3.18g–3.07g.

Khusrau Malik (AH 555–82 / AD 1160–86)

9 coins

Fig. 61.43 – IOLC.6744. Copper alloy jital, minted in Kuraman. *Obverse*: Bull seated to left. Devanagari inscription *śrī Samantadeva*. *Reverse*: Arabic inscription *Malik al-sultan al-'azam abu'l-malik Khusru*. 2.63g, 13mm. Tye 1995, p. 109, type 117.

Total 7 coins: 3.2g–3.1g (2), 2.87g–2.43g (5).

Fig. 61.44–5. Copper alloy jital, minted in Lahore. *Obverse*: Arabic inscription *Khusru Malik* encircled by dotted border. *Reverse*: Arabic inscription *al-sultan al-'azam Suraj al-daula*. Similar type see **F526/1a, Pl. 11.12**; Tye 1995, p. 100, type 120.

Fig. 61.44. Wilson 1841, p. 433, Coins pl.XX.16. 13mm. Coin not traced.

Fig. 61.45 – IOLC.6746. 3.2g, 13mm.

Total 2 coins: 3.2g, 3.14g.

Ghurid

176 coins

Ghiyāth al-dīn Muḥammād b. Sām (AH 559–99 / AD 1163–1203)

Fig. 62.1 – IOLC.6722. Copper alloy jital, minted in Taliqan. *Obverse*: Horseman to left. *Reverse*: Arabic inscription *Taliqan al-sultan al-mu'azam*. 2.42g, 14mm. Tye 1995, p. 111, type 131.

Mu'izz al-dīn Muḥammād b. Sām (AH 569–99 / AD 1173–1203; supreme sultan 599–602 / 1203–6)

37 coins

Fig. 62.2. Silver double dirham, minted in Ghazni. *Obverse and Reverse*: Three lines of circular inscription, citing Ghiyāth al-dīn and Mu'izz al-dīn Muḥammād b. Sām. 28mm. Wilson 1841, p. 438, no. 8, Coins Pl. XX.35. Coin not traced.

Fig. 62.3. Silver dirham minted in Ghazni. *Obverse*: Centre and margin *kalima* inscribed in Arabic. *Reverse*: Arabic inscription citing sultan. Margin: mint; date off flan. 28mm. Wilson 1841, pp. 437–8, no. 8, Coins Pl. XX.29. Coin not traced.

Fig. 62.4–6. Copper alloy jital, minted in Ghazni. *Obverse*: Arabic inscription *Mu'izz al-duniya* in a square within a circle; a scroll within each outer quarter section. *Reverse*: Arabic inscription *wa al-dīn* in a square within a circle; a scroll within each outer quarter section.

Fig. 62.4 – IOLC.6787. 2.96g, 12mm.

Fig. 62.5. 15mm. Wilson 1841, p. 433, no. 28, Coins pl. XX.14. Coin not traced.

Fig. 62.6 – IOLC.6788. 2.83g, 13mm.

Total 20 coins: 3.98g–3.01g (9), 2.98g–2.16g (11).

Fig. 62.7 – IOLC.5271. Hexagonal copper alloy jital, minted in Ghazni (?) *Obverse*: Arabic inscription *Mu'izz al-duniya*. *Reverse*: Arabic inscription *wa al-dīn*. 2.48g, 14mm. Wilson 1841, p. 433, no. 31, Coins pl. XX.17.

Fig. 62.8 – IOLC.7429. Copper alloy jital, minted in Ghazni (?). *Obverse*: Faint traces of an Arabic inscription. *Reverse*: Hexagonal star (seal of Solomon) with dots in each triangular point and an Arabic inscription in the centre *ibn Muḥammād Sām*. 1.13g, 18mm. Tye 1995, p. 120, type 188.

Fig. 62.9 – IOLC.6738. Copper alloy jital, minted in Kuraman. *Obverse*: Six-petalled flower in twelve-pointed star (seal of Solomon). *Reverse*: Arabic inscription in centre *al-sultan al-'azam*; and in encircling margin. 2.17g, 12mm. Tye 1995, p. 118, type 176.

Total 8 coins: 2.83g–2.17g (6), 1.95g (2).

Fig. 62.10 – IOLC.6765. Copper alloy jital, minted in Kuraman. *Obverse*: Bull standing to left. *Reverse*: Arabic inscription *al-sultan al-'azam Mu'izz al-duniya wa al-dīn*. 2.63g, 12mm. Tye 1995, p. 118, type 178.

Total 4 coins: 3.13g (1), 2.68g–2.36g (3).

Fig. 62.11 – IOLC.6739. Copper alloy jital, minted in Kuraman. *Obverse*: Arabic inscriptions in centre and in encircling margin. *Reverse*: Arabic inscription *al-sultan Muḥammād* in a hexagonal star. 2.69g, 10mm.

Total 2 coins: 2.75g, 2.69g.

Fig. 62.12 – IOLC.6741. Copper alloy jital, minted in Kuraman. *Obverse and Reverse*: Worn Arabic inscription *al-sultan [al-'azam] Muḥammād b. Sām* encircled by **xox** band. 2.9g, 12mm.

Fig. 62.13 – IOLC.6810. Copper alloy coin, minted in Kuraman. *Obverse*: Bull standing to left. Devanagari inscription *śrī sama*. *Reverse*: Arabic inscription *al-sultan 'azam abu'l-muzaffar Muḥammād b. Sām*. 2.68g, 13mm.

Fig. 62.14 – IOLC.7434. Copper alloy jital, minted in Lahore. *Obverse*: Arabic inscription *Mu'izz* within circle with dotted border. *Reverse*: Arabic inscription *'adl* within circle with dotted border. 3.34g, 11mm. **F526/1a, Pl. 11.13**, p. 63

Catalogue of Coins | 205

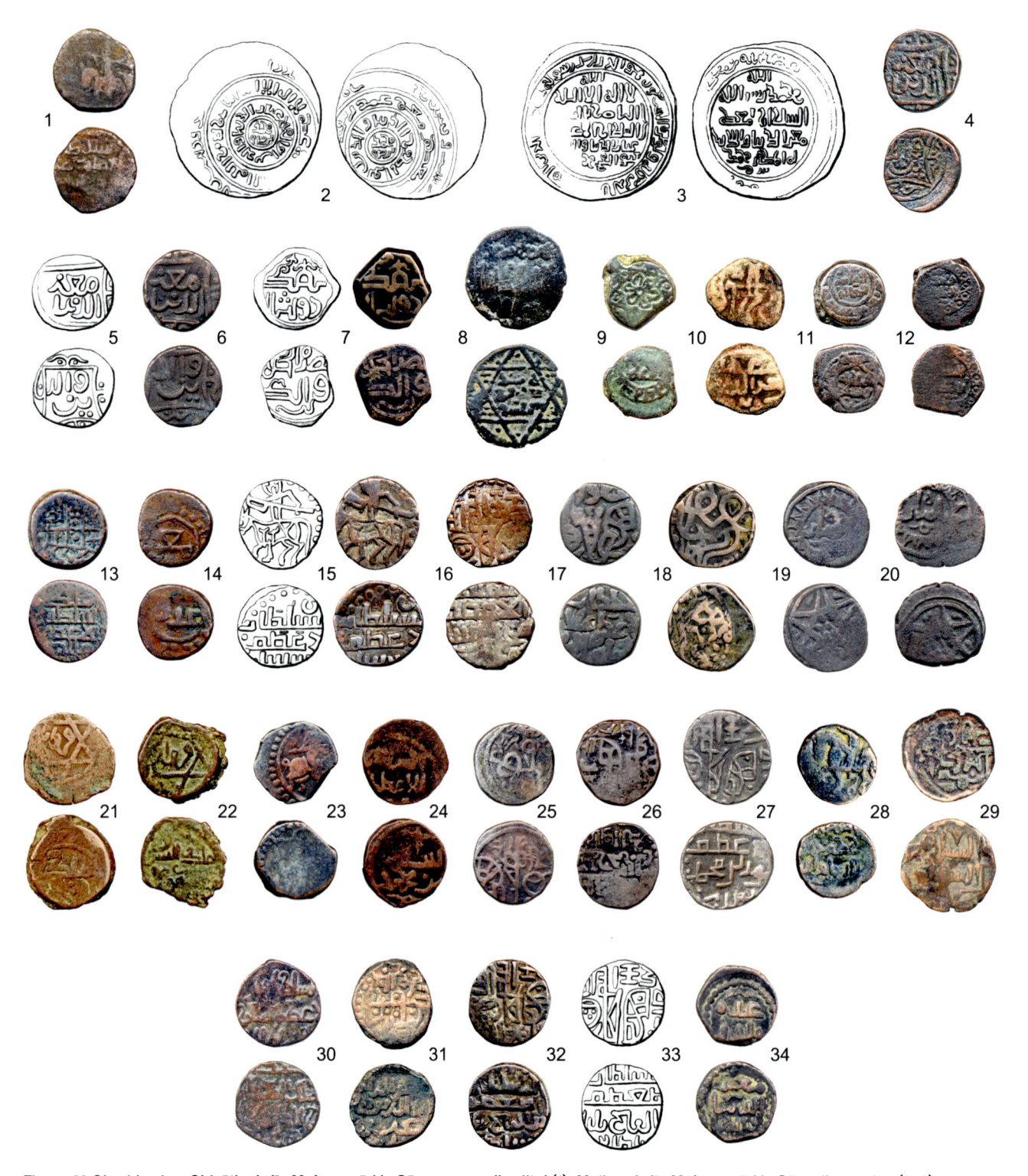

Figure 62 Ghurid coins. Ghiyāth al-dīn Muḥammād b. Sām copper alloy jital (1); Muʿizz al-dīn Muḥammād b. Sām silver coins (2–3), copper alloy jitals (4–14, 17), silver alloy jital (15), silver-plated jital (16); Anonymous (17–20); Malik al-Sharq (21–2); Bahaʾ al-dīn Sām (23–4); Jalal al-dīn ʿAli b. Sām silver coins (25–6); Ghiyāth al-dīn Maḥmūd silver coin (27); Taj al-dīn Yildiz copper alloy jitals (28–34)

above. Tye 1995, p. 120, type 192; Goron and Goenka 2001, p. 18, type D16.

Total 3 coins: 3.34g–3.08g (2), 2.85g (1).

Fig. 62.15 – IOLC.6809. Silver alloy jital, minted in Lahore. *Obverse*: Horseman to left. Inscription off flan *Reverse*: Arabic inscription *al-sultan al-ʿazam Muḥammād b. Sām*. 3.52g, 15mm. Wilson 1841, p. 433, Coins pl.XX.7. Tye 1995, p. 119, type 182.

Fig. 62.16 – IOLC.6802. Silver-plated copper alloy jital, minted in Lahore. *Obverse*: Horseman to right.

Devanagari inscription *śrī hamirah*. *Reverse*: Arabic inscription *al-sultan al-ʿazam Muḥammād b. Sām*. 3.28g, 16mm. Goron and Goenka 2001, p. 17, type D12.

Fig. 62.17 – IOLC.6723. Copper alloy jital, minted in Lahore. *Obverse*: Horseman to right. Devanagari inscription *śrī hamirah*. *Reverse*: Arabic inscription *al sultan al-ʿazam Muḥammād b. Sām*. 3.45g, 14mm.

Anonymous – in the name of Muḥammād b. Sām

Fig. 62.18 – IOLC.6868. Copper alloy jital, minted in

206 | *Charles Masson: Collections from Begram and Kabul Bazaar, Afghanistan, 1833–1838*

Bamiyan. *Obverse*: Bull seated to left. Devanagari inscription *śrī ma mehemeta same*. *Reverse*: Horseman to right. Devanagari inscription *śrī hamirah*. 3.32g, 14mm.
Total 3 coins: 3.32g–3.18g (2), 2.93g (1).

Anonymous – Bamiyan (13th century)
Fig. 62.19–20. Copper alloy jital, minted in Bamiyan (?) *Obverse*: Arabic inscription within circle of sun-rays. *Reverse*: Hexagonal star with a flower of six dots in the centre. Tye 1995, pp. 145, type 362.
Fig. 62.19 – IOLC.7437. 1.91g, 13mm.
Fig. 62.20 – IOLC.7438. 2.07g, 14mm.
Total 6 coins: 2.65g–2.07g (5), 1.91g (1).

Malik al-Sharq (king of the east)
Unidentified local ruler – probably Ghaznavid from Bamiyan – minting coins at Begram. See also **Fig. 62.8** above.
Fig. 62.21–2. Copper alloy jital, minted in Parwan (Begram). *Obverse*: Arabic inscription *Parwān* in the centre of a hexagonal star. *Reverse*: Arabic inscription *malik al-sharq* (king of the east).
Fig. 62.21 – IOLC.7421. 3.38g, 14mm.
Fig. 62.22 – IOLC.7423. 2.84g, 14mm (with an additional illegible inscription below).
Total 7 coins: 3.38g (1), 2.94g–2.18g (6).

Baha' al-dīn Sām (AH 588–602 / AD 1192–1206)
Fig. 62.23 – IOLC.6727. Copper alloy jital, minted in Bamiyan. *Obverse*: Horseman to right. *Reverse*: Arabic inscription in cartouche *al-sultan al-'azam Baha al-duniya wa al-dīn*. 2.75g, 15mm.
Fig. 62.24 – IOLC.7101. Copper alloy jital, minted in Balkh. *Obverse*: Arabic inscription *Sām b. Muḥammād*. *Reverse*: Arabic inscription *Balkh al-sultan al-'azam baha' al-duniya wa al-dīn*. 2.68g, 15mm. Tye 1995, pp. 115, 168, type 157.
Total 2 coins: 2.96g, 2.68g.

Jalal al-dīn 'Ali b. Sām (AH 602–11 / AD 1206–15)
Fig. 62.25 – IOLC.6728. Silver alloy coin, minted in Bamiyan. *Obverse*: Seated bull to right. Traces of Devanagari inscription. *Reverse*: Horseman to left. Traces of Devanagari inscription; Arabic *jalal* on rump. 3.44g, 12mm. Tye 1995, pp. 117, 168, type 169 3.
Fig. 62.26 – IOLC.5409. Silver alloy coin, minted in Bamiyan. *Obverse*: Horseman to left. Devanagari inscription *śrī hamirah*. *Reverse*: Arabic inscription *'adil al-sultan al-'azam Jalal al-duniya wa al-dīn*. 2.89g, 12mm. Tye 1995, pp. 117, 168, type 167.2.
Total 9 coins (types vary): 3.44g–3.38g (3), 2.92g–2.38g (6).

Ghiyāth al-dīn Maḥmūd (AH 602–9 / AD 1206–12)
Fig. 62.27 – IOLC.6724. Silver alloy coin, minted in Lahore. *Obverse*: Horseman to right. Devanagari inscription *śrī hamira*. *Reverse*: Arabic inscription *'adil al-sultan al-'azam Maḥmūd b. Muḥammād b. Sām*. 3.38g, 14mm. **F526/1a, Pl. 11.5**, see p. 63 above. Tye 1995 p. 114, type 149; Goron and Goenka 2001, p.18, type D20.

Taj al-dīn Yildiz, Governor of Ghazni (AH 602–11 / AD 1206–15)
Fig. 62.28 – IOLC.7485. Copper alloy jital, minted in Ghazni. *Obverse*: Horseman to left. *Reverse*: Arabic inscription *al-malik al-mu'azzam Taj al-duniya wa al-dīn Yildiz*. 2.60g, 13mm. Tye 1995, pp. 121, 169, type 197.
Fig. 62.29 – IOLC.6872. Copper alloy jital, minted in Ghazni. *Obverse*: Arabic inscription in cartouche *abduh al-malik*. *Reverse*: Arabic inscription in a cartouche *al-sultan [al-shahid (?)]*. 3.08g, 13mm. Tye 1995, pp. 122, 169, type 203.
Fig. 62.30 – IOLC.6871. Copper alloy jital, minted in Ghazni. *Obverse*: Arabic inscription *al-malik al-mu'azzam Taj al-duniya wa al-dīn Yildiz*. *Reverse*: Arabic inscription *al-sultan al-'azam Mu'izz al-duniya wa al-dīn*. 2.88g, 15mm. Tye 1995, pp. 17, 121, 169, type 199.
Total 71 coins: 3.18g–3.01g (25), 2.99g–2.63g (46).
Fig. 62.31 – IOLC.6749. Copper alloy jital, minted in Kuraman. *Obverse*: Bull standing to left. Devanagari inscription *śrī Samanta*. *Reverse*: Arabic inscription *Mu'izz al-duniya wa al-dīn 'abduh Yildiz*. 3.33g, 13mm. Tye 1995, pp. 122, 169, type 200.
Total 6 coins: 3.12g–3.11g (2), 2.58g–2.22g (2), 1.65g–1.61g (2).
Fig. 62.32–3. Copper alloy jital, minted in Lahore. *Obverse*: Horseman riding to right. *Reverse*: Arabic inscription *al-sultan al-mu'azam abu'l fath Yildiz al-sultan*. Goron and Goenka 2001, p. 18, type D27; Tye 1995, pp. 122, 169, type 201.1.
Fig. 62.32 – IOLC.7473. 3.38g, 15mm.
Fig. 62.33. Wilson 1841, p. 433, no. 23, Coins pl. XX.9. Coin not traced.
Total 3 coins: 3.38g, 3.01, 2.84g.
Fig. 62.34 – IOLC.6725. Copper alloy jital, minted in Lahore. *Obverse*: Arabic inscription *'abduh Yildiz* and small acanthus scroll with dotted border. *Reverse*: Arabic inscription *Mu'izz al-duniya wa al-dīn* with dotted border. 3.18g, 14mm. Tye 1995, pp. 122, 169, type 204.

Khwarazm Shah

'Ala al-dīn Muḥammād b. Tekish (AH 596–617 / AD 1200–20)
Fig. 63.1. Wilson 1841, p. 437, no. 1, Coins pl. XX.28. Gold dinar minted in Ghazni, AH 616. 29mm. Purchased Kabul bazaar. Coin not traced. There are, however, 21 India Office Collection gold dinars of the same type consecutively registered as IOC.1643–IOC.1663 which are probably identifiable as some of the 'considerable number of similar coins' acquired by Masson in Kabul bazaar (Wilson 1841, p. 437).
Fig. 63.2 – IOLC.6878. Copper alloy jital, unknown mint. *Obverse*: Arabic inscription in centre *bin sultan*, encircled by an Arabic inscription in margin *al-sultan al-'azam 'Ala al-duniyā wa al-dīn Muḥammād*. *Reverse*: Arabic inscription *Allāh la ilah illa Allāh Muḥammād rasul al-Nasir*. 2.91g, 16mm. Tye 1995, pp. 129, 171, type 248.
Total 5 coins: 3.59g–3.05g (2), 2.91g–2.71g (3).
Fig. 63.3 – IOLC.7404. Copper alloy jital, unknown mint. *Obverse*: Arabic inscription in centre *Muḥammād*, encircled by Arabic inscription in margin *al-sultan al-'azam*

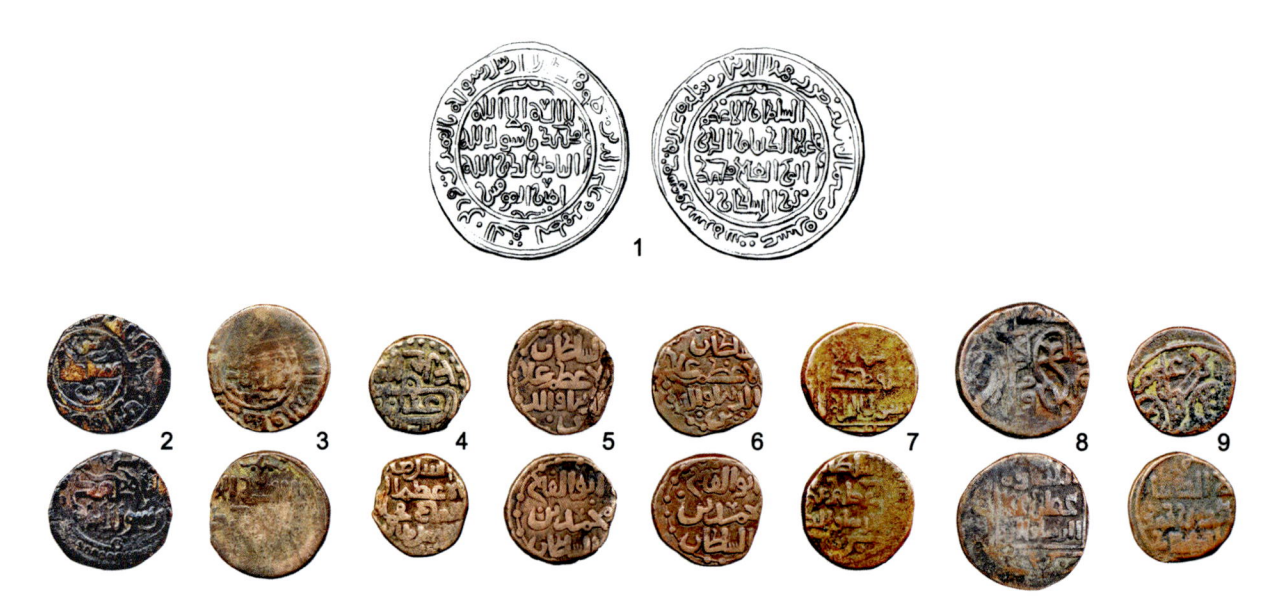

Figure 63 Khwarazm Shah coins. ʿAla al-dīn Muḥammād b. Tekish gold dinar (1), copper alloy jitals (2–9)

ʿAla al-duniya wa al-dīn. *Reverse*: Arabic inscription *la ilah illa Allāh Muḥammād rasul Allāh*. 3.31g, 15mm. Tye 1995, pp. 132, 172, type 274.

Fig. 63.4 – IOLC.6750. Copper alloy jital, minted in Ghazni. *Obverse*: Bull standing to left in dotted border. Devanagari inscription *śrī Samantadeva*. Arabic inscription *Ghazna* on rump. *Reverse*: Arabic inscription *al-sultan al-ʿazam abu'l-fath Muḥammād bin al-sultan*. 2.94g, 11mm. Tye 1995, pp. 135, 172, type 294.

Total 6 coins: 3.09g (1), 2.94g–2 23g (5).

Fig. 63.5–6. Copper alloy jitals, minted in Ghazni. *Obverse*: Arabic inscription *al-sultan al-ʿazam ʿAla al-duniya wa al-dīn*. *Reverse*: Arabic inscription *abu'l-fath Muḥammād b. al-sultan*. Tye 1995, pp. 133, 172, type 283.

Fig. 63.5 – IOLC.7112. 2.89g, 13mm.
Fig. 63.6 – IOLC.7131. 2.91g, 14mm.

Total 465 coins: 3.55g–3g (260), 2.99g–2.04g (205), 1.8g (1).

Fig. 63.7 – IOLC.7245. Copper alloy jital, minted in Bamiyan. *Obverse*: Arabic inscription in square frame *la ilah illa Allāh Muḥammād rasul Allāh*. *Reverse*: Arabic inscription in cartouche *al-sultan al-ʿazam ʿAla al-duniya wa al-dīn*. 2.96g, 15mm. Tye 1995, pp. 133, 172, type 276.

Fig. 63.8 – IOLC.7912. Copper alloy jital, minted in Bamiyan. *Obverse*: Horseman riding to right. Arabic inscription *Muḥammād bin sultan Bamiyan*. *Reverse*: Arabic inscription in square cartouche *al-sultan al-ʿazam ʿAla al-duniya wa al-dīn*. 3.37g, 18mm. Tye 1995, pp. 127, 170, type 236.

Total 2 coins: 3.37g, 2.68g. See also **F526/1a, Pl. 11.8** (pp. 62–3 above).

Fig. 63.9 – IOLC.7916. Copper alloy jital, minted in Qunduz. *Obverse*: Horseman riding to right. Arabic inscription *al-sultan al-ʿazam*. *Reverse*: Arabic inscription *Qunduz ʿAla al-duniya wa al-dīn Muḥammād al-sultan*. 2.92g, 14mm. Tye 1995, pp. 126, 170, type 233.

Total 4 coins and a fragment: 2.92g–2.36g.

Ilkhanid (1256–1353)

Fig. 64.1 – IOLC.5214. Silver coin. Unattributed local ruler. *Obverse*: Arabic inscription. *Reverse*: Arabic inscription. 1.18g, 17mm.

Total 2 coins: 1.23g, 1.18g.

Fig. 64.2 – IOLC.5183. Copper alloy coin; overstrike. Unattributed mint/ruler. *Obverse*: Arabic inscription in square Kufic, encircled by a wide decorative border. *Reverse*: Inscription encircled by dotted border. 3.69g, 26mm.

Total 11 coins: 9.84g (1), 4.86g–4.01g (4), 3.86g–3.02g (4), 2.32g–2.25g (2).

Uljaytu (1304–16)

Fig. 64.3 – IOLC.5212. Silver-plated copper alloy coin; overstrike; unattributed mint. *Obverse*: Traces of a central inscription in a triangle overstruck on one within a circle. *Reverse*: An inscription within a cinquefoil. 3.34g, 23mm.

Total 1 coin and a fragment: 3.34g, 2.16g.

Timurid (1370–1500)

Anonymous unregulated civic coinage

Fig. 64.4 – IOLC.5220. Copper alloy falus, minted in Kandahar. *Obverse*: Deer to left, surrounded by Persian inscriptions and arabesques. *Reverse*: Goose to right (?) surrounded by Persian inscriptions and arabesques. 9.41g, 29mm.

Fig. 64.6 – IOLC.5227. Copper alloy falus, minted in Kabul AH 877 / AD 1419. *Obverse*: Persian inscription in centre of a hexagonal star. *Reverse*: Ornamental star-shape with a central inscription, dated 877. 3.21g, 18mm.

Total 27 anonymous coins: 4.42g (1), 3.99g–3.09g (6), 2.93g–2g (13), 1.97g–1.27g (5), 0.75g (1).

Fig. 64.7 – IOLC.5248. Copper alloy falus, minted in Kabul. *Obverse*: Arabesques. *Reverse*: Persian inscription *Kabul*. 1.53g, 16mm.

Total 4 coins: 2.98g–2.81g (2), 1.53g–1.48g (2).
Unattributed 3 coins: 5.66g, 3.94g, 2.76g.

Aq-Qoyunlu (Turkmen of the White Sheep 1378–1508)

Fig. 64.8 – IOLC.5202. Copper alloy countermarked coin, unknown mint. *Obverse*: Worn inscription with a countermark. *Reverse*: Worn. 2.12g, 21mm.

Total 15 coins: 5.14g (1), 4.66g–4.32g (2), 3.7g–3.41g (2), 2.74g–2.07g (6), 1.96g–1.47g (4).

Figure 64 Ilkhanid coins. Unattributed (1–2); Uljaytu silver-plated coin (3). Timurid anonymous civic copper alloy falus (4–7). Aq-Qoyunlu countermarked coin (8), Mu'izz al-dīn Jahangir overstrike (9). Wali Muḥammād b. Jani of Astrakhan white metal plated coin (10). Durrani coins. Maḥmūd Shah (11); anonymous civic copper alloy falus (12). Barakzai anonymous civic copper alloy falus (13–14). Unattributed civic copper alloy coins: Afghanistan (15–16), Iran (17). Zengid of Mosul Badr al-dīn Lu'lu' (16). Ottoman Maḥmūd II silver 20 para (17)

Mu'izz al-dīn Jahangir (AH 848–85 / AD 1444–51)
Fig. 64.9 – IOLC.5275. Copper alloy uniface coin; overstrike. *Obverse*: A symbol roughly resembling a fish (?) within a feathered square, enclosed by a square frame with two straight and two scalloped sides. In the left field are a dotted flower and a zero. *Reverse*: Traces of the worn undertype with a large, irregular incuse mark. 8.82g, 29mm. Mitchiner 1977, p. 267, type 1796 (?).

Janids of Astrakhan (1599–1785; successors to the Shaybanid dynasty in Central Asia)

Wali Muḥammād b. Jani (AH 1014–16 / AD 1605–11)
Fig. 64.10 – IOLC.5278. White metal plated coin, minted in Bukhara. *Obverse*: Persian inscription *Muḥammād Khan Wali Bahadur* in a square dotted frame. *Reverse*: Persian inscription (?) in a square dotted frame. 4.4g, 27mm. Mitchiner 1977, p. 285, type 1994.

Total 2 coins: 4.4g, 4.21g.

Durrani (1774–1823)

Maḥmūd Shah (AH 1223–33 / AD 1808–17)
Fig. 64.11 – IOLC.5256. Copper alloy coin, minted in Ahmadshahi (Kandahar). *Obverse*: Part of a Persian inscription flanked by small dotted flowers. *Reverse*: Small dotted flowers. 2.7g, 12mm.

Total 2 coins: 13.33g, 2.7g.

Catalogue of Coins | 209

Anonymous unregulated civic coinage

Fig. 64.12 – IOLC.5276. Hammered copper alloy falus minted AH 1229 / AD 1813, in Kabul. *Obverse*: Flower between two swords. *Reverse*: Ornamental inscription and date *Kabul falus 1229*. 7.8g, 19mm. Valentine 1911, pp. 62–3, no. 10.

Total 2 coins: 7.94g, 7.8g.

Barakzai (1824–38)

Anonymous unregulated civic coinage

Masson left Afghanistan in 1838, which provides a cut-off date for the anonymous unregulated coins issued by municipal and provincial governors in his collection.

Fig. 64.13 – IOLC.5257. Hammered copper alloy falus minted in Kabul. *Obverse*: Sword encircled by floral scrolls within a dotted border. *Reverse*: Part of an inscription surrrounded by floral scrolls. 9.25g, 21mm.

Fig. 64.14 – IOLC.5261. Hammered copper alloy falus minted in Kabul. *Obverse*: Flower and sword. *Reverse*: Inscription; small dotted flowers. 2.25g, 15mm.

Total 7 coins: 9.25g (1), 5.57g (1), 4.82g–4.67g (2), 2.87g–2.25g (2), 1.27g (1).

Afghanistan

Anonymous/unattributed civic coinage

Fig. 64.15 – IOLC.7742. Copper alloy falus, minted in Ahmadshahi (Kandahar). Unattributed. *Obverse*: Leaf between two swords. *Reverse*: Traces of an inscription. 9.09g, 20mm.

Fig. 64.16 – IOLC.7741. Unattributed copper alloy falus, minted in Afghanistan (?). *Obverse*: Persian inscription. *Reverse*: Worn Persian inscription, dated AH 809 / AD 1409. 7.61g, 20mm.

Total 13 coins: 11.36g (1), 10.97g (1), 9.09g (1), 7.61g (2), 5.8g–5.26g (2), 4.97g–4.63g (2), 3.16g (1), 2.82g–2.38g (3).

Iran

Anonymous unregulated civic coinage

Fig. 64.17 – IOLC.5254. Copper alloy falus. *Obverse*: Worn Persian inscription. *Reverse*: Worn Persian inscription *zarb 1210* (AD 1797). 3.97g, 22mm.

Zengid of Mosul

Badr al-dīn Lu'lu' (1234–59)

Fig. 64.18 – IOLC.5270. Copper alloy dirhem, minted in Mosul. *Obverse*: Diademed head facing to left within a square dotted border; a star in the lower left corner. *Reverse*: Arabic inscription citing the 'Abbasid caliph al-Mustansir, the Zengid ruler Lu'lu', and the Ayyubid sultans al-Kamil and al-Ashraf. 5.37g, 23mm.

Ottoman

Maḥmūd II (1808–39)

Fig. 64.17 – IOLC.5281. Silver 20 para, minted in Constantinople AH 1223, year 24 / AD 1808. *Obverse*: Tughra within chain wreath, encircled by floral border. *Reverse*: Arabic inscription (regnal year, mint and date) within chain wreath, encircled by floral border. 0.72g, 18mm.

Part 4: Catalogue of Gems, Seals and Amulets

Elizabeth Errington, Wannaporn Kay Rienjang and Chantal Fabrègues

Prior to 1837, Masson only records his acquisition of three engraved gems in his official correspondence with the East India Company (December 1834: **E161/VII f. 25**). The remaining statements of quantities all date from the period 15 October 1837 to 30 June 1838. The two principal amounts – duplicated in several lists – are 33 gems and beads collected up to 15 October (**Vol. II, E161/VII ff. 30, 32**) and 57 engraved gems collected 15 October to 30 June 1838 (**Vol. II, E161/VII f. 33, 36**), If added altogether (3 + 33 + 57), these provide a total of 93, which is very close to the 92 engraved gems now attributed to Masson in the Museum.

However, in one of his private inventories drawn up in the 1840s after his return to London (**Vol. II, F526/1**k), Masson lists 8 gems dispatched 11 December 1834, plus 3 dispatched 1 December 1835; then 33 for 15 October 1837, followed by 18 for 30 June 1838, providing a total of only 62 for the whole lot. This is further complicated by the fact that an unspecified number among 100 gems donated in 1943 and formerly belonging to Henry Haversham Godwin-Austen, are said in the acquisition registers to have been collected by Masson (p. 12 above). The similarities in subject matter, style and materials shared by some examples within the two groups tend to confirm this attribution (**Fig. 65**), but since it cannot be confirmed, the Godwin-Austen examples are only listed, with a link to their individual records on www.britishmuseum.org/research/collection_online, when comparable with confirmed Masson gems.

The collection includes 1 glass and 92 stone intaglios, 34 of which are engraved with Arabic or Persian inscriptions and are thus grouped here under Islamic seals. Of the remaining 59 gems, one is possibly a Christian amulet (**Fig. 71.1**), Another figural example dating from *c.* 1st century BC–1st century AD, was re-inscribed in Persian in the 17th–18th century (**Fig. 66.12**), while two seals have Hebrew and Devanagari inscriptions respectively (**Fig. 68.15–16**). The rest (55 intaglios) are carved with images, some of which are accompanied by inscriptions in Pahlavi, Kharoshthi and Bactrian. As the motifs and inscriptions are incised on the surface, the intaglios may have retained their function as seals, although their common use also as jewellery has been acknowledged since the 6th century BC in the Greek world (Boardman 1997). A few intaglios are set in later plain silver ring mounts (**Fig. 68.1–2, 9**; **Fig. 70.5**). Seven have a suspension hole (**Fig. 66.3–8**; **Fig. 68.8**) and many have a flat base with bevelled edges suggesting they were intended either as a pendant seal or as a mount for a finger or signet ring.

All the images in **Figs 66–70** are enlarged on a scale of 2:1, unlike the rest of the material catalogued (**Figs 71–134**) which is illustrated actual size.

Non-Islamic seals and intaglios

The 59 non-Islamic gems include a garnet cameo of a female head (**Fig. 66.1**), a flat octagonal sard seal already mentioned, with a later Persian inscription on the reverse (**Fig. 66.19**); a Christian (?) amulet dated *c.* 5th–7th century (**Fig. 71.1**); and two later seals, one 17th-century Jewish, with a Hebrew inscription, the other early 19th-century Hindu with a Devanagari inscription (**Fig. 68.15–16**). The images include a wide range of subjects, from deities, human figures and portraits, to plants and animals.

Figure 65 Carnelian intaglio, Godwin-Austen collection 1943,1009.24 (comparable to Figs 68.10–12)

Materials used largely comprise gemstones in the quartz family. The majority of the intaglios are of chalcedony, an opaque and translucent quartz. The varieties of chalcedony include carnelian (17 examples), sard (3 examples) and nicolo. Additional types of quartz used are amethyst and rock crystal. Garnet is popular (17 examples), whereas lapis lazuli and glass are rare (one example each: **Figs 68.8**, **67.9** respectively). Being of relatively hard stone, intaglios worked in quartz and garnet were most likely engraved using rotating metal tools coated with an abrasive such as emery and perhaps mounted with diamond chips (Boardman 1997, p. 78; Callieri 1997a, p. 165; Sax and Meeks 2011, p. 185). The engraved surface is usually oval, with few rectangular or circular and one octagonal. There is a mixture of carved motifs on flat and convex faces, except for those classified as Sasanian, where almost all have their motifs carved on the flat face. Based on features such as subject, style and carving techniques, the intaglios broadly represent the various cultural groups who ruled in eastern Afghanistan from the late Achaemenid to the medieval Islamic period (c. 4th century BC–13th century AD).

Two intaglios have features which may place them towards the end of the Achaemenid period (**Fig. 66.2–3**). They show the use of a point, a technique which produces rounded depressions on the carved surface characteristic of Persian-Hellenistic seals of the late 4th century BC (Callieri 1997, p. 85). Four intaglios in the collection exhibit portrait heads in the manner popular among Hellenistic and Roman traditions. The portrait bust on a green chalcedony intaglio (**Fig. 66.11**) moreover resembles that depicted on the Greco-Bactrian king Eucratides I (174–155 BC). Classical deities also feature as subject matter. These include Tyche, Nike (Victory) and Eros (Cupid).

In addition, the collection possesses an intaglio carved with a standing Heracles with a club and lion-skin (**Fig. 67.13**), in the same manner as that depicted on coins from the time of the Greco-Bactrian king Demetrius (c. 200–190 BC), down to the Kushan king Kujula Kadphises (c. AD 50–90; **Figs 34–5**) and more rarely, Huvishka (c. AD 151–90).

Inscriptions in Pahlavi, used on coins of the Kushano-Sasanians and Sasanians, are engraved alongside subjects on four intaglios, all in a distinctive style from those carved with classical figures (**Fig. 68.1–4**).

Four intaglios may be grouped to the Hun period (c. 4th–6th century). They show figures, generally human busts, whose design and details resemble those depicted on coins of the Kidarite Huns of the 4th century and the Alkhan Huns of the late 4th–5th century (**Fig. 68.8–12**). The similarity between motifs and rendering as shown on coins current in Afghanistan and intaglios found there, in combination with the engraving of scripts used in this region, suggest some connections between coins and glyptic art. This also suggests that workshops for glyptic art were likely to have existed in Afghanistan during the above periods.

Islamic seals and intaglios

As with non-Islamic intaglios, the majority of the 36 Islamic examples in the Masson collection are made of gemstones in the quartz family, with translucent and opaque chalcedony making up the largest portion. Varieties of chalcedony include carnelian (the most popular: 16 examples), jasper (4 examples), and more rarely sardonyx and sard (2 examples each). The only transparent quartz used is rock crystal. Another relatively hard gemstone is garnet, although there is only one Islamic seal of this material in the collection (**Fig. 69.17**). Softer stones include haematite (3 examples) and lapis lazuli (one example). The collection also has one glass cameo (**Fig. 71.5**), as well as one brass and four copper alloy seals (**Fig. 71.6–10**).

Almost all of the intaglios are engraved with inscriptions alone. Only in few instances are the inscriptions depicted alongside motifs, which include a star (**Fig. 70.1–4**), Solomon's knot (**Fig. 69.13**), St George on horseback (**Fig. 70.6**) and flower-like dots with a leafy frond (**Fig. 71.8**). The majority of inscriptions are in Arabic, three are in Persian, one in Arabic and Persian and one in pseudo-Kufic. All but four inscriptions (**Fig. 71.2–5**) are engraved in reverse, so their intended use was as seals. The contents of the inscriptions include simple phases or a motto (*'ālama*), phases with reference to God, verses from the *Qur'ān*, and names of individuals (see also Porter 2011, pp. 35–83).

Most seals are oval or rectangular in shape. Less popular shapes are circular (2 examples), octagonal (4 examples) and straight-sided oval (4 examples). None of Islamic seals have a suspension hole or are perforated. Many of them have a flat back and bevelled edges, suggesting they were intended as settings for rings.

Like the non-Islamic intaglios, the engraving on relatively hard stones was likely to have been made using rotating metal tools coated with an abrasive. According to an analysis of tool marks left on engraved surface of selected Islamic seals by Margaret Sax and Nigel Meeks, early, intermediate and late Islamic seals (8th–20th century) were engraved using lathe-mounted rotary wheels (Sax and Meeks 2011, p. 188).

Metal seals

In addition to gems, the collection has 75 copper alloy seals of various sizes, forms and iconography. There is also a single terracotta seal (**Fig. 72.1**). The pre-Islamic period presents a wide variety of forms. In the stepped pyramid type (**Fig. 72**), the motifs are carved on the flat base, with the superstructure serving as a handle, usually pierced for attachment. Box-seals comprise a double cube, pierced longitudinally, with an image on each of the remaining four sides (**Fig. 75**). Other forms have one or two, usually pierced, lugs on the back (**Fig. 74**). Although some may have been used as seals, others may have been intended perhaps as ornaments such as buttons (**Fig. 74.17**). The motifs include geometric designs, animals (lion, horse, elephant, ibex, stag, zebu, griffin and dragon) as well as human figures and deities.

One intaglio depicts a seated figure reminiscent of the Buddha in meditation (**Fig. 73.5**). Kushan deities such as Oesho (in the guise of Shiva) and classical figures such as Heracles are also included (**Fig. 75.9**). A figure seated in an ascetic's hut (**Fig. 74.8**) resembles depictions on Gandharan sculptural reliefs (e.g. Bhattacharyya 2002, pp. 133, 137, nos 583, 620), while the three-leafed vegetal form above the shoulder of the bust on **Fig. 74.31** is a crude representation of the flaming shoulders found on Kushan, Kushano-Sasanian and Alkhan coins.

Two are inscribed: one in Greek (? **Fig. 74.24**), the other in Kharoshthi (**Fig. 74.29**).

In contrast, metal Islamic seals are restricted to only five altogether and are all inscribed: one in pseudo-Arabic, another in pseudo-Kufic (**Fig. 71.9–10**), a third in Persian dated AH 1080 / AD 1669/70 (**Fig. 71.8**). The latest are two of identical type: one with a Persian inscription (**Fig. 71.7**), the other dated in Urdu AH 1154 / AD 1741 (**Fig. 71.6**). Overall however on stylistic, iconographic and inscriptional grounds, the majority of the metal seals belong to the period *c.* 1st century BC–6th century AD. They have strong affiliations with finger-rings of the same period, many of which no doubt also functioned as signet rings (**Figs 78–83**).

Gems *c.* 4th century BC–6th century AD (scale 2:1)

Fig. 66.1 – 1880.3562. IM.Gems.27. Garnet cameo in bas-relief of the facing head of a woman, her hair gathered in two bunches of curls above the forehead and swept back over the ears. Flat on the back with a bevelled edge suggesting it was originally set in a ring. Chipped on one side of the face, around the chin and on the back. Indo-Greek/Roman, *c.* 1st century BC–3rd century AD. 10mm x 9.5mm. Errington 1999, p. 228, pl. 7.3.

Fig. 66.2 – 1880.3488. IM.Gems.13. Oval carnelian intaglio, flat on both sides with a bevelled edge, depicting a goddess (Anahita?) wearing a crown and standing in profile, arms outstretched, facing a lion. The quite high relief is carefully executed, but with no attempt to disguise the use of the point, which produces rounded depressions characteristic of Persian-Hellenistic seals. Worn; the engraved face is scratched and chipped. Achaemenid, *c.* 4th century BC. 20mm x 17mm x 3mm. Callieri 1997, no. 4.4, p. 85, pl. 12.

Fig. 66.3 – 1880.3489. IM.Gems.10. Slightly oval, carnelian scaraboid: a flat face with a convex back and a large circular suspension hole pierced longitudinally; depicting a lion emerging in profile from behind a mound of stones surmounted by a tree. In moderate relief, quite carefully executed, but the use of the point characteristic of Persian-Hellenistic seals is undisguised. Chipped in several places, including the lion's paw. Achaemenid, *c.* 4th century BC. 21mm x 17mm x 11mm.

Callieri (1997, no. 4.15, pp. 89–90, pl. 13) notes that the motif of the tree rising from a stylised mountain is also found on Indian punch-marked coins (i.e. Mauryan period, *c.* 269–187 BC, see Gupta and Hardaker 2014, pp. 248, 262, marks 115, 329).

Fig. 66.4 – 1880.3547. IM.Gems.17. Oval seal pendant, in amethyst or quartz with violet reflections, convex on both sides, with a small circular hole pierced longitudinally; showing a winged, galloping horse in profile. The hooves show the undisguised use of the point characteristic of Persian-Hellenistic seals. Considerable interior exfoliations; chipped. Persian-Hellenistic, *c.* 4th–3rd century BC. 16mm x 20mm x 10mm. Callieri 1997, no. 4.9, p. 87, pl. 12.

Fig. 66.5 – 1880.3555. IM.Gems.35. Oval seal pendant, in light purple amethyst, convex on both sides, with a small circular suspension hole; showing a prancing horse in profile. Executed in moderate relief with undisguised use of the point characteristic of Persian-Hellenistic seals for the muzzle, hoofs and leg joints. Internal exfoliation. Persian-Hellenistic, *c.* 4th–3rd century BC. 16mm x 11mm x 7mm. Callieri 1997, no. 4.8, p. 87, pl. 12.

Fig. 66.6 – 1880.3604. IM.Gems 61. Oval pale chalcedony cabochon-cut seal, with a convex face showing a seated bull. A small suspension hole is pierced horizontally. Persian-Hellenistic, *c.* 4th–3rd century BC. 14mm x 17mm x 9.5mm.

Fig. 66.7 – 1880.3605. IM.Gems.62. Oval pale chalcedony cabochon-cut seal, flat face with a convex back and a large suspension hole pierced longitudinally; showing a winged griffin. Chipped on the top left face behind the griffin's head and around the suspension hole. Persian-Hellenistic, *c.* 4th–3rd century BC. 19.5mm x 27mm x 21mm; face: 17.5mm x 21mm.

Fig. 66.8 – 1880.3606. IM.Gems.63. Oval pale chalcedony cabochon-cut seal, flat face with a convex back and a large suspension hole pierced longitudinally; showing a crudely rendered bird. Marked with ingrained scratches. Persian-Hellenistic, *c.* 4th–3rd century BC. 17.3mm x 22.7mm x 19mm; face: 13.5mm x 16mm.

Fig. 66.9 – 1880.3579. IM.Gems.44. Oval light-coloured garnet intaglio, strongly convex face with a flat back; showing a walking horse in profile. The seal is carefully finished and the engraved horse naturalistic in treatment. Scored with two small marks at the top edge. Indo-Greek or Kushan (?) *c.* 1st century BC–2nd century AD. 8mm x 11mm x 3mm. Callieri 1997, no. 1.27, p. 53, pl. 3; Errington 1999, pp. 212, 228, pl. 7.18.

Fig. 66.10 – 1880.3576. IM.Gems.41. Rectangular almandine garnet intaglio, convex face with rounded ends and a strongly concave back, the right side is broken and missing. The extant fragment shows a griffin in profile, harnessed by a man on foot. Indo-Greek/Roman (?) *c.* 1st century BC–3rd century AD. 12mm x 13mm x 2mm. Callieri 1997, no. 1.25, p. 52–3, pl. 2.

Fig. 66.11 – 1880.3727. IM.Gems.26. Oval chrysoprase (green chalcedony) intaglio, slightly convex face (?) with a

Figure 66 Garnet cameo head (1). Gemstone intaglios *c.* 4th–3rd century BC (2–8). 2nd century BC–3rd century AD (9-11). 1st century BC–1st century AD re-engraved *c.* 17th–18th century (12)

214 | *Charles Masson: Collections from Begram and Kabul Bazaar, Afghanistan, 1833–1838*

bevelled edge, depicting the bust of a man wearing a Macedonian helmet to left. The image resembles the portrait bust on the coins of the Greco-Bactrian king Eucratides I (174–155 BC), see **Fig. 24.11–24**. Slightly chipped on the back. Indo-Greek (?) 2nd–1st century BC. 14mm x 10mm.

Fig. 66.12 – 1880.3563. IM.Gems.29. Rectangular semi-transparent sard intaglio, flat face with the corners subsequently cut off to make it octagonal; the reverse being re-engraved in the Islamic period. The original image shows Tyche (right) with a cornucopia facing Nike, who is descending to crown her with a wreath. On the back a Persian nastaliq inscription in high relief:

عبد الله
ابن مرتضی

'Abdallāh b. Murtaḍā

Indo-Greek/Islamic, c. 1st century BC–1st century AD/17th–18th century. 15mm x 11.5mm x 2.5mm. Callieri 1997, no. 1.10, p. 47, pl. 1; Porter 2011, p. 84, no. 364.

Fig. 67.1 – 1880.3599. IM.Gems.56. Oval almandine garnet intaglio, with a flat face and concave back; showing a trotting ibex to left. Indo-Scythian (?) c. 2nd–1st century BC. 7mm x 8mm x 2mm.

Fig. 67.2 – 1880.3583. IM.Gems.48. Oval carnelian intaglio, flat on both sides with a bevelled edge on the back; showing an eagle in three-quarters view with wings outstretched, its head turned backwards and holding a palm frond in one talon. Similar to 1880.3543, from the relic deposit of Hadda stupa 10 (see **Vol. I, pp. 191–2, Fig. 279.22**). Roman, c. 1st–4th century AD. 10mm x 9mm x 2.5mm. Callieri 1997, no. 1.29, p. 54, pl. 3.

Fig. 67.3 – 1880.3584. IM.Gems.49. Oval orange-yellow chalcedony intaglio, having a convex face with a flat back; depicting a bearded male bust to left. Roman, c. 1st–4th century. 10mm x 11mm x 3mm.

Callieri (1997, no. 1.16, p. 49, pl. 2) notes that the depiction on this seal resembles an impression on a sealing from Cyrene, the ancient Greek and Roman city in Libya.

Fig. 67.4 – 1880.3545. IM.Gems.15. Oval carnelian intaglio, flat on both sides with a bevelled edge on the face; showing a clean-shaven, naturalistic bust in profile. Roman, c. 1st–3rd century. 19mm x 15mm x 3.5mm. Callieri 1997, no. 1.15, p. 49, pl. 2; Errington 1999, pp. 212, 228, pl. 7.9.

A similar seal in the Godwin-Austen collection was probably also originally acquired by Masson (see britishmuseum.org/collection_online 1943,1009.34). **Fig. 67.5 – 1880.3548.** IM.Gems.18. Oval amber-coloured chalcedony intaglio, flat on both sides with a bevelled edge on the back; showing a female bust in profile, her hair bound by a fillet and brushed forwards into a thick curled roll with a fringe around the face and neck. The shoulders are covered with drapery. Fractured diagonally across the lower half. Roman, c. 1st–2nd century AD. 13mm x 11mm x 2mm. Errington 1999, p. 212, 228, pl. 7.12.

Callieri (1997, no. 1.19, p. 50, pl. 2) notes that the depiction on this seal resembles an impression on a sealing from Libya.

Fig. 67.6 – 1880.3554. IM.Gems.34. Oval polished, pyrope-almandine garnet intaglio, flat on both sides with a bevelled edge on the back; showing a winged female bust to right, in fairly high relief, possibly of Artemis (Diana) or Nike (Victory). Slightly chipped to the right of the head. Roman, c. 1st–3rd century. 11mm x 8mm x 2mm. Callieri 1997, no. 1.11, pp. 47–8, pl. 1; Errington 1999, p. 212, 228, pl. 7.4.

Fig. 67.7 – 1880.3553. IM.Gems.33. Lower part of an oval, highly polished, almandine garnet intaglio, having a flat face with a slightly convex back; showing a helmeted bust, probably of Athena. The top half has broken off at eyebrow level and is missing. Roman, c. 1st–3rd century. 10mm x 13mm x 2mm. Callieri 1997, no. 1.13, p. 48, pl. 1.

Fig. 67.8 – 1880.3552. IM.Gems.32. Oval semi-transparent sard intaglio, flat on both sides with a bevelled edge on the back; showing a winged nude Eros (Cupid) in profile, holding a branch in one hand and a helmet (?) in the other. Roman, c. 1st–3rd century. 12mm x 10.5mm x 2mm. Callieri 1997, no. 1.20, pp. 50–1, pl. 2.

Fig. 67.9 – 1880.3565. IM.Gems.36. Oval intaglio in yellow glass, having a slightly convex face with a flat back; showing a standing female figure wearing a chiton and raising her right hand towards her face. Very worn. Roman, c. 1st–3rd century. 18mm x 13mm x 2mm. Callieri 1997, no. 1.26, p. 53, pl. 2.

Fig. 67.10 – 1880.3577. IM.Gems.42. Oval irregular cabochon-cut, garnet intaglio, having a convex face with a concave back; showing a winged Nike (Victory), wearing a chiton, polos and diadem and holding a wreath and a palm branch; a Kharoshthi inscription beside the wing, and at the bottom: *Aspaḍunai* ([to] Aśvaduna). Kushan (?) c. 1st–2nd century AD. 11mm x 9mm x 3mm.

Callieri (1997, no. 5.1, p. 91, pl. 14) notes that the only evidence in Gandhara for the concave-convex section of this seal is found on nine possibly imported Roman garnets from Sirkap (Marshall 1951, vol. II, p. 650, no. 71.a-i, pl. 207, no. 10.a-i). The present gem could therefore be a Roman import to which the inscription was added later.

Fig. 67.11 – 1880.3582. IM.Gems.47. Broken garnet intaglio, flat on both sides, the lower half missing, executed in fairly high relief; showing the helmeted figure of Athena, with a scarf billowing behind her, holding a spear in her hand. Roman, c. 1st–3rd century. 10mm x 11mm x 3.5mm. Callieri 1997, no. 1.5, pp. 23, 44–5, pl. 1.

A similar seal in the Godwin-Austen collection was probably also originally acquired by Masson (see britishmuseum.org/collection_online 1943,1009.18).

Fig. 67.12 – 1880.3559. IM.Gems.22, Oval cabochon-cut almandine garnet intaglio, having a convex face with a flat back and a worn surface; showing a standing goddess, wearing a polos and chiton, holding a branch and cornucopia. The crown identifies the goddess as Tyche or Hariti. The garnet is somewhat opaque with internal faults; the lower rim slightly chipped. Kushan, c. 1st–3rd century. 13mm x 11mm x 4mm. Callieri 1997, no. 7.8, p. 108, pl. 19; Errington 1999, p. 212, 228, pl. 7.2.

A similar seal in the Godwin-Austen collection was probably also originally acquired by Masson (see britishmuseum.org/collection_online 1943,1009.38).

Fig. 67.13 – 1880.3544. IM.Gems.11. Oval carnelian intaglio, flat on both sides with a bevelled edge; showing a standing figure of Heracles with a club and lion-skin.

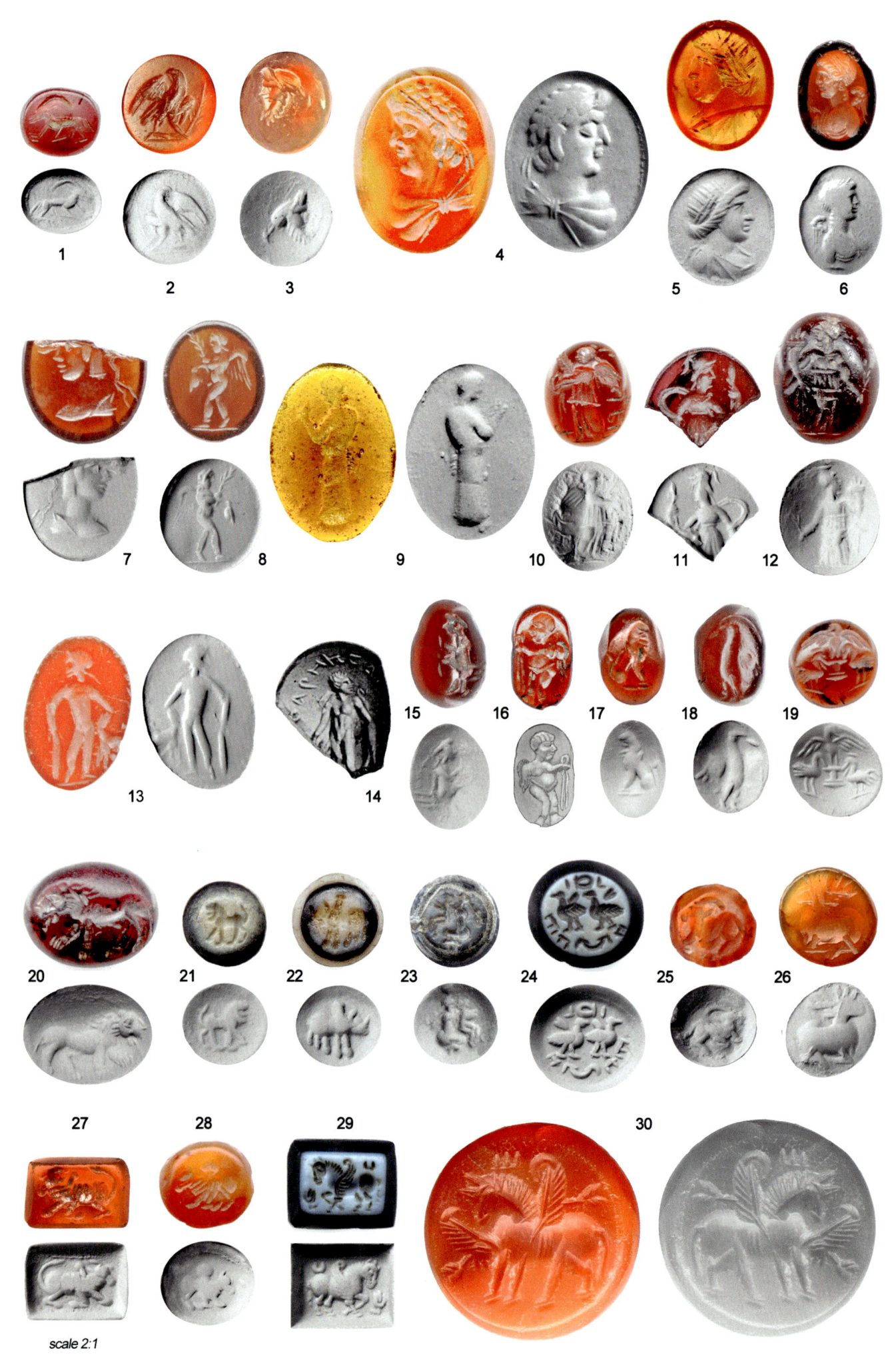

Figure 67 Indo-Greek, Roman, Kushan and Sasanian intaglios *c.* 1st century BC–6th century AD

216 | *Charles Masson: Collections from Begram and Kabul Bazaar, Afghanistan, 1833–1838*

Chipped all around the rim. Kushan, *c.* 1st–3rd century. 15mm x 11mm x 3mm. Callieri 1997, no. 5.4, p. 92–3, pl. 14; Errington 1999, p. 212, 228, pl. 7.1.

The image closely resembles depictions of Heracles on coins of the first Kushan king, Kujula Kadphises. A similar seal in the Godwin-Austen collection was probably also originally acquired by Masson (see britishmuseum.org/collection_online 1943,1009.39).

Fig. 67.14 – 1880.3989. IM.Gems.73. Broken oval sard intaglio, with a convex face and concave back; engraved with a finely executed nude male figure holding a fish (?). Part of a Bactrian inscription (?) οαρμησαι (*oarmēsai*) around the top section of the seal. Broken, with the bottom part missing. Kushan (?). 9mm x 7.5mm. Bivar 1968, p. 9, pl. I.5; Davary 1982, p. 114, sig. 66.

Accompanied by a 19th-century red wax sealing. The intaglio was not found during the registration process of Masson seals in 1998, and has not surfaced subsequently. A clear image of it is published in Bivar 1968. Its publication by Davary suggests it was lost/mislaid between 1982 and 1998.

Fig. 67.15 – 1880.3578. IM.Gems.43. Elongated oval, irregular cabochon-cut, garnet intaglio, with an extremely convex face and a flat back; showing a crudely executed, draped, standing figure in profile, wearing a flat hat or helmet (?) and holding a staff. Three parallel horizontal lines extend behind the figure at thigh level. Moderate relief perfunctorily engraved, lacking finish and detail; *c.* 1st–5th century. 11mm x 8mm x 5mm. Callieri 1997, no. 6.1, p. 99, pl. 16.

A similar figure of a helmeted Zeus, holding a sceptre with right arm outstretched, occurs on Indo-Parthian coins of Sasan (AD 64–70). A better executed helmeted figure with a staff is also found on intaglio 1880.3542, from Hadda stupa 10 (**Vol. I, pp. 191–2, Fig. 279.21**).

Fig. 67.16 – 1880.3597. IM.Gems.54. Small, oval, low cabochon-cut, pyrope-almandine garnet intaglio, with a slightly convex face and a flat back; showing a standing nude, winged Eros (Cupid) holding a diadem. Moderate relief and perfunctorily engraved; lacks finish and detail. Similar in style to **Fig. 67.15**; *c.* 1st–5th century. 11mm x 8mm x 3mm.

Fig. 67.17 – 1880.3988. IM.Gems.74. Elongated oval, high cabochon-cut, pyrope-almandine garnet intaglio, having a convex face with flat back, depicting a lion seated to right; *c.* 1st–3rd century. 9.6mm x 7mm x 3.2mm.

According to IM.Gems.74: 'Sard. Indistinct intaglio figure, small'. M. Willis noted in 1998: 'Found with other Masson seals in a box. Description does not match, but it was the only seal left over'.

Fig. 67.18 – 1880.3596. IM.Gems.53. Oval almandine garnet intaglio, cabochon-cut with a flat back; engraved with a standing bird; *c.* 1st–3rd century. 10mm x 8mm x 3mm.

Fig. 67.19 – 1880.3598. IM.Gems.55. Oval almandine garnet intaglio, with a slightly convex face; showing a bird standing on a pedestal, facing to the front, with wings displayed; flanked on either side by a long-legged bird with a curved neck and large beak resembling a pelican or perhaps a stork; *c.* 1st–3rd century. 8.5mm x 9mm x 3mm.

Fig. 67.20 – 1880.3551. IM.Gems.28. Oval garnet intaglio, having a highly convex face with a flat back, showing a walking lion. Slightly chipped rim with internal breaks. Kushano-Sasanian, *c.* 3rd–4th century. 10mm x 14mm x 5mm. Callieri 1997, no. 7.52, p. 125, pl. 27; Errington 1999, pp. 212, 228, pl. 7.19.

A similar seal has the Bactrian legend κοþοοχοορνο (*kašofarno* or *košofarno*: Davary 1982, p. 114, sig. 69) and is dated by Bivar (1968, p.13, pl. IV.6) to the Kushano-Sasanian period or later. See also Callieri (1997, p.125, cat. no. 7.51) for another seal of the same type in the Victoria and Albert Museum (IM 50-01932), said to have been found near Jalalabad in 1842.

Fig. 67.21 – 1880.3601. IM.Gems.58. Small, circular nicolo intaglio, having a slightly convex face with bevelled edges; engraved with a standing lion. Kushano-Sasanian (?) *c.* 3rd–5th century. 9mm x 4mm.

Fig. 67.22 – 1880.3600. IM.Gems.57. Small, circular nicolo intaglio, having a flat face with a bevelled edge; showing a crudely engraved humped bull. Kushano-Sasanian (?) 3rd–5th century. 9mm x 4mm.

There are also two similar seals in the Godwin-Austen collection which were probably also originally acquired by Masson (see britishmuseum.org/collection_online 130966 and 130954).

Fig. 67.23 – 1880.3602. IM.Gems.59. Small, circular nicolo intaglio, having a flat face with bevelled edges, indistinctly engraved with a seated woman holding the stick-like figure of a child. Kushano-Sasanian (?) *c.* 3rd–5th century. 9mm x 4mm.

Fig. 67.24 – 1880.3566. IM.Gems.37. Oval nicolo intaglio, having a flat face with bevelled edges, showing two birds walking to left and an illegible Pahlavi inscription. Sasanian, *c.* 3rd–5th century. 11mm x 12mm x 3.5mm. Errington 1999, p. 228, pl. 7.22.

Fig. 67.25 – 1880.3615. IM.Gems.75. Circular carnelian intaglio, having a whitish worn upper surface and a flat face with a bevelled edge chipped along the back; engraved with an ibex seated to left. Sasanian (?) *c.* 3rd–5th century. 9mm x 2.4mm.

A similar seal in the Godwin-Austen collection was probably also originally acquired by Masson (see britishmuseum.org/collection_online 130996).

Fig. 67.26 – 1880.3585. IM.Gems.50. Oval carnelian intaglio, flat on both sides with a bevelled edge on the back side; engraved with a stag seated to left. Similar in execution to **Fig. 68.5**. Sasanian (?) *c.* 5th–6th century. 10mm x 11mm x 2mm.

Fig. 67.27 – 1880.3581. IM.Gems.46. Rectangular orange chalcedony intaglio, flat on both sides with a bevelled edge; showing a humped bull walking to left, its tail in the air. Sasanian, *c.* 4th–5th century. 7mm x 12mm x 3.5mm. Callieri 1997, no. 2.22, p. 64–5, pl. 5.

Two similar seals in the Godwin-Austen collection were probably also originally acquired by Masson (see britishmuseum.org/collection_online 130966 and 130970).

Fig. 67.28 – 1880.3586. IM.Gems.51. Oval carnelian intaglio, flat on both sides with a bevelled edge; engraved with a humped bull walking to left. Sasanian, *c.* 4th–5th century. 9mm x 11mm x 3mm.

Similar seals have also been found in Sogdia: Callieri 1997, no. 2.21, p. 64, pl. 5.

Fig. 67.29 – 1880.3561. IM.Gems.24. Rectangular nicolo intaglio, having a flat face with a bevelled edge; showing the winged horse Pegasus facing a vegetal motif to left; a crescent in the upper right field. Sasanian (?) *c.* 4th–5th century. 11.5mm x 9mm. Errington 1999, pp. 212, 228, pl. 7.21.

Fig. 67.30 – 1880.3500. IM.Gems.12. Circular amber-coloured carnelian intaglio, showing a winged horse in fairly high relief, its wings pinned by arrows (?). Above the head, a monogram. Internal exfoliation; outer rim chipped. Sasanian (?) *c.* 4th–5th century. 22mm x 5mm. Callieri 1997, no. 2.25, p. 65, pl. 6.

A similar seal in the Godwin-Austen collection was probably also originally acquired by Masson (see britishmuseum.org/collection_online 130958).

Fig. 68.1 – 1880.3608. IM.Gems.65. Oval nicolo intaglio with a flat face; engraved with a female facing bust, encircled by a minute Pahlavi inscription. Set in a later plain silver ring. Sasanian. *c.* 4th–5th century. 14mm x 13mm x 6.4mm x 19.25mm.

A seal in the Bibliothèque Nationale, Paris (BN 1975.251.3, ex Le Berre collection) shows a facing bust with the same hairstyle and drapery held in place by a circular clasp on one shoulder (Gyselen 1993, p.102, no.20.G.2, pl. XV.20.G.2). Bivar 1968, p. 21, pl. XXVIII.6; Errington 1999, pp. 212, 228, pl. 7.7.

Fig. 68.2 – 1880.3550. IM.Gems.25. Circular nicolo intaglio, flat on both sides with a bevelled edge on the front; in a metal setting with a perforated lug; showing a female bust to left, with ribbons trailing from her hair. Pahlavi characters in front of the face, of which only *p* is recognisable (see Gignoux in Callieri 1997, p. 307, no. 2.20, where he suggests the engraved characters could possibly be read as [']*p*[*zwn*], 'growth, increase'). Sasanian, *c.* 4th–5th century. 11mm x 10mm x 3mm. Callieri 1997, no. 2.20, p. 63–4, 307, pl. 5; Errington 1999, pp. 212, 228, pl. 7.6.

Fig. 68.3 – 1880.3567. IM.Gems.38. Rectangular nicolo intaglio, having a flat face with a bevelled edge; showing the heads of a man and woman facing each other; between them a Pahlavi inscription *biyahin*. Sasanian, *c.* 2nd–5th century. 9mm x 12mm x 4mm. Bivar 1968, p. 21, pl. XXVIII.4.

Fig. 68.4 – 1880.3614, IM.Gems.72. Oval carnelian intaglio, having a flat face; engraved with a nude, standing young woman (?), her hair drawn back into a large bun. One hand is raised, holding a flower (?) in front of her face; the other holds a ring or diadem down at her side. Pahlavi inscriptions on each side. Sasanian, *c.* 3rd–5th century. 12mm x 11mm x 1.5mm. Bivar 1968, p. 21, pl. XXVIII.9.

A similar seal in the Bibliothèque Nationale, Paris (BN 1971.511) shows a clothed female with a flower and the Pahlavi legend 'Mōrūdēy (?) son of Čihrid' (Gyselen 1993, p.77, no.10.A.4, pl. I.10.A.4); other examples of the same subject hold a variety of different objects, including a diadem (Gyselen 1993, pl. I.10.A).

Fig. 68.5 – 1880.3568. IM.Gems.39. Oval carnelian intaglio with a flat face; showing a ram before a bearded figure in a long coat and hat, holding a staff. Behind the man is a fire altar. Chipped along the top edge. Sasanian, *c.* 5th–6th century. 12mm x 13mm x 2mm. Bivar 1969, BD 16, pl. 5 (OA 5).

The same subject is found on seven seals in the Bibliothèque Nationale and Musée du Louvre, Paris (Gyselen 1993, p. 88, pl. IX.16.4–10), five examples (pl. IX.16.5–9) being very similar in execution except that the position of the ram and human figure are reversed.

Fig. 68.6 – 1880.3587. IM.Gems.52. Oval carnelian intaglio with a convex face; engraved with a palmate leaf encircled by its stem which terminates in a small triangle; *c.* 3rd–5th century. 9mm x 10mm x 3mm.

Fig. 68.7 – 1880.3580. IM.Gems.45. Circular carnelian intaglio, having a flat face with reversed bevelled edge; showing a bull kneeling to right; *c.* 3rd–5th century. 12mm x 2mm.

Fig. 68.8 – 1880.3564. IM.Gems.30. Nearly circular intaglio in lapis lazuli, having a slightly convex face with a flat back; showing a clean-shaven male bust to left. At the right edge is a circular suspension hole. Kidarite, *c.* 5th century. 16mm. Göbl 1967, I, p.249, G50; III, pl. 87.50; Errington 1999, pp. 212, 228, pl. 7.10.

Callieri notes the similarity of the treatment of the male figure to that used on Hun seals (1997, no. 7.41, pp. 120–1, pl. 25).

Fig. 68.9 – 1880.3609. IM.Gems.66. Oval nicolo intaglio with a flat face; depicting a bust in profile, with chin-length hair brushed forwards into a thick curled roll and fringe around the face and neck. The drapery of a garment covering the shoulders is indicated by incised lines around the neck. Set in a later plain silver ring. Kidarite, *c.* 5th century. 16.2mm x 14.7mm x 6mm x 20mm. Errington 1999, p. 228, pl. 7.8.

Fig. 68.10–12. Three oval carnelian intaglios, convex face with a flat back; showing the profile bust of a man with a moustache and chin-length hair brushed forwards into a thick curled roll with a fringe around the face and neck. The chest is rendered in four segments. The same hairstyle is found on silver coins issued by Kidara Kushanshah and is worn by an archer depicted with Alkhan and Kidarite huntsmen on horseback on a silver plate from Swat (Errington 2010, pp. 156–7, figs 1–2). A related gem (1880.3560) has an Alkhan Hun tamgha and is from the Hadda stupa 10 relic deposit, dated by coins found with it to the 5th century (**Vol. I, pp. 191–2, Fig. 279.19**). Kidarite, *c.* 5th century.

Fig. 68.10 – 1880.3549. IM.Gems.20. 11.5mm x 11mm x 3mm. Callieri 1997, no. 7.29, p. 116, pl. 22; Errington 1999, pp. 212, 228, pl. 7.13.

Fig. 68.11 – 1880.3558. IM.Gems.19. 14mm x 11mm x 3mm. Callieri 1997, no. 7.35, p. 118, pl. 23 (misnumbered 1880.3549, IM.Gems.20); Errington 1999, pp. 212, 228, pl. 7.11.

Fig. 68.12 – 1880.3595. IM.Gems.21. Slightly chipped along the left edge. 14mm x 12mm x 3mm. Callieri 1997a, pp. 172, 175, no. 10/12.

Fourteen similar seals in the Godwin-Austen collection were probably also originally acquired by Masson (see **Fig. 65** and britishmuseum.org/collection_online 1943,1009.18, 1943,1009.21–32, and 1943,1009.36).

Fig. 68.13 – 1880.3546. IM.Gems.16. Oval garnet intaglio, having a convex face with a bevelled edge and flat back; showing a male bust to left, above a feathered design

Figure 68 Sasanian, Hun c. 3rd–6th century and later 17th–19th century seals

Catalogue of Gems: Cameos, Seals and Amulets | 219

resembling two horizontal wings; inscribed personal name μοζδακο (Mozdako) in Bactrian in the left field. Slightly chipped along the top and bottom edge. The detail of a bust emerging above a feathered design also occurs on Alkhan coins. Hun, *c.* 5th–6th century. 19mm x 14mm x 3.5mm. Callieri 1997, no. 7.40, p. 120, pl. 24; 1997a, pp. 172, 175, no. 10/13.

Fig. 68.14 – 1880.3501. IM.Gems.14. Oval intaglio in rock crystal, having a highly convex face with a flat back; showing the busts of a man and woman facing each other. Badly chipped beneath the busts. Callieri notes the similarity of the treatment of the male figure to that used on Hun seals. Hun, *c.* 5th–6th century. 16mm x 19mm x 4mm. Callieri 1997, no. 7.46, p. 123, pl. 26.

Fig. 68.15 – 1880.3661. IM.IsGems.26. Octagonal sard seal; flat face, with a Hebrew inscription in three lines: Eliezer son Yissachar Segal, Z'L (May his memory be for a blessing). The inclusion of a surname suggests the inscription belongs to the early modern period. Reading courtesy of Mark Geller and Sacha Stern. Jewish. *c.* 17th century. 16mm x 12.5mm.

Fig. 68.16 – 1880.3610. IM.Gems.67. Rectangular carnelian intaglio, having a flat face with bevelled edges, chipped along the top and engraved with a three-line Devanagari inscription: *satguru sahāya* (an invocation asking for the guru's intercession); *jalasa rāya* (the name of the individual who seeks help). But as with the first oddly written *sa*, here too the engraver has left out a vowel sign and/or has transposed *la* and *sa*. 'Jasala Rāya' or 'Jaisala Rāya' would make more sense. Reading courtesy of Shailendra Bhandare. Hindu, early 19th century. 14mm x 17mm x 3.5mm. Wilson 1841, p. 54, fig. 12, Antiquities pl. IV.12. Accompanied by an ink imprint on paper made by Masson (**F526/1**).

Islamic gems (scale 2:1)

Fig. 69.1 – 1880.3668. IM.IsGems.33. Nearly circular carnelian cameo, bevelled towards the back. One line of angular Arabic script, apparently not reversed, but not decipherable. 8mm x 7mm.

Fig. 69.2 – 1880.3642. IM.IsGems.7. Rectangular pink-orange carnelian seal, slightly white as a result of burial or weathering; flat on both sides with bevelled edges. A cursive Arabic inscription with two arrow motifs above:

وفا هب

He has placed his trust in him

13mm x 11mm x 4.5mm. Porter 2011, p. 74, no. 314.

Fig. 69.3 – 1880.3643. IM.IsGems.8. Rectangular carnelian seal, flattish on both sides with bevelled edges and a Persian (?) name in cursive script:

روشنائي / روستائي

Rūstā'ī / Rawshanā'ī (?)

The name is unclear. Rawshanā'ī means 'luminosity' in Persian. 14mm x 11mm x 4.5mm. Porter 2011, p. 39, no. 67.

Fig. 69.4 – 1880.3644. IM.IsGems.9. Rectangular orange carnelian seal, flat on both sides with bevelled edges. Arabic inscription in two lines of angular script with forked terminals. These are joined together to form a line through the tops of both Allāhs:

لله

محمد بن علي ولي الله

To God / Muḥammad b. 'Alī is the friend of God

18mm x 11mm x 2.5mm. Porter 2011, p. 57, no. 203.

Fig. 69.5 – 1880.3663. IM.IsGems.28. Rectangular carnelian seal, with a flat face and convex back; damaged top left. Two lines of Arabic script, with a star above. The terminals of the letters are slightly forked.

علي بن الحسن

الحسن بن الحسين

'Alī b. al-Ḥasan / al-Ḥasan b. al-Ḥusayn

10mm x 9mm x 3.5mm. Porter 2011, p. 42, no. 94.

Fig. 69.6 – 1880.3645. IM.IsGems.10. Oval bright orange carnelian seal, flat on both sides with bevelled edges. Three lines of angular Arabic script. The flat projections from the terminals are joined together to form horizontal lines at the tops of the letters *lam* and *alif*. The words on the first line are continuously joined.

ما شاء الله

قال[ة] الا بالله

استغفر الله

As God wills / there is no power except in God / ask forgiveness of God.

17mm x 12mm x 3mm. Porter 2011, p. 69, no. 277.

Fig. 69.7 – 1880.3649. IM.IsGems.14. Straight-sided oval carnelian seal, flat on both sides with bevelled edges. One line of angular Arabic script with forked terminals:

فائد

Fā'id

16mm x 10mm x 3mm. Porter 2011, p. 44, no. 106.

Fig. 69.8 – 1880.3650. IM.IsGems.15. Oval carnelian seal, with a flat face, bevelled edge and a concave back. Three lines of angular Arabic script with forked terminals:

لله

محمد بن عبد الله

يثق

In God Muḥammad b. 'Abdallāh trusts

17mm x 13mm x 3mm. Porter 2011, p. 52, no. 165.

Fig. 69.9 – 1880.3664. IM.IsGems.29. Oval carnelian seal, flat on both sides with bevelled edges. One line of angular Arabic script with forked terminals:

لكل اجل كتاب

For each period a book is revealed

18mm x 11mm x 3mm. Porter 2011, p. 68, no. 273.

Fig. 69.10 – 1880.3666. IM.IsGems.31. Oval carnelian seal, with a flat face, slightly concave back and straight sides. One line of angular Arabic script:

حمدان بن عبد الله

Ḥamdān b. 'Abdallāh

14mm x 9mm x 3mm. Porter 2011, p. 38, no. 61.

Fig. 69.11 – 1880.3667. IM.IsGems.32. Oval carnelian cabochon-cut seal, with a convex face and flat back. One line of angular Arabic script:

حنان بن ساعون

Ḥannān (?) Sā'ūn

11mm x 7mm x 6mm. Porter 2011, p. 39, no. 62.

Fig. 69.12 – 1880.3669. IM.IsGems.34. Oval carnelian cabochon-cut cut seal, having a convex face and flat back with bevelled edges. One line of angular Arabic script:

Figure 69 Inscribed Islamic gems

Catalogue of Gems: Cameos, Seals and Amulets | 221

هلل انبت

We have repented to God

12mm x 9mm x 6mm. Porter 2011, p. 64, no. 242.

Fig. 69.13 – 1880.3662. IM.IsGems.27. Rectangular carnelian seal, flat on both sides and bevelled towards the front. Two interlaced hexagram Solomon's knot motifs between the extended verticals of an undecipherable Arabic inscription in angular script. 15mm x 10mm.

Fig. 69.14 – 1880.3640. IM.IsGems.6. Oval carnelian seal, having a slightly convex face and flat back with bevelled edges and a cursive Arabic inscription, dated 187 (probably AH [1]187 / AD 1773/4):

يثق بربه العلي عبده حسين بن علي

١٨٧

His servant Ḥusayn b. 'Alī believes in God on high

16mm x 10mm x 2mm. Porter 2011, p. 110, no. 518.

Fig. 69.15 – 1880.3647. IM.IsGems.12. Oval chalcedony seal, flat on both sides with bevelled edges. Grey and white, possibly damaged by weathering or burial. One line of angular Arabic script with a dotted margin:

العز لله

Glory belongs to God

17mm x 12mm x 5mm. Porter 2011, p. 73, no. 307.

Fig. 69.16 – 1880.3656. IM.IsGems.21. Circular pale purple chalcedony seal, flat on both sides with bevelled edges. The cursive Arabic inscription has dots. It is symmetrically arranged around a central square and is enclosed within a circular frame of double lines. A knot motif above the *jīm* of *Sayanjalī*.
Centre:

الا بالله وما توفيقي

My success can only come through God (*Qur'ān* 11: 88)
Compartments:

دان علايا مظهر العجائب / تجدهُ عونا لك
في النوائب / كل هم و غم
سينجلي / بولايتك ياعلي اي علي يا علي

Call upon 'Alī, manifester of miracles, you will find him a help to you in adversity, all care and grief will clear away through your friendship, O 'Alī, O 'Alī, O 'Alī.

25mm x 4.5mm. Porter 2011, p. 89, no. 381.

Fig. 69.17 – 1880.3641. IM.IsGems.6a. Oval garnet cabochon-cut intaglio, having a convex face with a slightly concave back. An Arabic inscription in angular script with forked terminals. The *nūn* of *bin* extends out into a foliate terminal:

سهل بن ساكان

Sahl b. Sākān

11mm x 7mm x 4.7mm. Porter 2011, p. 40, no. 73.

Fig. 70.1 – 1880.3652. IM.IsGems.17. Rectangular black haematite seal, flat on both sides with bevelled edges. One line of angular Arabic script, with forked terminals. The words are joined in a continuous line. The initial *mīm* floats above the line. Stars above and below the inscription:

علي بن محمد

'Alī b. Muḥammad
Analysis of tool marks by Margaret Sax and Nigel Meeks revealed that this seal was engraved using a rotary wheel. Damaged bottom right; c. 9th century. 15mm x 10mm x 4.5mm. Porter 2011, p. 43, no. 96; Sax and Meeks 2011, p. 186.

Fig. 70.2 – 1880.3651. IM.IsGems.16. Rectangular black haematite seal, flat on both sides with bevelled edges. Three lines of angular Arabic script. The central Muḥammad is large and bold, with forked terminals, and the *qāf* of *yathiq* loops upwards. There are stars on either side of the top line:

بالله يثق
محمد
يفدع بالله ام اليطق

In God Muḥammad trusts. He withstands with God's [support] that which cannot be borne
Damaged in places. 18mm x 15mm x 3.8mm. Porter 2011, p. 55, no. 185.

Fig. 70.3 – 1880.3653. IM.IsGems.18. Rectangular black haematite seal, having a flat face and uneven back with bevelled edges (corner chipped). Two lines of angular Arabic script. A crescent is above the first line:

بالله عبد الله
يثق

In God 'Abdallāh trusts

14mm x 11mm x 4mm. Porter 2011, p. 50, no. 151.

Fig. 70.4 – 1880.3665. IM.IsGems.30. Rectangular black jasper seal, having a flat face and uneven back with bevelled edges. One line of angular Arabic script with forked terminals. The words are joined to form a continuous line. A star below the inscription:

محمد بن احمد

Muḥammad b. Aḥmad

8mm x 4.5mm x 3mm. Porter 2011, p. 45, no. 120.

Fig. 70.5 – 1880.3659. IM.IsGems.24. Oval brown and white sardonyx seal, with a flat face, set in a plain silver finger-ring of a later date. Two lines of angular-cursive Arabic script:

احمد بن سرويه

'Aḥmad b. Sarawayh (?)

13mm x 9mm x 6mm. Porter 2011, p. 36, no. 43.

According to Venetia Porter, there are a number of possibilities for the father's name. Sārawayh with the *alif* omitted is one, Sārūya is another, e.g. a Sārūya b. Farkhān (AH 116 / AD 734) ruled as one of the Ispahbads of Ṭabaristān and Gīlān (Zambaur 1927, p. 186). Alternatively, an initial letter *shīn* is possible, as in Shīrawayh (Aṣfar b. Shīrawayhī was the first Dailamite general in Iran, see Canard EI²)

Fig. 70.6 – 1880.3635. IM.IsGems.1. Oval red jasper seal, flat on both sides with unevenly bevelled edges. Engraved with the figure of St George on horseback to right, holding a cross and with a dragon at his feet. Cursive Arabic inscriptions around the sides:

سلطان ملك
موفـق (؟)

Sultan, king or kingship
Possibly another word *muwafaq* ('fortunate') is made up of the dragon's body and the horse's tail. 12th–13th century (?). 17mm x 14mm x 4mm. Porter 2011, p. 82, no. 358.

Fig. 70.7 – 1880.3636. IM.IsGems.2. Oval red jasper seal with a flat face, uneven back and bevelled sides. Three

scale 2:1

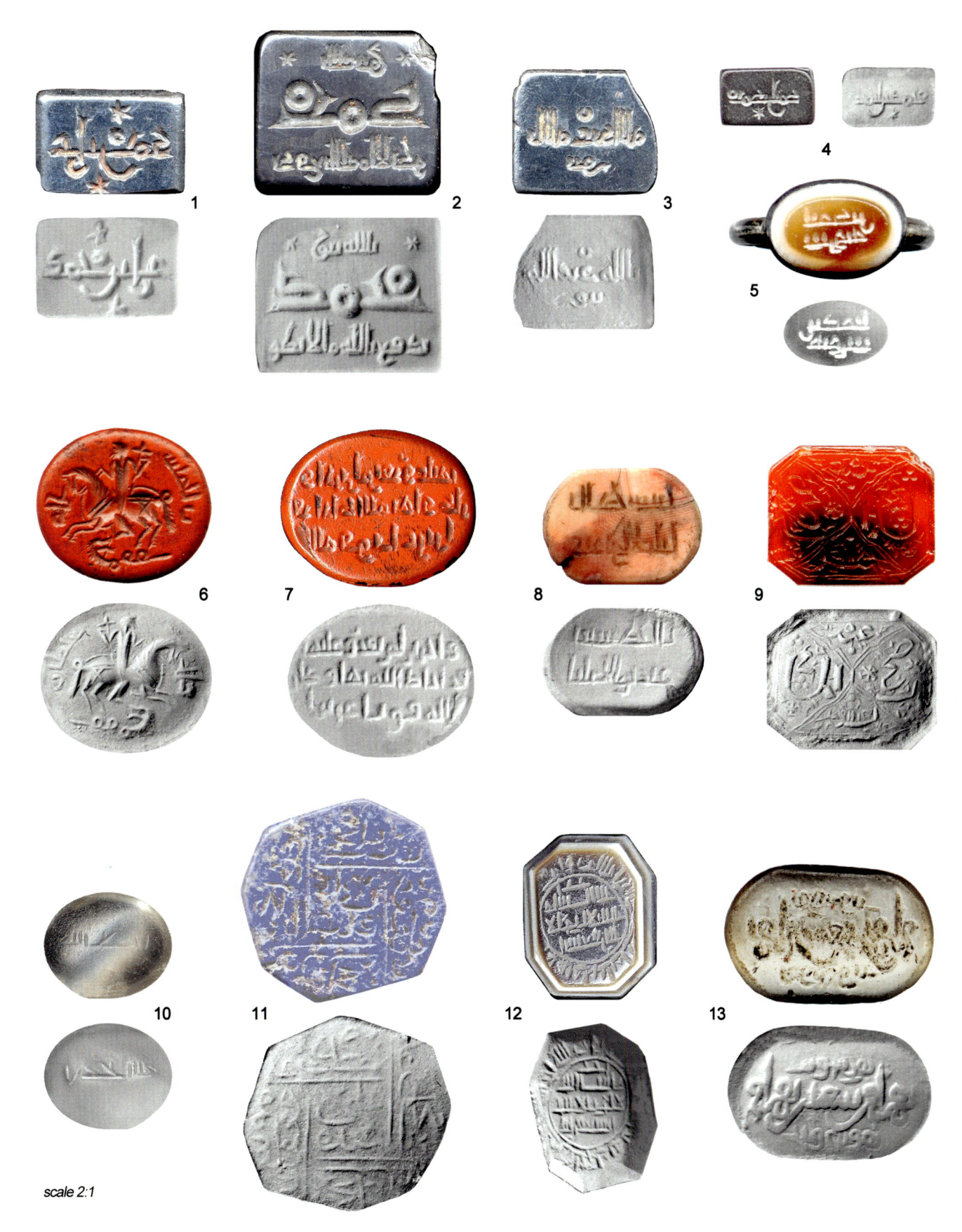

Figure 70 Inscribed Islamic gems

lines of cursive Arabic script. A small crescent above the *qāf* of *yughraq*.

آوخرتي لم يدع وعليها
قد اجاط الله بهم وكان
الله قويا عزيرا

There is no avoiding my end. God has encompassed it and God is strong and able to enforce his will
(From *wa kāna: Qurʾān*, 33: 25).
19mm x 14mm x 5mm. Porter 2011, p. 71, no. 288.

Fig. 70.8 – 1880.3648. IM.IsGems.13. Straight-sided oval, pale red jasper (?) seal, flat on both sides with bevelled edges. Two lines of Arabic inscription in angular script. Undeciphered. 11mm x 10.25mm.

Fig. 70.9 – 1880.3658. IM.IsGems.23. Octagonal sard seal with surface divided diagonally into four quarters filled with Arabic inscriptions mixed with floral motifs. Undeciphered. 16mm x 13mm.

Fig. 70.10 – 1880.3657. IM.IsGems.22. Oval rock crystal seal with a worn and indistinct Arabic inscription in angular script. 25mm x 20mm.

Fig. 70.11 – 1880.3638. IM.IsGems.4. Octagonal, lapis lazuli seal, flat on both sides with bevelled edges, with cursive Arabic inscription symmetrically arranged around a central square which is formed out of the four returns of the letter *yāʾ* of ʿAlī:
Centre:

علي عبده   His servant ʿAlī

Compartments (anti-clockwise from the top), the Twelve Imams:

محمد حسن
محمد حسين علي
موسى جعفر علي
محمد حسن علي

Muḥammad Ḥasan ʿAlī / Mūsā Jaʿfar ʿAlī / Muḥammad Ḥusayn ʿAlī / Muḥammad Ḥasan ʿAlī.
17.5mm x 19mm x 2.5mm. Porter 2011, p. 88, no. 377.

Fig. 70.12 – 1880.3654. IM.IsGems.19. Octagonal brown and white sardonyx seal, with high bevelled sides, cut down. Arabic inscriptions in angular script in the centre field and around the margin.
Margin:

قل هو الله احد [الله الصمد] لم يلد ولم يولد ولم يكن
له كفوا

Say 'He is God, the one and only [the eternal absolute], he does not beget nor is he begotten and [there is] none like unto him'
(*Qurʾān*, 112: 1–4).
Centre:

احد
ام شاء الله
قال قوة الا بالله
استغفر الله

None [end of verse 4 of *sūra* 112]. As God wills, there is no power except in God, ask forgiveness of God.
15mm x 12mm x 5.5mm. Porter 2011, p. 70, no. 282.

Fig. 70.13 – 1880.3639. IM.IsGems.5. Rock crystal cabochon-cut seal; a convex face and flat back with rounded edges, with inscriptions on both sides in Arabic and Pahlavi. The concurrent use of both scripts occurs extensively on Arab-Sasanian coins of the Umayyad and early ʿAbbasid periods, and both inscriptions on this seal are therefore likely to have been engraved at the same time.
Side A: Pahlavi above and below Persian name in angular cursive script, with a star below:

بهرام بن سعيد بن بهرام

Bahrām b. Saʿīd b. Bahrām
Pahlavi: *farrokha* 'good fortune'; *pʾkyck* 'pure'
Side B: Arabic script in angular style and crudely inscribed. After the Abū is an extra *alif*. A possible alternative is Abūʾl Qādir:

ابو احمد (؟)   Abū Aḥmad, or   حمدن Hamdān
(with the *alif* omitted)

20mm x 12mm x 6mm. Porter 2011, p. 85, no. 370; Walker 1941, pp. 1–158.

Inscribed cameos, amulets and metal seals (scale 1:1)

Fig. 71.1 – 1880.3603. IM.Gems.60. Christian amulet (?). Oval green heliotrope (bloodstone) intaglio with bevelled edges, depicting a mythical beast with the head of a donkey, body and wings of a bird, and four (?) legs; surrounded by potent and simple crosses and, upper left, three Greek letters ΛPH or ΛPI +.

The Islamic equivalent is the Buraq, the winged horse/donkey/mule associated with Muḥammad's *isra* (night journey from Mecca to Jerusalem and back) and with his ascent to heaven. But the crosses and Greek letters suggest the image is Christian, *c*. 5th–7th century. 15mm x 21mm x 4.5mm. Errington 1999, p. 228, pl. 7.20.

Fig. 71.2 – 1880.3660. IM.IsGems.25. Hexagonal carnelian intaglio, flat on both sides, with a blurred and illegible Persian inscription inlaid in white enamel. 13.5mm x 13mm.

Fig. 71.3 – 1880.3646. IM.IsGems.11. Oval flat carnelian intaglio with bevelled edges. The Arabic inscription is not reversed and therefore not intended as a seal, but is not decipherable. 16mm x 11mm.

Fig. 71.4 – 1880.3655. IM.IsGems.20. Rock crystal amulet with tourmaline (?) inclusions. Oval slightly convex face and a flat back with bevelled edges. Cursive Arabic inscriptions divided into sections by the four returns of the letter *yāʾ* of ʿAlī:

اللهم صل على محمد و علي و فاطم
والحسن والحسين و علي و محمد و
جعفر و موسى وعلي و محمد و علي
والحسن و محمد

O God! Bless Muḥammad and ʿAlī / and Fāṭima, and al-Ḥasan and al-Ḥusayn, and ʿAlī / and Muḥammad and Jaʿfar, and Mūsā, and ʿAlī / and Muḥammad, and ʿAlī, and al-Ḥasan and Muḥammad.
38mm x 24mm x 6mm. Porter 2011, p. 151, no. A72.

Fig. 71.5 – 1880.3637. IM.IsGems.3. Oval glass cameo, flat on both sides, with purple bas-relief Arabic inscription on a white ground:

ليس ينجي من القدر حزم ولا ي و الحذر

Neither a firm decision nor caution can save one from fate. 27mm x 20mm x 4mm. Porter 2011, p. 163, no. A108.

Fig. 71.6–7. Box '9'. Cast copper alloy buttons (?). A rectangular frame with a bevelled edge and sloping, stepped sides. The inscription is not reversed and therefore not intended as a seal. The square attachment on the reverse has broken off. Readings courtesy of V.S. Curtis and Gul Rahim Khan.

Fig. 71.6 – 1880.3878.a. The incised Urdu inscription gives a name and date: *Shāh Karam Nī Parvīn* (or the Persian month *Farva[r]din*) *1154* (AD 1741). 14mm x 13mm x 7mm.

Fig. 71.7 – 1880.3878.b. Box 9. An incised Persian inscription: *yā imām Husayn* (Oh Imam Husayn). 18th century. 3mm x 11mm x 7mm.

Fig. 71.8 – 1880.3634. IM.Metal.1 / OA+14379. Flat circular brass seal resembling a Mughal coin, dated AH 1080 / AD 1669/70. Within a double line border, a cursive Persian inscription, with clusters of flower-like dots and a leafy frond in the background:

لطف الله شد ز مهر حسین ۱۰۸۰

1080. The favour of God comes from the love of Ḥusayn 28mm x 1mm. Porter 2011, p. 121, no. 582.

Fig. 71.9 – 1880.3920. Box 9. Cast, brass-washed copper alloy domed seal, with a single-word pseudo-Arabic (?) inscription beginning *mim-he* (?) within a circular border containing a row on incised dots. The upper, domed surface has a central, pierced hole, perhaps where a stem was attached, and incised lines running from the centre to the edges. 12mm x 3mm.

Fig. 71.10 – 1880.3925. Box 9. Large fragment of a cast copper alloy seal (?) with a pseudo-Kufic inscription in the centre, encircled by an inscription in smaller letters possibly reading 'Muḥammad' and *la illa*; *c.* 8th–10th century. 34.8mm x 30.4mm x 8.4mm.

Terracotta seal

Fig. 72.1 – 1880.3770. IM.Metal.152. Burnished square terracotta seal, with tapering sides, pierced for suspension. On the square seal surface, a hare standing to right, with a pseudo-Kharoshthi (?) inscription of four (?) letters below. 2nd century BC–2nd century AD (?). 11mm x 16mm.

Copper alloy pyramidal seals

Fig. 72.2 –20. Square pyramidal seals with sloping or stepped sides and a pierced cylindrical stem, cast in copper alloy and engraved on the base; *c.* 2nd–6th century.

Fig. 72.2–8. IM.Metal.152.

Fig. 72.2 – 1880.3745. A winged horse (probably Pegasus), walking to right; Sasanian (?) *c.* 5th–6th century. 11.5mm x 9mm.

The motif is popular on late Sasanian seals (Bivar 1968, pls XX.1–8, XXIV.7).

Fig. 72.3 – 1880.3707. An ibex (?) with long horns, standing to right, with a small, three-leafed twig in front. Sasanian (?) *c.* 5th–6th century. 11mm x 7mm.

For another example of the same subject, see **Fig. 72.15**, where the antlers show clearly that a stag is intended and the symbol in the right field is a taurine.

Fig. 72.4–5. Seals showing a humped bull standing to right, with a vertical ellipsoidal mark in front and a flattened crescent above; *c.* 2nd–6th century. Another example is in the Cambridge Ridgeway collection (CMAA.1927.1192).

Fig. 72.4 – 1880.3749. 0.9mm x 10mm.

Fig. 72.5 – 1880.3708. 13mm x 10mm.

For a clearer depiction of the same subject, see **Fig. 72.14**, where in front of the bull is a taurine and above a crescent.

Fig. 72.6 – 1880.3746. A standing lion to right, with tail raised. In front is a taurine and above a crescent. 10mm x 7.5mm x 8.5mm.

Fig. 72.7–10. Seals with a schematically rendered standing lion to right and a flattened crescent above.

Fig. 72.7 – 1880.3748. 12mm x 9mm.

Fig. 72.8 – 1880.3747. In front of the lion is an ill-defined mark, possibly a taurine symbol. 12mm x 10mm.

Fig. 72.9 – 1880.3752. IM.Metal.151. The image of a lion (?) with a taurine symbol (?) in front. 13mm x 10mm.

Fig. 72.10 – 1880.3753. IM.Metal.151. A standing lion to right, with a small circle above. 10mm x 8mm.

Fig. 72.11 – 1880.3750. IM.Metal.152. Seal with the stem broken at the point where it was originally pierced. The worn image shows either a lion with a crescent above or a stag (?) walking to right and cursorily rendered. 7mm x 8mm.

Fig. 72.12 – 1880.4100. Box 2.a. The worn face depicts an animal standing to right with a flattened crescent above. 8mm x 7mm x 6mm.

Fig. 72.13–15. Seals engraved with the image of a stag to right and a vertical mark in front.

Fig. 72.13 – IOLC.7551. K.358. 10mm x 10mm x 15mm.

Fig. 72.14 – 1880.3981.h. Box 4.b. 8mm x 11mm.

Figure 71 Inscribed cameos, amulets and metal seals

Figure 72 Terracotta seal (1) and copper alloy pyramidal seals (2–26)

Fig. 72.15 – 1880.3751. IM.Metal.152. A taurine symbol in front of the stag. 11mm x 7.5mm x 8.5mm.
Fig. 72.16 – 1880.3743. IM.Metal.152. A humped bull walking to left, a taurine symbol in front and a crescent above. 11.5mm x 11mm.
Fig. 72.17 – 1880.3744. IM.Metal.151. A bird to right on a branch (?). 10mm x 9mm.
Fig. 72.18–20. IM.Metal.151. Seals with a leaf frond between two vertical lines.
Fig. 72.18 – 1880.3756. 9mm x 8mm.
Fig. 72.19 – 1880.3754. 12mm x 10mm.
Fig. 72.20 – 1880.3755. 9mm x 10mm.
Fig. 72.21–6. Oval seals with flaring sides and a pierced stem, cast in copper alloy; c. 2nd–6th century.
Fig. 72.21 – 1880.3759. IM.Metal.152. A standing lion to right, a vertical line in front and a flattened crescent above. 12mm x 6mm x 14mm.
Fig. 72.22 – 1880.3760. IM.Metal.151. A schematically rendered standing lion to right, a flattened crescent above. 9mm x 6mm x 8mm.
Fig. 72.23 – 1880.3761. IM.Metal.152. An indistinct, schematically rendered seated lion (?) to left. 11mm x 6mm x 9.5mm.
Fig. 72.24–5. Seals with a leaf frond between two vertical lines.
Fig. 72.24 – 1880.3758. IM.Metal.151. 11mm x 5mm x 9mm.
Fig. 72.25 – 1880.3757. IM.Metal.151. 12mm x 7.5mm x 14.5mm.
Fig. 72.26 – IOLC.7552. K.359. Seal engraved with a row of three stars or flowers. 10mm x 6mm x 10mm.

Miscellaneous copper alloy seals
Fig. 73.1 – 1880.3790.n. IM.Metal.141. Large broken ring seal with knobbed shoulders and a large roughly oval bezel engraved with the auspicious symbols of two fish, a vase of plenty and a conch; c. 1st century BC–1st century AD. 15.8mm x 19.9mm x 25.4mm.

Fig. 73.2 – 1880.3800. IM.Metal.152. Oval seal with sloping sides and a long stem terminating in a loop. On the face is the schematic image of a stag, standing to left. 14mm x 16mm x 21.5mm.

Fig. 73.3 – 1880.3763. IM.Metal.151. Small, square seal with a long, tapering stem joined to a large trefoil looped handle. On the face is a grid incorporating a pseudo-inscription. 22mm x 7.5mm x 13mm.

Fig. 73.4 – 1880.3762. IM.Metal.151. Thick circular seal with a pierced rounded lug. On the face is a five-petalled flower made of punched circles joined by lines to the centre, with four smaller circles in the interstices. 13mm x 14.5mm x 5mm.

Fig. 73.5 – 1880.3628. IM.Metal.162. Circular seal with a large rectangular lug, pierced with a large hole for suspension. On the slightly convex face, a schematic representation of the Buddha (?), seated in *padmāsana*; to the right a vase with an elongated neck, to the left a flower bud on a long stem; A piece is missing from the lower edge; with incrustations. *c.* 2nd–4th century. 12mm x 4mm; lug: 8mm x 7mm. Callieri tentatively dates the seal to the Kushan period (1997, no. M1, p. 132, pl. 30; 1997a, pp. 172–3, 175, no. 10/17).

Cast copper alloy seals with pierced lugs

Fig. 74.1–8. Square seals with a lug centre back.

Fig. 74.1 – 1880.3620. IM.Metal.10. Brass-washed (?) with a standing lion to right. 1st century AD. 15.5mm x 15mm x 3mm; lug: 7.2mm x 3.3mm x 3mm. Wilson 1841, p. 54, fig. 9, Antiquities pl. IV.9; Callieri 1997, no. M15, pp. 136–7, pl. 33; Errington 1999, p. 228, pl. 7.30.

Fig. 74.2 – 1880.3702.b. IM.Metal.141. A crudely executed image of an ibex standing to right. The loop at the back has broken off. 15mm x 15.2mm x 1.1mm.

Fig. 74.3 – 1880.3702.a. IM.Metal.141. An elephant, trunk and right leg raised, walking to the left within a dotted border. On the back, the remains of a wide loop. 10.8mm x 11mm x 2.8mm.

Fig. 74.4 – 1880.3767. IM.Metal.152. Thick brass-washed seal, with a smooth back and no trace of any means for attachment. On the face is a horned goat (?) moving to left, with its tail in the air. 11mm x 11mm x 4mm.

Fig. 74.5 – 1880.3766. IM.Metal.151. Rectangular seal with a long-necked bird, wings extended; traces of a lug. 15mm x 12.8mm x 2.5mm.

Fig. 74.6 – 1880.3769. IM.Metal.151. Thick seal, with a slightly broken lug. The image is very worn, with only traces of lines. 12mm x 13mm.

Fig. 74.7 – 1880.3765. IM.Metal.151. Rectangular seal with two standing figures in long robes (possibly male and female) facing each other with a vertical line between them. 15mm x 15.5mm x 1.6mm; lug: 5mm.

Fig. 74.8 – 1880.3674. IM.Metal.8. A tree with palm-like fronds in the centre, flanked on one side by a figure seated in an ascetic's hut, and on the other a small animal (possibly a goat) with three birds above. The seated figure resembles depictions of ascetics in huts found on Gandharan reliefs. The face is worn; *c.* 2nd–4th century. 18mm x 16mm x 3.3mm x 13.6mm x 10.3mm x 9mm. Wilson 1841, p. 54, fig. 8, Antiquities pl. IV.8

Fig. 74.9–15. Circular seals with a lug soldered centre back.

Figure 73 Miscellaneous copper alloy seals

Fig. 74.9–10. IM.Metal.152. Within a circle, a seated stag with large ears and antlers, its head turned backwards.

Fig. 74.9 – 1880.3777. On the back are traces of a design, possibly depicting the flames of a fire altar and attendant, indicating reuse perhaps of a former coin (?). 19mm.

Fig. 74.10 – 1880.3808. A flattened loop is soldered on the back. 17mm.

Fig. 74.11 – 1880.3781. IM.Metal.152. Seal and pierced lug cast in one piece; depicting a dragon with gaping jaws to left. 18mm.

Fig. 74.12 – 1880.3782. IM.Metal.152. Within a circle, a lion seated to left, with head raised and tongue sticking out. 19mm.

Fig. 74.13 – 1880.3805. IM.Metal.152. Disc or seal, with a pierced hole in the centre where a lug was once attached. On the face is a griffin with a curled tail, seated to right. 24mm.

Fig. 74.14 – 1880.3806. IM.Metal.152. Very worn with only traces of an animal, probably a lion, seated to right. A broken pierced lug on the back. 11mm.

Fig. 74.15 – 1880.3807. IM.Metal.151. A human figure walking to left, carrying a large, unidentified object. 14mm.

Fig. 74.16 – 1880.3780. IM.Metal.152. Brass-washed circular disc with the image of a goat (?) standing to left. The reverse is covered with stippling. 11mm.

Fig. 74.17 – 1880.3784. IM.Metal.151. Brass-washed circular seal with two thin lugs, each pierced twice. On the face are two crudely executed fish swimming in opposite directions within a roughly hatched border. 19mm.

Fig. 74.18–27. Oval seals with two pierced lugs on the back. The Cambridge Ridgeway collection (CMAA.1927.1192) has two seals of this type.

Fig. 74.18 – 1880.3773. IM.Metal.151. Brass-washed; with a lion (?) seated to left. One lug is broken. 10.6mm x 12.7mm x 6mm.

Catalogue of Gems: Cameos, Seals and Amulets | 227

Fig. 74.19 – 1880.3774. IM.Metal.152. A bull walking to right, with an incised curved line above. 13mm x 11mm.

Fig. 74.20 – 1880.3772. IM.Metal.152. Schematic image of wavy lines and a winged horse (?). 12mm x 11mm.

Fig. 74.21 – 1880.3771. IM.Metal.152. Brass-washed; with a winged dragon standing to right. 12mm x 13mm.

Fig. 74.22–3. IM.Metal.151. A quadruped with large ears and an upright tail, walking to the right. Two wings or tusks (?) extend from the chest.

Fig. 74.22 – 1880.3775. 13.6mm x 12mm.

Fig. 74.23 – 1880.3776. 14mm x 12mm.

Fig. 74.24 – IOLC. 7547b. A musk deer (?) with tail raised, walking to right. One lug is broken. 12mm x 10mm.

Fig. 74.25 – 1880.3778. IM.Metal.151. Brass-washed; both lugs broken. On the worn face is a standing bare breasted female figure in a long skirt, facing to front, her right arm outstretched, left hand on hip, cradling an object (perhaps a palm frond) executed as a row of three dots; *c.* 3rd–4th century. 11.5mm x 13.8mm x 5.5mm. For similarly executed figures, see **Fig. 81.16**.

Fig. 74.26 – 1880.3632. IM.Metal.149. A figure in a short tunic and trousers (?) running to right and holding a large notched club. Behind the head is a reversed *f*-shape possibly representing the Greek letter φ (*ph*) or Kharoshthi *ga*; *c.* 2nd–4th century. 13mm x 11.5mm x 3mm; lugs: 7mm x 5mm x 6mm. Callieri 1997, no. M3, p. 132, pl. 30.

Fig. 74.27 – 1880.3629. IM.Metal.146. An elephant and rider to right, with a prominent s-shaped diadem (?) behind. The right half of one lug is missing. Kushan (?) *c.*1st–3rd century. 16.4mm x 13.7mm. Callieri 1997, no. M4, pp. 132–3, pl. 30; 1997a, pp. 172, 175, no. 10/16.

Fig. 74.28 – 1880.3783. IM.Metal.151. Brass-washed circular seal, with a large attachment ring at the back, cast in one piece. On the face is a male deity (?), with a halo, standing to front, his upper torso turned to the right. He holds a fly whisk (?) in his left hand and a club in his right. Kushan (?) *c.* 3rd–4th century. 15.8mm x 13mm. The execution of the figure resembles those found on **Fig. 75.9** and **Fig. 79.1** dating to the Kushan period.

Fig. 74.29 – 1880.3619. IM.Metal.9. Thin, oval seal, pierced at the top, depicting a female dancer (possibly a *nāgī* or serpent divinity), standing with one foot in front of the other, and one hand on her hip. The other arm is raised, with two bangles round the wrist and she holds a round object (perhaps a cymbal) in her hand. A long, sinuous scarf snakes in a large loop above one shoulder and along either side of her body. A Kharoshthi inscription in four characters names the owner, Balaka. Kushan (?) *c.* 1st–2nd century. 16mm x 14mm x 1mm. Callieri 1997, no. M7, p. 134, pl. 31.

On a comparable image on a signet ring from Swat, the woman holds a parrot in her right raised hand, while her scarf arcs behind her shoulder (Nasim Khan 2006, p. 55, figs 47–8). This rendering is characteristic of early 1st-century Mathura sculptures (Sharma 1976, figs 23, 57, 79). It occurs in Gandhara on a toilet tray found at Taxila in Sirkap stratum I (Marshall 1951, p. 496, pl. 144, no. 70). The figure's stance recalls that of Salabhanjika on a 1st–2nd-century sculpture from Mathura (Czuma 1985, pl. 216, no. 69) and on Gandharan sculptures (Zwalf 1996, p. 208, nos 232, 349, 352).

Fig. 74.30 – 1880.3630. IM.Metal.147. Circular seal with the bust to left of a bearded man in profile, wearing an ear-ring and necklace of beads, his hair schematically rendered as two rows of short parallel lines. On the back is an elongated, tapering and pierced lug set off-centre; *c.* 3rd–5th century. 15.3mm x 14.7mm. Callieri 1997, no. M11, p. 135, pl. 32; Errington 1999, p. 228, pl. 7.38.

Fig. 74.31 – 1880.3631. IM.Metal.148. Circular seal with a slightly domed back, depicting a roughly executed bust to left of a man in profile, with stippled hair and beard. The three-leafed vegetal forms above each shoulder are reminiscent of the flames and plumes found in this position on Kushan, Kushano-Sasanian and Alkhan coins. A flattened, semi-circular lug on the reverse is pierced with a small hole for suspension; *c.* 3rd–5th century. 19mm x 2mm; lug: 9.5mm x 8.5mm x 1.6mm. Callieri 1997, no. M10, p. 135, pl. 32; Errington 1999, p. 228, pl. 7.39.

Fig. 74.32 – 1880.3834.b. IM.Metal.160. Circular bezel for a seal or intaglio, with two pierced lugs for attachment on the back; *c.* 1st century AD. 15.6mm x 3.5mm.

Fig. 74.33–5. Shallow cup-shaped bezels for seals or intaglios, with two lugs for attachment on the back, both pierced twice; *c.* 1st century AD.

The late 1st-century BC–early 1st-century AD Indo-Scythian/Indo-Parthian level at Sirkap, Taxila, produced similar oval bezels, but for rings (Marshall 1951, p. 583, pl. 180, nos 127–9). That these objects were for seals is suggested by cast copper alloy seals of the same form (see **Fig. 74.18–27** above). There are a further three examples in the Cambridge Ridgeway collection (CMAA.1927.1192).

Fig. 74.33 – 1880.3834.c. IM.Metal.160. 16.5mm x 4.7mm x 4mm x 10.5mm.

Fig. 74.34 – 1880.3834.d. IM.Metal.160. One lug is slightly broken. 17.2mm x 15.4mm.

Fig. 74.35 – 1880.3981.l. Box 4. 16.4mm x 14.5mm.

Fig. 74.36–7. Cast, circular bell-shaped copper alloy mount for a gem or stone, with a short stem and attachment loop. Two more examples are in the Cambridge Ridgeway collection (CMAA.1927.1192). **Fig. 74.36 – 1880.3764.** IM.Metal.151. 10mm x 11mm.

Fig. 74.37 – 1880.3820.g. IM.Metal.160. The loop is broken. 12mm x 9mm.

Box seals

Copper alloy seals pierced lengthwise, with representations in intaglio on each of the four sides; *c.* 1st–5th century.

Fig. 75.1 – 1880.3624. IM.Metal.134. Images of (1) a standing winged (?) female figure; (2) a seated lion; (3) a hare or a horned animal looking backwards; (4) a horse. Each image is framed by a recessed line. 12.5mm x 6.8mm x 6.5mm.

Callieri identifies the standing winged figure as Nike (?) 'in profile to left with a beribboned crown (?)'. He sees the hare as a 'horned quadruped (caprid?)'. Callieri 1997, no. M23, p. 139, pl. 36 (misnumbered IM.Metal.135, 1880.3625).

Fig. 75.2 – 1880.3625. IM.Metal.135. Images of (1) a standing figure holding a staff and a shield (?); (2) a peacock; (3) a standing lion; (4) a nesting bird. Corroded in patches: conserved and cleaned November 2009. 12.8mm x 8.16mm x 8.5mm. Callieri 1997, no. M24, pp. 139–40, pl. 36 (misnumbered IM.Metal.136, 1880.3626).

Figure 74 Cast copper alloy seals with pierced lugs

Catalogue of Gems: Cameos, Seals and Amulets | 229

Fig. 75.3 – 1880.3627. IM.Metal.137. Images of (1) a stag standing before a tree; (2) a standing (?) animal; (3) a seated lion; (4) a seated winged griffin. 16mm x 11.5mm x 11mm. Badly corroded in patches: conserved and cleaned November 2009. Callieri 1997, no. M25, p. 140, pl. 37.

Fig. 75.4 – 1880.3626. IM.Metal.136. Images of (1) a lion (?) to right; (2) a vase with three sprays and possibly a small bird perched on the lip; (3) a man riding an elephant to right (?); (4) a figure, possibly the Buddha, seated in meditation under an arched canopy. 15mm x 9mm x 9mm. Callieri 1997, no. M22, p. 139, pl. 35 (misnumbered IM.Metal.134, 1880.3624). For a discussion of the *pūrṇaghaṭa* motif, see **Fig. 83.7–9**. For other examples, see https://research.britishmuseum.org/research/collection_online/search.aspx IOLC.7565, IOLC.7772.

Fig. 75.5 – 1880.3621. IM.Metal.132. Images of (1) a lion; (2) an ibex; (3) two (?) confronted birds; (4) a winged (?) Nike standing to right, holding a beribboned diadem. Kushan; *c.* 2nd–4th century. 17.6mm x 10mm x 9.8mm. Callieri 1997, no. M20, p. 138, pl. 34; Errington 1999, pp. 211, 228, pl. 7.24.

Fig. 75.6 – 1880.3622. IM.Metal.131. Images of (1) a lion; (2) a stag; (3) a bird with head to right; (4) a schematically executed winged (?) Nike standing to right, holding a beribboned diadem (?). Kushan; *c.* 2nd–4th century. 14.26mm x 9mm x 9mm. Callieri 1997, no. M19, p. 138, pl. 34; 1997a, pp. 173, 176, no. 10/18.

Comparison between **Fig. 75.5–6** shows an almost identical choice of subject matter (lion, stag/ibex, bird) for three of the faces, which are, moreover, arranged in the same sequence. The visible lines on the fourth face also correspond closely with those on the better executed standing figure here, indicating that the same representation of a winged (?) figure holding a diadem and staff is intended. See **Fig. 79.1** for a similar figure.

Fig. 75.7 – 1880.3670. IM.Metal.138. Worn and corroded representations of a lion walking to left; a standing figure; a nesting bird; and a standing ibex (?). 13mm x 9mm x 8.5mm. Conserved and cleaned November 2009.

Fig. 75.8 – 1880.3623. IM.Metal.133. Images of (1) three birds in procession; (2) a standing figure holding a diadem; (3) a facing bull's head with a bird (?) between the horns; (4) a long-necked bust in profile with stippled hair tied with a diadem, the ties hanging down behind the head; *c.* 5th century. 13.84mm 7mm x 7.1mm. Callieri 1997, no. M21, pp. 138–9, pl. 36.

Similar portrait busts with stippled hair or head-dress occur on copper alloy coins of the Kidarite/Alkhan Hun period (*c.* 5th century) found at the shaivite cave site of Kashmir Smast, Peshawar Valley, Pakistan (Nasim Khan *et al.* 2008, pp. 111, 133, nos 217, 221, 327). See also **Fig. 74.31** above.

Fig. 75.9 – 1880.4073. IM.Metal.130. Images of (1) a three-headed, standing Kushan god Oesho, in the guise of Shiva; (2) a standing male and female figure (Oesho and Ommo?/Pārvatī) facing each other and clasping hands; (3) a man in Kushan dress worshipping at a fire altar; (4) Heracles standing, holding a club. 3rd–4th century. 18mm x 10.5mm x 10.5mm.

The good condition of the seal suggests that it was probably purchased in Kabul bazaar rather than found at Begram. Cribb 1997, fig. 17; Rosenfield 1967, pl. xvi; Errington and Curtis 2007, pp. 113–14, fig. 95; Jongeward *et al.* 2012, p. 134, fig. 4.14.

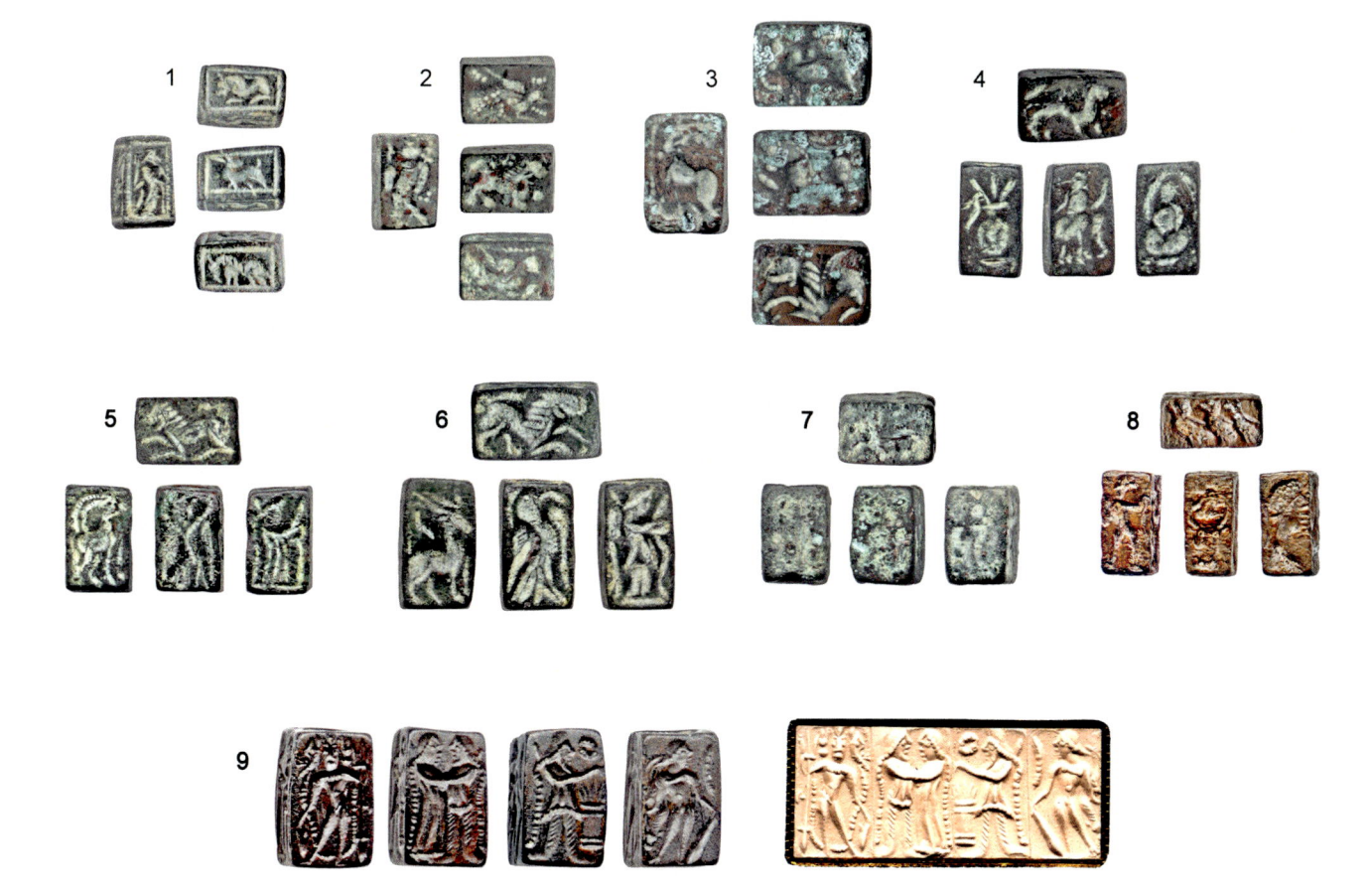

Figure 75 Box seals *c.* 1st–5th century

Catalogue of Gems: Cameos, Seals and Amulets | 231

Part 5: Catalogue of Ornamental Metalwork and Miscellaneous Artefacts

Chantal Fabrègues with Elizabeth Errington, Kirstin Leighton-Boyce and Wannaporn Kay Rienjang

The Masson collection includes a vast range of ornaments and jewellery, mostly of copper alloy and in a fragmentary condition. Finger- and signet-rings are most numerous: 281 of the total 415 are included here (**Figs 78–92**). There are also a great number of pins of various kinds, especially ones with bird finials (**Figs 94–100**). Birds also feature on phial stoppers, as buttons or bracteates and as decorative fittings (**Figs 101, 117, 128**). Many are highly stylised, even to the extent of becoming flat double-headed U-shapes (**Fig. 98–9**), but some are executed naturalistically in the round (raven, duck, hoopoe, peacock, parrot: **Fig. 100**).

The earliest material appears to date from *c.* 3rd–2nd millennium BC; then there is a hiatus, with the bulk of the finds belonging to the period *c.* 4th century BC–13th century AD. As far as Begram is concerned, this date range is mirrored in the coin finds from the site and it can be assumed that all the earlier Bronze Age material, together with finds from the later 13th to the early 19th century, was acquired in Kabul bazaar. To this group can be added most of the silver and the rare gold artefacts.

A defining feature of the copper alloy Begram pieces is the baked mud deposit coating the majority, which were collected from the site after being washed out during the annual rains. They mostly retain this patina, as – unlike the coins – few have been cleaned or conserved. From this it follows as a broad rule of thumb, that not only the cleaner, but also the better preserved artefacts, are from Kabul bazaar.

As already stated in the preface (pp. 1–2 above), there is general lack of comparable dated or provenanced material from archaeological excavations at other sites, which makes it difficult to identify or arrange many of the objects in any firm chronological sequence. For this reason, the catalogue is arranged thematically, according to related subject matter, with stamps, Bronze Age seals, signet- and finger-rings following on from the gems and seals catalogued above. The principal groups of artefacts are broadly classified as follows:

Stamps **Fig. 76**
Bronze Age stamps and seals **Fig. 77**
Signet- and finger-rings **Figs 78–92**
Brass-washed and incised fragments **Fig. 93**
Human figures **Fig. 94**
Pins, kohl/antimony rods, spatulas, ear cleaners **Figs 95–102**
Phial stoppers **Fig. 101**
Ear-rings **Figs 103–4**
Vase with dolphin handles pendants **Fig. 105**
Beads **Figs 106–7**
Pendants **Figs 108–16**
Buttons **Figs 117–18**
Bracteates and pierced elements **Fig. 119**
Bangles **Figs 120–1**
Buckles **Fig. 122**
Belt and riveted fittings **Fig. 123**
Riveted and pierced elements **Fig. 124**
Washers and pierced elements **Fig. 125**
Nails, tacks and studs **Fig. 126**
Lids **Fig. 127**
Bird fittings **Fig. 128**

Vessel fittings **Fig. 129**
Striated fragments **Fig. 130**
Spoons **Fig. 131**
Dies **Fig. 132**
Arrowheads **Fig. 133**
Fragments of uncertain function; chains **Fig. 134**
Miscellaneous stone and other objects **Fig. 135**

Stamps
Fig. 76.1 – 1880–4136.a. IM.Metal.151. Copper alloy stamp, with concentric circles incised on the head, and a hole through the end of the shaft. 16mm x 35mm.
Fig. 76.2 – 1880–4136.c. IM.Metal.151. Copper alloy stamp or fastener (?), with concentric circles incised on the head and a thin, broken shaft. 14mm x 10mm.
Fig. 76.3 – 1880–4136.b. IM.Metal.151. Copper alloy stamp with a short, flat shaft and traces of a design on the rounded head. 19mm x 18mm.

Bronze Age stamps or seals
Fig. 77.1 – 1880.3710.a. IM.Metal.154. Cast copper alloy openwork seal or stamp, comprising five wide spokes with projecting rims, radiating from a circular hub also encircled by a flange. The outer rim is mostly missing and two spokes are broken. The back is flat, with the remains of an attachment loop in the centre; *c.* 2000 BC–1500 BC. 30.7mm x 3.7mm.
Fig. 77.2 – 1880.3710.b. IM.Metal.154. Cast copper alloy openwork seal or stamp, with one broad, and four narrow raised spokes radiating from a flat, circular hub on which remains part of the raised outline of a Maltese cross; *c.* 2000 BC–1500 BC. 23.9mm x 16mm x 4mm.
Fig. 77.3 – 1880.3710.c. IM Metal 154. Cast copper alloy rim fragment of a large, circular seal or stamp; flat on the reverse, with the remains of ridged design comprising a V-shape and two parallel line; *c.* 2000 BC–1500 BC. 24mm x 12.2mm x 3.6mm.

Fig. 77.1–3 belong to the large class of compartmented seals which are characteristic of the Bactria-Margiana Archaeological Complex (BMAC, also known as the Oxus Civilization), the modern archaeological designation for a Bronze Age culture located along the upper Amu Darya (Oxus River) in present-day Turkmenistan, Afghanistan, southern Uzbekistan and western Tajikistan. The BMAC may have extended as far as southern Afghanistan and Baluchistan, which have also yielded artefacts typical of the culture. Compartmented seals have been found in large numbers in these areas, both from clandestine diggings in the 1970s (Pottier 1984; Tosi 1988, fig. 11; Salvatori 1988) and from scientific excavations. Known sites where examples have been excavated are: Namazga on the banks of the Murghab river (Masson and Sarianidi 1972), Togolok (Sarianidi 1990) and Gonur Tepe in Margiana (Sarianidi 1993, 2002), Dashly Tepe (Masson and Sarianidi 1972) and Mundigak (Casal 1961) in Afghanistan, Dabar Kot, Rana Ghundai, Shahi Tump (Amiet 1977, p. 117), and the Mehrgarh-Sibri complex in Baluchistan (Sarianidi 1993, p. 37).

The seals depict geometrical motifs, like the three examples here, and also floral motifs, crosses, animals such

Figure 76 Stamps

as goats, snakes and scorpions, birds (primarily eagles with spread wings), human figures and fantastic dragons. **Fig. 77.1, 3** closely resemble some examples from plundered tombs in Bactria, now in the Louvre Museum (Amiet 1988b, p. 168, fig. 13.h, l) and **Fig. 71.3** is also similar to an example said to come from southern Bactria, now in a private collection (Salvatori 1988, p. 183, fig. 49, bottom right).

Impressions of such seals have been found on pottery. Scholars disagree about their use. It has been suggested that they were used for administrative control of trade and production (Hiebert 1994, p. 380); were related to a well-organised trade system which involved transporting and transacting goods over long distances (Salvatori 1988, p. 163); were symbols of power and property, or, since a large number have similar images, they may have served as amulets protecting their owners from evil rather than as symbols of ownership (Sarianidi 2002, p. 41).

Compartmented seals have been variously dated to the end of the 3rd/beginning of the 2nd millennium (Amiet 1977, p. 119, Salvatori 1988), or to the first half of the 2nd millennium BC (Tosi 1988, p.123, Sarianidi 1993, p. 36). According to Amiet (1977, p. 117; 1988, pp. 166, 169), they originated in Iranian Sistan: at Shar-i-Sokhta their development can be charted throughout the 3rd millennium BC from steatite prototypes and it is only here and at Shahdad, on the other side of the Lut desert in the region, that they are known to have been used as marks on pottery (Hakemi and Sajjadi 1988, pp. 145, 150). Sarianidi considers this a purely local invention (2002, p. 41). The Masson seals were probably acquired in Kabul bazaar.

Fig. 77.4 – IOLC.7545. K.352. Cast copper alloy stamp in the shape of a flower with twelve-petals, executed in raised outline around a circular hole in the centre, with traces of a lug in the centre of the back. *c.* 1900–1700 BC. 30mm x 30mm. Begram.

A similar compartmented copper alloy seal with a star motif (BM 1993,0129.6) from Margiana (ancient Merv) or Bactria, is dated by Asko Parpola *c.* 1900–1700 BC (Callieri 1997a, pp. 51, 53, no. 3/17).

Fig. 77.5 – IOLC.7546. K.353. Fragment of a large, cast copper alloy stamp or seal, with raised, curved lines around a circle which has a drilled hole in its centre. On the reverse, the hole forms the centre of a large broken lug. 30mm x 22mm; *c.* 1900–1700 BC.

Fig. 77.6 – 1880.3871.a. Box 9. Cast copper alloy mould or stamp in the shape of a six-pointed star. One side is flat, the other has a ridge dividing the star into two triangles,

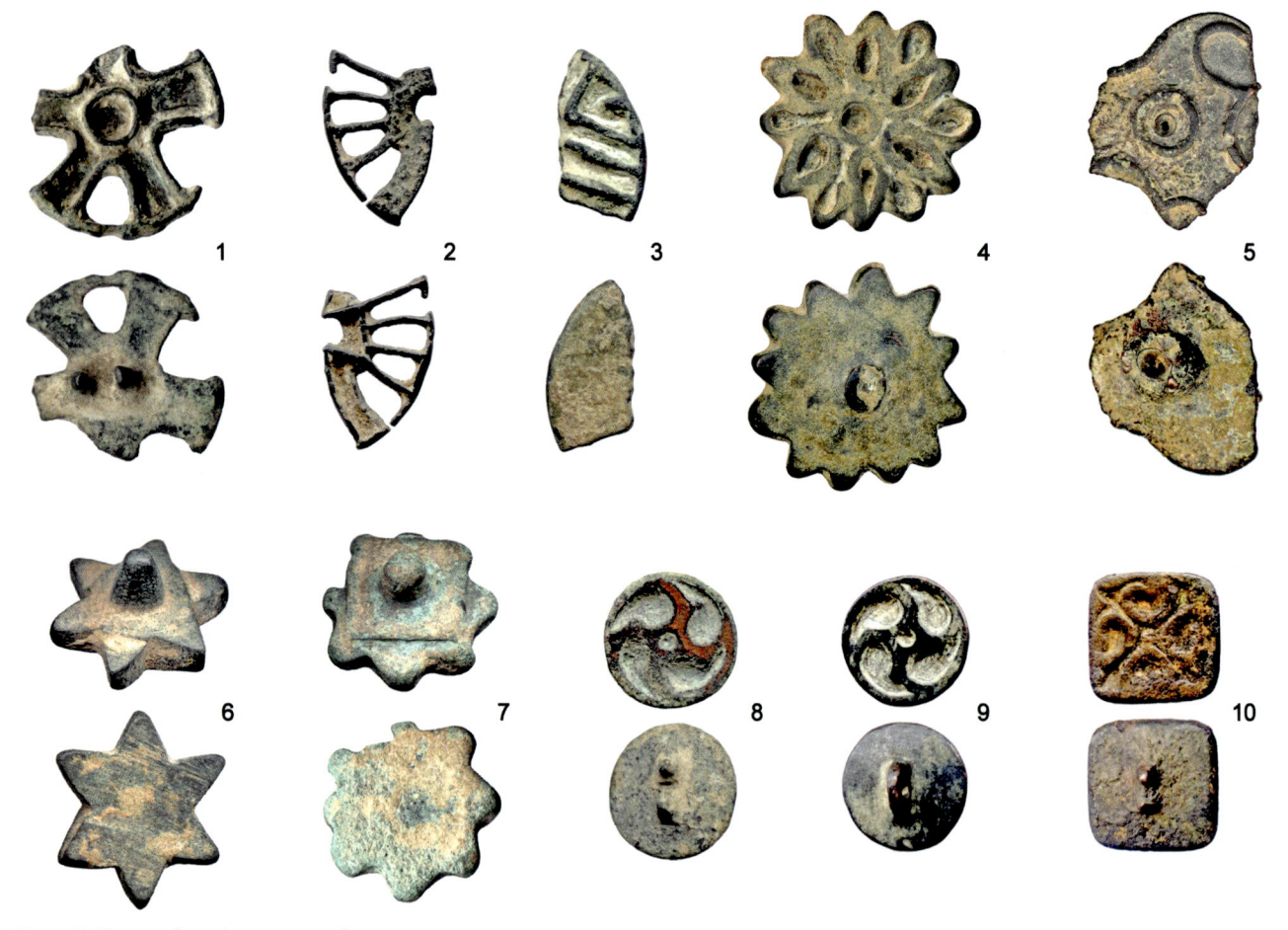

Figure 77 Bronze Age stamps or seals

with a prominent cone-shaped lug in the centre. 26.3mm x 14.7mm; *c.* 2000–1500 BC.

A similar example (seen on the art market *c.* 2007) was said to come from Bactria and dated *c.* 2nd millennium BC.

Fig. 77.7 – 1880.3871.b. Box 9. Cast copper alloy mould or stamp in the shape of a flower with eight petals. One side is flat, the other has a superimposed square fitting within the petals, with a prominent rounded lug in the centre. 25mm x 10.4mm; *c.* 2000–1500 BC.

A similar example was a surface find at Gonur Tepe, a Bronze Age oasis settlement of ancient Margiana, Turkmenistan, a BMAC site (Sarianidi 1993, pl. VI.i).

Fig. 77.8–9. IM.Metal.154. Two cast copper alloy circular seals or buttons, with a pierced lug on the reverse. On the front, four curved spokes in the rough approximation of a swastika radiate from a circular hole in the centre; *c.* 3000 BC–2000 BC.

A similar swastika-like motif is found on late 3rd–early 2nd-millennium BC funerary pottery from Shahi Tump and Bampur-Makran (Cardi 1966; Fairservis 1975, pp. 222, 226, figs 55, 57).

Fig. 77.8 – 1880.3710.e. The lug on the back is broken. 18.4mm x 3.6mm.

Fig. 77.9 – 1880.3710.f. 17mm x 2.6mm.

Fig. 77.10 – 1880.3710.d. IM.Metal 154. Cast copper alloy, square seal (?) with rounded corners and a small, broken lug on the back. The obverse design comprises an incised saltire, with a raised heart-shape in each of the four interstices; *c.* 1500 BC. 18.3mm x 17.6mm x 2.3mm.

A similar motif appears on a circular seal with a long, pierced handle sold at auction in 2005. It was said to come from Bactria and was dated *c.* 1500 BC (Malter Galleries Auction 5 December 2005, lot 1228.1).

Signet- and finger-rings

Rings 1: *c.* 1st century BC–1st century AD

Fig. 78. IM.Metal.141 (unless otherwise stated). Copper alloy rings, cast in one piece, with a broad and flat engraved circular or oval bezel and a shank (flat within; the outer profile slightly curved) which spreads to the edge of the bezel and fits the finger. The bezel is raised beyond the outline of the shank, making it appear as a separate plate fastened to the shank, which it is not. This is a Greek type of finger-ring found from the second half of the 4th century BC down to the Hellenistic period (Boardman, 2001, p. 214, type XI, pl. 217).

Fig. 78.1–4. The roughly circular bezels are engraved with a winged Nike standing to left, wearing a double chiton. She holds a beribboned wreath in her extended right hand and a palm frond (her other attribute) in the crook of her left arm. 1st century AD.

There is another ring with the same image in the Cambridge Ridgeway collection (CMAA.1927.1192).

Nike occurs on coins from the time of Menander (*c.*155–130 BC; **Fig. 26.11–14**), but the ring image is similar to representations of this divinity on Indo-Parthian coins of Gondophares (*c.* AD 32), Sarpedones, Orthagnes (*c.* AD

234 | *Charles Masson: Collections from Begram and Kabul Bazaar, Afghanistan, 1833–1838*

52–64) and Abdagases (c. AD 52–64; see **Fig. 32.20**; Mitchiner 1975–6, vol. 8, types 1082–3, 1088, 1096–103, 1106). The same image occurs on a round malachite gemstone set in a silver mount with an attachment loop from Tillya Tepe burial 5, dated 1st century AD (Sarianidi 1985a, fig. 5.10, Ill.72, p. 46); and on a bronze finger-ring with a leaf-shaped bezel from Gandhara in the Aman ur Rahman collection (Aman ur Rahman and Falk, 2011, no. 06.06.08).

Fig. 78.1 – 1880.3702.g. Complete brass-washed ring. 15.5mm x 18mm.

Fig. 78.2 – 1880.3702.h. Bezel and a small part of the shank. 15.2mm x 13mm; shank: 4.7mm x 1.9mm.

Fig. 78.3 – 1880.3702.i. Brass-washed bezel and a small part of the shank. 15.8mm x 14mm; shank: 3.9mm x 1.8mm.

Fig. 78.4 – 1880.3702.j. Roughly circular bezel and part of the shank. 16.3mm x 14.2mm; shank: 4mm x 1.6mm.

Fig. 78.5–12. The bezel shows a schematic bare-breasted female figure, standing to front with one knee bent. Her raised right hand holds an object – probably a wreath – with an undulating streamer hanging down to the ground. Above her left arm is a fan of three or four straight lines. She wears a tiara (?), a scarf over her left arm and falling to her feet, and a garment resembling trousers reaching down to the knees. The drapery is indicated by finely incised parallel lines across her legs. Parallel lines across her right forearm may indicate bracelets.

There is another ring with the same image in the Cambridge Ridgeway collection (CMAA.1927.1192).

Copper finger-rings with a raised oval bezel engraved with a similar motif were found at Taxila: one at Sirkap in the early 1st-century AD Indo-Parthian stratum, Block C, and one at Dharmarajika, north-east of the monastic quarter F (Marshall 1951, p. 648, nos 48, 52, pl. 198.48, 52). Marshall identifies the figure on the Dharmarjika specimen as a dancing figure (Shiva?) with a snake or bow and wearing a lion-skin. He confusingly dates this example as 'early medieval', even though its twin (pl. 198.48) was found in the 1st-century levels at Sirkap. A further example was discovered in tomb 284 of the Kushan necropolis of Tup Khona, southern Tajikistan (Litvinsky and Sedov 1984, fig. 11) and at the 1st-century AD site of Yotkan in Khotan, Xinjiang (Stein 1921, p. 100, pl. V, Yo.010.e).

Fig. 78.5 – IOLC.7554. K.362. 14mm x 13mm.

Fig. 78.6 – 1880.3702.l. 16.3mm x 4.4mm x 2mm.

Fig. 78.7 – IOLC.7554. K.361. 15mm x 14mm.

Fig. 78.8 – 1880.3702.s. The head-dress is depicted as three vertical lines. 16.2mm x 6.4mm; shank: 2.7mm.

Fig. 78.9 – 1880.3702.k. 14mm x 2.3mm x 1.6mm.

Fig. 78.10 – 1880.3702.m. 16.5mm x 18.8mm; shank: 4.6mm x 2.5mm.

Fig. 78.11 – 1880.3702.n. 16.4mm x 15.2mm; shank: 5.2mm x 2.26mm.

Fig. 78.12 – 1880.3706.b. Oval bezel. The motif is worn. 13.3mm x 10.7mm; shank: 5mm x 1,5mm.

Fig. 78.13–15. The bezel is engraved with a schematic, bare-breasted female figure represented facing, with her legs slightly flexed and her arms akimbo (?). An undulating scarf around her shoulders hangs loosely on either side down to her feet.

A signet-ring depicting the same figure was included in the relic deposit of Bimaran stupa 2, suggesting a date of c. 1st century AD for images of this kind (**Vol. I, Fig. 119.16**). A related image appears on the flat oval bezel of copper finger rings from various sites. One was found in the Indo-Scythian/Indo-Parthian levels at Sirkap, Taxila (Marshall 1951, p. 658, pls 198.51, 207.18), another is from an unspecified site in Gandhara (Aman ur Rahman and Falk 2011, TM 07.08.04) while others come from the Xinjiang site of Niya (Stein 1921, p. 268, pl. XXIX, N.0012; 1907, pls LI, DK.004, LII, N.0014.g). 1st century AD.

Fig. 78.13 – 1880.3702.d. Round bezel: 3mm x 13.6mm; shank: 3.5mm x 1.3mm. Errington 1999, p. 232, pl. 11.4.

Fig. 78.14 – 1880.3702.e. Small round bezel: 9.2mm x 2.5mm x 3.6mm.

Fig. 78.15 – 1880.3788.m. Small oval bezel. 10mm x 8mm; shank: 3.3mm x 1.3mm.

Fig. 78.16 – 1880.3702.f. The schematic female figure stands beneath a leafy arch which is depicted by a line and an outer row of dots and dashes. 14.3mm x 15.9mm; shank: 4.2mm x 1.7mm. Errington 1999, p. 232, pl. 11.3.

A duplicate is in the Cambridge Ridgeway collection (CMAA.1927.1192).

Fig. 78.17–18. A female figure in Indian attire stands to front under an arch represented by a line between two rows of dots. Her left hand is on her hip and holds an object looking like a stick which rests on the shoulder. Her right arm is raised upwards from the elbow. She is bare-breasted, with the lower garment rolled around the waist. Her hair is tied to one side in a bun and she wears ear-rings.

The image brings to mind female figures on terracotta plaques of the Sunga period (2nd–1st century BC) which are roughly rectangular with a rounded top and are decorated along the edge with a row of large dots or flowers. The dotted arch forms a frame for the figure. Examples come, for instance, from Dig in Rajasthan, Rajghat in Delhi and Boral near Calcutta (Poster 1986, fig. 28; Chandra 1971, fig. 454; Biswas 1981, pl. XX a). Hair arranged in a side bun also occurs on terracottas of the same period from Kausambi and Chandraketugarh (Ashton 1950, pl. 4, fig. 46; Ghosh 1965, pl. A). It is furthermore found on sculptures from Butkara in Swat, which are attributable on stylistic grounds to the early Gandhara school, c. 1st century AD (Faccenna and Taddei 1964, pls DCLXIV/MAI 4640, DCLXV/MAI 3157). The finger-rings probably belong to the same period.

Fig. 78.17 – 1880.3702.u. The bun and the ear-rings are clearly visible, although their exact form cannot be ascertained. 7.4mm x 14.7mm; shank: 4.1mm x 1.8mm.

Fig. 78.18 – 1880.3702.v. Partly defaced. 14.5mm x 12.5mm; shank: 5mm x 3.3mm.

Fig. 78.19 – 1880.3702.q. Copper alloy signet-ring showing two bare-breasted women standing side by side, holding hands, the other hand resting on the hip. Their hair is arranged in a side bun. They wear a scarf looped over one shoulder and hanging down to the feet. The drapery folds of the lower garment hanging from the waist are rendered as finely incised parallel lines across the legs. The image shows affiliations in the arrangement of the garment with the figures depicted above (**Fig. 78.13–16**) and affiliations in

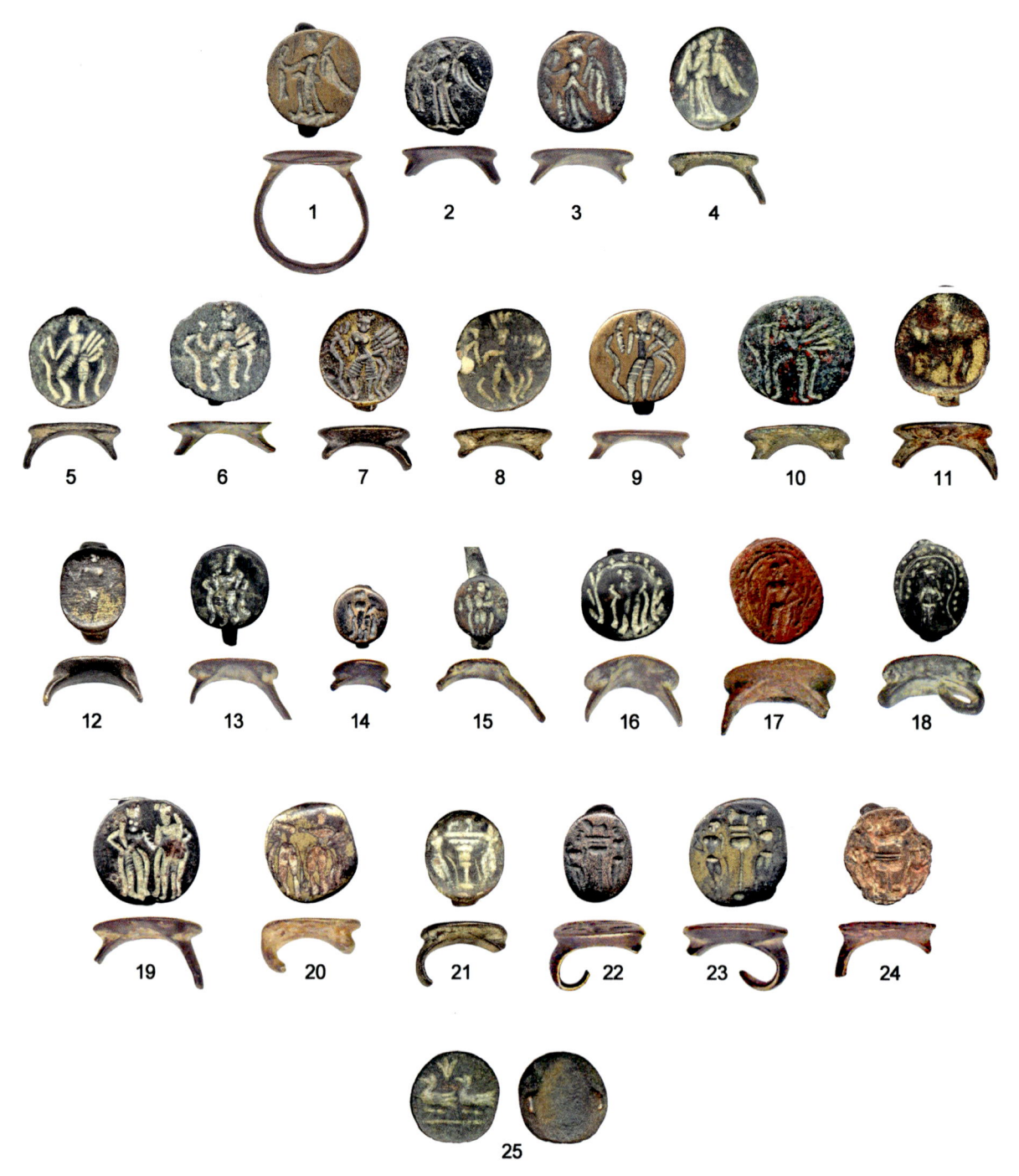

Figure 78 Signet- and finger-rings 1: *c.* 1st century BC–1st century AD

their rendering to the figures in **Fig. 78.5–11**. This suggests a comparable date of the 1st century AD. 16.7mm x 17.9mm; shank: 4.3mm x 1.8mm.

Fig. 78.20 – 1880.3702.0. Brass-washed copper alloy ring depicting two female (?) figures standing arm in arm, the free hand resting on the hip, with loose drapery folded over the arm and hanging down to the feet. 15.7mm x 15.5mm; shank: 5.4mm x 2.2mm.

Fig. 78.21–4. The design shows two bare-breasted women wearing a garment gathered at the waist and standing on either side of a slender column with a bulbous base and capital surmounted by a stepped abacus which supports a lion standing to left.

The motif of the column surmounted by a lion recalls the pillars bearing the edicts of the Mauryan emperor Ashoka (*c.* 269–232 BC) which were erected all over India at sites such as Lauriya-Nandangarh (Thapar 1997, pp. 5–6). Pillars similarly mounted with seated lions were also erected beside stupas at Buddhist sites such as Saidu Sharif I in Swat, dated 1st–5th century (Faccenna and Callieri 2003, pp. 311, 314, fig. 21), the lion being a symbol of the Buddha, lion of the Shakya clan (Rowland 1953, pl. 8). The column as represented on the finger-rings has exact counterparts on reliefs carved on the 1st-century BC northern gateway of stupa 1 at Sanchi (Heinrich 1965, fig. 59), on 1st century BC pillars at Bodh Gaya (Coomaraswamy 1935, pillars 21–2, 64, 92), and on a caitya pillar of the Early Phase at Amaravati (Barrett 1954, pl. IX.2). The women on the ring may be interpreted as worshipping the Buddha through circumambulation of the pillar, as is depicted on a sandstone relief from Mathura attributable to the 1st century AD (Klimburg-Salter 1995, fig. 95a; Lucknow State Museum J.268).

Fig. 78.21 – 1880.3702.x. Copper alloy. Oval bezel. 13.8mm x 12.9mm; shank: 4.7mm x 1.8mm.

Fig. 78.22 – 1880.3702.y. Brass-washed ring. 14.7mm x 11.3mm; shank: 2.9mm x 4.5mm.

Fig. 78.23 – 1880.3702.z. Brass-washed ring, 17.7mm x 15.8mm; shank: 4.2mm x 2.4mm.

Fig. 78.24 – 1880.3788.a. Broken round bezel. Whereas the attendants are represented in full, only the top of the column surmounted by a large bulbous capital topped by a large lion is depicted. 15.2mm x 14.8mm; shank: 5.3mm x 2.3mm.

Fig. 78.25 – 1880.3702.r. Round flat bezel depicting two ducks swimming to left, with a tulip-like bud in the upper ground. Only stubs of the shank survive; *c.* 1st century AD. 14mm.

Rings 2: *c. 1st century* AD *and Islamic (?)*

Fig. 79.1 – 1880.3633. IM.Metal.150. Copper alloy signet-ring fragment, cast in one piece, comprising a flat rectangular bezel with a bevelled edge and concave back to fit around a finger. The surviving stubs of the shank are flat inside and slightly convex outside. The image depicts a seated male bearded figure in a cloak and long-sleeved robe, with his head in profile, arms outstretched and legs in three-quarter view. He holds an unidentifiable object in his left hand and a shaft, probably a sceptre, in his right. His hair is brushed forward from the crown into a row of curls around his face and neck. 14mm x 10mm; shank: 2.3mm x 3.2mm. Callieri 1997, no. M2, p. 132, pl. 30.

The figure resembles that on coins of Parthian kings, particularly from the time of Phraates IV (*c.* 38–2 BC) and Artabanus II (*c.* AD 10–38) down to the 3rd century (Loginov and Nikitin 1996, p. 49, figs 1.4–5, 1.37, 46; Errington and Sarkhosh Curtis 2007, p. 48, fig. 50). The affinities with images of kings who reigned around the beginning of the 1st century AD, suggests an early date perhaps in the Parthian period. However, similarities in the hairstyle and in execution between this ring and the seal **Fig. 75.9** suggest that it could also be of Kushan date.

Fig. 79.2–5. IM.Metal. 141. Copper alloy signet-rings, cast in one piece. The shank is flat inside, slightly convex outside. The bezel is oval, slightly domed with a moulded rim, and engraved. The type is attested at Takht-i-Sangin in south Tajikistan where it may belong to the 1st century AD (Zeimal 1985, p. 95, fig. 222, left: IOT 82).

Fig. 79.2 – 1880.IOLC.7557. K.364. Within a dotted border is a schematic female figure, her hair in a top-knot. 17mm x 9mm. The figure is stylistically close to that on finger-ring **Fig.78.14**).

Fig. 79.3 – 1880.3788.g. The bezel is engraved with a woman standing to front. An undulating scarf wrapped round her shoulders hangs down loosely either side to her feet. The figure resembles that on finger-ring **Fig.78.13**.

Fig. 79.4 – 1880.3788.e. Brass-washed copper alloy. The worn face has a draped figure standing to left with the left arm extended: possibly a winged Nike holding a beribboned wreath, within a double-lined border; *c.* 1st century AD. 14.2mm x 11.7mm; shank: 3.2mm x 1.8mm.

Fig. 79.5 – 1880.3788.f. Engraved with a winged Nike to right, dressed in a chiton and holding a wreath in her right hand. 14mm x 10.3mm; shank: 3.4mm x 1.2mm.

A comparable figure occurs on a bronze signet-ring in the Aman ur Raman collection (Aman ur Rahman and Falk 2011, no. 06.06.08) and on a seal found at Sirkap, Taxila, in the *c.* 1st century BC–1st century AD stratum III (Marshall 1951, II, p. 682, no. 42; III, pl. 207.29).

Fig. 79.6–10. IM.Metal. 141. The rings share a similar profile to those above, but the presence of a Persian inscription on **Fig. 79.9** indicates that the type continued into the Islamic period, *c.* 8th–10th century.

Fig. 79.6 – 1880.3788.j. Engraved with a five-pointed star. 7.5mm x 12.7mm; shank: 2.8mm x 1.6mm.

Fig. 79.7 – 1880.3788.k. Engraved with an uncertain motif, either floral or a seated bird. 13.5mm x 9.5mm.

Fig. 79.8 – 1880.3788.i. The worn traces of engraved undulating and straight lines resemble a winged dragon, but are probably a Persian or Arabic inscription. 14mm x 10mm; shank: 2.3mm x1mm.

Fig. 79.9 – 1880.3788.h. The blundered (?) Persian inscription reads *akhir* ('recent' or 'recently'); reading courtesy of Vesta Curtis). 9mm x 15.3mm; shank: 2.8mm x 1.5mm.

Fig. 79.10 – 1880.3812.c. Copper alloy rounded circular bezel, cast in one piece with a thick shank, and engraved with unidentified C-shapes and lines. 16mm x 3mm x 9mm x 2mm.

Rings 3: *c. 1st century* BC*–4th century* AD

Fig. 80.1–3: Fragments of copper alloy signet-rings, cast in one piece with a raised bezel, sharply bevelled at the point where it joins a thick shank, plano-concave in section. This

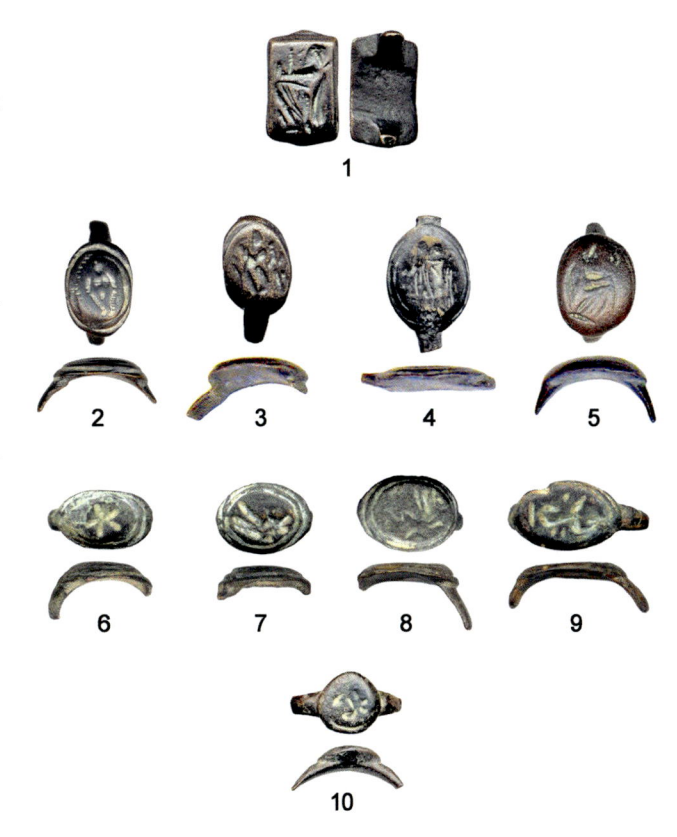

Figure 79 Signet- and finger-rings 2: *c.* 1st century AD (1–5); Islamic (?) (6–10)

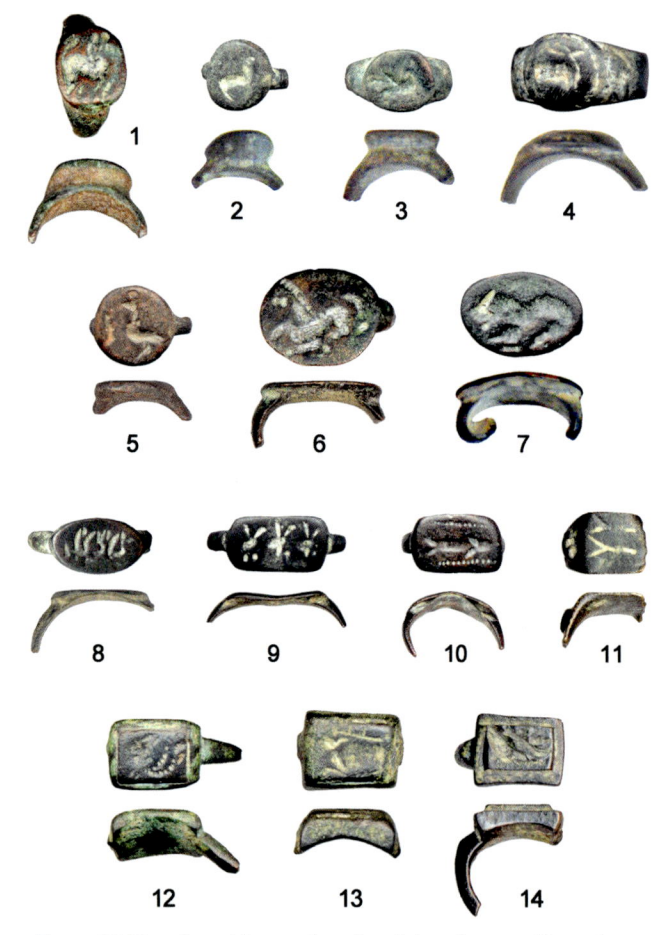

Figure 80 Signet- and finger-rings 3: *c.* 1st century BC–4th century AD

type of finger-ring was found at Sirkap, Taxila, in the 1st-century AD Indo-Parthian stratum (Marshall 1951, p. 648, nos 48–9) and in late 2nd century BC–1st century AD tombs at Tulchar in Tajikistan (Mandel'stham 1966, pl. LVI.8).

Fig. 80.1 – IOLC 7556. K.363. The oval bezel is engraved with the image of a quadruped walking to right. The animal has large round ears, a long muzzle and neck, with raised wings behind, thin legs and a raised tail. It resembles a winged horse (Pegasus) on a bronze copper bezel found at Sirkap, Taxila, in the *c.* 1st century BC–1st century AD stratum III (Marshall 1951, p. 648, no. 43, pl. 207.27). 16mm x 9mm. For a similar figure see **Fig. 74.22**.

Fig. 80.2 – 1880-3788.c. IM.Metal.141. The round bezel is engraved with a worn image, possibly of a deer, but the front legs and other details are missing. The shank is narrow and roughly rectangular in section; *c.* 1st century AD. 8.5mm x 4.9mm; shank: 2.7mm.

Fig. 80.3 – 1880.3788.d. The oval bezel has the worn image of a bird (?). The shank is thick and widens at the shoulders. 8.2mm x 9.9mm; shank: 6.7mm x 2.7mm.

Fig. 80.4 – 1880.3812.f. Cast copper alloy signet-ring with a rounded oval bezel and a wide, broken shank; engraved with a seated stag to right, encircled by a dotted border. 13.7mm x 10.4mm x 4mm; shank: 8mm.

Fig. 80.5 – 1880.3788.n. Copper alloy signet-ring, cast in one piece, with a flat circular bezel engraved with a long-necked bird facing a slightly curved frond to left. 10.7mm x 2.9mm x 14mm.

Fig. 80.6 – IOLC 7553. K.360. Copper alloy signet-ring, cast in one piece; the flat oval bezel has a recumbent lion to left; *c.* 3rd–4th century AD. 18mm x 12mm.

The depiction resembles that of a walking lion on an intaglio from Jalalabad in the Victoria and Albert Museum (IM 50-01932; see Callieri 1997, p. 125, no. 7.51), and another in the Masson collection (**Fig. 67.20**). A similar seal is dated *c.* 3rd–4th century on the basis of its Bactrian legend *kasofarno* or *kosofarno* (Bivar 1968, p. 13, pl. IV, 6; Davary 1982, p. 114, sig. 69).

Fig. 80.7 – 1880-3788.b. IM.Metal.141. The oval bezel has a recumbent lion to left. 11mm x 17mm; shank: 3.9mm x 2.1mm.

Fig. 80.8–10. IM.Metal. 141. Copper-alloy signet-rings cast in one piece, with a thin flat bezel merging into the shank (which is flat in section on the inside; round on the outside).

Fig. 80.8 – 1880.3788.o. The oval bezel has a pseudo-Pahlavi (?) inscription, or three very schematic birds to right. 13.4mm x 7.2mm; shank: 2.9mm x 1.5mm.

Fig. 80.9 – 1880.3799.b. The rectangular bezel has a row of three birds flying to right. 20mm x 14.2mm x 7mm; shank: 2.3mm.

The birds perhaps represent geese (*haṃsa*), a common Buddhist motif found on the copper alloy so-called 'Kanishka reliquary', dated by a coin or cast of a coin of Huvishka (AD 151–90) to *c.* late 2nd century (Errington 2002a). A similar motif is depicted on finger-ring **Fig. 82.13**.

Fig. 80.10 – 1880.3799.c. The rectangular bezel depicts an elongated fish between two rows of dots. 13mm x 7.8mm; shank: 1.3mm.

Fig. 80.11 – 1880.3790.t. Fragment of a cast copper alloy finger-ring with wide, sloping shoulders decorated with a knob and broadening into a flat, thin rectangular bezel incised with two horizontal Y-shaped lines probably representing a pair of fish. 12.7mm; bezel: 8.2mm x 9.6mm.

Fig. 80.12 – 1880.3799.e. Cast copper alloy finger-ring with traces of brass-wash and a rectangular bezel depicting a bird (?) within an incised frame. The shank is semi-circular in section, slightly widening at the shoulders. 18mm; bezel: 12.8mm x 9.5mm.

Fig. 80.13 – 1880.3816.x. IM.Metal.141. Rectangular bezel of a cast copper alloy signet-ring, originally brass-washed. The central section is raised above the surrounding edge and has an engraved recumbent stag to left. 14.6mm x 10.5mm x 4mm.

Fig. 80.14 – 1880.3816.w. IM.Metal.141. Cast copper alloy finger-ring. The surviving shoulder is roughly triangular in section and abuts a thick rectangular, stepped bezel depicting a bird (?) to right with a leafy branch. 18.2mm; bezel: 12.4mm x 9.5mm.

A similar finger-ring, attributed to the early Sasanian period, was found at War Kabud, Iran (Musche 1988, p. 307, pl. CVII, type 5). This form of bezel also occurs in rings from Corinth (Davidson 1952, p. 239, pl. 104, no. 1898) and in one from an unspecified place in Iran or Israel (Content 1987, p. 38, no. 11). All are dated to the 9th–11th century.

Rings 4: *c.* 1st century BC–6th century AD; Islamic (?)

Fig. 81.1–20. IM.Metal.141 (unless otherwise stated). Cast copper alloy finger-rings with a shank widening at the shoulders into a flat, elliptical bezel. Two varieties may be distinguished. In the first, the shank and the shoulders are thin and roughly rectangular in section (e.g. **Fig. 81.1–3**). This ring type first appears in the Greek world during the 7th–6th century BC and continues down into the Roman period. Examples dating from the 5th century BC and from the 1st–2nd century AD have been found in Asia Minor (Konuk and Arslan 2000, nos 177–85) while examples in iron dated *c.* late 4th-century–145 BC have been found at Ai Khanum (Frankfort 1984, p. 65, nos 27–49).

In the second variety, the shank is plano-convex in section widening into thick shoulders that are either curved or perpendicular to the elliptical bezel (e.g. **Fig. 81.6–8**). This is a type found all over the Roman Empire. One example engraved with a *triratna* symbol was found at Taxila (Marshall's Photographic Archives). Others engraved with human figures or animals were excavated in Bactria from the late 2nd century BC–1st century AD necropolis at Tulchar in the Bishkent valley, Uzbekistan (Mandel'stham 1966, pl. LXVI.15–16, 20) and from tombs at Takht-i Sanguin in Tajikistan (Zeimal 1985, p. 95, no. 222). At Palmyra, some specimens were found in Tomb F of the south-eastern necropolis, dated AD 128–222 (Higuchi and Saito 2001, fig. 74.14–15). Parthian Iran also yielded examples (Musche 1988, p. 221, pl. LXXVII, 1.3.4–5 and pl. CVIII). Finger-rings of this type have been discovered as far east as Kucha and Yulduz-Bagh on the border of the Taklamakan Desert (Stein 1928, pp. 826, 828, pl. CXI, Kucha.0122, Kucha.06, Yul.075). From Mogul Ghundai in Baluchistan, Pakistan, comes an example attributed to the Kushan or the Gupta period (Stein 1929, pl. 12).

Fig. 81.1 – 1880.3788.r. The bezel shows an image in relief of a woman standing to front, with legs crossed and her head to left. Her hair is tied in a bun at the nape of her neck. She wears a garment around her thighs, leaving the rest of her body bare. Her right arm is bent at elbow and she holds a wreath above a small pillar or altar. Her left arm is akimbo with traces of drapery falling from it; *c.* 1st century BC–1st century AD. 17.8mm x 7.8mm x 2mm.

Fig. 81.2–3. The bezels show the relief image of a naked ithyphallic man and woman embracing. This is the Greek motif of Eros and Psyche or Aphrodite, examples of which occur at Sirkap, Taxila, on a gold brooch (Marshall 1951, p. 632, no. 98, pl. 191.u) and on a carnelian seal in a gold frame (Marshall 1951, p. 681, no. 30, pl. 207, nos 11, 11a), both from the 1st-century AD Indo-Parthian stratum. The motif further appears at Shaikhan Dheri on a clay impression (Dani 1965–6, pl. XLVI.3).

Fig. 81.2 – 1880.3788.s. 18.3mm x 8.9mm x 3.6mm.
Fig. 81.3 – 1880.3788.t. 18.3mm x 8.8mm x 1.9mm.
Fig. 81.4 – 1880.3799.z. The bezel shows a worn female figure to right, wearing a helmet and a short chiton, possibly Nike or Athena. 18.2mm x 8.6mm x 4.1mm x 1.6mm.

Fig. 81.5 – 1880.3789.n. The bezel is engraved with a dancing female figure standing to front, left leg crossed over the right. Her hair is bound in a side knot. She is naked, apart from anklets, a garment around her hips and a scarf which falls in loose folds on either side of her body. She is adorned with anklets. Her right hand rests on her hip; the left is raised and holds an uncertain object; *c.* 1st century AD. 17mm x 10mm; shank: 4.1mm x 1.3mm. A similar finger-ring was found at Sirkap, Taxila, in the 1st century AD Indo-Parthian stratum (Marshall 1951, p. 648, no. 46, pl. 198, no. 46 and pl. 207, no. 33). For another example, see **Fig. 74.29**.

Fig. 81.6 – 1880.3932.a. IM 26 / SKM 1074. The bezel has the engraved image of a closed door and an archway supporting three branches of leafy foliage. 20.2mm x 14.4mm; shank: 6.9mm x 1.7mm.

Fig. 81.7 – 1880.3789.p. The brass-washed engraved bezel depicts a winged Nike standing to left, wearing a helmet and a chiton. Her extended right hand holds a wreath with floating ribbons and a palm frond (her other attribute) is cradled in her left arm. 11.6mm x 11.4mm; shank: 2.7mm x 1.6mm.

A similar image, but closer stylistically to the Greek classical prototypes, appears on a malachite intaglio found in the early 1st-century AD burial 5 at Tillya Tepe in Afghanistan (Sarianidi 1985a, fig. 5.10, Ill.72). Owing to its crude style, the present finger-ring is probably of a later date, i.e. possibly Kushan period, *c.* 3rd–4th century. For a similar execution of the figure, see **Fig. 79.1**.

Fig. 81.8 – IOLC.7562. K.369. Worn and unidentified image; possibly fighting animals (?) 18mm x 9mm.

Fig. 81.9 – 1880.3788v. The bezel is engraved with a man to right, wearing a short tunic and cloak tied around his neck. He holds a bunch of flowers. On either side of his legs are a star (to left) and a taurine (to right). The curving hemline of the tunic resembles that found on coins of Kushan kings from the time of Kanishka II (*c.* AD 230–46) onwards; *c.* 3rd–4th century AD. 14.6mm x 8.9mm; shank: 3.7mm x 1mm.

Fig. 81.10 – 1880.3788.u. The bezel has a schematic engraved image of a man, walking to left, dressed in a short tunic and trousers and holding a rod. 17.8mm x 8.5mm; shank: 3.3mm x 1mm.

Fig. 81.11 – 1880.3789.q. Brass-washed copper alloy. The bezel has a crudely engraved human figure running with arms outstretched, beneath an arch executed as a series of short hatched lines and dots. 1.6mm x 9.5mm; shank: 2.1mm x 1.3mm.

Fig. 81.12 – 1880.3789.f. The bezel is elliptical; the shoulders curved. The engraved face has a dotted arch and ground line within which is a squat helmeted (?) figure running to left with arms slightly bent and looking backwards. 18.5mm x 8.3mm x 1.9mm.

Fig. 81.13 – 1880.3812.a. Female (?) head facing left, with her hair gathered in a bun at the nape of the neck. She wears a necklace and ear-rings. 12.5mm x 11.2mm; shank: 5mm x 2mm.

Fig. 81.14–16. Cast copper alloy finger-rings with an elliptical bezel engraved with classical motifs, but of such rough workmanship, it is tempting to attribute them to a later date, perhaps 3rd–4th century AD.

Fig. 81.14 – 1880.3788.x. The shank is flat and the shoulders slope. The broken bezel depicts the standing figures of a man to left, with a himation around his shoulders and hanging down on his right side, facing a woman in a long, pleated chiton, and holding up an object between them. Both heads are missing. The folds of the woman's garment are rendered as a series of incised lines. 15.3mm x 12.1mm; shank: 4.8mm x 1.4mm.

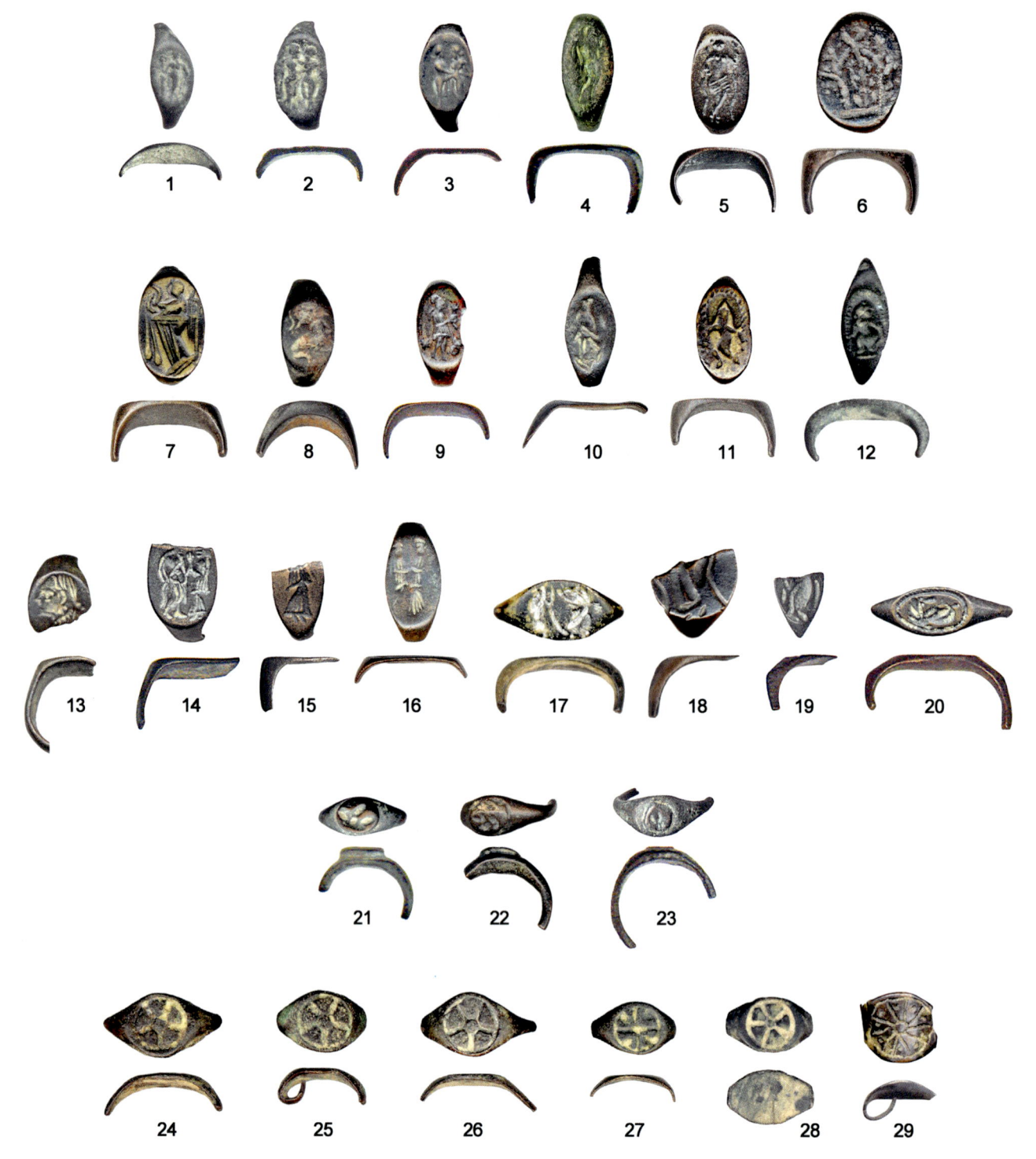

Figure 81 Signet- and finger-rings 4: *c.* 1st century BC–6th century AD; Islamic (?) (29)

Fig. 81.15 – 1880.3789.o. Brass-washed copper alloy. The shank is semi-circular in section and the shoulders perpendicular to the broken bezel. The fragment shows a woman from the shoulders downwards, turned to right, with the folds of her chiton rendered as a series of incised lines. 12.5mm x 9mm; shank: 3.8mm x 1.5mm.

Fig. 81.16 – 1880.3788.w. Brass-washed copper alloy. The shank is almost flat and the shoulders slope. The bezel depicts two women standing side by side, dressed in long chitons, rendered as a series of incised lines. 17.8mm x 9.4mm; shank: 4mm x 1.3mm.

Fig. 81.17 – 1880.3789.h. The worn image is unidentifiable; possibly two facing figures. 10mm x 18.9mm; shank: 2.4mm.

Fig. 81.18–20. Cast copper alloy signet-rings with a flat oval bezel, the sloping shoulders angled to a sharp point at the junction with the shank, which is triangular in section.

A finger-ring with a shank of similar profile, but with a hollowed oval bezel for an inlay, was found in Building I of the Tepai Shakh necropolis in Tajikistan. This building yielded coins of Kanishka I, Vasudeva and Kanishka III which suggests for its content a date range of 2nd–3rd century AD.

Fig. 81.18 – 1880.3789.i. Bezel and shoulder fragment. The extant part shows lower part of a standing female figure, turned to left, clad in a long dress and scarf. 19.4mm x 14.8mm.

Fig. 81.19 – 1880.3789.j. As above but the woman is turned to right. 13mm x 8.5mm.

240 | *Charles Masson: Collections from Begram and Kabul Bazaar, Afghanistan, 1833–1838*

Fig. 81.20 – 1880.3789.k. Brass-washed copper alloy signet-ring with a flat bezel depicting a distinct, but unidentifiable image, perhaps a floral motif, within a border of dots. 8mm x 14.7mm x 2mm.

Fig. 81.21–3. Cast copper alloy finger-rings comprising a shank that widens into flat elliptical shoulders, with a small raised bezel in the centre. This variety occurs in Kurgan IV, Tomb 1 at Tulchar, dated late 2nd century BC–1st century AD (Mandel'stham 1966, pl. LVI.6).

Fig. 81.21 – 1880.3812.d. The raised bezel is oval with a punched floral motif. 5.8mm x 7.6mm x 3.7mm; shank: 6.6mm.

Fig. 81.22 – 1880.3812.k. The raised bezel is oval with a similar floral (?) motif. 4.8mm x 7.5mm; shank: 6.8mm x 2.5mm.

Fig. 81.23 – 1880.3812.e. The raised bezel is circular with traces of an incised lines. 4.8mm; shank: 17.6mm x 6.7mm x 1.6mm.

Fig. 81.24–8. Cast copper alloy finger-rings with a shank plano-convex in section and of uniform thickness widening on the shoulders into a flat, elliptical bezel, decorated with an engraved circle containing a five-petalled flower. Romano-Byzantine (?).

Fig. 81.24 – 1880.3789.b. 20.8mm x 10mm x 2.6mm.
Fig. 81.25 – 1880.3789.c. 15.9mm x 10mm x 4mm.
Fig. 81.26 – 1880.3789.d. 20.4mm x 10.5mm x 2mm.
Fig. 81.27 – 1880.3789.e. 15mm x 8.7mm x 3mm.
Fig. 81.28 – IOLC.7560. K.367. 15mm x 8mm.
Fig. 81.29 – 1880.3981.o. Box 4.b. Fragment of a finger-ring of sheet silver. The flat, narrow shank expands into an elliptical bezel with an incised sun symbol within a circle. Ten rays divide the background into equal segments, each decorated with a punched dot. 13mm x 12mm x 4mm.

A comparable motif occurs on a 10th–12th century finger-ring from Corinth (Davidson 1952, no. 1931).

Rings 5: c. 1st century BC–3rd century AD

Fig. 82. IM.Metal.141 (unless otherwise stated). Mainly elliptical bezels engraved with figures of animals.

Fig. 82.1–8. Copper alloy signet-rings, cast in one piece, with a broad shank (plano-convex in section) widening into thick shoulders that are perpendicular to the large, flat, oval bezel. 1st–3rd century AD.

Fig. 82.1 – 1880.3790.a. An engraved stag with large antlers, standing to right. 18.6mm x 12.2mm x 5.9mm x 1.7mm.

Fig. 82.2 – 1880.3790.c. The worn image of a winged griffin, standing to right. 14.2mm x 9.6mm; shank: 5.6mm x 2.8mm.

Fig. 82.3 – IOLC.7563. K.370. The image of a horse (?) with the head turned backwards over an S-shaped body. The distorted stance of the animal is reminiscent of Scythian Animal Style. 1st century BC (?) 18mm x 8mm.

An animal running and looking backwards is depicted on a round copper seal found at Sirkap, Taxila, in the 1st-century BC–1st-century AD Indo-Scythian stratum (Marshall 1951, p. 680, no. 17, pl. 208.40).

Fig. 82.4 – 1880.3789.w. The worn image of a lion (?) walking to left. 10.3mm x 18.9mm x 3.8mm x 1mm.

Fig. 82.5 – 1880.3789.s. Broken bezel depicting a lion (?) with long legs and tail, standing to left, with a small taurine symbol above. The shank is slightly triangular in section. 12.6mm x 9.8mm; shank: 5.1mm x 1.4mm.

Fig. 82.6 – 1880.3789.v. Broken bezel with the head, mane and paws of a recumbent lion to right. 13.5mm x 9.1mm.

Fig. 82.7 – 1880.3789.x. The bezel is engraved with the image of a rampant lion (right) attacking a bull or a zebu (left). 12.3mm x 20.9mm; shank: 5.6mm x 2.2mm.

Fig. 82.8–10. The shoulders and the bezel are thin and curved.

Fig. 82.8 – 1880.3789.z. Broken bezel with a pair of confronting birds on either side of a small pile of parallel horizontal lines. 15.4mm x 9.2mm.

Fig. 82.9 – 1880.3788.y. Brass-washed broken oval bezel, engraved with a pair of stylised fish tied together within an incised border. 11.5mm x 11.5mm; shank: 4.5mm x 1.1mm.

Fig. 82.10 – 1880.3789.a. Fragment of a large bezel engraved with the forepart of a reclining lion to left within a dotted border. 15.2mm x 14mm.

Fig. 82.11 – 1880.3902.a. IM 21 / SKM 1100. A dragon to left within a dotted border. Cleaned and conserved. 1st–3rd century AD (?). 12.6mm x 15.6mm; shank: 4.5mm x 1.6mm.

Fig. 82.12 – 1880.3788.z. The image of a cockerel to left within a circle. 13.4mm x 11.2mm; shank: 5mm x 1.6mm.

Fig. 82.13 – 1880.3790.e. Signet-ring, with thick shoulders perpendicular to a flat, rectangular bezel depicting a row of four birds in flight to right, above a row of dots. 10.9mm x 18mm; shank: 2.6mm x 1.4mm.

Fig. 82.14–15. Cast copper alloy finger-rings with an almond-shaped bezel, thick shoulders and a shank triangular in section. A ring of this type, with a Gupta Brahmi inscription, was found in the stupa court at Bhamala, Taxila, and attributed to the 5th century AD (Marshall 1951, pp. 396, 648, no. 56, pls 198.576, 208.58). Another, also in bronze and engraved with a winged figure holding a rython (?), was found in Building IV at Tepai Shakh, Tajikistan, and may belong to the last phase of the necropolis (4th–5th century).

Fig. 82.14 – 1880.3789.r. Bezel fragment showing the forepart of a recumbent griffon-like creature, but without wings. 12mm x 10.5mm; shank: 5.4mm x 2.5mm.

Fig. 82.15 – 1880.3812.b. Fragment with the repeated motif of an eight-pointed star between two moon-shaped incisions separated by a vertical line and framed by a line running parallel to the bezel's edge. 13.2mm x 11mm; shank: 4.5mm x 2mm.

Fig. 82.16 – 1880.3812.l. Complete finger-ring cut out in one piece from a copper alloy sheet, with an open shank which widens at shoulder level into a rounded bezel. This shows a bird with flapping wings to right and a double row of punched dots beneath the curve of the body. Sasanian or early Islamic (?). 11.6mm x 14mm; shank: 20mm x 3.5mm x 1.5mm.

Similar examples were found at Qasr-i Abu Nasr, Iran (Whitcomb 1985, fig. 66.o, n).

Fig. 82.17–18. Cast, brass-washed copper alloy finger-rings. The shank is circular in section, widening and

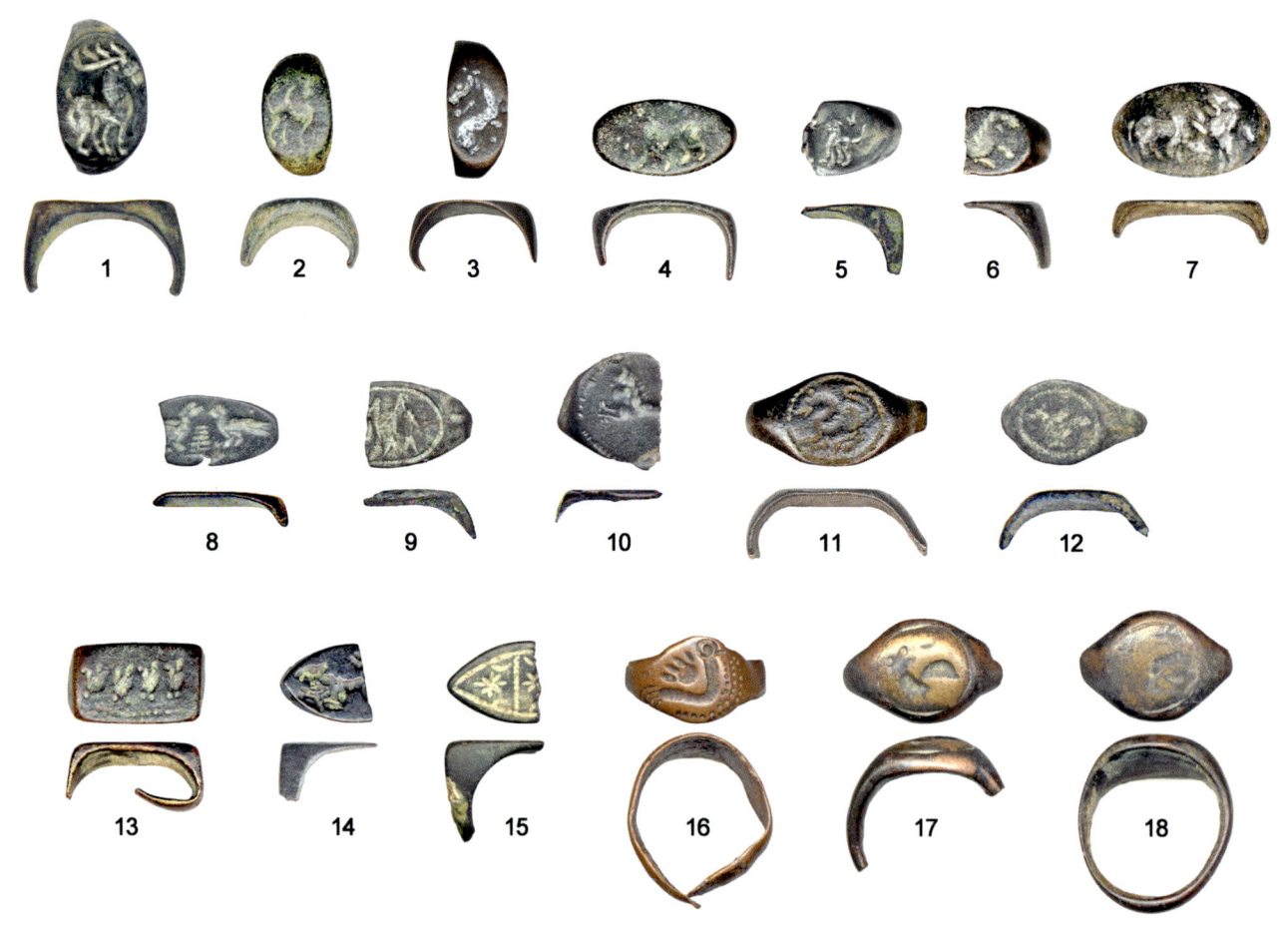

Figure 82 Signet-rings 5: *c.* 1st century BC–3rd century AD

thickening into a domed elliptical bezel decorated with a motif within an incised circle. Probably Sasanian.

Fig. 82.17 – 1880.3812.i. The bezel has a punched motif of a cockerel to left. 14mm x 4.7mm x 23.75mm.

Fig. 82.18 – 1880.3812.h. Complete finger-ring. The worn bezel has only traces of a motif. 14.7mm x 4mm; shank: 21mm x 1.4mm.

Rings 6: c. 3rd–12th century

Fig. 83. IM.Metal.141 (unless otherwise stated).

Fig. 83.1 – 1880.3790.w. Complete brass-washed copper alloy signet-ring. The shank broadens towards the notched shoulders and slightly raised rectangular bezel, which depicts a schematic female figure, possibly a winged (?) Nike, walking to right with arms extended, holding a diadem. 7.2mm x 13.7mm x 21mm.

Fig. 83.2–3. Cast copper alloy signet-rings, with knobbed, notched shoulders and a rectangular, slightly raised bezel.

Fig. 83.2 – 1880.3706.o. IM.Metal.145. A dotted border frames the engraved image of a dancing woman, her head turned to left and her body to front, with her right leg crossed over the left. Her left hand rests on her hip; the right holds up an uncertain object. Her hair is tied in a bun at the back of her head. She wears a necklace and bangles. 20.6mm x 11.7mm x 26mm.

Fig. 83.3 – 1880.3790.s. Broken bezel showing a 'vase of plenty' (*pūrṇaghaṭa*). 16.2mm x 10.4mm x 8.7mm.

Fig. 83.4-5. Copper alloy signet-rings cast in one piece with a shank, semi-circular in section, widening into flat shoulders. The join with the slightly raised round bezel is defined by a notch. Within an incised circular border a winged Nike is depicted standing to left, her extended arms holding a beribboned diadem. Rings of this type were found in south Tajikistan and dated 1st century (Zeimal 1985, p. 95, no. 227).

Fig. 83.4 – 1880.3790.f. Oval bezel minus the shank, with a schematic engraved Nike. 13mm x 15.2mm.

Fig. 83.5 – 1880.3790.g. 14mm x 16mm x 22.5mm.

Fig. 83.6–8. Copper alloy signet-rings cast in one piece, with a shank semi-circular in section, flat notched shoulders and an oval bezel depicting within a dotted border a 'vase of plenty' (*pūrṇaghaṭa*) with incised lines above indicating foliage. The simplified oblique lines on either side derive from the depiction of tendrils signifying growth and fruitfulness, but here seem to represent diadem ribbons; *c.* 1st–4th century AD. For another example, see **Fig. 75.4**.

The *pūrṇaghaṭa* or *pūrṇakalaśa* is a common motif in Hindu, Jain and Buddhist art. It is one of the eight *aṣṭamangala* (auspicious signs) symbolising abundance, like the cornucopia in Greek and Roman art. Its use is attested from *c.* 1st century BC onwards. It was particularly prevalent in early Buddhist art, occurring on 1st-century BC–1st-century AD reliefs from Bharhut, Sanchi, Mathura and Amaravati; on 2nd-century reliefs from Nagarjunakonda and Anuradhapura; and on 1st–2nd-century Gandharan reliefs from Swat and the Peshawar Valley (Sivaramamurti 1974, fig. 244; Marshall and Foucher 1947; Vogel 1930, pl. VII.15; Barrett 1954, pl. IX.29; Longhurst 1938, pl. 31c; Boisselier 1978, p. 110, fig. 24; Faccenna and Taddei 1964, vol. II.3, pl. DCXIVa, W.S. 27; Tissot 1985, pl. XVI.8).

Figure 83 Signet-rings 6: *c.* 3rd–12th century

An identical bulbous vase with a long, narrow neck and lines emerging above a broad rim occurs on 6th-century Alkhan Hun copper alloy coins found at Kashmir Smast in the Peshawar Valley. On the coins the flanking tendrils have also become ribbons, but are more realistically depicted. Earlier coins in the series and Alkhan silver coins bearing the title ξαβοχο show a trident or three flowers instead of the 'foliage' lines (Nasim Khan *et al.* 2008, pp. 89, 168–9, nos 489–91; Göbl 1967, pl.28.101). It later occurs on the reverse of 7th-century Nepalese coins with Kuvera, god of wealth, on the obverse (Rhodes, Gabrisch and Valdettaro 1989, pp. 45–7, pls. 8–9), and survives in the form of the Tibetan *bumpa* (urn of wisdom) and in Hindu *kumbha* rituals.

Similar finger-rings were found in Ferghana (Litvinsky 1986, p. 88, fig. 17; Gorbunova 1986, pls XXXVIII.4, XLIII.1, 11), at Lop Nor (Stein 1921, fig. 117.2), Lou-Lan and Niya (Stein 1921, vol. 2, p. 430, pl. XXIX, L.A. 0094; and p. 248, pl. XXIX, N XII–XXVII 002–003 respectively).

Fig. 83.6 – 1880.3790.o. 22.9mm x 15.6mm x 11.3mm x 4.6mm.

Fig. 83.7 – 1880.3790.p. Brass-washed. 20.8mm x 12.1mm.

Fig. 83.8 – 1880.3790.q. 16.8mm x 13.7mm; shank: 5.4mm x 1.7mm.

Fig. 83.9 – 1880.3799.f. Cast copper alloy signet-ring, with a shank (semi-circular in section), flat notched shoulders and a circular bezel engraved with a lion to right. 12.6mm x 14mm x 17.4mm.

Fig. 83.10–12. Copper alloy signet-rings, cast in one piece, with a shank semi-circular in section, flat notched shoulders and an oval bezel depicting a recumbent animal encircled by an incised oval border.

Fig. 83.10 – 1880.3790.k. A lion to left. The frame is decorated with short incisions. 21mm x 13.8mm x 11mm.

Fig. 83.11 – 1880.3790.l. The worn image of a winged dragon (?) to left. 26mm x 19.6mm x 12.6mm.

Fig. 83.12 – 1880.3790.m. A winged-dragon (?) to right. 23.2mm x 14.2mm x 10mm.

Fig. 83.13–15. Cast copper alloy signet-rings, with a shank (semi-circular in section), flat notched shoulders and an oval bezel depicting a hare with long ears, running to left, within an incised oval border.

Fig. 83.13 – 1880.3790.h. Bezel fragment. 20mm x 13mm.

Catalogue of Ornamental Metalwork and Miscellaneous Artefacts | 243

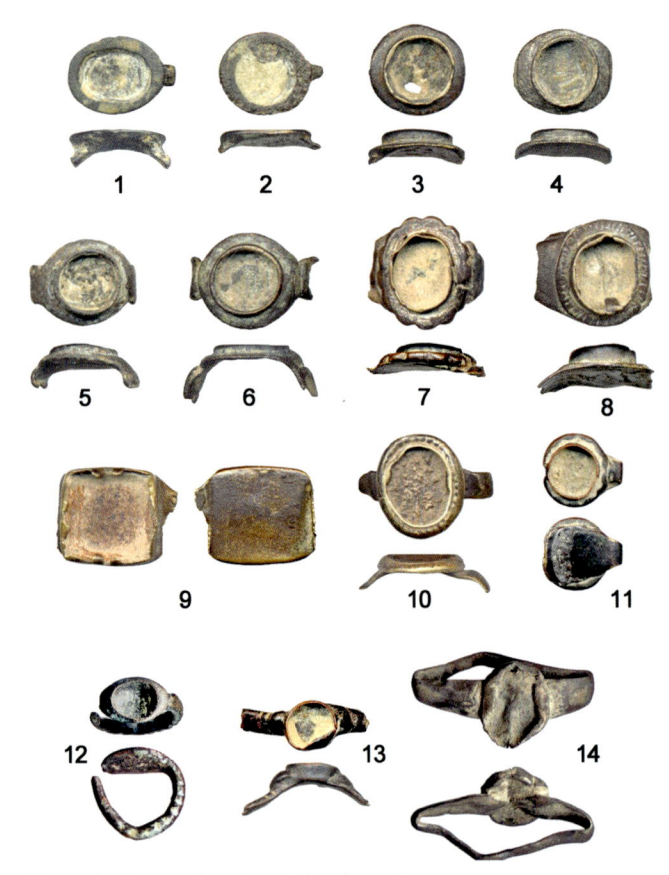

Figure 84 Finger-rings 7: *c.* 3rd–11th century

Fig. 83.14 – 1880.3790.j. Brass-washed bezel fragment. 14mm x 13.8mm x 9.6mm.

Fig. 83.15 – 1880.3790.i. Brass-washed. 14.45mm x 15.85mm x 17.5mm.

Fig. 83.16–19. Copper alloy signet-rings, cast in one piece, with a shank (semi-circular in section), flat notched shoulders and a rectangular bezel.

Fig. 83.16 – 1880.3790.u. A schematic bird to left, within a rectangular incised frame. 7.80mm x 12.15mm x 8.4mm.

Fig. 83.17 – 1880.3790.v. The surface of the bezel shows traces of decoration, but is badly degraded. 20.5mm x 11.4mm x 7.8mm

Fig. 83.18 – 1880.3928.a. The bezel is incised with long-necked bird (possibly a goose) to right. 8.4mm x 11.6mm x 17.3mm.

Fig. 83.19 – 1880.3816.w. The surviving shoulder is roughly triangular in section, slopes down to form an angle with the shank, and abuts a thick rectangular, two-stepped bezel with a bird (?) to right in high relief and a branch with three leaves above. 9.5mm x 12.4mm x 18.2mm.

Finger-rings with a rectangular stepped bezel occur at various periods. One, found at War Kabud, Iran, is attributed to the early Sasanian period (Musche 1987B, p. 307, pl. CVII, type 5). Others belong to the early Islamic period: examples from Corinth and Gurgan, are dated 11th–12th century (Davidson 1952, no. 1898); and from Iran 9th–11th century (Content 1987, p. 38, no. 11).

Rings 7: *c.* 3rd–11th century

Fig. 84.1–2. IM.Metal.141. Copper alloy finger-rings, cast in one piece with a thin shank, semi-circular in section, above which rises a large, flat bezel. This is edged with a plain band, which creates a shallow cell for a stone or paste insert.

A comparable finger-ring was found at Yalangtush Tepe in Naos 3, Room 2, which contained two coins of Kanishka I (Rtveladze 1983, p. 134, fig. 10, 19). The necropolis was in use between the late 1st and early 3rd century AD.

Fig. 84.1 – 1880.3811.b. The bezel is oval. 10.5mm x 13.2mm x 13.7mm.

Fig. 84.2 – 1880.3811.c. The bezel is roughly circular. 11mm x 12.7mm x 14.2mm.

Fig. 84.3–8. IM.Metal.141. Copper alloy finger-rings, cast in one piece. The shank widens into flat shoulders which join a bezel with a flat outer edge and a raised inner rim for a stone or paste insert.

Fig. 84.3 – 1880.3811.e. Circular bezel and cell. 12mm x 13.3mm x 13.3mm.

Fig. 84.4 – 1880.3811.f. Circular bezel and cell, with traces of gilding. 11.3mm x 11.5mm x 13.5mm.

Fig. 84.5 – 1880.3811.g. Oval bezel and circular cell with traces of gilding. 13.4mm x 12.5mm x 14.6mm.

Fig. 84.6 – 1880.3811.h. Oval bezel and circular cell. The shoulders are pinched and have a raised oval rim, probably for additional inserts. There are traces of gilding. 12.8mm x 18.8mm.

Fig. 84.7–9. IM.Metal.141. Copper alloy finger-rings with a shank, flat in section, broadening at the shoulders to the width of the bezel which is soldered to it.

Fig. 84.7 – 1880.3811.j. The oval bezel has a scalloped edge, with a raised inner rim for a stone or paste insert. 15mm x 13.3mm x 3.2mm x 16mm.

Fig. 84.8 – 1880.3811.l. The oval bezel has a flat outer edge engraved with radiating lines. This surrounds a raised inner rim for an insert. Traces of gilding. 14.3mm x 13mm x 3.3mm x 16mm.

Fig. 84.9 – 1880.3811.k. The remains of a broad flat shank is attached to a square cell of the same width, the outer rim of which is damaged. 17mm x 12mm.

Fig. 84.10–11. Copper alloy finger-rings with the widened ends of a flat shank soldered to a flat bezel with a raised inner rim for holding a stone or paste insert.

Fig. 84.10 – 1880.3811.m. IM.Metal.141. The bezel is oval, encircled by a band of beading; with traces of gilding. 14mm x 12mm x 1.5mm x 3.5mm x 0.65mm x 18.8mm.

Fig. 84.11 – 1880.3930.b. Box 8. The bezel is almost circular with the raised rim for an insert encircled by an outer ring of scalloped decoration. 11mm x 9.8mm x 9.2mm x 2.3mm.

Similar bezels in silver, one inlaid with carnelian, the other possibly sard, were found in the relic deposit of Hadda stupa 10, for which the accompanying coins suggest a date of 4th–5th century AD (**Vol. I, pp. 185–7, 189, Fig. 283.13, 15**).

Fig. 84.12–13. Cast copper alloy finger-rings with a thick oval bezel with a cavity for an inlay. The shank is circular in section and segmented by short incised lines to simulate beading.

A similar finger ring was found in the Seth-Abad necropolis, 6–7km as the crow flies from Begram. Three Hun coins found in the necropolis date it to the late 5th– early 6th century (Ghirshman 1946, pp. 3–4, fig. 3.c).

Fig. 84.12 – 1880.3933. IM.Metal.159. 6mm x 8mm x 18mm.

Fig. 84.13 – 1880.3840.a. IM.Metal.160. 5.5mm x 8mm x 9mm.

Fig. 84.14 – 1880.3811.n. IM.Metal.141. Copper alloy finger ring, cast in one piece, comprising a circular setting for an inlay and part of the shank, semi-circular in section, with a small knob on each shoulder and two horizontal incisions marking the shank below. 10th–11th century (?). 6.7mm x 7.4mm x 18mm x 3mm.

Fig. 84.15 – 1880.3932.b. IM 26 / SKM 1074. Complete, but squashed silver finger-ring. The shank widens towards the shoulders and has cut, pointed ends soldered to the back of a circular bezel with a raised outer rim forming a cell for an inlay. 10th–11th century (?). 9.5mm x 11.4mm; shank: 25.2mm x 5.2mm.

Rings 8: c. 3rd–11th century

Fig. 85.1 – 1880.3811.a. IM.Metal.141. Copper alloy finger-ring, cast in one piece. The shank is plano-convex in section and edged on either side by a narrow, flat band. It widens gradually towards the bezel, which has an oval depression with a raised rim for a paste or stone insert, flanked on either side by a small circular cavity, probably also for inlays. 8mm x 9.4mm x 2.2mm.

A comparable finger-ring was found at Yalangtush Tepe, Uzbekistan, in Room 2 of Naos III, together with coins of Wima Kadphises, Kanishka I and Huvishka. They suggest a 2nd-century date for the contents of the tomb (Pugachenkova and Rtveladze 1978, fig. 6.43). Another comparable specimen (without lateral depressions) was found in Tomb 190 of the Tup Khona necropolis, Tajikistan (Litvinsky and Sedov 1984, pl. II.12).

Fig. 85.2–4. IM.Metal.141. Finger-rings of copper alloy, cast in one piece, with a shank plano-convex in section widening gradually into an elliptical bezel which has a circular depression in the centre for an inset stone or paste inlay. This type of finger-ring is of Roman origin, found all over the Roman Empire from the 1st century AD onwards. Examples attributed to the 2nd–3rd century were found at Corinth (Davidson 1952, pl. 102.1812) and others attributed to the 2nd–4th century were found at Sardis (Waldbaum 1983, no. 846). In Bactria, examples from Dal'verzin Tepe (Pugachenkova and Rtveladze 1978, p. 111, fig. 79), the Yalangtush Tepe necropolis (Rtveladze 1983, figs 4, 6) and Surkh Kotal (Fussman and Guillaume 1990, p. 121, pls 5, VIII.232) are dated late 1st–early 3rd century.

Fig. 85.2 – 1880.3799.j. 10.2mm x 10.4mm x 20.5mm.

Fig. 85.3 – 1880.3799.k. 11mm x 11mm x 16.5mm.

Fig. 85.4 – 1880.3799.l. Traces of gilding. 8.7mm x 10.5mm x 16.8mm.

Fig. 85.5–10. IM.Metal.141. Copper alloy finger-rings, cast in one piece. The shank gradually widens into an elliptical bezel with a circular or oval depression for an inset stone or paste inlay of about the same size as the bezel. Corinth yielded an example attributed to the 3rd century AD (Davidson 1952, pl. 102.1811); examples from Sardis are attributed to the Late Roman period (Waldbaum 1983, no. 845); and those from tomb 4 at Hasani-Mahaleh in Iran are dated 1st–3rd century (Musche 1988, p. 226, pl. LXXX, 3.2).

In Bactria, a similar specimen was found at Surkh Kotal (Fussman and Guillaume 1990, p. 121, pls 5, VIII.233).

Fig. 85.5 – 1880.3799.o. The bezel is circular. 11mm x 12mm x 17mm.

Fig. 85.6 – 1880.3799.p. The bezel is oval. 10.6mm x 14.5mm x 20.2mm.

Fig. 85.7 – 1880.3799.q. The bezel is oval. 10mm x 14mm x 21.7mm.

Fig. 85.8 – 1880.3799.r. The bezel is oval, the shank and shoulders are triangular in section. 10.6mm x 16mm x 23.4mm.

Fig. 85.9-10. The oval depression for an inlay is exactly the same width as the bezel. A similar finger-ring was found in Room 2 of Naos III of the Yalangtush Tepe necropolis, Uzbekistan, dated late 1st–early 3rd century (Rtveladze 1983, fig. 10.21).

Fig. 85.9 – 1880.3799.x. 18.7mm x 15.5mm x 10.8mm.

Fig. 85.10 – 1880.3799.u. 21.5mm x 16.6mm x 9.5mm.

Fig. 85.11 – 1880.3799.t. The bezel and the depression for the inlay are lozenge-shaped, the shank and the shoulders are triangular in section. 22.2mm x 14.6mm x 10.5mm.

Comparable finger-rings were found in Room 2 of Naos III of the Yalangtush Tepe necropolis, Uzbekistan, dated late 1st–early 3rd century (Rtveladze 1983, fig. 10.17) and in western Ferghana, Tajikistan (Litvinsky 1986, p. 88, no. 31).

Fig. 85.12 – 1880.3799.i. Cast copper alloy finger-ring, with a narrow, flat shank that abruptly expands into an elliptical bezel with a wide circular depression filled with the remains of a paste (?) inlay. 17mm x 12mm.

An iron example with bronze inlay was found in Building II of the Tepai Shakh necropolis, dated by coins to the 2nd–3rd century AD (Litvinsky and Sedov 1983, p. 156, no. 144, 21, pl. XXX.18). Others attributed to the 3rd–8th century and originating from Iran are in the Nasser Khalili collection (Raby 1993, no. 56).

Fig. 85.13 – 1880.3706.r. IM.Metal.145. Cast copper alloy finger-ring. The shank widens at the shoulders into an oval bezel with a raised edge encircling a central depression for a paste or stone insert. 23mm x 16.5mm x 12.5mm.

Fig. 85.14–16. IM.Metal.141. Copper alloy finger-rings, cast in one piece, with a shank (plano-convex in section), slightly wider shoulders and a rectangular bezel with rounded corners and a raised outer edge forming a shallow cell for an insert.

Fig. 85.14 – 1880.3790.x. 16mm x 9mm.

Fig. 85.15 – 1880.3790.y. 15mm x 9mm.

Fig. 85.16 – 1880.3706.p. IM.Metal.145. The rectangular bezel is filled with a degraded paste inlay. 18mm x 10.3mm x 7.2mm.

Fig. 85.17 – 1880.3812.r. Copper alloy finger-ring, cast in one piece. The shank is a little wider at the shoulders which are flat, notched at the top and attached to a slightly raised oval bezel. This contains a round depression for an inset stone. 8mm x 9mm x 17mm.

Fig. 85.18 – 1880.3812.x. Cast copper alloy finger-ring. The flat, wide shoulders are decorated with five parallel incised lines which adjoin the rim of a hemispherical depression for a stone insert. It has a hole at the bottom. 8mm x 8mm x 11mm.

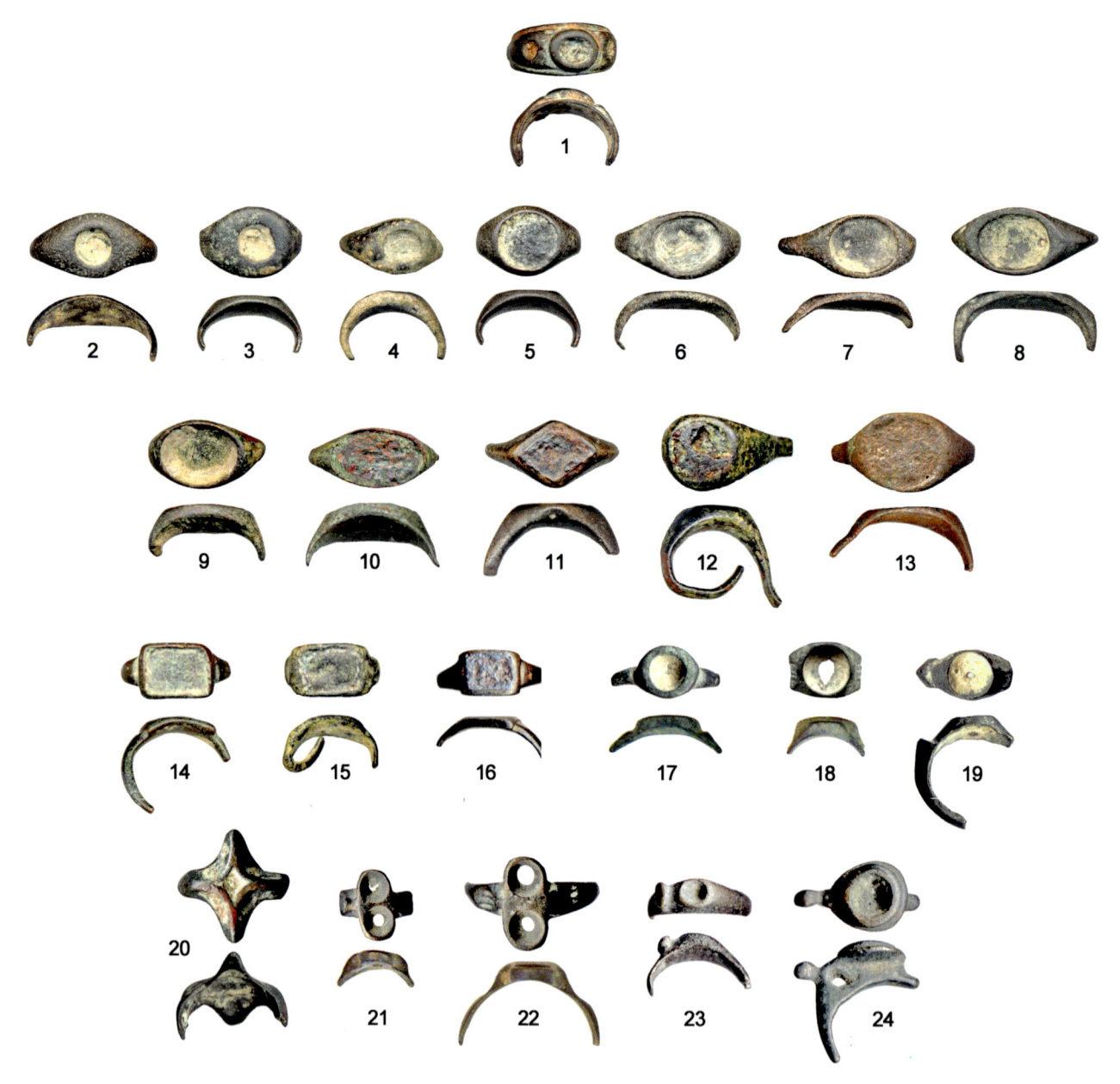

Figure 85 Finger-rings 8: *c.* 3rd–11th century

Fig. 85.19 – 1880.3812.w. Copper alloy finger-ring, cast in one piece. The shank is triangular in section and the shoulders are cut flat and deeply notched. The bezel takes the form of a truncated cone with a large hemispherical depression for an inlay. 7mm x 8mm x 17mm.

A fragment of finger-ring with a comparable bezel, dated 9th–10th century was found in Khwarazm (Research Center for Silk Roadology 1996, p. 31). The accentuated knob-like projection on the shank occurs on 10th–12th-century finger-rings found at Corinth (Davidson 1952, nos 1888, 1890).

Fig. 85.20 – 1880.3812.z. Fragment of a cast copper alloy finger-ring. The shoulders widen into a bezel in the form of an elongated lozenge, perpendicular to the shank, with concave sides and rising in ridges to form a small, similarly lozenge-shaped depression, perhaps originally containing an inlay. 17mm x 15.5mm x 18mm.

Fig. 85.21–2. Two fragments of cast copper alloy finger-rings. The oblong bezel is set at right angles to the shank, and contains two hemispherical depressions (with circular holes in the base) for stone inserts.

Fig. 85.21 – 1880.3812.y. 11mm x 6mm x 11mm.

Fig. 85.22 – 1880.3934. 21mm x 8mm x 14mm. The flat shoulders are engraved with three parallel lines.

Fig. 85.23–4. In these two finger-rings one of the shoulders has a projecting rounded knob. This type of ring was fashionable during the Sasanian period. It is found on a 5th–6th-century signet-ring formerly in the Nelidow collection (*Hofkunst van de Sassanieden* 1993, p. 282, no. 137); and on finger-rings from Iran attributed to the 7th–9th century (Raby 1993, p. 190, nos 42–3). Others in the Zucker collection are assigned to the late Sasanian period (Content 1987, p. 31, no. 1). There are also 6th–8th century examples from Pendjikent, Tajikistan (Belenitsky *et al.* 1973, p. 85, fig. 52) and from Kuva in the Ferghana valley, Uzbekistan (Bulatova 1972, p. 129, fig. 3).

Fig. 85.23 – 1880.3812.t. Cast copper alloy finger-ring. The almost flat shank widens towards an oval depression, designed for a stone inset. A small oval knob with rounded edges rises from one shoulder. 16mm x 4.5mm x 3.5mm.

Fig. 85.24 – 1880.3812.v. Cast copper alloy finger-ring.

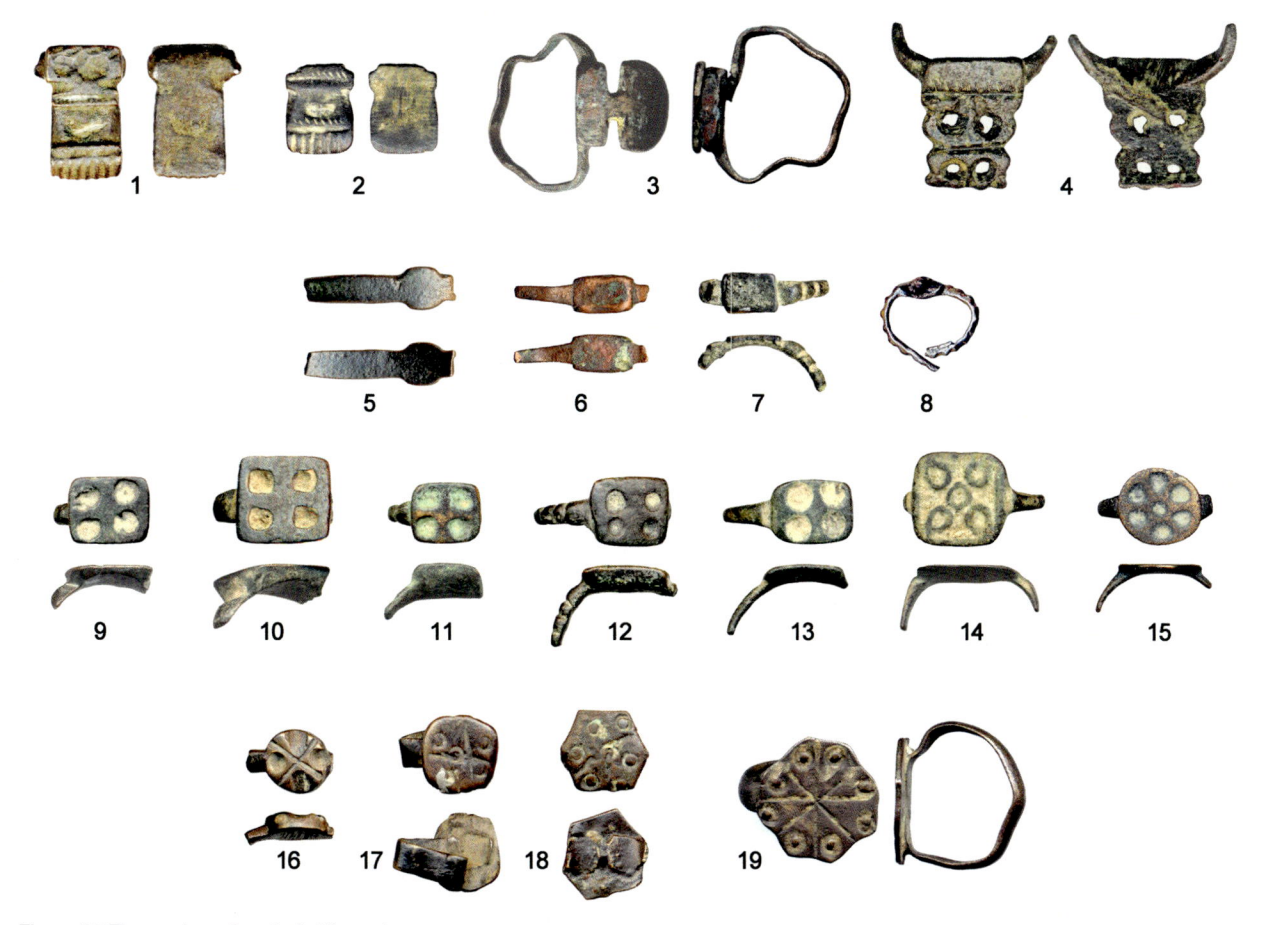

Figure 86 Finger-rings 9: *c.* 2nd–6th century

The oblong bezel rises on a broad stem from the shank and has a hemispherical depression, surrounded by a raised rim, for an inset stone. A section of the shank rises from one shoulder to meet the edge of the bezel, leaving a circular hole, and branches away to terminate in a small knob. 10mm x 12mm x 20mm x 6mm. The Cambridge Ridgeway collection (CMAA.1927.1192) has a similar ring.

Similar holes below the bezel occur on 12th-century finger-rings found at Corinth (Davidson 1952, nos 1981–2).

Rings 9: *c.* 2nd–6th century

Fig. 86.1–4. Finger-rings consisting of a hoop with a projection attached to one side. This form corresponds to that of Roman key-rings found throughout the Empire from the 1st century AD onwards. (http://romanlocks.com/Keys). A ring of this type, with a projecting symbol of Ahuramazda, found at Seleucia, is dated *c.* AD 40–115/16 (Musche 1988, p. 231, pl. LXXXII, type 9). An intact example recovered from the burial ground of Yalangtush Tepe (Naos 2, Room 1), Uzbekistan, possibly belongs to the late 2nd century, as the tomb also contained a coin of the Kushan king Huvishka (*c.* AD 151–91; Rtveladze 1983, pp. 126–7, 129, fig. 4; Göbl 1984, type 176–9). Another, with a flat, rectangular projection pierced with a slit and decorated with incised lines, from Sardis, is tentatively dated 4th–7th century (Waldbaum 1983, pl. 49.870).

Fig. 86.1 – 1880.3687.t. IM.Metal.25 / IM 8 / SKM 1069. Cast copper alloy bezel fragment, with traces of the shank merging with the top edge of a rectangular, moulded projection. The opposite end is curved and ornamented with a band of parallel vertical ridges resembling a comb. In the centre of the front is a crescent-shaped incision banded on either side by a horizontal row of raised dots. 17.3mm x 10mm x 4.7mm.

It is similar to the bezel from the intact ring found at Yalangtush Tepe and is therefore probably of the same date, *c.* late 2nd century AD.

Fig. 86.2 – 1880.3835. IM.Metal.160. Cast copper alloy, thin, rectangular fragment, possibly part of a finger-ring bezel, with traces of gilding and divided into three horizontal sections with a crescent-shaped depression in the centre, flanked above and below by an incised line and a row of short diagonal hatchings. The top is broken; the bottom edge has a band of vertical parallel lines. The back is flat and undecorated. 12mm x 9.3mm.

Fig. 86.3 – 1880.3836. IM.Metal.160. Complete copper alloy finger-ring. The shank is rectangular in section and open at the top where it is soldered to the rectangular base of a flat, shield-shaped projecting bezel. This is semi-circular along the bottom, with a deep rectangular notch on either side. The surface of the bezel is plain. The shank has been squashed and the bezel is slightly bent. 16.5mm x 11.6mm; shank: 20.4mm x 2.7mm.

Fig. 86.4 – 1880.3687.s. IM.Metal.25 / IM 68, 17 / SKM 1069. Cast copper alloy finger-ring. The remains of a shank (semi-circular in section) is attached to the top of a projecting rectangular bezel. It is divided by incised lines into three bands, the top one plain; the remaining two with scalloped sides and each pierced with two holes. 18mm x 14mm (plaque).

The ornament is stylistically close to a horse harness found at Qanat Tepe, Nishapur, and is probably of similar date, c. 9th–10th century (Allan 1982, no. 137).

Fig. 86.5–8. IM.Metal.145. Fragmentary finger-rings with a narrow shank and a thin bezel.

Fig. 86.5 – 1880.3706.d. A smooth fragment of a plain, small, hexagonal bezel and a flat shank. 20.2mm x 4mm–5.8mm.

Fig. 86.6 –1880.3706.m. A flat, worn, rectangular bezel and a flat shank. 18.2mm; bezel: 9mm x 5mm.

Fig. 86.7 – 1880.3706.q. A flat, undecorated rectangular bezel with a degraded paste inlay (?) and a notched shank. 5.5mm x 7.6mm x 17.7mm.

Fig. 86.8 – 1880.3977.e. IM 33 / SKM 1103. Small, squashed silver finger-ring (?) with a flattened oval bezel. The notched shank is now broken, but the ends originally overlapped and were soldered together. 13mm; bezel: 6mm x 3mm.

Fig. 86.9–13. IM.Metal.141. Copper alloy finger-ring, cast in one piece, with a narrow shank plano-convex in section and a square or rectangular bezel bearing four small circular depressions, which might have been intended for stone or paste inlays. Probably Romano-Byzantine. 4th–6th century.

Fig. 86.9 – 1880.3811.o. 9mm x 11.2mm x 14mm x 3mm.

Fig. 86.10 – 1880.3811.r. The bezel is thick, and the shank almost flat. 11.5mm x 12.7mm; shank: 17.2mm x 4.5mm.

Fig. 86.11–12. The shank is notched along its outer edge, creating the effect of beading.

Fig. 86.11 – 1880.3811.t. 8mm x 9.6mm; shank: 14mm x 2.4mm.

Fig. 86.12 – 1880.3811.u. 11.8mm x 9.3mm; shank: 18.8mm x 3mm.

Fig. 86.13 – 1880.3811.v. 8.6mm x 11.6mm x 2mm x 18mm.

Fig. 86.14 – 1880.3811.w. Copper alloy square bezel with rounded corners and part of the shank. The face of the bezel has been moulded, or cut away, to leave five raised circles and an outer raised border. 14.2mm x 12.6mm x 1mm x 19.2mm.

Fig. 86.15 – IOLC.7571. K.378. Part of a copper alloy shank and a flat circular bezel, with engraved circles forming a six-petalled flower. 17mm x 10mm.

Fig. 86.16–18. Fragments of cast copper alloy finger-rings. The face of the bezel is divided by an incised saltire.

Fig. 86.16 – 1880.3811.x. Circular bezel and part of the shank flat on the inside, semi-circular on the outside. Each quarter delimited by the cross has a deep indentation extending to edge of the bezel. 8.5mm x 2.5mm x 12mm.

A comparable finger-ring (with an additional punched depression in the centre), dated 11th–12th century, was found at Corinth (Davidson 1952, no. 1973).

Fig. 86.17 – 1880.3811.y. Roughly hexagonal bezel soldered to a flat shank. The face has a roughly incised cross and a punched dot slightly off-centre, encircled by another four dots. There are traces of silver plating. 10.5mm x 10.5mm x 1.5mm x 14.5mm.

The circles recall that the dot in circle motif – said to provide protection from the 'evil eye' – is widespread on 4th–6th-century Roman finger-rings (Davidson 1952, nos 1850–1, 1878, 1894) and still found on 10th–12th-century rings (Davidson 1952, nos 1887, 1886, 1978).

Fig. 86.18 – 1880.3811.z. Hexagonal bezel and a flat shank, of which only the soldered section on the back of the bezel survives. The face of the bezel is engraved with seven circles, one in the centre and six others roughly placed in each angle of the hexagon. 12.7mm x 10.7mm x 1.5mm x 11.3mm.

Fig. 86.19 – 1880.3879. IM.Ring.5. Complete cast copper alloy finger-ring. The shank is broad, thin, plano-convex in section, with its ends flattened and soldered onto a roughly octagonal bezel with a scalloped outer edge. The surface is divided into eight sections by incised lines radiating from the centre, and each containing a dot in circle motif. 18th–19th century. Kabul bazaar. 16mm x 16.8mm x 1mm; shank: 20mm x 4mm.

Finger-rings with a scalloped outer edge are found dating from the Byzantine period and also from the 12th century (Davidson 1952, nos 1952, 1967).

Rings 10: c. 3rd–13th century

Fig. 87.1–3. IM.Metal.141. Cast copper alloy finger-rings with a thick domed bezel. This type of ring occurs at Qasr-i Abu Nasr (Musche 1988, pl. CVII).

Fig. 87.1 – 1880.3812.n. A thick domed lozenge-shaped bezel, with traces of an engraved design. 8.3mm x 11mm x 4mm x 16.7mm.

Fig. 87.2 – 1880.3812.o. A thick domed oval bezel with traces of radial engraved lines around the edge. 17.5mm x 9mm x 13mm.

Fig. 87.3 – 1880.3812.p. A roughly circular, domed bezel, engraved with dots and lines in a radiating geometrical pattern. 6.4mm x 2.5mm x 2.7mm x 12.8mm.

Fig. 87.4 – 1880-3813.a. Cast copper alloy finger-ring. The square brass-washed bezel forms an inverted pyramid above the shank and depicts a stag standing to the left. 7.5mm x 8.5mm x 9mm x 16mm.

A similar ring, said to come from the Middle East, in the Nasser Khalili collection, is attributed to the 7th–9th century (Raby 1993, no. 38).

Fig. 87.5 – 1880-3813.b. Cast copper alloy finger-ring. The circular bezel is linked to the shank by a short, concave cylindrical column. The shank is square in section and slightly ribbed, broadening at the shoulders to form an oblong below the bezel, which has a worn motif surrounded by dots. 9mm x 7mm x 12mm.

A ring with a similar profile, but in which the cylinder flares out to form a square, was found in Uzbekistan and dated 9th–10th century (*Culture and Art of Ancient Uzbekistan* 1991, fig. 679). In another example, in the Zucker collection, the cylinder is higher and crowned with a garnet. It is attributed to the Seljuq period, c. 11th–12th century (Content 1987, no. 46).

Fig. 87.6 – 1880.3872. IM.Ring.1. Complete silver finger-ring with an open shank, semi-circular in cross-section, the ends soldered to a flat, hexagonal oblong bezel. This is decorated with a diagonal band containing an embossed S-shaped vegetal scroll with a four-petalled flower in the centre. 18th–19th century. Kabul bazaar. Bezel: 10.2mm x 14.2mm; shank: 22mm x 4.2mm.

The scroll motif frequently appears on 12th–13th century finger-rings, such as examples from Iran in the Harari collection (Hasson 1987, nos 60–1).

Fig. 87.7 – 1880.3874. IM.Ring.3. Complete finger-ring carved in one piece from mottled carnelian (?), with white impurities over much of the shank and part of the bezel. The shank is triangular in cross-section and notched on either side of a small protuberance at the base and three times on each shoulder. The bezel is a flat, pointed oval which slopes inwards to join the shoulders. Timurid or Safavid, *c.* 14th–18th century. Kabul bazaar. Bezel: 8mm x 15mm; shank: 14mm x 21mm.

The ring shows affinities to other carnelian examples, also with a pointed oval bezel, which differ only in that the shank has a spur at its base and the shoulders are without notches. One found at Corinth is wrongly assigned to the Roman period (Davidson 1952, pl. 107.1989). Another in the Zucker collection (Content 1987, p. 112, fig. 67) is attributed to the Timurid period (late 14th–15th century). Other specimens in the Zucker collection, although with a circular bezel, have a similar shank of triangular cross-section with a spur at the base and three notches on the shoulders (Content 1987, nos 76, 78). They are attributed to the Safavid period (16th–18th century).

Fig. 87.8–10. IM.Metal.160. Fragments of cast copper alloy finger-rings (?) triangular in cross-section, tapering towards the outer edge and decorated on the two faces with a repeated dot in circle motif.

A similar, but complete ring was found at Qanat Tepe, Nishapur, and dated *c.* 9th–13th century (Allan 1982, pp. 166, 175, no. 171- MMA 40.170.203). Part of a comparable lapis lazuli ring, with one side flat, the other slightly convex and ornamented with four small, gold inset circles, was found at Yoktan, Khotan (Stein 1921, p. 116, pl. IV, Yo. 00101. A).

Fig. 87.8 – 1880.3853.a. 19.5mm x 3mm x 2mm.
Fig. 87.9 – 1880.3853.b. 20mm x 3mm x 2mm.
Fig. 87.10 – 1880.3853.c. 21mm x 4mm x 1mm.

Rings 11: with pseudo-Arabic, c. 8th–11th century

Fig. 88.1–5. Cast copper alloy finger-rings with a shank, rectangular in section, broadening into thin, curved shoulders which merge smoothly into a roughly rectangular bezel. A finger-ring of this type, dated 8th–14th century, was found at Ghubayra, Iran. (Bivar 2000, p. 108, pl. 70a, no. B6/74-457).

Fig. 88.1–2. IM.Metal.145. The bezel is narrow and undecorated.

Fig. 88.1 – 1880.3706.x. 13mm x 4mm.
Fig. 88.2 – 1880.3706.f. 14mm x 6.7mm.
Fig. 88.3 – 1880.3876. IM.Ring.6. Complete silver finger-ring with an undecorated bezel. 20mm x 10mm x 9mm.
Fig. 88.4 – 1880.3813.d. IM.Metal.141. The surface of the square bezel is worn; the shoulders have an incised circular motif with radiating lines. 11mm x 18mm.
Fig. 88.5 – 1880.3813.i. IM.Metal.141. The bezel has an engraved pseudo-Kufic inscription comprising three

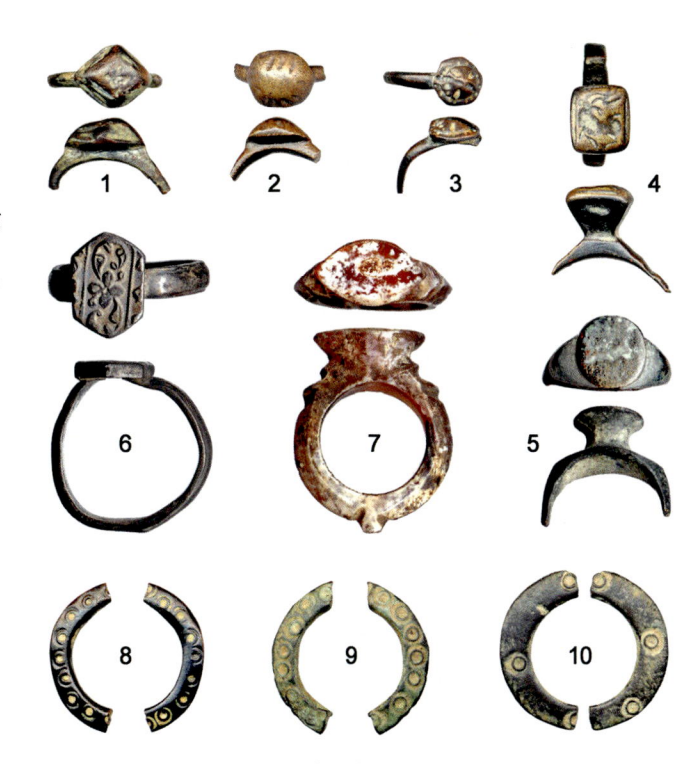

Figure 87 Finger-rings 10: c. 3rd–13th century

horizontal lines, each surmounted by regularly spaced, short vertical incisions. On the shoulders are four curved lines in two pairs resembling brackets: (). 8.5mm x 9mm x 19mm.

Fig. 88.6–16. Copper alloy finger-rings, cast in one piece, with a shank either rectangular or plano-convex in section, sloping shoulders and a raised, flat, mostly rather thick, rectangular bezel. This is an Islamic type, with examples, attributed to the 9th–10th century, being found in Iraq (Raby 1993, pp. 24, 189, no. 41) while others, attributed to the 10th–11th century, were found at Kiev (Darkevich 1976, pl. 39, no. 21).

Fig. 88.6–7. The junction of the undecorated bezel with the shoulders is at a sharp angle.

Fig. 88.6 – 1880.3817.f. IM.Metal.145. 12mm x 9mm x 7mm.

Fig. 88.7 – 1880.3813.m. IM.Metal.141. Square bezel. 7.5mm x 13.5mm.

Fig. 88.8 – 1880.3981.p. Box 4.b. Cast, silver alloy rectangular bezel and part of the shoulder. The bezel is heavily scratched and retains traces of solder, suggesting the ring originally had a mount/setting for a gem. Traces of incised motifs survive on the shoulder. 16mm x 12mm x 10mm.

Fig. 88.9 – 1880.3817.d. IM.Metal.145. Worn square brass bezel with stray incisions. 10mm x 13mm.

Fig. 88.10 – 1880.3813.l. IM.Metal.141. The bezel is undecorated. 15mm x 12mm x 8.5mm.

Fig. 88.11 – 1880.3813.o. IM.Metal.141. The bezel has incised traces of three vertical lines; with a bisected lozenge on the shoulders. 14mm x 8mm x 6mm.

Fig. 88.12 – 1880.3813.n. IM.Metal.141. The rectangular bezel is engraved with a pseudo-Arabic (?) inscription. The shoulder has concentric comma-shaped incisions. 12mm x 9mm x 8mm.

Fig. 88.13 – IOLC 7582. K.390. Bezel engraved with two identical, superimposed lines of a pseudo-Kufic

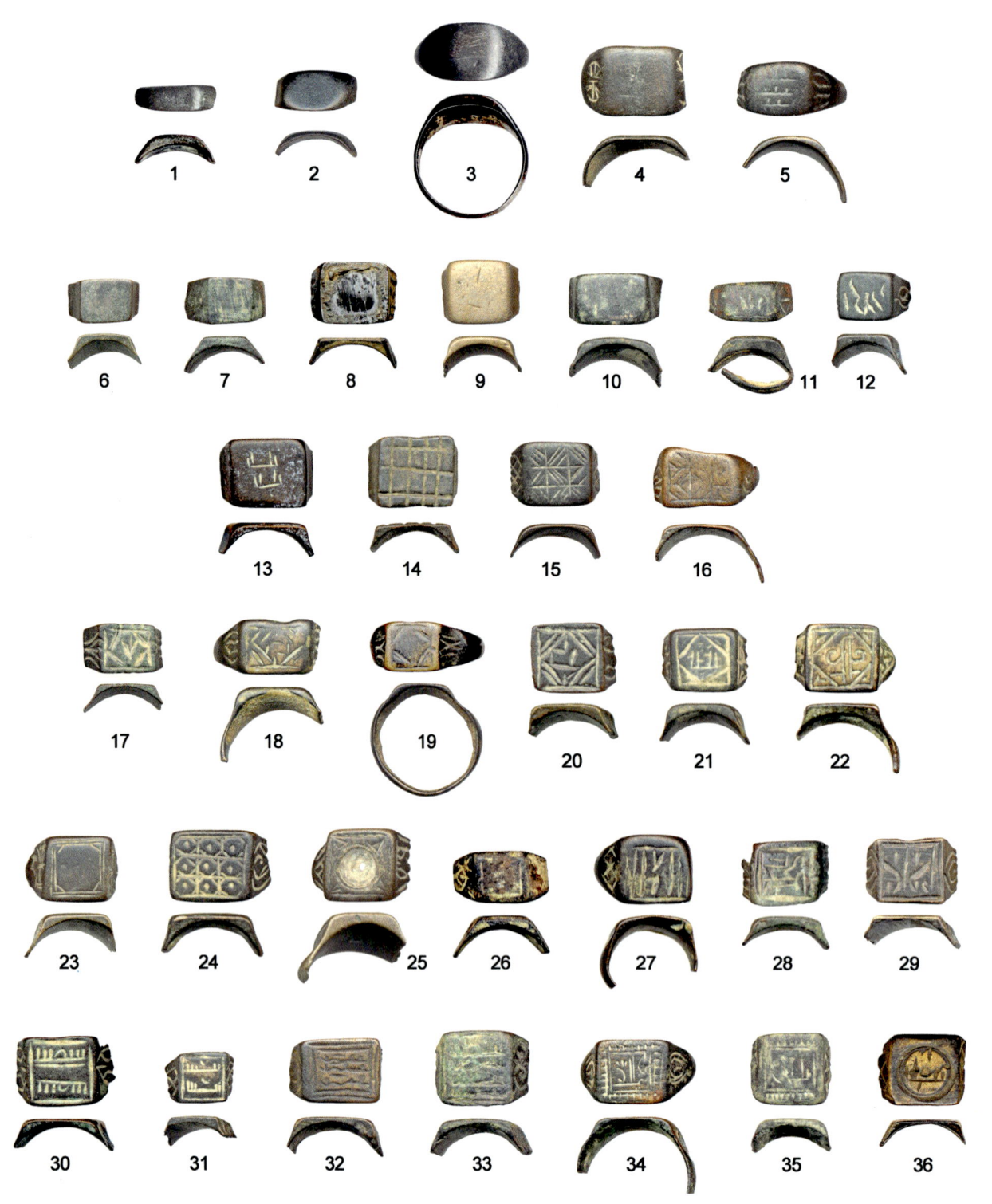

Figure 88 Finger-rings 11: with pseudo-Arabic inscriptions *c.* 8th–11th century

inscription, comprising a horizontal line surmounted by vertical short incisions. 16mm x 11mm.

Fig. 88.14 – 1880.3814.c. IM.Metal.141. Rectangular bezel engraved with a rough grid of three horizontal lines bisected by four vertical lines. 15mm x 12.5mm x 11.5mm.

Fig. 88.15–16. Rectangular bezels with an incised grid of nine squares each bisected with diagonal lines zigzagging to form lozenges.

Fig. 88.15 – 1880.3813.h. IM.Metal.141. The diagonals comprise three lines. The shoulders have an incised grid of lozenges. 14mm x 10mm x 8mm.

Fig. 88.16 – 1880.3817.b. IM.Metal.145. The diagonals comprise two lines. The shoulder motif is similar to **Fig. 88.25**. 11mm x 10mm x 5.5mm.

Fig. 88.17–35. IM.Metal.141. The bezel has a motif or inscription framed by an incised square or rectangle; additional incised decoration on the shoulders.

Fig. 88.17 – 1880.3813.r. An incised triple leaf frond within a lozenge, bordered by a rectangle. A simplified honeysuckle motif is incised on the shoulder. 13mm x 9mm x 8mm.

Fig. 88.18 – 1880.3813.w. Traces of a pseudo-Arabic inscription within a roughly incised lozenge framed by a

250 | *Charles Masson: Collections from Begram and Kabul Bazaar, Afghanistan, 1833–1838*

rectangle. The shoulders have two facing pairs of concentric curved lines. 18mm x 11mm x 10.5mm.

Fig. 88.19 – 1880.3813.q. Complete finger-ring. The bezel is engraved with a lozenge within a square; the shoulders with an X between two curved lines. 20mm x 8mm x 9mm.

Fig. 88.20 – 1880. 3813.x. A pseudo-Arabic inscription framed by a double lozenge within a square. The shoulders have two pairs of facing curved incisions resembling brackets. 11mm x 12mm x 14mm.

Fig. 88.21 – 1880.3813.y. *Allah* (?) inscribed in Arabic framed by a lozenge within a square. The one shoulder has an incised motif resembling ram's horns; the other the Persian letter *jā* (probably part of a name). 10mm x 10.5mm x 14mm.

Fig. 88.22 – 1880. 3813.z. A pseudo-Arabic inscription, set within a lozenge and outer square with a dot or small incised mark within each angle. The shoulders have a stylised leaf motif within a triangle. 11mm x 12mm x 18mm.

Fig. 88.23 – 1880.3814.a. The outer edge of the bezel has an incised double border, with short diagonal lines cutting across the four corners to form an octagon. The shoulders have four roughly incised horizontal lines banded by three regularly spaced, vertical double lines, with a few curved incisions below. 10.5mm x 11mm x 15mm.

Fig. 88.24 – 1880.3814.d. The face is divided into an incised grid of nine squares, each containing a hexagon with a dot in the centre. The shoulders are engraved with two facing pairs of concentric curved lines. 12mm x13mm x 17mm.

Fig. 88.25 – 1880.3814.b. The outer edge of the bezel is defined by an incised square, with small triangles inside each corner abutting an engraved circle. This surrounds a perforated hemispherical depression designed for an inset stone, now missing. The shoulders have an incised lozenge motif. 18mm. 12mm x 11.5mm x 18mm.

Fig. 88.26 – IOLC.7581. K.389. The remains only of a worn incised square border. The shoulders have an incised circle with radiating lines. 16mm x 8mm.

Fig. 88.27 – 1880.3814.g. Engraved Arabic numerals, 7 (٧) and 6 (٦) flanked by a vertical line on either side; set within a square border. The shoulders have a pair of incised lozenges. 11mm x 12mm x 16mm.

Fig. 88.28 – 1880.3814.e. A pseudo-Arabic inscription within a square. The shoulders have four evenly spaced incised lines within a triangle. 10mm x 11.5mm x 14.5mm.

Fig. 88.29 – 1880.3814.f. A rectangular incised border containing a central vertical line flanked on either side by an addorsed S-shape, possibly a pseudo-Arabic inscription (?). The shoulders are engraved with two concentric circles with a dot in the centre. 10.5mm x 11mm x 15mm.

Fig. 88.30 – IOLC.7584. K.392. The bezel is engraved with a mirrored pair of lines of a pseudo-Arabic inscription and the shoulders with the mirrored motif resembling a '6'. 16mm x 11mm.

Fig. 88.31 – 1880.3814.i. The square incised border contains a two-line pseudo-Kufic inscription comprising the same word repeated twice. The shoulders have part of a lozenge divided into four quarters. 8mm x 11.5mm.

Fig. 88.32 – 1880.3814.j. The same line of a pseudo-Arabic inscription is repeated three times, within a border of double lines. The shoulders have a set of concentric comma-shaped incisions with a dot at the centre. 10.5mm x 13mm x 15.5mm.

Fig. 88.33 – 1880.3814.k. The same line of a pseudo-Arabic inscription repeated four times, within an incised border. The shoulders have a double scroll motif. 12mm x 16mm.

Fig. 88.34 – 1880.3814.l. A pseudo-Arabic inscription within an incised double square, the outer one ornamented with regularly spaced, short, perpendicular lines. The shoulders have a pair of concentric curved lines on either side of a vertical line. 10mm x 11mm x 20mm.

Fig. 88.35 – 1880.3814.m. A pseudo-Arabic inscription within an incised frame, which is bordered top and bottom by a row of small triangles. The shoulders each have traces of a lozenge (?) motif. 11mm x 13mm.

Fig. 88.36 – 1880.3902.e. IM 21 / SKM 1100. The square bezel is engraved with a pseudo-Arabic inscription within a deep double circle with a drill hole in its centre. The shoulder has a grid of incised squares. 12mm x 9mm

Rings 12: Islamic, c. 10th–12th century.

Fig. 89.1–5. Cast copper alloy finger-rings with broad, faceted shoulders and a hexagonal bezel. Islamic, 12th century.

Fig. 89.1 – 1880.3814.x. IM.Metal.141. A brass-washed, roughly hexagonal bezel, with a large hemispherical depression for a stone insert in the centre, framed by incised lines. The shoulders also have traces of incised decoration. 10mm x 10mm x 14mm.

Fig. 89.2 – IOLC.7586. K.394. A plain, flat, elongated hexagonal bezel, with faceted shoulders. 15mm x 9mm.

Fig. 89.3 – 1880.3814.s. IM.Metal.141. The bezel is engraved with a lozenge divided by diagonals into four squares. 10mm x 11mm x 13mm.

Fig. 89.4 – 1880.3902.f. IM 21 / SKM 1100. The thick outer edge of the bezel is ornamented with segments of two parallel lines separated at each angle of the hexagon by a vertical line. The face of the bezel has an incised pseudo-Arabic inscription within a circle. 14mm x 14mm x 5mm.

Fig. 89.5 – 1880.3814.z. IM.Metal.141. Complete finger-ring. The shank (semi-circular in cross-section) flattens and widens at the shoulders which curve slightly upwards to a hexagonal bezel. This is incised with a pseudo-Arabic inscription of one word repeated (with small variation) twice. 9mm x 9mm x 17mm x 1mm.

Fig. 89.6–12. IM.Metal.141. Fragments of cast copper alloy finger-rings. The shank (semi-circular in cross-section) flattens and widens at the shoulders which merge into a thickened, roughly circular bezel, with a corrugated outer rim. A finger-ring of this type from Corinth is dated to the 12th century (Davidson 1952, p. 240, pl. 105.1904).

Fig. 89.6 – 1880.3815.k. The bezel comprises only a large circular pierced depression for an inset stone. The depression is encircled by a border of etched triangles resembling rays. One shoulder has two small incised triangles butted against a line. 11mm x 15mm.

Fig. 89.7 – 1880.3815.p. The shoulders widen into a

Figure 89 Islamic finger-rings 12: *c.* 10th–12th century

thin, roughly circular, worn bezel, which has indented notches around its edge. 16mm x 12mm.

Fig. 89.8 – 1880.3815.c. A slightly thickened, roughly circular bezel, scalloped round the edges and incised with a horizontal row of three lozenges between parallel lines. 11.5mm x 11.5mm x 14mm.

Fig. 89.9 – 1880.3815.a. Incised with a pseudo-Arabic inscription of one word, appearing (with small variation) twice (similar inscription to **Fig. 89.5**). 11.5mm x 11.5mm x 14mm.

Fig. 89.10–11. A thickened, roughly square, notched bezel, incised with a stylised bird to right, within a circle.

Fig. 89.10 – 1880.3815.j. The shoulders have an incised acanthus leaf motif. 21mm x 12mm x 12mm.

Fig. 89.11 – 1880.3815.i. The shoulders have traces of incised decoration. 16mm x 12mm x 11mm.

Fig. 89.12 – 1880.3815.q. A thin bezel incised with two lines of pseudo-Kufic inscription within a circle decorated with alternating rays and notches around the edge. The fragmentary shoulders have two incised lozenges inserted one within the other. 12mm x 13mm x 16mm.

Fig. 89.13–17. The bezels have an accurately engraved circle, with a drill hole at the bottom of a small round cavity in the centre marking the compass point. Regularly spaced notches around the circle give the bezel a scalloped edge.

Fig. 89.13 – 1880.3815.l. An incised line of pseudo-Arabic within the circle. The shoulder has incised lines and crosses. 11mm x 12mm x 15mm.

Fig. 89.14–15. The bezels have an incised pseudo-Arabic inscription within a double circle, with alternating rays and scalloped notches around its edge. The shoulders have an incised double triangle.

Fig. 89.14 – 1880.3815.m. 13mm x 12mm x 19mm.
Fig. 89.15 – 1880.3815.n. 12mm x 16mm.
Fig. 89.16 – 1880.3817.o. IM.Metal.145. The scalloped notches around the edge of the bezel are wide and deep, emphasising the impression of a rayed circle around the worn pseudo-Arabic inscription in the centre. The shoulder has traces of incised lines. 12mm x 12mm x 16mm.

Fig. 89.17 – 1880.3815.r. The roughly oblong bezel is edged with deeply indented notches. Within the circle is a roughly incised lozenge with concave sides. The small round cavity encircling the drill hole in the centre may have contained an inlay. The surviving shoulder is undecorated. 10mm x 12mm x 18mm.

Fig. 89.18–23. The bezel is incised with a rough circle containing a stylised bird with flapping wings. An image of a bird occurs on a silver signet-ring attributed to the 12th century in the Harari collection (Hasson 1987, p. 50, no. 58) and on another attributed to the Seljuq period (11th–12th century) in the Zucker collection (Content 1987, p. 79, no. 40).

Fig. 89.18 – 1880.3815.d. 11mm x 11mm x 17mm.
Fig. 89.19 – 1880.3815.e. 12mm x 12mm x 21mm.
Fig. 89.20 – 1880.3815.f. 10.5mm x 11mm x 15mm.
Fig. 89.21 – 1880.3815.g. 10.5mm x 11mm x 14mm.
Fig. 89.22 – IOLC.7588. K.396. The bird is reduced to an abstract design of incised oval and overlapping S-shapes. 15mm x 12mm.

Fig. 89.23 – 1880.3815.h. The bird is reduced to a series of lines within a circle with a flat notched rim. 11mm x 12mm x 14mm.

Rings 13: Islamic, *c.* 12th century.
Fig. 90.1–4. IM.Metal.141. Cast copper alloy finger-rings with a shank, plano-convex in section, broadening into flat shoulders and a slightly raised circular bezel. Islamic, *c.* 12th century.

Fig. 90.1 – 1880.3814.w. The worn bezel has an incised horizontal scroll motif between two pairs of parallel lines. 9mm x 10mm x 17mm.

Fig. 90.2 – 1880.3814.v. An incised horizontal band with two addorsed curved lines forming a scroll between two pairs of parallel lines. The shoulders have two incised concentric semi-circles with a marked compass point. 12mm x 17mm.

Fig. 90.3 – 1880.3817.n. IM.Metal.145. The bezel has a pseudo-Arabic inscription. The shoulders have traces of incised decoration. 11.5mm x 17mm.

Fig. 90.4 – 1880.3814.y. The flat bezel has a pseudo-Arabic inscription. The shoulders have an incised double lozenge motif. 12mm x 18mm.

Fig. 90.5–8. IM.Metal.141. Cast copper alloy finger-rings with a shank (plano-convex in section) broadening into a circular bezel incised with one or two concentric circles and with a small, round cavity, possibly for an inlay, in its centre.

Fig. 90.5 – 1880.3815.w. The thick bezel rises above the shank. It is incised with two wide concentric rings which may have been inlaid and has a central small depression for a paste or stone insert. 11mm x 17mm.

Fig. 90.6 – 1880.3815.v. A dot in circle in the centre, within an outer concentric circle lightly incised around the edge of the bezel. The central dot is pierced by a tiny hole, possibly for attaching an insert. 11mm x 17mm.

Fig. 90.7 – 1880.3815.u. The bezel is incised with a dot in circle motif. On the shoulders are three regularly spaced small holes each within an incised circle. 13mm x 21mm.

Fig. 90.8 – 1880.3815.x. The bezel is incised with a circle around a central cavity which is pierced by a tiny hole. A small prong protrudes at each of the four quarters of the bezel. The shoulders are decorated with a downward fan of three lines. 16mm x 15mm x 18mm.

Rings 14: with pseudo-Arabic, c. 8th–12th century

Fig. 91.1–4. IM.Metal.141. Cast copper alloy Islamic finger-rings. The shoulders are pinched at their juncture with the circular bezel. Two small prongs protrude from the circumference of the bezel at the centre points between the shoulders. 12th century.

Fig. 91.1 – 1880.3815.y. Worn, with traces of three incised parallel lines, probably of a pseudo-Arabic inscription. 13mm x 12mm x 15mm.

Fig. 91.2 – 1880.3815.z. Worn, with a mirror-image pseudo-Arabic and leaf-like incised marks transposed on either side of a horizontal line, within two concentric circles. 15mm x 13mm x 18mm.

Fig. 91.3 – 1880.3817.p. IM.Metal.145. An incised pseudo-Arabic inscription within two concentric circles; very worn at one side. 14mm x 13mm x 15mm.

Fig. 91.4 – 1880.3877. IM.Metal.160. A flattened circular bezel fragment with an incised band of two lozenges each set within a square. 14mm x 11mm x 15mm. For another example of the same lozenge design, see **Fig. 89.8**.

Fig. 91.5–8. Cast copper alloy Islamic finger-rings, with pinched shoulders and a rectangular bezel, which has an incised pseudo-Arabic inscription within a rectangular frame. A small knob protrudes from the centre of the top and bottom edges of the bezel.

Fig. 91.5 – 1880.3816.a. IM.Metal.141. The inscription is banded by a small toothed design above and below. 11mm x 12mm x 15mm.

Figure 90 Islamic finger-rings 13: c. 12th century

Fig. 91.6 – 1880.3816.b. IM.Metal.141. The inscription is placed within a rectangular border comprising a small toothed design. 11mm x 11mm x 17mm.

Fig. 91.7 – 1880.3936. IM 42 / SKM 1122. The bezel has a wide border of short parallel lines. 15mm x 10mm x 1mm.

Fig. 91.8 – 1880.3816.g. IM.Metal.141. Worn incised lines of a pseudo-Arabic inscription within a frame. 13mm x 11mm x 17mm.

Fig. 91.9–12. IM.Metal.141. Cast copper alloy finger-rings with a narrow shank and a rectangular bezel with a pseudo-Arabic inscription of two straight lines and nine dots within an incised border. A small knob protrudes from the mid-point of the bezel sides. Islamic, 8th–12th century (?).

Fig. 91.9 – 1880.3816.c. 11mm x 11mm x 14mm.
Fig. 91.10 – 1880.3816.d. 11mm x 11mm x 16mm.
Fig. 91.11 – 1880.3816.e. 11mm x 12mm x 18mm.
Fig. 91.12 – 1880.3902.d. IM 21 / SKM 1100. 9mm x 13mm x 2mm.

Fig. 91.13 – 1880.3873. IM.Ring.2. Complete cast copper alloy finger-ring, with traces of silver inlay. The flat rectangular bezel is knobbed at the corners and at the mid-point of the sides. Around the plain rectangle in the centre is a band of damascened arabesques, with a rope-pattern along its outer edge. The shoulders broaden towards the bezel, then are pinched at the point where they are soldered to it; and are incised with floral designs. 16mm x 16mm; shank: 22mm x 4mm. Purchased in Kabul bazaar.

A comparable finger-ring found in north-western Iran is dated 12th–13th century (Raby 1993, p. 221, no. 215).

Fig. 91.14–17. Cast copper alloy finger-rings with a hexagonal bezel which has bevelled edges, knobbed at each corner. The shank, semi-circular in cross-section, broadens at the shoulders which are pinched at their junction with the bezel.

Finger-rings of this hexagonal form in the Zucker collection are attributed to the 11th–12th century-Seljuq period (Content 1987, p. 81, nos 42–3). Further specimens are in the Nasser Khalili collection. One from Anatolia or Syria, with a scroll border and a pseudo-Arabic inscription, is attributed to the 12th century (Raby 1993, p. 221, no. 217); two other examples from Anatolia or the Caucasus, also with a scroll border but without an inscription, are dated

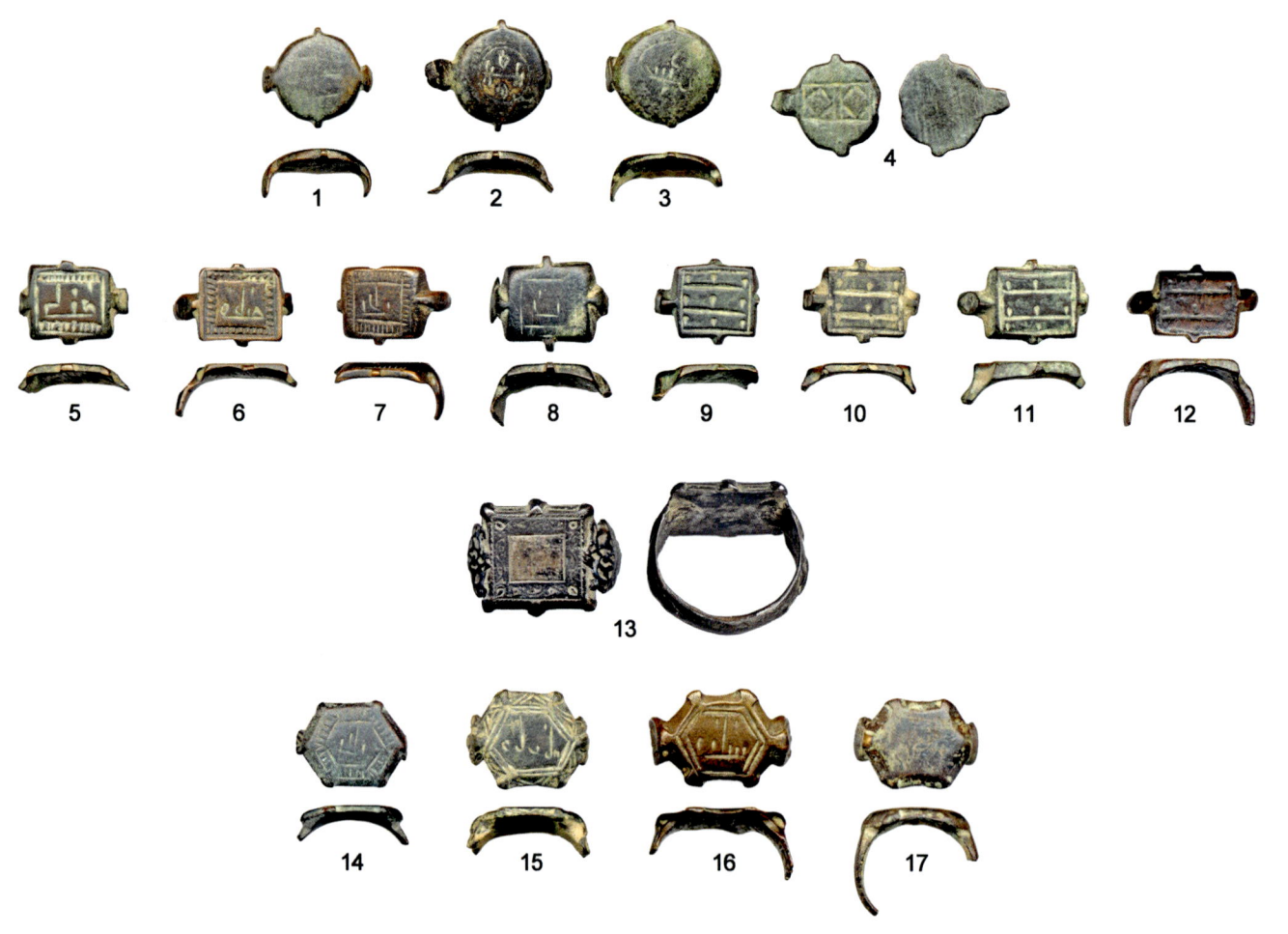

Figure 91 Finger-rings 14: with pseudo-Arabic inscriptions *c*. 8th–12th century

12th–13th century (Raby 1993, nos 214, 220); a final example from Anatolia or the Caucasus, with an inscription within a plain border, is dated 13th century (Raby 1993, no. 219).

Fig. 91.14 – IOLC.7589. K.397. The ring is broken at the shoulders. The bezel has a pseudo-Kufic inscription within a wide border of short parallel lines. 16mm x 12mm.

Fig. 91.15 – 1880.3816.i. IM.Metal.141. An incised and gilded cursive pseudo-Arabic inscription set within a roughly hexagonal border of double lines. The bevelled edges between the knobs of the bezel are incised with double chevrons to form a six-pointed star, with raised triangles at the juncture of the bezel with the shoulders. 13mm x 16mm x 17mm.

Fig. 91.16 – 1880.3816.v. A gilded pseudo-Kufic inscription set within a hexagonal border of double incised lines. The shoulders are incised with double lines roughly in the shape of a lozenge. 13mm x 18mm x 20mm.

Fig. 91.17 – 1880.3816.h. The surviving section of shank broadens below the shoulder, then narrows again slightly at the juncture with the bezel. The edges of the hexagonal bezel are scalloped; its face worn, with a trace of gilding at one edge where it joins the shoulder. 12mm x 14mm x 18mm.

Rings 15: with pseudo-Arabic, *c*. 10th–11th century

Fig. 92.1–7. IM.Metal.141. Small finger-rings with a circular bezel and pinched shoulders; *c*. 10th–11th century.

Figs. 92.1-2. The bezel is flat with an incised horizontal band of double-lined chevrons between two parallel lines.

Fig. 92.1 – 1880.3816.k. 9mm x 14mm.

Fig. 92.2 – 1880.3816.l. 8mm x 14mm.

Fig. 92.3 – 1880.3816.m. The bezel has an incised rectangle containing a chevron. 8.5mm x 15mm.

Fig. 92.4 – 1880.3706.n. IM.Metal.145. The bezel is undecorated. 9.5mm x 14mm.

Fig. 92.5 – 1880.3816.o. The bezel is incised with three parallel lines of a repeated pseudo-Arabic inscription. 8.5mm x 11.3mm.

Fig. 92.6 – 1880.3816.j. The outer edge of the bezel is corrugated and its surface is engraved with one line of a pseudo-Arabic inscription. 11.5mm x 15mm.

Fig. 92.7 – 1880.3816.n. The bezel has a domed centre surrounded by a flat edge. 11.5mm x 13.2mm x 4.7mm x 17.5mm.

Fig. 92.8–14. Cast copper alloy finger-rings pierced with holes on the shoulders.

Fig. 92.8 – 1880.3814.q. IM.Metal.141. Hexagonal bezel, with a double-line incised border. The shoulders are ornamented with incised vertical lines and pierced with two holes below. 7mm x 10mm x 14mm.

Fig. 92.9 – 1880.3814.r. Hexagonal bezel, with a small, incised, wave-like motif of two identical lines, framed by a border comprising an incised line edged with a row of small, regularly spaced notches. One of the shoulders is perforated by a hole, with the edge of a second hole below, across which the shank has broken away. The other shoulder is undecorated. 8mm x 10.5mm x 13mm.

Fig. 92.10 – 1880.3817.h. IM.Metal.145. Worn

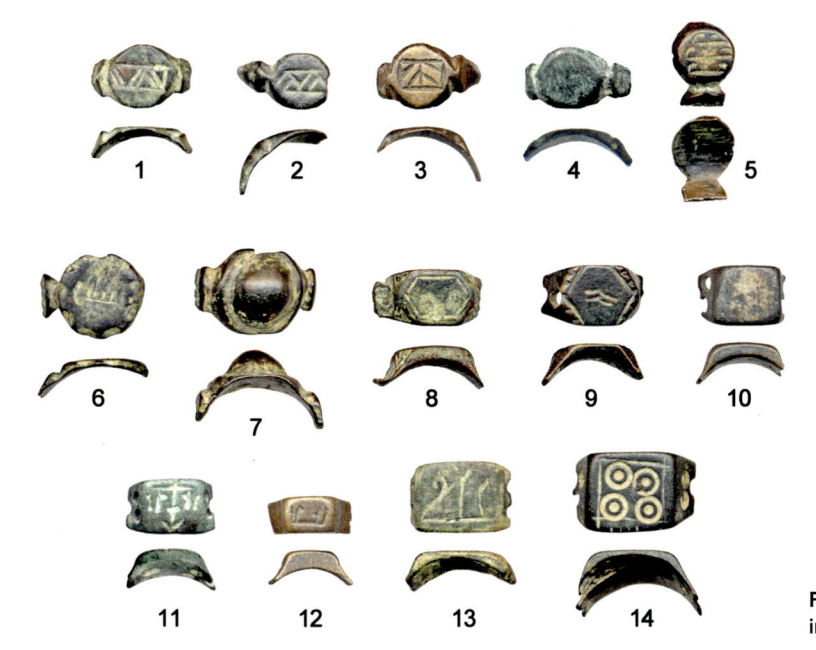

Figure 92 Finger-rings 15: with pseudo-Arabic inscriptions *c.* 10th–11th century

abraded rectangular bezel. The shoulders are pierced with two juxtaposed holes. 7.5mm x 8mm x 11mm.

Fig. 92.11 – 1880.3981.q. Box 4.b. The thick, rectangular bezel is incised with an arrow and transverse line in the centre, flanked on either side by two letters of a pseudo inscription. The shoulders each have two intact drilled holes and the remains of a third at the point where the shank is broken. 12mm x 7mm x 2mm.

Fig. 92.12 – 1880.3813.p. IM.Metal.141. Narrow rectangular bezel with a pseudo-Arabic inscription. The shoulders are each pierced with two holes. 11mm x 7mm x 4.5mm.

Fig. 92.13 – 1880.3814.n. IM.Metal.141. Rectangular bezel with a large pseudo-Arabic inscription. The broad shoulders are each pierced with two circular holes. 9mm x 12mm x 14mm.

Fig. 92.14 – 1880.3814.o. IM.Metal.141. Flat rectangular bezel, with the shoulders narrowing towards the shank. The bezel is engraved with four dot in circle motifs set within an incised square. The shoulders are each pierced with three holes. 11mm x 11mm x 16mm.

Brass-washed elements

Fig. 93. Brass-washed copper alloy discs decorated with engraved semi-circles emanating from each corner, filled with hatching and forming a lozenge in the centre; *c.* 9th–13th century. This decoration is found on a series of rings ranging from the Late Roman/Byzantine period (*c.* 4th–7th century) down to the 13th century (http://www.ancientresource.com/lots/ancient_jewelry/jewelry_rings.htm: viewed 28 Sept. 2019).

Fig. 93.1 – 1880.3839.c. IM.Metal.160. Bezel of a finger-ring with rounded corners and the remains of a soldered shank on the back. 13.4mm x 16.5mm x 0.6mm.

Fig. 93.2 – 1880.3997. SKM 1067 (?). Square top of a lid (?) with the remains of a slightly recessed lip on the back. 12mm x 12.mm x 0.5mm.

Fig. 93.3 – 1880.3839.b. IM.Metal.160. Oval concave disc with the remains of a shank (?) on one side; decorated with an incised cross dividing the ground into four, with semi-circular designs between the outer edges. The back is corroded. 13.2mm x 16.6mm x 1.6mm.

Fig. 93.4 – 1880.3839.a. IM.Metal.160. Circular disc with an incised zig-zag band across the centre, flanked on either side by three cross-hatched semi-circles. Stubs of flanges around the edge on the back suggest that it may have been an amulet case. 17.2mm x 0.6mm.

Plaque

Fig. 94.1 – 1880.3728. Miniature copper alloy plaque showing the front and rear view of a headless female figure standing beside a smaller female attendant with a grotesque head. The larger figure holds a flower in her right hand, her left resting on a plinth. The attendant appears to be walking towards her, but with her head turned to face the viewer; *c.* 1st–3rd century AD. 12.3mm x 12mm x 1.7mm.

Pins and finials

Fig. 94.2 – 1880.3711.o. IM.Metal.155. Copper alloy ornamental hair- or dress-pin head in the form of a woman in Greek dress. The figure stands on the square abacus of a capital with her left leg bent slightly forward, right hand on hip and left arm at her side. She wears a long belted dress, with a himation draped over her left shoulder and around her hips. The folds of the garments are rendered in parallel bands. Her hair is rolled back and gathered in a top knot on the crown of her head. The shaft is broken and missing. 1st century BC–early 1st century AD. 35mm x 10mm. Errington 1999, p. 229, pl. 8.1.

Figure 93 Brass-washed elements

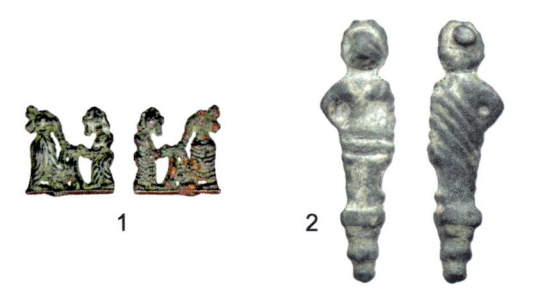

Figure 94 Plaque and pin with female figures

Pin heads in the form of a figure were common in the Greek and Roman world, the most prevalent choice of subject being Aphrodite. Gold examples attributed to the 2nd century BC with a representation of the Greek goddess leaning against a pillar have been found, for instance, at Karpenisi in central Greece and in Syria (Higgins 1980, p. 171, pl. 53g; G&RJC.3034). In Egypt, a 3rd–2nd-century BC silver specimen was brought to light at Alexandria (Hoffman and Davidson 1965, p. 192, figs 72a-b), while at Galjub, bronze models were found among the trading stock of a Hellenistic goldsmith (Ippel 1922, pl. III.7). A finial more comparable to the Begram pin belongs to a bronze perfume dipper dated 4th–3rd century BC from Etruria. It takes the form of a woman in a *himation* standing on an abacus with her right leg slightly bent, her left hand on the hip and her right arm at her side. (Metropolitan Museum 23.160.88).

In the eastern world, besides the Begram example, four intact bronze pins with heads representing the same subject have been found. Two were discovered during excavations at Sirkap, Taxila. One, with both hands on hip, was recovered from the 1st-century BC Indo-Scythian stratum; the other, with the left hand on the hip and the right raised (to grasp her hair?) comes from the early 1st-century AD Indo-Parthian stratum (Marshall 1951, p. 586, nos 227–8, pl. 173.y, p, pl. 182.c, pp. 12, 15). A third example with her arms hanging downwards was also found during excavations at Butkara I (Callieri and Filigenzi 2002, fig. 10). A fourth (possibly an antimony rod) was collected in the Kashmir Smast area and is without archaeological context. The figure is semi-nude and holds the hem of her shawl which has slid down her lap (Nasim Khan 2006, p. 207, no. 30, fig. 216).

It may be, as Marshall suggests, that the Taxila figures can be identified as Aphrodite. The same representation may also be intended in the Butkara, Kashmir Smast and Begram examples. All these bronze pins are of local manufacture, but certainly derive from Greek examples introduced south of the Hindu Kush, in Gandhara and Swat by the Bactrian Greeks. They all seem to belong to the same artistic trend. They may therefore be attributed to a similar period as the Sirkap examples and dated *c.* 1st century BC–1st century AD. The attribution of such a date for the Begram pin receives support from the same way the drapery is rendered in close parallel folds, as on toilet-trays and schist sculptures from the Indo-Scythian–Indo-Parthian stratum at Sirkap, Taxila (Marshall 1951, pls 144.63, 145.77, 212.8, 213.9–11, 13).

Hair- or dress-pins

Fig. 95.1 – 1880.3676.b. IM.Metal.12. Cast two-pronged hair-pin crowned by a pair of small confronted s-shaped birds. Sasanian, *c.* 3rd–6th century. 40mm x 19mm.

A similar two-pronged hair-pin was excavated from the Sasanian levels at Merv (personal communication St J. Simpson). The type may go back to the Hellenistic period. A double pronged example from Macedonia with a finial comprising two S-shaped addorsed snakes is attributed to the 4th century BC (Hoffmann and Davidson, 1965, no. 73).

Fig. 95.2 – 1880.3819.c. IM.Metal.160. Two-pronged hair-pin (?) the top and tips missing; cast in copper alloy with traces of silver plating. Islamic, *c.* 8th–12th century (?) 28mm x 12mm.

Fig. 95.3 – 1880.3819.a. IM.Metal.160. Copper alloy pin, with a flat, broken shaft, topped by a cupped washer with a small hole in the centre. 21mm x 7mm. Sasanian, *c.* 5th–7th century.

The ornament may belong to the same artistic trend as a pin consisting of shaft surmounted by a small ring from Qasr-i Abu Nasr in Iran and attributed to the 5th–7th century (New York Metropolitan Museum of Art 36.30.72).

Fig. 95.4 – 1880.3976.a. IM 14 / SKM 1104. Cast copper alloy pin finial in the shape of a small hand with splayed fingers, narrowing at the wrist to the width of a shaft. Roman, 2nd–3rd century AD. 17.4mm x 12.5mm x 3.7mm.

A large number of hair-pins with a finial in the shape of a hand with outstretched fingers have been found in Bactria. Bone examples, dated 1st–2nd century AD, were recovered at Khalchayan and at Dal'verzin Tepe; others, dated to the 4th century, were recovered at Ak Tepe II and Zar Tepe. This type of hair-pin originates from the Roman world, where it first appeared around the 1st century AD and remained in use until the end of the Roman Empire. It is the most widely distributed group of Roman hair-pins. Specimens have been found in Egypt, Pompeii, Hungary, Switzerland, England and elsewhere (for an extensive bibliography, see Bartus 2012, pp. 205–35). The Begram specimen is probably an import from the West. Bactria yielded other varieties of hand finials, all of which also originate from the Roman Empire: a hand with the index raised and the other fingers bent, a hand holding an apple or an egg. There are two pin finials, still retaining their shafts, and with different hands (one holding an object), in the Cambridge Ridgeway collection (CMAA.1927.1192).

Fig. 95.5 – 1880.3682.a. IM.Metal.21. Cast copper alloy hand with three fingers raised and the index finger and thumb touching. The palm is modelled, the back of the hand is smooth. Traces on the bottom edge indicate that it may have been attached to a shaft. Sasanian, *c.* 4th–6th century. 21mm x 16mm x 3mm. Errington 1999, p. 230, pl. 9.16. A duplicate is in the Cambridge Ridgeway collection (CMAA.1927.1192).

The ritual hand gesture is a symbol of reverence in front of a king or divinity and also of assurance from the god. It frequently occurs in Sasanian art. The god Varhran (Verethragna) on a capital from Kermanshah and the goddess Anahita on a capital from Bisitun, both attributed to the time of Khusrau II (AD 591–628), are represented making the gesture (Compareti 2006, figs 4, 13). It is depicted on numerous seals (Bivar 1968, pl. XV.8–9: ME 1861,0628.12, 1967,0220.3; Bivar 1969, pp. 67–8, pl. 9.1–6; Gyselen 1993, pl. VI, 10.F.2, F.12; Brunner 1978, p. 122, nos

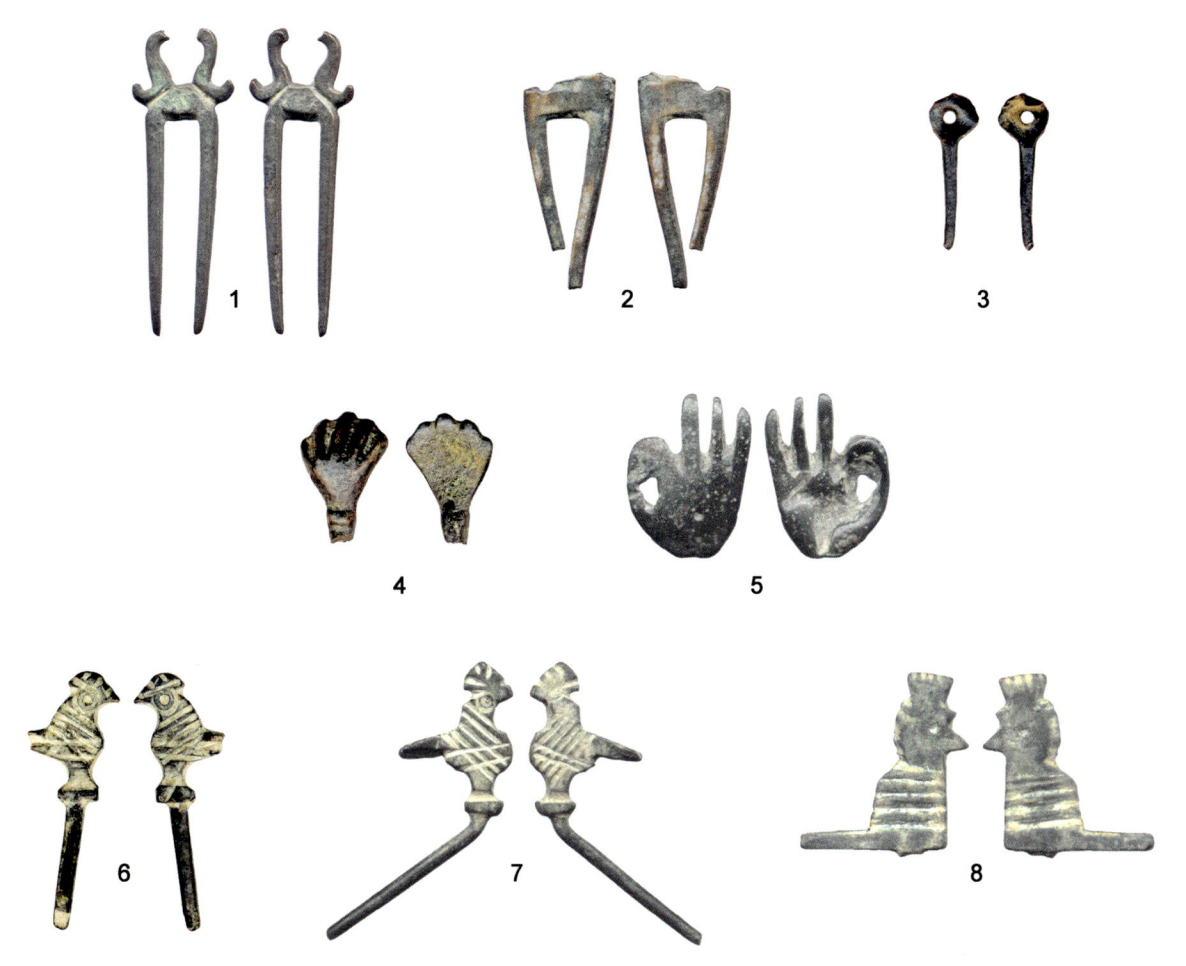

Figure 95 Hair- or dress-pins with bird and hand finials

49, 64; Demange 2006, no. 153). Its use may have continued into the Islamic period. A right hand attached to a pin, the thumb and index finger touching, with the palm gilded, the back of the hand nielloed with silver inlay, was found at Madraseh Tepe, Nishapur (Allan 1982, p. 104, no. 186). The ornament can only be loosely dated 8th–12th century.

Fig. 95.6–7. Two copper alloy pins with finials in the shape of a flat, stylised cockerel with a comb and pointed tail; decorated on the body with a series of incised parallel diagonal lines and crossed by two horizontal ones; c. 1st century BC–1st century AD.

The pins are stylistically close to a bone hair-pin from the Indo-Scythian/Indo-Parthian stratum III at Sirkap, Taxila (Marshall 1951, p. 657, no. 30, pl. 206.14).

Fig. 95.6 – IOLC.5459. K.212. The eye is a punched circle and dot. The tip of the tail and the end of the shaft are missing. 35.mm x 10mm.

Fig. 95.7 – 1880.3681.k. IM.Metal.20. The eye is a punched circle and dot. The shaft is bent at 45° and the tip is missing. 42mm x 17mm. Errington 1999: p. 229, pl. 8.21.

Fig. 95.8 – 1880.3895. Copper alloy-pin finial in the shape of a flat, stylised bird (possibly representing a hoopoe) with an erect crest or comb, pointed beak and an incised dot for the eye. The straight tail extends horizontally from the body, which is decorated with incised bands. The shaft is missing. 4th century AD. 25mm x 23mm x 3.9mm.

The Cambridge Ridgeway collection has two identical examples (CMAA.1927.1192).

A similar pin was found at Iavanskoe (Garavkala, Tajikistan) in a layer dated by Kushano-Sasanian coins and a fragment of pottery stamped with the face of Hormizd II to the 4th century (Zeimal 1985, p. 138, no. 368).

Bird finials for kohl or antimony rods

Fig. 96.1–2. IM.Metal.156. Cast copper alloy kohl or antimony rods with stylised bird finials decorated with dot in circle motifs. 2nd–1st millennium BC or 3rd–6th century AD.

A rod with a stylistically comparable finial was seen in the trade (http://bcgalleries.com.au, Item code 06529, 2006) together with a cosmetic phial in which it is said to have been found. The phial had a tripod base, a cable-like moulding around the almost spherical body and a projecting lip. The items were said to come from the Bactria-Margiana Archaeological Complex and dated to the 2nd–1st millennium BC. Further examples of similar phials with kohl rods of a type well attested during the Bronze Age tend to give weight to the proposed dating.

However, the discovery by Stein of such a phial in one of the cairns at Moghul Ghundai in the Zob River Valley, North-West Frontier Province, Pakistan is worth noting (Stein 1929, pl. M.vii.a; Fairservis 1975, pp. 358–9, fig. 74).

The dating of these cairns is controversial. Some scholars consider them to be possibly associated with the Aryan movement into the subcontinent, while others, like Stein and Fairservis, based on the date of some other items in the cairns, place them in the Kushan or Gupta period,

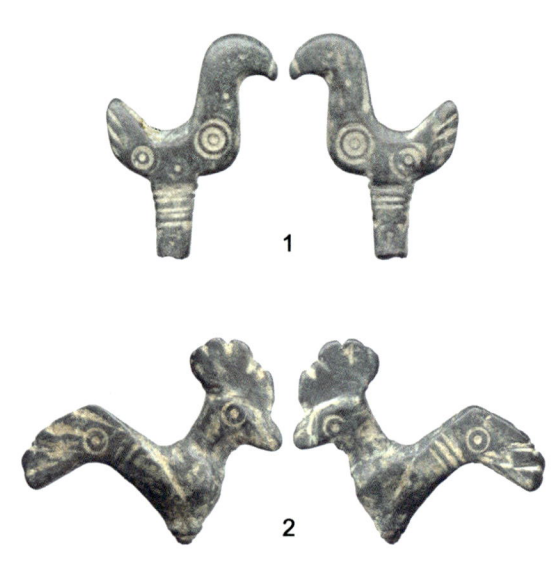

Figure 96 Bird finials for kohl or antimony pins

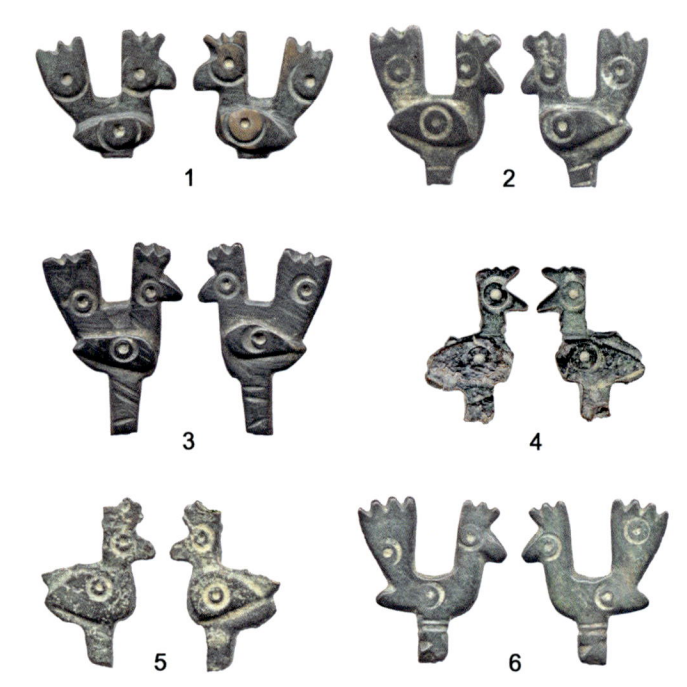

Figure 97 Pins with stylised cockerel finials

c. 3rd–6th century. This may be therefore the period to which the Begram rods belong.

The dot in circle motif has a long life. It originates in the Bronze Age, when it appears in the Indus Civilization, for instance, on *c.* 2nd-millennium BC ivory objects from Mohenjo-daro (Dikshit 1927, pl. XXI.b; Marshall 1931, pl. CXXXII.38, 42, 45) and in the Bactrian Civilization (Amiet 1988a, pp. 133–4). It continues, maybe without interruption, into the early Islamic period. It is found, for instance, on 6th–2nd-century BC ivory plaques from various sites in India and at Taxila; on 5th–4th-century BC bone and ivory objects from Bhir Mound; on 1st-century BC–1st-century AD objects from Sirkap (Ghosh 1989, p. 263; Marshall 1951, pl. 199.12–14); on 6th–8th-century objects from Penjikent (Zeimal 1985, p. 212, nos 547, 549) and on Seljuq objects (Erginsoy 1978, fig. 183a).

Fig. 96.1 – 1880.3712.s. The bird has a rounded head, short beak and an upward tail. The beak and tail feathers are delineated by incised lines, the eye by a single dot. The body is decorated with two punched dot in circle motifs on each side. Only a short section of the shaft survives. It is square in section and has a dot in circle motif topped by parallel incised lines. 30mm x 23mm.

Fig. 96.2 – 1880.3712.r. A cockerel in the round, with a large comb and pointed beak. The tail feathers turn downwards, forming an inverted v-shape. The shaft is completely missing. A punched dot in circle marks each eye and, together with three incised lines, also decorates the tail. 25mm x 35mm.

Pins with stylised cockerel finials

Fig. 97.1–6. Flat cast copper alloy pins with a finial in the shape of stylised cockerel. The neck is short; the head has a prominent beak and erect comb; the tail is turned upwards and slightly fanned. The wings are rounded at the front, narrowing towards the back and stand slightly proud of the body, which also tapers to a point at the back. Three punched dot in circle motifs form the eye and decorate the wing and tail on each side. The shaft is wide and flat and marked with incisions. Islamic, *c.* 8th–12th century. (Wilson 1841, p. 54, fig. 13, Antiquities pl. IV.13).

The type survived for centuries. A modern silver pin from Herat acquired at Kabul has a finial of similar general shape (Janata 1981, fig. 68.6).

Fig. 97.1 – 1880.3711.k. IM.Metal.155. The shaft is missing. 19mm x 16mm. Errington 1999, p. 229, pl. 8.16.

Fig. 97.2 – 1880.3711.l. IM.Metal.155. Only a stub of the shaft survives and is decorated with two incised lines at its junction with the finial. 21mm x 18mm. Errington 1999, p. 229, pl. 8.15. A duplicate is in the Cambridge Ridgeway collection (CMAA.1927.1192).

Fig. 97.3 – 1880.3712.k. IM.Metal.156. 25mm x 17mm.

Fig. 97.4 – IOLC.5467. K.220. Fragment, with the tail and most of the shaft missing. 21mm x 12mm.

Fig. 97.5 – 1880.3711.j. IM.Metal.155. Fragment, with the tail and most of the shaft missing. 22mm x 15mm. Errington 1999, p. 229, pl. 8.17.

Fig. 97.6 – 1880.3712.m. IM.Metal.156. The wings are not defined. The short shaft is decorated with a notch topped by two parallel incised lines. 23mm x 20mm.

Pins with angular stylised bird finials

Fig. 98.1–6. Cast copper alloy pins with a finial representing an angular stylised bird with a curved crest and pointed beak. The body is more or less right angled at the front, tapering to a point at the back and displays scratches resulting from the manufacturing process. The tail is upright and fanned. Islamic, *c.* 8th–12th century.

There are no exact counterparts, only variants of the type. One from Nishapur, with a round head and a thin curved beak is dated 8th–12th century (Allan 1982, fig. 155). Another, illegally exported, confiscated by UK Customs in 2005 and returned to the Kabul Museum, has a head and crest forming a triangle in the profile. It was accompanied

Figure 98 Pins with angular stylised bird finials

Catalogue of Ornamental Metalwork and Miscellaneous Artefacts | 259

by antimony rods dated 8th–12th century (same type as **Fig. 103.7, 9, 11**). The two types are likely to be contemporary. An example of unknown provenance in the Bumiller collection has a high crest in the form of a cross and its body ending in a fish tail. It is tentatively attributed to the 10th century (Dahncke 1992, p. 178, BC-872).

Fig. 98.1 – 1880.3681.b. IM.Metal.20. The surface is decorated on both sides with three punched dot in circle motifs. 39mm x 27mm.

A duplicate is in the Cambridge Ridgeway collection (CMAA.1927.1192).

Fig. 98.2 – 1880.3711.f. IM.Metal.155. 23mm x 27mm.
Fig. 98.3 – IOLC.5463. K.216. 25mm x 28mm.
Fig. 98.4 – 1880.3712.g. IM.Metal.156. 25mm x 28mm.
Fig. 98.5 – 1880.3681.a. IM.Metal.20. The head has a forked crest and pointed beak, but no detailing. 33mm x 21mm.
Fig. 98.6 – 1880.3711.g. IM.Metal.155. The stunted head is abnormally small, with a short neck and a tiny pointed beak and crest. 20mm x 20mm.

Fig. 98.7–11. Cast copper alloy hair- or dress-pins with a finial in the form of a bird with an angular U-shaped body, a comb, curved, pointed beak and spread upright tail, but little or no detailing. The flat shafts are all broken and missing to a greater or lesser degree. Islamic, c. 10th–11th century (?) No parallels from a dated context have been found.

Fig. 98.7 – IOLC.5464. K.217. The tail mirrors the head. The bottom of the body is incised with two pairs of parallel lines. 32mm x 28mm. The Cambridge Ridgeway collection (CMAA.1927.1192) has a further two examples.

Fig. 98.8 – 1880.3712.j. IM.Metal.156. The tail and shaft are missing. A pair of diagonal lines are incised across the chest, with another single line at the base of the tail. 29mm x 22mm.

Fig. 98.9 – 1880.3681.c. IM.Metal.20. The tail and part of the shaft are missing. A diamond-shape in relief marks the point where the shaft joins the body. 29mm x 22mm.

Fig. 98.10 – 1880.3712i. IM.Metal.156. The tail and most of the shaft are missing. A diamond-shape in relief marks the point where the shaft joins the body. 20mm x 20mm.

Fig. 98.11 – IOLC.5465. K.218. The splayed tail mirrors the outline of the head. Most of the shaft is missing. The mould flashing has not been removed. 28mm x 20mm. A duplicate is in the Cambridge Ridgeway collection (CMAA.1927.1192).

Fig. 98.12 – 1880.3711.c. IM.Metal.155. The comb is erect, and the splayed tail mirrors the outline of the head. 25mm x 23mm.

Fig. 98.13 – 1880.3712.f. IM.Metal.156. The crest is erect and the tail ends in three fanned feathers. 27.2mm x 23.7mm. A duplicate is in the Cambridge Ridgeway collection (CMAA.1927.1192).

Pins with U-shaped finials

Fig. 99.1–5. Flat U-shaped finials representing a stylised bird, with an almost identical head and tail resembling two addorsed bird heads with an erect crest. On both sides there are scratches resulting from the manufacturing technique and three small punched dot in circle marks for the eye, on the tail and in the middle of the body respectively. Islamic; c. 9th–11th century.

There are three examples of the same type in the Cambridge Ridgeway collection (CMAA.1927.1192).

Fig. 99.1 – IOLC.5462. K.215. The shaft is missing. 22mm x 25mm.

Fig. 99.2 – 1880.3712.b. IM.Metal.156. Zigzag incised lines decorate the short shaft. 33mm x 24mm.

Fig. 99.3 – 1880.3711.b. IM.Metal.155. A few cross-hatched lines decorate the short shaft. 33mm x 20mm. Errington 1999, p. 229, pl. 8.14.

Fig. 99.4 – 1880.3711.a. IM.Metal.155. Broken unfinished fragment lacking punched decoration and still retaining traces of mould flashing; no shaft survives. 20mm x 21mm.

Fig. 99.5 – 1880.3819.f. IM.Metal.160. The base of the U and the space between its uprights are not as rounded as in the other examples. The beak and tail are missing. A spike only remains. This could either be a fragmentary specimen of the same type under consideration here, or a new type with two spikes. 28mm x 12mm.

Pins with stylised peacock finials

Fig. 99.6 – 1880.3712.h. IM.Metal.156. Finial in the shape of a peacock, with an erect crest, down-turned wings and a raised tail with splayed feathers. The shaft is completely lost. Islamic, c. 8th–12th century. 26mm x 26mm.

The wings are similar to those of the phial stopper **Fig. 101.12**.

Fig. 99.7 – 1880.3713.h. IM.Metal.29. The finial is a stylised peacock, with an erect crest and a tail of three splayed feathers. The eyes are marked by a dot in circle. The same motif is stamped on the body and tail on one side and on the body on the other. The top of the short shaft is incised with parallel lines 37mm x 22mm.

Fig. 99.8–9. A flat, stylised bird with the head missing. It has a tail of three splayed feathers. The wings stand slightly proud of the body on both sides and have a round hole for an inset stone. Some notches can be seen on either side of the top of the shaft. Islamic, c. 8th–12th century.

A complete example sold on the antique market provides evidence that the head was that of a peacock.

Fig. 99.8 – 1880.3675. IM.Metal.11 / SKM 1098. 44mm x 18mm x 5mm. Wilson 1841, p. 54, fig. 15, Antiquities pl. IV.15, misidentified as an axe.

Fig. 99.9 – 1880.3711.h. IM.Metal.155. Most of the shaft is missing. 27mm x 18mm. Errington 1999, p. 229, pl. 8.18.

Pins with naturalistic bird finials

Fig. 100.1 – 1880.3712.o. IM.Metal.156. Pin finial in the shape of a duck in the round with wing feathers rendered as oblique incisions on either side of a horizontal line. Only a short section of the shaft survives. Islamic, 8th century (?). 23mm x 18mm x 4.3mm. A duplicate is in the Cambridge Ridgeway collection (CMAA.1927.1192).

No other counterpart has been found, but an allied pin with a finial in the shape of a cockerel from Kashmir Smast

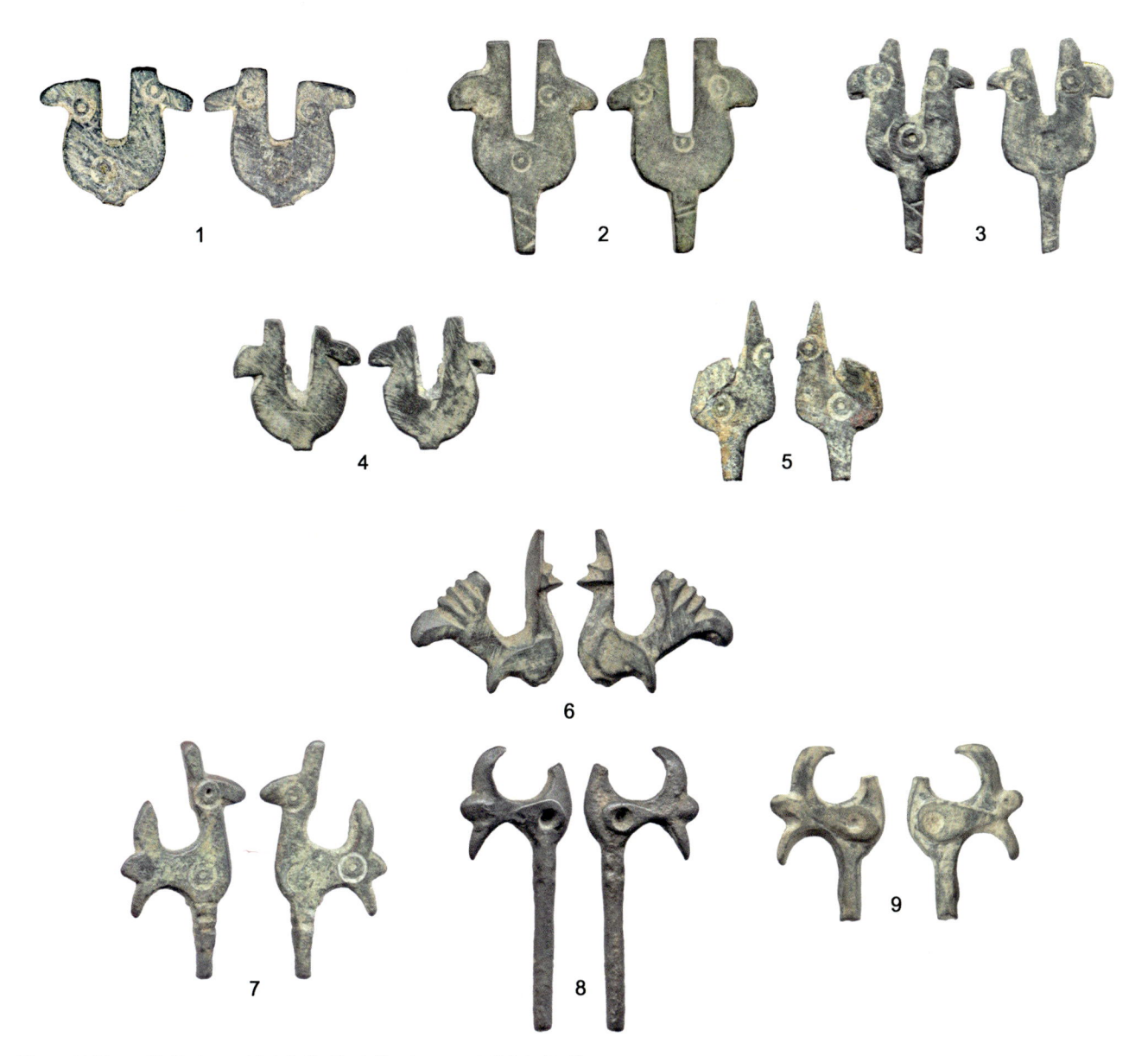

Figure 99 Pins with U-shaped finials (1–5); stylised peacock finials (6–9)

also has its wing feathers rendered in the same way (Nasim Khan 2006, p. 207, no. 27, fig. 213). Finds from this site can only be broadly dated from numismatic evidence to the 2nd–13th century. However, the occurrence of similarly executed feathers on an 8th-century ceramic duck from Penjikent in Tajikistan may be of some chronological significance (Zeimal 1985, p. 203, no. 512).

Fig. 100.2 – 1880.3681.j. IM.Metal.20. Pin with a finial in the shape of a small duck, with a long neck and a groove along the top of the head. The body is flat on top, with incised diagonal lines along the sides defining the wings, and ending in a pointed tail. Only the tip of the round shaft is missing. 37mm x 15mm. Errington 1999, p. 229, pl. 8.7.

The rendition of the wings echoes **Fig. 100.1** which suggests a similar c. 8th-century date.

Fig. 100.3–5. Cast copper alloy pin with a finial in the shape of a bird in the round. It has a body tapering towards the tail and well defined wings with the feathers indicated.

Fig. 100.3 – 1880.3712.p. IM.Metal.156. The bird is a peacock with an erect crest, a small curved beak, deep socketed round eye and a long neck. The tail and shaft are missing. Islamic, c. 10th–12th century. 28.5mm x 13.4mm x 6.5mm.

Two similar pin finials are known. One was excavated from the early site of Qanat Tepe, Nishapur, and dated 8th–12th century (Allan 1982, pp. 61–2, 71, fig. 70). The other was purchased by Stein at the Keriya oasis east of Khotan, and according to him appears to be the head of a kohl or antimony rod (Stein 1907, vol. 1, p. 469, pl. LI, Ker.001).

Fig. 100.4 – 1880.3681.h. IM.Metal.20. The finial is in the shape of a long-necked goose. The eye is depicted as an incised dot; the wings are clearly defined, but the tail is missing. The details are obscured by wear. Only the thickened, rectangular junction between the shaft and the finial survives. It has two parallel incised lines at either end and a notch in each corner of the central section. It is similar to that in **Fig. 100.2**. Islamic, c. 10th–12th century. 41mm x 18mm. Errington 1999: p. 229, pl. 8.6. A duplicate is in the Cambridge Ridgeway collection (CMAA.1927.1192).

Fig. 100.5 – 1880, 3681.l. IM.Metal.20. Worn and broken pin with the head missing. The thickened junction between the finial and shaft is square in section and

Catalogue of Ornamental Metalwork and Miscellaneous Artefacts | 261

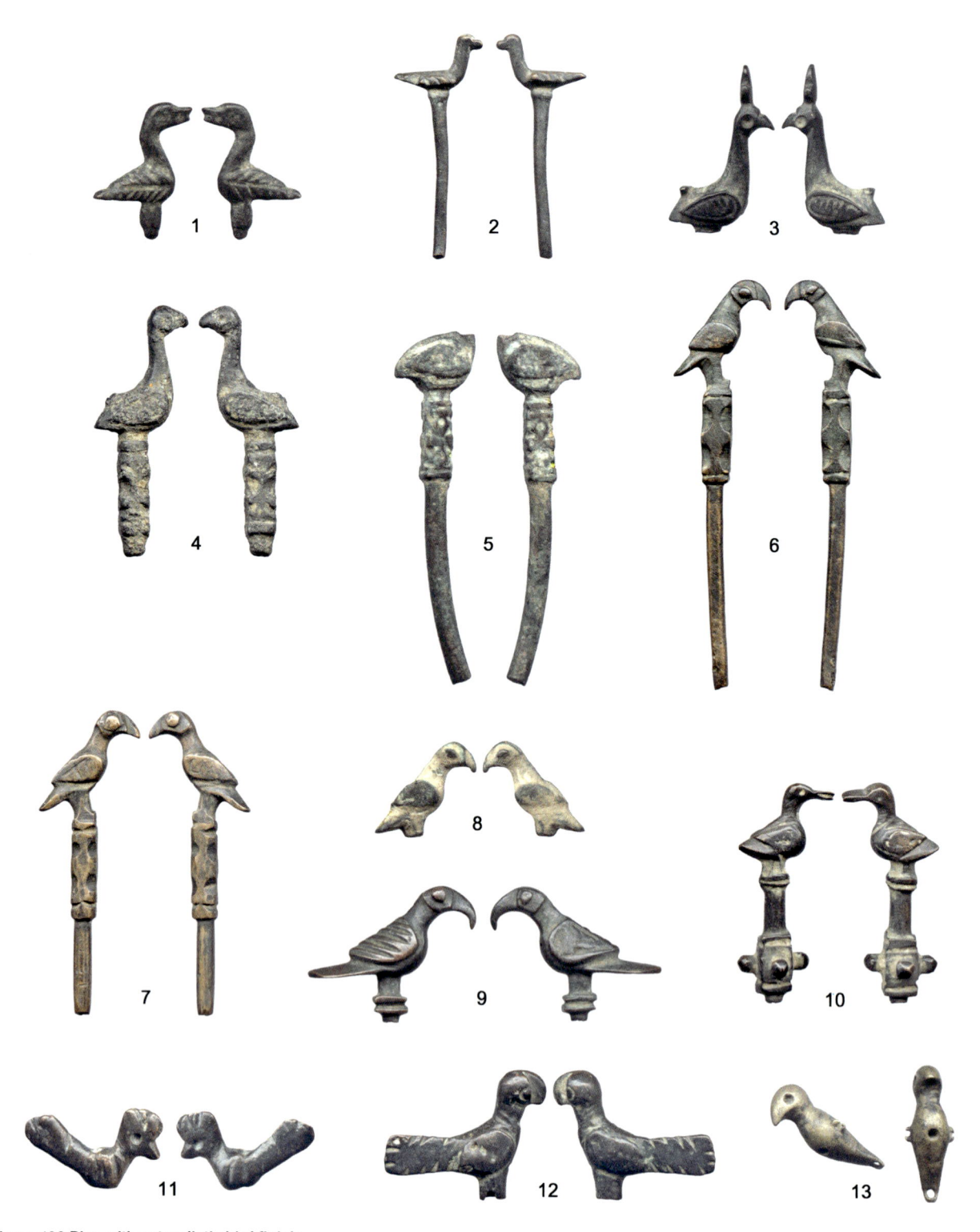

Figure 100 Pins with naturalistic bird finials

decorated between double bands with dot in diamond shapes. The thinner main shaft is curved and circular in section with the end missing. The upper shaft resembles that of a kohl stick found at Nishapur (Allan 1982, nos 83–4). See also **Fig. 102.1** for a similar shaft. Islamic, c. 10th–12th century. 57mm x 15mm. Wilson 1841: Antiquities pl. IV.4.a.

Fig. 100.6–9. Cast copper alloy kohl or antimony rods with a finial in the shape of a bird in the round, resembling a raven with a curved beak and bulbous eyes. The wings are clearly defined; the tail is flattened and points downwards. Where it survives, the bottom half of the shaft is round, while the banded junction with the finial is square in section, and notched at each corner to form diamond shapes. The pristine condition of **Fig. 100.6–7, 9** suggests they were bought in Kabul bazaar, while the deposits on **Fig. 100.8** indicate that it was probably collected from Begram.

A pin with a similar shaft and finial has been found in Bactria and attributed to the Bronze Age (Salvatori 1988, p. 184, fig. 83). However, a pin of the same type was excavated from Pit K (dated c. 8th–14th century) at Ghubayra, Iran (Bivar 2000: pp. 17, 109, no. B7/71-045, fig. 55, pl. 71a). Furthermore, the rendering of the wings is comparable with that of a bird pin from Madraseh Tepe, Nishapur, dated 8th–13th century (Allan 1982, pp. 70–1, fig. 68).

262 | *Charles Masson: Collections from Begram and Kabul Bazaar, Afghanistan, 1833–1838*

Fig. 100.6 – 1880.3681.g. IM.Metal.20. 68mm x 18mm. Errington 1999: p. 229, pl. 8.9.

Fig. 100.7 – 1880.3681.f. IM.Metal.20. 50mm x 18mm. Errington 1999: p. 229, pl. 8.10.

Fig. 100.8 – 1880.3712.n. IM.Metal.156. Uncleaned, 20mm x 16mm.

Fig. 100.9 – 1880.3673. IM.Metal.7. The slightly splayed tail ends in a point. The wings are rounded at the front, taper to a point at the back and join together at a sharp angle along the top. One is decorated with diagonal parallel grooves, the other with an acanthus scroll. The legs are fused into a short, round shaft standing on a double-banded square plinth, below which was the round pin shaft, now lost. 23mm x 30mm x 8mm. Wilson 1841, p. 54, fig. 16, Antiquities pl. IV.16: misidentified as 'iron handle of a key'.

Fig. 100.10 – 1880.3681.i. IM.Metal.20. Pin with a finial in the shape of a life-like duck. The round shaft is decorated with a thicker rectangular section with a boss on each side centred between two grooves. The shaft below this point is missing. Islamic, *c.* 8th–14th century. 36mm x 17mm. From Kabul bazaar (?). Errington 1999: p. 229, pl. 8.4.

A duplicate is in the Cambridge Ridgeway collection (CMAA.1927.1192).

Fig. 100.11–12. The two finials may have once decorated bronze vessels. They very much resemble those which adorn the lids of Arabic teapot dallah, dated 16th or 19th century.

Fig. 100.11 – 1880.3712.q. IM.Metal.156. Cast copper alloy bird in the round, resembling a hoopoe with crest raised, a long tail, pointed beak and dot for the eye. It is pierced vertically through the body for suspension. Islamic, *c.* 8th–14th century. 24mm x 14.8mm x 6.2mm. From Kabul bazaar (?).

Fig. 100.12 – 1880.3711.m. IM.Metal.155. Finial in the shape of a parrot in the round, with notched decoration along the edges of the flat tail. The bird sits on a cylindrical section with a hole in its centre into which a pin or attachment tab was originally inserted. Islamic, *c.* 8th–14th century. 27mm x 22.5mm x 7.2mm. From Kabul bazaar (?).

Fig. 100.13 – 1880.3713.f. IM.Metal.156. Cast brass-washed copper alloy finial in the shape of a bird in the round, with a curved beak, two drilled holes for the eyes, two pierced broken lugs for the wings, a pierced lug at the tip of the tail, and a hole drilled on the underside for attachment to a pin (?). 23mm x 9mm.

Miscellaneous pins

Fig. 101.1 – 1880.3687.o. IM.Metal.25 / IM 68 / SKM 1069. Flat, rectangular, cast copper alloy finial fragment of a double-pronged (?) pin, decorated on one side with a large punched dot and double circle between three smaller dot in a single circle motifs. Islamic, *c.* 8th–10th century. 25mm x 12mm. No counterpart has been found.

Fig. 101.2 – 1880.3819.e. IM.Metal.160. Flat, copper alloy pin head with a brass (?) wash and a large punched dot in circle motif on the front. Only a stub of the shaft survives. 16mm x 13mm x 1mm. Islamic, *c.* 8th–10th century.

Fig. 101.3 – IOLC.5461. K.214. Flat, cast copper alloy pin with a pointed head decorated with a punched circle and dot on one side. 24mm x 10mm. Islamic, *c.* 8th–10th century.

A duplicate is in the Cambridge Ridgeway collection (CMAA.1927.1192).

Fig. 101.4 – 1880.3849. IM.Metal.160. Flat, copper alloy pin fragment. The shaft has rudimentary bead and reel notches; the head is oval with a smaller recessed oval in the centre of both sides, and surmounted by a triangle with curved sides meeting in a point at the top. Both surfaces are covered with fine parallel machine-made striations. Islamic, *c.* 10th–11th century. 26.8mm x 15.8mm x 1.6mm.

For similar striations see **Fig. 130**.

Fig. 101.5–6. Cast copper alloy pin fragments. The square head has a cut-out V-shape along the top and is notched around the edges of one side to represent a six-pointed star.

Fig. 101.5 – 1880.3713.i. IM.Metal.156. The rectangular shaft has slightly rounded front edges. The front of the head is worn, with only traces of notched edges. The back is plain with the V-shape cut into its top edge. 23.5mm x 3mm; head: 9mm x 10mm. A duplicate is in the Cambridge Ridgeway collection (CMAA.1927.1192).

Fig. 101.6 – 1880.3909.a. 8. The shaft is missing. The head has a cut-out V-shape into the top edge of the front. The back has multiple striation marks. 9mm x 8mm x 2mm.

For similar striations see **Fig. 130**.

Ear-cleaner

Fig. 101.7 – 1880.3819.d. IM.Metal.160. Copper alloy ear-cleaner with a thin, broken shaft, semi-circular in section, and a flat, rounded head; *c.* 1st century AD (?). 19mm x 6mm

Spatula-shaped pins

Fig. 101.8 – 1880.3713.j. IM.Metal.156. Flat, copper alloy hair- or dress-pin with a splayed and notched trilobate top, decorated only on one face of the surviving upper shaft with a notched motif banded by parallel incised lines; *c.* 1st century AD (?). 54mm x 21mm x 1mm.

A similar splayed and notched pin fragment, but decorated with three dot in circle motifs, is in the Cambridge Ridgeway collection (CMAA.1927.1192). The decoration of the shaft has a counterpart in a flat bronze rod from the 1st-century AD Indo-Scythian stratum at Sirkap, Taxila (Marshall 1920, p. 20, no. 9, pl. XXIV.17). The same stratum contained a hair-pin with a finial decorated with dot in circle motifs (Marshall 1951, pl. 182, p. 14). The Masson pin may belong to the same period.

Fig. 101.9 – 1880.3687.p. IM.Metal.25 / IM 68 / SKM 1069. Flat, copper alloy splayed pin in two pieces, notched along the top and decorated on one side with dot in double circle motifs and incised parallel lines. There are diagonal scratch marks on the undecorated reverse. Islamic, 10th century (?) 24mm x 16mm. No counterpart has been found.

Spatula

Fig. 101.10 – 1880.3681.d. IM.Metal.20. Copper alloy pin or antimony rod with a wide, flat shaft slightly curved and ridged at the end to form a spatula. The finial is in the shape of a flat, stylised bird with a comb, pointed beak and upright tail. A repeated incised dot in circle motif decorates both sides: two on the shaft, two on the tail, one on the chest and

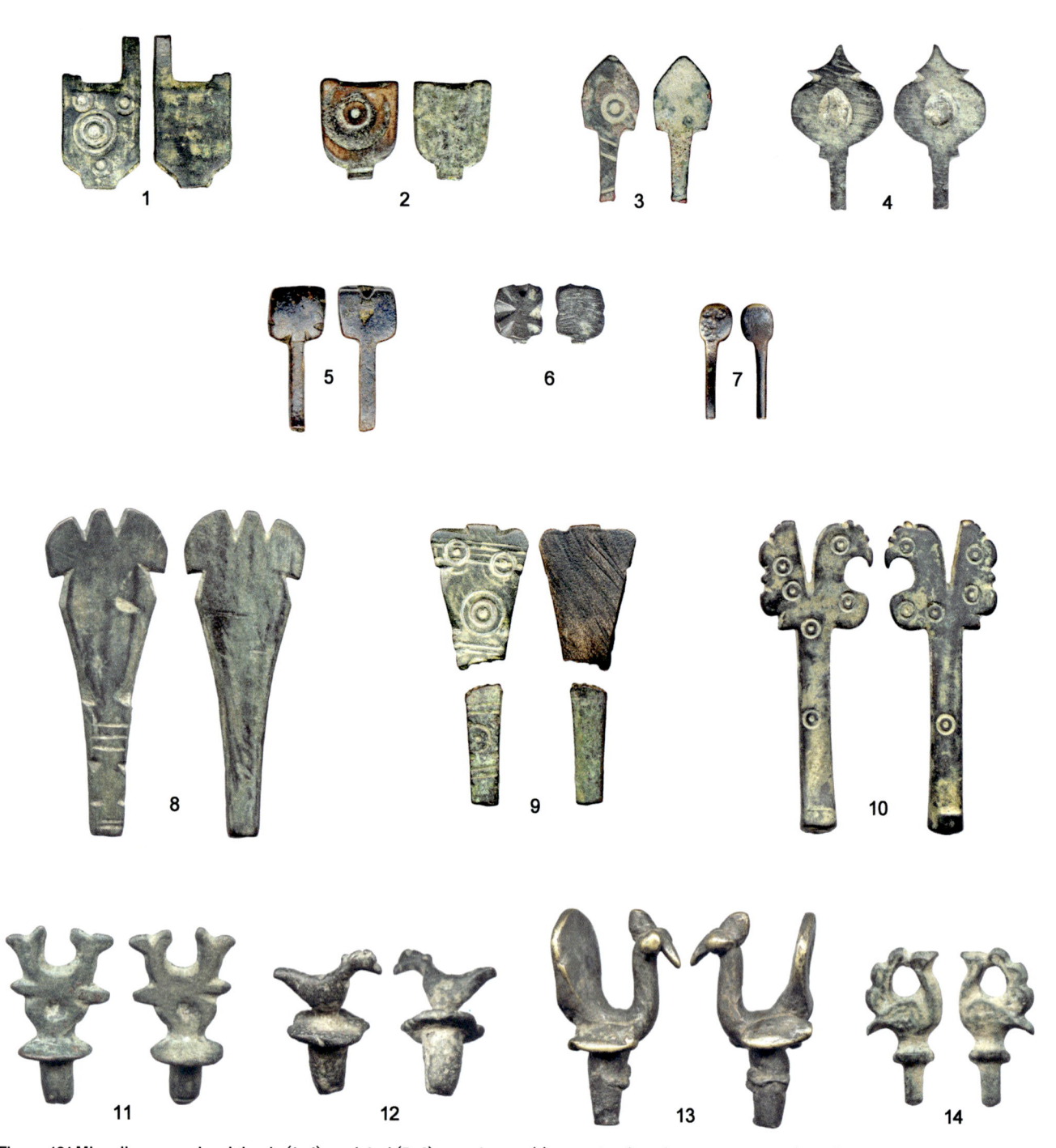

Figure 101 Miscellaneous pins: Islamic (1–4); undated (5–6); ear cleaner (7); spatulas (8–10); phial stoppers (11–14)

one marking the eye. 1st–6th century AD. 50mm x 20mm. Errington 1999: p. 229, pl. 8.12.

Phial stoppers
Fig. 101.11 – 1880.3711.n. IM.Metal.155. Stopper with a finial in the shape of a *triratna* (Three Jewels: symbolising the Buddha, *Dharma* and *Sangha*) surmounting a wheel and set on the circular, concave top of a short plug. 1st century AD. 30mm x 18mm; plug: 12.5mm.

Several stoppers of this type were excavated from the 1st century AD Indo-Parthian stratum at Sirkap, Taxila, (Marshall 1951, p. 587, no. 251, pl. 182.g-m). The *triratna* commonly appears on early Indian and Gandharan Buddhist sculptures and in Indo-Parthian jewellery and objects from Sirkap (Marshall 1951, pl. 180, no. 117, pl. 191, no. 101, pl. 195, no. 147, pl. 197, no. 24, pl. 177, no. 364).

Fig. 101.12 – 1880.3713.g. IM.Metal.156. The finial is a bird with a small comb and tail, resting on the circular, concave top of a short, conical plug. Early 1st century. 24.6mm x 18mm; plug: 14.5mm.

The stopper is stylistically related to the examples from the 1st century Indo-Parthian stratum at Sirkap.

Fig. 101.13 – 1880.3681.m. IM.Metal.20. Brass antimony or kohl phial stopper with a short plug. The finial depicts a peacock with a small crest and a fanned, upright tail. 1st century. 36mm x 22mm. Errington 1999. p.229, pl.8.5.

A comparable example was excavated from the early 1st-century Indo-Parthian stratum at Sirkap (Marshall 1951, p. 587, pl. 173, no. 182,i, pl. 182, nos 242, 247).

Fig. 101.14 – 1880.3711.i. IM.Metal.155. Stopper in the shape of a stylised peacock, the neck arched and the

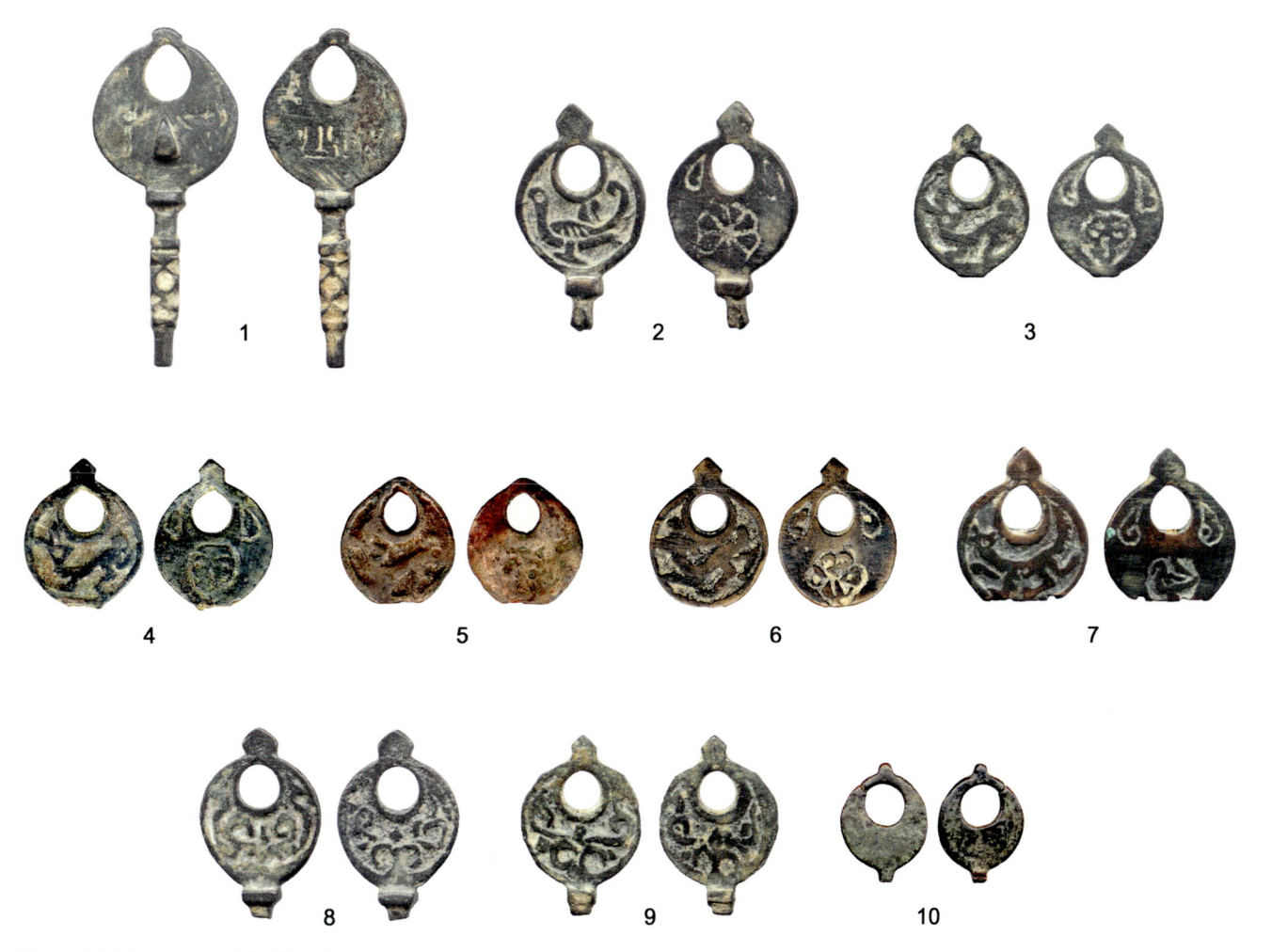

Figure 102 Islamic period clothing pins

scalloped tail curved over the back to touch the head. The wings curve downwards to end in a point. The bird rests on a reel-shaped base surmounting a slender plug. 8th century. 26mm x 13mm (finial). A duplicate is in the Cambridge Ridgeway collection (CMAA.1927.1192).

The date is suggested by the stopper's resemblance to a pin finial from an 8th-century burial at Ush-At in south Kyrgyzstan (Zadneprovsky 1975, fig. 26). The tail of the bird is similarly scalloped and forms a circle with its arched neck. The rendering may have its roots in the late Sasanian artistic repertoire, in which birds, usually pheasants, but also ducks, peacocks and cockerels, are commonly represented in this way, e.g. on the garment of an elephant rider on a 6th–7th-century relief at Taq-i-Bustan, Iran (Baldwin 1970, p. 6, fig.5); on 7th–8th-century textiles from Central Asia (*L'image tissée* 2006, figs 9, 15); on 6th–7th-century Sasanian silver vessels (Grabar 1967, no. 32; Trever and Lukonin 1987, nos 24, 26, 30); and on a later 8th–9th-century Central Asian gold plate (Brentjes and Vasilievsky 1989, p. 159).

Clothing pins

Fig. 102.1–10. IM.Metal.142. Cast copper alloy pins with a flat, ovate or round head, a circular or oval eye cut out at the top and a small pentagonal projection at the apex. Most of the shafts are missing. Islamic, *c.* 11th–13th century.

No exact parallel has been found. However, the shape is a rounder version of drop-shaped pendants with a similar eye e.g. **Fig. 114.1** and an example from Qanat Tepe, Nishapur, dated *c.* 9th–13th century (Allan 1982, pp. 70–1, no. 65). A lotus bud appears on pendants **Fig. 112.9** (*c.* 9th–11th century) and **Fig. 113.1** (*c.* 10th century); and an Arabic inscription in a rectangular cartouche on pendants **Fig. 113.2** (*c.* 11th–12th century), **Fig. 113.3** and **Fig. 113.5** (*c.* 11th–13th century).

Fig. 102.1 – 1880.3703.h. One side has a triangle in high relief, flanked by traces of incised decoration; the other with traces of an incised pseudo-Kufic inscription. The top of the shaft is square, the lower shaft round. 48mm x 21mm. Errington 1999 p. 230, pl. 9.4.

Fig. 102.2 – 1880.3703.g. One side depicts a sitting bird with a long, curled tail; the other has an incised spatulate leaf on either side of the eye and an eight-petalled flower below. The top of the shaft is square, the lower shaft round. 31.5mm x 19.2mm. Errington 1999, p. 230, pl. 9.3.

The spatulate leaf is similar in shape to that on 12th–13th-century ceramic wares (Pope and Ackerman 1964–5, p. 2696, fig. 904k). The floral decoration on the reverse also occurs on pendant **Fig. 113.4**, dated 10th–12th century. There is a broken example with the same reverse in the Cambridge Ridgeway collection (CMAA.1927.1192).

Fig. 102.3–4. One side depicts a hare looking backwards; the other has a rosette below the eye and a foliate motif on either side. None of the shafts survive.

The animals in the chase motif developed in the mid-12th century (Erginsoy 1978, p. 52). Running hares decorate 12th–13th-century bronzes from Khwarazm now in the

Catalogue of Ornamental Metalwork and Miscellaneous Artefacts | 265

Kabul and Ghazni museums (Melikian-Chirvani 1975, figs 2–4).

Fig. 102.3 – 1880.3703.c. 21mm x 17mm.

Fig. 102.4 – 1880.3819.j. IM.Metal.160. 21.3mm x 17.6mm.

Fig. 102.5 – 1880.3703.d. Worn and pitted fragment, with traces of an animal on one side. 18mm x 17mm.

Fig. 102.6 – 1880.3703.e. One side depicts a dog (?) running to left; the other has two foliate motifs and a six-petalled flower. 21.5mm x 17.5mm.

Fig. 102.7 – 1880.3703.f. One side depicts a wolf (?) with a long, shaggy tail, looking backwards; the other has a foliate motif on either side of the eye and a bird in the round cartouche below. The bottom of the finial is lost. 22mm x 19.3mm. Errington 1999 p. 230, pl. 9.1.

The animal resembles that on pendant **Fig. 113.5**, dated 11th–12th century.

Fig. 102.8–9. Both sides are decorated with arabesques.

Fig. 102.8 – 1880.3703.a. 27mm x 18mm.

Fig. 102.9 – 1880.3703.b. 25mm x 17.4mm. Errington 1999, p. 230, pl. 9.

Fig. 102.10 – 1880.3819.k. IM.Metal.160. Small, worn, with no visible decoration. 16.7mm x 12.5mm.

Ear-rings

Fig. 103.1–2. Copper alloy ear-rings of thin wire with a loop at one end, strung with three beads separated by coiled wire spacers. Similar ear-rings of thin wire and strung beads are found in the Roman Empire during the 1st century AD, but without the coiled spacers (Marshall 1911, pl. LIII.2565, 2567). They are also found during the early Islamic period at Takht-i Sulaiman, Iran, 10th–11th century (Gladiss 1998, p. 95, no. 25); at Sayram-Su in Chimkent, Central Asia, 10th–11th century (Lester 1991, p. 22, fig. 4) and at Corinth, 12th century (Davidson 1952, pl. 108, no. 2014), but in all these examples the beads are made of two joined hemispheres, which tends to preclude a dating to the early Islamic period. One example from Corinth includes beads of the same type as **Fig. 103.2** (Davidson 1952, pl. 108, no. 2004). Roman or early Islamic (?).

Fig. 103.1 – 1880.3687.m. IM.Metal.25 / IM 68 / SKM 1069. Ear-ring strung with three cast faceted beads alternating with two wire spacers (one only intact). 18mm x 5mm.

Fig. 103.2 – 1880.3717.h-i. IM.Metal.160, IM.Metal.159. Two fragments of a wire ear-ring with small strung beads. The larger fragment has an attachment loop at one end and two beads; the smaller has one bead and a section of coiled wire. Beads: 10mm x 9mm x 3mm.

Fig. 103.3–6. Open wire rings, thicker in the middle, with wire coiled around one or both ends; c. 1st–3rd century AD.

This type of ear-ring, which goes back to the 2nd millennium BC, is found in 1st-century BC–1st-century AD tombs at Dura Europos (Toll 1946, pls XXXVI, XXXVII, XLVI), 1st–2nd-century tombs at Sardis (Waldbaum 1983, pl. 47, no. 809) and in a 2nd-century hoard at Palmyra (Johnson 1931, p. 78, pl. XLVI, 1). Further east they are found in the early 1st-century Indo-Parthian stratum at Sirkap, Taxila (Marshall 1951, pl. 191, nos 33, 35) and inside a Gandharan reliquary (Kurita 2003, figs 764, 938); in a hoard buried in the 3rd century at Dal'verzin Tepe, Uzbekistan (Pugachenkova 1978, fig. 77); and in Tajikistan, in 1st-century BC–1st-century AD Kushan tombs at Tulchar (Mandel'shtam 1966, pl. LVIII.2, 23) and 1st–3rd century AD Kushan tombs at Tup Khona (Litvinsky and Sedov 1983, pl. II, nos 19, 22, 28–9, 33 4, 39, 47–8; Zeimal 1985, nos 292–3). During the early Sasanian period, the type is found at Tell Mahuz in Iran (Musche 1988, p. 295, pl. CII, 2).

Fig. 103.3 – 1880.3717a. IM.Metal.160. Copper alloy. The top of the ring is missing. Wire is coiled around both ends leaving the middle plain. 11mm x 2mm.

Fig. 103.4 – 1880.3717.b. IM.Metal.160. Misshapen copper alloy ring. One end of the wire is bent into a loop before coiling back around itself. The other plain end forms a thin prong for inserting into the attachment loop. 18mm x 3mm.

Fig. 103.5 – 1880.3717.g. IM.Metal.160. Copper alloy ring. One end of the wire was bent to form a loop (now broken) before coiling back around the end three times. 16mm x 13mm x 2mm.

Fig. 103.6 – IOLC.5445. K.186. Broken silver wire ring, bound with a twisted piece of wire at one end. 12mm x 2mm.

Fig. 103.7 – IOLC.5447. K.188. Ear-ring (?) made from a copper alloy strip curved into a rough circle and knotted at one end. 10mm x 3mm.

This example resembles a 1st–3rd-century ear-ring from Tup Khona, made of wire or a metal strip, with one end coiled into a loop into which the other end could be inserted (Litvinsky and Sedov 1984, pl. II.40).

Fig. 103.8 – 1880.3717.f. IM.Metal.160. Cast copper alloy open ring bound with three loops of wire at one end. 12mm x 1.5mm.

One example in gold was found in a 1st century BC–1st century AD tomb at Tulchar, Tajikistan (Mandel'shtam 1966, pl. LX) and another in bronze at Surkh Kotal, Afghanistan (Fussman and Guillaume 1990, fig. 234, pls 5, VIII). A further gold example of this type – differing only in that the looped end is embellished by a row of granules – was found at Kampyr Tepe, Uzbekistan, a 1st–2nd-century Kushan city (Pugachenkova et al. 1991, fig. 203).

Fig. 103.9 – 1880.3838.d. IM.Metal.160. Part of a small copper alloy ear-ring, flattened at one end, with a narrow prong at the other. 13.4mm x 2.2mm.

Fig. 103.10–17. Plain copper alloy open rings. The basic type was found in large numbers in the 1st-century BC–1st-century AD Tulchar necropolis (Mandel'shtam 1966, pl. LVIII). They were also found in the c. 5th-century relic deposit of Hadda stupa 10 (**Vol. I, Figs 278.21–6, 283.26–56**).

Fig. 103.10 – 1880.3880.g. IM.Metal.159. Small copper alloy hoop ear-ring, comprising a flat band narrowing to a point at either end. 10mm x 3mm (widest point).

Fig. 103.11 – 1880.3880.h. IM.Metal.159. Copper alloy hoop ear-ring with one tapering end. 21mm x 18mm x 2mm.

Fig. 103.12 – 1880.3880.i. IM.Metal.159. Plain copper alloy hoop ear-ring tapering at each end. 18mm x 20mm x 2mm.

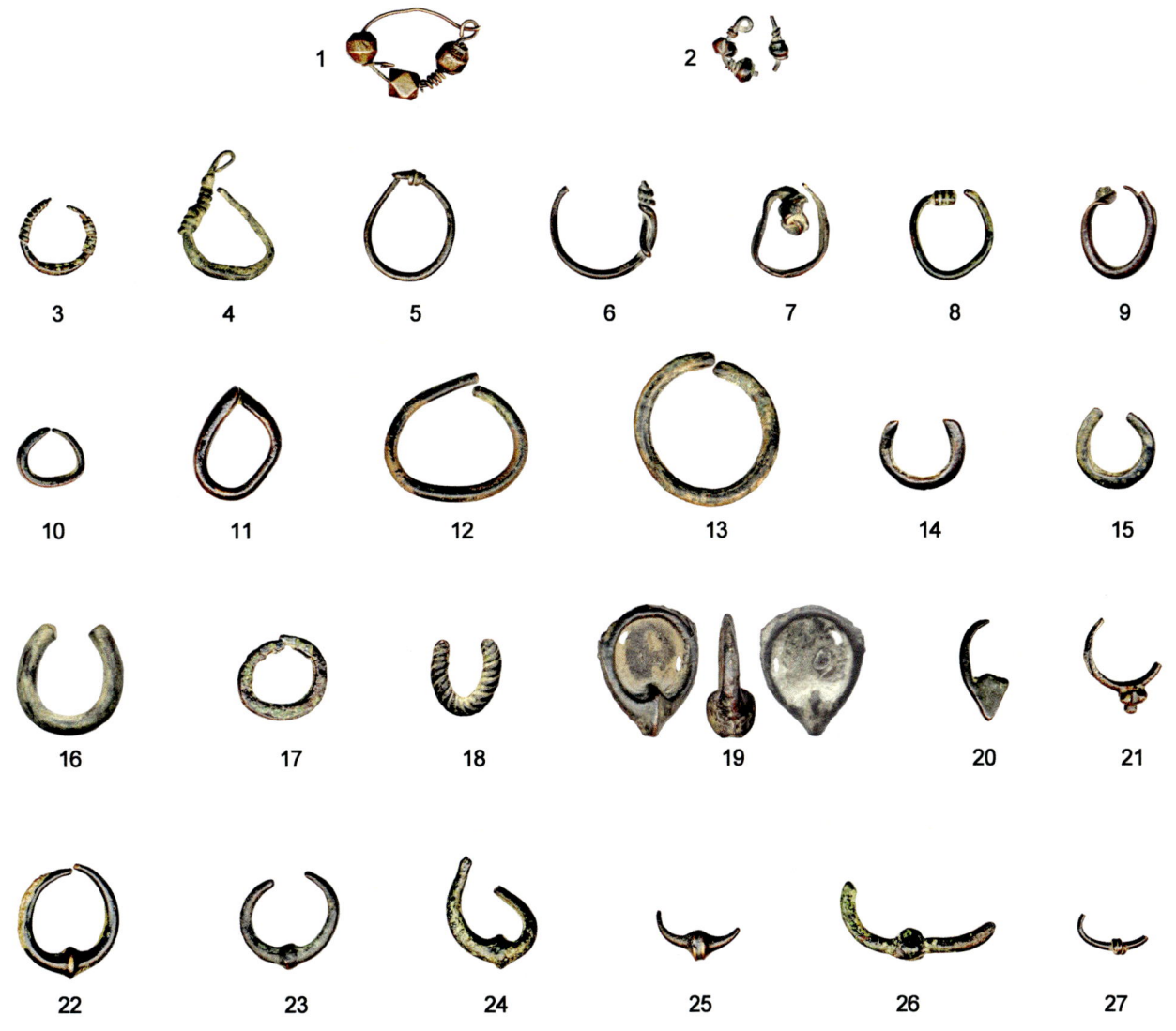

Figure 103 Ear-rings c. 1st–5th century

Fig. 103.13 – 1880.3890.a. Box 9. Plain open-ended silver alloy (?) ring. Uncleaned. 22mm x 2mm.

Fig. 103.14–15. IM.Metal.159. Two plain copper alloy hoop ear-rings.

Fig. 103.14 – 1880.3880.m. 12mm x 2mm.

Fig. 103.15 – 1880.3880.n. 12mm x 2mm.

Fig. 103.16 – 1880.3880.o. IM.Metal.159. Thick copper alloy hoop ear-ring. 16mm x 4mm.

Fig. 103.17 – 1880.3880.f. IM.Metal.159. Small, flat, copper alloy hoop ear-ring, decorated with notches on either side of the open ends. 13mm x 1.5mm.

Fig. 103.18 – 1880.3880.p. IM.Metal.159. Copper alloy hoop ear-ring with twisted rope decoration. 10mm x 2mm.

Fig. 103.19 – 1880.3713.a. IM.Metal.156 / SKM 1087. Unfinished casting of a copper alloy hoop ear-ring formed as an open ring with flaring ends joined together by a vertical rib along the junction. The bleed of excess metal in the centre and around the edge has not been removed. 2nd–3rd century AD. 18.5mm x 15mm x 7.4mm. Errington 1999, p. 229, pl. 8.22.

A similar ear-ring, but in gold and with a pearl attached at the mid-point of the hoop, was found in the 2nd–3rd-century Building I of the necropolis at Tepai Shakh (Litvinsky and Sedov 1983, p 151, pl. XXXIII.5).

Fig. 103.20 – 1880.3717.d. IM.Metal.160. Cast copper alloy fragment of a drop-shaped ear-ring with a solid lozenge at the mid-point. 14mm x 6mm.

Fig. 103.21 – 1880.3717.e. IM.Metal.160. Cast copper alloy hoop ear-ring fragment, decorated at the mid-point with a cluster of globules. 14mm x 12mm. 1st century AD or early Islamic (?).

Examples in gold or silver opening on the top attributed the 1st century AD were found at Nowruz-mahaleh in Iran, Ghazni and Uruk-Warka (Musche 1988, p. 56, pl. VIII, 1.5.1). Specimens opening on the side, one of them in gold, was found at Qasr-i Abu Nasr, old Shiraz (Whitcomb 1985, pl. 52, fig. 66.b).

Fig. 103.22–5. Cast copper alloy open rings thickening from each end towards the centre which is marked by one or two parallel and vertical ribs.

Ear-rings of this type were found in the 4th–5th-century tombs of the Tup Khona necropolis, Tajikistan (Litvinsky and Sedov 1984, pl. II.26–7; Zeimal 1985, no. 296).

Fig. 103.22 – 1880.3717.c. IM.Metal.160. 16mm x 4mm.

Fig. 103.23 – IOLC.5446. K.187. 10mm x 3mm.

Fig. 103.24 – 1880.3880.b. IM.Metal.159. Now bent out of shape. 17mm x 5mm.

Figure 104 Miscellaneous ear-rings *c.* 2nd–3rd century? (1–2); *c.* 12th–13th century (3–4)

Fig. 103.25 – 1880.3880.c. IM.Metal.159. 13mm x 4mm.

Fig. 103.26–7. Cast copper alloy rings with tapering ends and a globule at mid-point. No counterpart has been found.

Fig. 103.26 – 1880.3880.d. IM.Metal.159. Now bent out of shape. 23mm x 4mm.

Fig. 103.27 – 1880.3880.a. IM.Metal.159. The mid-point globule is formed by a double loop of thin wire. 10mm x 1mm.

Miscellaneous ear-rings

Fig. 104.1–2. Copper alloy ear-rings, cast in one piece, with a pendant and a hinged and pinned ring fastener. Kushan, 2nd–3rd century.

Fig. 104.1 – 1880.3713.b. IM.Metal.156 / SKM 1087. The U-shaped suspension ring is decorated on each face with three pseudo-rivets. It is slit and riveted at either end with the remains of the hinged ear fastener on one side. A convex stem joins it to a three-sided drop pendant ,with a recessed circle on each face. 24.7mm x 7.6mm (drop) x 2.9mm (top section).

Fig. 104.2 – 1880.3713.c. IM.Metal.156 / SKM 1087. The U-shaped suspension ring is slit and riveted at either end for the ear fastener. One rivet still survives. The pendant is three-sided, with a recessed circle on each of the oval faces and has a circular banded terminal ending in a knob. 8.3mm x 9.6mm (triangular section) x 9.6mm (top section) x 5.5mm (knob).

There is a duplicate in the Cambridge Ridgeway collection (CMAA.1927.1192). A similar ear-ring was found in Building I of the Tepai Shakh necropolis, which dated by coins to the 2nd–3rd century (Litvinsky and Sedov 1983, p. 151, pl. XXVIII.7).

Fig. 104.3–4 – 1880.3810. (**3**) IM.Metal.25 / IM 32 / SKM 1105; (**4**) IM.Metal.156 / IM 17. Pair of copper alloy ear-ring or necklace pendants cast in one piece. They have a flat pierced tang crossed at mid-point by a horizontal bar.

The pendant comprises an inverted tear-drop joined to a heart-shape (both for inlays, now missing), with a trefoil motif below. The pair were originally registered separately with groups of other miscellaneous material. 12th–13th century. 36.5mm x 10mm x 37.5mm x 10mm.

The trefoil motif at the base and the horizontal bar below the suspension ring are characteristic of Seljuq pendants. They occur in a crescent-shaped pendant from Nishapur (Allan 1982, no. 67), a pear shaped pendant from Khwarazm (Nerazik 1976, fig. 59,1) and below **Figs 113.3**, **114.1**.

A cruder version in the Cambridge Ridgeway collection (CMAA.1927.1192) combines the tear-drop/heart/trefoil motif with the double U-shaped attachment loop found on **Fig. 104.1–2**.

Fig. 104.4 – 1880.3820.d. IM.Metal.160. Cast copper alloy fragment of an ear-ring, with a heart-shaped inset for a stone and three globules below. 12th–13th century. 17mm x 9mm.

Ear-ring or necklace pendants

Fig. 105. IM.Metal.157. Copper alloy pendants in the shape of an amphora with two dolphins as handles; decorated with stippling. The amphora has a conical foot with a moulding above, a spherical body with a slightly flattened shoulder, narrow neck and moulded rim. The dolphins are stylised with a prominent dorsal fin, their tails attached to the shoulder of the vase; their heads joined with the rim and forming a hole for suspension. Late 1st century BC–1st century AD. Errington 1999, p. 229, pl. 8.26–31.

Fig. 105.1 – 1880.3714.l. 18mm x 11mm.
Fig. 105.2 – 1880.3714.g. 16mm x 11mm.
Fig. 105.3 – 1880.3714.c. The fins are missing; pierced for suspension. 17mm x 10.5mm.
Fig. 105.4 – 1880.3714.e. 18mm x 12mm.
Fig. 105.5 – 1880.3714.d. The top of the pierced suspension hole is broken. 18mm x 12mm.
Fig. 105.6 – 1880.3714.h. 18mm x 14mm.
Fig. 105.7 – 1880.3714.a. 18mm x 13mm.
Fig. 105.8 – IOLC.5483. K.264. 20mm x 15mm.
Fig. 105.9 – 1880.3714.b. 18mm x 14mm.
Fig. 105.10 – 1880.3714.i. The suspension hole is broken. 18mm x 16mm.
Fig. 105.11 – 1880.3714.f. 19mm x 11mm (13.6mm with attachment ring).
Fig. 105.12–17. The neck of the amphora and the dolphins are flat.
Fig. 105.12 – IOLC.5485. K.266. 19mm x 14mm.
Fig. 105.13 – 1880.3714.k. 22mm x 16mm.
Fig. 105.14 – IOLC.5484. K.265. 16mm x 12mm.
Fig. 105.15 – 1880.3713.l. IM.Metal.156. 17mm x 12mm.
Fig. 105.16 – 1880.3714.j. 18mm x 14mm.
Fig. 105.17 – 1880.3713.k. IM.Metal.156. The suspension hole is broken. 15mm x 11mm.

Pendants in the form of an amphora with handles in the shape of dolphins are of Hellenistic origin and first appeared around the 2nd century BC. They occur throughout the Hellenistic empire as a component in elaborate ear-rings and necklaces. A pair of ear-rings incorporating pendants of this type in the British Museum were found in a tomb at

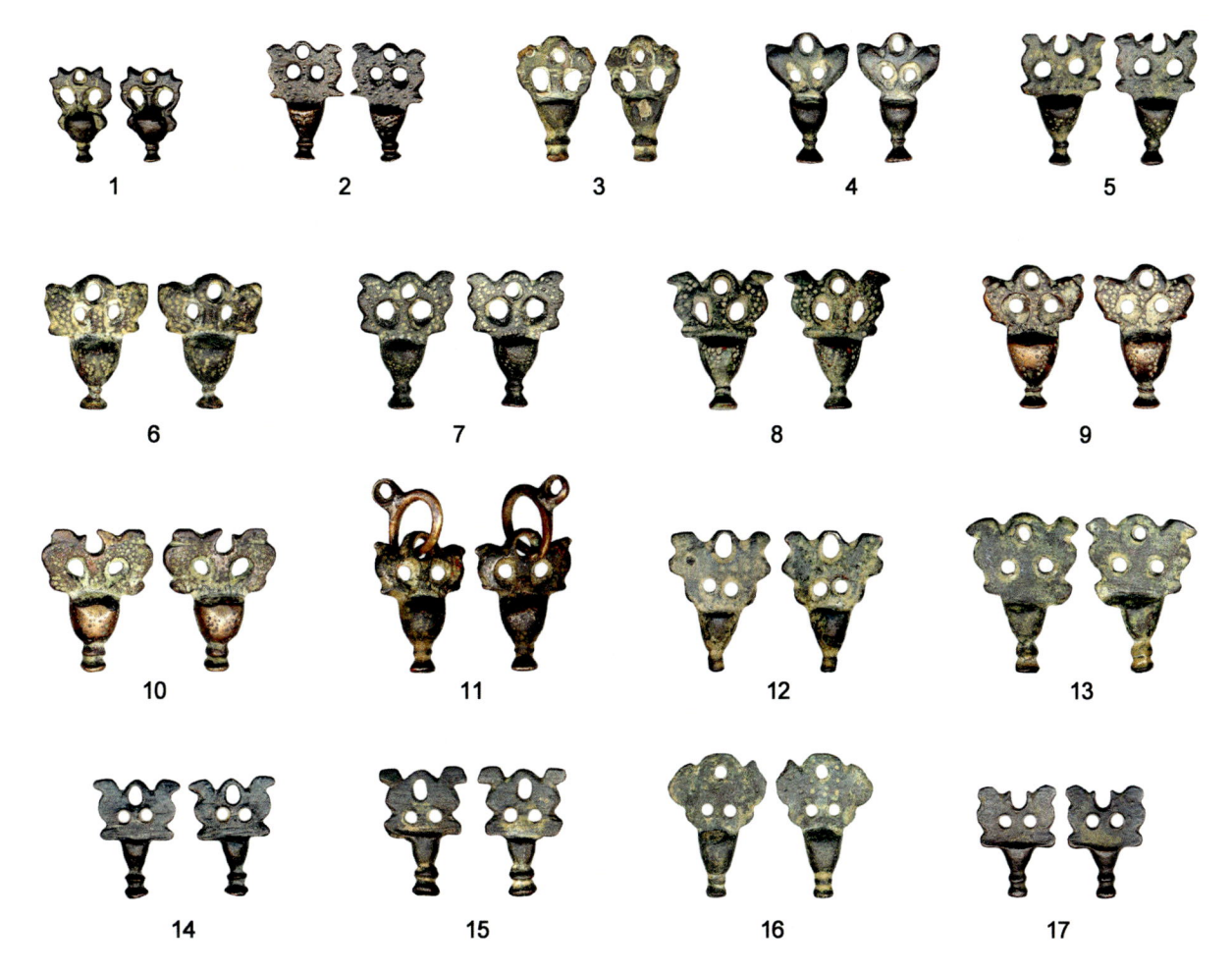

Figure 105 Ear-ring or necklace pendants

el-Ashmunein in Egypt and attributed to the 2nd century BC (Marshall 1911, nos 2332–3; 1904,0706.1). Also from Egypt is a gold example, found on a necklace together with gold Bes head pendants and mosaic beads (Christies, 7 Dec. 2011). From Syria come three in the de Clercq collection, including a pair from Amrit (De Ridder 1911, nos 269, 587– 8); one in the de Luynes collection (Fontenay 1887, p. 107); and another from Tortosa in the von Nelidow collection (Pollak 1903, pp. 76–7, 216, pl. XI).

A pair in a private collection of unspecified Bactrian provenance with a garnet body decorated at the shoulders with gold granulated triangles (Bopearachchi, Landes, Sachs 2003, no. 93) closely resemble 2nd–1st-century BC examples from Tortosa (De Ridder 1911, pp. 50, 59–61, 108–10, nos 270–89, 595–623). It seems possible therefore that the design could have been introduced into Bactria from Syria.

In most of the examples cited, the amphora body is of glass or precious stone, with a gold mount forming the base, neck and handles. One of three in the Miho collection, Japan, however, is entirely of gold (*Treasures of Ancient Bactria* 2002, fig. 188.e-g). The 1st-century AD burial 8 of barrow 55 at Kalinovka (Volgograd, south Russia) also yielded a gold example (*Scythian, Persian and Central Asian Art* 1969, p. 32, no. 32).

The necropolis of Tulchar, south-west Tajikistan, produced seven specimens with alabaster bodies mounted in gold, which show a regression from the Helenistic prototype in the form of the stylised dolphins (Mandel'stham 1966, pp. 124–6, pl. LIX.1–5, 7; 1969, pp. 525–34).

Further amphora pendants dated to the 1st–2nd century AD have been recovered from two necropolises close to Tulchar: one pair at Aruktau (Mandel'stham 1975, p. 52, no. 142, pl. XVIII.23) and two others in the burial ground BM V (Litvinsky and Sedov 1984, pp. 130–1, figs 31–2; Zeimal 1985, pp. 85, 106, nos 270–1, 273–4). Another pair was found in the burial ground of Ittifok, in the Parkhar region of south-east Tajikistan (Zeimal 1985, p. 85, 114, no. 314, IOT nos 215–16).

In Gandhara, a pair with turquoise amphora hanging from a gold flower are said to have been found in the 3rd-century BC stratum II of Bhir Mound, Taxila, but more credibly come from the 2nd–1st-century BC stratum I (Marshall 1951, pp. 106, 623, pl. 190.a). An example of the same type in the Victoria and Albert Museum is also said to be from the Taxila area, while another acquired at the same time is likely to be of similar provenance and date (Hallade 1968, p. 85, IS.16-1948, IS.19-1948, pl. IX). Yet another in the Fitzwilliam Museum, Cambridge (ANE. 9. 1970) and some in a private collection are attributed to Taxila (Tanabe 2008, nos VI 88–90).

In these Gandharan ear-rings, the dolphins have either been roughly cut from gold sheet, or they have a naturalistic appearance resembling the bronze dies recovered from the 1st century AD Indo-Parthian stratum at Sirkap (Marshall 1951, pl. 180, nos 153, 158). The dolphins in the Masson amphora pendants reflect these two tendencies. They can be

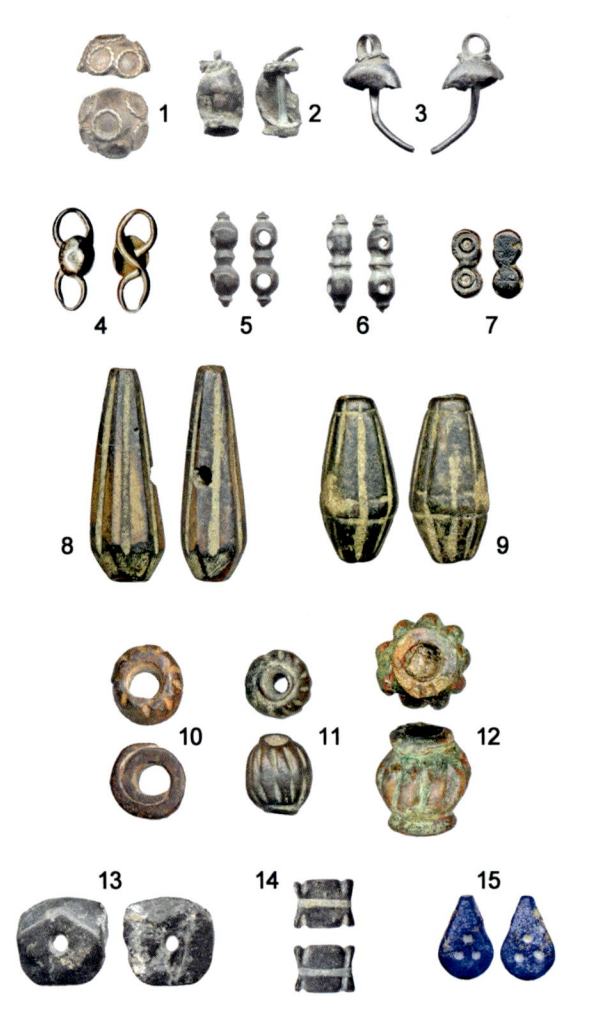

Figure 106 Beads and spacers

assumed on this basis belong to the same period, 1st century BC–1st century AD when there is evidence from Bactria and Gandhara that amphora pendants with dolphin handles were particularly in vogue.

Beads and spacers

Fig. 106.1 – 1880.3977.i. IM 33 / SKM 1103. Half a small, hollow silver sphere, possibly a bead (?) with an uneven rim; decorated on the outer surface with six small appliqué circles of twisted wire; *c.* 2nd–late 5th century. 10mm x 10mm. Kabul bazaar.

Fig. 106.2 – 1880.3981.x. IM 33 / SKM 1103 (?). Broken hollow hammered silver barrel bead, with a piece of wire threaded through its centre for an attachment loop at either end; *c.* 2nd–5th century. 10mm x 5mm. Kabul bazaar.

Fig. 106.3 – 1880.3981.w. IM 33 / SKM 1103 (?). Part of a hollow sphere of a hammered silver bead, with a wire threaded through its centre and soldered into a loop on the outer surface of the sphere; *c.* 2nd–5th century. 18mm x 8mm. Kabul bazaar.

Fig. 106.4 – 1880.3910. Box 8. Hollow domed copper alloy disc soldered to a length of wire twisted into a figure-of-eight, creating a loop on either side. 14mm x 5.6mm x 3mm.

Fig. 106.5–6. Cast copper alloy spacer beads, comprising a narrow moulding flanked on either side by a sphere, each pierced horizontally and with a tiny finial.

Fig. 106.5 – 1880.3825.a. IM.Metal.160. 13mm x 4mm.
Fig. 106.6 – 1880.3981.d. Box 4.b. 13mm x 4mm.

Fig. 106.7 – 1880.3823.f. IM.Metal.160. Copper alloy double bead made from two joined discs, each pierced horizontally and incised on one side with concentric circles. 9.3mm x 4mm x 2.4mm.

Fig. 106.8–9. Bi-conical faceted copper alloy beads, with a groove incised along the length of each face. Beads of this type are found in Khwarazm and dated 12th–13th century (Nerazik 1976, pl. 58.5, 16).

Fig. 106.8 – 1880.3823.d. IM.Metal.160. A circular hole is cut through the centre of one face, connecting at a right angle with the central perforation. 28.8mm x 9.3mm (maximum) x 4mm (minimum).

Fig. 106.9 – 1880.3823.e. IM.Metal.160. Two incised lines encircle the bead at its widest point and another at its narrowest. 22.5mm x 11.2mm (maximum) x 5.2mm (minimum).

Fig. 106.10 – 1880.3823.a. IM.Metal.160. Bead formed from a flat strip of copper alloy coiled around the central hole. The bead narrows in diameter towards one end, which is decorated with incised lines radiating around the central hole; the other end is cut flat. 5.6mm x 10mm.

Fig. 106.11 – 1880.3823.b. IM.Metal.160. Spherical copper alloy bead, decorated with regularly spaced incised lines. 10.6mm x 9.3mm.

Copper alloy beads of this type occur in Khwarazm *c.* 10th–12th century (Nerazik 1976, fig. 59.9)

Fig. 106.12 – 1880.3823.c. IM.Metal.160. Copper alloy bead, banded at each end by a slightly flared flange, with deeply incised vertical lines decorating the bulbous body. 13.7mm x 13.7mm.

Fig. 106.13 – 1880.3905. Box 8. Irregular square bead of serpentinite (?) drilled through the centre. The surface of the back is rough, probably originally flat; the front is faceted; *c.* 2nd–3rd century. 13mm x 11mm x 4mm.

A similar bead was found associated with objects from Wardak stupa 1, dated by its reliquary to year 51/AD 178 (**Vol. I, pp. 204–5, Fig. 307.8**) which suggests a possible similar date for beads of this type.

Fig. 106.14 – 1880.3909. b. Flat, rectangular bead of black serpentinite (?) with two longitudinal perforations. The surface on both sides is divided lengthwise by an incised line and notched top and bottom at either end, with slightly splayed sides. 8mm x 6mm x 2mm.

Fig. 106.15 – IOLC.5494. K.278. Drop-shaped lapis lazuli pendant. Pierced for suspension and decorated with three drilled holes on each side. 12mm x 8mm.

Triangular pendants of lapis lazuli, dated 10th–12th century, are found in Khwarazm. They probably had an amuletic value (Nerazik 1976, p. 105).

Pendants and beads with radiating spikes

Fig. 107.1 – 1880.3705.p. IM.Metal.143. Cast copper alloy, four-armed cross with knobbed tips; one ending in a flattened, pierced lug for suspension. The remains of a raised oval in the centre on two opposing sides suggests that it originally had six arms. 29.7mm x 19.2mm x 5.6mm.

Fig. 107.2 – 1880.3713.e. IM.Metal.156. Cast copper alloy cruciform pendant with six arms. One arm, slightly longer than the rest, is flattened and pierced at the tip for suspension. The attached wire loop is soldered to a globule

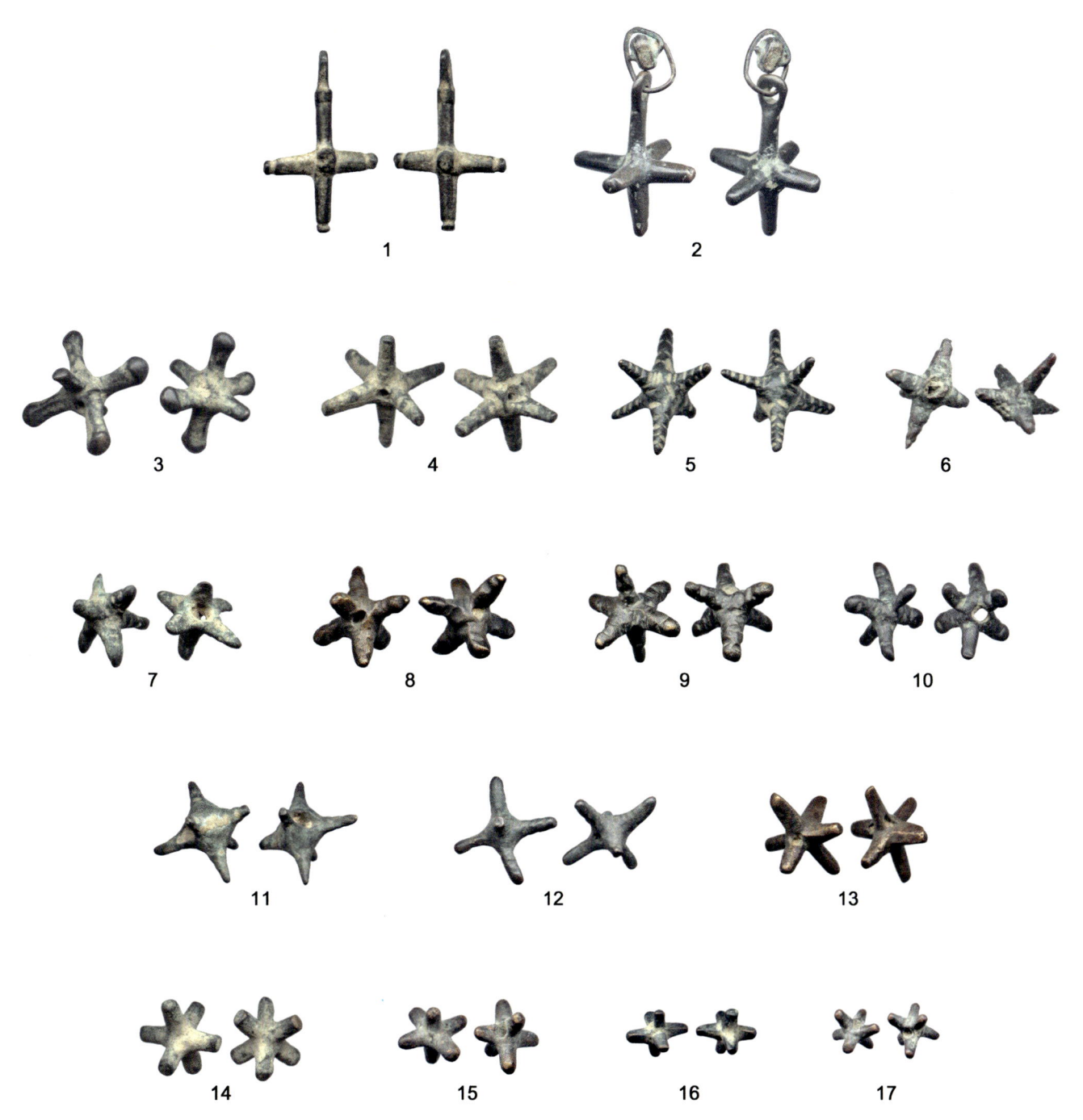

Figure 107 Pendants and beads with radiating spikes

or bead at one end. 28.3mm x 22.5mm x 11mm (loop) x 6mm (bead). Errington 1999, p. 229, pl. 8.40.

Fig. 107.3–17. IM.Metal.143. Cast copper alloy beads pierced through the centre for attachment and with six radiating spikes, mostly with rounded tips and each decorated with incised parallel lines. The graded size of the examples suggests they were possibly strung together as a necklace; *c.* 1st–6th century. Errington 1999, p. 229, pl. 8.39–43. Four more examples are in the Cambridge Ridgeway collection (CMAA.1927.1192).

Fig. 107.3 – 1880.3705.i. 23mm x 17.8mm.
Fig. 107.4 – 1880.3705.a. 24.3mm x 22.5mm.
Fig. 107.5 – 1880.3705.b. The tip of one arm has broken off. 24.5mm x 18.3mm.
Fig. 107.6 – 1880.3705.n. The sixth arm is missing. 17.5mm x 14.1mm.
Fig. 107.7 – 1880.3705.d. 17.5mm x 16.4mm.
Fig. 107.8 – 1880.3705.k. 19.6mm x 18.8mm.
Fig. 107.9 – 1880.3705.l. 19.8mm x 16.9mm.
Fig. 107.10 – 1880.3705.c. 18.5mm x 16.2mm.
Fig. 107.11 – 1880.3705.e. 19.1mm x 17.4mm.
Fig. 107.12 – 1880.3705.o. 19mm x 9.4mm.
Fig. 107.13 – 1880.3705.j. 18.8mm x 16.6mm.
Fig. 107.14 – 1880.3705.m. 15.6mm x 14.9mm.
Fig. 107.15 – 1880.3705.f. 14mm x 12mm.
Fig. 107.16 – 1880.3705.g. 10.2mm x 9.5mm.
Fig. 107.17 – 1880.3705.h. 10.5mm x 8.8mm.

Amulet pendants

Cast copper alloy amulet pendants in the form of human figures with an attachment loop on the flat reverse, *c.* 1200–750 BC. The unsoiled condition and suggested date indicate they were acquired in Kabul bazaar.

Fig. 108.1–2. A figure standing to front. Both arms are

Catalogue of Ornamental Metalwork and Miscellaneous Artefacts | 271

bent at the elbow, holding in each crook a palm leaf which fans out above each shoulder. The head is crowned with a small cap or topknot. The eyes are rendered as a dot in circle.

Fig. 108.1 – IOLC 5482. K.263. The legs are broken and missing. 20mm x 15mm.

Fig. 108.2 – 1880.3677b. IM.Metal.13. The elongated head is triangular in section with the nose extending from the top of the skull. There is a dot in circle device in the centre of the chest. The right leg is missing; the straight left leg is square in section and decorated with parallel incisions. 30mm x 15mm. Errington 1999, p. 229, pl. 8.38.

Fig.108.3 – 1880.3677a. IM.Metal.13. A figure standing to front with legs apart. The head and cap are triangular in section. The cap is pointed with a narrow rim and a tuft on the top. The nose and eyes and device in the centre of chest are rendered as a dot in circle. Lying across the shoulders and the back of the neck is a lizard-like animal with a large head and a tail. The right arm is bent at the elbow; the left hanging at the side. Worn parallel incisions are visible on the left leg. 29mm x 12mm. Errington 1999, p. 229, pl. 8.36.

Fig. 108.4 – 1880.3677c. IM.Metal.13. A human figure, standing with legs apart and both arms extended outwards from the body. The back of the head is a flat disc bearing an incised cross. The face is roughly oval with a pointed top. 29mm x 12mm. Errington 1999, p. 229, pl. 8.37.

Bronze, cast amulet pendants in the shape of a 3–4cm high standing human figure occur over a long period at various places in northern Iran and Central Asia. Few come from controlled excavations. Most have been purchased on the open market and have therefore neither a firm provenance nor date. With the exception of a few which have modelling, albeit crude, on the back, the majority have a flat back with a suspension loop attached. The legs are square in section, while the arms are occasionally extended, but more generally akimbo with the hands clasped at waist or chest level. Among the examples from clandestine excavations, six are in the Godard collection (De Waele 1982, fig. 149, nos 293–6, fig. 220, nos 399, 400), one in the Adam collection (Moorey 1974, p. 165, no. 145), and two in the Ashmolean Museum, Oxford (Moorey 1971, pl. 66, figs 429–30). Those in the Godard collection are undoubtedly from Iran since they were acquired by him when he was director of the archaeological services there between 1928 and 1960. De Waele shows that they come from northern Iran, i.e. south of the Caspian Sea, and attributes to them a date from the late 2nd to the beginning of the 1st millennium BC. Wilber (rugreview.com) gives Luristan, a region located between Mesopotamia (Iraq), Nehavend and ancient Elam (Khuzistan), as the provenance of the example in the Missouri Museum collection. This is because he bought it in Tehran soon after the plundering of Luristan which followed the chance discovery in 1928 of the first Lur burial.

According to Moorey, the example in the Adam collection, which he dates Iron Age I or II (*c.* 1200–750 BC), is supposed to have been found in Azerbaijan or Gilan, i.e. either east or south of the Caspian Sea. As for the Ashmolean Museum figures, he seems to suggest an origin in central Iran or Luristan and an 8th-century BC date, mentioning firstly, eight bronze specimens from burials of the 8th-century BC necropolis B at Sialk, near Kashan (central Iran), where they were placed on the chest of the deceased (Ghirshman 1938, p. 58, fig. 6, pl. XXVII.2, pl. LII, S.582, pl. LXXV, S.918, pl. LXXIII, S.939). Secondly, he notes that specimens recovered from burials in the Kazabad mound near Hulailan, Luristan, were claimed by Stein, on the basis of accompanying objects, to be no earlier than the 1st millennium BC (Stein 1938, pp. 331–2).

It should be noted that Moorey's connections are not entirely convincing, as Stein does not describe or illustrate the figures he found at Kazabad and, moreover, the Sialk examples are stylistically different from those in the Ashmolean Museum. Their sex is denoted: one is masculine, the others feminine. They are 5–6cm high, their arms are akimbo, their legs joined together and they have pierced suspension holes, indicating that northern Iran rather than Luristan is their most likely provenance. This view is consistent with the fact that excavations of Lur Bronze and Iron Age burials by Van den Berghe (1968, 1970a–b, 1973a–b), and more recently by Haerinck and Overlaert (2004), do not record any examples of such figures. Furthermore none appear among the antiquities from Luristan in the David Weill collection (Amiet 1976), nor in the published catalogues of the Graeffe collection (Godard 1954) and the Coiffard collection of Luristan bronzes (Amiet 1963), although these may not have been fully published.

Beyond their general shape, the Begram specimens share with these examples of probable northern Iranian origin some further details. So, for instance, **Fig. 108.2** and an example in the Ashmolean Museum (Moorey 1971, no. 430) both represent the eyes as a dot in circle and repeat the same motif on the chest. **Fig. 108.2** also has the same rendering of the nose and mouth as an example in the Godard collection (De Waele 1982, no. 296). It may be added that the stick and plume held by **Fig. 108.1–2** is not dissimilar from the depictions of the arms of female figurines, 9–14cm high, with a flat body, short legs, a large head with open eye-sockets and prominent pierced ears, which are reported from the Piravend region (north of Luristan) and attributed to the 8th century BC (Amiet 1976, fig. 230; Moorey 1971, fig. 211). Because of their artistic links with these figures from northern Iran, there is therefore little doubt that the Begram figures share a similar prototype. That they come from the same region and are of the same date is however not certain. Indeed, they display some features, such as the headdress and parallel incisions across the legs, which are not met with in the northern Iranian figures. They could accordingly have been produced locally. Furthermore, there is some evidence that figures of the same sort continued being made long after the 8th century BC. Burials in the Kara-bulak cemetery in Ferghana (eastern Uzbekistan), dated 2nd century BC–7th century AD (Gorbunova 1986, p. 177), have produced four examples, all 30mm high, standing with legs apart and square in section, the arms akimbo and the hands either on the hips or the belly. One has a pointed hat (Gorbunova 1986, pp. 143, 331, pl. LI.2–5). The early medieval city of Penjikent in Sogdia, western Tajikistan (Belenitsky *et al.* 1973, fig. 56.7), dated 6th–8th century (Formozov *et al.* 1977, p. 145), has yielded an example, also 30mm high, with a pointed hat and the arms ending in stumps. All have minimal face modelling with the mouth and eyes rendered as elongated holes. The back of the Penjikent example is also modelled. When compared with these Central Asian examples, the Begram anthropomorphic figures seem to be earlier and moreover closer to their northern Iranian counterparts. They may be tentatively dated *c*. 8th–2nd century BC.

Charms
Fig. 108.5 – 1880.3682.b. IM.Metal.21. Cast copper alloy charm in the shape of a miniature boot, with a pierced lug at the top; *c*. 1st millennium BC (?). 17.5mm x 12.4mm x 4.9mm. Errington 1999, p. 230, pl. 9.17.

A similar pendant has been found in north Luristan, Iran, and attributed to the beginning of the 1st millennium BC (De Waele 1982, p. 172, no. 272). Another specimen, found at Khurvin, Iran, has been dated 9th–8th century BC (Ghirshman 1964). Two comparable examples in the British Museum are said to come from Kirman (ex Sir Percy Sykes collection, 1921,0220.22–3). A final example was found at the Nishapur site of Falaki, which suggests a date *c*. 8th–13th century AD (Allan 1982, pp. 70–1, no. 67). However, Allan says that it is unique (p. 32), so it could be assignable to the 1st millennium BC, as could also the Begram pendant.

Fig. 108.6 – 1880.3682.c. IM.Metal.21. Cast copper alloy charm in the shape of a miniature jug with a handle; *c*. 8th century AD. 20.9mm x 12mm x 4.8mm. Errington 1999, p. 230, pl. 9.15.

A comparable charm from Pendjikent, Tajikistan, is dated 7th–8th century (Belenitsky *et al*. 1973, p. 92, fig. 56). Another found at Kurkat in north Tajikistan is dated 3rd–7th century (Negmatov 1979, p. 336, fig. 2).

Bells
Fig. 109.1 – 1880.3687.d. IM.Metal.25 / IM 32 / SKM 1105. Cast copper alloy, faceted bell with a rounded rim and surmounted by a flat, pierced lug. A circular hole near the apex of the bell probably served as the attachment point for the tongue (now missing); 3rd–6th century (?). 33mm x 21.7mm.

Fig. 109.2 – 1880.3687.e. IM.Metal.25 / IM 32 / SKM 1105. Cast copper alloy bell with a hole in the body for attaching the tongue and a pierced lug at the apex; *c*. 3rd–7th century. 18.2mm x 12.1mm.

Fig. 109.3 – IOLC.5486. K.267. Broken copper alloy bell-decorated with incised lines and a zig-zag pattern. It has a pierced lug for suspension, and is also pierced through the body. 20mm x 15mm.

Pendants attached to barrel beads
Fig. 110.1–4. IM.Metal.160. Cast copper alloy pendants, comprising a slightly domed disc with a flat reverse, attached either to a single barrel-bead or to two superimposed barrel-beads, pierced laterally, decorated with a horizontal ridge below and with an incised line at either end; *c*. 4th century BC (?).

The pendants resemble silver examples consisting of a hemispherical drop topped by a T-shape in a 4th-century BC necklace excavated from Bhir Mound, Taxila (Marshall 1951, p. 627, no. 55, pl. 192.c).

Figure 108 Amulet pendants (1–4); charms 5–6)

Fig. 110.1 – 1880.3820.a. 18mm x 11mm.
Fig. 110.2 – 1880.3820.b. The domed disc has a large notch at the base. 19mm x 11mm.
Fig. 110.3 – 1880.3820.c. IM.Metal.160. 26mm x 11mm.
Fig. 110.4 – 1880.3979. IM 57 / SKM 1096. 24.3mm x 10mm.
Fig. 110.5–6. Cast copper alloy, openwork obcordate pendant and fragment, triangular in section with three globules in the centre of the inner point of the inverted heart shape. A short, cylindrical, horizontally grooved stem at the top joins a spherical bead pierced laterally. The back is flat. Early 1st century AD.

Comparable pendants in gold occur on two necklaces excavated from the Indo-Scythian/Indo-Parthian stratum III at Sirkap, Taxila (Marshall 1951: p. 627, pl. 193, nos 57–8).

Figure 109 Bells

Catalogue of Ornamental Metalwork and Miscellaneous Artefacts | 273

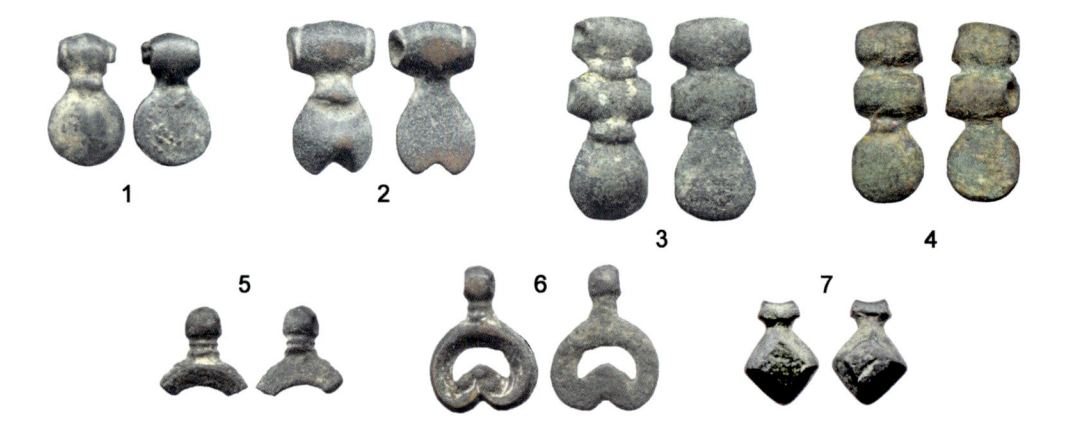

Figure 110 Pendants attached to barrel beads

The site also yielded obcordate bronze elements, all presumably dies, 'on which sheet-metal of gold, silver, copper or bronze could be hammered out with the help of punches and converted into pieces of jewellery' (Marshall 1951: pl. 179, no. 76; pl. 181, nos 184–6).

Fig. 110.5 – 1880.3981.a. Box 4.b. Fragment 10.6mm x 12mm x 2.6mm.

Fig. 110.6 – 1889.3713.d. IM.Metal.156. 19.5mm x 15mm x 2.5mm.

Fig. 110.7 – 1880.3682.d. IM.Metal.21. Cast copper alloy, lozenge-shaped pendant. The ring for suspension is broken with the result that the object resembles a vase. 1st–2nd century AD. 14mm x 10.2mm x 5.7mm. Errington 1999, p. 230, pl. 9.14.

A small blue glazed bead pendant of similar shape was found in 2nd–3rd century AD Building I of the Tepai Shakh necropolis in southern Tajikistan (Litvinsky and Sedov 1983, pl. XXXIII.31).

Pyramidal ornaments or amulets

Fig. 111.1–3. IM.Metal.153. Cast copper alloy ornaments or amulets in the form of a stepped pyramid on a square undecorated base, and surmounted by a flat ring which is pierced off-centre so that it is open at the top; *c.* 1st–3rd century AD. Although allied in form to pyramidal seals (**Fig. 72**), the lack of any image or means of attaching a gem on the base indicates that they never functioned as seals.

Fig. 111.1 – 1880.3709.a. The base has a small rounded foot at each corner. 25mm x 14.6mm x 5.8mm.

There is a duplicate in the Cambridge Ridgeway collection (CMAA.1927.1192). A similar example was found

Figure 111 Pyramidal ornaments or amulets

in a 1st–3rd-century tomb at Parkhar in south Tajikistan (Zeimal 1985, pp. 111, 113, no. 309). A more sophisticated example, in gold with three granules at each corner of the steps is in the Miho collection. It is attributed to the 3rd–2nd century BC (*Treasures of Ancient Bactria*, 2002, p. 136, fig. 189.e).

Fig. 111.2 – 1880.3709.b. 17.6mm x 11.6mm x 3.1mm.

Fig. 111.3 – 1880.3709.c. The base has a pair of random incised lines across it. 13.9mm x 7.3mm x 2.4mm.

Pendants *c.* 8th–12th century

Fig. 112.1 – IOLC.5491. K.275. Cast copper alloy square pendant, with two pierced lugs for suspension. The back is flat; the sloping sides form a bevelled edge probably for a paste infill; *c.* 8th–10th century. 24mm x 19mm.

Fig. 112.2 – 1880.3820.n. IM.Metal.160. Cast copper alloy square pendant, with two loops for suspension; decorated on the front with a punched dot and double circle encircled by eight smaller dot in circle motifs; *c.* 8th–10th century. 18.3mm x 16.3mm x 2.7mm.

Fig. 112.3 – 1880.3687.n. IM.Metal.25 / IM 32 / SKM 1105. Large flat copper alloy triangular pendant, with four regularly spaced pierced lugs along the base and a suspension ring at the apex, with two parallel mouldings below. Both sides are covered with manufacturing scratches and decorated with randomly punched dot in circle motifs. Islamic, *c.* 8th–10th century. 46.8mm x 36mm.

See **Fig. 96.1–2** for a discussion of the longevity of the dot in circle motif. It is found on a number of objects from Begram primarily of the Islamic period.

Fig. 112.4 – 1880.3903. Cast copper alloy pendant in the shape of a slightly convex leaf, with its tip and the top section of the lug missing and one side notched and damaged. The convex surface is decorated with three dot in circle motifs. Islamic, *c.* 8th–10th century. 33.5mm x 19.8mm.

Fig. 112.5 – IOLC.5490. K.274. Cast copper alloy pendant, with a trumpet-shaped floral motif flaring outwards from a bulbous horizontal moulding below the suspension ring. The floral motif was originally flat (now bent on one side) and is covered with fine manufacturing scratches; *c.* 8th–12th century. 28mm x 20mm.

Fig. 112.6 – 1880.3904.a. Box 9. Cast copper alloy talismanic pendant; drop-shaped with an elongated trefoil motif at the bottom and a pierced circle for attachment at

Figure 112 Islamic pendants *c.* 8th–13th century (1–6, 10–20); 18th–19th century (7–9)

the top. Both faces are covered with incised cursive Arab inscriptions: *bism allah rahman al-rahim* (in the name of God, the compassionate, the merciful). Islamic, *c.* 10th–13th century. 47.8mm x 12.3mm x 2.7mm. (Inscription read and translated by V.S. Curtis).

Fig. 112.7 – 1880.3685.e. IM.Metal.23. Crumpled and broken, hollow silver sheet metal pendant. It has a small attachment ring at the top, with a small disc in front, decorated with embossed dots; and a globular trefoil motif at the bottom. A diamond-shaped plaque with embossed dots decorates the upper body with a small plain embossed disc

below. 18th–19th century. 26.2mm x 6.2mm. From Kabul bazaar; associated in registration records with **Fig. 112.8**.

The ornament resembles, to some degree, bronze dies from Sirkap, Taxila (Marshall 1951, pl. 179, nos 46, 50–1). On some ear-rings from Sirkap and Bhir Mound, appliquéd discs are attached in a similar way to the front of the suspension rings (Marshall 1951, pl. 190, nos 1, 3–4), but the design persists, for it is also found on late Islamic ornaments from Kabul (Janata 1981, pls 28.3, 68.4).

Fig. 112.8 – 1880.3685.f. IM.Metal.23. Silver repoussé pendant made of two separate lozenge-shaped pieces,

Catalogue of Ornamental Metalwork and Miscellaneous Artefacts | 275

domed in the centre and decorated with a row of granules along the two lower flattened edges. A soldered ring at the top holds the two lozenges together. A chain of four links is attached to the ring; *c.* 18th century (?). 14mm x 11.8mm; 20.5mm (chain). From Kabul bazaar.

Similar ornaments have been recorded as part of a necklace, acquired in Kabul, which included coins of the Qajar king Fath 'Ali Shah (1797–1834) and also as ear-rings (Scerrato and Taddei 1963, pls XIII.125, IX.152; Janata 1981, pls 28.1, 28.3).

Fig. 112.9 – 1880.3825.b. IM.Metal.160. Silver chain with two small tear-drop shaped plates attached to one end. Possibly an ear-ring. 33.1mm x 3.3mm (chain); 5.4mm (plate).

This type of pendant appears in numerous Islamic pieces of jewellery, possibly of the 18th century, acquired at Ghazni, Afghanistan and Mingora, Swat, Pakistan (Scerrato and Taddei 1963, pl. XII.204; pl. XV.95, 336).

Fig. 112.10 – 1880.3904.b. Box 9. Small silver repoussé pendant with a mastic backing; lozenge-shaped with rounded angles, topped by a small rectangle decorated with a rosette, and a suspension loop. The surface is decorated with a lotus bud flanked on each side by a small six-petalled rosette and surrounded by small hemispherical globules; *c.* 9th–11th century (?). 18.8mm x 10.3mm. From Kabul bazaar.

Fig. 112.11–13. Three cast copper alloy pendant beads in the shape of a horizontally elongated hexagon, with a notched tube attached to the top edge for suspension; *c.* 8th–12th century.

Fig. 112.11 – 1880.3821.c. IM.Metal.160. The front has a circular hole for a stone insert in the centre. Both front and back are slightly rounded. 11.4mm x 18.7mm x 5.4mm.

Fig. 112.12 – 1880.3821.b. IM.Metal.160. The front is slightly rounded, the back flat. 9mm x 16.8mm x 4.4mm.

Fig. 112.13 – 1880.3981.c. Box 4.b. The front is slightly rounded, the back flat. 9mm x 14.3mm x 4mm.

Fig. 112.14–15. Two cast copper alloy beads or pendants; semi-circular in outline, with a straight top edge joined to a horizontal tube for suspension; *c.* 8th–12th century.

Fig. 112.14 – 1880.3821.a. IM.Metal.160. The suspension tube is notched. 10.7mm x 11.9mm x 3mm.

Fig. 112.15 – 1880.3981.b. Box 4.b. The front surface is decorated with an engraved triangular tree flanked by two birds (?). 15.8mm x 17mm x 3mm.

Fig. 112.16 – 1880.3821.d. IM.Metal.160. Cast copper alloy flat trapezoidal bead. The profile of the narrow suspension tube along the upper edge is concave at either end. In the centre of the front is a circular hole for a paste or stone insert, now missing; *c.* 8th–12th century. 11.6mm x 10.6mm x 3mm.

This bead is stylistically close to an 8th–13th-century bronze trapezoidal pendant, with a horizontal rib along its upper edge topped by two suspension rings, from Tepe Madraseh, Nishapur (Allan 1982, p. 96, no. 151).

Fig. 112.17–20. Cast copper alloy pendants; shield-shaped, curving down to a point in the centre, with a straight ridge across the top of the obverse, above which are two suspension loops. In the centre is a round depression for a stone or inlay. The back (including the loops) is flat and undecorated. Islamic, *c.* 12th–13th century.

No counterpart has been found. However, the horizontal ridge along their upper edge recalls the already cited pendant from Nishapur (Allan 1982, p. 96, no. 151). Suspension rings that are flat at the back, with a horizontal bar below are characteristic of the 12th–13th-century.

Fig. 112.17 – 1880.3686.a. IM.Metal.24. The hole contains a piece of glazed turquoise inlay. 14.8mm x 11.5mm. Errington 1999, p. 230, pl. 9.13.

Fig. 112.18 – 1880.3822.a. IM.Metal.160. 22.7mm x 18.4mm.

Fig. 112.19 – IOLC.5492. K.276. The depression is perforated. 19mm x 16mm.

Fig. 112.20 – IOLC.5493. K.277. In the centre of the obverse is an etched foliate design, and on the reverse, a three-lobed leaf pointing downwards. Both sides have traces of a white deposit. 18mm x 13mm.

Islamic crescent-shaped pendants

Fig. 113.1–5. IM.Metal.24. Flat, cast copper alloy pendants, the top edge divided into two crescents with a knob-like suspension ring at each end and the sides curving downwards to meet at a centre point along the bottom edge. Islamic, *c.* 9th–11th century.

Fig. 113.1 – 1880.3686.h. The surviving suspension ring forms a bulging knob at the front above a double moulding. In the centre of the obverse is a drop-shaped lotus bud, outlined and in high relief, flanked on either side by the cut-out image of a walking, caparisoned elephant. On the reverse are traces of a roundel with the drop on either side containing a half palmette. 40.5mm x 35.9mm x 5.4mm (thickness with drop). An intact duplicate is in the Cambridge Ridgeway collection (CMAA.1927.1192). Errington 1999, p. 230, pl. 9.10.

Suspension rings with a ridge below are characteristic of 10th–13th century Islamic pendants while lotus buds in high relief emphasised by a shallower outline appear on 8th–9th-century water bottles from Iran (Dahncke 1988, pp. 72, 76) and 10th-century examples from Khurasan (Melikian-Chirvani 1982, p. 41).

Fig. 113.2 – 1880.3686.f. IM.Metal.24. Brass-washed pendant. In the centre of the top is a small projection between two pierced circles; the edge then curves to a point at the sides which is also pierced (now broken on the left side). In the centre of the bottom edge is a small projecting round lug. The front has a prominent raised circular bezel for a stone or paste insert, flanked on either side by the cut-out design of a walking elephant carrying a palanquin. On the back is a roundel containing a walking hare (?) with a bird of prey on its back pecking at its head. Above is a rectangular cartouche with an Arabic inscription *al-malik al-malik* (king of kings) and in each of the upper corners a bird. Islamic, *c.* 10th–11th century. 44.7mm x 55.4mm x 5.4mm (with circular mount). Errington 1999, p. 230, pl. 9.11.

Fig. 113.3 – 1880.3686.g. Pendant (the left side missing). The surviving suspension ring has a notched moulding. The extant lower edge has a short, splayed, three-lobed projection in the centre. On the front is an arabesque in low relief of birds encircled by foliate scrolls. The tendrils form a heart enclosing a trifoliate leaf in the

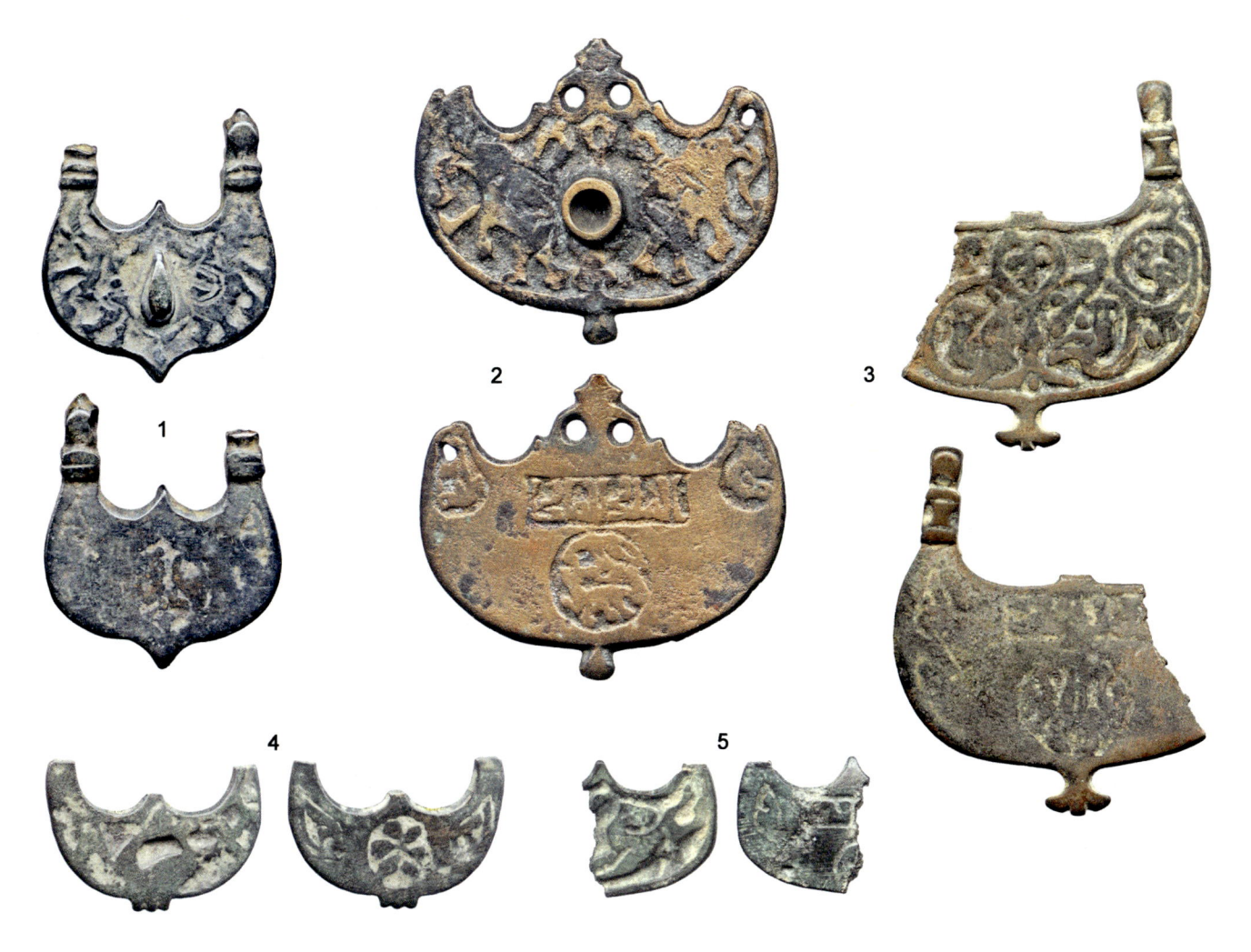

Figure 113 Islamic crescent-shaped pendants

upper centre of the design. The roundel on the reverse has two confronted birds in foliage, flanked on either side by a half palmette. The worn Arabic inscription in a rectangular cartouche above probably reads *al-malik al-malik* (king of kings). Islamic, *c.* 10th–11th century. 52.8mm x 47.6mm x 2.5mm.

The decorative motifs are characteristic of early Islamic metalwork. The trifoliate leaf within a heart-shape is found on an 11th-century bronze tray from Khurasan in the Kabul Museum (Melikian-Chirvani 1975, pl. VII, fig. 2), on an 11th–12th century flacon in the Bumiller collection (Bumiller 1993, p. 89, no. 110b, BC-708), and on a pair of 8th–13th-century heart-shaped ornaments found at the Nishapur site of Tepe Madraseh (Allan 1982, p. 64, nos 26–7). Stems enclosing a bird appear on an 8th–13th century incense burner acquired in Nishapur (Allan 1982, pp. 86–7, no. 102). The motif of a bird in a circular medallion also occurs on a 12th-century ewer from Khurasan (Melikian-Chirvani 1982, p. 85, no. 19).

Fig. 113.4 – 1880.3686.i. The two suspension rings are missing and the tip of the point at the centre of the upper edge is also broken. In the centre of the lower edge is a short schematic trefoil. On the front is a crudely executed bird (probably a peacock) flanked by vegetal motifs. The roundel on the reverse has a six-petalled flower in low relief, flanked on either side by a leaf. 21.6mm x 32.9mm x 1.9mm. Errington 1999, p. 230, pl. 9.12.

The decoration on the reverse is similar to that on pins **Fig. 102.4–6**.

Fig. 113.5 – 1880.3686.j. IM.Metal.24. Fragment. On the extant front is a running feline, with head looking backwards and legs extended, fitting the curved outline of the pendant. On the back are the remains of a roundel with an Arabic inscription in a rectangular cartouche above and flanked by a leaf. 19.6mm x 19.8mm.

Islamic drop-shaped pendants

Fig. 114.1 – 1880.3907.a. Box 9. Large, cast copper alloy, leaf-shaped pendant, with a centred smaller cut-out of the same shape immediately above a five-lobed projection at the base; and a pierced suspension lug at the top. On both sides the surface is decorated in shallow relief with a large rosette within a circle flanked on either side with arabesques. The cinquefoil projection at the base may contain the word *Allah*. Islamic, *c.* 10th–12th century. 72.3mm x 45.5mm.

A pendant of similar shape in the Berlin Museum für Islamische Kunst is said to come from the eastern Mediterranean, and is dated 9th–10th century (Gladiss 1998, p. 111, no. 50). A comparable pendant, of similar but inverted shape, was found at Qanat Tepe, Nishapur, and dated 8th–12th century (Allan 1982, pp. 70–1, no. 65). Two from Khwarazm (northern Uzbekistan) are dated 11th–13th and 12th–13th century respectively (Nerazik 1976, p. 105, fig. 59.2–3; Vishnevskaia 1963, fig. 4.26). The decoration recalls

Figure 114 Islamic drop-shaped pendants

a 10th–12th-century pendant from Uzbekistan (*CAAU* 1991, p. 157, no. 669).

Fig. 114.2–3. Cast copper alloy, drop-shaped pendants, rounded on the front with a flat reverse. Islamic, *c.* 10th–12th century.

Fig. 114.2 – 1880.3907.b. Box 9. The pendant has a rounded, slightly ridged projection at the bottom and a small moulding at the apex surmounted by a suspension ring. On the front are two worn horizontal bands filled with closely spaced vertical lines. The patina suggests it may have originally been brass washed. 52mm x 20.8mm x 4.9mm.

A similar pendant, dated 8th–mid 12th century, was found at the site of Sabz Pushan, Nishapur (Allan 1982, pp. 70–1, no. 66); another from Samarkand is dated 10th–12th century (*CAAU* 1991, vol. 2, p. 157, no. 670).

Fig. 114.3 – 1880.3686.c. IM.Metal.24. Pendant lacking its suspension ring. The division between the thicker triangular upper part and thinner curved lower part is marked on both sides by a prominent horizontal line. Each section on both sides is decorated with worn vegetal designs in low relief within a broad plain border. 38.7mm x 20.2mm x 2.7mm (upper section)

A 10th–12th century pendant from Uzbekistan has its surface partitioned horizontally and decorated with foliage in the same way (*CAAU* 1991, no. 668).

Fig. 114.4–5. Cast copper alloy pendants decorated

with vegetal motifs in shallow relief within a plain border.

Fig. 114.4 – 1880.3686.b. IM.Metal.24. Drop-shaped pendant, rounded on one face, flat on the other, with a ridge at the apex surmounted by a suspension ring and a small pointed projection at the base. Both faces are decorated in low relief within a wide border: the rounded side with an interlaced knot design; the flat one with an arabesque. Islamic, c.12th century. 50.5mm x 17.8mm x 5.5mm. Errington 1999, p. 230, pl. 9.5.

Interlaced foliate designs in repoussé with engraved details also occur on a bronze 12th-century tray from Ghor province, Khurasan, in the Muza-i Rawza, Ghazni (Melikian-Chirvani 1975, p. 59, pl. 1, fig. 5).

Fig. 114.5 – 1880.3686.d. IM.Metal.24. Cast copper alloy tetrahedron-shaped pendant with a small pierced lug at the base, which originally would have supported a pendant. The back is flat, its surface divided by an inverted T-shaped band, decorated with a vertical rope pattern. The two resulting upper triangles contain addorsed S-shaped scrolls; the pentagon below contains an arabesque. The front is divided into four triangular planes. The two elongated triangular surfaces are partitioned into three sections containing mirror S-shaped scrolls, a simplified rope pattern and a paisley motif. The two smaller planes below are also decorated. Islamic, c.10th–12th century. 40.6mm x 17.7mm x 6.5mm. Errington 1999, p. 230, pl. 9.6.

A 10th–12th-century pendant with comparable decoration was found in Uzbekistan (*CAAU* 1991, no. 669). The S-shaped sroll motif appears on two 12th-century bronze trays from Khurasan, now in the Herat Museum and Kabul Museum respectively (Melikian-Chirvani 1975, pp. 60–1, pl. 1, figs 7–8).

Fig. 114.6 – 1880.3686.e. IM.Metal.24. Cast copper alloy, angular drop pendant with a flat trapezoidal back, pointed at the base and with a pierced suspension lug at the apex. The front is divided into four inclined facets with a prominent vertical rib in the centre. The two outer facets are notched, giving an arrow-like appearance to the base of the pendant. Islamic, c.12th–13th century. 37.9mm x 12.1mm x 6.7mm. Errington 1999, p. 230, pl. 9.7.

The prominent central rib is found on 12th–13th-century mortars from western Iran and Seljuq Anatolia (Melikian-Chirvani 1982, p. 159, no. 67; Erginsoy 1978, fig. 200.b).

Miscellaneous pendants

Fig. 115.1 – 1880.3907.c. Box 9. Cast copper alloy, large, flat, leaf-shaped pendant with a pierced lug for attachment at the top. It is decorated on one side with an outlined arabesque comprising a bud with a bulbous tip and two curved stems radiating from the centre of the base. On the other side are seven lines of a worn and illegible (possibly pseudo-) Arabic inscription. Islamic, c. 12th–13th century. 50.5mm x 31mm.

No counterpart has been found, but several examples of the same shape are known. Some are decorated with two addorsed birds and Arabic inscriptions: one gold and one bronze example, both in private collections and said to come from Iran, are dated 12th–13th century (Hasson 1987, nos 42–3). Two others are in the Museum für Islamische Kunst,

Figure 115 Miscellaneous pendants

Berlin. One is attributed to Iran and dated 13th–14th century, while the other is said to be either from Iran or Anatolia and dated 13th century (Gladiss 1998, nos 57–8). An example decorated with a volute in relief was found at the site of Kara-Khoja, near Turfan (Stein 1928, p. 596, pl. LXXI.kao.03). A comparable vegetal motif occurs on metalwork from Mosul dated 1233–59 (Erginsoy 1978, figs 142, 144).

Fig. 115.2 – 1880.3907.d. Box 9. Cast lead pendant or amulet, with a large loop attached to the straight top. The plaque flares into three lobes resembling an inverted fleur-de-lis in outline. Both faces are covered with five lined rows of Devanagari script written upside down. Hindu (?). 19.3mm x 16mm. Worn with only a few letters are legible, especially on the back. The inscription was probably deliberately inscribed upside down so that it could be read by the wearer.

Two comparable ornaments in silver were acquired in Kabul (Janata 1981, pl. 6.2–3).

Fig. 115.3 – 1880.3671. IM.Metal.3. Silver enamelled inverted leaf-shaped pendant with two suspension loops. The design shows two crowned figures walking to the right, the one in front having apparently speared the winged dragon (?) depicted vertically and upside down before him. The figure behind holds a long club-shaped object. Both human figures carry quivers on their backs and have a V-shaped prong extending above one shoulder. The scene is flanked by a flower on either side and a vegetal scroll below. The royal blue enamelled ground is edged with a band of lighter turquoise blue, with details of the central design picked out in turquoise, green and orange enamel; *c.* 18th century. 33.8mm x 31mm x 32.7mm x 1.7mm. For similar floral sprays and crowned figures in similar dress, see **Fig. 116.3**

Fig. 115.4 – 1880.3907.e. Box 9. Cast, brass, bulbous drop-shaped pendant, pierced for suspension immediately below the pointed apex. The centre is decorated with shallow granulation arranged in zigzag bands and edged with finely coiled lines, within a border of banded granules, coils and punched circles. The reverse is plain. Some bronze corrosion on obverse; *c.* 14th–17th century. 29.9mm x 28mm.

A pendant of the same form, dated 17th century, was found in Anatolia (Gladiss 1998, no. 66).

Frog and circular pendants

Fig. 116.1 – 1880.3822.c. IM.Metal.160. Cast copper alloy pendant or charm in the shape of a frog. The suspension ring is broken. 12th century (?). 20.9mm x 13.2mm x 2.3mm.

Fig. 116.2 – 1880.3906. Box 9. Cast, circular copper alloy pendant showing a stylised frog encircled by two concentric friezes. The motifs of the inner frieze are defaced, but seem to comprise a pattern of alternating dots and lines. The outer, wider one is decorated with three framed, short, illegible Arabic – possibly Quranic – inscriptions, alternating with three circles each containing a bird. The reverse is plain. The broken suspension loop is flat at the back. Islamic, *c.* 12th century. 39mm x 43mm (with loop).

Two similar specimens, different only in an openwork frog in the centre encircled by a single frieze, are known. The first, again encircled by an illegible Arabic inscription, is from an unspecified site in Uzbekistan and is assigned to the 12th century (Abdullaev, Rtveladze and Sishkina 1991, p. 175, no. 705). The other has a frieze decorated with a moulded undulating line, and was found in the vicinity of the *c.* 1st–13th-century cave site of Kashmir Smast, in north-west Pakistan (Nasim Khan 2006, p. 209, no. 2, fig. 223). The resemblance between the Kashmir Smast, Begram and Uzbekistan pendants indicates a similarity in date; and further suggests that all three specimens could be Ghurid, since the sites where they were found were all part of the Ghurid empire in the 12th century.

It should be noted, however, that the frog motif dates back to remote antiquity. A miniature Bactrian seal in the shape of a hand has a frog on the palm (Sarianidi 1993, p. 33, pl. VI.f–g). The seal comes from an undated plundered grave, but resembles an early 2nd-millennium BC hand-shaped seal (a surface find at Gonur, in Margiana, Turkmenistan), with a circle in place of a frog on the palm (Sarianidi 1993, p. 33, pl. VI.d). The frog also appears on 3rd–2nd-century BC Indian punch-marked coins (Gupta and Hardaker 1985, series IV, nos 398–404). After this date, it is not traceable until its re-appearance in the Islamic period.

Fig. 116.3 – 1880.3684.a–b, IM.Metal.14. Two silver alloy circular pendants, each with an attachment loop and with the same repoussé design of a crowned figure to right, dressed in a calf-length tunic with a gathered skirt, and playing a pipe; floral sprays on each side; *c.* 18th century. 24mm x 30mm.

For similar floral sprays and crowned figures in similar dress, see **Fig. 115.3**.

Pseudo-coin pendants

Fig. 116.4–15. Cast copper alloy coin with a suspension loop that is flattened at the back. Ghurid, *c.* 12th century.

Fig. 116.4 – 1880.3738.c. *Obverse*: A band of dots and part of a circle filled with a grid of lozenge shapes each containing a dot in its centre. *Reverse*: Indistinct traces of a similar design. 13.6mm x 10.9mm.

Fig. 116.5 – 1880.3738.e. The off-flan design on both sides comprises a circle divided by oblique lines into a grid of differently shaped partitions each with a dot in its centre. 13.6mm x 10.4mm.

Fig. 116.6 – 1880.3822.b. IM.Metal.160. *Obverse*: Two concentric bands of dots with an indistinct meandering line below. *Reverse*: Undecorated. Islamic, *c.* 11th–13th century. 13mm x 10mm.

Fig. 116.7 – 1880.3739.d. *Obverse*: Two curved bands of dots with part of a pseudo-Arabic (?) inscription below. *Reverse*: Uneven, covered with striations and traces of illegible letters or motifs. 17.4mm x 14mm.

Fig. 116.8 – 1880.3739.b. Both sides are covered with striations and traces of lozenge shapes and dots. 16.9mm x 13.4mm.

Fig. 116.9 – 1880.3738.b. Coin of Ghurid Mu'izz al-dīn Muḥammād (1173–1203). *Obverse*: Schematic bull walking to left. *Reverse*: Traces of an inscription encircled by a dotted border. Kuraman mint (?), Tye 1995, p. 118, type 175 (?).

Fig. 116.10 – 1880.3739.a. *Obverse*: An off-centre circle of pseudo-Arabic inscriptions (?). *Reverse*: A grid of squares, each with a dot in the centre. Ghurid (?). 20.7mm x 17.5mm.

Pendants of this type, but decorated with talismanic Kufic letters and astrological signs, were found at Nishapur, and dated 8th–12th century (Allan 1982, nos 60–1).

Fig. 116.11 – 1880.3739.c. Traces of a brass wash. *Obverse*: A grid of squares, each with a dot, encircled by an outer zigzag band with a dot in each triangle. *Reverse*: A larger grid, each square containing a smaller one with a dot in its centre. 18mm x 14.5mm.

Fig. 116.12 – 1880.3738.d. Probably brass-washed. *Obverse*: Possible traces of Arabic (?) letters. *Reverse*: Worn and illegible. 16.4mm x 13.3mm.

Fig. 116.13 – 1880.3738a. Only worn traces of a design survive on both sides. 16.9mm x 13.5mm.

Fig. 116.14–15. Coin pendant with two attachment loops. Ghurid, *c.* 12th–13th century.

Fig. 116.14 – 1880.3736. One broken loop. The worn pattern suggests that the design may be that of a 'bull and horseman' coin of the post Shahi period. Comparable in size and execution with **Fig. 116.15**, which suggests it is of similar date. 22mm x 19.2mm. Tye 1995, p. 94, type 34 (?).

Fig. 116.15 – 1880.3737. Brass-washed. The design is off flan on both sides and comprises three lines of Kufic within a broad border, of which only the words *al-sultan al-sultan* are recognisable. Reading by V.S. Curtis. The title *al-sultan al-sultan* is found on coins of Mu'izz al-dīn Bahram (1240–

Figure 116 Frog (1), circular (2–3) and pseudo-coin pendants (4–15)

42), the seventh sultan to rule Delhi after its conquest by the Ghurid ruler Muḥammād b. Sām (1193–1206). 22.5mm x 19.7mm.

Bird buttons

Fig. 117.1 – 1880.3704.r. IM.Metal.144. Cast copper alloy button or ornament in the shape of a wingless bird with a smooth body ending in a pointed tail. The head emerges from a collar around the neck and it has a pierced lug for attachment on the underside. 18mm x 5mm.

Fig. 117.2–24. IM.Metal.144. Cast copper alloy buttons or ornaments in the shape of a bird, with a raised head, wings curved back in flight and a splayed tail; a pierced lug for attachment on the underside.

Fig. 117.2 – 1880.3704.h. Two incised lines form a saltire across the upper surface of the wings. The tip of one wing is missing. 17mm x 10mm.

Fig. 117.3 – 1880.3704.i. The neck is elongated and merges into a rounded head. Two incised lines form a V-shape across the upper surface of the wings. The tail is rounded, with an incised line across the underside. 25mm x 13mm.

Fig. 117.4 – 1880.3704.p. The lug is broken and the head is missing. The front curved edge of the wings has a series of regularly spaced notches. 16mm x 14mm.

Fig. 117.5 – 1880.3704.m. Two incised lines form a saltire across the worn surface of the wings and traces of notching are visible around the edge of the splayed tail. 22mm x 10mm. Errington 1999, p. 229, pl. 8.22.

Fig. 117.6 – IOLC.7542. K.349. The outer edges of the wings are decorated with short, parallel incised lines and there is an incised line across the rounded tail. 17mm x 12mm.

Fig. 117.7–9. Random incised lines decorate the upper surface. The splayed tail is lightly notched.

Catalogue of Ornamental Metalwork and Miscellaneous Artefacts | 281

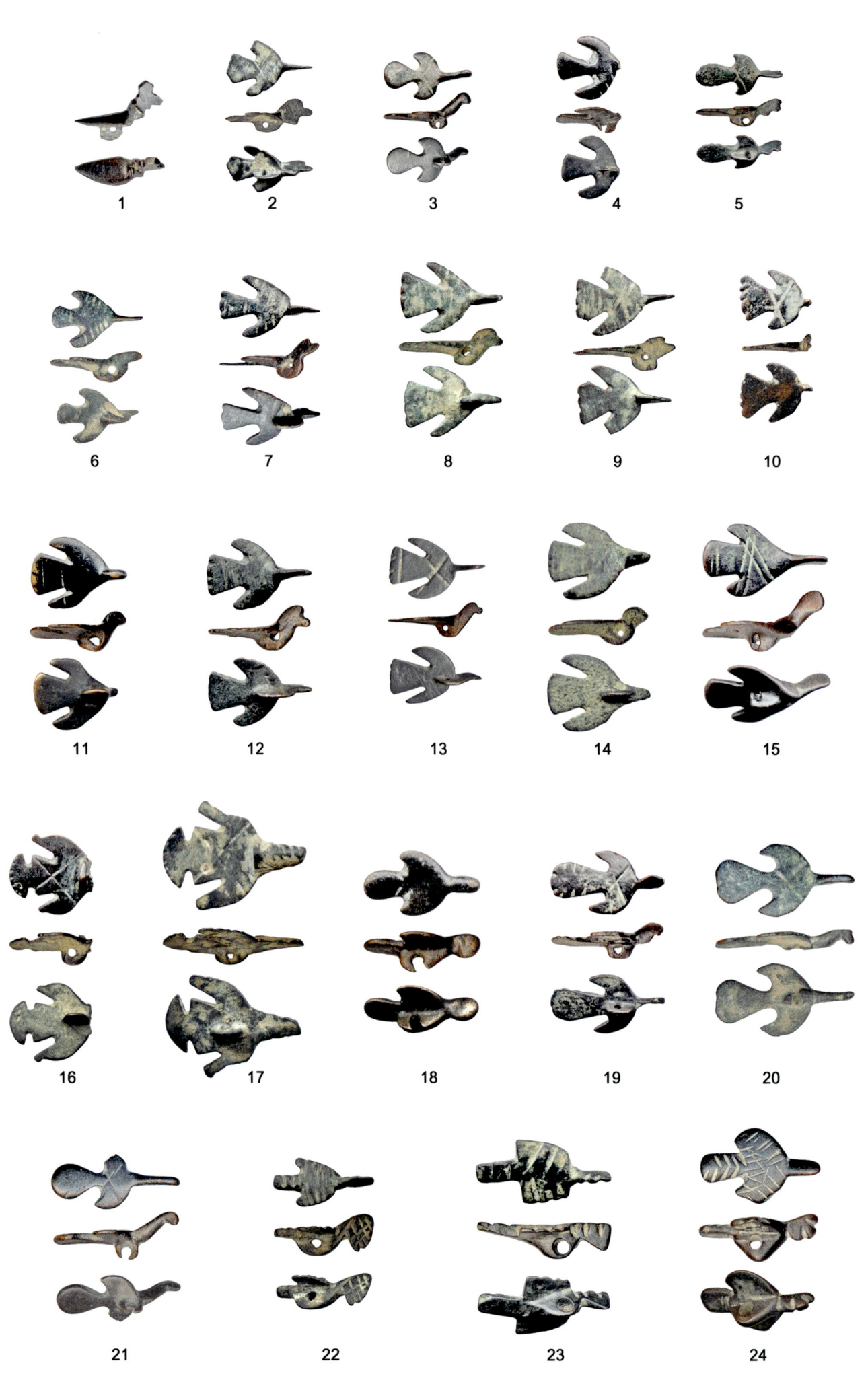

Figure 117 Bird buttons

282 | *Charles Masson: Collections from Begram and Kabul Bazaar, Afghanistan, 1833–1838*

Fig. 117.7 – 1880.3704a. 20mm x 13mm. Wilson 1841, p. 54, Antiquities pl. IV.5.

Fig. 117.8 – 1880.3704.c. 21mm x 13mm.

Fig. 117.9 – 1880.3704.d. 19mm x 13mm.

Fig. 117.10 – 1880.3704.e. Two incised lines form a saltire across the body and the tail is notched. The head and lug are missing. 14mm x 10mm.

Fig. 117.11–12. Two parallel, lightly incised lines across the notched tail.

Fig. 117.11 – 1880.3704.o. An incised line extends across part of one wing. The head is rounded and the beak not defined. 19mm x 13mm.

Fig. 117.12 – 1880.3704.l. 20mm x 15mm.

Fig. 117.13 – 1880.3976.b. IM 14 / SKM 1104. The upper surface has an incised saltire across the wings and a single line across the notched tail. 19.4mm x 12mm.

Fig. 117.14 – 1880.3704.k. Four parallel incised lines decorate the tail which is not notched. 18mm x 15mm.

Fig. 117.15 – 1880.3704.j. The longish neck merges into a rounded undefined head. The double-lined saltire is incised off centre, with another pair of parallel lines across the rounded tail. 25mm x 13mm. Errington 1999, p. 229, pl. 8.25.

Fig. 117.16–17. The wide, flat tail has short regularly spaced incised marks along its semi-circular edge, with a deep cut-out notch on either side and an incised saltire across the body.

Fig. 117.16 – 1880.3704.g. The head is missing. 15mm x 15mm.

Fig. 117.17 – 1880.3704.q. The head narrows to a point and has a series of four horizontal notches along its upper surface, giving it the appearance of a standing man in a coat and pointed hat. In addition to the saltire, there are two incised dots between the notches and the wings. 28mm x 22mm.

Fig. 117.18 – 1880.3704.n. A small thickset bird, with a round head, short wings, a rounded tail and a broken pierced lug. 25mm x 13mm.

Fig. 117.19 – 1880.3704.f. An incised saltire across the upper surface of the wings and short lines are etched along the edge of the rounded tail. The beak is missing. 22mm x 11mm.

Fig. 117.20–1. Bird with a long neck, round head, short wings with an incised saltire, and a rounded tail. The lug on the underside is broken.

Fig. 117.20 – IOLC.7541. K.348. Worn. 27mm x 13mm. There is another example in the Cambridge Ridgeway collection (CMAA.1927.1192).

Fig. 117.21– IOLC.7540. K.347. The tip of the left wing is missing. 25mm x 6mm.

Fig. 117.22 – 1880.3713.m. IM.Metal.156. A stylised bird with a large angular head, short squared tail and stubby wings; a large pierced lug on the underside. The upper surface of the body is decorated with roughly parallel incised lines, the head with crosshatching. 28mm x 13mm.

Fig. 117.23 – 1880.3704.b. IM.Metal.144. A stylised bird with an almost triangular head and wings that join at right angles to the narrow squared tail. Wide, regularly spaced lines are incised along the length of the tail, body and head. 25mm x 13mm. Errington 1999, p. 229, pl. 8.24.

Fig. 117.24 – IOLC.7543. K.350. A stylised bird with an angular head, stubby wings and a straight tail; a triangular pierced lug on the underside. The lower edge of the head is notched; the upper surface of the body is decorated with incised chevrons on the tail and crosshatching on the wings. 22mm x 15mm. The Cambridge Ridgeway collection (CMAA.1927.1192) has two examples of this type.

Buttons

Fig. 118.1–2. IM.Metal.25 / IM 32 / SKM 1105. Cast brass-washed copper alloy domed buttons, with a thick attachment bar extending across the back; *c.* 2nd century BC to 7th–8th century AD.

Ornamental examples of this type occur in the Hellenistic period at Qandahar and during the 1st century BC–1st century AD at Tulchar (**Fig. 118.1**). Similar buttons have been found examples occur during the 4th–5th century at Tup Khona Tajikistan (Litvinsky and Sedov 1984, pl. II.36, tomb 263). Similar buttons dated 7th–8th century have been found at Tureng Tepe, on the Gurgan plain, south of the Caspian Sea (Bourchalat and Lecomte 1987, pp. 175, 177, 197, pl. 100.4) and at Dzhety Asar 3 (Altyn Asar) in Kazakhstan (Levina 1971, p. 90, figs 19, 29).

Fig. 118.1 – 1880.3687.j. Incised lines radiate from a small central boss and terminate in punched dots around the rim. 15.8mm x 8.4mm.

A similar button has been found at Kandahar, Site F, in Phase III, dated to the Hellenistic period (McNicoll and Ball 1996, p. 272, fig. 209.1) and in late 2nd century BC–1st-century AD Kurgan XVI, tomb 13 at Tulchar (Mandel'sham 1966, pl. LV.17).

Fig. 118.2 – 1880.3687.i. A plain central boss encircled by a band of beading around the rim. 17.5mm x 6.6mm.

Fig. 118.3 – 1880.3834.a. IM.Metal.160. Cast copper alloy button, in the shape of a flower with eight petals (the tip of one broken); a pierced lug on the back for attachment. Islamic, *c.* 10th–11th century. 19mm x 8.2mm x 2.8mm.

A similar incised floral motif decorates the palmette-shaped belt-fitting **Fig. 123.8**, the form of which is typical of the early Islamic period.

Fig. 118.4 – IOLC.7544. K.351. Cast copper alloy, large flat circular button, with a lug at the back. The upper surface is completely worn; the back retains possible traces of Arabic inscriptions (?) suggesting it was made from a coin; *c.* 8th–10th century. 20mm.

Fig. 118.5 – 1880.3687.g. IM.Metal.25 / IM 68 / SKM 1069. Cast copper alloy flat button, in the shape of a seven-lobed flower, with an attachment loop on the back. The surface is worn, with traces of a punched dot in circle motif in each lobe. Islamic, *c.* 8th–10th century AD. 29.1mm x 7.1mm.

See **Fig. 96.1-2** for a discussion of the longevity of the dot in circle motif. The motif is also found on a number of other objects from Begram primarily of the Islamic period: (*cf.* **Fig. 112.3**, **Figs 97–9, 101, 108**).

Fig. 118.6 – 1880.3830.c. IM.Metal.160. Cast copper alloy button (?) in the form of a flower made up of six globular-petals with a domed centre. The hollowed reverse has red and yellow textile fragments adhering to it and

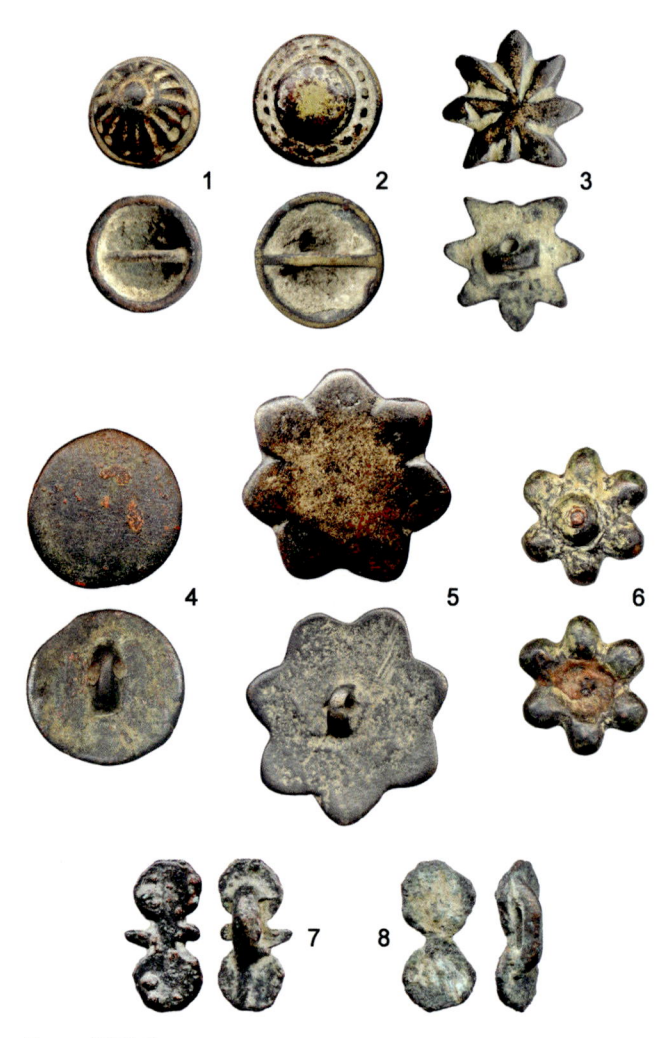

Figure 118 Buttons

traces of an attachment ring in the centre. 19.mm x 7.5mm.

Fig. 118.7–8. Cast copper alloy buttons or ornaments comprising two flat joined circles, with a lug soldered to the back.

Fig. 118.7 –3831.a. IM.Metal.160. A horizontal bar dissects the join between the two circles, creating a. rough butterfly shape. 20mm x 10.5mm.

Fig. 118.8 – 1880.3831.b. Box 8. Corroded. 19.8mm x 10.2mm.

Bracteates and miscellaneous pierced ornaments

Fig. 119.1 – 1880.3830.a. IM.Metal.160. Part of a silver bracteate (?) with a repoussé image of a male head in profile to left. 17mm x 1mm.

Fig. 119.2–3. Circular uniface cast copper alloy coin-like pierced discs. Within a double dotted border is the diademed head of a man resembling that found on the 'Heraus' coins of Kujula Kadphises (*c.* AD 40–90) and the Heliocles imitations of Wima Takto (*c.* AD 90–113). Kushan (?) *c.* 1st–2nd century (**Fig. 36.32-6**).

Fig. 119.2 – 1880.3734. Diademed male head to right. Broken on the left side and pierced lower right. 13mm.

Fig. 119.3 – IOLC.7749. Diademed male head to left. Pierced, with a slit, lower centre. A large lump of copper alloy is soldered to reverse. 15mm x 14mm.

Fig. 119.4 – 1880.3680. IM.Metal.4. A small, pierced circular bracteate or medallion, made of a double folded layer of gold sheeting, with the same repoussé image on both sides of a diademed bird standing to right, holding a pearl necklace in its beak. The proportions – a long neck and legs, plump body – identify it as a goose (*haṃsa*), which in Buddhism symbolises the wandering soul and the propagation of the Doctrine to all realms. Sasanian period, *c.* 6th–early 7th century. 14.5mm. Kabul bazaar.

The motif reproduces what Gasparini designates the 'Sasanian duck' (2014, p. 86, fig. 11). Similar representations of various birds and animals within a pearl roundel are found in stucco and on textiles of the late Sasanian period. Representations, for instance, of the mythical *senmurv* – a winged creature with a dog-like head and the tail of a peacock – occur on the coat of the Sasanian king, Khusrau II (AD 591–628) in the large grotto at Taq-i Bustan, Iran (Riboud 1983, pp. 92–105).

The Sasanian motif of a diademed bird with a string of beads in its beak spread from Iran into Afghanistan, northwards to Sogdia, and from there along the Silk Road eastwards to China. It is found on frescoes at the Buddhist caves of Bamiyan and Qizil in Xinjiang (Seipel 1996, p. 334, no. 197).

On the ceiling of the vestibule of Hall 1 at Bamiyan, roundels containing a pair of geese (?) face-to-face, holding the ends of a string of pearls in their beaks alternate with roundels containing a peacock, and are dated end of 6th–beginning of 7th century (Tarzi 1977, pp. 27, 155, pls A5, B55, D57.a-e). A comparable goose with a pearl necklace is also found together with the Alkhan tamgha on copper alloy coins inscribed *javati dharmaḥ* ('dharma may be victorious') in Brahmi. Examples have been found at the cave site of Kashmir Smast, north-west Pakistan (Nasim Khan *et al.* 2008, p. 129, nos 308–9; Vondrovec 2014, vol. I, p. 287, type GC-A 20).

Pearl roundels enclosing the representation of a similar goose/duck with a string of pearls in its beak and a floating ribbon around its neck are painted on a clay bench in Cave 60 at Qizil, and dated *c.* late 6th–early 8th century (Rowland 1974, pl. p. 162, p. 169; Combaz 1937, pl. 144; Tarzi 1977, p. 155, pl. D57.f). At Afrasiab in Sogdia (Uzbekistan), comparable roundels (differing only in that the ribbons floating behind the bird are held in its beak) decorate the robe of one of the dignitaries in the mural paintings on the west wall of the 'Hall of the Ambassadors', dated *c.* AD 660 (Azarpay 2014, p. 41, fig. 4).

A peacock, identifiable by its raised tail, is also represented in the stucco decorations from the late Sasanian complex at Ramavand (Barz Qawaleh) in Luristan province, Iran (Karamian and Farrokh 2017, p. 78, fig. 12); in frescoes dated *c.* late 6th–early 7th century at Varakhsha and Pendjikent in Uzbekistan (Rowland 1974, p. 93, fig. 42); in roundels on the pillow under the head of the giant Buddha in *Parinirvāna* in Mogao cave 158 at Dunhuang, constructed in AD 839 (Gasparini 2014, p. 86, fig. 11); and on 9th-century silks excavated at Astana in Turfan and at Dulan in Qinghai.

Fig. 119.5 – 1880.3830.b. IM.Metal.160. Fragment of a copper alloy bracteate with a repoussé flower encircled by dots, a dot between the tips of adjoining petals, and traces of gilding (?). 19mm x 10mm x 1mm.

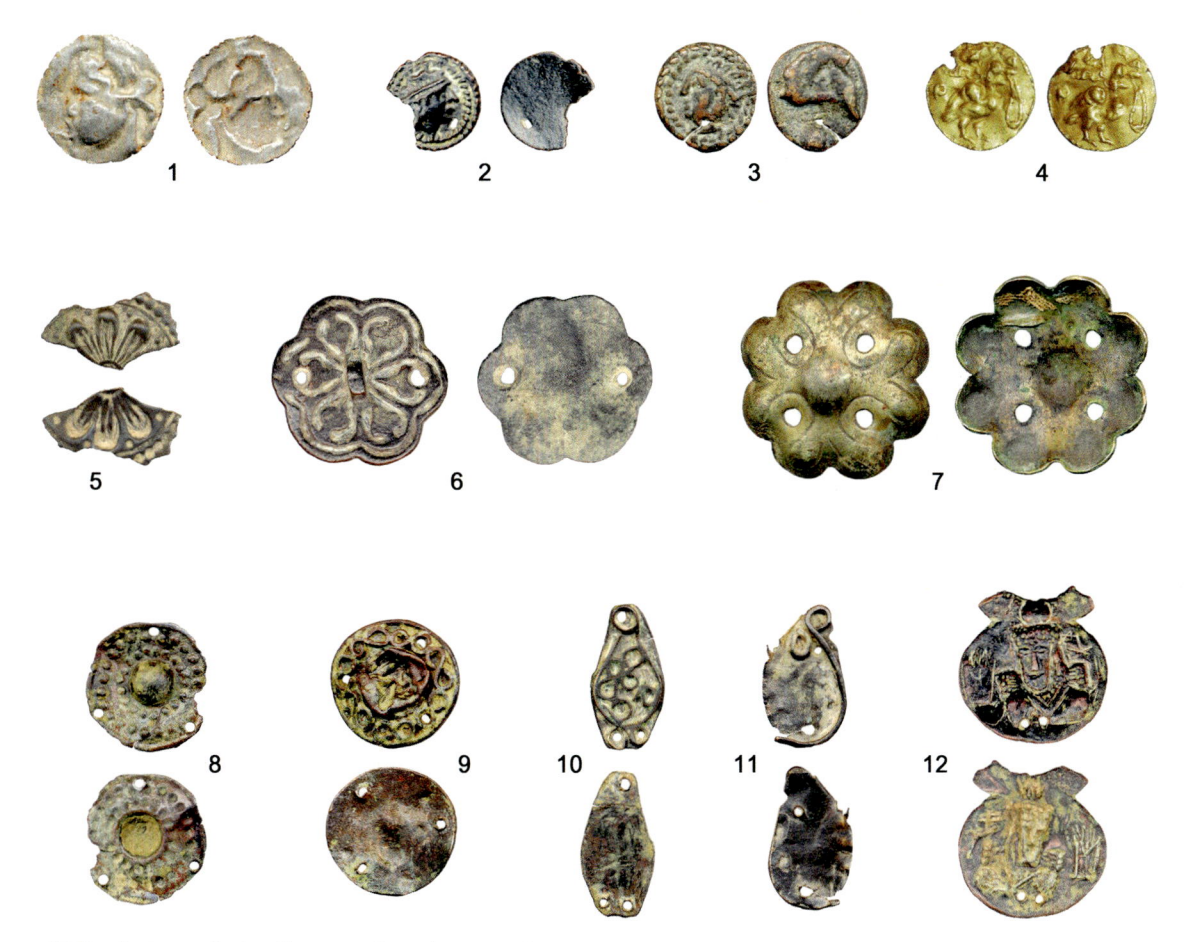

Figure 119 Bracteates and miscellaneous pierced ornaments

The fragment closely resembles the circular gold bracteates decorated with a rosette of the Late Classical and Hellenistic periods. Examples were found in Tomb 4 at Pella, Macedonia (Lilibaki-Akamati *et al.* 2011, p. 325), dated 4th century BC, and in a Scythian tomb at Tetranyna Mohyla, dated BC 350 (Reeder 1999, fig. 16). Further specimens in the Miho collection, Japan, are said to come from Bactria, but may be from Mir Zakah (*Treasures of Ancient Bactria* 2002, fig. 207a.).

Fig. 119.6 – 1880.3687.f. IM.Metal.25 / IM 32 / SKM 1105. Cast copper alloy bracteate in the form of a six-lobed flower with a projecting lug in the centre and pierced in two places. 24mm.

Fig. 119.7 – 1880.3687.h. IM.Metal.25 / IM 32 / SKM 1105. Domed bracteate of brass, with a nipple in the centre and eight lobes. Pierced with four holes and incised with a Maltese cross design with curving lines. A fragment of cloth adheres to reverse. 28mm.

Fig. 119.8 – 1880.3846.a. IM.Metal.160. Cast copper alloy disc, with a domed centre encircled by two rows of punched dots. There are three pierced holes for attachment. 2nd–1st century BC. 17mm x 2mm.

Similar examples in gold, perhaps from the Mir Zakah hoard, occur in the Miho collection (*Treasures of Ancient Bactria* 2002, p. 150, fig. 207b).

Fig. 119.9 – 1880.3846.b. IM.Metal.160. Cast copper alloy disc, with an appliqué domed centre, now squashed, encircled by an appliqué band of a running figure-of-eight decoration. There are three holes for attachment, pierced through centres of the figure-of-eight design. 17mm x 3mm.

Fig. 119.10 – 1880.3847.a. IM.Metal.160. Cut sheet metal copper alloy plaque, roughly oval, with flattened ends and traces of gilding. It has soldered appliqué decoration in the form of a drop-shaped wire outline enclosing six randomly placed circles. A hole is punched through at one end, and two at the other; each with an appliquéd wire circle around it. 24mm x 10mm x 1mm.

Fig. 119.11 – 1880.3847.b. IM.Metal.160. Cut sheet metal copper alloy teardrop-shaped plaque, with the remains of an appliquéd wire band around the edge, and curling back on itself to form a circle at the top, with a second appliquéd circle on the inside. There are two punched holes at the top and bottom respectively. 24mm x 11mm x 1mm.

Fig. 119.12 – 1880.3720. IM.Metal.163. Copper alloy oval plaque with the crowned repoussé bust of a Sasanian king to front. Two curved elements extending on either side of the globe at the top may conceivably represent wings or diadems. Pierced with two small holes at the bottom. Sasanian, *c.* 3rd–5th century. 20.5mm.

Bangles

Fig. 120.1 – 1880.3697. IM.Metal.127 / SKM 1087. Open-ended cast copper alloy, oval bangle, thickening and flaring at either end; *c.* 1st–3rd century AD. 68mm x 9.5mm x 3mm. Cleaned and conserved. Errington 1999: p. 230, pl. 9.19.

The type was used as an arm ornament or anklet at Sirkap, Taxila (Marshall, 1951, p. 578, no. 3, pl. 171.3) and in Bactria at Tillya Tepe, Afghanistan, during the 1st century AD (Sarianidi 1985b, p. 238, fig. 7) and at various other sites during the 1st–3rd century: Dal'verzin Tepe (Pugachenkova 1978, p. 94, fig. 73), Yalangtush Tepe (Rtveladze 1983, p. 134), and in Tajikistan Tepai Shakh and Tup Khona (Litvinsky and Sedov 1983, p. 155, pl. XXX.2–3; 1984, p. 216, pl. III.3, 5–6, 9–15).

Fig. 120.2 – 1880.3826.d. IM.Metal.160. Cast copper alloy bangle, rounded on the outside and open at the ends. 1st century BC–3rd century AD. 60mm x 6mm x 4.5mm. Cleaned and conserved.

Similar bangles were found in late 2nd-century BC–1st-century AD tombs at Tulchar, south-east Tajikistan (Mandel'shtam 1966, pl. LIV.10–11) and in 1st–3rd century tombs at Tup Khona (Litvinsky and Sedov 1984, p. 216, pl. III.13, 16, 24).

Fig. 120.3–21. Cast copper alloy bangle fragments.

Fig. 120.3 – 1880.3716.h. IM.Metal.159. Curved strip, possibly a bangle. 1st–3rd century. 58mm x 2mm.

An open bangle – with ends oval in section – was found at Babashov, south-east Turkmenistan, in late 2nd-century BC–1st-century AD kurgans (Mandel'shtam 1975, pl. XL.2) and in 1st–3rd-century tombs at Tup Khona (Litvinsky and Sedov 1984, p. 216, pl. III.11).

Fig. 120.4 – 1880.3900.d. IM.Metal.159. Bangle (?) fragment, flat in section, broken at one end; rounded and wider at the other end. 1st century BC–1st century AD. 29.4mm x 6.5mm–4mm x 2.7mm.

Fig. 120.5 – 1880.3912.f. IM.Metal.159. Fragment, widening and thickening towards one end, then narrowing to a point; the other end is broken. Late 2nd century BC–1st century AD. 38.2mm x 6.4mm x 3mm.

A bangle, with one flat end as in **Fig. 120.4** and the other tapering as here, was found in late 2nd-century BC–1st-century AD tombs at Tulchar (Mandel'shtam 1966, pl. LIV.13).

Fig. 120.6 – IOLC.5498. K.301. Fragment, broken at both ends; decorated with incised lines. 29mm x 5mm.

Fig. 120.7 – IOLC.7515. K.305. Fragment, broken at both ends. Curved, with a smooth inside edge and triangular profile; decorated with a faceted lozenge between two transverse bands. 25mm x 3mm.

Fig. 120.8 – 1880.3828.e. IM.Metal.160. Fragment, with a section of parallel transverse incisions and one deeper, incised groove. 20.2mm x 3.5mm.

Fig. 120.9 – IOLC.7525. K.331. Fragment, broken at both ends. Curved, and oval in profile, the inside is smooth and the outside ribbed with parallel transverse incisions across each alternate rib. 2nd–3rd century AD. 44mm x 5mm.

An example of this type in bronze was found at Yalangtush Tepe, in Naos II Room 1, which contained coins of Huvishka (Rtveladze 1983, fig. 4).

Fig. 120.10 – 1880.3828.f. IM.Metal.160. Fragment, flat on the inner surface and rounded on the outer, with a series of transverse incisions simulating a string of beads. 23.8mm x 3.4mm x 2.6mm.

Fig. 120.11 – 1880.3812.q. IM.Metal.141. Fragment of a bangle (?) with a ribbed shank, oval in cross-section, and a raised oval decorated with an engraved humped bull seated to the left. 9.5mm x 11.5mm x 25.5mm.

Fig. 120.12 – 1880.3828.g. IM.Metal.160. Fragment, round in section, with deep transverse incisions on the outside. 21.8mm x 4mm.

Fig. 120.13 – 1880.3828.i. IM.Metal.160. Fragment, flat on one side, rounded on the other, with transverse incisions and a scalloped edge. 5th century. 18.8mm x 4.9mm x 2.2mm.

A fragment of a copper bangle similar to this example was found at Taxila, in the monastic area of the Kunala stupa. It is attributed to the 5th century (Marshall, 1951, p. 352, p.578, no. 12, pl. 171.i).

Fig. 120.14 – IOLC.7526. K.332. Fragment, decorated on the outside with a band of faceted rectangles, each raised to a point in the centre. 5th century. 34mm x 10mm.

Fig. 120.15 – 1880.3828.h. IM.Metal.160. Fragment, deeply toothed on the outer surface. 19.2mm x 5.3mm x 4.1mm.

Fig. 120.16 – 1880.3828.j. IM.Metal.160. Fragment, , rounded on the other, with transverse incisions leaving a lozenge pattern, and a scalloped edge. 5th century. 33.5mm x 7.2mm x 2.6mm.

Fig. 120.17 – IOLC.7529. K.335. Fragment, broken at both ends. Flat and curved, decorated with incised vertical and V-shaped diagonal lines on the outside. 28mm x 5mm.

Fig. 120.18 – 1880.3687.u. IM.Metal.25 / IM 68 / SKM 1069. Copper alloy, notched bangle fragment, with an incised chevron pattern. 38mm x 7mm.

Fig. 120.19–21. Fragments decorated with raised lozenges each containing a dot in circle; *c.* 6th century.

The motif occurs at the end of an open bangle found in a 3rd-century Roman tomb at Rataria, Bulgaria (Ruseva-Slokoska 1991, no. 173). However, a similar motif also occurs on the bone handle of a knife from Penjikent, dated 6th century (Zeimal 1985, p. 212, no. 547).

Fig. 120.19 – 1880.3828.m. IM.Metal.160. The lozenges alternate with a pair of raised transverse lines. 26.5mm x 4.8mm x 2.3mm.

Fig. 120.20 – IOLC.7531. K.337. The lozenges alternate with three raised parallel lines. 25mm x 5mm.

Fig. 120.21 – 1880.3828.n. IM.Metal.160. 19.6mm x 5.8mm x 2mm.

Bangle fragments

Fig. 121.1–19. Cast copper alloy bangle fragments.

Fig. 121.1 – 1880.3828.o. IM.Metal.160. Flattened band with a row of overlapping punched dot in a circle motifs and incised lines. 4th century AD. 19mm x 8.5mm x 1.25mm.

Fig. 121.2 – 1880.3828.l. IM.Metal.160. Flattened band with three punched overlapping dot in circle motifs. 4th century. 10.9mm x 8.7mm x 1.7mm.

A similar fragment was found at Augusta Raurica, Switzerland, in a 4th-century Roman tomb (Riha 1990, 3.20, pl. 19, no. 550).

Fig. 121.3–4. Fragments with a double row of punched, overlapping dot in circle motifs between incised lines. 4th century.

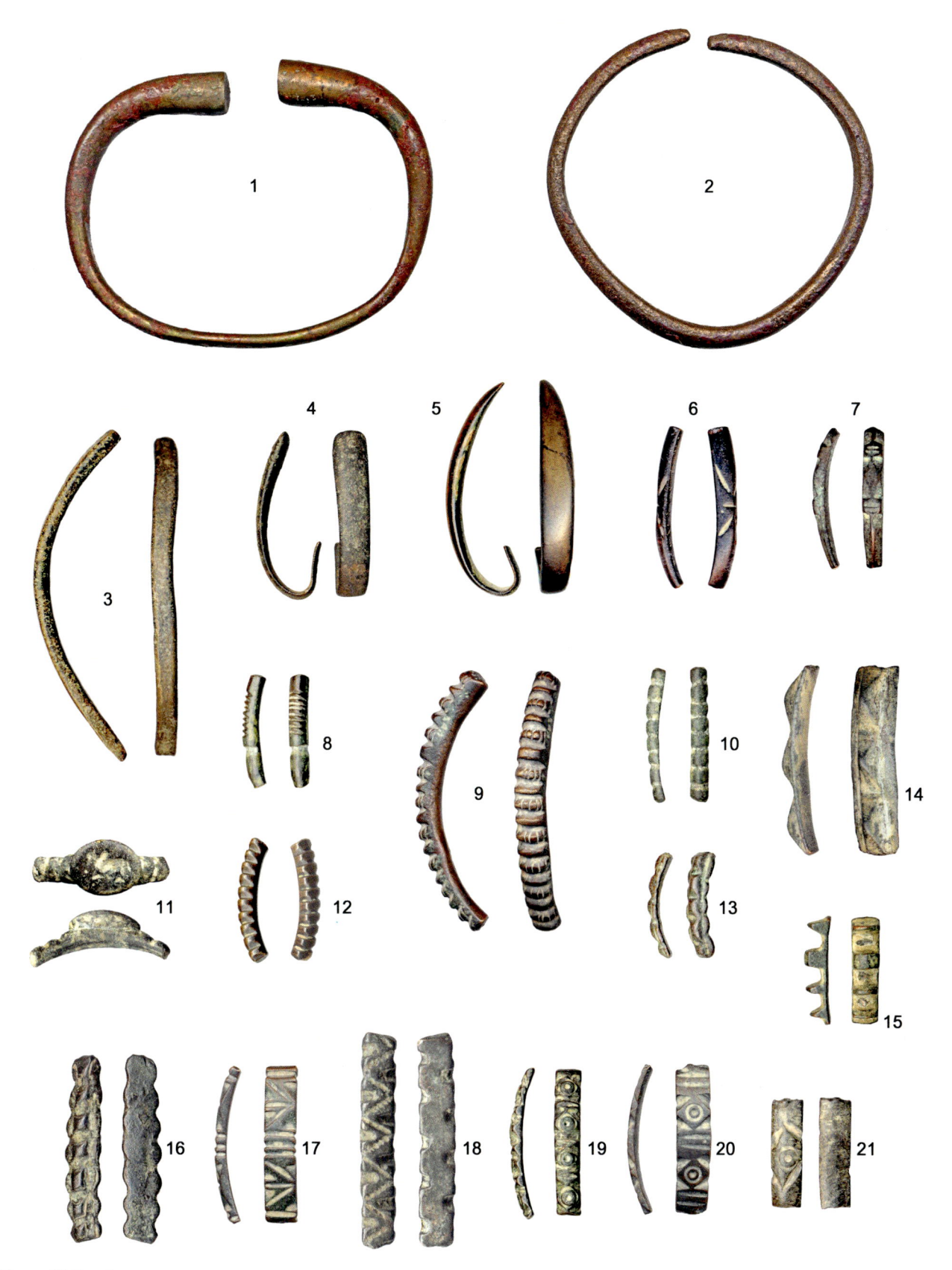

Figure 120 Bangles

Catalogue of Ornamental Metalwork and Miscellaneous Artefacts | 287

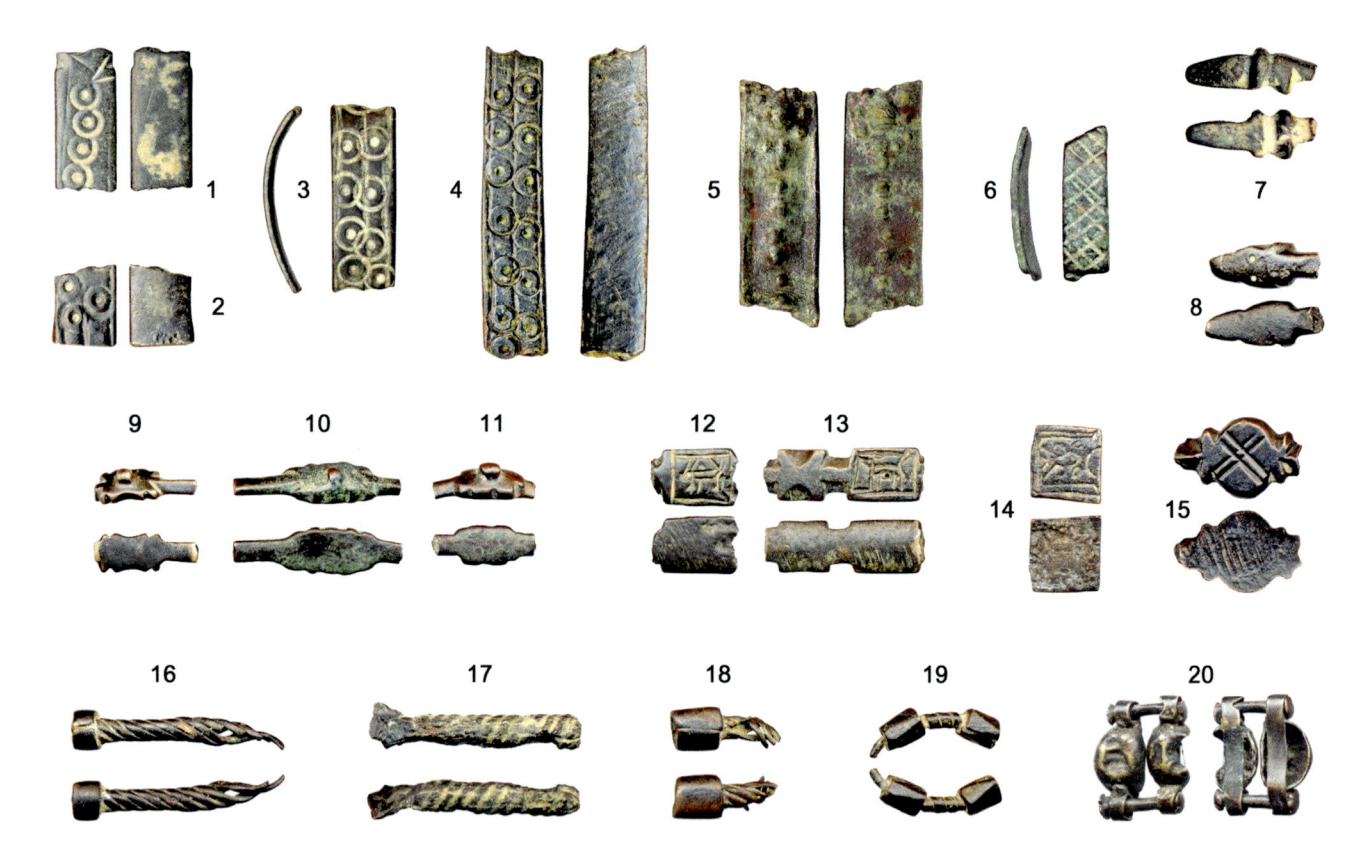

Figure 121 Bangle fragments

Fig. 121.3 – 1880.3828.p. IM.Metal.160. 25mm x 8.8mm x 1.5mm.

Fig. 121.4 – 1880.3916.b. IM.Metal.159. Flattened band. 41mm x 9mm x 1.6mm.

A similar fragment was found in a 4th-century Roman tomb at Augusta Raurica (Riha 1990, 3.20, pl. 19, no. 551).

Fig. 121.5 – 1880.3916.g. IM.Metal.159. Flattened band with raised edges and dots punched in an irregular line through from the reverse and, at one end, a larger dot surrounded by a circle of smaller ones. 33mm x 11mm x 2mm.

Fig. 121.6 – IOLC.7528. K.334. Fragment with incised cross-hatched decoration. 20mm x 5mm.

Fig. 121.7 – IOLC.7514. K.304. Terminal of an open-ended bangle which emerges from two thicker fused rings and narrows to a point. 18mm x 5mm.

Fig. 121.8 – 1880.3827. IM.Metal.160. Terminal of an open-ended bangle, in the form of a stylised snake head with two punched eyes. 1st century BC–1st century AD. 16mm x 6.2mm x 4.1mm.

Bangles with similar finials were found in Bactria in the kurgans of Aruktau, Babashov and Tulchar (Mandel'shtam 1975, pls XVIII.26, XL.5; 1966, pl. LIV.8). The type continues into the 3rd century with silver specimens from the Nikolaevo and the Chaoushevo treasures (Ruseva-Slokoska 1991, nos 160–1). Ruseva-Slokoska also mentions a 1st century AD silver example from the Schiller collection in Berlin.

Fig. 121.9–11. IM.Metal.160. Fragments of the same bangle (?) comprising a thin band of triangular section, and a wider, thickened, roughly rectangular section with indented edges and a knob protruding from the top.

Fig. 121.9 – 1880.3816.p. 14mm x 5mm x 3.5mm.

Fig. 121.10 – 1880.3829.a. 25mm x 6mm x 4mm.

Fig. 121.11 – 1880.3829.b. 14mm x 5.5mm x 4mm.

Fig. 121.12–13. Two fragments of the same bangle. Rectangular plates with incised decoration alternate with a square containing a saltire in high relief. A narrow band joins the elements together.

Fig. 121.12 – 1880.3914.a. IM.Metal.141. The rectangle depicts an angular hare standing to the left. 11.7mm x 7.7mm x 1.8mm.

Fig. 121.13 – 1880.3914.b. IM.Metal.160. The rectangle depicts an angular dog (?) standing to the left. 22.3mm x 7.2mm x 1.7mm.

Fig. 121.14 – 1880.3915. Box 8. Small, rectangular plaque of copper alloy, possibly part of a bangle (?) with incised decoration, including a palmette motif resembling a fish. 10.1mm x 9.7mm x 0.9mm.

Fig. 121.15 – 1880.3687.w. IM.Metal.25 / IM 68 / SKM 1069. Terminal of an open-ended bangle (?) comprising a flat oval disc with slightly bevelled edge and decorated with an incised double-lined saltire. On either side is a small, flattened moulding extending into a narrow, ridged band. The back is undecorated, but covered with a series of parallel striations. Islamic (?) c. 8th–10th century. 17mm x 11mm.

For similar striations see **Fig. 130**.

Fig. 121.16 – 1880.3828.a. IM.Metal.160. Bangle (?) fragment. Fragment of five twisted wires held together at one end by a capped bead. 29mm x 3mm; cap: 5.5mm.

Fig. 121.17 – 1880.3828.c. IM.Metal.160. Bangle (?) fragment formed of strands of wire twisted around a central core and fused together. 29.5mm x 4.6mm.

Fig. 121.18 – 1880.3828.b. IM.Metal.160. Fragment of six twisted wires held together at one end by a capped bead. 14.9mm x 3.2mm; cap: 5.7mm.

Fig. 121.19 – 1880.3828.d. IM.Metal.160. Bangle (?) fragment with two faceted beads threaded onto a wire. The space between the two is bound with a flattened strip twisted around the central core. 18.3mm x 2.1mm; beads: 4.1mm.

Fig. 121.20 – 1880.3687.l. IM.Metal.25 / IM 68 / SKM 1069. Hammered brass-washed copper alloy ornament, possibly a bracelet (?) comprising two hollow domed ovals, each with a narrow band at the back and looped top and bottom, through which a pin secures the two pieces together. 16mm x 7mm.

Buckles and strap fittings

Fig. 122.1 – 1880.3937.a. Box 9. Cast lead buckle comprising an outer open ring with ends in the form of a bird attached to a small oval transverse bar with a crescent-shaped loop below for attachment to a narrow strap. Parthian or Sasanian. 23.9mm x 18.3mm x 2.7mm.

The outer ring recalls Parthian buckles in which this section consists of two confronted animal heads (Ghirshman 1979, pl. IV.1); while a further example from Corinth is tentatively attributed to the Byzantine period (Davidson 1952, pl. 115, no. 2248). The inner section resembles that of some Sasanian buckles (Ghirshman 1979, pl. VII.1).

Fig. 122.2–4. Two cast copper alloy belt clasps and the fragment of a third, comprising a rectangular strap slot, with small projecting knob at each corner, attached by a short bar to a circle pierced in the countersunk centre by an oblong hole to receive the projecting boss of the other (missing) half of the clasp. *c.* 10th–11th century.

A comparable intact example, comprising both parts of the clasp, was found at Tepe Madraseh (C9, well 2), Nishapur, a site dated 8th–13th century (Allan 1982, pp. 66–7, no. 38). It only lacks projecting knobs on the top corners of the rectangular slot. A second example, found at Corinth, is attributed to the Byzantine period or later (Davidson 1952, p. 115, no. 2247). A third, in which the circle is decorated with an incised scroll pattern and the central hole is T-shaped, was found at Sardis in Anatolia. It is identified as a lock plate and also thought to be Byzantine (Waldbaum 1983, pl. 24, no. 388).

Fig. 122.2 – 1880.3937.b. Box 9. 25.9mm x 14.8mm.

Fig. 122.3 – 1880.3937.c. Box 9. 29mm x 16.5mm.

Fig. 122.4 – 1880.3937.d. Cast copper alloy fragment comprising the rectangular strap slot, with a small projecting knob at each corner, and part of the bar which once attached it to the circular part of a belt clasp. 13.7m x 11.9mm.

Fig. 122.5 – IOLC.7591. K.399. Cast copper alloy buckle; thickened and pointed in the front, with bulbous sides. The tongue and the centre of the bar are missing but traces of the original transverse pin remain in the holes drilled through the points of attachment to the rectangular strap slot; *c.* 8th–13th century. 28mm x 23mm.

A number of buckles of the same type have been found at various sites. Several examples from Penjikent are dated 8th century (Belenitsky *et al.* 1973, fig. 54.2; Zeimal 1985, p. 210, no. 537). One example from Nishapur Village Tepe is dated 8th–13th century (Allan 1982, pp. 66–7, no. 37), while others from the Mazar-tagh of Khotan are undated (Stein 1928, p. 95, pl. VI, M.Tagh.017).

Fig. 122.6 – IOLC.7590. K.398. Cast copper alloy buckle, comprising a C-shaped front, fluted sides and a straight bar at the back; with a trace of gilding on the inner side edge. The tongue is missing; *c.* 10th–11th century. 28mm x 34mm.

One comparable example from Iran or Central Asia is dated 10th–11th century (Darkevitch 1976, pl. 40, 4), another from Turkey is dated 7th–11th century (Brentjes and Vasilievsky 1989, p. 161).

Fig. 122.7 – 1880.3841. IM.Metal.160. Copper alloy buckle fragment, cast in one piece with the remains of an oblong opening in the centre. One side is straight; the top flares outwards, curving on the inner side to form the bar (now broken); *c.* 8th century. 17mm x 16.2mm x 2.5mm.

The almost complete buckle **Fig. 122.6** provides the prototype for reconstructing this fragment.

Fig. 122.8 – 1880.3713.n. IM.Metal.156. Copper alloy buckle cast in one piece with a narrow opening in the centre. One side is straight; the top and bottom flare outwards to a point beyond the curved outer edge of the other side or bar, to which the remains of a wide, flat prong is attached. 22mm (widest) x 15.2mm (widest) x 7.1mm (prong).

Fig. 122.9 – 1880.3937.e. Box 9. Copper alloy, hinged clasp, with drill holes for the hinge; attached to a flat curved decorative element with a V-shaped prong in the centre. Cast in one piece. 24.2mm x 19.9 x 3.2mm.

Fig. 122.10 – 1880.3937.f. Box 9. Cast copper alloy, rectangular buckle with rounded corners. A bead and reel motif in the middle of each of the longest sides covers the drill holes for the buckle bar, now broken off and missing. A raised leaf motif in the middle of each of the shortest sides has a recessed central rib to hold the tongue in place, flanked on either side with parallel incised lines. 32.7mm x 24.4mm x 4.5mm. *c.* 10th–13th century.

Fig. 122.11 – 1880.3937.h. Box 9. Cast copper alloy rectangular strap fitting, decorated with a small disc in the centre of the front face. 23.1mm x 14.8mm x 3.5mm.

An example from Corinth, with a knob instead of a disc, is attributed to the Byzantine period (Davidson 1952, pl. 115, no. 2228).

Fig. 122.12 – 1880.3937.g. Box 9. Cast copper alloy plain rectangular strap-fitting. 18.6mm x 16.2mm x 2mm.

Fig. 122.13 – IOLC.7592. K.400. Small square cast copper-alloy strap fitting with notched decoration on three sides. 10mm x 10mm. *c.* 8th–13th century.

Fig. 122.14 – 1880.3716.c. IM.Metal.159. Hammered silver tongue of a buckle. 21mm x 3mm.

Fig. 122.15 – 1880.4117.e. Fragment of a cast copper alloy hinged component; one end broken, the other, thicker end cut out in the centre and pierced to hold a tongue. 22mm x 8mm x 3.mm.

Belt and other riveted fittings

Fig. 123.1–3. IM.Metal.160. Copper alloy, D-shaped belt-fitting, cast in one piece with an open oblong slot and one or two rivets on the reverse; *c.* 7th–8th century.

Similar fittings have been found at Penjikent in Tajikistan (Belenitsky *et al.* 1973, fig. 54; Zeimal 1985, p. 211, nos 538–9) and others acquired at Kucha in the Tarim Basin, Xinjiang (Stein 1928, p. 826, pl. CXI, Kucha.011; Huashan *et al.* 1987,

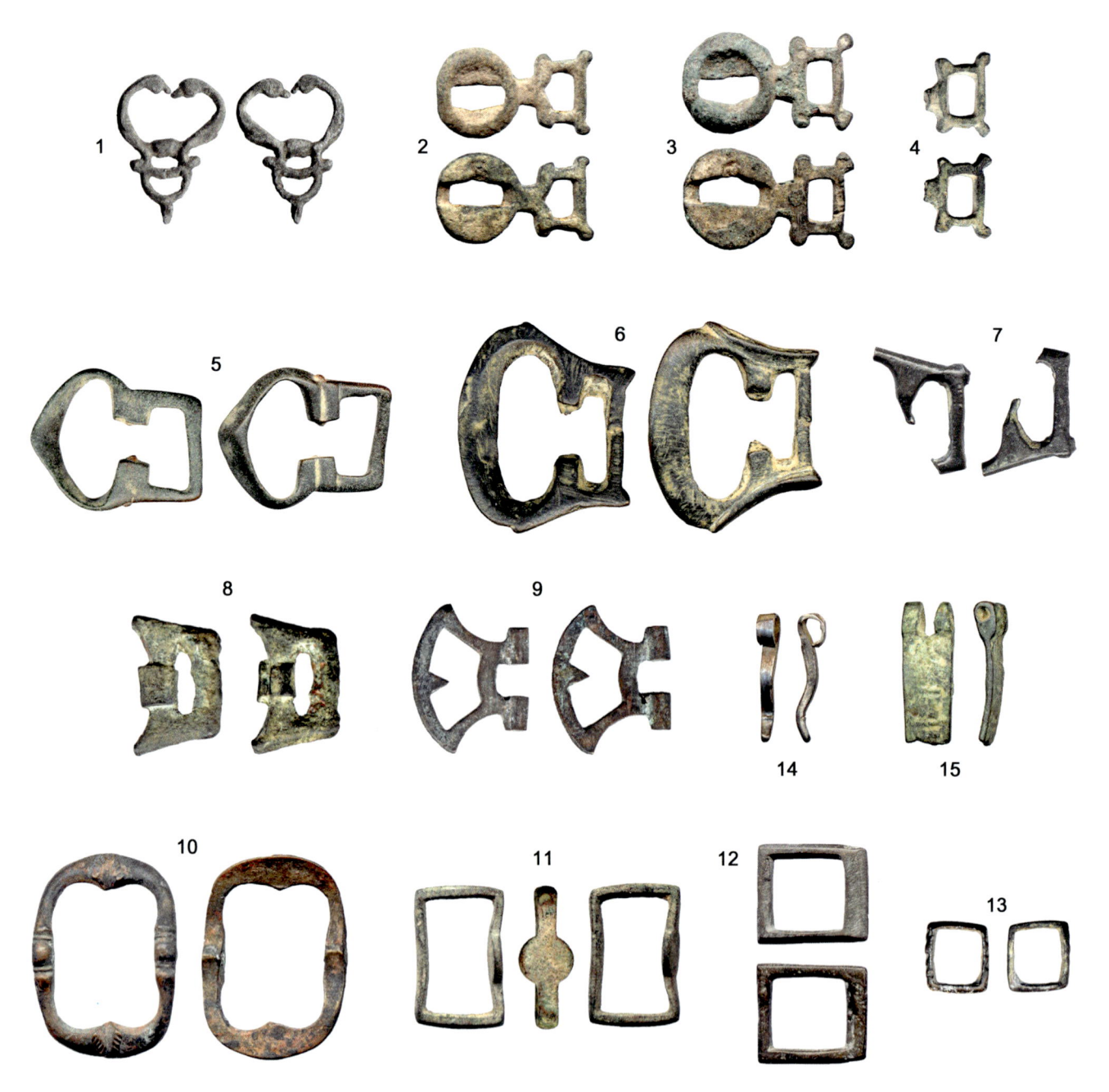

Figure 122 Buckles and strap fittings

pl. XXIX.v). Comparable examples have also been found at Toprak Kala in Khwarazm, Uzbekistan (Tolstov 1953, fig.42.3; Research Center for Silk Roadology 1996, p. 32).

Fig. 123.1 – 1880.3842.a. One rivet on the reverse. 16.4mm x 12.2mm x 1.9mm; rivet: 3mm.

Fig. 123.2–3. The outer edge is bevelled; the back hollow. The bleed of excess metal into the slot during casting has not been removed.

Fig. 123.2 – 1880.3842.b. Two lugs on the reverse of the rounded end, one still attached to a small square of thin copper alloy sheet. 19mm x 14.4mm x 2.8mm; lug: 4.8mm.

Fig. 123.3 – 1880.3842.c. Traces of a rivet in the centre of the reverse. 18.8mm x 14.8mm; rivet: 2.5mm.

Fig. 123.4–5. Cast copper alloy, D-shaped belt fittings, with an oblong slot, scalloped and a bevelled rounded outer edge.

Fig. 123.4 – IOLC.7593. K.401. It has two rivet holes. The front is flat, the back slightly recessed; *c.* 7th–8th century. 16mm x 19mm.

Fig. 123.5 – IOLC.7594. K.402. Two lugs on the reverse of the rounded end, one still riveted to a small square of thin copper alloy sheet; *c.* 7th–8th century. 14mm x 22mm.

Fig. 123.6 – 1880.3938.a. Box 9. Cast copper alloy belt-fitting (?) comprising two conjoined rings, the one smaller than the other, slightly pointed on the inside and decorated on the outside with two small projecting knobs. Two rivets on the reverse. 26mm; large ring: 15.8mm; small ring: 10.1mm; rivets: 2.4mm, 2.8mm. It is stylistically related to buckles **Fig. 122.2–4** and therefore probably of the same period; *c.* 8th–12th century.

Fig. 123.7 – 1880.3938.b. Box 9. Cast copper alloy stylised palmette with an oval cut-out in the centre, flanked by two backward curving sepals, and a rounded above terminating in a small trefoil at the tip. On the back are the

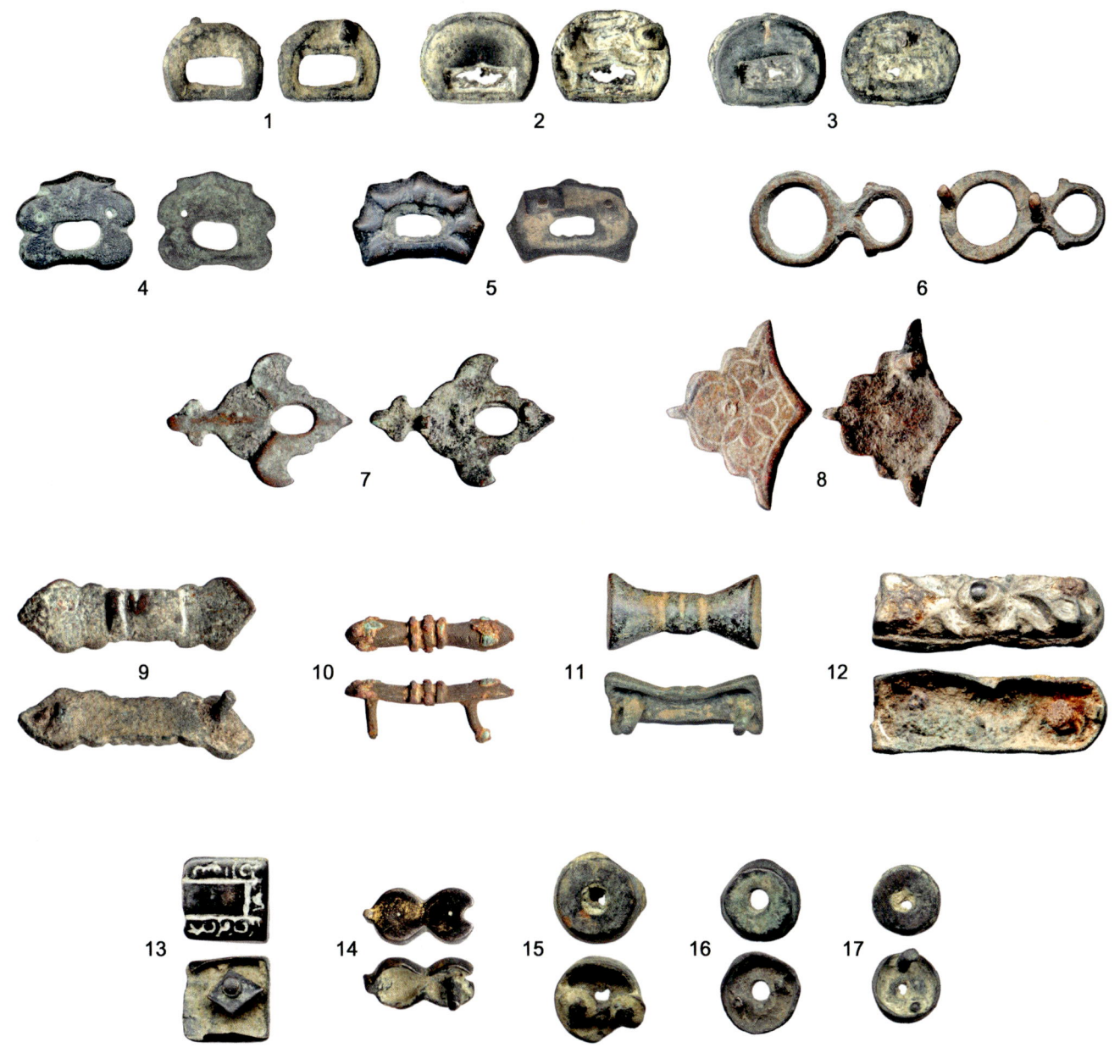

Figure 123 Belt and other riveted fittings

remains of two broken loops. Islamic, *c.* 10th–12th century. 30mm x 21mm.

The small trefoil relates it to pendants **Figs 112.6** and **114.1**, dated 10th–12th century. The motif is popular on Islamic pottery of the 11th–15th century (Jenkins 1983, nos 21–3, 27, 36, 39). It also occurs in a Qur'an produced in Cairo in 1304 (Wilson 1998, fig. 76).

Fig. 123.8 – 1880.3938.c. Box 9. Cast copper alloy appliqué ornament in the shape of a splayed palmette with an incised border and a seven-petalled flower in the centre immediately below a small punched rivet hole. Two rivets on the reverse. Islamic, *c.* 10th–11th century. 22.7mm x 30mm; rivets: 4.4mm.

The form is similar to the top section of a 8th–12th century bronze fitting for furniture from Qanat Tepe, Nishapur (Allan 1982, p. 95, no. 147). It is stylistically comparable to 10th–11th-century bronze fittings (Darkevich 1976, pl. 39. 2–3).

Fig. 123.9 – 1880.3939.a. Box 9. Cast copper alloy, bent ornamental appliqué strip, with a rivet at either end of a flat reverse (one now broken), The central bar is hemispherical in section, with incised banding. The flat terminals are scalloped twice on the sides and end in a point; their surfaces decorated with traces of incised decoration contained within the outline of a heart. 38.6mm x 11.5mm x 4.2mm; rivet: 4.8mm.

Fig. 123.10 – 1880.3939.b. Box 9. Cast copper alloy, appliqué ornament, with a long rivet at either end of a flat reverse. The front comprises three prominent rings in the centre; with a faceted bar on either side that gradually increases in diameter, and then decreases more sharply to a point. 27mm x 4.9mm; rivets: 4.2mm, 6.7mm.

Fig. 123.11 – IOLC.7595. K.403. Cast copper alloy, hollow appliqué ornament, possibly a belt-fitting, in the shape of a bow, hemispherical in section, with a narrow centre divided into two bands and flanked on either side by a trapezium. There are two rivets on the reverse. 25mm x 10mm.

Fig. 123.12 – 1880.3939.c. Box 9. Cast copper alloy belt-fitting with traces of gilding (?). The edge of the hollow, oblong case is rounded at one end, with a rectangular tab at mid-point. The opposite end is straight, with a corresponding small section of the edge cut away in mid-point. The moulded foliate decoration is in high relief and comprises a small boss with an inset garnet or red glass in the centre, flanked on either side by a heart and acanthus leaves. A rivet perforates each heart shape and extends through the back; *c.* 7th–10th century. 37.8mm x 12.9mm x 7.9mm.

Comparable examples, in the shape of an oblong case with foliate decoration in high relief, but with a slightly pointed end instead of a rounded one, have been found in various areas: in Iran, where they are attributed to the Seljuq period (1050–1221; Erginsoy 1978, fig. 64) or to the 10th–11th century (Darkevich 1976, pl. 39.13); in Central Asia where they are attributed to the Turks or Seljuqs and dated 7th–11th century (Brentjes and Vasilievsky 1989, p. 161); at Tajik, a Buddhist site south-east of Kucha, dated *c.* 7th–10th century (Stein 1928, p. 823, Taj.01, pl. CXI); and at Yarkhoto, Turfan, in a datable context of *c.* 7th–8th century (Stein 1921, pp. 1168, 1175, pl. VII, Y.K.i.001).

Fig. 123.13 – 1880.3843.a. IM.Metal.160. End section of a hollow, rectangular casing with an incised Arabic inscription around the outer edge. On the back, a single rivet is riveted to a lozenge-shaped piece of thin, copper alloy sheet. Islamic, *c.* 10th–12th century. 20mm x 13.6mm x 4mm; rivet: 5mm.

Fig. 123.14 – 1880.3843.b. IM.Metal.160. Cast copper alloy, hollow casing comprising two joined discs with traces of gilding. On diametrically opposite sides of the rim, one disc is notched and the other has a small raised tab. One rivet survives in the centre back of the notched disc and there are traces of a second rivet along the bottom edge of the other disc. 17.6mm x 8.7mm x 3.2mm; rivet: 5.3mm.

Fig. 123.15–17. IM.Metal.160. Cast copper alloy hollow discs with a large hole in the centre, slightly outward sloping sides and two rivets on the reverse. 8th–9th century.

An example attributed to the 8th century was found at Penjikent (Belenitsky *et al.* 1973, fig.54) and another at Samarra to the 9th century (Iraq Department of Antiquities 1940, pl. CXLII).

Fig. 123.15 – 1880.3843.c. A large semi-circle is cut out of the side. The rivets still each have a small square washer of thin sheet metal. 14.3mm x 5.3mm; rivet: 7.8mm.

Fig. 123.16 – 1880.3843.d. 12.6mm x 2.8mm.

Fig. 123.17 – 1880.3843.e. The disc is straight-sided with one intact rivet and the remains of another. 10.8mm x 3.5mm; rivet: 6.5mm.

Decorative fittings

Fig. 124.1 – 1880.3940.a. Box 9. Cast copper alloy appliqué ornament with a lozenge in the centre divided into four raised quarters, flanked on either side by a vertical band with a crenelated outer edge. The back is slightly hollow, with a rivet in the centre. 11.4mm x 8.6mm x 2mm; rivet: 23mm.

Fig. 124.2 – 1880.3941. Box 8. Cast copper alloy, flat X-shaped appliqué ornament with bevelled edges, two notches in the middle of each of the two straight sides, and the remains of a broken rivet through the centre; *c.* 10th–11th century. 15.3mm x 12.mm.

A similar example dated *c.* 10th–11th century, is from the Kama River region (a tributary of the Volga and part of its navigable river trade route) in Russia (Kazakov 1991, p. 138, pl. 44.88).

Fig. 124.3 – 1880.3940.b. Box 9. Cast brass flat crescent, decorated with incised arcs and lines on the face. On the back are traces of a rivet; *c.* 10th–11th century. 14.1mm x 16.2mm x 2.7mm.

Similar examples of larger size are from the Kama River region (Kazakov 1991, p. 138, pl. 44.86–7).

Fig. 124.4 – 1880.3940.c. Box 9. Cast copper alloy stud in the shape of a six-petalled flower, with a rivet in the centre of the back. 14mm x 2.6mm; rivet: 6.4mm.

Fig. 124.5 – 1880.3940.d. Box 9. Cast copper alloy hemispherical stud in the shape of an eight-petalled flower, with a rivet in the centre of the back. 10.7mm x 4.8mm; rivet: 4.5mm.

Fig. 124.6 – 1880.3843. f. IM.Metal.160. Cast copper alloy flat stud, decorated with incised lines radiating from a circle which is divided into quarters by an incised cross. On the back are traces of a lug or rivet. 11mm x 9.8mm x 1.5mm.

Fig. 124.7 – 1880.3843.g. IM.Metal.160. Cast copper alloy, circular stud (?), with a nipple in the centre. On the back are traces of a large circular lug (?). 12mm x 3.7mm; lug: 6mm.

Fig. 124.8 – 1880.3843.h. IM.Metal.160. Cast copper alloy hollow casing or stud rounded at one end and straight (possibly broken off) at the other; the remains of a rivet on the back. 13mm x 10.5mm x 2mm.

Fig. 124.9 – 1880.3843.i. IM.Metal.160. Cast copper alloy hollow circular stud, with the remains of a rivet on the reverse. 14.5mm x 3mm.

Fig. 124.10 – 1880.3809. IM.Metal.151. Copper alloy circular stud, engraved with a whorl of three semi-circles; a small rivet on the back. 12mm.

Fig. 124.11 – IOLC.7600. K.409. Cast copper alloy relief-moulded plaque with a small rivet hole. The upper part resembles a *triratna* resting on a scroll, with a long central prong. The reverse is flat. 27mm x 24mm.

Fig. 124.12 – IOLC.7601. K.410. Cast copper alloy ornamental plaque; shaped in relief, the upper part resembling a *triratna* resting on a scroll, with a long central prong flanked below by addorsed curled elements. The upper left-hand prong is broken; the rivet for attachment is still in place; the reverse is flat. 27mm x 14mm.

Fig. 124.13 – 1880.3686.l. IM.Metal.24. Cast copper alloy appliqué ornament, probably a buckle fitting, in the shape of a shield, with a bevelled edge that retains traces of gilding. The flat surface is decorated with two incised, mirrored, leafy scrolls. It is pierced by three holes; the one in the centre retains a bent rivet. Islamic, *c.* 10th–11th century. 14.9mm x 18.3mm.

A small ornament of the same shape from Sardis is tentatively attributed to the Ottoman period (Waldbaum 1983, no. 714). The motif of two mirrored scrolls occurs on a large number of small fittings of the 9th–11th century (Kyzlasov 1969, p. 108, fig. 40; Kazakov 1991, p. 130, fig. 44; Brentjes and Vasilievsky, 1989, p. 161).

Fig. 124.14 – 1880.3943.a. Box 9. Cast copper alloy heart-shaped fitting, with a bar across the top and a rivet

Figure 124 Decorative fittings

hole in the centre. The design is delineated with a thick incised line and there are traces of silver (?) in the grooves; *c*. 10th–11th century. 16mm x 14.4mm.

Small heart-shaped fittings were particularly fashionable between the 10th–11th century. Examples have been found in the Kama River region, Russia (Kazakov 1991, pp. 132–5, pl. 44.24–6, 31–45), and in Khwarazm (Nerazik 1976, fig. 61). Specimens from the Tuva region are dated 9th–10th century (Kyzlasov 1969, p. 108, fig. 40; Kazakov 1991, p. 130, fig. 44. Others from Central Asia are dated 7th–11th century (Brentjes and Vasilievsky, 1989, p. 161).

Fig. 124.15 – 1880.3943.b. Box 9. Cast copper alloy belt-fitting with scalloped edges matching a row of round hollows along either side, and ending in a point at the top. In the centre are two rivet holes; *c*. 8th century. 21mm x 11.4mm x 2.3mm.

In outline it is comparable to a belt-fitting with two lugs on the back from Penjikent, dated 8th century (Belenitsky *et al*. 1973, fig. 54).

Fig. 124.16 – IOLC.7599. K.408. Fragment of a cast copper alloy plaque with notched sides and a hole for attachment at one end; broken at the other end (?); decorated on the upper surface with two parallel incised lines. 14mm x 8mm.

Fig. 124.17 – 1880.3954. Box 9. Cast copper alloy clasp, comprising a tongue, which broadens round a central fastening hole and ends in a point, attached by a hinge to a smaller hollow plate with a central hole for attachment. 31mm x 8.5mm x 3mm.

Fig. 124.18 – 1880.3961. Box 8. Cast copper alloy plaque, roughly triangular, with indented edges, two lobes at the top, and a rivet hole below; decorated with two incised transverse lines and two circular depressions, perhaps for inlays. The rectangular base is broken at both sides. 16mm x 13mm x 1mm.

Sheet metal pierced objects

Fig. 125.1 – 1880.3820.m. IM.Metal.160. Rectangular pendant of copper alloy sheeting with a cut saw-tooth lower edge and a punched hole in the centre of the top for suspension. Broken on one bottom corner, with multiple scratches on both sides. 24.5mm x 25.7mm.

It may be intended to represent a comb, which since earliest times had a talismanic value.

Fig. 125.2 – 1880.3844.a. IM.Metal.160. Roughly rectangular piece of copper alloy sheeting, with a small hole close to one corner and diagonally opposite, a larger hole, which has partly cut away the edge of the plaque. Both sides are corroded and possibly show traces of punch marks. 17mm x 14mm x 1.2mm.

Fig. 125.3 – 1880.3845.b. IM.Metal.160. Copper alloy square plaque, with a hole through the centre. 13.5mm x 13mm x 2mm.

Fig. 125.4 – 1880.3949. Box 8. Copper alloy rectangular plaque, with a short, flared stem ending in a domed head projecting from one side. Originally there were three holes for attachment, one centred at the base of the stem, the other two at the opposite corners (one now missing). The stem has traces of gilding. 19.5mm x 10.5mm x 0.5mm; stem: 5.5mm.

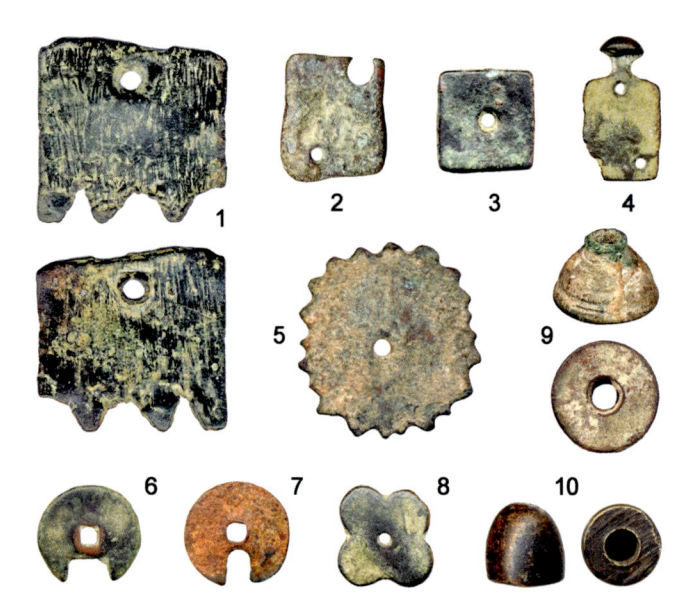

Figure 125 Sheet metal pierced objects

Fig. 125.5 – 1880.3945. Box 9. Copper alloy disc with a hole through the centre and a toothed edge. 18mm x 1mm.

Fig. 125.6 – 1880.3843.l. IM.Metal.160. Copper alloy disc or washer, with a square hole through the centre and a rectangular section cut out of the side. 14mm x 1mm.

Fig. 125.7 – 1880.3944.b. Box 8. Copper alloy disc or washer, with a round hole through the centre and a U-shaped section cut out of the side. 14.5mm x 1mm.

Fig. 125.8 – 1880.3845.a. IM.Metal.160. Copper alloy plaque resembling a simplified flower with four lobes and a hole through the centre. 13mm x 13mm x 2mm.

Fig. 125.9 – 1880.3947.a. Box 9. Solid, cast copper alloy hemisphere, with incised bands encircling the dome, and a wide hole through the centre, enclosed by a short collar at the top. 9mm x 14mm; hole:3.5mm.

Fig. 125.10 – 1880.3947.b. Box 9. Solid, domed cap of cast copper alloy, flat at the base. In the centre is a circular hole, extending through most of the dome. 10mm x 11mm; hole: 4mm.

Nails, tacks and studs

Fig. 126.1 – 1880.3952. Box 9. Cast copper alloy object resembling a spinning top; comprising a thin disc, with a conical protuberance rising from the centre of the top, and a long, thin pin extending from the centre underneath. Both sides of the disc are decorated; the underside with two concentric bands of geometric decoration in low relief; the upper surface with a ring of small studs. 19mm x 17.5mm.

Fig. 126.2 – 1880.3843.j. IM.Metal.160. Cast copper alloy hollow circular stud with pin. 7.5mm x 5mm; pin: 9mm.

Fig. 126.3–4. Box 9. Copper alloy stud, with a hollow, domed head and tapering pin.

Fig. 126.3 – 1880.3951.a. 10mm x 9mm.

Fig. 126.4 – 1880.3951.b. 13mm x 9mm.

Fig. 126.5 – IOLC.7611. K.446. Copper alloy nail or tack; comprising a broken circular head with an uneven upper surface (possibly raised decoration), moulded onto a shaft with a broken tip. 20mm x 12mm.

Fig. 126.6 – 1880.3868.b. IM.Metal.160. Cast copper alloy rivet. 12mm x 8mm.

Fig. 126.7 – 1880.3977.m. IM 33 / SKM 1103. Twisted S-shaped shaft of a silver nail (?) with one flattened and one pointed end. 17mm x 2mm.

Fig. 126.8 – 1880.3977.l. IM 33 / SKM 1103. Bent silver nail with a blunt point and a small, flat, square head. 13mm x 2mm x 3mm.

Lids

Fig. 127.1 – 1880.3959.a. Box 9. Broken oval lid of cast copper alloy with traces of silvering. The upper surface is covered with floral decoration in low relief around a central rosette. The flange on the underside of the lid is set 3mm in from the rim. 60mm x 55mm x 5mm.

Fig. 127.2 – 1880.3990.m. Box 11 / J.14. Cast copper alloy fretwork lid, with an oval, domed body and a wide flat rim above a recessed lip. There is a circular hole at the apex, four tiny holes around the rim and a further two on the upper surface for attachment. 10th–11th century. 48mm x 30mm x 15mm.

There is no counterpart, but domed lids with a flat rim were common during the early Islamic period. Examples have been found at the 8th–13th century site of Nishapur (Allan 1982, p. 161, nos 162–5). An 8th–10th-century example in the Aron collection has a bird finial (Allan 1986, no. 26) as does **Fig. 128.4** and this may have once also been the case here.

Fig. 127.3 – 1880.3687.k. IM.Metal.25 / IM 68 / SKM 1069. Thin, domed, circular lid (?) hammered in copper alloy with a folded edge on the inside rim, which is decorated with evenly spaced incised lines; partly broken. 20.2mm x 4.5mm.

Fig. 127.4 – 1880.3959.b. Box 9. Circular disc of cast copper alloy with traces of silvering. The upper surface has a running band of linked dot in circle motifs around a central circular hole. A flange on the underside is set 2.5mm in from the rim, suggesting that this was a lid. 16mm x 3.5mm.

Fig. 127.5 – IOLC.7609. K.443. Copper alloy flat oval lid (?) with a thick wire handle looped through two regularly spaced holes and bent at right angles on the back. 24mm x 11mm.

Figure 126 Nails, tacks and studs

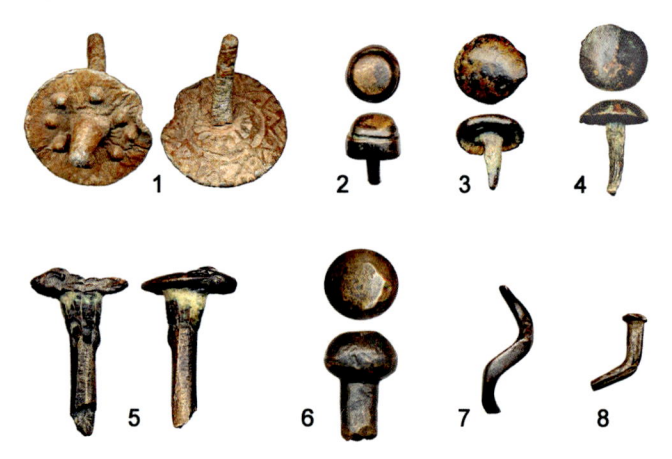

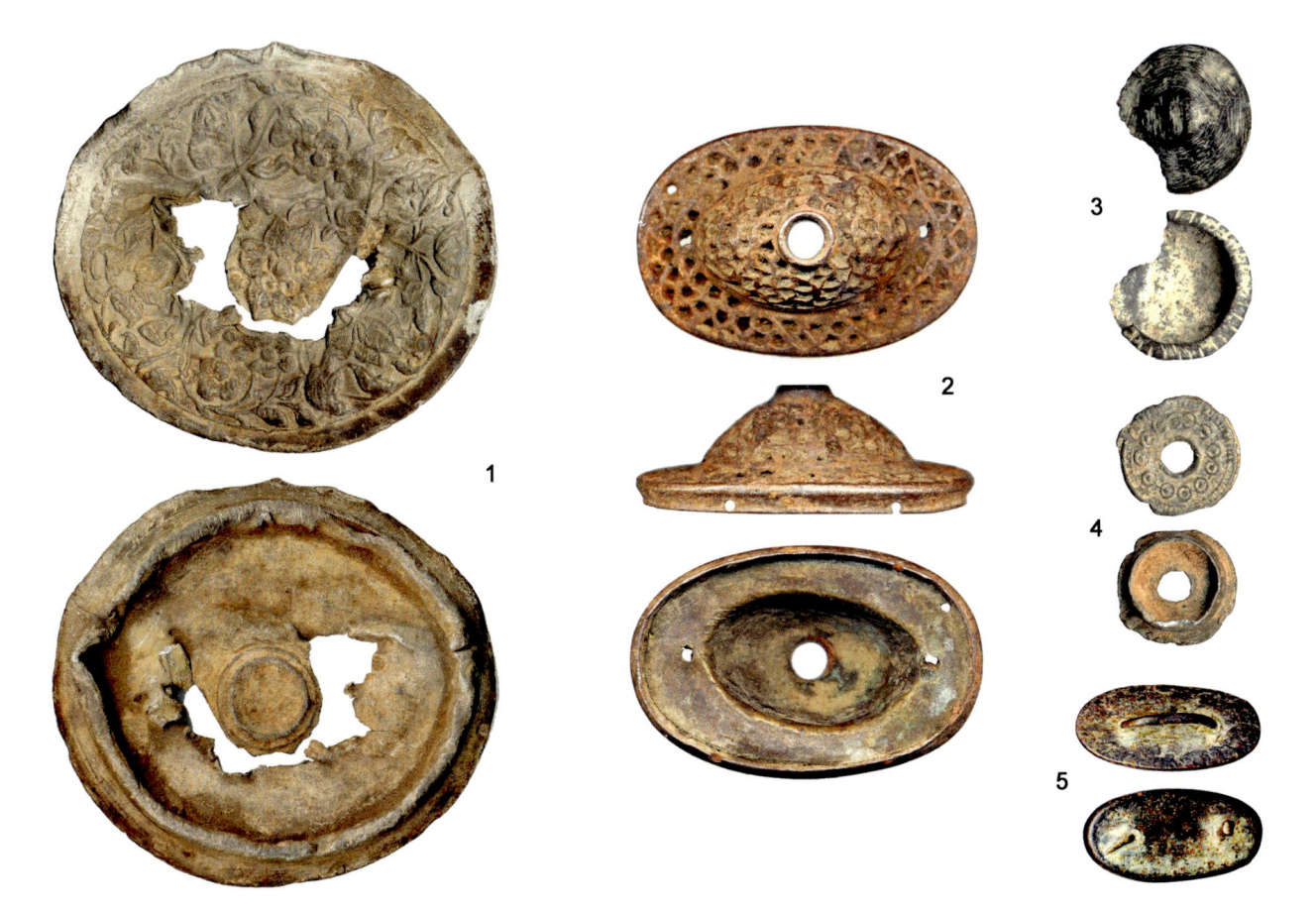

Figure 127 Lids

Ornamental birds

Fig. 128.1 – 1880.3672. IM.Metal.6. Solid cast copper alloy bird with long neck, triangular comb, curved beak and wings, but missing a tail. There is a large recess at the bottom for a shaft to attach it to a vessel or incense burner. 11th–12th century. 45.5mm x 35mm x 16.6mm. Wilson 1841, p. 53, fig. 9, Antiquities pl. III.9.

The form of the bird is typical of Seljuq bronzes. A comparable, complete bird is fixed to the top of a Seljuq incense burner dated 11th century (Bodur 1987, fig. 84). A bird finial with a comparable head was found at 8th–13th-century Nishapur (Allan 1982, fig. 155).

Fig. 128.2 – 1880.3713.p. IM.Metal.156. Cast copper alloy, slightly curved, ornamental foot, topped by a bird with a large head and a pointed wing or tail. The outer face is decorated with random incised lines and a punched dot in circle for the eye. The inner face has a lug at neck level for attachment to some object, possibly the top of an oil lamp handle. 11th–12th century. 44mm x 9.5mm; bird: 29mm.

Fig. 128.3 – 1880.3686.m. IM.Metal.24. Cast copper alloy flat plaque in the shape of a hawk with an incised decorative band around the neck and a circle on the body containing an interlocking Soloman's knot. Broken across the base. 10th–11th century. 60mm x 24mm x 3.2mm. Errington 1999 p. 230, pl. 9.8.

The Soloman's knot is a typical motif of Samanid Khurasan (AD 819–1005) where it appears on a large number of 10th-century bronzes (Melikian-Chirvani 1975, IV.2, pls V.1, VI.2; 1982, p. 44, no. 5), as well as some acquired in Kabul (Bumiller 1993, p. 93, fig. 37; Dahncke 1992, vol. 4, p. 82, no. 203a). The motif also occurs on a series of ewers bearing the name of the same craftsman, Ahmad. They are attributed to the first half of the 11th century and come from Ghazni, Qal'a-i Qakhqakha III, northern Tajikistan, Yaryk-depe 2, south-eastern Turkmenistan, and the Sogdian site of Chaghaniyan (http:www.transoxiana.org/Eran/Articles/ilyasov.html, pls II.1, III.2, III.3, IV.1–3).

Fig. 128.4 – 1880.3687.b. IM.Metal.25 / IM 68 / SKM 1069. Domed, pierced lid of an incense burner cast in copper alloy, surmounted by a bird; with a pierced lug for attaching a hinge. 10th–11th century. 40mm x 32mm.

Vessel fittings

Fig. 129.1 – 1880.3687.r. IM.Metal.25 / IM 68 / SKM 1069. Hollow finial fragment, resembling the dome and superstructure of a miniature stupa, with a recessed section around the bottom edge for fitting into a base; perhaps from the lid of a reliquary; cast in copper alloy; c. 3rd–6th century AD. 31.5mm x 10.3mm.

Fig. 129.2–3. Box 9. Cast copper alloy finials. The pear-shaped body has a collar and domed knob at one end and a flaring, flat, roughly circular base at the other, but with no obvious means of attachment. 8th–10th century.

A comparable finial decorated the apex of the domed lid of an 8th-century ewer (Migeon 1927, II, p. 29, fig. 227) and the handle of a 9th–10th-century ewer (Bodur 1987, p. 81, A1).

Fig. 129.2 – 1880.3959.c. A band of moulding separates the body from the base. 27.5mm x 10mm (base diameter).

Fig. 129.3 – 1880.3959.d. There is an indentation, just off-centre, in the base. 22mm x 8.5 (base diameter).

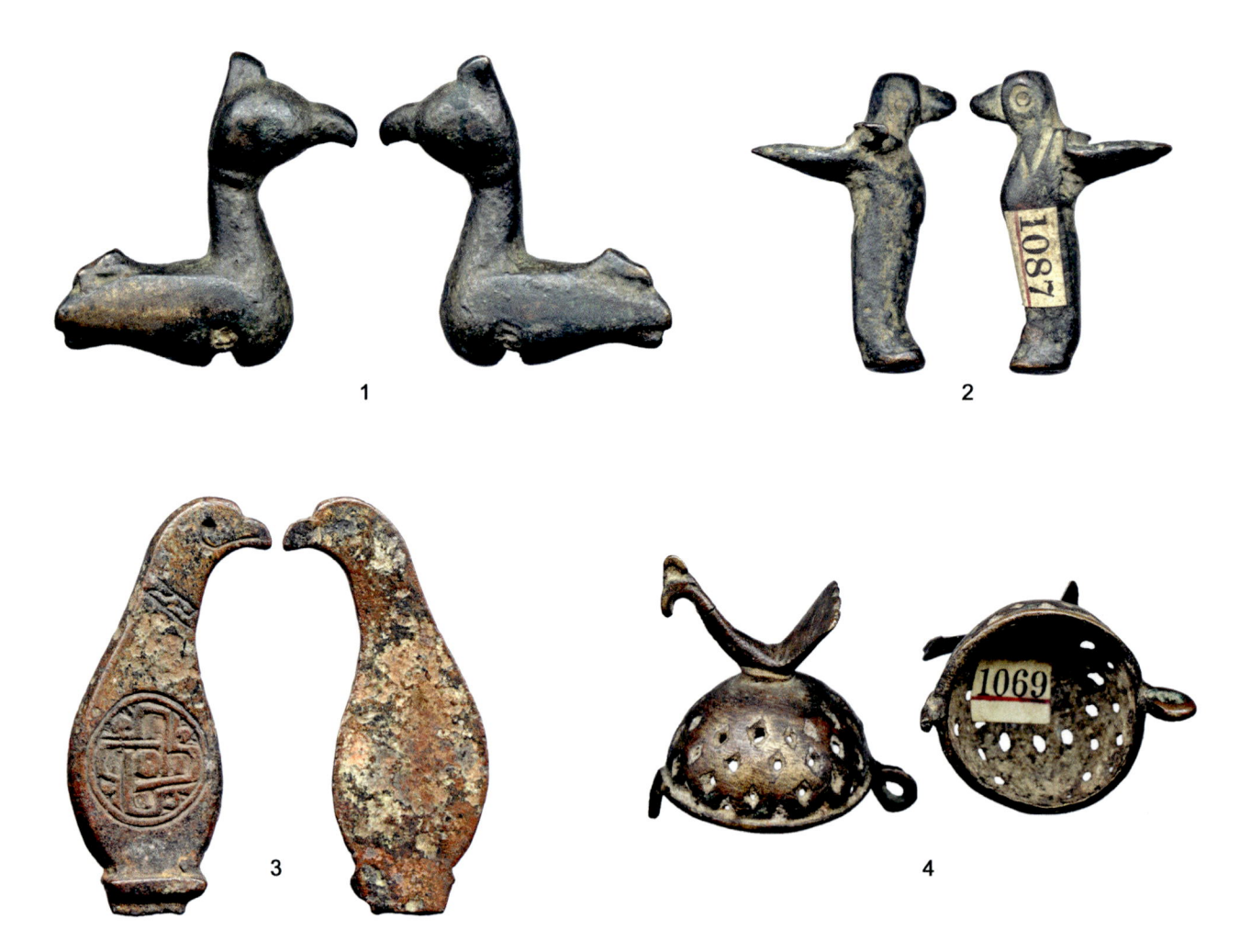

Figure 128 Ornamental birds

Fig. 129.4 – 1880.3990.g. Box 11, J.14. Flaring, elongated neck and shoulder of a hammered copper alloy vessel. 62mm x 35mm (base) x 20mm (rim).

Fig. 129.5 – 1880.3990.j. Box 11, J.14. Cast copper alloy, intact curved leg from a tripod vessel or small brazier (?). The form is splayed at the top, narrowing into an arched slender leg and terminating in a small foot. 58mm x 18mm.

Fig. 129.6 – 1880.3990.k. Box 11, J.14. Cast copper alloy ornamental handle (?), in the form of an open, elongated trefoil, pointed at the tip and with two holes for attachment at right angles to the base. 50mm x 27mm.

Striated fragments

Fig. 130.1–4. Flat copper alloy fragments, the back covered with multiple striations resulting from the manufacturing process. Similar striations or scratches occur, often together with the dot in circle motif, on ornaments of the 10th–11th century such as pins **Fig. 101** and pendants **Fig. 112.3**. Islamic, 10th–11th century.

Fig. 130.1–2. Fragments of lozenge-shaped plaques with rounded corners, decorated in the centre with an incised roundel containing a Solomon's knot, flanked by a punched dot in circle motif. For documentation of this motif, see **Fig. 128.3**.

Fig. 130.1 – 1880.3686.k. IM.Metal.24. There is a small lozenge-shaped projection attached to the bottom corner and a tiny hole at the place of the remaining dot, perhaps for a nail to fix the element on a wooden box. 29.2mm x 21mm.

Fig. 130.2 – 1880.3850.a. IM.Metal.160. 22.6mm x 30mm.

Fig. 130.3 – 1880.3850.b. IM.Metal.160. Fragment with a curved edge ending in a point; decorated with an incised roundel containing a Solomon's knot (?) encircled by five randomly punched dot in circle motifs (three complete). 22.4mm x 19.2mm.

Fig. 130.4 – 1880.3850.d. IM.Metal.160. Roughly triangular fragment, with one curved edge and floral decoration in shallow relief. 19.7mm x 23.8mm.

Spoons

Fig. 131.1–2. Cast copper alloy spoons with a shallow bowl and a short section of a flat handle. The point where the two join is decorated on the front with incised horizontal lines and forms a thicker reinforcement triangle on the back of the bowl.

Fig. 131.1 – IOLC.7662. The bowl is slightly pointed at its tip. The surviving section of the handle is marked by an incised line at the point where it joins the bowl. 11th–13th century. 43mm x 37mm.

A similarly shaped bowl of a spoon, but decorated with a punched dot in circle motif, was excavated on the eastern slope of the Citadel at Ghubayra, Iran (Area C, Grid no.K96d, Layer 2), dated c. 11th–13th century (Bivar 2000, pp. 39–40, 104, 387, no. B3/72-224, pl. 64.e).

Fig. 131.2 – IOLC.7663. Spoon fragment. Part of the bowl and handle with four incised lines at the join. 11th–13th century. 25mm x 18mm.

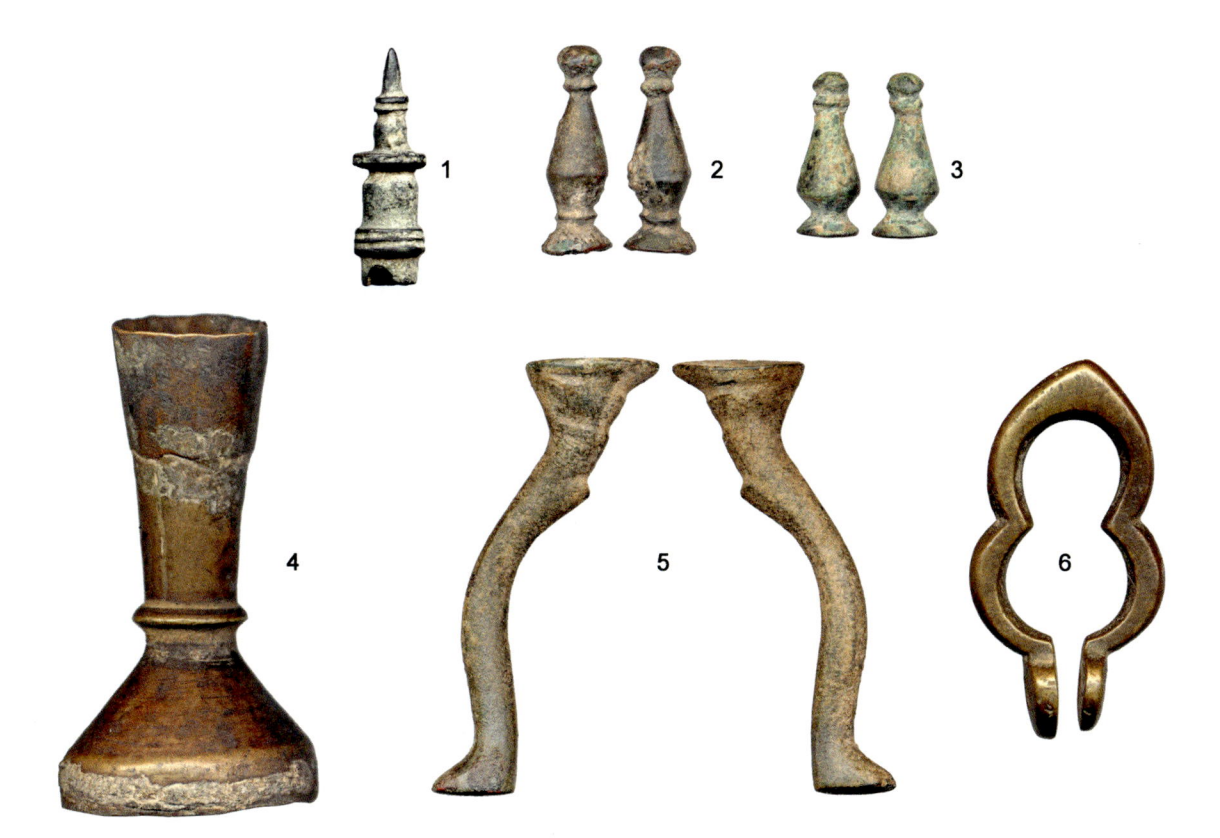

Figure 129 Vessel fittings

Fig. 131.3 – 1880.3715.a. IM.Metal.158. Copper alloy spoon with an oval hammered thin bowl, slightly split at the tip. The short section of the handle, is flat at its junction with the bowl and tapers along the surviving length of its shaft. 8th–13th century. 41mm x 22mm.

A spoon with a similar bowl, but with a handle that is round in section was found at Nishapur Village Tepe, dated c. 8th–13th century (Allan 1982, pp. 90–1, fig. 117).

Fig. 131.4 – 1880.3715.b. IM.Metal.158. Cast copper alloy, shallow, elliptical bowl of a spoon, with a stub of the handle and scratches on the reverse. 11th–14th century. 30mm x 24mm.

Fig. 131.5 – 1880.3715.c. IM.Metal.158. Cast copper alloy bowl and part of the handle of a small spoon with a thick, flattened rim. At the junction with the bowl, the handle is decorated with an incised line and two notches. 11th–14th century. 20.5mm x 14.6mm.

A similar spoon to **Fig. 131.4–5** was excavated from the citadel at Ghubayra, Iran (Area C, Grid no. H1c, Pit G), dated c. 11th–14th century (Bivar 2000, pp. 18, 103, no. B3/71-18, pl. 63.b).

Dies

Fig. 132.1 – 1880.3687.a. IM.Metal.25 / IM 32 / SKM 1105. Cast copper alloy die for a lobed boss in the shape of a domed eight-pointed star, with a hole in the apex. 1st century or 6th–7th century. 42mm x 12mm.

Two examples of smaller size, one with eight points, the other with six, were found at Sirkap, Taxila in the 1st-century AD Indo-Parthian stratum (Marshall 1951, p. 582, pl. 179.89, 93). Another with nine points was found at Kandahar, Site F, Phase VIIb2, and dated to the late 6th–early 7th century (McNicoll and Ball 1996, p. 272, fig. 209.2).

Fig. 132.2 – 1880.3963. IM.Metal.159. Cast copper alloy, crescent, square in section, with a thick centre tapering to a point at either end. Islamic, c. 12th–13th century. 10mm x 2.8mm x 3mm.

A similar example was found in Khwarazm, Uzbekistan (Research Center for Silk Roadology 1996, p. 32).

Fig. 132.3–4. Box 9. Two cast copper alloy crescents, lozenge-shaped in section, with a thick centre tapering to a sharp point at either end. Islamic, c. 12th–13th century.

Figure 130 Striated fragments

Catalogue of Ornamental Metalwork and Miscellaneous Artefacts | 297

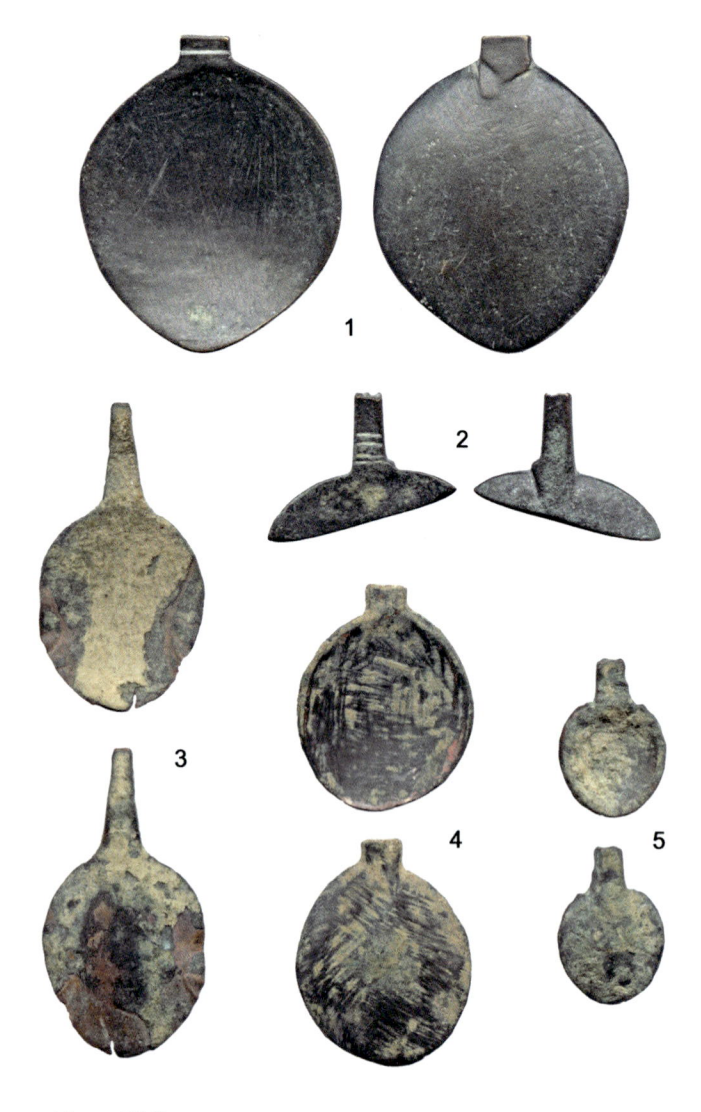

Figure 131 Spoons

A similar example was found in Room 17 of the 'palace' on the citadel (Area C, Grid N98a, layer 2) at Ghubayra Iran (Bivar 2000, p. 108, pl. 70.b, no. B6/74–457) and dated *c.* 14th century. Khwarazm yielded several specimens, one dated 12th–13th century (Vishnevskaia 1963, p.60, fig. 4.24; Research Center for Silk Roadology 1996, pp. 31–2; Nerazik 1976, fig. 62.2–4). Another example was acquired by the Pelliot Mission at Tongouz Bagh, in the Kucha region (Huashan *et al.* 1987, pl.XXX.1).

Fig. 132.3 – 1880.3965. 18.4mm x 20.3mm x 6.5mm (thickest point).

Fig. 132.4 – 1880.3966. 26.3mm x 21mm x 7.5mm (thickest point).

Fig. 132.5 – 1880.3967. Box 9. Cast copper alloy, heart-shaped die with a prominent central raised section. 26mm x 21mm x 10.3mm.

Fig. 132.6 – 1880.3678.a-c. IM.Metal.15. Three solid copper alloy moulds for sheet metal repoussé ornaments in the shape of a fish; *c.* 1st–7th century (?). 24mm x 8mm. Errington 1999: p. 229, pl. 8.33–5.

Fish-shaped bronze dies with a pair of fins on either side of the body were found in the 1st-century AD Indo-Parthian stratum at Sirkap, Taxila. This stratum also produced a belt or girdle of three rows of repoussé gold fish stamped on such dies (Marshall 1951, p. 522, pl. 179, 0. 79; pl. 180, no. 109; p. 630, no. 78, pl. 194b). The British Museum has another three dies in the shape of a fish with a fin on either side near the tail, but with scales represented by a herring-bone pattern (1921,0220.31–3). . They come from Kirman and are undated but could be Sasanian. An ear-ring acquired at Ispahan with four pendants in the shape of a fish shows that the motif was still in use during the Islamic period (Scerrato and Taddei 1963, pl. VIII.59).

Fig. 132.7 – 1880.3968. Box 9. Cast copper alloy, triangular die (?); rounded on one side, with a stepped ridge on the other. 34.6mm x 21.5mm x 9.4mm.

Arrowheads

Fig. 133.1–6 – 1880.3683.a-f. IM.Metal.22. Six cast copper alloy trilobate arrowheads of different types. Indo-Greek (?), *c.* 2nd century BC. Errington 1999, p. 230, pl. 9.20–3.

Copper alloy trilobate arrowheads, with or without barbs and with pierced sockets, are most commonly said to be Greek. From the numismatic evidence, it appears that the period of concentrated Greek occupation of Begram dated from the time of Apollodotus I, Eucratides I and Menander (180–130 BC).

Copper alloy examples definitely predate the Kushan period at the site. Arrowheads of similar shapes to **Fig. 133.1–4**, but all of iron, were excavated in considerable numbers from Begram II and III, which Ghirshman dates to the Kushan (*c.* AD 127–246) and Kushano-Sasanian (*c.* AD 246–390) periods respectively (Ghirshman 1946, pp. 26, 30, pls XXI.16, XXXVI.BG290a-b, XLVIII.BG464).

Fig. 133.1–2 – 1880.3683.a-b. With short, pierced sockets and without barbs. 30mm.

Fig. 133.3–4 – 1880.3693.c-d. Barbed, with sockets extending the length of the core. 33mm.

A similar example with three barbs was found at Ghiaur Kala in Turkestan (Pumpelly 1908, I, pt II, p. 198, fig. 51.7); another was acquired at Kucha (Stein 1928, p. 824, pl. CXI, Kucha 069).

Fig. 133.5 – 1880.3693.e. With a short socket and without barbs, but with two notched lobes. 33mm.

Fig. 133.6 – 1880.3693.f. Triangular in section with moulded pseudo-tangs fused to a pierced socket. The tip is broken. 33mm.

Miscellaneous decorative elements (function uncertain)

Fig. 134.1 – 1880.3791. Box 8. Small lead, crescent-shaped plaque, with a short central stem ending in a trefoil tip. 12mm x 10mm.

Fig. 134.2 – 1880.3687.q. IM.Metal.25 / IM 68 / SKM 1069. Square copper alloy plaque comprising a cross pierced with five holes and a ridged lozenge in each of the four interstices. Islamic (?) *c.* 8th–10th century. 15mm x 15mm.

The fragment relates stylistically to open-work items identified as parts of a horse harness from Nishapur (Alan 1982, nos 131–9).

Fig. 134.3 – 1880.3858.a. IM.Metal.160. Fragment of a cast copper alloy open-work plaque; slightly convex with small notched detailing on the smooth pierced surface. The

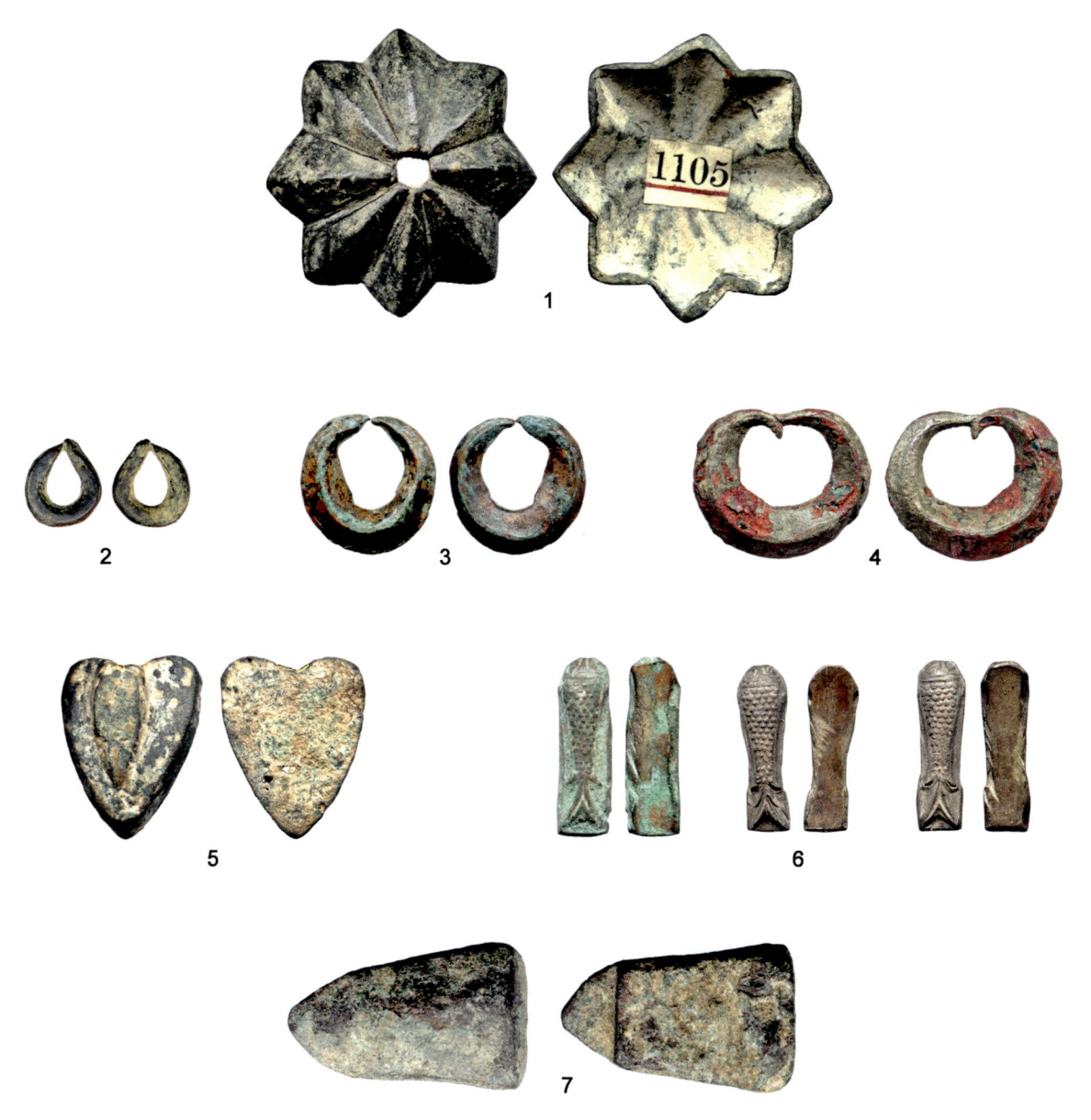

Figure 132 Dies

edges are cut to form a lozenge, separated by wide transverse bands from the broken section below and the rounded tip above. 29.5mm x 11mm x 1mm.

Similar, but much larger open-work plaques formed part of a horse harness at Nishapur (Allan 1982, pp. 92–3, nos 136 –7).

Fig. 134.4 – IOLC.7539. K 346. Unfinished (?) copper alloy flower, with two partial drill-holes and a central star-shaped boss of brass on the front; the back plain. Possibly intended as a spacer for a necklace or pendant. 13mm.

Fig. 134.5 – 1880.3824. IM.Metal.160. Flat, copper alloy plaque with concave sides, perhaps a die, decorated with a winged standing figure, perhaps Nike, in low relief on the front; the back is undecorated. 1st century AD. 14.2mm x 12.3mm (maximum) x 7.6mm x 2mm (minimum).

Spacers in the form of a sheaf commonly occur in necklaces of the Hellenistic period where they alternate with a rosette (Fabrègues 1991, pp. 178, 180). Examples in terracotta were found at the Bhir Mound, Taxila (Marshall 1951, p. 462, no. 146, pl. 136.0). Plain gold examples form part

Figure 133 Arrowheads

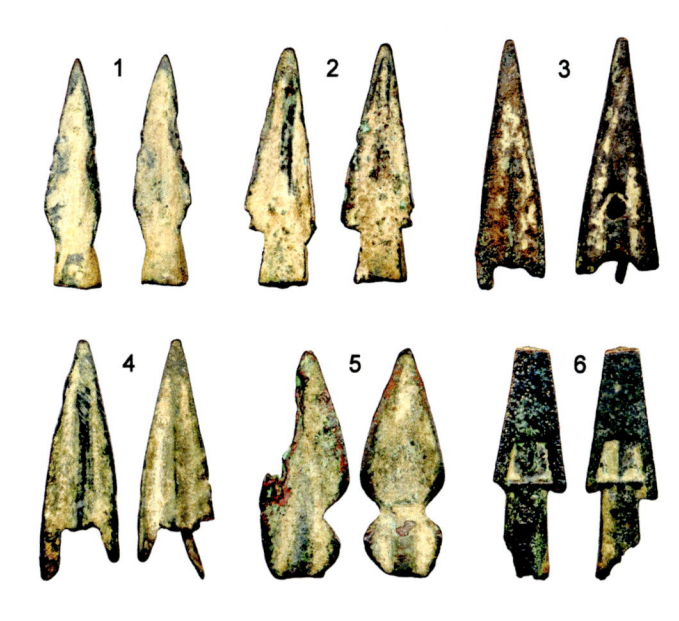

Catalogue of Ornamental Metalwork and Miscellaneous Artefacts | 299

Fig. 134.11 – 1880.3685.g. IM.Metal.23. Small silver loop of fused globules resembling beads. 9mm x 7mm x 2mm.

Fig. 134.12 – 1880.3685.d. IM.Metal.23. Piece of thick silver wire coiled at one end. 22mm x 1.5mm x 4mm.

Fig. 134.13 – 1880.3825.d. IM.Metal.160. Two links of a copper alloy chain. 22mm x 7.1mm.

Fig. 134.14 – 1880.3972.a. IM.Metal.159. Two loops of copper alloy wire linked together. 22.5mm x 5.5mm x 1mm.

Wire fittings

Fig. 134.15 – 1880.3955.b. Box 9. Copper alloy ring, the ends soldered together. Attached to the ring is a loop, which appears to have originally been the end of a shaft. 16.5mm x 15.5mm x 2mm.

Fig. 134.16 – 1880.3816.s. IM.Metal.141. Strip of copper alloy, the ends bent round to join each other and abut the centre of the strip, forming two contiguous rings, with traces suggesting that a further piece of copper alloy was soldered to it. 16.5mm x 8.5mm x 5.5mm.

Fig. 134.17 – 1880.3854.b. IM.Metal.160. Coiled strip of cast copper alloy, broken off at the outer end. 20mm x 14mm x 4mm.

Fig. 134.18 – 1880.3854.a. IM.Metal.160. Two interlocking rings of cast copper alloy; the larger is roughly circular, with the ends overlapping, the smaller is drop-shaped, the ends abutting. 30mm x 18mm.

Fig. 134.19 – 1880.3955.a. Box 9. Strip of copper alloy wire, which has been looped around a closed circular ring and twisted to form a short rope-like shaft. 35mm x 3mm; ring: 9.5mm.

Weights

Fig. 135.1–2. IM.Metal.160. Cubical weights of the Indus Valley type; made of steatite (?); *c.* 2100 BC.

Fig. 135.1 – 1880.3718.a. 11mm x 3.58mm.

Fig. 135.2 – 1880.3718.b. 9mm x 2.55mm.

Miscellaneous

Fig. 135.3 – 1880.3990.d. Box 11 / J.14. Faceted and polished ball of serpentinite. 16mm.

Fig. 135.4 – 1880.3485. IM.Metal.5 / SKM 402. Copper alloy astragalus, probably used as a gaming piece. Eastern Roman Empire (?), 1st–2nd century AD. 24mm x 11mm x 10mm. Wilson 1841, p. 53, fig. 10, Antiquities pl. III.10; Errington 1999, p. 230, pl. 9.18.

For similar examples from the Roman world, see www.britishmuseum.org Collection Online 1772,0311.176 (bronze); 1814,0704.1091 (onyx); 1841,0704.1134 (rock crystal).

Fig. 135.5 – 1880.3607. IM.Gems.64. Oval grey baked clay amulet plaque with a pointed apex; showing Mahākāla (an aspect of Shiva considered a protector deity in Nepalese and Tibetan Buddhism). The figure has three heads, six arms and four legs. His visible attributes include a staff and possibly a skull-cup. The lower part of a chakra or wheel can be seen between his legs. Buddhist, 11th century, originating from Tibet or Nepal (?). 17.64mm x 13.2mm. Errington 1999, p. 234, pl. 13.2.

Purchased in Kabul bazaar. The British Museum registration slip IM.Gems.64 incorrectly identifies this

---

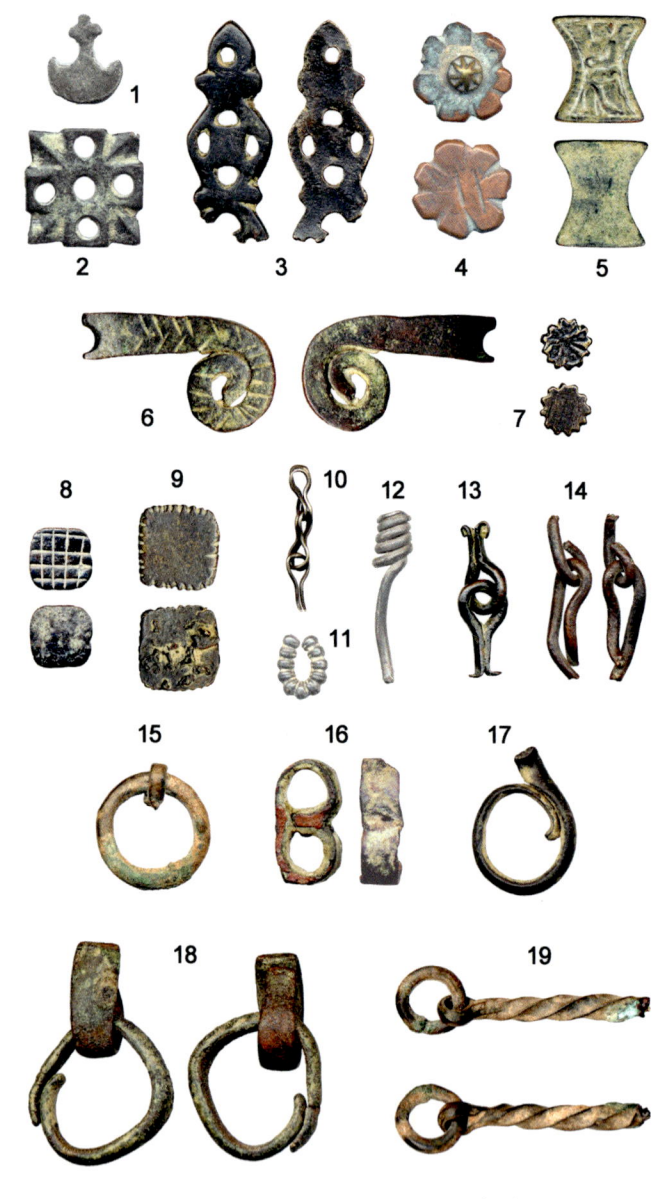

Figure 134 Miscellaneous decorative elements (1–9), chains and wire (10–14), wire fittings (15–19)

of a necklace from burial 5 at Tillya Tepe, Afghanistan (Sarianidi 1985a, fig. 5.3).

Fig. 134.6 – 1880.3858.b. IM.Metal.160. Flat strip of cast copper alloy, Broken off on either side of a semi-circular hole through the centre at one end; narrowing and curving into a spiral at the other and decorated with incised lines on the front. 26mm x 14.5mm x 1.5mm.

Fig. 134.7 – 1880.3830.d. IM.Metal.160. Cast copper alloy flat, circular plaque with a toothed edge and flower design on one side; smooth and undecorated on the other. 7mm x 2mm.

Fig. 134.8 – 1880.3981.i. Small, square plaque of thin silver (?) alloy, decorated with an incised grid on one side.

Fig. 134.9 – 1880.4117.h. Box 8. Thin, square, copper alloy plaque; smooth and flat on one side, with a notched edge; traces of solder (?) on the reverse. 11mm x 1mm.

Chains and decorative wire

Fig. 134.10 – 1880.3825.c. IM.Metal.160. Three links of a silver chain. 21mm x 3.5mm.

Figure 135 Weights (1–2), miscellaneous objects (3–9), stone ornaments (10–12), counters or tallies (13–14), glass (15–18)

object as having been found in 'Nandara tope (circa 1837)'. The correct clay sealing from Nandara stupa 1 is 1880.3891.e (**Vol. I, pp. 128–9, Fig. 162.4**).

Fig. 135.6 – 1880.3866. IM.Metal.160. Cylindrical rod of copper alloy, with (?) a brass wash, with a short section of narrower diameter and one end, and opening into a ring at the other. Possibly a key. 41mm x 15mm (ring) x 7mm (rod).

Fig. 135.7 – 1880.3676.a. IM.Metal.12. Bodkin cast in copper alloy with one round and one elongated eye and a globule on the point; decorated along the shaft with zigzag lines on one side and dots and crosses on the other. 56mm x 3mm.

Fig. 135.8 – IOLC.7624. K.461. Cast copper alloy triangular fragment of a Chinese mirror, with one curved and two cut straight sides. On the front is a band of moulded relief, flanked on either side by short hatched lines, and containing the remains of three Chinese characters (one complete). Flat on the back. Han dynasty (206 BC–AD 220) c. 1st century AD. 25mm x 17mm. Identified by Lutz Ilisch.

Catalogue of Ornamental Metalwork and Miscellaneous Artefacts | 301

The fragment has the same design (but maybe not the same inscription) as the two mirrors found in Tillya Tepe burials 5–6 respectively (Sarianidi 1985a), another dated AD 6 (Loewe 2001–2, p. 239, fig. 1) and a fourth example in the British Museum (1989,1211.1).

Fig. 135.9 – 1880.3676.c. IM.Metal.12. Miniature comb-shaped copper alloy key with five teeth and the remains of a shaft attached to one corner. The shaft is square in section, with two ridges and a broken loop. 12mm x 12mm x 6.8mm x 3.4mm.

Stone ornaments

Fig. 135.10 – 1880.3611. IM.Gems.69. Rectangular pale green jade plaque with a thick border framing the top and two sides. The panel in the centre shows a vegetal stem with three curling offshoots and beside it, a flying crane. The plaque is pierced a hole in each of the two top corners. On the back are three pairs of evenly spaced, smaller holes, each *c.* 4mm in depth and possibly for attachment to a belt. Western Liao dynasty, *c.* 12th–13th century AD. 38mm x 50mm x 9mm. Errington 1999, p. 228, pl. 715.

The plaque is part of a current British Museum scientific research project on Chinese jade.

Fig. 135.11 – 1880.3612. IM.Gems.70. Alabaster *yoni* ('source of life', symbol of the goddess Shakti, consort of Shiva), carved as a raised C-shape embellished with chevrons on a plain rectangular base, with a projecting lug for suspension (broken). In the centre is a circular hole for inserting the *lingam* (missing). On the back between two bands of chevrons is the name 'Ali Farrukh (?) inscribed in Persian. Additional mirror image inscriptions around the sides are blundered, but appear to begin (left side) *lā ī[lā]* ... i.e. There is no god but God alone and Muḥammād is his messenger (Inscriptions read by V.S. Curtis and Gul Rahim Khan). 30mm x 27.7mm x 7mm; lug: 5.5mm.

Fig. 135.12 – 1880.3613. IM.Gems.71. Pentagonal, brown-yellow fossilised limestone pendant, pierced at the narrowest point at the top for suspension. The front is slightly rounded, sloping on either side from the thickest point in the centre towards the rounded edges; the back is flat. 19th century. 46.5mm x 27mm x 10.3mm x 12.6mm x 8.3mm.

Counters or tallies

Fig. 135.13–14. Two rectangular cast copper alloy counters or tallies (?) with rounded corners and thick grooved lines dividing the surface area into equal sections.

Fig. 135.13 – IOLC.7670.1. K.612. A central groove divides the surface into two halves. 28mm x 17mm.

Fig. 135.14 – IOLC.7670.2. K.613. A grid of one vertical and two horizontal grooves divides the surface into six sections. 32mm x 19mm.

Glass

Fig. 135.15 – 1880.3828.t. IM.Metal.160. Teardrop-shaped ornament, or pendant, cast in opaque, uncoloured glass. Flat on one side, with a raised nipple on the other. 23mm x 15mm.

Fig. 135.16 – 1880.3828.s. IM.Metal.160. Flat, circular disc cast in opaque green glass; possibly an inlay or a board game counter. 12mm.

Fig. 135.17 – 1880.3828.u. IM.Metal.160. Flat, circular disc of ivory. Smooth on the front, but uneven on the back suggesting it may have been an inlay, rather than a board game counter. 14mm.

Fig. 135.18 – 1880.3828.v. IM.Metal.160. Flat, circular disc cast in opaque uncoloured glass; possibly an inlay or a board game counter. 10mm.

Concluding Remarks

This third volume on the Masson collection manuscripts, records and artefacts in the British Library and British Museum completes the survey of his archaeological work on the Buddhist sites of Afghanistan, and his acquisitions from Begram and Kabul bazaar. It is easy to forget that his discoveries were made in the 1830s, almost two centuries ago, at the very beginning of research in the field. Inevitably some of his theories have not survived the test of time, but it is remarkable how much he got right and the value of his detailed documentation has increased exponentially. In fact, the significance of his unpublished records only emerged with the utilisation by the Masson Project of this previously overlooked rich British Library resource.

Despite being the culmination of two decades of research on the Project, the Begram publication is not envisaged as the end of work on the subject, but hopefully will act merely as a springboard for future research by others. Many avenues are still open to investigation. Known collections in the Cambridge Fitzwilliam Museum and Museum of Archaeology and Anthropology, and the uncharted numismatic collection inherited by the Indian Museum, Kolkata, have only been referred to in passing here and remain uncatalogued. Even in the British Museum, work still needs to be done on the India Office coin collections (IOC and IOLC), while the identification and dating of many of the small metal artefacts remain uncertain.

Restricting the search to archaeological records and the British Museum collections as the Project has done, excludes a vast array of unique Masson manuscripts held by the British Library. These include all his sketches of the Salsette and Elephanta cave temples, Afghan towns and buildings (including a series illustrating the Bala Hisar at Kabul), drafts of articles and a large part of the miscellaneous ephemera of **F526/1–2**. Much of the official and political correspondence has also been omitted here, but is duplicated in East India Company records held by the UK National Archives at Kew and by central and regional archives throughout India.

In terms of Begram, Masson's finds supplement those of the Délégation archéologique française en Afghanistan a century later, by offering a broader numismatic remit than that provided by the French excavations, which were largely restricted to the Kushan levels. In contrast, the coins Masson collected range from *c.* 4th century BC to the early 13th century AD. In lieu of any future excavations, they indicate that the city was earlier under Indo-Greek rule, particularly during the reigns of Eucratides and Menander, but these and earlier levels have yet to be revealed. The coins further indicate that the site was probably still occupied until the Mongol invasions under Genghis Khan (1206–27). But the range of material also raises a number of queries, including the precise location of the Islamic period Parwan mint and how it corresponds to the known site of Begram. So there are many unanswered questions yet to explore, which it is hoped that Masson and his collections from Begram will help to elucidate.

In acknowledgement of his immense achievement, it seems only fitting that Masson should have the last word (see Appendix 1).

Appendices

Three supplementary documents are reproduced in appendix form. The first and most substantial Appendix 1 is a transcription of Masson's copious annotations in his personal copy of *Ariana Antiqua* held by the Bodleian Library, Oxford.

Appendices 2–3 are manuscripts from a box of miscellaneous Masson papers in the British Library (**F526/1**), which concern his acquisitions from Begram and Kabul:

Appendix 2 (**F526/1m**) is an East India Company Bombay Government receipt for the collections made between 19 October 1836 and December 1838. Compiled by J.P. Willoughby, Secretary to the Bombay Government in 1840–1, it is the only independent list of Masson's last collections prior to shipment to London. The distinctive handwriting of this manuscript and its sub-division of the coins and objects into 'Bags' I–XVII and A–G (**Fig. 142**) has enabled the identification of two stray bags in the India Office holdings of the British Library – marked F and k in the same hand (**Fig. 5**) – as part of this specific collection from Masson (see pp. 11–12, 14).

Appendix 3 (**F526/1n**) is a summary list by Masson of an estimated total of all his collections made during the entire period (1833–8). The watermark on the paper dates this compilation of data to 1843 or later.

Appendix 4 is a list of standardised spelling of personal and place names and 19th-century common transcriptions of names – such as the misreading of Bactrian H and Þ – being mistaken for K and R, resulting inter alia in 'Okro' (Oesho) and 'Ardokro' (Ardochsho).

Appendix 5 lists the British, South Kensington and India Museum inventory and accession numbers.

Appendix 1: Masson's Annotated Copy of *Ariana Antiqua*

Piers Baker with Elizabeth Errington

Professor Wilson would have done essential service in pointing out which was which – in which he has really bewitched the subject – or signally failed (Masson's annotated copy of *Ariana Antiqua*, p. 439: see p. 325 below).

Introduction

The year before Masson returned to London, his 'Memoir on the Topes and Sepulchral Monuments of Afghanistan' was published as Chapter II in H.H. Wilson's *Ariana Antiqua. A Descriptive Account of the Antiquities and Coins of Afghanistan* (London 1841).

Masson's own copy of *Ariana Antiqua* survives in the Bodleian Library in Oxford (Shelfmark Afghan 1 d 1). It is signed by Masson on the title page (**Fig. 136**), and it contains his extensive annotations.

This copy passed through at least two other hands before reaching the Bodleian Library via the Oxford Indian Institute, to which it was bequeathed by B.H. Baden-Powell.[1] Affixed to the inside of the front endpaper is the catalogue entry for the sale at which he acquired it, annotated 'Bought Oct. 1897. BHBP'.

The previous owner recorded on another page (before the title page) that he bought it at the sale of 'coins, medals &c.' of the Revd W.C. Neligan at Sotheby's on 15 November 1881. He replaced in it, as he records, two imperfect plates with those from the copy of the work previously owned by Major W.E. Hay, and had them bound in (by Morrell in 1890)[2] with some notes from that copy, which he then sold.

Masson annotated well over half of its 470 pages and 21 plates. Some of the annotations are personal – even bitter, reflecting his treatment at the hands of the East India Company and in particular '*the interference of Captn Wade*' (**p. v**). In the annotations to the Preface, for example, he sets the record straight as regards the Bombay government's support for his research in Afghanistan, and what he thought of the apparently generous presentation of 200 copies of the book to his mother. In the chapter he wrote himself, he corrects minor details and adds further thoughts, illustrating his continuing interest and research. In the remainder, he challenges Wilson on numerous occasions, e.g. '*Could Wilson seriously make this remark?*' (**p. 421**) – and suggests many corrections to Wilson's text, to the extent that one wonders if he would have accepted inclusion of his material in the volume if he had been given the option. He also uses the book to write out various copies and transcriptions of Kharoshthi inscriptions and Kharoshthi and other coins legends illustrated, giving further evidence of his continuing research. Many of his comments and amendments have stood the test of time.

Most of the annotations are in ink, almost always in a neat hand, but some are in pencil and written less carefully. Some of the pencilled comments are overwritten by much neater and usually longer annotations in ink (e.g. **p. 8**), and vice versa (e.g. **p. 57**), so use of ink or pencil cannot be taken as an indication of the order in which Masson added his comments. Where the annotations are in pencil, this is indicated in the transcript.

A complete digitised copy of *Ariana Antiqua*, with the library stamp of the Bibliothèque cantonale et universitaire de Lausanne, is at https://books.google.co.uk/books?id=oLgWAAAAQAAJ; the text can be searched, so

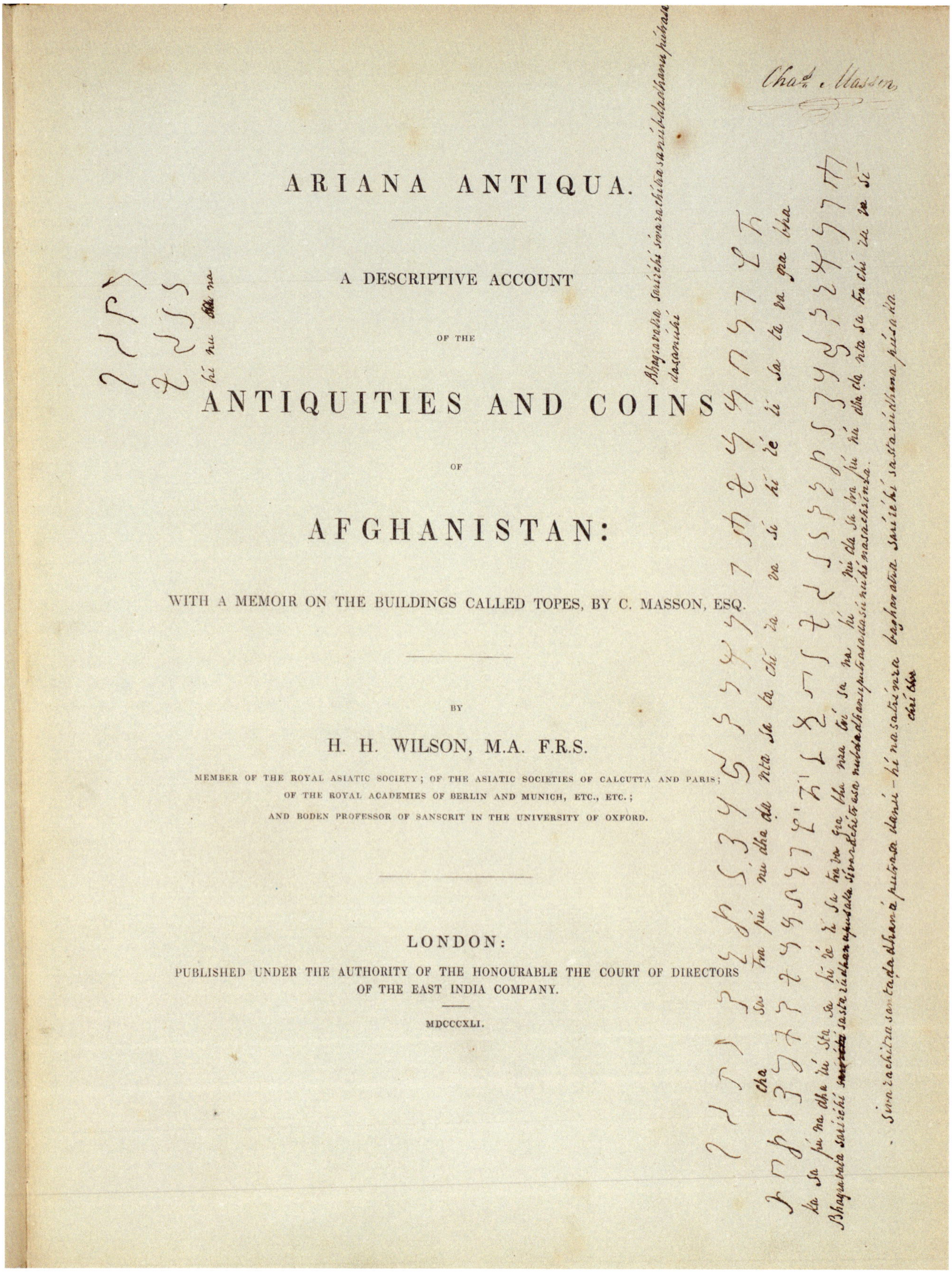

ARIANA ANTIQUA.

A DESCRIPTIVE ACCOUNT

OF THE

ANTIQUITIES AND COINS

OF

AFGHANISTAN:

WITH A MEMOIR ON THE BUILDINGS CALLED TOPES, BY C. MASSON, ESQ.

BY

H. H. WILSON, M.A. F.R.S.

MEMBER OF THE ROYAL ASIATIC SOCIETY; OF THE ASIATIC SOCIETIES OF CALCUTTA AND PARIS;
OF THE ROYAL ACADEMIES OF BERLIN AND MUNICH, ETC., ETC.;
AND BODEN PROFESSOR OF SANSCRIT IN THE UNIVERSITY OF OXFORD.

LONDON:

PUBLISHED UNDER THE AUTHORITY OF THE HONOURABLE THE COURT OF DIRECTORS
OF THE EAST INDIA COMPANY.

MDCCCXLI.

Figure 136 *Ariana Antiqua* title page: Masson's signature and Kharoshthi transcriptions. © Bodleian Library

may be useful to consult alongside Masson's marginalia transcribed here, where in the interest of space only brief references to the printed text are usually given. In the transcriptions that follow, minor comments or changes that do not affect the sense are generally omitted. As in the rest of the volume, Masson's and other 19th-century spellings, particularly of place names, have been standardised throughout (e.g. Begram for Béghram and Beghrám, Hadda for Hidda, Jalalabad for Jelalabad, Peshawar for Peshawer) and their variations listed in Appendix 5. However, Wilson's preferred use of Greek forms (such as Eukratides, Heliokles, Herakles) and Masson's for the Roman versions (Eucratides, Heliocles, Hercules) have been kept. The various spellings they use in transliterating coin legends are also retained e.g. *Sams-ud-din Mahomed / Mohomad / Mohammed bin Sam* (pp. 327–8, nos 25–7, 29, 35 below).

In the transcription that follows excerpts of the original *Ariana Antiqua* text are given in quotation marks, while Masson's annotations appear in italics. Comments within the quotations of Wilson and Masson's notes appear in square brackets. Cross references to page numbers in *Ariana Antiqua* are in bold.

Transcription of annotations

Title page

Masson signed the title page *Chas Masson*, and recorded his reading of the Kharoshthi text on the steatite reliquary from Bimaran 2 (illustrated in Antiquities pl. II, see **Vol. I, pp. 104–5, Fig. 117**), copying the characters and giving a transliteration. This is followed by a rendering of the text as: *Bhagravata saríréhí sasta rúdhan apusaka sivarachítrasa nubdadhanuputrasadasúnúhínasachrínra / Siva rachitra santada dhaná putrasa danú – hí nasatrínra baghavatra saríréhí sastarúchana púsaka;* and above the Kharoshthi *Bhagravatra saríréhí sovarachítra sanúbdadhanu pútrasa dasanúhí*.

There is a further small group of Kharoshthi characters with transliteration on the left of the page (**Fig. 136**).

Provenance

Interesting for its information on the provenance of the Bodleian's copy of the book, the following page has a book sale catalogue entry, cut out and pasted in, which reads:

> 938 Wilson (H.H.) Ariana Antiqua, Descriptive Account of the Antiquities and Coins of Afghanistan, *map and plates (2 slightly imperfect), uncut* 1841
>
> ** Mr C. Masson's (who was the principle compiler of the Work) own copy, with numerous MS. Notes and Corrections in his autograph (*several being signed*). It also contains the list of Subscribers, omitted in almost all other copies, with additional names in MS.

Below this is a note by the purchaser:

> *Bought at the sale of coins, medals &c of the Revd W.C. Neligan at Sotheby's 15/11/81 for £ E.E.-* [a copy of the sale catalogue in the British Museum Coins and Medals library is annotated with a sale price of £2, and the buyer's name is Mitchell]. *The 2 imperfect plates have been replaced from the copy of Major W.E. Hay (whence also the few ms notes herewith) which I bought at Sotheby's 9/8/1880 & since sold.*

This fine & unique copy is Mr Masson's own, with his autograph and numerous ms notes, all very important. Some of these notes have his initials 'C.M.' (p: 242, 334, 347 &c); others are signed (p: 125, 183). The list of subscribers, with ms additions, contained in this copy, is usually missing.

This work is the best extant account of ancient Bactria (modern Afghanistan); it is a very rare and valuable book, quite out of print.

Below: *Bound by Morrell,^{2} working to my own instructions. I. 93 V $^E/_L$ [?]^3*

Across the next page, pasted in, on laid paper, with a circular library stamp 'Indian Institute', is written *Masson's copy / £2.16.0.*^{4}

Below, pasted in separately, is a further book sale catalogue entry:

> 3144 WILSON (H.H.) ARIANA ANTIQUA, A Descriptive Account of the Antiquities and Coins of Afghanistan with a Memoir on the Topes by C. Masson, *26 plates of coins and antiquities, new half green morocco gilt, morocco corners, top edge gilt*, VERY RARE 4to.1841
>
> ** Charles Masson's own copy, with numerous MS. notes and corrections by him, many signed; and MS notes with two seals from Major Hay's copy [bound in at the beginning of the volume]; and the list of subscribers (usually wanting), with MS additions.

And further below, a library stamp 'Indian Institute Oxford'; and below again, in pencil: *Bought Oct. 1897* [initials] *BHBP*. Pasted to the inside of the front cover is the Indian Institute, Oxford's library label, with the note 'B.H. Baden-Powell bequest', the shelfmark and the subsequent note 'Conveyor Room'.

List of subscribers

There follows the rare list of subscribers, which begins with The Queen (2 copies), The Queen Dowager (5 copies) and Prince Albert (1 copy). Then follow the Archbishop of Canterbury and the Duke of Northumberland. Others on the list include the Hon. Mountstewart Elphinstone, General Sir Charles Napier, Col Sir Henry Pottinger and Godfrey Vigne. The printed name of Dr Simes, Cheltenham, is amended in mss to Dr Swiney. Among the handwritten additions at the end are the Duke of Devonshire and the Library of the Imperial Palace, Vienna.

Masson's annotations to Wilson

Preface

p. v
Against 'At an early period of his researches, Mr Masson proposed … to <u>transfer his actual</u> [Masson's underlining] and all future collections to the East India Company': *Mr Masson proposed to the Bombay Gov^t, if furnished with funds to expend such funds in researches on account of the Gov^t, of course to hand them over the results – when eventually Mr Masson learned that the Gov^t consented to advance money, Mr Masson voluntarily transferred to Gov^t the collections made at his own expense and then in his possession. They comprised relics from Topes at Darunta, the first years' collection of coins from Begram – besides other and various antiquities.*

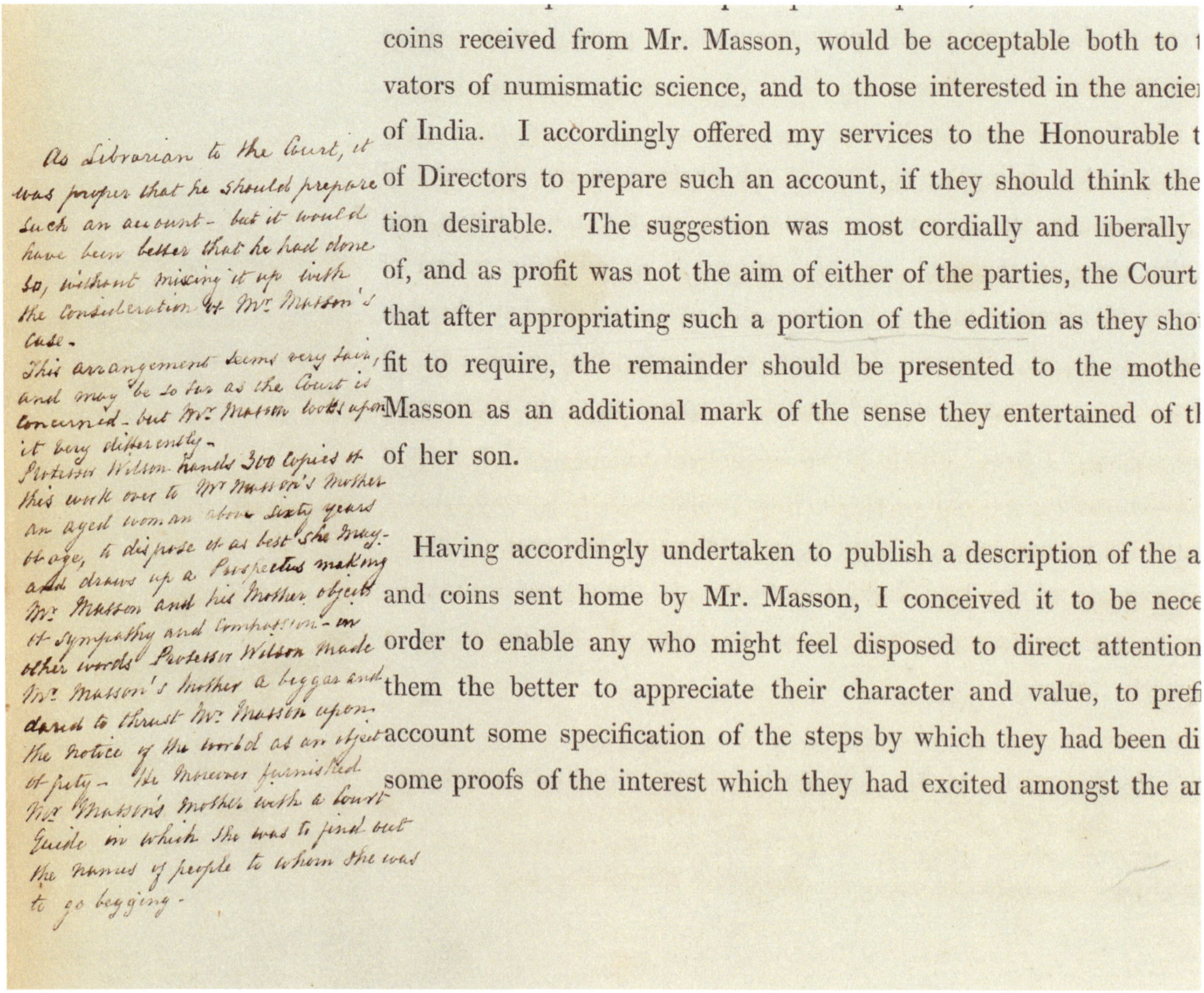
coins received from Mr. Masson, would be acceptable both to t
vators of numismatic science, and to those interested in the ancie
of India. I accordingly offered my services to the Honourable t
of Directors to prepare such an account, if they should think the
tion desirable. The suggestion was most cordially and liberally
of, and as profit was not the aim of either of the parties, the Court
that after appropriating such a portion of the edition as they sho
fit to require, the remainder should be presented to the mothe
Masson as an additional mark of the sense they entertained of tl
of her son.

Having accordingly undertaken to publish a description of the a
and coins sent home by Mr. Masson, I conceived it to be nece
order to enable any who might feel disposed to direct attention
them the better to appreciate their character and value, to prefi
account some specification of the steps by which they had been di
some proofs of the interest which they had excited amongst the ar

Figure 137 Masson's annotations on p. vi. © Bodleian Library

The Bombay Govt was willing to have defrayed the cost of the operations and authorized Mr Masson to appropriate for such purpose one half of the sums remitted to him – but the interference of Captn Wade prevented this arrangement being available to Mr Masson – consequently Mr Masson conducted his researches throughout at his own cost.

Against 'Mr Masson was employed … on behalf and at the expense of the East India Company': *a falsehood.*

p. vi

Against 'I accordingly offered my services to the Honourable the Court of Directors to prepare such an account [of the principal antiquities, and of the whole of the coins received from Mr Masson]': *As Librarian to the Court, it was proper that he should preface such an account – but it would have been better that he had done so, without mixing it up with the consideration of Mr Masson's case.*

Against 'the Court resolved, that after appropriating such a portion of the edition as they should think fit to require [right margin, in pencil: *200 copies*], the remainder should be presented to the mother of Mr Masson as an additional mark of the sense they entertained of the merits of her son' (**Fig. 137**): *This arrangement seems very fair, and may be so as far as the Court is concerned – but Mr Masson looks on it very differently.*

Professor Wilson hands 300 copies of this work over to Mr Masson's mother an aged woman above sixty years of age, to dispose of as best she may – and draws up a Prospectus making Mr Masson and his mother objects of sympathy and compassion – in other words Professor Wilson made Mr Masson's mother a beggar and dared to thrust Mr Masson upon the notice of the world as an object of pity. He moreover furnished Mr Masson's mother with a Court Guide in which she was to find out the names of people to whom she was to go begging.

p. vii

Against 'I therefore requested him [Mr Masson] to favour me with a more particular report of his operation': *Prof Wilson applied first to Mr Masson through the channel of Captn Wade, and received no reply. He then applied through the channel of Colonel Pottinger and was provided with what he wanted.*

pp. viii–ix & fn. 1

Against 'the able [Masson's underlining] geographer to the East India Company, Mr Walker' Masson has put '?' and, in the footnote against 'the probable route of Craterus was not by the Bolan but by the Gundara Pass': *can it be called a pass at all?*

Chapter I: Account of the Progress of Bactro-Indian Numismatic and Antiquarian Discovery, and Observations on the Edifices, called Topes

p. 6

Against 'There were not many private individuals in India,

who had the means or opportunities of forming collections of coins': *why not?*

p. 7
Against 'There is still no other public collection of the same kind [as the Asiatic Society's museum] in Bengal': *why should there be?* – 'and it is believed that a museum of any order is still wholly wanting at the other Presidencies': *Bombay has now one. 1845.*

Against 'There were two collections … of coins …, [one] by Colonel Mackenzie, which was purchased for the Company on his death': *what sum was given for it.*

Against Wilson's comment at the bottom of the page indicating the limited numismatic material available in the early 1830s, Masson writes *It is now worth while to refer to this account – to see how little or that nothing was then known, and to be satisfied of the value of what has been done since.*

p. 8
Against 'The zealous interest which Mr. Prinsep … <u>learned</u> [from Wilson] to take in the subject of Indian Numismatics': *did Prinsep <u>learn</u> from Wilson?*

Below (in pencil) original side-lined: *modest!*

Against the continuing passage on the influence of Wilson's work: *very modest*; [and in ink]: *Mr Masson saw Wilson's Paper in Kabul for the first time in 1836 – Mr Masson's collections were commenced in 1832.*

Against mention of the discovery of coins by General Ventura: *Ventura's operations had the merit of being voluntary ones.*

p. 9
Against 'Lieutenant Burnes, during his onward journey [to Bukhara], continued to avail himself of such opportunities as offered of collecting coins, and obtained several of great interest and value': *he did not avail himself – the two or three coins he brought from Bukhara were selections from a bag full !! so little was he aware of their value or even of what they were.*

p. 10
Against 'Mr Prinsep translated Professor Schlegel's Observations on the History of Bactria, illustrated by the coins discovered by Colonel Tod': *The Journal in which this translation appeared I saw at Kabul, it having been sent there to await Dr Gerard's arrival. Finding I could throw much light on the subject from the number of my coins and from their state of preservation, I hastily drew up a memoir (that below alluded to) for Dr Gerard to forward to Prinsep.*

p. 11
Against 'It may here be observed, that Mr Masson continued his researches at this place during the four succeeding years, and collected in this interval above thirty thousand coins': *Mr Masson's researches at Begram extended from 1833 to 1838. His collection comprised nearly or quite 120,000 silver and copper coins, a very few gold ones and a very few engraved gems; also many thousands of rings, seals brass and copper – cylinders and other antiquities.*

p. 12
Against '<u>The far greater proportion</u> [of copper coins; Masson's underlining], judging from Mr. Masson's own collection, must have been too much injured by time and corrosion to have had any other than metallic value' (in pencil): *hardly fair remark - or hardly true – the Begram coins infinitely surpass in preservation those found in India.*

p. 14
Against 'the legends on these coins, written in a barbarised form of Greek, were completely deciphered by Mr Prinsep': *Mr Masson in Kabul had done the same from his coins.*

p. 16
Against coins '<u>collected by Dr Gerard and [Lt Burnes]</u>': *Dr Gerard's coins were given to him by the Nawab Jabar Khan who begged them from Mr Honigberger.*

Against 'Amongst the coins of Mohan Lal is specified a tetradrachm of Euthydemus, as remarkable for its rich relief and exquisite workmanship': *Gerard to advance Mohan Lal's credit gave him this and other coins. The Euthydemus Gerard procured at Bukhara with some other antiquities.*

p. 19
Against a quotation of Prinsep on his taking further than Masson the deciphering of the Kharoshthi alphabet: *This is true – and Mr Masson did not seriously pursue the investigation because it would have been nearly useless, without means of reference, or in ignorance of the language.*

And below, in pencil (added separately, in a less neat hand): *how easy all this was – I did not follow it up as I should have otherwise done from wanting the means of reference to the language employed. Still while easy the merit is presumed great because the result is important – yet little, in fact nothing, more than determining a few letters of the alphabet has been yet effected with the simple fact that the language is Pali or as it is called in Persian works Pahlavi.*

p. 20
Against Prinsep 'determined the language to be, as he had always thought it likely to be, an Indian dialect <u>of Sanskrit origin</u>, to which the designation of Prakrit or Pali might be applied': *Mr Prinsep, I thought, found the language to be Pali or Pahlavi.*

p. 24 (in pencil)
Against 'A misappropriation made by the same distinguished numismatist, Pellerin, was more excusable, although it furnishes a warning against confidence in erudition': *very necessary.*

p. 25 (in pencil)
Against 'M. Jacquet's notice was … finally interrupted … by his premature death': *alas! Poor Jacquet!*

p. 26
Against 'A less elaborate but ingenious and talented account of General Allard's coins … was … drawn up by M. Jacquet': *Jacquet's account is of more value than M. Rochette's.*

p. 27
Against 'It is not surprising … that upon a subject so novel nothing should have been yet published in London beyond

the few observations addressed by myself [Wilson] to the Numismatic Society, printed in the Numismatic Journal, January, 1838': *An account giving no information beyond what was to be found in the Bengal Journals* [of the] *Asiatic Society.*

p. 31
Against 'Manikyala … Its geographical position leaves little doubt of its being the site of … Taxila': *Yet it is not positively the site of Taxila.* Wilson was wrong.

p. 36
Against 'These [Roman] coins are therefore of great chronological value, and determine the construction of [a stupa at Mera-ka-dheri near the village of Manikyala, excavated by Court (1834)] … to have taken place at a period not very long subsequent to the æra of Christianity': *Such coins do not exactly fix the age of a monument, although it must of course be subsequent, because they may have been curiosities at the time of deposit. However, they assign a limit to the antiquity of a monument and are therefore useful discoveries. M. Court's Tope is most likely more modern than Professor Wilson intimates.*

p. 41 (in pencil)
Against 'the Raja dug a cave … for the purpose of depositing in it images of the Buddha, with a vessel of brass, in which were deposited two of the bones of the Thacur … and over this cave was erected a place of worship, probably a tope, for the veneration of the Magas': *Compare this with what Wilson writes page 45+ where he insists that all the Topes covered relics real or supposed of the Buddhas – this Chittagong inscription proves that they all did not.*

p. 43
Against the list of coins found in stupas: *The genuine coins of Kanerkes [Kanishka] have never been found, I mean those with the Nanaia and Helios types. The coins found are the Rao Kanerki family. There have also been found in Topes with the coins of the Kadphises family, if such they be, or the okro [Oesho] figure and bull coins. Plate XI, figs 1 to 8.*

p. 45
Against 'The tope … of Topharamaya': *Tope of Rama?*

Against 'Lieutenant Burnes, Mr Masson, and M. Court, adopting the notions that prevail amongst the peoples of the country [Masson's underlining], are inclined to regard them as regal sepultures; but I am disposed with Mr. Erskine and Mr. Hodgson, and, I believe, with those learned antiquaries who have treated on the subject in Europe, to regard them as dahgopas on a large scale, that is, as shrines enclosing an protecting some sacred relic, attributed, probably with very little truth or verisimilitude, to Sakya Sinha or Gautama, or to some inferior representative of him, some Bodhisatwa [Bodhisatva], some high-priest or Lama of local sanctity': *Mr Masson regards some as royal sepultures others as saintly sepultures, others again as possibly shrines.*

p. 46
Against 'Clemens of Alexandria', in pencil: *? Is this Clemens the St Clemens or a pseudo-Clemens.*

p. 47 (in pencil)
Against 'From this [i.e. Clemens'] testimony we must conclude that in the first or second century of the Christian æra there were buildings of this description in the countries on the north-west of India': *We must not conclude before the genuine age of this Clemens is ascertained – what might be conceded to the testimony of a saint may not be possibly due to a pretender of later date.*

p. 50
Against 'it is to be hoped that the season is not very remote when intelligent and enterprising Englishmen may follow unrestrictedly the footsteps of Mr Masson … prosecuting the researches he has so zealously and ably commenced': *Why was Mr Masson himself to be prevented from continuing researches he had 'so zealously and ably commenced'? Did Professor Wilson know that Mr Masson was to be prevented?*

Antiquities pls I–IV, in pencil: small Kharoshthi annotation on pl. I, then on its reverse and on pl. II, extensive copies and transcriptions of Kharoshthi inscriptions – both pages badly foxed (**Fig. 138** and note on the title page, **Fig. 136** above).

Chapter II: Masson's Memoir on the Topes and Sepulchral Buildings of Afghanistan

p. 55
Last paragraph, 'in others [the stones] seem to have been collected from the skirts of the surrounding hills' corrected to: *in others they are found in the state as selected.*

p. 56
'In raising these enormous structures … it became necessary at certain stages … to allow the masses … to subside, as is now observed in the elevation of an ordinary mud wall', amended to: *a precaution still adopted in the elevation.*

Against 'Whether these layers mark the several periods of repose … or whether they have a mystical allusion': *Professor Ritter has broached a theory on this subject*; 'dimensions regulated on a fixed principle' amended to: *fixed principles.*

p. 57
After 'Others even exceed or fall short of these dimensions': *but in all of them, doubtless* [corrected in pencil to: *it is probable that*] *the height was regulated by the circumference or vice versa.*

11th line, 'interior' elevation corrected to: *inferior.*

Referring to 'many topes have contiguous to them large oblong areas … which seem … to have been intended for reservoirs of water': *The popular belief.*

'These areas may have some other meaning not yet understood': *It has since occurred to me that these hollowed mounds may be explained* – the sentence is left unfinished, but see **p. 101** below: *these hollowed mounds may have some reference to religious usages.* The structures are monasteries.

Against 'The topes of Hadda display incongruities, to be explained, as that spot may be the more recent as well as more general [corrected to *the more indiscriminate*] of the three important ancient places of sepulture'.

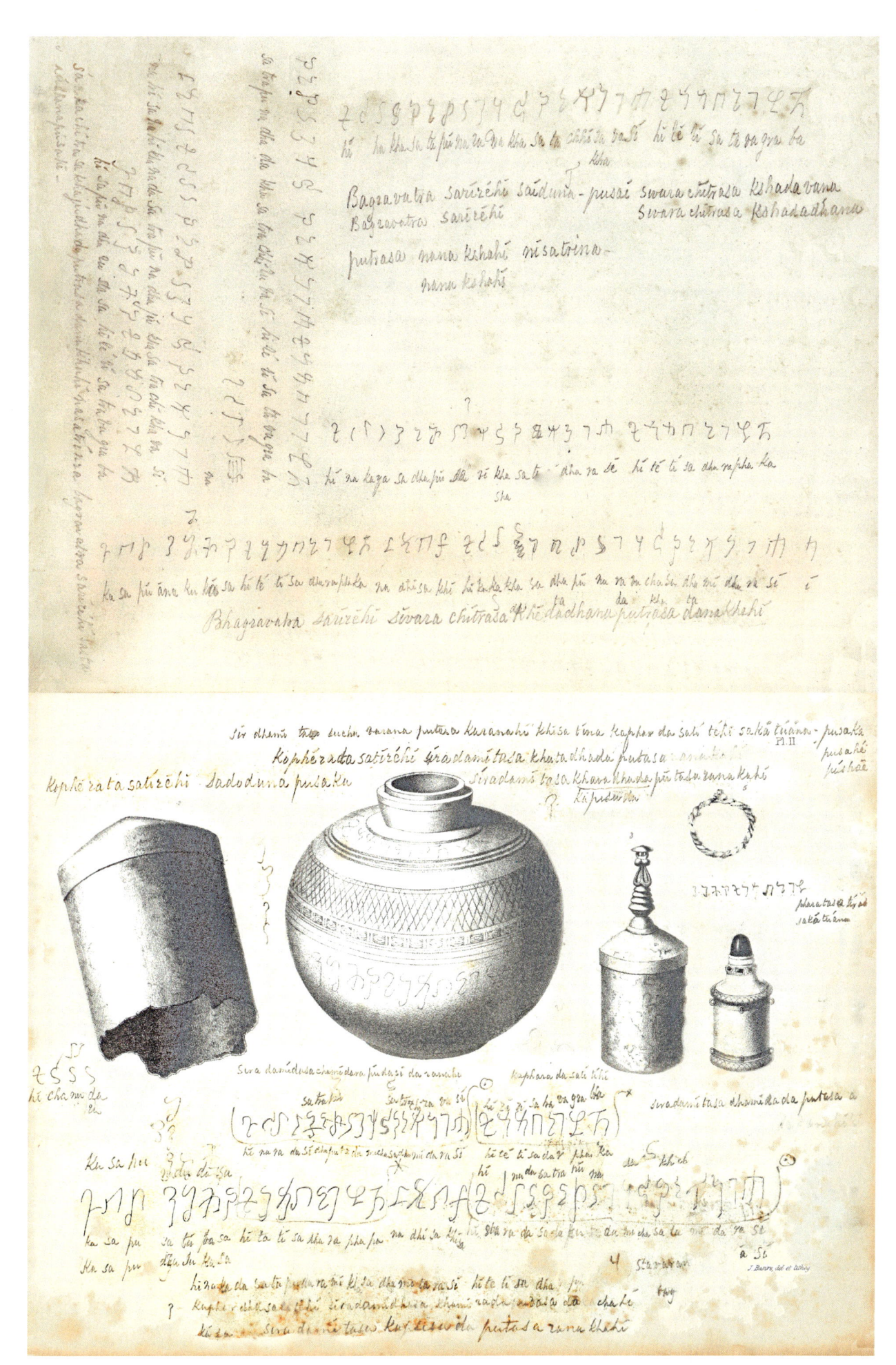

Figure 138 Masson's annotations on Antiquities Plate II. © Bodleian Library

Appendix 1 | 311

p. 60
11th line, 'In one or two instances' corrected to: *In three instances.*

p. 61
1st line 'If such were composed of hewn stone' amended to: *If, for instance, the mass* 'were composed'.

p. 65
Against 2nd line 'The probability is that no coins would be discovered': *Was I correct or not in this conjecture?*

p. 71 (in pencil)
Against the description of the Bimaran stupa 2 gold reliquary: *casket &c. £15.*

p. 75
8th line 'six copper coins ... two of the smaller, and four of the ordinary sized monies': 'four' wrongly corrected to six (Bimaran stupa 4, Soter Megas coins; see **Vol. I, p. 114, Fig. 129.1–6**).

After 'The coins [in Bimaran 4] yielded were of the early currency of the prince they indicate': *as proved by the youthful aspect of their busts.*

p. 78
Against Wilson's footnote 'Mr Masson has not given any authority for this historical fact [regarding the] title Choranes': *Vide Xenophon in his Hellen, where he states that the younger Cyrus was sent into Asia Minor with the title of ΧΟΡΑΝΟΣ / Choranes implying commander in chief* [*Hellenica* 1.4: caranus ('lord')].

p. 81
7th line: 'each circular arch [in the 'encircling belt' of Surkh Tope] being alternated by one of three sides' amended to: *by a triangular one* [*sic*: trapezoidal].

p. 83
Masson has drawn a box round the story of the 'cunning man of Delhi', and written at the bottom of the page: *Subject for a note and reference to a Review or critique in the Athenæum.*

p. 84
Against 'The figures on the clay were very similar ... and probably were, like them, personifications of NANAIA and HΛIOC, or of the sun and moon': *The types displayed merit particular attention with reference to the religious faith of the parties under whose auspices the structure was raised – If Buddhist, what had they to do with figures of Nanaia and Helios – If Mithraic the gold casket in the neighbouring tope of Bimaran has to be accounted for – Was their faith a mixed one?*

p. 86
On the lack of skulls associated with other human bones: *Herodotus Melpomene Cap. IX/V* [4.64] *'Every Scythian drinks the blood of the first person he slays: the heads of all the enemies who fall by his hand in battle, he presents to his king – this offering entitles him to a share of the plunder, which he could not otherwise claim'.*

Melpe Cap I XXIII [4.73]. *The above are the ceremonies observed in the interment of their kings: as to the people in general when any one dies, the neighbours place the body on a carriage, and carry it about to the different acquaintance of the deceased; these prepare some entertainment for those who accompany the corpse, placing before the body the same as before the rest. Private persons, after being thus carried about for forty days, are then buried. They who have been engaged in these rites &c &c.*

Last line 'constructed with much care' amended to: *constructed with great care.*

p. 88
Section headed 'Tope of Bár Robát' (Barabad): Bár amended incorrectly to *Behár* throughout.

'Numerous caves ... may probably relate to a celebrated Tappa [Khwaja Lahori], or mound, on the plain on the other side of the river', corrected to: *south of the river.*

At foot of page: *Has not this Tumulus been opened by Lt. Pigou? Vide Journal As. Socy in Bengal* (Pigou 1841, pp. 381–6).

p. 89
Against 'numbers of pisolithic pebbles, called sárcham, or "small shot", by the natives': *Zarcheum is the name of a hill pass mentioned by Diodorus* [XIV.46.6] *in his account of the progress of Semiramis from Baghistan on to Ecbatana. Sarcham is the name of a village in the Kafilan Koh range separating Azerbijan from Hamsah. Note: ascertain whether or not at this Persian Sarcham, these pisolitic pebbles are found – as that would account for the name. Pisolitic pebbles are now supposed by geologists to be triturated coral. True they are white and red – the latter sometimes very dark and they are semi transparent.*

p. 99
Against 'Adjacent to [Tepe Khwaja Lahori] are many tumuli, particularly near a hamlet named Chakanór': *Is Chakanor a corruption of Sakya Nur? the light of Sakya. Vide Fahian* [Faxian] *and Huin Thsang* [Xuanzang].

p. 101
On the 'topes of Chahár Bágh': *It has before been pointed out that these hollowed mounds may have some reference to religious usages – and that they remind us of similar vestiges in modern Persia and of the ancient Persian temples which were always uncovered.*

p. 105
On the 'monuments' of Hadda and the 'unsatisfactory' tradition linking them with 'Raja Udí [who] has attained a great traditionary fame in the countries between Jalalabad and the Hydaspes': *The country between the Indus and the Hydaspes / Jhelam was anciently called Yaudheya or Udíyana* [Udyana is actually modern Swat] *– and may have* [been] *the seat of extensive power at some time – whence perhaps the origin of the traditionary Raja Udí.*

p. 108 (in pencil)
Valuations of finds in £–s–d:

13 copper coins	*1–6*
Rings &c.	*5–0*
Silver casket	*1–0–0*
4 Sasanian [coins]	*4–0*

Chrystal?	1–0–0
Silver casket	2–0–0
Golden casket	20–0–0
Golden beads	3–0–0
[Total]	27–10–6

p. 109

Against the list of finds from Hadda stupa 10 (**Vol. I, pp. 177–91, Figs 278–83**), further valuations (in pencil):

5 gold solidi of the eastern emperors Theodosius, Marcian, and Leo.	*Value say*	£6–0–0
2 gold (alloyed) Kanauj coins.		1–4–0
202 silver coins of what we have been accustomed to call, I think unjustly, Sasanian coins.		10–2–0
1 gold ring set with engraved gem.		5–0–0
1 gold ring set with sapphire.		3–0–0
1 gold ring, without gem.		2–0–0
7 gold rings, plain with 2 fragments.		8–0–0
1 gold cylindrical case, small.		1–0–0
2 engraved gems, very interesting and beautiful ones.		5–0–0
3 rubies, plain gems.		3–0–0
7 gems, various.		1–15–0
13 beads, various.		1–0–0
13 gold ornaments.		
1 fragment sadap, or mother-of-pearl.		
1 fragment coral bead.		
1 silver ring set with gem.		15–0
62 silver rings, plain,		15–0–0
1 silver cylindrical case, without cover.		2–6
Sundry fragments of rings, silver ornaments, beads, &c.		2–0–0
11 copper coins.		1–0
		64–19–6
		27–10–6
		£92–10–0

Against fn. 3, Wilson's comment on the 202 silver 'Sasanian' coins (in ink): *Professor Wilson in consequence of this observation has laconically remarked in a note 'They are undoubtedly Sasanian coins' yet in the text of his work has failed to appropriate any one of them of which he has presented designs. I adhere to the opinion that they are not Sasanian or at least the Sasanians of Persia – I believe indeed that they are not Sasanian at all.* They include Sasanian and Alkhan Hun coins (see **Pls 13–14** above).

p. 110

Against 'It were needless to enter fully upon the nature of the various coins deposited, as they have been transmitted for more mature consideration': *Which I regret to say the want of sufficient powers by the literary men connected with the Honble East India Company – combined with worse motives has operated to prevent.*

p. 111

Pencil sketch of Hadda Stupa 8a reproduced in **Vol. I, p. 172, Fig. 267**.

p. 113

Funeral jars from Hadda 'The greater portion are of common baked potters' ware, but a few occur of a stronger species': *a stronger fabric.*

'Idols, etc.' of Hadda, corrected (in pencil then inked): 'The bodies are sometimes painted with red lead, and *more* rarely covered with gold leaf: they appear to have been interred in apartments, of which fragments are also found. I know not whether *or not* coins were *regularly* deposited with the idols but in the course of my search for them two or three Indo-Scythic [Kushan] coins *of the lower series* were detected'.

p. 116

'Section V. Topes of Koh Daman and the Kohistan' inserted: 'The next [stupa] occurs at' *Tope* 'Dara' *(the Tope valley) about twenty-five miles from Kabul*.

p. 117 (in pencil)

A long multiplication sum, with an apparent error at the start:

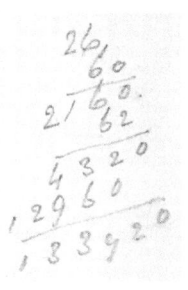

Chapter III: Ancient Notices of Ariana

p. 119

Against 'The extent of the kingdom founded by the successors of the Greek governors of the province of Bactria considerably exceeded the limits assigned to the province by classical geographers': *incorrectly expressed – many princes reigned not* [as] *successors of the Greek governors of Bactria – neither was but one kingdom formed.*

Against 'the Bactrian monarchy comprised not only Transoxiana': *it does not follow – other monarchies than the Bactrian flourished.*

Against 'the coins to be hereafter described show that there must have been several distinct dynasties': *exactly – which nullifies the foregoing remarks and assumptions.*

Against 'The country was … partitioned amongst different branches from the original stem': *it does not follow from the original stem.*

Against 'In its undivided form it was in all likelihood co-extensive with the modern kingdom of Kabul, and with the Ariana of the ancients': *Is the kingdom of Kabul equivalent to the ancient Ariana?*

p. 120

Against 'The denomination of Ariana has perhaps been rarely used with the precision it deserved either by ancient writers or their modern expounders': *Modest at all events – what could Professor W. know about Ariana beyond what he learned from ancient writers – from whom he must have got the very name? – did he as regards <u>modern</u> expounders learn anything from C.M's mss.*

Against the equation of Ariana and Iran: *it is true that the term Ariana is preserved in Iran, but it is in error applied to the country now bearing it – and Ariana never was the proper appellation of ancient Persia – which was Fars, Pars, Persia &c.*

Against 'the western limit [of Ariana]': *what becomes of Persia then? It is beyond the limits of Ariana.*

Against 'that is, taking in the whole of Yazd and Kirman, but excluding Fars': *very good – what has Fars to do with Ariana?*

Against 'The northern boundary is said to be the Paropamisadae mountains': *consequently to the north excluding Bactria and its parallel regions.*

p. 121
Against Strabo's linkage of 'some of the eastern Persians, and the Bactrians and Sogdians, with the people of Ariana below the mountains' because of 'the affinity of their languages' (XIV.11): *a very important fact – before I believe asserted by Herodotus and which the Professor need not wrest or contort to suit his own views. The speech spoken was no doubt Pali, of which the Sanskrit is descended, being the offspring of the Indian Pali current when Strabo wrote – vide columns and inscriptions in India.*

Against 'According to Manu, Arya-vartta, "the country of excellent men", extends between the Himalaya and the Vindhya mountains': *What authority is Manu for the ancient Ariana?*

p. 122
Against the 'Zend form … of the ancient Persian term for … west of the Indus [is] … Eriene-veejo … Sanskrit Arya-vartta, or varsha. M. Burnouf gives it the appellation Airyana': *Burnouf and Zend!*

Against 'the word Aniran on the coins of the Sasanian kings of Persia': *excellent!*

Against 'Arya, which the coins of the Sasanian princes denominate Iran': *what Sasanian coins?*

Against 'it would of course follow, that the country being that of the ancient Persians, the Persian language would be spoken in it': *vague, loosely and incorrectly set forth.*

Against 'If the language of Persian was Zend, this would have been used throughout Ariana; and its strong affinity to Sanskrit would justify the extension of Strabo's remarks even to the Indians of the Paropamisadae and the west bank of the Indus': *the same – the language was Pali.*

p. 123
Against 'It is, therefore, not at all unlikely that the people of Ariana …did … employ a similar form of speech': *Professor W. confirms Strabo!! Did Strabo need his confirmation?*

Against 'and that the affinity is a valid argument for regarding them as one people – the inhabitants of ancient Iran or Persia': *how were they inhabitants of Persia?*

Against 'with such reservation only as a regard for possibility imposes' (regarding the historical tradition): *wonderful – possibility!!!*

Against 'Mohammedan writers of the ninth and tenth centuries': *mind – of the 9th and 10th centuries – the Professor must be quizzing.*

Against 'According to [the Mohammedan writers], and in consistency with classical notices, the greater portion of Ariana was Iran or Persia': *In consistency with classical notices!!! What a lie!!!*

p. 124
Against 'Zoroaster, whom classical and oriental writers concur in designating as a native of Bactria or Balkh': left margin *or Zoroaster!!! fie Professor W!!!* right margin *classical again!!!*

Against 'These traditions, as well as the similarity of name, identify Gushtasp, … with the Darius Hystaspes of the Greeks': *identify! rather too strong a word!!*

p. 125
Against 'the tribes … of the Paropamisadae are termed [in Hindu tradition] Gandháras, of which modern Kandahar possibly preserves a vestige': *I should think unlikely. C.M.*

Against (following on from the above) 'but those of Bactria or Balkh are apparently intended by Bahlíkas': *The Bahlíkas, I suspect, were the natives of Bamiyan, and to the south of Bactria. C.M.*

Against 'the passages [in some of the Puranas] are obscure and, in all probability, corrupt:' *Why corrupt? There could be no object in corruption. C.M.*

Against 'These notices are of no great value': *The notices are of every value. C.M.*

p. 130
Against 'Parikanii' (one of the tribes mentioned by Herodotus, in pencil): *Par-i-kan / Feather pluckers;* against 'Orthokorybantes': *see Jacquet.*

p. 134 (in pencil)
Against 'the valleys of the Indian Caucasus …form a very extensive tract of country, which is yet but imperfectly known to us, never having been traversed by Europeans': *Ah Wilson, you are a bad rogue.*

Against 'the information collected under the direction of M. Court, and complied by him from the reports of the surveyors he employed': *a wrong term or calculated to mislead – Court hated the surveyors* (Wilson is correct: Court employed local men to survey the Peshawar Valley for archaeological sites, as he was unable to visit the region himself, see Court 1839).

p. 135
Against fn. 2, on the Mahabharata story of the gold-making ants: *Meru and Manduru … Is not Pipilikas the name of a people – the people of Pipílí? Shahbag Gharí [Shahbazghari] and Kapur di Gharí [Kapurdighari] are on the plain of Mardan which is the country intersected by the river which falls into the Indus at Atak [Attock]. It is inhabited by Yuzafzais and has the territory of Peshawar to the South – the district of Hashtnagar to the west, Buner to the north and the Indus separating it from Pakkali to the east. The Khasas are clearly the Khas. The Ekayanas might be the Kaians.*

p. 136
Against 'Wilford transferred [Kaspatyrus] to the Jhelum, in which he had the countenance of a modern town, Kashab-pur': *Wilford was wrong. Kashab – or rather Kushab being a modern term.*

Against fn. 2 (in pencil), on the 'Paktyiens': *the Baktiari.*

314 | *Charles Masson: Collections from Begram and Kabul Bazaar, Afghanistan, 1833–1838*

p. 147
Against 'From Armenia to the boundaries of Parthia was the range called Parakhoathras': *Parachoara – the delightful hills.*

p. 153
Beside the second paragraph, distance calculations, possible related to the adjacent discussion of 'Drangiana'.:

1000 – 114 – 600
500
57000 (57 = 171 miles

1000 – 114 – 600
600
68400 (68
8400
114
68
182 miles

Against the discussion of 'Prophthasia': *'Phrada, urbs in Drangis quam Alexander Propthasiam nominavit, ut Charax in sexto chronichorum' Stephanus* [Byzantinus].

p. 155
Against the discussion of the 'Ariaspæ': *The Ariaspí were a people of Zaranga – in one sense therefore they might be called Zarangæ. Herodotus calls them Orosangai perhaps a diminution of Orozaranggai. The Greeks translated their name the equivalent of which is now found in the same country in Bakhtiyari or friend in need.*

Against 'Hukairya': *Hukairya might become in popular language Hurya or Oro-(úrú).*

Against fn. 3 (in pencil): *In Orosangai may be concealed Khorsandí that is pessandi or 'approved of'.*

p. 157 (in pencil)
Top of page: *4120 Stadia*

Against 'the site of a city … the remains of which, M. Court says, are to be seen on the Arghasan river': *? precisely the same ruins are to be seen as to the east of Kabul – a large and high mound hollowed in the centre at the summit and with caves in its sides – built also in stages.*

Against 'Alexandria, which is usually considered to be Kandahar': *Kandahar is Alexandria.*

Against fn. 3 'some confusion in the name of the Arachotus, as if it was the same with the Kophen [river]' *possible.*

p. 158 (in pencil)
Against 'Beest or Bost': *Beest is correct.*

Against 'Purali river': *Query – is not the Arabis the river of Hingohl* (Hingol River in south-eastern Baluchistan; see also Masson 1843, pp. 390–1).

Against 'Hor or Haür': *Hor-mása.*

Against fn. 5 'Pliny calls the Oritæ Ichthyophagi, and observes they speak a language of their own': *how true is Pliny.*

p. 159 (in pencil)
Against 'The whole of the northern chain was called Caucasus by the Greeks': *?*

Against 'an extensive tract [the Hindu Kush and Paropamisadae mountains], very important, perhaps, for the elucidation of Bactrian history, has yet to be explored': *by whose fault?*

p. 161 (in pencil)
Against 'Burnes suggests that Zariaspa may be traced in Shehr Subz; but that would be to transfer it to Sogdiana': *Shehr-i-aspa / City of the Horde / Haibak? / Shebrgahn? Khulm?*

p. 162 (in pencil)
Against 'Atarmes': *river of Termes* [Termez].

Against 'The Dargis follows the course of the Gori or river of Kunduz; but no great reliance can be placed on Ptolemy's geography': *?*

p. 164
Against 'Pasikæ': *Pasika – Pashai?*

Against 'Augali': *Augali – Ogal is a name as Ogal Shams.*

p. 165 (in pencil)
Against Nautaka: *Nawa taka / the taka or hill of Nawa / Nau*
There follow calculations, ending with *miles 6½*.

p. 169
Against 'On the borders of Bactria … is the district of Choarene, the nearest country to India occupied by the Parthians' and link to the route of Craterus *apud* Strabo: *Was Choarene by chance the Kharan to the SW of Kalat of Baluchistan. It would have or might have fallen in the route of Craterus.*

p. 173 (in pencil)
Herat Kandahar	*371*
Kandahar Kabul	*309*
Kabul Peshawar	*205*
	885

Further distance calculations in the bottom margin, as in the right margin of p. 171 and at the top of p. 175.

Against fn. 1, quotation from Strabo (XI.8.9) in Greek, Masson writes out the Latin: *Sequitur quæ recta it per Bactrianam, et montis transcensum in Ortospana per trivium e Bactris apud Paropamisadas.*

p. 181
On the geography of the Hindu Kush and Sir Alexander Burnes' observation 'that the everlasting snows of the Hindu Kush had been surmounted before reaching Bamiyan': *Neither Hajikak or Kalu are considered parts of the Hindu Kush, which is the high range above Ghorband, and of which Bamiyan is south or south west. The snows he crossed of Hajikak are not everlasting.*

Against 'a corroboration of the assertion of Diodorus, that Alexander built other cities, each a day's journey from Alexandria': *not cities – rather stations or posts.*

Against, in Wilson's discussion of possible sites of Alexandria ad Caucasum, 'he [Masson] mentions various indications of extensive sites of ancient cities in the Kohistan and the Koh-daman; the latter of which, from its very appellation, the "mountain skirts", comes recommended by its agreement with the "sub-Caucasian" position of Alexandria': *but unfortunately they are not the mountain skirts of the Caucasus.*

p. 182
Against 'the Pass of Khoshal, which is open throughout the year': *not so.*
　Against 'Nicea': *Nikæa – Kabul.*

p. 183 (in pencil, partly illegible, see **Fig. 139**)
Against the discussion of the identification of the river Kophen, to which Alexander went from Nikæa: *Rennell apparently influenced by the marches of Tarmashirin Khan [1331–4]⁵ and Taimur [Timur, 1336–1405] upon India fancied that Alexander had followed the same route – and finding a Gomul – Go-mal in modern geography – concluded it was the Ko-phen of ancient geography; in this he conceived …[?] further borne out from the fact that the marches of all these conquerors led to the very same point in the west of the Punjab – Alexander almost certainly went to Patton [?] where also Taimur went, one of the high roads to India that [went] through Sangala in Alexander's days and through Jalum [Jhelum] in modern days leading to the same point at which the Satadrus or Sutlej was to be crossed. Yet Rennel while not taking into due notice all the intermediate points between Alexander's starting place, Alexandria ad Caucasum, and Sangala and above all being unmindful that Alexander on account of the season followed the northern route or that as close to the hills as possible, no doubt placed him in the southern, or which may be called the lower route, in error – C. Masson.*
　As to mere similarity of name – there is a river called Ko or Kow – in Laghman. Chaˢ Masson.

p. 185
Against the beginning of the second paragraph, referring to 'where the Panjshir river becomes the Kabul river', the original annotation *in Laghman* is overwritten and amended to *in Jalalabad.*
　Against 'sending Hephæstion and Perdiccas to the country of Peukelaotis': *Pushkalavatí – (Hashtnagar) / or Pushkala (Peshawar).*

p. 186
Against 'Lassen considers the Khoes to be the Káma or Khonar [Kunar] river': *probably right.*

p. 194 (in pencil)
Against 'travellers have been impressed with the coincidence between the structures [bridges] of the Sikh prince and the Macedonian conqueror … Alexander, it is generally admitted, crossed at the usual place, or opposite to Attok [Attock]': *of course the travellers knew what the Macedonian structure was – still the professor ventures to affirm their due. Alexander crossed the Indus higher up as Arrian asserts – where it was widest and smoothest – and therefore as Arrian says easier to be bridged – Attok then may or may not have existed.*

p. 195 (in pencil)
Against 'Chin-ab … Chandrabhága … Sandabala … which name … was changed as a term of ill omen': *the water of Chin … is this not a puerile surmise.*
　Against the discussion of the Ravi: *is it called the Iraotee by the natives? I never heard it called otherwise by them than Râví. C.M.*

p. 199 (in pencil)
Against 'the Sivis … are usually associated with the people of the north-west, or of the Punjab': *Sehwan – properly Sivistân or the lands of the sivi [?] tree.*
　Against 'Multan, or, as it is still called by the people, Mallithán': *It is not still called so – but Mallithán is said to be a more ancient term.*
　Against 'Rennel … would have placed the capital of the Malli on the Ravi': *And Rennel was right I think or nearly so.*

p. 200 (in pencil)
On the location of the capital of the Malli being at or near Multan, with footnote referencing Burnes: *Burnes no very good authority.*
　Against the reference to Salya, monarch of the Madras: *Is Salya the Sangala of coins and Rajput traditions?*
　Against 'the Oxydrakæ, whose name and situation … are traceable in Ooch': *Ooch or Uch happens to be a Turkic term for city.*

p. 201 (in pencil)
Against Alexander halted near the confluence of the Ravi and Chenab where 'he received the submission of … the Oxydrakæ' and of other tribes: *Oxydraea is in fact a Greek rendering of Ak-Sudruku or the White Sudras. Is not Chenab – the water or river of China?*
　Abastani – the inhabitants of or near the Takht Suliman.
　'Xathri' – Zathraustes [i.e.] Zathi – the inhabitants of the western banks of the Indus. Did they come down the Chenab – or the Indus? They were not Kshatriyas then.
　<u>*'Abastani / Apa-sthánas'*</u> *– the more likely indication.*
　Sogdi – Soda?
　Against the site of 'the city of the Sogdi': *near Chaipur and Jhellum Kot.*

p. 202 (in pencil)
Against 'the Sogdi of Arrian … are the Sodræ of Diodorus': *Sudra or Soda*
　Against 'An interesting memoir by … Captain McMurdo … on the lower course of the Indus' [McMurdo 1834, pp. 21–44]: *McMurdo's Memoir is most ingenious, but he endeavoured to prove, I think, too much. There can be little doubt that the Purana Deria was once a great branch of the Indus – but not the main branch, at least not in the time of Alexander.*
　Against 'the bed of the river … known as the Purana Deria, or "old river"': *This may or may not be true. It is singular that Khairpur the present capital in the past is distant from the Indus as well as Alore or the known site thereof – there is a query also whether Rorí be not the visitable and ancient Alore or A-Rora – from the ancient Mohomedan sepulchres at it might be so inferred.*
　Against 'It is also asserted by the Mohammedan chroniclers': *by what historians?*

p. 203 (in pencil)
Against 'Bukkur was constructed out of its ruins. This was of course a comparatively recent event': *doubtful*; against 'if there is any truth in these statements': *good.*
　Against 'the city of the Sogdi must have … been transmuted into an Alexandria. That traces of such an Alexandria did exist…': *but it was higher up at the confluence of the Punjab rivers with the Indus.*

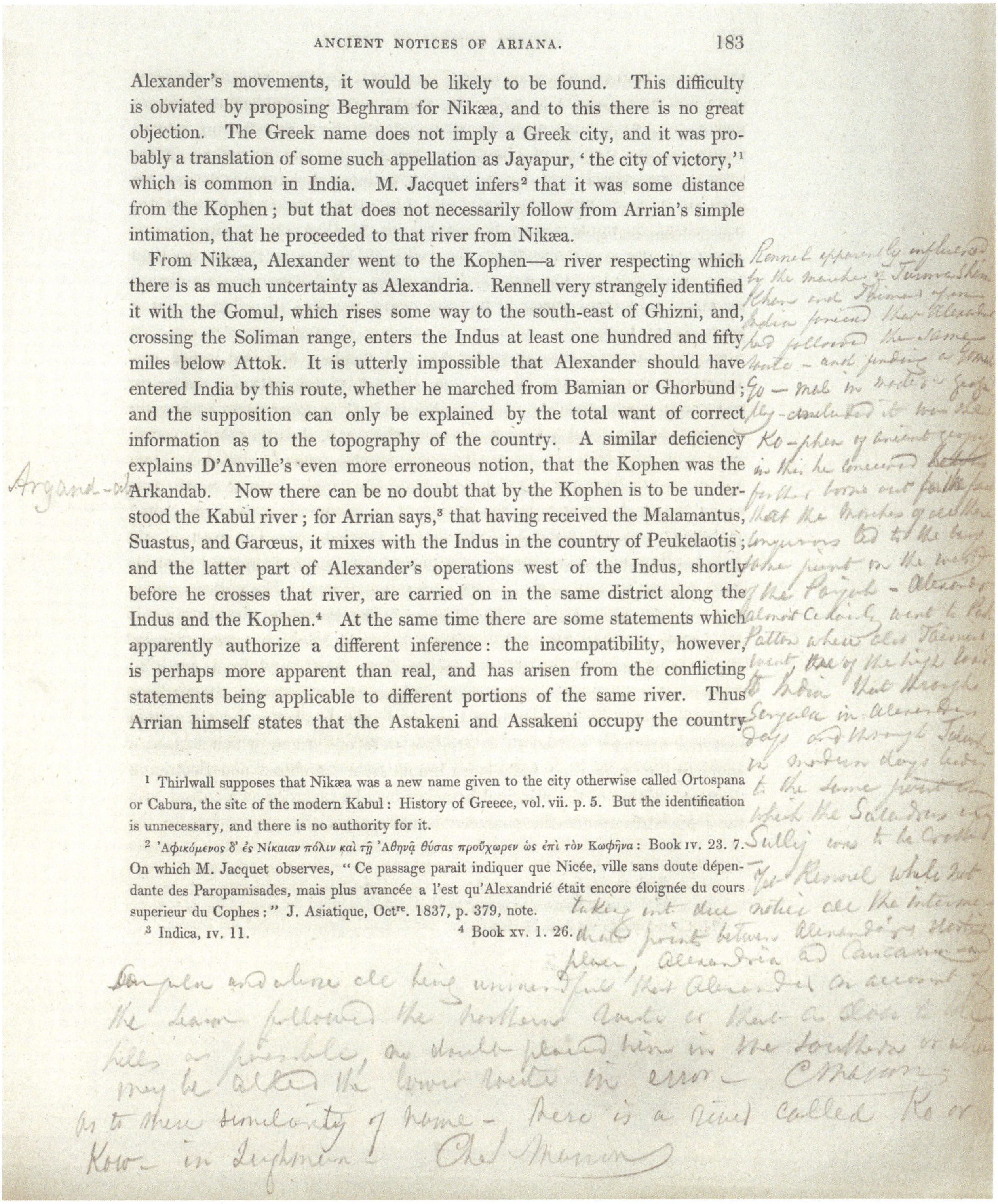

ANCIENT NOTICES OF ARIANA. 183

Alexander's movements, it would be likely to be found. This difficulty is obviated by proposing Beghram for Nikæa, and to this there is no great objection. The Greek name does not imply a Greek city, and it was probably a translation of some such appellation as Jayapur, 'the city of victory,'[1] which is common in India. M. Jacquet infers[2] that it was some distance from the Kophen; but that does not necessarily follow from Arrian's simple intimation, that he proceeded to that river from Nikæa.

From Nikæa, Alexander went to the Kophen—a river respecting which there is as much uncertainty as Alexandria. Rennell very strangely identified it with the Gomul, which rises some way to the south-east of Ghizni, and, crossing the Soliman range, enters the Indus at least one hundred and fifty miles below Attok. It is utterly impossible that Alexander should have entered India by this route, whether he marched from Bamian or Ghorbund; and the supposition can only be explained by the total want of correct information as to the topography of the country. A similar deficiency explains D'Anville's even more erroneous notion, that the Kophen was the Arkandab. Now there can be no doubt that by the Kophen is to be understood the Kabul river; for Arrian says,[3] that having received the Malamantus, Suastus, and Garœus, it mixes with the Indus in the country of Peukelaotis; and the latter part of Alexander's operations west of the Indus, shortly before he crosses that river, are carried on in the same district along the Indus and the Kophen.[4] At the same time there are some statements which apparently authorize a different inference: the incompatibility, however, is perhaps more apparent than real, and has arisen from the conflicting statements being applicable to different portions of the same river. Thus Arrian himself states that the Astakeni and Assakeni occupy the country

[1] Thirlwall supposes that Nikæa was a new name given to the city otherwise called Ortospana or Cabura, the site of the modern Kabul: History of Greece, vol. vii. p. 5. But the identification is unnecessary, and there is no authority for it.
[2] Ἀφικόμενος δ' ἐς Νίκαιαν πόλιν καὶ τῇ Ἀθηνᾷ θύσας προὔχωρεν ὡς ἐπὶ τὸν Κωφῆνα: Book IV. 23. 7. On which M. Jacquet observes, " Ce passage parait indiquer que Nicée, ville sans doute dépendante des Paropamisades, mais plus avancée a l'est qu'Alexandrié était encore éloignée du cours superieur du Cophes:" J. Asiatique, Oct^re. 1837, p. 379, note.
[3] Indica, IV. 11.   [4] Book XV. 1. 26.

Figure 139 Masson's annotations on p. 183. © Bodleian Library

Against 'The whole of the river's course at present, from Bukkur to Mithan-kote, is skirted by jungle': *rivers are in it. C.M.*

Against the last line of the page, 'It is not easy to conjecture an Indian original for Musikanus': *The term Kanus [is] common in these parts – might have been khanu or house now replaced by tandu (?)*

Against fn. 3, quoting Lt Wood on the 'healthy and luxuriant appearance' of the crops around Alore: *common place remarks of no meaning – applicable to any part of cultivated Sind.*

p. 204 (in pencil)
Against 'Craterus had been despatched across the Indus': *Craterus most likely was detached from Bukkur or Alore*; against 'that he had returned is evident': *did he return? Did he not go to Kirman?*

p. 205 (in pencil)
Against 'The capital of Musikanus was upon the river, and it was therefore not Sehwan': *? Sehwan may almost be called so.*

Against 'Sehwan stands close under the Lakhi mountains, and presents many vestiges of antiquity, especially its castle': *hardly mountains / the castle is not.*

Appendix 1 | 317

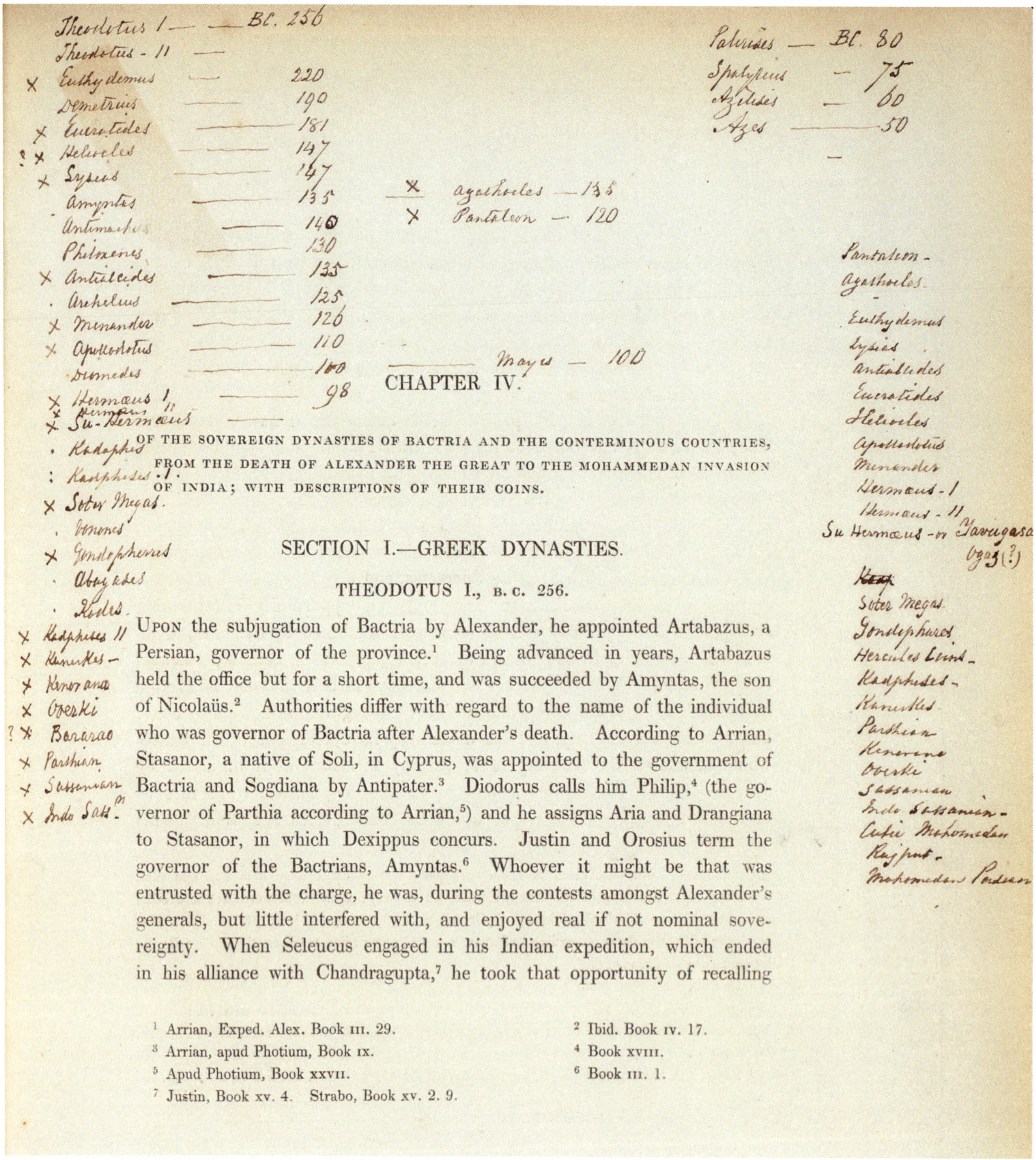

CHAPTER IV.

OF THE SOVEREIGN DYNASTIES OF BACTRIA AND THE CONTERMINOUS COUNTRIES, FROM THE DEATH OF ALEXANDER THE GREAT TO THE MOHAMMEDAN INVASION OF INDIA; WITH DESCRIPTIONS OF THEIR COINS.

SECTION I.—GREEK DYNASTIES.

THEODOTUS I., B.C. 256.

Upon the subjugation of Bactria by Alexander, he appointed Artabazus, a Persian, governor of the province.[1] Being advanced in years, Artabazus held the office but for a short time, and was succeeded by Amyntas, the son of Nicolaüs.[2] Authorities differ with regard to the name of the individual who was governor of Bactria after Alexander's death. According to Arrian, Stasanor, a native of Soli, in Cyprus, was appointed to the government of Bactria and Sogdiana by Antipater.[3] Diodorus calls him Philip,[4] (the governor of Parthia according to Arrian,[5]) and he assigns Aria and Drangiana to Stasanor, in which Dexippus concurs. Justin and Orosius term the governor of the Bactrians, Amyntas.[6] Whoever it might be that was entrusted with the charge, he was, during the contests amongst Alexander's generals, but little interfered with, and enjoyed real if not nominal sovereignty. When Seleucus engaged in his Indian expedition, which ended in his alliance with Chandragupta,[7] he took that opportunity of recalling

1 Arrian, Exped. Alex. Book III. 29.
2 Ibid. Book IV. 17.
3 Arrian, apud Photium, Book IX.
4 Book XVIII.
5 Apud Photium, Book XXVII.
6 Book III. 1.
7 Justin, Book XV. 4. Strabo, Book XV. 2. 9.

Figure 140 Masson's annotations on p. 215. © Bodleian Library

Against 'the palpable objection to the identity of Sehwan and Sindomana was apparent': *Sivistan – Sehwan – Persian* [?] *I will follow.*

Against fn. 3, the city that Diodorus [XVII.103.1] calls 'Harmatelia': *Mabélí.*

p. 206 (in pencil)
Against 'Moeris, the Raja of Pattalene': *Mír? Or Mír Rais?*

p. 207 (in pencil)
Against 'Bhambora': *Bhampora – a contraction of Bhamanpura*

p. 208 (in pencil)
Against 'the bay of Krokala': *Was not Krokala an island?*

Against 'his description of … Krokala identifies it beyond question with Karachi': *does it?*

p. 209 (in pencil)
Against the river bed of the Puran lying 'a long way east of the [river] Narra': *Strangely confused.*

Against 'he states that it flows to the south': *then his description is worthless – for the Purana was east of the present Indus and the Narra is west – unless Narra be applied to more arms of the river than one.*

p. 210 (in pencil)
Against 'Kori … more properly Khári': *more properly? Khor is the universal name for saltwater creek along the coast.*

p. 211 (in pencil)
Against (Wilson quotes Lt Wood) "supposing the Pinyari to have been the eastern arm of the Delta in the days of the Greeks, then we should fix the site of Pattala, where now stands the modern town of Jerk": *very ill fitted for such a site.*

Against 'Without pretending, therefore, to affirm that the northernmost point of the Delta was so far north as the Bahmanabad of McMurdo, it may be assumed conjecturally': *Just like H.H. Wilson.*

Following on from the above, 'It can scarcely be expected that any site shall be proposed to which no objections will apply': *Captⁿ Baker deputed by Lord Ellenborough will put probably these matters right – by a good survey.*

p. 212 (in pencil)
Against 'The truth of the legend [on Potala being the 'original site of the Sákyas'] may be questioned': *Why questioned? and then comes the not improbably admitting there may be truth in it.*

Against 'In the realm of Sigertis, we have very probably the name of the country mis-stated as that of the prince': *Si-gard? The fort of Si or Seh – which may be Sehwan.*

Against 'we might propose Tri-gartta for Si-gertis, but that the name belongs to a principality in the north of India … Kach-cha': *then why propose it? What affinity or analogy is there between Sigertis and Kach-cha?*

Against 'Su-rasthra …, the country adjacent to the kingdom of Sigertis on the east, or the modern Gujarat': *? the modern Gujarat.*

p. 215
In the margins and above the chapter heading (**Fig. 140**):

	Theodotus I	BC 256						
	Theodotus II					*Palirises*	BC 80	
X	*Euthydemus*	220				*Spalyrius*	75	
	Demetrius	190				*Azilises*	60	
X	*Eucratides*	181				*Azes*	50	
?X	*Heliocles*	147						
X	*Lysias*	147						
	Amyntas	135	X	*Agathocles*	135		*Pantaleon*	
	Antimachus	140	X	*Pantaleon*	120		*Agathocles*	
	Philoxenes	130					-	
X	*Antialcides*	135					*Euthydemus*	
.	*Archelius*	125					*Lysias*	
X	*Menander*	126					*Antialcides*	
X	*Apollodotus*	110					*Eucratides*	
	Diomedes	100		*Mayes*	100		*Heliocles*	
X	*Hermæus I*	98					*Apollodotus*	
X	*Hermæus II*						*Menander*	
X	*Su- Hermæus*						*Hermæus I*	
.	*Kadaphes*						*Hermæus II*	
:	*Kadphises .I.*						*Su Hermæus – or Yavugasa Ugaz (?)*	
X	*Soter Megas*							
.	*Vonones*						*Soter Megas*	
X	*Gondopherres*						*Gondophares*	
.	*Abagases*						*Hercules coins*	
.	*Kodes*						*Kadphises*	
X	*Kadphises II*						*Kanerkes*	
X	*Kanerkes*						*Ooerki*	
X	*Kenorano (Korano)*						*Sasanian*	
X	*Ooerki*						*Indo Sasanian*	
?X	*Bararao*						*Kufic Mahomedan*	
X	*Parthian*						*Rajput*	
X	*Sasanian*						*Mahomedan Persian*	
X	*Indo Sasⁿ*							

Chapter IV: Of the Sovereign Dynasties of Bactria and the Coterminous Countries

p. 221 Euthydemus (in pencil)
In top right margin: *My impression from the reading of Polybius [X.49] is that Euthydemus encamped on the Murghab and defeated there fell back upon Zariaspa (Balkh).*

Against 'Antiochus admitted the reasonableness of the plea, and … crossed the Caucasus': *As Antiochus crossed the Caucasus – the scene of operations must have been to the north of it and of the Paropamisas* [sic].

p. 222
Against 'Some of the coins are of a less careful execution': *It is more likely they are the coins of Scythic chiefs who displaced Euthydemus in Sogdiana. On the coins of Euthydemus is first noticed the type of the horse / sacred to the sun the divinity or emblem thereof of the Massagetæ (Scythians).*

p. 225 (in pencil)
Against '9, 10. Tetradrachm': *apparently rude Pali* (Coins pl. I.9–10: Euthydemus imitations acquired by Alexander Burnes in Bukhara).

There follow copies and transcriptions of Kharoshthi characters (also in bottom margin).

Against '13. Tetradrachm': *the Hercules is worthy of remark, as being the prototype of other forms which follow* (Coins pl. I.11: acquired by Karamat 'Ali in Kabul).

p. 226 (in pencil)
Against 17–19. (**Fig. 23.5, 7–8**) 'They were all found by Mr. Masson at Begram, and have not yet been met with elsewhere': *they have at Jalalabad.*

Against the last lines 'portrait … of Hercules, or … of Jupiter': *most likely – and it is worthy of notice that the horse (we know to have been sacred to the Sun) is on the reverse whence on the very earliest coins we possess of provincial or foreign currency – we discern an intimation of solar worship.*

p. 227 Seleucid – Antiochus III (in pencil)
Against '20. … R[everse]. Standing figure of Apollo': *This line is valuable as giving the type afterwards found on the coins of Apollodotus* (Coins pl. II.1; **Fig. 23.4**).

Against 'It was among Mr. Masson's last supply of coins from Begram and Kabul': *This sentence is one of the proofs of this book having been written at different periods – the coin was procured in 1836; my last supply was the collection of 1838 arriving in England 1840.*

p. 228 Demetrius (in pencil)
Against 'Bayer therefore concludes that [Demetrius] never reigned in [Bactria]': *Wilson here gives a very good proof that the assertions of learned men are not always to be taken for granted.*

p. 229 (in pencil)
Against 'It may be inferred that the conquests of Demetrius were made not whilst he was king, but in his father's lifetime': *This would be consistent with the appearance of the coins of Euthydemus south of the Hindu Kush.*

p. 230 (in pencil)
In top margin: *210 BC. Allow Demetrius to have been 15+58 = 73.*

Against 'Demetrius … gave the appellation of Euthydemia to …Sagala, on the Hydaspes': *Apollodotus may have captured Hisephami* (?)

p. 231 (in pencil, partly indistinct)
Against 'There seems no reason … to adopt the supposition … that there were two different princes of the name of Demetrius': *that Lysias a son of Demetrius recovered dominion in Kabul. Demetrius probably ascended the Bactrian throne on the demise of his father – then possessing himself of Arachosia marched upon Sind and the Punjab – Eucratides whatever his origin profited by his absence and seized upon Bactria – Demetrius' forces in Arachosia marched against Eucratides – besieged him as related – and in Armenian testimony sought refuge with Val Arsaces of Armenia.* [Repeats] *Lysias a son of Demetrius recovered Kabul.*

p. 242
'On the Arianian alphabet': *The appearance of Páli legends on the coins of Eucratides and the Bactrian kings, in my opinion, does not indicate a change but an accession of territory – neither a decline but an increase in power. The fact however is so far important, that it would seem to show that the peculiar alphabet employed was in use only in the regions south of the Hindú Kush or it may be to the south of the Oxus, a question which unfortunately I was not permitted to clear up. The absence of this alphabet on the circular and better coins of the earlier of these kings does not absolutely prove that it was not used in the countries north of the Hindu Kush, for such coins are most likely of metropolitan coinage and beyond doubt imitations of the Syro Macedonian currency. The coins with Pâlí legends, almost always square, were therefore provincial coins and issued probably from provincial mints. C.M.*

p. 243
Against 'Vowels': Kharoshthi characters and transcriptions.

p. 244
Against 'Consonants. K': *which Masson pointed out to Prinsep in a Memoir of 1836.*

Against 'The same in Agathokleia': *erroneous, the name of Agathokleia is not rendered in Pali – the coin being of Strato* (Masson also, in the left margin, gives his own transcriptions of the Kharoshthi characters representing KPA and KΛA).

p. 245
Against 'It is doubtful if the cerebral class of letters of the Nagari alphabet has any representatives in the Bactro-Indian alphabet': *It has since been proved to have cerebral letters.*

Against 'There is no doubt … much confusion in the forms representing t and d … and the ordinary form of r': *This seeming confusion has been removed.*

pp. 250–62 and on the table opposite p. 262
Kharoshthi characters and transcriptions in the margins.

p. 262
Against 'a well-defined alphabet of the Semitic family': *Is there any real difference between the Semitic and Aramean families? Discovery seems to prove not and goes far to show the distinction was unnecessary.*

Against 'It is not Sanskrit, but Prakrit': *It is Pali or Prakrit if it so pleases Prof. W. to style it.*

Against 'The letters can scarcely be Bactrian, or we should probably have met with specimens on the coins of … princes of … Bactria': *Are not specimens found in the coins of Eucratides, Menander and Apollodotus, historically known as kings of Bactria?*

p. 265 Heliocles

Against 'This is, no doubt, the character [as son] in which [Heliocles] appears upon the coin in question [Coins pl. XXI.7]': *Unluckily however for this theory the portraits of Heliocles and Eucratides on this coin give the negative to it. Heliocles appears aged – Eucratides appears young – Heliocles I presume was the father of Eucratides therefore the son of Eucratides would again be named Heliocles – and the various coins we have of Heliocles "King" belong I infer to this son.*

Against fn. 1, a translation of the Latin (in pencil): *'He carried the empire of the Parthians from Mount Caucas, many peoples being reduced to slavery, to the river Euphrates'.*

p. 266 (in pencil)

Line beginning 'The silence of history … hints furnished' annotated to *facts preserved* 'by the coins'.

Against 'We have for the period of probably about a century, at least twelve princes of genuine Greek nomenclature': *With the view of treating these princes – the Begram collections had a value which Wilson does not mention perhaps because I had pointed it out. They seemed to show what princes had or had not ruled in that spot – and my third memoir unpublished by Prinsep had the coins there found classed with that particular object in view* (**F526/1a**, see above pp. 39–42).

Against 'all conjectures … must be liable to so many sources of error, that they cannot be offered with courage or confidence. It is necessary … for the sake of perspicuity, to adopt some principle of classification': *They had better then be not offered / how[ever] necessary for perspicuity, when by his own confession all conjectures must be liable to so many sources of error – they would not be for the sake of but to the utter confusion of all perspicuity.*

At the foot of the page Masson gives his own chronological list of kings in response to Wilson's list on p. 267:

BC 256–240	Theodotus I [Diodotus]		Agathocles		
BC 240–220	Theodotus II		Pantaleon	BC 256–220	
BC 220–190	Euthydemus		Euthydemus	BC 220–190	
BC 190–140	Demetri Demetrius		Lysias		
			Antialcides	BC 190–180	
	Eucratides		Eucratides	BC 180–147	
	Heliocles, son of Eucratides		Heliocles	BC 147–127	*Greek empire restricted [?] in Bactriana*
			Menander	BC 126–100	*– Azes*
			Apollodotus	BC 100–75	
			Hermæus	BC 75–40	
		Kadaphes	Hermæus II	BC 40–20	*Scythians possess themselves [?] of Kabul*
		Kadphises			

p. 267 (in pencil)

Against 'the uncertainty which must attach to all deductions from such narrow premises': *narrow? are such premises if concurring and undeniable – slight or unreal ones? Wilson is the numismatologist – his cold regard is very unlike the keen and vivid glance which at a moment on the basic inspection of a coin seizes its interest and provenance from its style even of its age.*

Against the left hand column of kings: *Nonsense – the coins of Lysias and Antialkides must not be separated. The coins of Amyntas and of Agathocles according with each other may not be referred to Bactriana.*

Against the names of kings in the table: '?' against all except Euthydemus, Lysias, Eukratides, Antialkides, Menander, Apollodotus, Hermæus and Su-Hermæus; '*K*' against all without the '?'.

Against Diomedes: *Diomedes very probably a descendant of Demetrius.*

Against Agathokles / Pantaleon bracketed together: *from India? / Menander / Apollodotus / Archebius*

p. 279 Antialcidas

No. 5 (Coins pl. II.13, see **Fig. 27.9**), against 'it can scarcely be anything else than a club': *I have a coin which plainly shows the palm branch.*

Archebius

Against 'silver coins … Jupiter' type and titled 'Dikæos … ally him to the family of Eukratides': *Heliocles*.

Against 'Menander, to whom therefore he must be subsequent': *all this does not follow.*

Against 'The copy of the attitude is so exact that it may be intended for the portrait of Menander': *if so intended – the legend would have expressed it.*

p. 280

Against '2. Hemidrachm [Coins pl . XXI.10] … clears up the difficulty as to the name': *I think not.*

Menander

Against the date given for Menander (BC 126): *?*

Hypanis amended to *Hypasis?*

Masson writes the full quotation from Strabo XI.11.1 (in Latin), and gives an English translation at the foot of p. 281.

p. 281 (in pencil)

Against 'the drachms of Menander and Apollodotus': παλαιαι δραχμαι [old drachms] *he* [the author of the *Periplus*] *calls them.*

Against coins of Menander 'are obtained in the Punjab, but apparently they are brought thither for sale': *?*

Against 'Colonel Todd … discovered his coins of Apollodotus and Menander on the Jumna': *Plenty in Gujarat.*

p. 282
Against 'the style of [Menander's] coins is evidence of his being subsequent not only to [Euthydemus], but to Eukratides and Heliokles', in pencil: *certainly.*

p. 283
Against 𐨨𐨞𐨡𐨯 (copied in margin): *ma-na-da-sa / Mena(n) dasa.*

p. 285
Against 'in none does the face bear the character of age. The attitude of the combatting king occurs on a coin of Alexander', in pencil: *this is gratifying to know.*

Against copper coin no. 7 (Coins pl. IV.3, see **Fig. 26.1**): a further copy and transcription of the Kharoshthi rendering of Menander.

p. 288 Apollodotus I
Against 'That Apollodotus was close upon a barbarized period is confirmed by the coin … in which his title appears to be "king of kings", and his costume is Scythian [i.e. Kushan]': *A single specimen may establish a fact – as for instance if we had no other testimony we might receive it as evidence of the existence of a king – but with regard to the coinage of King Apollodotus, with so many excellent specimens, we must treat the solitary specimen as an exception – and looking at its inferior fabric we may well suspect the circumstances under which it was struck. Suppose Apollodotus wrested some obscure province or even if not obscure yet distant province from the Parthian monarch of the day, say even in Lower India, the coinage might have been inferior such as this specimen would denote. That Apollodotus was near a barbarized period I think not altogether proved from this coin even if the legend be so unmistakeable as M. Rochette assumes it to be. The titles Basileus Ba— were old ones with the Parthian monarchs at the time of Apollodotus.*

p. 291
Against 'un des derniers monumens numismatiques du regne d'Apollodote': *si elle est véritablement une médaille d'Apollodote…*

Diomedes
Against 'use of a common title is no positive evidence of identity of dynasty': *son or relative of Demetrius?*

p. 298 Agathocles
Against 'Agathokles was of Greek and of Bactrian origin … Suyasas must have been a Hindu': *still not one of the Professor's Hindus.*

p. 303 'Barbaric princes'
Against 'Yu-chi [Yuezhi] were expelled about BC 200': *a little before 150 BC – say 175 BC. / Euthydemus then reigning in Bactria.*

Against 'Su': *the Su – perhaps the Su or Sy-evi (Sui or Suevi) of Ptolemy.*

Against 'The Su, also called Szu, Se, Sai and An-szu': *therefore they may be the Asoi of Pliny.*

Against 'These events must have occurred some time anterior to BC 126': *122 BC is the date of Chang-kian's mission, 109 BC the date of his return / Heliocles then reigning in Bactria – the son of Eucratides.*

p. 304
Against 'M. Remusat states that … [the Yuezhi] had … subjugated the An-szu before the visit of Chang-kian: *M. Remusat says no such thing. / M. Remusat says in the first century of our era – which makes a difference of at least 150 years – 122 <u>Before</u> Christ Chang-kian's mission / 25–50 <u>After</u> Christ the subjugation of the An-Szu.*

Against 'Kao-fu, or Kabul': *Why is Kao-fu – Kabul? Might it not be Ka-va, Ka-wa as applied to Kâwa Zamin.*

p. 305
Against 'the immigrant tribes … were branches of that great Turkish race': *Very doubtful – it is contrary to all ancient testimony to believe that the Getæ or Massagetæ were Turkí tribes or nations – Pliny states that the more ancient writers call them Aramæi. It is well observed by Gosselin[6] that this remark of Pliny agrees with that of Posidonius quoted by Strabo – lib I, cap II. 'He who, according to me, reasons best, is Posidonius, who seeks the signification of names, in the affiliation and common origin of people. Following him, Armenians, Syrians and Avars, by dialect, their manner of life, their features and especially by their proximity, appear to be the same race -for instance Mesopotamia, where we meet with a mixture of the three people, and where their resemblance is the most striking.*

In like manner the Assyrians, Arians and Aramæans have much resemblance, whether between themselves or with the other people we have just cited, for those who we call Syrians call themselves Aramæans, to which term resemble the names of Armeni Arab and Erembe.'

p. 307 'Su-Hermaeus' / Kujula Kadphises
In top margin: Persian text in fn. 3 of p. 306 copied out and transcribed.

Against 'It is not impossible that we have traces [in the Su-Hermæus coins] of the very prince to whom the conquest is ascribed by the Chinese': *It will not be impossible, but it will even be probable that we have perhaps something more than traces of the very prince to whom the conquest is ascribed by the Chinese if in the legend, I mean the Bactro Pali legend, common to the coins of Su Hermios with the Hercules type and the [Kujula] Kadphises Kosola coins with the same Hercules type which appear to give the name of Yaruga or Yuga, we may detect an affinity with the names given by the Chinese Yun-Kao-Ching perhaps Yuga-Sena or the native or Bactro-Pali legends of the Kadaphes coins. I can say nothing having never met with them perfect.*

p. 308
Against 'Zathou Kozolou Kadaphes': *of the pure or holy Kosala Kadaphes the Korano [Kujula Kadphises the Kushan].*

At the foot of the page and on the following page (p. 309), various Kharoshthi transcriptions.

p. 309
Against (last line): 𐨐𐨪𐨣𐨯 *this legend appears to be wrong – no coin of the Hercules and club (if such it*

be) bearing the Pali word Maharajasa – as the legend appears to be [legend then written out, changing the first word (to the right) and transcribing it *sa-da-phi-ma-dha* with *na-thí* as alternatives under the second and third characters (from the left)].

p. 310
Against 'These coins [of Su-Hermaeus] are found … in the topes': *These coins not found in the Topes.* Masson is mistaken here. The relic deposit of Hadda stupa 3 includes two Kujula Kadphises coins of this type (see **Vol. I, p.167, Fig. 256.13–14**).

p. 311 'Uncertain names' / Wima Takto
Against 'M. Rochette attributes these coins to Heliokles', in pencil: *They are so unless 'these coins may be the issue of a Barbarian or Saka prince of the time of Heliokles who imitated the … coins of that king'.*

p. 312 'Coins of uncertain names' (in pencil)
Against 'Rochette conjectures that they are intended for coins of Heliokles': *Independently I had arrived at the same conclusion – forced indeed upon me by observing that the type of a copper coin found by M. Court as figured by Prinsep was identical with that of the celebrated coin described by Mionnet.*

Against the paragraph describing coin no. 5 (Coins pl. VIII.17), a unique silver coin of the Indo-Scythian satrap Zeionises: *misplaced here I think.*

p. 313 Maues (in pencil)
Against 'they seem to intimate that … this prince is connected … with Menander and Apollodotus': *no such thing – they only prove that the same provinces or cities were under the rule of the several kings at various periods.*

p. 316 Spalirises (in pencil)
Against the Kharoshthi: *Legend incorrectly given; it is* [copied then transcribed] *kaligudamasa* (actually *spalirihasa*: Coins pl. VIII.12; see **Fig. 29.4**).

p. 318 Spalirises and Spalagadama (in pencil)
Against the Kharoshthi: *Legend again wrong. It is* [copied then transcribed] *Balagadamasa for the name / the titles are sa trapusa ha la ba* (actually *spalahoraputrasa … spalagadamasa*: Coins pl. VIII.13; see **Fig. 29.3**).

p. 321 Azes
Against 'It may be a question … whether Azes should not be regarded rather as a native of India than of Scythia': *Whether a native of India or not – Azes was a king of Gandhara – and the modern Kabul was not under his rule.*

p. 322 (in pencil)
Against 'from the frequency with which some of his coins are found in the topes': *no coin of Azes was ever found in a Tope.*

p. 331 (in pencil)
Against 'These coins [of Indo-Scythian satrap Mujatria] are very numerous in all the collections, and have been found in most of the topes in considerable quantity': *not in considerable quantity – four in one – and one or two in another* (Bimaran stupas 2 and 5; Hadda stupa 3 respectively, see **Vol. I, Figs 117.1–4; 136.20–4; 256.27–8**).

p. 334 Soter Megas
Against the record of a Soter Megas 'silver' drachm (Coins pl. IX.9): *I also sent home a silver coin of this class, if not more than one – C.M. / Court was keeping one.* These are clearly all forgeries. There are no silver Soter Megas issues.[7]

p. 347 'Miscellaneous Arsacid Kings' (Sanabares)
Against 'These are from a considerable number of coins [of Sanabares, see **Fig. 33.2–8**] found by Mr. Masson at Begram': *They were not found at Begram, but were procured in a large parcel from the bazaar of Kabul, and probably brought from Turkestan.*

Against 'the unique gold coins of Diodotus and Euthydemus': *It must be borne in mind that the very fact that these two gold coins, although unique to <u>us</u>, having been found, puts it beyond doubt that both Diodotus and Euthydemus had a coinage of gold and so had possibly all the Greco-Bactrian kings. C.M.*

Against 'The solitary instance of a genuine silver coin of [Wima] Kadphises' (**Fig. 38.3**): *Not so – as proved by the solitary instance noted – two coins silver of Kadphises passed through my hands. Silver coins of Ermaios with the Hercules type and of the nameless great king were also found by me – and of the latter or nameless king, M. Court found a gold coin. C.M.* Apart from **Fig. 38.3**, these are again all forgeries (see **p. 334** above).

p. 349 Kushan
Against 'an immense copper coinage': *In the time of the Indo-Scythic [Kushan] princes of Kabul – the copper mines for that country were extensively worked and upon a very superior and even scientific system.*

Against 'The copper coins of [Wima] Kadphises and Kanerkes [Kanishka] are found in considerable quantities': *? if fact – Wilson must I think refer to the lowest series of the Indo-Scythic coinages and not to the monies of Kadphises and Kanerkes.*

Against 'ΚΑΔΦΙCΗC': *Basileus Oohmo Kadphises / Ovohemo / Voemo / Ovoemo* [Wima].

p. 351 (in pencil)
Against 'This is by no means an unusual form of the divinity, and is the type here represented': *The figure and bull have in other coins (later coins) the legend Okro [ΟΗÞΟ] – whence therefore this insisting upon Saiva being intended – what is more probable is that Saiva is nothing more than the Hindu or Sabean Okro.*

p. 354 Wima Kadphises
In the top margin, Masson copies and transcribes the Kharoshthi legend printed in the first paragraph, continuing at the top of p. 355 below.

p. 355
Against the description of coin no. 7, **Pl. XI.9** (**Fig. 38.3**): *? whether belonging to [Wima] Kadphises – the Greek legend appears to be BACIΛEUL AKCUΛKHIC / basileus aksulkeis/akstakeis / the Pali legend is singular – maharaja – rajadiraja vríma kadaphísasa.*

Against 'It has the singularity of being the only silver coin of the Indo-Scythian kings yet found': *Not so – an undoubtedly genuine silver coin of the Hermios [Hermaeus] Hercules type was sent home by me. C.M.* (see also **p. 347** above).

p. 357
Against the description of coin no. 16, Coins pl. XI.14 (**Fig. 34.5**); in pencil: *Should not be included here – with the coins of [Kujula] Kadphises.*

Against 'the entire Greek legend is ΖΑΘΟΥ ΚΟΖΟΛΥ ΚΑΔΑΦΕΣ ΚΟΓΑΝΟ': *To this Greek version of the legend – the Bactro-Pali counterpart is best accommodated – I mean the Bactrian legend common to the Hercules coins. Zatho stands for dharmathesasa or dharmaphedasa – Kosolu for Kujula – Kadphises for nothing – because the name on the Hermios and Kadphises Kosolu coins is Yuga or Yavaya – while it responds to that of Kadphises on the pure Kadphises coins – KOPANO [Kushan] is the equivalent of Satrapusha.*

p. 361 Kanishka
Against 'A term of frequent occurrence upon both the gold and copper coins is OKPO' [OHÞO]: *why is not OKPO [Oesho] the Pahlaví that is, Pali Aukhra – as in Aukhuramazd / Ormazd / &c. (i.e. Ahuramazda).*

Against 'Ugra also, although it is an appellation of Siva', in pencil: *Okro – the equivalent of the Persic Akra.*

p. 363
Against the discussion of 'Bibi Nani, or Lady Nani': *whether the Assa Mahí, the Great, the universal Mother or Eve – is or not Nanaia may be matter of speculation – under the hill at Kabul no doubt once sacred to her and now known by her name Assa Mahi is a spot and village still called Nanachi – also beyond Ghazni on the road to Kandahar are two villages the Great and little Naní.*

p. 365
Against 'a coin having upon it the figure of Siva': *does not this passage establish that the Siva of the Hindu Pantheon and the Okro or Ardokro [Ardochsho] of the Indo Scythics are one and the same personage or deity?*

p. 374 Huvishka
Against 'Komaro is … the name of the [Indian] deity of war': *The God of Kaddea Gama, whose temple is near to Leawawa in Ceylon – is called by the Cingalese Kande Keomareyo – he is described as having six heads, twelve hands &c &c – and represented as both standing and seated on a peacock – so much for the name IKANDO KOMAPO – the initial I being probably C or S as in the case of the Spalirises coins. The Hindus who call this deity their own, have his name Scanda Kumara.*

Against 'the Aswini-kumaras': *Sir W. Jones [1788] says 'the two Cumars (Kumaras) are the Castor and Pollux of India' – 'On the chronology of the Hindus' – As. Res. Vol. 2, p. 105.*

p. 380 Vasudeva imitations (in pencil)
Against 'Uncertain or "Ardokro" coins of the Indo-Scythic series … have been … denominated by Mr. Prinsep … "link" coins': *did not Swiney or Stacey denominate them 'link' coins?*

p. 381 Sasanian (in pencil)
Against 'we have ample evidence of the influence, and possibly the authority, of Sasanian princes in the presence of their coins in Afghanistan': *doubtful. if a genuine Sasanian coin be met with at or near Kabul it is clearly an accidental coin – that is a foreign coin, one which was never current.*

p. 382 (in pencil)
Against 'From Kabul and the neighbourhood … Mr. Masson has reaped an abundant harvest of Sasanian coins': *Are they Sasanian? The greater part I think not.*

Against 'the coins of … princes in a costume and of features very different from those of the Sasanian kings in general ([Coins] pl. XVI, fig. 18) [see **Pl. 14**, *Fig. 7* above]': *These are the particular coins* (Alkhan, from Hadda stupa 10, see **Vol. I, Fig. 282**).

p. 383
Against 'Coins which … are undoubtedly of the later Sasanian kings', in pencil: *??? see under.*

Against 'We do not find amongst the Sasanian coins of Kabul any of the coins of Ardashir': *The Armenian writers say that the Pahlavís have three tribes – the Surenis – the Aspahapatis, and the Karanis – and the two former placed Ardashir son of Sasan (truly son of Papal vide inscriptions) on the throne. The Pahlavis were so named from the birth place Pahl – is not this the Chinese Pho-lo or Balkh.*

Then for the word Sasan – it clearly was not the name of the father of Ardashir.

p. 384 (in pencil)
In the left margin, Masson writes a list of the Sasanian kings.

p. 387 (in pencil)
Against Shapur 'was engaged in hostilities with Bactria'; or, fn. 1, 'Carmania': *he may have been engaged both in war with Bactria and with Carmania.*

Against 'We can scarcely … admit … that a branch of the Arsacidan dynasty was then reigning at Balkh': *This fact is curious and not improbable – Balkh was occupied by the Getae centuries before the age of Sapor.*

p. 391
In the right margin, Masson writes the names of a series of Sasanian monarchs in Pahlavi script and transliteration.

p. 400 'Indo-Sasanian'
Against coin no. 30, Coins pl. XXI.22 (**Fig. 57.4–7**; Shahi Tegin) 'From one of two coins in the Masson collection': *I had <u>many</u> of these coins.*

p. 404 Punch-marked coins (in pencil)
Against 'The style of these pieces and the rudeness of their execution': *Why the style? Is their execution rude?*

p. 405 'Saurashhtran' / Western Satraps (in pencil)
Against 'None of them have been found in Afghanistan': *Two or three occur – rarely.*

p. 407 (in pencil)
Against 'Of the Gupta princes … we have authentic traces in the seventh century': *? if not earlier.*

p. 416 'Buddhist coins' / Local issues
Against 'Those which have the lion on the reverse [e.g. **Fig. 22.11–15**] are thought by Prinsep to bear an analogy to the copper coins of Agathokles': *I also thought the same, and before Prinsep – and think so still. C.M.*

p. 417 Gupta coins (in pencil)
Against 'it has been thought likely [the 'rude coins of this class … belonged to the Rajas of … Kanauj']… but they have been obtained in many other situations': *Wilson likes to be safe.*

Against 'A banner with a bird, probably the Garuda': *why not an owl?* (Wilson is correct).

Against 'the figures represent Rama and Sitá: *? as to Rama and Sita.*

p. 418
Against 'we have the prototype in those coins which bear the legend Ardokro'[Ardochsho]: *the prototype of the Ardokro figure is found on a coin of Azes – that is the seated figure – see fig 12 Plate 7* [**Fig. 30.18**]. *If on later coins of unquestionably Hindu or Brahmanical princes, it should, as Wilson would have it, represent Lakshmi or Durga – it can only prove that Lakshmi and Durga, the one or the other or both, as the case may be, are but adaptations of the Mithraic Okro or Ardokro – and this would go far to prove that the actual Hindu that is Brahmanical mythological system is nothing more [than] one naturally resulting from the amalgamation of previous systems known in India – such as the Greek and Mithraic for instance, not to speak of others.*

p. 421 (in pencil)
Against 'Vikramaditya … It would be highly interesting if this coin could be considered as the coin of the great patron of Hindu literature … Vikramaditya, king of Ujayin, BC 56 ': *Could Wilson seriously make this remark? Vikramaditya of Ujayin must have flourished at least five centuries before the coin – a better query would have been – could it be considered a coin of Vikramaditya in whose reign the nine jewels flourished and in which the literature called Sanskrit was so much cultivated.*

p. 422
In the top left margin, Masson lists legends on Gupta coins:
Vikramaditya
Chandra Gupta
Sinha Vikrama
Majendra Sinha
Kumara Gupta
Samara Gupta
Samudra Gupta
Skanda Gupta

p. 427 (in pencil)
Against 'Durgá, who is intended by the sitting female': *If the sitting figure be Durga – then is Durga an Indian imitation of the Mithraic Nanaia?*

p. 429 'Rajput' / Turkic and Hindu Shahi
Vide p. 442. Vol 9 – As. Res. reprint in London 1809 [Colebrook 1809] *– VII. Inscription on copper plate found at Amgách'hi in Sultanpur – district of Dinajpur'. The seal affixed has the name Sri Vigraha pála déva*
princes named

1	Loca Pála
2	Dharma Pála
3	…………...
4	*Jaya Pála*
5	*Déva Pála*
6	…………...
7	…………...
8	?………….
9	Rája Pála
10	Pála Déva
11	Mahípála Déva
12	Nayapála Déva
13	Vigraha Pála Déva

Against 'Rajput Coins – Silver… 6–10 … Sri Syalapati deva', in pencil: *Bappa was called Syalapati.*

p. 439 'Conclusion'
Against 'It is impossible to imagine that the presence of Greek principalities upon the confines of India … failed to exercise some influence upon the arts and knowledge of the Hindus': *and upon the religion?*

Against 'The amount [of influence] may not have been considerable, but it was not likely to have been totally wanting; and … it is recognised by the Hindus themselves in the frequent allusions to the Yavanas': *P[rof]. Wilson elsewhere, i.e. in other works, states that the Yavana allusions have been interpolations.*

Against 'That barbarians succeeded to the Greeks in Bactria … was made known … by the Chinese scholars of Paris': *How made known? – was it not before known from classical authors? What the Chinese accounts did was to confirm and to illustrate what was previously known.*

Against 'In them we may trace several and successive dynasties of barbaric rulers, Saka, Getæ, Parthians, Huns and Turks': *If we may trace – P[rof]. Wilson would have done essential service in pointing out which was which – in which he has really bewitched the subject – or signally failed.*

p. 440
Against 'At the date of their [i.e. the barbaric rulers'] first establishment some of them apparently retained the divinities of the Greeks': *allusive I presume to the Hermaeus Hercules coins.*

Against 'others … endeavoured to combine the worship of fire with the polytheism of the Hindus': *allusive I presume to the Kadphises coins.*

Against 'different dynasties attempted to introduce … the deities of a form of Mithraic faith': *allusive I presume to the Kanerkes and Rao Kanerki coins.*

Against 'Hindu sovereigns, after a long interval, once more reigned in the country of the Paropamisadae': *it was a long interval.*

p. 449
At foot of page (Index, O–S): *Dhamapídasa Kujulakasa tra Kushanaya Vugasa*

Plates illustrating coins

As a typical example (**Fig. 141**) shows, Masson extensively annotated the illustrations of coins with transcriptions of legends, and attributions, sometimes (as here) copying and transcribing some of the legends on the blank facing pages, or adding other notes (the annotations are in pencil other than where noted. Indistinct annotations, copies of Kharoshthi legends and their transcriptions are omitted).

Plate V (**Fig. 141**; above coins):

8. *Yadaphes* (Wilson) [Kujula Kadphises; Kharoshthi legend on reverse copied around coin in ink; see p. 310; **Fig. 34.7**]

9. *Yadaphes* (Wilson) [part of Kharoshthi legend on reverse copied beside coin; **Fig. 34.10**]

10. *Yadaphes* (Wilson) [**Fig. 34.11**]

11. *Hermæus* [**Fig. 28.8**]

12. *Undopheres* [Gondophares; **Fig. 32.8**]

13. *Undopheres* [**Fig. 32.10**]

14. *Undopheres* [Anonymous imitation in name of Hermaeus; **Fig. 28.20**]

15. *Undopheres ?* [**Fig. 28.20**]

16. obverse *Gondophares*; reverse *Sharahetasa / doubtful* [part of monogram and legend copied below, annotated *Gondophares?* **Fig. 32.1**]

17. obverse *Gondophares*; reverse *Sharahetasa* [**Fig. 32.17**]

18. *Gondophares*; reverse *doubtful* [**Fig. 32.2**]

20. *Gondophares?*; reverse *Sharahetasa* [Sasan; **Fig. 32.28**]

Blank page facing Pl. V (**Fig. 141**)

The annotations are (at the top): *ΒΑΣΙΛΕΩΣ ΣΤΗΡΟΣΣΥ ΕΡΜΑΙΟΥ*

Centre: copies of Kharoshthi legends with transcriptions, the second also being translated:

Kujula-ka-satrapusha-daya-[?]vugasa dhamaphidasa
Pushana Yavgasa
Satrapy of Kosala. (Money) of the righteous Yavuga / Yavga
Ya-vu-ga-sa
Yun-kao-ching or Yugasenu

Plate VI (above / beside coins):

1. *Abagases?* [Swiney collection]

2. *Gondophares?* [below] *thura* [**Fig. 32.5**]

13. *APT / Artemis* [Azes II; **Fig. 30.1**]

14, 18–19. *Siva* [Azes II; **19**: **Fig. 30.2**]

15. *Dharma / (Buddha)* [Azes II, seated king; after Prinsep 1835, pl. XXIII.15]

16, 17. *Buddha* [Azes II; **16**: **Fig. 30.3**; **17**: Ventura collection]

Masson also writes *aya* against a number of coins on pls VI–VII where this appears in the Kharoshthi legend.

Plate VII (above / beside coins):

3. *suthu* [Azes II; **Fig. 30.10**]

5. *Artemis* [Azes I; Swiney collection]

8. *obverse – style of Apollodotus* [Azes II; **Fig. 30.21**]

9–10. *Apollodotus style* [**10**:] *Ayasa* [Azes II; **Fig. 30.22**]

12. [obv.] *original or prototype of Ardokro* [rev.] *Apollo*; Masson draws the left-hand monogram, writing *nisra / aya* below it. [Azes II; **Fig. 30.18**]

13, 14. *Azes* [II; **Fig. 30.29–30**]

17. *doubtful* [Swiney collection]

Blank page facing Plate VIII

Coins found in stupa deposits – see **Vol. I**

Tepe Darunta	*Great Nameless King and inferior Hercules coins*
Chaharbagh	[Wima] *Kadphises and Rao Kanerki* [Kanishka I]
Hadda	*miscellaneous*
Shévaki	[Wima] *Kadphises*
Gul Dara	[Wima] *Kadphises* [and] *Rao Kanerki ko Rano* [Huvishka]
Wardak	*Inferior* [Wima] *Kadphises or Bull and standing figure type*
Kurd Kabul	*Inferior*
Manikyala	

Copy of monogram to right of figure on reverse of coin no. 1: *shégashu*

Plate IX (above coins):

1. *Kodes or Hyrkodes* [Swiney collection]

2. *Kodes* [reverse] *Ardothro* [Mohan Lal collection]

3–7. *Kodes* [Mohan Lal; Karamat 'Ali]

8–22. *nameless* [Soter Megas; **Figs 36–7**]

Plate X (above coins):

1–4, 6. *nameless* [Soter Megas; **Figs 36–7**]

5, 7–21. *Kadphises* [Wima Kadphises: **Fig. 38.7–8, 10–11, 13**: gold coins from Guldara stupa, see **Vol. I, Fig. 69.1–6**]

Plate XI (above coins):

1–2, 12. *Kadphises?* Wilson [**1–2**: Vasudeva I; **12**: Kujula Kadphises: **Fig. 34.18**]

3–8, 13. *Kadphises?* [**3–8**: Vasudeva I and imitations; **13**: Kujula Kadphises: **Fig. 34.19**]

10. *Kadphises* [reverse] *Kayadaphasayn[-]as* [Kujula Kadphises: **Fig. 34.14**]

14. *Kadaphes* [Kujula Kadphises: **Fig. 34.5**]

Plate XII (above / below coins):

5. *Rao – Nano – Rao – Kanerki(?) Korano* [Court collection]

13. *of the King Nerk?* [Kanishka I: **Fig. 39.14**]

Blank page facing Plate XII

Raona – no – Rao – Kanerki – ko – rano
Rao – nano – rao – Kanerki – Korano
The great – the very great Kanerkes the Korano
The holy – the very holy Kanerkes the Korano

Plate XIII

The plate lacks figure numbers. Coins numbered by Masson, but in sequence across the page by rows, not always corresponding with Wilson's numbering on **pp. 370–2**)

In top margin: *Page 370*

Below coin no. **3**: *Rao – Nana – Rao – Nake – Korano* [Kanishka I: **Fig. 41.18**]

In margin (legend on Buddha coins **1–3**): *ΒΑVΔΑ – ΑΚΑΜΑ*

Baudha Akama
Boudha Akama

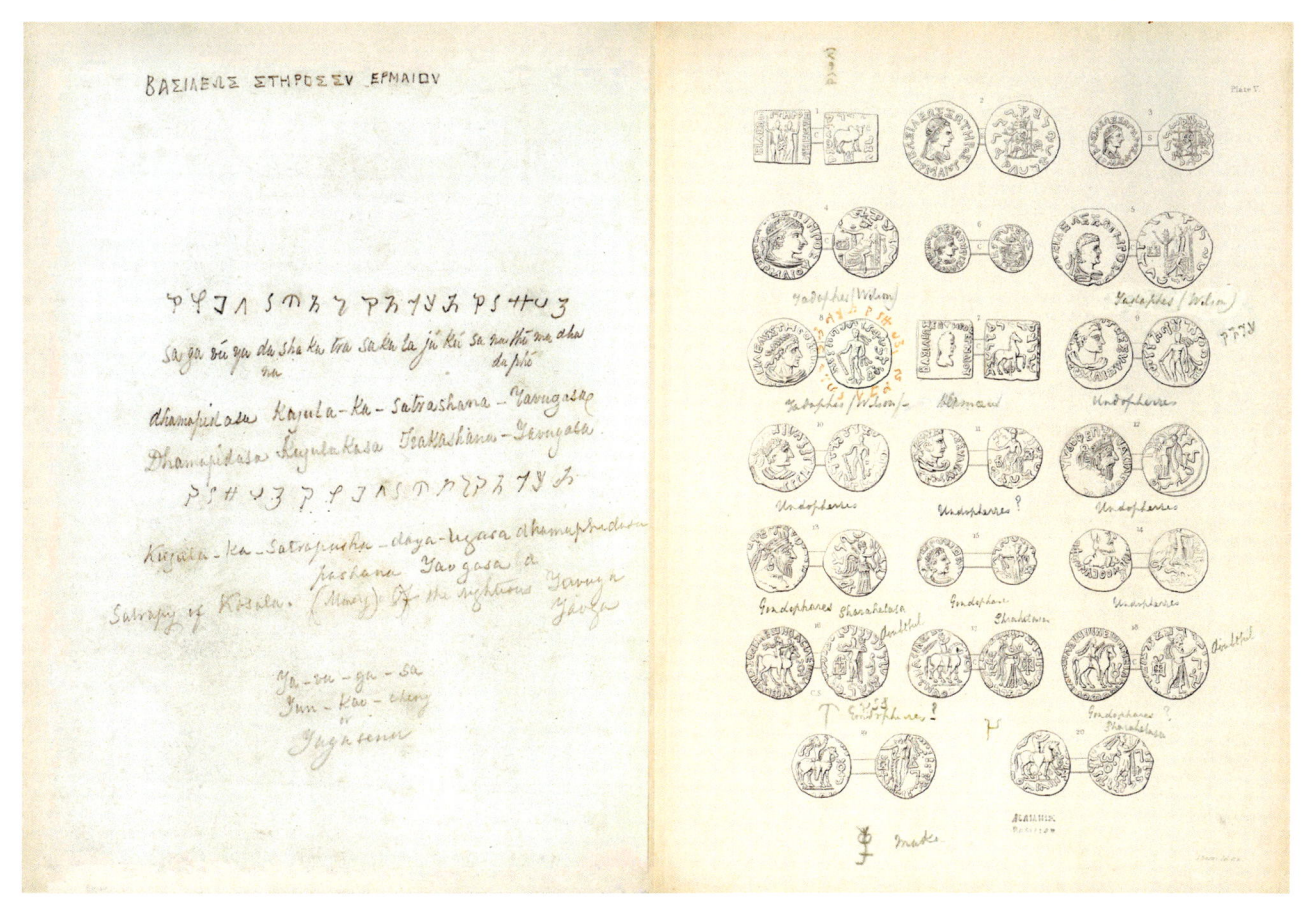

Figure 141 Annotations to and opposite Coins pl. V. © Bodleian Library

Below Masson coin no. **11** (**p. 372**, no. 9, pl. XIII.12), [Huvishka: **Fig. 44.20**]
Rao – Nana – Rao Nake Korano
The righteous Rao – the Korano of Nake (Nikea)

Plate XIV
In top margin: *Page 373*
Around coin no. **12** (in ink): *Raono rao*; below: *I have no doubt that Wilson's view of this corrupt Greek legend being intended for Rao Nano Rao* [Kushano-Sasanian in name of Vasudeva: **Fig. 51.1**]
Above coin no. **13** (in ink): *Rao Nana rao Boooho Korano* [in pencil]: *OOKP / OOHPI* [Kushano-Sasanian, in name of Vasudeva: **Fig. 51.3**]
Above / below coin no. **16**: [p.] *379 / Here Wilson is I think very deficient.* [Kushano-Sasanian Peroz I: **Fig. 51.5**]

Plate XVIII Gupta coins – not Masson collection.
Above coins (mostly following legends in Wilson's text):
3. *Chandra Gupta*
4. Beside coin: *Chandra*; [reverse] *Sri Vikrama*
5. *Sinha Vikrama*
6. *Samu* [reverse] *Parukram*
7–8. *vijaya* (**7**) *360 +* AD
9–10. *Samudra?*
12. [illegible] *Jayati Mahendra Gupta*
13. *Sri Skanda?*
14. *Kumara Gupta type*
16–17. *Mahendra Gupta*
18. Around reverse image: *Sri Prakrama Deva*

Plate XIX
Above coins (mostly following legends in Wilson's text, and bracketing coins according to Wilson's groupings):
[Turkic (Kabul) Shahi and Hindu Shahi coins]
Heading: *Sri Samagu deva [Samantadeva] – Bhíma*
6, 9. *Sri Syalapati deva* [Spalapatideva; **Fig. 58.1, 3**]
10–11. *Samagu deva* [Samantadeva; **Fig. 58.24**]
12. *Sri Vanka deva* [Vakkadeva; **Fig. 58.12**]
13. *Sri Syalpati deva?* [Spalapatideva; **Fig. 58.7**]
14. *Sri Hari?* [Spalapati imitation; **Fig. 58.11**]
[Delhi Sultanate coins]
15–17. *Samagu deva* [reverse] *Sri Raja*
18. *Asavari Sri Samagu deva* [reverse] *Sri Prithwi Raja deva*
19. *Sri Samagu deva* [reverse] *Madana Pala deva*
20. *Asavari Sri* [reverse] *Srí*
21. *-ta deva*
22. *Sri Samagu ma*
23. *Madhava (Sri) Sama* [reverse] *Sri Madana (Pala)*
24–6. [& bracketed with **27**]: *Sri Mohommed Sam* [reverse *Sri Hamira*
28. *Sri Sams-ud-din* [reverse] *Sri Mohommed?*
29–30. *Sri Sams-ud-din* [reverse] *Sri Mohommed?*
31. *Sri Sams-ud-din* [reverse] *Sri Hamíra*
32, 33. *Sri Sams-ud-din*
34. *Asavari Sri* [reverse] *Sri Raja*
35, 36. *Sri Mohammed bin Sam* [reverse] *Sri Hamira*
37. *Sams-ud-din Mahomed*[8]
38. *Nazir ud dunia* [Nasir al-dīn Muḥammād b. Hasan Qarlugh]
39. *Al Sultan al Azim Abul Muzaffar Ibrahim / Sri Samagu* ['adil al-sultān al mu'azam abul' muzaffar Ibrahim: Nasir al-daula Ibrahim (Ghaznavid) / Samantadeva]

Plate XX
Above coins (mostly following legends in Wilson **pp. 433–8**):

3. *Sri Mahomed Sams-ud-din / Sri Hamíra* [Muḥammād b. Sām (Ghurid)]

4. *Ala ud din Mohammed (Khwarism) / Sultan Azim al Sultan* ['Ala al-dīn Muḥammād b. Tekish (Khwarazm) / al-sultān al-'azam]

5. *Sri Samagu deva* [Samantadeva] */ Shah al Sultan Azim Abul Muzaffar Ibrahim* [Ghaznavid: the legend given for a different issue of the same ruler is repeated, see Coins pl. XIX.39 above. This coin reads 'adil nasir al-daula wa zahir al-millat Ibrahim: **Fig. 61.23**]

6. *Azim Maiz ud dunia wa ud din* [al-'azam mu'izz al-duniyā wa al-dīn abū'l muzaffar: Muḥammād b. Sām]

7. *Sultan al Azim Mohammed bin Sam* [al-sultān al-'azam Muḥammād b. Sām: **Fig. 62.15**]

8. *Ala ud din Mohammed (Khwarism) / Mahomed Sultan* ['Ala al-dīn Muḥammād b. Tekish (Khwarazm)]

9. *Azim al Fateh Bulbun Sultan* [sic: al-sultān al-mu'azam abū'l fatḥ Yildiz al-sultān: Tāj al-dīn Yildiz, Ghurid governor of Ghazni; **Fig. 62.33**]

10. *Maiz ud dunia* [Mu'izz al-duniyā Muḥammād b. Sām]

11. *Al Sultan*

12. *Azim Abul Muzaffar Ibrahim* [al-mu'azam abul' muzaffar Ibrahim: Nasir al-daula Ibrahim (Ghaznavid)]

13. *Altamsh* [Shams al-dīn Iltutmish, sultan of Delhi]

15. *Abul Fateh Mohammed al Sultan / bin Mohammed (Khwarism)* [abū'l fatḥ Muḥammād al-sultān / b. Muḥammād (Khwarazm)]

16. *Al Sultan al Moazim / Al seraj al daulet* [al-sultān al-'azam Suraj al-daula] *Khosru Malek* [Khusrau Malik; **Fig. 61.44**]

17. *Nasir ud dunia wa du din* [Mu'izz al-duniya /wa al-dīn Muḥammād b. Sām; **Fig. 62.7**]

20. *Maiz-du-dunia wa du din / al Sultan Altamsh* [Mu'izz al-duniyā wa al-dīn / al-sultān Iltutmish (Delhi)]

21. *Adel al Sultan al Azim Muzaffar Ibrahim* ['adil al-sultān al-mu'azam abūl' muzaffar Ibrahim: Nasir al-daula Ibrahim]

22. *Sri mad Govinda Chandra deva* [Govindachandradeva (Kanauj); **Fig. 59.13**]

23. *Sri mad Jadjeya deva* [Gangeyadeva (Kalachuri); **Fig. 59.14**]

24. *Sri mad Kumara Pala deva* [Kumarapaladeva (Yadava); **Fig. 59.15**]

25. *Sri mad Mir Mahomed Sam* [śrī mahamada biṇi sāma: Muḥammād b. Sām; **Fig. 59.18**]

26. *Sri mad Mir Mohammed Sam* [śrīma hamīra mahamada sāmaḥ: Muḥammād b. Sām; **Fig. 59.19**]

27. *Mohamed Chhám* [śrīma hamīra mahamada sāmaḥ: Muḥammād b. Sām; **Fig. 59.20**]

28. *Ghazni* [AH] *616* [Muḥammād b. Tekish, (Khwarazm): **Fig. 63.1**]

29. *Mahomed ben Sam / Ghazni* [Muḥammād b. Sām: **Fig. 62.3**]

30. *Abul Kasim Mahmud Sabektigin* [Sebuktegin (Ghaznavid): **Fig. 60.18**]

31. *Mahmud* [I (Ghaznavid): **Fig. 60.22**]

32. *Masaud* [Mas'ūd (Ghaznavid): **Fig. 61.3**]

33. *Modud* [Mawdūd I (Ghaznavid): **Fig. 61.9**]

34. *Bahram Shah* [Ghaznavid]

35. *Mahomed bin Sam* [Muḥammād b. Sām: **Fig. 62.2**]

36. *Baghdad – 188 Hijra* [below] *Harun al Rashid*

Notes

1 Presumably Baden Henry Baden-Powell, CIE (1841–1901), variously Conservator of Forests for the Punjab, Vice-Chancellor of the University of the Punjab (1883–5) and Chief Court Judge for Lahore (1886–9). He returned to England in 1896, lived in Oxford and died at the age of 59. He was buried in St Sepulchre's Cemetery, Oxford.

2 The London bindery founded by W.T. Morrell, c. 1861.

3 Possibly indicating the type or cost of binding.

4 The price could also be read as £2.10.00.

5 He campaigned in India in 1327 and became ruler of the Mongol Chagatai Khanate in 1331.

6 P.F.J. Gosselin (1751–1830) was a commentator on classical geographers.

7 For a discussion on forgeries in Court's collection, see Errington 1995, p. 415, figs 3.F, H-L; 4.

8 Masson's spellings appear to vary, though it is often unclear whether and 'a' or 'o' is intended.

Appendix 2: F526/1m. EIC receipt of Masson's Collections 19 October 1836 to December 1838

F526/1m. List of Coins &co.
EIC Bombay Government documentation of receipt of Masson's collections 19 October 1836 to December 1838, compiled by J.P. Willoughby (Secretary to Bombay Government). Watermark: SE & Co. 1838 (**Fig. 142**).

A. 1 bag containing:
1 bag 25 gold coins.
1 bag 25 silver coins.
1 bag 36 copper coins.
6 engraved stones.
In Mr Masson's note of 7th December 1838 stating that they cost 270 Rs and were purchased from his own funds, the copper coins are not mentioned.

B. 1 bag gold [and] silver coins &co &co from Begram. 10 bags collected since 1838:
1 bag 57 silver coins.
Green bag 7 gold coins.
Green bag 45 silver coins.
1 bag 73 silver coins.
1 bag 216 silver, very small coins.
1 bag 117¼ tolas very small coins [1.37kg]
1 stone with Muhammadan effigy.
1 bag silver fragments 4½ tolas [52.48g].
1 bag silver coins 3¾ tolas [43.74g] & 1 bag copper coins.
1 bag fragments of stone &co.

C. 1 bag fragments of stone and sand.

D. 1 bag [containing]:
1 bag 1064 copper coins T.H.P.
1 bag 563 copper coins T.H.P.
1 bag 257 copper coins T.H.P.
1 bag 660 copper coins T.H.P.

E. 1 bag containing 12 bags:
1 bag 6 copper coins H.P.
1 bag 98 copper coins H.P.
1 bag 29 copper coins H.P.
1 bag 62 copper coins H.P.
1 bag 31 copper coins.
1 bag 192 copper coins.
1 bag 58 copper coins.
1 bag 8 copper coins.
1 bag 32 copper coins.
1 bag 37 silver coins.
1 bag 190 silver coins.
1 bag 72 silver coins.

F. 1 bag containing 9 bags. Gold, silver coins &co from Bazaar Kabul collected since November 1838.
1 piece marble.
1 bag small stone.
1 red bag engraved glass &co.
1 red bag 59 gold coins.
1 bag 6 copper coins.
1 bag 1 gold ring & engraved stone.
1 bag 21 silver coins.
1 bag 67 silver coins.
1 bag 43 silver coins.

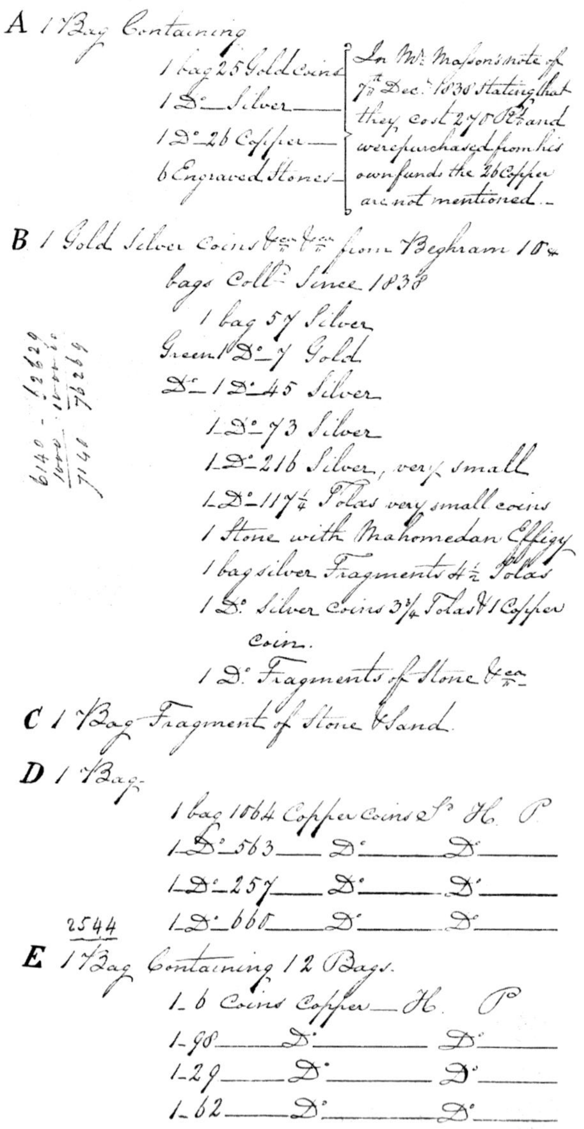

[Handwritten list on left side of page, transcribed as legible:]

A. 1 Bag containing
  1 bag 25 Gold coins ⎫ In Mr Masson's note of
  1 Do Silver   ⎪ 7th Dec 1838 stating that
  1 Do 26 Copper   ⎬ they cost 270 Rs and
  6 Engraved Stones   ⎪ were purchased from his
                      ⎭ own funds the 26 Copper
                        are not mentioned.

B. 1 Gold Silver Coins &c &c from Begram 10+
   bags Colld Since 1838
     1 bag 5½ Silver
     Green Do 1 Gold
     Do 1 Do 45 Silver
     1 Do 73 Silver
     1 Do 216 Silver, very small
     1 Do 117½ Tolas very small coins
     1 Stone with Mahomedan Effigy
     1 bag silver Fragments 4½ Tolas
     1 Do Silver coins 3½ Tolas & 1 Copper coin.
     1 Do Fragments of Stone &c

6140 12620
      11000
7140 7326¼

C. 1 Bag Fragment of Stone & Sand.

D. 1 Bag
     1 bag 1064 Copper coins So H P
     1 Do 563   Do   Do
     1 Do 257   Do   Do
     1 Do 660   Do   Do
   2544

E. 1 Bag Containing 12 Bags.
     1. 6 Coins Copper — H P
     1. 98   Do   Do
     1. 29   Do   Do
     1. 62   Do   Do

Figure 142 MSS F526/1m, f. 1

G. 1 bag containing copper fragments, brass elephant &co. In Box no. 11.
2 bags containing 4041¼ tolas [47.14kg] copper coins.
1 bag said to contain 1706 copper coins.
1 bag said to contain 906 copper coins.
1 bag said to contain 889 copper coins.
1 bag said to contain 6668 copper coins.
1 bag said to contain 2165 copper coins.
1 bag said to contain <u>435</u> copper coins.
                  12769

1 bag said to contain 52 copper coins.
1 bag said to contain 83 copper coins.
1 bag said to contain 530 copper coins.
1 bag said to contain 58 copper coins.
1 bag said to contain 49 copper coins.
1 bag said to contain 172 copper coins.
1 bag said to contain 56 copper coins.
1 bag said to contain 118 copper coin.
1 bag said to contain 65 copper coins.
1 bag said to contain 34 copper coins.
1 bag said to contain 870 copper coins.
1 bag said to contain 60 copper coins.
1 bag said to contain 4 copper coins.
1 bag said to contain 16 copper coins.
1 bag said to contain 829 copper coins.
1 bag said to contain 3245 copper coins.
24 bags   18955

Signed John Williams, President
True copy, signed L.R. Read, Chief Secretary to Government
True copy, P.M. Melvill, Political Agent in Kutch [1840–1]

Appendix 3: F526/1n. Masson's Summary List of Collections 1833–8

F526/1n. Watermark: Wade 1843

Gold coins from Kabul

1834	Indo-Scythic, Kadphises, Kanerki & Ooerki [Wima, Kanishka, Huvishka]	6
1835		7
1835	small	1
1836	(of 1836 I have no account)	
1837		13
1835	Kufic & Muhammadan, Khwarazm, Ghurid & Ghazni	1
1836		103
1837		37
1835	Kanauj Pala series	1
1836		1
1837		17
1837		6
1837	Early fire worshippers	1
1837	Kanauj Gupta series	1
1835	Roman Trajans	2

In 1838, for which I have no account, I yet find statements of 93 gold coins procured from Kabul; there were more, but even these I cannot classify.

1838	Of various kinds	93
1834	Byzantine	1

Silver coins from Kabul – Bactrian drachms & hemi-drachms

1834	Menander	111
	Apollodotus	7
	Antimachus	6
	Hermaeus	1
	Alexander	1
1835	Menander, Apollodotus, Antimachus	74
1835	Various Menander, Apollodotus, Hermaeus, Antialcidas &c. di-drachms, drachms &c.	29
1837	Antiochus tetradrachms	2
	Eucratides tetradrachms	1
	Menander	9
	Apollodotus	2
	Antimachus	3
	Heliocles	1
	Antialcidas	1
	Archebius	1
	Hermaeus	8
	Azes	4
	Nameless Great King	1
	Hermaeus Kujula Hercules type	1
	Euthedemus tetradarachms	5
	Menander	1
	Apollodotus	2
	Hermaeus	1

1834	Sasanian	18
1835		26
1835		125
1836		17
1837		60
1837		48
1837	Arsacid or early fireworshippers	1
1834	Horseman & bull Spalapatideva series	24
1835		120
1837		34
1837		8
1834	Kufic & Muhammadan, Khwarazm, Ghurid, Ghazni, Tartar &c. &c.	13
1835		98
1836		1
1837		288
1837		21
1836	Square coins, emblems sun moon & chaitya	1
1837		37
1837		6
1836	Kodes	1
1836	Kanauj Pala series	1
1836	Athenian	1
1837	Saurashtian	8
1837	Kanauj Pala series	1
1834	Dubious, or at the time unassignable	1
1835		10
1837		7
1834	Indo-Scythic [Wima] Kadphises	1
	Here again the deficiency of 1836 occurs, and for 1838 without the ability to classify, I can only adduce a partial total	
1838	Of various kinds, Bactrian &c.	801

From Kabul

1835	Intaglios	3
1837		33
1837		8
1838		2
1838		1
1838	Peshawar	1
1838	Gold ring with cameo (superb)	1
1835	Figures	2
1837	Silver ornament	1
1837	Brass idol	1
1837	Stone idols	3
1837	Brass chair or throne	1
1837	Circular brass ornament & figure	1

1837	Square brass ornament	1
1838	Brass antiques	3
1838	Jade ornaments	2

Copper coins

1834	Kabul	410
1834	Jalalabad	248
1835	Kabul	c. 5000
1835	Peshawar	c. 400
1837	Kabul	c. 4000
1838	Kabul – number unknown	–

With regard to these copper coins, [for] 1836 & 1838 the collections are unknown, but as they continually increased, it may be reckoned that the bazaar of Kabul supplied altogether from 20,000 to 25,000 copper coins.

From Begram
Gold coins

1836		–
1837	Kanouj Pala series	6
1838	Indo-Scythic	1
1838	Indo-Scythic	1

Silver coins

1837	Bactrians, Menander, Apollodotus, Hermias, Antialcidas &c.	18
1837	Various in kind – square punched, Cufic &co, but the greater proportion minute coins [3 of 3069 overwritten]	3,069
1837	Bactrian a few and [various, as above]	560
1838	Bactrian a few and [various, as above]	2,338
1838		142

The collection from Begram was continued to a later period in 1838 than the totals above extend to. Consequently they are imperfect. The collection for 1836 also was not counted, but it comprised a Demetrius.

1834	Intaglios	8
1838	Intaglios – number unknown, say	6
1838	Silver rings	3
1838	Intaglios	30

Copper coins

1833		1,878
1834		1,930
1835		2,500
1836	[estimated]	3,474
1837	[estimated?]	30,345
1837		3,930
1838	[estimated]	16,759
1838	[estimated]	1,800

The amounts here are incomplete.

Copper & Brass Rings, Seals &co.

1834	Many, but numbers unknown	
1835		
1836		
1837		256
1837	Many, but numbers unknown	
1838		816
1838		148

Brass Figures, Ornaments &co.

| 1837 | These are figures of birds, animals &co. co. with fibula &co. | 370 |

Cylinders

| 1837 | [Rectangular bronze cylinder seals] | 8 |

These, perhaps miscalled cylinders, were parallelogram brass or copper square tubes – each side having a figure or device cut into it. Many were found every year, but [only] in this instance in 1837 is the number preserved.

The imperfect data of the Begram collections give as totals:

Gold coins	8
Silver coins	6,127
Copper coins	62,616
Copper & brass rings &co.	1,220
Copper figures, ornaments &co.	370
Copper cylinders	8
Intaglios &co.	17
Silver rings	30

The prime cost of the above, which was only given in or charged to Government was about Rs 2000 or as nearly may be £200.

Appendix 4: List of Standardised Spelling and Transcribed Names

Adelphoros; Adelphortus	Spalagadama
Ambēr (Greek)	Anbēr (Pahlavi)
Antialcides; Antialkides	Antialcidas
Archelius	Archebius
Ardokro	Ardochsho
Ases; Asos; Asus; Azos; Azus	Azes
Azilisus	Azilises
Balochistan	Baluchistaj
Bámíân; Bamian	Bamiyan
Banir	Buner
Bararao	Vasudeva
Baryzaga	Barygaza
Béghrám; Beghrám	Begram
billion	billon
Bokhara	Bukhara
Boorj	Burj
Brahminical	Brahmanical
Canyacubja	Kanyakubja (Kanauj)
Chinab	Chenab
Cufic	Kufic
Daroonter; Duroonter; Duroonto; Deronta; Darounta; Durúnter	Darunta
dusht	*dasht*
Ermaios; Hermios	Hermaeus
Farwān	Parwan
Genghiz	Genghis Khan
Ghiznah; Ghizni; Ghuzni	Ghazni
Ghuznavi	Ghaznavid
Ghor	Ghurid
Gundai	Ghundai
Gondopherres	Gondophares
Gujarāt, Guzerat	Gujarat
Gyaur Kala (old Merv)	Ghiaur Kala
Hidda; Hiddah	Hadda
Ipalirisus; Spalyrises	Spalirises
Jabbar Khan; Jabber Khan	Jabar Khan
Jelalabad; Jelálábád; Jellalabad	Jalalabad
Jalum; Jhélam; Jhellum	Jhelum
Juzjān (Arabic)	Gozgān
Kabal; Kâbal; Kâbul	Kabul
Kadaphes	Kadphises
Kalat; Kelat	Qalat
Kanerkes; Kanerkos	Kanishka
Kannauj; Kanoj	Kanauj
Karahichi; Qaracheh; Qaracha	Karacheh; Karratcha
Kerman	Kirman
Kenorano; Korano	Kushan
Khedree; Khedri	Khedari
Khele; Kheyl	Khel
Khwojeh; Khwajeh	Khwaja
Killah Bulend; Qal'a Bulend	Killa Bolend
Koh Butcher	Koh-i Bacha

Khonar	Kunar
Khosru Malek	Khusrau Malik
Khwarism	Khwarazm
Kosolo; Kosolu	Kujula
Lysius; Ausius	Lysias
Mahigir	Mahighir
Mahomed; Mohammed	Muhammad
Mahmood	Mahmud
Masaud	Mas'ud
Modud	Mawdud
Nagree	[Deva]nagari
Neyshabur	Nishapur
Nowab; Nuwab	Nawab
Nyscea; Nysæan; Nysean	Nysa; Nysian
Okro	Oesho
Ookmo	Wima
Ooerki	Huvishka
Paropamisus	Paropamisadae
Pehlevi; Pehlivi; Pehlvi	Pahlavi
Perwan; Parwān; Farwān	Parwan
Peshawer; Peshawur	Peshawar
Phrahates; Phraortes	Phraates
Sabaktagin	Sebuktegin
Samagu deva	Samantadeva
Sanscrit	Sanskrit
Sassan	Sasan
Sassanian	Sasanian
Sinde	Sind
Syalapati deva	Spalapatideva
Taimur	Timur
tamga	tamgha
Tapa; Tappa; Tuppeh; Tupper	Tepe
Theodotus	Diodotus
Tope Durrah; Top Darrah	Topdara
Turkistan	Turkestan
Unad-Pherros; Undopheres; Pherros	Gondophares
Vanka deva	Vakkadeva
Vicramaditya	Vikramaditya
Visma-mitra	Vishvamitra
Wullee Mahomed	Walli Muhammad
Yezd	Yazd

Appendix 5: British Museum, India Museum and South Kensington Museum Inventories

In addition to the current British Museum registration numbers, the objects from the Masson collection in the Department of Asia can have up to three more historical inventory numbers relating to their initial accession into the East India Company's India Museum (IM) and subsequent transfer via the South Kensington Museum (SKM) to the British Museum (BM IM) in 1880–2.

Key:

IM: India Museum no. These numbers are written in ink on the pink underside of small shallow trays inherited from the India Museum and containing the objects (**Vol. I, Fig. 8**). They are linked to small rectangular loose tickets bearing a pencilled India Museum number, e.g. 'No. 67', many of which are no longer with their correct IM trays.

SKM: **South Kensington Museum no.** These numbers were allocated to the IM trays of objects on their transfer to South Kensington *c.* 1880. They appear as large printed numbers stuck to the IM trays or, in some cases, to the actual objects (**Vol. I, Fig. 8**). They are also listed in the *India Museum. Inventory of the Collection ... transferred to the South Kensington Museum* (SKM/IM 1880, pp. 25–9, 157, 179).

BM IM: British Museum India Museum no. Numbers with the prefix 'IM' and the addition 'Gems', 'Rings' or 'Metal', were allocated when the India Museum objects entered the British Museum *c.* 1880. Some were transferred directly from the India Office; others went first to the South Kensington Museum and received a SKM number before being sent on to British Museum.

Box no.: The relic deposits – still mostly in their India Museum trays – were stored in 7 boxes until registration for the Masson Project. These have been arbitrarily numbered 1–7. Modern plastic boxes arbitrarily numbered 8–11 contained fragments that were clearly from Begram (e.g. **Fig. 6**), but had never been allocated an IM.Metal number.

Trays 'A' and 'B' are larger unnumbered trays found in Box 2 (a) and Box 4 (b). These were white with a blue trim and contained smaller India Museum trays together with a mix of loose items, including some stray pieces unlikely to be from the relic deposits but most probably from Begram or Kabul.

India Museum / South Kensington inventory numbers			
IM	SKM	BM reg.	Description
14	1104	1880.3976.a-b	Splayed hand finial; bird button
-	1067	1880.3997	Lid
21	1100	1880.3902.a-f	6 'rings and portions of rings. Metal'
26	1074	1880.3932.a-b 1880.3936	3 finger-rings; 1 with pseudo-Arabic inscription
33	1103	1880.3977.a-e	'Fragments of metal ornaments'; rings
42	1122	1880.3936	Ring bezel
57	1096	1880.3979	Pendant with 2 barrel attachment beads

BM IM.Gems: India Museum gems		
No.	BM reg.	Description
10	1880.3489	Lion with tree on mound
11	1880.3544	Carnelian standing Heracles
12	1880.3500	Carnelian winged horse with arrows
13	1880.3488	Carnelian goddess facing a lion
14	1880.3501	Rock crystal busts of man and woman
15	1880.3545	Carnelian male bust
16	1880.3546	Garnet male bust, Bactrian inscription
17	1880.3547	Amethyst or quartz galloping horse
18	1880.3548	Chalcedony female bust
19	1880.3558	Carnelian Hun male bust
20	1880.3549	Carnelian Hun male bust
21	1880.3595	Carnelian Hun male bust
22	1880.3559	Almandine garnet standing Tyche
24	1880.3561	Nicolo winged horse
25	1880.3550	Nicolo female bust
26	1880.3727	Chrysoprase helmeted bust
27	1880.3562	Garnet cameo head
28	1880.3551	Garnet walking lion
29	1880.3563	Sard Tyche and Nike / Persian inscription
30	1880.3564	Lapis lazuli male bust
32	1880.3552	Sard winged Eros
33	1880.3553	Almandine garnet broken helmeted female
34	1880.3554	Pyrone-almandine garnet winged female
35	1880.3555	Amethyst horse
36	1880.3565	Yellow glass standing female figure
38	1880.3567	Nicolo male bust facing female, inscribed
39	1880.3568	Carnelian ram and standing man
41	1880.3576	Garnet griffin and man
42	1880.3577	Garnet winged Nike, inscribed
43	1880.3578	Garnet standing figure
44	1880.3579	Carnelian horse
45	1880.3580	Carnelian kneeling bull
46	1880.3581	Chalcedony humped bull
47	1880.3582	Garnet broken helmeted Athena
48	1880.3583	Carnelian eagle
49	1880.3584	Chalcedony bearded male bust
50	1880.3585	Carnelian seated stag
51	1880.3586	Carnelian humped bull
56	1880.3599	Garnet ibex
57	1880.3600	Nicolo humped bull
58	1880.3601	Nicolo standing lion
59	1880.3602	Nicolo seated woman and child
60	1880.3603	Heliotrope winged donkey
61	1880.3604	Chalcedony seated bull
62	1880.3605	Chalcedony winged griffin
63	1880.3606	Chalcedony bird
64	1880.3607	Clay amulet plaque
65	1880.3608	Nicolo female facing bust, inscribed
66	1880.3609	Nicolo male bust
67	1880.3610	Carnelian Devanagari inscription
69	1880.3611	Chinese jade plaque
70	1880.3612	Alabaster yoni with Persian inscription
71	1880.3613	Fossilised limestone pendant
72	1880.3614	Carnelian standing female, inscribed
73	1880.3989	Sard male figure with fish, inscribed. Now lost
74	1880.3988	Pyrope-almandine garnet seated lion
75	1880.3615	Carnelian seated ibex

BM IM.IsGems: India Museum Islamic gems		
No.	BM reg.	Description / Inscription
1	1880.3635	Jasper. St George and the dragon
2	1880.3636	Jasper. There is no avoiding my end …
3	1880.3637	Glass. Neither a firm decision nor caution …
4	1880.3638	Lapis lazuli. His servant 'Alī …
5	1880.3639	Rock crystal. Arabic and Pahlavi inscriptions
6	1880.3640	Carnelian. His servant Ḥusayn b. 'Alī
6a	1880.3641	Garnet. Sahl b. Sākān
7	1880.3642	Carnelan. He has placed his trust in God
8	1880.3643	Carnelian. Persian name Rūstā'ī / Rawshanā'ī
9	1880.3644	Carnelian. Muḥammad b. 'Alī is the friend of God
10	1880.3645	Carnelian. As God wills …
11	1880.3646	Carnelian cameo, undecipherable inscription
12	1880.3647	Chalcedony. Glory belongs to God
13	1880.3648	Jasper. Undeciphered
14	1880.3649	Carnelian. Fā'id
15	1880.3650	Carnelian. In God Muḥammad b. 'Abdallāh trusts
16	1880.3651	Haematite. In God Muḥammad trusts …
17	1880.3652	Haematite. 'Alī b. Muḥammad
18	1880.3653	Haematite. In God 'Abdallāh trusts
19	1880.3654	Sardonyx. Say 'He is God, the one and only' …
20	1880.3655	Rock crystal. O God! Bless Muḥammad and 'Alī
21	1880.3656	Chalcedony. My success can only come …
22	1880.3657	Rock crystal. Worn indistinct Arabic inscription
23	1880.3658	Sard. Undeciphered Arabic inscriptions
24	1880.3659	Sardonyx. 'Aḥmad ibn Sarawayh (?)
25	1880.3660	Carnelian/white enamel inlay. Undecipherable
26	1880.3661	Sard Hebrew inscription
27	1880.3662	Carnelian. Undecipherable Arabic inscription
28	1880.3663	Carnelian. 'Alī b. al-Ḥasan …
29	1880.3664	Carnelian. For each period a book is revealed
30	1880.3665	Jasper. Muḥammad b. Aḥmad
31	1880.3666	Carnelian. Ḥamdān b. 'Abdallāh

BM IM.Rings: India Museum rings		
No.	BM reg.	Description/inscription
1	1880.3872	'Silver ring with hexagonal bezel and floral design – Persian style; without inscription'
2	1880.3873	'Silver ring with square bezel with projections on. corners and sides – Persian style'
3	1880.3874	Mottled carnelian ring with a pointed oval bezel
5	1880.3879	Bronze ring with flower-shaped bezel
6	1880.3876	Silver ring. Plain flat bezel continuous with hoop

BM IM.Metal: India Museum miscellaneous metal objects		
No.	BM reg. no.	Description
1	1880.3634	'Bronze signet seal. Inscription (reversed) of Lutfullah 1080. … in the shape of a Persian coin of the 17th century'
3	1889.3671	Silver enamelled pendant: 2 figures with dragon
4	1880.3680	Gold bracteate with diademed goose
5	1880.3485 / SKM 402	Astragalus (Wilson 1841, Antiquities pl. III.10)
6	1880.3672	Bird plaque
7	1880.3673	Bird finial of a pin: (Wilson 1841, Antiquities pl. IV.16)
8	1880.3674	Square seal with lug: Ascetic seated in hut (Wilson 1841, Antiquities pl. IV.8)
9	1880.3619	Oval seal: female dancer with Kharoshthi inscription
10	1880.3620	Square seal with lug: lion to right (Wilson 1841, Antiquities pl. IV.9)
11	1880.3675 / SKM 1098	Bird pin with the head missing (Wilson 1841, Antiquities pl. IV.15; misidentified as an axe)
12	1880.3676	Bodkin
13	1880.3677	3 amulets: human figures with an attachment loop
14	1880.3684	2 silver alloy circular pendants: crowned figure to right
15	1880.3678	3 moulds in the form of a fish
20	1880.3681, 1880.3713	13 bird finials for pins and phial stoppers (1880.3681.e; see **Vol. I, Fig. 278**, Hadda 10)
21	1880.3682	3 charms: hand, boot, jug and vase-shaped pendant fragment
22	1880.3683	6 arrowheads
23	1889.3685	'Small silver objects from Begram (8)' (1880.3685.a-c: rings from Hadda 10?)
24	1880.3686	'Bronze appliqué ornaments and pendants apparently belonging to a suit of Muhammadan armour about the period of the Muhammadan conquest of Kabul (870 AD). Kufic inscription on two pieces … From Begram'.
25	1880.3687 / IM 68 / SKM 1069; 1880.3810 / IM 32 / SKM 1105	'Bronze ornaments, bosses of shield, a hinged cover pierced with holes and surmounted by a bird resembling in shape a helmet [1880.3687.b] &c'. A label with IM.Metal.25 states: 'apparently from Begram. Bronze fragments of appliqué ornament with holes for fixing to shields &c. Three are pendant shaped with holes for suspension [1880.3687.d-e, n]. One (SKM 1105 [1880.3687.a]) is the boss of a shield'. SKM 1069 is pasted on 1880.3687.b. SKM register no.1069 / IM.68: 'Rings, seals and fragments of metal ornaments'
127	1880.3697 / SKM 1087	'A bronze bangle or wristlet, thickened at the ends which nearly meet. From an unspecified tope or from Begram'. SKM 1087 label is pasted onto bird 1880.3713.p; see IM.M 156
130	1880.4073	Box seal with Kushan figures: Wesho, standing couple, man at fire altar, Heracles
131	1880.3622	Box seal with lion, stag, bird, winged Nike
132	1880.3621	Box seal with lion, ibex, 2 birds, winged Nike
133	1880.3623	Box seal with 3 birds, standing figure with diadem, bull's head 9?), bust in profile
134	1880.3624	Box seal with winged figure, lion, hare (?), horse
135	1880.3625	Box seal with standing figure, peacock, lion, nesting bird
136	1880.3626	Box seal with lion, vase, elephant rider, seated man under arch
137	1880.3627	Box seal with stag, animal (?), lion, winged griffin
138	1880.3670	Box seal with lion, standing figure, nesting bird, ibex (?)
141	1880.3702; 1880.3788 – 1880.3790; 1880.3799, 1880.3811 – 1880.3816	IM.Metal.141: 'Box containing a large number of bronze rings or broken bezels of rings with traces of legends or figures on most of them. From Begram'.
142	1880.3703.a-h	'Bronze heads of pins (8) … with designs, patterns, figures of animals &c. on the sides. From Begram'
143	1880.3705	'Bronze pendants or ornaments in the form of a cross with four horizontal arms. Some are pierced for suspension at the end of the upright; some have round knobs at the ends of the 6 arms (16 altogether)'
144	1880.3704	'Bronze pendants (16) in the shape of birds with wings expanded, a loop below for suspension. From Begram about 1835'
145	1880.3706, 1880.3817	'A collection of fragments of bronze rings & bezels of rings without designs or inscriptions. From Begram 1835'
146	1880.3629	Oval copper alloy seal with 2 lugs; elephant rider to right
147	1880.3630	Circular copper alloy seal with lug; male bust to left

148	1880.3631	Circular copper alloy seal with lug; bearded male bust to left
149	1880.3632	Oval copper alloy seal with 2 lugs; running figure with club to right
150	1880.3633	Rectangular copper alloy signet-ring bezel; seated figure to left
151	1880.3744, 1880.3752 – 1880.3758; 1880.3760, 1880.3762 – 1880.3766, 1880.3769, 1880.3773, 1880.3775 – 1880.3776; 1880.3778 – 1880.3779; 1880.3783 – 1880.3784; 1880.3807, 1880.3809, 1880.4136	'A collection of 22 bronze seals with various figures, leaves, flowers & miscellaneous. From Begram'
152	1880.3707 – 1880.3708; 1880.3743, 1880.3745 – 1880.3751; 1880.3759, 1880.3761, 1880.3767, 1880.3770 – 1880.3772; 1880.3774, 1880.3777, 1880.3780 – 1880.3782; 1880.3800, 1880.3805 – 1880.3806; 1880.3808	'A collection of 21 bronze seals with figures of animals and birds. From Begram'
153	1880.3709	'3 charms or amulets in the shape of a square based stupa in several tiers surmounted by a crescent. From Begram'
154	1880.3710	'6 bronze stamps for impressing designs'.
155	1880.3711	'Bronze ornamental pin-heads of which 14 are shaped like birds and one is a human figure. From Begram'
156	1880.3712, 1880.3713 / SKM 1087; 1880.3810	'35 bronze pin-heads mostly shaped like birds of various kinds. From Begram'
157	1880.3714	'12 small bronze pendants of a peculiar shape; one has a ring for suspension. From Begram'
158	1880.3715	'3 bronze bowls of spoons'
159	1880.3716, 1880.3870, 1880.3972, 1880.3880	'Miscellaneous bronze objects from Begram not otherwise classified … Pieces of wire &c.'
160	1880.3717 – 1880.3718; 1880.3818 – 1880.3831; 1880.3833 – 1880.3850; 1880.3852 – 1880.3854; 1880.3856 – 1880.3866; 1880.3868	'Miscellaneous bronze objects from Begram. Pieces of bronze used as appliqué ornament &c. Masson Coll. From India Museum'
161	1880.3719	[65] 'Small fragments of bronze [and 2 of lead] from Begram. No definite shape'
162	1880.3628	Circular copper alloy seal with rectangular lug, seated Buddha
163	1880.3720	Oval plaque with 2 wings; bust of Sasanian king
Box 2.a (tray A)	1880.4100	Copper alloy pyramidal seal
Box 4.b (tray B)	1880.3981	Uncleaned fragments in unnumbered tray in box with relic material
Box 8	1880.3895, 1880.3905, 1880.3909 – 1880.3910, 1880.3915, 1880.3928, 1880.3930, 1880.3941, 1880.3944, 1880.3949, 1880.3961	Unnumbered box of miscellaneous Masson collection ornaments and fragments
Box 9	1880.3867, 1880.3871, 1880.3881, 1880.3890, 1880.3902, 1880.3904, 1880.3906 – 1880.3907; 1880.3925, 1880.3937 – 1880.3940; 1880.3943, 1880.3945, 1880.3947, 1880.3951 – 1880.3952, 1880.3954 – 1880.3955; 1880.3959, 1880.3965, 1880.3968	Unnumbered box of miscellaneous Masson collection ornaments and fragments
Box 11 J.14	1880.3990	Unidentified box of undocumented miscellaneous ornament fragments together with a small tag marked 'J.14'; now designated Box 11. Probably Masson collection, but lacks proof to assign it definitely as such

References

Abbreviations

BM: British Museum

BMC: British Museum Catalogue
    Greek (Attica, Megaris, Aegina): Head 1888
    Greek (Parthia): Wroth 1903
    India (Ancient): Allan 1936
    India (Greek and Scythic): Gardner 1886
    Oriental (Arab-Sassanian): Walker 1941

BMJC: F.H. Marshall (1911) *Catalogue of the Jewellery, Greek, Roman and Etruscan in the Department of Greek and Roman Antiquities*, British Museum, London

CAAU: *Culture and Art of Ancient Uzbekistan* 1991, Exhibition Catalogue, 2 vols, Moscow

CMAA Cambridge Museum of Archaeology and Anthropology (Ridgeway Collection 1827.1192)

CRAI: *Comptes Rendus de l'Academie des Inscription et Belles-Lettres*

EI²: *Encyclopaedia of Islam* (2nd edition)

IM: India Museum of the East India Company in London (closed in 1878)

IOC: India Office Collection of coins transferred to the British Museum 1882

IOLC: British Library India Office Loan Collection of coins and finds transferred to the British Museum 1995 and 2007

JASB: *Journal of the Asiatic Society of Bengal*

JRAS: *Journal of the Royal Asiatic Society*

MDAFA: Mémoires de la Délégation archéologique française en Afghanistan

MSS Eur.: European Manuscripts, British Library India Office Collections

NAI: National Archives of India, Political Consultations nos 45–7, 23 January 1835, § 13.

Proc. ASB: Proceedings of the Asiatic Society of Bengal

SKM: South Kensington Museum (later renamed the Victoria and Albert Museum)

Vol. I: E. Errington *et al.* (2017) *Charles Masson and the Buddhist Sites of Afghanistan: Explorations, Excavations, Collections 1832–1835*, British Museum Research Publication 215 (https://doi.org/10.48582/charlesmasson_vol1)

Vol. II: E. Errington *et al.* (2017) *The Charles Masson Archive. British Library, British Museum and Other Documents relating to the Masson Collection*, British Museum Research Publication 216 (https://doi.org/10.48582/charlesmasson_vol2)

See also www.britishmuseum.org Collection Online: Charles Masson

Archival sources

British Library

MSS Eur. European Manuscripts, India Office Collections:

E161/VI: MSS Eur. E161/VI (Kaye & Johnston 636) Masson Manuscripts, Correspondence VI, to Masson (copies).

E161/VII: MSS Eur. E161/VII (Kaye & Johnston 637) Masson Manuscripts, Correspondence VII, from Masson (copies), ff. 3–6, 11, 13–15, 20–2, 25–7, 29–33, 36, 38–40.

E169/I: MSS Eur. E169/I (Kaye & Johnston 656 [1–18]) Masson Manuscripts, Miscellaneous, part I.

E169/II: MSS Eur. E169/II (Kaye & Johnston 656 [19]) Masson Manuscripts, Miscellaneous, part II.

F526/1–2 Masson Papers, India Office Collections:
Two separate bundles boxed together in 1961: one 'found in a box

with other miscellaneous papers in 1958'; the other 'discovered in the Newspaper Room in 1958 by Mrs M.C. Poulter (archivist)'.

F526/1: 'Coins &co. purchased since 15 October 1837 and in my hands' (copy of E161/VII f. 32, with additional comments [added in brackets] to **E161/VII ff. 31–2: Vol. II, p. 66**).

F526/1a: 'Analysis of the Begram coins with reference to plates', 30ff.

F526/1c: 'Particulars of coins &c. procured from Begram from 8 November 1837 to 30 June 1838', 1f.

F526/1d: 'Particulars of coins &c. procured from the bazaar of Kabul from 8 November 1837 to 30 June 1838', 1f.

F526/1e: 'Coins &co. forwarded from Kabul by C. Masson [Begram 1833–8]', 1f.

F526/1f: 'List of coins A', 2ff.

F526/1g: 'List of coins B', 2ff.

F526/1h: **'Descriptive catalogue of select coins in the cabinet of Mr Masson', 12ff.

F526/1i: 'List of coins [in Masson's] 1st Cabinet', 2ff.

F526/1j: 'List of coins collected from Begram in the Kohistan of Kabul, conjectured to be the site of Alexandria ad Caucasum', 3ff.

F526/1k: Untitled lists of silver, copper and gold coins collected from Begram, Kabul bazaar and elsewhere 1833–8, 4ff.

F526/1m: EIC receipt of Masson's collections 19 October 1836 to December 1838.

F526/1n: Masson's summary list of collections 1833–8.

G41: MSS Eur. G41 Drawings of the caves of Jalalabad and Kabul, with descriptions (c. 1850 from original sketches made in 1833–5).

G43: MSS Eur. G43 Drawings of the cave temples on the island of Salsette and Elephanta, Mumbai (c. 1850 from original sketches made in 1841).

E/4 Bombay Dispatches: East India Company, General Correspondence with India

E/4/1057 [prev. LXII]: *Bombay Dispatches*, 6 Nov. 1833 – 25 June 1834, pp. 790-1: Masson, Mr. American: Memoranda on countries of Central Asia obtained from, to be transmitted to Supreme Government.

E/4/1062 [prev. LXVII]: *Bombay Dispatches*, 5 January 1838 – 31 May 1838, pp. 789–839: Proceedings relating to Mr Masson's researches into coins and antiquities of Afghanistan.

E/4/1065 [prev. LXX]: *Bombay Dispatches*, 4 September 1839 – 25 March 1840, pp. 1279, pp. 1346–7: Reference, Mr Masson. Afghanistan: coins and antiquities collected by Mr Masson; collection of coins and antiquities sent to England and proceedings and remarks respecting.

E/4/1066 [prev. LXXI]: *Bombay Dispatches*, 1 April 1840 – 2 September 1840, p. 834: Reference, Mr Masson.

E/4/1068 [prev. LXXIII]: *Bombay Dispatches*, 7 April 1841 – 1 September 1841, pp. 587–8, 602: Reference, Mr Masson. Receipt of collection of Mr Masson (antiquarian), acknowledged.

E/4/1069 [prev. LXIV]: *Bombay Dispatches*, 8 September 1841 – 2 March 1842, pp. 408–9, 598–9: Afghanistan, research into antiquities of. Application from Mr Masson (antiquarian), for transmission of copper coins to agent in London.

E/4/1070 [prev. LXV]: *Bombay Dispatches*, 9 March 1842 – 6 July 1842, p. 597–8: Donation to Mr Masson, and arrangements respecting passage money.

P/ Bombay Political Proceedings

P/387/71: *Bombay Political Proceedings*, 11 March – 1 April 1835: Bombay Political Consultations 12, no. 780, 1 April 1835.

- *Extract Masson's letters to Pottinger, No. 5* [copy: E161/VII f. 8]: Memorandum accompanying letter of 9 October 1834, of relics &co., held by Charles Masson for the Bombay Government.
- *Extract Masson's letters to Pottinger, No. 6* [copy: E161/VII ff. 16–22]: Memorandum accompanying letter of 11 December 1834, of relics, coins &co. despatched from Kabul.

P/387/–: *Bombay Political Proceedings*, 1836: Bombay Political Consultations, 29 June 1836.

P/388/58: *Bombay Political Proceedings*, 28 March – 18 April 1838, Bombay Political Consultations, no. 1440, 4 April 1838: 'Particulars ... of coins &co. forwarded to Pottinger, 15 October 1837' [copy: E161/VII ff. 31, 33].

P/389/18: *Bombay Political Proceedings*, 23 October – 13 November 1839: Bombay Political Consultations, 13 November 1839.

East India Company *Court Minutes*: Decisions by Court of Directors.

IOR/B/233 *Court Minutes*, 15 October 1856 – 8 April 1857: East India Company Court of Directors Resolution 11 February 1857.

British Museum

Department of Coins and Medals

Acquisitions Medal Room 10 February 1838: 116 Bactrian and Indo-Scythic coins presented by the Hon. East India Company.

Acquisitions Coins 13 August 1857: 118 coins purchased from Major Cunningham.

Acquisitions Coins 1882: India Office Collection presented by the Rt Hon. the Secretary of State for India in Council.

Coin Catalogues 1845 (Arc p15) May 1845: presented by the Court of Directors of East India House; 59 coins.

Register of Coins and Medals, September 1835: purchased from M. Honigberger, 24 coins. Reg. 1835,0901.1–24.

Register of Coins and Medals 10 February 1838: presented by East India Company, 116 coins. Reg. 1838,EIC.1–116.

Register of Coins and Medals 18 July 1843: purchased from East India Silk Company 9 coins. Reg. 1843,0718.1–9.

Register of Coins and Medals, vol. III, 14 June 1845, pp. 14–15: 59 'Sasanian coins presented by the Hon. East India Company'. Reg. 1845,EIC.1–59.

Register of Coins and Medals [1882]: India Office Collection presented by India Office, 2420 coins. Reg. IOC.1–2420.

Central Archives
BM-TM: British Museum Trustees Minutes
BM-OP: British Museum Original Papers

Masson
BM-OP 20–6–1847, Ellis to Hawkins introducing Masson.
BM-TM–10–7–1847, Standing Committee, 10 July 1847, no. 7288. Ludlow to Ker suggesting employment of Masson.

India Museum transfer – Masson Collection:
CE 3/40 **BM-TM 23–7–1881**, Standing Committee, 23 July 1881, vol. XL, nos 15713–14.

CE 3/40 **BM-TM 25–3–1882**, Standing Committee, 25 March 1882, vol. XL, no. 15936.

CE 3/40 **BM-TM 14–10–1882**, Standing Committee, 14 October 1882, nos 16128–9

CE 3/43 **BM-TM 11–7–1885**, Standing Committee, 11 July 1885, vol. XLIII, no. 17084.

CE 3/49 **BM-TM 10-2-1900**, Standing Committee, 10 February 1900, vol. XLIX, nos 1103–4.

CE 3/49 **BM-TM 10-3-1900**, Standing Committee, 10 March 1900, vol. XLIX, no. 1127.

CE 4/179 **BM-OP 18-7-1881**, no. 3117, 18 July 1881.

CE 4/180 **BM-OP 11-10-1882**, no. 4595: Report by Franks, 11 October 1882.

CE 4/199 **BM-OP 30-1-1900**, no. 286, 30 January 1900.

Fitzwilliam Museum Library, Cambridge

FW 1906 Letters from F.W. Thomas, Librarian, India Office, regarding proposed transfer of coins from the India Office Collection to the Fitzwilliam Museum.

FW 27-7-1906 Thomas to W.G. Searle, Keeper of Coins and Medals, Fitzwilliam Museum.

FW 11-8-1906 Thomas to M.R. James, Director, Fitzwilliam Museum.

FW 19-11-1906 Thomas to James.

FW 15-11-1912 Thomas to S.C. Cockerall, Director, Fitzwilliam Museum

References

Abdullaev, K.A., Rtveladze, E.V. and Sishkina, G.V. (1991) *Culture and Art of Ancient Uzbekistan*. Exhibition Catalogue, 2 vols, Moscow.

Album, S. (1992) 'An Arab-Sasanian dirham hoard from the year 72 Hijri', *Studia Iranica* 21, pp. 161–95, pls XXI–XXXII.

Album, S. (2011) *Rare Coins Auction* 27, lot 214, pp. 40–1.

Allan, J. (1936) *A Catalogue of the Indian Coins in the British Museum. British Museum. Catalogue of the Coins of Ancient India*, London.

Allan, J.W. (1982) *Nishapur: Metalwork of the Early Islamic Period*, Metropolitan Museum of Art, New York.

Allan, J.W. (1986) *Metalwork of the Islamic World. The Aron Collection*, London.

Alram, M. (1986) *Iranisches Personennamenbuch: Nomina Propria Iranica in Nummis*, Vienna.

Alram, M. (1999/2000) 'A hoard of copper drachms from the Kāpiśa–Kabul region', *Silk Road Art and Archaeology* 6, pp. 129–50.

Alram, M. (2008) 'Ein Schatzfund Hephthalitischer Drachmen aus Baktrien', *Numismatische Zeitschrift* 116/117, *Festscrift für Günther Dembski zum 65. Geburtstag*, pp. 253–68.

Alram, M. (2016) *Das Antlitz des Fremden. Die Münzprägung der Hunnen und Westtürken in Zentralasien und Indien*, Vienna.

Alram, M. and Gyselen, R. (2012) *Sylloge Nummorum Sasanidorum Paris–Berlin–Wien*. II. *Ohrmazd I – Ohrmazd II*, Vienna.

Alram, M. and Pfisterer, M. (2010) 'Alkhan and Hephthalite coinage', in M. Alram, D. Klimburg-Salter, M. Inaba and M. Pfisterer (eds), *Coins, Art and Chronology II. The First Millennium C.E. in the Indo-Iranian Borderlands*, Vienna, pp. 13–38.

Alram, M., Klimburg-Salter, D., Inaba, M. and Pfisterer M. eds (2010) *Coins, Art and Chronology II. The First Millennium C.E. in the Indo-Iranian Borderlands*, Vienna.

Aman ur Rahman and Falk, H. (2011) *Seals, Sealings and Tokens from Gandhara*, Wiesbaden.

Amiet, P. (1963) 'Les bronzes du Luristan de la collection Coiffard', *La Revue du Louvre et des Musées de France*, XIIIème année, pp. 11–90.

Amiet, P. (1976) *Les Antiquités du Luristan. Collection David-Weill*, Paris.

Amiet, P. (1977) 'Bactriane proto-historique', *Syria* LIV, pp. 89–121.

Amiet, P. (1988a) 'Elam and Bactria', in G. Ligabue and S. Salvatori (eds) *Bactria. An Ancient Oasis from the Sands of Afghanistan*, Venice, pp. 127–40.

Amiet, P. (1988b) 'Antiquities of Bactria and outer Iran in the Louvre collection', in G. Ligabue and S. Salvatori (eds) *Bactria. An Ancient Oasis from the Sands of Afghanistan*, Studies and Documents, vol. III, Venice, pp. 159–80.

Anon. *Periplus of the Erythraean Sea* (see Casson 1989).

Archer, M. (1969) 'Charles Masson', *British Drawings in the India Office Library*, London, pp. 248–53.

Arrian, *History of Alexander and Indica*, tr. P.A. Blunt, 2 vols: I. *Anabasis of Alexander*, books I–IV; II. *Indica*, books V–VII, ed. J. Henderson, Loeb Classical Library, London–Cambridge, Mass. 1976–83 (I repr. 1989; II repr. 2000).

Ashton, L. ed. (1950) *The Art of India and Pakistan. A Commemorative Catalogue of the Exhibition held at the Royal Academy of Arts, London, 1947–8*, London.

Azarpay, G. (2014) 'The Afrasiab murals: a pictorial narrative reconsidered', *The Silk Road* 12, pp. 49–56.

Bagram District Parwan Province (2004) – Forum Valka.cz https://forum.valka.cz/attachments/5461/bagram_1_.pdf [viewed 31-10-2017].

Baldwin, C.R. (1970) 'Sasanian ducks in a western manuscript', *Gesta* 9.1, pp. 3–10.

Ball, W. and Gardin, J.-C. (1982) *Archaeological Gazetteer of Afghanistan*, Paris.

Barrett, D. (1954) *Sculptures from Amaravati in the British Museum*, London.

Bartus, D. (2012). 'Roman hairpins representing human hands. Typology and symbolism', *Firkak II. Fiatal Romai Koros Kutatok II. Konferenciakötete* (2007. Oct. 9–10, Visegrad; 2009, Nov. 20–22, Komaron), Györ, pp. 205–34.

Becatti, G. (1955) *Oreficerie antiche dalle Minoiche alle Barbariche*, Rome.

Belenitsky, A.M., Bentovich, I.B. and Bol'shakov, O.G. (1973) *Srednevekovyi gorod Srednei Asii* [The Medieval Cities of Central Asia], Leningrad.

Bernard, P. (1982) 'Alexandrie du Caucase ou Alexandrie de l'Oxus', *Journal des Savants*, pp. 217–42.

Bernard, P. (1985) *Les monnaies hors trésors – questions d'histoire Gréco-Bactrienne*, Paris.

Bernard, P. (2002) 'L'œuvre de la Délégation archéologique française en Afghanistan (1922–1982)', *CRAI* 146, pp. 1287–323.

Bernard, P. (2011) 'The Greek colony at Aï Khanum and Hellenism in Central Asia', in F. Hiebert and P. Cambon (eds), *Afghanistan. Crossroads of the Ancient World*, British Museum exhibition 3 March – 1 July 2011, London, pp. 81–129.

Bernard, P., Pinault, G.-J. and Rougemont, G. (2004) 'Deux nouvelles inscriptions grecques de l'Asie centrale', *Journal des Savants*, pp. 227–356.

Bhandare, S. (2018) 'Numismatics and "the Other" – investigating coinage and "Greekness" at Taxila', in H.P. Ray, *Buddhism and Gandhara*, London, pp. 70–103.

Bhatia, P. (1973) 'Bull/horseman coins of the Shahis, c. AD 650–1026', *Proceedings of the Indian History Congress* 34, vol. I, pp. 50–61.

Bhattacharyya, D.C. ed. (2002) *Gandhāra Sculpture in the Government Museum and Art Gallery, Chandigarh*. (In the light of the International Colloquium held in 1998), Chandigarh.

Biswas, S. (1981) *Terracottas of Bengal*, New Delhi.

Bivar, A.D.H. (1968) *Kushan and Kushano-Sasanian Seals and Kushano-Sasanian Coins: Sasanian Seals in the British Museum*, London.

Bivar A.D.H. (1969) *Catalogue of the Western Asiatic Seals in the British Museum. Stamp Seals II: The Sasanian Dynasty*, London.

Bivar, A.D.H. (1970) 'The sequence of Menander's drachmae', *JRAS*, pp. 123–36.

Bivar, A.D.H. (2000) *Excavations at Ghubayrā, Iran*, London.

Boardman, J. (1997) 'Greek seals', in D. Collon (ed.) *7000 Years of Seals*, London, pp. 74–87.

Boardman, J. (2001) *Greek Gems and Finger Rings*, London.

Bodur, F. (1987) *Türk Maden Sanati* [The Art of Turkish Metalworking], Istanbul.

Boisselier, J. (1978) 'Asie du Sud-est. Sri Lanka', *La Grammaire des formes et des styles. Asie*, Fribourg, pp. 99–130.

Bombay Dispatches (1834) Bombay Political Department, Political Consultations 1230/183, 16 April, no. 6, pp. 781–90.

Bopearachchi, O. (1991) *Monnaies gréco-bactriennes et indo-grecques. Catalogue raisonné*, Paris.

Bopearachchi, O. (1993) *Catalogue of Indo-Greek, Indo-Scythian and Indo-Parthian coins of the Smithsonian Institution*, Washington.

Bopearachchi, O. (1995) 'Découvertes récentes de trésors indo-grecs: nouvelles données historiques', *CRAI* 139, pp. 611–30.

Bopearachchi, O. (1997) 'The posthumous coinage of Hermaios and the conquest of Gandhara by the Kushans', in R. and B. Allchin, N. Kreitman and E. Errington (eds), *Gandharan Art in Context*, Cambridge, pp. 189–213.

Bopearachchi, O. (1999) 'Recent coin hoard evidence on pre-Kushana chronology', in M. Alram and D. Klimburg-Salter (eds), *Coins, Art, and Chronology. Essays on the Pre-Islamic History of the Indo-Iranian Borderlands*, Vienna, pp. 99–144.

Bopearachchi, O. (2001 [2003]) 'Les données numismatiques et la datation du bazaar de Begram', *Topoi* 11/1, pp. 411–35.

Bopearachchi, O. (2015) *From Bactria to Taprobane. Selected Works of Osmund Bopearachchi*, vol. 1: *Central Asian and Indian Numismatics*, New Delhi.

Bopearachchi, O. and Aman ur Rahman (1995) *Pre-Kushana Coins in Pakistan*, Karachi.

Bopearachchi, O., Landes, C. and Sachs, C (eds) (2003) *L'archéologie de l'Asie Centrale*, Lattes.

Bosworth, C.E. (1996) *The New Islamic Dynasties. A Chronological and Genealogical Manual*, Edinburgh (repr. 2004).

Bosworth, C.E. (2008) 'The appearance and establishment of Islam in Afghanistan, in É. de la Vaissière (ed.), *Islamisation de l'Asie central – Processus locaux d'acculturation du VIIe au XIe siècle. Cahiers de Studia Iranica* 39, pp. 97–114.

Bourchalat, R. and Lecomte, O. (1987) *Fouilles de Tureng tepe sous la direction de Jean Deshayes. 1. Les periodes Sassanides et Islamiques*, Mémoire 74, Paris.

Bracey, R. (2012) 'Policy, patronage and the shrinking pantheon of the Kushans', in V. Jayaswal (ed.), *Glory of the Kushans: Recent Discoveries and Interpretations*, New Delhi, pp. 197–217.

Brentjes, B. and Vasilievsky, R.S. (1989) *Schamanenkrone und Weltenbaum – Kunst der Nomaden Nordasiens*, Leipzig.

British Museum Collection Online: http://www.britishmuseum.org/research/collection_online/search.aspx.

Brunner, C.J. (1978) *Sasanian Stamp Seals in the Metropolitan Museum of Art*, New York.

Bulatova, V. (1972) *Drevnyaya Kuva* [Ancient Kuva], Tashkent.

Bumiller, M. (1993) *Flügelschalen und Flakons. Typologie frühislamischer Bronzen der Bumiller Collection*, Schriften des Museums für Frühislamische Kunst in Bamberg, vol. 3, Panicale.

Bumiller, M. (2001) *Tropfenförmige Anhänger. Typologie frühislamischer Bronzen der Bumiller Collection*, Schrifften des Museums für Frühislamische Kunst in Bamberg, vol. 6, Bamberg.

CAAU (1991) *Culture and Art of Ancient Uzbekistan*, exh. cat., Moscow.

Callieri, P. (1997) *Seals and Sealings from the North-West of the Indian Subcontinent and Afghanistan (4th century BC–11th century AD). Local, Indian, Sasanian, Graeco–Persian, Sogdian, Roman*, Naples.

Callieri, P. (1997a) 'Indian seals before Islam', in D. Collon (ed.), *7000 Years of Seals*, London, 1997, pp. 161–76.

Callieri, P. (2001 [2003]) La presenta via commerciale tra l'India e Roma attraverso l'Oxus e il Mar Caspio: nuovi dati di discussione', *Topoi. Orient–Occident* 11/1, pp. 537–46.

Callieri, P. (2010) 'Bīrkoṭ-ghwaṇḍai in the post-Kushan period', in M. Alram, D. Klimburg-Salter, M. Inaba and M. Pfisterer (eds), *Coins, Art and Chronology II. The First Millennium C.E. in the Indo-Iranian Borderlands*, Vienna, pp. 371–87.

Callieri, P. and Filigenzi, A. (2002) *Il maestro di Saidu Sharif. Alle origini dell'arte del Gandhara*, Rome.

Cambon, P. (1996) 'Fouilles anciennes en Afghanistan (1924–1925). Païtâvâ, Karratcha', *Arts Asiatiques* 51, pp. 13–28. http://www.persee.fr/doc/arasi_0004-3958_1996_num_51_1_1383.

Cambon, P. (2006) 'Begram, ancienne Alexandrie du Caucase ou capitale kouchane', in *Afghanistan: les trésors retrouvés. Collections du musée national de Kaboul*. Paris, pp. 81–111.

Cambon, P. et al. (2006) *Afghanistan: les trésors retrouvés. Collections du musée national de Kaboul*, Musée national des Arts asiatiques-Guimet exhibition 6 December 2006–30 April 2007, Éditions de la Réunion des musées nationaux, Paris.

Cambon, P., Giraudier, V. and Trouplin, V. (2018) *De l'Asie à la France libre: Joseph & Marie Hackin, archéologues et compagnons de la Libération*, Paris.

Canard, M. (EI²) 'Aṣfar b. Shīrawayhī, *Encyclopaedia of Islam* (2nd edition).

Cardi, B. de (1966) 'Excavations at Bampur, a third millennium settlement in Persian Baluchistan', *Anthropological Papers of the American Museum of Natural History* V, no. 51. 3, New York, pp. 233–355).

Carl, J. (1959) 'Le bazar de Begram', in J. Hackin, J. Carl and J. Meunié, *Diverses recherches archéologiques en Afghanistan (1933–1940)*, MDAFA VIII, Paris, pp. 82–102.

Casal, J.M. (1961) *Fouilles de Mundigak*, MDAFA XVII, Paris.

Casson, L. (1989) *The Periplus Maris Erythraei. Text, with Introduction, Translation and Commentary*, Princeton.

Chandra, M. (1971) 'Terracottas in Bharat Kala Bhavan', in A. Krishna (ed.), *Chhavi: Golden Jubilee Volume Bharat Kala Bhavan 1920–70*, Benares, pp. 1–15.

Chandra, R.G. (1964) *Studies in the Development of Ornaments and Jewellery in Proto-Historic India*, Varanasi, 1964,

Chapman, J.S. (1841) 'Gems found at Beghram', *JASB* X, pp. 613–14, plate facing p. 614.

Coarelli, F. (1962) 'The painted cups of Begram and the Ambrosian Iliad', *East and West* 13, pp. 317–35.

Colebrooke, H.T. (1809) 'On ancient monuments containing inscriptions', *Asiatic Researches* 9, (London repr.), pp. 398–453.

Collon, D. ed. (1997) *7000 Years of Seals*, London.

Combaz, G. (1937) *L'Inde et l'Orient classique*, Paris.

Compareti, M. (2006) 'Iconographical notes on some recent studies on Sasanian religious art with an additional note on an Ilkhanid monument by Rudi Favaro', *Annali ca Foscari* XLV.3, pp. 163–200.

Conolly, E.B. (1840) 'Gems from Kandahar', *JASB* IX, pp. 97–99

Content, D.J. (1987) *Islamic Rings and Gems: The Zucker Collection*, London.

Coomaraswamy, A.K. (1935) *La sculpture de Bodhgaya*, Ars Asiatica XVIII, Paris.

Court, C.-A. (1827) 'Itinerary of a journey from Persia to Kabul made in the year 1826', in Grey, C. (1929) *European Adventurers of Northern India, 1785 to 1849*, ed. H.L.O. Garrett, Lahore, appendix II, pp. xxvii–xlviii.

Court, C.-A. (1834) 'Further information on the topes of Mánikyála, being the translation of an extract from a manuscript memoir on ancient Taxila', *JASB* III, pp. 556–62 (repr. Thomas 1858, vol. I, pp. 138–41).

Court, C.-A. (1839) 'Collection of facts which may be useful for the comprehension of Alexander the Great's exploits on the western banks of the Indus, *JASB* VIII, pp. 304–13, map.

Court, C.-A. (MSS) *Mémoires manuscrits du général Claude-Auguste Court*, 5 vols, Musée des Arts asiatiques Guimet, Paris, ref. 64836.

Cribb, J. (1983) 'Investigating the introduction of coinage in India – a review of recent research', *Journal of the Numismatic Society of India* XLV, Varanasi, pp. 80–101.

Cribb, J. (1985) 'Dating India's earliest coins', in M. Taddei and J. Schotsmans (eds), *South Asian Archaeology, 1983*, Naples, pp. 535–54.

Cribb, J. (1993) 'The Heraus coins: their attribution to the Kushan king Kujula Kadphises, ca. AD 30–80', in M. Price, A. Burnett and R. Bland (eds), *Essays in Honour of Robert Carson and Kenneth Jenkins*, London, pp. 107–134.

Cribb, J. (1999/2000) 'Kanishka's Buddha image coins revisited', *Silk Road Art and Archaeology* 6 (*Papers in Honour of Francine Tissot*), pp. 151–89.

Cribb, J. (2002) 'Coins reported from Akra', *Ancient Pakistan* 15, pp. 65–84.

Cribb, J. (2005) 'The Greek kingdom of Bactria, its coinage and its collapse', in O. Bopearachchi and M.-F. Boussac (eds), *Afghanistan, ancient carrefour entre l'est et l'ouest*, Turnhout, pp. 207–25.

Cribb, J. (2007a) 'Rediscovering the Kushans', in E. Errington and V. Sarkhosh Curtis, *From Persepolis to the Punjab. Exploring Ancient Iran, Afghanistan and Pakistan*, London, pp. 179–210.

Cribb, J. (2007b) *Money as a Marker of Cultural Continuity and Change in Central Asia.*, Oxford.

Cribb, J. (2010) 'The Kidarites. The numismatic evidence', in M. Alram, D. Klimburg-Salter, M. Inaba and M. Pfisterer (eds), *Coins, Art and Chronology II. The First Millennium C.E. in the Indo-Iranian Borderlands*, Vienna, pp. 91–146.

Cribb, J. (2014) 'The Soter Megas coins of the first and second Kushan kings, Kujula Kadphises and Wima Takto', *Gandharan Studies* 8, pp. 77–133.

Cribb, J. (2015) 'Dating and locating Mujatria and the two Kharahostes', *Journal of the Oriental Numismatic Society* 223, pp. 26–48.

Cribb, J. (2018) 'Numismatic evidence and the date of Kanishka I', in W. Rienjang and P. Stewart (eds), *Problems of Chronology in Gandhāran Art*, Oxford.

Cribb, J. (2019) 'Charles Masson's finds from Begram and identifying the Islamic mint of Farwān', *Journal of the Oriental Numismatic Society* 238, pp. 5–11.

Cribb, J. and Bracey, R. (at press) *Catalogue of Kushan Coins in the British Museum*, London.

Cribb, J., Farid Khan and Amanullah (2012) 'Late Kushan copper hoard (?) from the collection of the S.R.O. in Directorate of Archaeology and Museums Khyber Pakhtunkhwa', *Ancient Pakistan* XXIII, pp. 117–43.

Culture and Art of Ancient Uzbekistan (1991) Exhibition Catalogue, 2 vols, Moscow.

Cunningham, A. (1840a) 'Notes on Captain Hay's Bactrian coins', *JASB* IX, pp. 530–44.

Cunningham, A. (1840b) 'Extracts from letters to the Asiatic Society', Proc. ASB, 4 November 1840, *JASB* IX, p. 860.

Cunningham, A. (1842) 'Second notice on some new Bactrian coins', *JASB* XI, pp. 130–7.

Cunningham, A. (1845) 'Notice of some unpublished coins of the Indo-Scythians', *JASB* XIV, pp. 430–41.

Cunningham, A. (1862) Extract of a letter to E.C. Bayley, Proc. ASB, May 1862, *JASB* XXXI, pp. 303–8.

Cunningham, A. (1868) 'Coins of Alexander's successors in the East', *Numismatic Chronicle*, new ser. 8, pp. 93–136, 181–213, 257–83.

Cunningham, A. (1869) 'Coins of Alexander's successors in the East', *Numismatic Chronicle*, new ser. 9, pp. 28–46, 121–53, 217–46, 293–318.

Cunningham, A. (1870) 'Coins of Alexander's successors in the East', *Numismatic Chronicle*, new ser. 10, pp. 65–90, 205–36.

Cunningham, A. (1872) 'Coins of Alexander's successors in the East', *Numismatic Chronicle*, new ser. 12, pp. 157–85.

Cunningham, A. (1873) 'Coins of Alexander's successors in the East', *Numismatic Chronicle*, new ser. 13, pp. 187–219.

Cunningham, A. (1884) *Coins of Alexander's Successors in the East*, London (repr. articles in *Numismatic Chronicle* 1868–73).

Cunningham, A. (1888) 'Coins of the Indo-Scythian king Miaüs or Heraüs', *Numismatic Chronicle*, 3rd ser. 8, pp. 47–58, 199–248.

Cunningham, A. (1889) 'Coins of the Tochari, Kushâns, or Yue-ti', *Numismatic Chronicle*, 3rd ser. 9, pp. 268–311.

Cunningham, A. (1890) 'Coins of the Sakas', *Numismatic Chronicle*, 3rd ser. 10, pp. 103–72.

Cunningham, A. (1891) *Coins of Ancient India from the Earliest Times down to the Seventh Century AD*, London.

Cunningham, A. (1892a) 'Coins of the Kushans, or Great Yue-ti', *Numismatic Chronicle*, 3rd ser. 12, pp. 40–82, 98–159.

Cunningham, A. (1892b) *Coins of the Indo-Scythians*, London (repr. articles *Numismatic Chronicle*, 3rd ser. 8–12, 1888–92).

Cunningham, A. (1893) 'Coins of the Later Indo-Scythians, Introduction and Later Kushâns', *Numismatic Chronicle*, 3rd ser. 13, pp. 93–128, pp. 166–77, 184–202.

Cunningham, A. (1894) 'Coins of the Later Indo-Scythians – Ephthalites, or White Huns', *Numismatic Chronicle*, 3rd ser. 14, pp. 243–93.

Cunningham, A. (1895) *Later Indo-Scythians. Ephthalites, or White Huns*, London (repr. articles in *Numismatic Chronicle*, 3rd ser. 13–14, 1893–4).

Curiel, R. (1953) 'Le trésor du Tépé Maranjān. Une trouvaille de monnaies sasanides et kušano-sasanides faite près de Caboul', in R. Curiel and D. Schlumberger, *Trésors monétaires d'Afghanistan*, MDAFA XIV, Paris, pp. 170–5.

Curiel, R. and Schlumberger, D. (1953) 'Le trésor de Mir Zakah près de Gardēz', in R. Curiel and D. Schlumberger, *Trésors monétaires d'Afghanistan*, Paris, pp. 65–100.

Curtis, J. (1976) 'Parthian gold from Nineveh', *British Museum Yearbook* I, pp. 46–66.

Curtis, V.S. (2001) 'Parthian belts and belt plaques', *Iranica Antiqua* XXXVI, pp. 299–327.

Czuma, S.J. (1985) *Kushan Sculpture: Images from Early India*, Cleveland.

Dahncke, M. (1988) *Frühislamische Bronzen der Bumiller Collection*, vol. 1, Panicale.

Dahncke, M. (1992) *Bumiller Collection: Frühislamische bronze-Öllampen und ihre Typologie*, vol. 2, Panicale..

Dalton, O.M. (1964) *The Treasure of the Oxus*, 3rd ed. London.

Dani, A.H. Dani, A.H. (1965-6) 'Shaikhan Dheri excavation (1963 and 1964 seasons)', *Ancient Pakistan* II, pp. 17–113.

Darkevich, V.P. (1976) *Khudozhestvennyi Metall Vstoka VIII–XIII vv* [Fine eastern metalwork of the 8th to the 13th centuries], Moscow.

Davary, G.D. (1982) *Baktrish. Ein Wörterbuch auf Grund der Inschriften, Handschriften, Münzen und Siegelsteine*, Heidelberg.

Davidson, G.R. (1952) *Corinth XII. The Minor Objects*, Princeton.

De Blois, F. (2006) 'Du nouveau sur la chronologie Bactrienne post-hellénistique: l'ère de 223–224 ap. J.C.', *CRAI* 2, pp. 991–7.

De la Vaissière, É. (2018) 'L'ère kouchane des documents bactriens', *Journal Asiatique* 306(2), pp. 281–4.

De Ridder, A. (1911) *Collection de Clercq*, Catalogue VII, part 1, *Les bijoux*, Paris.

De Saxcé, A. (2011) 'Jouveau-Dubreuil et l'archéologie du sous-continent indien', in M. Royo, M. Denoyelle and E. Champion (eds), *Du voyage savant aux territoires de l'archéologie*, Paris, pp. 291–310.

De Waele, E. (1982) *Bronzes du Luristan et d'Amlash. Ancienne Collection Godard*, Louvain-La-Neuve.

Demange, F. (2006) *Les Perses Sassanides. Fastes d'un empire oublié (224–642)*, Musée Cernuschi, Musée des arts de la ville de Paris, 5 September–30 December, Paris.

Desmond, R. (1982) *The India Museum 1801–1879*, London.

Deyell, J. (1990) *Living Without Silver – The Monetary History of Early Medieval North India*, Delhi.

Dikshit, K.N. (1927) 'Western Circle. Mohenjo-daro', *Archaeological Survey of India Annual Report 1924–25*, Calcutta, pp. 20, 63–72.

Diler, O. (2009) *Islamic Mints*, Istanbul.

Diodorus Siculus, *Library of History*, tr. C.H. Oldfather, vols 4–8, books XIV–XVII, Cambridge, MA, London, 1989.

Dobbins, K.W. (1970) 'The question of the imitation Hermaios coinage', *East and West* 20, pp. 307–27.

Dobbins, K.W. (1972) *Coinage and Epigraphy of the Śakas and Pahlavas: a Reconstruction of the Political Chronology and Geography of the Indo-Iranian Borderlands 130 BC to AD 70* (PhD thesis, Australian National University).

Dussubieux, L. and Gratuze, B. (2001 [2003]), 'Analyse quantitative de fragments de verre provenant de Begram', *Topoi. Orient–Occident* 11/1, pp. 451–72.

Erginsoy, Ü. (1978) *Islam Maden Sanatinin Gelişmesi* [Development of Islamic Mining Art], Ankara.

Errington, E. (1995) 'Rediscovering the coin collection of General Claude-Auguste Court: A Preliminary Report', *Topoi* 5/2, pp. 411–24.

Errington, E. (1997) 'The British East India Company Collection', in P. Callieri, *Seals and Sealings from the North–West of the Indian Subcontinent and Afghanistan (4th century BC – 11th century AD)*, Naples, pp. 18–23.

Errington, E. (1999) 'Rediscovering the collections of Charles Masson', in M. Alram and D.E. Klimburg-Salter (eds), *Coins, Art and Chronology. Essays on the pre–Islamic History of the Indo-Iranian Borderlands*, Vienna, pp. 207–37.

Errington, E. (2001 [2003]) 'Charles Masson and Begram', *Topoi. Orient–Occident* 11/1, pp. 1–53.

Errington, E. (2002a) 'Numismatic evidence for dating the "Kaniṣka" reliquary' (with an appendix on the inscription by H. Falk), *Silk Road Art and Archaeology* 8, pp. 127–46.

Errington, E. (2002b) 'Ancient Afghanistan through the eyes of Charles Masson: the Masson Project at the British Museum', *International Institute for Asian Studies Newsletter*, March, pp. 8–9.

Errington, E. (2002c) 'Discovering ancient Afghanistan. The Masson Collection', *Minerva* 13/6, Nov/Dec, pp. 53–5.

Errington, E. (2010) 'Differences in the patterns of Kidarite and Alkhan coin distribution at Begram and Kashmir Smast', in M. Alram, D. Klimburg-Salter, M. Inaba and M. Pfisterer (eds), *Coins, Art and Chronology II. The First Millennium C.E. in the Indo-Iranian Borderlands*, Vienna, pp. 147–68.

Errington, E. *et al.* (2017) *Charles Masson and the Buddhist Sites of Afghanistan: Explorations, Excavations, Collections 1832–1835*, British Museum Research Publication 215, London (https://doi.org/10.48582/charlesmasson_vol1).

Errington, E. *et al.* (2017) *The Charles Masson Archive. British Library, British Museum and Other Documents relating to the Masson Collection*, British Museum Research Publication 216, London (https://doi.org/10.48582/charlesmasson_vol2).

Errington E. and Cribb J. eds (1992) *The Crossroads of Asia. Transformation in Image and Symbol in the Art of Ancient Afghanistan and Pakistan*, Cambridge.

Errington E. and Sarkhosh Curtis, V. (2007) *From Persepolis to the Punjab. Exploring Ancient Iran, Afghanistan and Pakistan*, London 2007 (repr. 2011; 2nd repr. as *From Persia to Punjab*, Mumbai 2014).

Fabrègues, C. (1991) *The Jewellery on the Gandhara Sculptures in Schist and its Chronological Significance*, PhD. thesis, School of Oriental and African Studies, London University.

Faccenna, D. and Callieri P. (2003) 'The Buddhist sacred area of Saidu Sharif I', *Ancient Civilizations from Scythia to Siberia. An International Journal of Comparative Studies in History and Archaeology* IX, pp. 307–80.

Faccenna, D. and Taddei, M. (1962–4) *Sculptures from the Sacred Area of Butkara I (Swat, W. Pakistan)*, IsMEO Reports and Memoirs II.2–3, Rome.

Fairservis, W.A. (1975) *The Roots of Ancient India*, 2nd ed. rev., Chicago.

Falk, H. (2016) 'Two new Kṣaharāta Kṣatrapas', *Journal of the Oriental Numismatic Society* 227, pp. 10–12.

Fehèrvāri, G. (1980) *Islamic Metalwork of the Eighth to the Fifteenth Centuries in the Keir Collection*, London.

Fenet, A. (2010) *Documents d'archéologie militante. La mission Foucher en Afghanistan (1922–1925)*, Mémoires de l'Académie des Inscriptions et Belles-Lettres 42, Paris.

Field, H. and Prostov, E. (1948) 'Recent excavations at Khwarazm', *Ars Islamica* 13–14, pp. 139–48.

Fishman, A. and Tod, I. (2018) *The Silver Damma – On the Mashas, Daniqs, Qanari Dirhams and Other Diminutive Coins of India 600–1100 CE*, Nasik.

Fontenay, E. (1887) *Les Bijoux anciens et modernes*, Paris.

Formozov, A.A., Jacenko, I.V., Belenitsky, A.M. and Darkevic, V.L. (1977) *Proizvedeniya iskusstva v novykh nakhodkakh sovetskikh arkheologov* [Works of art recently discovered by Soviet archaeologists], Moscow.

Foucher, A. (1925) 'Notes sur l'itinéraire de Hiuan-tsang en Afghanistan', in *Études asiatiques publiées à l'occasion du 25e anniversaire de l'École française d'Extrême-Orient*, Paris, pp. 257–84.

Foucher, A. (1942) *La vieille route de l'Inde: de Bactres à Taxila*, MDAFA I, Paris.

Frankfort, H.P. (1984) *Fouilles d'Aï Khanoum. III. Le sanctuaire du temple a niches indentées. 2. Les trouvailles*, MDFA XXVI, Paris.

Fussman, G. (1970) 'Inscriptions kharoṣṭhī du Musée de Caboul', *Bulletin de l'Ecole française d'Extrême-Orient* 57, pp. 43–56.

Fussman, G. (2008) *Monuments bouddhiques de la région de Caboul – Kabul Buddhist Monuments*, MDFA XXII, Publications de l'Institut de civilisation indienne, fasc. 76.1–2, Paris.

Fussman, G. and Guillaume, O. (1990) *Surkh Kotal en Bactriane. II. Les monnaies – Les petits objets*, MDFA XXXII, Paris.

Fussman, G. and Thierry, F. (2001) *Raoul Curiel (1913–2000): un savant dans son siècle*, Paris.

Gardner, P. (1886) *The Coins of the Greek and Scythic Kings of Bactria and India in the British Museum*, London.

Garg, S. (2016) 'New light on Charles Masson' in V. Widorn, U. Franke and P. Latschenberger (eds) *South Asian Archaeology and Art. Contextualizing Material Culture in South and Central Asia in Pre-Modern Times*, Papers from European Association for South Asian Archaeology and Art 20th conference, Vienna 2010, Turnhout, pp. 203–11.

Gasparini, M. (2014) 'Sino-Iranian textile patterns in trans-Himalayan areas', *The Silk Road* 14, pp. 84–96.

Gerard, J.G. (1833) 'Continuation of the route of Lieutenant A. Burnes and Dr Gerard, from Peshawar to Bokhára', *JASB* II, pp. 1–23.

Gerard, J.G. (1834a) 'Proposal to the Society to employ Masson to continue research in Afghanistan', Proc. ASB, April 1834, no. 28, *JASB* III, p. 195.

Gerard, J.G. (1834b) 'Memoir on the topes and antiquities of Afghanistan', *JASB* III, pp. 321–9.

Ghirshman, R. (1938) *Fouilles de Sialk près de Kashan*, vol. II, Paris.

Ghirshman R. (1946) *Bégram. Recherches archéologiques et historiques sur les Kouchans*, MDAFA XII, Cairo. https://archive.org/details/MIFAO79.

Ghirshman, R. (1962) *Parthes et Sassanides*, Paris.

Ghirshman, R. (1964) *Persia from the Origins to Alexander the Great*, London.

Ghirshman, R. (1979) 'La ceinture en Iran', *Iranica Antiqua* XIV, pp. 167–96.

Ghosh, A. (1948) 'Taxila (Sirkap), 1944–45', *Ancient India* 4, pp. 41–84.

Ghosh, A. (1965) 'Indian Archaeology 1962–63: A Review', *Archaeological Survey of India*, New Delhi.

Ghosh, A. ed. (1989) *An Encyclopedia of Indian Archaeology*, vol. 1, New Delhi.

Gill, S. (2001 [2003]) 'Procédés narratifs dans les ivoires de Begram', *Topoi. Orient–Occident* 11/1, pp. 515–35.

Gladiss, A. von (1998) *Schmuck im Museum für Islamische Kunst*, Berlin.

Göbl, R. (1967) *Dokumente zur Geschichte der iranischen Hunnen in Baktrien und Indien*, 4 vols, Wiesbaden.

Göbl, R. (1971) *Sasanian Numismatics*, Braunschweig.

Göbl, R. (1976) *A Catalogue of Coins from Butkara I (Swat, Pakistan)*, Rome.

Göbl, R. (1984) *System und Chronologie der Münzprägung des Kušānreiches*, Vienna.

Göbl, R. (1993) 'Supplementa Orientalia III', *Numismatica e Antichità Classiche* XXII, pp. 229–42.

Godard, Y. et al. (1954) *Bronzes du Luristan, Collection E. Graeffe. Exposition du 6/7 au 26/9/1954 au Gemeente Museum*, La Haye.

Gorbunova, N.G. (1986) 'The Culture of Ancient Ferghana VI century BC–VI century AD', *BAR International Series* 282.

Gorbunova, N.G. (1992) 'Early nomadic pastoral tribes in Soviet Central Asia during the first half of the first millennium AD', in G. Seaman (ed.), *Foundations of Empire: Archaeology and Art of the Eurasian Steppes*, Los Angeles, pp. 34–50.

Gorin A.N. and Dvurechenskaya, N.D. (2018) *Katalog Monet Kreposti Uzundara (Yuzhnyi Uzbekistan) – Materialy Tokharistanskoy Ekspeditsii Vypusk* XI [Catalogue of the Coins of the Uzundar Fortress (South Uzbekistan) – Materials of the Tokharistan Expedition Issue XI], Tashkent.

Goron, S. and Goenka, J.P. (2001) *The Coins of the Indian Sultanates. Covering the Area of Present-Day India, Pakistan and Bangladesh*, New Delhi.

Goukowsky, P. (1989) 'Alexandrie de l'Oxos ou Alexandrie du Caucase?', *Mélanges Pierre Lévêque*, vol. 2, Anthropologie et société, Besançon, pp. 245–66.

Grabar, O. (1967) *Sasanian Silver. Late Antique and Early Medieval Arts of Luxury from Iran*, Ann Arbor.

Grenet, F. (2006) 'Nouvelles données sur la localisation des cinq Yabghus des Yuezhi. Arrière plan politique de l'itinéraire des marchands de Maès Titianos', *Journal Asiatique* 294, pp. 325–41.

Grey, C. (1929) *European Adventurers of Northern India, 1785 to 1849*, ed. H.L.O. Garrett, Lahore.

Guillaume, O. (1990) *Analysis of Reasoning in Archaeology – the Case of Graeco-Bactrian and Indo-Greek Numismatics*, Delhi (tr. O. Guillaume, *L'analyse des raisonnements en Archéologie: le cas de la numismatique Gréco-Bactrienne et Indo-Grecque*, Paris 1987).

Gul Rahim Khan (2007) 'Kanishka coins from Taxila', *Gandharan Studies* 1, pp. 119–48.

Gul Rahim Khan (2010) 'Copper coins of Vasudeva and successors from Taxila', *Gandharan Studies* 4, pp. 39–161.

Gul Rahim Khan (2014) 'Soter Megas coins from Taxila', *Gandharan Studies* 8, pp. 135–59.

Gul Rahim Khan and Cribb, J. (2012) 'Coins of Kujula Kadphises from Taxila', *Gandharan Studies* 6, pp. 81–219.

Gupta, P. (1989) *Geography from Ancient Indian Coins & Seals*, New Delhi.

Gupta, P.L. and Hardaker, T.R. (1985) *Ancient Indian Punchmarked Coins of the Magadha-Maurya Kārshāpana Series*, Nasik.

Gupta, P.L. and Hardaker, T.R. (2014) *Punchmarked Coinage of the Indian Subcontinent. Magadha-Mauryan Series*, rev. ed. Nasik.

Gyselen, R. (1993) *Catalogue des sceaux, camées et bulles sassanides de la Bibliothèque Nationale et du Musée du Louvre I. Collection générale*, Paris.

Hackin, J. (1954) 'Les fouilles de Begram (1939)', in J.-R. Hackin, J. Carl and P. Hamelin, *Nouvelles recherches archéologiques à Begram, ancienne Kâpicî (1939–1940)*, 2 vols, MDAFA XI, Paris, pp. 11–16.

Hackin, J. and Carl, J. (1933) *Nouvelles recherches archéologiques à Bamiyan*, MDAFA III, Paris.

Hackin, J. and Hackin, J.-R. (1939) *Recherches archéologiques à Bégram (chantier no. 2, 1937)*, 2 vols, MDAFA IX, Paris.

Hackin, J., Carl, J. and Hamelin, P. (1954) *Nouvelles recherches archéologiques à Bégram, ancienne Kâpicî (1939–1940)*, 2 vols, MDAFA XI, Paris.

Hackin, J.-R., Carl, J. and Meunié, J. (1959) *Diverses recherches archéologiques en Afghanistan (1933–1940)*, MDAFA VIII, Paris.

Haerinck, E. and Overleat, B. (2004) 'The Iron Age III Graveyard at War Kabud, Pusht-i Kuh, Luristan (Luristan Excavation Documents, V)', *Acta Iranica* 42, Leuven.

Hakemi, A. and Sajjadi, S.M.S. (1988) 'Shahdad excavations in the context of the Oasis civilization', in G. Ligabue and S. Salvatori (eds), *Bactria. An Ancient Oasis from the Sands of Afghanistan*, Venice, pp. 143–53.

Hallade, M. (1968) *Gandhara Art of North India and the Graeco-Buddhist Tradition in India, Persia and Central Asia*, London.

Hamelin, P. (1952) 'Sur quelques verreries de Begram', *Cahiers de Byrsa* 2, pp. 11–25.

Hamelin, P. (1953) 'Matériaux pour servir a l'étude des verreries de Bégram', *Cahiers de Byrsa* 3, pp. 121–56.

Hamelin, P. (1954) 'Matériaux pour servir à l'étude des verreries de Begram (suite)', *Cahiers de Byrsa* 4, pp. 153–83.

Hardaker, T.R. (1999) *The Mashaka Fractional Coinage of Ancient India, A Type Catalogue*, Nasik.

Hasson, R. (1987) *Early Islamic Jewellery*, Jerusalem.

Hay, W. (1840) 'Account of coins found at Bameean' and 'Note on the above by the officiating secretary [Torrens]', *JASB* IX, pp. 68–75.

Head, B.V. (1888) *Catalogue of Greek Coins in the British Museum: Attica, Megaris, Aegina*, vol. 22, ed. R.S. Poole, London.

Heinrich, G.F. (1965) *Buddhistische Kunst Indiens*, Leipzig.

Herodotus *Melpomene Cap. The Persian Wars*, book 4, tr. G. Rawlinson, ed. B.J. Butterfield, 1942. http://www.parstimes.com/history/herodotus/persian_wars/melpomene.html.

Hiebert F. (1994) 'Production evidence for the origin of the Oxus Civilization', *Antiquity* 68, pp. 372–87.

Hiebert, F. and Cambon, P. eds (2011) *Afghanistan. Crossroads of the Ancient World*, catalogue of British Museum exhibition 3 March – 3 July, London.

Higgins, R. (1980) *Greek and Roman Jewellery*, London, 2nd ed.

Higuchi, T and Saito, K. (2001) *Tomb F – Tomb of BWLH and BWRP: Southeast Necropolis Palmyra, Syria*, Research Center for Silk Roadology, 2 vols, Nara.

Hill, J.E. (2009) *Through the Jade Gate to Rome – A Study of the Silk Routes during the Later Han Dynasty 1st to 2nd Century CE – An Annotated Translation of the Chronicle on the 'Western Regions' in the* Hou Han Shu, Cooktown.

Hoffman, H. and Davidson, P.F. (1965) *Greek Gold. Jewellery from the Age of Alexander*, Mainz.

Holt, F. (1988) *Alexander the Great and Bactria: The Formation of a Greek Frontier in Central Asia*, Leiden (repr. 1995).

Huashan, C., Gaulier S., Maillard M., Pinault, G. (1987) 'Sites divers de la région de Koutcha. Epigraphie koutchéenne', *Mission Paul Pelliot. Documents archéologiques* VIII, Paris.

Hulsewé, A.F.P. and Loewe, M.A.N. (1979) *China in Central Asia, the Early Stage: 125 BC – AD 23: An Annotated Translation of Chapters 61 and 96 of the History of the Former Han Dynasty*, Leiden.

Icomos 24.03.2005 'Actions in Afghanistan', *Heritage at Risk 2004/2005*, pp. 26–31: http://www.international.icomos.org/risk/2004/afganis2004.pdf.

Ilyasov, J.Y. 'Bronze ewers of craftsman Ahmad', http:www.transoxiana.org/Eran/Articles/ilyasov.html.

Imperatorskaya Arkheologicheskaya Kommissiya [Imperial Archaeological Commission] (1906) *Al'bom risunkov, pomeshchennykh v otchetakh Imperatorskoi Arkheologicheskoi Kommissii za 1882–1898* [Album of illustrations from the reports of the Imperial Archaeological Commission for the years 1882–1898], St Petersburg.

Ingholt, H. and Lyons, I. (1957) *Gandhāran Art in Pakistan*, New York.

Ippel, A. (1922) *Der Bronzefind von Galjub*, Berlin.

Iraq Department of Antiquities (1940) *Excavations at Samarra 1936–1939*, vol.1, *Architecture and Mural Decoration*, Baghdad.

Itina, M.A. ed. (1979) *Kocevniki na granicach Khorezma* [The nomads on the frontiers of Khwarazm], Moscow.

Jacquet, E. (1836) 'Sur les découvertes archéologiques faites par M. Honigberger dans l'Afghanistan [1]', *Journal Asiatique*, 3ème sér. II, pp. 234–77, pls I–XIII; http://gallica.bnf.fr/ark:/12148/bpt6k931286.image.langEN.r=journal%20asiatique.swf.

Jacquet, E. (1837) 'Sur les découvertes archéologiques faites par M. Honigberger dans l'Afghanistan [2]', *Journal Asiatique*, 3ème sér. IV, pp. 401–40; http://gallica.bnf.fr/ark:/12148/bpt6k93130r/f1.image.langEN.

Jacquet, E. (1838) 'Sur les découvertes archéologiques faites par M. Honigberger dans l'Afghanistan [3]', *Journal Asiatique*, 3ème sér. V, pp. 163–97, pl. XIII; http://gallica.bnf.fr/ark:/12148/bpt6k931313/f163.image.

Jacquet, E. (1839) 'Sur les découvertes archéologiques faites par M. Honigberger dans l'Afghanistan [4]', *Journal Asiatique*, 3ème sér. VII, pp. 385–404, pls XIV–XV; https://ia600309.us.archive.org/6/items/s3journalasiatiq07sociuoft/s3journalasiatiq07sociuoft.pdf.

Janata, A. (1981) *Schmuck in Afghanistan*, Graz.

Jansari, S. (2012) 'Roman coins from the Mackenzie Collection at the British Museum', *Numismatic Chronicle* 172, pp. 93–104.

Jansari, S. (2013) 'Roman coins from the Masson and Mackenzie Collections at the British Museum', *South Asian Studies* 29.2, pp. 177–93; http://dx.doi.org/10.1080/02666030.2013.833762.

Jarrige, J.F. (1973) 'La fin de la civilisation harappéenne', *Paleorient*, pp. 263–87.

Jenkins, M. (1983) *Islamic Pottery. A Brief History*, The Metropolitan Museum of Art, New York.

Johnson, J. (1931) 'Jewellery', in P.V.C. Baur and M.I. Rostovtzeff (eds), *The Excavations at Dura-Europos conducted by Yale University and the French Academy of Inscriptions and Lettres. Preliminary Report of the Second Season of work 1928–29*, New Haven, pp. 78–82.

Jones, W. (1788) 'On the chronology of the Hindus' *Asiatick Researches* 2, pp. 88–114.

Jongeward, D. and Cribb, J. (2015) *Kushan, Kushano-Sasanian, and Kidarite Coins. A Catalogue of Coins from the American Numismatic Society*, New York.

Jongeward, D., Errington, E., Salomon, R. and Baums, S. (2012) *Gandharan Buddhist Reliquaries*, University of Washington Gandharan Studies series, Seattle.

Justin [Justinus, Marcus Junianus], *Prologues. Epitome of the Philippic History of Pompeius Trogus*, tr. J.C. Yardley, intro. R. Develin, Philological Association Classical Resources 3, Atlanta 1994.

Karamian, G. and Farrokh, K. (2017) 'Sasanian stucco decorations from the Ramavand (Barz Qawaleh) excavations in the Lorestan province of Iran', *Historia i Swiat* 6, pp. 69–88.

Kaye, G.R. and Johnston, E.H. (1937) *Catalogue of Manuscripts in European Languages Belonging to the Library of the India Office*. vol. II, part II: *Minor Collections and Miscellaneous Manuscripts* London: section II, nos 631–57, 'The Masson Papers', pp. 1272–82.

Kazakov, E.P. (1991) *Bulgarskoe selo X-XIII vekov nizovii Kamy* [Bulgar village of the 10th–13th centuries in the lower Kama River area], Kazan.

Klimburg-Salter, D.E. (1995) *Buddha in Indien. Die frühindische Skulptur von König Aśoka bis zur Guptazeit*, Vienna.

Konow, S. (1929) *Kharoshthi Inscriptions.* Corpus Inscriptionum Indicarum II.1, Calcutta.

Konuk, K. and Arslan, M. (2000) *Ancient Gems and Finger Rings from Asia Minor. The Yuksel Erimtan Collection*, Ankara.

Kovalenko, S. (1995/6) 'The coinage of Diodotus I and Diodotus II, Greek kings of Bactria', *Silk Road Art and Archaeology* IV, pp. 17–74.

Kritikos, P.G. and Papadaki, S.P. (1967) 'The history of the poppy and of opium and their expansion in antiquity in the eastern Mediterranean area', *Bulletin of Narcotics* 19.3, pp. 17–38; http://rbedrosian.com/hpop.htm.

Kurita, I. (1988) *Gandhāran Art. I. The Buddha's Life Story, II*, Tokyo.

Kurita, I. (2003) *Gandharan Art: Ancient Buddhist Art Series*, rev. ed. 2 vols, Tokyo.

Kuwayama, S. (1974) 'Kapisi Begram III: Renewing its dating', *Orient* 10, pp. 57–78.

Kuwayama, S. (1991a) 'The Hephthalites in Tokharistan and northwest India', *Zinbun: Annals of the Institute for Research in*

Humanities, Kyoto University 24, 1991, pp. 89–134 (repr. Kuwayama 2002, pp. 107–39).

Kuwayama, S. (1991b) 'The horizon of Begram III and beyond: a chronological interpretation of the evidence for monuments in the Kapiśi–Kabul–Ghazni region', *East and West* 41, pp. 79–120 (repr. Kuwayama 2002, pp. 173–99).

Kuwayama, S. (1992) 'The inscription of Ganeśa from Gardez and a chronology of the Turki Shahis', *Journal Asiatique* 279/3–4, pp. 267–87 (repr. Kuwayama 2002, pp. 249–59).

Kuwayama, S. (1998) 'Not Hephthalite but Kapiśan Khingal: identity of the Napki coins', in A.K. Jha and S. Garg, *Ex Moneta: Essays in Numismatics, History and Archaeology in Honour of Dr David W. MacDowall*, New Delhi, pp. 331–49 (repr. Kuwayama 2002, pp. 208–21).

Kuwayama, S. (1999) 'Historical notes on Kāpiśī and Kābul in the sixth–eighth centuries', *Zinbun: Annals of the Institute for Research in Humanities, Kyoto University* 34, pp. 25–77.

Kuwayama, S. (2002) *Across the Hindu Kush of the First Millenium. A Collection of the Papers*, Kyoto.

Kuwayama, S. (2010) 'Between Begram II and III. A blank period in the history of Kāpiśī', in M. Alram and D. E. Klimburg-Salter (eds), *Coins, Art and Chronology II: The First Millennium C.E. in the Indo-Iranian Borderlands*. Vienna, pp. 283–97.

Kyzlasov L.R. (1969) *Istoriya Tuvy v srednie veka* [The History of Tuva in the Middle Ages], Moscow.

L'image tissée. Textiles de l'Antiquité a la Renaissance. Exposition/Vente du 23 février au 2 avril 2006, www.lesenluminures.com.

Lafont, J.-M. (1987) 'La présence française dans le royaume sikh du Penjab, 1822–1849', thèse d'Etat 1 June, Université de Paris III–Sorbonne Nouvelle.

Lafont, J.-M. (1992) *La présence française dans le royaume sikh du Penjab, 1822–1849*, Paris.

Lafont, J.-M. (2007) 'From Taq-i Bustan to Lahore: French and Italian officers in Persia and the Punjab 1816–46', in Errington and Sarkhosh Curtis, *From Persepolis to the Punjab. Exploring Ancient Iran, Afghanistan and Pakistan*, London 2007 (repr. 2011; 2nd repr. as *From Persia to Punjab*, Mumbai 2014).

Lane Poole, S. (1876) *The Coins of the Mohammadan Dynasties in the British Museum, Classes III–X*, vol. II, ed. R.S. Poole, London.

Lassen, C. (1838) *Einleitung zur Geschichte des Griechischen und Indoskythischen Könige in Bactrien, Kabul und Indien, durch Entzifferung der Alt-kabulischen Legenden auf ihren Münzen*, Bonn (English tr. Lassen 1840).

Lassen, C. (1840) *Greek and Indo-Scythian Kings and their Coins*, tr. T.H.E. Röer, with commentary by H. Torrens, Calcutta (repr. C. Lassen, 'Points in the history of the Greek and Indo-Scythian kings in Bactria, Cabul and India, as illustrated by deciphering the ancient legends on their coins', *JASB* IX, 1840, pp. 251–76, 339–78, 449–88, 627–76, 733–65).

Lecuyot, G. (2013) *Fouilles d'Aï Khanoum IX. L'habitat*, MDAFA XXXIV, Paris.

Leriche, P. (2007) 'Bactria, land of a thousand cities', in J. Cribb and G. Herrmann (eds), *After Alexander, Central Asia before Islam*, Oxford pp. 121–53.

Lerner, J. (2018) 'A prolegomenon to the study of pottery stamps from Mes Aynak', *Afghanistan: The Journal of the American Institute of Afghanistan Studies* 1.2, pp. 239–56.

Lester, A. (1991) 'A Fatimid hoard from Tiberias', in Na'ama Brosh (ed.), *Jewellery and Goldsmithing in the Islamic World*, International Symposium, The Israel Museum, Jerusalem, 1987, pp. 21–9.

Levina, L. (1971) *Keramika nizhnei i srednei Syrdary v I tysyacheletii n.e.* [Pottery of the lower and middle Syr Darya in the 1st millennium CE], Moscow.

Lilibaki-Akamati, M., Akamatis, I.M., Chrysostomou, A. and P. (2011) *The Archaeological Museum of Pella*, Athens.

Li Rongxi (tr.) (1996) *The Great Tang Dynasty Record of the Western Regions*, Berkeley.

Litvinsky, B.A. (1986) *Antike und frühmittelalterliche Grabhügel im westerlichen Fergana-Becken, Tadzikistan*, Munich.

Litvinsky, B.A. and Mukhtidinov, Kh. (1969) 'Antichnoe gorodishche Saksanokhur (yuzhnyi Tadzhistan). Sovetskaya arkheologiya' [The ancient urban site of Saksanokhur (southern Tadzhikistan)], *Sovetskaya Arkheologiya* 2, pp. 160–78.

Litvinsky, B.A and Tursunov N.O, (1974) 'The Leninabad krater and the Louvre Sosibios vase (Neo-Attic art and Central Asia)', *East and West*, n.s. 24.1–2, pp. 89–110.

Litvinsky, B.A. and Sedov, A.V. (1983) *Tepai Shach. Kul'tura i svyazi Kushanskoy Baktrii* [Tepa-i Shakh. The culture and international connections of Kushan Bactria], Moscow.

Litvinsky, B.A. and Sedov, A.V. (1984) *Kul'ty i rituały kushanskoy Bactrii* [Cults and rituals of Kushan Bactria], Moscow.

Liu Jucheng (1989) *Zhongguo Guqian Lu*, Beijing.

Loewe, M. (2001–2) 'Dated inscriptions on certain mirrors (AD 6–105): genuine or fabricated?' *Early China* 26/27, pp. 233–56.

Loginov, S.D. and Nikitin, A.B. (1996) 'Parthian coins from Margiana: Numismatics and history', *Bulletin of the Asia Institute* 10, pp. 39–51.

Longhurst, A. (1938) 'The Buddhist Antiquities of Nâgârjunakonda', *Memoirs of the Archaeological Survey of India* 54, Delhi.

L'or des Amazones (2001) *L'or des Amazones: peuples nomades entre Asie et Europe, VIe siècle av. JC – IVe siècle apr. JC*, Paris.

MacDowall, D.W. (1968) 'The Shahis of Kabul and Gandhara', *Numismatic Chronicle* 7th ser. VIII, pp. 189–224.

MacDowall, D.W. (1985) 'The successors of the Indo–Greeks at Begram', in J. Schotsmans and M. Taddei (eds), *South Asian Archaeology 1983*, Rome, pp. 555–65.

MacDowall, D.W. (1991) 'The Hazarajat hoard of Indo-Greek silver drachms', *Pakistan Archaeology* 26, pp. 188–98.

MacDowall, D.W. and Callieri, P.-F. (2004) *A Catalogue of Coins from the Excavation at Bir-Kot-Ghwandai 1984–1992*, Rome.

MacDowall, D.W. and Taddei, M. (1978) 'The Pre-Muslim Period', in F.R. Allchin and N. Hammond (eds), *The Archaeology of Afghanistan*, London, pp. 233–299.

Mackay, D. (1949) 'The jewellery of Palmyra and its significance', *Iraq* XI, pp. 160–87.

Mackay, E.J.H. (1938) *Further Excavations at Mohenjo-daro*, New Delhi.

Mackay, E.J.H. (1943) *Chanhu-daro Excavations 1935–36*, American Oriental Series, vol. 20, New Haven.

MacLean, D.N. (1989) *Religion and Society in Arab Sind*, Leiden.

Maheshwari, K.K. (2010) *Imitations in Continuity: Tracking the Silver Coinage of Early Medieval India*, Nasik.

Mairs, R. (2014) 'Achaemenid Ai Khanoum', *Archäologische Mitteilungen aus Iran und Turan* 46. pp. 1–19. pdf academia.edu.

Malek, H.M. (2019) *Arab-Sasanian Numismatics and History during the Early Islamic Period in Iran and Iraq – The Johnson Collection of Arab-Sasanian Coins*, London.

Mandel'stam, A.M. (1966) *Kochevniki na puti v Indiyu* [Nomads on the way to India], Trudy Tadzhikskoy Arkheologicheskoy Ekspeditsii [Proceedings of the Tajik Archaeological Expedition] 5, Moscow–Leningrad.

Mandel'stham, A.M. (1969) 'Archäologische Bemerkungen zum Kushana-Problem in Beitrage zur Alten Geschichte und deren Nachleben', *Feschrift für Franz Altheim zum 6. Okt 1968*, Berlin, pp. 525–34.

Mandel'stham, A.M. (1975) *Pamyatniki kochevnikov kushanskogo vremeni v severnoy Baktrii* [Monuments of nomads of Kushan times from northern Bactria], Trudy Tadzhikskoy Arkheologicheskoy Ekspeditsii [Proceedings of the Tajik Archaeological Expedition] VII, Leningrad.

Marshall, F.H. (1911) *Catalogue of the Jewellery, Greek, Roman and Etruscan in the Department of Greek and Roman Antiquities*, British Museum, London.

Marshall, J. (1902–3) 'Excavations at Charsadda', *Archaeological Survey of India Annual Report*, pp. 141–84.

Marshall, J. (1920) 'Excavations at Taxila', *Archaeological Survey of India Annual Report 1914–15*, Calcutta.

Marshall, J. (1931) *Mohenjo Daro and the Indus Civilization*, London.

Marshall, J. (1951) *Taxila*, 3 vols, Cambridge.

Marshall, J. and Foucher, A. (1947) *The Monuments of Sanchi*, Calcutta.

Masson Manuscripts, British Library India Office Collections MSS Eur. (listed in E.H. Kaye and E.H. Johnston, *Catalogue of Manuscripts in European Languages*, vol. II, part II, section II; M. Archer, *British Drawings in the India Office Library*, London 1969, pp. 248–53).

Masson, C. (1834) 'Memoir on the ancient coins found at Beghrám, in the Kohistán of Kábul', *JASB* III, pp. 153–75.

Masson, C. (1836a) 'Second memoir on the ancient coins found at Beghrám, in the Kohistán of Kábul', *JASB* V, pp. 1–28.

Masson, C. (1836b) 'Third memoir on the ancient coins discovered at a site called Beghrám in the Kohistán of Kábul', *JASB* V, pp. 537–48.

Masson, C. (1841) 'A memoir on the buildings called topes', in H.H. Wilson, *Ariana Antiqua. A Descriptive Account of the Antiquities and Coins of Afghanistan*, London (repr. Delhi 1971), pp. 55–118, Coins pls I–XXII.

Masson, C. (1842) *Narrative of Various Journeys in Balochistan, Afghanistan and the Panjab*, 3 vols, London (repr. Karachi 1974).

Masson, C. (1843) *Narrative of a Journey to Kalat. Including an Account of the Insurrection at that Place in 1840, and a Memoir on Eastern Balochistan*, vol. 4 of *Narrative of Various Journeys in Balochistan, Afghanistan and the Panjab*, London (repr. Karachi 1977).

Masson, V.M. and Sarianidi V.I. (1972) *Central Asia. Turkmenia before the Achaemenids*, New York–Washington.

Maximova, M.I. (1979) *Artiuchovskii kurgan* [Artiukhovsky barrow], Leningrad.

Maxwell-Jones, C. (2015) *Typology and Chronology of Ceramics of Bactra, Afghanistan 600 BCE–500 CE*, PhD thesis, University of Michigan.

McCrindle, J.W. (1893) *The Invasion of India by Alexander the Great*, London.

McMurdo, J. (1834) 'Dissertation on the river Indus', *JRAS* I, pp. 21–44.

McNicoll, A.W. and Ball, W. (1996) 'Excavations at Kandahar 1974 and 1975: The first two seasons at Shahr-i Kohna (Old Kandahar) conducted by the British Institute of Afghan Studies', *British Archaeological Reports, International Series no. 641*, Oxford.

Mehendale, S. (1997) *Begram: New Perspectives on the Ivory and Bone Carvings*, PhD thesis, University of California, Berkeley.

Mehendale, S. (2001 [2003]) 'The Begram ivory and bone carvings: some observations on provenance and chronology', *Topoi. Orient–Occident* 11/1, pp. 485–514.

Mehendale, S. (2005) *Begram: New Perspectives on the Ivory and Bone Carvings*, Berkeley.

Mehendale, S. (2011) 'Begram: At the heart of the Silk Roads', in F. Hiebert and P. Cambon (eds), *Afghanistan: Crossroads of the Ancient World*, London, pp. 131–44.

Melikian-Chirvani A.S. (1975) 'Les bronzes du Khorâssân 3', *Studia Iranica* 4, pp. 187–205.

Melikian-Chirvani, A.S. (1982) *Islamic Metalwork from the Iranian World: 8th–18th Centuries*, Victoria and Albert Museum Catalogue, London.

Melzer, G. (2006) 'A copper scroll inscription from the time of the Alchon Huns, (in collaboration with L. Sander)', in J. Braarvig, P. Harrison, J.-U. Hartmann, K. Matsuda, L. Sander (eds), *Buddhist Manuscripts III (Manuscripts in the Schøyen Collection)*, Oslo, pp. 251–78.

Menninger, M. (1996) *Untersuchungen zu den Gläsern und Gipsabgüssen aus dem Fund von Begram, Afghanistan*, Würzburger Forschungen zur Altertumskunde, Bd. I, Würzburg.

Meunié, J. (1954) 'Begram, chantier 2, 1939', in J.-R. Hackin, J. Carl and P. Hamelin, *Nouvelles recherches archéologiques à Begram, ancienne Kâpicî (1939–1940)*, 2 vols, MDAFA XI, Paris, pp. 7–9.

Meunié, J. (1959a) 'Begram – fouille de 1938', in J. Hackin, J. Carl and J. Meunié, *Diverses recherches archéologiques en Afghanistan (1933–1940)*, MDAFA VIII, Paris, pp. 103–6.

Meunié, J. (1959b) 'Une entrée de la ville à Begram', in J. Hackin, J. Carl and J. Meunié, *Diverses recherches archéologiques en Afghanistan (1933–1940)*, MDAFA VIII, Paris, pp. 107–113.

Meyer, K. and Brysac, S. (2001) *Tournament of Shadows. The Great Game and the Race for Empire in Asia*, London.

Migeon, G. (1927) *Manuel d'art musulman. Arts plastiques et industriels*, II, Paris.

Mill, W.H. (1834) 'Supplement to the historical remarks on the Allahabad inscription no. 2', *JASB* 3, pp. 339–44.

Mitchiner, M. (1975–6), *Indo-Greek and Indo-Scythian Coinage*, vol. 8. *The Indo-Parthians. Their Kushan Neighbours*, London.

Mitchiner, M. (1976) *Indo-Greek and Indo-Scythian Coins*, 9 vols, London.

Mitchiner, M. (1977) *Oriental Coins and their Values. 1. The World of Islam*, London.

Mitchiner, M. (1978) *Oriental Coins and their Values. 2. The Ancient and Classical World, 600 BC–AD 650*, London.

Mitchiner, M. (1979) *Oriental Coins and their Values. 3. Non-Islamic States & Western Colonies AD 600–1979*, London.

Moorey, P.R.S. (1971) *Catalogue of the Ancient Persian Bronzes in the Ashmolean Museum*, Oxford.

Moorey, P.R.S. (1974) *Ancient Persian Bronzes in the Adam Collection*, London.

Moorey, P.R.S. (1994) *Ancient Mesopotamian Materials and Industries: The Archaeological Evidence*, Oxford.

Morris, L. (2017) 'Revised dates for the deposition of the Begram hoard and occupation at the New Royal City', *Parthica* 19, pp. 75–104.

Mosanef, F. and Saffar, M.T. (2013) 'An Umayyad dirham of Tokharistan' *Journal of the Oriental Numismatic Society* 217, p. 8.

Murray, C. (2016) *Sikunder Burnes: Master of the Great Game*, Edinburgh 2016.

Musche, B. (1988) *Vorderasiatischer Schmuck zur Zeite der Arsakiden und der Sasaniden*, Leiden–Cologne.

Narain, A.K. (1957) *The Indo-Greeks*, Oxford.

Nasim Khan, M. (2001) 'Exploration and excavation of the earliest Śivaite monastic establishment at Kashmir Smast', *Ancient Pakistan* XIV, pp. 218–309.

Nasim Khan, M. (2006) *Treasures from Kashmir Smast (The Earliest Śaiva Monastic Establishment)*, Peshawar.

Nasim Khan, M., Errington, E. and Cribb, J. (2008) *Coins from Kashmir Smast. New Numismatic Evidence*, Peshawar.

Negmatov, N.N. (1979) 'Nekotorye i perspektivy arheologii severnogo Tadzhikistana v svjazi s sozdaniem gosudarstva. Kratkiye rezul'taty rabot 1974 g' [Some perspectives of archaeology of northern Tajikistan in connection with the emergence of the state. Brief results of work in 1974], *Arkheologicheskie raboty v Tadzhikistane* XIV *(1974 god)*, Dushanbe.

Nehru, L. (2004) 'A fresh look at the bone and ivory carvings from Begram', *Silk Road Art and Archaeology* 10, pp. 97–150.

Nerazik, E.E. (1976) *Sel'skoe zilishche v Khorezme (I–XIV vv)* [Rural dwellings in Khwarazm in the 1st–14th centuries], Moscow.

Nezafati, N and Pernicka, E. (2012) 'Early silver production in Iran', *Iranian Archaeology* 3, pp. 37–45.

Nicolini, G. (2001/4) 'Pendants d'oreille en or de la periode hellenistique tardive au Musée du Louvre', *Revue archeologique*, 31, pp. 3–35.

Norris, E. (1846) 'On the Kapur-di-Giri rock inscription', *JRAS* VIII, pp. 303–14.

Obel'chenko, O.V. (1961) 'Lyavandaksky molgilnik' [Lyavandasky barrow], *Istoria material'noy kul'tury Uzbekistana* [History of the Material Culture of Uzbekistan] 2, pp. 12, 157–9.

Obel'chenko, O.V. (1974) 'Kurgannye mogil'niki epokhi Kushan v Bukharskom oazise' [Kurgan barrows of the Kushan epoch in the Bukhara oasis] in *Central Asia in the Kushan Period*, vol. 1, Moscow.

Olivieri, L.M. (2018) 'Physiology and meaning of pottery deposits in urban contexts (Barikot, Swat): Archaeological field notes with an addendum on the lásana/λάσανα pottery forms', *Ancient Pakistan* XXIX, pp. 123–39.

Olivieri, L.M. et al. (2014) *The Last Phases of the Urban Site of Bir–kot–ghwandai (Barikot).The Buddhist Sites of Gumbat and Amluk–dara (Barikot)*, ACT Reports and Memoirs II, Lahore.

Olivier-Utard, F. (1997) *Politique et archéologie: histoire de la Délégation archéologique française en Afghanistan, 1922–1982*, Paris.

Ousley, W. (1800) *The Oriental Geography of Ebn Haukal, an Arabian Traveller of the Tenth Century*, London.

Paiman, Z. (2018) 'Le monastère de Qol-e-Tut à la lumière des fouilles archéologiques', *Afghanistan: The Journal of the American Institute of Afghanistan Studies* 1.1, pp. 95–121.

Paiman, Z. and Alram, M. (2013) *Tepe Narenj à Caboul, ou l'art bouddhique à Caboul au temps des incursions musulmanes*, Publications de l'institut de civilisation indienne fasc. 82, Paris.

Parpola, A. (1997) 'Seals of the greater Indus Valley', in D. Collon (ed.), *7000 Years of Seals*, London, pp. 51–3.

Petrie, C.A., Magee, P. and Nasim Khan, M. (2008) 'Emulation at the edge of empire: the adoption of non-local vessel forms in the NWFP, Pakistan during the mid-late 1st millennium BC', *Gandhāran Studies* 2, pp. 1–16.

Pfisterer, M. (2013) *Hunnen in Indien – Die Münzen der Kidariten und Alchan aus dem Bernischen Historischen Museum und der Sammlung Jean-Pierre Righetti*, Vienna.

Philostratus, *The Life of Apollonius of Tyana. The Epistles of Apollonius and the Treatise of Eusebius*, tr. F.C. Conybeare, 2 vols, London–New York 1912.

Pigou, R. (1841) 'On the topes of Darunta and caves of Bahrabad', *JASB* X.1, pp. 381–6.

Pirazzoli-t'Serstevens, M. (2001 [2003]) 'Les laques chinois de Begram. Un réexamen de leur identification et leur datation', *Topoi. Orient–Occident* 11/1, pp. 473–84.

Pollak, L. (1903) 'Goldschmiedarbeiten' in *Besitz Sr. Excellenz A.J. von Nelidow*, Leipzig.

Polybius, *Histories*, F. Hultsch, *The Histories of Polybius*, tr. E.S. Shuckburgh, London, 1889, www.archive.org.

Pope, A.U. and Ackerman, P. eds (1964–5) *A Survey of Persian Art, From Prehistoric Times to the Present*, 13 vols, 2nd ed., London.

Porter. V. (2011) *Arabic and Persian Seals and Amulets in the British Museum*, Research Publication 160, London.

Poster, A.G. (1986) *From Indian Earth: 4000 Years of Terracotta Art*, Brooklyn Museum exhibition, New York.

Pottier, M.-H. (1984) *Matériel funéraire de la Bactruane méridionalede l'Age du Bronze*, Paris.

Prinsep, H.T. (1844) *Historic Results from Bactrian Coins: Discoveries in Afghanistan*, London.

Prinsep, J. (1833a) 'On the Greek coins in the cabinet of the Asiatic Society', *JASB* II, pp. 27–41 (repr. Thomas 1858, vol. I, pp. 7–22).

Prinsep, J. (1833b) 'Note on Lieutenant Burnes' collection of ancient coins', *JASB* II, pp. 310–18, pl. VII (repr. Thomas 1858, vol. I, pp. 23–44, and as 'Mr. James Prinsep's notes', appendix to A. Burnes, *Travels into Bokhara*, 1834, vol. II, pp. 463–73).

Prinsep, J. (1833c) 'Bactrian and Indo-Scythic coins – continued', *JASB* II, pp. 405–16 (repr. Thomas 1858, vol. I, pp. 45–62).

Prinsep, J. (1835a) 'Further notes and drawings of Bactrian and Indo-Scythic coins', *JASB* IV, pp. 327–48, pls XIX–XXV (repr. Thomas 1858, vol. I, pp. 176–94, pls XIII–XVIII).

Prinsep, J. (1835b) 'On the connection of various ancient Hindu coins with the Grecian or Indo-Scythic series', *JASB* IV, pp. 621–43 (repr. Thomas 1858, vol. I, pp. 195–200, 224–31, 277–88).

Prinsep, J. (1836a) 'New varieties of Bactrian coins engraved as pl. XXXV, from Masson's drawings and other sources', *JASB* V, pp. 548–54 (repr. Thomas 1858, vol. I, pp. 352–9, pl. XXVIII).

Prinsep, J. (1836b) 'New varieties of the Mithraic or Indo-Scythic series of coins, and their imitations', *JASB* V, pp. 639–57 (repr. Thomas 1858, vol. I, pp. 360–96).

Prinsep, J. (1836c) 'New types of Bactrian and Indo-Scythic coins engraved as pl. XLIX', *JASB* V, pp. 720–4 (repr. Thomas 1858, vol. I, pp. 397–401, pl. XXXII).

Prinsep, J. (1837) 'Note on the facsimiles of inscriptions from Sanchí near Bhilsa, taken for the Society by Captain Ed. Smith, Engineers', *JASB* VI, pp. 451–77.

Prinsep J. (1838) 'Additions to Bactrian numismatics and discovery of the Bactrian alphabet', *JASB* VII, pp. 636–855 (repr. Thomas 1858, vol. II, pp. 125–44).

Prinsep, J. (MSS) 'James Prinsep Oriental Coins', 3 vols, Ashmolean Museum, Oxford, Hebenden Coin Room Archives, Arch. Ash. fol.18.

Proc. ASB (1836), Proceedings of the Asiatic Society, January, *JASB* V, p. 54.

Proc. ASB (1838) 'V. Coins and relics from Bactria', Proceedings of the Asiatic Society, December, *JASB* VII, pp. 1047–50.

Proc. ASB (1839a) Proceedings of the Asiatic Society, May, *JASB* VIII, p. 74.

Proc. ASB (1839b) 'Literary and antiquities', Proceedings of the . Asiatic Society, December, *JASB* VIII, p. 341.

Proc. ASB (1845) 'Report on Shahbazgarhi inscription from Royal Asiatic Society, London', Proceedings of the Asiatic Society, May no. IX, *JASB* XIV.I, pp. xxxix–liv.

Pugachenkova, G.A. (1978) *Les trésors de Dalverzine-Tépé*, Leningrad.

Pugachenkova, G.A. (1989) 'The terra-cotta horses of Bactria-

Tokharistan: semantics and image,' *Bulletin of the Asia Institute* 3, pp. 15–19.

Pugachenkova, G. and Rempel, L.I. (1991) 'Gold from Tillia-tepe', *Bulletin of the Asia Institute* 5, pp. 11–25.

Pugachenkova, G.A. and Rtveladze, E.V. eds (1978) *Dalverzintepe: Kushanskiy gorod na iuge Uzbekistana* [Dal'verzintepe: Kushan city in south Uzbekistan], Tashkent.

Pugachenkova, G.A., Takamatsu K. *et al.* (1991) *Drevnosti yuzhnogo Uzbekistana* [Antiquities of southern Uzbekistan], Tokyo.

Pumpelly, R. ed. (1908) *Explorations in Turkestan. Expedition of 1904*, Washington DC.

Raby, J. ed. (1993) *Ornament and Amulet: Rings of the Islamic Lands*, The Nasser D. Khalili Collection of Islamic Art XVI, London.

Rapin, C. (1992) *Fouilles d'Aï Khanoum VIII, La trésorerie du palais hellénistique d'Aï Khanoum. L'apogée et la chute du royaume grec de Bactriane*, MDAFA XXXIII, Paris.

Rapin, C. (2001) 'La tombe d'une princesse nomade à Koktepe près de Samarkand', *CRAI*, January–March, pp. 34–92.

Rapin, C. (2013) 'On the way to Roxane: the route of Alexander the Great in Bactria and Sogdiana (328–327 BC)', in G. Lindström, S. Hansen, A. Wieczorek, M. Tellenbach (eds), *Zwischen Ost und West. Neue Forschungen zum antiken Zentralasien*, Archäologie in Iran und Turan 14, Darmstadt, pp. 43–82.

Rapson, E.J. (1904) 'Ancient silver coins from Baluchistan', *Numismatic Chronicle* 4th ser. IV, pp. 311 – 25.

Rapson, E.J. (1905) 'Notes on Indian coins and seals, part VI', *JRAS*, pp. 783–814.

Reece, R. (2003) *Roman Coins and Archaeology: Collected Papers*, Wetteren.

Reeder, E. ed. (1999) *Scythian Gold: Treasures from Ancient Ukraine*, New York.

Rehman, A. (1979) *The Last Two Dynasties of the Śāhis – Analysis of the History, Archaeology, Coinage and Palaeography*, Islamabad.

Research Center for Silk Roadology ed. (1996) Kodai Horazumu no kenkyū. 'Amudariya karyūbu o chūshin to shite' [Research on ancient Khwarazm centring on the downstream part of the Amudarya], *Bulletin of the Research Center for Silk Roadology* 2, Nara.

Rhi, J. (2008) 'Changing Buddhism', in *Gandhara. The Buddhist Heritage of Pakistan. Legends, Monasteries, and Paradise*, Unesco exhibition, Bonn–Berlin–Zurich Nov. 2008 – Jan. 2010, Mainz 2008, pp. 242–8.

Rhodes, N.G, Gabrisch, K. and Valdettaro, C. (1989) *The Coinage of Nepal from the Earliest Times until 1911*, London.

Rhys Davids, T.W. (tr.) (1890–4) *The Questions of King Milinda* [*Milindapañha*], The Sacred Books of the East, F.M. Müller, vols 35–6, London–Oxford 1879–1900.

Riboud, K. (1983) 'Brief comments on the depiction of the simurgh', *National Museum Bulletin, New Delhi* 4–5, pp. 92–105.

Riha, E. (1990) *Das römischen Schmuck aus Augst und Kaiseraugst*. Augst, Römermuseum (Forschungen in Augst 10).

Rochette, R. (1835) 'Supplément à la notice sur quelques médailles greques inédites des rois de la Bactriane et de l'Inde', *Journal des Savants*, 1835, pp. 1–35.

Rosenfield, J.M. (1967) *The Dynastic Arts of the Kushans*, Berkeley–Los Angeles.

Rosen Stone, E. (2008) 'Some Begram ivories and the South Indian narrative tradition: New evidence', *Journal of Inner Asian Art and Archaeology* 3, pp. 45–59.

Rosu, A. (1969) 'L'oeuvre de Joseph Hackin, bibliographie', *Bulletin de l'Ecole française d'Extrême-Orient* 55, pp. 233–44.

Rowland, B. (1953) *The Art and Architecture of India*, London.

Rowland, B. (1974) *Asie Centrale*, Paris.

Rtveladze, E.V. (1983) 'Mogil'nik kushanskogo vremeni Yalangtush-tepe' [A Kushan burial ground at Yalangtush Tepe], *Sovetskaya Arkheologiya* 2, Moscow, pp. 125–43.

Rtveladze, E. (1993/4) 'Coins of the Yuezhi rulers of northern Bactria', *Silk Road Art and Archaeology* 3, pp. 81–96.

Ruseva-Slokoska, L. (1991) *Roman Jewellery. A Collection of the National Archaeological Museum, Sofia*, Sofia.

Rütti, B. (1998) 'Begram, 356 n. Chr', in F. Müller *et al.* (eds), *Mille Fiori. Festschrift für Ludwig Berger zu seinem 65. Geburtstag*, Augst, pp. 193–200.

Salomon, R. (1998) *Indian Epigraphy. A Guide to the Study of Inscriptions in Sanskrit, Prakrit, and the other Indo-Aryan Languages*, New York.

Salvatori, S. (1988) 'Early Bactrian objects in private collections', in G. Ligabue and S. Salvatori (eds) *Bactria. An Ancient Oasis from the Sands of Afghanistan*, Venice, pp. 181–7.

Sarianidi, V. (1985a) *Bactrian Gold from the Excavations of the Tillya-Tepe Necropolis in Northern Afghanistan*, Leningrad.

Sarianidi, V. (1985b) *The Golden Hoard of Bactria from the Tillya-Tepe Excavations in Northern Afghanistan*, New York.

Sarianidi, V. (1993) 'Excavations at southern Gonur', *Iran* XXXI, pp. 25–39.

Sarianidi, V. (2002) 'The palace and necropolis of Gonur', in G. Rossi-Osmida (ed.), *Margiana. Gonur Depe Necropolis. 10 Years of Excavations by Ligabue Study and Research Centre*, Florence, pp. 17–49.

Sax, M. and Meeks, N.D. (2011) 'Methods of engraving', in V. Porter, *Arabic and Persian Seals and Amulets in the British Museum*, Research Publication 160, London, pp. 185–8.

Scerrato, U. and Taddei, M. eds (1963) *Mostra di Monili dell'Asia dal Caspio all'Himalaya*, Palazzo Brancaccio, 10 April–10 May, Istituto Italiano per il Medio ed Estremo Oriente, Rome.

Schlegel, K.F. (1808) *Über die Sprache und Weisheit der Indier* [On the Language and Wisdom of India], Heidelberg.

Schindel, N. (2004) *Sylloge Nummorum Sasanidorum Paris–Berlin–Wien. III. Shapur II. – Kawad I./2. Regierung*, Vienna.

Schindel, N. (2010) 'The era of the Bactrian documents: a reassessment', *Gandharan Studies* 5, pp. 1–10.

Schlumberger, D. (1953) 'L'argent grec dans l'empire achéménide', in R. Curiel and D. Schlumberger, *Trésors monétaires d'Afghanistan*, Paris, pp. 1–64.

Schwarz, F. (1995) *Sylloge Nummorum Arabicorum. Tübingen. Gazna/Kabul XIV d Hurasan IV*, Tübingen.

Scythian, Persian and Central Asian Art from the Hermitage collection, Leningrad, Tokyo National Museum 6 April–1 June 1969, Tokyo.

Seipel, W. (1996) *Weirauch und Seide. Alte Kulturen an der Seidenstraße*, Vienna.

Sellwood, D. (1980) *An Introduction to the Coinage of Parthia*, London.

Senior, R. (1999) *The Coinage of Hermaios and its Imitations Struck by the Scythians*, CNG, London.

Senior, R. (2000) *A Catalogue of Indo-Scythian Coins. An Analysis of the Coinage*, 3 vols, Glastonbury.

Senior, R. (2001) *Indo-Scythian Coins and History*, 3 vols, London.

Senior, R. (2006) *Indo-Scythian Coins and History*, vol. 4, London.

Seyrig, H. (1953) 'Antiquités de la nécropole d'Emèse', *Syria* 29, pp. 204–50.

Shakur, M.A. (1947) *A Dash Through the Heart of Afghanistan, Being Personal Narrative of an Archaeological Tour with the Indian Cultural Mission*, Peshawar.

Sharma, R.C. (1976) *Mathura Museum and Art: A Comprehensive Pictorial Guide Book*, Mathura.

Sims-Williams, N. (2008) 'The Arab-Sasanian and Arab-Hephthalite coinage: a view from the East', *Cahiers de Studia Iranica* 39, pp. 115–30.

Sims-Williams, N. (2010) *Iranisches Personennamenbuch II. Iranische Personennamen, fasc. 7. Bactrische Personennamen*. Iranische Onomastik 7, Sitzungsberichte der Phil.-hist. Klasse der Österreichischen Akademie der Wissenschaften 806, Vienna.

Sims-Williams, N. (2012) *Bactrian Documents from Northern Afghanistan*, vol. I: *Legal and Ecomomic Documents* (rev. 2007 ed.), London.

Sims-Williams, N. and Cribb, J. (1995/6) 'A new Bactrian inscription of Kanishka the Great', *Silk Road Art and Archaeology* 4, pp. 75–142.

Sims-Williams, N. and de Blois, F. (2018) *Studies in the Chronology of the Bactrian Documents from Northern Afghanistan*, 1834, Vienna.

Sircar, D.C. (1966) *Indian Epigraphical Glossary*, Dehli.

Sivaramamurti, C. (1974) *L'art en Inde*, Paris.

SKM/IM 1880: South Kensington Museum (1880) *India Museum. Inventory of the Collection of Examples of Indian Art and Manufactures transferred to the South Kensington Museum*, Science and Art Department of the Committee of Council on Education, London.

Smith, D.S. (2000) 'Early Central Asian imitations I: the coinage of Eukratides I', *The Celator* 14.7, July, pp. 6–20.

Smith, D.S. (2001) 'Early Central Asian imitations III: coinage of Heliokles I and the Kushan connection', *The Celator* 15.11, November, pp. 6–16.

Smith, V.A. (1898) 'Numismatic notes and novelties, no. III', *JASB* LXVII.1, pp. 130–40, pl. XIV.

Smith, V.A. (1906) *Coins of Ancient India: Catalogue of the Coins in the Indian Museum Calcutta*, Calcutta.

Sotheby, Wilkinson and Hodge (1887) *Catalogue of ... Indo-Scythic, Hindu and Indian Coins, sold on behalf of the Government of India*, 6 August, pp. 54–62.

Stein, M.A. (1907) *Ancient Khotan. Detailed Report of Archaeological Explorations in Chinese Turkestan*, 2 vols, Oxford.

Stein, M.A. (1921) *Serindia. Detailed Report of Explorations in Central Asia and Westernmost China*, 5 vols, Oxford (repr. Delhi 1980, 4 vols).

Stein, M.A. (1928) *Innermost Asia. Detailed Report of Exploration in Central Asia, Kan-Su and Eastern Iran*, 4 vols. Oxford. (repr. New Delhi 1981).

Stein, M.A. (1929) 'An archaeological tour in Waziristan and Northern Baluchistan', *Memoirs of the Archaeological Survey of India* 37, Calcutta, pp. 46–9.

Stein, M.A. (1938) 'An Archaeological Journey in Western Iran', *Geographical Journal* 92, pp. 331–2.

Stephanus Byzantinus, *Stephanos Peri Poleön; Stephanus de Urbibus*, Jonge (pub.) 1678.

Strabo, *Geographia*, books XI, XV, tr. H.L. Jones, *The Geography of Strabo* V, ed. G.P. Gould, Loeb Classical Library 8 vols, London–Cambridge, Mass. 1968 (5th repr.).

Taddei, M. (1999) 'Chronological problems with Buddhist unbaked-clay sculpture from Afghanistan and surrounding areas', in M. Alram and D. Klimburg-Salter (eds), *Coins Art and Chronology: Essays on the pre-Islamic History of the Indo–Iranian Borderlands*, Vienna, pp. 391–7.

Taj Ali (2001) 'Archaeological survey of District Mardan in the North-West Frontier Province of Pakistan,' *Ancient Pakistan* XIV, pp. 55–172.

Tanabe, K. (1986) 'Sculptures of Palmyra', *Memoirs of the Ancient Orient Museum* I, Tokyo.

Tanabe, K. ed. (2000) *Gandhara and Silk Road Arts: The Hirayama Ikuo Collection*, Tokyo.

Tanabe, K. (2008) *Gandharan Art from the Hirayama Collection*, Kodansha.

Tarn, W.W. (1938) *The Greeks in Bactria & India*, Cambridge (2nd ed. 1951; 3rd ed. Chicago, 1997).

Tarzi, Z. (1977) *L'architecture et le décor rupestre des grottes de Bamiyan*, 2 vols, Paris.

Thapar, R. (1997) *Aśoka and the Decline of the Mauryas*, Delhi (rev. ed.).

Thomas, E. (1847) 'On the coins of the kings of Ghazni', *JRAS*, pp. 267–387.

Thomas, E. (1849) 'The Pehlví coins of the early Mohammedan Arabs', *JRAS* 12, pp. 253–347.

Thomas, E. ed. (1858) *Essays on Indian Antiquities, Historic, Numismatic, and Palaeographic, of the late James Prinsep, F.R.S. Secretary to the Asiatic Society of Bengal*, 2 vols, London.

Tissot, F. (1985) *Gandhâra*, Paris.

Tissot, F. (2006) *Catalogue of the National Museum of Afghanistan 1931–1985*, Unesco Paris.

Tod, J. (1826) 'An account of Greek, Parthian, and Hindu medals found in India', *Transactions of the Royal Asiatic Society of Great Britain and Ireland* I.2, pp. 313–42.

Tod, J. (1829) 'On the religious establishments of Mewar', *Transactions of the Royal Asiatic Society of Great Britain and Ireland* II.1, pp. 270–325.

Toll, N.P. (1946) 'The Necropolis', in M.I. Rostovtzeff et al. (eds), *The Excavations at Dura-Europos conducted by Yale University and the French Academy of Inscriptions and Letters. Preliminary Report of the Ninth Season of Work 1935–1936*, part II, New Haven–London.

Tolstov, S.P. (1953) *Auf den Spuren der Altchoresmischen Kultur*, Berlin.

Torrens, H. (1840) 'Note on Kandahar gems', *JASB* IX, pp. 100–6.

Torrens, H. (1842) 'Note on Kandahar gems', *JASB* XI, pp. 137–48, pls 1–3.

Tosi, M. (1988) 'The origin of early Bactrian civilization', in G. Ligabue and S. Salvatori (eds), *Bactria. An Ancient Oasis from the Sands of Afghanistan*, Venice, pp. 109–23.

Treasures of Ancient Bactria (2002) Miho Museum Exhibition Catalogue 20 July–18 August; 1 September–15 December, Kyoto.

Trever, K.V. and Lukonin, V.G. (1987) *Sasanidskoe serebo. Khudozhestvennaya kul'tura Irana III–VIII vekov. Sobranie Gosudarstvennogo Ermitazha* [Sasanian silver. Artistic culture of Iran in the 3rd to the 8th centuries. Collection of the State Hermitage], Moscow.

Turner, P.J. (1989) *Roman Coins from India*, London.

Tye, R. and M. (1995) *Jitals. A Catalogue and Account of the Coin Denomination of Daily Use in Medieval Afghanistan and North West India*, South Uist.

Valentine, W.H. (1911) *Modern Copper Coins of the Muhammadan States of Turkey, Persia, Egypt, Afghanistan, Morocco, Tripoli, Tunis, etc.*, London.

Van den Berghe, L. (1964) *La nécropole de Khurvin*, Istanbul.

Van den Berghe, L. (1967) 'La nécropole de War Kabud ou le déclin d'une civilisation du bronze', *Archeologia* 18, Oct., pp. 49–61.

Van den Berghe, L. (1968) 'La nécropole de Bani Surmah. Aurore d'une civilisation de bronze', *Archeologia* 24, Sept.–Oct., pp. 53–63.

Van den Berghe, L. (1970a) 'La nécropole de Kalleh Nisar', *Archeologia* 32, Jan.–Feb., pp. 65–73.

Van den Berghe, L. (1970b) 'Luristan. Prospections archéologiques dans la région de Badr', *Archeologia* 36, Sept.–Oct., pp.10–21.

Van den Berghe, L. (1973a) 'Le Luristan à l'Age du Bronze. Prospections archéologiques dans le Pusht-i Kuh central', *Archaeologia* 63, Oct., pp. 25–36.

Van den Berghe, L. (1973b) 'Le Luristan à l'âge du fer. La nécropole de Kutal-I-Gugul', *Archeologia* 65, Dec., pp. 17–29.

Vats, M.S. (1940) *Excavations at Harappa*, Calcutta.

Vishnevskaia, O.A. (1963) 'Archeologitseskie razvedki na

srednevekovykh poseleniyakh levoberezhnogo Khorezma' [Archaeological surveys of the Medieval settlements of the left-bank Khwarazm], in S.P. Tolstov (ed.), *Materiale Khorezmskoi ekspeditsii*, tom. 7. *Polevye issledovaniya Khorezmskoy ekspeditsii v 1958–61 gg.'* vyp. II. Pamyatniki srednevekovogo vremeni. Etnografitseckie rabote [Materials of the Khwarazm Expedition 7. Field research of the Khwarazm expedition in 1958–61, issue II. Monuments of the Medieval period. Ethnographic reseach], Moscow, pp. 54–72.

Vitkevich, I.V. (1983) 'Zapiska, sostavlennaya po 3 rasskazam Orenburgskogo Lineinoga Batal'ona No. 10 Praporshchika Vitkevicha otnositel'no puti ego v Bukharu i obratno' [A note compiled from the stories told by Vitkevich, ensign in the 10th Orenburg Manoeuvre Battalion, of his journey to Bukhara and back], in N.A. Khalfin (ed.), *Zapiski o Bukharskom Khanstve* [Notes on the Bukharan Khanate], Moscow.

Vogel, J.P. (1930) 'La sculpture de Mathurâ', *Ars Asiatica* XV, Paris–Brussels.

Vondrovec, K. (2010) 'Coinage of the Nezak', in M. Alram, D. Klimburg-Salter, M. Inaba and M. Pfisterer (eds), *Coins, Art and Chronology II. The First Millennium C.E. in the Indo-Iranian Borderlands*, Vienna, pp. 169–90.

Vondrovec, K. (2014) *Coinage of the Iranian Huns and their Successors from Bactria to Gandhara (4th to 8th century CE)*, 2 vols, ed. M. Alram and J. Lerner, Vienna.

Waldbaum, J.C. (1983) *Metalwork from Sardis. The Finds through 1974*, Harvard.

Waleed Ziad (2006) 'The Treasures of Kashmir Smast', *Journal of the Oriental Numismatic Society* 187 (Spring), pp. 14–33.

Walker, J. (1941) *British Museum. A catalogue of the Arab-Sassanian Coins (Umaiyad governors in the East, Arab-Ephthalites, 'Abbasid governors in Tabaristan and Bukhara)*, vol. 1, London.

Walker, S. and Higgs, P. (2001) *Cleopatra of Egypt: from History to Myth*, London.

Walsh, E.H.C. (1939) *Punch-Marked Coins from Taxila*, Delhi.

Walters, H.B. (1926) *Catalogue of Engraved Gems, Greek, Etruscan and Roman in the British Museum*, London.

Whitcomb, D.S. (1985) *Before the Roses and Nightingales: Excavations at Qasr-i Abu Nasr, Old Shiraz*, Metropolitan Museum of Art, New York.

Whitehead, R.B. (1947) 'Notes on Indo-Greeks', *Numismatic Chronicle*, pp. 92–115.

Whitehead, R.B. (1950) 'Notes on the Indo-Greeks. Part III', *Numismatic Chronicle* 6th ser. 10, pp. 205–32.

Whitehouse, D. (1989) 'Begram, the Periplus and Gandharan art', *Journal of Roman Archaeology* 2, pp. 93–100.

Whitehouse, D. (2001 [2003]) 'Begram: the glass', *Topoi. Orient–Occident* 11/1, pp. 437–49.

Whitteridge, G. (1986) *Charles Masson of Afghanistan. Explorer, Archaeologist, Numismatist and Intelligence Agent*, Warminster.

Wilber, D.N. http://rugreview.com/orr/11-5-34.htm 'Luristan bronzes'.

Wilson, E. (1998) *British Museum Pattern Books. Islamic Designs*, London.

Wilson, H.H. (1832) 'Description of select coins, from originals or drawings in the possession of the Asiatic Society', *Asiatick Resarches* XVII, pp. 559–606.

Wilson, H.H. (1841) *Ariana Antiqua. A Descriptive Account of the Antiquities and Coins of Afghanistan: with a Memoir on the Buildings called Topes, by C. Masson, Esq.*, London (repr. Delhi 1997).

Wilson, H.H. (1850) 'On the rock inscriptions of Kapur di Giri, Dhauli and Girnar', *JRAS* XII, pp. 153–251.

Wingham, A. (1896) 'Analysis of specimens of oriental metal-work', *Journal of Indian Art and Industry* VI, pp. 85–8.

Wroth, W. (1903) *British Museum. Catalogue of the Coins of Parthia*, London.

Wypyski, M.T. (1992), 'Technical analysis of Gandhara glass medallions', in E. Errington and J. Cribb (eds), *The Crossroads of Asia. Transformation in Image and Symbol in the Art of Ancient Afghanistan and Pakistan*, Cambridge, pp. 281–3.

Xenophon, *Hellenica*, vol. I, books 1–4, *Xenophon in Seven Volumes*, tr. C.L. Brownson, Loeb Classical Library, London, Cambridge MA, 1918 (www.perseus.tufts.edu).

Yapp, M.E. (1980) *Strategies of British India. Britain, Iran and Afghanistan 1798–1850*, Oxford.

Yazdī, 'Ali (Sharaf al-Din) *Zafarnāmah*, ed. A. Urunbaev, Tashkent 1972.

Yu Taishan (2014) *A Concise Commentary on Memoirs on the Western Regions in the Official Histories of the Western and Eastern Han, Wei, Jin and Southern and Northern Dynasties*, Beijing.

Zadneprovsky, Y.A. (1975), 'Raskopki Katakombnogo Mogil'nika Ush-At v Yuzhnoi Kirgizii v 1973 g' [Excavations of the Ush-At catacomb cemetery in 1973], *Uspechi srednea ziatskoi archeologii vupusk I* [Successes of Central Asian Archaeology issue 1], Leningrad, pp. 53–5.

Zambaur, E. de (1927) *Manuel de généalogie et de chronologie*, Hannover.

Zeimal, E.V. ed. (1985) *Drevnosti Tadzhistana. Katalog vistavki, Izdatel'stvo Donish* [Tajikistan Antiquities Exhibition Catalogue, Donish Publishing House], Dushanbe.

Zeimal, E.V. (1994) 'The circulation of coins in Central Asia during the early Medieval period (fifth to eighth centuries AD)', *Bulletin of the Asia Institute* 8, pp. 245–67.

Zeimal, E. (1999) 'Tillya-Tepe within the context of Kushan chronology', in M. Alram and D. Klimburg-Salter (eds), *Coins Art and Chronology: Essays on the pre-Islamic History of the Indo–Iranian Borderlands*, Vienna, pp. 230–44.

Zhang, L. (2011) 'Chinese lacquerwares from Begram: date and provenance', *International Journal of Asian Studies* 8, pp. 1–24.

Zwalf, W. (1996) *A Catalogue of Gandhāra Sculpture in the British Museum*, 2 vols, London.

Websites

http://romanlocks.com/Keys. Section Warded Ring Keys, Images.

http://www.ancientresource.com/lots/ancient_jewelry/jewelry_rings.htm: seen 27/9/2019.

Contributors

Elizabeth Errington, leader of the Masson Project and former Curator of pre-Islamic coins of South and Central Asia, British Museum, is an authority on 19th-century archaeological records of Buddhist and related sites in Gandhara and Afghanistan.

Joe Cribb, former Keeper of Coins and Medals, British Museum, Adjunct Professor, Hebei Normal University, Honorary Research Associate, Heberden Coin Room, Ashmolean Museum and a Trustee of the Ancient India and Iran Trust, is an expert on Asian currencies, specialising in the coinages of ancient Afghanistan and Pakistan.

Lauren Morris, currently a postdoctoral researcher at the BaSaR 'Beyond the Silk Road' project (ERC-AdG) at Albert-Ludwigs-Universität Freiburg. She defended her PhD dissertation, 'The Begram Hoard and its Context' at Ludwig-Maximilians-Universität Munich in 2017, and is currently preparing it for publication.

Piers Baker, Masson Project researcher, currently an independent scholar and a Trustee of the Corpus Inscriptionum Iranicarum. He was a Research Fellow at the British Institute for Afghan Studies in Kabul in the late 1970s, subsequently completing a PhD on the history and archaeology of the Bamiyan valley, with a particular focus on Shahr-I Zohak.

Paramdip Khera, former Masson Project researcher, Curator of Islamic Coins and of the Islamic coins at the British Museum Project. She is currently Project Officer for the Two Centuries of Indian Print Project at the British Library. Her area of expertise and interest includes Islamic, Indo-Islamic and Sikh coins.

Chantal Fabrègues, independent scholar and Masson Project researcher. She is an authority on the jewellery and ornaments of ancient Gandhara and Afghanistan and is currently preparing a comprehensive study of the subject for publication.

Kirstin Leighton-Boyce, Masson Project researcher, former Museum Assistant, Department of Coins and Medals, and Curator of the Money Gallery, British Museum. Her wide-ranging interests include the ancient artefacts of Afghanistan. She is now an art therapist.

Wannaporn Kay Rienjang, Masson Project researcher, currently Lecturer in Archaeology, Thammasat University, Bangkok, and Assistant of the Gandhara Connections Project at the Classical Art Research Centre, Oxford. Her research focuses on the art and archaeology of ancient Afghanistan and Pakistan and Indian Ocean Trade.

Index

Index notes: page locators in *italic* refer to Figures, Plates and Tables

'Abbasid (AH 132–923 / AD 749–1258)
  coins catalogued, 113, 200, *201*, 210
  inscribed gem, *223*, 224
  by name of issue *see* al-Manṣūr
'Abd Allāh (*c.* 10th century), 201, *201*
'Abd al-Rashīd (AH 440–3 / AD 1049–52), *203*, 204
Abdagases (*c.* AD 52–70)
  coins catalogued, *151*, 152
  DAFA finds, *32–3*
  historical context, 89, *93*, 99, 102–3
'Abdallāh b. Khāzim (*c.* AH 64–73 / AD 684–92), *122–4*, *126*, 193, *194*
Abrashahr mint, 111, *111*, *119*, 121, 122, *122*, 193
Achaemenid
  bent bars, 88, 93, 98
  coins, *117*, 118, 129
  gemstone intaglios, 212, 213, *214*
'Adelphortus' *see* Spalagadama
aegis, 138–40
Afghanistan anonymous/unattributed civic coinage, *209*, 210
Agathocles (*c.* 190–180 BC), 47, 71, 74, 322
  coins, 41, *42*, 43, 45, *133*, 134
  historical context, 85, 87, 88, 95–6
  mint, 94
Ahmad b. Sahl (AH 303–8 / AD 915–20), 113
Ahmad b. Yusuf (AH 333–48 / AD 945–59), 116
al-Manṣūr (AH 136–7 / AD 754–5), 200, *201*
Alexander the Great (336–323 BC), 82–3, 93, 94, 118
  post-Alexander coins, 88, 93, 132, *133*
Alexandria ad Caucasum *see* Begram
Alkhan coins, 31, 64–8, *79–80*, *107*, 107–8, *117*, 183–8, *184*, *187*, 243, 313, 324
  by names of issue *see* Toramana I; Toramana II; Mihirakula; Narendra; *see also* Hun coins
  Kashmir Smast, 243
Alkhan seals, 212, 218, 220, 228, 230
  tamgha, 218, 284
Alptekin (AD 954–66), 113
'Ala al-dīn Muḥammād b. Tekish, *see* Muḥammād b. Tekish
'Amr b. al-Layth (AH 265–88 / AD 879–901), 200, *201*
Amirs of Sind (AH 256–399 / AD 870–1009), 201–2
  by names of issue *see* 'Abd Allāh, Da'ud; 'Umar b. al-'Ala
amulets, 224, *225*
animal motifs
  boar head, 39, 141
  buffalo head, 186
  bull
    coins, 109, *109*, 139, 154, 161, 177–8, 179, 182, 183, 196–7, 204–7, 208
    ornamental items, 280, 286, 310, 323
    seals and intaglios, 213, *216*, 217, 218, *219*, 225
    see also zebu
  camel, 55, 146, 154, 161
    bull-camel coin type, 103, 104, *160*
  deer, 46, 208
  dog, 266, 284, 288

dragon, 222, 227, 228, 237, 241, 243, 279
elephant
    goad, 140, 163, 170, 171, 173
    rider, 61, *72*, 173, 228, 265, *338*
frog, 280, *281*
goat, 163, 227
griffin, 213, *214*
hare, 225, 243, 265–6, 276, 288
    as 'horned quadruped', 228
horse
    Buraq, Islamic equivalent, 244
    horse rider, 156–7, 159
    Pegasus, *216*, 218
    walking horse, 213, *214*
    winged horse, *216*, 218
ibex, 215, *216*, 217, 225, 227, 230
lion
    finger rings, 236, *236*, 237, 238, *238*
    lion surmounting a column, 236, *236*, 237
    seals and intaglios, 213, *214*, *216*, 217
lion-skin, 141, 145, 154, 156, 235
panther, 41, *95*, 134
running feline, 277, *277*
stag seated, *216*, 217
wolf, *265*, 266
zebu, 131, 135, 142, 145, 146, 148, 149, 186
see also bull
Antialcidas (*c.* 115–95 BC)
    coins catalogued, *141*, 141–2
    coins, gold and silver, 91, *92*, 331
    DAFA finds, *32–3*
    historical context, 88, *93*, 97, *100*
    Masson's analysis, 40, 41–3, 72, 75
    Mir Zakah finds, 98, *100*
Antimachus I (*c.* 180–170 BC), 69, 91, *95*, *95*, *96*, *133*, 134
Antimachus II (*c.* 160–155 BC), 98
    coins catalogued, *133*, 134, *136*, 137–8
    dispersal, 128
    historical context, 88, 91, *95*, *96*, *96*
    Masson's analysis, *54*, 55
antimony rods, 257–8, *258*
Antiochus III Megas (223–187 BC), *36*, *37*, 72, 74, 80, 87, 88, 94, 132, 320
Apollodotus I (*c.* 180–160 BC), *36*, *37*, 39, 40, 41, 53, 55, 128
    coins catalogued, *133*, 135–7
    DAFA finds, *32–3*
    monograms and tamghas, *69*
Apollodotus II (*c.* 80–65 BC), 37, *144*, 145
    copper coin imitation, 102
Apraca stratega *see* Aspavarma, 149, *149*
Aq-Qoyunlu (Turkmen of the White Sheep 1378–1508), 208, *209*
Arab governors *see* 'Abdallāh b. Khāzim; Ahmad b. Sahl; Muṣ'ab b. al-Zubayr; Salm b. Ziyād; Tamim b. Zayd al-Qayni; 'Ubaydallāh b. Ziyād; 'Umar b. 'Ubaydallāh; *see also* Arab-Sasanian coins
Arab-Hephthalite/Arab-Bactrian coins, 110
Arabic inscriptions
    coins, 275, *275*
        pseudo-Arabic, 249–52

seals and intaglios, 220–5
    pseudo-Arabic, 213, 225
Arab-Sasanian coins
    coins catalogued, 127, 191–3, 200
    hoard of Sasanian, Arab-Sasanian and Ghar silver drachms, *119–26*
    imitations i.n.o. Khusrau II, 191, *192*, 196
    Masson's analysis, 110
Archebius (*c.* 90–80 BC)
    coins from Mir Zakah, 98
    silver coins, 51, *52*, 97, 143, 321
Ardashir I (AD 223–40), *106*, 180, *181*
Ardashir II (AD 379–83), *106*, 107
Ariana Antiqua, Masson's annotations, 306–7
    to Wilson's Preface, 307–8
    to Chapter I: Account of the Progress of Bactro-Indian Numismatic and Antiquarian Discovery, and Observations on the Edifices, called Topes, 308–10
    to Chapter II: Masson's Memoir on the Topes and Sepulchral Buildings of Afghanistan, 310–13
    to Chapter III: Ancient Notices of Ariana, 313–19
    to Chapter IV: Of the Sovereign Dynasties of Bactria and the Coterminous Countries, 320–5
    to Plates, 311, 326–8
arrowheads, 298, *299*
Arslan Shah (AH 509–10 / AD 1116–17), *203*, 204
Artabanus II (*c.* AD 10–38), 237
Ashmolean collection, 124–6
Ashoka (*c.* 269–232 BC), 236
Asiatic Society of Bengal, 11, 13, 15, 17
    see also Journal of the Asiatic Society of Bengal
Aspavarma (*c.* AD 33–64), 76, 89, 102, 149, *149*
astrogalus (gaming piece?), 300, *301*
Azes dynasty, 55, 57, 85–6, 102
    monograms, 47–9, *48*
Azes I (*c.* 46–1 BC), 53
    coins catalogued, *145*, 146
    coins from Mir Zakah, *99*
    era, 80
    historical context, 47, 49, 53, *76*, 80, 86, 97, 102, 104, 323
    imitations, 90, 102
        DAFA finds, *32–3*
    Masson's analysis, *48*, *54*, 55
Azes II (*c.* AD 16–30)
    coins catalogued, 146–8
    coins from Mir Zakah, *99*
    historical context, 49, 97, 326
    imitations, 83, 102, 104
    IOLC examples, 90
    Masson's analysis, *48*, 53, *54*, 55, 57
Azilises (*c.* 1 BC–AD 16), 55, *76*, 86, 102, *145*, 146

Bactria Yuezhi coins, 153, *153*
Bactrian coinage, *88*
    historical context, 106–7
    see also Bactrian inscriptions
Bactrian documents, 110, *112*, 112–13
Bactrian dynasty (*Ariana Antiqua*), 313, 314, 318–25
Bactrian era, 108, 110, *111*
Bactrian inscriptions

alphabet, 18–19
coins, 163, *164*, 165, 180–6, 193, 196
non-coin artefacts, 217, *219*, 220, 238
see also Bactrian coinage
Bactrian language, 18–19
Bactrian monograms, 69–70
Badr al-dīn Lu'lu' (AH 631–57 / AD 1234–59), *209*, 210
Baghdad mint, 113, 200
Baha' al-dīn Sām (AH 588–602 / AD 1192–1206), *206*, 207
Bahram Shah (AH 511–45 / AD 1117–50; AH 547–52 / AD 1152–7), *203*, 204–5
Baker, Piers, 35, 354
Balkategin (AH 355–62 / AD 966–73), 113
Bamiyan, 284
    coins, 208
        anonymous, *206*, 207
        Ghurid, 116, *206*
bangles, 285–6, *287*
    fragments, 286, *288*, 288–9
Barabad, 312
Barakzai unregulated civic coinage, *209*, 210
Barthoux, Jules (1881–1965), 7, 21
Baṣra mint, *111*, 120–1, *125*
battle-axe, 53, 146, 161
beads and spacers, 270, *270*
beads with radiating spikes, 271, *271*
Bean, Captain J.D.D., 5
Begram
    ancient name (Kapisa), *10*, *332*, *333*
    Burj Abdullah (citadel), *v*, *8*, 8–9, 20, 26, 29, 31, *33*
    coin enumerations see coin enumerations
    DAFA excavations see Délégation archéologique française en Afghanistan
    maps and aerial views, *6*, *7*, *8*
    Masson's discovery (July 1833), 5–9
        coin descriptions, 9–10
        identification as Alexandria ad Causcasum, 10, 17–18, 92–3
        non-coin finds, *10*, *332*, *333*
        reigning princes (195 BC–AD 50), *47*
    see also Begram monetary history; Masson collection history
Begram mint, 96, 97, 168, *169*, 170
    coins possibly attributed to, *172*, *174*
Begram monetary history, through Masson's archive and collection, 86
    coins following Saffarid conquest, 113–16
    data, 92–118
        Alkhan Hun and Turkic coins, *107*
        coins in use at Genghis Khan invasion, *117*
        early Indo-Greek copper coin comparisons, *96*
        finds according to Masson's three reports, *87–90*
        Kabul Shahi coins, *109*
        Kushano-Sasanian, Sasanian, Kidarite copper coins, *106*
        later Indo-Greek copper coin comparisons, *100*
        silver coins, use according to Bactrian documents, *112*
        stages in development of early Indo-Greek coins, *95*
    see also Begram
    gold and silver coins, 91
    miscellaneous coins, 116–17
    peaks of coin survival, 117–18
    periods
        Achaemenid, 93
        Bactrian and Indo-Greek, 94–7
        Hindu Shahi, 109
        Hun, Alkhan, Nezak, 107–9, 183
        Indo-Parthian and Parthian, 102–3
        Indo-Scythian, 100–102
        Islamic, 109–10, 112–13
        Kushan, 103–6
        Kushano-Sasanian and Kidarite, 106–7
        post-Alexander, 93
        post-Mauryan, 93–4
        Turkic Kabul Shahi, 107–9, 183
        Ya'qub b. al-Layth's conquest to Mongol invasion, 113, 116
    see also Begram
bells, 273, *273*
belt fittings, 289–92
    palmette, 283, 290, 291
Berre, Marc Le see Le Berre, Marc
Bēsut (c. AD 695–9), *111*, 112
Bibliothèque Nationale, Paris, 218
Bimaran
    (Stupa 2), 18, 148, 235, 307, 312, 323
    (Stupa 3), 47, 49, 148, 150
    (Stupa 4), 312
    (Stupa 5), 46, 49, 51, 148, 150, 323
bird motifs
    birds, 277
        bird buttons, 281–3
        ornamental, 295, *296*
    cockerel, 241, *242*, 257
    finials, 258, *258*, 260
    duck, 236, 260, 261, 263
    eagle, 43, 58, 215, 233, *337*
    goose, 208, 244, 261
        haṃsa, 238, 284
        or 'Sasanian duck,' 284, *285*
    hair- or dress-pins, 255, *256*
    mythical *senmurv*, 284
    naturalistic pin finials, 261–3, *262*
    owl, 132, 140
    parrot, 228, 263
    peacock, 131, 228, *231*, 277, 284, 324, *338*
        phial stoppers, *264*, 264–5
        pin finials, 260–1, *262*
    pheasant, 265
    raven, 262
    stylised bird (possibly hoopoe), 257, *257*
Bīshāpūr mint, *111*, *119*, *120*, *123–4*, *126*, 191, 193
bodkin, 301, *301*
boot charm, 273, *273*
bosses, 263, 283, 292, 297, 299, *338*
bracteates and pierced ornaments, 284–5
Brahmanical classification, 9, 63, 72, *73*, *78*, 80, 82–3, 196, 323
Brahmi inscriptions, 18, 41, 55, 68
    coins, 95, 108, 131, 134, 149, 183, 186, 188, 196, 198

Index | 357

Hadda Stupa 10 coins, *67–8*
    non-coin artefacts, 241, 284
brass-washed items, 225, 227–8, *229*, 235, 236, 237, 238, 239–44, 255, *255*, 263, 280, 283, 301
British Library, 3, 303
    India Office Collections, 13, 17, 90
    Masson Manuscript *see* Masson Manuscript F526/1a
British Museum, 17
    coin acquisitions (1838 and 1845), 15
        registration numbers, *336–9*
        tabulation of IOLC donation, *106*
    copper alloy object and coin fragments, *14*
    correspondence of coins illustrated in Masson's analysis of the Begram coins, *74–80*
    IOLC *see* India Office Loan Collection
Brownlow, Charles, 3–4
buckles and strap fittings, 289, *290*
Buddha depictions, 310
    coins, 23, 58, 105, 165, *166*, *167*, 168, 326, 339
    ornamental items, 227, *227*, 230, *231*, 236, 284
Buddhist coin deposits, 16
Buddhist reliefs, 27
Bukhara, 4, 309
    mint, 113, 209
Burj Abdullah, *v*, *8*, 8–9, 20, 26, 29, 31, *33*, *see also* Begram
Burnes, Alexander (1805–41), 5, 11, 84, 110, 309, 310, 315, 316, 320
Butkara, 235
    Stupa I, 112, 256
buttons, 283–4, *284*
    bird buttons, 281–3
Byzantine coins, 331
Byzantine ornamental items, 241, 248, 255, 289

Calliope, 143
Cambridge Museum of Archaeology and Anthropology (CMAA), 17, *see also* Ridgeway collection
Carl, Jean, 21–2, 24–5
cameos, 211, *214*, 224–5, *225*
carnelian artefacts
    gems *see* gems (*c.* 4th century BC–6th century AD)
    intaglio, 224, *225*
    ring, 249, *249*
Chach satrap *see* Zeionises
Chahamana dynasty (7th–12th century), 117, 198, *199*
Chahar Bagh Stupa 4, 161
chains, 300, *300*
chair back *in situ*, Begram, *25*
Charikar, 6, 9, *10*, 39, 40, 55, 57, 103, 128, 135, 139, 161
charms, 273, *273*, *338*
Chaulukya dynasty (*c.* AD 543–753), 198
    see Gadhaiya paisa
Chinese coins, 116–17, 198, *199*
Chinese mirror fragment, *301*, 301–2
coin enumerations, DAFA excavation, *32–3*, *93*
coin enumerations, Masson's collection
    Alkhan Hun and Turkic coins, *107*
    Begram finds according to Masson's three reports, *87–8*
    breakdown of coin quantities from Begram by century, *117*

coins collected from Begram, years 1833, 1834 and 1835, *72–3*
comparison coins from the India Office Loan Collection, *88–90*
comparison of early Indo-Greek copper coins, *96*
correspondence of coins illustrated in Masson's analysis, *74–80*
EIC receipt of Masson's collections (F526/1m), *329–30*
gold and silver coins
    from Begram (1837 and 1838), *92*
    Masson archival records of, *92*
    Sasanian, Arab-Sasanian and Ghar silver drachms, *119–26*
    use of silver coins according to the Bactrian documents, *112*
Kabul hoard, distribution by mint and date, *111*
Kabul Shahi coins, *109*
Kushano-Sasanian and Kushano-Sasanian style Kidarite copper coins, *106*
Masson's summary list of collections (1833–8) F526/1n, *331–3*
Masson's recorded quantities, collected 1833–8, *10*
    silver and copper coins (1833–8), *12*
    summary of the range of coins, *118*
    weighed coins in Boxes I and II, *12*
    see also Masson Manuscript (F526/1m), *329–30*
coin enumerations, Mir Zakah, *98–9*, *100*
coins by name *see* individual names of issue
coins by period *see* individual dynastic periods
coins, anonymous
    Bamiyan (13th century), 207
    i.n.o. Muḥammād b. Sām, 206–7
    imitations i.n.o. Hermaeus, 143, *144*, 145
    attributed to Toramana II, 186, *187*
    unregulated civic coinage, 208, *209*, 210
coins, Masson's analysis *see* Masson Manuscript F526/1a and individual names of issue
coins, miscellaneous, 116–17, 198
conch shell, 185, 188, 226
control marks, 178–9, *180*, 196, 197
cornucopia motif, 142, 148, 149, 159, 173, 178, 180, 183, 185, 215, 242
countermarked coins, 15, 103, 110, 112–13, *119–26*, 191, *192*, 196, 208, *209*
counters or tallies, *301*, 302
Court, Claude-Auguste (1793–1880), 4, 82, 310, 314, 315, 323
Cribb, Joe, 81, 127, 354
Cunningham, Alexander (1814–93), 16, 19, 58, 94, 104
    articles in *Numismatic Chronicle*, 85–6
    collection, 110, *119*, *121*, *123*, *124*, 127
Cupid (Eros), 212, 215, 217, 239

DAFA *see* Délégation archéologique française en Afghanistan
Da Yuezhi *see* Yuezhi
Da'ud (*c.* 10th century), 201, *201*
Dal'verzin Tepe, 29, 245, 256, 266, 286
Darābjird mint, *111*, *119*, *120*, *125*, *126*
Darunta stupas, 50, *51*, 102, 103, 148, 156, 307, 326
Dasht Maysān mint, *111*, *121*

decorative fittings, 292–3, *293*
    heart-shaped, 293
    miscellaneous (function uncertain), 298–300, *300*
Deh Rahman Stupa 1, 148
Délégation archéologique française en Afghanistan (DAFA),
    excavations at Begram, 20–34
    (Site 1) 'Bazar,' *21*, 21–2, 24, 26, 28, 29, 30, 32
    (Site 2), 20, 22–6, *25*, 27, 28, 29–30
        methodology of the Hackin-era excavations, 22
        Plan of (Le Berre), *23*
        Qala, 22, 23–4, 27, 28
    (Site 3), 26, 31, 32
    (Site B), *26*, 26–7, 29
    Sites
        plan of, *8*
        synthesis of coin finds, 32–3
    Begram I, 29
    Begram II, 29–30
    Begram III, 30–1
    excavators' interpretations, debate on, 28
    finds, *93*, 103
        (Rooms 1–9), 23
        (Room 10), 23, *24*
        (Room 11), 23, *24*
        (Room 13), 24, *24*
            catalogue errors, 26
        (Room T), 24, 27
        synthesis of coin finds, *32–3*
    Ghirshman excavations (1941–2), 26–7, 29
    Hackin excavations (1936–40), 21–4
        documentation and publication record, 24–6
        methodology, 22
    maps and aerial views, *6*, *7*, *8*
    New Royal City, 21
    Qala, 23
    surveys (1923–5), 20–21
Demetrius I (*c*. 200–190 BC), *36*, 134, 212, 320
Devanagari inscriptions
    coins, 196–9, 202, 204–7, 208
    seals, 211, *219*, 220
dies, 297–8, *299*
    in the shape of a fish, 298, *299*
Diodorus (*c*. 90–30 BC), 312, 315, 318
Diomedes (*c*. 95–90 BC), *52*, *76*, 97, 142, 322
    DAFA finds, *32–3*
    Masson's analysis, 53, 55
    monograms, motifs, inscriptions, 51, 69, 142, *142*
Dost Muhammad Khan (1826–39, 1843–63), 4–5
Durrani coins, 209–10

ear cleaner, 263, *264*
ear-ring or necklace pendants, 268–70
ear-rings, 266–8
    miscellaneous, 268, *268*
East India Company (EIC)
    army, 3
    Bombay Dispatches (E/4/1065), 4, 11, 13, 15
        collections acquired, *10*, 14–15
        documentation of receipt, 329–30
        silver drachms (Kabul 1834), *119–24*

items passed to British Museum, 107, 191
    Masson's comments on, 307–8
    see also India Museum, London
East India House *see* India Museum, London
Eden, Emily (1797–1869) coin collection, *124–6*
'Ermaios the elder' / the 'younger,' 43
Eros (Cupid), 212, 215, 217, 239
Errington, Elizabeth, 3, 35, 81, 127, 354
Eucratides I (*c*. 174–145 BC), 39–40, 69
    coins catalogued, 135–7
    DAFA finds, *32–3*,
    historical context, 84, 85, 86, *95*, 95–6, 135–7, 212, 215
    imitations, 101–2, 137, 154, *155*
Euthydemus I (*c*. 230–200 BC)
    coins catalogued, *113*, 114
    DAFA finds, *32–3*
    historical context, 80, 87, 94, 320
    Masson's analysis, *36*, 37, 74
Euthydemus II (*c*. 190–185 BC), 96
excavations of DAFA *see* Délégation archéologique française
    en Afghanistan

Fabrègues, Chantal, 211, 232, 354
falus, 113, 208, *209*, 210
Fasā mint, *111*, *125*
Ferghana, 243, 245, 246, 272
finials *see* pins: and finials
fire altar, 57–8
fish motifs, 238
    dies in the shape of a fish, 298, *299*
    dolphins, 268–70, *269*
Fitzwilliam Museum, 16, 17, 86, 90, 93–4, 110, 113, *120–21*, *123–4*, 138–9, 269
foliate motifs
    'vase of plenty' (*pūrṇaghaṭa*), 242, *243*
    geometrical floral, 233
    palmate leaf, 218, *219*
    palmette shaped, 288
    S-shaped vegetal scroll, 248–9, *249*
    spatulate leaf, 265, *265*
    trifoliate leaf within a heart-shape (Islamic), 277
    triple leaf frond within lozenge, 250, *250*
Foucher, Alfred (1865–1952; Director of DAFA 1922–34), 20–1
Franks, A.W. (1826–97), 16
French excavations at Begram *see* Délégation archéologique
    française en Afghanistan
Fromo Kesaro, (*c*. AD 738–45), 107, 113

Gadhaiya paisa, *62*, *63*, 198, *199*
Gahadavalas of Kanauj coins, 198, *199*
Gandhara coins, 29, 30, 93, 97, 101, 104, 106–7
    mint, 105, *106*, 173, *174*, *181*, 182–3
Gandhara ornamental items and design, 227, 228, 235, 256, 264, 266, 269–70
Gandhari *see* Kharoshthi
Gangeyadeva (*c*. 1015–40), 61, 199, *199*
Gaofu, 101
gems *c*. 4th century BC–6th century AD
    amethyst or quartz, galloping horse, 213, *214*

Index | 359

amethyst, prancing horse, 213, *214*
carnelian
    bull kneeling, 218, *219*
    bust with chin-length hair, 218, *219*
    eagle, 215, *216*
    goddess (Anahita?), 213, *214*
    Heracles, 212, 215, *216*, 217
    humped bull walking, *216*, 217
    ibex seated, *216*, 217
    lion, 213, *214*
    naturalistic bust, 215, *216*
    palmate leaf, 218, *219*
    ram and figure with staff, 218, *219*
    stag seated, *216*, 217
    winged horse, *216*, 218
    woman holding flower (?), 218, *219*
chalcedony
    bearded male, 215, *216*
    bird, 213, *214*
    humped bull walking, *216*, 217
    seated bull, 213, *214*
    winged griffin, 213, *214*
chrysoprase, with man, 213, *214*, 215
garnet
    Eros, *216*, 217
    facing head of a woman, 213, *214*
    griffin, 213, *214*
    helmeted Athena, 215, *216*
    helmeted female bust, 215, *216*
    lion and walking lion, *216*, 217
    male bust over feathered design, 218, *219*, 220
    standing bird, *216*, 217
    standing figure, *216*, 217
    standing goddess, 215, *216*
    trotting ibex, 215, *216*
    walking horse, 213, *214*
    winged female bust, 215, *216*
    winged Nike, 215, *216*
lapis lazuli, clean-shaven male bust, 218, *219*
nicolo
    female facing bust, 218, *219*
    female with ribbons, 218, *219*
    humped bull, *216*, 217
    man and woman facing, 218, *219*
    Pegasus, *216*, 218
    standing lion, *216*, 217
    two birds walking, *216*, 217
    woman and child, *216*, 217
rock crystal, man and woman facing, *219*, 220
sard
    nude male holding a fish (?), *216*, 217
    Tyche and Nike, *214*, 215
    winged nude Eros, 215, *216*
yellow glass, standing female, 215, *216*
see also gems, Islamic; seals and intaglios
gems, allocation numbers at transfer to the British Museum, *337*
gems, Islamic, 212, 220–4
    black and red jasper, 222, *223*, 224
    black haematite, 222
    carnelian, 220, *221*, 222
    garnet, 222
    rock crystal, *223*, 224
    sard, *223*, 224
    sardonyx, *223*, 224
    see also gems *c*. 4th century BC–6th century AD
Gerard, James G. (1795–1835), 4, 84, 110, 309
Ghar rulers *see* Bēsut; Skag Gōzgān; Zhulād Gōzgān
    silver drachms, *124*
Ghaznavid coins, catalogued, 113, 202–5
    by names of issue *see* 'Abd al-Rashīd; Alptekin; Arslan Shah; Bahram Shah; Balkategin; Ibrahim; Ibrahim b. 'Abd al-Ghaffar; Ismā'īl b. Sebuktegin; Khusrau Malik; Khusrau Shah; Maḥmūd I; Manṣūr; Mas'ūd I; Mas'ūd III; Mawdūd I; Muḥammad b. Maḥmūd; Sebuktegin
Ghenghis Khan (1206–27), 92
Ghiaur Kala, 289
    mints *see* Merv mints
Ghirshman, Roman (1885–1979), 20, 25, 26–7, 29
Ghiyāth al-dīn Maḥmūd b. Muḥammad (AH 602–9 / AD 1206–12), *206*, 207
Ghiyāth al-dīn Muḥammad b. Sām (AH 559–99 / AD 1163–1203), 205–6, *206*
Ghurid coins, 63, 77–8, 116, 205–7, *206*
    i.n.o. Muḥammad b. Mas'ūd, 116
    Muḥammad b. Sām versions of Kalachuri and Yadava gold coins, *199*, 199–200
    by names of issue *see* Baha' al-dīn Sām; Ghiyāth al-dīn Maḥmūd b. Muḥammad; Ghiyāth al-dīn Muḥammad b. Sām; Jalal al-dīn 'Ali b. Sām; Mu'izz al-dīn Muḥammad b. Sām; Taj al-dīn Yildiz
Ghurid ornamental items, 280–1
glass, *301*, 302
gods/goddesses
    Apollo, 37, 132
    Ardochsho, 27, 49, 159, *160*, 178–90, 183, *184*, 198, 324, 325
    'Ardokro', 304, 324, 325, 326, 334
    Artemis, 134, 215
    Athena, *95*, 132, *133*, 138–40, 146, 149, 150, 215, *337*
    Athsho, 163, 165, 167, 170, 171, 173
    Demeter, 142
    Dionysus, *95*, 134
    Dioscuri, 15, 39, 40, 42–3, *95*, 101, 135
    Lakshmi, 46, 61, 198–9, 325
    Mahākāla, 300
    Miiro, Mioro, Myro, 58, 165, 167–8, 171, 173
    Nana, Nanaia, Nanashao, 58, 61, *72*, 77, 163, 165, 167, 170, 172
    Nike, 41, 46. *95*, 101–2, 104, 137–8, 140–1, 146, 149–50, 152, 212, 215, 228, 230, 234, 237–9, *238*, 242
    Oado, 165, 168, 170, 173, 175
    Oesho, 18, 31, 49, 57, 58, 61, 76–8, 159, *160*, 163 165, 167–8, 170–1, 173, 213, 230
    and bull, 26, 31, 161, 177, 180, 182
    'Okro', 18, 61, 304, 310, 323, 324, 325, 335
    Pharro, *58*, *168*, *173*
    Poseidon, 53, 134, 145
    Shakti, *301*, 302
    Shiva, 235, 300

Subhadra, 41, 134
Tyche, 40, 102, 212, 215, *337*
Visakha (Bizago), 168
Yakshi, 53, 145
Zeus, 137, 142, 143, 146, 150, 152, 154, 161
    enthroned Nicephorus, 141
see also human figure motifs
Godwin-Austen collection, 17, 211, *212*, 215, 217
Gondophares (*c.* AD 32–58), 16
    coins catalogued, 149–50, *151*
    DAFA finds, *32–3*
    historical context, 83, 85, 101, 102–3
    Masson's analysis, *44*, 46–7, *54*, 57
    monograms, motifs, inscriptions, 234, 326
Govindachandradeva (*c.* AD 1114–55), 61, 198, *199*
Greco-Bactrian coins, 94
    coins catalogued, *133*, 134–8
    historical context, 94–5
    imitations, 135, *136*
    IOLC comparisons, *88*
    Masson's analysis, *36*, 37, 51–61
    monograms, *70*
    by names of issue *see* Agathocles; Antimachus; Antimachus II; Apollodotus I; Demetrius I; Euthydemus I; Heliocles I; Pantaleon
Greco-Bactrian kings, 36–7, 41, 72
Greek inscriptions, 40, 41–3, *71*, 163, 228, *229*
'Guebre' (Kushano-Sasanian), *88*, 106–7, 180–3, *184*
Guldara, 57, 161
Gurjara-Pratihara (*c.* 900–1000), 198, *199*

Hackin excavations at Begram, 21–4
    documentation and publication record, 24–6
    under Ria Hackin, 24
Hadda, 16, 35, 44, 311, 312–13
    Stupa 10 coins, 67–8, 313
        Tope Kelan finds, 107
    Stupa 3 coins, 323
hair- or dress-pins, 255, 256, *256*, *257*
    ritual hand gesture finial, 256–7, *257*
Hamadān, *111*, *119*, *124*
Han Shu, 101
Haraat mint, *111*, *121*, *122*, *125*, *126*, 193
Hārūn al-Rashīd (AH 170–93 / AD 786–809), 200, *201*
Hazarajat, 10, 16, *92*, 128
    hoard coins catalogued, 134–5, 137–9
Hebrew inscriptions, 211, *219*, 220
Heliocles I (*c.* 145–130 BC), 72, *87*, *92*
    coins catalogued, *136*, 137
    coins from Mir Zakah, *98*
    historical context, 91, 95, 97, 100–1, 321
    imitations, *32–3*, *93*, *99*, 103–4
        DAFA finds, *32–3*
    correspondence of coins, 75
    of Wima Takto, *44*, 45, 47, *158*, 159, 284
Heliocles II (*c.* 110–100 BC), 97, *98*, 142, *142*
Hephthalite, 27, 108, 110, 112, 185
Herat, 3–4, 110, 258
Herat Museum, 279
Hermaeus (*c.* 90–70 BC), 18
    and Calliope, 143
    coins catalogued, 143, *144*
    DAFA finds, *32–3*,
    Hermaeus Hercules coins, 324, 325
    historical context, 321, 322
    imitations, 103, 104
        'Ermaios', 43, 45, 50
        Kujula Kadphises, 154, *155*, 323
        life time and anonymous, 43, 45, 143, *144*
        posthumous, 53–5, *54*, 100, 101, 102
Herodotus, 312, 314, 315
Higaksha (*c.* late 1st century AD), 37, 102, 149, *149*
Hindu Kush, 5, 41, 49, 96, 315
Hindu/Kabul Shahi (*c.* AD 859–990), 9, 31, 325, 327
    coins catalogued, 196–8
    historical context, 91, 109
    Masson's analysis F526/1a and reports, *62*, *63*, 91, 127–8
    by names of issue *see* Pala…; Samantadeva; Spalapatideva; Vakkadava
Honigberger, John Martin (*c.* 1795–1868), 46, 47, 51, 57, 161, 309
Hormizd I (*c.* AD 270–300), 180
    coins catalogued, *181*, 182, 189, *190*
    historical context, 106
Hormizd II (*c.* AD 300–3), 31, 257
    coins catalogued, 182, 189, *190*
    historical context, 107
Hou Han Shu, 101
human figure motifs
    amulet pendants, 271–3, *273*
    hand with outstretched fingers, 256, *257*
    plaque and pin with female figures, 225, *256*
    ritual hand gesture, 256–7, *257*
    gems, 215–16, 217, 218, *219*, 220
    rings *see* rings
    see also gods/goddesses
Hun coins, 12, 15, 16, *62*, 64, *65*, 78, 85, 86, 92, 106–9, *117*, 183–8, *184*, *187*
    see also Alkhan; Hephthalite; Kidarite; Nezak
Hun countermarks, 191
Hun seals, 212, 218, *219*
Huvishka (*c.* AD 151–90), 105, 161, 238, 246, 247, 286
    coins catalogued, 168–75, *177*
    DAFA finds, *32–3*
    imitations, *175*
    Masson's analysis, *56*, 58, *59*–60, 61, 77–8
    mint, 105, *172*, *173*, *174*
Hyrcodes (1st century AD), 5, 12, *153*, 153–4

Ibrahim (AH 451–92 / AD 1059–99), *203*, 204
Ibrahim b. 'Abd al-Ghaffar (AH 337–45 / AD 949–56), 113
Ilkhanid (AH 623–754 / AD 1256–1353), 66, *80*, 208, *209*
India Museum, London, 86, 200
    acquisition of Masson collections, 11, 12, 16–17, 90
    transfer to India Office (1869), 15
    transfers to British Museum (1880–2), 15, 101, 107, 341–2
        coins recorded, 139, 141–2
        inventory and accession numbers, *336–9*
Indian Museum, Calcutta/Kolkata, 16, 17, 86, 90, 101, 200
India Office Loan Collection (IOLC), 2, 13, 15, 17, *88*, 90

bags relating to Willoughby's list, 13, *13*, 329–30, *330*
contamination and mistaken inclusions, 90, 102–3
dispersal, 15–17
Indo-Greek coins, *88–9*
  coins catalogued, 138–45
  historical context, 91
    early Indo-Greek coins, 95–6
    later Indo-Greek coins, 96–7
      comparisons, *100*
    local coins contemporary with, 93–4
    stages in development of, *95*
  imitations, 100
  IOLC comparisons, *88*
  monograms, *70*
  by names of issue *see* Agathocles; Apollodotus II; Archebius; Diomedes ; Heliocles II; Hermaeus; Lysias; Menander I; Pantaleon; Philoxenus, Strato I; Theophilus; Zoilus
Indo-Greek period, *95*, 95–7
  coins from Mir Zakah, *98*
Indo-Parthian coins, *89*, 102–3, 149–52, *151*
  DAFA finds, *32–3*
  by names of issue *see* Abdagases; Gondophares; Sanabares; Sasan
Indo-Sasanian coins *see* Hun, Alkhan, Nezak and Turkic coins
Indo-Scythian coins, 16, *87–8*, 100–2
  coins catalogued, *136, 145*, 145–8
    imitations, 198
    monograms, *69*
    satraps, 148–9
  IOLC comparisons, *89*
  from Mir Zakah, *99*
  by names of issue *see* Azes I; Azes II; Azilises; Maues; Spalagadama; Spalahores; Spalirises; Vonones
  satraps *see* Aspavarma; Higaksha; Kharahostes; Mujatria; Zeionises
inscriptions *see* Arabic inscriptions; Bactrian inscriptions; Brahmi inscriptions; Devanagari inscriptions; Greek inscriptions; Islamic inscriptions; Kharoshthi inscriptions; Kufic inscriptions; Pahlavi inscriptions; Persian inscriptions; Urdu inscriptions
intaglios *see* seals and intaglios
IOLC *see* India Office Loan Collection
Iran unregulated civic coinage, 210
Ishpola stupa, 80
Ishtakhr mint, *119, 123*
Islamic coins, *60, 62, 66*
  (AD 870 to Mongol invasion), 113–16, *201, 203*
  coins catalogued, *192, 194–5*, 200–9
  early Islamic coins, 109–10, 112–13
  historical context, 109–10, 112–13
  Shahi-Islamic, IOLC comparisons, *90*
Islamic inscriptions: gems, seals and intaglios, 212, 220–4
Islamic ornamental items
  ear-rings, 266
  pendants
    crescent-shaped, 276–7, *277*
    drop-shaped, 277–9, *278*
  pins, 258–63, *264, 265*
  rings and Islamic type rings, 249, 251–3

Ismāʿīl b. Ahmad (AH 279–92 / AD 892–907), 113, 116
Ismāʿīl b. Sebuktegin (AH 387–8 / AD 997–8), 113, 116, *201, 202*

Jalāl al-dīn (Khwarazmshah) *see* Mangubarni
Jalal al-dīn ʿAli b. Sām (AH 602–11 / AD 1206–15), *206*, 207
Jalalabad, *10*, 37, 43, 82, 90, 100, 103, 148, 161, 238
  and region *see* Bimaran, Hadda
Janids of Astrakhan (1599–1785), 209, *209*
Jayy mint, *111, 119*, 191
Jephson, George, 3–4
Jibin, 101
Jihonika *see* Zeionises
Journal of the Asiatic Society of Bengal, 1, 127
  Masson's Memoir (1834), 5, 9, 10, 82, 86
  Masson's Second Memoir (1836), 7–9, 10, 17, 82–4, 91–2, 96, 128
  Masson's Third Memoir (1836), 35, 82–3, 86, 90, 101
  Masson Manuscript *see* Masson Manuscript F526/1a
  see also Asiatic Society of Bengal
Jouveau-Dubreuil, Gabriel, 21
Justin, 94

Kabul, *6, 7*, 109
  bazaar coins, 11, 12–13, 16, 128, 183
  parcels of coin from, 11
Kabul Arab-Sasanian coin hoard, 110
  distribution by mint and date, *111*
  Islamic coins, 200
  Khusrau II coins, 110, *111, 119*
  Sasanian, Arab-Sasanian and Ghar silver drachms, *119–26*
Kabul mint, 64, 82, 108
Kabul Museum, 279
Kalachuris of Tripuri, 199, *199 see also* Gangeyadeva
Kamari Stupa 2, 57, 161
Kanishka I (*c.* AD 127–51), 58, *59*, 163–8
  DAFA finds, *32–3*
Kanishka II (*c.* AD 230–46), *60*, 61
  DAFA finds, *32–3*
  imitations i.n.o., 178
Kanishka III (*c.* AD 267–72), *60*, 61, 179–80
Kanauj *see* Gahadavalas; Yasovarman
Kapisa, 5, 101–2, *see also* Begram
Karacheh (or Karratcha), 7, *7*, 8, 29
Karamat ʿAli, 4, 82, 110, 320
Kashmir coin imitations, 198
  mint, 103, 105, 173, *174*
Kashmir Smast, 108, 109, 117, 185, 230, 243, 256, 260–1, 280, 284
Kavad (Kushano-Sasanian), 63, *72, 79*, 112, 112–13, *181*, 182
Kavad I (1st reign AD 488–96), *190*, 191
  drachms named after, *112*, 112–13
key with five teeth, *301*, 302
Kharahostes (*c.* early 1st century AD), *54*, 55, 102, 148
Kharoshthi inscriptions
  Bactrian, 18–19, 40, 43
    Masson's copies of coin inscriptions, *71*
  coins, 141–9, 154, 156, 159, 161
  decipherment, 18–19

Masson's analysis, 40, 41, 43, 46, 51, 53, 71
Masson's annotations, *306*, 307, 309, 310, 320, 323, 326
non-coin artefacts, 228, *229*
Khera, Paramdip, 127, 200, 354
Khurasan, *111*, *119*, 121–3, *124*, *125*–6, 193
motifs, 276, 277, 279, 295
Khusrau I (AD 531–75), 107 *190*, 191
motifs and marks, 64
Khusrau II (AD 591–628)
coins catalogued, 110, *111*, 112, *190*, 191, 196
imitations, *120*, 191, 193, 196
DAFA finds, 31
motifs, 64, 256, 284
tabulation of Sasanian/Arab-Sasanian coin hoard, *119–20*, *124*
Khusrau Malik (AH 555–82 / AD 1160–86), 63, 116, *203*, 205
Khusrau Shah (AH 552–55 / AD 1157–60), *203*, 205
Khwarazm Shah, 16, 63, 66, 82, 92, 116, 117, *118*, 128
by names of issue *see* Muḥammād b. Tekish, Mangubarni
coins catalogued, *207*, 207–8
Kidara (*c.* AD 355–85), 68, *106*, 106–7, 183, *184*, 185
Kidarite coins, *106*, 106–7, 183–5, 212
by names of issue *see* Kidara; Orölano; Tobazino
see also Hun coins
Kidarite seal, 218; ring, 230
Killa Bolend (Qal'a-i Bulend), 6, 7–9
Kirmān, 273, 298, 317
Kirmān mint, *119*, *120*, 122, *123*, *125*, 191, 193
Koh-i Bacha, 6, 7–8
Koh-i Pahlawan, *v*, 7, 29, *see also* Koh-i Bacha
Koh-i Top *see* Koh-i Bacha
Kohistan, 5–7
kohl or antimony rods, 257–8, *258*
phial stoppers, 232, 260, 264, *264*, *338*
Kotpur Stupa 2, 51, 156
Kshaharata satrap *see* Higaksha
Kufic coins, 9, 63, 66, *72*, *78*, *80*, *88*, 200
Kufic inscriptions
coinage, 63, 208, *209*
non-coin artefacts, 280–1
pseudo-Kufic, 213, 249, 251, 254
Kujula Kadphises (*c.* AD 50–90), 46, *48*, 80, 118, 322–3, 326
coins in own name (catalogued), 103–4, 154–6, *157*
correspondence of coins, 76
DAFA finds, *32–3*
Hermaeus, 154, *155*, 323
historical context, 47, 83, 84, 85, 106, 118
inscriptions, 51–2, 100
Masson's analysis, 46–7, *48*, 50–1, *52*, 53–5, 72–3
motifs, 46, 212, 217
unofficial imitations, 156, *157*
Kumarapaladeva (*c.* 1145–71), *199*, *199*
Kushan coins (*c.* AD 50–352), 154–80
coins catalogued, 180–3
enumeration of collection (1833–5), 72
historical context, 106–7
early coins, 103–6
imitations, 183–5
IOLC comparisons, *89*
Soter Megas issues, 156–9

by names of issue *see* Huvishka; Kanishka I; Kanishka II; Kanishka III; Kujula Kadphises; Shaka; Vasishka; Vasudeva I; Vasudeva II; Wima Kadphises; Wima Takto
Kushan coins from DAFA excavation, 93
Kushan gems, seals and intaglios, 215–17
Kushan mint, 105, 118
Kushano-Sasanian coins, *99*
coins catalogued, 180–3, *184*
DAFA finds, *32–3*,
historical context, 85, 90, 97, 105–6, 112, *118*
imitations, 105
inscriptions, 327
IOLC comparisons, *90*
Masson's analysis, *62*, 63–4, *79*
by names of issue *see* Ardashir I; Ardashir II; Peroz I; Peroz II; Hormizd I; Hormizd II; Kavad; Meze; Shapur II; Varhran
see also 'Guebre'
Kushano-Sasanian seals and intaglios, 217

Lashkari Bazar, 109
Lassen, Christian (1800–76), 84–5, 316
Le Berre, Marc (d. 1978)
Begram collection, *98–9*, 218
plan of Site II, *23*, 26, 27
Leighton-Boyce, Kirstin, 127, 354
Lewis, James *see* Masson, Charles (1800–53)
lids, 294, *295*
local lion and elephant coins, 46–7, 72, 128
DAFA finds, *32–3*
Luristan, 272, 273, 284
Lysias (*c.* 120–110 BC), 75
coins catalogued, 141, *142*
historical context, 43, *47*, 85, 97, 320, 321
Masson's analysis, 41, *42*, 69

Mackenzie, Colin (1754–1821), 17, 309
Macnaghten, William Hay (1793–1841), 4, 5
Madraseh Tepe *see* Nishapur
mahadhama, 107
Maḥmūd b. Muḥammad *see* Ghiyāth al-dīn Maḥmūd
Maḥmūd I (AH 388–421 / AD 998–1030), 63, 116
coins catalogued, *201*, 202
Maḥmūd II (AH 1223–55 / AD 1808–39), *209*, 210
Maḥmūd Shah (AH 1223–33 / AD 1808–17), 209, *209*
Malik al-Sharq (king of the east), *206*, 207
Mallet, Louis, 15
Mangubarni/Mengubirti, *aka* Jalāl al-dīn (*c.* 1220–31), 116
Manikyala 'Tope' (Great Stupa), 58, 80, 112
Manṣūr (AH 362–6 / AD 973–7), 113
Manṣūr I b. Nūh (AH 350–65 / AD 961–76), 113, 200, *201*, 202
Mas'ūd I (AH 421–32 / AD 1031–41), 202, *203*
Mas'ūd III (AH 492–508 / AD 1099–1115), *203*, 204
Masson collection history
auction sales, 16, 128
Bombay Government letter (6 March 1839), 11
coins, summary of range, *118*
dispersal
East India Company acquisition, *10*, 14–15

Index | 363

documentation of receipt, 329–30
donation to British Museum, 15
Masson's comments on, 307–8
India Museum *see* India Museum, London
traced from February 1838 to 1906, 15–17
India Office 'residue', 15, 16, 17
IOLC *see* India Office Loan Collection
Masson's initiating system, 9–10
Masson's reports on Begram finds, 82–3
fate of estimated 60,000 to 80,000 coins, 11–15
Prinsep's use of, 83–4
scholars after Prinsep, 84–6
Masson's summary list, 331–3
estimates of coins, rings, seals and ornaments found, *10*, 10–11
non-coin artefacts, 16–17
recording and cataloguing, 127–8
Errington reconstruction, 90–1
following transportation to England and Masson's death, 86, 90
see also Begram; Masson papers and publications
Masson Manuscript F526/1a
(Plate 1) Recorded Greek Bactrian kings: Antiochus III, Euthydemus, Apollodotus I, Menander I, 36–7, 72
(Plate 2) Menander, Eucratides, *38*, 39–41
Unrecorded Greek Bactrian kings: Pantaleon, 41, 72
(Plate 3) Agathocles, Lysias, Antialcidas, Hermaeus, 41, *42*, 43, 45
(Plate 4) imitations of Wima Takto, local coins, punch-marked, Gondophares, *44*, 45–7
(Plate 5) Soter Megas, Azes II, Kujula Kadphises, 47, *48*, 49–51
(Plate 6), Kujula Kadphises, Archebius, Diomedes, Spalirises, *52*, 53
'doubtful or unknown names': Vonones, Azes II, Maues, Apollodotus I, Azes I, *52*, 53
(Plate 7), *54*, 80
Gondophares, Mujatria, Azes II, *54*, 57
Hermaeus posthumous imitations; Kujula Kadphises, 53, *54*
Vatashvaka, Antimachus II, Spaladagama, Azilises, Azes I, Kharahostes, *54*, 55
(Plate 8) Kushan: Wima Kadphises, Huvishka, Kanishka I, *56*, 57–61
(Plate 9) Kanishka I, Huvishka, 58, *59*, 61
(Plate 10) Huvishka, Vasudeva I, Kanishka II and imitation, Kanishka III, *60*, 61, 63
(Plate 11) Hindu Shahi, jitals, Gadhaiya paisa, Kushano-Sasanian, Parthian, Hun, *62*, 63–4, 80
(Plate 12) Alkhan Hun, Sasanian, Turki Shahi, Nezak uniface, Arab-Sasanian/Hepthalite, 64, *65*
(Plate 13) Napki Malka, Shri Shahi, Islamic, 64, *66*, *66*
Kufic, Muhammadan, 66
(Plates 14–15) 4 Hadda Stupa 10 coins, 66, *67–8*, 68
Alkhan, Sasanian, Kidarite, 68
(Plate 16) Monograms and tamghas, *69*
(Plate 17) Monograms on Bactrian, Indo-Greek and other coins, *70*
(Plate 18) Greek and Kharoshthi coin inscriptions, *71*
see also coin enumerations, Masson's collection

Masson papers and publications
annotations to *Ariana Antiqua* see *Ariana Antiqua*
'A memoir on the buildings called topes' (1841), 310–19
Narrative of Various Journeys (1842), 5–7, 9–10, 81
three memoirs (in *JASB*)
(1834), 5, 9, 10, 82, 86
(1836a), 7–9, 10, 17, 82–4, 91–2, 96, 128
(1836b), 35, 82–3, 86, 90, 101
see also Masson Manuscript F526/1a
Masson, Charles (1800–53)
death, 90
decipherment of Kharoshthi, 18
discovery of Begram, 5–10
early life and career, branded as spy, 3–5
on funding, 307–8
legacy, 17–19, 303
see also Masson collection history; Masson Manuscript F526/1a; Masson papers and publications
Mathura mint, 173
Maues (*c.* 75–65 BC), 80, 85, 100, 101, 102, 323
coins catalogued, 145, *145*
Mauryan coins, *130*, 131, 132, *132*
IOLC comparisons, *89*
see also Ashoka
post-Mauryan local coins, 93–4, *130*
punch-marked, *36*, 128–31
Mawdūd I (AH 432–42 / AD 1041–50), 202–204
Menander I (*c.* 155–130 BC)
coins catalogued, 138–41
copper alloy coins, 96–7, 128, 139–41
DAFA finds, *32–3*
historical context, 82, 83, 85–6, 87, 88, 95–8
Masson's analysis, *36*, 72, 74
monograms, 39, 97, 138–41
silver coins, *38*, 43, 91, *92*, 137–9
Merv al-Rudh mint *see* Merv
Merv mints
Anbēr, 110, *111*, 112, *124*, *126*
Margiana, 152
Merv al-Rudh, 110, *111*, *121–2*, *123*, *126*
Mes Aynak, 30
metal items, allocation numbers at transfer to the British Museum, *338–9*
Meunié, Jacques (1898–1967), 21–2, 23–4, 27, 31, *32*
Meze (Kushano-Sasanian), 63, 72, 79, *181*, 182
Mihirakula (*c.* AD 515–40), 186
mints listed, with signatures/marks, *111*, *119–26*
Mir Zakah, 96, 97, *98–9*, 285
comparison table of later Indo-Greek copper coins, *100*
monograms appearing in Masson Manuscript F526/1a, 96–7, 102
Antimachus II, 55
Apollodotus I, 37, *69*
Apollodotus II, 37
Archebius, 51
Azes II, 57
Azilises, 55, *69*
Bactrian, *69–70*
Diomedes, 51
'Ermaios the Elder' (Hermaeus life-time issues), 43, *47*

'Ermaios the Younger (?)' (Hermaeus posthumous
    imitations), 43, 45, *47*
Eucratides I, 39–40, *69*
Gondophares, 57
Huvishka, 58
Kharahostes, 55
Lysias, 41
Menander, 39, *69*, *96*
Mujatria, 57
Spalagadama, 55, *69*
Spalirises, 53
Wima Kadphises, 57
monograms on coins catalogued *see* individual names of issue
Morris, Lauren, 20, 354
motifs
    by design
        animal *see* animal motifs
        bird *see* bird motifs
        cornucopia *see* cornucopia
        fish motifs, 238
            dolphins, 268–70, *269*
            palmette shaped, 288
        foliate *see* foliate motifs
        gods and goddesses *see* gods/goddesses
        human figure *see* human figure motifs
        Solomon's knot, 212, 222, 296
        swastika, 131, 177, 180, 182, 183, 234
Muʿizz al-dīn Jahangir (AH 848–85 / AD 1444–51), 209, *209*
Muḥammād b. Maḥmūd (AH 421 / AD 1031; AH 432 / AD 1041), 202, *203*
Muḥammād b. Masʿūd (AH 558–88 / AD 1163–92), 116
Muḥammād b. Sām, Ghiyāth al-dīn (AH 559–99 / AD 1163–1203), 116, 205, *206*
Muḥammād b. Sām, Muʿizz al-dīn (AH 569–602 / AD 1173–1206), 61, 63, *78*, 198, *199*, 199–200, 205–6, *206*, 281, 328
    anonymous coins i.n.o., 206–7, *206*
    supreme sultan (1203–6), 116
Muḥammād b. Tekish, ʿAla al-dīn (AH 596–617 / AD 1200–20), 63, *78*, 82, 116, 117
Muʿizz al-dīn Muḥammad b. Sām *see* Muḥammad b. Sām
Mujatria (*c.* AD 60–80), 16, 49, *54*, 57, 80, 102, 323
    coins catalogued, 148–9, *149*
    DAFA finds, *32–3*
Muṣʿab b. al-Zubayr (*c.* AH 70 / AD 690), 64, 193, *194*
Musée Guimet, 22, 25–6, 28, *32–3*

nails, tacks and studs, 294, *294*
Nandara Stupa 1, 301
nandipada, 152, 159, 161, 177
Napki Malka ('king Nezak'), 66, 108
Narendra coins, 187, *187*
Narseh (AD 293–303), 189, *190*
Naṣr b. Ahmad (AH 301–31 / AD 914–43), 116
New Royal City *see* Begram
Nezak coins, 64, 65, 66, *72*, *80*, 107–8, 186. *187*
    by names of issue *see* Napki Malka; Nezak Malka; Shri Shahi
    see also Hun coins

Nezak Malka, 186, *187*
Nishapur, 258, 268, 273, 277, 280, 289, 294, 297
    horse harness, 298–9
    Madraseh Tepe, 257, 262, 276
    Qanat Tepe, 248, 249, 261, 265, 291
    Sabz Pushan, 278
Nizametdin, 4, 5
Nūh II b. Manṣūr (AH 365–87 / AD 976–97), 113, 200, *201*

Orlagno (Verethragna), 163
ornamental objects, miscellaneous, 300–2
    striated fragments, 296, *297*
Orölano (*c.* 4th century), 107
Ottoman unregulated civic coinage, *209*, 210
Oxus River, 233

Pahlavi inscriptions
    coinage, 106, 108, 182, 183, 186–8, 191
        Turkic silver drachms, 193, *195*, 196
    intaglio, 212, 218, *219*, 224
    Kharoshthi *see* Kharoshthi
    Masson's notes and annotations, 18, 63, 309, 324
        Prinsep on, 84
    pseudo-Pahlavi (?), rings, 238, *238*
Pala... (*c.* AD 850–1000), 196–7
Palmyra, 239, 266
Pantaleon (*c.* 190–185 BC)
    coins catalogued, *133*, 134
    DAFA finds, *32–3*,
    historical context, 85, 94, *95*, 95–6
    Masson's analysis, *38*, 41, 45, *75*
Papak (early 3rd century) ruler of Fars, 189, *190*
Paropamisadae, 37, 85, 100, 101, 314, 315, 325
Parthian coins, 45, 82
    coins catalogued, 152–3, *153*
    historical context, 45, 82–3, 86, 101, 102–3
    imitations
        DAFA finds, *32–3*
        Masson's analysis, 57, *62*, 63–4, *72*, *78–8*
        Masson's annotations, 321, 322
        Mir Zakah, *98*
    by names of issue *see* Artabanus II; Phraates III, Phraates IV, Phraates V
Parthian ornamental items and motifs, 237, 238, 239, 289
Parwan coins, 5, 7, 113, 116, 117, 200, 202, 207, 303
    mint, 113, 116, 117, 200, 202, 207, 303
Pegasus, 218, 225, 238
pendants
    c. 8th–12th century, 274–6, *275*
    amulet, 271–3, *273*
    amulet pendants, 271–3, *273*
    attached to barrel beads, 273–4, *274*
    frog and circular, 280, *281*
    of Hellenstic design, 268–70
    Islamic crescent-shaped, 276–7, *277*
    Islamic drop-shaped, 277–9, *278*
    miscellaneous, *279*, 279–80
    palmette, 276, 277, *277*
    pentagonal fossilised limestone, *301*, 302
    pseudo-coin, 280–1, *281*

Index | 365

pyramidal, 274, *274*
with radiating spikes, 270–1, *271*
Penjikent, 258, 261, 272–3, 286, 289, 292, 293
Peroz (AD 457, 459–84) Sasanian, *68*, 108, 112, 117, *119*
  coins catalogued, *181*, 189, 191, 192
Peroz (*c*. AD 350–5) Kidarite, *184*, 185
Peroz I (*c*. AD 245–70) Kushanshah, 31, 64, 105, 106, 180, 182
Peroz II (*c*. AD 303–30) Kushanshah, 64, *181*, 182
Persian inscriptions
  coins, 208–10
  non-coin artefacts
    cameos, amulets and metal seals, 225, *225*
    gems, 213–15, 220, *221*, 224
    nastaliq, 215
    re-inscribed, 211, *214*
    seals and intaglios, 211–13, 224
    signet- and finger-rings, 237, *237*, 238
    stone ornament, 302
phial stoppers, *264*, 264–5
Philostratus, 46, 101, 102
Philoxenus (*c*. 100–95 BC)
  coins catalogued, 142, *142*
  silver medal, 55
Phraataces *see* Phraates V
Phraates III (*c*. 69–57 BC), *98*
Phraates IV (*c*. 38–2 BC), 153, 237
Phraates V (*c*. 2 BC–AD 4) (or Phraataces), 46, 64, 103, 152, 153, 237
Phraötes (king of Taxila), 102
pilei (bonnets), 135
pins
  and finials, 255–7, *256*
    angular stylised bird finials, 258–60
    cockerel finials, *257*, 258, *258*
    hand with outstretched fingers, 256, *257*
    naturalistic bird finials, 260–3
    peacock finial, 260–1, *262*
    ritual hand gesture, 256–7, *257*
    stylised bird (possibly hoopoe), 257, *257*
    stylised peacock finials, 260, *261*
    U-shaped finials, 260, *261*
  miscellaneous, 263, *264*
  spatula-shaped, 263, *264*
plaques, 255, *256*
  clay amulet plaque, 300–1, *301*
  fragment, lozenge-shaped, 296, *297*
  jade, vegetal decoration with flying crane, *301*, 302
  miscellaneous, 298–300, *300*
  with human figures, 255, *256*
pottery, 23, 24
  stamped medallions, *22*, 28, 30
Pottinger, Henry (1789–1856), 4, 11
Prinsep, Henry Thoby (1783–1878), 13
Prinsep, James (1799–1840), 13
  Ariana Antiqua, 127
    Masson's annotations, 309, 320, 321, 323, 325
  collection, 110, *126*
  manuscripts, 18
  Masson Manuscript F526/1a, 37
  Masson's reports, 35, 83–6, 101–2, 127

punch-marked coins, *36*, *44*, 45–7, *75*, *89*, 93–4, 118, 128–31
pyramidal ornaments or amulets, 274, *274*

Qasr-i Abu Nasr (old Shiraz), 241, 248, 256, 267
Qul-i Nadir, 8, 29
Qul-i Tut, 30
Qurʾān, 212, 222, 224, 291

Rayy mint, *119*, *120*, *121*
Ridgeway collection, 17, 225, 227, 228, 234, 235, 256, 257, 258, 260–1, 263, 265, 268, 274, 276, 283
Rienjang, Wannaporn Kay, 127, 211, 232, 354
rings (ear-rings), 266–70
rings (signet- and finger-rings), 234–55
  allocation numbers at transfer to the British Museum, *337*
  assemblage quantities, Masson's records, *10*
  c. 1st century BC–1st century AD, 234–7
    bare-breasted female figures, 235–6, *236*
    female figure beneath leafy arch, 235, *236*
    female figure in Indian dress, 235, *236*
    Greek type, 234, *236*
    two ducks swimming, *236*, 237
    two females arm in arm, 236, *236*
    with winged Nike, 234, *236*
  c. 1st century AD (and Islamic)
    Nike, 237, *237*
    seated male bearded figure, 237, *237*
  c. 1st century BC–6th century AD, 238–41
    bare-breasted woman, 239, *240*
    dancing female figure, 238, *238*
    lion, 236, *236*, 237
    man facing woman, 238, *238*
    man holding flowers, 238, *238*
    Nike, 238, *238*
    resembling winged horse, 238, *238*
    running figures, 238, *238*
  c. 2nd–6th century, 247–8
  c. 3rd–11th century, 245–7
  c. 3rd–12th century, 242–4
    'vase of plenty' border, 242, *243*
    Nike (?), 242, *243*
    winged dragon, 243, *243*
  c. 3rd–13th century, 248–9
    mottled carnelian (?), 249, *249*
  c. 8th–11th century, with pseudo-Arabic, 249–52
    triple leaf frond within lozenge, 250, *250*
  c. 8th–12th century, with pseudo-Arabic, 253–4
    hexagonal form, 253–4, *254*
  c. 10th–11th century, with pseudo-Arabic, 254–5
  c. 12th century, Islamic, 252–5
    brass-washed elements, 255, *255*
rods, 257–8, *258*
  cylindrical rod (key?), *301*, 301
Roman coins, v, 15, 17, 103, 104, 310
  Augustus design, 154, *155*
  aurei, 161, 183
  Jansari research on, 17
Roman ornamental items
  bangles, 286, *288*, 289
  ear-rings, 266

gems, 213–15, *216*
miscellaneous, 300, *301*
pin finials, 256, *257*
rings, 239, 245, 247, 248
Royal Asiatic Society, 16, 18, 90
Rudrasena I (AD 200–22), 46
Rudrasena II (c. AD 256–78), 117, 149, *149*

Saffarid coins, 109, 113–16, *117*, 200, *201*
    by names of issue *see* 'Amr b. al-Layth; Ya'qub b. al-Layth; Taj al-dīn Naṣr b. Bahram Shah
Salm b. Ziyād (c. AH 60–3 / AD 680–3)
    coins catalogued, *192*, 193, *194*
    historical context, 112
    Masson's analysis, 64
    silver drachms, *121–2, 124, 125–6*
Samanid coins
    coins catalogued, 200–201
    historical context, 116, *117, 118*, 295
    Masson's sketches of, *114–15*
    by names of issue *see* Ismā'īl b. Ahmad; Manṣūr I b. Nūh; Naṣr b. Ahmad; Nūh II b. Manṣūr
Samantadeva (c. AD 850–900), *197*, 197–8, 327, 328
Sanabares (c. mid 1st century AD), *89*, 103, 152–3, *153*, 323
Sandan (c. AD 700–50), 79, 108–9, *195*, 196
Sanskrit, 53, 55, 309, 314, 321, 325
Sapalbizes (c. 2 BC–AD 20) local ruler in Bactria, 105, 153, *153*
Sardis, 245, 247, 266, 289, 292
Sasan (c. AD 64–70), 80, 103, *151*, 152, 217
Sasanian coins, 67, *68*, 189–91
    DAFA finds, *32–3*
    hoard of Sasanian, Arab-Sasanian and Ghar kingdom silver drachms, *119–26*
    by names of issue *see* Ardashir I; Ardashir II; Hormizd I; Hormizd II; Kavad I; Khusrau I; Khusrau II; Narseh; Peroz; Shapur son of Papak; Shapur II; Varhran IV; Varhran V; Yazdagird I; Yazdagird II; Yazdagird III
satraps *see* Higaksha; Kharahostes; Mujatria; Rudrasena I; Rudrasena II; Zeionises
Schlumberger, Daniel (1904–72; Director of DAFA 1945–65), 20, 27
    Curiel and Schlumberger (1953), 96, *96*, 97, *98–9*
Scythians, 100–2
seals and intaglios
    assemblage quantities, *10*
    box seals, 213, 228, 230, *231*
    cabochon-cut seals, 213, 220, 224
    cameos and amulets
        amulet, Christian (?), 211, *225*
        carnelian intaglios, 224, *225*
        garnet cameo of female head, 211, *214*
        glass cameo, 224–5, *225*
        heliotrope amulet of mythical beast, 224, *225*
        rock crystal amulet, 224, *225*
    inscriptions, 211–12
        Arabic, 220–5
        Bactrian, *219*, 220
        Devanagari, 211, *219*, 220
        Greek, *229*
        Hebrew, 211, *219*, 220
        Kharoshthi, *229*
        Pahlavi, 212, 218, *219*
        Persian, 213, 224, *224*, 225
            (?), 220, *221*
            nastaliq, 215
        Persian, re-inscribed, 211, *214*
        pseudo-Arabic, 213, 225, *225*
        pseudo-Kufic, 213, *225*
        Urdu, 213, 225, *225*
    intaglios, materials and working, 212
        cabochon-cut, 215, 217, 222
        haematite, 212
    Islamic, 212
    and non-Islamic, 211–12
    metal seals, 212–13, 227, *229, 231*
        box seals, 213, 228, 230, *231*
        brass seal, inscribed, 225, *225*
        buttons (?) inscribed, 225, *225*
        copper alloy domed seal, 225, *225*
        copper alloy, with pierced lugs, 213, 227–8, *229*
        miscellaneous copper alloy, 226–7, *227*
        pyramidal, copper alloy, 225–6, *226*
    sardonyx seal, 222, *224*
    terracotta seal, 213, 225, *226*
    see also gems *c.* 4th century BC–6th century AD; Islamic gems
Sebuktegin (AH 366–87 / AD 977–97), 113, 116, *201*, 202
Seleucus I (AD 977–97), 94, 132, *133*
Seljuqs, 116, 292
Shaboro, 72, 79, *see also* Shapur II
Shahbazgarhi rock inscription, 18
Shaka (c. AD 302–42), 106, 180, *180*
Shapur II (c. AD 309–79)
    coins catalogued, 189, *190*
        i.n.o. Kavad, 183
        Shaboro, 183
    correspondence of coins, 79
    historical context, 106–7, *107*, 108
    imitations, 67, *68*, 108
    coins with crown of, 185
    Masson's analysis, 64, 67, *68*
Shapur III (AD 383–8), 107, 108, 189, *190*
Shapur, son of Papak, 189, *190*
sheet metal pierced objects, 293–4, *294*
Shri Sero coins, 108, *see also* Turkic rulers
Shri Shahi coins, 31, *32–3*, 66, *80*, *93*, 117
    coins catalogued, *107*, 186, *187*, 188
    DAFA finds, *32–3*
    historical context, 107–8
    Masson's analysis, *66*
Sijistān mint, *111*, 120, 122, 123, *124–5, 126*
Sind coins, 12, 91, 201–2
    historical context, 109–10
    see also Amirs of Sind
Sirkap, Taxila, 228, 235, 237, 238, 239, 241, 256, 257, 263, 264, 266, 275, 286, 297, 298
Skag Gözgān (c. AD 674/679–95), 110, *111*, 112
Sogdia, 272, 284, 295, 314, 315, 320
Sogdian coins, 5, *153*, 153–4, 198, *199*; *see also* Hyrcodes
Soter Megas issues, 22

Index | 367

coins catalogued, 156–9
　DAFA finds, *32–3, 93*
　historical context, 83, 85–6, 90, 103–5, 312
　Masson's analysis, *48*
　　correspondence of coins, *75*
　Masson's annotations, 312, 323
　Wima Takto *see* Wima Takto
South Kensington Museum inventory, *336*
Spalagadama (*c.* 59–40 BC)
　coins catalogued, *145*, 146, 323
　DAFA finds, *32–3, 93*
　historical context, 100, 102
　Masson's analysis, 55
　Mir Zakah finds, *99*
Spalahores (*c.* 65–50 BC), *93*, *145*, 145–6
　DAFA finds, *32–3*
Spalapatideva (*c.* AD 750–850), 63, 109, 196–7, *197*
Spalirises (*c.* 50–40 BC), 53, 146
spatula, 263–4, *264*
spoons, 296–7, *298*
Spur (*c.* AD 746–53), 108, 109, 196
　silver dracmh i.n.o., 193, *195*
stamps, 233, *233*
　Bronze Age stamps or seals, 233–4
Steuart collection, 110, *125*, *126*
stone ornaments, *301*, 302
Strabo, 314, 315, 321
stratega, 149
Strato I (*c.* 125–110 BC), 97, *100*, 141, *142*
　DAFA finds, *32–3*
studs, 294, *294*
stupa relic deposits *see* Bimaran; Chahar Bagh; Deh Rahman; Guldara; Hadda; Ishpola; Kamari; Kotpur; Manikyala; Nandara; Surkh Tope; Tope-i Kutchera; Wardak
Surkh Kotal, 245, 266
Surkh Tope, 148, 312
Susa mint, *111*, *119*, *124*
swastika motif, 131, 177, 180, 182, 183, 234
Swat, 96, *96*, *100*, 218, 228, 242, 256, 276, 312
　Butkara, 112, 235, 256
　Saidu Sharif I, 236

tacks, 294, *294*
Taj al-dīn Naṣr b. Bahram Shah (AH 618–19 / AD 1221–2), 200, *201*
Taj al-dīn Yildiz, Governor of Ghazni (AH 602–11 / AD 1206–15), *206*, 207
tallies, *301*, 302
tamghas, *69*, 107–8, 150–3, 156–61, 168, 183–5
Tamim b. Zayd al-Qayni (*c.* AD 726–30), 110
Tarmashirin Khan (1331–4), 316
Tatarang Zar, 9
Taxila
　Bhamala finds, 241
　Bhir Mound finds, 269, 273, 299
　coin finds, 90, 91, 93–7, *100*
　　historical context, 46–7, 103–4, 105
　　'local Taxila' issues, 45, *72*
　Kunala stupa find, 286

Masson's annotation, 310
Sirkap finds, 228, 235, 237, 238, 239, 241, 256, 257, 263, 264, 266, 275, 286, 297, 298
Tegin (*c.* AD 706–39), 108, 109, 196
Tepai Shakh necropolis, Tajikistan, 240, 245, 268, 274
Tepe Khwaja Lahori, 312
Tepe Marajan, 107
Theophilus (*c.* 130 BC), 97, *100*
Thomas, Edward, 127
Tillya Tepe
　(burial 5), 235, 239, 300, 302
　(burial 6), 302
Timur (1370–1405), 18, 316
Timurid unregulated civic coinage, 208, *209*
Tobazino (*c.* AD 420), 107
Tope-i Kutchera, Darunta, 80, 148
Topes and Sepulchral Buildings of Afghanistan, 310–13
Toramana I (? *c.* AD 485–515), *184*, 186
Toramana II (*c.* AD 540–99), 108, 186, *187*
Tribhuvanagiri, 199, *199*
Tripuri, 199, *199*
triratna, 239, 264, 292, *293*
Tulchar necropolis tombs, 238, 239, 266, 283, 286, 288
Tup Khona necropolis tombs, 235, 245, 266, 267, 283, 286
Turkic Kabul and Hindu Shahi coins, *62*, 109, 196–7
Turkic rulers, 188–9, *192*
　(6th–7th century), 186–8
　(*c.* 8th century), 193, *195*, 196
　by names of issue *see* Fromo Kesaro; Sandan; Spur; Tegin; Shri Sero
Turkmen of the White Sheep, 208, *209*

'Ubaydallāh b. Ziyād (*c.* AH 52–62 / AD 672–82), 63, *79*, *111*, *120–5*, 191–3
Uljaytu (1304–16), 208, *209*
'Umar b. al-'Ala (*c.* 10th century), 201, *201*
'Umar b. 'Ubaydallāh (*c.* AH 67–72 / AD 687–92), *123*, *128*, 193, *194*
Umayyad caliphate (AH 41–132 / AD 661–750), 110, 224
unregulated civic coinage, 208, *209*, 210
Urdu inscriptions, 213, 225
Uzbekistan, 239, 245, 246, 247, 248, 266, 272, 277–9, 280, 284, 290, 297

Vakkadeva (*c.* AD 750–870), 197
Varhran (*c.* AD 330–59) i.n.o., 183, *185*
Varhran IV (AD 388–99), 67, 68, 189, *190*
Varhran V (AD 420–38), 64, 189, *190*
vase, 227, 230, 242, *243*
'vase of plenty' (*pūrṇaghaṭa*), 242, *243*
Vasishka (*c.* AD 246–67), 105, 178–9, *180*
　DAFA finds, *32–3*
Vasudeva I (*c.* AD 190–230), 61
　copper alloy coins, 105, *140*, *176*, 177
　gold coins, *176*, 177
　imitations i.n.o., 177–8, 180
　　DAFA finds, *32–3*
Vasudeva II (*c.* AD 272–97), 106
Vatashvaka (*c.* 2nd century BC), 55
vegetal scroll, 248–9, 280

Veh-Ardashir mint, *111, 119*, 191
Ventura, Jean-Baptiste (1795–1858), collection, 16, 40, 41, 45, 46, 55, 90, 309, 326
vessel fittings, 295–6, *297*
Victoria and Albert Museum, 90, 217, 238, 269
    South Kensington Museum inventory, *336*
Viradaman (father of Rudrasena II), 149
Vitkevich, Ivan (1808–39), 4–5
Vonones (*c.* 65–50 BC), *52*, 53, 145–6
'Voyage à travers la Perse centrale et l'Afghanistan' (Court), 4

Wade, Claude, 4
Wali Muḥammād b. Jani (AH 1014–16 / AD 1605–11), 209, *209*
Wardak Stupa I, 270
washers, 294, *294*
weights, 300, *301*
Western Satraps, 84, 324
    by names of issue *see* Rudrasena I; Rudrasena II
Willoughby, J.B., receipt of Masson's collections, 12–13, 329–30
Wilson, Horace Hayman (1786–1860), 127, 305, 307
    Ariana Antiqua see *Ariana Antiqua*,
Wima Kadphises (*c.* AD 113–27), 323, 326
    Begram collection, 72
    DAFA excavations, 22, 24, 27, *32–3*
    gold coins, 161, *162*
    historical context, 104–5
    Masson's analysis, *56*, 57
Wima Takto (*c.* AD 90–113), 323
    Begram collection, 72, *87*
    coins catalogued, 159–61
    Heliocles imitations of, *44, 158*, 284
    historical context, 83, 84, 103–4, 118
    Masson's analysis, 45, 47, 49
        correspondence of coins, *75–6*
    Soter Megas issues *see* Soter Megas issues
    tamghas, 69
wire fittings, 300, *300*
Witkiewicz, Jan, 4

Xuanzang, 20, 28, 118

Ya'qub b. al-Layth al-Ṣaffār (AH 247–65 / AD 861–79), 109, 113
Yadavas of Tribhuvanagiri, 199, *199 see* Kumarapaladeva
Yalangtush Tepe, 244, 245, 247, 286
Yasovarman of Kanauj (*c.* AD 713–36), 198
Yazd mint, *111, 119, 124*
Yazdagird I (AD 399–420), 189, *190*
Yazdagird II (AD 438–57), 64, *67, 68, 79*, 189, *190*
Yazdagird III (AD 632–51), 191, *192*
    era, 112, *119–20*, 196
Yildiz *see* Taj al-dīn Yildiz
Yoktan, Khotan, 235, 249
yoni, 302
Yuezhi, 29, 30, 43, 100–1, 153, 322

Zabulistan mint, 188
Zeionises (*c.* AD 30–50), 102, 149, *149*, 323
Zengid of Mosul, *209*, 210 *see also* Badr al-dīn Lu'lu'
Zhulād Gōzgān (*c.* AD 700–7), 110, *111*, 112, 189, 191, *192*, 193, *195*
Zoilus (*c.* 130–120 BC), 97